Food, Nutrition and the Prevention of Cancer: a Global Perspective

World Cancer Research Fund

American Institute for Cancer Research

Copyright © 1997 World Cancer Research Fund /
American Institute for Cancer Research

First published 1997 by the American Institute for Cancer Research,
1759 R St. NW Washington, DC 20009

ISBN: 1 899533 05 2

British Library Cataloguing in Publication Data
A catalogue record for this book is available from the British Library

Library of Congress Catalog Card No. 97–61549

Printed in the USA by BANTA Book Group, Menasha, WI 54952

Design: **Chris Jones, Design for Science, London**
Typesetting: **Paul Samat, using Bitstream Charter and Frutiger**

Graphics: **Mark Fletcher, Smith Ward Design Consultancy**
                   Jan Hawtin
Globes and maps: **Mountain High Maps**

Cover photographs from left to right, with thanks to:
Henry Sims/The Image Bank, Kenny Menczer,
Alan Becker/The Image Bank, Nevada Wier/The Image Bank,
Kenny Menczer, Chris Close/The Image Bank, Mark Romanelli/The
Image Bank, Regine M./The Image Bank
Food shots from Letraset Phototone Backgrounds

Food, Nutrition and the Prevention of Cancer: a Global Perspective

WORLD CANCER RESEARCH FUND
IN ASSOCIATION WITH
AMERICAN INSTITUTE FOR CANCER RESEARCH

World
Cancer
Research Fund

American
Institute for
Cancer Research

CONTENTS

O ver the last 15 years, a number of expert reports have reviewed the literature on diet and cancer and made recommendations designed to reduce the risk of cancer. This report builds on that earlier work and we acknowledge our debt to the many scientists responsible and, even more crucially, to the thousands of researchers whose findings, reviewed and assessed here, form the basis of our recommendations.

The report was commissioned by the Executive officers of the World Cancer Research Fund (WCRF) and the American Institute for Cancer Research (AICR) on behalf of the WCRF/AICR Board. We are grateful to the many organisations and individuals who have supported us in our work, as contributors, observers, advisers, consultants and reviewers, and to the Board and staff of the WCRF and the AICR, for their financial, technical, scientific, editorial and administrative support.

This report has some special features. As its title indicates, it is concerned explicitly with the primary prevention of cancer, and has a global perspective. We have emphasised those aspects of food and nutrition likely to reduce cancer risk, while giving due weight to those that may increase risk.

We have agreed on a consistent method to assess the various types of scientific evidence, so that the basis for our judgements can itself be evaluated by the reader. The dietary recommendations designed to prevent cancer, set out in chapter 8 and summarised on pages 522–523, are generally food-based, and either quantified or set out in clear language, so as to be useful to both policy-makers and the general public. The recommendations have been framed bearing in mind existing guidelines designed to prevent deficiency and infectious diseases, and to prevent non-infectious diseases other than cancer, especially cardiovascular diseases. The panel accepted a relatively broad brief which included consideration of factors related to diet, and we have concluded that relative body mass and degree of physical activity are both important in modifying the risk of cancer.

Our work has been done in the context of the terms of reference agreed at our initial meeting, which were:

- To review the scientific and other expert literature linking foods, nutrition, food preparation, dietary patterns and related factors, with the risk of human cancers worldwide.
- To devise a series of dietary and other recommendations suitable for all societies and designed to reduce the risk of human cancers.
- To evaluate the degree of consistency between such recommendations and those proposed for the prevention of coronary heart disease and other diseases.
- To consider both the feasibility and the policy implications of the global implementation of these recommendations.

We believe this report fulfils these terms of reference.

The burden of preventable suffering and death from cancer throughout the world is huge. Some of the cancers now most common in Europe, North America and Australasia are known to be largely preventable. Changes in society worldwide are accelerating and are liable, if unchecked, to increase the burden of cancer, most of all in Africa, Latin America and Asia.

As will become clear, evidence of causal links between food and nutrition and cancer is often sufficiently strong to be a basis for recommendations to policy-makers and to the general public. It is now apparent that, although genetic predisposition varies, the key factors determining whether or not people develop cancer are environmental. The two most important ways to reduce cancer risk are the avoidance of cancer-causing agents, of which tobacco is by far the most lethal, but which also include biological agents, viruses and bacteria, and the habitual consumption of diets high in those foods and drinks that protect against cancer. A principal purpose of this report has been to identify such diets.

We find that current data support previous findings that inappropriate diets cause around one-third of all cancer deaths.

We have chosen to take a positive approach in this report.

We estimate that recommended diets, together with maintenance of physical activity and appropriate body mass, can in time reduce cancer incidence by 30–40%. At current rates, on a global basis, this represents 3–4 million cases of cancer per year that could be prevented by dietary and associated means.

We believe that action to prevent cancer is rational, timely and important, and should be, therefore, a major priority and responsibility for international agencies, governments, industry, non-governmental organisations, medical and health authorities, and for all working in the public interest at international, national and community level.

Although derived from the scientific data, this report, with its dietary recommendations and public policy proposals, has been designed not so much as a work of reference but rather as a catalyst for change. Its target readership is policy-makers and opinion leaders worldwide. To this end, the substantive literature reviews and other scientific material at the centre of the report are made more accessible by means of appropriate summaries and explanatory text, written in plain language and amplified by graphics. This dual-level approach keeps faith both with the science and with the need to communicate the findings to those able and willing to translate science into action.

John D. Potter
on behalf of the panel
July 1997

PANEL

Chair
John D. Potter MBBS PhD
Fred Hutchinson Cancer Research
Center
Seattle, WA, USA

Members
Adolfo Chavez MD MPH
Instituto Nacional de la Nutricion
Mexico City, Mexico

Junshi Chen MD
Chinese Academy of Preventive
Medicine
Beijing, China

Anna Ferro-Luzzi MD
Istituto Nazional della Nutrizione
Rome, Italy

Tomio Hirohata MD DrSHyg
Nakamura University
Fukuoka City, Japan

W. P. T. James CBE MD FRCP FRSE
The Rowett Research Institute
Aberdeen, UK

Fred F. Kadlubar PhD
National Center for Toxicological
Research
Jefferson, AR, USA

Festo P. Kavishe MD
UNICEF Office of the Regional Director
of East Asia and Pacific Region
Phnom Penh, Cambodia

Laurence N. Kolonel MD PhD
University of Hawaii
Honolulu, HI, USA

Suminori Kono MD MSc
Kyushu University
Fukuoka City, Japan

Kamala Krishnaswamy MD
Indian Council of Medical Research
Hyderabad, India

**A. J. McMichael MBBS FFPHM
FAFPHM**
London School of Hygiene and
Tropical Medicine
London, UK

Sushma Palmer DSc
Center for Communications, Health
and the Environment (CECHE)
Washington, DC, USA

Lionel A. Poirier PhD
National Center for Toxicological
Research
Jefferson, AR, USA

Walter C. Willett MD DrPH
Harvard School of Public Health
Boston, MA, USA

Scientific adviser to AICR/WCRF
T. Colin Campbell PhD
Cornell University
Ithaca, NY, USA

OBSERVERS

The panel wishes to thank the
following representatives of UN and
other agencies who acted as observers,
attended relevant panel meetings, and
commented on drafts of the report in
progress.

**International Agency for
Research on Cancer,
Lyon, France**
Elio Riboli MD

**Food and Agriculture Organization
of the United Nations, Rome, Italy**
John R. Lupien PhD
William D. Clay
Valeria Menza

**World Health Organization, Geneva,
Switzerland**
Elisabet Helsing PhD
Mark Tsechkovski MD

**National Cancer Insitute,
National Institutes of Health,
Bethesda, MD, USA**
Peter Greenwald MD DrPH

CONTRIBUTORS AND CONSULTANTS

The panel wishes to thank the following scientists and other experts in public health who drafted original contributions to the report or who acted as consultants during panel meetings.

W. Robert Bruce MD PhD
University of Toronto
Toronto, Canada

John Burn MD FRCP
University of Newcastle-upon-Tyne
Newcastle-upon-Tyne, UK

Claudia Sanchez Castillo PhD
Instituto Nacional de la Nutricion
Mexico City, Mexico

Lawrence Fishbein PhD
Annandale, VA, USA

David Forman PhD
Centre for Cancer Research, University of Leeds
Leeds, UK

Geoffrey R. Howe PhD
Columbia University
New York, NY, USA

Richard Longhurst PhD
Commonwealth Secretariat
London, UK

Loic le Marchand MD PhD
University of Hawaii
Honolulu, HI, USA

D. J. Millward PhD DSc
School of Biological Sciences,
University of Surrey
Guildford, UK

Jane A. Pryer PhD
London School of Hygiene & Tropical Medicine
London, UK

Ann Ralph PhD
The Rowett Research Institute
Aberdeen, UK

Jose Romero MPH
Pan-American Health Organization (PAHO)
Mexico City, Mexico

Prakash Shetty MD PhD
London School of Hygiene & Tropical Medicine
London, UK

Noel W. Solomons MD
Centre for Sensory Impairment Aging and Metabolism (CESSIAM)
Guatemala City, Guatemala

Sherri O. Stuver ScD
Harvard School of Public Health
Boston, MA, USA

Benjamin Torún MD PhD
Institute of Nutrition of Central America and Panama (INCAP)
Guatemala City, Guatemala

Ron Walker PhD
University of Surrey
Guildford, UK

John H. Weisburger MD PhD
American Health Foundation
New York, NY, USA

Martin Wiseman MD
Department of Health
London, UK

REVIEWERS

The panel wishes to thank the following scientists who reviewed relevant chapters and sections of the report at different stages.

Herman Adlercreutz MD PhD
University of Helsinki
Haartmaninkatu, Finland

Yoon-Ok Ahn MD PhD MPH
Seoul National University College of Medicine
Seoul, Korea

Christine B. Ambrosone PhD
National Center for Toxicological Research
Jefferson, AR, USA

Katrine Baghurst PhD
Commonwealth Scientific and Industrial Research Organization (CSIRO)
Adelaide, Australia

Peter Baghurst PhD
Commonwealth Scientific and Industrial Research Organization (CSIRO)
Adelaide, Australia

Helmut Bartsch PhD
German Cancer Research Centre
Heidelberg, Germany

Franco Berrino MD
Epidemiology Instituto Nazionale Tumori
Milan, Italy

Sheila Bingham PhD
MRC Dunn Nutrition Centre
Cambridge, UK

Diane F. Birt PhD
University of Nebraska Medical Center
Omaha, NE, USA

William J. Blot PhD
International Epidemiology Institute
Ltd
Rockville, MD, USA

Roswell K. Boutwell PhD
University of Wisconsin School of
Medicine
Madison, WI, USA

Peter Boyle PhD
European Institute of Oncology
Milan, Italy

Tim Byers MD MPH
University of Colorado Health Sciences
Center
Denver, CO, USA

Kenneth K. Carroll PhD DSc
The University of Western Ontario
London, Canada

Carl Cerniglia PhD
National Center for Toxicological
Research
Jefferson, AR, USA

Samuel M. Cohen MD PhD
University of Nebraska Medical Center
Omaha, NE, USA

Michel P. Coleman BM MSc MFPHM
London School of Hygiene & Tropical
Medicine
London, UK

Pelayo Correa MD
Louisiana State University Medical
Center
New Orleans, LA, USA

Daniel W. Cramer MD
Brigham & Women's Hospital
Boston, MA, USA

Sandra J. Culp PhD
National Center for Toxicological
Research
Jefferson, AR, USA

John Cummings MD FRCP
Dunn Clinical Nutrition Centre
Cambridge, UK

Daniel R. Doerge PhD
National Center for Toxicological
Research
Jefferson, AR, USA

Gerard DuBois MD
Centre Hospitalier Universitaire
D'Amiens
Amiens, France

James S. Felton PhD
Lawrence Livermore National
Laboratory
Livermore, CA, USA

Robert A. Floyd PhD
Oklahoma Medical Research
Foundation
Oklahoma City, OK, USA

Silvia Franceschi
Aviano Cancer Center
Aviano, Italy

Shoji Fukushima MD
Osaka City University Medical School
Osaka, Japan

Hirota Fujiki MD PhD
Saitama Cancer Center Research
Institute
Saitama, Japan

Richard P. Gallagher MA FACE
British Columbia Cancer Agency
Vancouver, Canada

Catherine Giessler PhD
King's College
London, UK

Edward Giovannucci MD
Harvard School of Public Health
Boston, MA, USA

Marc T. Goodman PhD
University of Hawaii
Honolulu, HI, USA

John Groopman PhD
John Hopkins University School of
Hygiene and
Public Health
Baltimore, MA, USA

Stephen S. Hecht PhD
University of Minnesota Cancer Center
Minneapolis, MN, USA

Joseph H. Hotchkiss PhD
Cornell University
Ithaca, NY, USA

Jussi Huttunen MD
National Public Health Institute
Helsinki, Finland

Martijn B. Katan PhD
Wageningen Agricultural University
Wageningen, The Netherlands

David G. Kaufman MD PhD
University of North Carolina School of
Medicine
Chapel Hill, NC, USA

Linda C. Koo PhD
University of Hong Kong
Wong Chuk Hang, Hong Kong

Alan R. Kristal Dr PH
Fred Hutchinson Cancer Research Center
Seattle, WA, USA

David Kritchevsky PhD
The Wistar Institute of Anatomy and Biology
Philadelphia, PA, USA

Lawrence Kushi ScD
University of Minnesota School of Public Health
Minneapolis, USA

Maria Teresa Landi PhD
University of Milan
Milano, Italy

Jun Yao Li MD
Chinese Academy of Medical Sciences
Beijing, China

Ronald J. Lorentzen PhD
US Food and Drug Administration
Washington DC, USA

Albert B. Lowenfels MD
New York Medical College
Valhalla, NY, USA

James K. McDougall PhD
Fred Hutchinson Cancer Research Center
Seattle, WA, USA

Katherine A. McGlynn PhD
Fox Chase Cancer Center
Philadelphia, PA, USA

Barrie M. Margetts PhD
The Wessex Institute for Health Research and Development
Southampton, UK

James R. Marshall PhD
Arizona Cancer Center
Tucson, AZ, USA

Susan T. Mayne PhD
Yale University School of Medicine
New Haven, CT, USA

Anthony B. Miller MB, FRCP
University of Toronto
Ontario, Canada

Margaret Miller PhD
Center for Veterinarian Medicine, US Food and Drug Administration
Rockville, MD, USA

Nubia Munõz MD
International Agency for Research on Cancer
Lyon, France

Minako Nagao PhD
National Cancer Center Research Institute
Tokyo, Japan

Tom P. O'Connor PhD
University College Cork
Cork, Ireland

Yoshiyuki Ohno MD PhD
Nagoya University School of Medicine
Nagoya, Japan

D. Maxwell Parkin MD
International Agency for Research on Cancer
Lyon, France

Henry C. Pitot MD PhD
The University of Wisconsin
Madison, WI, USA

Miriam C. Poirier PhD
National Cancer Institute
Bethesda, MA, USA

Barry M. Popkin PhD
University of North Carolina
Chapel Hill, NC, USA

Nancy Potischman PhD
National Cancer Institute
Bethesda, MD, USA

Eddie Reed MD
National Cancer Institute
Bethesda, MD, USA

Bandaru S. Reddy PhD
American Health Foundation
Valhalla, NY, USA

Bill D. Roebuck PhD
Dartmouth Medical School
Hanover, NH, USA

Adrianne E. Rogers MD
Boston University School of Medicine
Boston, MA, USA

Nathaniel Rothman MD
National Cancer Institute
Bethesda, MD, USA

Paul Rozen MD
Tel Aviv Medical Centre
Tel Aviv, Israel

Daniel M. Sheehan PhD
National Center for Toxicological Research
Jefferson, AR, USA

Rashmi Sinha PhD
National Cancer Institute
Bethesda, MD, USA

Thomas J. Slaga PhD
University of Texas
Smithville, TX, USA

Marty Slattery PhD
University of Utah
Salt Lake City, UT, USA

Takashi Sugimura MD PhD
National Cancer Center
Tokyo, Japan

Michihito Takahashi MD PhD
National Institute of Health Sciences
Tokyo, Japan

Suketami Tominaga MD
Aichi Cancer Center Research Institute
Nagoya, Japan

Dimitrios Trichopoulos MD
Harvard Public School of Health
Boston, MA, USA

Cheryl Lyn Walker PhD
MD Anderson Cancer Center
Smithville, TX, USA

Shaw Watanabe MD
Tokyo University of Agriculture
Tokyo, Japan

Elizabeth K. Weisburger PhD
Bethesda, MD, USA

Yasushi Yamazoe PhD
Tohoku University
Sendai, Japan

Xihe Zhao
Chinese Academy of Preventive
Medicine
Beijing, China

Introduction

Those wishing to understand the relationship between food, nutrition and cancer, and to identify cancer as a largely preventable disease, are faced with several fundamental questions. This applies to all those individuals and agencies addressed by this report: to policy-makers in government, non-government agencies and industry; to research scientists, medical and health professionals, consumer advocates, and community workers; to editors, writers and journalists; and to individual citizens. These questions include: when is the evidence of a relationship between any aspect of food and nutrition and cancer strong enough to justify recommendations to policy-makers, health professionals and the general public? How can the importance of food and nutrition in the modification of cancer risk be compared with other lifestyle and environmental factors, and with the effects of genetic susceptibility, the play of chance and the ageing process? Why are the diets of industrialised countries and regions often identified as increasing the risk of various cancers, when the people who eat such diets generally live longer than people in the developing world? Can cancer be prevented by dietary or other means? If so how? We have attempted to address some of these questions in this report.

EARLY INTERPRETATIONS

The idea that nutrition is an important factor in the risk of cancer is not new. Yong-He Yan, living in the Song Dynasty (960–1279 AD), thought that poor nutrition was a cause of the condition we would now know as cancer of the oesophagus. Wiseman (1676) suggested that cancer might arise from 'an errour in Diet, a great acrimony in the meats and drinks meeting with a fault in the first Concoction' (digestion), and he advised abstention from 'salt, sharp and gross meats'.

Howard (1811) proposed that constipation was an important factor in cancer, basing his judgement on 40 years of clinical practice. Lambe (1815), a Fellow of the Royal College of Physicians of London, warned in his treatise on diet, cancer and other chronic diseases, against the danger of excess consumption of food in general and meat in particular. Bennett (1849), author of medical textbooks, wrote that 'the circumstances which diminish obesity, and a tendency to

the formation of fat, would seem, *a priori*, to be opposed to the cancerous tendency'.

By the early twentieth century, similar views were commonplace. Shaw (1907) advocated a prudent regime designed to reduce the risk of cancers, with more foods of vegetable origin, less foods of animal origin, and less alcohol, tea and tobacco. Roger Williams, in *The Natural History of Cancer* (1908), concluded that 'probably no single factor is more potent in determining the outbreak of cancer in the predisposed, than excessive feeding' and proposed that 'many indications point to the gluttonous consumption of proteids – especially meat – which is such a characteristic feature of the age, as likely to be specially harmful in this respect'. He also identified 'deficient exercise, and probably lack of sufficient vegetable food'.

During the first half of the twentieth century, two influential hypotheses on the environmental causes of cancer were developed. The first focused on occupational causes, notably exposure of workers to carcinogenic agents (Hueper, 1942). The second general theory focused on diet. The medical statistician and epidemiologist, Frederick Hoffman, a founder of the American Cancer Society (ACS) and the US National Cancer Surveys (which eventually led to the national network of cancer repositories – SEER), undertook a systematic review of the then current literature on diet and cancer (Hoffman, 1937). He concluded that 'excessive nutrition if not the chief cause is at least a contributory factor of the first importance'. He identified fatty, sugary foods, white bread and meat as possible specific factors.

Hoffman also undertook a systematic study of smoking and cancer, for the ACS and for insurance companies. He concluded (1931) that 'the inhalation of cigarette smoke… unquestionably increases the danger of cancer development'.

Early research proposing that cancer has nutritional and other environmental causes did not always rely merely on individual clinical observation. Walshe (1846) and Williams (1908) noted the effects of migration on cancer risk, as did Hoffman (1915) whose later work (Hoffman, 1937) also drew on his own multi-centre case-control study using 2,234 cancer cases and 1,149 controls, and referred to contemporary animal studies of the effects of different diets on transplanted tumour tissue.

Among the earliest formal epidemiological studies of diet and cancer were those by Orr (1933), who undertook an ecological study of oral cancer in India, and the other by Stocks (1933), who conducted a case-control study of cancer in England and Wales; each identified distortions of dietary patterns (especially low intakes of vegetables and fruit) as risk factors.

In the second half of the twentieth century, theories of the dietary origins of cancer tended to be increasingly discounted, in favour of alternative theories that cancer is either the result of random genetic error, exposure to viruses or exposure to specific chemical carcinogens. Laboratory research began to concentrate on the investigation of cellular and, ultimately, molecular carcinogenesis, as well as on the effectiveness of surgery, radiotherapy and chemotherapy, as cancer treatments. The index of the fifth edition of the standard textbook *Human Nutrition and Dietetics* (Davidson et al, 1972) included no reference to diet and cancer, and its text included only cursory reference to evidence that cancers of some sites may have some relationship with diet.

However, rates of incidence and death from various cancers continued to rise in industrialised countries (compare, for instance, Park, 1899 and Parkin et al, 1987) and epidemiological investigation indicated that this trend was not just a function of ageing. Further, studies of variations in cancer incidence from country to country, and in successive generations of people who migrated from one part of the world to another, strongly suggested that cancers are largely environmental in origin. In the second half of the twentieth century, a new body of experimental and epidemiological work (Tannenbaum and Silverstone, 1957; Doll, 1967) began to indicate that diet was indeed a major environmental factor affecting the incidence of cancers of a number of sites.

1950 TO 1980

In recent decades, increasing attention has been paid to various foods and nutrients as modifiers of cancer risk, and current thinking on diet and cancer is a synthesis of findings from epidemiological and experimental research.

Much early research on cancer was based on the idea that disease is caused by overexposure to specific discrete pathogenic factors. This concept, originating from late nineteenth century discoveries of the microbial agents of infectious diseases, has some application to chronic diseases (Stewart, 1968). Thus, excess intake of alcohol has been studied, initially with reference to upper aerodigestive cancers. Diets

high in fat have been thought to be an important factor in increased risk of some cancers more common in economically developed countries.

In the 1960s, the search for specific dietary causes of human cancer gained momentum as the experimental model of laboratory chemical carcinogenesis became widely used. There was a corresponding expectation that various specific chemical carcinogens would be identified in the human diet, as had been done in occupational cancer epidemiology, for example, with specific dyes, asbestos and benzene.

At the same time, descriptive and ecological epidemiology showed that the incidence rates of various cancers, including those of the oesophagus, pancreas, stomach, colon and rectum, varied greatly between countries and between regions within countries. Rates also varied over time and as people migrated from one country to another. For example, colon and breast cancer rates were noted to rise in Japanese migrants to the USA (Wynder and Shigematsu, 1967). These important findings showed that strong environmental influences were at work, and epidemiologists reasoned that these were likely to include diet.

The first reliable data for cancer incidence worldwide were collected by cancer registries set up for the purpose. The data were published initially by the International Union Against Cancer (UICC, 1965, 1970), and later by the International Agency for Research on Cancer. An early analysis of these data by Higginson and Muir (1973) noted that the incidence of most, if not all, cancers varied greatly in different countries and regions, and concluded, that '80 to 90 per cent of cancers are due to external factors and are thus theoretically preventable'.

A wide range of specific hypotheses about diet and cancer emerged during the 1970s. The investigation of these hypotheses was helped by the development of various biochemical and metabolic assays, most useful in ecological and prospective studies. Particular attention began to be paid to dietary fat, in light of its strong population-level association with cancer rates, and of the experimental evidence that fat induced cancer.

The distinguished Irish surgeon, Denis Burkitt, who identified the lymphoma that bears his name, developed the hypothesis that a lack of dietary fibre in the 'western' diet accounted for the rise of various chronic diseases, including colon cancer (Burkitt, 1969). But how could low-fibre, high-fat diets increase exposure to chemical carcinogens? To answer this question, epidemiologists and laboratory scientists, working in collaboration, proposed that the key biological events may involve bile acid metabolism, gut microbial ecology, chemical concentration and mucosal contact time (see, for example, Stephen and Cummings, 1980 for a synthesis of these ideas).

Meanwhile, laboratory scientists proposed that salt-pickled and other abrasive foods and drinks, in combination with a low vitamin C intake, made the gastric mucosa vulnerable to dysplastic change, and the gastric contents to carcinogenic nitrosamine production.

Insights into the multistage nature of carcinogenesis were derived from animal experiments early in the century and extended by increasingly sophisticated mathematical models of cancer risks. These set epidemiologists to thinking about types of dietary influences that did not entail direct damage to DNA. For example, the association of breast cancer with reproductive factors and sex hormone profile, the changes in risk with migration, the sex hormone differences between meat eaters and vegetarians, and animal experimental evidence showing modulation of carcinogen-induced mammary cancer by dietary fat, together suggested that diet may act indirectly on breast cancer by influencing hormonal and other metabolic processes. Other models followed.

Alcohol (that is, ethanol) was suspected of aiding the trans-membrane movement of chemical carcinogens (particularly those in tobacco smoke) in the mucosal cells of the upper aerodigestive tract, or else of impeding intracellular defences. Various micronutrients were proposed as reinforcing antioxidant defences, or switching on metabolic pathways that deactivated carcinogens.

AN EMERGING CONSENSUS

Interest in nutritional causes of cancer began to revive in the 1970s, at first in the USA. This was partly because overall cancer rates remained obstinately high while costs of treatment accelerated; partly because of the new evidence on diet and cancer; and partly because 'winning the war against cancer' was perceived as a national goal equivalent in importance to the earlier achievement of putting a man on the moon (Proctor, 1995).

The USA's National Cancer Act of 1971 required the National Cancer Institute (NCI), as a government agency, to investigate the relationship between nutrition and cancer. Following the revised Act of 1974, the NCI, jointly with the privately funded American Cancer Society (ACS), organised a symposium on 'Nutrition in the Causation of Cancer' (AACR, 1975). In his summary, Professor Mark Hegsted of the Harvard School of Public Health commended a prudent diet with 'less fat, less meat, less cholesterol and less food and more fruits, vegetables, and cereals, especially crude cereals'.

A further review by Wynder and Gori (1977) proposed that, for both men and women, the 'preventive potential' for all cancers was 80–90% and that diet accounted for 40% of all male cancers and 60% of all female cancers. It was suggested that key dietary causes of cancer, in general, included overeating, fat and meat. The fact that incidence of stomach cancer varies inversely with the incidence of breast and of colon cancer was interpreted as suggesting that high-fat, low-carbohydrate diets might protect against stomach cancer.

By the mid-1970s, descriptive, ecological and analytical epidemiological studies were providing a growing body of evidence on links between diet and cancer. The British epidemiologists Richard Doll and Richard Peto were commissioned by the US Congress to estimate to what extent cancer is avoidable. Their review, *The Causes of Cancer* (Doll and Peto, 1981), is still frequently cited. Formally, their conclusions apply only to the USA, but their references were from the world literature and, in the view of this and other expert panels, their interpretations have wide application.

Doll and Peto's review, which helped to reset the agenda for thinking on food, nutrition and cancer, included estimates of the extent to which cancer in general, and specific cancers, can be avoided by changes in diet.

Doll and Peto agreed that alcohol, in all forms, increases the risk of cancers of the upper aerodigestive tract and that this risk is exacerbated when drinkers smoke. They attributed approximately 3% of all cancer deaths to alcohol, while also stating that most of these deaths would be avoided if drinkers did not smoke. They concluded that environmental carcinogens, other than those in tobacco and diet, are relatively unimportant causes of cancer. This conclusion was based partly on ecological data which showed no coherent pattern (across various countries and regions) between cancer trends and the degree of external pollution.

The report by Doll and Peto anticipated that results of further research 'may well be' as follows: 'Diet will be shown to be a factor in determining the occurrence of a high proportion of all cancers of the stomach and large bowel as well as of the body of the uterus (endometrium), gall bladder and (in tropical countries) of the liver.' Diet may also prove to have a material effect on the incidence of cancers of the breast and pancreas and, perhaps through the anti-carcinogenic effects of various micronutrients, on the incidence of cancers in many other tissues. 'If this is so, it may be possible to reduce US cancer death rates by practicable dietary means by as much as 35% (for specific sites their estimates were: stomach and large bowel, 90%; endometrium, gallbladder, pancreas, and breast, 50%; lung, larynx, bladder, cervix, mouth, pharynx, and oesophagus, 20%; other types of cancer, 10%).'

This estimate of 35% Doll and Peto judged as 'plausible', while stressing the imprecision of the figures for individual cancers, and suggested that anything between 10 and 70% of all deaths from cancer may be caused by diets such as those consumed in the USA.

Aspects of diet mentioned in Doll and Peto's report as possibly protective against cancer included antioxidant vitamins, vegetables, such as carrots and leafy greens that are rich in these compounds, and bioactive microconstituents such as indoles and protease inhibitors. Fibre, or rather foods that make faeces bulky, were also cited as important. Aspects of diet mentioned as possible causes of cancer were overconsumption (cancers of the uterus and gallbladder in women), fat (cancers of the breast, colon and rectum) and meat (cancers of the colon and rectum). Those considered to be relatively unimportant causes of cancer were food additives (including colours and sweeteners), contaminants (apart from aflatoxin in relation to liver cancer), and methods of food preparation and storage that create carcinogens.

In 1982, the US National Academy of Sciences (NAS) published *Diet, Nutrition and Cancer*, commissioned by the NCI in 1980 (NAS, 1982). The 478-page volume, with well over 2,000 citations, was the first report of a multidisciplinary expert panel specifically on diet and cancer, the first to derive its findings from a thorough survey of epidemiological and experimental data, and the first to derive dietary recommendations designed to reduce the risk of cancer.

The report drew conclusions that informed the agenda for international and national agencies, that influenced patterns of research funding, and that added considerable impetus to the change in direction initiated by Doll and Peto.

A key passage in the NAS report has come to be generally accepted (Trichopoulos et al, 1996; Willett et al, 1996) and is endorsed by the panel of this present report: 'it is abundantly clear that the incidence of all the common cancers in humans is being determined by various potentially controllable external factors. This is surely the most comforting fact to come out of all cancer research, for it means that cancer is, in large part, a preventable disease.' Doll and Peto had concluded in related fashion: 'It is highly likely that the United States will eventually have the option of adopting a diet that reduces its incidence of cancer by approximately one-third, and it is absolutely certain that another one-third could be

preventing by abolishing smoking. These reductions would be roughly equivalent to the reduction in mortality from the infectious diseases brought about by improved hygiene and better health care delivery during the nineteenth century.'

The NAS report proposed six interim dietary guidelines 'both consistent with good nutritional practice and likely to reduce the risk of cancer'. These included recommendations to reduce intake of fat to 30% of total calories, to include fruits, vegetables and wholegrain cereals in the daily diet, to minimise consumption of salted and smoked foods, and to drink alcohol in moderation, if at all. Concern was expressed about carcinogens and mutagens in food.

Since 1982, a large number of reports and statements on diet and cancer or on diet and chronic diseases more generally have been published, and their conclusions in relation to cancer are tabulated in Appendix A.

The diet and cancer story is complex, if only because there are a large number of cancers of different types and sites. Further complexity has been created by the fact that different approaches to the study of cancer have been taken by scientists from separate disciplines. For example, much of the dietary causation of the cancers more common in economically developed countries tends to be seen in terms of metabolic and hormonal influences on carcinogenesis. By contrast, the dietary aetiology of cancers more common in developing countries tends to be seen in terms of chemical carcinogenesis; this involves dietary components and contaminants (for example, nitrosamines and mycotoxins) and deficiencies of specific microconstituents, as well biological agents such as the human papillomaviruses, the hepatitis viruses and the bacterium *Helicobacter pylori*.

During the 1980s and 1990s, several previously identified relationships between aspects of diet and cancer have been confirmed. Other relationships have emerged: for example, alcohol consumption has recently been consistently associated with an increased risk of cancer of the colon, rectum and breast (Kearney et al, 1995; Longnecker 1988, 1994). The recent body of evidence has reduced the importance of specific nutrients, for example, fat, in favour of foods, for example, meat. These and other examples, including the relatively much clearer evidence on the protective effect of regular physical activity, are reviewed and assessed in chapters 4–7 of this report.

Perhaps the most important finding that has emerged strongly in recent years, and is assessed in chapter 6.3, is that diets high in vegetables and fruits (and therefore in fibre, antioxidants and other bioactive microconstituents) are associated with reduced risk of most, if not all, epithelial cancers

(Steinmetz and Potter, 1991, 1996).

Correspondingly, the list of specific cancers the incidence of which is related to diet and factors related to diet has tended to increase (Willett and Trichopoulos, 1996). These include cancers of the mouth and pharynx (Marshall and Boyle, 1996), larynx (Riboli et al, 1996), oesophagus (Cheng and Day, 1996), lung (Ziegler et al, 1996), pancreas (Howe and Burch, 1996), stomach (Kono and Hirohata, 1996), colon and rectum (Potter, 1996a), breast (Hunter and Willett, 1996), endometrium (Hill and Austin, 1996), cervix (Potischman and Brinton, 1996), prostate (Kolonel, 1996), kidney (Wolk et al, 1996) and bladder (La Vecchia and Negri, 1996); these are all sites reviewed and assessed in this report.

During its four years of work, the panel responsible for this report came to the view that the most appropriate approach to the prevention of cancer by dietary means is to emphasise foods and drinks in the contexts of whole diets, within existing cuisines and cultures. For example, the traditional Mediterranean diet is, as a whole, a low-risk cancer diet relative to others in Europe, North America and other economically developed countries (Ferro-Luzzi, 1994), and it is defined by its food, regional climate and culture.

The panel also endorsed the view of others (Franceschi, 1994) that dietary diversity itself is probably a key factor in protection against cancer, especially in certain parts of the world and among impoverished populations. Diversity maximises the likelihood of more balanced as well as more adequate diets. Diets in poor rural populations around the world are often monotonous and marginal or even deficient in various microconstituents that may protect against some cancers (as well as the longer standing scourges of iodine, iron, and retinol/carotenoid deficiencies); cancers therefore, at least in part, can be seen as diseases of deficiency.

It is possible to construct four general patterns of the environmental causes of cancer (Potter, 1996b). Cancers generally more common in the past in the developed world, and which persist in the economically less developed world, can be seen as largely caused by either dietary deficiency, of which the root cause is insecure, or inadequate food supplies. Alternatively, they are caused by infection or infestation, also a manifestation of poverty. Cancers generally now more common in the economically developed world, and in urban areas elsewhere in the world, can be seen as largely caused by exposure to carcinogenic agents either singly or in combination, sometimes a consequence of industrialisation but always a consequence of the ubiquitous use of tobacco. The other general pattern is that of an excess of energy-dense foods in the context of physical inactivity, a situation that follows urbanisation. The first and the fourth patterns may be obverse sides of the same risk: an excess of fat and sugar-rich foods may produce a deficiency of protective dietary constituents almost as readily as a monotonous high-starch diet.

The diet and cancer relationship can be considered as part of a still larger picture, within an evolutionary framework (McMichael, 1994). Oxygen, released by photosynthesis, has accumulated in the lower atmosphere during the second half of Earth's existence. For aerobic organisms, including *Homo sapiens*, this oxygen is a double-edged sword: it enables efficient aerobic metabolism, but it also causes reactive damage to macromolecules. Terrestrial plants have evolved antioxidant defences against oxidative assault. These defences depend on certain elements (for example, selenium) and on the synthesis of complex molecules (for example, carotenoids and polyphenols).

Not surprisingly, many of these micronutrients have also become, through co-evolution, the antioxidant defences of the animals that eat those plants. Leaves and ripening fruits, the metabolically active parts of the plant, contain high levels of antioxidant vitamins. In contrast, seeds comprise dormant genetic material and energy stores and they have lower antioxidant concentrations. Because the evolutionary formative primate/hominid diet that shaped human biology was very high in antioxidant-rich leafy vegetables and fruit (Milton, 1993), human metabolism should therefore function best with diets high in foods rich in antioxidants. However, in most modern human populations, who have a relatively low intake of fresh vegetables and fruits, the daily oxidative assault from our oxygenated environment may be less well countered, thus facilitating carcinogenesis.

By its nature, in common with other subjects of research, the diet and cancer story remains incomplete. Data will continue to accumulate, and results of observational studies, metabolic studies and some large controlled trials are awaited. Recommendations based on an evolving science of food, nutrition and cancer will themselves evolve. This panel believes it is likely that new findings will strengthen and refine the evidence reviewed and assessed in this report.

BACKGROUND

CHAPTER ONE

Patterns of diet and cancer

The first lines of evidence suggesting that food and nutrition affect cancer risk come from examination of patterns of diet, and of patterns of cancer, at specific times and places.

The purpose of this chapter is to provide the reader with a sense of the diversity of human eating patterns, and the variation in cancer risks, across the world. These data are necessarily descriptive and broad. Causation cannot be inferred from a simple comparison of global dietary variations with worldwide patterns of cancer incidence. There is no attempt, in this chapter, to relate cancer outcomes to dietary patterns; the bulk of that evidence is provided in chapters 4–7.

This chapter is an overview of patterns of diet and patterns of cancer throughout the world. In the first section, historical and then recent dietary patterns are outlined. The diets of predominantly rural and pre-urban/industrial parts of the world within Africa, Latin America and Asia are described, followed by those of the industrialised world in Europe, North America and Australasia.

Cancer patterns are described in the second section. There is marked variation in the incidence of, and mortality from, many cancers in different regions and populations around the world, but certain general patterns can be identified. With important national and local exceptions, the economically developing countries of Africa, Latin America and Asia tend to have, in common, relatively high rates of cancers of the upper aerodigestive tract (of the mouth and pharynx, larynx and oesophagus), and of the stomach, liver (primary) and cervix.

In contrast, the economically developed countries of Europe, North America and Australasia tend to have, in common, relatively high rates of cancers of the colon and rectum, and of the hormone-related cancers of the female breast, the endometrium and the prostate. This pattern has now also emerged in urban areas of developing countries. Lung cancer, mainly caused by use of tobacco, is now the most common cancer throughout the world.

Cancer rates may change dramatically. For example, in most populations in the developed world, stomach cancer has been declining rapidly in recent decades, whereas rates of cancers of the colon, breast and prostate have been rising. Further variations in cancer patterns are seen in studies of migrants. Also, patterns of cancer are now changing rapidly within the economically developing world as populations age and become increasingly industrialised and urbanised. Such variations with time, migration and urbanisation indicate that cancer rates are strongly influenced by environmental factors, including diets, and that cancer is therefore largely preventable.

1.1 Patterns of diet

Dietary patterns have evolved throughout history and vary greatly in different parts of the world. In rural areas of economically developing countries, diets may depend solely on what a family or local community produces. As the use of cash is extended, a greater variety of foods becomes available in local markets or shops. In economically developed societies and in the urban areas of developing countries, diets are a reflection not only of food supplies grown and manufactured locally but also of those available nationally and internationally, and finally of market economies that ensure the availability of a wide choice of manufactured foods.

The diets typically consumed in rural areas of Africa, Latin America, Asia and Oceania often still rely on one or two staple cereal foods and may be fairly monotonous and bulky. Mostly, cereals are dominant, especially in the low-income countries of Asia, as well as in China and India. Rice dominates in Asia, wheat in north Africa, maize (corn) in Latin America, and maize and starchy roots in sub-Saharan Africa.

Foods of animal origin and added fats are eaten only occasionally in rural areas, exceptions being gatherer–hunter and pastoral communities, and populations who live by rivers and seas. Vegetables and fruits do not occupy a very important place in the diet. These diets include few industrially processed foods – such products are locally unavailable, or else beyond the reach of people living in subsistence economies.

As countries develop economically, consumption of the dominant staple cereal foods declines. The amount of fats and oils consumed tends to rise sharply. There is a consistent fall in the overall consumption of foods of plant origin and replacement with increasing amounts of foods of animal origin, notably meat, meat products and dairy products. Sugar consumption also generally increases rapidly.

Because, as a function of industrialisation and urbanisation, diets contain relatively more food of animal origin, and relatively less food of plant origin, such diets are correspondingly lower in fibre and other bioactive compounds found in food of plant origin. An ever-increasing proportion of food in industrialised societies is processed.

Within some of the most economically developed countries, this process has slowed and, for some population subgroups, it has reversed. Southern Europeans continue consumption of more red meat, total fats and sugar, but there is now a discernible trend in some northern European countries and within North America towards an increasing consumption of vegetables and fruits and somewhat decreasing consumption of red meat, fat, full-fat milk, other dairy products and sugar in the form of sucrose. This shift is most noticeable in countries where messages about nutrition and public health have been accepted by governments and promoted by health authorities and in the media.

HISTORICAL

The evolution of human diets has been shaped by climate, terrain, culture and other circumstances. The hominid line is estimated to have diverged from the ancestral line about 5–7 million years ago, with little subsequent physiological or metabolic change. The genus *Homo* evolved in the woodlands and savannahs of Africa about 2.5 million years ago. *Homo sapiens* appeared maybe 400,000 years ago. The human genome is only 2–3% different from that of plant-eating gorillas and chimpanzees.

Three different basic types of food system can be identified. The gatherer–hunter system stretches back to prehistoric times, and is not yet extinct. The peasant–agricultural system began about 10,000 years ago. The urban–industrial system is very recent, it has become typical in the world's richest countries only within the last few generations, and is now emerging in many other countries in economic transition.

GATHERER–HUNTER

Anthropological findings and recent studies of isolated groups such as Kalahari bushmen, Australian aborigines and Amazonian tribes suggest that *Homo sapiens* originally subsisted by gathering fruits, such as berries, and plants, such as leaves, tubers and pulses (legumes), together with meat obtained by scavenging and hunting. It is now generally accepted that the gathering (of plant foods, and also of insects and small living things) contributed a greater part of gatherer–hunter diets than meat from hunted animals (Eaton et al, 1988). Fish and other seafood from nutrient-rich estuaries have been more important in the relevant local areas; these are excellent sources of protein and minerals, and of the essential fatty acids needed for development of the brain (Crawford and Marsh, 1995).

The discovery of fire within the past million years enabled cooking which made roots digestible and meat soft. Subsequently, the use of smoking in fire enabled foods to be preserved for months. With the advent of early agriculture and animal husbandry, alternative methods of surviving food shortages were devised, such as sun-drying of meat, vegetables and fruits, salting, pickling and fermenting.

Salt, fat and sugar were all desired for different reasons. Salt is relatively scarce in foods in nature, and evolutionary pressure has led to highly sophisticated body mechanisms for extracting, absorbing and recycling sodium from foods. Fat is the most energy-dense component of food and so is valuable as the most efficient contributor to human fat stores needed as a source of energy in times of food shortage, in winter or during times of migration. The sweetness of sugar signals that fruits are ripe and that plant foods are safe to eat.

PEASANT–AGRICULTURAL

Over 10,000 years ago, people living in the Middle East region discovered that cereals (grains) could be cultivated, processed and subsequently cooked as breads and porridges, or dried. This enabled the sustenance of large populations. Sorghum and teff proved suitable for the dry regions of Africa, wheat became the principal crop in the Middle East, and barley and oats grew well in northern climates. Millet was developed as a staple crop in Asia; later rice became the principal cereal crop in wet Asian climates. As the Americas were inhabited, maize (corn) was discovered and used as a staple food.

Roots and tubers can often be left in the ground for long periods of time. Cassava became an important food in Africa. In the Americas, potatoes, yams, beets and turnips were cultivated. In warm climates, other starchy foods such as plantains and bananas were valuable sources of energy. Pulses such as beans, peas and other legumes were also recognised as crops that could be readily produced and stored.

Cultivation of cereals, roots, tubers, plantains and pulses enabled development of towns and cities where people probably ate less meat and fewer vegetables and fruits than gatherer–hunters and nomadic pastoralists, depending on climate and terrain. Various animals and birds have been domesticated and bred for food for thousands of years, and fish have been stocked in ponds and paddy fields. Traditionally, however, substantial amounts of flesh foods have been eaten usually only on special occasions, except by the rich. People living close to water have long eaten comparatively large amounts of readily available fish and seafood. Consumption of alcoholic drinks is variable – but, again, a function of an agrarian lifestyle.

Traditional lifestyles usually involve regular moderate physical activity; high levels of physical activity tend to be episodic, such as during planting and harvesting, and may cause seasonal weight loss.

Life expectancy at birth for pre-industrial peoples is generally much lower than among people living in industrialised societies. Most of the difference is in the death rates in infancy and early childhood, caused largely by infectious diseases, deficiency diseases and accidents – and, among young women, mortality in childbirth.

URBAN–INDUSTRIAL

Urban–industrial diets are very different from those involved with evolution of the human species (WHO, 1997). Food supplies, and thus diets in North America and Europe, were transformed in the late nineteenth century as an outcome of the industrial revolution, producing food on a mass scale. Much of this food was previously common only in the diets of wealthy people.

Steel roller mills, first developed in the 1870s, sifted and separated the component parts of wheat grains on an industrial scale, producing uniform quality white bread, from which the bran and germ was removed. White bread, like other refined cereal products, contains lower levels of fibre, essential oils, vitamins and minerals than wholegrain products.

Sugar refined from cane proved a valuable cash crop. From the 1870s on, the lifting of the sugar tax in Britain led to a spectacular increase in the availability of sugar, and the development of the biscuit, cake, chocolate, confectionery, jam and soft drink industries. Novel cuisines were devised, emphasising sweet foods for mid-afternoon tea and for 'pudding' at the evening meal. The habit of regular consumption of sugared, and otherwise sweetened, foods and drinks has since been exported to many countries all over the world.

Railways made it possible for vast tracts of America to be used for rearing cattle, and for the growth of the meat industry, using automated disassembly lines which turned animals into carcasses and thence into joints, or processed meat, then canned or conveyed in refrigerated railway cars and ships.

By these means, fatty meat from domesticated animals became an everyday food for all but the poorest people.

Encouraged by the discovery of Von Leibig in the mid-nineteenth century that animal protein promotes growth, a system of state-funded agricultural universities was set up in the USA to foster meat and dairy science and technology as the cornerstone of human nutrition. Livestock, originally left to graze or browse on marginal or fallow land, became reared increasingly intensively, and fed with cereals previously used as human food.

Consumption of fat rose in the industrialised world in the twentieth century, only partly as a result of the emergence of meat as an everyday staple food and the increase in consumption of full-fat milk, cheese and butter. Margarine, made initially by means of the industrial hydrogenation process in the early years of the twentieth century, represented an entirely new fat source. Hydrogenation, which converts mostly relatively unsaturated oils and soft fats into hard saturated fats, enables the manufacturer to produce a vast array of packaged foods which remain edible for a long period of time and thus can be kept on open shelves in shops for months.

Diets eaten in economically developed countries and urban areas of the developing world are relatively low in cereals, tubers and other starchy foods, and relatively high in sugar, fat, protein of animal origin, salt, and in meat, dairy products and alcohol. As societies become industrialised, consumption of starchy staples decreases and may decline from 50% or more of total energy intake to 25% or less. At the same time, consumption of fat increases and may

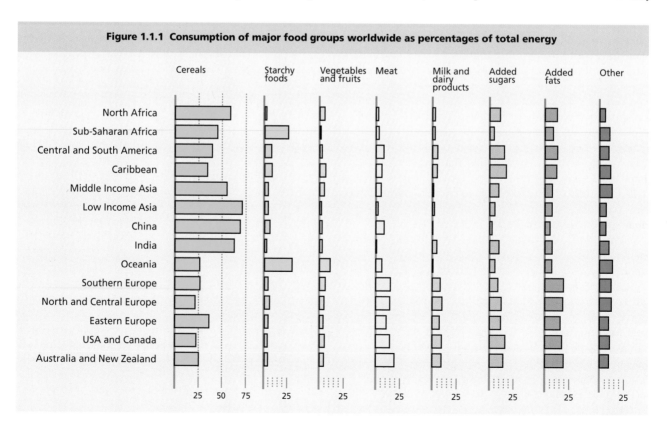

Figure 1.1.1 Consumption of major food groups worldwide as percentages of total energy

increase from less (sometimes much less) than 20% of total energy intake up to 40%. Meat, previously consumed only occasionally, becomes a centrepiece of main meals and a daily staple. Consumption of alcohol generally increases. As a result of any or all of these factors, diets generally become more energy dense. As an important adjunct, energy intake on a population basis decreases as industrialised societies become increasingly sedentary. Overweight and obesity, caused by a combination of energy-dense diets and lack of physical activity, become common.

Consumption of vegetables (excluding roots and tubers) and fruits is often more a function of climate and availability than of culture. Consumption of fresh vegetables and fruits has always been relatively high in the Mediterranean region and relatively low in northern and eastern Europe, for example. There are some signs, however, that consumption of fruits and fruit juices is increasing in relatively rich industrial regions, and this seems to relate to the availability of refrigerated distribution systems.

There are important exceptions to these broad generalisations. In particular, although modern industrialised diets are relatively salty, some diets, such as those eaten traditionally in Japan, Portugal and certain parts of China, include salted foods as staple or common items, and consequently also involve high salt intakes. Also, although alcohol consumption is generally higher in developed countries, it is high in some parts of the developing world.

CURRENT

What follows is an overview of current dietary patterns around the world.

WORLD

Global differences in consumption of the major groups as recorded for 1990 by the Food and Agriculture Organization of the United Nations (FAO) are shown in Figure 1.1.1. These food groups are broadly in line with those identified in chapter 6 of this report (and see Box 1.1.2).

The most striking evident difference is that, in Africa and Asia (apart from high-income Asian countries, notably Japan), half or more of all total energy is supplied by cereals or, less often, starchy roots or fruits. By contrast, in Europe and North America, less than one quarter of total energy is supplied by cereals. Consumption of added fats, alcohol, meat, dairy products and sweeteners is generally reciprocal with consumption of starchy staples. As one example, less (and often much less) than 10% of total energy comes from meat in the economically developing world whereas, in the economically developed world, including Australia and New Zealand, more than 15% of total energy comes from meat. Almost all of this is from domesticated animals.

The general tendency for consumption of cereal foods to decrease, and for that of added fats, alcohol, meat and dairy

Figure 1.1.2 World trends

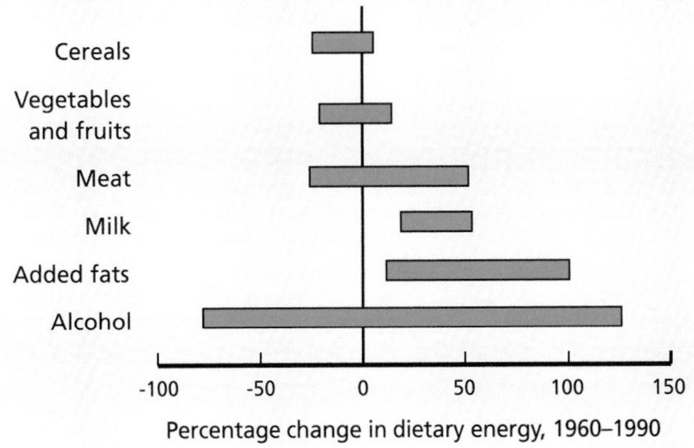

Percentage change in dietary energy, 1960–1990

Changes in the consumption of major food groups worldwide, 1960–1990. The bars indicate the range of the percentage changes in dietary energy. Added fats and milk shows striking increases.

BOX 1.1.1 FOOD BALANCE SHEETS

Food balance sheets are constructed by the FAO from national accounts of the supply and use of foods. Data are calculated from the food produced and imported for countries as a whole, minus food exported, fed to animals, or otherwise not available to humans, divided by the number of people in any country, to obtain average values per person (FAO, 1991).

Food balance sheets thus provide information about average food availability per head rather than about actual food consumption. Food availability information tends to overestimate food consumption in wealthy countries, such as the USA, where substantial amounts of food are wasted and fed to pets. It may also underestimate intake in any country where people grow food or raise animals in their back gardens or smallholdings, or forage or hunt for foods of plant and animal origin.

The highly aggregated nature of food balance sheets also masks variation in food intake between different population subgroups, and makes them insensitive to variations in consumption of specific foods and their relative importance within the diet. Such limitations and criticisms should not be overemphasised. For example, analysis of food balance sheets from China has confirmed that they are relatively accurate in these data and that they closely reflect major time and place trends in food availability for human consumption (Piazza, 1986).

The supply of different foods is expressed in this chapter as a percentage of total dietary energy supply (DES) because the amounts of different foods reported in food balance sheets represent the commodities as produced; there is no correction for the inedible portion or for wastage or losses. However, the nutrient and energy content of foods has been calculated to account for a proportion of edible material and for wastage and loss. This leads to an overestimation in most foods reported, which varies for different items, and so introduces a distortion into the apparent dietary profile. Expressing the data as the percentage contribution of each food group to total available energy attenuates these errors and reduces the distortion. Regional means have been weighted on the basis of the populations of individual countries. In the figures showing trends, changes in food supply in various regions of the world are shown as the percentage change in energy deriving from the specified food group in 1990 compared to the energy derived in 1960.

BOX 1.1.2 FOOD GROUPS

The following food groups have been used to analyse and present the data in this chapter. These have a fairly close resemblance to the groupings used in chapters 5 and 6 of this report.

1 Cereals (grains), that is, rice, wheat, barley, maize (corn), rye, oats, millet, sorghum
2 Roots, tubers and plantains, that is, cassava, sweet potato, potato, yam, plantain, banana
3 Vegetables and fruits, including olives, peanuts, sugar cane, but excluding roots, tubers, plantains, pulses (legumes), nuts and seeds
4 Meat
5 Milk and dairy products
6. Added sugars, including syrups and honey
7 Added fats, including vegetable oils (soybean, sunflower, rape, mustard and palm oils) and animal fats (butter, ghee, cream), but excluding oily foods eaten as such
8 Alcoholic drinks, excluding home-produced alcohol
9 Other, including pulses, nuts and seeds

products to increase, is shown in Figure 1.1.2 to be continuing throughout the world. Data are taken from comparison of FAO food balance sheets for 1961 and 1990 (see Box 1.1.1). On a global basis, the increase in consumption of added fats is striking. Consumption of total fats is increasing in all regions of the world, with the exception of Oceania (data not shown). Only in Africa is the consumption of alcohol not increasing. Consumption of vegetables and fruits shows little change.

AFRICA

Africa may be divided into two major regions: the north, or Saharan region, and the sub-Saharan region. The countries of north Africa are mostly middle-income economies and mainly Islamic. Most of the countries of sub-Saharan Africa are low-income countries, many of which have debt crises. Life expectancy remains low and child malnutrition high in many of these countries. Several still have problems of food security.

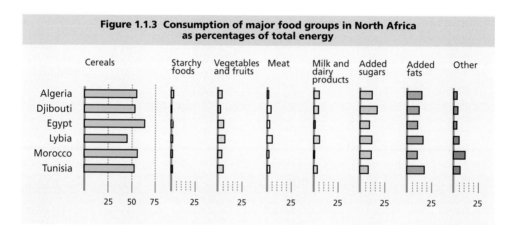

Figure 1.1.3 Consumption of major food groups in North Africa as percentages of total energy

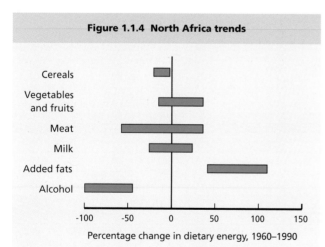

Figure 1.1.4 North Africa trends

Percentage change in dietary energy, 1960–1990

Changes in the consumption of major food groups in north Africa, in the period 1960–1990. This figure shows a small decrease in cereal consumption, a marked decrease in alcohol, and a large increase in added fats.

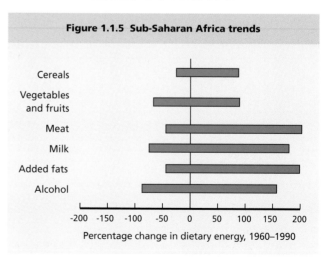

Figure 1.1.5 Sub-Saharan Africa trends

Percentage change in dietary energy, 1960–1990

Changes in the consumption of major food groups in sub-Saharan Africa, in the period 1960–1990. This figure shows large increases in the consumption of added fats, meat and milk.

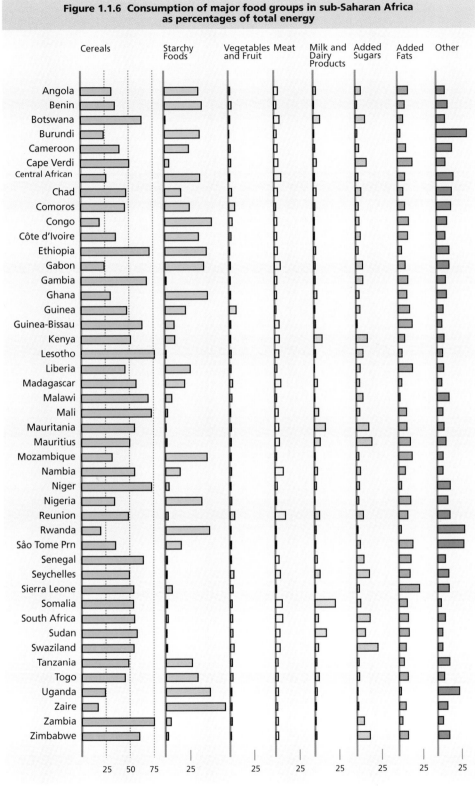

Figure 1.1.6 Consumption of major food groups in sub-Saharan Africa as percentages of total energy

oil. Meat and milk are present only in very small amounts (2–5% DES). The main types of meat are poultry, mutton and beef. The overall fat content of diet is not high and ranges from a high of 30% in Libya to about 16% in Morocco. Most of this is derived from the fats contained in meats, milk and dairy products, and oily food crops. Intakes of saturated fats are below 10% DES in all countries in this region. Vegetables, fruits and starchy roots supply between 3% DES (Djibouti) and 8% DES (Libya). In these Islamic countries little pork is eaten. Alcohol provides at most 0.5% DES in Djibouti and Tunisia.

Most sub-Saharan African diets are dominated by a single staple food, either a cereal or a starchy root. Figure 1.1.6 shows a roughly inverse relationship between the importance of these two foods in the diet. Cereals, such as maize, sorghum and millet, represent 65% of the total cereal production of sub-Saharan Africa.

Most sub-Saharan African diets have a low fat content. Added fats and oils provide only 6–11% DES in most countries and are mostly of vegetable origin. The types of vegetable oils are diverse. The contribution of total dietary fats to DES ranges from a very low minimum of 10% DES in Rwanda to a maximum of just over 30% DES in Somalia. Average meat consumption is low, at around 3% DES. Beef and pork are the most commonly consumed meats. Milk is consumed only in small quantities. Exceptions are countries of the Sudanese and Sahelian zones where nomadic pastoralists represent large sectors of the population.

Vegetables and fruits make a variable contribution to sub-Saharan African diets. In some countries, such as Rwanda

Figure 1.1.3 shows that cereals make the major contribution to DES in North Africa (45–65% DES). In most countries, the dominant type of cereal is wheat. Fats and oils contribute from 10% DES in Egypt and Morocco to 18% DES in Tunisia. These are almost all vegetable oils, notably olive

and Uganda, they contribute around 18% DES. This regional average is almost the highest in the world. In some areas, nuts and pulses are also an important part of the diet. There is a wide variation in alcohol consumption. The African average is low and some countries record almost zero consumption but, in other countries, consumption is high. High intakes are seen in Gabon, Cameroon and Burkina Faso. Home production of beer and other alcoholic drinks is a traditional practice in many areas.

Trends

Time-trend data for 1960–90 shown in Figure 1.1.4 reveal a small decrease in cereal consumption throughout north Africa, and a marked decrease in alcohol consumption, reflecting stricter adherence to Islamic law. Meat consumption has also tended to decrease (except in Egypt and Libya). Consumption of added fats and oils and thus total fat have risen. Intake of vegetables and fruits, and of dairy products, has not changed much. It is uncertain how far back the current sub-Saharan African dietary profiles reach. There is some documentation of the replacement in colonial times of indigenous cereals, such as sorghum and millet, with imported cereal varieties, such as maize, and the introduction of new crops, such as cassava (Bryceson, 1989). Time-trend data for 1960–1990 shown in Figure 1.1.5 reveal large increases in consumption of added fats, meat and milk.

LATIN AMERICA

Most Latin American countries (here including the Caribbean) have middle-income economies. The exceptions are Honduras, Guyana and Haiti, ranked as low-income economies.

This region has three dominant food cultures. In the Indo-Americas, along the mountains from Mexico through Central America to Colombia, Ecuador, Peru and Bolivia, the traditional staple foods are maize, beans and potatoes. In the

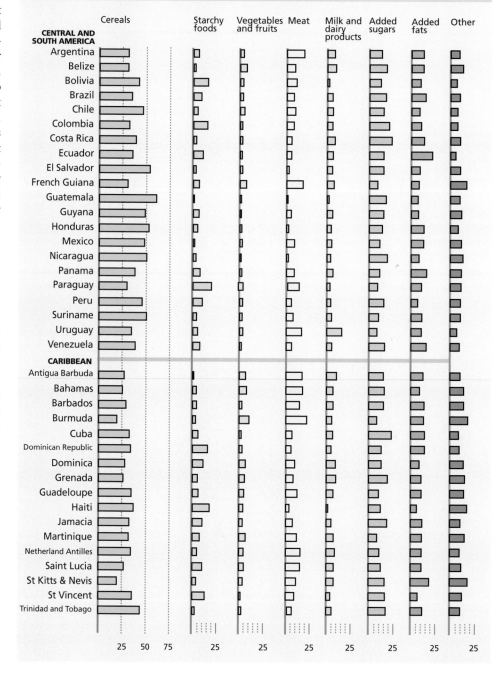

Figure 1.1.7 Consumption of major food groups in Latin America (including the Caribbean) as percentages of total energy

Tropi-Americas of Brazil, Venezuela and the Caribbean, traditional diets contain a large proportion of starchy roots and tubers. In the temperate prairies of South America, diets are high in animal foods but otherwise Mediterranean in nature.

Figure 1.1.7 shows that the diets of most countries in South America and the Caribbean are based on cereals. The proportion of DES ranges from under 20% in Bermuda to 50–60% in Nicaragua, Honduras, El Salvador and Guatemala. Starchy roots are important contributors to DES in some countries, such as Paraguay, Bolivia and Colombia.

There is a vast difference between the tiny amount of meat supplied in Central American countries such as Guatemala, Nicaragua, Honduras and El Salvador (< 3% DES), and the amounts available in the Bermudas, Argentina, Uruguay and Bahamas (18–22% DES). Beef is the main type of meat available in Argentina (14% DES) and Uruguay.

In Central America and in Brazil, Cuba and Paraguay, pulses are a relatively important part of the diet. Milk and dairy products are consumed in moderate amounts, representing on average 5% DES in most countries in the region.

Vegetables and fruits have an important place in the diets of most Caribbean countries where they contribute about 20% DES, with a large contribution from plantains and bananas. In many countries of South America, large quantities of fruits and starchy roots are consumed.

The average fat content of the diets in this region is not high (23–25% DES), but varies widely between countries. Thus Caribbean countries, Uruguay, Ecuador, Argentina, Panama and Mexico all have more than 30% DES from dietary fats, whereas Peru, Guatemala, Nicaragua, Haiti and Guyana have between 16% and 18% DES from fats. The dietary fats derive in almost equal proportions from added fats and oils and from non-separated fats.

Consumption of sugar is high in some countries. The highest consumption is found in Cuba and in Costa Rica (23–24% DES), followed by Colombia, Grenada, Jamaica, Nicaragua and others. In only a few countries is the supply of sweeteners less than 10% DES. Some sugar is used in the production of local alcoholic drinks. Average consumption of alcoholic beverages generally provides less than 3% DES.

Trends

Time-trend data for 1960–90 in Figure 1.1.8 show overall increases in meat, added oils and fats, and milk and dairy products. Meat availability has risen in most South American countries, except where it was already high (Argentina, Uruguay and Paraguay). Meat and milk supplies have decreased in the poorer countries of Central America. As in other economically developing regions, fats and oils have shown a marked increase. There has also been a small decrease in the consumption of vegetables and fruits, roots and tubers. Supply of alcoholic drinks has increased substantially almost everywhere.

ASIA

Asia is divided here into six major regions: Middle East Asia (MEA) includes Turkey, Israel, Syria, Lebanon, Saudi Arabia, Yemen, Iran and Iraq. These are all middle-income economies, except for the Yemen, a low-income country, and Israel, a high-income economy. Low-income Asia (LIA) includes Afghanistan, Bangladesh, Indonesia, Cambodia, Laos, Myanmar, Nepal, Pakistan, Sri Lanka and Vietnam. Middle-income Asia (MIA) includes North Korea, South Korea, Malaysia, the Philippines, Thailand. High-income Asia (HIA) includes Japan, Hong Kong and Singapore. India and China are classified as regions in themselves.

Figure 1.1.9 shows that cereals are the staple food of most Asian countries. Consumption varies inversely with income. The highest levels of consumption are recorded in low-income countries, with an average of 71% DES and a maximum of 84% DES in Bangladesh and Cambodia. In China, the proportion is 69% and in India, 63%. In middle-income countries and the Middle East, cereals provide about 55% DES; in higher-income countries, they provide about 40% DES. Most countries in the Middle East rely predominantly on wheat. Most other Asian countries consume rice almost exclusively. In India and China, however, cereal consumption is divided almost equally between rice and a combination of wheat and millet with some corn. There are large regional differences in both China and India. Cereals are generally supplemented by small quantities of pulses.

Asian diets generally contain few animal foods and only small amounts of vegetables and fruits, except in the Middle East and higher-income countries. The bulk of the Asian population consumes low-fat diets, but a marked increase in fat consumption has occurred in the Middle East, and in the more affluent countries, where diets are more diverse.

Intake of meat and meat products generally varies as a function of income, and is mostly low. Japan consumes about 6% DES as meat, and relies heavily on fish (7% DES).

In China, meat represents about 8% DES. In India, meat

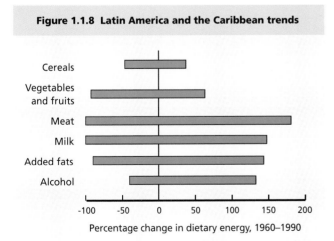

Figure 1.1.8 Latin America and the Caribbean trends

Percentage change in dietary energy, 1960–1990

Changes in the consumption of major food groups in Latin America and the Caribbean, in the period 1960–1990. This figure shows a small decrease in the consumption of vegetables and fruits, and a marked increase in fats.

Figure 1.1.9 Consumption of major food groups in Asia (subdivided into six major regions) as percentages of total energy

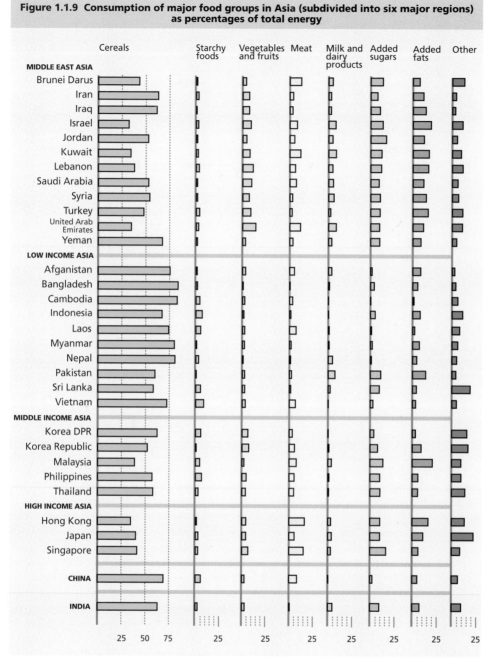

provides less than 1% DES. Low-income countries consume little meat. The average meat consumption in the Middle East is about 4% DES, with maximum values of 11–12% DES in the rich economies of the Arabian peninsula. The amounts of milk and dairy products consumed are generally low.

Consumption of vegetables and fruits also tends to vary as a function of income, ranging from 8% DES in the Middle East, to 5–6% DES in middle- and high-income countries; in the low-income region, this proportion drops to 2% DES.

The amount of total dietary fats is mostly low. High-fat diets, in excess of 30% DES, are consumed in Hong Kong, Israel, Kuwait and Malaysia. In contrast, the diets of Cambodia and Bangladesh (8%), North Korea and Vietnam (11%), Nepal and Laos (12%), Myanmar and the Philippines (14%) contain less than 15% DES from dietary fats.

The consumption of sugar and other sweeteners is moderately high, (except in low-income countries) with several consuming more than 10% DES.

Trends

Time-trend data for 1960–90 in Figure 1.1.10 show the most marked changes in diet in Asian countries. This reflects rapid industrialisation and urbanisation. Most countries show a decrease in cereal consumption, except for low-income countries where average consumption has been more stable. The most affluent countries show an increase in vegetable and fruit consumption. The consumption of milk and dairy products has increased in only a few countries.

Figure 1.1.10 Asia trends

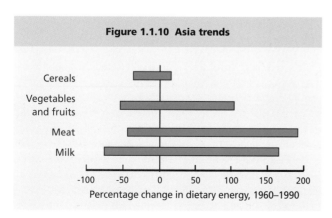

Percentage change in dietary energy, 1960–1990

Changes in the consumption of major food groups in Asia, in the period 1960–1990. Cereal consumption has decreased in most countries; vegetables and fruit consumption has increased in the more affluent countries.

Intake of meat has risen markedly in some countries: Japan (330%), China (342%) and South Korea (256%). In these and other high-income countries, consumption of saturated fatty acids has, consequently, also increased sharply. An increase in the consumption of added fats and oils has occurred in most countries.

OCEANIA

Oceania is a geographically vast region which comprises islands scattered across the Pacific. The countries are mostly middle-income economies. It is very sparsely populated.

Dietary patterns in Oceania are diverse. In some countries, colonialism or tourism has led to adoption of Western diets; in others, traditional diets are still consumed. Figure 1.1.11 shows that starchy foods are the staples in the region. Milk and dairy products are used little. Vegetables and fruits are mostly consumed in modest amounts and, in most countries, bananas are the main fruit eaten. Consumption of added fats, total fats, oils and sugar broadly varies as a function of income. Drinking of alcohol is low but increasing.

Trends

Time-trend data for 1960–90 in Figure 1.1.12 show rapid changes in diets. The current diets in this area are very different from those prevailing in this region three decades ago. Starchy roots are being replaced by cereals. There have also been increases in consumption of fats and oils, meat, milk and dairy products.

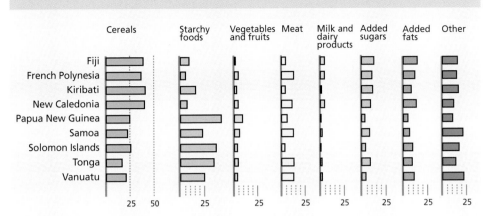

Figure 1.1.11 Consumption of major food groups in Oceania as percentages of total energy

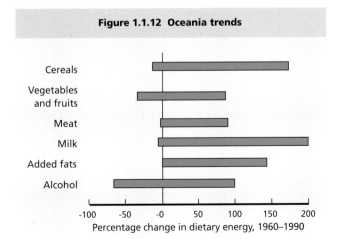

Figure 1.1.12 Oceania trends

Percentage change in dietary energy, 1960–1990

Changes in the consumption of major food groups in Oceania, in the period 1960-1990. Consumption of cereals is increasing as is consumption of meat, milk and added fats.

EUROPE

Europe is a relatively small but densely populated region. It is here divided into three regions: southern, north and central, and eastern.

Southern Europe

Countries of the southern European region, also known as Mediterranean countries (Greece, Italy, France, Portugal, Spain, former Yugoslavia), have for many years had diets identifiable as intermediate between traditional rural and industrial patterns. (Diets in the northern parts of Italy and France have a rather different nature.)

In the early part of this century, the diets of this region were characterised by four principal features. First, they were (and remain) high in vegetables and fruits, tubers and pulses. Second, wheat has long made up a large part of the energy content of these diets. Third, these cereal and pulse-rich diets have enabled settled societies to flourish with generally modest amounts of meat, although the diets of people living near the coast have historically been relatively rich in fish and seafood. The fourth, and unusual, feature of the diets of the Mediterranean region is the use of olive oil.

Figure 1.1.13 shows that cereals – mostly but not exclusively wheat – feature prominently in southern European diets, providing 25% DES. Edible fats and oils contribute 19% DES. Total dietary fats, including the unseparated fats from meats, milk and dairy products, contribute about 40% DES, ranging from 42–44% in Spain and France to 35–37% in Portugal, Malta and Italy.

Meat and meat products contribute on average 15% DES. The highest consumers are the Spanish with 20% DES from meats, mainly pork. The lowest consumers are in Italy and Malta (11–12%). Poultry is eaten only in modest amounts.

Vegetables and fruits are consumed in appreciable quantities in all southern Europe countries: on average, 6% DES. Sweeteners contribute about 9% DES. Alcohol consumption is high and ranges from 8% DES in Portugal to about 3% of DES in Greece.

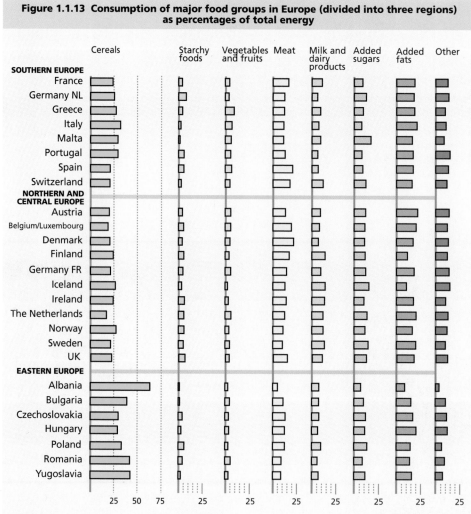

Figure 1.1.13 Consumption of major food groups in Europe (divided into three regions) as percentages of total energy

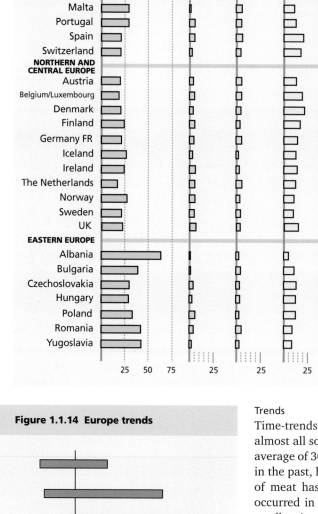

Figure 1.1.14 Europe trends

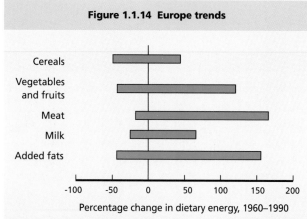

Percentage change in dietary energy, 1960–1990

Changes in the consumption of major food groups in Europe, in the period 1960-1990. See text for detailed changes in different regions of Europe.

Trends

Time-trends for 1960–90 show that cereal consumption, in almost all southern European countries, has declined by an average of 30%. Milk and dairy products, scarcely consumed in the past, have become much more popular. Consumption of meat has increased greatly. The record increases have occurred in Spain (250%) and Greece (about 160%). The smallest increase has been in France (about 20%). The high content of fats of the current southern European diets reflects these important trends of the last 30 years. The changes are most pronounced for those countries that, in the past, had the lowest consumption, such as Italy, Spain and Portugal (60–70%). There has been a small decline in alcohol consumption, the more so in countries that were previously the highest consumers. (Trends for Europe as a whole are shown in Figure 1.1.14.)

Northern and central Europe

Figure 1.1.13 shows that cereals, although still representing the single most important source of food energy, provide, on average, only 22% DES (range 18–28% DES) in the countries of northern and central Europe. This is the lowest contribution currently recorded among all the regions of the world. Wheat is the main cereal eaten, although some oats and rye are also consumed, particularly in Germany, Iceland and Finland.

Consumption of meat and meat products is high (14% DES), but there is a more than a twofold difference between countries: Denmark has the highest consumption of 24% DES, Sweden and Norway barely 10% DES. Intake of milk and dairy products is high: about 10% DES on average. Edible oils and fats provide about 19% DES on average, and represent about half the total dietary fats. These provide on average 39% DES, ranging from a maximum of about 44% DES in Denmark and Benelux, to a minimum of about 35% DES in Iceland and Finland. Saturated fatty acid content is generally high.

Vegetables and fruits are still consumed to a lesser extent than in southern Europe, contributing about 5% DES. Potatoes are important, notably in the UK, Ireland, Norway, Finland and the Netherlands. Generally, few fresh fruits are eaten.

Alcohol consumption is high. The lowest values are recorded in the Nordic countries (6% DES), except for Finland. The highest intakes are in Germany and Austria (8% DES).

Trends

Between 1960 and 1990 there was an increase in meat consumption in most countries. Milk consumption declined, especially in those countries that were major consumers in the early 1960s. The increase in intake of edible fats and total fats was modest (30–70%), compared with southern Europe. Intakes of vegetables and fruits have increased. Consumption of potatoes has declined almost everywhere. There has also been a general increase in alcohol consumption over the years, often in excess of 50%. (Trends for Europe as a whole are shown in Figure 1.1.14.)

Eastern Europe

The countries of eastern Europe – Albania, the former Yugoslavia, Romania, Bulgaria, Poland, the Czech Republic, Slovakia, Hungary, the former East Germany and the countries of the former Soviet Union – have recently undergone dramatic political and economic changes. These changes are very recent and few reliable statistics are available.

Figure 1.1.13 shows that cereals are the main dietary staple, accounting for about 37% DES. Edible fats and oils are next in importance as sources of dietary energy (16% DES), followed by meat and meat products (11% DES). Intake of total dietary fats is relatively low compared with other industrialised countries, ranging from about 20% DES in Albania to 37% in Hungary. The mean for the region is 31% DES. The amount of milk and dairy products (8% DES) is lower than in most other industrial countries.

Vegetables are consumed in small amounts. Potatoes and other starchy roots and pulses have a relatively important position in the diet. Fruits are not consumed in appreciable amounts. Alcoholic beverages (5% DES on average) are consumed in moderate amounts.

Trends

Time-trends for 1960–90 show that cereals and starchy foods have declined markedly throughout the region, and that total fats and animal foods have increased. The increase in the consumption of meats ranged from 30% to over 100%, that of total fats 15–60% and of alcohol 10–80%. More recent data indicate further changes, a consequence of severe political and economic difficulties experienced as these countries adjust to market systems. A decrease in the consumption of animal foods in eastern Europe was apparent in 1990 (Szostak and Sekula, 1991). In Russia, six national surveys have shown that the proportion of energy from fat consumed by adults dropped in a few years from 38% to 33%. (Zohoori et al, 1996). In Russia, there has been a recent steady decline in the percentage of energy from fats. Among elderly people (those aged 60 years and over), fat intake has declined from 36% to 30%. Although the fat intakes of children and non-elderly adults are over 30% DES, there have been steady declines in these groups also. (See Figure 1.1.14.)

NORTH AMERICA

North America includes the United States of America (USA) and Canada. The USA is relatively densely populated and Canada sparsely populated.

Figure 1.1.15 shows that the diets of the USA and Canada are similar in the contributions that the major food groups make to overall diet and in the highly diversified nature of the diets. No single food-group predominates. Cereals, as a group, make the largest single contribution to total DES (about 23%), but this is low in global terms. Wheat is the main type of cereal eaten (17% DES), with small amounts of

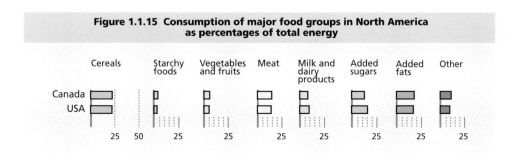

Figure 1.1.15 Consumption of major food groups in North America as percentages of total energy

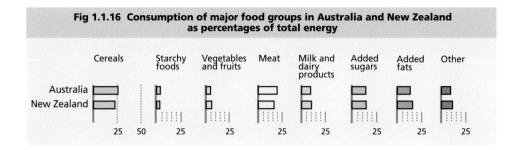

Fig 1.1.16 Consumption of major food groups in Australia and New Zealand as percentages of total energy

maize (3% DES) and rice (2% DES). Cereals are consumed largely as biscuits, crackers, breakfast cereals, cakes and pastries, and represent a major vehicle through which fats, oils and sweeteners find their way into the diet.

Quantitatively, the next most important contributors to DES are edible fats and oils (18% total DES), sweeteners (16% total DES), meat and meat products (14–15% total DES), milk and dairy products (about 10% total DES). Dietary fats provide 37% DES. Vegetables and fruits account for about 6% total DES. Alcohol contributes 5% DES, mainly as beer and wine.

Trends

Time-trends for the period 1960–90 show that intakes of cereals, meats and total fats have remained stable, whereas vegetable and fruit consumption has increased somewhat (10–20%) and that of milk and dairy products has declined (20–30%). The saturated fatty acid content of the diet fell (15–20%) and that of alcohol increased substantially (30%).

AUSTRALIA, NEW ZEALAND

Australia occupies a very large land mass, but is sparsely populated. New Zealand is a small island nation.

Figure 1.1.16 shows a diverse diet. Cereals, almost exclusively wheat, provide a quarter of the total dietary energy. The next important item is meat and meat products, which contribute about 20% DES. Milk and dairy products provide about 10% DES. Total fats provide about 36%, of which most (38%) are represented by hidden fats, a reflection of the high consumption of meat.

The consumption of vegetables and fruits provides about 5% DES. Consumption of sugar (14% DES) and alcoholic beverages (5% DES) is high.

Trends

Time-trends for 1960–90 show a modest decline in meat consumption, but no other remarkable change.

1.2 Patterns of cancer

It is likely that cancer has always been a human disease. Accounts of diseases that were probably cancer are found in early writings. European and North American medical records from the eighteenth to the first half of the twentieth century suggest that the incidence of cancer increased with urbanisation, although some of this apparent increase may have been due to ageing populations and better diagnosis.

Reliable global records began in the second half of the twentieth century with the establishment of cancer registries. Cancer is a major cause of death throughout the world and, in the developed world, is generally exceeded only by cardiovascular disease. An estimated 10 million new cases and over 7 million deaths from cancer occurred in 1996.

The incidence of cancers of some sites is known to change over time, sometimes rapidly. For example, throughout the world, the incidence of stomach cancer has generally declined in recent generations, whereas the incidence of oesophageal and lung cancer has increased. The incidence of cancers of the colon and rectum, breast and prostate increase in parallel with economic development.

As developing countries become urbanised, patterns of cancer, including those cancers that are strongly associated with diet, also tend to shift towards those of economically developed countries. Such changed patterns, which may be marked, are also observed among migrants from one part of the world to another. Changes in patterns of cancer with time, urbanisation and migration provide strong circumstantial evidence that the chief causes of most cancers are environmental, including dietary and lifestyle factors.

HISTORICAL

Evidence of cancer has been found in fossilised animal bones and in mummified human remains. Early medical writings dating back to the period of Ancient Egypt describe diseases that are likely to have been cancers. Hippocrates described diseases that probably were cancers of the stomach, rectum, breast, uterus, skin and other sites. However, the incidence rates of cancer, and the patterns of occurrence of different types of cancer, were unknown until relatively modern times. Nonetheless, some anecdotal accounts are informative.

It has often been said that cancer was rare among gatherer–hunter and pastoral peoples living in remote parts of the world, such as the Himalayas, the Arctic and equatorial Africa, when these were first visited by explorers and missionaries (Williams, 1908; Bulkley, 1927; Schweitzer, 1957). A summary of these early accounts can be found in *Cancer Wars* (Proctor, 1995). Such accounts have been taken to mean that cancer was generally rare in early history. The

African explorer, Dr David Livingstone, suggested that cancer is a 'disease of civilisation' (Maugh, 1979). Practically nothing is known about rates or patterns of cancer until careful records were first kept in Europe in the eighteenth century. These suggest that, historically, cancer might have been a relatively uncommon disease.

The Collection of the Yearly Bills of Mortality for London from 1657 to 1758, for example, listed 2 million deaths, of which around 0.25% were recorded as from cancer (Hoffman, 1915). The register of Market Deeping in Lincolnshire, England, between 1711 and 1723 listed two deaths out of a total of 387 as being from cancer (Newman, 1896). Until modern times, cancer, as we now understand it, was probably often confused with ulcers, benign tumours and other diseases. Further, such figures, no doubt, did not include many cancers of internal organs though those of the breast, for instance, were detectable and well described. Finally, these data describe populations whose life expectancy at birth was much lower than now. (This, of course, does not mean that there were no old people; life expectancy at birth is determined largely by early perinatal and childhood deaths.)

The question of whether cancer, in general, increases as a function of industrialisation has been debated since the beginning of the industrial revolution, and the accompanying development of medicine, public health and population surveys.

The idea that cancer is more common specifically in urban areas was much discussed in the nineteenth century, in the USA, France, Italy, Britain and elsewhere (Le Conte, 1842; Tanchou, 1843; Scotto and Bailar, 1969). The French physician, Stanislaus Tanchou, proposed Tanchou's law – that cancer increases according to the intensity of human civilisation. At the end of the nineteenth century, the American surgeon, Roswell Park, claimed that cancer was the one major disease that was steadily on the increase, citing statistics from England and Wales indicating a fivefold increase in cancer deaths from 1840 to 1896 (Park, 1899). The counter-argument was that the apparent increase in cancer rates accompanying industrial society merely reflected improved diagnosis, notably of cancers of internal organs, and more accurate methods of recording (Dublin, 1937).

A report of the US Census in 1906 recorded a 'steady increase' in cancer death rates, and a 1909 report noted that cancer accounted for 4% of all deaths. In 1915, the statistician, Frederick Hoffman, in his book *Mortality from Cancer Throughout the World* claimed that death from cancer was increasing 'at a more or less alarming rate throughout the entire civilised world', estimating that the global death rate from cancer was in the region of half a million a year. By the 1930s, it was apparent that age-adjusted death rates from cancer were rising in the USA (Roush et al, 1987). Later studies (Clemmeson, 1950; WHO, 1955; Wynder et al, 1959; Higginson, 1960) showed that cancer rates varied enormously throughout the world and that overall incidence was higher among urban populations.

CURRENT

What follows is an overview of current patterns of cancer around the world.

Reliable data on the incidence of cancer depend on accurate and comprehensive recording of cases in defined populations, good quality diagnosis, proper disease classification, and reliable population censuses by sex and age. The information presented here must be treated with some caution: survival rates from cancer are affected by the quality of diagnosis and treatment, so some geographical variation in cancer mortality may be a consequence of the international variability in medical services and some variations in incidence are an artefact of differences in the availability of diagnostic tools. Further, diagnostic practices and disease classification change over time.

WORLD

Global data on cancer incidence are presented in Tables 1.2.1 and 1.2.2. The International Agency for Research on Cancer has estimated that, in 1996, over 10 million new cases of cancer occurred, and over 7 million people died from cancer (WHO, 1997). Globally, among men, the eight most common cancers in order of incidence are now those of the lungs, stomach, colon and rectum, prostate, mouth and pharynx, liver, oesophagus and bladder. In order of mortality, lung and stomach cancer remain first and second, followed by liver, colon and rectum, oesophagus, mouth and pharynx, prostate and then lymphomas. Among women, the eight most common cancers in order of incidence are now: breast, cervix, colon and rectum, stomach, lung, mouth and pharynx, ovary and endometrium. In order of mortality, the order is again different: breast and stomach are followed by lung, colon and rectum, cervix, primary liver cancer, oesophagus, and mouth and pharynx.

For men and women taken together, the 12 most commonly occurring cancers in 1996 were lung, stomach, breast, colon and rectum, mouth and pharynx, liver, cervix, oesophagus, prostate, lymphomas, bladder and leukaemia. The 12 cancers which in 1996 were the most common causes of cancer death worldwide were lung, stomach, liver, colon and rectum, oesophagus, breast, mouth and pharynx, cervix, prostate, bladder, ovary and endometrium. All of these cancers are believed to be related to diet, including lung cancer where, of course, cigarette smoking is established as the

---

BOX 1.2.1 AGE STANDARDISATION OF CANCER RATES

Cancer rates change and generally increase with age. The overall rate of a particular cancer in a given population is thus influenced by the age distribution of the population. For example, if two populations actually have the same risk of breast cancer at each age, but one population is older than the other (a greater proportion of the women are in the older age groups), then the crude rate of breast cancer in the older population will be higher.

To compensate for this influence of the age distribution of the population on overall cancer rates when two or more populations are being compared, age-standardised (also called age-adjusted) rates are used. These compute rates for different populations as though they all had the identical age distribution. When this is done, differences in rates cannot be attributed to an effect of different age structures in the populations being compared. Here, all incidence and mortality rates have been standardised to the 'World Standard Population' (Parkin et al, 1992).

Age group	Number	Age group	Number
<1	2,400	45–49	6,000
1–4	9,600	50–54	5,000
5–9	10,000	55–59	4,000
10–14	9,000	60–64	4,000
15–19	9,000	65–69	3,000
20–24	8,000	70–74	2,000
25–29	8,000	75–79	1,000
30–34	6,000	80–84	500
35–39	6,000	85+	500
40–44	6,000	**All**	**100,000**

TABLE 1.2.1 ESTIMATED NUMBERS OF NEW CASES AND DEATHS FROM CANCER WORLDWIDE 1996 – MEN				
CANCER SITE	NEW CASES (THOUSANDS)	PER CENT OF TOTAL	DEATHS (THOUSANDS)	PER CENT OF TOTAL
Lung	988	18.6	878	22.4
Stomach	634	11.9	518	13.2
Colon, rectum	445	8.4	257	6.6
Prostate	400	7.5	204	5.2
Mouth and pharynx	384	7.2	237	6.1
Liver	374	7.1	370	9.4
Oesophagus	320	6.1	305	7.8
Bladder	236	4.4	107	2.7
Other	1,531	28.8	1,043	26.6
Total	**5,312**	**100.0**	**3,919**	**100.0**

Source: WHO, 1997

TABLE 1.2.2 ESTIMATED NUMBERS OF NEW CASES AND DEATHS FROM CANCER WORLDWIDE 1996 – WOMEN				
CANCER SITE	NEW CASES (THOUSANDS)	PER CENT OF TOTAL	DEATHS (THOUSANDS)	PER CENT OF TOTAL
Breast	910	18.2	390	12.2
Cervix	524	10.5	241	7.6
Colon, rectum	431	8.6	253	7.9
Stomac	379	7.6	317	9.9
Lung	333	6.7	282	8.8
Mouth and pharynx	192	3.8	129	4.1
Ovary	191	3.8	125	3.9
Endometrium	172	3.4	68	2.1
Other	1,874	37.4	1,387	43.5
Total	**5,006**	**100.0**	**3,192**	**100.0**

Source: WHO, 1997

major risk factor (NAS, 1989; WHO, 1997).

The predominant cancers in the economically developing world contrast with those of the economically developed world. Lung cancer is now the most common cancer in both. Countries in Africa, Latin America and Asia have, in common, relatively high rates of cancers of the upper aerodigestive tract, stomach, liver and cervix, whereas countries in Europe, North America and Australasia have, in common, relatively high rates of cancers of the colon and rectum, breast, prostate and endometrium.

AFRICA

Five regions of Africa are identified in Figure 1.2.1: north, or Saharan; and, of the sub-Saharan countries, south, east, west and middle. Rates of oesophageal cancer are much higher in southern Africa than elsewhere on the continent. The rates of lung cancer in both southern and northern Africa are also higher than elsewhere. Rates of stomach cancer are lower in north and western Africa. Rates of female breast cancer are much higher in north Africa, but rates of prostate

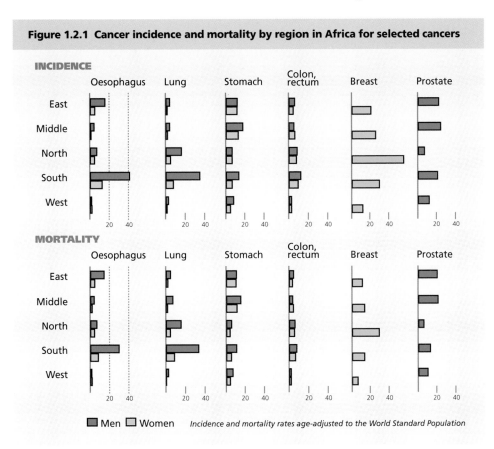

Figure 1.2.1 Cancer incidence and mortality by region in Africa for selected cancers

■ Men ☐ Women   *Incidence and mortality rates age-adjusted to the World Standard Population*

cancer are much lower.

Rates of cancers of the colon and rectum, breast and prostate are low throughout Africa compared with western Europe and North America, but people with these cancers are more likely to die than in western Europe and North America. Intercountry comparisons of cancer incidence in Africa are limited because of the lack of established cancer registries.

LATIN AMERICA

Regional incidence and mortality rates for cancer in Latin America are shown in Figure 1.2.2. Compared with Central America, South America shows higher rates of oesophageal, stomach, colorectal, lung (men) and breast cancer, but similar rates of lung (women) and prostate cancer. Incidence rates for cancers of the oesophagus and stomach in South America are higher than those among the white populations of North America, but rates of colorectal, lung, breast and prostate cancers are lower.

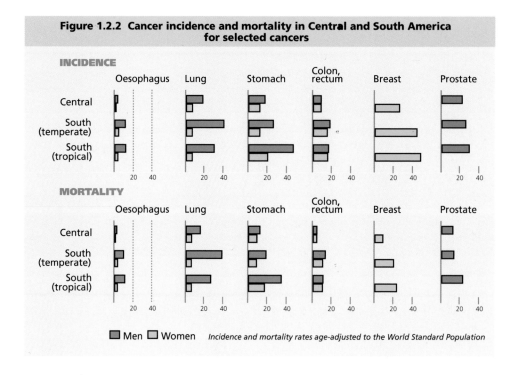

Figure 1.2.2 Cancer incidence and mortality in Central and South America for selected cancers

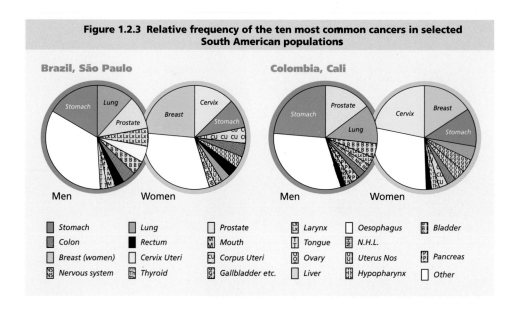

Figure 1.2.3 Relative frequency of the ten most common cancers in selected South American populations

TABLE 1.2.3 CANCER INCIDENCE IN SELECTED REGISTRIES IN THE CARIBBEAN, CENTRAL AND SOUTH AMERICA, 1983–1987

COUNTRY	REGION OR POPULATION	OESOPHAGUS		LUNG		STOMACH		COLON/RECTUM		BREAST	PROSTATE
		MEN	WOMEN	MEN	WOMEN	MEN	WOMEN	MEN	WOMEN	WOMEN	MEN
Martinique	All	13.7	2.5	11.0	3.0	24.9	10.6	9.2	8.8	28.2	48.2
Cuba	All	5.2	1.7	44.3	15.7	9.8	5.0	13.7	14.6	35.0	27.3
Costa Rica	All	3.8	1.2	12.7	4.7	46.9	21.3	9.1	9.6	26.7	23.7
Colombia	Cali	3.6	1.6	24.6	9.8	36.3	19.9	8.0	9.2	34.8	26.1
Brazil	Goiania	9.8	2.6	26.0	11.6	28.2	14.9	13.4	12.7	40.5	29.0
Ecuador	Quito	4.4	0.5	8.3	3.9	29.5	22.7	8.7	8.4	26.2	23.0
Paraguay	Asuncion	11.2	1.7	18.2	3.6	14.4	5.8	7.3	10.6	36.3	22.0
Peru	Trujillo	1.0	0.6	9.5	4.2	28.9	26.4	6.0	9.0	28.3	19.9

Incidence and mortality rates in the tables and figures in this chapter are rates per 100,000, adjusted to the World Standard Population

TABLE 1.2.4 CANCER MORTALITY IN CENTRAL AND SOUTH AMERICA, 1983–1987

COUNTRY	OESOPHAGUS		LUNG		STOMACH		COLON[a]		BREAST	PROSTATE
	MEN	WOMEN	MEN	WOMEN	MEN	WOMEN	MEN	WOMEN	WOMEN	MEN
Mexico	1.9	0.8	14.9	5.8	9.8	7.8	2.2	2.3	7.1	8.9
Costa Rica	4.1	1.6	15.7	5.9	46.0	22.5	4.3	4.2	12.3	14.4
Chile	8.3	3.7	21.8	5.9	35.3	14.7	4.2	4.6	12.7	12.4

[a] Does not include rectum

For the six cancer sites in the figure, the incidence rates do not differ remarkably between the temperate and tropical regions of South America, except for stomach cancer which occurs at a higher rate in the tropical zones, and lung cancer in men which is reported more in the temperate zones.

Differences in the incidence of the six cancer sites among various registries of Latin America are shown in Table 1.2.3. Rates of colorectal and breast cancer are low. Stomach cancer shows great variability, with a fourfold difference between Cuba and Costa Rica.

Cancer mortality rates for Mexico, Costa Rica and Chile are compared in Table 1.2.4. Except for lung cancer, the rates in Mexico are noticeably lower. This may reflect substantial under-reporting of cancer on death certificates in Mexico.

The relative frequency of the ten most common cancers in the registries of São Paulo in Brazil and Cali in Colombia are shown in Figure 1.2.3. Among men, lung cancer shows a similar proportion of cancers in both populations, but stomach and prostate cancers contribute more to male cancer in Cali than São Paulo. Among women, cervical cancer accounts for 22% of all cancers in Cali, but only 13% in São Paulo, where breast cancer accounts for 24% of all cancers in women.

ASIA

Asia is divided rather differently in Figure 1.2.4 compared with chapter 1.1. Here the division is into eastern (itself divided into three groups: China, Japan and other), south-eastern, southern and western. Rates of oesophageal cancer are much higher in China than elsewhere. Rates of stomach cancer are much higher in eastern Asia and are especially high in Japan. Rates of colorectal cancer are low throughout Asia compared with North America and western Europe: the rates in Japan, the highest in Asia, are similar to those in eastern Europe. Rates of lung cancer among men are

TABLE 1.2.5 CANCER INCIDENCE IN SELECTED REGISTRIES IN ASIA, 1983–1987

COUNTRY	REGION OR POPULATION	OESOPHAGUS		LUNG		STOMACH		COLON/RECTUM		BREAST	PROSTATE
		MEN	WOMEN	MEN	WOMEN	MEN	WOMEN	MEN	WOMEN	WOMEN	MEN
Japan	Osaka	8.4	1.8	41.5	11.7	73.6	32.7	26.5	16.4	21.9	6.6
China	Shanghai	14.9	6.4	53.0	18.1	51.7	21.9	17.8	15.6	21.2	1.7
Hong Kong	All	18.1	3.6	78.7	32.6	22.1	11.2	35.5	26.0	32.3	7.6
Singapore	Chinese	10.9	2.7	69.7	21.9	34.7	15.6	35.4	28.6	31.6	7.6
	Malay	1.2	0.9	34.0	12.1	6.4	5.4	15.1	12.1	23.2	11.0
	Indian	3.2	3.4	20.7	5.2	15.9	7.5	15.8	16.9	34.0	11.0
Thailand	Chiang Mai	4.1	2.7	40.5	29.5	11.6	6.0	9.9	7.7	13.7	4.0
Philippines	Manila	3.1	2.3	53.4	16.3	13.5	8.1	18.7	15.0	49.7	16.9
India	Bombay	11.4	8.4	14.0	3.0	7.3	4.3	6.4	5.1	24.6	6.9
	Madras	7.6	6.3	8.5	1.4	15.1	6.7	3.9	3.4	19.9	2.1
Israel	All Jews	1.4	1.1	28.3	9.6	14.6	7.5	35.9	30.5	64.7	17.5
Kuwait	Kuwaitis	3.7	1.7	14.5	4.8	4.1	2.0	4.3	4.5	17.2	4.4
	Non-Kuwaitis	1.9	1.9	44.9	12.7	14.4	5.9	7.3	9.3	35.6	10.5

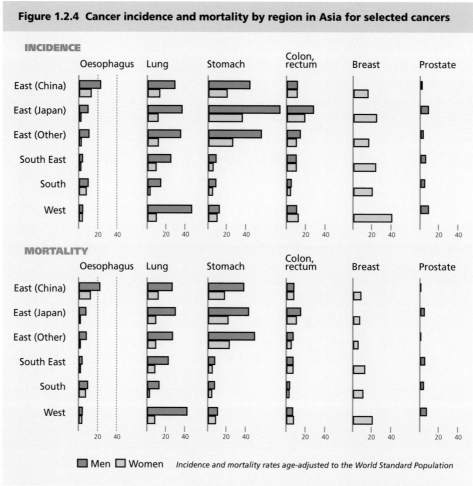

Figure 1.2.4 Cancer incidence and mortality by region in Asia for selected cancers

INCIDENCE

MORTALITY

■ Men □ Women   *Incidence and mortality rates age-adjusted to the World Standard Population*

TABLE 1.2.6 CANCER MORTALITY IN ASIA, 1983–1987

COUNTRY	OESOPHAGUS		LUNG		STOMACH		COLON[a]		BREAST	PROSTATE
	MEN	WOMEN	MEN	WOMEN	MEN	WOMEN	MEN	WOMEN	WOMEN	MEN
Japan	6.9	1.1	27.7	7.7	40.8	19.0	7.8	5.9	5.8	3.3
Hong Kong	11.2	2.0	55.9	23.9	11.5	6.5	9.4	6.9	8.7	2.7
Singapore	8.8	2.5	55.3	18.9	24.0	11.3	11.2	10.9	13.2	4.2
Israel	1.6	0.9	23.8	7.8	9.9	5.0	11.5	9.7	23.5	8.4

[a] Does not include rectum

lower than in North America and western Europe; the rates in southern Asia are especially low, even for the region. Rates of breast and prostate cancer in Asia are generally low by comparison with Western populations.

A remarkable range of incidence for each of six common cancers is seen in Asia (Table 1.2.5). For example, stomach cancer rates among men are very low in India (Bombay) and Kuwait (Kuwaitis), but ten times higher among men in Japan (Osaka). Similarly, the incidence of breast cancer is very low in Thailand (Chiang Mai), Kuwait (Kuwaitis) and India (Madras), but over three times higher among urban Philippine women and Jewish women in Israel, respectively.

Cancer mortality rates for Japan, Hong Kong, Singapore and Israel, four high-income countries in Asia, are shown in Table 1.2.6. For these populations, the incidence/mortality ratios are generally comparable to those in the USA and western Europe.

The relative frequencies of the ten most common cancers in two Asian populations (Bombay in India and Osaka Prefecture in Japan) are shown in Figure 1.2.5. The distributions in the figure are notably different. In Osaka, stomach cancer accounts for nearly one-third of all male cancers, followed by lung, liver and cancers of the colon and rectum in that order. In Bombay, cancers of the mouth and pharynx account for 18% of all male cancers, followed by cancers of

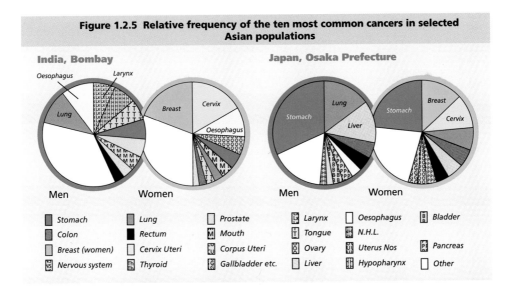

Figure 1.2.5 Relative frequency of the ten most common cancers in selected Asian populations

India, Bombay

Japan, Osaka Prefecture

Legend:
- Stomach
- Colon
- Breast (women)
- Nervous system
- Lung
- Rectum
- Cervix Uteri
- Thyroid
- Prostate
- Mouth
- Corpus Uteri
- Gallbladder etc.
- Larynx
- Tongue
- Ovary
- Liver
- Oesophagus
- N.H.L.
- Uterus Nos
- Hypopharynx
- Bladder
- Pancreas
- Other

the lung, oesophagus and larynx. Among women, stomach, colorectal and lung cancers contribute more to total cancer incidence in Japan than in India, where cervical and oesophageal cancers are proportionally more significant; breast cancer is prominent in both populations.

OCEANIA

Cancer incidence and mortality in Oceania is considered in two groupings: Melanesian populations and Micronesian/Polynesian populations (Figure 1.2.6). Except for lung and prostate cancers, for which the incidence and mortality rates are much higher among the Micronesians/Polynesians than the Melanesians, the rates in the two groups are not remarkably different.

The less favourable incidence-to-mortality ratios for colorectal, breast and prostate cancers compared with North America no doubt reflect under-reporting of incident cases, later diagnosis of cases and limited facilities for treatment.

Some comparative data among Melanesian and Polynesian populations are shown in Table 1.2.7 (Taylor et al, 1985). With few exceptions, Polynesian rates are much higher than those of Melanesians. The rates for a particular ethnic group across countries are similar; higher rates for Polynesians in New Zealand and Hawaii compared with the Cook Islands/Niue are, in part, an artefact of less complete case ascertainment in Niue.

TABLE 1.2.7 CANCER INCIDENCE IN SELECTED REGISTRIES IN OCEANIA, 1983–1987

COUNTRY	REGION OR POPULATION	OESOPHAGUS MEN	OESOPHAGUS WOMEN	LUNG MEN	LUNG WOMEN	STOMACH MEN	STOMACH WOMEN	COLON/RECTUM MEN	COLON/RECTUM WOMEN	BREAST WOMEN	PROSTATE MEN
Fiji	Melanesian	1.8	–	5.5	1.4	7.7	2.0	7.3	5.1	20.1	5.0
New Caledonia	Melanesian	12.5	–	34.3	14.2	15.6	6.8	7.9	2.3	16.6	3.7
Cook Islands/ Niue	Polynesian	10.6	–	71.1	4.7	24.0	14.6	15.9	9.7	45.3	15.9
New Zealand	Polynesian	6.1	0.7	110.4	80.7	33.7	20.3	23.1	18.9	61.4	36.5
Hawaii	Polynesian	11.2	1.3	94.6	28.6	40.2	17.8	42.1	19.3	95.0	40.8

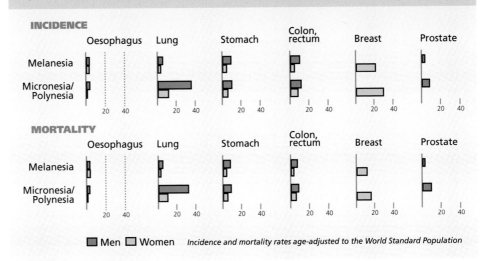

Figure 1.2.6 Cancer incidence and mortality by region in Oceania for selected cancers

INCIDENCE

MORTALITY

Men Women Incidence and mortality rates age-adjusted to the World Standard Population

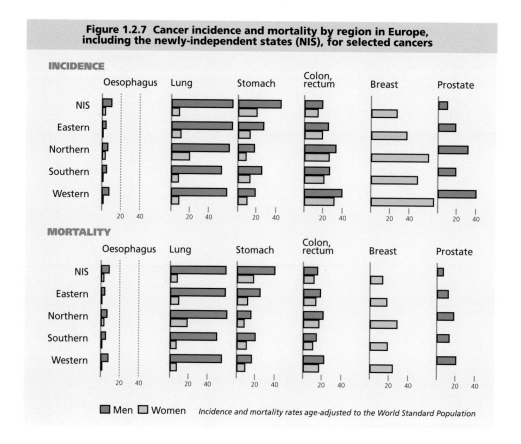

Figure 1.2.7 Cancer incidence and mortality by region in Europe, including the newly-independent states (NIS), for selected cancers

Men ☐ Women   *Incidence and mortality rates age-adjusted to the World Standard Population*

EUROPE

Incidence and mortality rates for Europe are compared in Figure 1.2.7. These show Europe divided into southern, western, northern and eastern countries, and countries of the former Soviet Union.

The incidence of lung cancer is high throughout the region, with the male rates uniformly much higher than the corresponding female rates. By comparison with North America, incidence rates for stomach cancer in Europe are relatively high, notably in southern and eastern Europe, and highest of all in the former USSR. The pattern for colorectal cancer is the reverse: the incidence among men is high in western Europe, but much lower in eastern Europe and the former USSR. Similarly, the incidence of breast cancer is high in western Europe but lower in eastern Europe and the former Soviet Union. Generally, rates for colorectal, lung (especially in women), breast and prostate cancers are somewhat lower than in North America.

Mortality rates generally parallel the corresponding incidence rates. Because many cancer patients survive their illness, mortality rates are necessarily lower than the corresponding incidence rates (the exceptions in the table for oesophageal cancer in men are no doubt a statistical anomaly – but also reflect the very high case-fatality rate in this cancer). The discrepancies between incidence and mortality rates are greater for breast, prostate and colorectal cancers, which have better survival rates than oesophageal, stomach and lung cancers.

Incidence rates in several European countries are shown in Table 1.2.8 (Parkin et al, 1992). As would be expected, the range of rates across countries is wider than that for the broader regions. There tends to be a high degree of homogeneity among the countries within a particular region of Europe. More impressive, however, is the range in rates that is reported within single countries that have more than one cancer registry (only one registry per country is shown in the table). For example, breast cancer rates within Italy vary twofold between the Latina region in the south of Italy (low) and Varese in the north (high). For stomach cancer, the intracountry range in Italy is more than twofold among men.

Similar comparisons for cancer mortality by country in Europe are shown in Table 1.2.9. Mortality tends to follow the incidence patterns. Incidence-to-mortality ratios vary by country in many instances. For example, the breast cancer incidence to mortality ratio in the Netherlands is 2.6, whereas in Hungary it is 1.4. A higher incidence-to-mortality ratio for a particular cancer reflects a higher rate of screening, a higher proportion of patients diagnosed at earlier stages of the disease and better access to high-quality treatment.

The comparative importance of specific cancers in different countries of Europe is illustrated in Figure 1.2.8 which shows the relative frequency of the ten most common

TABLE 1.2.8 CANCER INCIDENCE IN SELECTED REGISTRIES OF EUROPE AND THE NEWLY-INDEPENDENT STATES

COUNTRY	REGION OR POPULATION	OESOPHAGUS		LUNG		STOMACH		COLON/RECTUM		BREAST	PROSTATE
		MEN	WOMEN	MEN	WOMEN	MEN	WOMEN	MEN	WOMEN	WOMEN	MEN
UK	Birmingham	5.5	3.6	75.0	18.8	22.3	8.7	38.0	25.4	63.4	25.0
France	Somme	19.3	1.0	64.6	3.9	14.5	6.5	35.6	21.9	55.4	28.6
Netherlands	Maastricht	3.7	0.9	83.4	9.1	16.6	6.3	36.0	27.4	68.1	29.6
Germany	Saarland	6.1	0.8	69.6	7.3	20.4	11.5	40.5	29.4	56.3	28.9
Switzerland	Vaud	8.0	2.4	58.2	9.8	11.5	4.4	32.2	23.1	70.8	34.2
Italy	Florence	3.1	0.8	64.2	8.9	40.2	19.1	38.7	27.8	65.4	22.0
Spain	Zaragoza	4.6	0.4	42.2	3.6	20.9	9.4	20.3	14.2	39.5	17.6
Norway	All	2.6	0.8	33.9	9.7	15.7	8.0	35.6	28.2	54.8	43.8
Sweden	All	3.2	0.9	25.2	9.5	12.7	6.5	29.4	24.2	62.5	50.2
Denmark	All	3.9	1.3	58.5	23.1	12.5	5.7	37.6	30.1	68.6	29.9
Iceland	All	4.0	2.2	35.4	25.9	28.8	9.9	27.7	20.9	69.7	52.4
Finland	All	3.3	2.2	65.8	7.6	20.3	11.2	22.1	17.3	52.5	36.1
Poland	Warsaw	5.2	0.9	65.2	16.4	21.5	8.6	21.2	16.1	38.7	11.9
Slovakia	All	5.6	0.5	79.1	7.8	27.1	12.2	34.2	20.5	34.5	19.9
Hungary	Szabolcs	5.7	0.5	69.6	9.1	26.4	9.3	20.8	16.6	29.6	14.3
Romania	Cty Cluj	1.9	0.4	36.9	6.1	26.1	10.7	15.0	10.4	31.1	9.9
Belarus	All	4.4	0.5	55.6	5.3	46.7	20.1	17.9	13.3	24.7	9.0
Latvia	All	4.3	0.6	63.2	7.3	34.1	15.5	19.4	14.7	32.1	15.3
Estonia	All	5.0	0.7	67.0	7.7	37.0	18.6	23.7	18.3	33.9	18.8
Russia	St Petersburg	11.1	3.7	77.6	9.1	52.8	25.3	34.2	25.9	40.6	13.9

TABLE 1.2.9 CANCER MORTALITY RATES IN EUROPE, 1983–1987

COUNTRY	OESOPHAGUS		LUNG		STOMACH		COLON[a]		BREAST	PROSTATE
	MEN	WOMEN	MEN	WOMEN	MEN	WOMEN	MEN	WOMEN	WOMEN	MEN
England and Wales	6.7	3.0	64.2	19.3	14.8	6.0	12.5	10.4	29.2	14.8
Scotland	8.9	4.0	78.5	26.3	14.3	7.3	13.4	11.2	27.8	13.0
N Ireland	5.6	2.9	56.4	15.4	14.8	6.3	15.6	12.5	26.2	13.7
Ireland	6.4	3.7	50.3	17.6	14.1	7.0	15.7	13.4	26.1	15.4
France	12.4	1.0	44.9	4.4	10.6	4.3	12.4	8.0	19.3	16.5
Belgium	4.6	1.0	79.0	6.8	13.5	6.5	13.3	11.1	26.3	17.4
Netherlands	4.2	1.4	76.3	8.2	15.0	6.1	13.8	11.4	26.4	17.0
Germany[b]	4.7	0.8	49.0	7.0	17.0	8.9	14.2	11.7	22.5	16.3
Austria	3.7	0.5	47.6	8.4	20.5	9.9	13.4	10.0	21.9	15.6
Switzerland	5.8	1.0	48.3	6.5	11.5	5.3	12.7	8.6	25.2	21.7
Italy	4.7	0.8	57.9	6.9	20.4	9.5	9.8	6.9	20.4	11.6
Greece	1.8	0.5	48.0	6.4	10.5	5.4	4.9	4.5	15.2	7.9
Spain	5.4	0.7	39.3	3.6	16.2	7.7	7.1	5.4	15.0	12.7
Portugal	5.8	1.4	23.5	3.8	25.8	12.7	8.5	6.5	16.3	12.5
Norway	2.4	0.6	29.5	8.1	12.1	6.3	11.0	9.7	18.1	20.8
Sweden	2.9	0.8	24.2	8.6	10.1	5.3	10.0	8.0	18.0	18.9
Denmark	4.5	1.3	54.8	20.7	9.9	5.0	14.2	12.4	27.4	17.8
Finland	2.9	1.9	56.8	6.2	16.0	8.9	7.0	5.9	16.4	16.9
Poland	4.9	0.9	64.7	8.2	26.0	9.8	5.7	4.6	15.1	9.2
Czechoslovakia[c]	3.7	0.5	73.3	7.8	21.5	10.1	14.0	9.1	19.9	12.8
Hungary	5.7	0.6	69.2	12.0	25.9	11.3	14.1	10.9	21.4	15.6
Yugoslavia	3.9	0.8	44.0	7.2	18.5	8.7	5.4	4.2	14.1	8.3

[a] Does not include rectum
[b] Former Federal Republic (W Germany)
[c] Separate data for the Czech Republic and Slovakia not available

cancers in two areas of Europe (Warsaw in Poland, and Birmingham in the UK) (Whelan et al, 1990). Among men, stomach and laryngeal cancers comprise a greater proportion of total cancer incidence in Poland than in England, whereas lung, prostate, and colorectal cancers contribute a larger share of the cancer burden in England. Among women, cervical and gallbladder cancers account for a larger proportion of the total in Poland, whereas breast and colon are larger contributors to total cancer incidence in England.

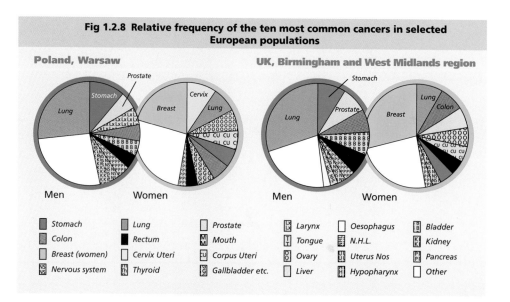

Fig 1.2.8 Relative frequency of the ten most common cancers in selected European populations

Poland, Warsaw — Men, Women

UK, Birmingham and West Midlands region — Men, Women

Legend:
- Stomach
- Colon
- Breast (women)
- Nervous system
- Lung
- Rectum
- Cervix Uteri
- Thyroid
- Prostate
- Mouth
- Corpus Uteri
- Gallbladder etc.
- Larynx
- Tongue
- Ovary
- Liver
- Oesophagus
- N.H.L.
- Uterus Nos
- Hypopharynx
- Bladder
- Kidney
- Pancreas
- Other

NORTH AMERICA

Cancer incidence and mortality rates among the white populations of the USA and Canada are generally comparable. Overall, the rates of colorectal, lung, breast and prostate cancers are higher for North America than western Europe, whereas the rates of stomach cancer are lower (Figure 1.2.9).

Relatively slight differences in cancer incidence are seen within either the USA or Canada when comparisons are limited to a single ethnic group, although a few exceptions can be found; for example, Newfoundland has stomach cancer rates in men twice those of the other provinces of Canada, all of which have similarly low rates (Parkin et al, 1992). When comparisons are made across ethnic groups, however, substantial differences can be seen. Table 1.2.10 compares incidence among six different ethnic groups in the USA. The incidence of oesophageal cancer is much higher in African-Americans, and the incidence of stomach cancer is much higher in Japanese and Koreans, compared with the other ethnic groups. Rates of colorectal cancer are low in Filipinos and especially low in Koreans. Lung cancer rates are remarkably high in African-Americans, lower in whites and much lower among Asians. Breast and prostate cancer rates are especially low in Koreans, but the rates of prostate cancer in all Asian groups are low in comparison with the rates in whites and blacks.

Figure 1.2.9 Cancer incidence and mortality in North America for selected cancers

INCIDENCE

North America — Oesophagus, Lung, Stomach, Colon/rectum, Breast, Prostate (scales 20, 40)

MORTALITY

North America — Oesophagus, Lung, Stomach, Colon/rectum, Breast, Prostate (scales 20, 40)

■ Men □ Women   *Incidence and mortality rates age-adjusted to the World Standard Population*

TABLE 1.2.10 CANCER INCIDENCE IN SELECTED REGISTRIES OF NORTH AMERICA, 1983–1987

COUNTRY	REGION OR POPULATION	OESOPHAGUS MEN	OESOPHAGUS WOMEN	LUNG MEN	LUNG WOMEN	STOMACH MEN	STOMACH WOMEN	COLON/RECTUM MEN	COLON/RECTUM WOMEN	BREAST WOMEN	PROSTATE MEN
Canada	All	4.2	1.3	68.5	23.9	12.4	5.4	44.4	33.7	71.1	51.4
USA	SEER[a]										
	White	4.0	1.3	64.3	29.9	8.0	3.5	46.5	33.2	89.2	61.8
	Black	13.9	3.6	90.0	28.1	12.4	5.6	38.6	32.3	65.0	82.0
USA	Los Angeles										
	Japanese	5.7	0.1	34.9	17.5	29.7	13.8	54.5	39.5	72.7	32.9
	Chinese	2.9	0.8	42.6	18.2	13.0	7.9	36.0	23.5	48.7	19.8
	Filipino	0.6	0.7	30.8	10.8	4.0	3.7	22.9	15.6	52.2	28.6
	Korean	2.8	0.5	38.3	12.4	41.5	22.9	12.3	12.4	16.9	8.9

[a] Surveillance, Epidemiology and End Results Program, consisting of a 10–12% sample of the population from 10 regions of the USA

TABLE 1.2.11 CANCER MORTALITY RATES IN NORTH AMERICA, 1983–1987

COUNTRY	OESOPHAGUS		LUNG		STOMACH		COLONa		BREAST	PROSTATE
	MEN	WOMEN	MEN	WOMEN	MEN	WOMEN	MEN	WOMEN	WOMEN	MEN
Canada	4.2	1.1	55.8	17.7	8.7	3.9	13.3	10.6	23.9	15.7
United States – whites	3.7	0.9	55.3	21.5	5.0	2.2	15.1	10.8	22.4	14.2
United States – non-whites	10.7	2.8	68.8	19.3	9.8	4.5	15.4	12.4	21.8	26.5

a Does not include rectum

Figure 1.2.10 Relative frequency of the ten most common cancers in selected North American populations

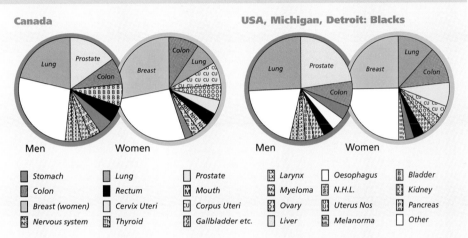

The incidence rates for Canada (all ethnic groups combined, but consisting primarily of whites) are generally similar to those for white Americans. The mortality rates for all white Canadians and Americans are also very similar (Table 1.2.11). Incidence-to-mortality ratios generally are more favourable for whites than blacks – reflecting more screening, earlier diagnosis and better access to treatment facilities.

The relative frequency of the ten most common cancers for two population groups in North America is shown in Figure 1.2.10. For the black population of Detroit, the proportion of all cancers contributed by lung, prostate, colon (women) and cervix is greater than in the population of Canada. In contrast, cancer of the bladder and uterus, non-Hodgkin lymphoma and melanoma contribute proportionately more to the total incidence in Canada.

AUSTRALIA, NEW ZEALAND

Cancer incidence and mortality rates for Australia and New Zealand are shown in Figure 1.2.11. These rates are comparable to those in North America, although the rates of lung, breast and prostate cancer are somewhat lower in Australia. The incidence-to-mortality ratios for breast and prostate can-

cers are noticeably less favourable (2.7 and 2.4, respectively) than North America (6.8 and 3.8, respectively). This may reflect a higher rate of cases detected by screening rather than substantially different diagnosis or treatment.

There is little difference in the rates among the different states within Australia, or between the white populations of Australia and New Zealand for the six cancer sites in Table 1.2.12. However, whereas the incidence rates of breast, prostate and oesophageal cancers are quite comparable between New Zealand Maoris (Polynesian population) and non-Maori people, stomach and lung cancer incidence is much higher and colorectal cancer is much lower among the Maoris of both sexes. It is notable that rates of female breast cancer are high among both Maori and non-Maori people in New Zealand. As seen in Table 1.2.13, mortality rates for all of these cancers are very similar in Australia and New Zealand.

The relative frequency of the ten most common cancers in South Australia (Australian state) and the non-Maori population of New Zealand is shown in Figure 1.2.12; the patterns do not differ substantially, except that bladder cancer is a more important cancer among Australian than New Zealand men.

Figure 1.2.11 Cancer incidence and mortality in Australasia for selected cancers

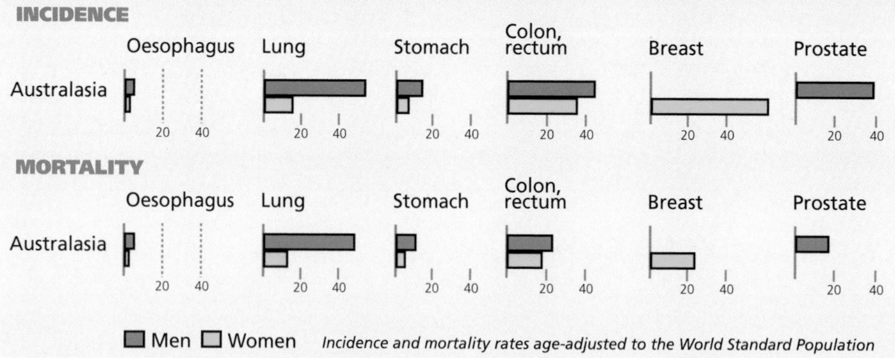

INCIDENCE

Oesophagus   Lung   Stomach   Colon, rectum   Breast   Prostate

Australasia

MORTALITY

Oesophagus   Lung   Stomach   Colon, rectum   Breast   Prostate

Australasia

■ Men □ Women   *Incidence and mortality rates age-adjusted to the World Standard Population*

TABLE 1.2.12 CANCER INCIDENCE IN SELECTED REGISTRIES OF AUSTRALASIA, 1983–1987

COUNTRY	REGION OR POPULATION	OESOPHAGUS		LUNG		STOMACH		COLON/RECTUM		BREAST	PROSTATE
		MEN	WOMEN	MEN	WOMEN	MEN	WOMEN	MEN	WOMEN	WOMEN	MEN
Australia	New South Wales	4.0	2.3	52.7	13.4	11.8	5.2	43.4	32.0	59.6	39.0
	South	3.9	1.6	46.5	12.2	12.8	4.3	40.1	30.3	56.1	42.0
	Western	3.9	1.7	53.5	16.0	13.1	5.2	40.8	31.5	58.5	39.8
New Zealand	Maori	7.0	1.0	119.1	62.2	25.3	20.4	23.6	19.5	64.0	37.3
	Non-Maori	5.3	2.4	51.7	15.7	12.3	5.2	51.3	42.8	64.3	35.4

TABLE 1.2.13 CANCER MORTALITY IN AUSTRALASIA, 1983–1987

COUNTRY	OESOPHAGUS		LUNG		STOMACH		COLONa		BREAST	PROSTATE
	MEN	WOMEN	MEN	WOMEN	MEN	WOMEN	MEN	WOMEN	WOMEN	MEN
Australia	4.4	1.7	46.3	11.4	9.1	4.0	15.7	12.5	20.6	16.0
New Zealand	4.7	1.9	49.0	14.8	10.7	4.8	15.8	15.5	26.3	17.2

a Does not include rectum

Figure 1.2.12 Relative frequency of the ten most common cancers in selected Australia and New Zealand populations

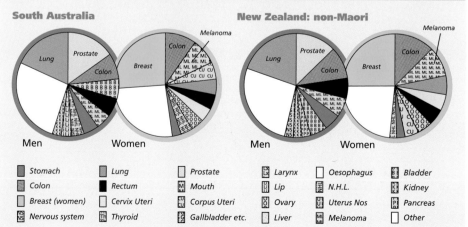

South Australia

New Zealand: non-Maori

Men   Women   Men   Women

■ Stomach   ■ Lung   □ Prostate   Larynx   □ Oesophagus   Bladder
■ Colon   ■ Rectum   Mouth   Lip   N.H.L.   Kidney
□ Breast (women)   □ Cervix Uteri   Corpus Uteri   Ovary   Uterus Nos   Pancreas
NS Nervous system   Thyroid   Gallbladder etc.   Liver   Melanoma   □ Other

CHANGING PATTERNS OF CANCER

Rates of cancers of many sites have changed, in some cases remarkably, in recent decades. Rates of some cancers have increased and rates of others decreased, overall or in some parts of the world. Consistent data on trends in cancer incidence and mortality in many regions are now available (Coleman et al, 1993). Overall trends tend to be consistent throughout the world, but the degree of change can vary substantially from area to area.

Changes in cancer incidence over time largely reflect corresponding changes in environmental exposure. Dramatic shifts indicate that disease rates may respond remarkably quickly to such changes, and all the more so if a number of relevant environmental factors vary at the same time.

Trends in incidence are summarised for six cancer sites identified as diet-related between 1960–70 and 1985 from information supplied by a number of cancer registries. For more information about dietary and other causes of these cancers and others, see the relevant sections of chapter 4. Information about these six cancer sites is followed by a summary of data on changes in patterns of cancer among migrants, and as a result of urbanisation in the economically developing world.

SPECIFIC SITES

OESOPHAGUS

Rates of oesophageal cancer have generally increased in most parts of the world (Figure 1.2.13). The increase has been most marked in western Europe and in North America. There is general agreement that the risk of oesophageal cancer is increased by smoking, and that regular drinkers of alcohol who also smoke are at especially high risk.

LUNG

Rates of lung cancer have also generally increased throughout the world with sharp increases for women almost everywhere (Figure 1.2.14). Incidence of lung cancer varies mainly with rates of smoking. Rates among men have also generally increased but have begun to decline in some developed countries. In some populations, the increases have been dramatic, for example, a 268% increase over the period 1970–85 among women in Alberta, Canada. Most of these changes can be attributed to increased rates of smoking in these populations, itself a consequence of greater availability, promotion and aggressive marketing of cigarettes to young people and, particularly, young women.

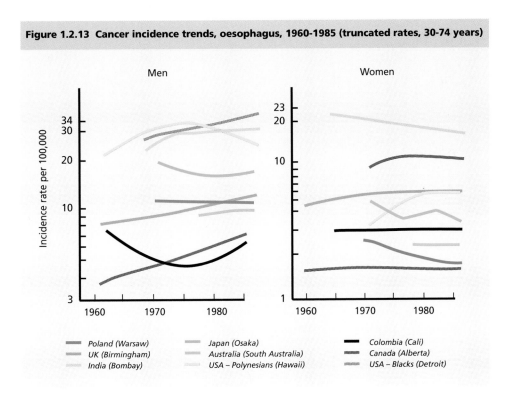

Figure 1.2.13 Cancer incidence trends, oesophagus, 1960-1985 (truncated rates, 30-74 years)

Men

Women

Incidence rate per 100,000

Poland (Warsaw)	Japan (Osaka)	Colombia (Cali)
UK (Birmingham)	Australia (South Australia)	Canada (Alberta)
India (Bombay)	USA – Polynesians (Hawaii)	USA – Blacks (Detroit)

Figure 1.2.14 Cancer incidence trends, lung, 1960-1985 (truncated rates, 30-74 years)

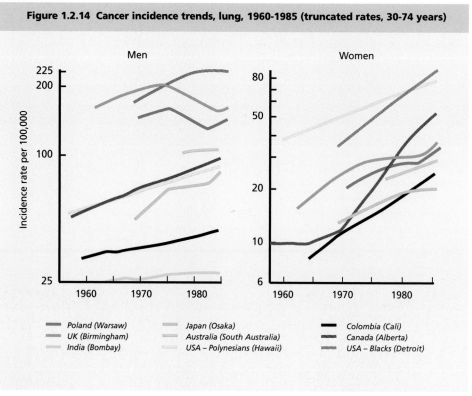

Figure 1.2.15 Cancer incidence trends, stomach, 1960-1985 (truncated rates, 30-74 years)

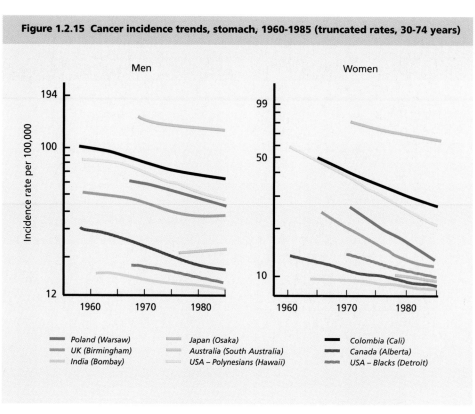

**Figure 1.2.16 Cancer incidence trends, colon and rectum, 1960-1985
(truncated rates, 30-74 years)**

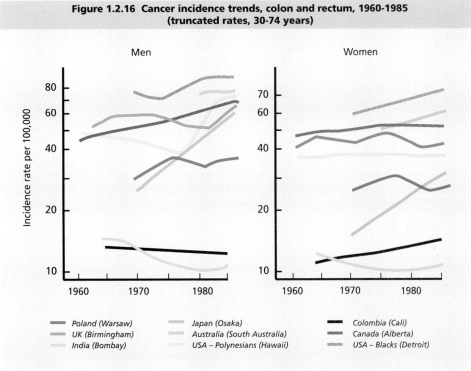

Men

Women

Poland (Warsaw)
UK (Birmingham)
India (Bombay)
Japan (Osaka)
Australia (South Australia)
USA – Polynesians (Hawaii)
Colombia (Cali)
Canada (Alberta)
USA – Blacks (Detroit)

**Figure 1.2.17 Cancer incidence trends, breast, 1960-1985
(truncated rates, 30-74 years)**

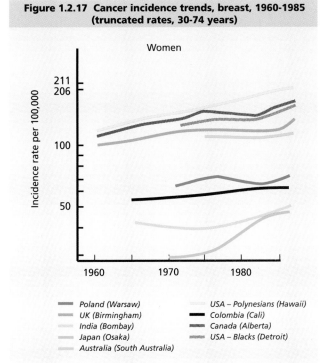

Women

Poland (Warsaw)
UK (Birmingham)
India (Bombay)
Japan (Osaka)
Australia (South Australia)
USA – Polynesians (Hawaii)
Colombia (Cali)
Canada (Alberta)
USA – Blacks (Detroit)

**Figure 1.2.18 Cancer incidence trends, prostate, 1960-1985
(truncated rates, 30-74 years)**

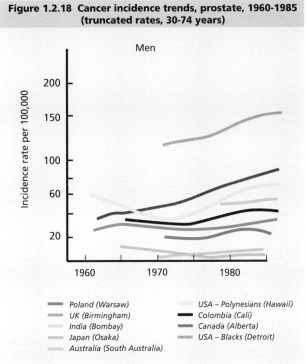

Men

Poland (Warsaw)
UK (Birmingham)
India (Bombay)
Japan (Osaka)
Australia (South Australia)
USA – Polynesians (Hawaii)
Colombia (Cali)
Canada (Alberta)
USA – Blacks (Detroit)

STOMACH

Rates of stomach cancer have generally been decreasing throughout the world (Figure 1.2.15). Overall, the decrease has been of the order of 30% between 1960 and 1985. Of the regions included in the figure, India, China and North America have the lowest rates. There is general agreement that risk of stomach cancer is reduced by diets high in vegetables and fruits, and increased by high-salt diets, among other factors.

COLON AND RECTUM

Incidence rates of colorectal cancer have generally increased (Figure 1.2.16). Highest rates in the regions represented in the figure are seen in North America; lowest rates occur in India and Colombia. The greatest change has occurred in Japan, where the incidence has increased almost threefold. Cancers of the colon and rectum are, with stomach cancer, those most closely associated with diet. There is general agreement that risk of colorectal cancer is reduced by diets high in vegetables and unrefined plant foods, and by exercise.

BREAST

Incidence rates of breast cancer have also increased overall (Figure 1.2.17). Rates of breast cancer are low in developing countries and high in developed countries, and are increasing in parallel with industrialisation. Of the countries included in the figure, the increases have been greatest in Japan and Hawaii. One factor that increases risk of breast cancer is early menarche, itself thought to be associated with urban–industrialised diets.

PROSTATE

Rates of this male hormone-related cancer which, like breast cancer, is generally low in the developing world and high in the developed world, have also increased (Figure 1.2.18). Rates are particularly high and tending to rise in North America, most of all among black people in the USA. This cancer is also identified as related to diet, and higher risk has been associated with diets high in meat and animal fat.

MIGRANTS

Migrants share a common genetic background with their parents as well as their children. Changes in the patterns of cancer, as people of the same genetic background move from one part of the world to another, provide evidence on the extent to which the causes of cancers are environmental. In such migrant populations, compared with those who stay home (sedantes) the difference between the rate (say, in the home country) and the higher rate (in the new country) may indicate the extent to which changes in relevant environmental factors influence risk.

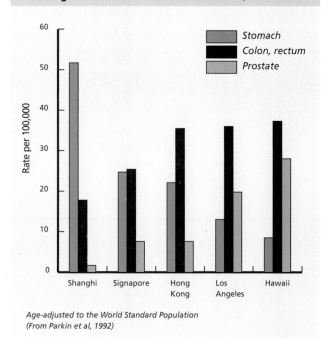

Figure 1.2.19 Cancer incidence for selected cancers among Chinese men in different countries, 1983–1987

Age-adjusted to the World Standard Population
(From Parkin et al, 1992)

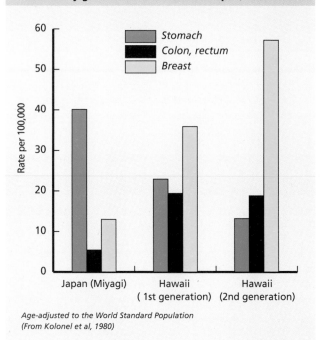

Figure 1.2.20 Cancer incidence for selected cancers in Japanese women by generation in Hawaii and Japan, 1968–1977

Age-adjusted to the World Standard Population
(From Kolonel et al, 1980)

Studies of cancer patterns among migrant populations are therefore of great interest, and have stimulated further epidemiological studies designed to identify the relative contribution of different environmental factors, including diet, to cancer risk.

Migrant studies provide compelling evidence that cancer is principally determined by environmental factors, including diet. Patterns of cancer among migrant groups as they move from country to country often change faster than those within any country. Patterns of diets also change over time as a result of migration, sometimes dramatically.

Some examples of changes in patterns of cancers identified as being diet-related among migrant groups are shown in Figures 1.2.19–1.2.22. Of these, Figure 1.2.19 shows rates of cancer incidence for selected sites among Chinese men in several locations (Parkin et al, 1992). Rates of stomach cancer decreased as this population group moved from Shanghai to other south-east Asian locations (Singapore and Hong Kong) and to the USA (Los Angeles and Hawaii). Rates of this cancer were four to six times higher in Shanghai compared with the USA; rates in Singapore and Hong Kong were intermediate. The story for prostate cancer was even more dramatic: rates increased 10–15 times or more between Shanghai and the USA, again with intermediate rates in Singapore and Hong Kong. With cancer of the colon and rectum, rates increased as much as twofold among the migrants. Among Chinese men, stomach cancer was 30 times more common than prostate cancer in Shanghai, whereas prostate cancer was over three times more common than stomach cancer in Hawaii.

Contrasts in patterns of cancer among women over successive generations are shown in Figure 1.2.20 for Japanese women who migrated to Hawaii (Kolonel et al, 1980). Stomach cancer rates dropped by almost a half in the first generation (the migrants themselves) in Hawaii and by over two-thirds in the second generation (the migrants' children). By sharp contrast, rates of breast cancer increased almost three times in the first generation in Hawaii and were between four and five times higher in the second generation. Cancer of the colon and rectum increased almost four times in the first generation but did not increase further in the second generation.

A somewhat different pattern was seen among first-generation Japanese migrants in Brazil, where rates of stomach cancer in women were only slightly lower, and rates of colon cancer only slightly higher, but rates of breast cancer were much higher than in Japan (Tsugane et al, 1990). In these groups, stomach cancer was three times more common than breast cancer in Japan whereas, for the second generation of migrants to Brazil, breast cancer was over five times more common than stomach cancer.

Cancer rates may change fast among migrants in a new country. For example, deaths from breast cancer among Italian migrants to Australia have been shown to be half that of Australian-born women averaged over the first five years in the host country, whereas after 17 years the rates of death were the same as those of native Australians (Figure 1.2.21) (McMichael and Giles, 1988). Figure 1.2.22 shows the effect of time in Australia on stomach cancer mortality among migrants to Australia from Yugoslavia, Poland, England, Italy and Greece, where, generally, rates dropped over time (McMichael et al, 1980).

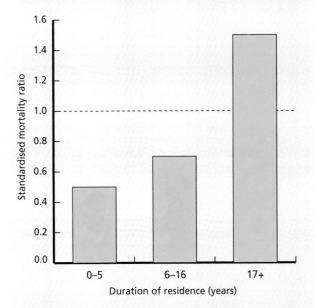

Figure 1.2.21 Breast cancer mortality ratios for Italian women migrants by duration of residence in Australia, 1962–1971

Age-adjusted to the World Standard Population   Australian-born= 1.0
(From McMichael and Giles, 1988)

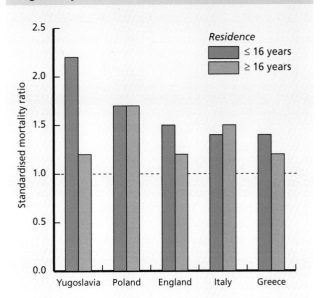

Figure 1.2.22 Stomach cancer mortality ratios for European migrants by duration of residence in Australia, 1962–1976

Adults ≥ 30 years, age- and sex-adjusted to the World Standard Population
Australian-born= 1.0
(From McMichael et al 1980)

URBAN AREAS OF ECONOMICALLY
DEVELOPING COUNTRIES

Migrant studies provide impressive circumstantial evidence that common cancers have important environmental causes. So, too, do the phenomena now widespread in Africa, Latin America and Asia, known as the demographic, nutritional and epidemiological transitions, which have been the subject of recent observational studies (Popkin, 1993).

Division of the world into economically developing and developed regions and countries, or alternatively into the south and the north, has a broad correspondence to economic and other realities. People who live in Africa have, on average, a far lower income than people who live in North America, to take an obvious example. On the other hand, people who live in a number of industrialised countries in eastern Europe and the former USSR, conventionally designated as economically developed, have a lower average income than people who live in high-income countries in Asia, such as Singapore and Japan.

More importantly from the point of view of this and other reports on food, nutrition and public health, economically developing countries in many parts of the world are now in a state of rapid transition and, in recent years, all the more so as they respond to market forces. The phenomenon whereby people in western Europe moved off the land into cities, following the Industrial Revolution in the eighteenth and nineteenth centuries, with consequent changes in patterns of diet and of disease, is now occurring within many countries in the economically developing world, but at a very much more rapid rate.

Data of the type summarised in this chapter so far, from the Food and Agriculture Organization, to identify patterns of diet, and from cancer registries, to identify patterns of cancer, are mostly highly aggregated. Although useful, these data are from some years past, and so do not reflect very recent changes in patterns of diet or cancer. Further, many of the data reflect regional and national trends, and are often not sensitive enough to detect shifts within countries.

There is now strong evidence that very recent and accelerating shifts of population from rural areas to cities within economically developing countries is being followed not only by corresponding major changes in dietary patterns, but also in patterns of chronic diseases, including cancer. This trend has been highlighted by the 1997 World Health Report (WHO, 1997).

Broadly, economic development and the rapid growth of cities in Africa, Latin America and Asia are having the effect of changing diets in urban and peri-urban areas, from traditional patterns based on starchy staples and relatively low consumption of meat, dairy products and fats and oils, to

urban–industrial patterns. These diets are more energy dense, with lower consumption of staple starchy foods, and relatively high consumption of fat, meat and meat products, and processed foods that often contain substantial amounts of fat and/or sugar. There is also a tendency for alcohol consumption to rise (FAO, 1989; WHO, 1997). There is, in addition, a corresponding switch from occupations involving regular, although sometimes seasonal physical activity, to a sedentary way of life.

The nutritional profile of urban, as compared with rural, diets in developing countries varies, partly according to the economic status of families and individuals. The diets of urban people with relatively high incomes become more diverse; more vegetables and fruits, and milk and dairy products are consumed, and a variety of fresh and processed foods and drinks are available in shops and markets and from street vendors. On the other hand, people who are forced into cities because of extreme poverty and insecurity, who live in very crowded circumstances in peri-urban areas such as the *favelas* of Rio de Janeiro and São Paulo in Brazil, may consume diets lower in starch and higher in fats, oils and sugar, without any countervailing benefits.

Studies carried out in various parts of the economically developing world show that the very rapid transition to urban–industrial diets and lifestyles within Africa, Latin America and Asia is followed by a rapid epidemiological transition, whereby chronic diseases of the sort that are common in Europe, North America and Australasia become much more prevalent. In some cases these changes have not been accompanied by marked decreases in the rates of the already endemic cancers, for example, those of stomach, liver and cervix, nor in the prevalence of deficiency and infectious diseases.

In the higher-income countries of Asia, cancer patterns in urban areas are now approximating to those of established industrial economies in the West. For example, incidence of cancers of the breast, colon, prostate and ovary approximately doubled in Singapore between the 1970s and the 1990s (WHO, 1997).

In India, cancers associated with Western diets and lifestyles are also becoming more common. There are indications of rising incidence of cancers of the lung, colon and rectum, previously relatively low in comparison to western countries (Gopalan, 1997).

More details of these trends are given in chapter 9.2 of this report. Between 1996 and 2020, the total number of cases of cancer in the developing world is predicted to double and, in the developed world, to increase by 40% (WHO, 1997). The sharp increase in rates of cancer particularly in the economically developing world amounts, in the view of the panel, to a global public-health emergency.

CHAPTER TWO

Diet and the cancer process

Cancer involves fundamental biological processes concerning disordered cell replication and cell death, and disorganisation of organ structure: it may be that cancer is the price humans pay for their flexible genome and evolutionary development.

The roles of food and nutrition in the processes that protect against and promote cancer are outlined in this chapter.

The first section explains the nature of cancer, how it is categorised, and why certain cancers are more common in childhood and others in adult life. The main causes of cancer are outlined in the second section.

The rest of the chapter describes the steps in the cancer process and shows how each may be affected by diet, obesity, physical activity, etc. Modification of risk by dietary factors can occur at different stages of the cancer process. For example, they may reduce the effects of environmental carcinogens, damage DNA directly or indirectly, and either promote or inhibit the progression of cancer.

It is sometimes thought that food and nutrition affect cancer risk only inasmuch as diets may contain specific carcinogenic substances. While various carcinogens have been identified in foods and drinks, these appear to contribute only slightly to the overall impact of diet on cancer risk. First, the story of the role of food and nutrition in the modification of the cancer process is much more complex. Second, the most important effects of diet may be mediated by actions that inhibit the cancer process.

The detailed information in this chapter reflects an explosion of recent insights into the workings of cells and the cancer process itself. The chapter ends with a figure which gives a graphical outline of the different stages at which diet may modify the cancer processs.

The specific mechanisms by which individual constituents of diet affect the cancer process are often not fully understood, and no doubt many remain to be identified. However, existing knowledge gives key insights into the cancer process, which should, in turn, inform recommendations designed to prevent cancer.

Chair

Professor John D. Potter
*Fred Hutchinson Cancer
Research Center
Seattle, USA*

Panel Members

Dr Adolfo Chavez
*National Institute of Nutrition
Mexico City, Mexico*

Dr Junshi Chen
*Chinese Academy of
Preventive Medicine
Beijing, China*

Professor Anna Ferro-Luzzi
*National Institute of Nutrition
Rome, Italy*

Professor Tomio Hirohata
*Nakamura University
Fukuoka City, Japan*

Professor Philip James
*The Rowett Research Institute
Aberdeen, UK*

Dr Fred F. Kadlubar
*National Center for Toxicological
Research
Arkansas, USA*

Dr Festo Kavishe
*UNICEF, East Asia and
Pacific Region
Phnom Phen, Cambodia*

Professor Laurence Kolonel
*University of Hawaii
Hawaii, USA*

Professor Suminori Kono
*Kyushu University
Fukuoka City, Japan*

Dr Kamala Krishnaswamy
*National Institute of Nutrition
Hyderabad, India*

Professor A.J. McMichael
*London School of Hygiene and
Tropical Medicine
London, UK*

Professor Sushma Palmer
*Center for Communications,
Health and the Environment
Washington DC, USA*

Dr Lionel Poirier
*National Center for
Toxicological Research
Arkansas, USA*

Professor Walter Willett
*Harvard School of Public Health
Boston, USA*

Scientific Adviser to AICR/WCRF

Professor T. Colin Campbell
*Cornell University
Ithaca, USA*

*This correspondence originated
in the office of:*

☐ AICR
*1759 R St NW,
Washington, DC 20009
Tel   (202) 328-7744
Fax   (202) 328-7226*

☐ WCRF
*105 Park Street
London W1Y 3FB
Tel: (0171) 343 4200
Fax: (0171) 343 4201*

Cancer can be prevented...

That's a vital message in today's world. In 1996 the World Health Organization estimated that 10 million new cases of cancer occurred around the world. Over just the next five years that number is expected to increase to 14.7 million cases.

Cancer must be prevented...

The growing burden of cancer, not just in industrialized nations, but in developing nations around the world, is a health problem which can not and should not be ignored. The enclosed report, Food, Nutrition and the Prevention of Cancer: A Global Perspective, is an important step in the process of making cancer prevention not just a concept, but a reality. And while it's clear that we still can not prevent every case of cancer, there is now overwhelming evidence that the majority of cancers are preventable.

This report, the most comprehensive review of diet and cancer research from a global perspective to date, was more than 3 years in development. The project has involved an expert panel of 15 of the world's leading researchers in diet and cancer, more than 100 peer reviewers, and participants from the World Health Organization (WHO), the U.S. National Cancer Institute (NCI), the Food and Agriculture Organization (FAO) and the International Agency for Research on Cancer (IARC). More than 4,500 research studies were reviewed for this report, and case studies from a number of representative countries are included.

The development of Food, Nutrition and the Prevention of Cancer: A Global Perspective has been a joint project of the World Cancer Research Fund (WCRF) and the American Institute for Cancer Research (AICR). It is being made available, at no cost, to thousands of researchers, policy makers and health educators around the world. This report presents new dietary guidelines for cancer prevention, new public policy recommendations for cancer prevention, and a thorough review of the science behind its findings.

It is a report which will help set a new foundation for research, public policy and health education in the field of diet and cancer. On behalf of the World Cancer Research Fund and the American Institute for Cancer Research, I am proud to be able to provide you with a complimentary copy of this important document.

Together we can make cancer prevention a reality that can save millions of lives.

Sincerely,

Marilyn Gentry
President

P.S. Additional copies can be ordered by completing the order form attached to the enclosed envelope.

Cancer is similar to other chronic diseases, such as coronary heart disease, and to infectious and deficiency diseases because the chief underlying causes are environmental. Among these causes, food and nutrition are important modifiers of cancer risk. Cancer is, however, different from other diseases, in that changes in the genetic information coded in the DNA of cells are fundamental to its nature.

This does not mean that cancer is largely an inherited disease, although a small, as yet unquantified, proportion of cancers results directly from the inheritance of predisposing genes. Rather, a fundamental part of the cancer process involves damage to the DNA of the cells making up the cancerous mass. This damage accumulates over time: rogue cells replicate further and escape the mechanisms that are usually in place to protect the organism from the growth and spread of such cells. These protective mechanisms are both internal (the body's own systems) and external (the environment, including food and nutrition).

Cancer can be regarded as a disease of cells; it is characterised by an excess of cells beyond the number needed for normal function of the body organ affected. Cancer almost always occurs in a specific body organ such as the lung, the liver or the breast, and the causes of these different cancers are often different.

Molecular and cell biologists are interested largely in events taking place in the cell, but physicians and surgeons treat the disease by focusing on the specific organ involved. In contrast, the cancer epidemiologist takes account of the differences in the patterns of, and risks for, specific cancers across whole populations, and attempts to identify the underlying causes of these differences, whether they exist in relation to factors such as dietary and exercise habits, tobacco, alcohol and other drug use, race, ethnicity, geography, family history or occupation.

Two features of cancer help in the understanding of the role of diet in the disease process. First, cancer is a rare disease at the cellular level. Up to 30% of all individuals in the developed world will present clinically with one of a wide variety of cancers at some time in their lives. However, if the number of cells at risk (in each human there are about 10,000,000,000,000 or 10^{13} cells) is taken into account, and, given that in general none or only one of these cells grows and replicates to present as a clinical cancer, it is obvious that this is a disease that only rarely escapes normal protective systems.

The second point is that DNA is liable to both change and damage; this is central to its capacity to evolve and adapt. If DNA could not be changed by forces in the environment, there would be no variation in genetic potential to allow nat-ural selection to occur. Cancer is, in a real sense, the price we pay for the long-term adaptability of the human species.

2.1 THE NATURE OF CANCER

Cancer is a disease that has been known about since ancient times (Pitot, 1986). The word is derived from the Latin for 'crab' and appears to have been first described in a collection of works (500 BC to AD 200) ascribed to Hippocrates and other Greek physicians. They recognised the clinical presentation of a variety of tumours and classified them as either carcinos or benign growths, which were circumscribed and did not spread, or as carcinomas or crab-like growths, which invaded surrounding tissue and caused the death of the patient. The term 'neoplasm' was coined later by Galen (AD 200) who defined cancers as new growths that were 'contrary to nature'.

The ability of neoplasms to migrate to other tissues or organs and form additional tumours was also recognised and described as a *metastasis* – from the Greek word meaning to change places. However, from these early times, and throughout the Middle Ages, cancer was generally regarded with other diseases as a consequence of alterations in the four bodily humours (blood, phlegm, yellow bile and black bile) which defined the central attributes of individual physiology and, when out of balance, pathology.

The formation of cancer cells, as such, was not appreciated until the development of the compound microscope in the nineteenth century and its application to pathology (the study of diseased tissues). Cell theory was developed extensively in the first half of the nineteenth century by a number of scientists including Schwann, Reichert, Remak and Virchow. One of this group, Johannes Müller, a German physiologist, observed that tumours, like all living things, were composed of individual cells. However, he noted that cancer cells appeared to be quite different from normal cells and often resembled those found in rapidly growing embryos.

By 1865, Thiersch had concluded that tumours of the inner and outer linings of the body (epithelial tumours) arose from normal epithelial cells. The next important step was the differentiation of tumours into those of inflammatory and non-inflammatory origin by von Recklinghausen in the 1860s; this distinction then became ever clearer as the role of bacteria in infectious disease became increasingly established.

By the early twentieth century, further developments in microscopic pathology and the surgical treatment of cancer led to the study of tumours as a separate scientific discipline called oncology. James Ewing, a US pathologist, defined neoplasms as autonomous new growths of tissue comprising an abnormal group of cells which grow in a manner that is not in coordination with surrounding normal tissue. This definition, espoused in the 1920s, provided a biological basis for understanding the cancer cell, and led to our modern classification of tumours according to their tissue of origin, their growth properties, and their capacity to invade other tissues, to metastasise and, ultimately, to cause death.

INITIAL OBSERVATIONS ON FOOD, NUTRITION AND CANCER

Compared with the recognition of cancer as a distinct disease state, the recognition of diet as a possible contributor is of more recent origin. In 1914, Peyton Rous observed that the restriction of food consumption delayed the development of tumour metastases in mice. In the 1920s and 1930s, the accumulation of vital statistics by insurance companies showed an association between obesity and mortality from cancer in different organs. In the 1930s, exploration of the role of diet in human cancers began and, even at that stage, evidence emerged of the capacity of a higher intake of plant foods to reduce the risk of cancer (Stocks and Karn, 1933). By 1940 (Tannenbaum, 1940), the protective effects of under-feeding on tumour formation in experimental animals were recognised.

In the 1980s, Doll and Peto (Doll and Peto, 1981) attempted the first relative quantification of the environmental contributions of a variety of factors such as diet, tobacco, alcohol, occupation and radiation. This work was notable for at least two reasons. First, despite the wide range of estimates of the contribution that diet makes to the cause of cancer, it was identified as being plausibly comparable with tobacco. Second, although the authors identified some very specific agents (some synthetic antioxidants) as perhaps having a preventive influence on cancer, dietary patterns were identified largely by their contribution to increased risk. This present report focuses, in addition, on those factors in diet which, from current evidence, protect against cancer.

CANCER AND CELLS

As stated above, the adult human body is composed of about 10^{13} cells. As it starts from a single cell (the fertilised ovum), it is clear that the multiplication of cells is an essential, normal function. In the embryo and fetus, cell replication builds all the organs, systems and parts that make up the body. During infancy, childhood and adolescence, cell division allows the achievement of adult size. Following injury, the multiplication of cells works towards the regeneration and repair of the damaged tissue.

Throughout life, there is a regular turnover of the cells of many different parts of the body. These include:

- the linings of all body organs that interact with the environment: for example, the skin, the respiratory tract, the digestive organs and the white cells which combat infection;

- the organs that secrete products either within the body or externally: for example, the breast, the endocrine organs, the liver and pancreas;

- the organs that cycle in intermittent readiness for reproduction, particularly the lining of the uterus, the endometrium, and the organs that produce reproductive cells, the testis and ovary.

Cell division is fundamental to the function of all adult systems except the nervous system, muscles and bones. Even bones retain the capacity for cell replication if broken.

A fundamental feature of tumours (or neoplasms) is an increase in the number of cells beyond the requirements of the growth, repair and reproduction of the host. Tumours fall into two categories: benign and malignant (Pitot, 1986). Benign tumours are characterised by their relatively slow growth, encapsulation and non-invasiveness, and microscopic similarity to the normal surrounding tissue. Cells from a benign tumour are generally of uniform size and shape and their nuclei appear normal and contain the usual number and arrangement of chromosomes (the genetic material of the cell that contains the DNA). In contrast, malignant tumours usually exhibit rapid growth and invade adjacent normal tissues. Cells from a malignant tumour are often large and of abnormal shape. Under the microscope, cancer cells often resemble embryonic or undifferentiated cells (anaplastic), but they may also have aberrant nuclei and an abnormal number of chromosomes. The presence and nature of the malignant tumour at the time of clinical presentation give the diagnosis of cancer; treatment is determined by the body organ involved, the tumour type, its growth and the degree of spread. Together, the disease and its treatment predict prognosis and survival.

The naming and classification of a tumour are determined not only from its benign or malignant status but also from the cell type and tissue of origin. In general, the suffix '-oma' attached to a cell or tissue type (for example, papilloma) signifies a benign tumour, whereas malignant tumours are described as: carcinomas, if derived from epithelial tissue (for example, adenocarcinoma); sarcomas, if derived from mesenchymal tissue; or the term 'malignant' is added (for example, malignant melanoma).

THE GROWTH OF CANCER

The growth of a malignant tumour usually destroys surrounding tissue, induces increased blood vessel formation to supply nutrients to the multiplying cancer cells, and eventually may spread to distant tissues – metastasis.

Metastasis involves the release of cancer cells into the blood or lymphatic circulation; from here they may reach and colonise other organs and grow into secondary tumour masses. These metastatic cells are not just random cells that break off from the main tumour mass; in fact, they are already adapted for growth at new body sites, although the mechanism is not well understood. The growth of a malignant tumour often continues at the expense of the host, resulting in wasting or starvation of the body, called cachexia, although this may, in part, be a defence mechanism against the cancer.

Metastatic cancers that have spread to several tissues (for example, brain, lung, bone marrow and blood vessels) impair organ function and the immune response, with a resultant susceptibility to infection; they produce tissue damage, necrosis and bleeding, any of which can lead to death of the host (Pitot, 1986). It is usually the distant and widespread nature of the disease that is ultimately lethal, not the original tumour. Early detection of the tumour (for example, by screening) and its complete removal usually result in a better outcome than late detection. Prevention of the process altogether constitutes the best solution.

As cancer occurs only in cells that are replicating, the pattern of cancers is quite different in children and adults. In early life, the brain, nervous system, bones, muscles and connective tissue are all still growing, and cancer is much more common in these tissues in children than in adults. On the other hand, the common adult tumours predominantly involve epithelial linings and are rare in children. Leukaemias and lymphomas (tumours of the immune system) occur throughout life, although their nature differs depending on whether they occur early or late.

2.2 CAUSES OF CANCER

The fact that each cancer arises from a single cell provides evidence that, once the abnormal behaviour arises, the capacity for such behaviour is handed on to the daughter cells. This, in turn, shows that cancer is a disease that fundamentally involves the structure and function of DNA.

THE IMPORTANCE OF DNA

Abnormalities of DNA can arise in a variety of ways, although not all of the processes are fully understood. Sources of abnormalities include the following:

- A gene that is essential to the long-term stability of DNA or to the proper control of cell replication can be inherited in an abnormal form from one parent. Such abnormalities are rare but appear to account for a relatively larger proportion of cancers in children and young adults.

- DNA can be damaged at any time in life by agents in the environment such as radiation and substances (both synthetic and natural) in our food, water, air and workplace. It is clear that, in a very high proportion of

---

BOX 2.1 ABNORMALITIES OF METHYLATION OF DNA

Why both increases and decreases of methylation of DNA can increase the risk of cancer

Hypermethylation

Gene (normally without methyl groups) ⇓ Gene + methyl groups	Protein needed for cell or tissue func tion Loss of needed protein

Hypomethylation

Gene + methyl groups (normally methylated) ⇓ Gene (loss of methyl groups)	No production of protein inappropriate for specific cell of tissue Production of inappropriate protein

---

individuals, cells are capable of eliminating this damage or its consequences. Individuals who are exposed to constant high levels of DNA-damaging agents for prolonged periods, such as cigarette smokers, or those who have inherited a poor capacity to repair DNA damage, are at particularly high risk.

- Sometimes, the DNA of a gene that is important in the control of cell function is shut down (hypermethylated) or inappropriately expressed as a result of loss of methyl groups (hypomethylated) rather than damaged.

- A fourth way in which abnormalities can arise involves the function of DNA. In this case, there may be over- or under-expression of growth-controlling factors or their receptors. Many human cancers may result from a combination of damage to the DNA, change in the expression of specific genes and loss of growth control.

There is one important piece of evidence to support the concept that most human cancers arise from interaction between the environment (including diet, smoking, etc.) and the genetic material of cells, and not from simple inherited predispositions; this derives from the observation that migrants rapidly acquire (sometimes even within the migrating generation) the cancer risk profile of the host country, rather than keeping the rates of their country of origin (see also chapter 1). As rates of cancer of different body sites vary worldwide, this means that risk is not determined solely by inherited factors. Some environmental (including dietary) exposures, some of the genetic and acquired predispositions and some of the metabolic processes central to the development of cancer are described below.

As seen from the perspective of the experimental biologist, current concepts of the aetiology (pattern of causation) of human cancer have generally focused on three agents: viruses, radiation and chemicals. Epidemiologists tend to separate out dietary patterns as a specific separate cause, although part of the dietary story overlaps with that of chemicals.

AGENTS

Infection (viruses)

Cancer-causing viruses have been studied extensively in experimental animals, and their mechanisms of action have provided critical insights into the cancer process. In fact, it was these efforts that led to the discovery of both viral and cellular cancer genes, called oncogenes, which can be activated by viruses, radiation or chemical carcinogens (see below).

Epidemiological studies have implicated viruses as an aetiological agent only in certain cancers. These include the Epstein–Barr virus (a cause of Burkitt lymphoma and nasopharyngeal carcinoma), hepatitis B and C viruses (causes of liver cancer), human papillomaviruses (causes of cervical cancer) and the human T-cell leukaemia viruses. There is a growing body of evidence that the bacterium *Helicobacter pylori* is a causal agent in stomach cancer.

Radiation

Ultraviolet radiation, in the form of sunlight, has long been recognised as the major cause of human skin cancer. With the exception of malignant melanoma, skin cancers are seldom fatal and can easily be treated by surgery. Exposure to ionising radiation (X-rays, γ-rays, etc.), on the other hand, is important in a variety of cancers, particularly those involving the blood and lymphatic systems, but also those of the breast, thyroid and brain.

Although populations in Japan have developed neoplastic disease as a result of the use of nuclear weapons, recent human exposure to ionising radiation has been limited to medical X-rays or radiation therapy, cosmic rays, radioactive airborne pollutants (including those from nuclear accidents and weapons testing) or to workers in specific occupations (for example, the nuclear industry). Altogether, it is estimated that only about 3% of all cancer deaths result from some form of radiation (Tomatis et al, 1990).

Chemical carcinogens (including tobacco-derived agents)

The role of chemical carcinogens in human cancer was first suggested in the eighteenth and nineteenth centuries by clinical observations that prolonged contact with soot, coal tar, pitch, shale and petroleum oils led to the increased occurrence of cancers of the skin, lungs and other tissues. However, it was not until the early 1900s that the chemical nature of these organic substances became known, with the synthesis of dibenz[a,h]anthracene as the first pure chemical carcinogen and the characterisation of benzo[a]pyrene as the major carcinogenic constituent of coal tar. Experimental carcinogenesis in animals was established following the demonstration that these pure chemicals (collectively called polycyclic aromatic hydrocarbons) could induce the formation of skin cancer in rodents as a result of direct application (Searle, 1984).

Another class of chemicals, the aromatic amines, was also recognised at this time as being carcinogenic. These compounds were then in widespread commercial use as intermediates in the synthesis of dyes and as antioxidants in rubber and lubricating oils. By 1895, a German physician, Ludwig Rehn, suggested that occupational exposure to aromatic amines led to the development of urinary bladder cancer. Rehn made some insightful comments on the potential mechanism of tumour induction: 'one can only imagine that substances were present in solution in the urine discharged from the kidneys and that these caused a tumor to form by means of a chemical stimulus'. However, it was not until 1938 that aromatic amines were shown experimentally to induce bladder tumours in the dog.

Throughout the twentieth century, either as a result of experimental studies on laboratory animals or from known exposures in humans, other classes of chemical compounds were shown to be carcinogenic. The most important chemicals for the population cancer burden are the many carcinogenic constituents of tobacco smoke. Others include products derived from combustion and organic synthesis; and substances present in food as normal constituents, as microbial contaminants and, or that are formed during food preparation (for example, nitroaromatic hydrocarbons, nitrosamines, hydrazines, triazenes, halogenated hydrocarbons, pyrrolizidine alkaloids, alkenylbenzenes, mycotoxins and heterocyclic amines). In addition, it is now recognised that carcinogens may be produced endogenously through physiological processes such as inflammation, oxidative stress, nutritional and hormonal imbalances, and repetitive tissue injury (Ames, 1983; Cohen and Ellwein, 1991).

Today, it is estimated that environmental factors are primarily responsible for 70–90% of all human cancers (Doll and Peto, 1981;Tomatis et al, 1990). This does not imply that environmental and exogenous chemicals, as such, cause most human cancers, but rather that specific environmental agents – both those with the capacity to interact with DNA and those that have other influences on the function and replication of cells – may contribute significantly to the development of this disease. In this context, not only are occupational exposures and tobacco smoke considered to be part of the environment, but so, too, is diet.

THE ROLE OF FOOD AND NUTRITION

Throughout the 1930s and 1940s, the modifying effects of diet upon cancer induced in animals by purified chemicals were shown repeatedly (Poirier et al, 1986; Doll, 1992). This interest in the interaction between dietary constituents and cancer-causing agents and processes is perhaps not surprising, because many of these early investigators had studied in departments of agricultural chemistry or nutrition, and many of the hypotheses proposed centred on the nutritional deficiencies that were believed to be provoked by carcinogenic compounds.

During this period, essential nutrients that were shown to inhibit chemically induced tumours included vitamin A (retinol), which was shown to inhibit carcinoma formation in epithelial tissues by polycyclic aromatic hydrocarbons, and riboflavin, which inhibited liver cancer caused by azo dyes in rats (Poirier et al, 1986). In this environment, the observation that a single dietary deficiency of choline induced liver cancer in rats, even in the apparent absence of an exogenous carcinogen, was not totally unexpected.

The earliest epidemiological studies to suggest protective dietary patterns were conducted by Stocks and Karn in the UK and Orr in India. These studies (both published in 1933) were the first to suggest that diets high in vegetables and fruits were associated with a reduced risk of cancer in a variety of organs.

Since these early investigations, an enormous wealth of information has been compiled which shows that specific dietary factors can significantly alter the likelihood of induction of cancer by known carcinogens in a variety of tissues and organs. Moreover, dietary modulation of the cancer process has been found to apply to whole classes of chemicals. The nutrients showing modulatory effects in experimental cancer include: macronutrients (fats, carbohydrates, protein and fibre); vitamins (folic acid, riboflavin, β-carotene, retinol, α-tocopherol and vitamin B_{12}); and minerals (selenium, zinc, magnesium and calcium). Many of these modulatory effects observed in animals have also been reported in human epidemiological studies.

2.3 CARCINOGENESIS

ANIMAL MODELS

The mechanisms of chemical carcinogenesis have been studied extensively in animal models and have been categorised into at least three stages: initiation, promotion and progression (Harris, 1991; Pitot and Dragan, 1994). However, in experimental systems, it is possible to ensure that initiation, promotion and progression are the consequence of exposure to specific, sequential, ordered and non-overlapping agents. For humans, or any other free-living animal, none of these conditions is likely to occur. Individual steps towards malignancy occurring in a predictable order in an experimental setting may have counterparts in the natural world; but in human cancer, rather than three discrete processes, there is likely to be an accumulation of genetic changes and variations in proliferation rate which lead to loss of cellular and tissue homeostasis. It is more probable, in the natural world, that the cells with differing degrees of dysplastic and neoplastic behaviour will be present together in the target organ. Also, it is clear that some exposures (for example, tobacco smoke) contain agents that act early (initiation) and late (progression) in the cancer process.

HUMAN CARCINOGENESIS

For human carcinogenesis, particularly in relation to the interactions with diet, the process of carcinogenesis can be envisaged as a series of events (including the three stages originally identified in animals):

- Exposure to the relevant agent(s)

- Metabolism of the agent(s)

- Interaction between the agent(s) and the cell constitutents (especially the DNA) at risk – initiation

- Repair of the DNA damage, death of the cell or persistence and replication of a clone of abnormal cells within the tissue

- Growth of this abnormal clone into a definable focus of pre-neoplastic cells – promotion

- Growth of the tumour and its spread to other parts of the body – progression.

The host's susceptibility and its defences interact with, and modify, every stage of this process.

2.4 EXPOSURE TO AGENTS

Humans are exposed to a variety of known carcinogens in tobacco (smoking, chewing and snuff), in the workplace, the wider environment, diet (including those from food preparation, storage and spoilage) and alcoholic drinks (Figure 2.1). It is not yet established what proportion of human cancers is accounted for by such specific known carcinogens. Parkin et al (1985) have estimated that 15% of all cancers are caused by tobacco smoke and this, coupled with knowledge of smoking and cancer, must be regarded as strong evidence that directly-acting carcinogens account for a significant and measurable proportion of the worldwide cancer burden. A smaller, but more uncertain, proportion appears to be caused by industrial carcinogens such as benzene and asbestos. Viruses and bacteria, as noted above, are central to the aetiology of some important cancers.

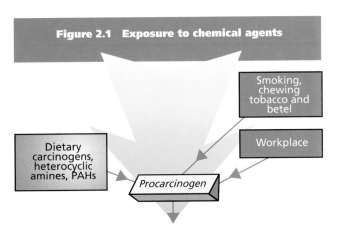

Figure 2.1   Exposure to chemical agents

Smoking, chewing tobacco and betel

Workplace

Dietary carcinogens, heterocyclic amines, PAHs

Procarcinogen

Viruses and radiation work by routes different from these exposures

THE ROLE OF FOOD AND NUTRITION

The major difficulty in deciding on the role of carcinogens is that there is currently considerable uncertainty about how often exposure to carcinogens occurs and how effective the defences against such exposures are. Is the important step the failure of the defence mechanisms rather than the exposure? A second source of uncertainty is the evidence that promotional agents, as opposed to DNA-damaging substances and processes, are central to human cancer. Finally, there is a growing body of evidence to show that DNA damage can also be induced by the normal metabolic functions that produce oxygen radicals (see Box 2.2).

BOX 2.2 OXYGEN RADICALS

It is now increasingly thought that some DNA damage can occur as a result of the normal functions of the body and its cells. Oxygen is crucial to our whole metabolism. Many cellular processes require oxygen. Sometimes oxygen and other small molecules (e.g. hydroxyl groups, –OH) become electron-deficient. These oxygen radicals (also called radical oxygen species, ROS) can, like other carcinogens, react with DNA and, if these adducts are not repaired, they may induce mutations.

The following are some known and suspected dietary carcinogens: aflatoxins (found in mouldy food), heterocyclic amines (meat cooked at very high temperatures), *N*-nitroso compounds (found in some spoiled foods, protein foods and perhaps generated endogenously); and polycyclic aromatic hydrocarbons (products of combustion and found in cooked foods and dark beer). These are discussed further in chapter 4.

2.5 METABOLISM OF AGENTS

Chemical carcinogens, the agents responsible for direct DNA damage, are found in a structurally diverse array of chemical classes. A common property of most of these carcinogens is their ability to become strong electrophiles (electron-deficient molecules) after biotransformation by normal human metabolic enzymes. Such electrophiles tend to react readily with nucleophilic (electron-rich) molecules such as proteins and DNA.

Although some carcinogens are directly electrophilic (for example, alkylating and acylating agents), most are converted to their electrophilic derivatives through normal cellular metabolism. This process is known as metabolic activation and sometimes occurs in several steps. Understanding of this process was developed, in large part, by the work of James and Elizabeth Miller. The electrophilic metabolite that binds to cellular DNA is termed an 'ultimate carcinogen' (Simic and Bergtold, 1991). Activation is a normal enzymatic process (so-called phase I enzymes, including the cytochrome P450 system) that converts a particular

chemical into a more water-soluble, but reactive, form that can then bind to cell macromolecules such as DNA, RNA, proteins and lipids (Figure 2.2).

This whole process developed primarily to make foreign compounds more water soluble and therefore more readily excreted in urine, that is, to detoxify the compounds; the body is not trying to make carcinogens.

Enzymes involved in the metabolic activation of chemical carcinogens are those normally involved in the oxidation, reduction and conjugation of dietary constituents, endogenous hormones, drugs and other foreign compounds. As the levels of carcinogen-activating enzymes and carcinogen detoxification mechanisms can differ appreciably between different tissues, between species and between individuals within species, each chemical carcinogen may induce a unique spectrum of tumours in different experimental animals and across human populations.

Phase II detoxification enzymes are also involved in the handling of a variety of chemicals in food, and they can be turned on (induced) by a variety of plant compounds. This tendency to induce enzymes may account for the capacity of some plant constituents to reduce cancer in humans and experimental animals. If the enzymes are already induced by more benign plant compounds, they are more readily able to detoxify the more carcinogenic agents in the diet.

Detoxification can occur at each step in this metabolic pathway, either as a result of reaction with nucleophilic compounds not crucial to cell function (for example, glutathione), or by conversion to stable metabolites that can readily be excreted. The efficiency of detoxification can be a critical factor in determining the carcinogenic potency of a particular agent.

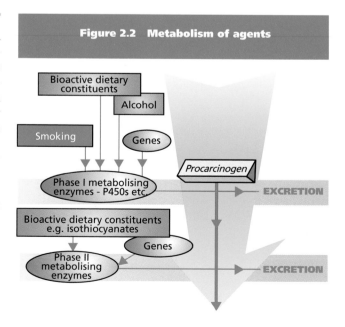

Figure 2.2 Metabolism of agents

THE ROLE OF FOOD AND NUTRITION

Although a large number of dietary intervention studies have been undertaken in experimental animals, far fewer have been devoted to examining the effects of diet on carcinogen metabolism. Among the first were the studies by the Millers showing the capacity of the B vitamin, riboflavin, to increase inactivation of the carcinogen N,N-dimethyl-4-amino-azobenzene (butter yellow – an azo dye once used as a colouring agent in butter) in rats (Miller and Miller, 1953). Subsequently, it has been shown that dietary components can impede carcinogenesis by the following:

■ Blocking the metabolic activation that is controlled by the enzymes that catalyse oxidation or conjugation reactions

■ Increasing metabolic detoxification by similar processes

■ Providing alternative targets for the electrophilic metabolites

For example, using 2-acetylaminofluorene as an experimental carcinogen, the addition of methyl donors (for example, choline) to the diets of rats deficient in these compounds resulted in a decrease in the activated compound and in tumour occurrence (Poirier, 1987). Similarly, limiting the bioavailability of sulphate to rats suppressed the tumorigenicity of an azo dye (Weisburger et al, 1972). Compounds found in a range of plants, particularly members of the cabbage family (Cruciferae), are potent inducers of phase II enzymes (Huang et al, 1994).

Other examples involve calorie restriction and selenium feeding, which have been shown to inhibit binding to DNA by aflatoxin B_1 in the livers of rats (Chou et al, 1992; Shi et al, 1994). Selenium also decreased the metabolic activation of 2-acetylaminofluorene in the livers of rats and increased its detoxification (Poirier et al, 1986)

A wide variety of bioactive compounds and their derivatives has been shown to inhibit carcinogenesis in a number of experimental systems involving initiation, promotion and progression (Ho et al, 1994; Huang et al, 1994), and foods that contain abundant quantities of these substances – largely foods of plant origin – have consistently been shown to be associated with a lower risk of cancers at almost every site (Steinmetz and Potter, 1991a). A major mechanism of action is thought to involve their ability to increase expression (enzyme induction) of critical detoxification enzymes that are responsible for decreasing the bioavailability of potentially DNA-damaging carcinogens (Steinmetz and Potter, 1991b). In particular, phytochemicals (chemicals of plant origin) have increased the cellular levels of glutathione, glutathione transferase and glucuronyl transferase to facilitate the destruction of reactive electrophiles and oxidants into innocuous, excretable metabolites.

An increase in detoxification enzymes induced by dietary components tends to decrease overall metabolic activation of carcinogens and carcinogenesis in experimental animals. However, it is still not clear whether reduction in human carcinogenesis occurs because of such increased detoxification and decreased DNA damage.

2.6 INITIATION

Initiation is made up of a series of events whereby an exogenous or endogenous carcinogen induces alterations in the genetic make-up of the cell; this results in a lesion that can be inherited and which confers upon that cell the potential for neoplastic growth. This usually occurs after metabolic activation of a procarcinogen (Figure 2.3).

Figure 2.3 Initiation

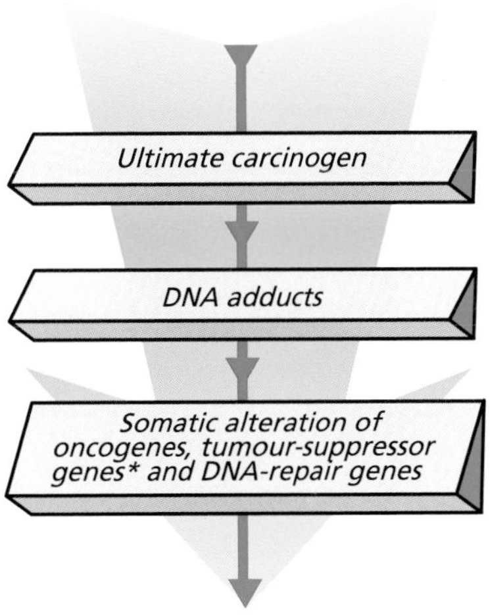

Ultimate carcinogen

DNA adducts

Somatic alteration of oncogenes, tumour-suppressor genes* and DNA-repair genes

* Some viruses act by inhibiting tumour-suppressor proteins and not by causing DNA damage

The chemistry of a wide variety of carcinogens has been extensively studied (Kadlubar and Beland, 1985). The relative potency of carcinogens appears to be determined by the stability of the adducts formed with DNA and by the ability to induce heritable alterations in the target genes (Hemminki et al, 1994). The binding of a carcinogen to proteins, not DNA, generally accounts for the vast majority of carcinogen residues bound to molecules – sometimes with high specificity. If such proteins include important growth controllers or their receptors, this could suggest non-DNA-interacting mechanisms as additional roles for electrophiles in cancer (this kind of interaction with proteins is well established in viral carcinogenesis). In addition, carcinogen binding to nuclear histones (proteins that surround and interact with DNA) and acidic proteins has also been documented. The intimate association of these proteins with chromatin (molecules containing DNA, RNA and proteins), and their pivotal role in the control of gene expression, certainly suggest that the modification of nuclear proteins by ultimate carcinogens could result in the induction or repression of proteins controlling cell replication, growth or differentiation.

Finally, blood proteins such as serum albumin and haemoglobin, the oxygen-carrying substance in red blood cells, often trap electrophilic metabolites of carcinogens. For serum albumin, this may occur in the liver (where albumin is synthesised) or in the extracellular fluid or blood plasma (where albumin is the predominant protein). As a result of its abundance in the body, binding of carcinogens to serum albumin may be an important detoxification reaction.

For similar reasons, binding of carcinogens to haemoglobin may also be regarded as a detoxification process. Indeed, for several different carcinogens, covalent binding to haemoglobin can be in the range of 1–10% of the dose administered. Accordingly, the high level of carcinogen that binds to blood proteins and its relative availability have resulted in the development of sensitive analytical methods for its detection in human populations, as a means of assessing exposure to chemical carcinogens.

BOX 2.3 DNA ADDUCTS, REPAIR AND MUTATION

Adducts

The structure of DNA can be altered if other molecules become chemically bonded to it, particularly to various nitrogens and oxygens. Such adducted molecules include hydroxyl groups (-OH), methyl groups (-CH$_3$) and larger compounds including heterocyclic and aromatic amines and polycyclic aromatic hydrocarbons. Such adducts are important for several reasons. Firstly, they distort the shape of the DNA molecule, potentially causing mistranslations. Secondly, when the DNA reproduces itself (replicates), an adducted base can be misread causing a mutation in the new strand. Thirdly, repair of bulky adducts can result in breakages of the DNA strand which can, in turn, result in mutations or deletions of genetic material.

Repair

The structure of translated DNA is such that each sequence of three bases (triplet) codes for a particular amino acid. The reproducibility and fidelity of the structure is ensured by the fact that they are only two legitimate pairings. If a wrong base is incorporated into one strand, the relevant DNA-repair system recognises the error by reading the other strand and cuts out and replaces the wrong base. If the cell, and therefore the DNA, replicates before it is repaired, the mutation becomes fixed in one of the two resulting cells and therefore, in any and all of its daughter cells. Mutations are therefore more likely to occur if cells are reproducing more rapidly (less time for repair) or if DNA repair mechanisms are defective.

There are other kinds of repair mechanisms for more extensive DNA damage (strand breaks, deletions, etc) and failure of these can also result in changes in the structure of the DNA.

Mutations and deletions

Mutations and deletions in key molecules such as oncogenes, tumour-suppressor genes and DNA-repair genes can therefore follow adduct formation and faulty repair. Such mutations and deletions are known key steps in carcinogenesis.

The reaction of ultimate carcinogens with the individual nucleic acids of DNA or RNA involves two general types of macromolecular damage: strand breakage and carcinogen–base adduct formation (Hemminki et al, 1994). Both are known to occur after carcinogen exposure in vivo, and both adduct formation and strand breakage (see Box 2.3) are believed to play a critical role in the initiation and promotion of the neoplastic process, when damage occurs in specific genes involved in growth control or repair of DNA.

Many of the carcinogen–base adducts formed have the potential to cause miscoding (that is, mutations) during replication. Such modifications can also give rise to large insertions or deletions in the nucleic acid sequence. In each of these cases, the fixation of the lesion by faulty repair mechanisms or as a consequence of cell replication represents a heritable change: the altered base is misread, the mistake is inherited by the daughter cells, and the gene no longer codes exactly (or at all) for the protein.

Unless DNA alterations are repaired effectively, they become permanent changes during the next cell division and are thus propagated from cell to cell during normal tissue growth and development. It is important to note that not all DNA alterations lead to neoplasia. To become an 'initiated' cell, the carcinogen-induced alteration must be one that eventually allows the cell to grow and reproduce autonomously, and become independent of the control of the surrounding normal cells.

GENETIC ALTERATION

There are at least four types of genetic alteration induced by environmental (including dietary) or endogenously formed carcinogens that could lead to cancer.

■ The first is somatic mutation, involving the covalent binding of carcinogens to DNA as the initial step. Direct support for this hypothesis comes from the strongly electrophilic nature of ultimate carcinogens, the ability of these compounds to bind covalently to DNA in vivo and in vitro, and the fact that faulty repair or persistence of the carcinogen–base adduct is known to result in a mutation. Moreover, carcinogens are directly mutagenic in microbial and mammalian test systems and on purified DNA. Mutation after covalent binding is strongly supported by the more recent discoveries that tumours induced by chemical carcinogens often contain single-base (point) mutations in genes that control cell growth (see below). Moreover, tumour promotion and progression, which can be strongly modified by nutritional status, may also involve formation of endogenous carcinogens such as reactive oxygen species (for example, hydroxyl radicals) and products of lipid peroxidation (for example, crotonaldehyde, malondialdehyde, 4-hydroxy-2-nonenal).

■ A second mechanism for tumour induction is also a consequence of DNA damage; it involves facilitated entry of a cancer-causing (oncogenic) DNA virus. Indeed, there are several experimental studies that show that chemical carcinogens and oncogenic viruses can act synergistically to transform cells into a neoplastic state. In an analogous manner, such DNA damage can also allow enhanced or unscheduled expression or inactivation of genes controlling cell growth.

■ A third mechanism involves the ability of carcinogens to react with RNA through covalent binding or induction of RNA damage; this then becomes transcribed into DNA, resulting in mutations or changes in gene expression. In fact, high levels of the enzyme that synthesises DNA from RNA, reverse transcriptase, are produced by the oncogenic RNA viruses (such as HTLV-I), which could likewise act together with carcinogens.

■ Fourth, modification by carcinogens of the enzymes that carry out DNA synthesis, the DNA polymerases, is known to decrease the fidelity of replication and repair. This will result in replication of DNA where the errors are allowed to persist (error-prone replication) and subsequent mutations. In an analogous manner, the carcinogenic metals, presumably through ionic interactions with DNA polymerases, are known to cause mismatching of the DNA bases and subsequent mutations.

Genetic damage can occur anywhere in the genome. It is probably crucial for the development of cancer only when what is damaged are the genes that control the proliferation and survival of the cell itself. Damage to proto-oncogenes and tumour-suppressor genes (as well as the genes that control DNA repair) is, therefore, the most important.

The discovery of 'oncogenes' which, when mutated, are capable of inducing transformation, and of functional opposites of oncogenes – the 'tumour-suppressor genes' – provides a unifying concept for the DNA-damaging parts of the cancer process and the loss of growth control. Both classes of genes, which together number over 100, are responsible for regulating the growth and differentiation of cells in a coordinated manner within the tissue (Weinberg, 1994), almost the antithesis of Ewing's definition of neoplasia.

PROTO-ONCOGENES

It is probably worth noting that the term 'oncogene' was applied after it was realised that these genes contained almost identical (homologous) DNA sequences to those found in DNA tumour viruses, but before it was recognised that these were not yet oncogenes (literally cancer genes). In fact, only after mutation of the DNA or over-expression of the gene, which results in a protein that is abnormal or over-abundant, is a continuous signal transmitted which tells the cell to replicate, thus leading to uncontrolled cell growth. Oncogenes or 'proto-oncogenes' (describing their non-mutated state) are crucial to the control of normal cell replication.

BOX 2.4 PROTO-ONCOGENES

The proteins produced by these genes are growth-controlling molecules. When these are mutated they are known as oncogenes and frequently allow unchecked proliferation of the cells. *(The accelerator is stuck.)*

It is now recognised that viral oncogenes (in cancer-causing viruses) evolved by acquiring a portion of the normal cellular proto-oncogene and placing it within the region of the viral replicative sequence.

There are several families of proto-oncogenes variously involved in biochemical signalling between and within cells and in the control of cell replication. On the basis of their location within the cell and the nature of the proteins that they code, cellular proto-oncogenes can be classified into four general categories (Anderson et al, 1992): protein kinases, the G-proteins, the nuclear proto-oncogenes and growth factors.

It is important to remember that this classification is not intended to imply that the different types of proto-oncogenes function independently of each other, either in their normal role or in carcinogenesis. On the contrary, it has been shown that, in different cells and tissue types, the coordinated activation or over-expression of more than one oncogene (for example, *ras* and *myc*) is often required to confer the full potential for neoplastic growth.

The mechanisms of activation of cellular proto-oncogenes into transforming oncogenes include at least three different processes: somatic mutation, gene over-expression, and gene rearrangement. The first two are thought to be important in the early stages of cancer, whereas the third seems to be important in the later stages known as progression. Somatic mutations serve as a primary mechanism for the activation of the *ras* proto-oncogenes, and result in permanent structural changes in the G-proteins, such that GTP hydrolysis is impaired and the protein remains in the activated state; this then transmits a continuous and uncontrolled (rather than an intermittent and controlled) stimulus to cell growth and replication.

It is now apparent that these *ras* mutations can arise as a consequence of the reaction of chemical (including dietary) carcinogens with the DNA in the coding sequence of the proto-oncogene and almost universally at one of three specific codons. Indeed, the point mutations observed in the mutated oncogenes of cancers are seen in mutagenicity test systems and match those induced by carcinogen–DNA adduct formation.

The initiation step in many tumours, including common human cancers such as those of the colon and pancreas, appears to be closely related to carcinogen-induced mutations of the *ras* family of oncogenes.

Another mechanism (which can be functionally equivalent to an activated oncogene) involves gene over-expression. In this, a normal proto-oncogene is expressed or amplified at a high level for a prolonged period of time, at an inappropriate time during cell growth, or in a tissue that ordinarily does not express the gene. Gene over-expression can also occur as a result of carcinogen-induced point mutations or genetic rearrangements (see below) in the non-coding, control sequences of proto-oncogenes. In addition, tumour promoters, which serve to disrupt cell physiology, appear to interfere in the cascade of normal cellular controls including proto-oncogenes, so that gene products are then expressed in an uncoordinated manner.

An additional mechanism for proto-oncogene activation is genetic rearrangement; this frequently involves the translocation of genetic material between chromosomes. Such genetic rearrangements may arise spontaneously or as a consequence of carcinogen-induced DNA damage; they are thought to be important in tumour progression. Such genetic abnormalities are known to exist in germline cells of some individuals and are believed to form the basis for genetically determined susceptibility to specific types of cancer.

TUMOUR-SUPPRESSOR GENES

Tumour-suppressor genes (see Box 2.5) code for a heterogeneous group of proteins, the absence of which (as a result of either the loss of both copies of the coding DNA or the protein itself after the formation of complexes with viral or other proteins) allows the cell to replicate without the usual checks on the integrity of the cell and its genome. The existence of tumour-suppressor genes has long been inferred from laboratory studies in which malignant tumour cells were fused with normal cells; the resultant hybrid cells displayed normal characteristics. A clear demonstration of this phenomenon involved the introduction of teratocarcinoma cells from one mouse strain into early embryos of another strain. The offspring retained the genetic markers and developed the physical characteristics of both strains; however, they did not develop malignant tumours, indicating that the cancer cells had indeed reverted to a normal phenotype in the presence of a normal copy of the tumour-suppressor gene.

BOX 2.5 TUMOUR-SUPPRESSOR GENES

The proteins produced by these genes prevent the cell from reproducing at inappropriate times or when the DNA is extensively damaged. When these are mutated or lost, the cell can still reproduce when its DNA is damaged. *(The brakes have been lost.)*

Another line of evidence for tumour-suppressor genes came from studies on the genetic basis of certain human cancers, namely retinoblastoma of the eye and Wilms' tumour of the kidney. Both cancers were first noted to arise in association with loss of genetic material on chromosomes 13 and 11, respectively. Subsequently, it became clear that the cancers arise from cells that lack not only the proper function of the inherited (abnormal) gene but also the second (normal) copy, so that they are completely without the protein product of the relevant gene.

It is now well established that certain individuals, who have an inherited defect in one of a number of tumour-suppressor genes, for example, *Rb* (the retinoblastoma gene), *p53* (associated with the Li–Fraumeni syndrome), *WT1*, *WT2* (the Wilms' tumour genes) or *APC* (the familial polyposis coli gene), have a much higher risk of specific tumours and develop them at a much earlier age than do people in the general population. The process always involves the loss of function of the remaining intact copy of the gene in those cells that become cancerous.

It is now also clear that many sporadic tumours undergo the same process; cells in genetically non-susceptible individuals must, however, lose both copies of the gene (both are normal at birth) before the cells can become neoplastic. This is a more significant issue for the overall population burden of cancer and for environmental influences on carcinogenesis. It is central, for instance, in colon cancer where it appears that most of the cells in the non-familial cancers have lost both copies of the *APC* tumour-suppressor gene. It has also become clear, very recently, that the second copy of a tumour-suppressor gene can become inactivated, not just by mutation, but also by silencing the gene through hypermethylation (addition of extra methyl groups); this is known to occur, for instance, in the development of kidney cancer in about 20% of those who have a germline mutation of the von Hippel–Lindau (*VHL*) gene. (See Box 2.1.)

As with the mutation of proto-oncogenes to an activated state after DNA damage, loss of tumour-suppressor gene function involves, in a high proportion of cases, interaction between DNA and some damaging agent. What proportion of this damage is a consequence of exposure to diet, tobacco smoke, industrial carcinogens, etc., and what proportion is a consequence of endogenously produced oxygen radical damage, is not established.

THE ROLE OF FOOD AND NUTRITION

Both macro- and micronutrients and other bioactive constituents of the diet have been shown to alter the various stages of carcinogenesis (Becci et al, 1979; Wood et al, 1983; Newberne and Rogers, 1986; Poirier et al, 1986; Kritchevsky and Klurfeld, 1987; Pariza, 1987; Sawada et al, 1990; Birt et al., 1992; Newmark and Lipkin, 1992; Wattenberg, 1992; Yuspa, 1994). Although, in recent years, a large number of important animal experimental studies have examined the role of diet in the modulation of tumour promotion, relatively few studies have examined modulation of initiation by diet. A few illustrative examples are given here; more are discussed in chapter 4.

The initiation of mammary carcinogenesis in female rats has been found to be inhibited by treatment with a protein-rich or selenium-supplemented diet; conversely, initiation was enhanced by pre-treatment with a high-fat diet. Furthermore, a high-fat diet enhanced the initiation of skin tumour formation in mice treated with a chemical carcinogen, DMBA (dimethylbenzanthracene), and energy restriction was shown to suppress liver tumour formation in rats given aflatoxin B_1.

A high animal protein (casein) diet enhanced the expression of a hepatitis B viral (HBV) antigen in HBV-containing transgenic mice (Hu et al, 1994). Similarly, the *p53* tumour-suppressor gene has been shown to undergo several alterations during carcinogenesis by dietary deficiency of methyl groups. The gene becomes hypomethylated and shows increased expression and increased DNA strand breaks (Christman et al, 1993; James et al, 1994a). The resulting liver tumours show a pattern of mutations (Smith et al, 1993) consistent with those seen in a large proportion of human cancers (Harris, 1993).

In addition, the increased expression of *ras* and *myc* oncogenes in the livers of rats fed diets deficient in methyl groups may be reversed by later supplementation of the animals with methyl donors (Wainfan and Poirier, 1992; Christman et al, 1993; Poirier, 1994).

The development of human colon tumours appears to correlate inversely with the intake of folate (Giovannnucci et al, 1993; Glynn and Albanes, 1994), and likewise a deficiency of folate enhances the development of colon tumours in dimethylhydrazine-treated rats (Glynn and Albanes, 1994). Folate and/or choline deficiency induces mutations both in vivo and in vitro, causes chromosomal and DNA single-strand breaks (James et al, 1994a; Glynn and Albanes, 1994), and inactivates the tumour-suppressor gene *p53* (Harris, 1993; James et al, 1994a).

Thus, the mechanisms of nutritional modulation of the early stages of carcinogenesis are consistent not only with biochemical and pharmacological endpoints but also with the molecular pathogenesis of this disease.

2.7 DNA REPAIR

As ultimate carcinogens (including those derived from diet) are electrophilic, they bind to electron-rich DNA, forming covalently bound adducts. Subsequent replication or error-prone repair of this modified DNA can result in mutations; these are structural changes in the genetic material that are inherited in the daughter cells of these damaged cells. (See Box 2.3). Such structural changes can involve the substitution of an incorrect base (point mutation), the addition or deletion of genetic material (frameshift or missense mutations), or even DNA strand breakage, with resultant aberrations in the pattern and organisation of the chromosomes (for example, karyotypic abnormalities, sister chromatid exchange or micronucleus formation) (Figure 2.4).

If such a process occurs in the ovum or sperm of an organism, germ-cell mutations arise and can be passed on to children. If mutations occur in other cells of the body, then they may be propagated as the somatic cell mutations characteristic of almost all tumours.

In addition to the mechanisms of detoxification of compounds before they interact with DNA, effective repair of carcinogen–base adducts can also serve as a critical detoxification mechanism. Several enzymatic processes are now understood that allow a carcinogen-modified base to be

Figure 2.4 DNA repair

DNA adducts

Genes

Somatic alteration of oncogenes, tumour-suppressor genes and DNA-repair genes

DNA repair

NORMAL DNA

removed by cleavage of its glycosyl bond, conversion back to the original base, or its excision along with neighbouring nucleotides and subsequent replacement with a newly synthesised sequence.

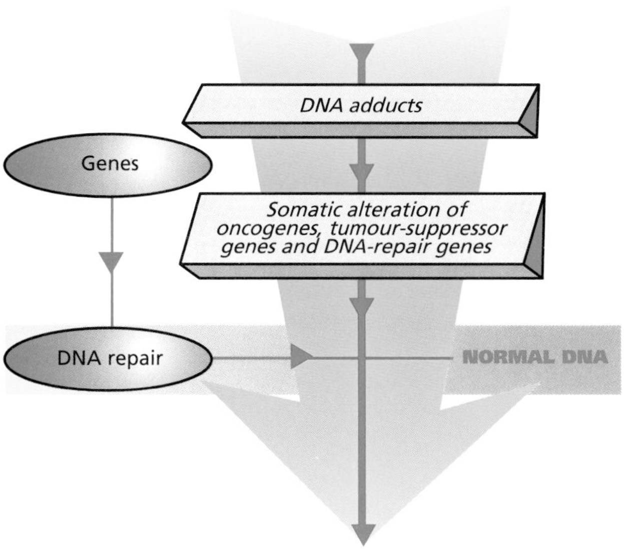

In this regard, several studies have shown that, when DNA–carcinogen adducts are formed in tissues that are not susceptible to carcinogenesis by a specific known agent, such adducts are often rapidly repaired. However, in tissues that have been shown to be the target of the carcinogen, specific carcinogen–base adducts usually persist in the DNA or reach a high steady-state level upon chronic exposure to the carcinogen. With aflatoxin B_1, for example, it has been estimated that steady-state levels of one adduct per 10^6 normal bases in the liver corresponds to a 50% incidence of hepatocellular carcinomas.

DNA repair enzymes (Radman and Wagner, 1993; Wei et al, 1994) are likely to play a critical role in determining the steady-state level of carcinogen–DNA adducts and their probability of serving as mutagenic lesions (see Box 2.3 and below). It is currently believed that there at least 25 different enzymes involved in DNA repair processes in humans. Many of these were discovered by the identification of rare hereditary disorders involving defective excision or base repair, or chromosomal instability, for example, xeroderma pigmento-

BOX 2.6 DNA-REPAIR GENES

DNA-repair genes produce proteins that ensure that damage to DNA is constantly repaired. When one of these genes is mutated, either in the germline or somatically, increasing DNA damage can accumulate in the affected cell(s). If a mutated or over-expressed proto-oncogene is like a stuck accelerator, and if loss of function of a tumour-suppressor gene is like lost brakes, *mutation of a DNA repair gene is comparable to having no mechanic.*

sum, Cockayne syndrome, ataxia telangiectasia, Fanconi anaemia and Bloom syndrome.

However, there is now epidemiological evidence that indicates that reduced DNA-repair capacity is associated with an increased prevalence of skin and brain cancer in the general population. Moreover, recent studies show that individuals with defective genes involving 'mismatch DNA repair' (one kind of DNA repair that corrects abnormalities of base pairing across the DNA strands) are at high risk for several cancers, including hereditary non-polyposis colon cancer (HNPCC).

DEATH OF THE DAMAGED CELL

If DNA damage has occurred as a consequence of exposure to exogenous carcinogens or endogenously generated oxygen radicals, and if the damage has persisted and been fixed in a clone of daughter cells by cell replication, it is still possible for the cells to die. All cells are equipped with a cell-suicide mechanism (programmed cell death), which ensures the death of that cell if the DNA is damaged beyond repair. Such a situation will not occur with a single point mutation but can arise as further loss of DNA occurs – deletions, strand breakage and whole chromosome loss. At some point in this accumulation of damage, the cell undergoes cell-cycle arrest and enters into the process known as apoptosis, involving break-up of the DNA and death of the cell. It is distinguished from the cell death associated with tissue trauma or necrosis by producing no inflammatory response.

It is now clear that the failure of some cancer cells to undergo apoptosis is the consequence either of loss of function of *p53* and other genes that control the cell-cycle checkpoints, or loss of the integrity of the machinery, controlled by the *bcl*-2 family of genes, of the apoptotic process itself.

THE ROLE OF FOOD AND NUTRITION

There are currently no data to suggest that any dietary exposures are related directly to the efficiency of the process of DNA repair.

There are also no established dietary agents that alter the apoptosis pathway in vivo. However, there are recent data to suggest that volatile short-chain fatty acids (produced in the colon by the fermentation of fibre and complex carbohydrates) may induce apoptosis in colon cancer cell lines in vitro (Hague et al, 1993; Hague and Paraskeva, 1995). Fibre and volatile fatty acids are thought to be important in colon carcinogenesis, so this may prove to be an important mechanism of action for a relatively late-acting dietary constituent. Research on this process may reveal other late-acting dietary modifiers of cancer in this and other organs.

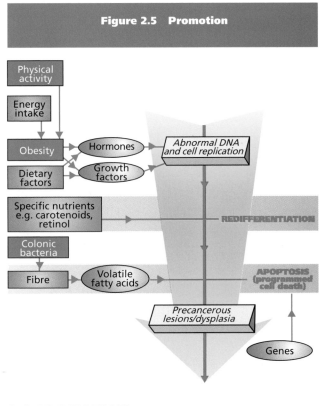

Figure 2.5   Promotion

2.8 PROMOTION

The next stage in the cancer process is called promotion. This involves alterations in gene expression and cell proliferation which transform the initiated cell into a discernible population of cancer cells. The concept of tumour promotion was elucidated largely by the discovery of chemicals that have no appreciable carcinogenic activity on their own but greatly enhance tumour development when given in conjunction with a carcinogen (Figure 2.5).

Such tumour promoters arise from diverse chemical classes such as the phorbol ester derivatives (naturally occurring plant constituents widely used in animal carcinogenesis experiments), certain barbiturate drugs, chlorinated hydrocarbons from industrial or agricultural sources, alcohol and endogenous hormones. In addition, high or low levels of essential dietary constituents have themselves been shown to exhibit tumour-promoting activity (Becci et al, 1979; Wood et al, 1983; Newberne and Rogers, 1986; Poirier et al, 1986; Kritchevsky and Klurfeld, 1987; Pariza, 1987; Sawada et al, 1990; Birt et al, 1992; Newmark and Lipkin, 1992; Wattenberg, 1992; Yuspa, 1994); classic tumour-promoting activity has been observed in rodents fed high dietary levels of protein (Wattenberg, 1992), fats and/or calories (Poirier et al, 1986; Kritchevsky and Klurfeld, 1987; Pariza, 1987) or low levels of methionine or choline (Sawada et al, 1990).

Tumour promoters do not appear to act by direct interaction with or binding to DNA; in experimental animals, continued application of tumour promoters usually results in more tumours. However, tumour promoters are especially potent in their ability to cause cellular replication and to exert profound changes in gene expression which alter controls on cell growth. Tumour promoters may also indirectly increase oxidative stress and lipid peroxidation, which leads to further DNA damage and its consequences.

These events are manifested by changes in the structural appearance and organisation (morphology) of cells within a tissue, by increases in their growth rate or mitosis, and by the extent to which these cells succeed or fail in becoming fully and normally functional (differentiation). Overall, promotion is thought to occur as a consequence of continued exposure to exogenous chemical carcinogens, which can produce further DNA damage, or tumour promoters (which promote growth with or without DNA damage), or to result from the body's own (endogenous) mechanisms producing changes in nutritional and hormonal status.

LOSS AND GAIN OF FUNCTION

The mutation of an oncogene (only one hit is necessary to contribute towards malignant behaviour) and the loss of the control exerted by a tumour-suppressor gene (here loss, mutation or silencing of both copies is necessary) could both be the consequences of the kinds of direct-acting carcinogens discussed above.

The other mechanisms that involve over-expression of an oncogene, the hypermethylation of a normal tumour-suppressor gene, or the complexing of a normal tumour-suppressor protein by a virus, are clearly more complicated and involve mechanisms both with and without interaction with DNA.

Moreover, it has also become apparent that the different classes of proto-oncogenes and the tumour-suppressor genes represent a network of functionally related genes that exert intricate controls over growth processes. As this cellular machinery becomes damaged by exposure to carcinogens and tumour promoters (including those in the diet), radiation, etc., tumorigenic potential is increased.

Finally, the capacity to repair the DNA damage in any one of these genes or even, of course, in the genes that code for the DNA repair proteins themselves, will also influence the overall likelihood of any one cell or individual developing cancer. There are still other inherited genes associated with an increased risk of cancer that do not yet clearly fall into the oncogene, tumour-suppressor or DNA repair gene classes. *BRCA-1*, associated with a markedly increased risk of breast cancer, is a possible example. Its mode of action is not established and almost nothing is yet known about the way in which environmental factors, such as diet, or host factors, such as hormones, interact with it. *BRCA-1* proteins belong to a highly conserved family of proteins called grannins, which undergo cleavage at the C-terminal end to yield short bioactive peptides that stimulate cell growth.

THE ROLE OF FOOD AND NUTRITION

The effects of diet on experimental tumour promotion have largely been investigated in four organ systems: mouse skin, rat mammary gland, rat intestine, and rat and mouse liver (Becci et al, 1979; Wood et al, 1983; Newberne and Rogers, 1986; Kritchevsky and Klurfeld, 1987; Pariza, 1987; Sawada et al, 1990; Birt et al, 1992; Newmark and Lipkin, 1992; Wattenberg, 1992; Yuspa, 1994). Findings from such investigations indicate that increased ingestion of fats and/or calories markedly enhances tumour promotion in most tissues examined (Poirier et al, 1986; Kritchevsky and Klurfeld, 1987; Pariza, 1987; Birt et al, 1992). Nutrients that have shown protective effects against tumour promotion are selenium and vitamin D.

The promotion of pre-cancerous tumours in the livers of rats (by feeding of a diet with 20% casein – the protein in milk) was inhibited if in subsequent feeding the casein level was dropped to 5% or was replaced by 20% plant protein.

Moderate deficiencies of the major dietary methyl donors, methionine and choline, have been shown to enhance liver tumour formation in rodents very markedly (Poirier et al, 1986; Sawada et al, 1990). Choline deficiency causes a rise in the hepatic contents of diacylglycerol, a second messenger that increases cell proliferation (Zeisel, 1992).

Finally, the efficacy of specific nutrients in delaying the progression of pre-cancerous lesions from one stage to the next can be seen in such disparate organs as the liver (with methyl donors being protective) and urinary tract (retinoids). Retinoids are also established in humans as agents capable of reducing the likelihood of a second primary cancer in the upper aerodigestive tract (for example, oropharynx, larynx, oesophagus) in those already treated for cancers in this part of the body. There is good evidence to suggest that this chemotherapeutic approach to secondary prevention acts late in the process of carcinogenesis and, in fact, slows down or prevents promotion.

The beneficial or adverse effects of dietary components on tumour promotion and progression are frequently accompanied by decreased or increased levels, respectively, of oxidative damage in the target tissues (Poirier et al, 1986; Wattenberg, 1992). Considerable speculation has thus centred on the possible role of oxidative damage to DNA in tumour promotion and progression (Ames, 1991; Simic and Bergtold, 1991). Evidence has accumulated indicating the direct formation of oxidised DNA bases in vivo and their association with increased consumption of calories.

Calorie restriction has been shown to suppress the expression of the H-*ras* oncogene in the pancreas of rats as well as the formation of spontaneous tumours in 'transgenic knock-out' mice – mice with a *p53* tumour-suppressor gene that has been rendered non-functional by genetic engineering techniques (Hass et al, 1993; Hursting et al, 1994); again this suggests mechanisms with and without interaction with DNA. Evidence for a role for obesity in human cancers has been found in studies of breast, endometrium, colon and kidney tumours. Physical activity, which maintains lean body mass as well as influencing several other systems in the body, especially endocrine and immunological function, is very consistently associated with a lower risk of colon cancer and, probably, breast cancer.

More recent studies have provided evidence that oxidation of membrane lipids can also eventually lead to DNA damage (Bartsch et al, 1994). It is now apparent that each stage of carcinogenesis may be advanced further by carcinogen-induced DNA damage, as well as by a variety of mechanisms that influence the behaviour but not the structure of DNA. These latter are called epigenetic mechanisms.

There are at least three categories of epigenetic alterations induced by carcinogens or nutritional factors that could lead to neoplasia. The most widely accepted of these involves viewing cancer as essentially a disease of cellular differentiation, with exogenous and endogenous carcinogens and/or nutritional factors acting to alter the critical cellular proteins that control these processes.

Examples of such protein modification include the binding of carcinogens either to histones and other nuclear proteins crucial to the normal DNA function, or to protein kinases which may cause the cell to express behaviours (even in the absence of obvious DNA damage) that are consistent with progression towards the behaviour of a malignant cell. Viral proteins (for example, those produced by the human papillomaviruses, the probable causal agents in cervical cancer) can bind to human cellular proteins (tumour-suppressor proteins) in a way that allows the uncontrolled growth of cells, even in the absence of any direct DNA changes. Finally, nutritional status (particularly choline, methionine, folate or carotenoid deficiency) can cause changes in gene expression in abnormal cell types, and this can result in the loss of control of tissue growth.

A second epigenetic mechanism involves carcinogen binding to RNA polymerases or to transfer RNA (tRNA), which can result in changes in the codons that specify amino acid synthesis in proteins. Such an amino acid substitution could also alter the structure and function of critical proteins controlling cell growth and differentiation.

Third, it should be recognised that many chemicals and host factors may be regarded as co-carcinogenic because they function as tumour promoters, provide a hormonal stimulus or depress the immune response; each of these may encourage previously existing initiated cells to proliferate and progress towards the development of a benign or malignant tumour.

The role of these epigenetic mechanisms in tumour development is now known to be complicated by association with several types of endogenously caused DNA damage known to occur in vivo (Poirier et al, 1986; James and Swendseid, 1989; Meuth, 1989; Hinrichsen et al, 1990; Randerath and Randerath, 1994). These types of damage include: single-strand breaks, chromosomal breaks, hypomethylation, abnormal base insertion, base oxidation and adduct formation.

Each of these can result in abnormal gene expression or gene mutations. Moreover, each form of damage can be enhanced by dietary manipulation alone. In most instances, the dietary changes involved also result in an enhancement of tumour formation. For example, fragile chromosomes are produced in human lymphocytes during folate deficiency, and respond to folate treatment. Similarly, a diet deficient in folic acid, as well as in the methyl donors methionine and choline, increases DNA single-strand breaks in the lymphocytes of rats.

The demonstration of DNA hypomethylation in the livers of methyl-deficient rats was made only one year after it became clear that dietary methyl insufficiency caused liver cancer in this species. The long-term feeding of methyl-deficient diets to rats or the chronic application of tumour promoters to mouse skin has led to increased levels of 8-hydroxyguanine (an oxidised DNA base) in the liver and epidermal DNA, respectively. On the other hand, calorie restriction leads to decreased levels of 8-hydroxyguanine and other oxidised DNA bases. Lipid peroxidation, induced by chemicals or by nutritional alterations, may enhance the formation of etheno-, propano-, and malondialdehyde adducts of DNA (Bartsch et al, 1994; Chaudhary et al, 1994; Kim et al, 1994; Nath and Chung, 1994). Thus, specific changes in dietary patterns can result in identifiable genetic damage known to be associated with both the early stages of carcinogenesis, including adduct formation and DNA breaks, and epigenetic changes that influence the later growth and clonal expansion of abnormal cells.

Finally, it is important to note that no single genetic or epigenetic mechanism can account for all the steps in carcinogenesis in a single tissue, and certainly cannot account for the variety of routes that different tissues take to neoplasia. Indeed, it is likely that there is a number of possible mechanisms, even in the same tissue and with the same agents in the transition from normal to transformed cells and thence to cancer. The role and site of action of many probable agents – both those that increase and those that decrease the likelihood of cancer – still have to be elucidated.

2.9 PROGRESSION

The last stage of the cancer process, progression, involves the increased growth and expansion of a population of initiated and promoted cancer cells from a focal lesion to an invasive tumour mass, often accompanied by an increasingly abnormal complement of genetic material. DNA damage is widespread in this late stage with loss, breakage and duplication of multiple chromosomes. Progression leads ultimately to metastasis, whereby tumour cells migrate to distant sites in the body (Figure 2.6).

As noted above in the section on proto-oncogenes, one mechanism for proto-oncogene activation is genetic rearrangement; this frequently involves the translocation of genetic material between chromosomes. The result is either production of an altered gene product or the enhanced or uncoordinated expression of the proto-oncogene that has been translocated away from its normal (upstream) genetic controlling sequences. These genetic rearrangements may arise as the result of oxygen-radical damage or as a consequence of carcinogen-induced DNA damage, and are thought

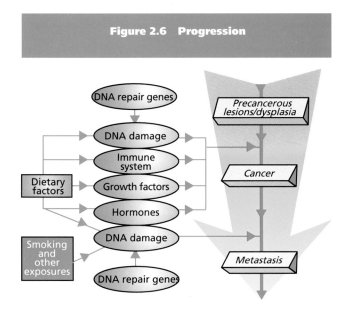

Figure 2.6   Progression

to be important during tumour progression.

As is the case for tumour-suppressor genes, such genetic abnormalities are known to exist in the germline of some individuals and are believed to form the basis for genetically determined susceptibility to specific types of cancer.

THE ROLE OF FOOD AND NUTRITION

The role of food and nutrition, including carcinogens, in this final stage of tumorigenesis is not yet clear. Recent studies show that many chemical carcinogens and tumour promoters can give rise to the formation of reactive oxygen species (for example, hydroxyl radicals) that can cause DNA damage and chromosomal breakage; this is one mechanism that has been linked to the development of a fully malignant cancer. Agents that induce the early mutations may also contribute to the later stages of total disorganisation of the tumour cell genome, and the loss of control of proliferation and apoptosis. Although evidence for dietary agents that act in this way is lacking so far, epidemiological data on smoking suggest that tobacco-associated carcinogens could act both early and late in the cancer process.

Figure 2.7 *overleaf* integrates the cancer processes described above into one flow diagram.

FIGURE 2.7 DIET AND THE CANCER PROCESS
Current knowledge about some of the interrelationships of food, nutrition and other factors, and how these may affect the cancer process, is summarised in here. As the science develops, pathways may become more complex, and are likely to be drawn with more confidence.

At the earliest stages in the cancer process, known individual dietary carcinogens, such as heterocyclic amines, polycyclic aromatic hydrocarbons and *N*-nitroso compounds, may contribute directly to the body's carcinogenic load. Such compounds are found in cooked foods, cured and spoiled food, and some alcoholic drinks. The extent to which such dietary carcinogens may initiate the cancer process depends on the general quality of diets. If diets are high in vegetables and fruits, the availability of a large number of bioactive compounds is increased; these induce detoxification enzymes which, in turn, reduce the exposure of DNA to carcinogens.

In the intermediate stages of carcinogenesis, in which there is growth of the initiated clone of cells, it is probable that energy balance and turnover are critical in maintaining normal cell behaviour or allowing expansion of the abnormal cells. Leanness reduces risk and obesity increases the likelihood of tumorigenesis, probably through the action of specific hormones and growth factors. This, in turn, suggests a role for total energy intake and physical activity in the cancer process.

Later in the cancer process, when DNA damage is again central, vegetables and fruits provide folate, a major source of physiological methyl donors reducing the likelihood of DNA hypomethylation and chromosome breakage. In the specific case of the colon, fibre may be fermented by the colonic bacteria producing volatile fatty acids; these may increase the probability that abnormal cells will undergo programmed cell death – apoptosis. Antioxidants are widespread in foods of plant origin and may reduce the generation of oxygen radicals; these radicals are believed to play a role in the later stages of the cancer process during the gross disorganisation of DNA. Energy-dense diets that contain substantial amounts of fat may create more reactive metabolites, including lipid peroxides and oxygen radicals.

Through such chemical changes, the constituents of diet and connected factors, methods of food processing, specific foods and drinks, as well as diets as a whole, have a part to play in all the stages of the cancer process. Together with this, there is interplay between environmental factors, and predisposition, both inherited and acquired, and this may vary at different stages of life.

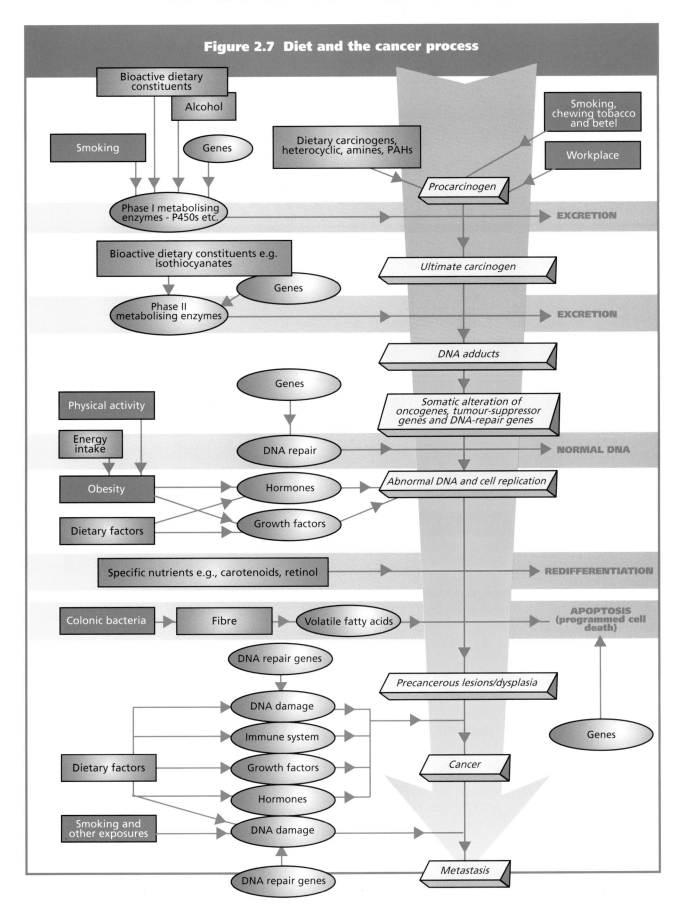

Figure 2.7 Diet and the cancer process

CHAPTER THREE

Scientific evidence and judgement

Cancer is largely a preventable disease; the incidence of cancer can be substantially reduced by means of diet.

The basis for these judgements is set out in this chapter. Methods used to investigate the links between food, nutrition and cancer are summarised, and their strengths and weaknesses outlined. Explanations are given of how findings from many different kinds of studies may amount to sufficient proof of causal relationships between food, nutrition and cancer.

The first section summarises different types of epidemiological study. These include: descriptive and ecological studies and studies of populations over time, cohort and case-control analytical studies conducted at the individual level, and controlled trials of different agents and diets in selected groups. The second section outlines the means by which energy intake, body mass, physical activity, dietary constituents, foods and drinks, and methods of food processing can be assessed. The third section describes experimental studies, and short-term studies in humans designed to identify mechanisms by which aspects of diet may affect the risk of cancer.

No study design stands alone. In science, as in other disciplines relevant to public policy, there is no absolute proof. Instead, analogous with legal process, corroborative findings from various sources can form a solid basis for recommendations designed to improve public health. The strongest evidence indicating that food and nutrition modify the risk of cancer comes from a combination of different types of epidemiological enquiry, supported by experimental findings, and by identification of plausible biological pathways. The panel's assessments of the relative merits of the different types of scientific evidence are made at the end of each section.

Recommendations to policy-makers and to individuals on the primary prevention of cancer require sound evidence that consequent actions will be effective. The fourth section shows how the impact of food and nutrition on the risk of cancer in populations can be assessed, as a basis for effective quantified recommendations. Finally, the fifth section of the chapter explains the methods the panel has used, in chapters 4 to 7, to review and assess the evidence.

3.1 EPIDEMIOLOGICAL STUDIES

Epidemiological research describes and seeks to explain the distribution of health and illness within human populations. Knowledge of the causes of human cancer comes primarily from epidemiological studies which compare population groups or categories of individuals who share some common characteristic.

The methods used are based mainly on comparative observations made at the level of whole populations, special groups (such as migrants or vegetarians), or individuals within a population, who are investigated by methods using varying degrees of control. By relating differences in circumstances and behaviour to differences in the incidence of disease, associations that may be causal are identified.

Every type of epidemiological study has particular strengths and weaknesses. Confident judgements are normally only possible when the lines of different types of evidence converge. A necessary basis for public policy is reliable knowledge of what happens when people are exposed to different environmental factors; public health policy will continue to rely primarily on the findings of epidemiology.

DESCRIPTIVE STUDIES

The descriptive epidemiology of cancer includes data on incidence, mortality and risk. The most basic information about cancer comes from statistics on cancer incidence and mortality, as summarised in chapter 1. Cancer incidence rates are usually specified by sex and age. Cancer mortality rates are more widely available than cancer incidence rates, as the former can be derived from routinely collected national data on causes of death.

Information from cancer incidence and mortality rates has limitations. Differences in incidence rates or changes in these rates over time can be due to differences in screening intensity or changes in diagnostic criteria. On the other hand, cancer mortality rates, at least for some cancers, can also be altered by screening programmes and effective therapies.

Cancer risk is the probability of developing cancer during a specified time. Sometimes this is expressed as risk within an average lifetime as, for example, the one in eight probability of a woman in the USA being diagnosed with breast cancer.

CORRELATION STUDIES

The simplest type of study for exploring the relationship between diet and cancer is the correlation or ecological study. This investigates diet and cancer at the population level, and entails comparisons of cancer rates with consumption of nutrients, foods or other aspects of diet.

The first systematically gathered evidence on diet and cancer to suggest that the principal causes of most cancers are environmental in origin, and that diet may be a major environmental factor, came from correlation studies. The conclusions and recommendations of statements and reports on diet and cancer published up to the early 1980s, notably the NAS report *Diet, Nutrition and Cancer* (NAS, 1982) placed substantial reliance on correlation studies, together with migrant and animal studies, and evidence of biological plausibility (see below).

Some correlations between dietary constituents and cancer risk are remarkably strong. For example, the international correlation between meat intake and the incidence of colon cancer has been measured as 0.85 for men and 0.89 for women (Armstrong and Doll, 1975), meaning that most of the difference in rates of this cancer can be accounted for, on a statistical basis, by differences in meat consumption.

An obvious limitation of most correlation studies is that, while they may suggest a relationship between a specific environmental factor (such as an aspect of diet) and disease, the actual causal relationship may be with a different, diet-associated, confounding factor (Kinlen, 1983).

For instance, diets high in meat (of the type eaten in industrialised societies) are associated with an increased risk of some cancers common in such societies. But diets high in meat are also likely to be high in fat, and may also be high in sugar and alcohol; in addition, people who eat such diets are relatively likely to have high incomes, live in urban areas and lead sedentary lives. Unless data on exposure to relevant dietary and non-dietary factors other than meat are available, and these factors are allowed for, it is not possible, in this instance, to be sure that meat is the key factor affecting cancer risk.

Further, a lack of correlation between an aspect of diet and disease may disguise an actual relationship, because of possible varying genetic predisposition in different populations. So correlation studies may give false-positive results (data suggesting a relationship with cancer where none exists) or false-negative results (data suggesting no relationship where, in fact, one does exist).

Another problem with the simpler type of correlation study is that the 'exposure' data may sometimes relate only weakly to the subpopulation of individuals at risk of disease. One example is alcohol and breast cancer. As stated in chapter 4.11, alcohol consumption is related to an increased risk of breast cancer. Interpretation of correlational data on alcohol intake and breast cancer is complicated, however, because it is generally the men who consume most of the alcohol in any population, whereas it is the women who develop breast cancer. In cases like this, correlation studies need to collect data on relevant population subgroups divided, for example, by sex, as has been done in China (Chen et al, 1990).

Furthermore, correlation studies (certainly across countries) cannot be independently reproduced, and independent replication is an important part of the scientific process. Although the dietary information can be elaborated and the analyses can be refined, the data in a repeat analysis will not really be independent. Even as more information becomes available over time, the populations, their diets and the confounding variables will be similar.

However, correlation studies have special strengths, especially when conducted between populations, either internationally or cross-culturally among contrasting populations within a country. One reason why such studies are valuable is because interpopulation ranges in intake of foods and dietary constituents are sometimes wider than, or different from, intrapopulation ranges. For example, within industrialised countries virtually all individuals consume between 23% and 50% of their calories in the form of fat (Willett et al, 1992), whereas the mean fat intake for whole populations throughout the world varies from less than 15% to 42% of calories (WHO, 1990).

Studies of wide ranges of dietary intake are an important means of identifying relationships between food and nutrition and the risk of disease, if only because levels of intake that modify disease risk may be above or below the ranges found in specific populations. For example, cross-cultural epidemiological studies, both of settled populations and of migrants, supported by other human and animal data, indicate that the risk of coronary heart disease increases with increasing intake of saturated fat, whereas studies conducted within relatively homogeneous populations may show little, if any, correlation between saturated fat consumption and incidence of coronary heart disease.

This superficially puzzling finding may be explained by the fact that the ranges of fat intake within populations are sometimes too narrow to detect an effect. This is why dietary goals designed to prevent coronary heart disease commonly recommend levels of saturated fat intake below those consumed by most individuals within industrialised societies (WHO, 1982, 1990). Alternatively, the relationship seen in cross-sectional studies may be due to other factors associated with affluence, such as a sedentary lifestyle and obesity.

The same issue may apply to data on food, nutrition and cancer risk, and may have the same implications. Cross-cultural correlation studies may, thus, provide a test of the validity of the findings of studies conducted among relatively homogeneous populations. Such studies also have other strengths. Average national diets are likely to be more stable over time than the diets of individual people; for most countries, the changes in dietary intakes over a decade or two are relatively small. Also, the disease rates on which international studies are based are usually derived from relatively large populations and are therefore subject to only small random errors. However, the quality of assessment and recording of disease may vary a great deal between countries.

Much can be learned from international comparative studies of food, nutrition and cancer (and other diseases). The very different living conditions, and the vast variety of foods of plant and animal origin throughout the world, enable dietary factors that are associated with cancers in one relatively homogeneous region or country to be tested subsequently in very different countries. Thus, in North America and northern Europe, many environmental factors can obscure or distort dietary causes of cancer, despite rigorous attempts to adjust for such non-dietary factors. If, however, the same evidence of relationships between diet and cancer emerges in entirely different cultural and dietary contexts, the credibility of findings within one region or country is reinforced.

Associations between aspects of diet and cancer found in correlation studies are most likely to point to a causal relationship when the populations studied are known to consume much the same diet over long periods of time, when the associations show consistent trends across different levels of analysis (populations, subpopulations, migrant groups, for example), and when they are biologically plausible.

Correlation studies may compare populations at a common point in time. They may also compare single populations over a period of time. These are called secular trend studies.

Major changes in the rates of a disease within a population over time provide evidence that non-genetic factors play an important role in that disease. In Japan, for example, the rates of colon cancer have risen dramatically since 1950 (Aoki et al, 1992). Analysis of the secular trends in putative dietary risk factors may then suggest explanations. While secular changes clearly demonstrate that environmental factors, which may include diet, are primary causes of this disease, genetic susceptibility factors may still influence which individuals become affected within a population.

SPECIAL EXPOSURE GROUPS

Subgroups within a population that consume unusual diets provide an additional opportunity to learn about relationships between dietary factors and cancer. These may simply be compared with the general population or studied on an individual basis. Such groups are often defined by religious or ethnic characteristics. In addition, the special populations often live in the same general environment as the comparison group, which may reduce the number of alternative explanations for any differences that might be observed. For example, colon cancer mortality among the largely vegetarian Seventh-day Adventists is only about half that expected on the basis of the mortality rate within the population at large (Phillips et al, 1980). This observation supports the hypothesis that diets containing large amounts of meat increase the risk of colon cancer.

Findings based on special exposure groups are subject to some of the same limitations as correlation studies. Many factors, both dietary and non-dietary, are likely to distinguish these special groups from the comparison population. Thus, another possible explanation for the lower colon cancer incidence and mortality among the Seventh-day Adventist population is that differences in rates are attributable to a lower intake of alcohol or to a higher consumption of vegetables. Studies of special exposure groups can, however, control for such confounding factors.

MIGRANT STUDIES

Migrant studies enable assessment of whether the correlations observed in ecological studies are due to genetic or environmental factors. As mentioned in chapter 1, populations migrating between areas with different cancer incidence rates acquire the rates characteristic of their new location for most cancers, often after only one or two generations.

Such findings prove beyond reasonable doubt that genetic factors cannot be primarily responsible for the large differences in cancer rates in different regions and countries. Cancers whose incidence shifts with migration are, to that extent, diseases with environmental causes. Where incidence rates among immigrants actually overshoot the rates of the new host country, as in pancreatic cancer among Polish migrants to Australia or colon cancer among the Japanese in Hawaii, it is plausible that this represents a difference in the proportion of susceptibles to the environmental factor(s) among the new migrants compared with those born locally.

The importance of migrant evidence for establishing environmental causes has been emphasised in a number of reports on diet and cancer risk. For example, with particular reference to correlation and migrant studies, the major study by Doll and Peto (1981), noted international differences in death from cancer of a large number of sites, approximating to those reviewed and assessed in this report, and estimated the percentage of these deaths that might be attributed to various factors, including diet. This analysis was done with specific reference to the USA but may be taken to apply elsewhere.

Thus, the great variation in deaths from colorectal cancer and in stomach cancer in different parts of the world, and lack of evidence of non-dietary causes of these cancers, led Doll and Peto to the estimate that 90% of deaths from these cancers might be avoidable by feasible dietary means. (Subsequent evidence of associated and non-dietary factors, such as physical activity in the case of colon cancer and bacterial infection in the case of stomach cancer, would probably modify such estimates.) The 'best estimate' proposed by Doll and Peto, based on the evidence then available, was that perhaps 35% of all cancer deaths are caused by diet (excluding alcohol, estimated as causing a further 3% of all cancer

deaths). A corresponding percentage of cancer deaths was identified as avoidable by dietary means.

Doll and Peto emphasised, however, that such a figure was a 'guesstimate' and that between 10% and 70% of all cancer deaths might be attributable to diet, although their estimates of the role of diet in deaths from cancers of specific sites—of the pancreas, gallbladder, breast, and endometrium (all 50%), and of the mouth and pharynx, larynx, oesophagus, lung, cervix and bladder (all 20%), as well as colorectal and stomach cancers—were made with comparative confidence.

CASE-CONTROL STUDIES

The preceding sections have examined 'big picture' variations in cancer and diet at the population or subpopulation levels. Most recent epidemiological research on food, nutrition and cancer has been done in a more detailed, resource-intensive fashion by collecting information at the level of the individual. Sets of individuals are compared, in case-control, cohort or cross-sectional studies. Information from these forms of epidemiological research is statistically more powerful than that gathered from population studies.

Many of the weaknesses of correlation studies can be avoided in case-control studies. Known or suspected potential confounding factors can be controlled or eliminated in the study design, or controlled in the data analysis.

In case-control studies, patients with a specific type of cancer (the cases) and a comparable group of people without cancer (the controls) are identified from the same known (or presumed) source population. Information is then obtained from each case and control subject, often by interview about their earlier diets. It may then become evident that the cancer patients report (say) higher levels of consumption of alcohol than the control subjects. The possibility that this finding is confounded by (say) smoking – because drinkers often also smoke – can be dealt with by analysing the results for smokers and non-smokers separately, or by adjusting the analysis of the alcohol/cancer relationship for smoking behaviour. If the result of such analysis showed no difference in alcohol intake between the cancer cases and controls, this would be evidence that alcohol was not a cause of that particular cancer.

Large case-control studies, with several hundred or more cases and a similar or larger number of controls, can deal with many confounding factors in this way.

Case-control studies have some weaknesses of their own. Individuals may misreport their habitual past diets; if cases and controls differ in the accuracy of their dietary recall, the ensuing comparison will be biased. Also, some individual aspects of diet, especially nutrient content, may not vary greatly within a population, so case-control studies may not show wide ranges of cancer risk within that population.

A range of risk between half and twice the average risk is often as much as can be expected between the lowest and highest consumption levels. However, such ranges have major public health significance where certain cancers are important causes of death, and can also suggest, by reference to cross-cultural correlation studies or by extrapolation, that radical dietary change may bring even greater benefits.

Another common problem is that controls are often people with another disease, because hospital patients are convenient subjects to study; their disease might also be diet-related. In such situations, the study results could be seriously biased, and may often not show a clear difference between cases and controls. For such reasons, the results of different case-control studies of diet and cancer are sometimes inconsistent.

COHORT STUDIES

In prospective cohort studies, the diets of a large group of healthy individuals are assessed and the group is then followed over time, usually for a decade or more, during which time a number of cohort members will develop cancer. The relationship of those cancers to specific characteristics of individual diets is then analysed.

Prospective cohort studies avoid most of the methodological problems of other epidemiological studies. They also provide the opportunity to obtain repeated assessments of diet at regular intervals, which improves the validity of individual dietary assessment and enables examination of the effects of diet on various cancers and on diseases other than cancer. Cohort studies also enable the collection and storage of tissue samples for subsequent analysis in relation to the occurrence of cancer (see 3.3).

The main limitations of prospective studies are practical. Even for common diseases, such as colon or breast cancer in industrialised societies, it is necessary to enrol tens of thousands of subjects to have reasonable statistical power to determine relative risks. Hence, such studies are expensive. They are, therefore, of value mainly as means of investigating diseases common in economically developed countries. They are not a practicable means of investigating relatively uncommon diseases.

Cohort studies also usually depend on the use of self-administered food-frequency questionnaires (see Box 3.2). Limitations on the validity of questionnaire assessment of usual diet are essentially the same as for case-control studies. Cohort studies may have other limitations. In some circumstances, the cohort of people selected from the population at large may be more homogeneous in lifestyle (and dietary habits) than a random sample of the total population. For logistical reasons, the age range of cohort populations is often more restricted than that of case-control studies. If exposures are associated with different levels of risk at different ages (age interactions), this will be less obvious in the cohort study (Slattery et al, 1995). As a result of their prospective design, with diet being assessed before the occurrence of cancer, there is little likelihood of selection or recording bias in cohort studies.

Prospective cohort studies that have published data on diet and cancer include the Nurses' Health Study (about 95,000 women), the California Adventists' Study (about 40,000 men and women), the New York State Cohort (about 80,000 men and women), the Canadian Breast Cancer Screening Cohort (about 56,000 women), the Health Professionals Follow-up Study (about 52,000 men), the Iowa Women's Study (about 42,000 women) and the Dutch Health Study (about 130,000 men and women).

As diets within single populations are likely to be too homogeneous to allow complete study of relationships with disease, international and cross-cultural studies are of special value. In Europe, a large multicentre prospective cohort study (EPIC), and in the USA and Australia two large multi-ethnic cohort studies, are due to be published around the year 2000.

CONTROLLED TRIALS

Controlled trials use a control group of people given an inactive substance, and an intervention group given dietary constituents that may affect cancer risk. This is as close as epidemiology gets to the experimental designs used in animal studies; controlled trials of diet are somewhat like trials used to test drugs.

For obvious ethical reasons, the study of factors believed to increase the risk of disease in humans cannot usually be studied experimentally by deliberately exposing groups of people to the risk factor. It is unlikely, for example, that trials could be conducted to examine the effect of alcohol on the risk of human breast cancer, other than to examine the metabolic, especially hormonal, consequences of short-term administration of alcohol to healthy volunteers.

BOX 3.1 DIET: TIME OF EXPOSURE, TIME OF MEASUREMENT

The assessment of diet and its relationship with disease is complicated by time. In general, it is not yet known when diet is most relevant in the cancer process. This factor probably varies from cancer site to site. For some cancers, diet may be important during childhood, even though the disease occurs decades later. For other cancers, it may be that diet may act as a late-stage promoting or inhibiting factor; thus intake over a continuous period up to just before diagnosis may be important.

Ideally, data on dietary intake at different points before diagnosis could help to resolve these issues. But people rarely make clear changes in their diets at identifiable points in time; more typically, eating patterns evolve over periods of years. In case-control studies, epidemiologists often direct questions about diet to a period several years before diagnosis of the disease in the hope that the diet at that point will represent, or at least be correlated with, diet during the critical period in cancer development.

Diets of individuals tend to be correlated from year to year, so that imprecision in identification of critical periods of exposure may not be serious. In North America at least, for most nutrients, correlations for repeated assessments of diet at intervals from one to about ten years are of the order of 0.6–0.7, with decreasing correlations over longer intervals. These correlations are similar to other biological measurements made in free-living populations, such as serum cholesterol and blood pressure (Willett, 1990a).

The preferred experimental method is the randomised controlled trial in which people are assigned to an intervention or control group at random. The strength of evidence from experimental studies is increased if they are conducted 'blind', meaning the subjects do not know whether they belong to the intervention or to the control group, or 'double-blind', meaning that the investigators do not know either. The study may use a 'cross-over' design, meaning that half-way through the study, subjects are switched from one exposure/treatment to the other.

Such trials usually test the effects of varying levels of supplementation with dietary microconstituents (as pills or by other means). Blind or double-blind trials are usually impossible with foods or dietary macroconstituents, which are recognisable. Non-blind studies that require substantial changes in behaviour, such as giving up familiar foods and substituting new foods, are typically much more difficult, because this requires continuous personal instruction and a high level of commitment by the participant.

The principal strength of a randomised trial is that potentially confounding variables should be distributed at random between the treatment and control groups, thus minimising the possibility of spurious differences in outcome because of extraneous factors.

Such trials among humans are best justified after considerable data have been collected to ensure that benefit is reasonably probable and that an adverse outcome is unlikely. Controlled trials are particularly useful as a means of evaluating hypotheses that microconstituents of diet, such as vitamins or trace elements, can prevent cancer, because these microconstituents can be formulated into pills or capsules.

Controlled trials have limitations. The time between the change in the level of a dietary factor and any expected change in the incidence of disease is usually uncertain. Trials should therefore be of long duration. Nonetheless, if an effect is not found, it can always be argued that the follow-up was of insufficient duration. It is questionable whether trials of sufficient size, duration and degree of compliance could be conducted to evaluate hypotheses that involve major changes in eating patterns, such as a major reduction in fat intake.

In non-blind studies of foods, the control group may adopt the dietary behaviour of the treatment group if the treatment diet is thought by them to be beneficial. Such trends, which occurred in the US Multiple Risk Factor Intervention Trial of coronary disease prevention (Multiple Risk Factor Intervention Trial Research Group, 1982) may obscure a real benefit of the treatment.

People who agree to participate in trials tend to be relatively health conscious and highly motivated; people who, on the basis of their dietary intake, are at high potential risk, and thus susceptible to intervention, are liable to be underrepresented. Hence, the generalisability of the results is limited. For example, if low folate intake is thought to be a risk factor for colon cancer and a trial of folate supplementation is conducted among a health-conscious population including few individuals with low folate intake, the trial might show no effect simply because the study population was already receiving the full benefit of this nutrient from diet. In such an instance, it would be useful to measure dietary intake of folate before starting the trial.

Controlled trials designed to assess how aspects of diet may prevent cancer, and that use synthesised and concentrated microconstituents of diet such as vitamins and trace elements are called chemoprevention trials. Examples include the trial of upper gastrointestinal cancer prevention in China, which used a combination of vitamins and minerals (Blot et al, 1993) and the Finnish trial of α-tocopherol and β-carotene (Alpha-Tocopherol, Beta-Carotene Cancer Prevention Study Group, 1994).

Such trials may yield strong evidence of the effect of a specific factor. However, as they are often based on epidemiological studies that have shown protective effects of a group of foods, there is always a possibility that the actual active agent or combination of agents in the foods has not been used in the trial. Also, even if the active agent is used, an effect may well be missed in a limited-duration trial if the agent acts at an early stage in carcinogenesis, which may be several decades before diagnosis.

Results of intervention studies should be interpreted with caution. Such studies attempt to intervene in, as yet, only partly understood biological pathways, in special populations of adults (usually at high risk of disease), and therefore at what may be a late, although preclinical, stage of the cancer process, or else when pre-cancerous lesions are present. The agents used, while apparently protective as contained within foods, may have unexpected effects in isolation, especially in doses higher than those found in normal diets.

META-ANALYSIS AND POOLED ANALYSIS

Unless an epidemiological study is sufficiently large, modest but potentially important associations can be missed simply because of the inadequate statistical power of the study. The techniques of meta-analysis and of pooled analysis have been developed to provide summaries of selected collections of studies. Meta-analysis and pooled analysis may select only prospective studies, or other studies judged to be of relatively high quality. Both have obvious strengths but, unless they include all relevant studies from a systematic literature review using comparatively objective criteria for selection, they can repeat or even magnify the bias of individual studies. A further potential problem is whether data from different studies are fully comparable: for example, different studies may use different quantified cut-off points for 'high' or 'low' intake or for quartiles or quintiles of intake, or even not use quantified measures.

In meta-analyses of studies concerned with diet and cancer, the results of a collection of published studies are statistically summarised, to produce a single estimate of the extent to which aspects of diet modify risk. Pooled analyses go back to the original primary data of published studies, enabling analysis using the same methods, which typically vary in published papers. Other details, such as dose–response relationships, can also be evaluated more fully.

The panel assessed the relative value of epidemiological evidence as follows:

■ Population correlation studies can and often do provide suggestive evidence enabling more rigorous investigation but, in isolation, they should generally not be considered strong evidence for causation. However, when confounding factors can be controlled, or when cross-cultural studies assess wide ranges of exposure to dietary variables, or when their findings are backed by experimental and other data, correlation studies make an important contribution to the overall evidence of causal relationships between food and nutrition and cancer risk.

■ Population studies of migrants, as well as of secular trends and special exposure groups, show that the chief causes of most cancers are environmental. Their findings may strengthen evidence produced by correlation studies.

■ Case-control studies may produce evidence that is significant in isolation. Such evidence is strengthened when corroborated in different studies conducted in a number of centres and, in particular, by consistent results from populations with different patterns of diet and of cancer. Consistent results from case-control studies corroborate evidence from other epidemiological studies and from experimental and other data.

■ Cohort studies of prospective design may produce evidence that is of special significance for common cancers. Evidence of associations between diet and cancer gained from cohort studies is strengthened when these are international or cross-cultural. Results from cohort studies are both significant in themselves and as corroboration of evidence from other epidemiological studies and from experimental and other data.

■ Controlled trials in which intervention shows a beneficial effect are good evidence that the agents used are protective. Controlled trials are not, however, an epidemiological 'gold standard'. Studies in which intervention shows no effect, or even a detrimental effect, do not show that the agents used are irrelevant or harmful in the context of whole diets, or among normal, healthy populations. The results of intervention studies should not be treated as refutation of evidence from other types of epidemiological study, especially when such other evidence is backed by data from animal studies and identification of plausible biological pathways. Intervention studies in which microconstituents have no effect or even seem to increase cancer incidence do, however, provide strong

evidence against the use of such agents, singly or in combination, as dietary supplements.

■ In general, individual-based case-control, cohort and controlled intervention trials provide more powerful evidence that associations between food and nutrition and cancer risk are causal. Findings of population studies, especially when they are controlled for confounding factors, are cross-culturally consistent, and are backed by other evidence, can, however, also provide important evidence of causal links. The strongest evidence comes from consistent findings using different types of epidemiological studies in diverse populations.

3.2 NUTRITIONAL ASSESSMENT

The sheer complexity of human diets represents a daunting challenge to anyone contemplating a study of its relationship to cancer. The foods and drinks everybody consumes each day contain literally thousands of chemicals, some well known, others little known and unmeasured.

Recent research into food, nutrition and cancer has expanded and developed nutritional science itself. Conventionally, and largely for historical reasons, dietary constituents have been classified as macronutrients (energy, protein, fat, carbohydrates and their fractions) or micronutrients (vitamins, minerals and trace elements).

Nutritionists, who, until recently, were mostly concerned with avoidance of deficiency diseases, have usually investigated the relationship between diet and disease in terms of this nutrient-based classification, and have tended to regard 'food' as a subject for dietitians and other paramedical workers. Epidemiologists, whether trained as nutritionists or physicians or not, have often not felt constrained by such conventions, and investigate foods, nutrients and other dietary factors at various levels of detail. Many dietary and associated factors not historically of interest to nutritionists are now identified as important in modifying cancer risk.

ENERGY INTAKE AND BODY MASS

Early experimental work on cancer emphasised the importance of factors associated with diet, notably energy intake, energy balance, and body size and mass (including obesity), as well as physical activity.

There is good evidence, summarised in various sections of chapter 4 and in chapter 5.1, that energy imbalance leading to overweight and obesity increases the risk of some cancers. But it does not necessarily follow that high energy intake itself increases cancer risk: energy intake reflects factors other than over- or undereating in relation to requirements. Inter-individual variation in total energy intake is largely due to differences in body size and in physical activity (Willett, 1990a).

Most nutrient intakes are correlated with total energy intake; therefore, much of the variation in the intake of specific nutrients relates to factors such as body size and physical activity, which may in themselves affect the risk of disease. When total energy intake is related to the risk of cancer, for example in cases where physical activity is protective, failure to account for total energy intake in the analysis can confound associations with specific nutrients and result in misleading findings. Unfortunately, total energy intake has not been measured or appropriately accounted for in many studies on diet and cancer, making the interpretation of these studies unclear.

The example of coronary heart disease is instructive. Higher total energy intake is related to reduced risk of heart disease, because physical activity is protective. Given that energy intake is correlated with intake of dietary macroconstituents in general, it follows that high consumption of saturated fat may seem to be protective, whereas in fact this constituent of diet is agreed to increase the risk of heart disease.

This seeming paradox disappears when the measure of fat consumption is expressed in relation to total dietary energy intake. Thus, adjustment for total energy intake is fundamentally necessary to avoid misleading conclusions about nutrients. The most commonly employed method is division by total energy to show not the amount of the dietary constituent, but its percentage of total energy or calories. Thus, in the case of saturated fat, the key measure is not grams consumed so much as the percentage of total calories.

Valid estimates of weight and height can be obtained by questioning, including by recall of several decades earlier. Thus, estimates of obesity can be obtained easily for large prospective investigations or retrospectively in the context of case-control studies.

DIETARY CONSTITUENTS

Many studies on diet and cancer examine the possible relationship of dietary constituents with cancer risk, as reflected in chapter 5. These constituents include not only macronutrients and micronutrients but also bioactive compounds that have not traditionally been considered relevant to public health.

For example, epidemiological evidence that diets high in vegetables and fruits protect against cancers of a number of sites has encouraged various animal and other experiments. These suggest that the protective factors are not only a number of microconstituents that may be grouped together and termed antioxidants (carotenoids, vitamins C and E, and the mineral selenium), but are also an unknown number and combination of microconstituents of foods of plant origin, now commonly known as bioactive compounds.

An advantage of representing diets in terms of specific constituents is that such information can be related directly to fundamental knowledge of biology (metabolism, cellular responses, hormonal changes, and so forth).

BOX 3.2 MEASUREMENT OF DIETS

Traditionally, studies designed to assess the relationship between food, nutrition and health status or disease outcome have involved weighing and measuring all foods and drinks consumed. Such laborious techniques make studies of a large number of people impossible. However, simplified and standardised methods for assessing dietary intake have now been developed and validated. These have enabled a better understanding of the importance of diet to cancer risk.

In the '24-hour recall' method, the basis of most national nutrition surveys, subjects are asked to report their food intake during the previous day. Interviews are conducted by nutritionists or trained interviewers. This method has the advantages of requiring no training or literacy and minimal effort on the part of the participant. The most serious limitation of the 24-hour recall method is that dietary intake is highly variable from day to day.

Dietary records or food diaries are detailed meal-by-meal recordings of the types and quantities of food and drink consumed during a specified period, typically 3–7 days. The method places a considerable burden upon the subject, thus limiting its application to literate people who are also highly motivated. The effort involved in keeping diet records may increase consciousness of food intake and encourage an alteration in diet. However, diet recording has the distinct advantage of not depending on memory and of allowing direct measurements of portion sizes. Dietary records reduce the problem of day-to-day variation, by taking the average of a number of days; in addition, weekday/weekend variability, which in some societies is high, can be accounted for.

Short-term recall and diet-record methods are generally expensive, may be unrepresentative of usual intake, and are inappropriate for assessment of past diet. For these reasons, many investigators now use food frequency questionnaires, which include a food list and a frequency response section for subjects to report how often each food was eaten. Diets tend to be reasonably well correlated from year to year, and subjects are usually asked to describe their frequency of using foods with reference to the preceding year. Food frequency questionnaires are easy for literate subjects to complete, often as a self-administered form. Processing is readily computerised and inexpensive so that even prospective studies involving repeated assessments of diet among tens of thousands of subjects are feasible.

Dietary questionnaire methods are validated by comparison with more elaborate methods. Dietary records are particularly attractive because they do not depend on memory and, when weighing scales are used to assess portion sizes, do not depend on the perception of the amount of foods eaten.

Validation studies generally show that the degree of measurement error derived from food frequency questionnaires is similar to that from other methods (Willett, 1990a).

Central to the measurement of diets for studies of chronic disease are the issues of the timing of exposure and timing of measurement (see Box 3.1) and the methods of measurement (see Box 3.2).

FOODS, DRINKS AND FOOD PROCESSING

The use of foods and drinks to represent diet has several practical advantages when examining relationships with disease. When there is some reason to believe that some constituent of diet is associated with risk, but a specific hypothesis has not been formulated, an examination of the relationship of foods and food groups with the risk of disease, as in chapter 6, will provide a means of exploring the data. Associations observed with specific foods may lead to a hypothesis relating to a defined chemical substance.

For example, observations that higher intakes of green and yellow vegetables are associated with reduced rates of lung cancer have led to the hypothesis that the antioxidant β-carotene might protect DNA from damage caused by short-lived, highly reactive, molecular species, referred to as free radicals (Peto et al, 1981). The finding by Graham et al (1978) that intake of cruciferous vegetables is inversely related to the risk of colon cancer supported the suggestion that indoles or isothiocyanates, bioactive compounds contained in these vegetables, may be protective (Wattenberg and Loub, 1978). When, as may happen, such hypotheses are not supported by further research, it does not follow that diets as such are unrelated to disease risk; rather, some other constituents of diet may turn out to be the key factors.

Epidemiological analyses based on foods and drinks, as distinct from dietary constituents, are generally more applicable to dietary recommendations because individuals and institutions determine nutrient intake largely by their choice of foods. Even if the intake of a specific dietary constituent is convincingly shown to be related to the risk of disease, this is not sufficient information on which to make dietary recommendations. Foods are extremely complex mixtures of different constituents that may compete with, antagonise or alter the bioavailability of any single constituent nutrient contained within them.

The best approach to epidemiological studies of relationships between diet and disease combines analyses of dietary constituents with those of foods and drinks, singly and in combination. In this way, a potentially important finding is least likely to be missed. Moreover, the case for causality is strengthened when an association is observed with overall intake of a dietary constituent and also with more than one food source of that constituent, particularly when the food sources are otherwise different. This provides multiple assessments of the potential for other constituents to confound; if an association was observed for only one food source of the constituent, other factors contained in that food would tend to be similarly associated with disease. For example, the hypothesis that alcoholic drinks increase the risk of breast cancer is strengthened by observing not only an overall association between alcohol intake and the risk of breast cancer, but also by observing independent associations with intakes of both beer and spirits. This makes it less likely that some factor other than alcohol in just one of these drinks is responsible for the increased risk.

Further, it is evident that the risk of cancers of some sites is modified not only by the balance of dietary constituents and foods and drinks, but also by the means by which foods are processed, as reviewed in chapter 7. Thus, the study of, say, frying or salting, conventionally the province of the food technologist or cook, has become an important part of the work of the research scientist concerned with diet and cancer.

The panel assessed the relative value of dietary assessment as follows:

■ The most effective approach to the examination of the relationship between food and nutrition and cancer is to conduct analyses at all levels of: individual dietary constituents; foods and drinks; food groups; methods of food processing; and diets as a whole.

3.3 BIOLOGICAL AND EXPERIMENTAL STUDIES

Studies using biological measures and experimental designs may be carried out on humans or animals, or on human, animal or microbial material or cell cultures. Unlike most epidemiological studies, experimental studies entail more than observation. The scientist controls the system under investigation, making measured interventions in different subsets of the study population (humans, animals, tissues, cells), and compares the outcome between those subsets. The outcome may be cancer incidence in a human trial of chemoprevention; metabolic change in a short-term trial in human volunteers; indicators of cancer risk in studies of human cells; tumour incidence in an animal experiment; or altered biological activity in studies of tissues or cells.

Evidence from observational epidemiology using self-reported exposure measures can be supported by including data on human biology – physiological and biochemical markers and measures of molecular processes. It can be further strengthened by data from experimental studies – human, animal or in vitro. Both epidemiological and experimental studies can stimulate complementary investigations using the other mode. Overall, epidemiology backed by cogent experimental and biological findings can provide strong evidence of causal relationships between diet and cancer.

BIOMARKERS

Analysis of biological materials, such as plasma, other tissue or DNA, is becoming widely used in human studies, as well as in non-human models, to improve understanding of the relationships between food and nutrition and cancer. In principle, biological indices ('biomarkers') can be used to improve the measurement of exposure, host susceptibility or early (pre-cancer) outcomes.

Biomarkers can be identified at a variety of different stages in the cancer process. These include: biomarkers of exposure to factors that may increase risk, for example, polycyclic aromatic hydrocarbons or alcohol; through biomarkers of the early stages of cancer, such as changes in cell proliferation or gene expression; to identifiable early manifestations of cancer, such as aberrant crypt foci in the colonic mucosa. Overlying all of these are biomarkers of susceptibility, both genetic, such as a germline mutation in a tumour suppressor gene, for example, *BRCA-1* or *APC*, or a polymorphism in a carcinogen-metabolising enzyme, for example, *NAT2* or *GSTM1*, and acquired, for example, specific hormone levels, insulin levels or waist-to-hip ratio.

Data on exposure biomarkers derived from human studies have the advantage of not depending on the memory or knowledge of the subject. For example, urinary sodium may be a better measure of sodium intake than any method of diet recording, because most of the sodium in diets eaten in economically developed countries is contained in processed foods in very variable amounts. It is an additional advantage that many blood measurements can be made on specimens including those collected and stored for other purposes, thus allowing estimates of exposures to be made at any time, including when new tests become available. Such new data can then be incorporated into an existing data set.

However, biomarkers are not always reliable indicators of intake. For example, even when the levels of a nutrient can be measured in tissue (including blood), these levels are often highly regulated homoeostatically, and thus reflect dietary intake poorly. Levels of retinol, calcium and sodium in blood are good examples. As with dietary intake, the blood levels and urinary excretion rates of some other nutrients can fluctuate substantially over relatively short periods of time, hence a single measurement may not provide a good reflection of long-term intake.

Further, biomarkers are often inappropriate in case-control studies because, in the presence of cancer, the levels of nutrients in tissue may alter due to the cancer itself, its treatment or to changes in diet (Wald et al, 1986).

Molecular epidemiology investigates biomarkers of cancer risk by detecting and measuring DNA damage, especially the formation of 'adducts' and their associated genetic mutations (McMichael, 1994). Genetic damage or 'fingerprinting' caused by aflatoxins, polycyclic aromatic hydrocarbons, oxidising agents and other carcinogens on genes has been identified. Measurement of genetic damage, and corresponding measurements of DNA repair proficiency, can help to elucidate the effects of food and nutrition on the cancer process (Schulte and Perera, 1993; Groopman et al, 1994).

Biomarkers of susceptibility to cancer can also be measured, especially the inborn genetic variations (polymorphisms) at a particular gene locus. For example, there is accumulating evidence that an individual's acetylator status, which determines their capacity to metabolise potentially carcinogenic heterocyclic amines, influences the risk of colon cancer. Rapid acetylators appear to be at increased risk of colon cancer (Vineis and McMichael, 1996), and this may reflect their pattern of metabolic response to heterocyclic amines in cooked meat. There is some recent evidence that the combination of above-average consumption of meat, especially if well cooked, with rapid acetylator status entails a particularly elevated risk of colon cancer (Roberts-Thomson et al, 1996). The identification of susceptibility genotypes by DNA analysis is also becoming increasingly feasible. For example, acetylator status can be determined by direct genotyping of DNA in white blood cells. There are many other such polymorphisms, especially of the P450 enzymes.

Measures of cellular proliferative activity may also be revealing. As cell proliferation is a critical step in cancer cell formation, dietary factors that slow down cell proliferation could have a profound effect on human cancer, by delaying tumour promotion and progression so that a detectable cancer never develops within a human lifetime.

Another important process in the study of the cancer process is apoptosis, or programmed cell death, which is under genetic control but is also affected by environmental, including dietary, exposures. This is the process that ensures the death of unwanted cells, or those with very damaged DNA, in multicellular organisms. It is of major importance in the development of the organism, and appears to play a major role in ridding the body of cells on the pathway to cancer. The balance between apoptosis and cell proliferation is likely to be critical in determining whether a cancer will develop.

Eventually, investigation at the molecular and submolecular levels may identify the genetic mechanisms by which environmental factors, including food and nutrition, affect cancer risk. This, in turn, could strengthen the appropriate public health strategies. Molecular methods may also enable individuals in countries with a well developed clinical medical infrastructure to be screened for inherited or acquired vulnerability to cancer.

PRE-CANCEROUS STATES

Cancers of some sites, including those of the oesophagus, stomach, colon, breast and cervix, may be preceded by pre-cancerous states that can be diagnosed, and that are known to increase the risk of cancer itself. Given the long time-course of most cancers, investigation of such precursor lesions may cast light on the causation of the related cancers. Evidence on the effect of food and nutrition on some of these pre-cancerous states is assessed in chapter 4.

For example, almost all colon cancers develop from

adenomatous polyps of the colon, and data on the relationship between diet and these polyps is also relevant to colon cancer (see chapter 4.10). There are a number of histologically different adenomatous polyps. Determining risk factors for those that develop into cancer will enable identification of risk factors for the early stage of the cancer itself and so allow early intervention.

ANIMAL MODELS

Laboratory animals are used to test the effect of food and nutrition on cancer. Animals randomly assigned into a number of subgroups may be fed diets of varied or different composition over a period of time, with all other controllable factors held constant, to see which dietary constituents decrease or increase cancer rates. They may be exposed to different levels of nutrients (for example, fat or fibre) or to differing doses of suspected carcinogens (such as pesticides or food additives), the effect of which is then measured. They may have tumours initiated by irradiation, viruses or other known chemical carcinogens: the effect of dietary constituents on the promotion and progression of such tumours may then be investigated.

Animal models are also used to assess potential toxicological hazards as a means of guiding regulations and guidelines that specify the levels of exposure agreed to be safe in the environment and in food supplies.

The two main advantages of animal studies are that laboratory conditions can be accurately controlled in ways impossible in any normal human environment, and that genetic variability between individuals can largely be avoided. It is prudent to regard the results of animal tests as indicative of the possible effect of a dietary component, a food or a dietary pattern on the risk of human cancer; many insights into the cancer process have been gained by these means. Salient data from animal studies are incorporated into the literature reviews in chapter 4.

However, laboratory animals are not miniature humans. Anatomy, physiology and biochemistry vary markedly across species. Some substances known to be mutagenic or carcinogenic in animal models do not affect humans, and vice versa. For example, aflatoxin B_1, a known human liver carcinogen, does not induce hepatocellular carcinoma in mice, even at very high doses. Further, some of the factors that make laboratory studies attractive, such as early maturation and short lifespan, can make extrapolation to humans problematic.

Animal studies also have other limitations. In order to obtain statistically significant results, carcinogens and nutrients are both commonly administered to animals in doses far higher than in any conceivable real-life equivalent. Even if such a substance is proved to induce tumours or to modify cancer risk in animals, this may occur only in concentrations never found outside laboratory conditions (Ames et al, 1987; Hoel et al, 1988).

Animal studies may allow identification of specific dietary factors that modify cancer incidence, and can help to identify biological pathways by which dietary factors, believed to modify cancer risk, have their effect. As foods may contain thousands of constituents, sharply focused laboratory work, impractical or impossible within human populations, may provide hypotheses to guide epidemiological research, and reveal modifiable pathways to cancer in humans.

IN VITRO STUDIES

Many substances that cause mutations in micro-organisms also cause mutations in mammalian cells, and may also induce cancer in animals and human beings. This observation underlies the usefulness of bacterial mutagenicity tests (such as the Ames test), which have been widely used to study the biological effects and presumptive carcinogenicity of substances, including dietary components. As these short-term tests are relatively easy to carry out in a laboratory, and their results can be available in a few days at low cost, they have been widely used to study the effects of components of human diets.

Such tests give leads to human research, help to explain biological mechanisms of action and add plausibility to other findings. However, their results cannot and should not be extrapolated directly to human beings (Ames et al, 1987).

For example, important human carcinogens, such as asbestos or alcohol, are not mutagenic. These may act in other ways, such as by affecting the permeability of host tissues to carcinogens, by altering hormonal balances that inhibit or promote tumour growth, by changing the immune response of the host, or by affecting the rate of cell division. As these non-genotoxic activities are not replicated in bacterial or other mutagenicity testing systems, false-negative results will be produced: no mutagenicity is detected despite carcinogenic potential in humans. False-positives can also occur if a dietary constituent is mutagenic in microbes but not mutagenic or carcinogenic in humans. However, the sensitivity of such tests in identifying known chemical carcinogens is high, and they have contributed substantially to our knowledge of carcinogenesis.

BIOLOGICAL PATHWAYS

Epidemiological and experimental evidence indicating a causal association between an aspect of diet and cancer is strengthened when a biological pathway or mechanism by which the cancer process may be modified is identified, and when this mechanism is biologically plausible. Indeed, it can be argued that epidemological data, however strong and consistent, are an inadequate basis for any definite judgement of causality unless supported by mechanistic evidence.

The reverse, however, does not apply: the identification of a mechanism, even when biologically plausible, is not in itself sufficient evidence, simply because mechanisms can be adduced to support an almost infinite variety of hypotheses.

Data on mechanisms may derive from any type of experimental study: of humans, animals or in vitro studies of cells. Such data are incorporated in the reviews in chapter 4. For example, the mechanisms by which salt irritates and damages the gastric mucosa and potentiates carcinogens at a later stage of the stomach cancer process, support and strengthen evidence that diets containing a substantial amount of salt and salted food increase the risk of stomach cancer (Correa, 1992). Again, evidence indicating that alcohol influences oestrogen metabolism strengthens the likelihood that the repeatedly observed relationship between alcohol intake and increased risk of breast cancer is causal (Reichman et al, 1993). Other examples where mechanistic data, particularly that derived from animal and in vitro studies, are valuable include the extensive findings on a wide variety of bioactive compounds that currently provide possible explanations for the lower rates of cancers of various sites that are associated with diets high in vegetables and fruits.

Cell biology provides increasing insights into the genesis of cancer, enabling an increasing understanding of the steps that lead from normal cell division, through the initiation of cancer cells, to the growth, proliferation, and invasion of these cells, and finally to their distant spread. Physiological, cellular and genetic studies provide evidence of many biological pathways whereby environmental factors, including diet, may modify the cancer process (WCRF, 1993).

The panel assessed the relative value of biological and experimental studies as follows:

■ Biomarkers of cancer susceptibility, whether genetic or acquired are beginning to emerge as useful tools in cancer research. Data from analysis of biomarkers, if interpreted cautiously, can provide useful information that may support epidemiological and experimental evidence. Well-directed use of molecular biomarkers in epidemiology is likely to give valuable insights into the influence of dietary factors on cancer risk, for both normal and susceptible individuals and populations.

■ Pre-cancerous lesions can, when investigated, produce useful or even strong evidence that dietary factors affect the risk of cancer itself.

■ Animal models may produce data that guide and support epidemiological studies, and identify mechanisms that may also apply in humans, but do not, in isolation, provide good evidence of relationships between human diets and human cancer risk.

■ Microbial mutagen-testing data may guide and support epidemiological studies, but do not in themselves provide good evidence on human cancer risk, and should be interpreted with more caution than animal data.

■ Mechanisms, when identified and when biologically plausible, are important evidence of causal relationships between food and nutrition and cancer when corroborative of strong epidemiological and other evidence but, in isolation, are insufficient to assess human risk.

3.4 MEASUREMENT OF RISK

The findings of science have a profound impact on public policy and therefore on the way we live. Legislators and other policy-makers need to be reasonably sure that recommendations based on scientific evidence are sound, important, and feasible.

There are agreed methods to judge when the findings of epidemiology, supported by data from experimental and other studies, amount to good evidence of causal relationships between environmental factors and disease outcome.

Evidence that some aspect of diet certainly or probably modifies cancer risk is intrinsically important scientifically; ordinarily, it is significant for policy-makers and the general public only if the causal relationship can also be shown to be important. Scientists concerned with public health therefore also estimate the extent to which dietary factors may affect cancer incidence. This is done by assessing the strength of the association between exposure and disease; the absolute risk (which depends on the strength of the causal association and the prevalence of the disease); population-attributable risk (which depends on the strength of the causal relation and the prevalence of the exposure); and dose–response data (the extent to which risk decreases or increases with increasing exposure).

Such calculations can be a reliable basis for public health policies that are likely to reduce the incidence of cancer, and for advice to the general public, expressed in quantified terms.

CAUSATION

Dietary recommendations designed to prevent cancer are made on the basis that there is sufficient evidence of a causal relationship between relevant aspects of diet and cancer risk.

The concept of causation is used as a tool to understand the world and the way it works, without necessarily thinking about what 'cause' means. Causation is an interpretation placed on an observed association of events. The causal process can never itself be directly observed; it is always inferred. Scientists in any discipline, physical, chemical or biological, whether doing an active experiment or observing a natural system, cannot absolutely prove causation, and it is always possible that further research will produce evidence that changes conclusions. Nonetheless, scientists can be more or less confident of the causal interpretations that they place on associations observed as a result of research, depending on its type and quality (Marmot, 1986).

Epidemiological, experimental and other studies of food, nutrition and cancer, in common with similar work in the health sciences, produce evidence of associations between environmental exposures and disease outcomes. Following the criteria for causality first set out by Bradford Hill (Hill, 1965; IARC, 1990), it is generally agreed that associations can be judged to be causal in nature when exposures precede outcomes, and when associations are consistent, unbiased, strong, graded, coherent, repeated, predictive and plausible.

For example, as reviewed and assessed in chapter 4.9, there is a variety of epidemiological evidence from correlation, case-control and cohort studies that dietary aflatoxin (produced by a mould in certain foods stored in warm moist conditions) is linked with primary liver cancer in humans. Aflatoxin is a potent carcinogen in some experimental animal studies. Mechanisms have also been identified: it is known that aflatoxin binds to cellular DNA, forms promutagenic adducts on guanine bases in DNA, and is associated with a distinctive mutation of the *p53* tumour suppressor gene, known to be important in the development of many cancers (Hsu et al, 1991). Thus, the data from different types of epidemiological studies, from animal studies and from identification of plausible mechanisms all point to a conclusion that aflatoxin increases the risk of primary liver cancer.

As another example, reviewed in chapter 4.5, in a very large number of case-control and cohort studies, people consuming higher amounts of vegetables and fruits have experienced lower risk of lung cancer than those who consume lower amounts of these foods, even with careful adjustment for cigarette-smoking. In addition, levels of β-carotene in prospectively-collected blood samples have consistently been inversely associated with the risk of lung cancer. However, β-carotene may be only a marker for other correlated constituents of vegetables and fruits.

The number of such constituents that may plausibly reduce the incidence of lung cancer is large and includes compounds that can block the activation of environmental carcinogens (for example, isothiocyanates), act as antioxidants to reduce or prevent DNA damage (for example, various carotenoids), or modify methylation or reduce chromosomal breaks (folic acid). In several large intervention trials, pharmacological doses of β-carotene failed to reduce the incidence of lung cancer and may have even increased risk. These findings strongly suggest that β-carotene is not responsible for the observed benefit of vegetable and fruit consumption.

Thus, in this example, epidemiological evidence to support a benefit of vegetables and fruits is strong and there is abundant biological plausibility for a preventive/protective role for numerous constituents of these foods. However, at this time, although it is not known which combination of these constituents or which mechanisms explain the epidemiological findings, the body of evidence is convincing that vegetables and fruit protect against lung cancer.

Consistent epidemiological data, preferably backed by evidence of biological plausibility, may, by itself, be sufficient evidence to infer causality. Most knowledge of cancer causation, and hence prevention by modification of environmental factors other than diet, is based primarily on epidemiological findings supported by biological plausibility. These include: cigarette smoking (cancers of the mouth and pharynx,

oesophagus, lung, pancreas, bladder); solar radiation (skin); ionising radiation (most cancers); asbestos (lung); occupational exposures to carcinogens (bladder, skin, leukaemia); arsenic in water supplies (skin); viral infections (Burkitt lymphoma, cervix, liver) and exogenous hormones (breast, endometrium).

QUANTIFICATION OF RISK

The quantification of risk of any disease is an essential basis for public health policy planning, and indeed for individual decision making. It is not enough to know that the risk of cancer is affected by diet. The key question is: by how much? If consumption of alcohol increases the risk of cancer of the breast, and diets high in vegetables decrease the risk of various cancers, to what extent may the incidence of cancer on a population basis be affected by these factors, and how can individuals best make judgements that involve changes in their diets and lifestyles? Assessment of risk helps to answer such questions.

The strength of a relationship between a risk factor and the occurrence of disease is commonly expressed in terms of relative risk. This is the ratio of risk (or incidence) of a disease among people with a particular characteristic (such as, say, high meat intake) to that among people without that characteristic (in this example, those with no or low meat intake). Relative risks below 1.0 – an inverse association – imply a protective effect: a relative risk of, say, 0.5 for high vegetable consumption implies a halving of risk. Relative risks above 1.0 indicate an increased risk.

The higher the relative risk, the stronger the evidence for causal relationships: a relative risk of, say, 2.0 for high meat consumption implies a doubling of risk, whereas a relative risk of, say, 12.0 for a combination of certain levels of drinking and smoking not only implies a twelvefold increase in risk but is also powerful evidence of causation.

Absolute risk is also important. Small relative risk values, when consistent, are important when the number of affected people is large. A large relative risk of a rare cancer amounts to only a small absolute risk, which may reasonably be considered not very significant either by public health planners or by individuals assessing their own lifestyles. By contrast, a small relative risk may amount to a large absolute risk when a cancer is common. For example, an increased risk of 10% implied by a relative risk of, say, 1.1, amounts to very many extra cases of colon and breast cancer in Europe and North America, where these cancers are very common. Assessment of small relative risks depends on the size and quality of the studies in which such risks are found. Small relative risks may amount to strong evidence if consistently found in large, well-designed studies.

QUANTIFICATION OF RECOMMENDATIONS

Policy-makers and the general public need to know the extent to which cancer may be prevented by dietary means. They also need to know the most effective dietary means by which cancer may be prevented. The judgement that vegetables and fruits protect against various cancers is not in itself very useful. The question is, what amount of vegetables and fruits?

Dose–response data describe how the degree of exposure to relevant environmental factors (dose) affects the risk of disease (response) (Rose, 1992). In the case of food and nutrition, any effect on cancer risk is complex: generally it is a factor of the relative balance of dietary constituents within diets as a whole, over a prolonged period of time, perhaps several decades.

Comparison of the results of large numbers of epidemiological studies conducted in different societies, in which intake and dose–response relationship have been estimated on a population or individual basis, provides a robust range of information that enables relatively reliable setting of quantified goals, as specified in chapter 8.

Thus, in the case of vegetables and fruits, the recommendation to eat at least five portions or at least 400 grams a day, which has been made in a number of reports on diet and cancer, will be rational and well-justified if studies consistently show that the risk of cancers of a number of sites is substantially reduced when vegetables and fruits are habitually consumed at or above the recommended levels. Evidence for still greater protection above this level and greater risk below corresponds to a relatively simple model of dose–response for a protective factor. Within limits, the more the better.

A dose–response graph corresponding to the effect of an aspect of diet on cancer risk may not start at zero, and may not be monotonic. A number of dietary constituents, including various vitamins and minerals, are known to be protective against various diseases up to certain levels, but also to be toxic in high doses; this may explain why some intervention trials using supplements of microconstituents believed to be protective against cancer as contained in foods have been ineffective. The investigators undertaking such trials may have assumed a straight-line dose–response curve ('the more, the better') whereas in fact, the dose–response curve may be more complex.

Dietary recommendations designed to prevent cancer should, if possible, be consistent for all cancers, and should preferably also be consistent with recommendations designed to prevent other diseases. However, the dose–response to a particular aspect of diet may vary in the cases of different cancers, and also between cancer and other diseases. Take alcohol, as an example. The evidence summarised in chapters 4 and 5 indicates that alcohol increases the risk of oesophageal cancer only among regular drinkers, and that this risk is increased by smoking; that alcohol increases the risk of primary liver cancer, but only indirectly, through liver cirrhosis, and thus usually as a result of heavy drinking of alcohol. However, the risk of breast cancer is increased in what seems to be a straight-line dose–response starting with the smallest amount of alcohol. On the other hand, small amounts of alcohol are now identified as protective against coronary heart disease (although not against other diseases of the circulation system).

BOX 3.3 METHODS OF ESTABLISHING THE DOSE–RESPONSE CURVES

Dose–response graphs have been prepared as a means of summarising the quantitative results of case-control and cohort studies. The graphs show changes in the relative risk (or odds ratio) of cancer at a particular site for different levels of intake of dietary constituents, or different levels of associated factors.

The plots show not only the direction of the association, that is, whether the risk of cancer increases or decreases with exposure, but also allow estimations of levels of exposure that may reduce risk in order to help quantify specific public health recommendations.

Most of the dose–response material appears in the Assessment sections of chapters 5, 6 and 7.

Method for preparing dose–response graphs

■ Data were used only from methodologically sound case-control studies with 200 cases or more, or from cohort studies with 100 cases or more. For some cancer sites more restrictive criteria on study size were used.

■ For each study, the relative risks or odds ratio for different exposures, as given in the study, was plotted on a logarithmic scale. Where the level of exposure was open-ended (usually the uppermost category in the study), specific consistent rules were adopted. If no quantile cut-offs were provided, the information was sought from the author. (Some otherwise relevant studies had to be omitted when the information was unobtainable.)

■ Where a study gave separate results for men and women, these results are shown as separate lines on the graphs.

■ Rules were established to ensure comparability across studies and to adjust for major causal exposures that may be confounders, for example, tobacco for cancer of the larynx; body mass index for breast cancer.

■ A logarithmic scale was used so that the visual distance above and below the reference category line (RR or OR =1) is comparable. Thus an OR of 2.0, which represents a doubling of the risk is the same distance from the reference line as an OR of 0.5, which represents a halving of the risk.

■ The individual plots were then adjusted to a common baseline, usually the lowest exposure common to all studies, by moving each curve to pass through RR or OR =1 at this exposure. This allows comparison between studies.

Interpretation

■ When plotted in this way, the data can be interpreted as follows, taking the example of lung cancer and vegetable intake. As consumption goes up from 100 g/day to 500 g/day the risk of lung cancer decreases by about 60%, irrespective of the background rate in the population and taking into account sex, age and smoking status. As a further example, for stomach cancer, increasing intakes of both vegetables and fruits are associated with a decreasing risk of stomach cancer. A reduction of 60% is seen across the range of vegetable consumption from 100 g/day to 350 g/day, and fruit consumption from 50 g/day to about 300 g/day.

THE HEALTH OF NATIONS

The task for scientists concerned with improvement of public health in the field of food and nutrition and cancer, notably when advising policy-makers, is not only to identify aspects of diet that modify cancer risk, but also to estimate the extent to which cancer can be prevented by feasible dietary change, on a population basis. Such estimates are most likely to be translated into policy action if they indicate the possibility of substantial benefit.

To estimate the 'population-attributable risk', information about the profile of exposure of the population is needed, along with the estimate of the relative risk associated with that exposure (preferably expressed in dose–response fashion). In the case of diet and cancer, the population attributable risk may indicate the number and/or proportion of cancers preventable within a population if everybody at increased risk were to consume diets associated with lower risk.

For example, if regular alcohol consumption doubles the risk of oesophageal cancer, and one-third of the population are regular alcohol drinkers, then the drinkers (33%) and non-drinkers (67%) would have equal numbers of oesophageal cancers. Because half the cancers in the drinkers are due to alcohol consumption, then one-quarter of all oesophageal cancers in that population are attributable to alcohol consumption.

Extending estimates across diverse populations can be done in two ways: first by assuming that the documented dose–response relationships (often available for only a few populations) can be extrapolated beyond the range of the observed data; second, by deriving a dose–response relationship from international and other cross-cultural multi-population data. Either approach entails risky assumptions. Problems include variations in the definition of terms and in data quality between countries; uncontrolled inter-population confounding; and the fact that populations may vary in their susceptibility.

Calculations of the population-attributable risk are likely to be most reliable when results from intra-population studies are consistent with those from cross-cultural studies. When significant discrepancies occur between these two types of estimate, this fact should be acknowledged explicitly in the risk-assessment process.

From the policy-maker's perspective, a key public health task is to estimate the extent to which a population's cancer risk would be shifted if the mean and range of population exposure were substantially displaced towards lower-risk exposures using effective policies designed for such a purpose (WHO, 1982; Rose, 1992).

The role of food and nutrition in the prevention of cancer is complex, and the risk of cancer is characteristically modified by a number of environmental factors, including diet, that may interact with each other.

When a disease is believed to have one sole or chief environmental cause, estimates of the population-attributable risk can be made with relative confidence and precision.

Thus, estimates of the number of preventable deaths caused by cigarette smoking, both from lung cancers worldwide and within specific regions and countries, may be expressed fairly precisely as, for example, X deaths a year in the UK and Y deaths a year in China, following the general agreement that cigarette smoking is the chief cause of this cancer. The potential for lives saved from epidemic infectious and deficiency diseases may also be expressed precisely, on the assumption that such diseases have one cause and one cure.

The more the attributable burden of diet-related cancer within populations can be quantified, and the better this can be done, the more useful and influential this information will be in policy making. However, the risk of chronic diseases, including cancers of most sites, is typically modified by a number of environmental factors, of which diet may be just one; various aspects of diet may be relevant, some decreasing the risk, others increasing it. Further, risk factors may interact with each other, resulting in higher rates than might be expected by simply summing these risks.

For example, it is now recognised that smoking, high blood pressure and high levels of serum cholesterol act synergistically to increase the risk of atherosclerosis. Thus, in North America, the risk of coronary heart disease is eight times higher if all three factors are present, this increase being greater than the sum of the three separate risks. Similarly, the risk of cancers of the upper aerodigestive tract is increased by alcoholic drinks, but synergistically increased if drinkers also smoke.

Furthermore, a large number of environmental factors is believed to affect the risk of cancers of different sites to varying degrees. Factors that modify the risk of primary liver cancer, breast cancer and melanoma are believed not to have a great deal in common; and the aspects of diet associated with the relatively low incidence of some cancers (of the colon and rectum, for example) are associated with the relatively high incidence of other cancers (of the stomach, for example).

The estimation of the contribution made by any major individual risk factor, such as food and nutrition, to cancer risk therefore requires some boldness, and is normally appropriately expressed as a relatively broad range.

The panel assessed judgements of causation and estimates of risk as follows:

- Causal relationships between food and nutrition and cancer risk can be reliably inferred when epidemiological evidence is consistent, unbiased, strong, graded, coherent, repeated, predictive and plausible. Such evidence is strengthened by corroborative experimental and other biological data.

- The relative risk of cancer is most important when the degree of risk is high. However, in the case of common cancers, and a high prevalence exposure, consistently elevated but low to moderate relative risks may also be important.

- Dietary recommendations are most useful when quantified. The estimation of the dose–response relationship between dietary factors and cancer risk provides a valuable guide to quantified dietary recommendations.

- Public health policies are well served by estimates of the risk of cancer attributable to diet on a population basis. These are a valuable tool for policy-makers, who are then able to make rational decisions about the allocation of resources: between policies designed for the primary prevention of cancer by dietary as compared with other means; between policies designed to prevent cancer as compared with other diseases; and between the primary prevention of cancer by dietary means, and screening, treatment and palliative care.

3.5 JUDGING THE EVIDENCE

In order to review and assess the scientific evidence as a basis for dietary recommendations designed to prevent cancer, the panel has agreed to use uniform methods and terminology.

Throughout the report, matrices are used to summarise the panel's judgements on the strength of evidence of relationships between food and nutrition and cancer. Judgements are based first on the consistency, strength and quality of epidemiological evidence, then on experimental and other biological evidence, including identification of plausible mechanisms. When substantial evidence from different types of epidemiological study gives consistent results, and when there is supportive evidence from experimental and other biological research, this is judged to amount to convincing evidence of a causal relationship or, if somewhat weaker, evidence that a causal relationship is probable.

Convincing evidence of causal relationships, and evidence of probable causal relationships, usually provide sufficient bases for dietary recommendations directed to policy-makers and the general public; these are set out in chapter 8.

TERMINOLOGY

In assessing the relationship between food and nutrition and cancer, this report uses a uniform language and method to interpret the scientific evidence. Therefore, the reader should be able to follow the panel's thinking. Judgements based on the criteria here are used throughout chapters 4–7, and the dietary recommendations made in chapter 8 are derived from those judgements.

The following terms are used to denote four levels of the strength of scientific evidence of causal relationships: convincing; probable; possible and insufficient.

EVIDENCE	DECREASES RISK	NO RELATIONSHIP	INCREASES RISK
Convincing			
Probable			
Possible			
Insufficient			

The following terms are used to make judgements on causal relationships: decreases risk; no relationship; and increases risk.

PRESENTATION

The panel's judgements are consistently presented in a graphical form. In chapters 4–7, summaries of the evidence on cancer sites, dietary constituents, foods and drinks, and food processing are accompanied by matrices in which the panel's judgements are summarised, see above, (with footnotes where appropriate).

'Convincing' means that the evidence of a causal relationship is conclusive. 'Probable' means that the evidence is strong enough to conclude that a causal relationship is likely. Convincing evidence is a sufficient basis for dietary recommendations to policy-makers, health professionals and the general public. Evidence of probable decreased or increased risk is usually also a sufficient basis for dietary recommendations.

'Possible' means that a causal relationship may exist, but the evidence is not strong enough to generate recommendations primarily derived from the evidence on food, nutrition and cancer. 'Insufficient' means that there is suggestive evidence, but that this is too scanty or imbalanced to make any more positive judgement. The box 'insufficient, no relationship' is not used.

JUDGEMENTS

The nature and quality of the evidence on food, nutrition and cancer vary enormously, given the number of cancer sites, the complexity of diet, the variety of study designs and the great number of hypotheses that have been tested over the years. This is an additional reason why a standard set of terms, with agreed, although flexible, criteria, is considered by the panel to be a useful means of assessing and judging evidence.

The model matrix below includes entries for a (non-existent) cancer site, showing how entries may be placed. It should be emphasised that the terms used are shorthand and, in an important sense, should not be taken literally. For example, to judge that the evidence that vegetables and fruits decrease risk is convincing does not mean that one apple will prevent cancer; to judge that meat probably increases risk does not mean that vegetarianism is essential.

EVIDENCE	DECREASES RISK	NO RELATIONSHIP	INCREASES RISK
Convincing	Vegetables and fruits		
Probable	Physical activity	Alcohol	Meat
Possible	Vitamin C	Tea	High body mass
Insufficient			Animal fat

By analogy, the statement that smoking causes lung cancer does not mean that one cigarette is a death sentence.

Words and phrases such as those used in the matrix below, and in the matrices in chapters 4–7, really mean 'diets relatively high in vegetables and fruits'; or 'regular physical activity'; or 'diets relatively high in vitamin C'; or 'diets containing substantial amounts of (red) meat', or 'body mass (BMI) above a specified level'.

The literature reviews included in chapter 4 frequently use terms such as 'diets high in vegetables and fruits', while the matrices use the shorthand words or phrases. In most cases, a major task for the panel (in common with other expert groups convened for such purposes) has been to define such words and phrases by means of the dietary goals set in chapter 8. This is done after examination of the totality of the evidence reviewed and assessed in chapters 4–7.

For example, take one entry in the model matrix above, that for vegetables and fruits. Different types of epidemiological study may (and do) show that populations and individuals who consume relatively large amounts of vegetables and fruits as an habitual and important part of their diets have a relatively low risk of cancers of various sites.

Part of the purpose of dose–response analyses is to compare results from different studies, to judge the optimum quantity of vegetables and fruits required as a means of preventing cancer, and to generate reliable quantified recommendations (see chapter 8). If the great majority of studies that show an association between the intake of vegetables and fruits and the decreased risk of cancer found a small protective effect above intakes of 300 grams/day, but a larger protective effect above 400 grams/day, and also found that the greater the intake of vegetables and fruits, the greater the protection, this could be the basis for a dietary goal of 'at least 400 grams/day', which, in turn, would provide a definition for the term 'vegetables and fruits' in the matrix.

That is to say, the process of assessment and judgement may itself generate a more precise use of terms. This process is sometimes facilitated by existing reviews of the literature that have already graded the evidence (as has, for example, been done in the case of physical activity and colon cancer). Often, though, such reviews do not already exist, and the results of epidemiological studies can themselves be difficult to compare; in such cases, dietary guidelines are best expressed in terms of fairly broad ranges of intake.

WEIGHING THE EVIDENCE ACROSS STUDY TYPES

Relatively simple population studies, typically a starting point for more detailed and better controlled epidemiological research, may provide suggestions which, like circumstantial evidence in a court of law, can often be interpreted in different ways. Evidence from correlation and migrant studies cannot, in isolation, amount to more than a possible causal relationship.

Greater reliance is placed on aggregate evidence from individually based case-control and cohort studies and, where feasible, controlled intervention trials. When the results of such studies are repeatedly consistent, this strengthens the case for causal links. Given the accumulation of epidemiological evidence in recent years, most weight is given to human studies that have been carefully designed and controlled. Associations between aspects of diet and cancer amount to a convincing or probable causal relationship only when evidence from a substantial number of such studies clearly points in one direction.

Data from experimental studies in animal models may reinforce human evidence but, in isolation, can be no more than insufficient evidence, unless supported by identification of plausible biological pathways (mechanisms), in which case a judgement of 'possible' may be made. Similarly, identification of plausible mechanisms whereby aspects of diet could modify cancer risk may reinforce epidemiological evidence but, in isolation, can be no more than insufficient evidence.

STRENGTH OF EVIDENCE

The panel has decided to use a relatively flexible method to review and assess the evidence on food, nutrition and cancer, as outlined here.

Such a method has obvious strengths but, when confined to case-control and cohort studies, it discounts population-based studies and, partly for that reason, favours data from the economically developed parts of the world. Also, single-population case-control and cohort studies with the greatest statistical power may produce results with limited biological relevance.

Additionally, although relatively few, large, well-designed and controlled trials may produce strong and consistent conclusions that could therefore provide conclusive evidence, in other cases evidence may rightly be judged to be sufficiently strong to be a basis for recommendations despite coming from a mass of smaller studies, some of which are confused or contradictory and require more interpretation. Similarly, the extent to which experimental data and identification of plausible biological mechanisms can be held to reinforce or strengthen a judgement of a causal link cannot readily be formulated, but has been generally considered in the light of the strength and consistency of the epidemiological evidence.

A report just as this, with a global scope, has to accept that the nature and quality of the data from different examples of any one type of study, and from different parts of the world, vary greatly. Given that costly studies are not likely to be carried out in many parts of the world in the foreseeable future, such data may be best assessed by an international panel whose members not only collectively represent a range of disciplines but also have long-standing knowledge of conditions in different parts of the world.

The terms used in this report to denote the relative strength of evidence of a causal link are based on the following criteria. For individual studies, the relative strengths of associations are treated as follows:

■ 'Strong': a strong association is one where the relative risk (or odds ratio) is greater than 2.0 or less than 0.5, and is statistically significant.

■ 'Moderate': a moderate association is one where the relative risk (or odds ratio) is greater than 2.0 or less than 0.5, but not statistically significant, or else 1.5–2.0 or 0.5–0.75 and statistically significant.

■ 'Weak': a weak association is one where the relative risk (or odds ratio) is 1.5–2.0 or 0.5–0.75, but not statistically significant, or else less than 1.5 or greater than 0.75 and statistically significant. No association is thought to exist for relative risks (or odds ratios) between 0.75 and 1.50 that are not statistically significant.

To summarise a body of evidence, the following terms are used:

■ 'Convincing': epidemiological studies show consistent associations, with little or no evidence to the contrary. There should be a substantial number of acceptable studies, (that it, for dietary variables more than 20 studies)preferably including prospective designs, conducted in different population groups, controlled for possible confounding factors. Dietary intake data should refer to time preceding occurrence of cancer. Any dose–response relationships should be supportive of a causal relationship. Associations should be biologically plausible. Laboratory evidence is usually supportive or strongly supportive.

■ 'Probable': epidemiological studies showing associations are either not so consistent, with a number and/or proportion of studies not supporting the association, or else the number or type of studies is not extensive enough to make a more definite judgement. Mechanistic and laboratory evidence are usually supportive or strongly supportive.

■ 'Possible': epidemiological studies are generally supportive, but are limited in quantity, quality or consistency. There may or may not be supportive mechanistic or laboratory evidence. Alternatively, there

are few or no epidemiological data, but strongly supportive evidence from other disciplines.

■ 'Insufficient': there are only a few studies, which are generally consistent, but really do no more than hint at a possible relationship. Often, more well-designed research is needed.

If a significant portion of the data is inconsistent, amounting to possible or insufficient evidence of a causal relationship, the inconsistent evidence is noted as such. In some cases, the data are extremely limited and/or inconsistent: for such relationships, no judgement can be made.

In deriving the recommendations, more attention is given to evidence of relationships between foods and drinks and cancer risk, than to evidence on dietary constituents. (Alcohol is an exception to this general rule.) This decision has been taken with the possibility of confounding factors in mind: data, however strong and consistent, that seem to connect any dietary constituent to cancer risk may turn out, in fact, to relate to other constituents which may have not been controlled for, or which may not be susceptible to measurement. This applies in particular to microconstituents present in complex combinations in foods notably of plant origin, many of which may have potent biological activity, but also to carbohydrate, fat, protein and their subfractions. For the very heterogeneous nutrient 'carbohydrate', the panel has chosen not to make any judgement on carbohydrate as a whole, but rather to review and assess starch, fibre and sugar as separate entities.

Consequently, judgements on dietary constituents, apart from alcohol, are rated as evidence, at most, of a probable causal relationship. The exception is made for alcohol because it is so intimately and exclusively related to the drinks of which it is a part. For some very specific exposures, notably those associated with residues and additives, the panel has generally relied on assessments and judgements made by the International Agency for Research on Cancer (IARC) and regulatory bodies (see Box 3.4).

Tables encompassing a summary of all the available literature are presented in the relevant chapters for each relationship judged to be convincing or probable. In addition, where some issues have been particularly controversial in the literature (for example breast cancer and fat) we also present a tabular summary of the studies carried out to date.

The panel agreed the following methods as a means of judging the scientific evidence:

■ Plain language terms with ordinary meanings, and consistent graphical presentation, are used uniformly throughout the text, in order to review and judge the scientific evidence clearly.

■ The assessment of the evidence on food, nutrition and cancer, used throughout the text, involves a two-step process. First, the epidemiological evidence is assessed.

The International Agency for Research on Cancer (IARC) has established criteria for combining epidemiological and experimental data to evaluate the potential for human carcinogenicity of specific chemical compounds. These are classified by IARC (1993) as:

1 Carcinogenic to humans
2A Probably carcinogenic to humans
2B Possibly carcinogenic to humans
3 Not classifiable
4 Probably not carcinogenic to humans.

The IARC classifications and criteria are particularly useful when the extent of human exposure is limited, and are appropriately cautious, because human exposures should reasonably be restricted whenever modest suspicion exists for carcinogenic potential. In this report, they have been used in assessment of the evidence on specific dietary carcinogens, notably alcoholic drinks (see chapter 5.5) and those related to food processing (chapter 7).

The IARC criteria have also influenced the panel in its assessment of the scientific evidence on dietary constituents, foods and drinks, and methods of food processing other than those mentioned above. They do not, however, have complete application to the field of food, nutrition and cancer. First, epidemiological research into many aspects of diet and cancer has developed so fast since the late 1970s and 1980s that human data themselves can now often provide strong evidence of causal links. Second, the IARC criteria were developed largely to assess single agents that were believed to be carcinogenic, whereas most aspects of diet that plausibly increase cancer risk are not carcinogens. Third, the study of food, nutrition and cancer is also concerned with aspects of diet that protect against cancer, and this report deliberately emphasises the potential benefits of healthy diets. It is not obvious that these are susceptible to the type of analysis devised by IARC to identify carcinogenic compounds.

Second, if this supports a causal association, experimental and other evidence and biological plausibility are evaluated.

- Evidence of causal relationships between an aspect of diet and cancer risk may be judged to be convincing; the evidence may show a probable causal relationship; or else may show a possible causal relationship; or evidence may be insufficient. With the exception of alcohol, evidence of causal relationships between dietary constituents (as opposed to the foods of which they are constituents) and cancer is judged as, at most, probable.

- Judgements of convincing and of probable causal relationships usually justify recommendations designed to prevent cancer to policy-makers and the general public.

IMPLICATIONS

Prevention of cancer is and should be a high priority for policy-makers and the general public, worldwide.

Far-sighted policy-makers, aware that human diets have changed rapidly and radically as a result of industrialisation since the nineteenth century, and continue to do so with increasing pace, as a result of urbanisation and the internationalisation of economies, production and trade, will want to know the likely impact on public health of a wholesale shift in population diet. This requires both a sober and an imaginative approach to health risk assessment.

In most regions and countries of the world, comprehensive and high-grade epidemiological research data do not exist. Those who make and influence policy in the economically developing regions and countries in Africa, Latin America and Asia cannot patiently await the emergence of such local information, even if this were to prove adequate as a guide to reducing the increasingly heavy burden of preventable chronic disease that is pressing on the people in their countries.

Countries in the economically developed regions in Europe, North America, Australasia, and other relatively rich industrialised regions and countries, possess established research programmes and health care infrastructure. In such countries, there is an equally urgent need to assess the importance of recommendations designed to prevent cancer.

PART II

CANCERS, NUTRITION AND FOOD

CHAPTER FOUR

Cancers

The 18 sections of this chapter concern cancer sites which, together, account for about 80% of both total global cancer incidence, and of total global deaths from cancer. It is designed to bring the story of the relationship of food and nutrition with cancer up to date, by means of reviews which, given the volume of evidence that has now accumulated, are necessarily succinct, and by judgements based on these reviews, derived from criteria agreed by the panel.

The sequence of the sections in this chapter has a rough correspondence either with the body's anatomy, or else with sites that have some features in common, for anatomical, metabolic, hormonal or other reasons.
For ease of access, comparison and review, the structure of all sections of this chapter is consistent. First, the evidence and the panel's judgements are presented in words and by means of matrices. Entries in the matrices summarise the strength of evidence in favour of, or against, interpreting associations as causal. The criteria for the interpretation of the scientific evidence, and explanations of the terms used in the matrices, are outlined in chapter 3.

The text in each section then continues with an introduction which includes basic data on the cancer reviewed, together with a summary of global incidence patterns, pathogenesis and judgements made by previous expert panels where these are of special interest.

The main text of each section consists of literature reviews which, by also following a consistent structure, enable the reader to compare data within sections of this chapter and between this chapter and chapters 5 to 7. The reviews follow the sequence of the report itself: thus, reviews of dietary constituents (the subject of chapter 5) are followed by reviews of foods and drinks (chapter 6) and finally of food processing (chapter 7). Reviews of dietary constituents follow the internal sequence of chapter 5, with macroconstituents first (energy and related factors, carbohydrate, fat, protein, alcohol) and then microconstituents (vitamins, minerals, and other bioactive compounds). The sections on foods and drinks, and on food processing are similarly structurally consistent with chapters 6 and 7.

The reviews themselves usually also follow a standard sequence, reviewing the epidemiological data first, in the order discussed in chapter 3, with studies done at the level of individual exposure and outcome first and ecological (correlational) studies next. Experimental studies and possible mechanisms are then reviewed. Tables summarising the literature are also included, usually where the panel judges that evidence of a causal relationship is convincing or probable.

The first four sections concern cancers of the upper aerodigestive tract — mouth and pharynx, larynx, nasopharynx and oesophagus. Cancer of the mouth and pharynx is the fifth most common cancer in the world. Highest rates of cancers of the upper aerodigestive tract taken together are found in India, China, elsewhere in Asia, and in northern France.

The fifth section concerns lung cancer, now the most common cancer worldwide. Cancers of the stomach, pancreas and gallbladder are reviewed in the next three sections. Of these, stomach cancer is the second most common cancer worldwide and, with colorectal cancer, the other main cancer of the digestive tract, has been most strongly associated with diet. Cancers of the pancreas and gallbladder are relatively uncommon but usually fatal. Primary liver cancer, the sixth most common cancer worldwide, and most common within Africa and Asia, is reviewed in the ninth section.

The tenth section combines cancers of the colon and rectum, together the fourth most common cancer worldwide, and particularly common in developed countries and urban areas of developing countries.
The next six sections concern hormone-related or sex-specific cancers. Four of these – ovary, endometrium (lining of the uterus), cervix and prostate – are sex-specific. Thyroid cancer is also a hormone-related cancer.
Breast cancer is most common cancer of women worldwide, and is particularly common in developed countries and the urban areas of developing countries. Cancers of the ovary and the endometrium are also more common in more affluent parts of the world. Prostate cancer, the ninth most common cancer worldwide, is increasingly common in the developed world and the urban areas of the developing world.

Sections seventeen and eighteen concern the two urinary tract cancers – kidney and bladder.

4.1 Mouth and pharynx

Cancer of the mouth and pharynx is the fifth most common incident cancer and the seventh most common cause of death from cancer, throughout the world. An estimated 575,000 cases occurred in 1996, accounting for 5.6% of all new cancers.

Incidence of mouth and pharyngeal cancer is relatively high in the developing world, notably in India and elsewhere in Asia, and it is more common in men.

The panel has reached the following conclusions. The evidence that diets high in vegetables and fruits decrease the risk of mouth and pharyngeal cancer is convincing. The evidence that alcohol increases the risk of this cancer is convincing, and risk is further increased among drinkers of alcohol who smoke.

The panel notes that diets high in vitamin C, as contained in fruits and other foods of plant origin, possibly decrease the risk of this cancer; and that regular drinking of the herbal infusion maté possibly increases risk, plausibly because it is commonly drunk very hot.

Established causes of mouth and pharyngeal cancer are smoking, chewing of tobacco and chewing of betel.

The most effective means of preventing mouth and pharyngeal cancer is not to use tobacco or betel. The most effective dietary means of preventing mouth and pharyngeal cancer are consumption of diets high in vegetables and fruits, and avoidance of alcohol.

FOOD, NUTRITION AND CANCER OF THE MOUTH AND PHARYNX

In the judgement of the panel, the dietary constituents and the foods and drinks listed below modify the risk of cancer of the mouth and pharynx. Judgements are graded according to the strength of the evidence.

EVIDENCE	DECREASES RISK	NO RELATIONSHIP	INCREASES RISK
Convincing	Vegetables and fruits		Alcohol
Probable			
Possible	Vitamin C		Maté
Insufficient			

For an explanation of the terms used in the matrix, see chapter 3.

INTRODUCTION

INCIDENCE PATTERNS

Cancer of the mouth and pharynx is the fifth most common cancer in the world. In 1996, an estimated 575,000 new cases were diagnosed worldwide (WHO, 1997), accounting for 5.6% of all new cancers.

Incidence of mouth and pharyngeal cancer is twice as common in the developing world, where nearly 80% of cases occur. In developed countries, recent trends show an increase in incidence and mortality in Europe, Japan and Australia.

Cancer of the mouth and pharynx is twice as common in men as women.

Five-year survival rates are generally between 70 and 80%. In 1996, mortality attributable to cancer of the mouth

BOX 4.1.1 ESTABLISHED NON-DIETARY FACTORS AND CANCERS OF THE MOUTH AND PHARYNX

The following non-dietary factors increase the risk of cancers of the mouth and pharynx:

■ Smoking tobacco
■ Chewing tobacco or betel

and pharynx was estimated at 366,000 people, 5.1% of all cancer deaths (WHO, 1997).

PATHOGENESIS

Cancers of the mouth and pharynx include those of the tongue, the gums and floor of the mouth, other parts of the

MOUTH AND PHARYNGEAL CANCER estimated rates of cancer incidence by sex and area

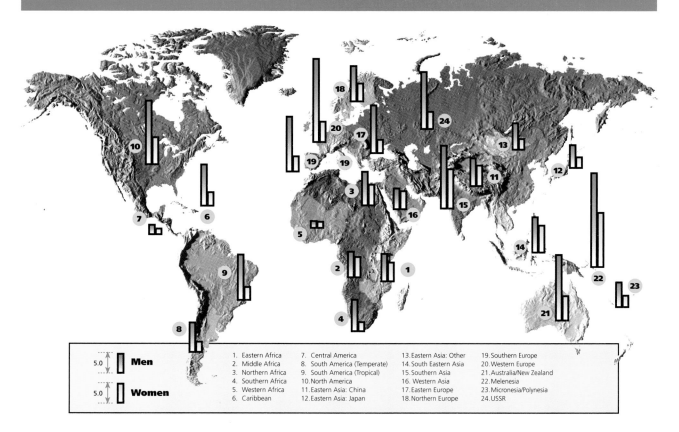

1. Eastern Africa	7. Central America	13. Eastern Asia: Other	19. Southern Europe
2. Middle Africa	8. South America (Temperate)	14. South Eastern Asia	20. Western Europe
3. Northern Africa	9. South America (Tropical)	15. Southern Asia	21. Australia/New Zealand
4. Southern Africa	10. North America	16. Western Asia	22. Melenesia
5. Western Africa	11. Eastern Asia: China	17. Eastern Europe	23. Micronesia/Polynesia
6. Caribbean	12. Eastern Asia: Japan	18. Northern Europe	24. USSR

mouth, and the pharynx. Cancers of the lip (predominantly influenced by sunlight and smoking) and of the salivary glands are not considered here.

Key epidemiological clues to the pathogenesis of cancer of mouth and pharynx are its striking male excess (it is between two and six times more common in men than in women, although some populations, particularly in India, show high rates in women) and its association with tobacco (both smoked and chewed) and betel nut (chewed).

In common with other upper aerodigestive cancers, tobacco and alcohol probably act as sources of direct-acting agents that damage DNA; there is a multitude of carcinogens in tobacco – both chewed and smoked – and the first metabolic product of alcohol acetaldehyde, can adduct to DNA. Further, alcohol can facilitate the entry of tobacco carcinogens into cells as a result of its solvent properties. Finally, both alcohol and tobacco damage cells, thus inducing a compensatory hyperproliferation that increases the likelihood of persistence of unrepaired DNA damage across generations of cells. Thermal damage and deficiencies in specific microconstituents will accelerate this process. Ultimately, an abnormal clone emerges; leucoplakia is a known precancerous lesion of the oral mucosa and represents the intermediate stage of the progress into frank carcinoma. Leucoplakia is a reversible lesion, but further DNA damage, probably involving proto-oncogenes and tumour-suppressor genes, will ultimately result in oral cancer.

JUDGEMENTS OF OTHER REPORTS

The WHO report, Diet, *Nutrition and the Prevention of Chronic Diseases* (WHO, 1990) concluded that consumption of alcoholic drinks was causally related to cancers of the mouth and pharynx, and that smoking also causes cancer at these sites. In addition, case-control studies of oral cancers have 'shown an increased risk associated with infrequent ingestion of fruit and vegetables'.

REVIEW

4.1.1 DIETARY CONSTITUENTS

4.1.1.1 Alcohol

The evidence linking alcohol consumption and the cancers of the upper aerodigestive tract – mouth and pharynx, nasopharynx, larynx and oesophagus – are extensive and consistent. An increased risk of cancer of the mouth and pharynx has been reported from each of six retrospective cohort studies (Sundby, 1967; Hakulinen et al, 1974; Monson and Lyon, 1975; Jensen, 1979; Robinette et al, 1979; Schmidt and Popham, 1981) and five prospective cohort studies (Klatsky, 1981; Kono et al, 1985; Adami et al, 1992; Chiesa, 1993; Chyou et al, 1995). The relative risk was increased in all studies (RR = 1.3–8.6), particularly in those of alcoholics in Norway (Sundby, 1967), Canada (Schmidt and DeLint, 1972; Schmidt and Popham, 1981) and Finland

(Hakulinen et al, 1981), with five retrospective and four prospective studies reporting statistically significant results. In Japan, a prospective cohort study among doctors found that, after adjusting for tobacco consumption, the risk of cancer of the mouth, pharynx, oesophagus and larynx (as a combined category) increased with increasing daily alcohol intake (RR = 8.6) (Kono et al, 1983, 1985, 1986). Results of these cohort studies are shown in Table 4.1.1.

Nineteen case-control studies that have examined the relationship between alcohol consumption and the risk of cancer of the mouth and pharynx are shown in Table 4.1.2. The earliest case-control studies were carried out in the USA (Wynder et al, 1962; Vincent and Marchetta, 1963; Keller and Terris, 1965), Sri Lanka (Hirayama, 1966) and France (Schwartz et al, 1962). Their initial observations of an increased risk with increased consumption of alcohol (OR = 1.3–7.2) have been confirmed by other studies in the USA (Gridley et al, 1990), Europe (Brugere et al, 1986; Tuyns et al, 1988; Franceschi et al, 1991; La Vecchia et al, 1991), and Puerto Rico (Martinez, 1992); these associations persisted when other risk factors, including smoking, were controlled for. In studies where different levels of alcohol consumption were examined, the risk increased with increasing consumption. In two other studies, both in India (where the prevalence of alcohol consumption, particularly relative to tobacco chewing and smoking, is low), no significant association was observed (Sankaranarayanan et al, 1989; Nandakumar et al, 1990).

A re-analysis of a study of US veterans (Rothman and Keller, 1972) found a synergistic interaction between alcohol and tobacco to be associated with the risk of cancer of the mouth and pharynx (Keller and Terris, 1965); individuals with high exposure to alcohol and tobacco had a relative risk of 15.6 compared with those who neither smoked nor drank alcohol. These results have subsequently been corroborated by other studies, although the exact nature of the interactive relationship (additive, multiplicative, etc.) remains unclear (Wynder et al, 1957a; Graham et al, 1977; Elwood et al, 1984; Olsen et al, 1985b; Tuyns et al, 1987; Spitz et al, 1988). It is noteworthy that a doubling of the cancer risk occurred in non-smokers who consumed at least 1.6 oz/day (36 g/day) of alcohol (Rothman and Keller, 1972). This demonstration of an effect of alcohol, independent of smoking, upon risk of cancer of the mouth and pharynx has been confirmed in studies from Canada (Elwood et al, 1984) and southern Europe (Tuyns et al, 1988).

Strong geographical correlations have been reported in France between mortality from liver cirrhosis and alcoholism and cancers of the mouth, pharynx and stomach (Lasserre et al, 1967). As they abstain from drinking as well as smoking, studies of Seventh-day Adventists have provided some further evidence. The rates of occurrence of cancers of the mouth, larynx and oesophagus in this group, both in the USA (Wynder et al, 1957a; Lemon et al, 1964; Phillips et al, 1980) and in Denmark (Jensen, 1979), are lower than in the general population.

In all of the ecological studies there is a recurrent diffi-

AUTHOR, YEAR AND PLACE	SIZE OF COHORT: NO. OF CASES	GROUP	RELATIVE RISK (95% CONFIDENCE INTERVAL)	SEX/AGE	ADJUSTMENT SMOKING HISTORY	OTHER VARIABLES
Sundby, 1967 Norway	1,722 men: 13[f] 1,722 men: 9[g] 1,722 men: 22[h]	alcoholics vs Oslo inhabitants	5.0 (2.6–8.6)*[d] 4.4 (2.1–8.5)*[d] 4.8 (3.0–7.2)*[d]	Y	N	N
Hakulinen et al, 1974 Finland	205,000 men: 3[g]	alcoholics	5.7 (1.2–16.5)*[d]	Y	N	N
Monson and Lyon, 1975 Massachusetts, USA	1,382: 13[h]	chronic alcoholics	3.3 (1.8–5.6)*[d]	Y	N	N
Robinette et al, 1979 USA	4,401 men: 14[h]	US veterans, alcoholics	2.2 (1.1–4.6)*[d,i]	Y	N	N
Jensen, 1980 Denmark	4,401 men: 18[f] 4,401 men: 12[g] 4,401 men: 30[h]	brewery workers	1.4 (0.2–2.3)** 1.9 (1.0–3.4)** 1.3 (0.9–1.7)**	Y	N	N
Schmidt and Popham, 1981 Canada	9,889 men: 24[h]	alcoholics vs Ontario population	4.2 (2.7–6.3)*[d] 7.2 (5.0–10.7)*[d]	Y	94% cohort smokers	N
Klatsky, 1981 USA	87,926: 15[h]	alcoholics vs US veterans Kaiser-Permanente	4.0 (1.7-7.9)*[d]	Y	Y	N
Kono et al, 1986 Japan	5,477: 18[h]	Japanese doctors	8.6 (6.9–10.6)*[d]	Y	Y	Y
Adami et al, 1992 Sweden	9,353: 500[h]	2+ oz/day vs occasional drinkers alcoholics	men 3.9 (2.7–5.5)* women 7.0 (1.4–20.3)*	Y	N	Y
Chiesa, 1993 Milan	167[j]	drinker vs non-drinker 1+ drinks/day vs none	1.0 (0.5–2.0)* 1.9 (0.7–5.3)*	N	N	N
Chyou et al, 1995 Hawaii	7,995 men: 521	25+ oz/month alcohol vs non-drinker	4.7 (2.6–8.3)*[e]	Y	Y	N
		361 oz/month beer vs non-drinker	3.7 (2.0–6.7)*[e]			
		4+ oz/month wine vs non-drinker	3.8 (1.8–8.2)*[e]			
		4+ oz/month spirits vs non-drinker	3.6 (2.0–6.6)*[e]			

* p < 0.05 for trend and/or for comparison of lowest vs highest consumption level
** p ≥ 0.05 for trend and for comparison of lowest vs highest consumption level
[d] confidence interval calculated by a 1991 IARC Working Group
[e] adjusted for one or more of the following factors
[f] oral cancer only
[g] pharyngeal cancer only
[h] oral and pharyngeal cancer
[i] 90% confidence interval
[j] oral leucoplakia
[k] standard incidence ratio and 95% confidence incidence
[l] upper aerodigestive tract – also includes oesophageal cancer and laryngeal cancer

culty. Alcohol consumption tends to be associated with other behaviours (especially cigarette smoking and certain aspects of diet) which may also influence the risk of developing cancer of these sites. Such confounding can only be satisfactorily addressed through direct and deliberate measurement of the relevant exposures and behaviours in studies of individuals.

For a given level of estimated ethanol intake, there is no clear difference in the risk associated with specific types of alcoholic drinks. Although an early study in the USA found the highest alcohol-related relative risk in whisky drinkers (Wynder et al, 1957a), subsequent studies have reported similar risks of cancer of the mouth and pharynx among drinkers of different types of wine, beer, whisky and mixed drinks (Keller and Terris, 1965).

There is little other animal experimental evidence that alcohol is an oral carcinogen (Rogers and Connor, 1991).

Several pathways for the biological mechanisms by which alcohol might affect the development of cancer of the mouth and pharynx have been proposed. Ethanol may damage cells, particularly cells in the upper gastrointestinal tract, and may modify the permeability of cell membranes thereby hastening the entry of carcinogens, or it may alter cell metabolism, thus leading to enhanced damage. Further, alcoholic beverages may contain other toxic and carcino-

TABLE 4.1.2 ALCOHOL CONSUMPTION AND THE RISK OF CANCERS OF THE MOUTH AND
PHARYNX: CASE-CONTROL STUDIES

AUTHOR, YEAR, AND PLACE	NO. OF CASES	TYPE OF ALCOHOL	COMPARISON[a]	ODDS RATIO (95% CONFIDENCE INTERVAL)[c]	SEX/AGE	ADJUSTMENT SMOKING HISTORY	OTHER VARIABLES
Wynder, 1957 New York, USA	462[g] men	all types – 1 drink = 8 oz beer, 4 oz wine, or 1 oz whisky	>6 drinks/day vs never	5.2 (2.2–12.4)*[e]	Y	N	N
	81[h] men			7.7 (1.9–31.2)*[e]	Y	N	N
Vincent &Marchetta, 1963, Buffalo, USA	42[g]	ethanol	>2 oz (47 g) vs non-drinkers	men 9.7 (3.0–31.9)*[e] women (41.03.4–495.3)*[e]	Y	N	N
	40[h]			men 52.5 (12.7–217.0)* women 82.0 (14.0–481.2)*			
Keller & Terris, 1965 New York, USA	134[f] men	all types	38+ g/day vs <9.5g/day	3.7 (1.7–7.8)*[e]	Y	Y	Y
Hirayama, 1966 Sri Lanka	227[g]	all types	drinkers vs non-drinkers	1.5 (0.9–2.8)**	N	N	Y
Martinez, 1969 Puerto Rico	278[g]	beer, wine, spirits	5+ drinks/day vs <1/day 1+ drinks/day vs none (women)	men 2.8 (1.1–7.0)*[e] women 0.8 (0.2–3.6)**[e]	Y	Y	Y
	39[h]		5+ drinks/day vs <1/day	men 14.7 (2.4–89.7)**[e]			
Feldman, 1975 New York, USA	96[f] men	all types	140+ g/day vs <70	4.5 (na)*	Y	Y	N
Bross, 1976 Buffalo, USA	145[g] men	beer, wine, spirits	30+ drinks/month vs non-drinkers	3.4 (1.7–6.6)*[e]	Y	Y	N
Graham, 1977 Buffalo, USA	548[g]	wine, beer, spirits converted to oz of ethanol	14+ drinks/week vs <1/week	2.7 (1.9–3.7)*	N	N	N
Williams, 1977 USA	172[g]	any alcohol	51+ oz/year vs non-drinkers (<1 drink/week)	men, lip and tongue, 1.4 (na)**[d] women 9.7 (na)*[d] men, gum and mouth, 3.7 (na)*[d] women 1.5 (na)*[d]	Y	Y	Y
	65[h]	any alcohol	51+ oz/year vs non-drinkers	men 6.2 (na)*[d]			
Winn, 1984 North Carolina, USA	227[g] women	all types converted to g ethanol/day	any vs none	0.5 (0.2–1.6)**[d]	Y	N	Y

genic substances. Finally, consumption may compromise nutritional status in ways that increase susceptibility to cancer (Rogers and Connor, 1991).

Data from numerous cohort and case-control studies have shown increased risk with higher alcohol consumption, irrespective of the type of alcoholic drink. Mechanisms for the effect have been proposed. The risk of these cancers is greatly increased among those who both drink alcohol and smoke.

Evidence that high alcohol intake increases the risk of cancer of the mouth and pharynx is convincing.

4.1.1.2 Vitamins

Carotenoids

One case-control study of pharyngeal cancer reported a statistically non-significant odds ratio of 0.8 for higher intake of carotenoids (Rossing et al, 1989), whereas another study of oral precancerous lesions reported an odds ratio of 3.0 (p < 0.05) (Prasad et al, 1985). One case-control study of oral leucoplakia (a known precancerous lesion)(Ramaswamy et al, 1996) found that participants with oral leucoplakia had significantly lower serum levels of β-carotene than normal controls.

Short-term intervention studies in Indian tobacco chewers found that, within 3–6 months, β-carotene (180 mg/week) (as well as retinol) reduced precancerous oral leucoplakia as well

Author, year, and place	No. of cases	Type of alcohol	Comparison[a]	Odds ratio (95% confidence interval)[c]	Sex/age	Adjustment Smoking history	Other variables
Elwood, 1984 British Columbia Canada	133[g] men	all types converted to oz ethanol/day	20+ oz/day vs <1 oz/week	4.5 (na) na	Y	Y	Y
	87[h]		450+ g/week vs <24 g/week	12.1 (na) na			
Olsen, 1985 Denmark	32[h]	all types	150+ g/week vs <150 g/week	1.8 (0.7–3.3)**[d]	Y	N	N
Brugere, 1986 France	756[f] men	all types	160+ g/day vs 0–39 g/day	lip 10.5 (4–27.7)*[e] tongue, mouth, gum 70.3 (42.8–115.4)*[e]	Y	Y	N
Tuyns, 1988 Europe	282[h] men	all types	121+ g/day vs 0–20 g/day	hypopharynx 12.5 (6.3–25.0)*[d]	Y	Y	Y
	118[h]			epilarynx 10.6 (4.4–25.8)*[d]			
Franco, 1989, Brazil	232[g]	Cachaca	>2,000 kg/life vs <1 kg/life	mouth 8.5 (2.5–29.4)*[d]	Y	Y	Y
			>2,000 kg/life vs <1 kg/life	6.7 (2.2–20.3)*[d]			
Sankaranarayanan, 1989, India	228[g]	any alcohol	>1/day vs none 20+ drinking years vs none	3.2 (2.3–6.7)*[d] 3.7 (2.1–6.3)*[d]	Y	N	Y
Oreggia, 1991 Uruguay	57[g] men	wine hard liquor total alcohol	201+ ml/day vs 0 201+ ml/day vs 0 201+ ml/day vs 0	5.8 (1.7–19.8)*[d] 3.3 (1.1–9.4)*[d] 11.6 (3.3–40.7)*[d]	Y	Y	Y
La Vecchia, 1991 Italy	105[g]	any alcohol	h vs l tertile	3.8 (2.0–7.0)*[d]	Y	Y	Y
Francheschi, 1991 Italy	104g	wine	84+ glasses/wk vs 0–6 glasses/wk	6.8 (2.4–19.3)*[d]	Y	Y	Y
		beer	14+ glasses/wk vs 0 glasses/wk	1.0 (0.5–1.9)*[d]			
		hard liquor	7+ glasses/wk vs 0 glasses/wk	0.5 (0.3–1.0)*[d]			
		all liquor	60+ glasses/wk vs <19 glasses/wk	3.0 (1.4–6.6)*[d]			

* p < 0.05 for trend and/or for comparison of lowest vs highest consumption level
** p ≥ 0.05 for trend and for comparison of lowest vs highest consumption level
[a] h = highest, l = lowest
[c] na – information is unclear or not available from the article
[d] adjusted for one or more of the following: race, residence, religion, education, socio-economic status, other dietary factors
[e] confidence interval calculated by a 1991 IARC Working Group
[f] pharyngeal cancer and oral cancers together
[g] oral cancer
[h] pharyngeal cancer

as the frequency of micronucleated cells (Stich et al, 1991). Although recurrence of lesions occurred eight months after cessation of supplementation, recurrences were prevented by giving smaller amounts of either β-carotene or retinol over extended periods of time (12 months). Studies in the USA also suggest that β-carotene supplementation (30 mg/day) significantly protects against oral precancerous conditions when given for 6 months (Garewal, 1995).

Animal studies that have examined the effect of various carotenoids on dimethylbenzanthracene (DMBA)-induced cancer of the salivary glands in rats have produced mixed results. Other experiments involving topical application of DMBA to the hamster buccal pouch (which is not, however, strictly analogous to the human oral mucosa), and subse-

quent application of carotenoids either topically, by injection or orally, have generally shown inhibition of tumours (Krinsky, 1991).

Data on supplementation trials aside, evidence relating to high dietary carotenoids and the risk of cancer of the mouth and pharynx is limited; no judgement is possible.

Vitamin C

Five case-control studies have examined the relationship between vitamin C intake and cancer of the mouth and pharynx; each of these has reported a statistically significant protective association (Marshall et al, 1983; Notani and Jayant,

Intervention studies in tobacco chewers and smokers with precancerous lesions have found a protective role for 'vitamin A', β-carotene and selenium, as well as for riboflavin and zinc (Stich et al, 1984).

The frequency of micronucleated cells decreased significantly with vitamin A and β-carotene (Stich et al, 1984) supplementation, and a cocktail of 'vitamin A', selenium, riboflavin and zinc led to a significant regression of precancerous lesions. A recent trial showed that supplementation with four nutrients – 'vitamin A', selenium, riboflavin and zinc – significantly reduced precursor lesions of the palate in a high-risk group of 'reverse smokers' (where the burning end is placed inside the mouth) (Prasad et al, 1995). Further, DNA adducts and micronucleated cells also decreased significantly, and the appearance of new lesions was prevented (Prasad et al, 1995). These data are provocative, but are too limited to provide the basis of a judgement.

1987; McLaughlin et al, 1988; Rossing et al, 1989; Gridley et al, 1990). Very generally, intake in the uppermost quantile of vitamin C consumption has been associated with an approximate halving of the risk of cancer of the mouth and pharynx (ORs = 0.3–0.6), and significant trends in at least one subgroup. One case-control study (Ramaswamy et al, 1996) found that serum vitamin C was lower in people with oral leucoplakia compared with normal controls.

High dietary vitamin C intake possibly decreases the risk of cancer of the mouth and pharynx.

Vitamin E

One case-control study of cancer of the mouth and pharynx (Barone et al, 1992) reported an OR of 0.4 (0.2–0.8) for longer consumption of vitamin E supplements (1–9 years vs never). Knekt et al (1991) reported that, in 12 case-control studies of cancer of the mouth, cases had, on average, serum levels of vitamin E that were 3% lower than those of controls. Ramasawamy et al (1996) found no significant difference in serum vitamin E levels between cases and controls.

Five animal studies of vitamin E and cancer of the buccal pouch in hamsters were reviewed in 1991 (Knekt et al, 1991). Each of these studies showed an inhibitory effect, both at high and low concentrations of vitamin E.

Although there are data on serum levels, evidence relating to high dietary vitamin E intake and the risk of cancer of the mouth and pharynx is very limited; no judgement is possible.

Folate

Mean serum levels of folate were significantly lower in cases of oral leucoplakia cases compared with normal controls in one case-control study (Ramasawamy et al, 1996).

Based on one study, no judgement is possible.

Retinol

Case-control studies of retinol and cancers of the mouth and pharynx have produced mixed results. Two such studies found that retinol intakes were associated with increased risk of cancers of the mouth and pharynx, with ORs of 1.6 and 4.5 and significant trends (McLaughlin et al, 1988; Gridley et al, 1992). In both, the association was stronger in men. Another case-control study of multiple cancer sites (Middleton et al, 1986), however, found retinol intakes to be associated with decreased risk of cancers of the mouth and pharynx, and a case-control study of cancer of the pharynx in the USA (Rossing et al, 1989) found no association with retinol intakes. Another study of people with oral leucoplakia (Ramaswamy et al, 1996) found that serum retinol levels were significantly lower in those with oral leucoplakia than in normal controls.

The evidence relating to high dietary intakes of retinol and the risk of cancer of the mouth and pharynx is inconsistent; no judgement is possible.

4.1.1.3 Minerals

Intervention trials in tobacco smokers and chewers with precancerous lesions have included selenium and zinc in combination with other nutrients, therefore making it difficult to separate the effects of the individual minerals. The available data on trial-based studies of these two nutrients is summarised in Box 4.1.2 (Stich et al, 1984; Krishnaswamy et al, 1993; Prasad et al, 1995).

Iron

One case-control study (Chyou et al, 1995) examined iron from food and supplements in relation to cancer of the mouth and found no association between dietary iron, supplemental iron, or the level of iron in nails and cancer of the mouth.

Based on one study, no judgement is possible.

Calcium

A population-based case-control study in the USA (Rogers et al, 1993), found no association between dietary, supplemental or nail level calcium and the risk of cancer of the mouth. In a cohort of Hawaiian Japanese men (Chyou et al, 1995), dietary calcium showed a protective association in men with aerodigestive tract cancers as a group, about 33% (30 of 92) of whom had cancer of the mouth and pharynx.

Evidence relating to high dietary intake of calcium and the risk of cancer of the mouth and pharynx is limited; no judgement is possible.

Zinc

Rogers and co-authors (1993) also explored the association between zinc and cancer of the mouth and found no significant relationship between any of their measures of zinc (diet, supplement, nail level) and such cancers.

Based on one study, no judgement is possible.

4.1.2 FOODS AND DRINKS

4.1.2.1 Cereals (grains)

Two case-control studies in the USA found a decreased risk associated with the consumption of cereals and cereal products (ORs of 0.5 and 0.9, with significant trends) (Winn et al, 1984; McLaughlin et al, 1988), but another found no association (Graham et al, 1977). Two studies conducted in Italy, one in India and one in China found an increased risk associated with the consumption of maize, polenta, rice, millet, bread or pasta, and ragi (Franceschi et al, 1990, 1992; Nandakumar et al, 1990; Zheng et al, 1993) (ORs = 1.8–31.2, with significant trends in all). One other study conducted in the USA found increased risk associated with the consumption of grains, but the association was not significant (Gridley et al, 1990).

> Evidence relating to diets high in cereals (grains) and the risk of cancer of the mouth and pharynx is inconsistent; no judgement is possible.

Wholegrain cereals

The relationship between cereal products and the risk of cancer of the mouth and pharynx may depend on the degree to which these products are refined. In several studies, wholegrain bread, wheat bread and pasta were associated with decreased risk (ORs = 0.1–0.8) (Winn et al, 1984; McLaughlin et al, 1988; Franceschi et al, 1992), however; only one of these showed a significant trend. If the consumption of wholegrain products shows decreased risk, whereas consumption of refined cereals has the opposite effect, it may, in part, be related to the additional nutrients contained in wholegrain products. As a result, diets dependent on one starchy staple and grossly deficient in various micronutrients may increase risk.

> Evidence relating to diets high in wholegrain cereals (grains) and the risk of cancer of the mouth and pharynx is limited; no judgement is possible.

4.1.2.2 Vegetables and fruits

One cohort study in Japan found a decreased risk of cancer of the mouth and pharynx with greater intake of green and yellow vegetables; the lower risk was observed to be independent of daily smoking, drinking and meat consumption (Hirayama, 1985).

Fifteen case-control studies that have examined vegetable and fruit consumption and the risk of cancer of the mouth are summarised in Table 4.1.3. Of these, thirteen have reported a statistically significant protective association for at least one vegetable and/or fruit category, with ORs ranging from 0.2 to 0.6 (Jafarey et al, 1977; Winn et al, 1984; Notani and Jayant, 1987; McLaughlin et al, 1988; Franco et al, 1989; Zheng et al, 1990; Franceschi et al, 1991, 1992; La Vecchia et al, 1991; Oreggia et al, 1991; Steinmetz and Potter, 1991; Gridley et al, 1992; Prasad et al, 1992).

Protective associations for vegetable and fruit consumption have remained significant after adjustment for smoking (or other forms of tobacco consumption, such as chewing) and high alcohol consumption, thought to be the two major causes of oral cancer. Five of seven studies that have examined vegetables as a broad category have reported protective associations (Jafarey et al, 1977; Notani and Jayant, 1987; Oreggia et al, 1991; Franceschi et al, 1992; Gridley et al, 1992); eight of ten have reported likewise for fruit (Winn et al, 1984; McLaughlin et al, 1988; Franco et al, 1989; La Vecchia et al, 1991; Franceschi et al, 1992; Gridley et al, 1992; Zheng et al, 1992). Typically, the frequency of intake showed an approximate halving of risk in daily versus less than daily consumers.

The evidence is most consistent for carrots, citrus fruits and green vegetables, for which four of four, four of five (Franco et al, 1989; Franceschi et al, 1991, 1992; La Vecchia et al, 1991) and six of eight studies (Winn et al, 1984; Franco et al, 1989; Gridley et al, 1992; La Vecchia et al, 1991; Franceschi et al, 1992; Zheng et al, 1992), respectively, have reported protective associations. The evidence for cruciferous vegetables is not as convincing; three of five studies have reported null associations (Gridley et al, 1992; Zheng et al, 1992, 1993). One Italian study showed a significant protective association for green peppers (Franceschi et al, 1991). Another study reported an increased risk for consumption of bok choy in China, but other vegetables and fruits were associated with reduced risk (Zheng et al, 1992).

An international ecological study (Herbet et al, 1993) used data from 59 countries and found a protective correlation between cabbage intake and oral cancer (based on food balance sheets and mortality data). In one of the earliest ecological observations on diet and cancer, Orr (1933) suggested that vegetable and fruit consumption determined differences in the risk of cancer of the mouth in India.

> Evidence that diets high in vegetables and fruits decrease the risk of cancers of the mouth and pharynx is convincing.

4.1.2.3 Pulses (legumes)

Five case-control studies of cancer of the mouth and pharynx examined for pulses; three reported decreased risk with increased intake and two reported increased risk. Protective associations were reported for women, but not men, in studies in the USA (Gridley et al, 1992) and Shanghai (Zheng et al, 1992) (ORs = 0.2, ns and 0.6, ns, respectively). In contrast, statistically significant ORs of 1.6 and 1.9 were reported for daily versus less than daily consumption of pulses in a study in India of cancers of the mouth and pharynx, respectively (Notani and Jayant, 1987). A study in Beijing reported an OR of 1.8 (0.8–4.0) for higher intake of lentils (Zheng et al, 1993); in another study in the USA, an OR of 1.3 (ns) was reported for higher consumption of legumes (McLaughlin et al, 1988).

One case-control study examined the relationship of intake of pulses to the development of second primary cancer, most

TABLE 4.1.3 VEGETABLE AND FRUIT CONSUMPTION AND THE RISK OF CANCERS OF THE MOUTH AND PHARYNX: CASE-CONTROL STUDIES

AUTHOR, YEAR, AND PLACE	NO OF CASES	TYPE OF VEGETABLES OR FRUIT	COMPARISON[A]	ODDS RATIO (95% CONFIDENCE INTERVAL)[B,C]	ADJUSTMENT SEX/AGE	SMOKING HISTORY	OTHER VARIABLES
Jafarey, 1977 Pakistan	204	Vegetables and fruits	na	prot assoc*	Y	Y	Y
Graham, 1977 New York, USA	584	Vegetables	na	na**	all men, age-matched	Y	Y
Marshall, 1982 New York, USA	425	Cruciferous vegetables	na	na**	all men, age-matched		
Winn, 1984 North Carolina, USA	227	Vegetables and fruits Green leafy vegetables Fresh fruits	21+ vs 0–10 servings/week	0.5 (0.3–0.8)* 0.7 (0.5–1.1)** 0.6 (0.4–0.8)	all women	Y	Y
Notani and Jayant, 1987, India	278	Vegetables and fruits	daily vs not daily	2.4 (1.4–4.0)* 0.9 (0.5–1.4)**	Y	Y	N
McLaughlin, 1988 USA	871	Vegetables and fruits	h vs l tertile	men 1.0 (na)** 0.4 (na)* women 0.8 (na)** 0.5 (na)*	Y	Y	Y
Franco, 1989, Brazil	236	Green vegetables Carotene vegetables/ fruits Citrus fruits	≥ 4 vs < 1 serving/week	0.7 (0.4–1.4)** 0.4 (0.2–1.0)** 0.5 (0.3–0.9)*	Y	Y	Y
Francheschi, 1991 Italy	302	Vegetables Carrots Cruciferous vegetables Fresh tomatoes Fresh fruits Citrus fruits	h vs l tertile	0.6 (na)* 0.5 (na)* 1.0 (na)** 0.5 (na)* 0.6 (na)* 0.7 (na)*	Y	Y	Y
La Vecchia, 1991 Italy	105	Green vegetables Carrots Fresh fruits	h vs l tertile	0.6 (0.3–1.2)* 0.4 (0.2–0.8)* 0.2 (0.1–0.4)*	Y	Y	Y
Oreggio, 1991 Uruguay	57	Vegetables and fruits	5 vs < 1 servings/week	0.2 (0.05–0.7)* 0.4 (0.1–1.3)*	all men	Y	Y
Francheschi, 1992 Italy	104	Green vegetables Carrots Fresh fruits	h vs l tertile	0.4 (0.2–0.8)* 0.4 (0.2–0.7)* 0.5 (0.3–0.8)*	all men	Y	Y
Gridley, 1992, USA	1,114	Vegetables and fruit	h vs l tertile	0.6 (na) na	Y	N	N
Prasad, 1992, India		Green leafy vegetables	h vs l tertile	1.8			
Zheng, 1992, China	204	Dark green vegetables Dark yellow vegetables Cruciferous vegetables Raw vegetables Citrus fruits	h vs l tertile	men 1.4 (na)** 0.3 (na)* 0.8 (na)** 0.5 (na)* 0.4 (na)*	not age-adjusted	Y	Y
		Dark green vegetables Dark yellow vegetables Cruciferous vegetables Raw vegetables Citrus fruits		1.2 (na)** 0.8 (na)** 1.5 (na)** 1.2 (na)** 0.4 (na)*			
Zheng, 1993, China	404	Carrots Tomatoes Oranges/tangerines	< 2/week vs <1/month	0.7 (0.3–1.8)** 0.5 (0.3–0.9)* 0.4 (0.4–0.7)*	Y	Y	Y

* p ≤ 0.05 for trend and/or for comparison of lowest vs highest consumption level
** p ≥ 0.05 for trend and for comparison of lowest vs highest consumption level
a h = highest, l = lowest
b 95% confidence interval; prot assoc, protective association; no assoc, no association; pos assoc, positive assocation
c na – information is unclear or not available from the article

of which were in the upper aerodigestive tract and lungs, in a group of patients with initial cancer of the mouth or pharynx (Day et al, 1994). Higher consumption was associated with a decreased risk of a second cancer.

Evidence relating to diets high in pulses and the risk of cancer of the mouth and pharynx is inconsistent; no judgement is possible.

4.1.2.4 Meat, poultry, fish and eggs
Meat
At least ten case-control studies have examined meat consumption in relation to the risk of cancer of the mouth and pharynx (Graham et al, 1977; Winn et al, 1984; Notani and Jayant, 1987; McLaughlin et al, 1988; Franco et al, 1989; Franceschi et al, 1991, 1992; La Vecchia et al, 1991; Oreggia et al, 1992; Gridley et al, 1992). Although one study observed a statistically non-significant protective association with fresh meat consumption (OR = 0.4) (La Vecchia et al, 1991), another reported a marginally significant, positive association for pork products (OR = 1.5) (Winn et al, 1984), and still others found no association (Notani and Jayant, 1987; McLaughlin et al, 1988; Franceschi et al, 1992).

Evidence relating to diets high in meat and the risk of cancer of the mouth and pharynx is inconsistent; no judgement is possible.

Fish
Fish consumption was associated with decreased risk of cancers of the mouth and pharynx in three of five case-control studies (ORs = 0.3–0.7) (Notani and Jayant, 1987; McLaughlin et al, 1988; La Vecchia et al, 1991). One (Winn et al, 1984) found fish consumption to be associated with a statistically significantly increased risk among women (OR = 1.5). The fifth found no association between fish consumption and the risk of cancer of the mouth and pharynx (Franceschi et al, 1991).

Evidence relating to diets high in fish and the risk of cancer of the mouth and pharynx is inconsistent; no judgement is possible.

Eggs
The association between egg consumption and cancer of the mouth and pharynx has been evaluated in several case-control studies, with equivocal results. Oreggia and colleagues (1991) found no association with cancer of the mouth or tongue. In Beijing (Zheng et al, 1993), egg consumption showed a statistically non-significant protective association with oral cancer (OR = 0.7, 0.4–1.3). La Vecchia and colleagues (1991) reported a statistically non-significant increased risk (OR = 1.5, 0.9–2.4) for egg consumption and cancer of the mouth and pharynx. Franceschi and colleagues (1991) found that those in the highest tertile for egg consumption had an OR of 1.6 for cancer of the mouth and pharynx, compared with those in the lowest tertile, and a statistically significant trend was noted.

Evidence relating to diets high in eggs and the risk of cancer of the mouth and pharynx is inconsistent; no judgement is possible.

4.1.2.5 Milk and dairy products
At least 10 case-control studies have examined the association between dairy products and risk of cancer of the mouth and pharynx (Graham et al, 1977; Winn et al, 1984; Notani and Jayant, 1987; McLaughlin et al, 1988; Franco et al, 1989; Franceschi et al, 1991, 1992; La Vecchia et al, 1991; Oreggia et al, 1992; Gridley et al, 1992). Cheese has been associated with both a statistically significantly decreased (OR = 0.6) (La Vecchia et al, 1991) and a significantly increased (Notani and Jayant, 1987; Franceschi et al, 1991) risk for cancer of the mouth and pharynx (OR = 1.9). Buttermilk was evaluated in only one study (Notani and Jayant, 1987), and showed a protective association (OR = 0.3). Results from the studies on milk have been mixed; one study found a significant protective association (La Vecchia et al, 1991) (OR = 0.3; Zheng et al (1993), in China, found a statistically non-significant protective association; Oreggia et al (1992) found no association between milk and cancer of either the mouth or tongue and Notani and Jayant (1987) found no association between milk and cancer of the mouth. McLaughlin et al (1988) found an increased risk (OR = 1.5) for higher consumption of dairy products, and a statistically significant trend among men, but not women. Jafarey et al (1977) did not report their odds ratios, but stated that the controls in their study had a significantly higher intake of dairy products than cases of cancer of the mouth and oropharynx. Winn et al (1984) found high consumption of dairy products was not related to the risk of cancer of the mouth and pharynx.

Evidence relating to diets high in milk and dairy products and the risk of cancers of the mouth and pharynx is relatively extensive but inconsistent; no judgement is possible.

4.1.2.6 Herbs, spices and condiments
Chillies
Red chillies show a positive association with cancer of the mouth and pharynx in at least one study; Notani and Jayant (1987) found a twofold increase with a dose–response relationship for the risk of cancer of the mouth and pharynx.

On the basis of one study, no judgement is possible.

Pepper
In some studies, red peppers showed a positive association with cancer of the mouth and pharynx (Notani and Jayant, 1987; Franco et al, 1989) (OR = 1.3-2.0). However, in other studies (Winn et al, 1984; Zheng et al, 1993), hot pepper consumption was not significantly related to oral and pharyngeal cancer risk (OR = 0.9-1.0).

The evidence relating to diets high in peppers and the risk of cancer of the mouth and pharynx is limited; no judgement is possible.

4.1.2.7 Coffee, tea, and other drinks

Coffee

A prospective study in Norwegian men, which adjusted for age, residence and tobacco smoking, reported no significant association between coffee consumption and the risk of cancer of the lip plus the mouth and pharynx (RR = 0.8 – 1.2) (Jacobson et al, 1986); however, these results were based on only 30 cases.

The results of case-control studies have been inconsistent. One such study in Italy showed a statistically significant association between coffee intake and a decreased risk of cancer of the mouth (OR = 0.3) and a statistically non-significant decreased risk of tongue cancer (OR = 0.6) (Franceschi et al, 1992), whereas another study in the USA showed no association (Graham et al, 1977). La Vecchia et al (1991) found a statistically non-significant protective association (OR = 0.8).

Evidence relating to high coffee intake and the risk of cancer of the mouth and pharynx is limited; no judgement is possible.

Tea

One case-control study of tea in Brazil reported a statistically non-significantly increased risk of cancer of the mouth with increased consumption (Franco et al, 1989); one in Italy showed a statistically non-significantly decreased risk for cancer of the tongue (OR = 0.8, 0.5–1.6), and a statistically significantly decreased risk for cancer of the mouth (OR = 0.4, 0.2–0.9) (Franceschi et al, 1992). A third study in India showed no statistically significant association (Notani and Jayant, 1987).

Evidence relating to high tea intakes and the risk of cancer of the mouth and pharynx is limited and inconsistent; no judgement is possible.

Maté

Maté is drunk as a tea, commonly in Brazil, Uruguay, and Argentina; it is drunk very hot through a metal straw. Maté appears to be an independent risk factor for oral cancers, with regular drinkers having an approximately twofold risk (De Stefani et al, 1988; Franco et al, 1989; Oreggia et al, 1991) compared with non-drinkers. The effect of temperature as such has not been reported in these studies. A significant dose–response association between daily intake of maté and the risk of cancer of the mouth and pharynx has been observed after adjustment for smoking and alcohol intake (De Stefani et al, 1988). As a result of its high prevalence in southern South America, maté drinking could account for up to 20% of cases of cancers of the mouth and pharynx in that region.

Regular maté drinking possibly increases the risk of cancers of the mouth and pharynx. As with the association between maté and risk of oesophageal cancer (see chapter 4.4), this may be a consequence of the temperature at which this beverage is usually consumed.

4.1.3 FOOD PROCESSING

4.1.3.1 Salt, salting and refrigeration

Salt

A population-based case-control study in Shanghai (Zheng et al, 1992) found an increased risk of cancers of the mouth and pharynx with consumption of salt-preserved meat and fish (ORs = 2.5 and 3.7 for men and women, respectively).

Based on one study, no judgement is possible.

4.1.3.2 Cured and smoked foods

Smoked foods

One Brazilian study (Franco et al, 1989) found no increase in the risk of oral cancer with smoked meat consumption, after adjustment for confounders. Another US study among women in North Carolina (Winn et al, 1984), found an increased risk from smoked meat and fish consumption with statistically significant ORs for smoked beef, smoked poultry and smoked fish of 1.8, 3.7 and 3.3, respectively for low (0–2/week) versus high (> 7.5/week) tertiles of intake.

Evidence relating to diets high in smoked foods and the risk of cancer of the mouth and pharynx is limited; no judgement is possible.

4.1.3.3 Cooking

Grilling (broiling) and frying

A study from Brazil (Franco et al, 1989) has shown an increased risk (OR = 5.3, 1.9–15.0) associated with charcoal-grilled meat (4 or more per week vs < 1/month). Zheng et al (1992) found an increased risk for cancer of the mouth and pharynx with consumption of deep-fried foods (OR = 1.2 for men, 2.2 for women).

Evidence relating to diets high in grilled, broiled and fried foods and the risk of cancer of the mouth and pharynx is limited; no judgement is possible.

4.2 Nasopharynx

Cancer of the nasopharynx is generally uncommon. Incidence is high in parts of China and elsewhere in south-east Asia.

The panel has reached the following conclusions. The evidence that diets high in Cantonese-style salted fish increase the risk of nasopharyngeal cancer is convincing.

Established causes of nasopharyngeal cancer are smoking and infection with the Epstein-Barr virus.

The most effective means of preventing nasopharyngeal cancer is not to use tobacco. The most effective dietary means of preventing nasopharyngeal cancer is avoidance of Cantonese salted fish.

FOOD, NUTRITION AND NASOPHARYNGEAL CANCER

In the judgement of the panel, the food listed below modifies the risk of cancer of the nasopharynx. The judgement is graded according to the strength of the evidence.

EVIDENCE	DECREASES RISK	NO RELATIONSHIP	INCREASES RISK
Convincing			Salted fish[a]
Probable			
Possible			
Insufficient			

For an explanation of the terms used in the matrix, see chapter 3.
[a] Data apply to Chinese and other populations where such foods are staples. Risk increases when such foods are often eaten very early in life.

INTRODUCTION

Nasopharyngeal cancer is predominantly a squamous carcinoma. It is frequently undifferentiated or poorly differentiated.

INCIDENCE PATTERNS

Nasopharyngeal carcinoma is a rare cancer in most parts of the world; the age-standardised incidence rate for either sex is generally less than 1 per 100,000 population. However, it is a common cancer in south-eastern China, including in Hong Kong where it is the second most common cancer, and in various other ethnic groups such as Malays and Filipinos living in south-east Asia (Singapore, Malaysia, Indonesia) and the USA. In China, there is a wide variation between incidence and mortality rates among different geographical regions; mortality rates range from 2–40 per 100,000 population. Mortality is 2–3 times higher in men than in women.

PATHOGENESIS

If the aetiology of nasopharyngeal cancer is similar to that of other epithelial sites, it seems plausible that there will be an environmental source of DNA-damaging agents, coupled with agents or processes that result in increased cell damage or increased cell proliferation. Plausible agents for the induction of DNA damage include Cantonese-style salted fish and perhaps other fermented foods, as well as tobacco smoke. Tobacco smoke can also act as a promoting agent as a result of its capacity to increase cell damage and reactive cell proliferation. The Epstein-Barr virus may also act as a proliferative stimulus – as may certain other chronic infections of the nasopharyngeal mucosa. For further information see Yu and Henderson (1996).

JUDGEMENTS OF OTHER REPORTS

Neither of the National Academy of Science reports, *Diet, Nutrition and Cancer* (NAS, 1982) and *Diet and Health* (NAS, 1989), nor the WHO report *Diet, Nutrition and the Prevention of Chronic Disease* (WHO, 1990) came to any conclusion about any relationship between dietary factors and the risk of nasopharyngeal cancer.

REVIEW

4.2.1 DIETARY CONSTITUENTS

4.2.1.1 Alcohol

The majority of studies on upper aerodigestive tract cancers and alcohol use have explored relationships at other sites. However, three case-control studies have reported results for nasopharyngeal cancer. One showed evidence of an increased risk (Nam et al, 1992), another found no relationship (Yu et al, 1985), and the last found a decreased risk (Sriamporn et al, 1992) associated with alcohol consumption.

> The evidence relating to alcohol consumption and the risk of nasopharyngeal cancer is limited and inconsistent; no judgement is possible.

4.2.2 FOODS AND DRINKS

4.2.2.1 Vegetables and fruits

No prospective studies of vegetable and fruit intake and nasopharyngeal cancer have been undertaken. Two case-control studies in China (Yu et al, 1989; Ning et al, 1990) have reported on vegetable and fruit consumption and the risk of nasopharyngeal cancer. Both found statistically significant protective associations for one or more vegetable and/or fruit categories. In general, associations with the consumption of vegetables and fruits have been in the direction of decreasing risk with higher intakes for the majority of risk estimates, with at least one fruit or vegetable in each study reaching statistical significance. Particularly striking protective associations were reported from one study in Guangxi, China (Yu et al, 1989) including odds ratios of 0.2, 0.3, and 0.3 (all $p < 0.05$) for higher intakes of carrots, tomatoes, and oranges and tangerines, respectively.

> The evidence relating to vegetables and fruits and the risk of nasopharyngeal cancer is very limited; no judgement is possible.

4.2.2.2 Pulses (legumes)

A case-control study of nasopharyngeal cancer in Guangxi, China (Yu et al, 1986) reported increased risk with greater intakes of fermented bean pastes. These associations were statistically significant for diet at one to two years of age, but not with diet at age twenty; odds ratios for diet at one to two years of age were 4.6 (1.8–11.4) and 3.6 (1.8–8.1) for fermented pastes from black beans and soya beans, respectively (Yu et al, 1986).

> Evidence relating to pulses and the risk of nasopharyngeal cancer is very limited; no judgement is possible.

TABLE 4.2.1 SALTED FISH CONSUMPTION AND THE RISK OF NASOPHARYNGEAL CANCER: CASE-CONTROL STUDIES

AUTHOR, YEAR, AND PLACE	NO. OF CASES	PERIOD OF EXPOSURE	COMPARISON[a]	ODDS RATIO (95% CONFIDENCE INTERVAL)[b,c]	SEX/AGE	ADJUSTMENT SMOKING HISTORY	OTHER VARIABLES
Henderson, 1976 California, USA	74	Current	na	no assoc**[d]	Y	N	Y
Henderson, 1978 California, USA	74	Current	1/week vs none >1/week vs none	2.1 (na)*[d] 3.1 (na)*[d]	Y	N	Y
Gesser, 1978 Hong Kong	108	During weaning	ever vs never	2.6 (na)*	Y	N	N
Armstrong, 1983 Malaysia	100	During childhood	ever vs never daily vs never	3.0 (na)*[d] 17.4 (na)*[d]	Y	N	Y
Yu, 1986 China	250	During weaning At age 10	ever vs never 1/week vs rarely	7.5 (3.9–14.8)* 37.7 (14.1–100.4)*	Y	N	N
Yu, 1988 China	128	During weaning At age 10	ever vs never weekly vs rarely	2.6 (1.2–5.6)* 1.4 (0.5–4.3)	Y	N	N
Chen, 1988 Taiwan	205	Before age 20	1–9/month vs never ≥10/month vs never	0.8 (na)** 1.5 (na)*	Y	N	N
Yu, 1989 China	306	During weaning At age 10	ever vs never daily vs never	2.1 (1.2–3.6)*[d] 2.4 (1.0–6.0)*[d]	Y	N	N
Ning, 1990 China	100	At age 10	1/week vs rarely	5.6 (na)**[d]	Y	N	N
Jeannel, 1990 Tunisia	80	Current	any vs none	1.5 (na)**[d]	Y	Y	Y
Sriamporn, 1992 Thailand	120	Current	weekly vs never	2.5 (1.5–5.2)*[d]	Y	Y	Y
Zheng, 1994 China	88	During weaning Ages 2–10	ever vs never weekly vs rarely	2.4 (na)*[d] 3.2 (na)*[d]	Y	N	Y

* p < 0.05 for trend and/or for comparison of lowest vs highest consumption level
** p ≥ 0.05 for trend and for comparison of lowest vs highest consumption level
[a] h = highest, l = lowest
[b] no assoc – no association
[c] na – information is unclear or not available from the article
[d] Matched or adjusted for one or more of the following: race, residence, other food items, occupation, education, socio-economic status

4.2.2.3 Herbs, spices and condiments

Harissa

The fiery condiment harissa, which is made up of red pepper, olive oil, garlic, caraway and salt, is consumed in north Africa.

A case-control study of nasopharyngeal cancer in Tunisia observed an increased risk with higher childhood consumption of harissa; increased risk was also observed for a stewing mixture composed of red and black pepper, garlic oil, caraway, and coriander (Jeannel et al, 1990). Direct weaning from breast milk to the typical adult diet (which includes harissa) was an additional risk factor in this population.

One study does not provide enough information on which to base a judgement.

4.2.2.4 Coffee, tea, and other drinks

Tea

Case-control studies that have examined tea consumption and the risk of nasopharyngeal cancers have generally found no association. One study in Taiwan (Lin et al, 1997), one in the USA (Henderson et al, 1976) and a third in Singapore (Shanmugaratnam et al, 1978) found that cases were not more or less likely to be tea drinkers than controls. Little information about the type of teas consumed was available in these early studies.

The data on nasopharyngeal cancer and tea consumption are limited; no judgement is possible.

4.2.3 FOOD PROCESSING

4.2.3.1 Salt, salting and refrigeration

Salted fish

Salted fish is prepared by treating fish with salt and drying it in the sun. Cantonese-style salted fish is usually softened by partial decomposition before or during salting. In the 1960s, it was observed that nasopharyngeal cancer in Hong Kong was higher in boat people than in house-dwellers (Ho, 1967). It was proposed that salted fish, a staple in the diets of boat people, was a cause of this cancer (Ho, 1971).

Eight case-control studies on Chinese, living in China (Yu et al, 1988, 1989; Ning et al, 1990; Zheng et al, 1994), Hong Kong (Gesser et al, 1978; Yu et al, 1986), Taiwan (Chen et al,

1988) and Malaysia (Armstrong et al, 1983) and four other studies, one in Tunisia (Jeannel et al, 1990), one in Thailand (Sriamporn et al, 1992) and two in the USA (Henderson et al, 1976, 1978) have investigated this hypothesis (Table 4.2.1). Although the studies used different approaches to the assessment of individual diet, all but three (Henderson et al, 1976; Chen et al, 1988; Jeannel et al, 1990) found statistically significant increased risk for nasopharyngeal cancer with higher intakes, with odds ratios ranging from 2.1 to 37.7. The findings also suggested that childhood exposure is particularly important (Armstrong et al, 1983; Yu et al, 1986, 1988, 1989; Zheng et al, 1994). The 1986 study reported by Yu et al found a significant dose–response relationship with more frequent consumption.

Experimental studies with rats have corroborated the salted-fish hypothesis. Rats fed cooked Chinese salted fish developed an increase in nasal and paranasal cavity tumours (Huang et al, 1978), and another study found a dose–response effect for salted fish consumption in rats (Yu et al, 1989). A similar observation was made in hamsters (Tricker et al, 1991).

The aetiological factors in the Cantonese-style salted fish have not been fully elucidated. Chemical analysis of salted fish shows the presence of various volatile carcinogenic nitrosamines (Huang et al, 1981; Tannenbaum et al, 1985; Song and Hu, 1988; Poirier et al, 1987). Zou et al (1994) found that N-dimethylnitrosamine (NDMA) and N-diethylnitrosamine (NDEA) were the predominant volatile nitrosamines in the salted fish, although N-nitrosopyrrolidine (NPYR) and N-nitrosopipperidine (NPIP) were also detected. Further analysis demonstrated that the concentrations of NDMA (0.290–0.866 mg/kg), NDEA (0.257–0.635 mg/kg) and total volatile nitrosamines (0.602—1.508 mg/kg) in salted fish samples collected from areas with nasopharyngeal cancer mortality of < 1, 1–< 2.5, 2.5–< 5.0 and > 5.0 per 100,000 population, respectively, showed significant (p < 0.01) positive correlations. Furthermore, salted fish nitrosated in a way that mimics the reaction in the stomach, produces a mutagenic response (Tannenbaum et al, 1985).

An alternative carcinogenic mechanism is suggested by the demonstration of activation of the Epstein-Barr virus by chemicals that are present in Chinese salted fish (Shao et al, 1988). Raised anti-virus antibody titres have been consistently demonstrated in people with nasopharyngeal cancer.

The epidemiological data, supported by experimental data and the identification of plausible agents – nitrosamines — provides convincing evidence that salted fish increases the risk of nasopharyngeal cancer, especially when eaten frequently in early childhood.

Salted vegetables
Salted mustard greens were significantly associated with increased risk of nasopharyngeal cancer in two case-control studies reported by Yu et al,(1986,1988). In the first study

(Yu et al, 1986), the result was no longer significant when intake of salted fish was accounted for. However, in the second study (Yu et al, 1988) the strong association remained after adjustment for salted fish intake.

The evidence relating to salt-preserved vegetables and nasopharyngeal cancer is currently limited; no judgement is possible.

Pickled and fermented foods
In the case-control study conducted in Tunisia (Jeannel et al, 1990), intake of pickled vegetables during childhood was associated with a significantly increased risk of nasopharyngeal cancer. However, the results were no longer significant when intake of other foods was accounted for in the analysis.

Other preserved foods associated with increased risk in early life include a range of fermented foods eaten by Chinese populations such as shrimp paste (OR = 3.2), salted duck egg (OR = 5.1), and fermented soya bean paste (OR = 2.7), as well as mouldy bean curd and fermented fish sauce (Yu et al, 1988, 1989). In north Africa, nasopharyngeal cancer has been associated with Quaddid (dried mutton preserved in olive oil), vegetables fermented in brine, and spicy foods, particularly if eaten early in life (Jeannel et al, 1990; Poirier et al, 1987).

The evidence on pickled and fermented foods hints at increased risk but is currently limited and non-specific; no judgement is possible.

4.3 Larynx

Cancer of the larynx is the fourteenth most common incident cancer throughout the world. An estimated 190,000 cases occurred in 1996, accounting for 1.8% of all new cancers.

Incidence of laryngeal cancer is relatively high in France, Italy and Spain, and it is much more common in men.

The panel has reached the following conclusions. Diets high in vegetables and fruits probably decrease the risk of laryngeal cancer. The evidence that alcohol increases the risk of this cancer is convincing, and, as with mouth and pharyngeal cancer, risk is further increased among drinkers of alcohol who also smoke.

An established cause of laryngeal cancer is smoking.

The most effective means of preventing laryngeal cancer is not to use tobacco. The most effective dietary means of preventing laryngeal cancer are consumption of diets high in vegetables and fruits, and avoidance of alcohol.

FOOD, NUTRITION, AND LARYNGEAL CANCER

In the judgement of the panel the dietary constituents and the foods and drinks listed below modify the risk of cancers of the larynx. Judgements are graded according to the strength of the evidence.

EVIDENCE	DECREASES RISK	NO RELATIONSHIP	INCREASES RISK
Convincing			Alcohol[a]
Probable	Vegetables and fruits		
Possible			
Insufficient	Carotenoids Vitamin C		

For an explanation of the terms used in the matrix, see chapter 3.
[a] Risk greatly increases if drinking is accompanied by smoking

INTRODUCTION

INCIDENCE PATTERNS

Cancer of the larynx is the fourteenth most common cancer in the world. In 1996, an estimated 190,000 new cases were diagnosed worldwide (WHO, 1997), accounting for 1.8% of all new cancers.

The incidence of laryngeal cancer varies widely around the world. Areas of high risk include France, Italy and Spain. The annual age-adjusted rates in men vary from a low of 0.93 per 100,000 to a high of 20.3. Approximately 60% of the global incidence of laryngeal cancer is found in developing countries.

Men account for 85% of the worldwide incidence of laryngeal cancer.

Five-year survival rates for laryngeal cancer are 50–60%. In 1996, mortality from cancer of the larynx was estimated at 99,000 people, 1.4% of all cancer deaths (WHO,1997).

PATHOGENESIS

Key epidemiological observations on the pathogenesis of laryngeal cancer include the marked male excess (perhaps five-fold more common in men) and the strong independent

BOX 4.3.1 ESTABLISHED NON-DIETARY FACTORS AND LARYNGEAL CANCER

The following non-dietary factor increases the risk of laryngeal cancer:

■ Smoking tobacco

and interacting associations with tobacco and alcohol. It seems plausible that tobacco smoke acts as a direct carcinogen-delivery system, with alcohol providing perhaps more ready access to cells for tobacco carcinogens via its solvent properties, and more DNA damage in its own right via its first metabolite acetaldehyde. Both alcohol and tobacco increase the likelihood of promotion because of their capacity to damage and kill cells, thus providing compensatory hyperproliferation and, ultimately, selection of a clone with a marked survival advantage. This may be the result of oncogene mutation, or loss of tumour-suppressor genes.

Whether the male excess is associated simply with greater consumption of alcohol and tobacco, a result of the larger adult male larynx (more tissue at risk), or a consequence of a critical exposure period at the time of pubertal laryngeal growth has not been established.

LARYNGEAL CANCER estimated rates of cancer incidence by sex and area

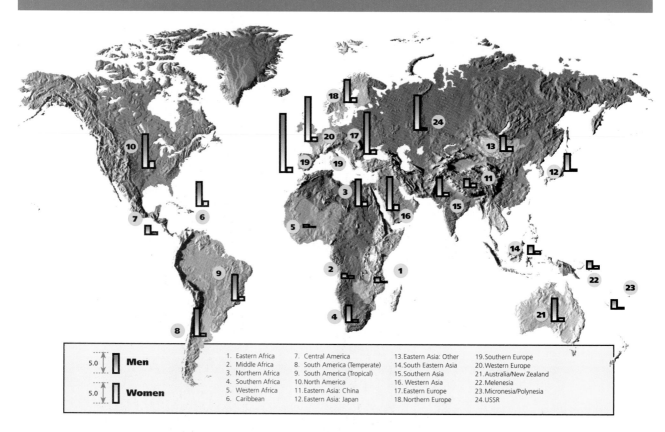

| 5.0 ↕ ▌ | **Men** |
| 5.0 ↕ ▌ | **Women** |

1. Eastern Africa	7. Central America	13. Eastern Asia: Other	19. Southern Europe
2. Middle Africa	8. South America (Temperate)	14. South Eastern Asia	20. Western Europe
3. Northern Africa	9. South America (Tropical)	15. Southern Asia	21. Australia/New Zealand
4. Southern Africa	10. North America	16. Western Asia	22. Melenesia
5. Western Africa	11. Eastern Asia: China	17. Eastern Europe	23. Micronesia/Polynesia
6. Caribbean	12. Eastern Asia: Japan	18. Northern Europe	24. USSR

TABLE 4.3.1 ALCOHOL CONSUMPTION AND THE RISK OF LARYNGEAL CANCER: COHORT STUDIES						
AUTHOR, YEAR AND PLACE	**SIZE OF COHORT: NO. OF CASES**	**GROUP**	**RELATIVE RISK (95% CONFIDENCE INTERVAL)**	**SEX/AGE**	**ADJUSTMENT SMOKING HISTORY**	**OTHER VARIABLES**
Sundby, 1967 Norway	1,722 men: 5	alcoholics vs Oslo inhabitants	3.1 (1.0–7.3)**d	Y	N	N
Hakulinen, 1974 Finland	205,000 men: 3	alcohol abusers	1.4 (0.3–7.2)**d	Y	N	N
Monsson, 1975, Massachusetts, USA	1,382: 6	chronic alcoholics	3.8 (1.4–8.2)*d	Y	N	N
Robinette, 1979, USA	4,401 men: 11	US veterans, alcoholics	1.7 (0.7–4.4)**	Y	N	N
Jensen, 1980, Denmark	4,401 men: 11	brewery workers	2.0 (1.4–4.9)*	Y	N	N
Schmidt, 1981, Canada	9,889 men: 12	alcoholics vs Ontario population	4.3 (1.4–4.9)*d	Y	94% cohort smokers	N
		alcoholics vs US veterans	4.5 (2.3–7.8)*d			
Adami, 1992, Sweden	9,353: 11	alcoholics	men 3.1 (1.5–5.7)*e women 23.2 (0.3–129.1)*e	Y	N	Y

* p < 0.05 for trend and/or for comparison of lowest vs highest consumption level
** p ≥ 0.05 for trend and for comparison of lowest vs highest consumption level
d confidence interval calculated by a 1991 IARC Working Group
e standardised incidence ratio and 95% confidence interval

JUDGEMENTS OF OTHER REPORTS

The WHO report, *Diet, Nutrition and the Prevention of Chronic Diseases* (WHO, 1990), concluded that consumption of alcoholic drinks was causally related to cancer of the larynx, and that smoking also causes cancer at this site. In addition, case-control studies of oral cancers have 'shown an increased risk associated with infrequent ingestion of fruit and vegetables'.

REVIEW

4.3.1 DIETARY CONSTITUENTS

4.3.1.1 Protein
Animal protein
Two case-control studies have examined the association between animal protein and the risk of laryngeal cancer. Freudenheim et al (1992) found an association between protein intake and increased risk of laryngeal cancer, which disappeared after controlling for energy intake. Another study, however, found an inverse association between a protein 'score' and the risk of laryngeal cancer; but the protein score was calculated from intakes of meat and meat products only, and low intakes of these foods were associated with generally poor nutrition (Zatonski et al, 1991).

Based on one study, no judgement is possible.

4.3.1.2 Alcohol
Studies of alcoholics have consistently shown that they have elevated risks of laryngeal cancer. Seven cohort studies of alcoholics have found relative risks in the range 1.4–23.2 (Sundby, 1967; Hakulinen et al, 1974; Monsson and Lyon, 1975; Robinette et al, 1979; Schmidt and Popham, 1991; Adami et al, 1992), with three reaching statistical significance (Monson and Lyon, 1975; Schmidt and Popham, 1991; Adami et al, 1992) (see Table 4.3.1). These studies, however, have lacked information on smoking habits – a well established cause of laryngeal cancer.

Seventeen case-control studies have found statistically significant increased risk of alcohol for laryngeal cancer. Odds ratios in these studies range between 1.8 and 330 (see Table 4.3.2). The first such study, by Wynder et al (1956) showed significantly higher alcohol consumption in cases compared to controls. In the highest category of alcohol intake (7 oz/day or more) the OR was 5.3 compared to non-drinkers. That finding has been confirmed by subsequent studies in Europe (Spaljkovic, 1971; Brugere et al, 1986; Tuyns et al, 1988; La Vecchia et al, 1990; Tavini et al, 1994) and North America (Hinds et al, 1979; Burch and Howe, 1981; Freudenheim et al, 1992; Hedberg et al, 1994) where studies have also reported a positive dose–response relationship between alcohol intake and cancer of the larynx.

In a large multi-centred study in Italy, Spain, Switzerland and France (Tuyns et al, 1988), significant increases in risk were observed with quantity of alcohol consumed, both for the supraglottic tumour locations (junctional area between larynx and pharynx) and for glottic (larynx) and subglottic

TABLE 4.3.2 ALCOHOL CONSUMPTION AND THE RISK OF LARYNGEAL CANCER: CASE-CONTROL STUDIES

AUTHOR, YEAR, AND PLACE	NO. OF CASES	TYPE OF ALCOHOL	COMPARISON[a]	ODDS RATIO (95% CONFIDENCE INTERVAL)[c]	SEX/AGE	ADJUSTMENT SMOKING HISTORY	OTHER VARIABLES
Wynder, 1956 New York, USA	209 men	whisky	>7 oz/day vs never	5.3 (2.5–11.2)[*e]	Y	Y	N
Vincent, 1963 Buffalo, USA	23	all types	47+ g/day vs <47 g/day	5.9 (2.4–14.3)[*e]	Y	N	N
Wynder, 1976 USA	224 men	all types	7+ oz/day vs <1 oz/day	2.3 (1.5–3.4)[*e]	Y	Y	N
Spalajkovic, 1976 France	200 men	all types	ever vs never	11.2 (6.9–18.2)[*e]	Y	N	N
Williams, 1977 USA	110	all types	51+ vs <50 oz/yr 51+ vs <50 oz/yr	men 2.3 (na)[*d] women 0.8 (na)[**d]	Y	Y	Y
Hinds, 1979 Washington State USA	47 men	units – 1 = 12 oz beer, 4 oz wine or 1oz spirits	6+ vs <1 unit/day	9.0 (2.4–34.1)[*]	Y	N	N
Burch, 1981 Ontario, Canada	184 men	all types	60+ g/day vs <24 g/day	4.8 (2.3–9.9)[*f]	Y	Y	N
Herity, 1981 Ireland	59 men	all types	heavy vs non-drinkers	3.2 (na) na	Y	N	N
Elwood, 1984 British Colombia Canada	154	all types	480+ g/week vs <24 g/week	extrinsic 6.5 (na) na[d] intrinsic 2.2 (na) na[d]	Y	Y	Y
Olsen, 1985 Denmark	326	beer	301+ g/week vs 0–100 g/week	4.1 (na) na	Y	Y	N
Zagranski, 1986 USA	87 men	all types	ever vs never	4.2 (1.4–12.4)[*]	Y	Y	N
Brugere, 1986 France	224 men	all types as calories consumed	160+ g/day vs 0–34 g/day 160+ g/day vs 0–39 g/day	supraglottis 42.1 (20.5–86.4)[*] glottis/subglottis 6.1 (3.4–10.9)[*]	Y	Y	N
De Stefani, 1987 Uruguay	107 men	wine hard liquor	any vs none any vs none	7.4 (3.0–18.1)[*] 4.0 (1.9–8.2)[*]	Y	Y	N
Tuyns, 1988 Europe Italy	727	all types	121+ g/day vs 0–20 g/day	2.6 (1.8–3.6)[*d]	Y	Y	Y
La Vecchia, 1990	110 men	all types	h vs l tertile	1.8 (na)[*d]	Y	Y	Y
Zatonski, 1990 Poland	249	vodka	regular vs irregular >30 yrs drinking vs non-drinker/non-smoker	10.4 (4.0–27.2)[*d] 330.3 (70.0–11.56)[*d]	Y	N	Y
Freudenheim, 1992 New York, USA	250 men	wine beer hard liquor any liquor	h vs l quartile h vs l quartile h vs l quartile h vs l quartile	1.1 (0.6–2.0)[**d] 2.7 (1.4–5.1)[*d] 2.2 (1.2–4.1)[*d] 3.5 (1.8–7.0)[*d]	Y	Y	Y
Tavini, 1994, Italy	367 men	all types	8+ drinks/week vs none	25.2 (na)[*d]	Y	Y	Y
Hedberg, 1994 Washington, USA	235	all types	42+ drinks/week vs <7 drinks/week	3.1 (1.2–7.9)[*d]	Y	Y	Y

[*] p < 0.05 for trend and/or for comparison of lowest vs highest consumption level

[**] p ≥ 0.05 for trend and for comparison of lowest vs highest consumption level

[a] h = highest, l = lowest

[c] na – information is unclear or not available from the article

[d] adjusted for one or more of the following: race, hospital, education, socio-economic status, residence, marital status, dental care, functional impairment due to alcohol use

[e] confidence interval calculated by a 1991 IARC Working Group

[f] 90% confidence interval

(endopharynx) sites, after adjusting for smoking, age, and area of residence (OR = 6.1–42.1).

The role of alcohol in laryngeal cancer appears to be independent of smoking, as illustrated above (Tuyns et al, 1988). Likewise, an increased risk of laryngeal cancer among non-smoking drinkers has been reported by Flanders and Rothman (1986) and in two Canadian studies (Burch and Howe, 1981; Elwood et al, 1984), where risk estimates ranged between 2.2 and 6.5 for non-smokers at the highest level of alcohol intake.

The joint effect of alcohol and tobacco has been investigated in many studies (Hinds et al, 1979; Burch et al,1981; Herity et al, 1981, 1982; Elwood et al, 1984; Olsen et al, 1985a; Flanders and Rothman, 1986; Zagraniski et al, 1986; Brownson and Chang, 1987; Splitz et al, 1988; Tuyns et al, 1988). A 'synergistic' effect between alcohol and tobacco in the induction of laryngeal cancer has been reported and, in the large study by Tuyns et al (1985), a multiplicative model provided an adequate description of the data. Although an early study suggested that the risk of laryngeal cancer is particularly high for whisky drinkers (OR = 5.3 for the highest level of intake) (Wynder et al, 1956), a significantly increased risk was also seen for wine and beer drinkers in this study. In further studies in North America (Wynder et al, 1976; Hinds et al, 1979; Burch et al, 1981), the relative risks seem to be similar for consumption of comparable amounts of wine, beer and spirits (ORs = 2.3–9.0). In a large case-control study in Denmark (Olsen et al, 1985), the only significantly increased relative risk was found for beer (OR = 4.1). Although no adjustment was made for the use of other beverages in any of these studies, the results indicate that alcoholic beverages increase the risk of laryngeal cancer irrespective of their alcohol content. The mechanisms involved may be similar to those proposed for oral and pharyngeal cancers, namely that ethanol may damage cells, modifying the permeability of cell membranes and permitting the entry of carcinogens. Additionally, cell damage may lead to increased replication. Finally, alcohol may contain other potentially carcinogenic substances, or may compromise nutritional status increasing susceptibility to cancer, for instance, via loss of antioxidant capacity.

The various anatomical parts of the larynx must be distinguished when considering aetiology. The endolarynx is exposed to inhaled agents, while the junctional area between the larynx and the pharynx is exposed to both inhaled and ingested agents, and therefore directly exposed to alcohol. There are some inconsistencies in relation to anatomical subsites of the larynx, with increased risk mostly limited to the extrinsic parts of the larynx directly exposed to alcohol, although it is worth remembering that, as a volatile substance, alcohol is present both in inspired and expired air.

The evidence that high alcohol consumption, irrespective of the type of beverage, increases the risk of laryngeal cancer, is convincing.

4.3.1.3. Vitamins
Carotenoids

Two case-control studies that have examined dietary carotenoids or a 'carotene index'; both reported statistically significant odds ratios of 0.5 for higher intake (Mackerras et al, 1985; Freudenheim et al, 1992). Another found that, compared to the highest intake group (> 1300 retinol equivalents), the three lowest quintiles were at significantly higher risk for laryngeal cancer (Estève et al, 1996). A study in China (Zheng et al, 1992) found a weak, non-significant decreased risk for the highest versus lowest tertile.

The evidence suggests that high dietary carotenoids may decrease the risk of laryngeal cancer, but is, as yet, insufficient.

Retinol

One case-control study of laryngeal cancer has found increased risk associated with higher retinol intakes (Freudenheim et al, 1992). Compared to the lowest quartile, all three of the upper quartiles were associated with statistically significantly higher risk for laryngeal cancer, with ORs of 3.2, 4.0, and 2.8 for the second, third, and highest quartiles, respectively. In a US study, Graham et al (1981) also found an increased risk for higher intakes (OR = 3.0, highest vs lowest tertile). Two further studies found risk to be unrelated to retinol intake (Mackerras et al, 1988; Estève et al, 1996).

The data on retinol and the risk of laryngeal cancer are limited; no judgement is possible.

Vitamin C

The studies by Freudenheim et al (1992) and Zheng et al (1992) reported on vitamin C intake. They both found non-significant protective associations, OR = 0.6 (0.3–1.3) for the highest compared with the lowest quartile of intake. Similarly, Graham et al (1981) found ORs of 0.4, p < 0.005 for the highest versus the lowest quartile of intake and ORs of 0.8 (0.5–1.4) for the highest versus the lowest tertile of intake. Again, the IARC multi-centre case-control study found that, compared to people in the lowest quintile, those with the highest level of vitamin C intake (>140 mg/day) were at a lower risk for laryngeal cancer (Estève et al, 1996).

The evidence suggests that vitamin C may decrease the risk of laryngeal cancer, but is, as yet, insufficient.

4.3.2 FOODS AND DRINKS

4.3.2.1 Vegetables and fruits
No prospective cohort studies of laryngeal cancer have reported on vegetable and fruit consumption. Results from nine case-control studies are shown in Table 4.3.3. Each of the studies that reported on the level of statistical significancer found a protective association for at least one category of vegetables and/or fruits; these studies were conducted in both developing and developed countries, including Uruguay (De Stefani et al,

TABLE 4.3.3 VEGETABLE AND FRUIT CONSUMPTION AND THE RISK OF LARYNGEAL CANCER: CASE-CONTROL STUDIES

AUTHOR, YEAR, AND PLACE	NO. OF CASES	TYPE OF VEGETABLES OR FRUIT	COMPARISON[a]	ODDS RATIO (95% CONFIDENCE INTERVAL)[c]	SEX/AGE	ADJUSTMENT SMOKING HISTORY	OTHER VARIABLES
Graham, 1981 New York, USA	374 men	vegetables	na	prot assoc	Y	N	N
		cabbage		ns**	age matched		
		broccoli		ns**			
		brussels sprouts		ns**			
Zemla, 1987 Poland	328 men	vegetables	na	prot assoc*	Y	N	N
DeStephani, 1987 Uruguay	107	vegetables	1/day vs <1	0.8 (0.5–1.3)**	Y	N	N
		fruit	1/day vs <1	0.4 (0.2–0.8)*			
Notani & Jayant, 1987 India	80 men	vegetables	1/day vs <1	0.4 (0.2–0.7)*	Y	N	N
		fruit	1/wk vs <1	0.5 (0.2–1.0)**			
La Vecchia, 1990 Italy	110	green vegetables	h vs l tertile	0.2 (na)*d	Y	Y	Y
		fresh fruits		0.3 (na)*d			
Zatonski, 1991 Poland	249 men	vegetables and fruits	h vs l tertile	0.3 (0.2–0.6)*d	Y	Y	Y
Maier, 1992 Germany	164 men	salad	1/week vs <1	0.5 (0.2–0.9)*	Y	Y	N
		fruit		0.6 (0.3–1.0)*			
Zheng, 1992 China	201	vegetables	h vs l tertile	men	Y	smoking, not alcohol	Y
		dark green vegetables		1.2 (na)*d			
		yellow vegetables		1.2 (na)*d			
		cruciferous vegetables		1.2 (na)*d			
		tomatoes		0.6 (na)*d			
		fruits		0.6 (na)*d			
		vegetables		women			
				1.1 (0.4–3.2)**d			
		dark green vegetables		0.9 (0.3–0.9)**d			
		yellow vegetables		0.5 (0.2–1.3)**d			
		cruciferous vegetables		3.0 (1.0–9.2)*d			
		tomatoes		1.1 (0.3–3.1)**d			
		fruits		0.5 (0.2–1.5)**d			
Esteve, 1996 Europe	1,147	vegetables	>350 vs <170 g	0.6 (0.4–0.9)*d	Y	Y	Y
		citrus fruit	>80 vs <20 g	0.5 (0.3–0.6)*d			
		other fruit	>250 vs <70 g	0.5 (0.4–0.8)*d			

* p < 0.05 for trend and/or for comparison of lowest vs highest consumption level
** p ≥ 0.05 for trend and for comparison of lowest vs highest consumption level
[a] h = highest, l = lowest
[b] prot assoc – protective association
[c] na – information is unclear or not available from the article
[d] matched or adjusted for one of the following: socio-economic status, education, total energy intake, residence

1987), India (Notani and Jayant, 1987), Poland (Zemla et al, 1987), Italy (La Vecchia et al, 1990), China (Zheng et al, 1992), the USA (Graham et al, 1991) and Germany (Maier and Beck, 1992). The most recent study was a multi-centre case-control study carried out in six regions of Europe, and included a total of 1,147 cases (Estève et al, 1996).

Of the studies that examined vegetables as a broad category, six reported protective associations (Graham et al, 1981; De Stefani et al, 1987; Notani and Jayant, 1987; La Vecchia et al, 1990; Maier and Beck, 1992; Estève et al, 1996) and each of six that examined fruit reported similarly (Graham et al, 1981; De Stefani et al, 1987; Notani and Jayant, 1987; La Vecchia et al, 1990; Zheng, 1992; Estève et al, 1996). Few data are available on any particular type of vegetable or fruit, although statistically significant odds

ratios of 0.5 or lower have been observed for higher intake of vegetables, fruits, green vegetables, salad, oranges and tangerines, and a vegetable and fruit score (Notani and Jayant, 1987; La Vecchia et al, 1990; Zatonski et al, 1991; Maier and Beck, 1992; Zheng et al, 1992; Estève et al, 1996). As with other cancers of the upper alimentary and respiratory tracts, tobacco smoking and high alcohol consumption are the two major risk factors for cancer of the larynx. In the majority of studies, protective associations for vegetable and fruit consumption remained after these factors were taken into account.

Diets high in vegetables and fruit probably decrease the risk of laryngeal cancer.

4.3.2.2 Pulses (legumes)

Two case-control studies of laryngeal cancer have reported weak non-significant decreases in risk with greater intake of pulses (Notani and Jayant, 1987; Zheng et al, 1992).

The data on pulses and laryngeal cancer are very limited; no judgement is possible.

4.3.2.3 Meat, poultry, fish and eggs

Meat

Case-control studies in India (Notani and Jayant, 1987), Italy (La Vecchia et al, 1990), China (Zheng et al, 1992) and Germany (Maier and Beck, 1992) suggest that meats, in general, are not associated with higher risk of laryngeal cancer. Notani and Jayant (1987) found no association between fresh meat and laryngeal cancer. La Vecchia (1990) reported that ham and salami were not associated, but that fresh meat was showed a positive association with laryngeal cancer, although not statistically significant. Zheng et al (1992) reported that liver consumption was associated with increased risk of laryngeal cancer, with a significant trend (OR = 2.2); however, the confidence limits for red meat intake included 1.0 (OR = 1.3).

The evidence on meat and laryngeal cancer is inconsistent; no judgement is possible.

Fish

Somewhat in contrast to meat consumption, higher fish consumption has, in some studies, been associated with a decreased risk for laryngeal cancer (Notani and Jayant, 1987; La Vecchia et al, 1990). A significant dose–response was seen in the study in northern Italy (La Vecchia et al, 1990). The multi-centre IARC study (Estève et al, 1996) found a statistically nonsignificant association with higher fish consumption. On the other hand, Zheng et al (1992) found no significant association with higher fish consumption.

The evidence on fish consumption and the risk of laryngeal cancer is limited; no judgement is possible.

Eggs

A higher risk of laryngeal cancer has been associated with increased egg consumption in two case-control studies (Notani and Jayant, 1987; Maier and Beck, 1992). Notani and Jayant (1987) reported statistically nonsignificant increases in laryngeal cancer using hospital or population controls (OR = 1.1–1.6), however; both confidence intervals included one.

The data on eggs and laryngeal cancer are very limited; no judgement is possible.

4.3.2.4 Milk and dairy products

Dairy products have shown protective associations in two case-control studies (Notani and Jayant, 1987; Maier and Beck, 1992). Buttermilk and other dairy products have shown odds ratios of 0.5 or less for high versus low consumption and risk of laryngeal cancer.

Evidence on milk and dairy products and the risk of laryngeal cancer is limited; no judgement is possible.

4.3.2.5 Herbs, spices, condiments

Chilli peppers

Red chilli powder, a spice commonly used in India, has been found, in one study, to be a risk factor when consumed in amounts greater than 100 g/month (Notani and Jayant, 1987). An OR of 3.4 (1.4–8.3) was seen for the highest compared to the lowest tertile of chilli powder use (p for trend = 0.10).

Based on a single study, no judgement is possible.

4.3.2.6 Coffee, tea and other drinks

Maté

In South Americans, the consumption of maté has been identified as an independent risk factor for laryngeal cancer, with a doubling of risk associated with regular consumption in each of two studies (De Stefani et al, 1987; Pintos et al, 1994). An adjusted OR of 2.2 (1.1–4.5) was seen for increased maté consumption in one study (Pintos et al, 1994). In the other, maté was associated with a threefold increase in risk for laryngeal cancer (De Stefani et al, 1987). In this study, maté use and smoking had a synergistic effect on the risk for laryngeal cancer. A similar effect was observed for maté and alcohol.

The data on maté and risk of laryngeal cancer are limited; no judgement is possible.

4.3.3 FOOD PROCESSING

4.3.3.1 Salt, salting and refrigeration

Salted foods

Salted and processed meat and fish, but not vegetables, when consumed daily, have been shown to increase the risk of laryngeal cancer (Zheng et al, 1992). This study found a dose–response relationship between higher intake of salted meat/fish and the risk of laryngeal cancer.

Based on only one study; no judgement is possible.

4.3.3.2 Cooking

Frying

Consuming deep-fried foods 'often' as opposed to 'never/occasionally' was found to increase the risk of laryngeal cancer in one study (OR = 2.2) although the result was not statistically significant (Zheng et al, 1992).

Based on only one study; no judgement is possible.

4.4 Oesophagus

Cancer of the oesophagus is the eighth most common incident cancer, and the fifth most common cause of cancer deaths, throughout the world. An estimated 480,000 cases occurred in 1996, accounting for 4.6% of all new cancers.

Incidence of oesophageal cancer is relatively high in China, elsewhere in Asia, and other developing regions, and it is more common in men.

The panel has reached the following conclusions. The evidence that diets high in vegetables and fruits decrease the risk of oesophageal cancer is convincing. The evidence that alcohol increases the risk of this cancer is also convincing, and, as with mouth and pharyngeal cancer, risk is further increased among drinkers of alcohol who smoke.

The panel notes that diets high in carotenoids and in vitamin C, found in vegetables and fruits and other foods of plant origin, possibly decrease the risk of oesophageal cancer; and that *N*-nitroso compounds, formed in preserved foods, possibly increase the risk of this cancer. The evidence that monotonous diets very high in cereals possibly increase the risk of oesophageal cancer is plausible because such diets are deficient in protective dietary constituents.

An established cause of oesophageal cancer is smoking.

The most effective way of preventing oesophageal cancer, is not to use tobacco. The most effective dietary means of preventing oesophageal cancer are consumption of varied diets high in vegetables and fruits, and avoidance of alcohol.

FOOD, NUTRITION AND OESOPHAGEAL CANCER

In the judgement of the panel, the dietary constituents and related factors and the foods and drinks listed below, modify the risk of cancer of the oesophagus. Judgements are graded according to the strength of the evidence.

EVIDENCE	DECREASES RISK	NO RELATIONSHIP	INCREASES RISK
Convincing	Vegetables and fruits		Alcohol
Probable			
Possible	Carotenoids Vitamin C		Cereals Maté [a] Very hot drinks [a] *N*-nitrosamines
Insufficient			Tea [a]

For an explanation of the terms used in the matrix, see chapter 3.
[a] These judgements possibly all represent increased risk associated with the consumption of very hot drinks.

INTRODUCTION

INCIDENCE PATTERNS

Cancer of the oesophagus is the eighth most common cancer in the world. In 1996, an estimated 480,000 new cases were diagnosed worldwide (WHO, 1997), accounting for 4.6% of all new cancers.

Areas of high risk include the 'oesophageal cancer belt', which runs from north-central China and spans westward through central Asia to northern Iran. The developing world accounts for 85% of the total global incidence. Other areas of high risk include parts of South America and south-east Africa.

Oesophageal cancer incidence is higher among males than females, with an estimated 320,000 cases (66%) occurring in males in 1996.

BOX 4.4.1 ESTABLISHED NON-DIETARY FACTORS AND OESOPHAGEAL CANCER

The following non-dietary factors increase the risk of oesophageal cancer:

■ Smoking tobacco
■ Barrett's oesophagus

The great majority of cancers of the oesophagus are squamous-cell carcinomas. In most countries the incidence of squamous-cell oesophageal carcinoma is higher in males than in females, and this difference increases with age. Primary adenocarcinoma of the oesophagus occurs either in conjunction with Barrett's columnar metaplasia in the lower oesophagus or from the mucous glands of the oesophagus (Schottenfeld, 1984).

Most oesophageal cancers occur in the middle and lower thirds of the oesophagus. However, earlier descriptive studies

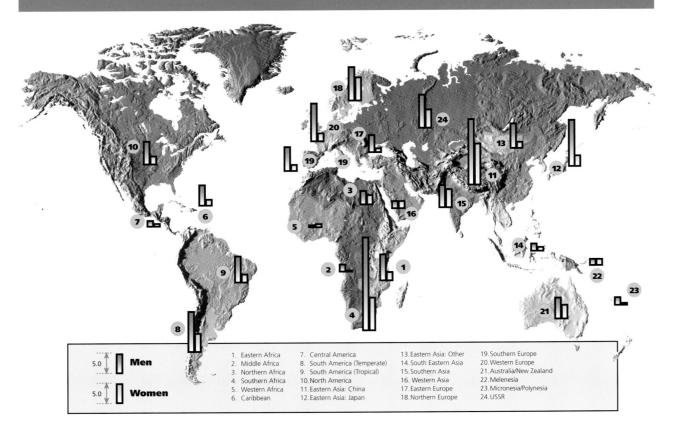

OESOPHAGEAL CANCER estimated rates of cancer incidence by sex and area

5.0 | Men

5.0 | Women

1. Eastern Africa
2. Middle Africa
3. Northern Africa
4. Southern Africa
5. Western Africa
6. Caribbean
7. Central America
8. South America (Temperate)
9. South America (Tropical)
10. North America
11. Eastern Asia: China
12. Eastern Asia: Japan
13. Eastern Asia: Other
14. South Eastern Asia
15. Southern Asia
16. Western Asia
17. Eastern Europe
18. Northern Europe
19. Southern Europe
20. Western Europe
21. Australia/New Zealand
22. Melenesia
23. Micronesia/Polynesia
24. USSR

in Sweden (Wynder et al, 1957) and historically in Scotland (Pearson, 1966; Schottenfeld, 1984) showed elevated proportions in the upper oesophagus in women. This unusual anatomical pattern was consistent with the occurrence of the nutrient deficiency-related Plummer-Vinson syndrome in women in these areas. This form of oesophageal cancer seems to be much less frequent than it was fifty years ago.

Survival rates for cancer of the oesophagus are poor, with 75% of patients dying within a year of initial diagnosis. Five-year survival rates are 5–10%. In 1996, mortality attributable to cancer of the oesophagus was estimated at 456,000 people, 6.4% of all cancer deaths (WHO, 1997).

PATHOGENESIS

Key epidemiological observations on the pathogenesis of oesophageal cancer include the very marked geographical variation in incidence, even over quite small distances, a male excess in low-risk countries that is absent in high risk areas, and the higher risk among lower socioeconomic groups. It appears that the environmental risk factors may vary, but the higher risk among those in poverty (and consuming more marginal diets) is a common factor everywhere.

It seems likely that, in some parts of the world, alcohol and tobacco act in a manner that is both independent and interactive in the aetiology of oesophageal cancer. Both can act to increase DNA damage, directly in the case of tobacco smoke, indirectly via a metabolite, acetaldehyde, in the case of alcohol. Further, both exposures can cause cell damage and death with resultant hyperproliferation and the likelihood of the emergence of an abnormal clone of cells with a proliferate advantage. This may be the result of mutated oncogenes or loss of tumour-suppressor genes including *p53*.

In other parts of the world, other exposures may take the place of the carcinogenic exposures – for example, opium residues and nitrosamines. Further, the causes of chronic cell damage and cell replication may include thermal damage from hot beverages, chronic nutrient deficiencies (see below) and various chronic proliferative lesions of currently unknown aetiology including Barrett's oesophagus.

The suggested pathway to oesophageal cancer, based on the natural history of the disorder as observed in high-risk areas is (analogously with stomach cancer):

Normal oesophagus ⇔ chronic oesophagitis ⇔ atrophy ⇔ dysplasia ⇒ cancer.

For more discussion, see Muñoz and Day (1996).

JUDGEMENTS OF OTHER REPORTS

The National Academy of Sciences report, *Diet, Nutrition and Cancer* (NAS, 1982), concluded that an increased risk of cancer of the oesophagus was associated with alcohol drinking, particularly in conjunction with cigarette smoking. Pickled and mouldy foods, deficiency of trace minerals and consumption of hot drinks were also associated with an increased risk. The frequent consumption of vegetables and fruit was associated with a decreased risk. The subsequent

report, *Diet and Health* (NAS, 1989), stated that cancer of the oesophagus was 'associated with the use of tobacco and alcohol individually, but especially with their combined use'. It also noted that preserved foods increased risk and that several vitamins and minerals were protective against oesophageal cancer, but the reasons for these relationships were not yet clearly established.

The WHO report, *Diet, Nutrition and the Prevention of Chronic Diseases* (WHO, 1990) concluded that 'epidemiological studies clearly indicate that drinking alcoholic beverages is causally related to cancer of the oesophagus' and that smoking also causes cancer at this site. It also stated that correlational studies had found positive associations between the risk of oesophageal cancer and low intakes of lentils, vegetables and fruits, animal protein and various vitamins and trace minerals. High intakes of pickled or salt-pickled, and mouldy foods, and consumption of foods and beverages at very high temperatures also increased the risk of oesophageal cancer.

REVIEW

4.4.1 DIETARY CONSTITUENTS

4.4.1.1 Protein

The observation that cancers of the oesophagus tend to be associated with traditional agrarian diets that are low in protein, and particularly animal protein, has led to the suggestion that very low intakes of animal protein may be implicated in carcinogenesis at this site.

One case-control study in France (Tuyns et al, 1987) and another in the USA (Ziegler et al, 1981) found that higher intakes of animal protein were associated with decreased risk of cancer of the oesophagus (ORs = 0.2 and 0.5, respectively, with statistically significant trends across categories of intake).

A cross-sectional survey in Southern Africa (Jaskiewicz, 1989) found higher intakes of animal protein were associated with a decreased incidence of mild cytological lesions. In these studies, however, higher levels of consumption of vegetables and fruits were also associated with decreased risk.

The evidence relating to intakes of animal proteins/foods and the risk of oesophageal cancer is limited; no judgement is possible.

4.4.1.2 Alcohol

Of all of the upper aerodigestive tract cancers, data on alcohol are most extensive for oesophageal cancer. Nine of 10 cohort studies and 18 of 21 case-control studies show increased risk associated with consumption of all types of alcoholic drink; 4 cohort studies and 15 case-control studies show statistically significant increases (IARC, 1988).

With the exception of the study of Dublin brewery workers (Dean et al, 1979), all retrospective cohort studies have

TABLE 4.4.1 ALCOHOL CONSUMPTION AND THE RISK OF OESOPHAGEAL CANCER: COHORT STUDIES

AUTHOR, YEAR AND PLACE	SIZE OF COHORT: NO OF CASES	GROUP	RELATIVE RISK (95% CONFIDENCE INTERVAL)[B,C]	SEX/AGE	ADJUSTMENT SMOKING HISTORY	OTHER VARIABLES
Sundby, 1967, Norway	1,722: 40	Alcoholics vs Oslo inhabitants	4.1 (2.9–4.6)*[d]	men, Y	N	N
Hakulinen, 1974, Finland	205,000: 101	Alcoholic abusers	5.7 (1.4–2.1)*[d]	men, Y	N	N
	205,000: 4	Alcoholics	4.1 (1.4–9.3)*[d]			
Monson and Lyon, 1975 Massachusetts, USA	1,382: 5	Chronic alcoholics	1.9 (0.4–5.5)**d	Y	N	N
Robinette, 1979, USA	4,401 men: 13	US veterans, alcoholics	2.0 (0.9–5.1)**d	men, Y	N	N
Dean, 1979, Dublin	3,000: 10	Brewery workers, cohort numbers an estimate	0.6 (0.3–2.1)**d	men, Y	N	N
Hirayama, 1979, Japan	265,118: 297	Patients in 29 health centers	beer 1.1 (na) na Sake 1.2 (na) na Whisky 1.7 (na) na Shochu 2.0 (na) na	Y	Y	N
Jensen, 1980, Denmark	4,401: 41	Brewery workers	2.1 (1.5–2.8)**	men, Y	N	N
Schmidt, 1981, Canada	9,889: 16	Alcoholics vs Ontario population	3.2 (1.8–5.2)*d 2.3 (1.3–3.8)*d	men, Y	94% cohort were smokers	N
Adami, 1992, Sweden	9,353: 26	Alcoholics vs US veterans alcoholics	men 6.9 (4.5–10.0)*e women 5.9 (0.1–32.6)*e	Y	N	N

* p < 0.05 for trend and/or for comparison of lowest vs highest consumption level
** p ≥ 0.05 for trend and for comparison of lowest vs highest consumption level
a h = highest, l = lowest
b 95% confidence interval; prot assoc, protective association; no assoc, no association; pos association, positive association
c na – information is unclear or not available from the article
d confidence interval calculated by a 1991 IARC Working Group
e standardized incidence ratio with 95% confidence interval

shown a two- to fourfold increase in risk of oesophageal cancer compared with rates for the general population. No information is available in these studies on tobacco smoking or other risk factors for oesophageal cancer. In a large study in Japan (Hirayama, 1979), after adjusting for smoking, relative risks of 1.7 and 2.0 were noted for whisky and shochu (a type of hard liquor) drinking, respectively. (Table 4.4.1)

At least 18 of the case-control studies have evaluated the effect of various alcoholic beverages adjusting for tobacco and nine for aspects of diet. Many of these studies have been carried out in countries where alcohol drinking is prevalent and, with the exception of two studies in South Africa (Bradshaw and Schonland, 1969, 1974), all reported increased risks with higher alcohol consumption. (Table 4.4.2.)

The risk of oesophageal cancer in relation to various types of alcoholic drinks is of interest. Most evidence suggests that it is the amount of alcohol consumed, rather than the particular drink (special attention has been paid to those with a high alcohol content) that determines risk of cancer; this applies both to the oesophagus and to other parts of the upper aerodigestive tract. However, there is some evidence that Calvados (a distilled beverage made from pears), in particular, may have a role in oesophageal cancer. This pear brandy is commercially produced, and made on farms for local use in the Calvados region of north-west France. It is a

hard liquor which, like other rough liquors made locally in many parts of Europe and elsewhere in the world, is notably abrasive when drunk (Tuyns et al, 1987).

Cachaca, a distilled sugar cane spirit, is the most common alcoholic drink in southern Brazil, where it accounts for 80% of alcohol consumed. Victora and colleagues (Victora et al, 1987) found that drinking cachaca is significantly associated with oesophageal cancer after adjusting for place of residence, smoking, and fruit and meat consumption. In relation to non-drinkers, those who had drunk 30 g or more per day for 50 years were 15 times more likely to develop oesophageal cancer. However, since cachaca is so popular in this area, it is difficult to determine if cachaca intake has an effect on oesophageal cancer independent of alcohol intake.

In three studies in the USA (Wynder and Bross, 1961; Pottern et al, 1981; Yu et al, 1988), increased risks were found both in whisky drinkers and in beer and wine drinkers – although the risk was greater in whisky drinkers. In Puerto Rico (Martinez, 1969), no differences in odds ratios were found for consumers of commercial rum only, of home-processed rum only, or of a mixture of beverages. The study of Danish brewery workers (Jensen, 1979) indicated that beer increases the risk of oesophageal cancer. In the north-western part of France where Tuyns and colleagues (Tuyns et al, 1979, 1987) carried out their case-control studies, further extended analyses, taking account of the sources of alcohol

TABLE 4.4.2 ALCOHOL CONSUMPTION AND THE RISK OF OESOPHAGEAL CANCER: CASE-CONTROL STUDIES

AUTHOR, YEAR, AND PLACE	NO OF CASES	TYPE OF ALCOHOL	COMPARISON[a]	ODDS RATIO (95% CONFIDENCE INTERVAL)[b,c]	ADJUSTMENT SEX/AGE	SMOKING HISTORY	OTHER VARIABLES
Wynder, 1957 New York, USA	150	All types – 1 unit = 18 oz beer, 8 oz wine or 2 oz spirits	> 12 units/day vs never	12.5 (1.5–78.4)*	men, Y	N	N
Martinez, 1969 Puerto Rico	163	All types – 1 unit = 18 oz beer, 8 oz wine or 2 oz spirits	5+ units/day vs < 1/day (men) 2+ units/day vs none (women)	men 7.7 (3.0–20.0)*e women 1.1 (0.3–4.6)**e	Y	Y	N
Bradshaw, 1969 South Africa	98	All types	ever vs never	0.9 (0.4–1.9)**e	Y	Y	N
Bradshaw, 1974 South Africa	196	All types	ever vs never	1.0 (0.6–1.8)**e	Y	Y	N
Bjelke, 1973 Minnesota, USA	52	Beer Wine Spirits	14+ vs < 1/month 1+ vs < 1/month 14+ vs < 1/month	4.4 (2.3–8.3)*e 0.5 (0.2–1.2)**e 2.1 (1.0–4.3)*e	Y	N	N
DeJong, 1974 Singapore	160	Samsu (hard liquor)	daily vs never < daily vs never	men 2.9 (na)* women 5.16 (na)*	Y	Y	N
Williams, 1977, USA	57	All types	50+ oz/yr vs none 50+ oz/yr vs none	men 1.4 (na) na[d] women 8.1 (na)*d	Y	Y	Y
Tuyns, 1977, France	200	All types	101+ g/day vs 0–20 g/day	18.3 (na) na	men, Y	Y	N
Tuyns, 1979, France	312	All types	81+ g/day vs none	11.6 (na) na	men, Y	Y	N
Pottern, 1981 Washington, DC, USA	90	All types	282+ g/day vs never drank > 5 glasses/week for > 1 month	7.5 (2.5–22.0)*	black men, Y	Y	N
Ziegler, 1981 Washington, DC, USA	120	All types as calories consumed	> 13,440 kcal/wk vs < 500	7.2 (2.5–20.8)*	men, Y	Y	N
Vasallo, 1985, Uruguay	185	All types	9+ g/day vs 0–39 g/day	7.6 (4.5–12.8)*	men, Y	Y	N
Victoria, 1987, Brazil	171	Cachaca	90+ g/day vs non-drinkers	8.2 (na)*d	men, Y	Y	Y
Decarli, 1987, Italy	105	All types	< 4 vs > 6 drinks/day	10.4 (4.4–24.9)*d	Y	Y	Y
Yu, 1988, Los Angeles USA	275	Beer Dinner wine Spirits All types	7+ cans/day vs none 4+ glasses/day vs none 4+ shots/day vs none 120+ g ethanol vs none	12.1 (4.1–35.4)*d 47.5 (5.1–440.8)*d 16.3 (6.3–42.1)*d 15.5 (5.9–41.1)*d	Y	Y	Y
Brown, 1988 South Carolina, USA	207	All types	> 9 oz ethanol/day vs none	incidence 3.6 (0.9–14.0)*d mortality 2.6 (1.2–5.6)*d	men, Y	Y	Y
La Vecchia, 1989, Italy	250	All types	> 8 vs 0 drinks/day	3.6 (0.9–13.0)	Y	N	N
De Stefani, 1990 Brazil	261	All types	250+ ml/day vs none	men 5.3 (2.7–10.2)*d	Y	Y	Y
Hanaoka, 1994, Japan	119	All types	150+ ml/day vs none	1.9 (0.7–4.9)*d	men, Y	Y	Y
Tavini, 1994, Italy	46	All types	414+ g/week vs < 53 g/week	5.9 (2.4–14.2)*d	Y	all non-smokers	Y
Hu, 1994, China	196	Hard liquor	8+ drinks/day vs < 4 drinks/day 114.5 litres/yr vs none	5.9 (1.4–21.0)*d 4.2 (2.1–8.6)*d	Y	Y	Y

* p < 0.05 for trend and/or for comparison of lowest vs highest consumption level
** p ≥ 0.05 for trend and for comparison of lowest vs highest consumption level
a h = highest, l = lowest
b 95% confidence interval; prot assoc, protective association; no assoc, no association; pos assoc, positive assocation
c na, information is unclear or not available from the article
d adjusted for one or more of the following: race, hospital, dietary factors, BMI, education, socio-economic status, residence
e confidence interval calculated by a 1991 IARC Working Group

consumption, found that beer, cider and wine had the strongest influence on risk – but it could not be ruled out that all types of beverages contributed to the risk in proportion to their alcohol content (Breslow and Day, 1980).

The joint actions of alcohol and tobacco in the aetiology of oesophageal cancer have been investigated in several studies (Tuyns et al, 1977b; 1979; 1987). They found a combined effect which fitted a multiplicative model.

Animal studies have been inconclusive because of the limitations of the experimental designs and methods used (IARC, 1988). Alcohol, as such, is not a direct-acting carcinogen or a promoter in animal models. Nevertheless, ethanol administered orally with carcinogens such as N-nitrosodiethylamine or N-nitrodi-n-propylamine resulted in enhanced incidence of oesophageal/forestomach tumours (Griciute et al, 1982; 1984).

The mechanism by which alcohol is causally related to cancer of the oesophagus is incompletely understood (IARC, 1988; Blot, 1992). Alcoholic beverages may contain carcinogens and other compounds; for example, compounds in alcoholic beverages can modulate DNA methylation, which would alter the susceptibility of DNA to mutational change (Yamada et al, 1992). Ethanol may facilitate the absorption of, or make mucosal cells more susceptible to, chemical carcinogens. Ethanol may affect the metabolism of carcinogens and thereby act as a carcinogen in tumours that are initiated by the action of carcinogens, particularly those in tobacco. Within the oesophageal mucosa, ethanol metabolism, itself, produces acetaldehyde. This is known to form adducts with macromolecules (for example DNA), is a carcinogen in experimental studies, and may act as a tumour promoter by increasing the proliferation of the epithelium (Mufti et al, 1989). There is evidence that acetaldehyde is genotoxic in humans (IARC, 1988). Studies in rats indicate that ethanol may act by promoting tumours initiated by N-nitroso compounds (Yang and Newmark, 1987).

The evidence that high alcohol consumption increases the risk of cancer of the oesophagus is convincing. This risk is markedly increased if drinkers of alcohol also smoke. While these data also suggest that Calvados, specifically, may increase risk of oesophageal cancer, the panel judges that any such effect is likely to be common to other abrasive liquors, and that the major effect is likely to be a function of total alcohol intake.

4.4.1.3 Vitamins
Carotenoids
Five case-control studies of oesophageal cancer have reported on carotenes, a carotene index, β-carotene, or a β-carotene index; each found a protective association, with odds ratios ranging from 0.2–0.8 (p < 0.05 in two studies) for higher intake (Ziegler et al, 1981; De Carli et al, 1987; Graham et al, 1990; Valsecchi, 1992; Hu et al, 1994). Valsecchi et al (1992) found that the combined effect of smoking and low β-carotene intake was nearly multiplicative.

High dietary carotenoid intake possibly decreases the risk of oesophageal cancer.

Vitamin C
Five studies, in the USA (Ziegler et al, 1981; Brown et al, 1988; Mettlin et al, 1981), France (Tuyns, 1983), and China (Hu et al, 1994), have examined vitamin C intake and the risk of oesophageal cancer and found statistically significant protective associations, with odds ratios for the highest levels of intake ranging from 0.4 to 0.6. The majority of these studies involved only men; one study that included both sexes reported odds ratios of 0.6 for each (Tuyns, 1983). All studies adjusted for alcohol consumption; three adjusted for smoking habits (Mettlin et al, 1981; Brown et al, 1988; Hu et al, 1994); another stated that such adjustment had no effect (Ziegler et al, 1981); and yet another was conducted in the west of France (Tuyns, 1983), where alcohol intake, rather than smoking was thought to be the primary risk factor.

Higher blood levels of ascorbic acid were correlated with a decreased risk of mortality from oesophageal cancer across counties in China (Chen et al, 1992).

High dietary vitamin C intake possibly decreases the risk of oesophageal cancer.

Folate and other lipotropes
There are some limited epidemiological data suggesting that folate deficiency, perhaps as part of a multiple micronutrient deficiency, may be a factor in the aetiology of cancer of the oesophagus. A case-control study involving 35 subjects found that early-diagnosed oesophageal cancer cases showed low mean blood levels of folic acid (p<0.01) and the relative risk between low folate intake and oesophageal cancer was 2.2 (p= 0.08) (Prasad et al, 1992). A cross-sectional study conducted in the Transkei (an area with a high incidence of oesophageal cancer) found a correlation between oesophageal cytological abnormalities and low plasma concentrations of folate, B_{12} and methionine (also of vitamins A and E) (Jaskiwickz et al, 1988).

The evidence relating to folate and other lipotropes and the risk of oesophageal cancers is limited; no judgement is possible.

Retinol
Three case-control studies have found increased risk (ORs > 2.0, with statistically significant trends) associated with higher retinol intakes (De Carli et al, 1987; Tuyns et al, 1987; Graham et al, 1990); however, two others found that higher retinol intakes were associated with a decreased risk of oesophageal cancer (ORs of 0.4 and 0.6) (Prasad et al, 1992; Middleton et al, 1986). Middleton's study in the USA (Middleton et al, 1986) found no association between retinol and oesophageal cancer in women.

An ecological study in China found no association between the retinol levels in pooled plasma samples and oesophageal cancer mortality rates (Guo et al, 1990).

It has been suggested that alcohol, a risk factor for upper

aerodigestive cancers, may have a synergistic effect with retinol on the risk of oesophageal cancer (Mayne et al, 1991).

The evidence relating to retinol and the risk of oesophageal cancer is inconsistent; no judgement is possible.

Vitamin E

There is only very limited evidence to suggest an association between vitamin E and oesophageal cancer. Only one case-control study has reported on dietary vitamin E and oesophageal cancer. Tuyns and colleagues (Tuyns et al, 1987) reported a significant protective association (OR = 0.3, 0.1–0.5) for dietary vitamin E (Tuyns et al, 1987). In areas with a high incidence of oesophageal cancer in China (Linxian) (Yang and Newmark, 1987) and South Africa (Ngobozana) (Van Helden et al, 1987), average serum levels of vitamin E have been observed to be lower than in areas of lower incidence.

The evidence relating to vitamin E and oesophageal cancer is limited; no judgement is possible.

Riboflavin

Riboflavin deficiency was identified as a strong risk factor (ORs in the range of 2.0) for oesophageal cancer in two case-control studies (Gao et al, 1994b; Thurnham et al, 1985), but not in another (Prasad et al, 1992). Prasad and colleagues (Prasad et al, 1992) found that riboflavin intake was greater in cases as compared to controls. Ziegler and associates (Ziegler et al, 1981) found that although higher riboflavin intake was associated with a decreased risk of oesophageal cancer (OR = 0.6), the foods that provided the bulk of the riboflavin intake were even more strongly associated with lower risk.

These data are limited and inconsistent; no judgement is possible.

4.4.1.4 Minerals

Selenium

One ecological study indicated that higher levels of dietary selenium may decrease the risk of oesophageal cancer (Krishnaswamy et al, 1993). In this Chinese study, mortality from oesophageal cancer and blood levels of selenium were correlated (R = –0.28, p < 0.05). In rats, when a diet deficient in many micronutrients was supplemented with selenium, tumour development was inhibited (Van Rensburg et al, 1985).

These data are very limited; no judgement is possible.

Iron

Iron deficiency has also been implicated as a possible risk factor for oesophageal cancer. The association between cancer of the oesophagus and Plummer-Vinson syndrome (difficulty in swallowing caused by the formation of webs of tissue across the upper oesophagus), for which iron deficiency is a risk factor, suggests that iron deficiency may be a risk factor for cancer of the oesophagus, possibly as part of a multiple deficiency state. There is some evidence of decreased risk of oesophageal cancer associated with meat consumption (see section 4.4.2.6).

These data suggesting that iron deficiency indirectly increases risk of oesophageal cancer are very limited; no judgement is possible.

Zinc

Some studies have indicated that higher levels of dietary zinc decrease the risk of oesophageal cancer. In a case-control study, Prasad and colleagues observed that patients with oesophageal cancer who were diagnosed early (studied because early in the course of the disease it is less likely that disease status will affect nutrient status) showed lower mean blood levels of zinc as compared with controls (Prasad et al, 1992). Zinc levels in the hair of Iranians at high risk of oesophageal cancer are very low (Ren and Han, 1991), and zinc deficiency, *per se*, is known to cause hyperplasia and parakeratosis in the oesophagus (Li, 1992).

Dong et al (1990) demonstrated that zinc deficiency increased the incidence of and shortened the lag time for chemically-induced oesophageal tumours in rats.

Evidence relating to dietary zinc intake and oesophageal cancer is limited; no judgement is possible.

4.4.2 FOOD AND DRINKS

4.4.2.1 Cereals (grains)

An association between the increased risk of cancer of the oesophagus and the consumption of cereal-based diets (maize, wheat, millet) has been observed in at least nine case-control studies in various parts of the world (including China, India, South Africa and Italy) (De Carli et al, 1987; Brown et al, 1988; Li et al, 1989; Yu et al, 1988; Wang, 1992; De Jong et al, 1974; Wahrendorf et al, 1989; Van Rensburg, 1981; Franceschi et al, 1990). These studies found increases in risk of the order of two- to sixfold with higher consumption.

In rats fed corn, wheat, sorghum, bananas or polished rice, oesophageal tumour yields were higher than in rats fed on millet, red sorghum, brown rice and potatoes (Van Rensburg et al, 1985). When the above diets were supplemented with B-complex vitamins and minerals such as zinc, selenium, magnesium and molybdenum, there was marked reduction in tumour incidence (Van Rensburg et al, 1986).

Maize (corn) is a poor source of B-complex vitamins, particularly riboflavin and niacin (Darby et al, 1977). Deficiency of such vitamins results in mucosal inflammation (Gopalan and Rao, 1975) which may predispose the epithelial tissue to malignancy. Another possible explanation is the presence of fungal contaminants, which may be present in grains stored in warm, moist conditions. A case-control study in China found consumption of mouldy grains to be associated with increased of oesophageal cancer (Thurnham et al, 1985).

There are some animal studies that found fungal contaminants to have a carcinogenic effect in laboratory mice.

Diets high in cereals possibly increase the risk of oesophageal cancer. However, any relationship between cereal consumption and oesophageal cancer is probably not with cereals as such, but with diets that are deficient in a number of protective microconstituents or contaminated with mycotoxins or both.

4.4.2.2 Roots, tubers and plantains

A case-control study among Singapore Chinese found a significant decrease in the risk of oesophageal cancer with higher consumption of both bananas and potatoes (De Jong et al, 1974), but it has been suggested that high consumption of these foods, not traditionally part of Chinese diets, could be a marker of a non-traditional lifestyle and thus of a lower exposure to suspected risk factors (Steinmetz and Potter, 1991). Brown et al (1988) also found potatoes to be associated with a decreased risk, but the association was not statistically significant (OR=0.7). Conversely, two case-control studies conducted in France (Tuyns et al, 1987) and the USA (Ziegler et al, 1981) have found the consumption of potatoes to be associated with increased risk (ORs ranging from 1.4 to 2.0), although it was non-significant in the former study. This study also found that higher consumption of bananas was associated with decreased risk, with a statistically significant OR of 0.6 (Ziegler et al, 1981).

The evidence relating to tubers, roots and plantains and the risk of oesophageal cancer is somewhat limited and inconsistent; no judgement is possible.

4.2.2.3 Vegetables and fruits

A cohort study of oesophageal cancer in Japan has shown a protective association between green and yellow vegetable consumption and the risk of oesophageal cancers; the association was apparent among smokers and drinkers, as well as among those who did not smoke and drink daily (Hirayama, 1985, 1986).

Twenty-two case-control studies have examined vegetable and fruit consumption in relation to cancer of the oesophagus; the methods and results of these studies are described in Table 4.4.3. Approximately half of the studies have been carried out in western countries and half in non-western countries, including China, Singapore, India, and Iran. Of these studies, 18 out of 22 have shown a statistically significant protective association for at least one vegetable and/or fruit category. In many of the studies, associations were adjusted for smoking (or other tobacco habits) and alcohol consumption, which are the major risk factors for oesophageal cancer in western societies; the protective associations for vegetables and fruit remained after controlling for these potentially confounding factors. One study calculated risk estimates for cancer at different anatomical locations within the oesophagus and found similarly protective associations for raw vegetables and fresh fruit throughout the oesophagus (Yu et al, 1988). The protective vegetables included green and yellow vegetables, tomatoes and leafy vegetables. Two of the studies showed a protective association with raw vegetables, with ORs of 0.6 and 0.4, (Cook-Mozaffari et al, 1979; Yu et al, 1988). In China, intakes of boiled vegetables (OR=1.3) and corn (OR=1.5), were associated with statistically significant increases in the risk of oesophageal cancer (Li et al, 1989; Wang, 1992).

The evidence for protective associations for vegetables (as a broad category), tomatoes, and citrus fruits has been very consistent, as each of five (De Carli et al, 1987; Notani and Jayant, 1987; Brown et al, 1988; De Stefani et al, 1990; Cook-Mozaffari et al, 1979), three (Brown et al, 1988; Cook-Mozaffari et al, 1979; Cheng et al, 1992), and four studies (Brown et al, 1988; Cook-Mozaffari et al, 1979; Cheng et al, 1992; Tuyns et al, 1987), respectively, that have examined these food categories have reported decreased risk for higher intakes. For allium vegetables, there is little evidence of a protective association, with each of four studies showing only null associations (Hu et al, 1994; Li et al, 1989; Cook-Mozaffari et al, 1979; Gao et al, 1994b). Increased risks associated with salt-pickled vegetables have been reported in two of three studies, with odds ratios of 13.1 and 3.6 for the highest versus the lowest intakes (Cheng et al, 1992; Wang, 1992).

Two studies of chronic oesophagitis (a probable cancer precursor) have shown protective associations for green vegetables and fresh fruit (Chang-Claude et al, 1990; Steinmetz and Potter, 1991); in contrast, a positive association for pickled vegetables has been observed (Wang, 1992).

The evidence that diets high in vegetables and fruits decrease the risk of oesophageal cancer is convincing.

4.4.2.4 Pulses (legumes)

Of six case-control studies that have examined pulses and the risk of oesophageal cancer, three reported decreased risk with increased consumption (ORs of 0.7) (Cook-Mozaffari et al, 1979; Prasad et al, 1992; Gao et al, 1994b), two reported increased risk (ORs of 1.1 and 1.3) (Notani and Jayant, 1987; Li et al, 1989), and one reported a slightly decreased risk for salted fermented soya paste, but slightly increased risk for soya products (ORs of 0.7 and 1.2, respectively) (Hu et al, 1994). One study in Shanxi, China, reported a statistically significant odds ratio of 0.3 for consumption of soya beans and soya bean products more than twice per week versus less than once per week (Wang, 1992); in the remaining studies, the associations were neither statistically significant nor particularly strong.

The evidence regarding pulses and risk for oesophageal cancer is limited; no judgement is possible.

TABLE 4.4.3 VEGETABLE AND FRUIT CONSUMPTION AND THE RISK OF OESOPHAGEAL CANCER: CASE-CONTROL STUDIES

Author, year, and place	No. of cases	Type of vegetable or fruit	Comparison[a]	Odds ratio (95% confidence interval)[b,c]	Sex/age	Adjustment Smoking history	Other variables
Wynder, 1961 New York, USA	150 men	green/yellow vegetables	na	prot assoc*	all males, age-matched	N	N
		fruit	na	prot assoc**			
DeJong, 1974 Singapore	160	bananas	weekly vs never	0.3 (na)*	Y	N	N
Cook-Mozaffari 1979, Iran	354 men	cooked green vegetables	>1/wk vs <1/wk	0.6 (0.4–0.9)*d	Y	N	Y
		raw green vegetables	>1/wk vs <1/wk	0.6 (0.4–0.9)*d			
		raw garlic	>1/wk vs <1/month	1.1 (0.8–1.6)**d			
		raw onions	>1/wk vs <1/month	0.7 (0.5–1.1)**d			
		raw tomatoes	>1/wk vs <1/wk	0.6 (0.4–0.9)*d			
		oranges	>1/wk vs <1/wk	0.6 (0.4–0.8)*d			
Zeigler, 1981 Washington, DC, USA	120	vegetables and fruit	h vs l tertile	0.6 (na)*d	Y	N	Y
		green vegetables	h vs l tertile	0.6 (na)*d			
		yellow vegetables	h vs l tertile	1.0 (na)**d			
		green leafy vegetables	h vs l tertile	0.5 (na)*d			
		fruit	h vs l tertile	0.5 (na)*d			
		citrus fruit	h vs l tertile	0.8 (na)**d			
Mettlin, 1981 New York, USA	147 men	vegetables and fruit	>80 vs 0–40/month	0.2 (na)*	Y	Y	N
DeCarli, 1987 Italy	105	green vegetables	>8 vs <6/wk	0.6 (0.3–1.5)**d	Y	Y	Y
		carrots	>8 vs <6/wk	0.6 (0.3–1.2)**d			
		fresh fruits	>1 vs <1/wk	0.3 (0.1–0.6)*d			
Notani, 1987 India	236	vegetables	daily vs not daily	0.4 (0.2–0.7)*d	Y	smoking not alcohol	Y
		fruits	>1/wk vs <1/wk	0.8 (0.5–1.3)**d			
Tuyns, 1987 France	743	fresh vegetables	h vs l quartile	0.6 (na)*d	Y	Y	Y
		citrus fruit	h vs l quartile	0.3 (na)*d			
		other fruit	h vs l quartile	0.7 (na)**d			
Victora, 1987 Brazil	171	fruit	frequency log days/month +1	0.7 (na)*d	Y	Y	Y
Wahrendorf, 1988 China	166	fresh fruits	>1/wk vs <1/wk	0.3 (0.2–0.6)*d	Y	smoking, not alcohol	Y
Yu, 1988 California, USA	275	raw vegetables/ fresh fruits	>4/wk vs <1/wk	0.4 (0.2–0.8)*d	Y	Y	Y
Brown, 1988 South Carolina, USA	207 men	vegetables	h vs l tertile	0.7 (0.4–1.3)**d	Y	Y	Y
		tomatoes	h vs l tertile	0.7 (0.4–1.4)**d			
		fruit	h vs l tertile	0.5 (0.3–0.9)*d			
		citrus fruit	h vs l tertile	0.5 (0.3–0.9)*d			
Li, 1989 China	1,244	fresh vegetables	>973 vs <483/yr	1.5 (1.2–1.0)**d	Y	smoking, not alcohol	Y
		dried vegetables	>111 vs <30/yr	0.8 (0.6–1.0)**d			
		pickled vegetables	>1/day vs never	no assoc**d			
		fresh fruit	>35 vs <0/yr	1.0 (0.8–1.2)**d			
DeStefani, 1990 Uruguay	261	vegetables	daily vs <1/wk	0.6 (0.3–1.0)**d	Y	Y	Y
		other fruit	daily vs <1/wk	0.3 (0.2–0.5)*d			

4.4.2.5 Nuts and seeds

A large case-control study of cancers of the oesophagus and gastric cardia in Linxian, in North Central China, reported a slightly increased risk with higher intake of legumes, nuts, and seeds; OR = 1.3, 1.0–1.6) for consumption greater than 122, versus less than 14 times per year (Li et al, 1989).

Based on one study, no judgement is possible.

4.4.2.6 Meat, poultry, fish, and eggs

Meat

Five case-control studies have examined the relationship between fresh meat consumption and oesophageal cancer;

the results are mixed (Ziegler et al, 1981; De Stefani et al, 1990; Yu et al, 1988; Tuyns et al, 1987; Tavini et al, 1994). A study in Milan, Italy, found non-significant increases in the relative risk in the upper tertiles of fresh meat consumption. Ziegler and colleagues (1981) reported on meat, fish, eggs and cheese as a group, and found no significant difference in odds ratios between high and low intakes. In a case-control study in Nebraska (Ward et al, 1997), high red meat consumption was associated with an increased risk of oesophageal cancer (OR = 2.0), and a significant dose–response was seen (p = 0.02). Among Los Angeles county residents (Yu et al, 1988), increased fresh meat consumption was associated with a statistically non-significant

Author, year, and place	No. of cases	Type of vegetable or fruit	Comparison[a]	Odds ratio (95% confidence interval)[b,c]	Sex/Age	Adjustment Smoking History	Other Variables
Wang, 1992 China	200	boiled vegetables	>7/wk vs <7/wk	1.3 (na)[**d]	Y	Y	Y
		pickled vegetables	some vs rarely	3.6 (1.1–18.4)[*d]			
		cabbage	>3/wk vs <2/wk	0.4 (0.2–0.9)[*d]			
Cheng, 1992 China	400	leafy vegetables	>daily vs <3/wk	0.4 (0.3–0.7)[*d]	Y	Y	Y
		pickled vegetables	>daily vs <1/yr	13.1 (2.6–67.0)[*d]			
		citrus fruits	>daily vs <1/yr	0.1 (0.02–0.4)[*d]			
Prasad, 1992 India	35	vegetables and fruits	several times/wk vs <1/wk	no assoc[**]	Y	N	N
Guo, 1992 China	640	fresh vegetables	h vs l tertile	0.8 (0.6–1.0)[**]	Y	smoking, not alcohol	N
		fresh fruits	h vs l tertile	0.9 (0.8–1.1)[**]			
Hu, 1994 China	196	fresh vegetables	h vs l quartile	0.6 (na)[*d]	Y	Y	N
		salted vegetables	h vs l quartile	0.7 (na)[**d]			
		pickled Chinese cabbage	h vs l quartile	0.7 (na)[**d]			
		fruits	h vs l quartile	1.5 (na)[**]			
Gao, 1994 China	902			men	Y	Y	Y
		vegetables	h vs l quartile	0.8 (na)[**]			
		dark green leafy vegetables	h vs l quartile	0.8 (na)[**]			
		dark orange vegetables	h vs l quartile	0.7 (na)[*]			
		cruciferous vegetables	h vs l quartile	0.8 (na)[**]			
		allium vegetables	h vs l quartile	1.1 (na)[**]			
		fruits	h vs l quartile	0.5 (na)[*]			
				females			
				0.9 (na)[**]			
				1.1 (na)[**]			
				0.6 (na)[*]			
				1.1 (na)[**]			
				1.1 (na)[**]			
				0.6 (na)[*]			
				0.6 (na)[*]			
Tavini, 1994 Italy	46	green vegetables	h vs l tertile	0.6 (0.1–0.8)[*d]	Y*all non-smokers	Y	Y
		fresh fruits	h vs l tertile	0.7 (0.3–1.7)[**d]			
Tomoyuki, 1994 Japan	141	green vegetables	h vs l quartile	0.8 (0.2–3.1)[**d]	Y	smoking,	Y
		yellow vegetables	h vs l quartile	2.3 (0.7–7.6)[**d]			
		fruit	h vs l quartile	0.5 (0.2–1.4)[**d]			

[*] p < 0.05 for trend and/or for comparison of lowest vs highest consumption level
[**] p ≥ 0.05 for trend and for comparison of lowest vs highest consumption level
[a] h = highest, l = lowest
[b] prot assoc – protective association; no assoc – no association; pos association
[c] na – information is unclear or not available from the article
[d] Matched or adjusted for one or more of the following: residence, BMI, socio-economic status, education, race, metal dust exposure, calories, tea consumption, family history, cachaca drinking, meat intake

increase in oesophageal cancer risk in the middle but not the upper tertile of consumption (OR = 1.5 and 1.0, respectively). In Uruguay (De Stefani et al, 1990), increased fresh meat intake was associated with a statistically non-significant decrease (OR = 0.6) in the risk of oesophageal cancer. In Calvados, France (Tuyns et al, 1987), meat was also protective; with risk decreasing across quartiles and OR of 0.2 in the highest quartile of intake. Further, there was a significant dose-response effect (p < 0.001).

It seems possible that, under some circumstances, meat provides specific micronutrients in otherwise somewhat deficient diets. Where diets are more varied, meat intake is neutral or even associated with increased risk. Nonetheless, the evidence relating to meat and the risk of oesophageal cancers is inconsistent; no judgement is possible.

4.4.2.7 Milk and dairy products

Five epidemiological studies have examined the association between the risk of oesophageal cancer and the consumption of milk or dairy products (Wynder et al, 1957; Ziegler et al, 1981; Notani and Jayant, 1987; Yu et al, 1988; Tuyns et al, 1987). Of these, one found a statistically significant protective effect for consumption of dairy products and eggs, combined (OR=0.5) (Ziegler et al, 1981), one recorded a statistically significant protective association with skimmed milk, but a statistically significant increase in risk with whole milk (ORs = 0.1 and 1.5, respectively) (Tuyns et al, 1987), and one noted a statistically significant protective association with buttermilk (OR=0.4) (Notani and Jayant, 1987). The other two did not report statistically significant findings. Dairy products may have a possible protective effect because these foods are good sources of a number of microconstituents, including riboflavin, zinc and perhaps calcium. Deficiencies of the first two of these have been noted in association with oesophageal cancer, although supplementation trials have, to date, been inconclusive about their benefit.

Evidence relating to milk and dairy products and the risk of oesophageal cancer is inconsistent; no judgement is possible.

4.4.2.8 Herbs, spices, condiments

Chillies

A high incidence of oesophageal cancer has been reported in Kashmir, India (Maqbool and Ahad, 1976). Investigation of the dietary habits of this population showed that the consumption of red chillies is two- to threefold higher in this population than in areas with low rates of oesophageal cancer in other parts of the country (Siddiqui et al, 1992).

When sundried (a process of preservation), red chillies acquire secondary amines such as pyrollidine; these are easily nitrosated in vivo in the presence of nitrites.

On the basis of this isolated ecological study, no judgement is possible.

Coffee

Coffee intake and the risk of oesophageal cancer was reviewed by an IARC Working Group (IARC, 1991). One case-control study in Italy reported no significant association with coffee intake (La Vecchia and Negri, 1989). A case-control study in Puerto Rico (Martinez, 1969) reported results for cancers of the mouth, pharynx, and oesophagus as a group. For men, a statistically significant increase in risk of oesophageal cancer (OR=2.7) was found for drinking hot coffee; the results were similar, but not statistically significant for women (Martinez, 1969). De Jong (1974), found no relationship for daily intake of coffee, however a statistically significant increase in risk was found for drinking burning hot coffee (OR=4.2).

The evidence on coffee drinking and the risk of oesophageal cancer is limited; no judgement is possible.

Tea

The relationship between tea intake and the risk of oesophageal cancer was reviewed by the IARC Working Group (IARC, 1991). The working group noted that studies have generally not distinguished between different types of tea, and that intake of other hot beverages was not considered in most studies. Five case-control studies have been conducted in Iran (Cook-Mozaffari et al, 1979), the USSR (Bashiron et al, 1968; Kaufman et al, 1965), Brazil (Victora et al, 1987), and Singapore (De Jong et al, 1974). Of these, only the Brazilian (Victoria et al, 1987) study showed no association. The others showed that drinking very hot tea was associated with a two- to threefold increase in risk; no effect of frequency of ingestion was seen. It is unclear, as in the case with the coffee anomaly noted above, whether it is the temperature of the beverage, rather than the beverage itself, that is associated with increased risk.

The evidence suggests that tea consumption may increase the risk of oesophageal cancer, but these data appear to describe an association with temperature not tea drinking per se; the evidence is, as yet, insufficient.

Maté

A clear statistically significant dose–response relationship has been reported between the amount of maté drunk each day and the risk of oesophageal cancer, with ORs ranging between 1.5 and 12.2 in South America (De Stefani et al, 1990; Victora et al, 1987; Vasallo et al, 1985). The risk increases significantly with duration of use. Further, the usually very high temperature at which this beverage is customarily consumed appears to be important. The mechanism may thus be mediated through thermal damage to epithelial tissue, probably as a predisposing and promoting factor.

When drunk regularly, maté possibly increases risk of oesophageal cancer, because of the temperature at which it is consumed.

Hot drinks

Nine case-control studies have suggested that beverages such as coffee, tea, and maté, when consumed at a very high temperature, increase the risk for oesophageal cancer (De Stefani et al, 1990; Victora et al, 1987; Vasallo et al, 1985; Martinez, 1969; De Jong et al, 1974; IARC, 1991; Bashiron et al, 1968; Kaufman et al, 1965). In particular, studies have shown that while frequency of ingestion was unimportant for some beverages, consuming very hot drinks increased the risk by as much as two- to fourfold for coffee and tea and twelvefold for maté.

Hot beverages may damage epithelial tissue. In laboratory animals, high temperatures are associated with development of precancerous lesions (Yioris et al, 1984).

Drinking very hot beverages possibly increases the risk of oesophageal cancer.

4.4.3 FOOD PROCESSING

4.4.3.1 Cured and smoked foods

N-nitrososamines

There has been much discussion, in the literature on oesophageal cancer, of the possible role of *N*-nitrosamines, especially in relation to oesophageal cancer in China (Lu et al, 1984; 1991). Relatively high levels (µg/kg) of nitrosamines and their precursors (nitrite, nitrate, and secondary amines) have been found in foods consumed in Linxian, China, an area well-known for its high risk of oesophageal cancer (age-adjusted male mortality around 160 per 100,000 population) (Singer et al, 1986). The addition of sodium nitrite to the local mouldy cornbread yielded *N*-nitrosodimethylamine, *N*-nitrosodiethylamine and *N*-nitrosomethylbenzylamine (*N*MBzA). A previously unknown carcinogenic nitrosamine, *N*-1-methylacetonyl-*N*-3-methylbutyl-nitrosamine was also found at levels of 0.2–0.3 mg/kg in local mouldy cornbread samples. The dietary intakes of total volatile nitrosamines and *N*MBzA respectively were higher in Linxian (634 and 107 µg/person/day) than in Yuxian (male age-adjusted mortality 27 per 100,000), a low risk county (285 and 0.2 µg/person/day); and *N*MBzA was found in 78% of the food samples collected from Linxian (Lu et al, 1991). *N*MBzA and *N*-nitrosarcosine (*N*SAR) were also found in gastric juice of local residents in Linxian (Lu et al, 1987).

The *N*-nitrosoproline (*N*PRO) test (Ohshima and Bartsch, 1981) was used to compare the endogenous formation of *N*-nitrosoamines in general populations of areas with different risks for oesophageal cancer. It was reported that the urinary excretion of *N*PRO in Linxian residents was significantly higher than that in Linxian (male age-adjusted mortality 35 per 100,000) residents (Lu et al, 1984). Wu et al (1993) found that the average amount of urinary excretion of *N*PRO and *N*SAR in the adult population was positively correlated with county mortality from oesophageal cancer in 69 rural Chinese counties with a wide range of mortality rates. These epidemiological data are supported by the finding of elevated levels of O^6- methylguanine adducts in oesophageal biopsy samples collected from residents in high risk areas of northern China (Umbenhauer et al, 1985).

There is evidence from animal experiments to support a role for *N*-nitrosamines in oesophageal cancer. In Linxian, China, feeding local mouldy foods and pickles to rodents induced epithelial hyperplasia and dysplasia of the esophagus (Yang, 1980). DNA adducts were formed when fetal oesophageal epithelia was cultured with *N*MBzA, and the transplantation of this treated fetal oesophageal epithelia caused tumour formation in BALB/C nude mice (Lu et al, 1991). Among the volatile *N*-nitrosoamines studied, *N*MBzA and *N*SAR have induced oesophageal tumour in mice and rats (Lu et al, 1991).

Although no causal association has been demonstrated, in vivo exposure to nitrosamines in high risk areas has been indirectly inferred from the presence of *N*-nitrosamines in gastric juice, from the urinary excretion of *N*-nitrosamino acids, from positive results to the in vivo proline test for endogenous nitrosation, and from the quantification of O^6 methylguanine adducts in oesophageal biopsy samples.

> Ecological evidence supported by experimental data suggests that exogenous dietary *N*-nitrosamine exposure and endogenous *N*-nitrosamine formation possibly increases the risk of oesophageal cancer.

4.4.3.3 Cooking

Animal foods grilled over an open fire (barbecuing) were associated with an increased risk of oesophageal cancer in two case-control studies, (Victora et al, 1987; De Stefani et al, 1990) but not in another (Brown et al, 1988). In one of the studies showing a positive association, although the estimate of risk associated with daily consumption was fairly high (OR=2.6), the confidence interval included 1.0 (25). Barbecued meats are known to contain carcinogens and mutagens formed by the pyrolysis of proteins; more studies are needed to evaluate this association. A case-control study in Nebraska (Ward et al, 1997) found that well-done meats were associated with a statistically non-significant increased risk for oesophageal cancer (OR=1.5).

> The evidence on cooking methods and the risk of oesophageal cancer is very limited; no judgment is possible.

4.5 Lung

Cancer of the lung is now the most common incident cancer and cause of cancer mortality, throughout the world. An estimated 1.3 million cases occurred in 1996, accounting for 12.8 per cent of all new cases of cancer.

Incidence of, and deaths from, this cancer are generally increasing throughout the world, mainly as a result of the increased global manufacture, marketing and advertising of cigarettes.

The panel has reached the following conclusions. The chief and overwhelming cause of lung cancer is use of tobacco, and smokers whose diet is protective nevertheless remain at high risk.

The evidence that diets high in vegetables and fruits protect against lung cancer is convincing. Carotenoids contained in foods of plant origin are probably also protective.

The panel notes that regular physical activity, and diets high in vitamin C, vitamin E and selenium, possibly reduce the risk of lung cancer, and that diets high in total fat, saturated fat and cholesterol, and also in alcohol, possibly increase risk.

The most effective means of preventing lung cancer is not to use tobacco. The most effective dietary means of preventing lung cancer is consumption of diets high in vegetables and fruits.

FOOD, NUTRITION AND LUNG CANCER

In the judgement of the panel, the dietary constituents and related factors, and the foods and drinks listed below, modify the risk of lung cancer, or else have no relationship with it. Judgements are graded according to the strength of the evidence.

EVIDENCE	DECREASES RISK	NO RELATIONSHIP	INCREASES RISK
Convincing	Vegetables and fruits[a]		
Probable	Carotenoids		
Possible	Physical activity Vitamin C Vitamin E Selenium	Retinol	Total fat Saturated/animal fat Cholesterol Alcohol
Insufficient			

For an explanation of the terms used in the matrix, see chapter 3.
[a] In particular, the evidence is most abundant and consistent for green vegetables and carrots, as well as for both vegetables and fruits generally.

INTRODUCTION

Lung cancer is the most common cause of death from cancer in North America and many northern European countries, and rates are increasing rapidly throughout the world, including Asia, Latin America and Africa. Cigarette smoking is universally recognised as the most important cause of lung cancer and is primarily responsible for these large increases. Even in countries where smoking rates have started to fall, lung cancer will remain a major form of cancer well into the next century because of the large number of former smokers. A number of occupational exposures, including asbestos, radon (particularly among miners), chromium, nickel and diesel exhaust, are also documented causes of lung cancer. However, the contribution of these factors to overall population rates is small compared with that of smoking, and the effects of at least some of these exposures appear to be

> **BOX 4.5.1 ESTABLISHED NON-DIETARY FACTORS AND LUNG CANCER**
>
> The following non-dietary factors increase the risk of lung cancer:
> - Smoking tobacco[a]
> - Asbestos exposure
> - Certain occupational exposures, e.g., nickel, radon, chromium
>
> [a]The panel emphasises that the main cause of lung cancer is smoking.

manifested primarily when combined with smoking.

The most common forms of lung cancer are squamous cell cancer or small-cell carcinoma and adenocarcinoma. As differences in aetiology have been hypothesised, these may merit separate examination in relation to dietary factors (Wynder and Hofman, 1994).

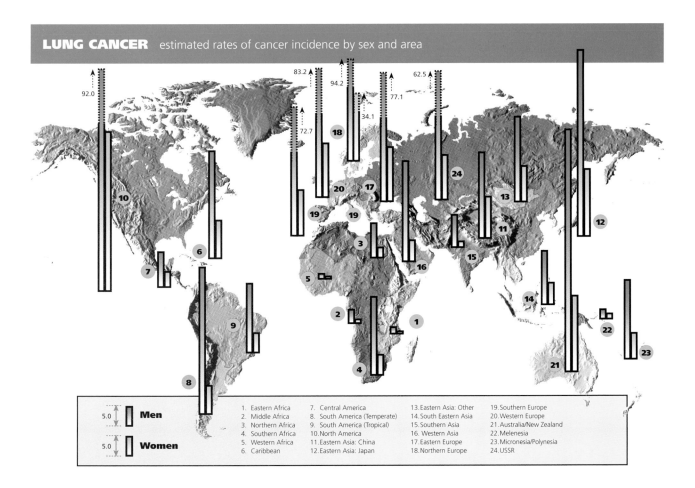

LUNG CANCER estimated rates of cancer incidence by sex and area

5.0 ▮ Men		5.0 ▯ Women

1. Eastern Africa
2. Middle Africa
3. Northern Africa
4. Southern Africa
5. Western Africa
6. Caribbean
7. Central America
8. South America (Temperate)
9. South America (Tropical)
10. North America
11. Eastern Asia: China
12. Eastern Asia: Japan
13. Eastern Asia: Other
14. South Eastern Asia
15. Southern Asia
16. Western Asia
17. Eastern Europe
18. Northern Europe
19. Southern Europe
20. Western Europe
21. Australia/New Zealand
22. Melenesia
23. Micronesia/Polynesia
24. USSR

INCIDENCE PATTERNS

Cancer of the lung is the most common cancer in the world. In 1996, an estimated 1,320,000 new cases were diagnosed worldwide (WHO, 1997), accounting for 12.8% of all new cancers.

Rates of lung cancer are highest in North America and Europe, and lowest in Africa, Asia and South America (Parkin et al, 1992). Eastern Europe has, at present, the highest national rates of lung cancer. Over 50% of lung cancer incidence (678,000 cases) occurred in the developed world in 1996. In some developed countries (such as Finland, the UK and the USA) the rates are now beginning to decline, as rates of smoking decline in these countries.

Incidence rates of lung cancer are far higher in men than in women, 75% of all new cases occur in men. This difference correlates with the difference in overall patterns of smoking between men and women. However, for the same lifetime exposure to tobacco, risks are similar in men and women.

The predominant risk factor for lung cancer is tobacco use. A lifetime smoker has a risk some 20–30 times that of a non-smoker. It is now generally accepted that passive exposure to tobacco smoke may increase risk by 30–50%.

Survival rates are low, with between 7 and 12% of cases surviving five years after initial diagnosis. In 1996, mortality attributable to lung cancer was estimated at 1,160,000 people, 16.3% of all cancer deaths (WHO, 1997).

PATHOGENESIS

In common with some other epithelial tissues, including the mouth, the upper aerodigestive tract, and the skin, the tissues of the lung and bronchi are exposed directly to a wide variety of environmental influences. The process of carcinogenesis in the lung almost certainly begins with one or more of the many compounds present in tobacco smoke (active or passive smoking) or in the air in the workplace causing DNA damage across the genome. Failure to repair this damage in a crucial tumour suppressor gene or oncogene begins the process that results in an expanding clone or abnormal cells. As only about 15% of smokers actually get lung cancer, the capacity of the lungs to protect themselves against these environmental insults is very high. This protective capacity, nonetheless, may vary as a result of inherited differences perhaps in the ability to metabolise carcinogens (Sellers et al, 1992); it certainly varies as a result of differences in dietary behaviours.

JUDGEMENTS OF OTHER REPORTS

Previous expert reports have concluded that low dietary levels of foods high in vitamin A and/or β-carotene (there has not always been a clear distinction) are associated with increased risk of lung cancer, particularly among heavy smokers (NAS, 1982). Frequent consumption of green and yellow vegetables, it has also been concluded, are protective against lung cancer (NAS, 1989).

REVIEW

Historically, the initial interest in diet and lung cancer in humans was motivated by experimental studies suggesting a protective effect of vitamin A. The focus then shifted to carotenoids and other antioxidants. Other factors, including dietary fats, cholesterol, and alcohol, have also been examined.

4.5.1 DIETARY CONSTITUENTS

4.5.1.1 Energy and related factors
Physical activity

A cohort study of longshoremen in San Francisco found decreased lung cancer mortality associated with high levels of work activity (relative risk (RR) = 0.6, adjusted for age, cigarette smoking and body mass index; p = 0.07 for trend) (Paffenbarger et al, 1987). The first United States National Health and Nutrition Examination Survey (NHANES I) study also suggested that higher non-recreational (i.e., occupational) physical activity, compared with inactivity, was related to lung cancer in men (RR = 0.5, 0.3–0.8; p = 0.02 for trend), whereas recreational activity was not associated with risk (RR = 1.1, 0.7–1.7); adjustment for smoking did not alter these findings (Albanes et al, 1989). In a cohort study of Japanese men in Hawaii, which used an index of physical activity based on the method used in the Framingham study, higher levels of physical activity were associated with moderately reduced risk of lung cancer (RR = 0.7, 0.5–1.0; adjusted for age, cigarette smoking and body mass index; p = 0.04 for trend) (Severson et al, 1989). Each of these cohort studies adjusted the physical-activity estimate for smoking; this is important because smokers are often less physically active than non-smokers.

One large case-control study in the USA found a weak association in the opposite direction (with a smoking-adjusted odds ratio (OR) = 1.3, 1.1–1.7; p < 0.01 for trend) for high, as compared with low, physical activity level (Brownson et al, 1991).

Three cohort studies of lung cancer have shown moderately decreased risk with higher levels of physical activity, after taking into account potential confounding by smoking habits, whereas one case-control study reported a weakly increased risk.

Higher levels of physical activity possibly decrease the risk of lung cancer.

4.5.1.2 Fat and cholesterol
Six cohort and six case-control studies have examined some aspects of dietary fat or cholesterol in relation to lung cancer.

Total fat

Of three cohort studies that examined total fat, one in Finnish men found a suggestion of increased risk (RR = 1.6, 0.8–3.1) for higher intake (Knekt et al, 1991b). The other two studies, in postmenopausal women in the USA and Japanese men in Hawaii, reported no associations (Chyou et al, 1993; Wu et al, 1994), although in the latter study diet was assessed by a single 24-hour recall, which may not be an accurate measure of long-term diet. In the studies in Finland and the USA, the risk estimates were adjusted for total energy intake.

Of four case-control studies that examined total fat, two studies in the USA and Hawaii reported an approximately twofold increase in risk that was statistically significant, with higher intake for men, but not for women (Byers et al, 1987; Goodman et al, 1988). On the other hand, a study of non-smoking women in the USA reported a strong increase in risk (energy-adjusted OR = 2.8; p = 0.02) (Alavanja et al, 1993). The remaining study in Canada reported a weak association (OR = 1.3, 1.0–1.6) for higher intake (Jain et al, 1990).

Thus, the cohort and case-control evidence regarding the relationship between total fat and lung cancer has produced mixed results. Two of three studies that adjusted for total energy intake have suggested increased risk with higher fat intake (Knekt et al, 1991b; Alavanja et al, 1993; Wu et al, 1994). All studies were restricted to non-smokers or adjusted for cigarette smoking, which may correlate positively with fat intake in some populations. Increased risk has been reported for both sexes, although two studies that included both men and women found stronger increases in risk for men (Byers et al, 1987; Goodman et al, 1988; Knekt et al, 1991b; Alavanja et al, 1993).

Five studies have examined risk associated with different types of dietary fat. Two found increases in risk for total fat to be largely attributable to saturated fat (Knekt et al, 1991b; Alavanja et al, 1993), another found increased risk with both saturated and unsaturated fats (Goodman et al, 1988), and the remaining studies reported no substantial increases in risk for either total or specific types of fat (Jain et al, 1990; Wu et al, 1994).

International ecological studies have shown positive correlations between total fat consumption and lung cancer rates in men (r = 0.7–0.8); correlations for women have generally been weaker (r = 0.3–0.4 (Carroll and Khor, 1975; Wynder et al, 1987; Hursting et al, 1990). In one of these studies, the correlation of lung cancer mortality with fat consumption (r = 0.8) was much stronger than that with tobacco use (r = 0.4); the correlation with fat remained after accounting for tobacco use, gross national product (GNP) and population size (p < 0.0001) (Wynder et al, 1987). Further ecological observations include that cigarette smoking in men is more prevalent, yet lung cancer mortality in men is lower, in Korea, China and Japan than in Belgium. Further, the degree to which the risk of lung cancer is affected by smoking appears to be lower in southern than in northern Europe; thus, it has been argued that smoking may interact with high consumption of animal fat, resulting in higher rates of lung cancer in northern Europe (Xie et al, 1991).

Experimental studies have shown that diets high in either saturated (beef tallow) or unsaturated (corn or sunflower oil) fat (20–25% of diet by weight), when fed *ad libitum*, increase the number of chemically induced or spontaneously metastasising lung tumours, compared with diets low in these fats (5%); the animals on the high-fat diets consumed more energy than those on the low-fat diets (Beems and van Been, 1984; Scholar et al, 1989). The tumour-enhancing effects were more pronounced with diets high in unsaturated fat than those high in saturated fat. Another study, using isocaloric diets, showed that diets high in polyunsaturated fat (corn oil) (23%) increased the number of metastases to a greater extent than a diet low in polyunsaturated fat (5%), and than diets high or low in monounsaturated (olive oil) or saturated (beef tallow) fat (Katz and Boylan, 1989).

Most of the xenobiotics found in tobacco smoke require metabolic activation before they exert genotoxic or carcinogenic activity. One of the different routes of transformation to their ultimate carcinogenic forms may involve peroxidase-dependent co-oxidation in the presence of various polyunsaturated fatty acids. The activity of these enzymes is high in lung tissue, so it is conceivable that specific compounds in tobacco smoke are more readily oxidised to their carcinogenic forms as a consequence of a high-fat diet (Wynder et al, 1987). The biological mechanism by which a high-fat diet might play a role in the aetiology of lung cancer could also involve effects on the cell membranes, the immune system or circulating hormone levels (Scholar et al, 1989).

Overall, the evidence regarding total fat and lung cancer is more abundant than for some other sites, but it is somewhat inconsistent. Ecological studies show a clear pattern of higher lung cancer rates with greater fat consumption; this appears to be largely independent of tobacco consumption. Cohort and case-control studies show either increased risk or no relationship; no studies have shown a statistically significant decrease in risk with higher total fat intake. Experimental studies show a tumour-enhancing effect of high-fat diets, regardless of type of fat, and this may be due to increased energy intake.

Diets high in total fat possibly increase the risk of lung cancer, but any effect of fat is minor compared to that of cigarette smoking.

Saturated/animal fat

Two cohort and four case-control studies of lung cancer have examined saturated or animal fat. One cohort study of Finnish men suggested increased risk (energy-adjusted RR = 1.6, 0.8–3.2); this association appeared to be largely attributable to butter consumption (Knekt et al, 1991b). This study further suggested that a high ratio of polyunsaturated to saturated fat (P:S ratio) in the diet was associated with decreased risk (energy-adjusted RR = 0.7, 0.4–1.1). On the other hand, no association was apparent for animal fat in a cohort of women in the USA (energy-adjusted RR = 0.8,

0.5–1.2) (Wu et al, 1994).

Results from the four case-control studies have consistently been in the direction of increased risk, with odds ratios ranging from 1.3 to 6.6 for higher intakes of saturated/animal fat (Goodman et al, 1988; Mettlin, 1989; Jain et al, 1990; Alavanja et al, 1993). A striking sixfold increase in risk (p = 0.005; adjusted for total energy intake) was reported for high saturated fat intake in non-smoking women in the USA (Alavanja et al, 1993).

One international ecological study found a weak positive correlation between saturated fat consumption and lung cancer incidence (r = 0.2; ns) (Hursting et al, 1990). Another study showed animal- , but not vegetable-fat consumption to be a predictor of lung cancer mortality (Xie et al, 1991); the effect of animal fat was independent of that of cigarette consumption.

Varying degrees of increased risk have been observed in almost all cohort and case-control studies.

Diets high in saturated/animal fat possibly increase the risk of lung cancer.

Monounsaturated fat

One cohort study of Finnish men reported no association between monounsaturated fat intake and the risk of lung cancer (energy-adjusted RR = 1.1, 0.6–2.1) (Knekt et al, 1991b).

Two case-control studies of lung cancer have examined intake of oleic acid. One study in Canada found no substantial association (OR = 1.2, 1.0–1.5) (Jain et al, 1990). Another study in non-smoking women in the USA found a strong increase in risk (energy-adjusted OR = 2.5; p = 0.07), although, as noted above, an even stronger increase in risk was observed for saturated fat in this study (Alavanja et al, 1993).

One international ecological study found no correlation between monounsaturated fat consumption and lung cancer incidence (r = 0.0) (Hursting et al, 1990).

The evidence relating to diets high in monounsaturated fat to the risk of lung cancer is too limited to support any conclusion; no judgement is possible.

Polyunsaturated/plant (vegetable) fat

One cohort study of Finnish men found no association between polyunsaturated fat intake and risk of lung cancer (energy-adjusted RR = 0.9, 0.5–1.5); however, a higher ratio of polyunsaturated to saturated fat (P:S ratio) in the diet was associated with a somewhat decreased risk (energy-adjusted RR = 0.7, 0.4–1.1) (Knekt et al, 1991b). Another cohort study in older women in the USA found a moderate decrease in risk with higher intake of vegetable fat (energy-adjusted RR = 0.7, 0.5–0.9); this association was stronger in smokers (Wu et al, 1994).

Three case-control studies of lung cancer that have examined unsaturated or polyunsaturated fat, or linoleic acid, have reported no substantial associations (ORs in the range 0.9–1.3; ns) for higher intakes (Goodman et al, 1988; Jain et al, 1990; Alavanja et al, 1993); one exception was an increase in risk with higher intake of polyunsaturated fat, observed for men only in a study in Hawaii (OR = 2.5, 1.4–4.4) (Goodman et al, 1988).

One international ecological study found no correlation between consumption of polyunsaturated fat and lung cancer incidence (r = 0.0) (Hursting et al, 1990).

The evidence relating to diets high in polyunsaturated/plant (vegetable) fat and the risk of lung cancer is inconsistent; no judgement is possible.

Cholesterol

At least four cohort studies of lung cancer have examined dietary cholesterol (Heilbrun et al, 1984; Knekt et al, 1991b; Shekelle et al, 1991; Wu et al, 1994); three of these have reported no association. The remaining study, which involved male Western Electric employees in Chicago, observed an increased risk with higher cholesterol intake (fat-adjusted RR = 1.9, 1.1–3.4) (Shekelle et al, 1991).

Of five case-control studies, three reported statistically significant increases in risk with higher cholesterol intakes, with ORs ranging from 1.6 to 2.2 (Hinds et al, 1983; Goodman et al, 1988; Jain et al, 1990). In two of these, an increased risk was observed for men, but not for women (Hinds et al, 1983; Goodman et al, 1988). In one study, the increase in risk was restricted to current heavy smokers but, because intakes of fat and cholesterol were highly correlated, it was not possible to show that the association for cholesterol was independent of that for fat (Goodman et al, 1988). In two studies, a plateau effect was apparent, such that, above certain levels of cholesterol intake, the risk of lung cancer did not increase further (Goodman et al, 1988; Jain et al, 1990). The two other case-control studies reported no statistically significant associations (ORs ranging from 0.9 to 2.0) (Byers et al, 1987; Alavanja et al, 1993).

Eggs, which are relatively unique in being a commonly consumed food that is a concentrated source of cholesterol, have been examined in several studies. One cohort study in Norwegian men found no statistically significant association (Kvåle et al, 1983). In the cohort study of Western Electric employees, mentioned above, the increased risk with total cholesterol appeared to be largely attributable to egg cholesterol (Shekelle et al, 1991). Conversely, in the case-control study in Hawaii, also mentioned above, the increased risk with higher cholesterol intake appeared to be stronger than that with egg consumption (Goodman et al, 1992). In another case-control study in Greece, no association with egg consumption was seen (Kalandidi et al, 1990).

An ecological study in Hawaii showed a positive correlation between intake of cholesterol and incidence of lung cancer among five ethnic groups (Kolonel et al, 1981).

In experimental studies, dietary cholesterol has been shown to increase the incidence of experimentally induced lung tumours substantially (McMichael et al, 1984).

The evidence regarding dietary cholesterol and lung cancer is somewhat mixed. One of four cohort studies and three of five case-control studies have shown moderate to strong increases in risk with higher intakes, and no studies have shown a statistically significant decrease in risk.

These data, along with those from ecological and experimental studies, show that diets high in cholesterol possibly increase the risk of lung cancer.

4.5.1.3 Alcohol

The relationship between alcohol intake and lung cancer has been examined in a number of cohort and case-control studies. Because alcohol drinking is strongly associated with smoking in most populations, a major methodological concern has been the possibility of incomplete control for confounding by cigarette smoking.

Of 17 cohort studies that have examined the relationship between alcohol intake and lung cancer (see Potter et al, 1992), only six have controlled for cigarette smoking. In the most recent of these six studies, which involved 109 cases of lung cancer among about 42,000 postmenopausal women in the USA, a strong increase in the risk of lung cancer was observed with higher alcohol intake; average intake was 10.2 g/day in those who eventually developed lung cancer, as compared with 3.6 g/day (p = 0.003) in those who did not (Potter et al, 1992). This difference was largely accounted for by differences in beer consumption (RR = 2.0, 1.02–3.8) for one or more, as compared with less than one, glass per week (adjusted for six categories of pack-years of smoking). In a cohort of Norwegian men, a strong increase in risk was reported with simultaneously high intake of alcohol and low intake of vitamins (RR = 3.7) (Kvåle et al, 1983). In a cohort of Japanese men in Hawaii, a moderate increase in risk was observed for those consuming 40 oz or more of alcohol per month (RR = 1.9) (Pollack et al, 1984). A study of Japanese male physicians reported increased risk with current alcohol consumption, but noted that the risk of lung cancer was highest among non-drinkers (Kono et al, 1986). This study, along with the study of US women, reported a U-shaped association, with the higher levels of risk in non-drinkers and heavy drinkers, compared with light and moderate drinkers. Another cohort study reported higher risk among the heaviest drinkers, although there was some evidence of residual confounding by cigarette smoking (Klatsky et al, 1981). The Framingham study reported no association between alcohol intake and lung cancer mortality (Gordon and Kannel, 1984). Thus, five of six cohort studies that adjusted for cigarette smoking have indicated some degree of increased risk with higher alcohol intake, albeit with important caveats in at least two studies.

Case-control studies generally have not reported substantial increases in risk with higher alcohol intake, after controlling for tobacco use (Schwartz et al, 1962; Williams and Horn, 1977; Herity et al, 1981; Mettlin, 1989).

A direct correlation between alcohol consumption and risk of lung cancer (r = 0.5–0.6) was suggested by a 1982 ecological analysis of data from 29 countries; this correlation with alcohol consumption was stronger than that with cigarette consumption (r = 0.2–0.4) (Potter et al, 1982).

In an experimental study of rats with chemically induced lung tumours, ethanol consumption caused a twofold increase in the incidence of tumours (Nachiappun et al, 1994).

One potential mechanism by which alcohol could increase the risk of lung cancer would be in acting as a solvent for carcinogens, particularly those in cigarette smoke. Alcohol has also been shown to induce changes in lung surfactant and in lipids in lung tissue in rodent models; such changes might increase susceptibility to carcinogenic agents (see Potter et al, 1982). Alcohol might further alter the oxidative capacity of liver enzymes that metabolise tobacco carcinogens or alter cellular metabolism, resulting in increased metabolic activation of procarcinogens (Bandera et al, 1992). Acetaldehyde, the initial metabolite of alcohol, has recently been shown to become bound to DNA in humans consuming alcohol; this form of DNA modification could serve to enhance the biological damage induced by carcinogens in tobacco smoke (Song and Vaca, 1997). Alternatively, although most epidemiological studies have attempted to control for the confounding effects of cigarette smoking, residual confounding may exist and thereby explain any observed associations for alcohol.

BOX 4.5.2 ANTIOXIDANT REQUIREMENTS OF SMOKERS

Smokers are at a higher risk of lung, as well as other cancers and other diseases, against which antioxidants may have a protective effect. Moreover, smokers tend to consume diets relatively low in antioxidants: smoking is associated with the consumption of diets including relatively fewer vegetables and fruits (Morabia and Wynder, 1990; Margetts and Jackson, 1993; McPhillips et al, 1994).

For these reasons, it could be argued that smokers should consume relatively high quantities of antioxidant nutrients, in the form of supplements, and that the more cigarettes smoked and the longer the duration of the habit, the higher the dose required.

There are a number of arguments against any such policy. First, smoking is the overwhelming cause of lung cancer, and any protective effect of antioxidants or other dietary factors is certain to be modest by comparison. Second, it would be unfortunate if smokers were encouraged to believe that they might continue their smoking habit safely if they were to take supplements. In fact, the Finnish and CARET trials do not show any protective effect of β-carotene or vitamin E supplements against lung cancer in well-nourished populations and it is certainly unknown which, if any, combinations or permutations of antioxidants might be protective. For now, the cessation of smoking and consumption of diets high in vegetables and fruit are the best recommendations.

TABLE 4.5.1 DIETARY CAROTENOID INTAKE AND THE RISK OF LUNG CANCER: COHORT STUDIES

AUTHOR, YEAR, AND PLACE	SIZE OF COHORT: NO. OF CASES	TYPE OF CAROTENOID	COMPARISON (HIGHEST VS LOWEST QUANTILES)	RELATIVE RISK (95% CONFIDENCE INTERVAL)	SEX/AGE	ADJUSTMENT SMOKING HISTORY	OTHER VARIABLES[a]
Shekelle et al, 1981 Chicago, USA	2,107 men: 33	Carotene	h vs l quartile	0.1* (na)	Y	Y	N
Kromhout, 1987 Zutphen, Holland	878 men: 63	β–carotene	h s l quartile	0.7 (0.4–1.3)	Y	Y	N
Knekt et al, 1991 Finland	4,538 men: 117						
non-smokers		Carotene	h vs l tertile	0.4* (na)	Y	Y	Y
smokers		Carotene	h vs l tertile	0.9 (na)	Y	Y	Y
Shibata et al, 1992 California, USA	11,580: 164						
men		β–carotene	h vs l tertile	1.1 (0.7–1.7)	Y	Y	N
women		β–carotene	h vs l tertile	0.6 (0.3–1.1)	Y	Y	N
Steinmetz et al 1993, Iowa, USA	41,387 women: 179	β–carotene	h vs l quartile	0.8 (0.5–1.4)	Y	Y	Y

* p ≤ 0.05 for trend or as compared with the lowest intake level
na not available
a Also adjusted for one or more of the following: residence, socio-economic staus, body mass index, height, energy, and fat intake

The balance of six cohort studies of lung cancer is consistent with increased risk with higher alcohol intake, but several case-control studies are not. Although most of these epidemiological studies controlled for cigarette consumption, the possibility of residual confounding remains. Biological mechanisms for an effect of alcohol have been proposed.

High alcohol intake possibly increases the risk of lung cancer, but any impact of alcohol consumption is minor compared with that of cigarette smoking.

4.5.1.4 Vitamins

Carotenoids

Numerous observational epidemiological studies have examined the relationship between carotenoid intake and lung cancer. Most of these studies reported on the intake of 'carotenoids' in general or 'β-carotene' specifically although, in fact, until recently, what was actually measured in most studies was a combination of α- and β-carotene, two carotenoids with vitamin A activity (see Box 4.5.2 and chapter 5.6 for more discussion of the assessment of vitamin A and carotenoid intake in epidemiological studies).

Five prospective studies of lung cancer have reported on carotenoid intake and are shown in Table 4.5.1; these studies involved cohorts in the USA (three studies), the Netherlands and Finland. Each study found an association in the direction of decreased risk, either overall or for either men or women; RRs ranged from 0.1 to 1.1 for higher intake. In two studies, the protective associations were statistically significant. Each of the five studies adjusted the risk estimates for carotenoids for smoking.

Eighteen case-control studies of lung cancer that have examined carotenoid intake are presented in Table 4.5.2.

These studies have been conducted in geographically diverse locations, including Singapore, Hong Kong, Italy, France, Greece, England, Canada, Hawaii and several other areas in the USA. Of the 34 ORs listed in Table 4.5.2 (some of the 18 studies reported separately for men and women or for more than one type of carotenoid), 15 signify a statistically significant decrease in risk with higher intake (six of these are from the same study in Hawaii, where strong protective associations were found for three individual carotenoids in both men and women). Seventeen ORs in Table 4.5.2 are less than 1.0, but are not statistically significant; two are 1.0 or more. Each of these case-control studies adjusted for cigarette smoking. Thus, the large balance of the case-control evidence on carotenoid intake and lung cancer is in the direction of a protective association.

In a 1992 review, Ziegler selectively considered six case-control studies that reported on carotenoid intake and used population or neighbourhood controls, rather than hospital controls; the smoking-adjusted odds ratios ranged from 0.4 to 0.8 for intakes in the highest tertiles or quartiles, thereby indicating decreased risk with higher intakes.

Some studies have examined carotenoid associations separately by sex, smoking status or histological type of lung cancer. These issues are somewhat interrelated, because a higher proportion of lung cancer in women, compared with men, occurs in non-smokers; also, a higher proportion of lung cancer in non-smokers (and therefore women), compared with smokers, is adenocarcinomas.

As smoking prevalence, and therefore lung cancer incidence, has been higher among men for much longer, some of the epidemiological studies have been of men only; others have involved both sexes, but generally fewer women. Three prospective and four case-control studies involved only men, and risk estimates ranged from 0.1 to 0.8 for higher intakes in these studies. One prospective and four case-control stud-

TABLE 4.5.2 DIETARY CAROTENOID INTAKE AND THE RISK OF LUNG CANCER: CASE-CONTROL STUDIES

AUTHOR, YEAR, AND PLACE	NO. OF CASES	TYPE OF CAROTENOID	COMPARISON (HIGHEST VS LOWEST QUANTILES)	ODDS RATIO (95% CONFIDENCE INTERVAL)	SEX/AGE	ADJUSTMENT SMOKING HISTORY	OTHER VARIABLES[a]
Kolonel et al. 1985, Hawaii, USA	364 men	Carotene	h vs l quartile	0.5 (0.3–0.8)	Y	Y	Y
	women	Carotene	h vs l quartile	1.7 (0.7–5.0)	Y	Y	Y
Samet et al, 1985 New Mexico, USA	447	Carotene	h vs l tertile	0.8 (0.6–1.1)	Y	Y	Y
Wu et al, 1985 California, USA	280	β–carotene	h vs l quartile	0.4 (1.2–0.9)	Y	Y	Y
Ziegler et al, 1986 New Jersey, USA	763 men	Carotene	h vs l quartile	0.8 (0.6–1.1)	Y	Y	Y
Bond et al, 1987 Texas, USA	308 men	Carotene	h vs l quartile	0.8 (0.3–1.7)	Y	Y	Y
Byers et al, 1987 New York, USA	296 men	Carotene	h vs l quartile	0.6* (na)	Y	Y	N
	154 women	Carotene	h vs l quartile	0.8 (na)	Y	Y	N
Pastorino et al 1987, Milan, Italy	47 women	Carotene	h vs l tertile	0.3 (0.1–1.1)	Y	Y	Y
Fontham et al 1988, Louisiana, USA	1,253	Carotene	h vs l tertile	0.9 (0.7–1.1)	Y	Y	Y
Ho et al, 1988 Hong Kong	50 men	β–carotene	h vs l quartile	0.3 (0.1–1.4)	Y	Y	N
Koo, 1988 Hong Kong	88 women[b]	β–carotene	h vs l tertile	0.7 (na)	Y	Y	Y
Dartigues et al 1990, France	106	β–carotene	> vs < 1,000 RE/day	0.2* (0.1–0.4)[c]	Y	Y	Y
Jain et al, 1990 Toronto, Canada	839	β–carotene	h vs l quartile	0.9 (na)	Y	Y	Y
Kalandidi et al 1990, Athens, Greece	160 women[b]	β–carotene	h vs l quartile	1.0 (0.6–1.6)	Y	Y	Y
Harris et al, 1991 Oxford, UK	96 men	Carotene	h vs l tertile	0.5 (na)	Y	Y	N
Candelora et al 1992, Florida, USA	124 women[b]	Total carotene	h vs l quartile	0.3* (0.1–0.6)	Y	Y	Y
		β–carotene	h vs l quartile	0.4 (0.2–0.8)	Y	Y	Y
		α–carotene	h vs l quartile	0.2* (0.1–0.4)	Y	Y	Y
		Lutein	h vs l quartile	0.9 (0.5–1.7)	Y	Y	Y
		Cryptoxanthin	h vs l quartile	0.4* (0.2–0.8)	Y	Y	Y
		Lycopene	h vs l quartile	0.6 (0.3–1.2)	Y	Y	Y
Dorgan et al, 1993 New Jersey, USA	1,951[d]	Carotene	h vs l tertile	0.8* (0.6–1.0)	Y	Y	Y
Le Marchand et al 1993, Hawaii, USA	230 men	β–carotene	h vs l quartile	0.5* (na)	Y	Y	Y
		α–carotene	h vs l quartile	0.4* (na)	Y	Y	Y
		Lutein	h vs l quartile	0.6* (na)	Y	Y	Y
		Lycopene	h vs l quartile	0.7 (na)	Y	Y	Y
		β–cryptoxanthin	h vs l quartile	0.9 (na)	Y	Y	Y
	102 women	β–carotene	h vs l quartile	0.3* (na)	Y	Y	Y
		α–carotene	h vs l quartile	0.5* (na)	Y	Y	Y
		Lutein	h vs l quartile	0.3* (na)	Y	Y	Y
		Lycopene	h vs l quartile	0.8 (na)	Y	Y	Y
		β–cryptoxanthin	h vs l quartile	0.9 (na)	Y	Y	Y
Mayne, 1993, 1994 New York, USA	413[b]	β–carotene	h vs l quartile	0.7 (0.5–1.0)	Y	Y	Y

* p ≤ 0.05 for trend or as compared with the lowest intake level
na not available
[a] Also adjusted for one or more of the following: residence, histological type, ethnicity, cholesterol intake, occupation, race, years of employment, education, vitamin supplements, number of live births, retinol intake, study phase, total calories, total energy intake, interviewer, religion, body mass index, income, occupational exposure to carcinogens, alcohol consumption
[b] Never smokers or non-smokers
[c] Epidermoid lung cancer
[d] Includes surrogate interviews

The assessment of vitamin A and carotenoid intake in most published epidemiological studies has been relatively crude and non-specific, resulting partly from limitations of data on food composition. In the earliest study on diet and lung cancer (Bjelke, 1975), findings for total vitamin A intake were reported. In many subsequent studies, total vitamin A was partitioned into preformed vitamin A (retinol) and carotenoids. Carotenoids include a large number of related compounds (including β-carotene, α-carotene, lycopene, lutein, zeaxanthin and many others), only some of which can be converted to retinol. Until recently, the usual method of estimating carotenoid intake was to use the published data for total vitamin A activity in foods and count this as carotenoid if the food was a vegetable or fruit. Sometimes these values have inaccurately been referred to as β-carotene only. These carotenoid values in fact include mainly α- and β-carotene, the two major carotenoids that can be converted to retinol, and therefore have vitamin A activity. These values do not include quantitatively important carotenoids such as lycopene or lutein, which are not converted to retinol. Most studies of carotenoid levels in sera also used these early methods which did not resolve individual carotenoids. More recently, comprehensive databases, based upon direct analysis of specific carotenoids in foods, have become available; these may eventually allow judgements regarding specific carotenoids, when sufficient studies using more precise food-composition data have accumulated.

Steinmetz et al, 1993). This lack of specificity for cancer involving the squamous epithelium suggests that carotenoids are acting through a mechanism other than (or in addition to) conversion to retinol, which is known to function in the normal differentiation of squamous epithelium.

At least two case-control studies have examined associations for five individual carotenoids, including α-carotene, β-carotene, lutein, lycopene and cryptoxanthin, based upon newly available analytical methods. A study in Hawaii reported a statistically significant decreased risk with increased intakes of α-carotene, β-carotene and lutein, but not of lycopene or cryptoxanthin (Le Marchand, 1993). In this study, the association between reduced risk and an index of total vegetable consumption was stronger than that for a variable summarising these three carotenoids. Another study of women in the USA found strong protective associations with α-carotene, β-carotene and cryptoxanthin, but not with lutein or lycopene; the strongest association was with α-carotene, for which an approximately fivefold lower risk was observed with intake in the uppermost quartile (Candelora et al, 1992).

Each of five nested case-control studies of lung cancer and carotenoid levels in prospectively collected sera has consistently shown a protective association (RRs = 0.4–0.6) for higher levels of β-carotene; the associations were statistically significant in four studies and trends were apparent in all five (Nomura et al, 1985; Menkes et al, 1986; Wald et al, 1988; Connett et al, 1989; Stahelin et al, 1991; see also Ziegler, 1992). (Table 4.5.3.) Regarding total carotenoids, one study reported a statistically significant odds ratio of 0.5 for higher blood levels (Connett et al, 1989). Almost all of the studies noted here matched on some measure of smoking status, suggesting that smoking does not account completely for the consistent and strong protective associations observed; smokers have been shown to have lower levels of serum carotenoids than non-smokers (see chapter 5.6).

In a review of studies of serum β-carotene levels, Comstock et al (1992) reported that, of ten cancer sites examined, the evidence for lung cancer was particularly striking, because prediagnostic levels were considerably lower for cases than controls in each of seven populations reviewed.

Few experimental data are available on carotenoids and lung cancer, as few animal models absorb carotenoids intact and the effects of cigarette smoking cannot be well simulated.

General mechanisms by which carotenoids may protect against lung and other cancers are discussed in chapter 5.6.

Three large intervention trials that have involved supplementation with β-carotene are described in Box 4.5.4. In two of these trials, small, but statistically significant, increases in incidence and mortality from lung cancer were observed in the group that took β-carotene supplements (in one of these trials, the active intervention group also took retinol supplements). In the third trial, no effect of supplementation with β-carotene was apparent. Currently, it is unclear whether β-

ies included women only, with risk estimates ranging from 0.3 to 1.0. In one prospective and three case-control studies that reported data separately for men and women, there was no evidence that the protective association was stronger in one sex (see Tables 4.5.1 and 4.5.2 for references).

Different prospective studies have shown protective associations for carotenoids to be stronger for either smokers (Shekelle et al, 1981) or non-smokers (Knekt et al, 1991a), so no conclusion can be reached on this point. One study of women reported odds ratios of 0.7 (ns) and 1.0 for ex-smokers and current smokers, respectively (Steinmetz et al, 1993). Three of four studies that were restricted to non-smokers reported protective associations, clearly suggesting that any protective effect is not limited to smokers (Koo, 1988; Kalandidi et al, 1990; Candelora et al, 1992; Mayne et al, 1994).

The association of carotenoids with specific histological types of lung cancer has been examined in several studies. In some studies that involved only or predominantly men, the protective association was limited to the squamous and/or small-cell types (Kvåle et al, 1983; Ziegler et al, 1984), whereas in others, the protective effect was seen also for the adenocarcinoma type (Byers et al, 1987; Le Marchand et al, 1989). Some studies only of women have suggested that the protective association for carotenoids is stronger for the adenocarcinoma (Wu et al, 1985) or large-cell types (Steinmetz et al, 1993). Thus, the observed protective association for carotenoids has not been consistently restricted to any one histological type, but rather observed for each histological subtype across various studies (see also Ziegler, 1992;

carotene from supplements is definitely harmful, although it is clear that there are no protective effects, at least not over periods of 4 to 12 years of supplementation. The amounts of β-carotene in the supplements used in intervention trials have been higher than those contained naturally in most diets, and β-carotene from supplements may have different biological properties from those of β-carotene consumed within intact foods. (See Box 4.5.4 for more detail.)

Overall, the extensive observational epidemiological data consistently show a weak to strong decrease in risk with higher dietary intakes of carotenoids. There is evidence to support a protective effect in both men and women; in non-smokers and smokers; and against each of the four histological types of lung cancer. However, the possibility that the observed decrease in risk is really attributable to some other component of carotenoid-containing foods (vegetables and fruits) cannot be discounted. No judgement can be made for any individual carotenoid at this point, because of the limitations of the laboratory analyses on which most of the data are based.

High dietary carotenoid intake probably decreases the risk of lung cancer.

This judgement does not apply to carotenoids from supplements, for which the evidence from supplement intervention trials does not support a protective effect and may suggest a harmful effect (see Box 4.5.4).

Vitamin C

At least six cohort studies have examined the relationship between vitamin C and lung cancer; all but one of these adjusted for cigarette smoking. A strong protective association was found within a Dutch cohort, RR = 0.4 (0.2–0.8) for the uppermost intake quartile (Kromhout, 1987). Two other studies, in Finland and the USA, found moderate to strong protective associations within certain subgroups. In the Finnish cohort, a protective association was observed within non-smokers, with relative risks of 0.3 (p ≤ 0.05) and 1.3 (ns) for the uppermost intake tertiles for non-smokers and smokers, respectively (Knekt et al, 1991a). In a cohort of elderly people in California, a moderate protective association was observed in women (RR = 0.6, 0.3–1.0, for uppermost intake quartiles), but not in men (RR = 1.1, 0.7–1.8) (Shibata et al, 1992). Two other cohort studies, in Norway and the USA, have found no appreciable associations between vitamin C intake and the risk of lung cancer, with relative risks of 1.2 (ns) and 0.8 (ns) for the highest levels of intake in the two studies, respectively (Kvåle et al, 1983; Steinmetz et al, 1993). In a sixth cohort study, which involved only 33 cases, those who developed lung cancer had reported lower vitamin C intakes at baseline than those who did not (91 vs 101 mg, respectively), although this difference was not statistically significant, nor was it adjusted for cigarette smoking (Shekelle et al, 1981).

At least 11 case-control studies of lung cancer have examined the relationship with vitamin C intake; each of these studies adjusted for cigarette smoking or was conducted entirely with non-smokers. Five of these studies found statistically significant moderate or strong protective associations

TABLE 4.5.3 STUDIES ON CAROTENOID LEVELS IN PROSPECTIVELY COLLECTED SERA AND THE RISK OF LUNG CANCER

AUTHOR, YEAR, AND PLACE	SIZE OF COHORT: NO. OF CASES	TYPE OF CAROTENOID	COMPARISON (HIGHEST VS LOWEST QUANTILES)	RELATIVE RISK (95% CONFIDENCE INTERVAL)	SEX/AGE	ADJUSTMENT SMOKING HISTORY	OTHER VARIABLES[a]
Nomura et al, 1985 Hawaii, USA	6,800 men[b]: 74	β–carotene	h vs l quintile	0.5* (0.2–1.3)	Y	Y	N
Menkes et al, 1986 Maryland, USA	25,802: 99	β–carotene	h vs l quintile	0.5* (na)	Y	Y	Y
Wald et al., 1988 London, UK	22,000 men: 271	β–carotene	h vs l quintile	0.4* (na)	Y	Y	Y
Connet et al, 1989[c] USA	12,866 men: 66	β–carotene	h vs l quintile	0.4 (na)	na	na	na
		Total caroteneoids	h vs l quintile	0.5 (na)	na	na	na
Knekt et al, 1990 Finland	36,265[d]: 766						
men		β–carotene	h vs l quintile	0.8* (0.5–1.1)	Y	Y	Y
women		β–carotene	h vs l quintile	1.0 (0.6–2.0)	Y	Y	Y
Stahelin et al, 1991 Basel, Switzerland	2,974 men[e]: 68[f]	β–carotene	h vs l quartile	0.6* (0.3–0.9)	Y	Y	Y

* p ≤ 0.05 for trend or as compared with the lowest serum level

na not available

a Also adjusted for one or more of the following: race, month of blood donation, duration of sample storage, plasma lipids, residence

b Japanese origin

c The Multiple Risk Factor Intervention Trial

d The Finnish Mobile Clinic Health Examination Survey

e The Basel Study

f Bronchus cancer

(ORs = 0.2 to 0.7 for higher intakes) (Fontham et al, 1988; Holst et al, 1988; Koo, 1988; Le Marchand et al, 1989; Candelora et al, 1992). Two further studies reported weaker and statistically non-significant associations in the direction of a protective effect (Kolonel et al, 1985; Kalandidi et al, 1990); in the study by Kolonel et al (1985) this effect was evident only in women, with a slight increase in risk observed in men. Four studies reported no substantial association between vitamin C intake and the risk of lung cancer (Byers et al, 1984; Hinds et al, 1984; Byers et al, 1987; Jain et al, 1990). No studies reported a statistically significant increased risk with higher vitamin C intake.

In a 1992 review on vitamin C and cancer by Block, nine of twelve studies of lung cancer (including both cohort and case-control studies) were noted to have reported results in the protective direction; these results were statistically significant in six studies. Of five studies that found statistically significant results for vitamin C and also examined β-carotene, a stronger protective association was suggested for vitamin C. It was also noted, however, that the main intent of most of these studies was to examine vitamin A or carotenoids, and that the dietary instruments employed may not have been designed to best assess vitamin C intake. In an earlier review on the same topic, Block (1991) noted that the median relative risk of lung cancer over ten studies was approximately 0.6 for higher intakes.

A prospective study of Swiss men found no differences in baseline levels of plasma vitamin C between those who subsequently died of lung cancer and those who did not; in this study, analysis of vitamin levels was conducted immediately after the blood was collected (Stahelin et al, 1991).

The antioxidant action of vitamin C provides a plausible biological mechanism by which it may protect against harmful substances in tobacco smoke and against other lung carcinogens (see also chapter 5.6).

Overall, most of six cohort and eleven case-control studies have found some degree of decreased risk of lung cancer with higher vitamin C intake, although these associations were in many cases only weak or moderate; no studies found a strong increase in risk.

It is conceivable that the observed decrease in risk is really attributable to some other component of vitamin C-containing foods (vegetables and fruits), and not to vitamin C itself.

Higher dietary vitamin C intake possibly decreases the risk of lung cancer.

Folate

As vegetables and fruits are the major sources of folate, insufficient intake of this vitamin might account, in part, for the protective effect of these foods. Although a potentially promising area, the relationship between folate intake and the risk of human lung cancer has not been extensively examined.

One case-control study found no association between folate intake and the risk of lung cancer (Bandera et al, 1991).

In a randomised trial among 80 smoking men with squamous metaplasia of the bronchus, a precancerous condition, high-dosage supplements of folic acid and vitamin B_{12} over 4 months led to an approximately twofold greater improvement in the cytological appearance of sputum than the placebo (Heimburger et al, 1988). As nutrients from supplements may have different biological properties from those consumed within intact foods, the evidence from studies of supplements have not been considered in the formulation of the panel judgements.

Biological mechanisms by which folate may protect against lung and other cancers relate to its function as a methyl donor and are discussed in chapter 5.6.

The evidence relating to dietary folate intake and the risk of lung cancer is very limited and non-specific; no judgement is possible.

Retinol

Earlier studies of vitamin A and lung cancer focused upon 'total vitamin A' or 'pre-formed vitamin A' (retinol), whereas studies within the past decade have focused more upon 'β-carotene' and 'carotenoids'. Evidence specific to total vitamin A or retinol is reviewed here. (See Box 4.5.3 for a discussion of the measurement of vitamin A and carotenoids in epidemiological studies.)

Two prospective studies of lung cancer have reported on total vitamin A intake. One study in Norway, involving 168 male cases, observed a moderate decrease in risk (RR = 0.7, ns, smoking-adjusted) (Kvåle et al, 1983), whereas the other in the USA, which included only 55 cases, found essentially no associations (RR = 1.0 for men and 0.9 for women) (Paganini Hill et al, 1987).

At least nine case-control studies of lung cancer have examined total vitamin A intake; these have reported mixed results. Three have found no substantial associations (OR = 0.7–1.2 for higher intakes) (Ziegler et al, 1984; Byers et al, 1987; Jain et al, 1990). The other six have found moderate to strong protective associations (OR = 0.4–0.7 for higher intakes), either overall, or within at least one subgroup (Mettlin et al, 1979; Gregor et al, 1980; Hinds et al, 1984; Samet et al, 1985; Ho et al, 1988; Le Marchand et al, 1989). One study of a UK population reported a statistically significant lower intake of vitamin A among male cases than male controls; in women, cases consumed more than controls, although the difference was not significant (Gregor et al, 1980). Another study in the USA reported decreased risk with higher intake for non-Hispanic (OR = 0.6, 0.4–1.0), but not for Hispanic (OR = 1.1, 0.6–2.0), whites (Samet et al, 1985).

Three prospective studies have reported on retinol or 'pre-formed vitamin A' intake. The largest of these, conducted among Finnish men and involving 117 cases, found a slight decrease in risk among non-smokers (RR = 0.7, ns; p for

BOX 4.5.4 DIETARY INTERVENTION TRIALS OF LUNG CANCER USING SUPPLEMENTS

Three major intervention trials using nutrient supplements have examined lung cancer as an endpoint. In 1994, results were published from the Alpha-Tocopherol, Beta-Carotene Cancer Prevention Study (ATBCCPS), a randomised intervention trial among approximately 29,000 male smokers in Finland (The Alpha-Tocopherol, Beta-Carotene Prevention Study Group, 1994). The study involved daily supplementation with either 20 mg β-carotene, 50 mg α-tocopherol (vitamin E), both or placebo for an average of 6 years; in this time period, 876 new cases of lung cancer occurred. The results of the trial were unexpected, in that the incidence of lung cancer was 18% higher (RR = 1.18; p = 0.01) among the men who took β-carotene supplements than among those who did not. Total mortality rate was also 8% higher (RR = 1.08; p = 0.02) among those who took β-carotene supplements. No difference in lung cancer incidence or overall mortality was apparent between those who took vitamin E supplements and those who did not.

The Physicians' Health Study (PHS) involved approximately 22,000 US physicians who were randomised into groups receiving either 50 mg β-carotene on alternate days or placebo (Hennekens et al, 1996). During an average of 12 years of supplementation, 170 new cases of lung cancer were diagnosed. No effect of β-carotene supplementation was apparent on lung cancer incidence, with 82 cases occurring in the supplementation group and 88 in the placebo group (ns). The relative risk of lung cancer for the β-carotene group was 0.9 (0.6–1.4); that for overall mortality was 1.05 (0.9–1.3). In this trial, only 11% and 39% of the participants were current and former smokers, respectively. When the analysis was restricted to current smokers (at baseline) the findings were similar to those for all participants (RR for lung cancer = 0.9, 0.6–1.4) with supplementation.

A third intervention trial, the Beta-Carotene and Retinol Efficacy Trial (CARET), involved approximately 18,000 men and women who were at higher risk of lung cancer, as a result of either smoking or occupational exposure to asbestos (Omenn et al, 1996). After an average of 4 years' daily supplementation with 30 mg β-carotene and 25,000 IU retinol combined, the trial was stopped 21 months early, as a result of unexpected findings that suggested harmful effects of the supplements. During the supplementation period, 338 new cases of lung cancer occurred (RR of lung cancer in the supplement group = 1.28, 1.04–1.57). The deleterious effect of the supplements appeared to be greater among asbestos workers and heavy smokers who continued to smoke during the trial, than among previously heavy smokers who had quit before the outset of the trial, although the differences between these groups were not statistically significant. The relative risk for death from any cause was 1.17 (1.03–1.33) for the supplement group. It was impossible to separate the effects of β-carotene from those of retinol in this study as they were given only in combination.

A fourth large intervention trial, the Women's Health Study, begun in 1992 and involving 40,000 female heath professionals in the USA, terminated the β-carotene arm of its supplement interventions in early 1996, directly following the release of the CARET and PHS results (Rower, 1996).

Thus, three large trials of β-carotene supplementation (one in combination with retinol) in well-nourished populations have provided no evidence of a protective effect against lung cancer and, in fact, two trials have shown increases in the risk of lung cancer and overall mortality. These findings were unexpected and troubling, and are inconsistent with results from studies of dietary or serum carotenoids, or of vegetables and fruits, which consistently support protective effects. Even within the ATBC-CPS, a protective association between baseline plasma β-carotene levels and lung cancer incidence was observed within the control group (ATBCCPS Group, 1994). Similarly, within CARET, participants with high pre-intervention levels of plasma β-carotene went on to have lower rates of cancer, irrespective of supplementation (Omenn et al, 1996). None of this evidence discounts the possibility that β-carotene, in the diet or plasma, may be a non-specific marker for lifestyles or dietary patterns that protect against cancer via pathways not involving β-carotene.

Chance is an unlikely explanation for such similar, but unforeseen, results from two large trials. Various explanations for the unexpected results of these trials have been suggested, although none has been well tested or accepted. The length of these three trials ranged from 4 to 12 years, which may not have been long enough to overcome lifelong exposures, and may have precluded the detection of protective effects against early stage events in a cancer with a long latency period. Nevertheless, supplementation in the PHS averaged 12 years. Further, beneficial effects might be difficult to achieve in the continuing presence of carcinogenic compounds in smokers. These hypotheses would explain a finding of no effect, but do not shed any light on the findings of increased risk in two trials involving predominantly heavy smokers. Also, the PHS reported no difference in effect on lung cancer incidence in current smokers, compared with former and non-smokers.

It could be that a disequilibrium is induced by excess β-carotene with respect to other nutrients and bioactive compounds. Serum β-carotene levels rose to 4–12 times the baseline levels in the supplemented groups in the three trials, signifying intakes far above the usual. Such high intakes of β-carotene might interfere with the absorption or metabolism of one or more of the other carotenoids or other plant constituents, which may have beneficial effects against cancer. β-Carotene has been further postulated to have pro-oxidant effects under certain non-physiological conditions (Omenn et al, 1996). Another hypothesis is that high levels of β-carotene may interfere with the normal apoptotic death of abnormal cells: bcl-2, an inhibitor of apoptosis, operates via an antioxidant pathway and it is possible that high doses of β-carotene mimic this effect (Potter, 1996). This mechanism might be particularly relevant in individuals with a large number of initiated cells, such as smokers, perhaps accounting for the difference between the CARET and ATBCCPS studies on the one hand (mainly long-term smokers) and the PHS findings on the other (only 11% and 39% smokers and ex-smokers, respectively).

Taken together, results of the ATBCCPS, PHS and CARET studies provide no evidence of benefit of β-carotene, vitamin E or retinol supplements against lung cancer in well-nourished populations, and provide some indication of adverse effects of β-carotene and perhaps retinol supplements, particularly in people at higher risk for lung cancer, such as heavy smokers. It is currently unclear whether β-carotene supplements are truly harmful.

trend), but a weak increase in risk among current smokers (RR = 1.4, p ≤ 0.10 for trend) (Knekt et al, 1991a). The study of an American cohort found RRs = 0.8 and 0.7, respectively, for men and women (Paganini Hill et al, 1987). In the Western Electric Study, an increase in risk was found (RR = 2.0), based on 33 male cases; in contrast, this study reported a strong decrease in risk with higher carotenoid intake (Shekelle et al, 1981). Thus, prospective studies of retinol have produced inconsistent results; notably, two of the three studies involved 55 or fewer cases.

At least 11 case-control studies have examined retinol or 'preformed vitamin A' intake; these have also produced inconsistent results. Five studies, in the USA and Canada, have reported no material associations (OR = 0.8–1.3) for higher retinol intakes (Ziegler et al, 1984; Wu et al, 1985; Fontham et al, 1988; Le Marchand et al, 1989; Jain et al, 1990). Three studies, in Italy, Hong Kong and France, have reported strong decreases in risk with higher intakes (OR = 0.2–0.5) (Pastorino et al, 1987; Koo, 1988; Dartigues et al, 1990). Another study, among non-smoking Greek women, reported a weak increase in risk (OR = 1.3, 0.98–1.8) (Kalandidi et al, 1990). An additional study, in British men, observed 11% higher average retinol intakes in cases than in controls, although statistical significance and risk estimates were not reported (Harris et al, 1991). The remaining study, in the USA, reported essentially no association among non-Hispanic whites, but a moderate increase in risk among Hispanic whites (OR = 1.7, 0.8–3.3) (Samet et al, 1985).

CARET, a dietary intervention trial that involved supplementation with retinol and β-carotene in individuals at higher risk of lung cancer, resulted in increased risk of lung cancer in the supplementation group, compared with the placebo group (Omenn et al, 1996). It was impossible to differentiate the effects of retinol from those of β-carotene in this trial (see Box 4.5.4 for more details). As the biological activity of retinol from supplements may be different from that from foods, and because of the fact that retinol was always given with β-carotene in this trial, these findings have not been taken into account in the panel's judgement on the effect of retinol from foods.

Retinol plays a role in the differentiation of epithelial cells and lack of normal differentiation is a characteristic of cancer cells; thus, it is theoretically possible that inadequate vitamin A may potentiate the development of lung and other cancer. (For more on retinol, see chapter 5.6.)

Overall, most epidemiological studies that have examined total vitamin A intake have reported either decreased risk with higher intake or no association. Of course, any data suggesting a protective effect of total dietary vitamin A may be reflecting an effect of carotenoids, rather than any effect of retinol itself; the evidence for carotenoids, as reviewed above, supports a probable decrease in risk with higher intakes. The studies that have examined 'preformed vitamin A' or retinol intake have shown inconsistent results, with many showing no statistically significant association. High dietary retinol intake possibly has no relationship with the risk of lung cancer.

Vitamin E

Relatively few epidemiological studies have examined dietary vitamin E intake, as a result of the methodological limitations discussed in chapter 5.6. One cohort study reported no difference in baseline dietary vitamin E intake between those who developed lung cancer and a selected control group (Connett et al, 1989). One case-control study of dietary vitamin E showed lung cancer cases to have lower intakes than controls (Lopez and Le Gardeur, 1982), whereas another showed no differences (Byers et al, 1987).

Pre-diagnostic serum levels of vitamin E have been shown to be lower in subsequent cases of lung cancer than controls in four of six populations studied. In two populations, levels were about 10% lower in cases; these differences were statistically significant whereas, in the remaining populations, differences were close to null (see Comstock et al, 1992).

Five case-control studies of lung cancer, which reported on blood levels of vitamin E were summarised in a 1991 review by Knekt (1991a). Four studies observed lower levels among cases than among controls (case-control differences ranged from 21% to 41%); the remaining study reported no association.

One of the intervention trials described in Box 4.5.3, the ATBCCPS, involved vitamin E supplementation to male heavy smokers and found no effect, compared with a placebo. The interpretation of these findings may be limited by the relatively low dose (50 IU per day) of the supplement and short duration (about 6 years on average) of the trial relative to the latency period in the development of lung cancer. In a recent case-control study restricted to non-smokers, use of vitamin E supplements was associated with reduced risk of lung cancer (OR = 0.6, 0.4–0.9); no details were available regarding dose or duration of use (Mayne et al, 1994).

As vitamin E from supplements may have different biological properties from those of vitamin E consumed within intact foods, the evidence from studies of supplements has not been taken into account in the panel's judgement on vitamin E and lung cancer.

General biological mechanisms by which vitamin E may protect against lung and other cancers are discussed in chapter 5.6.

High dietary vitamin E intake possibly decreases the risk of lung cancer.

4.5.1.5 Minerals
Selenium
Relatively few epidemiological studies have examined dietary selenium intake, as a result of the methodological limitations discussed in chapter 5.7. One cohort study of lung cancer in men, which examined dietary selenium intake, reported essentially null associations; odds ratios

were 1.0 and 0.8 (both ns) for the highest intake tertiles in smokers and non-smokers, respectively (Knekt et al, 1991a). As dietary assessment methods are generally inadequate to measure selenium status (see chapter 3), misclassification of selenium intake will tend to bias results towards the null.

Four prospective studies of lung cancer have examined serum selenium levels and one has examined levels of selenium in toenails. The four studies of serum selenium reported various relative risks of 0.3 (p = 0.001 for trend), 0.7 (ns; p for trend), 0.9 (ns; p for trend), and 1.4 (p = 0.07 for trend) for the highest quintiles; only the first study involved more than 100 cases (Menkes et al, 1986; Nomura et al, 1987; Coates et al, 1988; Knekt et al, 1990a). The most striking odds ratio of 0.3 was observed in a large study of Finnish men and was adjusted for smoking; this is important because smokers have been shown to have lower levels of selenium in the serum and toenails (Hunter et al, 1990a, b). In the study of levels of selenium in the toenails, which involved 317 cases of lung cancer within a large Dutch cohort, smoking-adjusted relative risks of 0.5 (0.3–0.8) and 0.4 (0.1–1.3) were reported for men and women, respectively (van den Brandt et al, 1993). Selenium levels in toenails are believed to be a more time-integrated measure of dietary selenium intake (see chapter 5.7).

In four of five additional prospective studies, lung cancer cases were found to have lower baseline serum selenium levels than people who remained free of the disease, even after controlling for the effects of smoking; each of these studies involved fewer than 40 cases (Willett et al, 1983; Salonen et al, 1984, 1985; Peleg et al, 1985; Virtamo et al, 1987; Ringstad et al, 1988).

Three case-control studies of lung cancer have generally shown protective associations for higher levels of selenium in blood, hair, urine and toenails (Poole, 1989; Bratakos et al, 1990; Tominaga et al, 1992). One study reported a strong decrease in risk with higher levels of toenail selenium in men (OR = 0.3, 0.1–1.0), but a strong increase in risk in women (OR = 3.2, 0.9–11.5) (Poole, 1989). Of course, in case-control studies, the possibility that selenium levels in cases of lung cancer reflect an effect of the disease, rather than a cause, cannot be discounted.

Ecological studies have shown an inverse association between estimated selenium intake and risk of numerous cancers, including lung cancer (Schrauzer et al, 1977).

A number of animal experimental studies have shown that selenium supplementation, usually at near toxic doses, suppresses the development of lung and other cancers (Ip et al, 1992; El-Bayoumy et al, 1993).

Most of the evidence regarding dietary selenium and lung cancer is constrained by limitations in assessment of dietary selenium (epidemiological studies), small numbers of subjects and therefore low statistical power (prospective studies of selenium levels in serum or toenails), the possibility of an effect of the disease on selenium levels (case-control studies of tissue selenium levels), or the use

of near toxic doses of selenium (experimental studies). Nevertheless, two large prospective studies of selenium levels in serum and toenails have observed strong protective associations. Most of the other data are at least consistent with decreased risk.

High dietary selenium intake possibly decreases the risk of lung cancer.

4.5.1.6 Other bioactive compounds

Isothiocyanates

Isothiocyanates are found in a number of foods and particularly in cruciferous vegetables. One particularly well-studied isothiocyanate is phenethyl isothiocyanate (PEITC). When added to diets of rats treated with the tobacco-derived nitrosamine 4-(methylnitrosoamino)-1-(3-pyridyl)-1-butan-one (NNK), PEITC was found to reduce lung tumour multiplicity, but not the number of tumour-bearing animals (Morse et al, 1989). Two less studied isothiocyanates, 3-phenylpropyl isothiocyanate (PPITC) and 4-phenylbutyl isothiocyanate (PBITC) were shown to reduce tumour multiplicity by 96% and the number of tumour-bearing animals by 60%.

The evidence relating to dietary isothiocyanates and the risk of lung cancer is limited; no judgement is possible.

Indoles

Indole-3-carbinol, found in cruciferous vegetables, has been shown in experimental studies to be an inhibitor of the activation of NNK, and to reduce the number of NNK-induced lung tumours (Morse et al, 1990). Inhibitors of carcinogen activation must be present at the time of exposure for the carcinogen to be effective; thus, they are not expected to be effective after smoking cessation.

The evidence relating to dietary indoles and the risk of lung cancer is limited; no judgement is possible.

4.5.2 FOODS AND DRINKS

4.5.2.1 Cereals (grains)

Experimental studies have shown that mice fed cereal-based diets develop fewer lung tumours than those fed a semipurified diet (Chung et al, 1993).

The evidence relating to cereals and the risk of lung cancer is limited to animal experimental studies; no judgement is possible.

4.5.2.2 Vegetables and fruits

Lung cancer is one of the sites for which a large number of prospective data are available regarding vegetable and fruit consumption.

Seven cohort studies have examined vegetable and fruit

consumption and are presented in Table 4.5.3. These studies have involved cohorts in Norway, the USA, Japan and the Netherlands; two studies involved men only, one women only, and four included both. Each of these studies showed protective associations for some vegetables or fruits. Most of the relative risks (23 of 31) presented in Table 4.5.4 for various types of vegetables and fruits are towards a protective association, although not all are statistically significant. No studies showed a statistically significant increase in risk for any type of vegetable or fruit. The strongest protective associations were those found for fruits in studies in the Netherlands and the USA, with people consuming the most fruit having only about 30% the risk of lung cancer of those consuming the least.

Seventeen case-control studies of lung cancer, which have examined vegetable and fruit consumption are presented in Table 4.5.5. Sixteen of these studies have reported statistically significant inverse associations for one or more vegetable and/or fruit categories, and almost all odds ratios (57 of 61) in Table 4.5.5 are towards a protective association, although not all are statistically significant. Similar to the cohort studies, no case-control studies showed a statistically significant increase in risk for any type of vegetable or fruit. The most striking odds ratios from various case-control studies were several in the range 0.1–0.3 for high consumption of vegetables, fruits, green vegetables, cruciferous vegetables, carrots or tomatoes (see Table 4.5.5).

Protective associations have been consistently shown for vegetables and fruit, together and separately, as shown in Tables 4.5.4 and 4.5.5. Three cohort and eight case-control

TABLE 4.5.4 VEGETABLE AND FRUIT CONSUMPTION AND THE RISK OF LUNG CANCER: COHORT STUDIES

AUTHOR, YEAR, AND PLACE	SIZE OF COHORT: NO. OF CASES	TYPE OF VEGETABLE OR FRUIT	COMPARISON (HIGHEST VS LOWEST QUANTILES)	RELATIVE RISK (95% CONFIDENCE INTERVAL)	SEX/AGE	ADJUSTMENT SMOKING HISTORY	OTHER VARIABLES[a]
Kväle et al, 1983 Norway	13,785 men: 168	Vegetables	h vs l quartile	0.5 (na)[b]	Y	Y	Y
		Tomatoes	h vs l quartile	0.5 (na)[b]	Y	Y	Y
		Carrots	h vs l quartile	0.6 (na)[b]	Y	Y	Y
		Cauliflower	h vs l quartile	0.5 (na)[b]	Y	Y	Y
		Fruits and berries	h vs l quartile	0.7 (na)[b]	Y	Y	Y
		Cabbage	h vs l quartile	0.6 (na)[b]	Y	Y	Y
Longde and Hammond, 1985 USA	1 million	Green salad	h vs l tertile	0.8 (na)	Y	Y	Y
		Fruit	h vs l tertile	0.6 (na)	Y	Y	Y
Hirayama, 1986 Japan	122,261 men: 1,454	Green and yellow vegetables	h vs l quartile	0.8* (na)	Y	Y	Y
	142,857 women: 463	Green and yellow vegetables	h vs l quartile	1.4 (na)	Y	Y	Y
Kromhout, 1987 Zutphen, Holland	878 men: 63	Fruit	h vs l quartile	0.3* (0.2–0.7)	Y	Y	N
		Citrus fruit	h vs l quartile	0.5* (0.2–1.0)	Y	Y	N
Fraser et al, 1991 California, USA	34,198[c]: 61	Fruit	h vs l tertile	0.3* (0.1–0.7)	Y	Y	N
		Green salads	h vs l tertile	0.7 (0.3–1.5)	Y	Y	N
		Cooked green vegetables	h vs l tertile	1.1 (0.4–2.9)	Y	Y	N
		Tomatoes	h vs l tertile	1.2 (0.5–3.0)	Y	Y	N
Shibata et al, 1992 California, USA	11,580: 94 men	Fruit and vegetables	h vs l tertile	1.2 (0.7–2.1)	Y	Y	N
		Vegetables	h vs l tertile	1.4 (0.8–2.3)	Y	Y	N
		Fruit	h vs l tertile	1.0 (0.6–1.7)	Y	Y	N
		Dark green vegetables	h vs l tertile	1.2 (0.7–1.9)	Y	Y	N
	70 women	Fruit and vegetables	h vs l tertile	0.6 (0.3–1.0)	Y	Y	N
		Vegetables	h vs l tertile	0.6 (0.3–1.0)	Y	Y	N
		Fruit	h vs l tertile	0.7 (0.4–1.2)	Y	Y	N
		Dark green vegetables	h vs l tertile	0.6 (0.4–1.2)	Y	Y	N
Steinmetz et al 1993, Iowa, USA	41,387 women: 179	Fruit and vegetables	h vs l quartile	0.5* (0.3–0.9)	Y	Y	Y
		Vegetables	h vs l quartile	0.5* (0.3–0.9)	Y	Y	Y
		Fruit	h vs l quartile	0.8 (0.4–1.2)	Y	Y	Y
		Green leafy vegetables	h vs l quartile	0.5* (0.3–0.8)	Y	Y	Y
		Carrots	h vs l tertile	0.7 (0.5–1.1)	Y	Y	Y
		Broccoli	h vs l quartile	0.7 (0.4–1.3)	Y	Y	Y
		Tomatoes	h vs l tertile	1.0 (0.6–1.6)	Y	Y	Y

* p ≤ 0.05 for trend or as compared with lowest consumption level
na not available
a Also adjusted for one or more of the following: residence, histological type, energy intake
b Squamous and small cell carcinoma
c Seventh-day Adventists
Note: This table includes any data available from the original study article on: vegetables and fruit (combined), vegetables (as a whole), fruits (as a whole), raw vegetables (as a whole), cruciferous vegetables, allium vegetables, green vegetables, citrus fruits, carrots or tomatoes. Any data on other vegetable or fruit items were not selected for the table

studies have examined vegetables as a whole; in seven of these, the highest consumers were found to have about 10–60% the risk of lung cancer of the lowest consumers. Six cohort and ten case-control studies have examined fruits as a whole, with 11 studies showing persons with the highest intakes to have about 30–70% the risk of those with the lowest intakes. Green vegetables and carrots are the specific types of vegetables which have the most available and consistent evidence. Sixteen cohort or case-control studies have examined green vegetable consumption, with ten showing the highest consumers to have about 30–60% the risk of the lowest consumers. For carrots, nine of eleven studies have found the highest consumers to have about 10–60% the risk of the lowest consumers. The majority of eight studies that examined cruciferous vegetables, either as a whole or as individual types, also found strong or moderate decreases in risk at the highest consumption levels.

In all of the lung cancer cohort and case-control studies, the fruit and vegetable associations were appropriately adjusted for cigarette smoking (see Tables 4.5.4 and 4.5.5). This reduces the possibility of observing a false protective association with vegetable and fruit consumption as a result of non-smokers consuming more vegetables and fruits than smokers, a phenomenon that has been documented in various populations (Morabia and Wynder, 1990; McPhillips et al, 1994).

One recent study examined the relationship of vegetable and fruit intake to cancer prognosis and survival in women who already had lung cancer: those who had eaten more vegetables and fruits before diagnosis had longer survival times than those who had eaten less (Goodman et al, 1992).

Experimental studies, which included orange or lemon oil in the diets of mice, have resulted in a reduction of over 80% in the yield of NNK-induced lung tumours (Wattenberg and Coccia, 1991). Another study showed that inclusion of 10–40% cabbage in the diets of mice resulted in increased activity of glutathione-S-transferase in lung tissue, as well as of other enzymes thought to be involved in the deactivation or excretion of potential carcinogens (Ansher et al, 1986).

Seven cohort and 17 case-control studies are almost entirely consistent with a protective effect of vegetables and fruits against lung cancer. The evidence is most abundant for green vegetables and carrots.

The evidence that diets high in vegetables and fruits decrease the risk of lung cancer is convincing.

4.5.2.3 Pulses (legumes)
One cohort study of lung cancer in Norway reported a decreased risk with greater intake of beans (RR = 0.4; ns); no association was found for peas (Kvåle et al, 1983).

A case-control study of lung cancer in Yunnan Province in China reported a strong decrease in risk with increased consumption of bean curd (OR = 0.4, p < 0.01 for trend for consumption more than 15.9 times per month versus fewer than

8.0) (Swanson et al, 1992). Another study in Hong Kong reported an increased risk for pulses, but a decreased risk for tofu and soy products (ORs = 1.7, ns and 0.3, 0.1–1.1, respectively) (Koo, 1988). A case-control study in Hawaii showed no material associations for peanut consumption (for men, OR = 1.1; for women, OR = 0.8, for more than 33 g/week, vs zero) (Goodman et al, 1992).

The evidence regarding pulses and the risk of lung cancer is limited, inconsistent and is not specific for any particular type of pulses; no judgement is possible.

4.5.2.4 Meat, poultry, fish and eggs
Fish
Only three epidemiological studies of lung cancer have examined intake of fish consumption. (Fatty fish are a main source of omega-3 fatty acids.) A cohort study in Norwegian men reported no statistically significant association between fish consumption and the risk of lung cancer (Kvåle et al, 1983). A case-control study in Hawaii reported no association in men (OR = 1.2, 0.7–2.0), but suggested a decreased risk in women with higher fish consumption (OR = 0.5, 0.2–1.4) (Goodman et al, 1992).

An international ecological study has shown a weak inverse correlation between consumption of omega-3 fatty acids from fish and lung cancer incidence (r = –0.3; ns) (Hursting et al, 1990).

The evidence relating to diets high in fish and the risk of lung cancer is too limited and non-specific to support any conclusion; no judgement is possible.

4.5.2.5 Coffee, tea and other drinks
Coffee
At least three cohort studies have examined the relationship between coffee drinking and lung cancer. One cohort study of Japanese men in Hawaii, which involved 110 cases of lung cancer, observed an increase in risk with higher coffee intake that became much weaker when adjusted for cigarette smoking (OR = 1.4 for five or more cups per day; p = 0.19 for trend) (Nomura et al, 1986). Another cohort study of men in the USA, which included 219 deaths from lung cancer after 20 years of follow-up, reported higher rates of lung cancer mortality in those who had consumed more coffee (smoking-adjusted RR = 2.4, 1.4–4.2, for more than six cups per day, compared with less than three). This association was confined almost entirely to current cigarette smokers and was not observed within ex- or non-smokers; consistent with the possibility of residual confounding by smoking (Chow et al, 1992). A third study among Norwegian men reported no association, after adjustment for cigarette smoking (Jacobsen et al, 1986).

A case-control study of lung cancer in New York (USA) reported no substantial association for regular coffee intake; intake of decaffeinated coffee was associated with a statistically significantly lower risk, which the authors thought

TABLE 4.5.5 VEGETABLE AND FRUIT CONSUMPTION AND THE RISK OF LUNG CANCER: CASE-CONTROL STUDIES

AUTHOR, YEAR, AND PLACE	NO. OF CASES	TYPE OF VEGETABLE OR FRUIT	COMPARISON (HIGHEST VS LOWEST QUANTILES)	ODDS RATIO (95% CONFIDENCE INTERVAL)	SEX/AGE	ADJUSTMENT SMOKING HISTORY	OTHER VARIABLES[a]
McLennan, 1977 Singapore	233	Vegetable index	h vs l index	0.4 (0.3–0.7)	Y	Y	Y
Mettlin, 1979 Buffalo, USA	292 men	Carrots	h vs l half	0.5* (na)	Y	Y	Y
Ziegler et al, 1986 New Jersey, USA	763 men	Vegetables	h vs l quartile	0.7* (0.5–1.0)	Y	Y	Y
		Green vegetables	h vs l quartile	0.7* (na)	Y	Y	Y
		Fruit	h vs l quartile	1.0 (na)	Y	Y	Y
Pisani et al, 1986 Lombardy, Italy	417	Carrots	h vs l quartile	0.3* (0.2–0.6)	Y	Y	Y
		Leafy green vegetables	h vs l quintile	0.8 (na)	Y	Y	Y
Bond et al, 1987 Texas, USA	308 men	Tomatoes	h vs l septile	0.4* (0.1–1.3)	Y	Y	Y
		Green vegetables	h vs l septile	0.5 (0.2–1.3)	Y	Y	Y
		Cruciferous vegetables	h vs l sextile	0.3* (0.0–3.3)	Y	Y	Y
		Carrots	h vs l septile	0.3* (0.1–1.2)	Y	Y	Y
Koo, 1988 Hong Kong	88 women[b]	Cruciferous vegetables	h vs l tertile	0.8 (na)[c]	Y	Y	Y
		Fresh leafy green vegetables	h vs l tertile	0.3 (0.1–1.0)	Y	Y	Y
		Carrots	h vs l tertile	0.1 (0.0–1.4)	Y	Y	Y
		Fresh fruit	h vs l tertile	0.6* (na)	Y	Y	Y
Fontham et al 1988, Louisiana, USA	1,253	Fruit	h vs l tertile	0.7* (0.5–0.9)	Y	Y	Y
		Vegetables	h vs l tertile	0.8 (0.6–1.0)	Y	Y	Y
		Fruit and vegetables	h vs l tertile	0.7* (0.6–0.9)	Y	Y	Y
		Carrots	h vs l tertile	0.6 (0.5–0.7)	Y	Y	Y
		Broccoli	h vs l tertile	0.6 (0.5–0.8)	Y	Y	Y
Le Marchand et al 1989, Hawaii, USA	230 men	Carrots	h vs l quartile	0.4* (na)	Y	Y	Y
		Tomatoes	h vs l quartile	0.4* (na)	Y	Y	Y
		Dark green vegetables	h vs l quartile	0.5* (na)	Y	Y	Y
		Cruciferous vegetables	h vs l quartile	0.5* (na)	Y	Y	Y
		Vegetables	h vs l quartile	0.4* (na)	Y	Y	Y
	102 women	Carrots	h vs l quartile	0.4* (na)	Y	Y	Y
		Tomatoes	h vs l quartile	0.3* (na)	Y	Y	Y
		Dark green vegetables	h vs l quartile	0.3* (na)	Y	Y	Y
		Cruciferous vegetables	h vs l quartile	0.2* (na)	Y	Y	Y
		Vegetables	h vs l quartile	0.1* (na)	Y	Y	Y
Mettlin, 1989 Buffalo, USA	569	Raw carrots	h vs l quartile	0.4 (0.3–0.7)	Y	Y	Y
		Raw broccoli	h vs l quartile	0.3 (0.2–0.6)	Y	Y	Y
		Spinach	h vs l quartile	0.6 (0.4–1.0)	Y	Y	Y
Jain et al, 1990 Toronto, Canada	839	Vegetables	h vs l quartile	0.6* (0.4–0.9)	Y	Y	N
		Fruit	h vs l quartile	1.1 (na)	Y	Y	N
Kalandidi et al 1990, Athens, Greece	160 women[b]	Vegetables	h vs l quartile	1.1 (0.4–2.7)	Y	Y	Y
		Fruit	h vs l quartile	0.3* (0.1–0.9)	Y	Y	Y

might be indicative of a healthier lifestyle in general among the controls (Mettlin, 1989).

The data regarding coffee drinking and lung cancer are limited; two of four analytical epidemiological studies have shown weak to strong increases in risk with higher consumption, after adjustment for cigarette smoking, although the possibility of residual confounding by smoking remains.

The evidence relating to high intakes of coffee and the risk of lung cancer is too limited to support any conclusion; no judgement is possible.

Tea

A prospective study of lung cancer among women in the USA found no association between tea consumption and risk of

lung cancer (RR = 1.1, 0.7–1.6) for two or more cups per day versus fewer than one per month) (Zheng et al, 1996). In a study of men and women in the Netherlands, which included 764 cases of lung cancer, tea consumption was initially associated with a moderate decrease in lung cancer risk, although this association disappeared after adjustment for cigarette smoking and several other factors; the relative risks before and after adjustment were 0.6 (p < 0.001 for trend) and 1.1 (0.7–1.6), respectively, for five or more cups per day, as compared with non-consumption (Goldbohm et al, 1996). In a third cohort of London men, an increased risk with greater tea consumption appeared to be mainly or entirely attributable to confounding by smoking (Kinlen et al, 1988).

International ecological studies have shown statistically significant positive correlations between lung cancer mortality or incidence and tea consumption in women (Stocks,

Author, year, and place	No. of cases	Type of vegetable or fruit	Comparison (highest vs lowest quantiles)	Odds ratio (95% confidence interval)	Sex/age	Adjustment Smoking history	Other variables[a]
Harris et al, 1991 Oxford, UK	96 men	Carrots	h vs l tertile	0.7 (na)	Y	Y	N
		Tomatoes	h vs l tertile	0.7 (na)	Y	Y	N
		Green vegetables	h vs l tertile	1.1 (na)	Y	Y	N
		Vegetable and fruit[d]	h vs l tertile	0.5 (na)	Y	Y	N
Swanson et al China	425 men	Dark green leafy vegetables	h vs l quartile	0.4* (na)	Y	Y	Y
		Tomatoes	h vs l quartile	0.7 (na)	Y	Y	Y
		Any fresh fruit	h vs l quartile	0.9 (na)	Y	Y	Y
		Oranges	h vs l quartile	0.7* (na)	Y	Y	Y
Candelora et al 1992, Florida, USA	124 women[b]	Vegetables	h vs l quartile	0.2* (0.1–0.5)	Y	Y	Y
		Green and yellow vegetables	h vs l quartile	0.4* (0.2–0.7)	Y	Y	Y
		Carrots	h vs l half	0.4 (0.2–0.6)	Y	Y	Y
		Tomatoes	h vs l half	0.7 (0.4–1.0)	Y	Y	Y
		Fruit	h vs l quartile	0.6* (0.3–1.1)	Y	Y	Y
		Citrus fruit	h vs l quartile	0.6 (0.3–1.1)	Y	Y	Y
Gao, 1993 Tokai, Japan		Raw vegetables	daily vs almost none/ sometimes	0.6 (0.4–1.0)		Y	
		Green vegetables	daily vs almost none/ sometimes	0.4 (0.3–0.7)		Y	
		Cabbage	≤ 3/wk vs almost none	0.4 (0.2–0.9)		Y	
		Fruit	daily vs almost none/ sometimes	0.5 (0.3–0.7)		Y	
Dorgan et al, 1993 New Jersey, USA	1,951[e]	Vegetables	h vs l tertile	0.7* (0.6–0.9)	Y	Y	Y
		Fruit	h vs l tertile	0.9 (0.7–1.1)	Y	Y	Y
Mayne et al, 1994 New York, USA	413[b]	Tomatoes	h vs l quartile	0.8 (na)	Y	Y	Y
		Greens	h vs l quartile	0.4* (na)[f]	Y	Y	Y
		Fresh fruit	h vs l quartile	0.4* (na)[f]	Y	Y	Y
		Raw vegetables	na	0.6 (0.4–1.0)	Y	Y	Y

* p ≤ 0.05 for trend or as compared with lowest consumption level
[na] not available
[a] Also adjusted for one or more of the following: education, vitamin supplements, live births, socio-economic status, dialect group, residence, race, ethnic group, income, respondent status, cholesterol intake, study site, total calories, occupation, study phase, religion, body mass index, total energy intake, interviewer
[b] Never smokers
[c] Adenocarcinoma plus large cell carcinoma
[d] Carotene-rich
[e] Includes surrogate interviews
[f] CI includes 1.0
Note: This table includes any data available from the original study article on: vegetables plus fruit (combined), vegetables (as a whole), fruits (as a whole), raw vegetables (as a whole), cruciferous vegetables, allium vegetables, green vegetables, citrus fruits, carrots, or tomatoes. Any data on other vegetable or fruit items were not selected for the table

1970; Armstrong and Doll, 1975).

In an experimental study, compounds in green tea have been shown to inhibit lung tumorigenesis induced by nitrosamines, perhaps via an antioxidant action (Chung et al, 1993). In another study, mice given decaffeinated green or black tea developed fewer lung tumours induced by NNK, a potent carcinogen in tobacco.

Three cohort studies have shown no effect of tea drinking on the risk of lung cancer, independent of the effect of smoking. Evidence relating to high tea consumption and the risk of lung cancer is limited; no judgement is possible.

4.6 Stomach

Cancer of the stomach is the second most common incident cancer and cause of cancer mortality, throughout the world. An estimated 1 million cases occurred in 1996, accounting for 10% of all new cases of cancer.

Incidence of, and deaths from, this cancer are generally decreasing throughout the world, most of all in the developed world. Stomach cancer is one of the two major cancers, the risk of which is commonly agreed to be modified mainly by food and nutrition.

The panel has reached the following conclusions. The evidence that diets high in vegetables and fruits protect against stomach cancer is convincing. The evidence that refrigeration protects against this cancer (by facilitating year-round consumption of vegetables and fruits and probably by reducing need for salt as a preservative) is also convincing. Vitamin C, contained in vegetables and fruits and other foods of plant origin, is probably protective.

Diets high in salt, added in manufacture and at table and in the form of

FOOD, NUTRITION AND STOMACH CANCER

In the judgement of the panel, the dietary constituents and related factors, the foods and drinks, and the methods of food processing listed below modify the risk of stomach cancer, or else have no relationship with it. Judgements are graded according to the strength of the evidence.

EVIDENCE	DECREASES RISK	NO RELATIONSHIP	INCREASES RISK
Convincing	Vegetables and fruits[a] Refrigeration[b]		
Probable	Vitamin C	Alcohol[c] Coffee Black tea Nitrates[e]	Salt Salting
Possible	Carotenoids Allium compounds Wholegrain cereals Green tea	Sugar Vitamin E Retinol	Starch[d] Grilled/barbecued meat and fish
Insufficient	Fibre Selenium Garlic		Cured meats N-nitrosamines

For an explanation of the terms used in the matrix, see chapter 3.

[a] In particular, the evidence is most abundant or consistent for raw vegetables, allium vegetables and citrus fruits.

[b] Indirectly, by reducing the use of salt and the risk of contamination.

[c] Alcohol is probably not related to stomach cancer as a whole, but may possibly increase risk of cancer of the gastric cardia specifically.

[d] See Boxes 5.2.1 and 5.2.2. for a discussion of starch and low micronutrient agrarian diets.

[e] From vegetables.

salted foods, probably increase the risk of stomach cancer.

The panel notes that diets high in wholegrain cereals, carotenoids, and allium compounds, and also green tea, possibly reduce the risk of this cancer; that regular consumption of meat or fish cooked by methods using direct flame possibly increase risk; and that alcohol possibly increases the risk of cancer of the gastric cardia.

The evidence suggests that monotonous diets very high in starchy foods possibly increase the risk of stomach cancer. It is concluded that this is probably because such diets are deficient in protective dietary constituents.

Regular consumption of coffee and black tea probably does not affect the risk of stomach cancer; likewise, alcohol does not affect risk, other than cancer of the gastric cardia.

An important established non-dietary cause of stomach cancer, is infection with the *Helicobacter pylori* bacterium, either independently or by interaction with dietary factors.

The most effective means of preventing stomach cancer is consumption of diets high in vegetables and fruits, and low in salt; and use of refrigeration for perishable foods, industrially and domestically.

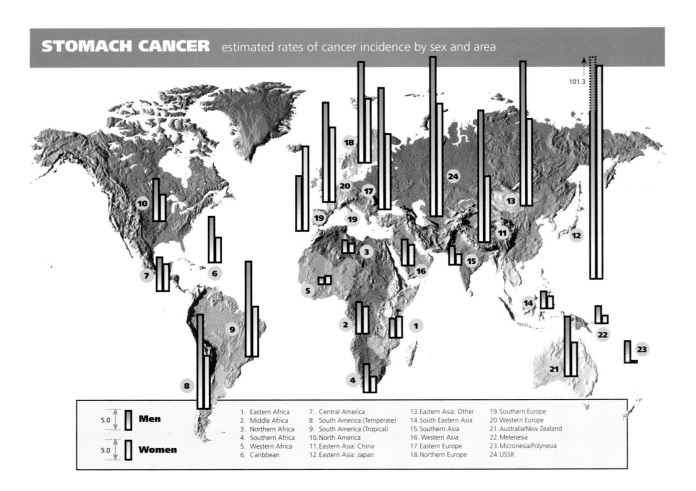

STOMACH CANCER estimated rates of cancer incidence by sex and area

101.3

5.0	**Men**
5.0	**Women**

1. Eastern Africa
2. Middle Africa
3. Northern Africa
4. Southern Africa
5. Western Africa
6. Caribbean
7. Central America
8. South America (Temperate)
9. South America (Tropical)
10. North America
11. Eastern Asia: China
12. Eastern Asia: Japan
13. Eastern Asia: Other
14. South Eastern Asia
15. Southern Asia
16. Western Asia
17. Eastern Europe
18. Northern Europe
19. Southern Europe
20. Western Europe
21. Australia/New Zealand
22. Melenesia
23. Micronesia/Polynesia
24. USSR

INTRODUCTION

INCIDENCE PATTERNS

Cancer of the stomach is the second most common cancer in the world. In 1996, it is estimated that there were over 1 million new cases diagnosed worldwide (WHO, 1997), accounting for nearly 10% of all new cancers.

Nearly two-thirds of all cases occur in developing countries, amounting to 639,000 cases in 1996. World statistics on stomach cancer mortality and incidence show a distinct geographical variation (Aoki et al, 1992; Parkin et al, 1992). The highest rates are found in Japan, Central and South America, and eastern Asia. In developed countries, rates have steadily declined, with Australia, Canada and the USA having the lowest rates. A reversal of this trend is, however, seen with cancers localised to the cardia (the upper part of the stomach).

Overall, stomach cancer rates are 50% lower in women (379,000 new cases in 1996) than in men (634,000 new cases in 1996) (Aoki et al, 1992; Parkin et al, 1992; WHO, 1997).

Migrants from high- to low-risk countries or areas, tend to maintain the high-risk characteristic of the population of origin, whereas the offspring acquire a risk closer to those of the host countries (Mirvish, 1983; Howson et al, 1986). Low socioeconomic status is consistently shown to be associated with high risk (Mirvish, 1983; Howson et al, 1986).

Survival in stomach cancer patients is poor, with a five-year survival rate of up to 20%. This figure improves to 60% if the tumour is localised to the stomach; however, very few cases are diagnosed at this stage (about 18%) due to the non-specific nature of the symptoms. In 1996, mortality attributable to stomach cancer was estimated at 835,000 people, 11.8% of all cancer deaths (WHO, 1997).

PATHOGENESIS

It is generally agreed that the chief factors affecting stomach cancer risk are environmental and, in particular, dietary.

Of non-dietary factors, *Helicobacter pylori* infection has recently been identified as an important cause of stomach cancer, as a result of the consistent association between the infection and stomach cancer, especially in prospective cohort studies (Forman, 1991). However, *H. pylori* infection in itself does not seem to be sufficient to cause stomach cancer, because the prevalence rates reach as high as 40–60% in several adult populations at low risk of stomach cancer, unlike the cancer itself, and show no difference between men and women (Forman, 1991; Eurogast Study Group, 1993).

As reviewed elsewhere (US Surgeon General, 1982) prospective cohort studies have consistently observed a small excess risk of stomach cancer among smokers compared with non-smokers, with a dose-response relationship in some studies. Recent studies have provided further support to the contention that cigarette smoking is a risk factor (Kono et al, 1987; Nomura et al, 1990; Kneller et al, 1991; Kato et al, 1992).

Correa (1988, 1992) has proposed a multistage model of gastric carcinogenesis, according to which different dietary and non-dietary factors are involved at different stages in the cancer process.

Several lines of evidence suggest that the precancerous lesions including chronic atrophic gastritis and intestinal metaplasia closely correlate with the geographical variation of stomach cancer. Chronic atrophic gastritis is known to confer an increased risk of stomach cancer. Metaplastic lesions surround carcinomas of the intestinal type, and small carcinomas arise in the metaplastic lesions. The following sequence is proposed by Correa (1988): normal mucosa; superficial gastritis; chronic atrophic gastritis; intestinal metaplasia; dysplasia, and carcinoma.

H. pylori infection and excessive salt intake are implicated in development of superficial gastritis and chronic atrophic gastritis. Salt may also exert a promoting effect at later stages. Carotenoids and other dietary components with antioxident capacity may suppress the progression from atrophic gastritis to carcinoma. Nitrosation (Correa 1988) and the formation of carcinogenic *N*-nitroso compounds (Mirvish 1983)may or may not be relevant to the process(Forman, 1991).

JUDGEMENTS OF OTHER REPORTS

The National Academy of Sciences report, *Diet, Nutrition and Cancer* (NAS, 1982) summarised evidence which suggested that raw vegetables, vitamin C and milk protect against stomach cancer, and that frequent consumption of smoked and salt-pickled foods and foods containing nitrates and nitrites might increase risk. The subsequent report, *Diet and Health* (NAS, 1989), identified low levels of consumption of fresh vegetables and fruits, and also intakes of large amounts of salt-preserved foods, as increasing risk of stomach cancer, concluding that 'dietary shifts away from this pattern could explain the great decline in stomach cancer mortality in the United States over the past 50 years'. This conclusion was repeated in the 1990 report *Diet, Nutrition and the Prevention of Chronic Diseases* (WHO, 1990).

BOX 4.6.1 ESTABLISHED NON-DIETARY FACTORS AND STOMACH CANCER

The following non-dietary factor increases the risk of stomach cancer:

■ Bacterial infection: *Helicobacter pylori*

4.6.1 DIETARY CONSTITUENTS

4.6.1.1 Carbohydrate

Total carbohydrate

Seven case-control studies and one cohort study have investigated the relationship between total carbohydrate consumption and stomach cancer; some have adjusted for total calorie intake (Buiatti et al, 1990; Ramon et al, 1993; Gonzalez et al, 1994; Hansson et al, 1994) or total food consumption (Risch et al, 1985) whereas others have not (Correa et al, 1985; Graham et al, 1990; Kneller et al, 1991). Risk estimates in these eight studies ranged from 0.6 to 1.6 for the uppermost consumption levels. The one prospective cohort study reported moderately increased risk with higher total carbohydrate intake, with an energy-unadjusted relative risk of 1.6 (< 0.05) for the uppermost consumption quartile (Kneller et al, 1991). Of five case-control studies with adjustment for total calorie or food intake, two found statistically significant moderate increases in risk (Risch et al, 1985; Ramon et al, 1993), two showed statistically significant (Hansson et al, 1994) or non-significant (Gonzalez et al, 1994) weak decreases in risk, and one study found virtually no association (Buiatti et al, 1990). Of two case-control studies not allowing for total calorie intake, one study found a statistically significant weak increase in risk with total carbohydrate consumption (Graham et al, 1990), and the other showed no material association (Correa et al, 1985).

The panel has decided that studies of total carbohydrate intake are unlikely to be meaningful, as a result of the important distinctions between different types of carbohydrates, especially starches and sugars. Therefore, the panel has decided to make no judgement on carbohydrate as such. Individual judgements are made in the following sections for starch, sugar and fibre.

Starch

Not all studies of carbohydrate consumption and stomach cancer have distinguished between different types of carbohydrate. Three case-control studies have estimated the consumption of starch, as separate from total carbohydrates, in southern Europe (Buiatti et al, 1990; Ramon et al, 1993) and the USA (Graham et al, 1990). Each of these studies observed a weak to moderate increase in risk with higher starch intake (ORs ranging from 1.3–1.6) these findings were statistically significant in two studies.

Some studies have examined starch-rich foods, rather than starch as such. As described in section 4.6.2.1 on cereals, at least 18 case-control studies of stomach cancer have examined intakes of various cereals or cereal-based products (Hirayama, 1971; Haenszel et al, 1972; Bjelke, 1974; Modan et al, 1974; Haenszel et al, 1976; Correa et al, 1985; Risch et al, 1985; Trichopoulos et al, 1985; La Vecchia et al, 1987; Kono et al 1988; You et al, 1988; Buiatti et al, 1989; Demirer

et al, 1990; Boeing et al, 1991; Gonzalez et al, 1991; Tuyns et al, 1992; Hansson et al, 1993; Ramon et al, 1993). Seven of eight studies that have examined broad food categories entitled 'cereals', 'grains', or 'starchy foods' have found weak to strong increases in risk with higher consumption (Bjelke, 1974; Modan et al, 1974; Risch et al, 1985; Trichopoulos et al, 1985; Demirer et al, 1990; Tuyns et al, 1992; Ramon et al, 1993). The evidence for specific cereals, or cereal-based products, such as rice, bread, or pasta, is less abundant and generally inconsistent. The only consistent evidence is with regard to wholegrain bread, for which the data support a possible protective effect against stomach cancer. For tubers and plantains, starchy foods that play a significant role in some diets, no judgement is possible regarding an effect on stomach cancer risk, because of very limited evidence (see section 4.6.2.2 on tubers and plantains).

It has been suggested that high-starch diets might cause damage to the gastric mucosa, but there is no experimental evidence to this effect (Howson et al, 1986). It has also been suggested that high-starch diets might be a factor in increased nitrosation and decreased mucous production because of their generally low protein content (Mirvish, 1983).

There is good evidence (see chapter 5.2) that a high starch intake is associated with increased risk of a number of cancers, not because of starch as such, but because high-starch diets eaten in impoverished regions may be deficient in a number of protective microconstituents. This does not, however account completely for the association between a high starch intake and stomach cancer in southern European countries.

Diets high in starch possibly increase the risk of stomach cancer. It is likely that this applies to starch in refined form.

Non-starch polysaccharides/dietary fibre

Five case-control studies of stomach cancer have reported on fibre intake. Two studies, in Canada (Risch et al, 1985) and Spain (Gonzalez et al, 1994), reported statistically significant decreases in risk with higher fibre intake, with total energy-adjusted or food-adjusted odds ratios of 0.4 in each. The three other studies, in Italy (Buiatti et al, 1990), Spain (Ramon et al, 1993), and Sweden (Hansson et al, 1994), reported no statistically significant associations. As discussed in section 4.6.2.1 on wholegrain cereals, wholegrain cereal products, which are fibre-rich foods, have been consistently associated with moderate to strong decreases in risk in several case-control studies (Trichopoulos et al, 1985; La Vecchia et al, 1987; Boeing et al, 1991; Tuyns et al, 1992; Hansson et al 1993).

Evidence suggests that diets high in fibre may decrease the risk of stomach cancer, but are as yet insufficient.

Sugar

One case-control study in Spain (Ramon et al, 1993) found an almost null association between simple carbohydrate consumption and the risk of stomach cancer. Seven case-control studies have addressed the relationship between sugar-rich products or sugar use and the risk of stomach cancer. Statistically significant increases in risk were found with higher consumption of sugar-rich products in Greece (Trichopoulos et al, 1985) and sugar use in Italy (La Vecchia, 1987), but the increase disappeared after adjustment for other dietary factors in both studies. A significant increase in risk also was observed for sweets in American blacks, but not in whites (Correa et al, 1985) and for oligosaccharide-rich products in Belgium (Tuyns et al, 1992). However, it is unclear whether these associations were independent of other dietary factors. One study in Canada (Risch et al, 1985) reported an increase in risk associated with chocolate consumption, independent of other dietary factors. Two studies, in Germany (Boeing et al, 1991) and Spain (Gonzalez et al, 1991), observed no material association between sugar-rich foods and stomach cancer.

These somewhat inconsistent data suggest that diets high in sugar possibly have no relationship with the risk of stomach cancer.

4.6.1.2 Protein

Total protein

Four case-control studies of stomach cancer have reported on total protein intake. Two studies in Italy (Buiatti et al, 1990) and the USA (Graham et al, 1990) demonstrated statistically significant increases in risk with higher total protein intake. In the former study, in which adjustment for total energy intake was performed, the increase in risk was strongest for cancer of the gastric cardia (Palli et al, 1992). The two other studies, in Spain (Ramon et al, 1993) and Sweden (Hanisson et al, 1994), found no statistically significant associations; adjustment for total energy intake was undertaken in the latter study.

The panel has decided that studies of total protein are unlikely to be meaningful because of the differences between the different types of protein. Therefore, the panel decided to make no judgement on total protein.

Animal protein

Three case-control studies of stomach cancer have specifically examined animal protein; the findings vary. One study in Italy (Buiatti et al, 1990) reported a strong increase in risk with animal, but not vegetable protein; adjustment for total energy intake was undertaken. When a subsite analysis was conducted within this study, a strong increase in risk was observed with higher animal protein intake for cancer of the gastric cardia (OR= 2.6, 1.2–5.8, for the uppermost quintile of intake) (Palli et al, 1992). A second study in Spain (Gonzalez et al, 1944) found no substantial association

(OR=1.4; ns; p for trend) after adjustment for total energy intake. A third study, in Spain (Ramon et al, 1993), also reported finding no association; no adjustment for total energy intake was made.

Kolonel et al (1981) found an increased risk of stomach cancer with higher intake of fish protein in Hawaii in a multi-ethnic correlation study, but this was thought to be a reflection of exposure to salted fish.

The evidence relating to diets high in animal protein and the risk of stomach cancer is limited; no judgement is possible.

Plant protein

The three case-control studies of stomach cancer mentioned in the previous section also examined vegetable protein intakes. The study in Spain reported a protective association (OR = 0.5, p<0.10 for trend for the uppermost quartile)(Gonzalez et al, 1994). The study in Italy reported no association for stomach cancer as a whole (Buiatti et al, 1990) but a moderate protective association for cancer at a specific subsite, the gastric cardia, (OR=0.5, 0.2–1.2 for the uppermost quintile of vegetable protein intake) (Palli et al, 1992). Each of these studies adjusted for total energy intake. The remaining study, in Spain, reported no association for vegetable protein and there was no adjustment for total energy intake (Ramon et al, 1993).

The evidence relating to diets high in plant protein and the risk of stomach cancer is limited; no judgement is possible.

4.6.1.3 Alcohol

In 1988, an IARC Working Group reviewed 12 case-control and 13 cohort studies, including those involving alcoholics and brewery workers, as well as those based on a general population; they concluded that there was 'little in the aggregate data to suggest a causal role for drinking of alcoholic beverages in stomach cancer'(IARC, 1988). Since that time, many more studies have been conducted.

Six population-based prospective studies of stomach cancer that have examined alcohol consumption are presented in Table 4.6.1. Two of these studies showed statistically significant increases in risk; the numbers of cases in these studies were small (Gordon et al, 1984; Kato et al, 1992). The remaining four studies showed no substantial association.

Reviewing six cohort studies of alcoholics and two cohort studies of brewery workers, the IARC Working Group (IARC, 1988) noted that the overall observed number of stomach cancer cases in these cohorts was 234, in comparison with 251 expected cases. In a subsequent cohort study of alcoholics in Sweden (Adami et al, 1992) the observed number of cases was 23, in comparison with 25 expected. Thus, there was no excess in stomach cancer incidence within these cohorts.

Twenty-six case-control studies that have examined alcohol intake are presented in Table 4.6.2; studies that exam-

TABLE 4.6.1 ALCOHOL CONSUMPTION AND STOMACH CANCER RISK: COHORT STUDIES

AUTHOR, YEAR AND PLACE	SIZE OF COHORT: NO. OF CASES	COMPARISON (HIGHEST VS LOWEST QUANTILE)	RELATIVE RISK (95% CONFIDENCE INTERVAL)	ADJUSTMENT SEX/AGE	OTHER VARIABLES[a]
Gordon et al, 1984 Framingham, Mass, USA	5,209: 28	na	positive assoc*	Y	Y
Kono et al, 1986, Japan	5,135 male physicians: 151	h vs l quintile	1.1 (0.6–2.1)	Y	N
Kneller et al, 1991, USA	17,633 white men[b]: 75	na	no assoc	Y	Y
Kato et al, 1992, Japan	9,753: 57	h vs l quartile	3.1 (1.4–6.9)	Y	N
Nomura, 1995, Hawaii, USA	8,006 men[c]: 250	h vs l quintile	1.2 (0.8–1.8)	Y	Y
Zheng et al, 1995, Iowa, USA	41,837 women[d]: 26	h vs l tertile	0.8 (0.3–2.2)	Y	Y

* $p \leq 0.05$ for trend or as compared with lowest consumption level
na not available
a Also adjusted for one or more of the following: smoking history, education, blood pressure, weight, lipo-proteins
b German and Scandinavian origin
c Japanese origin
d Post-menopausal women

ined only consumption of individual alcohol beverages, without mention of total alcohol intake, are not included. Seventeen of these studies show no material association between alcohol intake and risk of stomach cancer (Higginson, 1966; Graham et al, 1972; Haenszel et al, 1972; Bjelke, 1974a,b; Risch et al, 1985; La Vecchia et al, 1987; You et al, 1988; Buiatti et al, 1990; Kato et al, 1990; Agudo et al, 1992; Hoshiyama and Sasaba, 1992; Memik et al, 1992; Palli et al, 1992; Ramon et al, 1993; Hansson et al, 1994; Lee et al, 1995). Two studies, in the USA and France have shown statistically significant increases in risk with higher consumption (OR = 3.0 and 6.9, respectively, for the highest consumption levels) (Wu-Williams et al, 1990; Hoey et al, 1981); three further studies in the USA showed statistically significant increases in risk within particular subgroups, including blacks and men with adenocarcinoma of the cardia (Correa et al, 1985; Kabat et al, 1993; Vaughan et al, 1995). Two other studies reported weaker increases in risk that were not statistically significant (or statistical significance was not reported), (OR = 1.5 for the highest consumption quartile and OR = 4.9 for the highest consumption tertile) (Trichopoulos et al, 1985; Gonzalez et al, 1994). The two remaining studies showed decreased risk with higher consumption (Hu et al, 1988; Demirer et al, 1990).

Recent case-control studies have suggested a specific effect of alcohol on cancer of the gastric cardia. In the USA (Wu-Williams et al, 1990), a strong increase in risk of cancer of the gastric cardia was noted with higher alcohol consumption. Specific increases in cardia cancer risk with alcohol drinking were further noted in Italy (Palli et al, 1992) and Spain (Gonzalez et al, 1994). In Poland, heavy vodka drinking was found to be associated with an increased risk of cancer of the cardia, especially in smokers, as well as of non-cardia gastric cancer (Jedrychowski et al 1993). Three case-control studies in the USA (Kabat et al, 1993; Brown et al, 1994; Vaughan et al, 1995) have consistently shown that high alcohol consumption is associated with increased risk of adenocarcinoma of the oesophagus and gastric cardia combined.

A large number of cohort and case-control studies have investigated the relationship between alcohol and stomach cancer; the majority have found no association.

High consumption of alcohol probably has no relationship with the risk of stomach cancer.

However, recently accumulated evidence, including at least seven case-control studies, suggests that alcohol consumption possibly increases the risk of cancer of the gastric cardia.

4.6.1.4 Vitamins
Carotenoids

Two prospective cohort studies have examined carotenoid intake in relation to the risk of stomach cancer. One study of Japanese men in Hawaii reported a 37% lower (p = 0.15) intake of β-carotene and a 36 % lower (p = 0.11) intake of other carotenoids in those who developed stomach cancer (N = 111), than in those who remained cancer-free (N = 361) (Chyou et al, 1990). In the prospective Iowa Women's Health Study, in which 26 incident cases of stomach cancer were observed among about 35,000 women during 7 years of follow-up, relative risks of 0.6 and 0.3 were noted for the second and third tertiles of carotenoid intake, respectively, as compared with the lowest tertile (trend p < 0.05) (Zheng et al, 1995).

Eight case-control studies have examined dietary carotenoids in relation to the risk of stomach cancer. Six of these studies, in Canada, Italy, China, Spain and Sweden, have shown a statistically significant decrease in risk with higher intake (ORs = 0.3 to 0.6) (Risch et al, 1985; La Vecchia et al, 1987; You et al, 1988; Buiatti et al, 1990; Ramon et al, 1993, Hansson et al, 1994); one study in Germany reported no association (Boeing et al, 1991) and the remaining study in the USA reported odds ratios of 0.7 (0.4–1.1) for whites and 1.1 (0.7–1.7) for blacks separately

TABLE 4.6.2 ALCOHOL CONSUMPTION AND STOMACH CANCER RISK: CASE-CONTROL STUDIES

AUTHOR, YEAR AND PLACE	NO. OF CASES	COMPARISON (HIGHEST VS LOWEST QUANTILE)	ODDS RATIO (95% CONFIDENCE INTERVAL)	ADJUSTMENT SEX/AGE	OTHER VARIABLES[a]
Higginson, 1966, Kansas City, USA	93	na	no assoc	na	na
Haenszel et al, 1972, Hawaii, USA	220 Japanese	yes vs no	1.4 (na)	Y	Y
Graham et al, 1972, Buffalo, USA	160 men	na	no assoc	Y	Y
	68 women	na	no assoc	Y	Y
Bjelke, 1973, Norway	228	na	no assoc	na	na
Bjelke, 1973, Minnesota, USA	83	na	no assoc	na	na
Hoey et al, 1981, Lyon, France	40	na	6.9 (3.3–14.3)	na	na
Risch et al, 1985, Canada	246	na	no assoc	Y	Y
Correa et al, 1985, Louisiana, USA	189 whites	h vs l tertile	1.9 (1.0–3.4)	Y	Y
	187 blacks	h vs l tertile	2.2* (1.2–4.1)	Y	Y
Trichopoulos et al, 1985, Piraeus Greece	110	h vs l quartile	1.5 (na)	Y	Y
La Vecchia et al, 1987, Milano, Italy	206	h vs l tertile	1.2 (na)	Y	N
You et al, 1988, China	443	h vs l tertile	0.8 (0.6–1.1)	Y	Y
Hu et al, 1988, China	241	h vs l half	0.6 (0.4–0.9)	Y	Y
Wu-Williams et al, 1990 LA County, USA	137 men	h vs l quartile	3.0 (1.1–8.7)	Y	N
Kato et al, 1990, Japan	289 men	h vs l tertile	1.0 (0.7–1.4)	Y	Y
	138 women	h vs l tertile	0.7 (0.3–2.1)	Y	Y
Demirer et al, 1990, Ankara, Turkey	100	h vs l sextile	0.5 (na)	Y	Y
Buiatti et al, 1990, Italy	1,016	h vs l quintile	1.4 (1.0–1.9)	Y	Y
Agudo et al, 1992, Spain	234 men	h vs l quintile	1.2 (0.7–2.2)	Y	Y
	119 women	h vs l quartile	1.2 (0.3–6.3)	Y	Y
Memik et al, 1992, Turkey	252	h vs l quartile	0.9 (na)	Y	N
Palli et al, 1992, Italy	68[b]	h vs l quintile	1.4 (0.7–3.7)	Y	Y
Hoshiyama and Sasaba, 1992, Japan	294	h vs l quintile	1.0 (0.5–1.7)[c]	Y	Y
		h vs l quintile	1.3 (0.6–2.4)[d]	Y	Y
Kabat et al, 1993, USA	122 men[e]	h vs l quartile	0.7 (0.4–1.3)	Y	Y
	173 men[f]	h vs l quartile	2.3 (1.3–4.3)	Y	Y
	30 women[e]	h vs l quartile	0.9 (0.3–3.1)	Y	Y
	21 women[f]	h vs l quartile	3.8 (0.9–16.6)	Y	Y
Ramon et al, 1993, Barcelona, Spain	117	h vs l quartile	1.2 (0.7–2.9)	Y	Y
Hansson et al, 1994, Sweden	338	h vs l quartile	0.9 (0.6–1.4)[g]	Y	Y
Gonzales et al, 1994, Spain	29[h]	h vs l tertile	4.9 (0.7–36.3)	Y	Y
Lee et al, 1995, Korea	213	h vs l tertile	0.8 (0.4–1.5)	Y	Y
Vaughan et al, 1995 Washington State, USA	298[i]	h vs l quartile	1.8* (1.1–3.1)	Y	Y

* p ≤ 0.05 for trend or as compared with lowest consumption level

na not available

a Also adjusted for one or more of the following: ethnicity, socio-economic status, total food consumption, respondent status, income, smoking history, education, residence, study area, migration, family predisposition, total calorie intake, consumption of fruit, cooked vegetables, cold cuts and preserved fish, body mass index, race

b Gastric cardia cancer cases from Buiatti et al, (1990)

c Comparison with general population controls

d Comparison with hospital controls

e Adenocarcinoma of the distal stomach

f Adenocarcinoma of the cardia

g Twenty years before interview

h Gastric cardia cancer cases from Agudo et al, 1992

i Adenocarcinoma of the gastric cardia and oesophagus

(Correa et al, 1985).

Four prospective cohort studies have examined serum β-carotene in relation to subsequent risk of stomach cancer. In all four studies, after several years of follow-up, those who developed stomach cancer tended to have had lower levels of serum β-carotene at baseline than those who did not (Wald et al, 1988; Knekt et al, 1990; Stahelin et al, 1991; Nomura et al, 1995); in two studies, the difference was statistically significant. In a study of Swiss men, levels were 36% lower for cases (Stahelin et al, 1991); this was the only study in which blood samples were not stored, but were analysed immediately after collection, which is preferable to avoid degradation of carotenoids over time. In a study of Japanese men in Hawaii, a strong statistically significant protective association was reported (Nomura et al, 1995). In a study in Finland, levels were lower in cases for men (–10%)

but higher for cases for women (+28%) although for both sexes the differences were not statistically significant; this was the only study to involve women (Knekt et al, 1990).

A geographical correlation study in China reported inverse correlations between stomach cancer and serum levels of β-carotene (r = –0.24 in men and r = –0.20 in women) (Kneller et al, 1992).

Although several intervention trials using supplements have included β-carotene as part of a combination supplement (see Box 4.6.2), only two trials have examined the effects of β-carotene individually on stomach cancer risk; these were the trial among Finnish male heavy smokers and that among US male physicians, also described in Box 4.6.2. In the Finnish trial, more incident cases (70 vs 56) of stomach cancer occurred in the supplement group than in the placebo group (the difference was not statistically significant), thus suggesting no protective effect of β-carotene from supplements (The Alpha-Tocopherol, Beta-Carotene Prevention Study Group, 1994). In the US trial, the number of incident cases of stomach cancer was low; no difference was apparent between the supplement and placebo groups (19 vs 21 cases) (Hennekens et al, 1996). It should be borne in mind that the effects of a dietary constituent consumed from a supplement may be different to those when consumed from food (see Box 4.5.3).

In experimental studies, oral administration of β-carotene or canthaxanthin were shown not to affect the occurrence of gastric hyperplasia in animals given a chemical carcinogen, but were shown to suppress the incidence of gastric carcinoma (Santamaria et al, 1985, 1987). These data suggest that carotenoids may inhibit the later stages of gastric carcinogenesis.

Some studies have reported on carotenoids and precursor conditions for stomach cancer. One study showed lower dietary intake of β-carotene in people with severe chronic atrophic gastritis (The ECP-EURONUT-IM Study Group, 1992). People with gastric dysplasia have been shown to have lower levels of serum carotenoids than healthy controls (see review by Singh and Gaby, 1992). In China, people with intestinal metaplasia or dysplasia were found to have serum β-carotene levels about 10% lower than people without these conditions (Zhang et al, 1994).

Evidence from two cohort and six of eight case-control studies of carotenoid intake have shown that

carotenoids from foods are associated with decreased risk of stomach cancer. Four cohort studies of serum carotenoid levels also showed decreased risk with higher levels. Despite the consistent and abundant nature of this evidence, it cannot be ruled out that carotenoids are serving as proxies for other protective constituents of the same foods, i.e., mainly vegetables and fruits.

High dietary carotenoid intake possibly decreases the risk of stomach cancer.

Vitamin C

Two prospective studies that have examined vitamin C intake in relation to stomach cancer risk are presented in Table 4.6.3. In one cohort of Japanese men in Hawaii, no association was found (Chyou et al, 1990), whereas in a cohort of women in the USA, a 50% lower risk was observed for the upper two tertiles of vitamin C intake compared with the lowest tertile (p for trend < 0.16); this result was based on only 26 cases (Zheng et al, 1995).

Thirteen case-control studies that have investigated dietary intake of vitamin C and stomach cancer are shown in Table 4.6.4 (Bjelke, 1974a,b; Correa et al, 1985; Risch et al, 1985; La Vecchia et al, 1987; You et al, 1988; Buiatti et al, 1990; Graham et al, 1990; Boeing et al, 1991; Ramon et al, 1991; Palli et al, 1992; Gonzalez et al, 1994; Hansson et al, 1994). Twelve of these thirteen studies have reported protective associations (ORs in the range 0.3–0.6 for higher intake in each of the 10 studies reporting ORs), the protective association was statistically significant in nine studies. Adjustment was made for total energy intake in three studies (Buiatti et al, 1990; Gonzalez et al, 1994; Hansson et al, 1994); each of these reported a statistically significant protective association. One study in Sweden investigated dietary habits 20 years before interview, as opposed to the more recent diet queried in most studies, and reported an odds ratio of 0.4 (p < 0.05 for trend) for the uppermost quartile of vitamin C intake.

In a study of prospectively collected serum in Swiss men, those who died from stomach cancer (N = 20) over 12 years of follow-up had plasma vitamin C levels 20% lower at baseline than those who remained cancer-free (N = 2,421) (p< 0.05) (Stahelin et al, 1991). In this study, plasma vitamin levels were measured immediately after blood samples were

TABLE 4.6.3 VITAMIN C INTAKE AND STOMACH CANCER RISK: COHORT STUDIES

AUTHOR, YEAR AND PLACE	SIZE OF COHORT: NO. OF CASES	COMPARISON (HIGHEST VS LOWEST QUANTILE)	RELATIVE RISK (95% CONFIDENCE INTERVAL)	ADJUSTMENT SEX/AGE	OTHER VARIABLES[a]
Chyou et al, 1990, Hawaii, USA	8,006 men[b]: 111	na	no assoc	Y	na
Zheng et al, 1995, Iowa, USA	41,837 women: 26	h vs l tertile	0.5 (0.2–1.3)	Y	Y

[na] not available

[a] Also adjusted for: smoking history and total energy intake

[b] Japanese origin

TABLE 4.6.4 VITAMIN C INTAKE AND STOMACH CANCER RISK: CASE-CONTROL STUDIES

AUTHOR, YEAR AND PLACE	NO. OF CASES	COMPARISON (HIGHEST VS LOWEST QUANTILE)	ODDS RATIO (95% CONFIDENCE INTERVAL)	ADJUSTMENT SEX/AGE	OTHER VARIABLES[a]
Bjelke, 1973, Norway	228	na	negative assoc	N	N
Bjelke, 1973, Minneapolis, USA	83	na	negative assoc	N	N
Correa et al, 1985, Louisiana, USA	183 whites	h vs l quartile	0.5* (0.3–1.0)	Y	Y
	185 blacks	h vs l quartile	0.3* (0.2–0.7)	Y	Y
Risch et al, 1985, Canada	246	1g/day	0.4 (0.2–1.2)	Y	Y
La Vecchia et al, 1987, Milano, Italy	206	h vs l tertile	0.5* (na)	Y	Y
You et al, 1988, China	564	h vs l quartile	0.5 (0.3–0.6)	Y	Y
Buiatti et al, 1990, Italy	1,106	h vs l quintile	0.5* (0.4–0.7)	Y	Y
Graham et al, 1990, New York, USA	293	na	no assoc	na	na
Boeing et al, 1991, Germany	143	h vs l quintile	0.4* (0.2–0.8)	Y	Y
Palli et al, 1992, Italy	68[b]	h vs l quintile	0.4 (0.2–0.8)	Y	Y
Ramon et al, 1993, Spain	117	h vs l quartile	0.4* (0.2–1.0)	Y	Y
Gonzalez et al, 1994, Spain	354	h vs l quartile	0.6* (na)	Y	Y
Hansson et al, 1994, Sweden	338	h vs l quartile	0.7* (0.5–1.0)[c]	Y	Y
		h vs l quartile	0.4* (0.3–0.6)[d]	Y	Y

* p ≤ 0.05 for trend or as compared with lowest intake level

na not available

[a] Also adjusted for one or more of the following: energy intake, food consumption, education, residence, socio-economic status, respondent status, income, smoking history, ethnicity, intake of calories, hospital, migration, family predisposition, alcohol consumption

[b] Gastric cardia cancer cases from Buiatti et al, (1990)

[c] Adolescence

[d] Twenty years before interview

drawn, so the problem of degradation during storage was avoided.

A geographical correlation study in China has reported a weak inverse correlation between serum vitamin C levels and stomach cancer mortality in 65 counties (r = –0.26 in men and r = –0.06 in women) (Kneller et al, 1992).

Although some intervention trials have used combination supplements, including vitamin C (see Box 4.6.2), no trials have investigated the independent effect of vitamin C on the risk of stomach cancer.

Vitamin C has been shown to inhibit the intra-gastric formation of N-nitroso compounds. In animal studies, the inhibition of tumor formation has been observed when vitamin C is fed together with nitrite and amines or amides or with pre-formed carcinogens (Mirvish et al, 1983; Mirvish, 1986). Supplementation with vitamin C has been shown in at least two studies to decrease the mutagenicity of gastric juice in humans (see review by Singh and Gaby, 1991).

One case-control study of chronic atrophic gastritis, a condition associated with increased risk of gastric metaplasia, dysplasia and cancer, showed reduced risk with higher vitamin C intake (Fontham et al, 1986), whereas another in Japan found no relationship between vitamin C intake, as estimated from 11 foods, and the severity of gastric intestinal metaplasia (Nomura et al, 1982). Although there was no association between serum vitamin C levels and gastric precancerous lesions in Colombia (Haenszel et al, 1985), serum vitamin C levels were a statistically significant 20% lower in those with intestinal metaplasia or dysplasia than in those with superficial gastritis or chronic atrophic gastritis in China (Zhang et al, 1994). A few studies have shown people with

chronic atrophic gastritis to have lower concentrations of vitamin C in their gastric juice (see review by Singh and Gaby, 1991).

Overall, one of two cohort and 12 of 13 case-control studies that have examined dietary vitamin C have been extremely consistent in their findings of decreased risk of stomach cancer with higher intakes.

One prospective study of plasma vitamin C levels and one ecological study are also consistent; biological mechanisms for a preventive role of vitamin C against stomach cancer have been described. It is, however, possible that some other constituent of vitamin C-containing fruits and vegetables is responsible for the observed protective associations.

High dietary vitamin C intake probably decreases the risk of stomach cancer.

Vitamin E

One prospective cohort study of Japanese men in Hawaii examined the relationship between vitamin E intake and stomach cancer; no statistically significant association was found (Chyou et al, 1990). Another prospective study, of women in Iowa, reported a statistically non-significant decrease in risk among those with higher intakes of vitamin E, with a relative risk of 0.6 for the uppermost tertile of intake (Zheng et al, 1995).

Of six case-control studies of stomach cancer that have examined dietary vitamin E, two have shown statistically significant protective associations (OR = 0.6 for higher intake in each) (Buiatti et al, 1990; Hansson et al, 1994). The remaining studies reported no substantial associations (Risch et al, 1985; Buiatti et al, 1990; Graham et al, 1990; Ramon et al, 1993; Gonzalez et al, 1994; Hansson et al, 1994).

Two prospective cohort studies of serum or plasma concentrations of vitamin E and stomach cancer have been conducted; neither of these reported any appreciable difference in plasma vitamin E levels between people who developed stomach cancer and those who remained cancer-free (Stähelin et al, 1991; Nomura et al, 1995). One study adjusted for plasma lipid levels (Stähelin et al, 1991).

In an ecological study of 65 counties in China, weak positive correlations were noted between serum α-tocopherol levels and stomach cancer mortality rates (r = 0.23 in men and r = 0.13 in women) (Kneller et al, 1992).

Although several intervention trials using supplements have included vitamin E as part of a combination supplement (see Box 4.6.2), only one trial has examined the effects of vitamin E individually on stomach cancer risk; this was the trial among Finnish male heavy smokers (described in Box 4.6.2). After about 5 years of supplementation, more incident cases (70 vs 56) of stomach cancer occurred in the supplement group than in the control group (the difference was not statistically significant) (The Alpha-Tocopherol, Beta-Carotene Cancer Prevention Study Group, 1994). As discussed in Box 4.5.3, the effects of a dietary constituent consumed as a supplement may be different from those associated with the consumption of the same constituent in food.

A review of animal and in vitro experiments has shown that vitamin E can inhibit forestomach carcinogenesis in rats, although the relevance of these findings to humans is unclear, because this tissue is not directly analogous to human gastric tissue (Chen et al, 1988).

Men (but not women) with gastric dysplasia, a pre-cancerous condition for stomach cancer, have been shown to have lower levels of serum vitamin E than healthy controls (Haenszel et al, 1985). On the other hand, no material associations were shown between serum α-tocopherol levels and gastric pre-cancerous lesions, such as intestinal metaplasia and dysplasia, in Colombia (Haenszel et al, 1985) or China (Zhang et al, 1994).

Most of the evidence regarding vitamin E and stomach cancer suggests no relationship, although a few studies suggest decreased risk with higher intakes.

High dietary vitamin E intake possibly has no relationship with the risk of stomach cancer.

Retinol

In a prospective cohort study of women in the USA, a statistically non-significant protective association was reported between retinol intake and risk of stomach cancer (RR = 0.6, 0.2–1.7 for the uppermost tertile) (Zheng et al, 1995).

Seven case-control studies of stomach cancer have examined dietary retinol. Odds ratios for higher intakes ranged from 0.8 to 1.5 in these studies; in five studies the odds ratios were essentially null and not statistically significant (Risch et al, 1985; La Vecchia et al, 1987; You et al, 1988; Buiatti et al, 1990; Hansson et al, 1994). Only one study, in the USA, reported a statistically significant increase in risk (ORs = 3.1) (1.7–5.7) for men and 2.1 (1.1–4.1) for women for the highest consumption levels) (Graham et al, 1990). The remaining study reported a weak, statistically non-significant increase in risk (González et al, 1994).

Three prospective cohort studies, involving Japanese men in Hawaii, Finnish men and women, and Swiss men, have found no material difference in serum retinol levels between people who developed stomach cancer and those who did not (Knekt et al, 1990; Stahelin et al, 1991; Nomura et al, 1995).

In an ecological study of 65 counties in China, serum retinol levels were not correlated with stomach cancer mortality (r = –0.15 in men and r = 0.01 in women) (Kneller et al, 1992).

In another cross-sectional study in China that examined precancerous stomach lesions, no difference was found in serum retinol levels among people with chronic atrophic gastritis, intestinal metaplasia or dysplasia (precancerous conditions of different severity) (Zhang et al, 1994). Serum retinol concentrations were also shown to be unrelated to the prevalence of various pre-cancerous stomach lesions in Columbia (Haenszel et al, 1985).

One cohort and six of seven case-control studies have observed no statistically significant relationship between retinol intake and stomach cancer. Studies of serum or plasma retinol levels have also shown no relationship, although these studies do not provide data on retinol intake.

High dietary retinol intake possibly has no relationship with the risk of stomach cancer.

4.6.1.5 Minerals
Selenium

Three prospective cohort studies have investigated the relationship between serum or toenail selenium concentration and stomach cancer. One study of Japanese men in Hawaii found no material association, whereas a second study in Finland reported a protective association for both men and women (RR = 0.1; p = 0.002 for trend) for men (RR = 0.3; p = 0.15 for trend) for women (Nomura et al, 1987; Knekt et al, 1990). A third study in the Netherlands found a protective association with toenail selenium concentration for men (OR = 0.4, 0.2–1.0; p = 0.14 for trend), but no protective association for women (Van den Brandt et al, 1993). The risk estimates in each of these studies were based on relatively few cases, ranging from 22 to 72.

BOX 4.6.2 INTERVENTION TRIALS OF STOMACH CANCER USING SUPPLEMENTS

Four intervention trials have been concluded involving nutrient supplements and examining stomach cancer as an endpoint. Two trials were carried out in a rural county in China, where the rates of oesophageal and gastric cancers are among the highest in the world, and diets are marginally deficient in several micronutrients (Blot et al, 1993; Li et al, 1993). In one trial, the effects of four combinations of micronutrients, including retinol (5,000 IU) and zinc (22.5 mg); riboflavin (3.2 mg) and niacin (40 mg); vitamin C (120 mg) and molybdenum (30 μg); and β-carotene (15 mg), vitamin E (30 mg), and selenium (50 μg) were tested among about 30,000 adults aged 40–69 years. Five hundred and thirty-nine incident cases and 331 deaths from stomach cancer were observed during a 5-year period (Blot et al, 1993). A 16% lower incidence (0–29%) and 21% lower mortality (1–36%) were demonstrated among those receiving the combination supplements of β-carotene, vitamin E and selenium. No effect was found with the other supplement combinations, nor was any effect on the prevalence of gastric dysplasia apparent in a subgroup that underwent endoscopy (Taylor et al, 1994). Notably, the dosages of micronutrients given in this trial were lower than in some other trials.

In the other study in China, based upon more than 3,000 adults aged 40–69 years

with cytologically diagnosed oesophageal dysplasia, subjects were allocated to a group receiving either a daily multi-nutrient supplement containing 14 vitamins and 12 minerals or a placebo (Li et al, 1993). Over a 6-year period, slightly more incident cases (96 versus 81) and deaths (42 versus 35) from stomach cancer occurred in the supplement group, although these differences were not statistically significant.

A third intervention trial, among about 30,000 male smokers aged 50–69 years in Finland, assigned participants to one of four regimens with supplements of either (20 mg), vitamin E (50 mg), both or placebo (Alpha-Tocopherol, Beta-Carotene Prevention Study Group, 1994). Stomach cancer incidence over a period of 5–8 years was slightly greater among men receiving β-carotene than among those not receiving it (70 versus 56 cases), and also among those receiving vitamin E than among those not (70 versus 56 cases); these differences were not statistically significant.

A fourth trial included approximately 22,000 male physicians in the USA and involved supplementation with β-carotene (50 mg on alternate days) or placebo (Hennekens et al, 1996). After an average of 12 years, the number of incident cases of stomach cancer was low and almost equivalent in the supplement and placebo groups (19 vs 21 cases).

Another intervention trial did not examine stomach cancer as an endpoint as such, but rather antioxidant levels in plasma and gastric juice in 43 participants with pre-cancerous lesions of the stomach. After supplementation with different combinations of vitamin C (250–650 mg), β-carotene (6–15 mg), and vitamin E (75–200 mg) for 7 days (De Sanjosé et al, 1996), plasma levels of all supplemental nutrients were higher than at baseline, but levels of vitamin C in gastric juice were unchanged.

In summary, one intervention trial in China showed a combination supplement of β-carotene, vitamin E and selenium to be associated with lower risk of stomach cancer in a population known to be micronutrient-deficient. This should not be taken to indicate that supplements of these or other microconstituents are likely to be beneficial in populations or individuals where intake is adequate, not only for reasons detailed in chapter 3, but also because two further trials showed no protective effect of multi-nutrient or antioxidant supplements in high-risk groups with oesophageal dysplasia or heavy cigarette smoking patterns, respectively; in fact in each of these studies, stomach cancer rates were slightly higher in the supplement-taking groups.

In an ecological study in China (Kneller et al, 1992), serum selenium levels were shown to be inversely correlated with stomach cancer mortality (r = –0.33 in men and r = –0.39 in women). In this study, the inverse correlation remained highly statistically significant in multiple regression analysis including dietary β-carotene, vitamin C and other biochemical variables.

In a study of prevalent pre-cancerous stomach cancer lesions in China, including chronic atrophic gastritis, intestinal metaplasia and dysplasia (listed in order of increasing severity) serum selenium levels were found to be similar in people with chronic atrophic gastritis and dysplasia, but somewhat lower in people with intestinal metaplasia (p< 0.10) (Zhang et al, 1994). Another study, in the UK, reported no difference in serum selenium levels between cases with intestinal metaplasia and different groups of controls without this condition. One animal experiment has shown the incidence of N-methyl-N-nitro-N-nitrosoguanidine-induced cancer of the glandular stomach to be lower in rats fed a high-selenium diet, compared with those fed a low-selenium diet (Kobayashi et al, 1986).

The evidence suggests that high dietary selenium intake may decrease the risk of stomach cancer, but is as yet insufficient.

4.6.1.6 Other bioactive compounds
Allium compounds

Allium compounds are found in plants of the genus Allium, to which onions, garlic, leeks, chives, scallions and some 500 other species belong. Although there is no human evidence regarding allium compounds as such, there is substantial evidence regarding allium vegetables. The evidence that allium vegetables reduce risk of stomach cancer has been judged by the panel to be particularly consistent, with nine of eleven studies in the direction of a protective effect (see Table 6.3.2). Fewer studies have focused specifically on garlic, and the panel has concluded that the data are insufficient, but, if anything, support decreased risk with greater garlic consumption (see section 4.6.2.7 on garlic).

These studies include a recent prospective cohort study in the Netherlands (Dorant et al, 1996), in which a relative risk of 0.5 (0.3–0.95) was reported for those consuming 0.5 or more onions per day, compared with those not consuming onion. There was no relationship between garlic supplement use and stomach cancer in this prospective study. These studies further include a case-control study in China that specifically focused upon allium vegetables and reported an odds ratio of 0.4 (0.3–0.6) for consumption of > 65 versus < 32 grams per day (You et al, 1988; 1989). A protective association was seen for each allium vegetable examined, including garlic, garlic stalks, scallions, Chinese chives and onions.

One ecological study showed that an area in northern China, where garlic production is very high, had the lowest national mortality rate for stomach cancer. Another ecological observation showed an area of Georgia (USA), where Vidalia onions are grown, to have a stomach cancer mortality rate half that of the already low national average.

In vitro and animal studies of various allium compounds were reviewed by Dorant et al (1993). In general, results from in vitro studies have supported the hypothesis that specific allium compounds, including diallylsulphide, ajoene, allixin and allicin, have anti-mutagenic properties (Dorant et al, 1993). One animal study showed allylmethyltrisulphide to reduce the occurrence of chemically induced cancer of the forestomach, but not lung (Wattenberg et al, 1986). Other animal studies have shown various allium compounds to inhibit carcinogenesis at other sites (Dorant et al, 1993) (see also Chapter 5.8).

Regarding possible biological mechanisms by which allium compounds might exert their effect, studies of allylmethyltrisulphide in mice have shown increased activity of glutathione transferase (Wattenberg et al, 1986) and studies of diallylsulphide have shown various effects on cytochrome P450 enzymes (Yang et al, 1993). The antibacterial properties of allium compounds may provide another anticarcinogenic mechanism, particularly in the light of the growing evidence that *Helicobacter pylori* is an important risk factor for stomach cancer (Sivam et al, 1997). Inhibition of the bacterial conversion of nitrate to nitrite in the stomach, and subsequently the reduced formation of nitrosamines, may also be pertinent.

The evidence from epidemiological studies of allium vegetables is consistent with a decreased risk of stomach cancer, and plausible biological pathways have been identified.

Diets high in allium compounds possibly decrease the risk of stomach cancer.

Terpenoids
Limonene
D-Limonene is the terpenoid that has been studied the most in relation to cancer; it is the major component of the oil of citrus fruit peel and is used as a food flavouring agent. The evidence that citrus fruits protect against stomach cancer is particularly consistent, with 11 of 12 studies showing protective associations (see Table 6.3.2). However, the likelihood that limonene is responsible for this apparent beneficial effect is unclear, as citrus peel is not commonly consumed

along with the inner part of the fruit (nonetheless, some limonene is found in commercial orange juice), and other active compounds in citrus fruit, such as vitamin C, may be responsible for the apparent effect. IARC (1993) has graded D-limonene as non-classifiable with regard to its carcinogenicity to humans.

Citrus oils have been shown to inhibit the chemical induction of tumours of the forestomach in mice (Wattenberg, 1983). Other animal studies using citrus oils, or D-limonene itself, have resulted in inhibition or regression of chemically induced tumours of other sites (see Wattenberg et al, 1986; Hocman, 1989; Birt and Bresnick, 1991; Dragsted et al, 1993; and IARC, 1993).

Orange, lemon, grapefruit, and tangerine oils have been shown to induce the activity of glutathione transferase in the liver and small bowel in mice (Wattenberg, 1983), a potential mechanism for the observed inhibition of tumour formation. Additionally, terpenoids have been shown to inhibit the enzyme hydroxymethylglutaryl-CoA (HMG-CoA) reductase, which catalyses the rate-limiting step in cholesterol synthesis; as tumour cells accumulate and synthesise cholesterol faster than normal cells, terpenoids may suppress tumour growth by this mechanism (Elson and Yu, 1994).

Evidence from experimental studies and the identification of plausible biological pathways, together with evidence of protective effects of citrus fruits, suggests that diets high in terpenoids such as D-limonene may decrease the risk of stomach cancer, but, in the absence of epidemiological data, no judgement is possible.

4.6.2 FOODS AND DRINKS

4.6.2.1 Cereals (grains)

Four prospective cohort studies have examined associations between consumption of cereals (grains) and the risk of stomach cancer. One study in the USA (Kneller et al, 1991) found a moderate increase in the risk of stomach cancer with high consumption of cooked cereals, with a relative risk of 1.8 (p < 0.05 for trend) for the highest consumption. In another study, statistically non-significant increases in risk were noted for rice and noodles for Japanese living in Hawaii; no association was apparent for bread (Nomura et al, 1990). In two studies in Japan, rice consumption was not associated with the risk of stomach cancer (Hirohata, 1983; Hirayama et al, 1990).

At least 18 case-control studies of stomach cancer have examined intakes of various cereals or cereal-based products (Hirayama, 1971; Haenszel et al, 1972; Bjelke, 1974; Modan et al, 1974; Haenszel et al, 1976; Correa et al, 1985; Risch et al, 1985; Trichopoulos et al, 1985; La Vecchia et al, 1987; Kono et al, 1988; You et al, 1988a,b; Buiatti et al, 1989; Demirer et al, 1990; Boeing et al, 1991; Gonzalez et al, 1991; Tuyns et al, 1992; Ramon et al, 1993; Hansson et al, 1993). Seven of eight studies that have examined broad food categories called 'cereals', 'grains' or 'starchy foods' have found increased risk with higher consumption (Bjelke, 1974; Modan et al, 1974; Risch et al, 1985; Trichopoulos et al, 1985; Demirer et al, 1990; Tuyns et al, 1992; Ramon et al, 1993) with odds ratios ranging from 1.4 to 2.4; this increase was statistically significant in five studies (Modan et al, 1974; Risch et al, 1985; Trichopoulos et al, 1985; Tuyns et al, 1992; Ramon et al, 1993). One study in Italy examined 'pasta and rice' together, two predominant cereal foods in that country, and found a moderate increase in risk (OR = 1.7; p < 0.05) although another study in Italy found no association for consumption of 'bread and pasta' (Buiatti et al, 1989). In a study in Spain, the uppermost quartile of consumption of 'bread, pasta, and rice' was associated with decreased risk (OR = 0.6) (Gonzalez et al, 1991).

Six case-control studies that have specifically examined rice consumption in Japan, the USA and Spain have produced variable results (OR = 0.7 to 1.7 for higher consumption) (Hirayama, 1971; Haenszel et al, 1972, 1976; Correa et al, 1985; Kono et al, 1988; Ramon et al, 1993); four studies have reported associations in the direction of increased risk (Hirayama, 1971; Haenszel et al, 1972; Correa et al, 1985; Ramon et al, 1993); this increase was statistically significant in two studies (Haenszel et al, 1972; Ramon et al, 1993). Pasta consumption was associated with a statistically significant increase in risk in one case-control study in Greece (Trichopoulos et al, 1985). Consumption of polenta was found to be associated with increased risk in one study in Italy (OR = 2.3, p < 0.05 for intake in the uppermost tertile) (La Vecchia et al, 1987) whereas corn consumption was found not to be related to risk in a study in China (You et al, 1988).

Several studies have examined consumption of bread in general, or of different types of bread. Three studies, in Italy, Belgium and Germany, reported no material associations for 'bread' as a general category (La Vecchia et al, 1987; Boeing et al, 1991; Tuyns et al, 1992). The results from three studies that examined 'white bread' varied, with odds ratios ranging from 0.8 (ns) to 1.9 (p < 0.05) (Trichopoulos et al, 1985; Tuyns et al, 1992; Hansson et al, 1993); consumption of 'wholegrain', 'brown' or 'wholemeal' bread has been consistently associated with statistically significant decreased risk in four studies (Trichopoulos et al, 1985; Boeing et al, 1991; Tuyns et al, 1992; Hansson et al, 1993).

At the international level, there is a correlation between cereal consumption and increased risk of stomach cancer (r = 0.4–0.5) (Armstrong and Doll, 1975). In an ecological study of 65 counties in China (Kneller et al, 1992) consumption indices of wheat and millet consumption were moderately correlated with stomach cancer mortality. Rice consumption, however, was correlated with decreased mortality. In Japan, the consumption of rice correlates poorly with variation in stomach cancer mortality between prefectures, or with the declining trend in stomach cancer mortality (Hirayama, 1975; Howson et al, 1986).

The evidence regarding cereals and stomach cancer is abundant, but inconsistent, and somewhat suggestive of increased risk with higher consumption of cereals. However, this finding may be attributable to such diets being deficient in protective dietary constituents, either because they are monotonous and made up of one dietary staple, or because the cereals in the diet are mostly refined. In addition, it may be that different cereals have different effects on cancer risk. The evidence relating to cereals and the risk of stomach cancer is conflicting; no judgement is possible.

Wholegrain cereals

The relationship between cereal products and the risk of stomach cancer may depend on the degree to which these products are refined. A 1995 review of the literature on wholegrain intake and cancer (Jacobs et al, 1995) summarised seven case-control studies of stomach cancer, conducted in Italy, Belgium, Germany, Sweden, Poland, Greece and the USA, between 1985 and 1993, which examined consumption of wholegrain bread or pasta, wholemeal bread, non-white bread, brown bread or crisp bread (Trichopoulos et al, 1985; La Vecchia et al, 1987; Wu-Williams et al, 1990; Boeing et al, 1991a,b; Tuyns et al, 1992; Hansson et al, 1993). All but one of these studies consistently showed odds ratios of less than 1.0 for higher intake of wholegrain foods, compared with lower intake; in three studies, odds ratios of about 0.4 were observed for higher intakes. In three of these studies, no material associations were shown for 'white bread' or for 'bread' in general (Trichopoulos et al, 1985; Boeing et al, 1991; Hansson et al, 1993) and in one study a moderate increased risk was reported for 'white bread'(Tuyns et al, 1992).

The data regarding wholegrain cereals and stomach cancer, although somewhat limited in number, are almost entirely consistent.

Diets high in wholegrain cereals possibly decrease the risk of stomach cancer.

4.6.2.2 Roots, tubers and plantains

One prospective cohort study of stomach cancer in Japan examined potato consumption and reported increased risk with higher intakes (Hirohata et al, 1983).

An early case-control study in the USA showed a moderate increase in risk with greater potato consumption (Graham et al, 1972). However, no clear association has been observed in seven other studies (Acheson and Doll, 1964; Trichopoulos et al, 1985; La Vecchia et al, 1987; Boeing et al, 1991a; Tuyns et al, 1992; Hansson et al, 1993; Ramon et al, 1993) with odds ratios ranging from 0.8 to 1.4 (all ns) for the highest consumption levels; one further study reported decreased risk (OR = 0.6; ns) for the uppermost consumption quartile (Gonzalez et al, 1991).

One case-control study conducted in the USA found a

TABLE 4.6.5 VEGETABLE CONSUMPTION AND STOMACH CANCER RISK: COHORT STUDIES

AUTHOR, YEAR AND PLACE	SIZE OF COHORT: NO. OF CASES	TYPE OF VEGETABLE	COMPARISON (HIGHEST VS LOWEST QUANTILE)	RELATIVE RISK (95% CONFIDENCE INTERVAL)	ADJUSTMENT SEX/AGE	OTHER VARIABLES[a]
Hirayama, 1986, Japan	122,261 men: 3,414	Green and yellow vegetables	h vs l quartile	0.7* (na)	Y	N
	142,857 women: 1,833	Green and yellow vegetables	h vs l quartile	0.7* (na)	Y	N
Kneller et al, 1991, USA	17,633 men[b]: 75	Vegetables	h vs l quartile	0.9 (0.5–1.8)	Y	Y
		Cruciferous vegetables	h vs l quartile	1.3 (0.7–2.7)	Y	Y
Kato et al, 1992a, Japan	9,753: 57	Green-yellow vegetables	h vs l tertile	1.5 (0.8–3.1)	Y	na
		Other vegetables	h vs l tertile	1.2 (0.6–2.3)	Y	na
Kato et al, 1992b	3,914[c]: 45	Green-yellow vegetables	daily vs ≤ 2–3/week	0.8 (0.5–1.5)	Y	Y
		Raw vegetables	daily vs ≤ 1–2/month	0.8 (0.3–2.2)	Y	Y
Nomura et al, 1995 and Chyou et al, 1990	8,006 men[d]:					
	250	Vegetables	h vs l quartile	0.6* (0.3–0.9)	Y	N
Hawaii, USA	111	Green vegetables	h vs l quartile	0.7 (0.4–1.2)	Y	Y
		Cruciferous vegetables	h vs l half	0.7 (0.4–1.2)	Y	Y
Dorant et al, 1996	120,852	Onions	h vs l quartile	0.5* (0.3–1.0)	Y	Y
Holland[e]	139	Leeks	h vs l tertile	0.7 (0.4–1.1)	Y	Y

* p ≤ 0.05 for trend or as compared with lowest consumption level
na not available
a Also adjusted for one or more of the following: smoking history, residence, ethnicity, alcohol intake, vitamin C intake, beta-carotene intake, education, family predisposition
b Scandinavian and German origin
c Persons who underwent gastroscopic examination at baseline
d Japanese origin
e The Netherlands Cohort Study on Diet and Cancer

reduced risk with banana consumption (Correa et al, 1985); another in China found reduced risk with consumption of dried sweet potatoes (You et al, 1988).

In an ecological study in 65 counties in China (Kneller et al, 1992), consumption indices of potatoes, in common with cereals and grains, were moderately correlated with stomach cancer mortality. A non-significant association with increased mortality was noted for potatoes in Japan (Hirohata, 1983).

There are no animal experiments showing any relationship between consumption of tubers and the risk of stomach cancer, nor is there any known biological reason to suppose that tubers might increase risk.

Evidence relating to diets high in roots, tubers and plantains is inconsistent; no judgement is possible.

4.6.2.3 Vegetables and fruits

Stomach cancer is the most studied cancer with regard to vegetable and fruit consumption. Lung cancer and stomach cancer are thus the two sites for which the most prospective data are available. Six prospective cohort studies and 32 case-control studies have focused on this site; specific findings of these studies are detailed in Tables 4.6.5–4.6.8, which include results on ten groupings of vegetables and fruits, including all vegetables and fruits (combined), vegetables (as a whole), fruits (as a whole), raw vegetables (as a group), cruciferous vegetables, allium vegetables, green vegetables, citrus fruits, carrots and tomatoes.

Of the six cohort studies shown in Tables 4.6.5 and 4.6.7, three have reported a statistically significant protective asso-

ciation for one or more vegetable and/or fruit items or groups; these were the three studies with the largest number of cases of stomach cancer, 100–5,300 cases (Hirayama, 1986; Nomura et al, 1995; Dorant et al, 1996). One smaller study in Japan reported a statistically significant increase in risk with higher fruit intake (Kato et al, 1992a).

Of the 32 case-control studies in Tables 4.6.6 and 4.6.8, 27 studies reported a statistically significant protective association for one or more vegetable and/or fruit items or categories included in the tables; most of the remaining studies either reported protective associations that were not statistically significant or did not report on statistical significance. Most of the odds ratios or associations (130 of 153, i.e., 85%) in Tables 4.6.6 and 4.6.8 are in the protective direction, although not all are statistically significant. Only one case-control study showed a statistically significant increase in risk; this was shown for several individual vegetable items from one study in Japan (Tajima and Tominaga, 1986). The 32 studies were conducted in a variety of geographical locations with diverse dietary and cultural habits, including Japan, Greece, Poland, Italy, China, Turkey, England, Germany, Spain, Belgium, Sweden, and the states of Kansas, Louisiana, New York, and California in the USA.

Protective associations have consistently been shown for vegetables and fruit, collectively and separately, in epidemiological studies. Two cohort and eleven case-control studies have examined vegetables as a whole; in each of these, some degree of decreased risk was observed with higher consumption (statistically significant in six studies). The evidence for raw vegetables is particularly consistent and strong, with each of fourteen studies showing an association in the pro-

TABLE 4.6.6 VEGETABLE CONSUMPTION AND STOMACH CANCER RISK: CASE-CONTROL STUDIES

AUTHOR, YEAR AND PLACE	NO. OF CASES	TYPE OF VEGETABLE	COMPARISON (HIGHEST VS LOWEST QUANTILE)	ODDS RATIO (95% CONFIDENCE INTERVAL)	ADJUSTMENT SEX/AGE	OTHER VARIABLES[a]
Acheson and Doll, 1964 England	100	Tomatoes	h vs l quintile	no assoc	Y	N
Higginson, 1966	93	Raw vegetables	h vs l quartile	negative assoc	na	na
Kansas City, USA		Cooked vegetables	h vs l quartile	no assoc	na	na
Graham et al, 1972	160 men	Raw vegetables	na	negative assoc*	Y	Y
Buffalo, USA	68 women	Raw vegetables	na	negative assoc*	Y	Y
Haenszel et al, 1972	220 Japanese	Tomatoes	h vs l quartile	0.4* (na)	Y	Y
Hawaii		Onions	h vs l quartile	0.5* (na)	Y	Y
Bjelke, 1974, Norway	228	Vegetables	h vs l quartile	negative assoc	na	na
Bjelke, 1974, Minneapolis	83	Vegetables	na	negative assoc	na	na
		Tomatoes	na	negative assoc	na	na
Correa et al, 1985	90 whites	Vegetables	h vs l quartile	0.9 (0.6–1.4)	Y	Y
		Tomatoes	h vs l quartile	0.8 (0.5–1.3)	Y	Y
		Broccoli	h vs l quartile	1.0 (0.7–1.7)	Y	Y
		Spinach	h vs l quartile	negative assoc	Y	Y
	100 blacks	Vegetables	h vs l quartile	0.5* (0.3–1.0)	Y	Y
		Tomatoes	h vs l quartile	0.6 (0.3–0.9)	Y	Y
		Broccoli	h vs l quartile	0.5 (0.3–0.9)	Y	Y
		Spinach	h vs l quartile	negative assoc	Y	Y
Risch et al, 1985, Canada	246	Cruciferous vegetables	100g/day	0.7 (0.4–1.1)	Y	Y
		Pale green vegetables	100g/day	0.3* (0.1–1.1)	Y	Y
Trichopoulos et al, 1985	110	Vegetables	h vs l quartile	0.1* (na)	Y	Y
Piraeus, Greece		Onions	h vs l quintile	0.2* (na)	Y	Y
Tajima and Tominaga, 1985	93	Carrots	h vs l tertile	1.1 (na)	Y	N
Japan		Cabbage	h vs l tertile	2.2* (na)	Y	N
		Tomatoes	h vs l tertile	1.2 (na)	Y	N
		Onions	h vs l tertile	2.1* (na)	Y	N
		Spinach	h vs l tertile	2.5* (na)	Y	N
Jedrychowsky et al, 1986 Cracow, Poland	110	Vegetables	h vs l tertile	0.6 (0.3–1.5)	Y	Y
La Vecchia et al, 1987	206	Green vegetables	h vs l tertile	0.3* (na)	Y	Y
Milano, Italy		Cruciferous vegetables	h vs l tertile	1.2 (na)	Y	N
		Carrots	h vs l tertile	0.8 (na)	Y	N
		Tomatoes	h vs l tertile	0.7 (na)	Y	N
		Spinach	h vs l tertile	1.4 (na)	Y	N
Hu et al, 1988, China	241	Chinese cabbage	h vs l half	0.6 (0.4–0.8)	Y	Y
		Spinach	h vs l half	0.5 (0.3–0.8)	Y	Y
Kono et al, 1988, Japan	139	Raw vegetables	h vs l tertile	0.8 (na)[b]	Y	N
		Green-yellow vegetables	h vs l tertile	1.3 (na)[b]	Y	N
You et al, 1988, 1989, China	564	Fresh vegetables	h vs l quartile	0.4 (0.3–0.6)	Y	Y
		Scallions	h vs l tertile	0.6* (0.5–1.0)	Y	Y
		Garlic	h vs l tertile	0.5* (0.4–1.0)	Y	Y
		Chinese chives	h vs l tertile	0.5* (0.4–0.8)	Y	Y
		Onions	h vs l tertile	0.8 (0.8–1.4)	Y	Y
Buiatti et al, 1989, Italy	1,016	Raw vegetables	h vs l tertile	0.6* (na)	Y	Y
		Cooked vegetables	h vs l tertile	1.1 (na)	Y	Y
		Onion/garlic	h vs l tertile	0.8* (na)	Y	Y
Demirer et al, 1990 Ankara, Turkey	100	Raw yellow-green vegetables	h vs l half	0.1* (0.0–0.1)	Y	Y
Kato et al, 1990, Japan	289 men	Green-yellow vegetables	h vs l half	0.8 (0.6–1.1)	Y	Y
		Raw vegetables	h vs l tertile	0.6 (0.4–0.9)	Y	Y
	138 women	Green-yellow vegetables	h vs l half	0.8 (0.6–1.1)	Y	Y
		Raw vegetables	h vs l tertile	0.8 (0.5–1.5)	Y	Y
Graham et al, 1990	181 men	Raw vegetables	na	0.4 (0.2–0.8)	Y	Y
New York, USA		Carrots	na	protective assoc*	Y	Y
		Tomatoes	na	protective assoc*	Y	Y
		Onions	na	protective assoc*	Y	Y
	104 women	Onions	na	protective assoc*	Y	Y
Boeing et al, 1991, Germany	143	Vegetables	h vs l tertile	0.9 (0.5–1.4)	Y	Y
		Raw vegetables	h vs l tertile	0.6 (0.4–1.0)	Y	Y

AUTHOR, YEAR AND PLACE	NO. OF CASES	TYPE OF VEGETABLE	COMPARISON (HIGHEST VS LOWEST QUANTILE)	ODDS RATIO (95% CONFIDENCE INTERVAL)	ADJUSTMENT SEX/AGE	OTHER VARIABLES[a]
Gonzalez et al, 1991, Spain	354	Raw vegetables	h vs l quartile	0.8 (na)	Y	Y
		Cooked vegetables	h vs l quartile	0.5* (na)	Y	Y
		Onions	h vs l half	0.9 (0.6–1.4)[c]	Y	Y
		Tomatoes	h vs l quartile	0.9 (0.5–1.5)[c]	Y	Y
		Cruciferous vegetables	h vs l quartile	0.9 (0.6–1.4)[c]	Y	Y
		Spinach	h vs l half	1.7 (1.1–2.7)[c]	Y	Y
Boeing et al, 1991, Poland	741	Cabbage	h vs l tertile	0.6* (na)	Y	Y
		Tomatoes	h vs l tertile	0.8* (na)	Y	Y
		Cauliflowers	h vs l tertile	0.8 (na)	Y	Y
		Carrots	h vs l tertile	0.8 (na)	Y	Y
		Onions	h vs l tertile	0.7* (na)	Y	Y
		Vegetable score	h vs l tertile	0.6* (na)	Y	Y
		Spinach	h vs l tertile	1.0 (na)	Y	Y
Hoshiyama and Sasaba, 1992 Japan	294	Green-yellow vegetables	h vs l tertile	0.5* (0.3–0.8)[d]	Y	Y
		Raw vegetables	h vs l tertile	0.4* (0.2–0.7)[d]	Y	Y
		Green-yellow vegetables	h vs l tertile	0.7 (0.4–1.1)[e]	Y	Y
		Raw vegetables	h vs l tertile	0.4* (0.2–0.7)[e]	Y	Y
Jedrychowsky et al, 1992 Poland	741[f]	Green leafy vegetables	h vs l tertile	0.8* (0.6–1.0)	Y	Y
		Non-green vegetables	h vs l tertile	0.5* (0.4–0.7)	Y	Y
		Total vegetables	h vs l tertile	0.6* (0.5–0.8)	Y	Y
Memik et al, 1992, Turkey	252	Vegetables	h vs l tertile	0.6* (0.3–1.2)	Y	N
Palli et al, 1992, Italy	68[g]	Raw vegetables	h vs l tertile	0.4 (0.2–0.8)	Y	Y
		Cooked vegetables	h vs l tertile	1.5 (0.8–2.8)	Y	Y
		Onion/garlic	h vs l tertile	0.7 (0.3–1.4)	Y	Y
Tuyns et al, 1992, Belgium	449	Cooked vegetables	h vs l quartile	0.3* (0.2–0.5)	Y	Y
		Cooked leafy vegetables	h vs l quartile	0.3* (na)	Y	Y
		Cooked leeks	h vs l half	0.3* (na)	Y	Y
		Cooked carrots	h vs l half	0.6* (na)	Y	Y
		Cooked onions	h vs l half	0.3* (na)	Y	Y
		Cooked tomatoes	h vs l half	0.1 (na)	Y	Y
		Raw vegetables	h vs l quartile	0.4* (0.3–0.6)	Y	Y
		Raw leafy vegetables	h vs l quartile	0.3* (na)	Y	Y
		Raw tomatoes	h vs l tertile	0.7 (na)	Y	Y
Ramon et al, 1993, Barcelona Spain	117	Raw green vegetables	h vs l quartile	0.6* (0.3–0.8)	Y	Y
		Carrots	h vs l tertile	0.9 (na)	Y	N
		Cabbages	h vs l tertile	0.9 (na)	Y	N
		Tomatoes	h vs l tertile	1.0 (na)	Y	N
Hansson et al, 1993, Sweden	338	Total vegetables	h vs l quartile	0.5* (0.3–0.8)	Y	Y
		Carrots	h vs l quartile	0.6* (0.4–0.9)	Y	Y
		Broccoli	h vs l half	0.7 (0.5–1.1)	Y	Y
		Cabbage	h vs l half	0.7 (0.5–1.1)	Y	Y
		Onions	h vs l quartile	0.8 (0.6–1.2)	Y	Y
		Leeks	h vs l tertile	0.6* (0.4–0.9)	Y	Y
		Garlic	h vs l half	0.9 (0.6–1.2)	Y	Y
		Tomatoes	h vs l quartile	0.7* (0.5–1.1)	Y	Y
		Spinach	h vs l tertile	0.8 (0.6–1.2)	Y	Y
Lee et al, 1995, Korea	213	Cabbage	h vs l tertile	0.2* (0.0–0.3)	Y	Y
		Spinach	h vs l tertile	0.1* (0.0–0.3)	Y	Y

* p ≤ 0.05 for trend or as compared with lowest consumption level

[na] not available

[a] Also adjusted for one or more of the following: ethnicity, respondent status, education, income, smoking history, alcohol consumption, total food consumption, residence, study area, socio-economic status, migration, family predisposition, hospital, total calories, occupation, source of vegetables, other dietary factors

[b] Comparison with hospital controls. Data on general population controls not reported

[c] Also adjusted for individual food items within the reference group

[d] Comparison with general population controls

[e] Comparison with hospital controls

[f] Families of cases from Boeing et al, 1991

[g] Number of gastric cardia cases out of 923 GC cases from Buiatti et al, 1989

TABLE 4.6.7 FRUIT CONSUMPTION AND STOMACH CANCER RISK: COHORT STUDIES

AUTHOR, YEAR AND PLACE	SIZE OF COHORT: NO. OF CASES	TYPE OF FRUIT	COMPARISON (HIGHEST VS LOWEST QUANTILE)	RELATIVE RISK (95% CONFIDENCE INTERVAL)	ADJUSTMENT SEX/AGE	ADJUSTMENT OTHER VARIABLES[a]
Kneller et al, 1991, USA	17,633 men[b]: 75	Fruit	h vs l quartile	1.5 (0.8–2.9)	Y	Y
Kato et al, 1992a, Japan	9,753: 57	Fruit	h vs l tertile	1.9* (1.0–3.6)	Y	N
Kato et al, 1992b	3,914c: 45	Fruit	daily vs ≤ 1–2/month	0.6 (0.2–1.5)	Y	Y
Nomura et al, 1995 Hawaii, USA	8,006 men[d]: 250	Fruit	h vs l quartile	0.6* (0.4–1.0)	Y	N

* p ≤ 0.05 for trend or as compared with lowest consumption level
na not available
a Also adjusted for one or more of the following: smoking history, residence
b Scandinavian and German origin
c Persons who underwent gastroscopic examination at baseline
d Japanese origin

tective direction (statistically significant in nine) and five studies showing at least a 50% lower risk in those consuming the most raw vegetables (see Tables 4.6.5 and 4.6.7). Most of the studies that have examined green vegetables, carrots, or tomatoes have also found weak to strong decreases in risk at the highest consumption levels.

For salted and pickled vegetables, associations consistent with increased risk have often, but not always, been observed, particularly in non-Western populations (data not shown in the tables) (Hirayama et al, 1971; Haenszel et al,

TABLE 4.6.8 FRUIT CONSUMPTION AND STOMACH CANCER RISK: CASE-CONTROL STUDIES

AUTHOR, YEAR AND PLACE	NO. OF CASES	TYPE OF FRUIT	COMPARISON (HIGHEST VS LOWEST QUANTILE)	ODDS RATIO (95% CONFIDENCE INTERVAL)	ADJUSTMENT SEX/AGE	ADJUSTMENT OTHER VARIABLES[a]
Acheson and Doll, 1964 England	100	Oranges	h vs l quintile	no assoc	Y	N
Higginson, 1966 Kansas City, USA	93	Fresh fruit	h vs l quartile	negative assoc	na	na
Graham et al, 1972 Buffalo, USA	160 men	Fresh fruit	na	no assoc	Y	Y
	68 women	Fresh fruit	na	no assoc	Y	Y
Haenszel et al, 1972 Hawaii	220 Japanese	Fruit	na	no assoc	Y	Y
Bjelke, 1974, Norway	228	Fruit	na	negative assoc	na	na
Haenszel et al, 1976 Japan	783	Fruit	h vs l quartile	0.7* (na)	Y	Y
Correa et al, 1985 Louisiana, USA	189 whites	Fruit	h vs l quartile	0.5* (0.2–0.9)	Y	Y
	189 blacks	Fruit	h vs l quartile	0.3* (0.2–0.7)	Y	Y
Risch et al, 1985, Canada	246	Citrus fruit	100g/day	0.8* (0.6–0.9)	Y	Y
Trichopoulos et al, 1985 Piraeus, Greece	110	Fruit	h vs l quartile	0.8 (na)	Y	Y
		Lemons	h vs l quintile	0.2* (na)	Y	Y
		Oranges	h vs l quintile	0.3* (na)	Y	Y
Tajima and Tominaga, 1985 Japan	93	Oranges	h vs l tertile	0.9 (na)	Y	N
		Fruit	h vs l tertile	1.4 (na)	Y	N
Jedrychowsky et al, 1986 Cracow, Poland	110	Fruit	h vs l tertile	0.3 (0.1–0.6)	Y	Y
La Vecchia et al, 1987 Milano, Italy	206	Fresh fruit	h vs l tertile	0.5* (na)	Y	Y
		Citrus fruit	h vs l tertile	0.6* (na)	Y	Y
Kono et al, 1988, Japan	139	Mandarin oranges	h vs l tertile	0.6* (na)[b]	Y	N
		Fruit	h vs l tertile	0.6 (na)[b]	Y	N
		Mandarin oranges	h vs l tertile	0.7 (na)[c]	Y	N
		Fruit	h vs l tertile	0.5* (na)[c]	Y	N
You et al, 1988, China	564	Fresh fruit	h vs l quartile	0.6 (0.4–0.8)	Y	Y
Coggon et al, 1989 England	95	Fruit	h vs l tertile	0.4 (0.2–0.8)	Y	N
Buiatti et al, 1989, Italy	1,016	Citrus fruit	h vs l tertile	0.6* (na)	Y	Y
		Fresh fruit	h vs l tertile	0.4* (na)	Y	Y
Demirer et al, 1990 Ankara, Turkey	100	Citrus fruit	h vs l half	0.1* (0.0–0.1)	Y	Y
Kato et al, 1990, Japan	289 men	Fruit	h vs l tertile	0.8 (0.5–1.3)	Y	Y
	138 women	Fruit	h vs l tertile	0.8 (0.3–1.8)	Y	Y

1972; You et al, 1988; Kato et al, 1990, 1992; Lee et al, 1995) (see section 4.6.3.1 and chapter 7.5).

Nine studies have examined raw and cooked vegetables separately. Although a greater decrease in the risk was shown for cooked than for raw vegetables in two studies (Gonzalez et al, 1991; Tuyns et al, 1992) decreased risk was generally more evident for raw vegetables than for cooked (Higginson, 1966; Buiatti et al, 1989; Demirer et al, 1990) total (Boeing et al, 1991; Ramon et al, 1993), or other (Kono et al, 1988; Kato et al, 1990) vegetables in seven studies.

Particular attention has been focused on the relationship of consumption of allium vegetables to stomach cancer. One cohort and 11 case-control studies have examined consumption of allium vegetables, either as a group or as individual food items; the most commonly studied allium vegetable has been the onion. These studies took place in areas with diverse consumption patterns (types, as well as amounts of allium vegetables), including the Netherlands, Hawaii, Greece, Japan, China, Italy, the USA, Spain, Poland, Belgium, and Sweden. All but one of these 12 studies showed some degree of decreased risk, statistically significant in eight studies (see Tables 4.6.5 and 4.6.6). Six studies

showed people with the highest consumption of onions, leeks, garlic, chives and/or scallions have 20–60% the risk of those with the lowest consumption. Four studies have shown strong, statistically significant decreases in risk with greater consumption of onions. Allium compounds have been postulated to have an effect against stomach cancer via various mechanisms (see chapter 5.8 on Allium compounds).

Four cohort and 27 case-control studies have examined fruits as a whole; in 25 of these, odds ratios were less than 1.0 or a protective association was reported (statistically significant in 17 studies); nine studies showed that people with the highest intakes have about 20–50% the risk of those with the lowest intakes. For citrus fruit, eight of 14 studies have found the highest consumers to have about 10–60% the risk of the lowest consumers; four others found weaker decreases in risk (see Tables 4.6.7 and 4.6.8). Citrus fruits are rich in vitamin C, as well as in other lesser known bioactive compounds (see chapter 5.8); the consistency of the evidence regarding citrus fruits is compatible with the evidence on vitamin C, which the panel has concluded probably decreases cancer risk.

In most of the cohort and case-control studies, the fruit

Author, year and place	No. of cases	Type of fruit	Comparison (highest vs lowest quantile)	Odds ratio (95% confidence interval)	Adjustment Sex/Age	Other variables[a]
Wu-Williams, 1990 LA County, USA	137 men	Fruit	h vs l tertile	0.7 (0.3–1.7)	Y	N
Graham et al, 1990 New York, USA	289	Fruit	na	no assoc	na	na
Boeing et al, 1991 Germany	143	Fruit	h vs l tertile	0.6* (0.4–0.9)	Y	Y
		Citrus fruit	h vs l tertile	0.4* (0.3–0.7)	Y	Y
Gonzalez et al, 1991 Spain	354	Fruit	h vs l quartile	0.6* (na)	Y	Y
		Citrus fruit	h vs l quartile	1.0 (na)	Y	Y
Boeing et al, 1991 Poland	741	Fruit score	h vs l tertile	0.7* (na)	Y	Y
Hoshiyama & Sasaba 1992, Japan	294	Fruit	h vs l tertile	0.8 (0.4–1.4)b	Y	Y
		Fruit	h vs l tertile	0.4 (0.3–0.7)c	Y	Y
Jedrychowsky et al 1992, Poland	741d	Fruit	h vs l tertile	0.7* (0.6–0.9)	Y	Y
Memik et al, 1992 Turkey	252	Fresh fruit	h vs l tertile	0.5 (na)	Y	N
Palli et al, 1992, Italy	68e	Citrus fruit	h vs l tertile	0.3 (0.3–0.6)	Y	Y
		Fresh fruit	h vs l tertile	0.2 (0.1–0.5)	Y	Y
Tuyns et al, 1992 Belgium	449	Fresh fruit	h vs l quartile	0.6* (0.4–0.8)	Y	Y
		Citrus fruit	h vs l tertile	0.8 (na)	Y	Y
Ramon et al, 1993 Barcelona, Spain	117	Fruit	h vs l quartile	0.9 (0.2–1.1)	Y	Y
		Citrus fruit	h vs l tertile	0.5* (0.2–0.8)	Y	Y
Hansson et al, 1993 Sweden	338	Citrus fruit	h vs l quartile	0.5* (0.3–0.8)f	Y	Y
		Citrus fruit	h vs l quintile	0.7* (0.4–1.2)g	Y	Y

* p ≤ 0.05 for trend or as compared with lowest consumption level

na not available

a Also adjusted for one or more of the following: ethnicity, respondent status, income, smoking history, total food consumption, socio-economic status, education, residence, study area, migration, family predisposition, hospital, total calories, education, occupation, source of fruit, other food items

b Comparison with hospital controls

c Comparison with general population controls

d Families of cases from Boeing et al, 1991

e Number of gastric cardia cancer cases out of 923 GC total cases from Buiatti et al, 1989

f Adolescence

g Twenty years prior to interview

and vegetable associations were adjusted for various factors shown to be associated with stomach cancer risk, such as socioeconomic status, education, income or occupation, see Tables 4.6.7 to 4.6.8. Protective associations remained after adjustment for other dietary factors such as salty foods or starchy foods in some studies (Risch et al, 1985; La Vecchia et al, 1987; Coggon et al, 1989; Hansson et al, 1993; Ramon et al, 1993; Lee et al, 1995). Considering the methodological difficulties in dietary assessment in epidemiological studies and the relatively homogeneous nature of diet within most regions, it is remarkable that findings on vegetables and fruits have been reproduced with such consistency in so many studies.

In an international ecological study, vegetable consumption was shown not to be materially correlated with stomach cancer rates (r = 0.1–0.2) (Armstrong and Doll, 1975). But correlation studies within countries have provided evidence that vegetables and fruits are protective. In Colombia, consumption of vegetables and fruits was higher in villages at low risk of stomach cancer than in villages at high risk (Correa et al, 1983). Stomach cancer mortality rates in 65 counties in China were inversely correlated with the consumption of green vegetables (r = –0.44 in men and r = –0.36 in women), although not with fruit consumption (Kneller et al, 1992). In Japan, increasing consumption of fruits (not of vegetables) since the 1950s parallels the decline in stomach cancer mortality (Hirayama, 1990). Time-trend studies in Poland and the USA have also shown decreasing stomach cancer mortality over the same time period as increasing consumption of vegetables or fruit (Howson et al, 1986; Jedrychowski et al, 1986).

Studies of pre-cancerous lesions have shown protective associations with fruits and vegetables combined in USA (Fontham et al 1986), with vegetables excluding salted vegetables in China (Kneller et al, 1992), and with lettuce in Colombia (Haenszel et al, 1976); however, an increased risk was reported with higher intake of Moras, a highly acidic berry, in the last study. Fruits, green–yellow vegetables, or raw vegetables were not associated with chronic atrophic gastritis in a Japanese case-control study (Kato et al, 1990).

Animal studies in mice have shown that inclusion of orange and lemon oils in the diet greatly reduces chemically induced tumours of the forestomach (Wattenberg and Coccia, 1991). Another animal study showed that inclusion of 10–40% lyophilised cabbage in the diets of mice increases the activity, in the forestomach, of several enzymes involved in the metabolism of carcinogens, including glutathione-s-transferase, glutathione reductase, quinone reductase and others (Ansher et al, 1986). The relevance of these findings to humans is unclear, particularly as the forestomach of rodents is not directly analogous to the human stomach.

Fruits and vegetables contain many biologically active compounds that may be responsible for an anticarcinogenic effect against stomach cancer. These compounds and their potential bioactive mechanisms are reviewed in chapters 5.2 (fibre), 5.6 (carotenoids, vitamin C, folate and vitamin E), 5.7 (selenium), and 5.8 (other bioactive compounds).

The evidence that diets high in vegetables and fruits,collectively and separately, decrease the risk of stomach cancer is convincing.

The evidence for raw vegetables, allium vegetables and citrus fruits is particularly abundant and consistent for a protective effect. Any evidence not consistent with a protective effect relates almost entirely to salted and pickled vegetables.

4.6.2.4 Pulses (legumes)
One cohort study of stomach cancer in Hawaii reported a weak non-statistically significant decrease in risk with greater intake of tofu (Nomura et al, 1990). Seven of nine (78%) case-control studies of stomach cancer, which reported on pulses in general, on particular types of pulses or on tofu, found decreased risk with greater intakes, although many of these associations were weak and not statistically significant (Risch et al, 1985; You et al, 1988; Buiatti et al, 1989; González et al, 1989; Hoshiyama et al, 1992; Ramón et al, 1993; Lee et al, 1995). Two studies have shown statistically significant increases in risk, with ORs of 1.7 (Trichopoulos et al, 1985) and 4.2 (Tuyns et al, 1992) (see chapter 6.4) for higher intakes of beans. An ecological study in Columbia reported much higher intake of fava beans in certain villages with higher incidence of stomach cancer (Correa et al, 1983).

Epidemiological studies of stomach cancer in Japan, China and Korea have observed both protective and positive associations for consumption of fermented soybean paste (Kono et al, 1988; Lee et al, 1995) (see also chapter 6.4). Soybean paste or 'miso' is a rich, salty condiment made by combining soybeans and sometimes a grain, such as rice, with salt and a mould culture, and then ageing it for 1–3 years. In Japan, soybean paste is most often consumed in soup. Different associations for soybean paste in different populations might be explained by differences in salt content and mould contamination in different types of soybean paste.

Evidence relating to pulses and the risk of stomach cancer is limited; no judgement is possible.

4.2.6.5 Nuts and seeds
A case-control study of stomach cancer in Greece reported increased risk with higher nut consumption; the odds ratio for intake 10 or more times per month, versus never, was 2.8 (p < 0.01 for trend) (OR calculated from data in article) (Trichopoulos et al, 1985). A case-control study in Canada found no association for intake of 'seeds and legumes', with an OR of 0.9 (ns) for an increase of 100 g/day (Risch et al, 1985). A further case-control study in Japan reported decreased risk with increased nut intake; the OR was 0.5 (0.3–0.8) for consumption three or more times per month, versus never (Hoshiyama and Sasaba, 1992).

In an animal experiment, inclusion of poppy seeds in the diets of mice resulted in the inhibition of chemically induced stomach tumours (Aruna and Sivaramakrishnan, 1992).

Evidence relating to diets high in nuts and seeds is limited and conflicting; no judgement is possible.

4.6.2.6 Meat, poultry, fish and eggs
Meat

There is no evidence that meat, as such, is related to the risk of stomach cancer. Evidence of increased risk relates to cured and smoked meats, and to methods of cooking, as reviewed below in section 4.6.3.3.

4.6.2.7 Herbs, spices and condiments
Garlic
Intake of allium vegetables as a group, which includes garlic, as well as onions, scallions, leeks and chives, has been examined in many epidemiological studies of stomach cancer (see Tables 4.6.3 and 4.6.5). The evidence regarding allium vegetables is particularly abundant and consistent for stomach cancer, as compared with other sites, with nine of eleven studies having reported a protective association (see Table 6.3.2). As discussed in section 4.6.2.3, the panel has concluded that the evidence regarding allium vegetables as a group is particularly consistent for a protective effect against stomach cancer.

Fewer studies have looked specifically at garlic. In a prospective cohort study in the Netherlands, garlic supplement use was unrelated to risk (Dorant et al, 1996).

A case-control study in China (Tou et al, 1989) found that garlic consumption was associated with a decreased risk of stomach cancer, with an odds ratio of 0.7 (0.4–1.1) for consumption of more than 0.5 kg/year, compared with never; this study also showed a strong protective association for allium vegetables in general. A study in Italy similarly reported that people in the highest tertile of cooked garlic consumption have 40% of the risk of those in the lowest tertile (p < 0.001 for trend) (Buiatti et al, 1989). Another case-control study in Sweden reported no material association for garlic consumption more than once per month, compared with less frequently, for diet 20 years before interview (Hansson et al, 1993). A study in Spain similarly reported no association between garlic used as seasoning and stomach cancer risk (Gonzalez et al, 1991).

One ecological observation showed that the county in northern China with the lowest stomach cancer mortality is well known for its garlic production (You et al, 1989).

Garlic extracts and their chemical constituents (diallylsulphide and other allium compounds) have been shown to be anti-mutagenic in vitro and inhibitory in animal tumorigenesis as discussed in detail by Dorant and colleagues (Dorant et al, 1993). Garlic extracts have been shown to kill *Helicobacter pylori* in vitro at concentrations that are achievable in vivo with the consumption of 1–2 cloves per day (Siram et al, 1977). Several potential cancer-preventive mechanisms for sulphur-containing allium compounds unique to allium vegetables, are reviewed more fully in chapter 5.8.

The evidence suggests, if anything, that diets high in garlic decrease the risk of stomach cancer, but is, as yet, insufficient.

Chillies
A large case-control study of stomach cancer in Italy found higher consumption of chillies to be associated with decreased risk of stomach cancer (odds ratio 0.6, p < 0.001) (Buiatti et al, 1989), whereas another case-control study in Mexico found increased risk with high consumption, particularly for the intestinal type of stomach cancer (Lopez Carrillo et al, 1994). A further case-control study in Korea (Lee et al, 1995) demonstrated an increase in the risk associated with high consumption of hot pepper soybean paste stew; however, soybean paste stew as a whole was also associated with increased risk in this study (Lee et al, 1995).

In a human study, in which red pepper was administered intragastrically at a level of 0.1–1.5 grams, along with a test meal, gastric mucosal damage was apparent, as measured by gastric cell exfoliation and mucosal micro-bleeding (Myers et al, 1987).

Dried chillies, but not fresh chillies or chilli sauces, have been shown to contain volatile nitrosamines, which may be carcinogenic (Tricker et al, 1988). On the other hand, capsaicin, the pungent component of chilli peppers, has been shown to protect against aspirin-induced gastric mucosal damage in rats (Holzer et al, 1989). Capsaicin has further

TABLE 4.6.9 COFFEE CONSUMPTION AND STOMACH CANCER RISK: COHORT STUDIES

AUTHOR, YEAR AND PLACE	SIZE OF COHORT: NO. OF CASES	COFFEE EXPOSURE FACTOR	COMPARISON (HIGHEST VS LOWEST QUANTILE)	RELATIVE RISK (95% CONFIDENCE INTERVAL)	ADJUSTMENT SEX/AGE	OTHER VARIABLES[a]
Jacobsen et al, 1986	16,555: 147	Coffee	≥ 7 vs ≤ 2 cups/day	1.5**	Y	Y
Nomura et al, 1986	7,355 Japanese: 147	Coffee	≥ 5 vs 0 cups/day	no assoc**	Y	N

** p > 0.05 for trend and/or for comparison of highest vs lowest consumption level
[a] Adjusted for one or more of the following factors: residence

TABLE 4.6.10 COFFEE CONSUMPTION AND STOMACH CANCER RISK: CASE-CONTROL STUDIES

AUTHOR, YEAR AND PLACE	NO. OF CASES	EXPOSURE	COMPARISON (HIGHEST VS LOWEST QUANTILE)	RELATIVE RISK (95% CONFIDENCE INTERVAL)	ADJUSTMENT SEX/AGE	OTHER VARIABLES[a]
Higginson, 1966 Kansas, USA	93	Coffee	e	no assoc	N	N
Graham et al, 1967 New York, USA	276	Coffee	na	no assoc	Y	N
Tajima and Tominaga, 1985 Nagoya, Japan	93	Coffee	every day vs no habit of drinking	1.0	Y	N
Trichopoulos et al, 1985 Piraeus, Greece	110	Coffee and tea	h vs l quintile	positive assoc**	Y	Y
La Vecchia et al, 1989 Northern Italy	397	Coffee	≥ 3 vs 0–1 cups/day	1.3**	Y	Y
Memik et al, 1992 Turkey	252	Turkish coffee	≥ 4 vs 0–1 cups/day	no assoc	Y	N
Agudo et al, 1992 Spain	119 women	Coffee	consumer vs non-consumer	1.1 (0.5–2.1)	Y	Y
	235 men	Coffee	consumer vs non-consumer	0.9 (0.6–1.4)	Y	Y
Hansson et al, 1993 Sweden	338	Coffee	> 6200 vs <2200 ml/wk	1.1 (0.7–1.6)**	Y	Y

** p > 0.05 for trend and/or for comparison of highest vs lowest consumption level
na information not available or unclear from article
a Adjusted or matched for one or more of the following: time of interview, years of schooling, area of residence, socio-economic status, social class, education, marital status, alcohol consumption
b OR refers to consumption 20 years before interview. OR = 1.4 (0.8–2.2)* for consumption of > 3100 vs 0ml/wk in adolescence
c No significant differences between cases and controls in proportions reporting different levels of coffee consumption

been shown to lead to the release of an enteric substance, substance P, that accelerates transit time (Monsereenasorn et al, 1982; Silkoff et al, 1988), and thus might theoretically reduce the time of contact between the mucosa and any carcinogens in the gastrointestinal contents.

> The evidence relating to diets high in chillies and the risk of stomach cancer is fragmentary and conflicting; no judgement is possible.

4.6.2.8 Coffee, tea, other drinks

Coffee

Two prospective studies, involving cohorts of Japanese men in Hawaii and Norwegian adults, have found no statistically significant association between coffee consumption and the risk of stomach cancer (Nomura et al, 1986; Jacobsen et al, 1986); these studies are shown in Table 4.6.9.

In 1991, an IARC Working Group reviewed the evidence on coffee consumption and cancer risk and concluded that, of five case-control studies of stomach cancer, none showed any statistically significant associations; in one study in Greece the odds ratio was 3.2 (ns) for five cups per day, compared with one cup; odds ratios in the remaining four studies were between 1.0–1.3 for the highest consumption levels

TABLE 4.6.11 BLACK TEA CONSUMPTION AND STOMACH CANCER RISK: COHORT STUDIES

AUTHOR, YEAR AND PLACE	SIZE OF COHORT: NO. OF CASES	COMPARISON (HIGHEST VS LOWEST QUANTILE)	RELATIVE RISK (95% CONFIDENCE INTERVAL)	ADJUSTMENT SEX/AGE	OTHER VARIABLES[a]
Heilbrun et al, 1986, Hawaii, USA	7,833 men[b]: 136	h vs l tertile	1.0 (na)	Y	N
Kinlen et al, 1988, London, England	14,085 men: 172	h vs l quintile	2.5* (na)	Y	N
Goldbohm et al, 1996[c], Holland	58,279 men: 144	h vs l sextile	0.9 (0.5–1.8)	Y	Y
	62,573 women: 39	h vs l sextile	0.9 (0.5–1.8)	Y	Y

* p ≤ 0.05 for trend or as compared with the lowest consumption level
na information not available or unclear from article
a Adjusted or matched for one or more of the following: education, family predisposition, intake of coffee and vitamin C
b Japanese origin
c The Netherlands Cohort Study on Diet and Cancer

TABLE 4.6.12 BLACK TEA CONSUMPTION AND STOMACH CANCER RISK: CASE-CONTROL STUDIES

AUTHOR, YEAR AND PLACE	NO. OF CASES	COMPARISON (HIGHEST VS LOWEST QUANTILE)	ODDS RATIO (95% CONFIDENCE INTERVAL)	ADJUSTMENT SEX/AGE	OTHER VARIABLES[a]
Acheson and Doll, 1964, England	100	na	no assoc	Y	N
Higginson, 1966, Kansas City, USA	93	h vs l quartile	no assoc	na	na
Graham et al, 1972, Buffalo, USA	168 men	na	no assoc	Y	Y
	68 women	na	no assoc	Y	Y
Risch et al, 1985, Canada	246	na	no assoc	Y	Y
Trichopoulos et al, 1985, Piraeus Greece	110	h vs l quintile[b]	3.2 (na)	Y	Y
Tajima and Tominaga, 1985, Japan	93	h vs l half	0.8 (na)	Y	N
Demirer et al, 1990, Ankara, Turkey	100	h vs l sextile	0.6 (na)	Y	Y
Agudo et al, 1992, Spain	235 men	na	0.8 (na)	Y	Y
	119 women	na	1.8 (na)	Y	Y
Hoshiyama & Sasaba, 1992, Japan	294	h vs l tertile	1.4 (0.9–2.2)[c]	Y	Y
		h vs l tertile	1.2 (0.7–2.1)[d]	Y	Y
La Vecchia et al, 1992, Milano, Italy	564	h vs l half	1.0 (0.8–1.3)	Y	Y
Memik et al, 1992, Turkey	252	h vs l tertile	0.5* (0.3–1.0)	Y	N
Hansson et al, 1993, Sweden	338	h vs l quartile	0.7* (0.5–1.1)	Y	Y

* $p \leq 0.05$ for trend or as compared with the lowest consumption level
na not available
a Adjusted or matched for one or more of the following: ethnicity, total food consumption, education, residence, smoking history, socio-economic status, coffee consumption, total calories, consumption of fruit, vegetables, cold cuts and preserved fish
b Includes coffee
c Comparison with general population controls
d Comparison with hospital controls

(IARC, 1991; Higginson, 1966; Graham et al, 1967; Tajima and Tominaga, 1985; Trichopoulos et al, 1985; La Vecchia et al, 1989). Similarly, subsequent case-control studies in Spain, Turkey and Sweden have reported no substantial association between coffee consumption and risk of stomach cancer (Agudo et al, 1992; Memik et al, 1992; Hansson et al, 1993). These eight case-control studies are presented in Table 4.6.10.

Of two prospective and eight case-control studies, none has reported a statistically significant association between coffee consumption and risk of stomach cancer.

High consumption of coffee probably has no relationship with the risk of stomach cancer.

Tea
In a 1993 review of tea consumption and cancer that summarised 13 epidemiological studies of stomach cancer, four showed a protective association (two ecological and two case-control), two showed increased risk with higher consumption (one cohort and one case-control), and seven (all case-control) showed no relationship; these included studies of both green and black tea (see Yang and Wang, 1993).

In 1991, an IARC Working Group reviewed the available data regarding tea drinking and risk of stomach cancer. They noted that one cohort study showed an increased risk with higher consumption, which remained after adjustment for social class, and that four of five case-control studies showed no association.

In this report, an attempt is made to examine associations for green and black tea separately, because of the different constituents and potentially different biological effects of these different types of teas.

Green tea
Four of five case-control studies of green tea in Japan (Tajima and Tominaga 1985; Kono et al, 1988; Kato et al, 1990) and in China (Yu and Hsieh, 1991; Yu et al, 1995) have suggested a protective effect. Although a significant decrease in risk was found only among those consuming 10 cups or more per day in a Japanese study (Kono et al, 1988) a clear dose–response relationship was observed in a study in China (Yu et al, 1995). One case-control study in Japan observed no material associations for green tea(OR = 0.8, 0.5–1.3 for women, and 1.0, ns for men, for five or more cups per day, as compared with none) (Kato et al, 1990).

Several animal experiments have been conducted in which green tea infusions have been shown to reduce the incidence of experimentally induced stomach cancer (see Yang and Wang, 1993).

Polyphenol extracts of tea, especially of green tea, are known to have anticarcinogenic effects in animals (Yang and Wang, 1993). An animal study showed epigallocatechin, a principal component of green tea polyphenols, to inhibit chemical carcinogenesis in the glandular stomach (Yamane et al, 1995). Another study suggested that the anticarcino-

TABLE 4.6.13 SALT AND SALTED FOODS CONSUMPTION AND STOMACH CANCER RISK: COHORT STUDIES

AUTHOR, YEAR AND PLACE	SIZE OF COHORT: NO. OF CASES	TYPE OF SALTED FOOD	COMPARISON (HIGHEST VS LOWEST QUANTILE)	RELATIVE RISK (95% CONFIDENCE INTERVAL)	ADJUSTMENT Sex/Age	Other VARIABLES[a]
Nomura et al, 1990 Hawaii, USA	7,990 men[b]: 150	Table salt/shoyu	h vs l tertile	1.0 (0.6–1.6)	Y	N
Kneller et al, 1991, USA	17,633 men[c]: 75	Salted fish	h vs l tertile	1.9 (1.0–3.6)	Y	Y

[na] not available.
[a] Also adjusted for smoking history
[b] Japanese origin
[c] Scandinavian and German origin

genic effects of green tea catechins may be stronger than those of black tea polyphenols (Wang et al, 1992).

High consumption of green tea possibly decreases the risk of stomach cancer.

Black tea

Three prospective studies of stomach cancer which have examined consumption of black tea are presented in Table 4.6.11. One of these observed a moderate increase in risk with higher consumption in British men, which was partially, but not entirely, attributable to confounding by social class (Kinlen et al, 1988). A cohort study in the Netherlands reported a protective association which disappeared when adjusted for education, vitamin C intake, and other factors; odds ratios before and after multivariate adjustment were 0.7 (p = 0.15 for trend) and 0.9 (ns; p for trend), respectively (Goldbohm et al, 1996). A third study of Japanese men in Hawaii found no association (Heilbrun et al, 1986).

Another recent cohort study of American women reported decreased risk of all digestive tract cancers combined, with a relative risk of 0.7 (0.5–0.98) for two or more cups of black tea per day, compared with a monthly consumption or less (Zheng et al, 1996). No result was reported for stomach cancer specifically, because of the low number of stomach cancer cases, but the relative risk for all upper digestive tract cancers was 0.4 (0.1–1.4), based upon 47 total cases.

Twelve case-control studies that have examined black tea consumption, are shown in Table 4.6.12. Nine of these have shown no relationship to stomach cancer risk, with two studies in Turkey and Sweden showing statistically significant decreases in risk with higher intakes, and one study in Greece showing an increase in risk for higher intake of tea and coffee combined which was not statistically significant.

The majority of three cohort and 12 case-control studies have shown no association with the risk of stomach cancer risk, after controlling for potential confounding factors, such as social class or education.

High consumption of black tea probably has no relationship with the risk of stomach cancer.

4.6.3 FOOD PROCESSING

4.6.3.1 Salt, salting and refrigeration
Salt
A prospective study of stomach cancer which has examined intake of salt (Table 4.6.13) showed no association with intake of table salt or shoyu (Nomura et al, 1990).

Sixteen case-control studies that have reported on salt or salted foods are presented in Table 4.6.14. Eight of these have estimated overall dietary salt or sodium intake; of these, four, in the USA, Spain, Puerto Rico and Korea, have shown strong statistically significant increases in risk (OR = 2.1–5.0 for the highest intake levels) (Graham et al, 1990; Ramon et al, 1993; Nazario et al, 1993; Lee et al, 1995). The remaining four studies showed no substantial associations (Modan et al, 1974; Correa et al, 1985; Risch et al, 1985; You et al, 1988). It has been pointed out that starchy foods and diets associated with high rates of stomach cancer, including those in some European countries, contain substantial amounts of salt in bread and other staples; in places where starchy diets are not salty, as in some countries in Africa, stomach cancer rates are low (Joossens and Kesteloot, 1988).

Six of the studies in Table 4.6.14 have specifically examined the use of table salt, with three studies, in Belgium, England, and Poland, reporting statistically significant increases in risk, (OR = 1.6–6.2 for higher intakes) (Tuyns et al, 1988; Coggon et al, 1989; Boeing et al, 1991). Two other studies each reported statistically non-significant odds ratios of 1.5 for consumption in the upper half of the table salt intake distribution (Buiatti et al, 1989; La Vecchia et al, 1987); the remaining study reported no association (Boeing et al, 1991a).

Results from the Intersalt study of 24 countries showed a correlation between urinary sodium excretion and stomach cancer mortality (r = 0.7 in men and in women) (Joossens et al, 1993). The study included countries with high rates of sodium excretion and stomach cancer mortality, such as China, Colombia, and Japan, as well as with lower rates of salt intake and stomach cancer, such as Mexico, Iceland, Belgium, England, and Wales. The study produced similar findings for nitrate excretion, but the effect of sodium appeared to be stronger (Joossens et al, 1996).

TABLE 4.6.14 SALT AND SALTED FOODS CONSUMPTION AND STOMACH CANCER RISK: CASE-CONTROL STUDIES

AUTHOR, YEAR AND PLACE	NO. OF CASES	TYPE OF SALTED FOOD	COMPARISON (HIGHEST VS LOWEST QUANTILE)	ODDS RATIO (95% CONFIDENCE INTERVAL)	ADJUSTMENT SEX/AGE	OTHER VARIABLES[a]
Acheson and Doll, 1964 England	100	Salted/dried fish	h vs l quartile	1.7 (na)	Y	N
Hirayama, 1971, Japan	454	Salted vegetables	na	positive assoc*	Y	Y
Haenszel et al, 1972 Hawaii, USA	220 Japanese	Salted/dried fish	h vs l quartile	2.6* (na)	Y	Y
Bjelke, 19074, Norway	228	Salted fish	na	positive assoc	na	na
Modan et al, 1974 Tel Aviv, Israel	na	Salt	na	no assoc	na	na
Haenszel et al, 1976 Japan	783	Salted/dried fish	h vs l quartile	1.2 (na)	Y	Y
Correa et al, 1985	9 whites	Salt	h vs l quartile	1.2 (0.3–4.0)	Y	Y
Louisiana, USA	9 blacks	Salt	h vs l quartile	1.3 (0.4–5.0)	Y	Y
Risch et al, 1985, Canada	246	Salt intake	na	no assoc	Y	Y
Tajima & Tominaga, 1985 Japan	93	Salted/dried fish	h vs l half	2.0* (na)	Y	N
La Vecchia et al, 1987 Milano, Italy	206	Table salt	h vs l tertile	1.5 (na)	Y	N
Hu et al, 1988, China	241	Salted and fermented soya paste	h vs l half	1.5 (1.0–2.2)	Y	Y
Kono et al, 1988, Japan	139	Salty foods	h vs l tertile	1.4 (na)[b]	Y	N
		Salted fish	h vs l tertile	1.0 (na)[b]	Y	N
You et al, 1988, China	564	Salted fish	h vs l tertile	1.4 (0.8–1.5)	Y	Y
		Salted vegetables	h vs l half	1.1 (0.7–1.8)	Y	Y
		Salt intake	h vs l quartile	1.1 (0.8–1.4)	Y	Y
Tuyns, 1988, Belgium	293	Table salt	h vs l tertile	1.8* (1.2–2.8)	na	na
Coggon et al, 1989 England	95	Table salt	high vs low	6.2 (2.0–18.9)	Y	Y
Buiatti et al, 1989, Italy	1,016	Salted/dried fish	h vs l tertile	1.4* (na)	Y	Y
		Table salt	h vs l half	1.5 (1.3–1.9)	Y	Y
Graham et al, 1990	186 men	Sodium intake	h vs l quartile	3.1* (1.7–5.8)	Y	Y
New York, USA	107 women	Sodium intake	h vs l tertile	4.7* (2.3–9.6)	Y	Y
Demirer et al, 1990 Ankara, Turkey	100	Salted foods	h vs l half	3.8* (2.1–6.9)	Y	Y
Kato et al, 1990, Japan	289 men	Salted/dried fish	h vs l half	1.2 (0.9–1.7)	Y	Y
		Salted fish gut, cod roe	h vs l half	1.5* (1.1–2.1)	Y	Y
	138 women	Salted/dried fish	h vs l half	0.7 (0.5–1.0)	Y	Y
		Salted fish gut, cod roe	h vs l half	0.5 (0.3–1.0)	Y	Y
Boeing et al, 1991 Germany	143	Table salt	na	no assoc	Y	Y
		Pretzels, salty snacks	h vs l tertile	1.5 (1.0–2.2)	Y	Y
Boeing et al, 1991 Poland	741	Table salt	h vs l half	1.6 (1.2–2.3)	Y	Y
Gonzalez et al, 1991 Spain	354	Salted fish	h vs l half	1.5 (0.9–2.6)	Y	Y
Hoshiyama & Sasaba 1992, Japan	294	Salty foods	h vs l tertile	2.3* (1.5–3.4)[c]	Y	Y
		Salty foods	h vs l tertile	1.1 (0.7–1.9)[d]	Y	Y
Palli et al, 1992, Italy	68[e]	Salted/dried fish	h vs l tertile	1.7 (0.9–3.1)	Y	Y
Ramon et al, 1993 Barcelona, Spain	117	Salt intake	h vs l quartile	2.1* (1.2–7.1)	Y	Y
Nazario et al, 1993 Puerto Rico	136	Salt intake	h vs l quartile	5.0* (2.1–12.0)	Y	Y
Hansson et al, 1993 Sweden	338	Salted fish	h vs l quintile	1.3 (0.8–2.1)[f]	Y	Y
		Salted fish	h vs l quintile	0.8 (0.5–1.3)[g]	Y	Y
Lee et al, 1995, Korea	213	Salt intake	h vs l tertile	3.7 (1.1–12.5)	Y	Y
		Salted side dishes	h vs l tertile	4.5* (2.5–8.0)	Y	Y

* p ≤ 0.05 for trend or as compared with lowest consumption level

na not available

[a] Also adjusted for one or more of the following: ethnicity, income, occupation, residence, race, respondent status, smoking history, alcohol consumption, total food consumption, study area, socio-economic status, migration, family predisposition, hospital, education, total calories, other food items, length of refrigerator use, consumption of salad vegetables in summer and winter, fresh or frozen fruit, smoked meat or fish

[b] Comparison with hospital controls as opposed to general population controls

[c] Comparison with general population controls

[d] Comparison with hospital controls

[e] Number of gastric cardia cancer cases from Buiatti et al, 1989

[f] Adolescence

[g] Twenty years prior to interview

Similar descriptive features of stroke and stomach cancer, including worldwide distribution and secular trends, are consistent with salt intake as a factor in stomach cancer (Joossens and Geboers, 1981).

In Japan, the geographical variation in stomach cancer mortality was shown not to correlate with per capita salt consumption, as estimated in the national nutrition survey for nine districts (Kono et al, 1983) or 47 prefectures (Honjo et al, 1994).

High-salt diets have been shown to enhance chemically induced carcinogenesis in the glandular stomach of rats (Takahashi et al, 1983; Takahashi et al, 1984).

The biological pathways by which salt increases risk of stomach cancer have been well articulated (Correa, 1992). Although salt is not intrinsically carcinogenic, intake of salt (and salted foods) leads to damage of the mucosal protective layer in the stomach, and results in an inflammatory regenerative response, increased DNA synthesis and cell proliferation (Charnley and Tannenbaum, 1985; Ames and Gold, 1990). This typically enhances carcinogenesis induced by specific carcinogens since a higher cell-replication rate decreases the possibility of DNA repair. Mucosal damage may also increase the likelihood of entry of carcinogens into cells.

It has been suggested that the significant correlation between *H. pylori* carriage and international rates of stomach cancer (Eurogast Study Group, 1993), in contrast to high *H. pylori* carriage and low rates of stomach cancer in Africa (Holcombe, 1992), where salt intake is low, indicates that bacterial infection is a co-factor with salt, which enhances carcinogenesis after the gastric epithelium is damaged (Joossens et al, 1996).

In Colombia (Chen et al, 1990), high salt intake measured by sodium:creatinine ratio of a single urine sample was strongly associated with an increased prevalence of gastric pre-cancerous lesions, such as chronic atrophic gastritis and gastric dysplasia. In China, salt consumption and soy sauce consumption were related to elevated risk of dysplasia (Kneller et al, 1992). A hospital-based case-control study in the USA (Fontham et al, 1986) reported increased risk of chronic atrophic gastritis, with and without intestinal metaplasia, in association with self-reported heavy salt use.

Epidemiological and experimental data, and plausible biological pathways, amount to evidence that diets containing substantial amounts of salt probably increase the risk of stomach cancer.

Salting

A variety of salted foods has been associated with increased risk of stomach cancer. A prospective study suggested increased risk with higher intake of salted fish, although the increase was not statistically significant (Kneller et al, 1991). Twelve of the studies presented in Table 4.6.14 have examined consumption of salted fish, with three studies, in Hawaii, Japan and Italy, reporting statistically significant increases in risk with higher consumption (ORs = 1.4 to 2.6)

(Haenszel et al, 1972; Tajima and Tominaga, 1985; Buiatti et al, 1989). Another study in Japan showed a statistically significant 50% increase in risk for high consumption of salted fish gut and cod roe in men, but not women, and no association for salted/dried fish in general for either sex (Kato et al, 1990). Statistically non-significant increases in risk were observed in four further studies (ORs = 1.5 to 1.7 for higher intakes in studies reporting risk estimates) (Acheson and Doll, 1964; Bjelke 1974b; Gonzalez et al, 1991; Palli et al, 1992). The remaining four studies showed no association (Haenszel et al, 1976; Kono et al, 1988; You et al, 1988; Hansson et al, 1993).

Other case-control studies have examined consumption of salty foods in general, salted vegetables or other specific salty foods, such as soya paste or pretzels; these studies have, for the most part, found varying degrees of increased risk with higher levels of consumption (Hirayama et al, 1971; Hu et al, 1988; Kono et al, 1988; You et al, 1988; Demirer et al, 1990; Boeing et al, 1991a; Hishiyama and Sasaba, 1992; Lee et al, 1995) (see Table 4.6.14).

Japanese pickled vegetables are generally pickled with salt, and an association between pickled vegetables and increased risk has been noted in Japanese living in Hawaii (Haenszel et al, 1972), but not in Japan (Haenszel et al, 1976).

Throughout the world, there is a strong and consistent correlation between intake of salt and salted foods and incidence of stomach cancer and pre-cancerous lesions (Puffer et al, 1967; Montes et al, 1985). In an ecological study of 65 rural counties in China (Kneller et al, 1992) the consumption of salt-preserved vegetables was weakly associated with stomach cancer mortality.

In Japan, the consumption of dried fish was positively related to the severity of intestinal metaplasia in men but not in women (Nomura et al, 1982), although a hospital-based case-control study found no association of chronic atrophic gastritis with salted/dried fish, salted fish gut or salt pickled vegetables (Kato et al, 1990). In Italy, the consumption of salted/dried fish was related to an increased risk of severe chronic atrophic gastritis as determined by serum pepsinogen levels (Anonymous, 1992).

Intake of salted foods, as with salt, leads to damage of the protective mucosal layer in the stomach, and thereby may enhance carcinogenesis.

Epidemiological and experimental data, and plausible biological pathways, amount to evidence that diets high in salted foods probably increase the risk of stomach cancer.

Refrigeration

Ten case-control studies of stomach cancer have examined refrigerator use and are presented in Table 4.6.15. Nine of these studies found some degree of protective association with duration of use; these studies were conducted in Canada, the USA, England, Italy, Germany, Sweden, Turkey and Korea (Risch et al, 1985; Buiatti et al, 1989; Coggon et

TABLE 4.6.15 YEARS OF REFRIGERATION USE AND STOMACH CANCER RISK: CASE-CONTROL STUDIES

AUTHOR, YEAR AND PLACE	NO. OF CASES	COMPARISON (HIGHEST VS LOWEST QUANTILE)	RELATIVE RISK (95% CONFIDENCE INTERVAL)	ADJUSTMENT SEX/AGE	OTHER VARIABLES[a]
Correa et al, 1985, Louisiana, USA	391	na	no assoc	na	na
Risch et al, 1985, Canada	246	na	0.8* (0.7–1.0)	Y	Y
Buiatti et al, 1989, Italy	1,016	h vs l tertile	0.7 (0.5–1.0)	Y	Y
Coggon et al, 1989, England	94	h vs l quartile	0.5* (0.2–1.0)	Y	N
Demirer et al, 1990, Ankara, Turkey	100	na	negative assoc*	Y	Y
La Vecchia et al, 1990, Milano, Italy	464	h vs l quartile	0.5* (0.3–0.9)	Y	N
Graham et al, 1990, New York, USA	177 men	h vs l quartile	0.4* (0.2–0.8)	Y	Y
	98 women	h vs l tertile	0.7* (0.3–1.4)	Y	Y
Boeing et al, 1991, Germany	143	h vs l tertile	0.7* (0.4–1.4)	Y	Y
Hansson et al, 1993, Sweden	338	h vs l sextile	0.4 (0.2–1.0)	Y	Y
Lee et al, 1995, Korea	210	h vs l tertile	0.2* (0.1–0.4)	Y	Y

*$p \leq 0.05$ for trend or as compared with lowest number of years

na not available

a Also adjusted for one or more of the following: total food consumption, ethnicity, residence, migration, socio-economic status, family predisposition, hospital, body mass index, vegetable and fruit consumption, education

al, 1989; Demirer et al, 1990; Graham et al, 1990; Boeing et al, 1991a; Hansson et al, 1993; Lee et al, 1995). A protective association with ownership of a refrigerator was found in a study in Turkey (Demirer et al, 1990), but not in one in the USA (Correa et al, 1985).

The critical factor determining the effect of domestic refrigeration on reduced risk of stomach cancer may be length of use. In England, no effect was shown for 15–29 years of use, but the odds ratio decreased to 0.5 after 29 years of use (Coggon et al, 1989). In Italy, the odds ratio declined to 0.5 after 40 years of use (La Vecchia et al, 1990).

Refrigeration may lead to decreased risk of stomach cancer indirectly, via a concomitant decrease in intake of salty foods or via increased intake of vegetables and fruits, which can be preserved for longer periods via refrigeration. Use of refrigeration has been shown to be inversely correlated with use of salting, with other methods of food preservation using salt, such as curing and smoking, and with the volume of salt in diets. Also, there is a consistent correlation between the use of industrial and domestic freezing, chilling and refrigeration, and decline in rates of stomach cancer (and stroke) throughout the world (Joossens and Kesteloot, 1996).

Evidence that refrigeration decreases the risk of stomach cancer is convincing.

The effect can be seen as indirect or adventitious, but is important, all the more so given the prevalence of stomach cancer in the world.

4.6.3.2 Cured and smoked foods

Cured meats

A prospective study of Japanese men in Hawaii reported a RR of 1.3 (0.9–2.0) for high consumption frequency (5 times or more versus once or less per week) of ham, bacon, and sausage combined (Nomura et al, 1990). Another prospec-

tive study in the USA also found a weak, positive association with the consumption of bacon or side pork (Kneller et al, 1991); RRs (and 95% CIs) for < 3, 3–5, 6–13, and 14 times or more per month were 1.0 (referent), 1.7(0.9–3.3), 2.0 (1.0–3.9), and 1.4 (0.6–3.1), respectively. Six case-control studies of stomach cancer have examined the association with selected items of cured meats separately (La Vecchia et al, 1987; Boeing et al, 1991b; Tuyns et al, 1992) with cured meats as a whole (Gonzalez et al, 1991) or with a broader group of processed or preserved meats (Buiatti et al, 1989; Boeing et al, 1991a). In general, a small, significant or non-significant elevation in the risk was observed at the highest consumption level; reported RRs ranged from 1.0 (Boeing et al, 1991b) to 1.7 (Boeing et al, 1991a). (See also Box 4.6.4).

The evidence suggest that diets high in cured meats may increase the risk of stomach cancer, but is as yet insufficient.

Smoked foods

The regular intake of meat and/or fish preserved by smoking has been noted in areas with high stomach cancer mortality in Iceland, Hungary and Latvia (NAS, 1982). In most analytical studies, smoked foods have been considered together with other preserved foods. Of six-case-control studies investigating the association with smoked foods as a single item, two studies found a positive association with smoked fish in the USA (Bjelke, 1974a) and with smoked foods among blacks but not among whites in the USA (Correa et al, 1985). Others found no association in England (Acheson and Doll, 1964; Coggon et al, 1989) and non-significant reduced risk in Belgium (Tuyns et al, 1992) and Sweden (Hansson et al, 1993).

Any hot flame leads to the production of nitrosyl compounds. Exposure of foods to these nitrosyl vapours essentially has the same effect as curing with nitrate or nitrite

BOX 4.6.4 NITRATE, NITRITE AND N-NITROSO COMPOUNDS

The possibility that N-nitrosated compounds are involved in human cancer has been an issue for many years. There is extensive experimental evidence that these compounds are cancer causing in animals (IARC, 1974; 1982). The stomach is an established site for N-nitroso compound carcinogenesis in animals (Mirvish, 1983, 1986). Nitrate occurs naturally in plants, but can be higher in the presence of nitrate fertilisers. It can be found naturally in water supplies, and levels can be higher as a result of fertiliser run-off. Nitrate is found in food largely because it is used in 'cured' foods as preservative. Nitrate and nitrite are not themselves carcinogenic in animals (NAS, 1981). N-Nitroso compounds can be formed from both nitrite and nitrate via biological pathways that have been shown to occur in humans and animals; N-nitroso compounds can also form during the curing process. Accordingly, concern has been expressed that nitrite from cured meats, etc., nitrates in vegetables, as well as pre-formed nitrosamines, may be involved in gastric carcinogenesis.

One cohort study of stomach cancer that examined daily intake of nitrate-related compounds observed no statistically significant difference in intake between cases and controls (Chyou et al, 1993).

Seven case-control studies of stomach cancer, in the USA and Europe, have examined intake of nitrate, nitrite or nitrosamines (Correa et al, 1985; Risch et al, 1985; Buiatti et al, 1990; Boeing et al, 1991a; Palli et al, 1992; Gonzalez et al, 1994; Hansson et al, 1994). Of six studies that reported specifically on nitrate, four showed no material associations, whereas two reported statistically significant moderate to strong decreases in risk with higher intake. Of six studies that reported specifically on nitrite, two observed statistically significant increases in risk, whereas the other four reported no material associations. One study that examined intake of nitrosamines reported a strong increase in risk with higher intake, whereas another that reported on intake of dimethylnitrosamine observed no association.

Reviewing 15 correlation studies, based on variable measures of nitrate exposure in 10 countries, Forman (1989) showed that

the studies were equally divided: one-third showing increased incidence of stomach cancer with greater exposure, one-third showing decreased incidence, and one-third showing no association.

Although the consumption of nitrates from vegetables may theoretically provide substrate for the formation of N-nitroso compounds, the concomitant intake of other compounds including vitamin C (a known inhibitor of endogenous nitrosation of amines) plausibly counteracts any increased risk. A controlled feeding trial in human subjects showed that when the amino acid proline was consumed along with beet juice (a rich source of nitrate), a nitrosamine was formed, but when ascorbic acid or α-tocopherol were consumed in addition, the production of the nitrosamine was inhibited (Oshima and Bartsch, 1981).

Studies on nitrate concentrations in drinking water do not show a positive association with cancer risk and high levels of industrial exposure among fertiliser workers similarly were not associated with elevated risk of cancer of the stomach or any other site (Forman et al, 1985a,b).

Nitrate levels in gastric juice were shown to be progressively higher in subjects with more severe precancerous lesions in Colombia, whereas the nitrate concentrations were shown to decrease as the gastric lesions advanced to intestinal metaplasia and dysplasia in Louisiana blacks (Fontham et al, 1986). These authors hypothesised that the major sources of nitrate exposure in high risk areas of Colombia were drinking water, grains, and root vegetables, while nitrate exposure in Louisiana derived largely from leafy vegetables, which appear to be protective against stomach cancer.

The human evidence regarding vegetable consumption clearly supports a protective effect against stomach cancer and cancers of other sites, rather than an adverse effect (see section 4.6.2.3).

In the Intersalt study, in which 24-hour urinary excretion of nitrate was measured in 24 countries, higher urinary nitrate levels were associated with increased stomach cancer mortality (r = 0.57 in men and r = 0.56 in women) (Joossens et al, 1993). However, when the countries were stratified by sodium intake, this correlation was

confined to those countries with high sodium intake. In countries with low sodium intake, higher nitrate levels were associated with lower mortality. This ecological finding would suggest that the effect of nitrate, if any, varies with salt exposure and possibly other dietary factors.

Any association between nitrite-cured foods and stomach cancer may also be due to other aspects of preserved meat and fish (Risch et al, 1985; Buiatti et al, 1989).

Besides preformed N-nitroso compounds, intragastric formation of such compounds has been implicated in human gastric carcinogenesis (Mirvish, 1983; Forman, 1987). Urinary excretion of nitrosoproline after oral administration of proline, a measure of endogenous nitrosation, was shown to be higher in residents in an area with a high risk of stomach cancer than those of a low-risk area in Japan (Kamiyami et al, 1987) and Costa Rica (Sierra et al, 1993). Specific foods commonly consumed in high-risk populations such as fava beans in Columbia (Yang et al, 1984) and salted fish in Japan (Marquardt et al, 1977) have been reported to contain potent mutagens after in vitro nitrosation. Japanese salted fish after nitrosation was shown to induce adenocarcinomas of the glandular stomach in rats (Weisburger et al, 1980).

Nitrate intake from vegetables probably has no relationship with the risk of stomach cancer .

Evidence relating to intakes of nitrates from fertiliser residues is confused and inconsistent; no judgement is possible.

While current epidemiological evidence is weak, laboratory studies supported by evidence of plausible biological pathways shows a link between N-nitroso compounds and stomach cancer. Overall, the panel judges that N-nitroso compounds, as found notably in cured meats and other foods and salted foods, may be related to the risk of stomach cancer, but the evidence is, as yet, insufficient.

solutions. Smoked foods may also have carcinogenic poly-cyclic aromatic hydrocarbons at their surface.

Evidence relating to diets high in smoked foods is conflicting; no judgement is possible.

4.6.3.3 Cooking
Grilling (broiling) and barbecuing; frying

Although a Japanese study (Kono et al, 1988) observed no association between the risk of stomach cancer and any of the following: broiled fish, grilled meat, or beefsteak and hamburger separately and stomach cancer, a study in Korea (Lee et al, 1995) reported a relative risk of 6.3 (3.5–11.4) among those consuming broiled meat and fish frequently. A trend towards increased risk was also found with the use of grilling (broiling) in preparation in Italy (Buiatti et al, 1989).

A prospective study in Japan (Kato et al, 1992) also reported an increased mortality from stomach cancer associated with frequent consumption of broiled fish (RR = 1.8 for > 3 times/week versus < 1–2 times/month; p for trend = 0.16), and also with broiled meat (RR = 2.3; p for trend = 0.03). A study in the USA (Wu-Williams et al, 1990) noted a significant positive association with barbecued or smoked foods combined (RR = 2.5, 1.2–5.9 for two times or more a week versus less).

Although an increased risk with grilled (broiled) fish was shown to be independent of vegetables and other related factors in the Korean study (Lee et al, 1995), adjustment was not made for other risk factors in the other studies. However, a recent study in the USA shows increased risk for stomach cancer associated with barbecuing/grilling and preferences for well-done, red meat (Ward et al, in press).

Experimental evidence and plausible biological pathways are given in Box 7.6.1.

It is reasonable to assume that data on grilling (broiling) apply to some forms of barbecuing.

More than 30 years ago, Acheson and Doll (1964) questioned the ways of serving 48 food items among 100 cases of stomach cancer and 200 hospital controls in England, and reported that the consumption of fried foods was lower in cases than in controls (p = 0.05). Graham et al (1972) calculated a score of eating different fried meats, and found virtually no difference between 228 cases and 228 controls in the USA.

Three case-control studies on cooking and stomach cancer have noted a statistically non-significant modest increase in the risk with fried meat in the USA (Higginson, 1966), with fried meat and fried fish each in Turkey (Demirer et al, 1990), and with pan-fried meat or fish combined in Sweden (Hansson et al, 1993), but three other such studies found no association with: fried foods in the USA, Japan, Slovenia, and Iceland (Wynder et al, 1963); deep-fried foods in the USA (Wu-Williams et al, 1990); and with the frequency of frying any foods in Italy (Buiatti et al, 1989). A highly significant association with decreased risk was noted with consumption frequency of foods fried over open fire in Sweden (Hansson et al, 1993) and with fried meat and fish in Korea

(Lee et al, 1995). A Polish study reported an RR of 2.1 associated with consumption of fried versus boiled meat (Jedrychowski et al, 1992).

Although cooking meat, and fish at high temperatures results in the formation of heterocyclic amines (HCAs), there is a lack of experimental data linking HCAs to gastric cancer.

Diets high in meat and fish that has been grilled (broiled) and barbecued possibly increase the risk of stomach cancer.

Evidence relating to the consumption of fried foods and the risk of stomach cancer is conflicting; no judgement is possible.

4.7 Pancreas

Cancer of the pancreas is relatively uncommon. An estimated 200,000 cases occurred in 1996, accounting for 2% of all new cases of cancer.

In general, rates of this cancer are higher in economically developed societies. Pancreatic cancer is almost always fatal.

The panel has reached the following conclusions. Diets high in vegetables and fruits are probably protective against pancreatic cancer.

The panel notes that fibre and vitamin C, as found in foods of plant origin, are possibly also protective, and that diets containing substantial amounts of red meat and cholesterol possibly increase risk.

Alcohol, and regular consumption of coffee, probably do not affect risk of this cancer.

An established non-dietary cause of pancreatic cancer is smoking.

The most effective dietary means of preventing pancreatic cancer is consumption of diets high in vegetables and fruits and, possibly, only occasional consumption of red meat.

FOOD, NUTRITION AND PANCREATIC CANCER

In the judgement of the panel, the dietary constituents and related factors, the foods and drinks, and the methods of food processing listed below modify the risk of pancreatic cancer, or else have no relationship with it. Judgements are graded according to the strength of the evidence.

EVIDENCE	DECREASES RISK	NO RELATIONSHIP	INCREASES RISK
Convincing			
Probable	Vegetables and fruits	Alcohol Coffee	
Possible	NSP/fibre Vitamin C	High body mass Tea	High energy intake Cholesterol Meat
Insufficient			Sugar Eggs Cured and smoked meat and fish

For an explanation of the terms used in the matrix, see chapter 3.

INTRODUCTION

The pancreas consists of two separate functional entities: the endocrine part, producing insulin and glucagon, and the exocrine part that produces enzymes such as trypsin, chymotrypsin, amylase and lipase (Rutter, 1980; Go et al, 1986).

Pancreatic cancer is among the most rapidly fatal cancers and its presentation and clinical course are usually marked by severe pain. One-year survival rates are less than 20% and 5-year survival is essentially zero (American Cancer Society, 1993; US DHHS, 1990). There are no effective means of screening or early diagnosis. In this chapter, pancreatic cancer is considered synonymous with adenocarcinoma of the exocrine pancreas; endocrine tumours are rare. Over two-thirds of exocrine tumours occur in the head of the

BOX 4.7.1 ESTABLISHED NON-DIETARY FACTORS AND PANCREATIC CANCER

The following non-dietary factor increases the risk of pancreatic cancer:
■ Smoking tobacco

pancreas (Howard and Jordan, 1977; Cubilla and Fitzgerald,1978b; Mack and Paganini-Hill, 1981; Sener et al, 1991).

INCIDENCE PATTERNS

Cancer of the pancreas is the thirteenth most common cancer in the world. In 1996, an estimated 200,000 new cases were diagnosed worldwide (WHO, 1997), accounting for

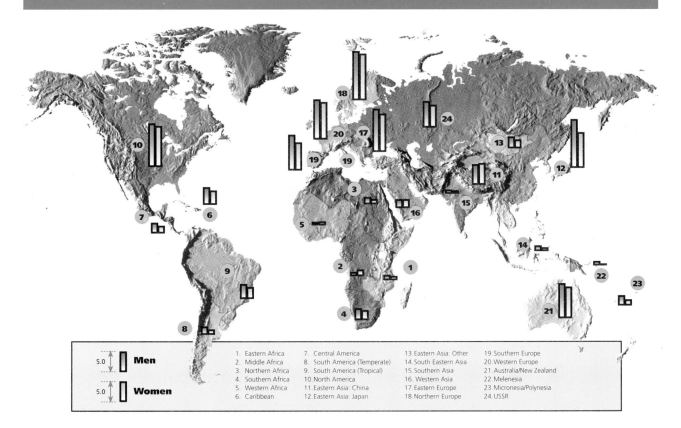

PANCREAS CANCER estimated rates of cancer incidence by sex and area

5.0 ⬍ ▮ **Men**	1. Eastern Africa	7. Central America	13.Eastern Asia: Other	19.Southern Europe
	2. Middle Africa	8. South America (Temperate)	14.South Eastern Asia	20.Western Europe
	3. Northern Africa	9. South America (Tropical)	15.Southern Asia	21.Australia/New Zealand
	4. Southern Africa	10.North America	16.Western Asia	22.Melenesia
5.0 ⬍ ▯ **Women**	5. Western Africa	11.Eastern Asia: China	17.Eastern Europe	23.Micronesia/Polynesia
	6. Caribbean	12.Eastern Asia: Japan	18.Northern Europe	24.USSR

nearly 2% of all new cancers.

There is substantial geographical variation in the incidence of pancreatic cancer with the highest rates being seen in the USA (particularly among black Americans) and similar Western populations (Riboli et al, 1992). The lowest rates are generally seen in Africa and some Asian countries, although Japan, which has seen a substantial increase in rates in recent decades, now has rates similar to those seen in the USA.

Men have approximately a one-third greater age-adjusted incidence rate than women (Parkin et al, 1993).

The highest mortality rates (Aoki et al, 1992) occur in northern Europe, including Britain, and in countries populated by migration from those areas. The corresponding rates in central and southern Europe are generally lower. Mortality rates in Japan are now similar to rates in Western countries (Aoki et al, 1992).

Survival rates for pancreatic cancer are among the worst for any cancer. Median survival is about 3 months (Axtell et al, 1976; Arnar et al, 1991; Riela et al, 1992). Most cases (perhaps 75–85%) present with relatively advanced disease and unresectable tumours. In 1996, mortality attributable to pancreatic cancer was estimated at 196,000 people, 2.8% of all cancer deaths (WHO, 1997).

PATHOGENESIS

The pancreas is, of course, intimately related to digestion and absorption, and it is reasonable to place diet high among the possible causal factors for pancreatic carcinoma (Willett and MacMahon, 1984a,b; Longnecker, 1990; Andersen et al, 1996). However, unlike every other part of the gastrointestinal tract, the pancreas is never exposed, either directly (mouth to anus) or indirectly (via the liver), to ingested or absorbed foods. Accordingly, the effects of diet on carcinogenesis in the pancreas are via changes in the internal metabolic environment of that organ, exposure to blood-borne agents or, more probably, both.

It appears probable that mutations in cellular proto-oncogenes and tumour-suppressor genes are central to pancreatic carcinogenesis. Numerous lines of evidence suggest that K-ras mutations are an early and important event (Alomoquera et al, 1988; Bos, 1989, 1990; Nagata et al, 1990; Shibata et al, 1990; Tada et al, 1990). Examples of such evidence include: the high proportion of malignant tumours with mutations in K-ras; the presence of the mutation in some pre-invasive lesions; the presence of the mutation in both primary and metastatic foci; and the reported amplification of the oncogene in some malignant tumours (Yamada et al, 1986; Parsa et al, 1988; Lemoine et al, 1992b) and cell lines (Hirai et al, 1985). The role of diet in this is not established, but there are some carcinogens, e.g., aromatic and heterocyclic amines (from diet and cigarette smoke), and some kinds of known DNA damage (particularly oxidative damage), which could produce such mutations.

JUDGEMENTS OF OTHER REPORTS

Earlier expert reports, for example, the National Academy of Sciences report, *Diet, Nutrition and Cancer* (NAS, 1982) and the subsequent report, *Diet and Health*, (NAS, 1989), were somewhat more ambivalent in their assessment of the evidence relating to specific dietary factors than is generally currently accepted; this reflects the availability of substantially more relevant studies since these reports were published.

REVIEW

4.7.1 DIETARY CONSTITUENTS

There is one caveat that relates to case-control studies of diet and cancer which is more relevant to pancreatic cancer than to other commonly studied sites. The very high early fatality rate for pancreatic cancer makes it difficult to identify and interview all patients before they become moribund or die of their disease. Accordingly, investigators have been forced to accept low response rates or to rely on proxy data sources, such as interviews with spouses, which may be a less reliable source of dietary information. Some studies have conducted stratified analyses, both including and excluding cases for whom proxy respondents were used. Most studies that have used proxy respondents for a proportion of the cases have used them for a similar proportion of the controls.

4.7.1.1 Energy and related factors
Energy intake
A large collaborative case-control study of pancreatic cancer, involving 802 cases from five studies in Australia, Canada, the Netherlands and Poland, and conducted under the auspices of the IARC (International Agency for Research on Cancer) SEARCH (Surveillance of Environmental Aspects Related to Cancer in Humans) Program, reported a strong dose–response increase in risk with increasing total energy intake (cigarette smoking-adjusted ORs of 1.2, 1.2, 2.0 and 2.1 (1.5–2.9; p < 0.0001 for trend) for increasing quintiles of intake) (Howe et al, 1992). The association was observed within both men and women, within groups of both proxy and non-proxy respondents, and was generally consistent across the five individual studies. The association appeared to be almost entirely attributable to an increase in risk with higher carbohydrate intake. In this study, as well as others (see Howe and Burch, 1996), no association was apparent between risk of pancreatic cancer and body mass, so any excess energy intake in cases would necessarily indicate higher physical activity, higher metabolic rate or over-reporting of energy intake by cases, compared with controls. In any case, as a result of this association with total energy intake, appropriate adjustment for energy intake is important to interpretation of results for specific nutrients.

Animal experiments have shown energy restriction to decrease pancreatic tumour incidence, even when experimentally induced by potent pancreatic carcinogens (Tannenbaum, 1959; Roebuck et al, 1981a; Pariza, 1987). This is true of experimental cancers at many other sites in animals.

Diets high in energy possibly increase the risk of pancreatic cancer.

High body mass

A prospective study involving a cohort of people who had received check-ups in the San Francisco area between 1945 and 1972, and were followed up for incidence of cancer, showed no strong associations between body mass index (BMI) or subscapular skin fold measurement and cancer of the pancreas, with smoking-adjusted relative risks of 1.02 (1.00–1.04) per unit increase (kg/m^2) and 1.12 (0.98–1.28 per inch, respectively (Friedman and Van den Eeden, 1993).

At least four case-control studies have examined BMI in relation to pancreatic cancer; none has found any association. From two studies reporting risk estimates, odds ratios ranged from 0.8 to 1.1 (all ns) for higher BMI (Ghadirian et al, 1991; Lyon et al, 1993); the other two studies reported no major differences in average or median BMI between cases and controls (Howe et al, 1990; Zatonski et al, 1991).

Based on these limited, but consistent, findings, high body mass possibly has no relationship with the risk of pancreatic cancer.

4.7.1.2 Carbohydrates

Total carbohydrate

At least seven case-control studies have examined the relationship between carbohydrate intake and pancreatic cancer. Five of these studies were part of the collaborative SEARCH study (described above), in which increased risk with higher carbohydrate intake was reported, with an overall energy- and smoking-adjusted odds ratio of 1.7 (1.3–2.4) (p < 0.01 for trend) for the highest quartile compared with the lowest; this analysis showed a steady dose–response relationship, with odds ratios of 1.0, 1.2, 1.4 and 1.7 for the four increasing quartiles (Howe et al, 1992; Howe and Burch, 1996). The results for carbohydrate were generally consistent across the five studies; four reported associations in the direction of increased risk, although in only two was the association statistically significant. In the combined SEARCH analysis the association with carbohydrate intake appeared to arise from both simple sugars and complex carbohydrates, with odds ratios of 2.8 (1.2–6.3) and 2.0 (0.95–4.3), respectively, for the highest quintiles compared with the lowest.

Two case-control studies in France and Greece, not included in the combined SEARCH analysis, do not show any evidence of increasing risk with higher consumption of carbohydrate, with odds ratios of 0.8 (0.6–4.1, adjusted for total fat intake) or 0.7 (0.4–1.1; p = 0.09 for trend, adjusted for total energy intake), respectively, per 83 g increase in daily intake (see Howe and Burch, 1996).

A number of case-control studies have reported increased risk with high-carbohydrate foods such as breads and cereals, white bread, and refined sugar. On the other hand, some studies have reported a decreased risk associated with wholegrain breads. The results of these studies were generally not adjusted for total energy intake, which limits their ability to be interpreted. (See sections below on sugar and 4.7.2.1 on cereals and wholegrain cereals).

No specific biological mechanism has been proposed for an effect of carbohydrate intake on pancreatic cancer risk. It has been postulated that dietary changes resulting from the onset of pancreatic cancer might lead to an increased proportion of carbohydrate in the diet, although this is speculative (see Howe and Burch, 1996).

Although there is some support from epidemiological studies that increased carbohydrate intake, particularly of the types typical to Western societies, may be associated with increased risk of pancreatic cancer, these data are not completely consistent and a specific biological mechanism is lacking. The panel has decided not to make a judgement on total carbohydrate, as a result of the distinctly different characteristics of different types of carbohydrates. Individual judgements are made in the following sections for starch, fibre and sugar.

Starch

A case-control study in Australia reported a weak protective association with intake of complex carbohydrate (OR = 0.7, 0.4–1.5, adjusted for total energy intake, for the highest quartile) (Baghurst et al, 1991). Another study in the Netherlands reported no statistically significant associations with higher intake of polysaccharides (energy-adjusted OR = 2.0 for women and 0.7 for men) (Bueno de Mesquita et al, 1990).

Some studies have reported increased risk of pancreatic cancer with high consumption of starch-rich foods, such as breads and cereals, although some have found protective associations for wholegrain breads. (See section 4.7.2.1 on cereals.)

The evidence relating to diets high in starch and the risk of pancreatic cancer is very limited; no judgement is possible.

Non-starch polysaccharides/dietary fibre

Six case-control studies of pancreatic cancer have investigated the relationship to fibre intake. Five of these studies showed moderate to strong protective associations, with energy-adjusted odds ratios ranging from 0.3 to 0.5 for the highest quartiles of intake; the association was statistically significant in three studies (see Howe and Burch, 1996). The combined analysis of the five SEARCH case-control studies demonstrated a steady decrease in risk with increasing fibre consumption (energy- and smoking-adjusted OR = 1.0, 0.7, 0.6 and 0.4; 0.3–0.6; p < 0.01 for trend, for increasing quartiles) (Howe and Burch, 1996). This association was independent of a protective association with vitamin C intake. This association with fibre was deemed, in the 1996 review by Howe and Burch, to be among the most consistent dietary associations for pancreatic cancer, along with protective associations for vegetables and fruit and for vitamin C. It should be noted that the term 'fibre' in most of the studies refers to NSP/dietary fibre and that the levels of consumption are those seen, in general, in Western societies.

As discussed in section 4.7.2.3, a number of studies have shown decreased risk of pancreatic cancer with higher consumption of vegetables and fruits; the panel has judged that greater consumption of vegetables and fruits probably decreases the risk of pancreatic cancer. Therefore, it is not clear whether fibre is simply acting as marker for such foods or is indeed specifically responsible for a decrease in risk. Of course other foods, notably cereals and legumes, also provide dietary fibre.

Diets high in NSP/dietary fibre possibly decrease the risk of pancreatic cancer.

Sugar

Pancreatic cancer has been associated with consumption of refined or simple sugar or sucrose in two out of four case-control studies, with odds ratios of 2.2 (1.1–4.6; p < 0.01 for trend), 2.0 (1.2–3.1), 1.2 (0.6–2.1) and 1.0 (0.8–1.3), respectively, for higher intakes (Raymond et al, 1987; Bueno de Mesquita et al, 1990; Baghurst et al, 1991; Kalapothaki et al, 1993). Another study reported increased risk with higher consumption of added sugar, particularly in women; (smoking-adjusted OR = 3.7, 1.5–9.1 for women and 1.3, 0.6–2.5 for men) (Lyon et al, 1993).

In an international ecological study, sugar consumption was the environmental variable most highly correlated with pancreatic cancer mortality in women (r = 0.6; p < 0.01) (Armstrong and Doll, 1975).

Evidence suggests that diets high in sugar may increase the risk of pancreatic cancer, but is, as yet, insufficient.

4.7.1.3 Fat and cholesterol

Total fat

A 1996 review by Howe and Burch discussed eight case-control studies of pancreatic cancer, which had reported results for total fat intake; these were conducted in Australia, Canada, the Netherlands, Poland, France, the USA and Greece. Three of these studies observed strong, statistically significant decreases in risk with higher intakes (OR = 0.3–0.4 for the uppermost intake quartiles); in another study, a weaker decrease in risk was observed (OR =0.7; 0.4–1.2). Two studies reported no association (OR = 0.9 and 1.1 for the highest intake quartile). The two remaining studies reported strong, statistically significant increases in risk (OR = 3.2 for the uppermost quartile and 12.9 for an

increase of 30 g/day, respectively). In both of these studies, the 95% confidence intervals were quite broad. The last observation comes from a study in France, based on only 69 cases. All studies, except for the last, adjusted for total energy intake, whereas the last adjusted for carbohydrate intake only. Adjustment for energy intake is critical to the interpretation of results for total fat, given the increase in risk with higher energy intake reported by most studies (see section 4.7.1.1 on Energy intake).

Five of these eight case-control studies were included in the collaborative SEARCH Program, described in section 4.7.1.1, in which a combined energy- and smoking-adjusted odds ratio of 0.8 (0.6–1.04, ns; test for trend) for the highest versus lowest quartile of fat intake was reported from an analysis including 802 cases (Howe and Burch, 1996).

The hypothesis that fat intake, particularly saturated/animal fat, might be associated with increased risk of pancreatic cancer was primarily generated by international correlation data showing rates to be high in countries with high saturated/animal fat intakes (Lea, 1967; Segi and Kurihara, 1972; Ghadirian et al, 1991d). On the other hand, Howe and Burch (1996), using carefully developed data and methods from Prentice and Sheppard (1990), calculated only a weak international correlation between total fat consumption and pancreatic cancer (r = 0.22, ns; for men).

Although ecological data have shown populations with higher fat consumption generally to have higher rates of pancreatic cancer, the case-control evidence is very mixed and does not support an increase in risk with higher intake.

The evidence relating to diets high in total fat and the risk of pancreatic cancer is markedly inconsistent; no judgement is possible.

Saturated/animal fat

Seven case-control studies of pancreatic cancer have examined the association with saturated fat. Three of the studies reported statistically significant (or borderline) decreased risk with higher saturated fat intake, with relative risks of 0.3 (0.1–0.8), 0.3 (0.1–1.0) and 0.2 (0.1–0.7) for intakes in the uppermost quartiles (Bueno de Mesquita et al, 1990, 1991; Baghurst et al, 1991; Zatonski et al, 1991; see also Howe and Burch, 1996); notably, the 95% confidence intervals were wide. In three studies, no substantial association was apparent, with statistically non-significant odds ratios ranging from 1.0 to 1.4 for higher intakes (Howe et al, 1990; Farrow and Davis, 1990; Kalaphothaki et al, 1993; see also Howe and Burch, 1996). In the remaining study, a statistically non-significant increase in risk was observed for the highest quartile of intake (OR = 1.9, 0.8–4.6) (Ghadirian et al, 1991). In six of these seven studies, the association for saturated fat intake was adjusted for total energy intake or intake of energy from other sources.

A combined energy- and smoking-adjusted odds ratio of 0.8 (0.6–1.2) for the highest quartile of intake of saturated fat was calculated based on the five case-control studies in the SEARCH Program.

Using carefully developed data and methods from Prentice and Sheppard (1990), Howe and Burch (1996) calculated a moderate correlation between saturated fat consumption and pancreatic cancer (r = 0.41, p = 0.09; for men).

Animal studies have reported an enhancement of chemically-induced preneoplastic lesions by a diet high in saturated fat (20% lard by weight) (Woutersen and van Garderen-Hoetmer, 1988a,b). The relevance of these findings to humans remains unclear.

Animal fat and saturated fat are intimately related in foods and in eating patterns with meat and with dietary cholesterol. A number of epidemiological studies have provided evidence of increased risk of pancreatic cancer with higher consumption of meat; the panel has judged that higher meat consumption possibly increases the risk of pancreatic cancer (see section 4.7.2.6 on Meat). Cholesterol might also be responsible for any increased risk with consumption of meat and animal foods; the panel has judged that higher cholesterol intake possibly increases the risk of pancreatic cancer (see section below on Cholesterol).

Overall, the epidemiological evidence relating to diets high in saturated or animal fat and the risk of pancreatic cancer is inconsistent; no judgement is possible.

Monounsaturated fat

Five case-control studies of pancreatic cancer have examined monounsaturated fat intake. One study in Poland found a strong decrease in risk with higher intake (OR = 0.1, 0.03–0.6; p = 0.02 for trend, for the uppermost quartile); this odds ratio was adjusted for smoking and for energy intake from other sources (Zatonski et al, 1991). In a study in the Netherlands, decreased risk was suggested in men, but not in women, with energy- and smoking-adjusted odds ratios of 0.4 (0.1–1.4) and 0.9 (0.3–2.9), respectively, for the uppermost quintiles of intake (Bueno de Mesquita et al, 1990). Three other studies have reported no material associations, with odds ratios ranging from 1.0 to 1.4 (NS) for higher intakes; each of these studies adjusted for smoking and two adjusted for total energy intake (Howe et al, 1990; Baghurst et al, 1991; Kalapothaki et al, 1993).

The evidence relating to diets high in monounsaturated fat and the risk of pancreatic cancer is limited and inconsistent; no judgement is possible.

Polyunsaturated/plant (vegetable) fat

Intake of polyunsaturated fat has been examined in six case-control studies of pancreatic cancer. Two studies, in Australia and Poland, have reported strong decreases in risk with higher intakes, after adjustment for smoking and energy intakes; the odds ratios from these studies were 0.4 (0.2–0.9; ns for trend) and 0.2 (0.06–0.6; p = 0.06 for trend), respectively (Baghurst et al, 1991; Zatonski et al, 1993). None of

the remaining four studies reported any statistically significant association, with odds ratios ranging from 0.7 to 1.4 for the highest intake levels (Bueno de Mesquita et al, 1990; Farrow and Davis, 1990; Howe et al, 1990; Kalapothaki et al, 1993). One study in the USA suggested a protective association for linoleic acid (OR = 0.6, 0.3–1.2; for the uppermost quartile), but no association for polyunsaturated fat in general (Farrow and Davis, 1990).

Several animal studies have shown that diets high in unsaturated fat, for example, 20% unsaturated fat by weight, increase the incidence of pancreatic tumours induced by various experimental methods, including strongly carcinogenic nitrosamines present in tobacco (Birt et al, 1981; Roebuck et al, 1981a, 1981b; O'Connor et al, 1989; Roebuck, 1992; Hoffmann et al, 1993). One study showed that a minimum portion of the diet, 4–8% by weight, must be made up of linoleic acid in order to produce the enhancing effects of unsaturated fat in azaserine-induced pancreatic cancer in rats (Roebuck et al, 1985). The relevance of these studies to the human situation remains unclear.

The evidence relating to diets high in polyunsaturated fat and the risk of pancreatic cancer is limited and inconsistent. Epidemiological studies have shown either decreased risk or no relationship; animal studies suggest increased risk; no judgement is possible.

Omega-3 fatty acids

One case-control study reported no association between intake of omega-3 fatty acids and the risk of pancreatic cancer (Farrow and Davis, 1990).

At least one animal study has shown an inhibitory effect of a diet high in omega-3 fatty acids (20% fish oil by weight) on chemically induced preneoplastic pancreatic lesions (O'Connor et al, 1989). This is in contrast to the tumour-enhancing effect seen for diets high in other unsaturated fats.

Evidence relating to diets high in omega-3 fatty acids and the risk of pancreatic cancer is very limited; no judgement is possible

Cholesterol

At least seven case-control studies of pancreatic cancer have examined dietary cholesterol. One study in Australia reported statistically significant increased risk with higher cholesterol intake (OR = 5.1, 2.4–10.9, for intake in the uppermost quartile) (Baghurst et al, 1991). Three other studies reported increases in risk that were not statistically significant, with odds ratios ranging from 1.5 (0.9–2.6) to 3.3 (0.9–12.1) for higher intakes (Bueno de Mesquita et al, 1990, 1991; Zatonski et al, 1991; Kalapothaki et al, 1993). The remaining three studies, in Canada and the USA, reported no association (Farrow and Davis, 1990; Howe et al, 1990; Ghadirian et al, 1991). In six of the seven studies, the association for cholesterol intake was adjusted for total energy intake and smoking.

Based on five of the above-mentioned studies in the SEARCH Program, a statistically significant increase in risk was observed for higher cholesterol intake (energy- and smoking-adjusted OR = 1.5, 1.1–2.0, for the uppermost quartile (Howe et al, 1992).

Some epidemiological studies have reported increased risk of pancreatic cancer with higher consumption of eggs, a substantial dietary source of cholesterol (Mills et al, 1988; Baghurst et al, 1991; Bueno de Mesquita et al, 1991). In general these studies have not distinguished between any effect of eggs and that of cholesterol as such.

Four of seven case-control studies of pancreatic cancer show an increased risk; the remaining three are null.

Diets high in cholesterol possibly increase the risk of pancreatic cancer.

4.7.1.4 Protein

Total protein

Eight case-control studies of pancreatic cancer have examined total protein intake; these have been reviewed by Howe and Burch (1996) and were conducted in Australia, Canada, the Netherlands, Poland, France, the USA and Greece. None of these studies showed a statistically significant risk estimate for the highest level of intake examined. The odds ratios ranged from 0.2 (0.02–1.8) for the uppermost quartile of intake in a study in Poland, to 2.1 (1.0–4.2) for the uppermost quartile in a study in the USA; many of the odds ratios were close to null. In most of these studies, the associations for protein intake were adjusted for total energy intake and smoking.

Five of the above-mentioned case-control studies were part of the SEARCH Program; the combined studies showed no association between protein intake and pancreatic cancer (energy- and smoking-adjusted OR = 0.9, 0.7–1.2, for the highest quartile) (Howe and Burch, 1996).

Animal studies have generally shown that dietary protein can modulate experimentally induced pancreatic carcinogenesis, but not in a consistent fashion; they further suggest a possible interaction with fat intakes, so that there is no effect when fat intake is low (Birt et al, 1983; Pour and Birt, 1983). One study in hamsters found incidence of experimentally induced and in situ carcinomas to be lower in the animals fed an 8% protein diet, compared with a 20% diet; the number of other lesions in the pancreas was also significantly higher in the hamsters fed the higher-protein diet (Kokkinakis and Scarpelli, 1989).

It has been suggested that protein might affect pancreatic tumourigenesis via over-stimulation of the pancreas by cholecystokinin (CKK) and secretin or by a protease/antiprotease imbalance, causing proteolysis in the pancreas, increased cell proliferation as part of the natural repair process, and subsequently increased opportunity for neoplastic change (see Farrow and Davis, 1990).

Although biological mechanisms have been proposed, eight case-control studies show inconsistent, but largely null, findings.

Because it is possible that there are differences between animal and plant proteins and their dietary sources, the panel has decided to make no judgement about diets high in total protein.

Animal protein

Each of the eight case-control studies mentioned above concerning total protein, which generally had null findings, was conducted within a population in which a large portion of total protein consumption came from animal protein. One case-control study in the Netherlands reported specifically on animal protein, but found no statistically significant associations (energy- and smoking-adjusted OR = 1.5, 0.8–3.1, for men and 1.0, 0.4–2.3, for women) (Bueno de Mesquita, 1990).

An international ecological study found that the factor most highly correlated with pancreatic cancer mortality in men was animal protein (r = 0.8) (Armstrong and Doll, 1975).

Evidence relating to diets high in animal protein and the risk of pancreatic cancer is very limited; no judgement is possible.

Plant protein

Plant protein was associated with a statistically non-significant decrease in risk of pancreatic cancer in a case-control study in the Netherlands (energy- and smoking-adjusted OR = 0.5 (0.2–1.5) and 0.7 (0.2–2.0) for the uppermost quintiles for men and women, respectively) (Bueno de Mesquita et al, 1990).

Evidence relating to diets high in plant proteins and the risk of pancreatic cancer is very limited; no judgement is possible.

4.7.1.5 Alcohol

It was first suggested by Dörken (1964), in discussing the findings of a case series, that alcohol abuse may increase the risk of pancreatic adenocarcinoma. Other early individual-level studies also suggested increased risk with alcohol consumption, but the results were subsequently questioned as a result of methods employed or lack of detail available about the procedures used (Burch and Ansari, 1968; Ishii et al, 1968; Lin and Kessler, 1981). In subsequent decades, the relationship between alcohol consumption and pancreatic cancer has been a focus of numerous studies. A 1986 review by Velema et al, encompassing seven case-control studies, three cohort studies and nine follow-up studies of groups with high alcohol intake, concluded that the evidence was insufficient for a causal relationship between alcohol and pancreatic cancer.

TABLE 4.7.1 ALCOHOL CONSUMPTION AND THE RISK OF PANCREATIC CANCER: COHORT STUDIES

AUTHOR, YEAR, AND PLACE	SIZE OF COHORT: NO. OF CASES	ALCOHOL EXPOSURE FACTOR	COMPARISON (HIGHEST VS LOWEST QUANTILES)	RELATIVE RISK (95% CONFIDENCE INTERVAL)	SEX/AGE	ADJUSTMENT SMOKING HISTORY	OTHER FACTORS[a]
Heuch et al, 1983 Norway	16,713: 63 incident cases	Alcohol use	≥ 14 times/month vs no or very limited use	2.7*[b]	Y	N	Y
Hiatt, 1988 California, USA	122,894: 48 incident cases	Alcohol	> 1 drink/day vs non-drinker	0.9 (0.3–2.7)	Y	Y	Y
Hirayama, 1989 Japan	122,261 males: 399 deaths	Alcohol	daily vs non-consumers	0.8	Y/N	N	N
Zheng et al, 1993 USA	17,633 white males: 57 deaths	Alcohol use	ever vs never	2.4 (1.1–5.5)	Y	Y	N
		Total alcoholic drinks	≥ 10 vs < 3/month	3.1 (1.2–8.0)	Y	Y	N
Shibata et al, 1994 California, USA	13,979: 65 incident cases	Alcohol (all types)	> 2 vs < 1 drinks/day	0.9 (0.4–1.9)**	Y	Y	N
Friedman and van der Feder, 1993 California, USA	175,000: 450 incident cases	Total alcoholic drinks	≥ 2 vs < 1 drinks/day	1.4 (0.9–2.0)**	Y	Y	Y
		Past heavy drinker	yes vs no	0.9 (0.6–1.3)**	Y	Y	Y

* $p \leq 0.05$ for trend and/or for comparison of highest vs lowest consumption level
** p 0.05 for trend and/or for comparison of highest vs lowest consumption level
[a] Adjusted or matched for one or more of the following: race, canton, income, residence, history of diabetes mellitus, Cajun ethnicity, respondent type, education level, alcohol consumption, meat consumption, total energy intake, coffee consumption
[b] Cases consumed less, on average, than controls

In 1988, an IARC Working Group evaluated the studies to that date. Of eight studies of cohorts of alcoholics that they evaluated, none showed a significantly elevated risk of pancreatic cancers. The Working Group noted that the observed number of cancer deaths resulting from pancreatic cancer in all the cohorts of alcoholics combined was 98, compared with about 84 expected; the pooled standardised mortality ratio (SMR) was 1.2 (0.9–1.4). Neither of two studies of cohorts of brewery workers in Dublin or Denmark showed any statistically significant increase in rates of pancreatic cancer. In only one of five further cohort studies of the general population was a statistically significant increase in risk observed for regular or heavy drinkers; most of these studies involved very few cases of, or deaths from, pancreatic cancer. Only one of 14 case-control studies showed increased risk among regular drinkers. It was therefore concluded that the consumption of alcoholic beverages was unlikely to be causally related to cancer of the pancreas (IARC, 1988).

Six prospective and 24 case-control studies that have examined alcohol consumption in relation to pancreatic cancer are presented in Tables 4.7.1 and 4.7.2. These include the studies reviewed by the IARC Group, as well as subsequent studies, with the exceptions that studies with fewer than 20 cases, and cohorts studies of alcoholics or brewery workers, are not included in the tables.

Two of the six prospective studies in Table 4.7.1 reported strong statistically significant increases in risk with higher total alcohol intake (Heuch et al, 1983; Zheng et al, 1993). For the study by Heuch et al, the IARC Working Group stated that it could not replicate the published relative risks. In a study of US men (Lutheran Brotherhood cohort), the strong increase in risk was adjusted for smoking and was present in both high and low consumers of meat, which was also a risk factor, although the dose–response pattern across levels of alcohol consumption was not smooth. The remaining four studies, including two that were by far the largest (Hirayama, 1989; Friedman et al, 1993), showed no material association. Of the six total studies, the two showing increased risk used a very low consumption level as their uppermost exposure category (for example, 14 or more times per month in the Norwegian cohort, ten or more times per month in the Lutheran Brotherhood cohort, compared with daily or two to three times daily in the other four studies); thus, there is no indication, when all studies are considered, that the highest levels of alcohol intake are associated with stronger increases in risk. Two studies examined the relationship for past drinkers, compared with non-drinkers; one reported increased risk for past drinkers, although this was not statistically significant (Hiatt et al, 1988); the other reported no association for past heavy drinkers (Friedman et al, 1993).

Of the 20 case-control studies in Table 4.7.2 that attempted to quantify alcohol consumption in some fashion, and for which information on the comparisons was available, none reported any statistically significant association; four of the odds ratios for higher consumption were at least 1.5 in these studies, eleven were between 0.75 and 1.5 (or there was said to be 'no association', but an OR was not quoted), and 10 were 0.75 or lower (the total number of ORs sums to more than 20 because some studies reported separate results for men and women). Of the remaining four studies, the earliest, involving Japanese men, reported a stat-istically significant increase in risk, but information on the specific comparison was not given; this association was not adjusted for smoking (Ishii et al, 1968, 1973). Another

TABLE 4.7.2 ALCOHOL CONSUMPTION[a] AND THE RISK OF PANCREATIC CANCER: CASE-CONTROL STUDIES

AUTHOR, YEAR, AND PLACE	NO. OF CASES	EXPOSURE	COMPARISON†	ODDS RATIO (95% CONFIDENCE INTERVAL)	SEX/AGE	ADJUSTMENT SMOKING HISTORY	OTHER FACTORS[b]
Ishii et al, 1968, 1973, Japan	311 men	Alcohol intake	na	positive assoc*	N	N	N
Wynder et al, 1973 USA	42 women	Alcohol consumption	e	no assoc	Y	N	Y
	100 men	Alcohol consumption	e	no assoc	Y	N	Y
Williams & Horm 1977, USA	85 women	Total alcohol	heavier vs non-drinkers	0.6**	Y	Y	Y
	901 men	Total alcohol	heavier vs non-drinkers	1.3**	Y	Y	Y
MacMahon et al, 1981 Massachusetts and Rhode Island, USA	149 women	Alcohol drinking	regular vs occasional	0.5 (0.3–1.1)	Y	N	Y
	218 men	Alcohol drinking	regular vs occasional	1.3 (0.6–2.6)	Y	N	Y
Manousos, 1981 Athens, Greece	50 women and men	Alcohol drinking	> 110g/day vs na	0.7 (0.3–1.3)	Y	N	N
Haines et al, 1982 California, USA	106 women and men	Alcohol consumption	na	no assoc	Y	N	Y
Durbec et al, 1983 Marseille, France	69 women and men	Alcohol intake	10 vs 0 g/day	1.2 (1.1–1.4)	Y	N	Y
		Duration of alcohol intake	10 vs 0 yr	0.7 (0.5–0.98)	Y	N	Y
Wynder et al, 1983 USA	122 women	Alcohol consumption	≥ 5 vs 0 oz/day	0.9 (0.3–2.1)	Y	Y	N
	153 men	Alcohol consumption	≥ 5 vs 0 oz/day	1.6 (0.9–2.6)	Y	Y	N
Kodama & Mori, 1983, Tokyo, Japan	84 women and men	Alcohol consumption	habitual daily vs others	0.6 (0.3–1.2)[l]	N	N	N
Gold et al, 1985 Baltimore, USA	201 women and men	Overall alcohol consumption	high vs low	0.6**[d]	Y	na	na
Mack et al, 1986 Los Angeles, USA	490 women and men	Alcohol intake	> 79 vs < 40 g/day	1.2 (0.7–2.2)[e]	Y	N	Y
Norell et al, 1986a Sweden	99 women and men	Alcohol	10 vs 0–1 g/day	0.6 (0.3–1.1)[f]	Y	N	Y
Falk et al, 1988 Louisiana, USA	160 women	Ethanol	≥ 3 beer equivalents/w vs non-drinker	0.6**	Y	Y	Y
	203 men	Ethanol	≥ 27 beer equivalents/w vs non-drinker	1.5**	Y	Y	Y
Cuzick and Babiker 1989, UK	216 women and men	Total alcohol consumption	≥ 14 units [g]/w vs never	1.7**[h,i]	Y	Y	Y
			ex-drinkers vs never	2.7*	Y	Y	Y
Clavel et al, 1989 Paris, France	63 women	Alcohol consumption	≥ 8 vs 0 drinks/day	0.3 (0.02–2.8)	Y	Y	Y
	98 men	Alcohol consumption	≥ 8 vs 0 drinks/day	0.6 (0.2–1.8)	Y	Y	Y
Olsen et al, 1989 Minnesota, USA	212 women	Total alcohol	≥ 4 vs 0 drinks/day	2.7 (1.0–7.3)	Y	Y	Y
Farrow and Davis 1990, Washington, USA	148 men	Alcohol consumption	≥ 15 vs 4 drinks/w	0.8 (0.5–1.4)	Y	Y	Y

study, for which information on the alcohol levels being compared was unavailable, reported no association (Haines et al, 1982). The other two studies examined 'ever' versus 'never' drinkers, but did not attempt to quantify intake; one study reported a statistically significant increase in risk for 'ever' drinkers (Lyon et al, 1992b), whereas the other reported no material association (Zatonski et al, 1993).

Two case-control studies reported on lifetime alcohol consumption; neither showed any material association (Bueno de Mesquita et al, 1991; Jain et al, 1991). Of two studies that examined duration of alcohol consumption, one in France reported a statistically significant decrease in risk with consumption for at least 10 years, compared with no consumption (Durbec et al, 1983); the other in Japan reported no material association for 40 or more years of drinking, compared with none (Mizuno et al, 1992). One study that compared ex-drinkers with 'never' drinkers reported a strong, statistically significant increase in risk, after adjustment for

smoking; this study also found a strong increase in risk with higher alcohol consumption among heavy smokers (OR = 5.6, p < 0.05, for 14 or more units per week vs never) (Cuzick et al, 1989). From five studies that reported risk estimates for women and men separately, higher alcohol intake was often associated with a decreased risk in women, but not men, although this pattern was not entirely consistent and none of the odds ratios was statistically significant (Williams et al, 1977; MacMahon et al, 1981; Wynder et al, 1983; Falk et al, 1988; Clavel et al, 1989).

Using a pooled analysis of three case-control studies from Italy, France and Switzerland (Raymond et al, 1987; La Vecchia et al, 1987; Clavel et al, 1989; Bouchardy et al, 1990) reported on 494 cases and 1,704 controls, and found no consistent association with consumption of total alcohol, wine, beer or spirits, or any evidence of a dose–response; the smoking-adjusted odds ratio for eight or more drinks per day, compared with less than two, was 0.8 (0.5–1.3).

Author, year, and place	No. of cases	Exposure	Comparison (highest and lowest quantiles)	Odds ratio (95% confidence interval)	Sex/Age	Adjustment Smoking history	Other factors[b]
Baghurst et al, 1991 Adelaide, Australia	104 women and men	Alcohol	> 18 vs 0 g/day	0.4 (0.2–0.9)[*]	Y	Y	N
Bueno de Mesquita et al, 1991 Netherlands	176 women and men	Total alcohol	≥ 128,971 vs < 22,471 g ethanol/lifetime	1.3 (0.7–2.4)[**]	Y	Y	Y
Ghadirian et al, 1991 Quebec, Canada	179 women and men	Total alcohol	h quintile vs never	0.7 (0.3–1.4)	Y	Y	Y
Jain et al, 1991 Toronto, Canada	249 women and men	Lifetime alcohol consumption	≥ 162,150 g vs none	0.9 (0.5–1.5)[**]	Y	Y	Y
Lyon et al, 1992[b] Utah, USA	149 women and men	Alcohol use	ever vs never	1.6 (1.1–2.4)[k]	Y	N	Y
Mizuno et al, 1992 Japan	124 women and men	Frequency of drinking alcohol	every day vs not at all	1.2 (0.6–2.7)	Y	N	N
		Age at first drinking alcohol	< 20 yrs vs no alcohol drinking	1.6 (0.6–4.2)	Y	N	N
			≥ 25 yrs vs no alcohol drinking	1.3 (0.5–3.0)	Y	N	N
		Years of drinking	≥ 40 yrs vs none	0.8 (0.4–1.7)	Y	N	N
Zatonski et al, 1993 Opole, Poland	110 women and men	Alcohol	ever vs never	1.2 (0.7–2.5)	na	na	na

[*] p ≤ 0.05 for trend and/or for comparison of highest vs lowest consumption level
[**] p > 0.05 for trend and/or for comparison of highest vs lowest consumption level
[†] w = week, g = grams, oz = ounces, yr = year
[na] information not available or unclear from article
[a] Table includes studies for which results for total alcohol intake or general alcohol consumption pattern were reported, and does not include studies for which only results on intake of specific alcoholic beverages were reported
[b] Adjusted or matched for one or more of the following: race, hospital, type of dwelling, carbohydrate intake, fat intake, duration of alcohol intake, respondent type, income, history of diabetes mellitus, fruit consumption, social class, degree of urbanization, foreign origin, educational level, coffee consumption, meat consumption, vegetable consumption, response status, total energy intake, place of residence, fibre intake, county of residence, institute
[c] No statistically significant differences between cases and controls in the frequency distribution of alcohol consumption, ranging from non-drinkers to 7+ units per day
[d] Association for overall alcohol consumption appeared to be attributable to wine consumption, with adjusted OR = 0.5 (0.3–0.8)[*] for ever vs never consumption
[e] OR = 2.7 (0.7–10.6) for 124 matched pairs directly interviewed
[f] 90% confidence interval
[g] unit = ½ pint (330 ml approx) of beer, 1 glass of wine, or 1 measure of spirits
[h] OR = 1.5 (statistically significant) for alcohol use 10 years prior to diagnosis/interview
[i] Positive association with alcohol was strongest among smokers; OR = 5.6 (statistically significant) among heavy smokers (> 20 cigarettes/day)
[j] OR = 2.3 (0.8–6.7) for subjects for whom spouses were the respondent
[k] Stated in original article that alcohol was not an important risk factor after adjusting for age, cigarette use, and coffee consumption
[l] OR taken from IARC Working Group, 1991

An international ecological analysis found alcohol consumption (1976) not to be an important correlate of pancreatic cancer mortality (1950–1969) (Yanai et al, 1979). An ecological analysis involving 41 of the US states, comparing pancreatic mortality (1957–1960) with per capita consumption of various alcoholic beverages (1960), found statistically significant correlations for spirits for both men and women (r = 0.4 and 0.6, respectively) after adjustment for consumption of beer, cigarettes and degree of urbanisation (Breslow and Enstrom, 1974). Another study that examined county-to-county variation in the USA found no consistent correlations (Blot et al, 1978), whereas a study in Japan found pancreatic mortality (1969–1971) to be significantly correlated with consumption of sake and whisky across prefectures, after adjustment for cigarette consumption (Kono and Ikeda, 1979). (See also Velema et al, 1986.)

In some animal models, alcohol has been shown to promote pancreatic carcinogenesis (Kuratsune et al, 1971), but not in others (Pour et al, 1983). In adult monkeys treated with N-nitrosodimethylamine preceded by ethanol, a twofold increase in the pro-mutagenic DNA lesion O^6-methylguanine in the pancreas was observed compared with monkeys not co-exposed to alcohol (Anderson et al, 1996).

Together with high fat intake, alcohol consumption is an important determinant of chronic pancreatitis, a suspected risk factor for pancreatic cancer (Paulino-Netto et al, 1960; Ishii et al, 1973). Thus, if, in spite of the generally null findings from most epidemiological studies, a true association were to exist between alcohol consumption and the risk of pancreatic cancer, the biological pathway might involve pancreatitis as an intermediate step. However, whether alcohol-induced pancreatitis is a causal risk factor for pancreatic cancer is unclear (Amman and Schueler, 1984; Amman et al, 1984; Lowenfels, 1984; Lowenfels et al, 1985, 1993), although idiopathic chronic pancreatitis clearly is (Lowenfels et al, 1993; Talamini et al, 1996).

Overall, the great majority of numerous epidemiological studies that have examined different aspects of alcohol consumption, including average and lifetime consumption, and duration, frequency and history of consumption, demonstrate no relationship.

High alcohol consumption probably has no relationship with the risk of pancreatic cancer.

4.7.1.6 Vitamins

Carotenoids

One cohort study in the USA has addressed the relationship of β-carotene intake to the risk of pancreatic cancer; no substantial association was observed (smoking-adjusted RR = 0.8, 0.4–1.4, for intake in the highest tertile) (Shibata et al, 1994).

Five case-control studies of pancreatic cancer have examined β-carotene intake (see Howe and Burch, 1996). None of these reported a statistically significant association; three of the reported odds ratios were less than 1.0 (ranging from 0.7 to 0.8), whereas three were greater then 1.0 (ranging from 1.1 to 1.7) (one study reported separate results for men and women, so there are six ORs from five studies). Each of the studies adjusted for smoking; most adjusted for total energy intake. For the four of these studies that were part of the SEARCH Program, a combined odds ratio of 0.7 (0.5–1.1) was calculated for intake in the uppermost quartile; this odds ratio was adjusted for smoking and for intakes of energy, vitamin C, fibre and cholesterol.

A prospective study in USA (Maryland) observed significantly lower baseline serum levels of lycopene (derived almost entirely from tomato-rich foods in American diets) in individuals who subsequently developed pancreatic cancer than in those who did not (Burney et al, 1989). Three studies of pre-diagnostic levels of serum β-carotene have produced mixed and statistically non-significant results with relation to subsequent pancreatic cancer (see Comstock et al, 1992).

Overall, the evidence relating to high dietary intakes of carotenoids and the risk of pancreatic cancer is inconsistent; no judgement is possible.

Vitamin C

One cohort study of pancreatic cancer in the USA reported an energy- and smoking-adjusted odds ratio of 0.8 (0.4–1.4) for higher intake of vitamin C (Shibata et al, 1994).

Each of seven case-control studies has shown a weak to moderate protective association between vitamin C intake and risk of pancreatic cancer (see Howe and Burch, 1996), with odds ratios ranging from 0.5 (0.3–0.9) in a study in Canada to 0.7 (0.03–14.7) in a study in Poland (ORs refer to the uppermost quantiles of intake). Each study adjusted for smoking; most adjusted for total energy intake. A statistically significant decrease in risk was also observed in the combined analysis of the five SEARCH studies, with an energy- and smoking-adjusted odds ratio of 0.6 (0.4–0.8) (also

adjusted for intakes of fibre and cholesterol). In a 1996 review of nutrition and pancreatic cancer, Howe and Burch concluded that the cumulative data for vitamin C were among the most consistent in relation to pancreatic cancer, along with those for vegetable and fruit consumption and fibre intake.

Animal studies have shown that vitamin C modulates the development of pancreatic cancer favourably (Woutersen and van Garderen-Hoetmer, 1988; Appel et al, 1991).

Overall, the epidemiological evidence regarding vitamin C and pancreatic cancer, one cohort and seven case-control studies, consistently shows some degree of decreased risk with higher intakes, although it cannot be entirely discounted that the protective association is actually due to some other substance(s) in vitamin C-containing foods, which are, in large measure, vegetables and fruits.

High dietary vitamin C intake possibly decreases the risk of pancreatic cancer.

Retinol

Seven case-control studies have reported on the relationship between retinol or total vitamin A intake and pancreatic cancer. Three studies observed no association (Farrow et al, 1990; Bueno de Mesquita et al, 1991; Ghadirian et al, 1991), whereas two reported increased risk with greater consumption, with odds ratios of 2.9 (1.4–6.2) for the uppermost quartile (p = 0.009 for trend) in a study in Australia (Baghurst et al, 1991), and 1.6 (p < 0.05) for more than about 35,000 RE (retinol equivalents) per month, compared with less than about 12,000, in a study in the USA (for men only; no association was found for women) (Falk et al, 1988). The two remaining studies found decreased risk with higher intakes, with odds ratios of 0.5 (0.2–1.5) for the uppermost quartile in a study in Poland (Zatonski et al, 1991), and 0.7 (0.6–0.9) for an increase of one standard deviation in total vitamin A intake in a study in Greece (Kalaphothaki et al, 1993). Each of these studies adjusted the retinol associations for smoking and for either total energy intake and other relevant aspects of diet.

Evidence from seven case-control studies on high dietary retinol intakes and the risk of pancreatic cancer are inconsistent; no judgement is possible.

Vitamin E

One case-control study of pancreatic cancer in Australia reported a strong decrease in risk with vitamin E intake in the uppermost quartile (OR = 0.4, 0.2–0.8; p = 0.006 for trend, adjusted for total energy intake and alcohol and tobacco usage) (Baghurst et al, 1991). Two other case-control studies showed no association (Bueno de Mesquita et al, 1991; Ghadirian et al, 1991).

In a review of studies of pre-diagnostic serum vitamin E levels in ten study populations, and subsequent cancer risk at ten sites, Comstock et al (1992) found the strongest association to be that with pancreatic cancer in a study of Finnish males; cases were found to have levels about 30% lower than controls. Essentially null associations have, however, been shown in two other populations.

Evidence relating to high dietary vitamin E intake and the risk of pancreatic cancer is very limited; no judgement is possible.

4.7.1.7 Minerals

Selenium

One case-control study in Australia reported a statistically non-significant protective association between dietary selenium intake and the risk of pancreatic cancer; the energy- and smoking-adjusted odds ratio for the highest intake quartile was 0.6 (0.3–1.2, ns; for trend) (Baghurst et al, 1991).

In a review of studies of pre-diagnostic selenium levels and risk of cancer at ten sites, Comstock et al (1992) reported the strongest finding from 24 reports to be an inverse association with pancreatic cancer in Finnish men; cases exhibited levels that were about 20% lower than controls. Another study also showed significantly lower levels in pancreatic cases, whereas a third study showed essentially no case-control difference.

High levels of dietary selenium (5 ppm) have been reported to stimulate the repair of single strand breaks of pancreatic DNA induced by bis(2-oxopropyl)-nitrosamine (Lawson and Birt, 1983). Another experiment showed palpable and histologically diagnosed pancreatic tumours to be less frequent in hamsters receiving a high level of selenium in their drinking water than in animals receiving a low level (Kise et al, 1990). Some other animal studies have shown that selenium supplementation enhances pancreatic carcinogenesis (Birt, 1989).

Evidence relating to high dietary selenium intake and the risk of pancreatic cancer is very limited; no judgement is possible.

Calcium

One case-control study of pancreatic cancer in the USA reported a protective association for calcium intake (energy- and smoking-adjusted OR = 0.5, 0.2–1.0, for the highest intake quartile) (Farrow and Davis, 1990). The authors of this study postulated that, if gut contents enter the pancreatic duct by reflux, then dietary calcium could exert a protective effect via a mechanism similar to that hypothesised for colon cancer, that is, calcium binds bile acids and fatty acids, and thereby reduces the irritating effect of these acids on the epithelium, the loss of the epithelial cells and resultant cell proliferation.

Evidence relating to high dietary calcium intake and the risk of pancreatic cancer is limited; no judgement is possible.

4.7.2 FOODS AND DRINKS

4.7.2.1 Cereals (grains)

The Lutheran Brotherhood Study, a prospective study involving a cohort of US men, reported no clear association between consumption of bread or cereals and risk of pancreatic cancer (Zheng et al, 1993).

Seven case-control studies have examined consumption of various cereals or cereal products. One study in the Netherlands, which reported on cereal products as a whole, found no association (OR = 1.1 for higher consumption); odds ratios for low- and high-fibre cereal products were 1.2 and 0.8, respectively (both ns) (Bueno de Mesquita et al, 1991). Similarly, a study in the USA reported no material association for consumption of breads and cereals combined (OR = 1.3, ns, for higher consumption) (Falk et al, 1988). On the other hand, another study in the USA reported increased risk with greater bread and cereal consumption (OR = 2.2, 1.2–4.1, for higher consumption) (Olsen et al, 1989). Each of these studies adjusted for smoking and for intake of either energy or other food groups, including meat and vegetables.

Bread as a whole or different types of bread have been examined in some studies. A study in Switzerland found bread as a whole to be associated with increased risk of pancreatic cancer (OR = 1.8, 0.9–3.5) for higher consumption, although this association was not statistically significant and was not adjusted for total energy intake (Raymond et al, 1987). A study in the USA reported increased risk with greater consumption of white bread, with an odds ratio of 2.3 (1.3–4.1) for two or more servings per week, compared with less than two; for wholegrain breads, however, the odds ratio was less than 1.0 (ns) (Gold et al, 1985).

The study of Falk et al (1988) examined rice intake and reported odds ratios of 1.5 and 1.2 (both ns) for higher intakes for men and women, respectively.

The evidence regarding diets high in cereals and the risk of pancreatic cancer is inconsistent, with most studies finding either no relationship or increased risk with higher intake of various cereal foods. As different cereals may have different effects on cancer risk, and because the effects of refined cereals may differ from those of unrefined (see section on wholegrain cereals below), the panel has decided to make no judgement on the relationship between cereals as a whole and the risk of pancreatic cancer.

Wholegrain cereals

The case-control study of Olsen et al (1989) in the USA, which reported a strong increase in risk with higher consumption of bread and cereals also reported that cases ate more white bread and less wholewheat bread than controls, suggesting that any increased risk was not attributable to wholewheat bread, and that intake of wholewheat bread was associated with decreased risk. Similarly, the case-control study of Gold et al (1985) in the USA found an increased risk with higher intake of white bread, but not wholegrain breads (OR < 1.0; ns). Another case-control study in the USA reported decreased risk in those who preferred wholegrain bread (OR = 0.7, 0.5–0.9), although it was noted that preference for wholegrain bread was correlated with consumption of more vegetables and fruits and less meat, two other potentially protective factors (Mack et al, 1986). In a study in Italy, no association was found for greater consumption of wholegrain bread or pasta (OR = 0.9, ns) (La Vecchia et al, 1990).

Four case-control studies of the risk of pancreatic cancer have found either no relationship or decreased risk with greater consumption of various wholegrain cereal foods, mainly breads.

Evidence relating to diets high in wholegrain cereals and the risk of pancreatic cancer is limited; no judgement is possible.

4.7.2.2 Roots, tubers and plantains

Three case-control studies of pancreatic cancer have examined the risk associated with higher consumption of potatoes. One study reported a protective association in women (p < 0.05), but not in men (Baghurst et al, 1991); another reported an increase in risk, although not statistically significant (OR = 1.5, ns) (Raymond et al, 1987); the third reported no association after adjusting for total energy intake and smoking (OR = 0.9, ns, for the highest quintile) (Bueno de Mesquita et al, 1991).

The evidence relating to diets high in potato and the risk of pancreatic cancer is limited and inconsistent; no judgement is possible.

4.7.2.3 Vegetables and fruits

At least 13 epidemiological studies have reported results on the intake of vegetables and/or fruits and risk of pancreatic cancer. General patterns of risk can be discerned from Tables 4.7.3 and 4.7.4, which show the results from three prospective and ten case-control studies, respectively.

The three prospective studies involved cohorts of, respectively, Seventh-day Adventists, white men, and elderly people, all in the USA; the number of cases in these studies was small, ranging from 40 to 65 deaths or incident cases. These studies showed both decreased and increased risk with higher consumption of various types of vegetables and fruits, although none of the associations was statistically significant (see Table 4.7.3).

Ten case-control studies of vegetable and fruit consumption, all conducted within Western societies, are shown in Table 4.7.4; nine of these have shown a statistically significant protective association for one or more vegetable and/or fruit items. Overall, there is a very consistent pattern of decreasing risk with increasing consumption of these foods. There is, however, substantial variation in the specific food items showing protective relationships, perhaps suggesting that there are more than a few active food components giving rise to the apparent protective effect. The two largest studies, with 490 and 363 cases, respectively, reported statistically significant decreases in risk with higher intakes of either all vegetables and fruits, or fruits only (Mack et al, 1986; Falk et al, 1988). Notably, many of these studies did not adjust for cigarette smoking, although statistically significant protective associations were found in almost all of the studies that did adjust for smoking. Three studies that adjusted for smoking reported high consumers of various types vegetables or fruits to have 30–50% of the risk of pancreatic cancer, compared with low consumers (Falk et al, 1988; Bueno de Mesquita et al, 1991; Lyon et al, 1993).

The epidemiological evidence is quite consistent for both

TABLE 4.7.3 VEGETABLE AND FRUIT CONSUMPTION AND THE RISK OF PANCREATIC CANCER: COHORT STUDIES

AUTHOR, YEAR, AND PLACE	COHORT SIZE NO. OF CASES AND DESCRIPTION	TYPE OF VEGETABLE OR FRUIT	COMPARISON[a]	RELATIVE RISK (95% CONFIDENCE INTERVAL)	ADJUSTMENT	
					SEX/AGE	SMOKING HISTORY
Mills et al, 1988 California, USA	34,000 Seventh-day Adventists: 40 deaths	Tomatoes	na	protective assoc**	na	na
		Fresh citrus fruits	na	protective assoc**	na	na
		Fresh winter fruits	na	protective assoc**	na	na
		Other fresh fruits	na	no assoc**	na	na
		Cooked green vegetables	na	positive assoc**	na	na
		Green salad	na	positive assoc**	na	na
Zheng et al, 1993 USA	17,633 white men: 57 deaths	Vegetables	h vs l quartile	no assoc**	na	na
		Fruits	h vs l quartile	no assoc**	na	na
Shibata et al, 1994 California, USA	13,979 elderly persons: 65 incident cases	Vegetables	≥ 4.7 vs < 3.2/day	0.8 (0.4–1.5)	Y	Y
		Fruits	≥ 3.6 vs < 2.4/day	0.9 (0.5–1.6)	Y	Y
		Dark green vegetables	≥ 0.5 vs < 0.1/day	1.2 (0.7–2.1)	Y	Y
		Yellow vegetables	≥ 0.8 vs < 0.4/day	0.6 (0.3–1.1)	Y	Y

* p ≤ 0.05 for trend and/or for comparison of highest vs lowest consumption level
** p > 0.05 for trend and/or for comparison of highest vs lowest consumption level
na information not available or unclear from article
[a] h = highest, l = lowest quantile

TABLE 4.7.4 VEGETABLE AND FRUIT CONSUMPTION[a] AND THE RISK OF PANCREATIC CANCER: CASE-CONTROL STUDIES

Author, year, and place	No. of cases	Type of vegetable or fruit	Comparison[a]	Odds Ratio (95% confidence interval)	Sex/age	Adjustment Smoking history	Other factors[b]
Gold et al, 1985 Baltimore, USA	201 women and men	Raw fruit and vegetables	≥ 5 vs < 5/w	0.6 (0.3–0.9)*	Y	N	N
Mack et al, 1986 Los Angeles, USA	490 women and men	Fresh fruits and vegetables	≥ 5 vs < 5/w	0.7 (0.5–0.9)*	Y	N	Y
Norell et al, 1986 Sweden	99 women and men	Vegetables	almost daily vs < 1/w	0.8 (0.4–1.6)[b]	Y	N	N
		Raw vegetables	almost daily vs < 1/w	0.6 (0.3–1.1)[b]	Y	N	N
		Fruits and juices	almost daily vs < 1/w	0.6 (0.3–1.3)[b]	Y	N	N
		Carrots	almost daily vs < 1/w	0.3 (0.2–0.7)[b]	Y	N	N
		Citrus fruit	almost daily vs < 1/w	0.5 (0.3–0.9)[b]	Y	N	N
Voirol et al, 1987 Switzerland	88 women and men	Vegetables	h vs l tertile	0.5*	Y	N	Y
		Fruit	h vs l tertile	0.6*	Y	N	Y
Falk et al, 1988 Louisiana, USA	363 women	Vegetables	≥ vs < median	0.9 (0.7–1.1)	Y	N	N
	160 women	Fruits and juices	≥ 64 vs < 25/m	0.5*	Y	Y	Y
	203 men	Fruits and juices	≥ 64 vs < 25/m	0.4*	Y	Y	Y
Olsen et al, 1989 Minnesota, USA	212 men	Cruciferous vegetables	≥ 9 vs ≤ 2/m	0.6 (0.3–1.0)	Y	Y	Y
		Non-cruciferous vegetables	≥ 32 vs ≤ 16/m	1.0 (0.5–1.7)	Y	Y	Y
		Fruits and juices	≥ 53 vs ≤ 21/m	0.9 (0.5–1.6)	Y	Y	Y
La Vecchia et al, 1990, Northern Italy	247 women and men	Green vegetables	h vs l tertile	0.8 (0.6–1.2)	Y	N	N
		Carrots	h vs l tertile	0.9 (0.6–1.2)	Y	N	N
		Fresh fruits	h vs l tertile	0.7 (0.4–0.98)	Y	N	N
Baghurst et al, 1991 Adelaide, Australia	52 women	Broccoli	c	protective assoc*	Y	N	N
		Brussels sprouts		protective assoc*	Y	N	N
		Carrots		protective assoc**	Y	N	N
	52 men	Tomatoes		protective assoc*	Y	N	N
Bueno de Mesquita et al, 1991	164 women and men	Vegetables	h vs l quintile	0.3*	Y	Y	Y
		Cooked vegetables	h vs l quintile	0.4*	Y	Y	Y
		Raw vegetables	h vs l quintile	0.4*	Y	Y	Y
		Cruciferous vegetables	h vs l quintile	0.3*	Y	Y	Y
		Tomatoes	h vs l quintile	0.7**	Y	Y	Y
		Carrots	h vs l quintile	1.3**	Y	Y	Y
		Fruits	h vs l quintile	1.1**	Y	Y	Y
		Citrus fruits	h vs l quintile	1.0**	Y	Y	Y
	89 women	Fruits	h vs l quintile	0.4**	N	N	N
Lyon et al, 1993 Utah, USA	60 women	Vegetables	high vs low	0.3 (0.1–0.7)*	Y	Y	Y
		Fruits	high vs low	0.4 (0.2–0.8)*	Y	Y	Y
	87 men	Vegetables	high vs low	1.0 (0.5–2.0)**	Y	Y	Y
		Fruit	high vs low	0.8 (0.4–1.6)**	Y	Y	Y

* p ≤ 0.05 for trend and/or for comparison of highest vs lowest consumption level
** p > 0.05 for trend and/or for comparison of highest vs lowest consumption level
na information not available or unclear from article
a h = highest, l = lowest, w = week, m = month
b Adjusted or matched for one or more of the following: region, place of residence, ethnic origin, blood glucose level, coffee, diabetes under treatment, race, examination site, date of first check up
c Adjusted for tobacco smoking and chewing, OR = 10.8 (statistically significant) for 18 male histologically-verified cases, for whom data on alcohol, smoking and chewing were available

vegetables and fruits, when examined separately. Six of seven studies examining vegetables as a whole reported risk estimates of less than 1.0 (for women, but not for men in one study), thus signifying a pattern of decreased risk with higher consumption. For fruits, eight of nine studies reported risk estimates of less than 1.0 (again, for women, but not for men in one study).

In a 1996 review of the literature on nutrition and pancre-

atic cancer, Howe and Burch concluded that 12 of 13 epidemiological studies (two cohort and ten case-control) showed some evidence of a protective association between vegetable and/or fruit consumption and pancreatic cancer. These studies, with one exception (Goto et al, 1990), are included in Tables 4.7.3 and 4.7.4.

One international ecological study of 18 countries found vegetable consumption to be inversely correlated with pancreatic cancer, but not with any of the other 13 cancers studied; fruit consumption was not related to any cancer (based on FAO food consumption data for 1954–1956 and mortality rates for 1966–1967) (Maruchi et al, 1977).

There is a wide variety of postulated mechanisms, many of which are complex, by which vegetables and fruits may lower risk of cancer at all sites (Wattenberg, 1985; Adlercreutz, 1990; Steinmetz and Potter, 1991b). (See chapters 5.2, 5.6, 5.8 and 6.3).

> There is substantial evidence from epidemiological
> studies that diets high in vegetables and fruits
> probably decrease the risk of pancreatic cancer.

4.7.2.4 Pulses (legumes)

One cohort study of pancreatic cancer in Seventh-day Adventists found an protective association for beans, peas and lentils (OR = 0.4, 0.2–1.1) (Mills et al, 1988), whereas another in Japan reported a positive association for intake of soybean paste soup (OR = 1.8, statistically significant). A case-control study in the Netherlands reported a null association for pulses (Buena de Mesquita et al, 1991).

In animals, it has been well established that ingestion of raw soy preparations, such as soy flour or soy-protein isolates, leads to preneoplastic and neoplastic pancreatic lesions. This effect is thought to be attributable to trypsin inhibitors, and possibly to other constituents of raw soy (see Gumbmann et al, 1989). The biological mechanism of trypsin inhibitors appears to involve excessive stimulation of cholecystokinin (CCK), which leads to pancreatic hypertrophy. One study in humans has shown greater release of CCK after ingestion of raw soy, than after ingestion of heat-treated soy. The relevance of the animal findings to humans is unknown, because few, if any, soy products are normally consumed raw by humans. One study in humans actually showed decreased release of CCK after prolonged ingestion of soy milk (heat-treated) (see Lu et al, 1995). Protease inhibitors are discussed further in chapter 5.8.

> Evidence relating to diets high in pulses and the risk of
> pancreatic cancer is limited and inconsistent; no
> judgement is possible.

4.7.2.5 Nuts and seeds

A case-control study in the Netherlands reported no association between intake of 'nuts and tasty snacks' and risk of pancreatic cancer (Bueno de Mesquita et al, 1991).

> Evidence relating to diets high in nuts and seeds and the
> risk of pancreatic cancer is very limited; no
> judgement is possible.

4.7.2.6 Meat, poultry, fish and eggs
Meat
Each of three prospective studies of pancreatic cancer that have examined meat consumption has found increased risk with greater consumption. In a cohort of Seventh-day

Adventists in the USA, in which 40 deaths from pancreatic cancer occurred, a relative risk of 2.3 (0.7–7.1) for current use of meat, poultry or fish was observed; meat was not examined separately from poultry and fish (Mills et al, 1988). In a larger cohort study in Japan, involving 399 deaths from pancreatic cancer, daily consumption of meat was also associated with increased risk, compared with non-consumption (Hirayama, 1989)). In a third cohort of white men in the USA, in which 57 deaths from pancreatic cancer occurred, higher intakes of meat were associated with increased risk (RR = 3.0, 1.2–7.5, for all meat and 2.4, 1.0–6.1, for red meat) (Zheng et al, 1993). In two of these studies, the associations for meat were adjusted for smoking (Mills et al, 1988; Zheng et al, 1993) and, in one, the increased risk with high total meat consumption was observed within all strata of cigarette smoking and alcohol drinking (Zheng et al, 1993).

Ten case-control studies of pancreatic cancer have examined some aspect of meat consumption; these studies have all been conducted in the USA or Europe (Gold et al, 1985; Mack et al, 1986; Norell et al, 1986; Raymond et al, 1987; Falk et al, 1988; Olsen et al, 1989; La Vecchia et al, 1990; Farrow and Davis, 1990; Bueno de Mesquita et al, 1991; Lyon et al, 1993). Some studies have examined meat as a whole, whereas others have examined only individual food items, so these data are not easily grouped for summarisation.

Of three studies that have reported on 'all meat' or 'total meat', two reported moderate to strong increases in risk with high consumption (smoking-adjusted OR = 2.5, 1.2–5.1, for >10 vs < 5 servings per week and 1.6, p < 0.05, for the highest vs lowest quintile) (Farrow and Davis, 1990; Bueno de Mesquita, 1991), and one reported no association (La Vecchia et al, 1990). A further study reported no association with high intake of 'meat from the butcher' (Raymond et al, 1987). One study in the USA, which reported specifically on red meat, found no substantial association in either men or women (OR = 1.4, ns, for high consumption in each) (Lyon et al, 1993).

Six studies have reported on beef consumption (Gold et al, 1985; Mack et al, 1986; Falk et al, 1988; Olsen et al, 1989; Farrow and Davis, 1990; Bueno de Mesquita et al, 1991), with mixed findings ranging from a strong increase in risk with high consumption (Farrow and Davis, 1990), to no association (Mack et al, 1986), to a protective association (Bueno de Mesquita et al, 1991). Seven studies that have reported on pork consumption have generally found increased risk with higher consumption (odds ratios ranging from 1.3 to 2.4 for high consumption) (Mack et al, 1986; Falk et al, 1988; Olsen et al, 1989; La Vecchia et al, 1990; Farrow and Davis, 1990; Bueno de Mesquita et al, 1991), with the exception of one study in Switzerland, which reported a decreased risk with an odds ratio of 0.6 (0.3–1.2) for higher intake of lean pork (Raymond et al, 1987).

Intakes of different processed meats have been examined in some studies. Various studies have reported increased risk with higher consumption of bacon, smoked ham, sausage and nitrated meats, but null associations have been reported for these and other processed meats in other studies (See also section 4.7.3 on Cured and smoked foods).

In their 1996 review of nutrition and pancreatic cancer, Howe and Burch concluded that, of 13 epidemiological studies (12 of these are discussed above), nine showed some evidence of increased risk with higher meat consumption, three showed no evidence of an association and one showed evidence of a protective association.

Thus, the balance of the epidemiological evidence is in the direction of increased risk of pancreatic cancer with higher meat consumption, although there is some inconsistency in the data and no particular type or category of meat emerges as specifically explaining the increased risk.

The epidemiological evidence regarding dietary fat suggests that neither total nor saturated fat is responsible for any increased risk with higher meat consumption; similarly the evidence on protein shows no association with risk. Thus, some other factor related to meat consumption might be responsible for the observed meat associations. Candidates include cholesterol (see section 4.7.1.3) and *N*-nitroso or heterocyclic aromatic compounds, which can be induced in meat by various forms of cooking or processing. If heterocyclic amines are carcinogenic for the human pancreas, then differences in cooking methods might explain some of the inconsistencies reported in the epidemiological literature regarding meat consumption (see section 4.7.3.3).

Diets high in meat possibly increase the risk of pancreatic cancer, perhaps particularly at the higher levels and with certain preparation methods commonly used in Western societies.

Poultry

One cohort study of men in the USA observed an increase in risk of pancreatic cancer with higher intake of chicken (RR = 1.9, 0.7–5.5, for the highest quartile, compared with the lowest) (Zheng et al, 1993).

Of four case-control studies, three have reported no association between intake of poultry or chicken and pancreatic cancer (Raymond et al, 1987; Olsen et al, 1989; Lyon et al, 1993); the other reported increased risk (OR = 2.5, 1.2–5.0) for chicken two or more times per week, compared with less than weekly (Farrow and Davis, 1990).

Evidence relating to diets high in poultry and the risk of pancreatic cancer is limited; no judgement is possible.

Fish

One prospective study of pancreatic cancer examined fish consumption and reported a relative risk of 1.4 (0.6–3.7, ns for trend) for the highest quartile of intake of all fish (Zheng et al, 1993).

Eight case-control studies have reported on fish consumption. One study in the Netherlands reported a moderate increase in risk with higher total fish intake (OR = 1.8, p <

0.05 for trend, for the highest quintile) (Bueno de Mesquita et al, 1991). Another study in the USA also reported a moderate increase in risk with higher seafood intake in men (OR = 1.9, p < 0.05 for trend) for consumption eight or more times per month, compared with less than twice; no association was seen in women (OR = 1.0) (Falk et al, 1988). On the other hand, a study in Australia found a protective association for fish, with cases reporting significantly lower intakes than controls (Baghurst et al, 1991). The remaining studies reported no statistically significant associations, with odds ratios for higher intakes of fish (in general, or fried/grilled or smoked) or shellfish ranging from 0.7 to 1.3 (Gold et al, 1985; Norell et al, 1988; Farrow and Davis, 1990; La Vecchia et al, 1990; Lyon et al, 1993).

Evidence relating to diets high in fish and the risk of pancreatic cancer is inconsistent; no judgement is possible.

Eggs

Two prospective studies of pancreatic cancer have examined egg consumption, with one study among Seventh-day Adventists finding a strong increase in risk with higher consumption, and the other study, among men in the USA, finding a non-significant decrease in risk; the relative risks were 2.5 (1.1–4.6, p = 0.05 for trend) for consumption three or more times per week, compared with less than weekly (Mills et al, 1988), and 0.7 (0.2–2.2, ns for trend) for the highest quartile of intake of eggs and dairy products combined, compared with the lowest (Zheng et al, 1993).

Of six case-control studies that have reported on egg consumption, two studies observed increased risk with higher consumption; in one study in the Netherlands, an odds ratio of 2.2 (p < 0.05; p < 0.05 for trend) for the highest quintile was reported (Bueno de Mesquita et al, 1991); in the other study, in Australia, cases consumed more boiled eggs and omelettes on average than controls (p < 0.05 for both) (Baghurst et al, 1991). The remaining four studies, in Italy and the USA, found no substantial association between egg consumption and pancreatic cancer risk (Gold et al, 1985; Mack et al, 1986; Farrow and Davis, 1990; La Vecchia et al, 1990).

Three of eight epidemiological studies have found increased risk of pancreatic cancer with higher consumption of eggs and the remaining studies have found no relationship.

The evidence suggests that diets high in eggs may increase the risk of pancreatic cancer, but is, as yet, insufficient.

4.7.2.7 Milk and dairy products

Neither of two prospective studies has reported any statistically significant association with either current use of whole milk (RR ≈ 1.0) (Mills et al, 1988), or high intake of dairy products and eggs combined (RR = 0.7, 0.2–2.2) (Zheng et al, 1993).

Of seven case-control studies that have examined intake of milk or any type of dairy product, only one study, in the USA, has found a statistically significant association; this was a strong increase in risk with higher consumption of dairy products in men (OR = 2.2, p < 0.05 for trend) for consumption more than 68 times per month, compared with fewer than 34 times; no association was apparent in women (Falk et al, 1988). Another study, in the USA, found weaker evidence of increased risk (OR = 1.5, 0.9–2.7) for intake of dairy products at least 39 times per month, compared with 16 times or fewer (Olsen et al, 1989). However, a further study, in Italy, found some evidence of decreased risk (OR = 0.7, 0.4–1.04) for intake of milk in the highest tertile, compared with the lowest (La Vecchia et al, 1990).

In four case-control studies that have examined dairy products as a comprehensive group, results have been mixed (OR = 0.8 (ns) to 2.2 (p < 0.05) for high consumption (Falk et al, 1988; Olsen et al, 1989; Bueno de Mesquita et al, 1991; Lyon et al, 1993). Three studies that have reported on milk independent of other dairy products have resulted in mixed, but relatively weak associations (OR = 0.7 (ns) to 1.5 (ns) for higher intake) (Raymond et al, 1987; Farrow and Davis, 1990; La Vecchia et al, 1990). Three studies that have examined cheese consumption have observed no relationship to risk (Farrow and Davis, 1990; La Vecchia et al, 1990; Bueno de Mesquita et al, 1991). One study also reported no association for consumption of fermented milk products specifically (Bueno de Mesquita et al, 1991).

Nine epidemiological studies of pancreatic cancer have examined some aspect of dairy product consumption, resulting in inconsistent but largely weak associations; no judgement is possible.

4.7.2.8 Coffee, tea and other drinks

Coffee

Pancreatic cancer, along with bladder cancer, has been one of the cancers studied in considerable depth for a possible effect of coffee consumption. In 1981, a case-control study generated interest when a two- to three-fold increase in risk with three or more cups of coffee per day was reported (MacMahon et al, 1981). Although the odds ratios were adjusted for smoking habits, the study was criticised for excluding potential controls with gastrointestinal disease, cancer, or diseases known to be associated with smoking or heavy alcohol consumption; these exclusions may have caused the pattern of coffee drinking in the control group to be different from that in the general population (Feinstein et al, 1981). In the subsequent decade, a multitude of studies examined the relationship between coffee drinking and pancreatic cancer.

La Vecchia et al (1987) conducted a pooled analysis of eight epidemiological studies up to that time (1,464 cases in total), excluding the hypothesis-generating study by MacMahon et al (1981), and calculated an odds ratio of 1.4 (1.1–1.8) for high coffee consumption, compared with non-consumption (adjusted for age, sex and smoking status).

Gordis (1990) reviewed 30 epidemiological studies addressing the relationship between coffee and pancreatic cancer, and concluded that the evidence did not support the hypothesis that coffee consumption increases the risk of pancreatic cancer. For six cohort studies, Gordis concluded that all are in agreement that there is no significant increase in pancreatic cancer risk associated with coffee consumption. For 14 case-control studies, Gordis argued that, overall, these studies did not identify coffee consumption as a major risk factor for pancreatic cancer, although results were somewhat inconsistent across studies. Some studies showed increased risk, but these associations were generally weak, lacking a dose–response pattern and/or applicable only to a particular subgroup (e.g., men or women, non-smokers or smokers, non-drinkers). Gordis also pointed out that the exclusion of individuals with smoking-related or gastrointestinal diseases from the control group in some studies may have caused the level of coffee consumption in the controls to be lower than would be expected in a group of healthy controls, thereby possibly creating an artefactual association between coffee consumption and the risk of pancreatic cancer.

In 1991, an IARC Working Group evaluated 21 case-control and six cohort studies (IARC, 1991); these were largely the same studies as those reviewed by Gordis. They concluded that none of the six cohort studies reported a statistically significant increase in risk and that any non-significant increase was reduced after adjustment for smoking. Regarding the 21 case-control studies, it was concluded that 12 showed increased risk; this increase was statistically significant in three and a dose–response relationship was apparent in two. A statistically non-significant increase in risk for the highest exposure group was the most common finding; this became weaker in some studies after adjustment for smoking. Seven studies reported no association and one reported a weakly protective association. The IARC Group concluded that the data as a whole suggested a weak positive relation between high levels of coffee consumption and pancreatic cancer, but that bias or confounding by cigarette smoking might account for the association. They further concluded that the data regarding decaffeinated coffee, which were fewer in number, were generally null.

Ten prospective studies and 26 case-control studies that have examined coffee consumption in relation to pancreatic cancer are shown in Tables 4.7.5 and 4.7.6. These include the studies reviewed by Gordis and IARC, as described above, as well as more recent studies. Only one of the ten prospective studies reported a statistically significant association; an increase in risk was found with daily coffee consumption, compared with non-daily, in a Japanese cohort in which 679 deaths from pancreatic cancer occurred; importantly, this association was not adjusted for cigarette smoking (Hirayama, 1989). Seven of the ten prospective studies in Table 4.7.5 involved fewer than 75 cases, thus the lack of statistically significant findings is not surprising and would still be compatible with a weak or moderate association. The two other large studies, with 450 and 127 cases, reported no association with more than six, compared with six or fewer

TABLE 4.7.5 COFFEE CONSUMPTION AND THE RISK OF PANCREATIC CANCER: COHORT STUDIES

AUTHOR, YEAR, AND PLACE	SIZE OF COHORT: NO. OF CASES	EXPOSURE FACTOR	COMPARISON	RELATIVE RISK (95% CONFIDENCE INTERVAL)	SEX/AGE	ADJUSTMENT SMOKING HISTORY	OTHER VARIABLES[a]
Snowdon, 1984 California, USA	23,912 Seventh-day Adventists: 71 deaths	Coffee consumption	≥ 2 vs < 1 cups/day	0.8 (0.4–1.6)[**]	Y	N[b]	N
Whittemore, 1985 USA	50,000 college alumni: 127 deaths	Coffee consumption in college	yes vs no	no assoc	Y	Y	N
Nomura, 1986 Hawaii, USA	7,355 Japanese men: 21 incident cases	Coffee intake	≥ 5 vs 0 cups/day	1.6[**]	Y	Y	N
Jacobsen, 1986 Norway	16,555 men and women: 63 incident cases	Coffee consumption	7 vs ≤ 2 cups/day	0.7[**c]	Y	N	Y
	13,664 men: 38 incident cases	Coffee consumption	7 vs ≤ 2 cups/day	0.7[**d]	Y	Y	Y
Mills et al, 1988 California, USA	34,000 Seventh-day Adventists: 40 deaths	Current use of regular coffee	≥ daily vs never	2.2 (0.6–8.0)[**]	Y	Y	N
		Past use of regular coffee	≥ daily vs never	0.7 (0.3–1.5)[**]	Y	N	N
Hiatt et al, 1988 California, USA	122,894 men and women: 48 incident cases	Coffee use	> 4 cups/day vs non-drinkers	0.7 (0.2–1.9)	Y	Y	Y
Hirayama, 1989 Japan	265,118 men and women: 679 deaths	Coffee consumption	daily vs non-daily	positive assoc[*e]	N	N	N
Zheng et al, 1993 USA	17,633 white men 56 deaths	Coffee consumption	≥ 7 vs < 3 cups/day	0.9 (0.3–2.4)	Y	Y	Y
Shibata et al, 1994 California, USA	13,979 elderly persons in a retirement community: 65 incident cases	Coffee consumption	≥ 4 vs < 1 cups/day	0.9 (0.3–2.8)[**]	Y	Y	N
Friedman and van den Tede, 1993 California, USA	175,000: 450 incident cases	Coffee	> 6 vs ≤ 6 cups/day	1.0 (0.7–1.2)[**]	Y	Y	Y

[*] p ≤ 0.05 for trend and/or for comparison of highest vs lowest consumption level
[**] p > 0.05 for trend and/or for comparison of highest vs lowest consumption level
[a] Adjusted or matched for one or more of the following: residence, ethnic origin, blood glucose level, diabetes under treatment, alcohol index, race, examination site, date of first check-up
[b] It is stated in the article that no significant or suggestive association was apparent after adjustment for cigarette smoking history via multivariate regression
[c] RR = 1.0 ** among 39 histologically confirmed cases
[d] RR = 0.9 ** among 22 histologically confirmed cases
[e] Pancreatic cancer mortality rates were 78.4 and 14.5 per 100,000 (p = 0.01) for daily and non-daily coffee consumers, respectively

cups per day, nor with a history of coffee consumption in college, respectively (Friedman et al, 1993; Whittemore et al, 1985).

Of the 26 case-control studies in Table 4.7.6, five reported a statistically significant increase in the risk of pancreatic cancer with greater coffee consumption. In individual studies, this association was observed for decaffeinated coffee only (Kessler 1981; Lin 1981), was not adjusted for smoking (Mack et al, 1986), was statistically significant either for only women (Clavel et al, 1989) or only men (Lyon et al, 1992), or was statistically significant only in heavy smokers, which would be compatible with the possibility of residual confounding by smoking (Lyon et al, 1992); the remaining study has been criticised for the exclusion criteria used in the selection of controls (MacMahon et al, 1981) (see above). Twenty studies reported no statistically significant associations; in three of these the odds ratios for higher consumption were at least 1.5, in twelve they were between 0.75 and 1.5 (or there was said to be 'no association', but an odds ratio was not quoted), and in five they were 0.75 or lower. Only

one study in Poland showed a statistically significant protective association for coffee consumption (Zatonski et al, 1993).

Eight case-control studies have examined consumption of decaffeinated coffee (see Table 4.7.6). One study reported a statistically significant increase in risk (Kessler 1981; Lin 1981), two reported increases in risk were not statistically significant (Hsieh et al, 1986; Gorham et al, 1988), four reported no substantial associations (La Vecchia et al, 1987; Farrow and Davis, 1990; Bueno de Mesquita et al, 1991; Ghadirian et al, 1991), and one reported a decrease in risk (for men, but not women) that was not statistically significant (Wynder et al, 1986). Changes in the processing and consumption of decaffeinated coffee during the 1970s and 1980s limit somewhat the ability to assess the relationship with pancreatic cancer risk in epidemiological studies.

In 1970, an ecological study comparing geographical variation in pancreatic cancer death rates and coffee consumption showed a correlation (higher intake with higher rates) (p = 0.008) (Stocks, 1970). Another international

TABLE 4.7.6 COFFEE CONSUMPTION AND THE RISK OF PANCREATIC CANCER: CASE-CONTROL STUDIES

Author, year, and place	No. of cases	Exposure	Comparison	Odds ratio (95% confidence interval)	Sex/Age	Smoking History	Other Factors[a]
MacMahon et al 1981, Massachusetts and Rhode Island, USA	369 women and men	Coffee drinking	≥ 5 vs 0 cups/day	3.2*	Y	N	N
			≥ 3 vs 0 cups/day	2.7 (1.6–4.7)	Y	Y	N
	151 women	Coffee drinking	consumers vs non-consumers	2.3 (1.2–4.6)	Y	N	N
Lin and Kessler, 1981, USA	109 women and men	Decaffeinated coffee consumption	[b]	positive assoc*			
		Regular coffee	na	no assoc	N	N	N
Severson, 1982 Washington, USA	22 women and men	Coffee consumption	yes vs no	1.0 (0.2–4.5)	Y	Y	N
Goldstein, 1982 California, USA	91 women and men	Coffee drinking	[c]	no assoc**	N	N	N
Wynder et al 1983, USA	122 women	Coffee drinking	≥ 6 vs 0 cups/day	1.0 (0.5–1.8)	Y	Y	N
	153 men	Coffee drinking	≥ 6 vs 0 cups/day	1.0 (0.6–1.8)	Y	Y	N
Kinlen & McPherson 1984, UK	216 women and men	Coffee consumption	daily vs never	0.9 (0.6–1.4)	N[d]	Y	Y
Gold et al, 1985 Baltimore, USA	201 women and men	Coffee drinking	≥ 3 vs 0 cups/day	1.7 (0.7–4.0)**	Y	Y	N
	103 women	Coffee drinking	≥ 5 vs 0 cups/day	2.9 (0.6–14.5)**	Y	N	N
	94 men	Coffee drinking	≥ 5 vs 0 cups/day	1.3 (0.02–76.8)**	Y	N	N
Wynder et al, 1986 USA	111 women	Caffeinated coffee consumption	≥ 3 vs < 1 cups/day	0.6**[e]	Y	N	Y
		Decaffeinated coffee consumption	≥ 3 vs < 1 cups/day	0.9 (0.4–1.9)	Y	N	Y
	127 men	Caffeinated coffee consumption	≥ 3 vs < 1 cups/day	1.5**[e]	Y	N	Y
		Decaffeinated coffee consumption	≥ 3 vs < 1 cups/day	0.7 (0.4–1.4)	Y	N	Y
Hsieh et al, 1986 Massachusetts and Rhode Island, USA	170 women and men	All coffee	≥ 60,000 vs 0 cumulative cups	1.5 (0.8–2.8)	Y	N	N
		Regular coffee	≥ 60,000 vs 0 cumulative cups	1.4 (0.8–2.7)	Y	N	N
		Decaffeinated coffee	≥ 6,000 vs 0 cumulative cups	1.6 (0.8–2.9)	Y	N	N
	87 women	Coffee drinking	≥ 5 vs 0 cups/day	2.2 (0.8–6.0)	Y	N	N
	85 men	Coffee drinking	≥ 5 vs 0 cups/day	2.4 (1.0–5.8)	Y	N	N
Mack et al, 1986 Los Angeles, USA	490 women and men	Coffee consumption	≥ 5 vs < 1 cups/day	2.0 (1.3–3.2)[f,g]	Y	N	Y
Norell et al, 1986 Sweden	99 women and men	Coffee intake	≥ 5 vs 0–1 cups/day	1.0 (0.4–2.6)[h]	Y	N	N
La Vecchia et al, 1987 Northern Italy	150 women and men	Coffee consumption	≥ 5 vs 0 cups/day	1.1 (0.4–2.7)	Y	Y	Y
		Decaffeinated coffee consumption	≥ 5 vs 0 cups/day	0.9 (0.4–1.9)	Y	Y	Y
Raymond et al, 1987 Switzerland	88 women and men	Coffee	≥ 1.4 vs 0 cups/day	1.3 (0.7–2.3)[h]	N	N	N
		Instant coffee	any vs 0 cups/day	1.4 (0.8–2.4)[h]	N	N	N
Falk et al, 1988 Louisiana, USA	160 women	Coffee drinking	≥ 8 cups/day vs non-drinker	0.9**	Y	Y	Y
	203 men	Coffee drinking	≥ 8 cups/day vs non-drinker	1.4 (0.8–2.5)**	Y	Y	Y
Gorham, 1988 California, USA	30 women and men	Regular coffee intake	≥ 3 vs < 3 cups/day	1.9**[i]	Y	Y	Y
		Decaffeinated coffee intake	≥ 1 vs < 1 cups/day	2.6 (0.8–8.6)[j]	Y	N	Y
Cuzick and Babiker, 1989, England	216 women and men	Coffee consumption	≥ 5 cups/day vs none	1.4**	Y	Y	N
Clavel et al, 1989 Paris, France	63 women	Coffee consumption	≥ 4 vs 0 cups/day	9.6 (1.3–70.7)*	Y	Y	Y
	98 men	Coffee consumption	≥ 4 vs 0 cups/day	2.1 (0.5–8.9)**	Y	Y	Y
Olsen et al, 1989 Minnesota, USA	212 men	Coffee consumption	≥ 7 vs < 1 drinks/day	0.6 (0.3–1.3)[k]	Y	Y	Y
Farrow & Davis, 1990 Washington, USA	148 men	Regular coffee consumption	≥ 6 vs 0 cups/day	1.1 (0.5–2.4)	Y	Y	Y
		Decaffeinated coffee consumption	regular drinkers vs non-drinkers	0.9 (0.4–1.9)	Y	N	N

AUTHOR, YEAR, AND PLACE	NO. OF CASES	EXPOSURE	COMPARISON[a]	ODDS RATIO (95% CONFIDENCE INTERVAL)	SEX/AGE	ADJUSTMENT SMOKING HISTORY	OTHER FACTORS[a]
Baghurst et al, 1991 Adelaide, Australia	104 women and men	Coffee	l	protective assoc**	Y	N	N
Bueno de Mesquita et al, 1991 Netherlands	176 women and men	Total coffee	≥ 11,840 vs < 6,193 litres/ lifetime	0.6 (0.3–1.2)**	Y	Y	Y
		Ground coffee	≥ 11,508 vs < 5,731 litres/ lifetime	0.8 (0.4–1.6)**	Y	Y	Y
		Instant coffee	≥ 618 vs 0 litres/lifetime	0.9 (0.5–1.7)**	Y	Y	Y
		Caffeinated coffee	≥ 11,769 vs < 6,098 litres/ lifetime	0.7 (0.3–1.5)**	Y	Y	Y
		Decaffeinated coffee	≥ 476 vs 0 litres/lifetime	1.1 (0.5–2.5)**	Y	Y	Y
Ghadirian et al, 1991 Quebec, Canada	179 women and men	Total coffee	highest quintile vs never drinkers	0.6 (0.2–1.6)**	Y	Y	Y
		Regular coffee	highest quintile vs never drinkers	0.8 (0.3–2.0)**	Y	Y	Y
		Decaffeinated coffee	highest quintile vs never drinkers	0.8 (0.3–1.9)**	Y	Y	Y
		Ground coffee	highest quintile vs never drinkers	0.8 (0.3–1.8)**	Y	Y	Y
		Ground decaffeinated coffee	highest quintile vs never drinkers	1.1 (0.2–5.8)**	Y	Y	Y
		Instant coffee	highest quintile vs never drinkers	0.7 (0.3–1.5)**	Y	Y	Y
		Instant decaffeinated coffee	highest quintile vs never drinkers	1.1 (0.4–2.9)**	Y	Y	Y
Jain et al, 1991 Toronto, Canada	249 women and men	Lifetime coffee consumption	≥ 1,110 cup-years vs none	0.9 (0.4–1.8)	Y	Y	Y
Lyon et al, 1992[b] Utah, USA	149 women and men	Coffee consumption	≥ 50,000 vs 0–2,000 cups/ lifetime	2.4 (1.2–4.9)[m,n]	Y	Y	Y
Mizuno et al, 1992 Japan	124 women and men	Coffee	every day (reference group) na)	0.8 (0.5–1.4)	Y	N	N
Zatonski et al, 1993 Opole, Poland	110 women and men	Coffee	ever vs never	0.6 (0.3–0.97)[o]	Y	Y	Y
		Coffee	highest quartile vs never	0.5 (0.2–1.0)[p]	Y	Y	Y

* p ≤ 0.05 for trend and/or for comparison of highest vs lowest consumption level

** p > 0.05 for trend and/or for comparison of highest vs lowest consumption level

na information not available or unclear from article

a Adjusted or matched for one or more of the following: tea consumption, race, hospital, year of interview, occupation, alcohol consumption, respondent type, residence, income, history of diabetes mellitus, fruit consumption, ethnicity, date of death, foreign origin, educational level, meat consumption, vegetable consumption, total energy intake, calorie- adjusted intake of protein, calorie-adjusted intake of calcium, consumption of other types of coffee (eg, regular, decaffeinated, ground, instant) fibre intake, religion, county of residence, institute

b More cases drank decaffeinated coffee than controls (41% vs 25%) (p < 0.001)

c The proportion of cases who were coffee drinkers was not different from the proportion of controls (82% vs 76%) (p > 0.10)

d ORs from sex-stratified analyses were similar for women and men

e OR calculated from data in original article

f OR = 3.4 (1.4–8.1) for 124 matched pairs directly interviewed

g For women the positive association was apparent for current or recent, but not never or ex-smokers; for men the association was apparent for both

h 90% confidence interval

i Association was apparent in ever, but not never smokers, with odds ratios of 4.3 (2.0–9.2) and 1.1 (0.0–5.8), respectively

j Association was apparent in ever, but not never smokers, with odds ratios of 5.5 (p < 0.05) and 1.0 (ns), respectively

k OR = 0.7 (0.3–1.6) for subjects for whom spouses were the respondents

l Cases consumed less coffee on average than controls (0.05 < p < 0.10)

m ORs from sex-stratified analyses were 1.7 (0.6–4.9) for women and 3.6 (1.3–10.0) for men

n ORs from smoking-stratified analyses were 1.7 (0.6–5.0) for never smokers and 6.7 (3.0–15.3) for those with ≥ 25 pack-years

o OR = 0.5 (0.3–1.2) for 31 directly interviewed cases

p OR = 0.3 (0.1–1.4) for 31 directly interviewed cases

ecological study, which examined per capita coffee consumption and pancreatic cancer mortality rates in 22 countries, reported a similar correlation (r = 0.6 for both men and women; p < 0.005), which remained statistically significant after adjustment for per capita consumption of total or saturated fat, cholesterol, cigarettes, tobacco or national income (r = 0.4–0.7; p < 0.05) (Binstock et al, 1983). An ecological study conducted within Italy reported moderate correlations between coffee consumption and pancreatic cancer mortality rates in 20 regions (r = 0.3 for men and 0.5 for women) (Decarli and La Vecchia, 1986).

An ecological time-trend analysis of coffee consumption (in the 1940s to 1960s) and pancreatic cancer mortality (in the 1950s to 1970s) in 16 countries showed correlations (r = 0.6 in men and 0.7 in women, adjusted for changes in smoking), although the strength of these associations was diminished after exclusion of Japan, where unusually marked post-war changes in both diet and pancreatic cancer rates had occurred (Cuckle and Kinlen, 1981). Time-trend comparisons within the USA and the UK have also shown increases in both coffee consumption and pancreatic cancer rates since the 1940s (Spector, 1981; Benarde and Weiss, 1982).

In an animal experiment, long-term coffee consumption had an inhibitory effect on dietary fat-promoted pancreatic carcinogenesis in rats and hamsters (Woutersen and van Garderen-Hoetmer, 1989).

Coffee contains caffeine and other methylxanthines that have been shown to be clastogenic in vitro. Readily oxidised phenolic compounds from coffee also act as catalysts for N-nitrosamine formation from nitrite salts at gastric pH (Challis and Barlett, 1975). Trichloroethylene, a solvent used in the extraction of caffeine in the production of decaffeinated coffee until 1977 was shown to be a bacterial mutagen and may be carcinogenic in mammals (see Wynder et al, 1986).

The possibility remains that the observed increase in risk with higher coffee consumption observed in some studies may be the result of residual confounding by smoking or dietary factors, for example, fruit consumption has been shown to be lower in heavy coffee drinkers (Falk et al, 1988), so an association with coffee consumption could feasibly be attributable to low fruit consumption; the panel has judged that higher fruit consumption probably decreases risk (see section 4.7.2.3).

Overall, a large amount of evidence has accrued on the relationship between coffee consumption and pancreatic cancer. Many of the analytical epidemiological data show no relationship. Few, if any, studies have shown a moderate or strong dose–response increase in risk that is also consistent across more than one subgroup, after appropriate adjustment for cigarette smoking; coherent criticism regarding the selection of comparison groups has also been a notable feature of some studies with positive findings.

High levels of coffee consumption probably have no relationship to the risk of pancreatic cancer.

4.7.2.12 Tea

A 1991 IARC Working Goup examined the evidence on tea consumption and risk of pancreatic cancer (IARC, 1991). They found most studies to show no significant association. It was concluded that three of four prospective studies showed no association (Heilbrun et al, 1986; Hiatt et al, 1988; Kinlen et al, 1988), whereas one documented a protective association (RR = 0.5, 0.3–0.9) for tea drinkers, compared with non-drinkers (Whittemore et al, 1983). It was further concluded that five of six case-control studies showed no association (MacMahon et al, 1981; Mack et al, 1986; La Vecchia et al, 1987; Raymond et al, 1987; Cuzik and Babiker, 1989), with the remaining study reporting a strong, statistically significant increase in risk with consumption of ten or more cups per day (OR = 2.6), compared with two or fewer (adjusted for smoking and coffee intake) in the UK (Kinlen and McPherson, 1984).

Since the IARC review, one cohort study of residents of a retirement community in the USA reported a protective association, with a smoking-adjusted relative risk of 0.4 (0.1–1.2) for two or more cups per day, compared with fewer than one cup per day (based on 63 cases) (Shibata et al, 1994); another cohort study, involving American (USA) women, reported no substantial association (smoking-adjusted RR = 0.8, 0.3–2.2; ns for trend) for two or more cups of tea per day, compared with consumption less than monthly (based upon 34 cases) (Zheng et al, 1996).

Of five case-control studies published since the IARC review, three, in Italy, the Netherlands and Canada, have shown no association between tea consumption and pancreatic cancer (Jain et al, 1991; Bueno de Mesquita et al, 1992; La Vecchia et al, 1992). Two other studies have shown protective associations. In one study in Poland, a smoking-adjusted odds ratio of 0.2 (0.1–0.5, p < 0.001 for trend) was observed for the highest quartile, compared with no consumption (Zatonski et al, 1993); in the other, in Japan, decreased risk was observed for daily consumption of black tea (OR = 0.5, 0.2–1.5), whereas increased risk was reported for heavy consumption of green tea (OR = 1.9, 1.1–3.6, for five or more cups per day) (Mizuno et al, 1992).

Although strong statistically significant associations have been observed in a few epidemiological studies, the possibility of confounding by smoking remains. Tea consumption may be associated with greater frequency of smoking in some populations and lesser frequency in others; therefore, the direction of the potential confounding may be different in various studies. In some populations, tea consumption may also be associated with dietary factors thought to be relevant to pancreatic cancer, for example, in women in the Iowa study, tea drinkers were more likely to be in the highest quartile of vegetable and fruit consumption (Zheng et al, 1996), so any association for tea consumption might be confounded by vegetable and fruit consumption, which has been judged by the panel as probably protecting against pancreatic cancer.

Tea contains compounds such as flavonoids and polyphenols which have been proposed to help protect against cancer; on the other hand, caffeine has been postulated to increase cancer risk (see chapter 6.9 for more detail).

Four of six cohort studies and eight of eleven case-control studies have shown no relationship between tea consumption and risk of pancreatic cancer. The remaining studies have shown mixed results, with most showing some degree of decreased risk, although these findings may be the result of residual confounding by smoking or vegetable and fruit consumption.

High tea consumption possibly has no relationship with the risk of pancreatic cancer.

4.7.3 FOOD PROCESSING

4.7.3.1 Additives
Nitrites and nitrates
Two case-control studies of pancreatic cancer, in Canada and Australia, have reported on dietary intakes of nitrate and nitrite. For nitrate, one study observed no significant association, whereas the other found a strong protective association; the energy- and smoking-adjusted odds ratios for the highest intake quartiles were 0.8 (0.4–1.8) and 0.5 (0.2–0.9, p = 0.03 for trend), respectively (Baghurst et al, 1991; Ghadirian et al, 1991). For nitrite, neither study found any substantial association, with odds ratios of 1.4 (0.5–4.1) and 0.9 (0.5–1.8) for the highest quartiles, respectively.

Evidence relating to nitrite and nitrate intake and the risk of pancreatic cancer is limited; no judgement is possible.

4.7.3.2 Cured and smoked foods
Intakes of different processed meats, including mainly cured and smoked meats, have been examined in some epidemiological studies. A cohort study of US men reported no statistically significant association with intake of salted or smoked meat or fish (RR = 1.5, 0.6–3.4, for higher consumption) (Zheng et al, 1993).

A case-control study in the USA reported a statistically non-significant increase in risk with higher consumption of bacon or sausage, but no association with bologna or salami, or smoked beef (Gold et al, 1985). A case-control study in Sweden also reported increased risk with intake of bacon or smoked ham once or more per week, compared with less than weekly (OR = 1.8, 1.0–3.4) (Norell et al, 1986). A third case-control study in the USA reported increased risk with higher intake of nitrated meats for men (OR = 2.8, 1.3–5.7), but not for women (OR = 1.1, 0.5–2.4) (Lyon et al, 1993).

Thus in general, four epidemiological studies have reported increased risk of pancreatic cancer with higher intake of specific smoked or cured meats or fish, although increased risk was not found for every type of smoked or cured meat or fish in each study; the increase in risk was also not always statistically significant.

Cured and smoked foods contain *N*-nitroso compounds, which can be activated in the liver and transported via the bloodstream to the pancreas; it is plausible that these compounds might play a role in human pancreatic cancer (Anderson et al, 1996). (See also chapter 7.5.)

The evidence suggests that diets high in cured or smoked meat or fish may increase the risk of pancreatic cancer, but is, as yet, insufficient.

4.7.3.3 Cooking
Grilling (broiling) and barbecuing, and frying
In a case-control study in Sweden (Norell et al, 1986) consumption of fried or grilled meat was associated with a marked increase in the risk; odds ratios for daily versus less than weekly were 13.4 (2.4–74.7) in comparison with population controls and 4.6 (1.2–18.2) in comparison with hospital controls. Fried or grilled fish was also associated with an increased risk of pancreatic cancer. There was no association with meat other than meat that had been fried or grilled. Deep-frying of foods has also been associated with increased risk in at least one case-control study (Farrow and Davis, 1990).

Humans who have consumed a meal of fried pork or bacon have been found to excrete detectable levels of mutagens in their urine (Baker et al, 1982). When fats are heated to high temperatures, such as in deep-frying, a variety of oxidative products is formed; some of these have been shown to increase pancreatic tumours in animal experiments (Sugimura, 1985; Tanaka et al, 1985). Tests in bacteria have shown burned and browned material from protein heated during the cooking of foods to contain highly mutagenic and carcinogenic heterocyclic amines (Sugimura and Nagao, 1982; Sugimura and Sato, 1983).

There are differences in the levels of heterocyclic aromatic compounds formed in meat and fish, depending upon the method, time and temperature of cooking (Felton and Knize, 1991). Frying and grilling cause formation of mutagenic compounds; boiling also produces mutagens, but far more slowly (Spingarn and Weisburger, 1979). In contrast, no mutagenic activity is produced by microwaving beef — even at three times the normal cooking period — whereas high levels of mutagens are formed by pan grilling (Nader et al, 1981). If heterocyclic amines are carcinogenic for the human pancreas, then differences in cooking methods might explain some of the inconsistencies reported in the literature for meat consumption and risk of pancreatic cancer.

The evidence relating to diets high in grilled and fried foods and pancreatic cancer is very limited; no judgement is possible.

4.8 Gallbladder

Cancer of the gallbladder is uncommon. There are no recent estimates of incidence.

The panel has reached the following conclusions. Evidence that food and nutrition affect the risk of gallbladder cancer is currently not substantial.

FOOD, NUTRITION AND GALLBLADDER CANCER

In the judgement of the panel the factor listed below modifies the risk of gallbladder cancer. Judgements are graded according to the strength of the evidence.

EVIDENCE	DECREASES RISK	NO RELATIONSHIP	INCREASES RISK
Convincing			
Probable			
Possible			Obesity[a]
Insufficient			

For an explanation of the terms used in the matrix, see chapter 3.
[a] Both Indirectly via increased risk of gallstones, and, possibly, directly.

INTRODUCTION

The gallbladder is a sac-like structure on the inferior surface of the liver that is about 8 cm long and 4 cm wide. The gallbladder stores the bile produced by the liver. Bile, when secreted into the intestine, aids digestion of fatty foods. Gallstones may precipitate out of solution as a result of a higher cholesterol-to-bile acid ratio in the bile, either a result of higher cholesterol secretion or of reduced bile salt production.

INCIDENCE PATTERNS

Most gallbladder cancers arise in the epithelium and are classified as carcinomas. The incidence of this cancer is low compared with other sites, even among those populations who are at highest risk, and accounts for about 1% of all cancer deaths. In high-risk populations, incidence in women is approximately double that of men but, in other populations, the rates are similar for men and women (Parkin et al, 1992). Incidence also varies geographically, with higher rates in certain areas of Latin America (Colombia, Peru, and Ecuador), Japan, and Eastern Europe (Poland, the Czech Republic, Slovakia, Hungary, and the former East Germany) (Parkin et al, 1992). In North America, high rates of gallbladder cancer have been noted in Hispanic and American Indian populations (Menck et al, 1975; Thomas, 1979). Survival from this cancer is poor (Young et al, 1984).

PATHOGENESIS

See Box 4.8.1 on gallstones and gallbladder cancer.

JUDGEMENTS OF OTHER REPORTS

Because the gallbladder is part of the gastrointestinal tract, it is plausible that dietary factors could contribute to the aetiology of cancer of this organ. In the 1982 report of the National Academy of Sciences *Diet, Nutrition and Cancer* (NAS, 1982), the paucity of data on this cancer was noted. No case-control studies of dietary factors and cancer of this site had been reported at that time, and the panel concluded that the evidence for a dietary aetiology was weak.

BOX 4.8.1 GALLSTONES AND GALLBLADDER CANCER

The only established risk factor for gallbladder cancer is a history of gallstones (Lowenfels et al, 1985; Kato et al,1990; Zatonski et al, 1992). Since several dietary or diet-associated risk factors have been proposed for gallstones, these relationships are briefly reviewed here.

Although obesity and high energy intake have been positively associated with the risk of gallstones in both cohort (Maclure et al, 1989) and case-control (Scragg et al, 1984) studies, there is little evidence in humans that high dietary fat and cholesterol, specifically, increase the risk of this condition (Bennion and Grundy, 1978a). In a case-control study in Australia, a positive association was found with increased intake of simple sugars in drinks and sweets (Scragg et al, 1984). In a similar study in Japan, increased risk was associated with the consumption of lettuce and cabbage and with a preference for salty foods (Kato et al, 1990). In contrast, alcohol consumption has been associated with a decreased risk of gallstones in some studies (Maclure et al, 1989; Scragg et al, 1984) but not others (Kato et al, 1990).

Only one study (Kato et al, 1990) reported findings separately by type of stone. In this study, a preference for oily foods was positively associated with cholesterol stones but inversely associated with pigment stones. Cholesterol stones are the predominant type in western countries, whereas pigment stones are most frequent in Asia. Nonetheless, incidence of cholesterol stones has been increasing recently in Japan (Bennion and Grundy, 1978a). In two studies, gallstone size, possibly reflecting the duration of exposure, was positively associated with risk of gallbladder cancer (Diehl, 1983; Lowenfels et al, 1989).

It is also of interest that a high prevalence of gallstones has been reported among American Indians and Hispanics in the USA (Bennion and Grundy, 1978a; Arevalo et al, 1987). Presumably diet and/or genetic factors influence gallstone formation by increasing the lithogenicity of bile (Bennion and Grundy, 1978a). Some constituents of lithogenic bile may be carcinogenic (Lowenfels, 1978).

4.8.1 DIETARY CONSTITUENTS

4.8.1.1 Energy and related factors

Energy intake

In a population-based case-control study of gallbladder cancer in Poland, total energy intake was associated with increased risk, with an odds ratio of 4.1 reported for the upper versus the lowest quartile (p < 0.01) (Zatonski et al, 1992).

On the basis of one study, no judgement is possible.

Body mass

Obesity is an established risk factor for gallstones, and gallstones are associated with an increased risk of gallbladder cancer (see Box 4.8.1).

Direct evidence that obesity increases the risk of gallbladder cancer comes from a large prospective cohort study in the USA, which found that gallbladder mortality rates were associated with obesity in women (Lew and Garfinkle, 1979).

In a case-control study in Poland, Zatonski et al (1992), noted an increase in risk of gallbladder cancer with obesity, again particularly among women.

The data from these two reports on obesity provide incomplete evidence for making a judgement. However, reports on positive associations of obesity with gallstone formation lend support to the findings, suggesting higher body mass may play a role – either direct or indirect – in gallbladder cancer.

Obesity possibly increases the risk of gallbladder cancer.

4.8.1.2 Carbohydrates

In a case-control study in Poland (Zatonski et al, 1992), no relationship was observed with intake of carbohydrates (OR = 1.2, p = 0.77).

On the basis of one study, no judgement is possible.

Non starch polysaccharides/ fibre

A lack of dietary fibre has been suggested as a possible cause of a variety of disorders prevalent among western societies, including cholesterol gallstones (Heaton, 1973). Direct evidence on the role of dietary fibre and gallbladder cancer is limited. In a case-control study in Poland, a weak protective effect was observed with high fibre consumption, OR = 0.31 (p = 0.089) (Zatonski et al, 1992).

On the basis of one study, no judgement is possible.

4.8.1.3   Fat and cholesterol

Total fat

One case-control study of biliary tract cancer in Japan reported increased risk with greater preference for 'oily foods', with an odds ratio of 3.3 (1.7–6.4); this study did not find positive associations for higher intakes of high-fat foods, such as meat, fried foods, or milk (Kato et al, 1989). A Polish case-control study observed no apparent trend with total fat intake and gallbladder cancer, and reported an OR of 0.86 (0.2–3.22, p = 0.91) (Zatonski et al, 1992).

In Japan, the incidence of gallbladder cancer has increased markedly in the past 30 years, during which time fat consumption and the frequency of cholesterol gallstones has also increased considerably, On the other hand, gallbladder cancer rates are higher in Japan than in the USA, even though dietary fat intake is higher in the USA (Tominaga and Kato, 1990).

The major risk factors for cancer of the gallbladder include a history of gallstones and obesity. To the extent that dietary fat contributes to either gallstone formation or obesity, it may indirectly increase the risk of gallbladder cancer. While most of the evidence supports no effect of dietary fat on gallstone formation (See Box 4.8.1), dietary fat may well lead to over-consumption of energy and subsequent obesity.

The evidence on total fat and the risk of gallbladder cancer is very limited; no judgement is possible.

Cholesterol

A Polish case-control study investigating gallbladder cancer found risk estimates to be greater than 1.0 for cholesterol, with an adjusted OR of 1.54 (0.5–4.7), (Zatonski et al, 1992). A study in Japan reported a possible protective association with eggs (see section 4.8.2.2).

On the basis of one study, no judgement is possible.

4.8.1.4 Alcohol

Although it has been suggested that alcohol is associated with a lower risk of gallstones in some studies (for example, Scragg et al, 1984; Maclure et al, 1989) but not all (Kato et al, 1990), the relationship with gallbladder cancer is much less clear. Chow et al (1994) found that alcohol was associated with a slightly reduced risk of gallbladder cancer but there was no evidence of a dose–response. Kato et al (1992), in contrast, reported an excess risk of biliary-tract cancer in association with high consumption of alcohol.

The evidence on high alcohol consumption and the risk of gallbladder cancer is inconsistent and very limited; no judgement is possible.

4.8.1.5 Vitamins

Vitamin C and vitamin E

In a case-control study of gallbladder cancer in Poland, possibly protective associations with both vitamin C and vitamin E intake were found (Zatonski et al, 1992). For vitamin C, the inverse association was statistically significant for the three highest consumption quartiles, OR = 0.29 (0.1–0.9). For vitamin E, the OR for the highest versus the lowest quartile of intake was 0.3 (0.1–0.96).

Based on only one case-control study, no judgement relating to vitamins C and E and the risk of gallbladder cancer is possible.

4.8.2 FOOD AND DRINKS

4.8.2.1 Vegetables and fruits
A study in Japan (Kato et al, 1989) reported a reduced risk of gallbladder cancer with frequent intake (ranging from daily to three times or more per week of: fruits OR = 0.3 (0.2–0.5); mushrooms, OR = 0.33 (0.1–0.9); boiled vegetables, OR = 0.37 (0.2–0.8) and salad, OR = 0.45 (0.2–1.00).

Based on a single study, no judgement is possible.

4.8.2.2 Meat, poultry, fish and eggs
Fish
A case-control study of cancer of the biliary tract in Japan reported decreased risk with greater consumption of fresh or salted fish, with odds ratios in the range of 0.1 to 0.4 (all p < 0.05) (Kato et al, 1989).

On the basis of one study, no judgement is possible.

Eggs
A case-control study of cancer of the biliary tract in Japan reported decreased risk with greater consumption of eggs, with odds ratios of 0.2 (0.1–0.5) and 0.4 (0.2–0.9) for gallbladder and biliary duct cancer, respectively (Kato et al, 1989).

On the basis of one study, no judgement is possible.

4.9 LIVER

Primary cancer of the liver is the sixth most common cancer and the third most common cause of death from cancer, throughout the world. An estimated 540,000 million cases occurred in 1996, accounting for 5.2 % of all new cases of cancer.

In general, rates of this cancer are much more common in developing societies, with China alone accounting for over half of all cases. Incidence is higher among men. Liver cancer is almost always fatal.

The panel has reached the following conclusions. The evidence that regular high consumption of alcohol increases the risk of liver cancer, by way of liver cirrhosis, is convincing; and contamination of food with aflatoxin probably increases risk.

The panel notes that diets high in vegetables possibly decrease the risk of liver cancer.

Established non-dietary causes of liver cancer are infection with the hepatitis B and hepatitis C viruses.

The most effective non-dietary means of preventing liver cancer is avoidance of exposure to hepatitis B and C viruses, and not to use tobacco. The most effective dietary means of preventing liver cancer is, if alcohol is consumed at all, limited consumption of alcohol, and avoidance of food liable to be contaminated with aflatoxin.

FOOD, NUTRITION AND PRIMARY LIVER CANCER

In the judgement of the panel, the dietary constituents, factors, the foods and drinks, and the methods of food processing listed below, modify the risk of primary liver cancer. Judgements are graded according to the strength of the evidence.

EVIDENCE	DECREASES RISK	NO RELATIONSHIP	INCREASES RISK
Convincing			Alcohol[b]
Probable			Aflatoxin contamination
Possible	Vegetables [a]		
Insufficient	Selenium		Iron

For an explanation of the terms used in the matrix, see Chapter 3.
[a] Not fruits
[b] Via liver cirrhosis caused by alcohol abuse

INTRODUCTION

Primary liver cancer includes hepatocellular carcinoma (HCC) as well as angiosarcoma, cholangiocarcinoma, and hepatoblastoma. Accounting for more than 90% of all cases (Cady, 1983), HCC is the predominant histological subtype on which most epidemiological investigations have focused. In this section, 'liver cancer' usually refers to primary HCC.

The other less common types of liver cancer are relatively rare in most parts of the world. Angiosarcoma has received some attention because of its link to certain environmental agents (IARC, 1987), including vinyl chloride (Makk et al, 1976), arsenic (Falk et al, 1981), and Thorotrast (a contrast medium formerly used with diagnostic X-rays) (Falk et al, 1979). Liver fluke infection may be an important risk factor for the development of cholangiocarcinoma in southeast Asia (Parkin et al, 1991).

> **BOX 4.9.1 ESTABLISHED NON-DIETARY FACTORS AND LIVER CANCER**
>
> The following non-dietary factors increase the risk of primary liver cancer:
> ■ Infection: Hepatitis B virus and Hepatitis C virus

INCIDENCE PATTERNS

Cancer of the liver is the sixth most common cancer in the world. In 1996 an estimated 540,000 new cases were diagnosed worldwide (WHO, 1997), accounting for 5.2% of all new cancers.

The geographical distribution of hepatocellular cancer varies greatly worldwide, perhaps more so than any other major tumour site. The disease is relatively uncommon in

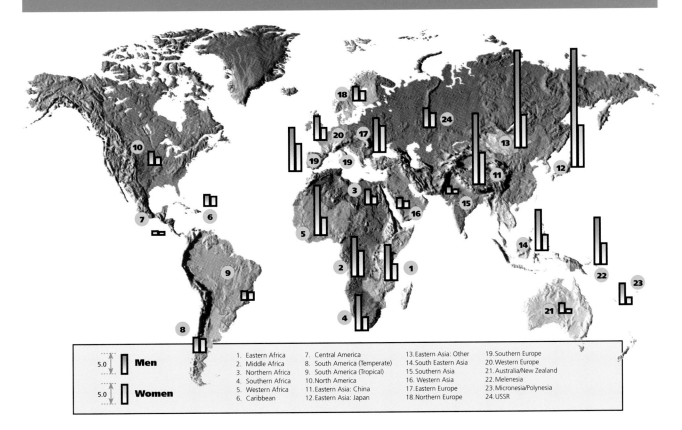

LIVER CANCER estimated rates of cancer incidence by sex and area

5.0 ↕ ■ **Men**	
5.0 ↕ ■ **Women**	

1. Eastern Africa
2. Middle Africa
3. Northern Africa
4. Southern Africa
5. Western Africa
6. Caribbean
7. Central America
8. South America (Temperate)
9. South America (Tropical)
10. North America
11. Eastern Asia: China
12. Eastern Asia: Japan
13. Eastern Asia: Other
14. South Eastern Asia
15. Southern Asia
16. Western Asia
17. Eastern Europe
18. Northern Europe
19. Southern Europe
20. Western Europe
21. Australia/New Zealand
22. Melenesia
23. Micronesia/Polynesia
24. USSR

developed countries. In the developing world, liver cancer is very common, accounting for more than 80% of the global cases; China alone accounts for 55% of the worldwide incidence.

Incidence among men is over twice that among women.

Infection with the hepatitis B virus is the predominant cause of liver cancer, with more than 80% of cases being the result of infection with this virus. Other risk factors include excessive alcohol consumption and exposure to aflatoxins.

Liver cancer has no effective treatment and survival rates are low, with only a 6% five-year survival rate in the USA; the survival rate may be lower still in developing countries. In 1996, mortality attributable to liver cancer was estimated at 536,000 people, 7.5% of all cancer deaths (WHO, 1997).

PATHOGENESIS

The major risk factor for liver cancer is chronic infection with hepatitis B or C virus. Hepatitis B is an established cause of liver cirrhosis and liver cancer, with overwhelming evidence based on ecological and analytical epidemiological studies, as well as on laboratory and animal investigations (Szmuness, 1978; Trichopoulos et al, 1982; Blumberg and London, 1985; Munoz and Bosch, 1987; Tabor and Kobayashi, 1992). Extensive information from around the world (IARC, 1987) has established an aetiological role for hepatitis B in the development of human liver cancer through chronic infection, as indicated by the expression of surface antigen (HBsAg) in serum. Hepatitis C more recently has been convincingly shown also to be associated with liver cancer. Recognition of the importance of hepatitis C in the development of liver cancer was initially made by studies in Japan (Liver Cancer Study Group of Japan, 1988; Okuda, 1991). Further studies have also demonstrated strong associations with hepatitis C infection (IARC, 1987).

Tobacco use is generally considered to pose a 'weakly or modestly positive' association with primary liver cancer, according to a recent review of 14 mostly case-control studies which show, on average, that heavy smokers have a relative risk (RR) for liver cancer of about 1.5 compared to non-smokers (Austin, 1991). However, there is some evidence that the increased risk is apparent mostly among HBsAg-negative liver cancer (Trichopoulos et al, 1987) and, thus, may be a contributing factor in areas where liver cancer is not virally-induced.

Exogenous steroidal hormone use may be relevant (Thomas, 1988; IARC, 1987), as may endogenous hormone levels (Stanford et al, 1991; Yu and Chen, 1993).

Chronic HBV infection can act as both an initiator and promoter of liver cancer. The host genome is altered as a result of integrating the viral DNA; deletion and rearrangement of host genes, as well as addition of HBV genes occurs.

These potentially mutating events can be augmented or mimicked by exposure to other agents including aflatoxins, specific industrial exposure and possibly tobacco smoke. The chronic viral infection also results in widespread cell death, and thus compensatory cell proliferation. This can lead to cirrhosis, but can also provide an environment in which cells with specific somatic genetic damage – particularly loss of *p53* and other tumour-suppressor genes – may have a growth advantage, and thus develop as an expanding clone.

Hepatitis C virus is an RNA virus that does not replicate through a DNA intermediate and is therefore active via a mechanism other than integration into host DNA. It does, however, cause chronic hepatitis and cirrhosis, thus minimally providing promotional/selection stimulus. For further detail, see London and McGlynn (1996).

JUDGEMENTS OF OTHER REPORTS

The 1982 report of the National Academy of Sciences, *Diet, Nutrition and Cancer* (NAS, 1982), identified aflatoxin as a risk factor for liver cancer, also saying that the evidence for a role of alcohol was extremely tenuous. The later report *Diet and Health* (NAS, 1989), also identified aflatoxin as a risk factor, and said that direct epidemiological evidence on alcohol was limited. The 1990 report of the World Health Organization, *Diet, Nutrition and the Prevention of Chronic Diseases* (WHO, 1990) concluded that alcohol is causally linked with liver cancer.

REVIEW

4.9.1 DIETARY CONSTITUENTS

4.9.1.1 Fat and cholesterol
Total fat
An international ecological study reported a positive correlation between consumption of total fat and the incidence of liver cancer (r = 0.5–0.6) (Rose et al, 1986).

In early animal studies, high-fat diets were shown to increase experimentally-induced liver tumour formation (Tannenbaum and Silverstone, 1949; Newberne and Zieger, 1978). In a more recent animal study, an increase was observed when either the polyunsaturated or saturated fat content was increased within isocaloric diets (Hietanen et al, 1990).

Intakes of different oils or fats were not related to the risk of liver cancer in two case-control studies (La Vecchia et al, 1988; Srivatanakul et al, 1991). In a case-control study in Greece (Hadziyannis et al, 1995), a significant increased risk of liver cancer was associated with an increase in average monthly consumption of total dietary oils and fats; the patterns of association for the food items comprising this group (butter, margarine, olive oil) were similar.

Increased intakes of dietary fat by experimental animals also appear to cause a relatively modest increase in liver tumour formation (Tannenbaum and Silverstone, 1949; Newberne and Zieger, 1978).

Evidence relating to diets high in total fat and the risk of liver cancer is limited; no judgement is possible.

4.9.1.2 Protein

Liver cancer occurs among populations whose intake of protein is relatively low. Currently there are no data from either human cohort or case-control studies on the relationship between protein intakes and the risk of liver cancer.

In a large correlation study, Armstrong and Doll (1975) found a decrease in the incidence of liver cancer with increasing intake of animal protein. For this reason it has been suggested that protein may be protective against liver cancer, (Crawford, 1971; Newberne and Rogers, 1971; Mandel et al, 1992). However, areas where protein intakes are low also commonly experience a higher prevalence of chronic hepatitis B infection and higher exposure to aflatoxins.

In a large ecological study of various regions in China (Campbell et al, 1990; Hsing et al, 1991), plasma cholesterol concentrations were strongly correlated with liver cancer mortality rates. Plasma cholesterol has been associated positively with the consumption of fat (USDHHS, 1988) and the animal protein casein (Sirtori et al, 1983; Terpstra et al, 1983), and negatively with the consumption of fibre and foods of plant origin (LSRO, 1985). Plasma cholesterol also increases during liver tumour promotion in experimental rats consuming dietary protein of animal origin (Wells et al, 1976; Youngman, 1990).

Experimental studies have shown that a decrease in dietary protein intake (Madhavan and Gopalan, 1968; Wells et al, 1976; Lee et al, 1977; Temcharoen et al, 1978) or replacement of animal protein with equivalent levels of plant protein (Schulsinger et al, 1989; Youngman and Campbell, 1992) causes a decrease in liver tumour formation. Because of very different growth rates and protein requirements, data from rat studies of protein should be treated with caution (see chapter 5.4).

The evidence relating to diets high in protein and the risk of liver cancer is limited and inconsistent, possibly due to differences in plant and animal protein, and their dietary sources; no judgement is possible.

4.9.1.3 Alcohol

A substantial number of epidemiological studies have documented a significant association between high alcohol intake and liver cancer. Two previous reports (IARC, 1988; Austin, 1991) reviewed the literature up to 1990 and suggested a moderate but consistent association between heavy drinking and liver cancer. Tables 4.9.1 and 4.9.2 include the results from those cohort and case-control studies, respectively, as well as the results from studies published more recently.

Despite variability in the amount of alcohol consumed at the highest levels, and in the classifications used and comparisons made, (alcoholics versus general population; drinkers versus non-drinkers) among the 18 cohort studies, almost all show increased risk (RRs = 1.0–35.1). Of the studies that reported on statistical significance or provided 95% confidence limits, 11 of 16 studies showed results that were statistically significant. ORs for the 19 case-control studies range between 0.6 and 12.0, with only two estimates being less than 1.0. Of the 17 studies that showed estimates greater than 1.0 and stated some measure of statistical significance, 14 were statistically significant. More moderate drinking of alcohol has not generally been associated with a strong increase in risk of liver cancer in these studies.

The one study that showed a decreased risk with increased alcohol intakes (Lu et al, 1988) used control patients who had been hospitalised for automobile injuries and, who thus, possibly, had higher levels of alcohol consumption than the population from which the cases arose.

A potential problem in many of these studies is the lack of control for important risk factors for liver cancer. Most studies did not control for chronic infection with hepatitis B virus (Sundby, 1967; Hakulinen et al, 1974; Monson and Lyon, 1975; Adelstein and White, 1976; Williams and Horm, 1977; Dean et al, 1979; Robinette et al, 1979; Jensen, 1980; Schmidt and Popham, 1981; Stemhagen et al, 1983; Yu et al, 1983; Hardell et al, 1984; Kono et al, 1986; Shibata et al, 1986; La Vecchia et al, 1988; Hirayama, 1989; Vall Mayans et al, 1990; Adami et al, 1992; Cordier et al, 1993; Goodman et al, 1995), and many did not control for smoking history (Sundby, 1967; Hakulinen et al, 1974; Monson and Lyon, 1975; Adelstein and White, 1976; Dean et al, 1979; Robinette et al, 1979; Jensen, 1980; Schmidt and Popham, 1981; Vall Mayans et al, 1990; Adami et al, 1992; Fukuda et al, 1993; Pan et al, 1993). The RRs from only two studies (Yu and Chen, 1993; Tsukuma et al, 1993) were adjusted for infection with HCV. In a subset of the subjects from the study by Tanaka et al (1992) additional adjustment for anti-HCV resulted in an RR of 2.1 (Tanaka et al, 1991).

In the cohort study by Adami et al (1992) patients who were diagnosed with alcoholism had a much lower risk of liver cancer than those diagnosed with liver cirrhosis only, but patients who were alcoholics and had cirrhosis had a similar risk to the patients with cirrhosis alone. In the Greek case-control study (Trichopoulos et al, 1987), no association was observed for heavy consumption of alcohol and the risk of liver cancer in cases without cirrhosis. In addition, in two studies from Japan (Tsukuma et al, 1993; Goodman et al, 1995), the RRs for subjects who had ceased drinking alcohol were higher than for those who were currently drinking; the interpretation of this observation was that those individuals may have stopped drinking alcohol because of the development of cirrhosis (Goodman et al, 1995). Thus, it would seem that the relevant exposure is alcohol drinking that leads to cirrhosis (Kew and Popper, 1984). Light and moderate alcohol consumption appear to have no major influence on the risk of liver cancer.

Excessive alcohol consumption, generally speaking, results in 'alcoholic liver disease' which proceeds through three progressively severe stages: fatty liver, alcoholic hepatitis, and cirrhosis (Lieber, 1993), ultimately leading to liver cancer by mechanisms not yet understood. Alcohol itself appears not to be able to induce (i.e. initiate) liver cancer in experimental animals, despite repeated investigations

TABLE 4.9.1 ALCOHOL CONSUMPTION AND THE RISK OF LIVER CANCER: COHORT STUDIES

AUTHOR, YEAR, AND PLACE	SIZE OF COHORT:	GROUP	EXPOSURE	COMPARISON	RELATIVE RISK (95% CONFIDENCE INTERVAL)	SEX/AGE	ADJUSTMENT SMOKING HISTORY	OTHER FACTORS[a]
Sundby, 1967	1,722:	Norwegian alcoholics	All alcohol	compared with Norwegian population	2.0 (nr)	Y	N	N
Hakulinen et al, 1974, Finland	205,000:	Finnish male alcohol misusers	All alcohol	observed number of cases vs expected number	1.5 (nr)*	Y	N	N
		Finnish male alcoholics	All alcohol	observed number of cases vs expected number	2.5 (nr) (ns)	N	N	N
Monson and Lyon 1975 Massachusetts, USA	1,139 men, 243 women	Chronic alcoholics	All alcohol	observed number of deaths vs expected number	1.0 (nr) nr	N	N	N
Adelstein and White, 1976 UK					5.8 (nr)*	N	N	N
Dean et al, 1979 Dublin, Ireland	881 men	Brewery workers	Stout/beer	observed number of deaths vs expected number	1.3 (nr) nr	Y	N	N
Jensen, 1980	4,401	Danish brewery workers			1.5 (nr)*	N	N	N
Schmidt and Popham, 1981 Canada	9,889 men	Alcoholics	All alcohol	observed number of deaths vs expected number	2.03 (nr) (ns)	Y	N	N
Oshima A et al, 1984, Japan	8,646 men	HBsAg positive men	All alcohol	heavy drinking (≥80 ml/d) (<27 ml/day)	8.0 (1.3–49.5)*	Y	Y	N
Kono S et al, 1986 Japan	5,135	Japanese male physicians	All alcohol	daily drinkers (≥2 gos/day) vs non-drinker	2.7 (1.0–6.8)*	Y	Y	Y
			All alcohol	ex-drinkers vs non-drinkers	1.4 (0.4–4.8) ns	Y	Y	N
Shibata et al, 1986 Japan	1,316	Japanese men	Shochu (distilled spirit)	≥2 units per day vs non-drinkers	14.3 (3.6–56.6)	Y	N	N
Hirayama, 1989 Japan	122,261 men 142,857 women		All alcohol	daily vs non daily drinking	1.69 (1.4–2.)*	Y	N	N
Ross, 1992 China	18,244 men		Ethanol	heavy (≥30 g/day) vs light consumers	1.8 (0.4–7.4) (ns)	N	Y	Y
Adami, 1992 Sweden	8,517 3,589 836	Alcoholics Cirrhotics Alcoholics with cirrhosis	All alcohol	expected vs observed no of liver cancer deaths	3.1 (1.6–5.3)* 35.1 (26.7–45.3)* 34.3 (17.1–61.3)*	N	N	N
Yu and Chen 1993, Taiwan	9,691 men		All alcohol	drinkers vs non-drinkers	4.3 (1.1–16.9)*	N	Y	Y
Tsukuma, 1993 Japan	917	Chronic liver disease patients	All alcohol	≥80 g/day vs < 80 g/day (current habit)	1.15 (0.35–3.78) (ns)	Y	Y	Y
				≥ 80 g/day vs < 80 g day (former drinkers)	1.66 (0.69–3.96) (ns)	Y	Y	Y
Goodman, 1995 Japan	36,133	Japanese from Hiroshima and Nagasaki	All alcohol	≥300 cc/week vs <135 cc/week	1.12			

* p < 0.05 for trend
nr not recorded
a also adjusted for one or more of the following: HBsAg+ve, aflatoxins, education, HCV infection, history of past liver disease, stage of disease

(IARC, 1988). Moreover, even though excessive alcohol intake is a cause of cirrhosis and even though cirrhosis is a 'common antecedent' (Anthony, 1977) of liver cancer, only about 10–30% of cirrhotic individuals eventually develop primary liver cancer (Rothman, 1980).

The interaction between alcohol consumption and other risk factors for liver cancer has been examined in a limited number of studies. With respect to chronic infection with hepatitis B, one study found an interaction with heavy alcohol drinking (Yu et al, 1991), and one did not (Cordier et al, 1993); in the former study, hepatitis C infection also interacted with alcohol consumption in the occurrence of liver cancer. However, one study found the risk of liver cancer to be further increased if those consuming greater amounts of alcohol were not chronically infected with hepatitis B (Fukuda et al, 1993). An interaction with heavier cigarette

TABLE 4.9.2 ALCOHOL CONSUMPTION AND THE RISK OF LIVER CANCER: CASE-CONTROL STUDIES

Author, Year, and Place	No of cases	Exposure	Comparison	Odds ratio (95% confidence interval)	Sex/Age	Smoking History	Other Variables[a]
Williams and Horm 1977, USA	men	Total alcohol, oz per year	heavy vs moderate consumption	2.75 (nr)	Y	Y	Y
	women	Total alcohol, oz per year	moderate consumption	5.05 (nr)	Y	Y	Y
Stemhagen et al 1983, USA	265: men	Alcohol	heavy drinkers vs abstainers	1.96 (0.75–5.10)	Y	Y	N
	women	Alcohol	heavy drinkers vs abstainers	5.57 (0.80–38.63)	Y	N	N
Yu et al, 1983, USA	78	Ethanol consumption	≥ 80g/day vs < 10 g/day	4.2 (1.3–13.8)			
Hardell et al, 1984 Sweden	102	All alcohol	> 370 ml spirits/week vs teetotallers	4.2 (1.8–10.8)			
Austin et al, 1986, USA	86	All alcohol	> 65 drink years vs never drinkers	3.3 (nr)	N	Y	N
Trichopoulos et al 1987, Greece	194	Ethanol (HCC and cirrhosis)	≥ 70 g/day vs < 10 g/day	1.2 (nr)	Y	Y	Y
		Ethanol (HCC, no cirrhosis)	≥ 70 g/day vs < 10 g/day	0.8 (nr)	Y	Y	Y
La Vecchia et al 1988, Italy	151	All alcohol	> 6 drinks per day vs < 4 drinks per day	1.43 (0.83–2.46)	Y	Y	Y
Lu et al, 1988, Taiwan	131	All alcohol	> 3 days/week vs none	0.62 (2.0–5.1)	Y	Y	Y
Tsukuma et al 1990, Japan	229	All alcohol	heavy drinkers 60g/day > 10 years	3.2 (2.0–5.1)	Y	Y	Y
Vall Mayans et al 1990, Spain	96	Ethanol	> 80 g/day vs 0 g/day	12.0 (nr)	Y	N	N
Yu et al, 1991, USA	74	Ethanol	≥ 60 drink years vs non-drinkers and ≤ 29 drink years	2.4 (1.2–5.0)	N	Y	N
Chen et al, 1991 Taiwan	200	All alcohol	habitual alcohol consumption vs non-habitual	3.37 (nr)	N	Y	Y
Srivatanakul et al Thailand	65	All alcohol	≥ 2 glasses/week vs occasional, non or ex drinkers	3.4 (0.8–14.6)	N	N	Y
Tanaka et al, 1992 Japan	204	All alcohol	current or ex drinker vs non-drinker	1.3 (0.9–2.0)	Y	N	N
			≥ 76.7 drink-years vs non-drinkers	1.9 (1.1–3.1)	Y	N	N
Mohamed et al 1992, South Africa	101	All alcohol	heavy drinkers vs light drinkers (men)	4.4 (1.4–14.1)	N	Y	Y
			heavy drinkers vs light drinkers (women)	1.6 (0.3–9.3)	N	Y	Y
Fukuda et al, 1993 Japan	368	Alcohol accumulated by age 40	60 drink years vs non-drinkers	3.23 (1.61–6.51)	N	N	Y
Pan et al, 1993 Taiwan	59	All alcohol	> 39.7 g/wk vs 0 g/wk	2.5 (nr)			
Tanaka et al, 1995 Japan	120	All alcohol	current/ex drinkers vs non-drinkers	2.1 (1.1–3.9)	Y	N	Y
			past history of heavy drinking vs no history	3.2 (0.8–13.6)	Y	N	Y

a adjusted for one or more of the following: race, sex, HBsAg status, education, area, cirrhosis, social class, family history, diet, betel nut chewing, HBV status, blood transfusion, history of hepatic disease

nr not recorded

smoking was also observed in three studies (Yu et al, 1983, 1991; Ross et al, 1992), but not in two others (Austin et al, 1986; Goodman et al, 1995).

The evidence that heavy and persistent drinking of alcohol, leading to cirrhosis and alcoholic hepatitis, increases the risk of primary liver cancer is convincing.

4.9.1.4 Vitamins

Carotenoids

A case-control study of 59 Taiwanese men who were HBV carriers and who had liver cancer (Pan et al, 1993) found no association between dietary β-carotene and the risk of liver cancer, controlling for age, education, ethnicity, occupation, alcohol consumption, and smoking. However, a weak dose–response was suggested for decreasing quartiles of serum β-carotene level and increasing incidence of liver cancer (OR=1.9, p=0.038 for the highest versus the lowest quartiles). In a case-control study of risk factors for liver cancer in Northern Italy (La Vecchia et al, 1988), the authors noted that a crude assessment of dietary carotenoids revealed OR=0.5 for the uppermost tertile of intake versus the lowest one, after adjustment for some possible confounders but not HBsAg status.

Evidence relating to high dietary carotenoid intake and the risk of liver cancer is limited; no judgement is possible.

Retinol

Two case-control studies of Taiwanese men have examined the role of serum retinol in the development of liver cancer; one study was among hepatitis B carriers (Pan et al, 1993) and one was nested within a cohort study (Yu and Chen, 1993; Yu et al, 1995). After adjustment for potential confounders, including infection (Yu et al, 1995), both studies found statistically significantly elevated odds ratios (ORs >4.0) for the lowest level of serum retinol concentration. In addition, the study by Pan et al (1993) reported a statistically significant increased risk of liver cancer associated with lower dietary retinol intake. As noted by the latter investigators, the possible effect of the malignancy on the biomarker cannot be excluded.

In the nested case-control study, interaction was assessed (Yu et al, 1995), and the effect of low serum retinol on liver cancer occurrence was much stronger among smokers (>10 cigarettes/day) (OR=6.7) and among HBsAg carriers (OR=14.1).

Animal studies have shown that dietary vitamin A may reduce the risk of hepatocellular carcinoma. Work by Maiorana et al (1980) showed that treating mice known to have a high incidence of spontaneous hepatoma with increasing doses of retinyl acetate decreased hepatoma rates in a dose-dependent manner. Studies on rats have also shown that vitamin A deficiency increases susceptibility to hepatoma induction (Suphakarn et al, 1983).

There are no human data on dietary retinol and serum retinol is not a marker of intake except at extremely low levels. Accordingly, although the serum retinol data are suggestive, no judgement is possible.

4.9.1.5 Minerals

Iron

Iron overload has been suggested as a risk factor for liver cancer. There are some animal data to support this hypothesis but it is unclear whether iron itself is directly involved in the cancer process or whether it acts indirectly via cirrhosis (Stal et al, 1995).

Directly relevant epidemiological data are limited to two ecological studies in China, both of which both found no association between biochemical markers of iron status and liver cancer mortality in humans (Hsing et al, 1991;

Chen et al, 1992).

Further evidence concerning iron and liver cancer has been obtained from a case-control study. Patients in whom hepatocellular carcinoma (HCC) developed without cirrhosis had significantly more frequent parenchymal iron excess than healthy controls, total iron scores significantly greater than controls, and significantly greater iron concentration in the liver. The authors (Turlin et al, 1995) suggested that these findings may indicate that liver cancer could be triggered by iron overload.

In humans, dietary-induced iron overload is relatively rare. It does occur in some southern African populations who drink large quantities of traditional beer brewed in iron pots, but is largely due to the condition of hereditary haemochromatosis in which excess iron is absorbed from either dietary sources or supplements. There is some evidence of a link between iron overload and hepatoma in these populations (Gangaidzo and Gordeuk, 1995; Gordeuk et al, 1993).

The possibility of some link between hereditary haemochromatosis and increased risk of liver cancer is supported in part by the findings of a study carried out in Germany (Niederau et al, 1996), in which a cohort of 251 haemochromatosis patients was followed up for 14.1 years. The observed mortality from liver cancer in the cohort was greater than expected, and liver cancers were associated with cirrhosis and increased amounts of mobilisable iron. Early diagnosis and therapy were shown to reduce the incidence of liver cancer.

Animal studies have shown that iron deficiency inhibits the development of liver tumours in rats (Yoshiji et al, 1992). One study by Kato et al (1996) found that a group of rats fed on an iron-adequate diet for 65 weeks developed liver tumours, whereas none of the paired rats fed an iron-deficient diet developed liver cancer over the same time period. Liver tumours have also been shown to be induced by iron overload in mice (Smith et al, 1995) and the authors suggested an iron-catalysed 'oxidative stress' mechanism. It has also been postulated that iron may act as a promoter of initiated hepatocytes in rats (Carthew et al, 1997) and that the same mechanism may operate in humans.

Iron has been shown to act as a cocarcinogen in vitro and in vivo (Hann et al, 1992).

There is a body of evidence that iron overload with diverse aetiologies may increase the risk of liver cancer. However, the evidence to suggest high dietary iron per se may increase the risk of primary liver cancer is, as yet, insufficient.

Selenium

While one correlational study of the incidence of liver cancer in Qidong County (Li et al, 1986) found rather strong decreased risk with higher serum selenium levels and grain selenium content, a larger study conducted across 65 counties in China observed no correlation between plasma selenium concentrations and liver cancer mortality (Hsing et al, 1991).

A chemoprevention trial in Qidong County has been conducted among residents 20 to 64 years of age, who were positive for HBsAg or who were from families at high risk of hepatoma (Han, 1993). The treatment group received 200 g/day of selenium via an enriched yeast preparation. Although details are lacking on randomisation and placebo-control, the rate of hepatoma was significantly lower among those receiving the intervention than among the controls ($RR=0.40$, $p<0.01$) after two-years of follow-up (Han, 1993).

Deficient intakes of selenium have been shown to increase hepatocarcinogenesis among experimental animals (Harr et al, 1972; Dauod and Griffin, 1978; (NAS, 1982); moreover, among rats and ducks exposed to aflatoxin B, administration of selenium reduced the incidence of hepatoma or precancerous liver nodules compared with control animals (Han, 1993).

The evidence suggests that dietary selenium may decrease the risk of liver cancer, but is, as yet, insufficient.

Folate and other methyl donors

Interest in lipotropes (choline, methionine, B_{12} and folate) first arose in 1932 (Best and Huntsman, 1932) when it was discovered that the fatty livers of depancreatised diabetic dogs could be alleviated by the feeding of 'lecithin' (phosphatidylcholine). Shortly thereafter it was reported that fatty livers could be prevented or reversed by the feeding of choline and, to some extent, by other dietary factors including methionine, folic acid and vitamin B_{12}.

Choline is an important dietary source of methyl groups and a precursor of phosphatidylcholine, the major phospholipid in mammalian membranes, as well as being a significant source of active methyl groups needed for the metabolism of fats (Orten and Neuhaus, 1982). It was originally known as a 'lipotrope nutrient' because it was capable of attracting fats away from the liver (Best et al, 1935).

Choline, methionine, folic acid and vitamin B_{12} interact in the regulation of the intracellular supply and metabolism of methyl groups. Lipotrope deficient or methyl-deficient diets have been shown to cause extensive liver damage, induce cell turnover and promote liver carcinogenesis in rats and certain strains of mice. However, the mechanisms have not yet been clearly elucidated.

Although extensive experimental work has been carried out in rodents, little is known about the effects of methyl insufficiency in humans. Christman et al (1993) have noted that although it is unlikely that human diets are as severely methyl deficient as those commonly used in laboratory settings, there is some evidence to suggest that diets in many parts of the world may be marginally deficient in lipotropes. Christman et al have also suggested that, in both rural and industrialised nations, excess intake of alcohol and/or administration of certain therapeutic drugs may induce conditions in which DNA methylation may be inhibited. Poirier (1994) has also noted that folate deficiency in humans may

contribute to a methyl insufficiency. This suggestion was linked to the discovery that patients with HIV infection had low levels of both s-adenosylmethionine and N-methyltetrahydrofolate in the cerebrospinal fluid (Surtees et al, 1990; Keating et al, 1991). It is likely that there may be some link between folate deficiency and liver cancer, given that alcohol induces both hepatotoxicity and folate deficiency in humans and experimental animals, and also that several clinical studies have shown some association between folate deficiency and dysplasia in cervical, bronchial and colonic epithelia (Butterworth et al, 1982; Heimburger et al, 1988; Lashner et al, 1989; Giovannucci et al, 1993).

The major developments prior to 1980, showing links between methyl group insufficiency and hepatocarcinogenesis in rodents, have been summarised in a review by Poirier (1994). This describes studies by Copeland and Salmon (1946) and Salmon and Copeland (1954) in which choline-deficient diets were shown to cause liver cancer in rats and mice. However, it was later postulated that the effects may have been due to the aflatoxin content of the rats' feed. Further work by Farber (1956, 1963); Shinozuka et al (1978); and Lapeyre and Becker (1979); demonstrated the importance of methyl-group metabolism.

Although the mechanisms for the carcinogenic potential of methyl-deficient diets have not been fully elucidated, work with rodents suggested a role for hypomethylation of DNA (Feo et al, 1987; Garcea et al, 1987; Chandar et al, 1989; Wainfan et al, 1989; Pascale et al, 1992; Wainfan and Poirier, 1992; Christman et al, 1993). Studies by Smith et al (1993) have shown a high frequency of mutations in the p53 tumour-suppressor gene in the DNA extracted from liver tumours in rats fed a choline-deficient diet. Other possible mechanisms include oxidative damage (Rushmore et al, 1984) and altered deoxynucleotide pool sizes (James et al, 1989).

Despite abundant experimental evidence from studies on rodents, and indirect speculation concerning humans, evidence from both epidemiological studies and controlled human trials is lacking. The human evidence that folate deficiency increases the risk of liver cancer is minimal; no judgement is possible.

4.9.2 FOODS AND DRINKS

A limited number of epidemiological studies have investigated the association between consumption of selected foods and food groups and occurrence of liver cancer. All have examined a number of different food items, although most have provided relative risk estimates only for those foods found to be significantly associated with liver cancer. A few of the studies did not control for the potentially important confounding effects of HBsAg (La Vecchia et al, 1988; Fukuda et al, 1993), or for hepatitis C viral infection (Lam et al, 1982; La Vecchia et al, 1988; Srivatanakul et al, 1991; Fukuda et al, 1993). Only one case-control study adjusted solely for age and gender (Fukuda et al, 1993). Only one study controlled for total food intake (Hadziyannis et al, 1995), a likely confounder of the association between dietary consumption and the risk of liver cancer. More specific comments concerning the reported results for specific foods are provided below.

In the study by La Vecchia et al (1988), the authors postulated that the inverse associations observed for food intake (none of the 14 food items increased liver cancer occurrence) might suggest an effect of a deficient diet on the development of liver cancer. Poor nutritional status would be more prevalent in populations of lower socioeconomic status, which might explain some of the international variation observed for this malignancy.

4.9.2.1 Cereals (grains)

In a case-control study by La Vecchia et al (1988) in Italy, a reduction of approximately 40% in the incidence of liver cancer was observed for the intermediate and high tertiles of wholegrain bread/pasta consumption; after including the other important food items in the multivariate model, the trend toward decreasing relative risk was not significant. By contrast, a recent case-control study in Greece reported no association between liver cancer and the consumption of cereals (Hadziyannis et al, 1995).

Correlation data from the large ecological study conducted in China suggested an inverse relationship between increasing daily intake of wheat and liver cancer mortality rates (Hsing et al, 1991); the association was strongest and statistically significant among men (r = –0.29) and persisted even after adjustment for HBsAg prevalence and total serum cholesterol.

Evidence relating to diets high in cereals and the risk of liver cancer is very limited and inconsistent; no judgement is possible.

4.9.2.2 Vegetables and fruits

The most consistent finding for food groups and the incidence of liver cancer is a decrease in risk associated with increased consumption of vegetables. Cohort studies in Japan (Hirayama, 1990) and Taiwan (Yu and Chen, 1993; Yu et al, 1995) reported evidence supportive of a decreased risk with higher vegetable consumption. In the latter study (Yu and Chen, 1993), there was a substantial increase in the relative risk of liver cancer among individuals consuming fewer than six meals with fresh vegetables per week, compared to those consuming more (RR=7.2, 1.5–33.8). In contrast, however, not eating meat was independently associated with an increased incidence of liver cancer (RR=3.7, 0.9–14.6); the authors of that study stated that these study subjects 'consumed mostly preserved vegetables and foodstuffs from beans' (Yu and Chen, 1993). The protective association found in Japan was with green–yellow vegetables (Hirayama, 1990).

A separate analysis of the cohort in Taiwan (Yu et al, 1995) found that the increased risk of liver cancer with low vegetable intake (fewer than six vegetable meals/week) was

observable in HBsAg carriers (RR=4.7, 2.0–11.1) but not noncarriers (RR=1.2, 0.3–5.4), and in smokers (RR=3.8, 1.7–8.5) but not nonsmokers (RR=0.9, 0.1–7.0). However, the 95% confidence intervals for these estimates are wide and overlapping.

Among the five case-control studies examining the association of food intake with liver cancer, three reported a decreased risk with higher levels of consumption of some type of vegetables (Lam et al, 1982; La Vecchia et al, 1988; Srivatanakul et al, 1991). The odds ratios were 0.6 or less. In two of these studies, conducted in Thailand and Italy, the association was statistically significant (La Vecchia et al, 1988; Srivatanakul et al, 1991). The Hong Kong study found a decreased risk with higher consumption of yellow vegetables, but not green vegetables (Lam et al, 1982). No association with frequency of intake of vegetables was observed in the other two case-control studies (Fukuda et al, 1993; Hadziyannis et al, 1995).

A minimal, statistically nonsignificant decrease in risk with higher consumption of fruits was reported in the study by Lam et al (1982). The case-control study from Italy also found a decrease in risk (OR=0.76) related to the highest tertile of fresh fruit consumption, but the trend was not statistically significant (La Vecchia et al, 1988). Two additional studies that considered intake of fruits reported no association with the risk of liver cancer (Srivatanakul et al, 1991; Hadziyannis et al, 1995).

Diets high in vegetables possibly decrease the risk of liver cancer. Evidence relating to diets high in fruits and the risk of liver cancer is limited; no judgement is possible.

4.9.2.3 Meat, poultry, fish and eggs

Meat

An increased risk was observed between daily meat consumption and liver cancer in the cohort study in Japan (Hirayama, 1990); this association was statistically significant and most apparent among men.

Frequency of meat consumption was not related to liver cancer in four case-control studies (La Vecchia et al, 1988; Srivatanakul et al, 1991; Fukuda et al, 1993; Hadziyannis et al, 1995). However, the results from the study of Chinese in Hong Kong (Lam et al, 1982) suggested a decreased risk of liver cancer with higher intake of pork.

No relationship between meat intake and the risk of liver cancer was reported in the large ecological study in China (Hsing et al, 1991).

Evidence relating to diets high in meat and the risk of liver cancer are limited and inconsistent; no judgement is possible.

Fish

The cohort study in Japan (Hirayama, 1990) and the case-control study in Italy (La Vecchia et al, 1988) showed decreased risks with increased intake of fish, albeit not statistically significant. No association was found in three other case-control studies (Srivatanakul et al, 1991; Fukuda et al, 1993; Hadziyannis et al, 1995).

In the correlational study conducted in China (Hsing et al, 1991), increased fish consumption was statistically significantly associated with increased liver cancer mortality rates (r=0.35, men; r=0.26, women).

Evidence relating to diets high in fish and the risk of liver cancer is limited and inconsistent; no judgement is possible.

Eggs

The two case-control studies that examined the effect of egg consumption on the incidence of liver cancer (La Vecchia et al, 1988; Fukuda et al, 1993) gave conflicting results. In the study in Italy (La Vecchia et al, 1988), a significant, moderately strong dose–response relationship was reported between higher frequency of intake and decreased risk of liver cancer. However, in the Japanese study, an increased risk of liver cancer was suggested for higher egg consumption among men only (OR=1.9, 1.3–2.7) (Fukuda et al, 1993), although adjustment was made solely for age.

Evidence relating to high egg consumption and the risk of liver cancer is limited and inconsistent; no judgement is possible.

4.9.2.4 Milk and dairy products

One case-control study (La Vecchia et al, 1988) reported a decreased risk of liver cancer with higher milk intake (OR=0.7, for the highest versus the lowest tertile). A case-control study in Japan (Fukuda et al, 1993) found a higher risk of liver cancer with a greater than average consumption of milk (OR=1.9, 1.3–2.7, in men; OR=2.6, 1.5–4.7, in women).

No association was found in relation to milk consumption in several other case-control studies (Hsing et al, 1991; Srivatanakul et al, 1991; Hadziyannis et al, 1995).

Evidence relating to diets high in milk and dairy products and the risk of liver cancer is limited and inconsistent; no judgement is possible.

4.9.2.5 Coffee, tea and other drinks

Tea

One cohort study has examined the relationship between tea consumption and the risk of liver cancer (Heilbrun et al, 1986). Subjects who consumed tea on at least two occasions per week were found to have a non-significantly decreased risk (RR=0.6) of liver cancer compared with subjects who almost never drank tea. Relative risks were adjusted for age at examination and alcohol consumption.

One study does not provide the basis for any judgement.

4.9.3 FOOD PROCESSING

4.9.3.1 Contaminants

DDT

Dicholorodiphenyltrichloroethane (DDT) is an organochlorine pesticide which was widely used between 1940 and 1960 as a general insecticide, and for the control of vector-borne diseases such as malaria. Despite DDT's major contribution to massive reductions in the number of malaria deaths in over 120 countries, its use is now banned or restricted in many countries because of its toxicity in many species and persistence in the environment. Human exposure via diet has been measurable in the past and residues persist in adipose tissue for decades.

There are no epidemological studies on dietary DDT intakes and liver cancer.

Experimental work in rodents has shown DDT to be a liver tumour-promoting agent. Several studies have shown that administration of DDT is associated with inhibition of the hepatic intercellular gap-junctional communication which may be an important mechanism of tumour promotion. The inhibition of communication between cells has been demonstrated in hamster embryo cells (Rivedal et al, 1994; Roseng et al, 1994), in rats (Tateno et al, 1994; Krutovskikh et al, 1995) and in cultured rat liver epithelial cells (Sigler and Ruch, 1993; Ruch et al, 1994). One study by Kostka et al (1996), which dosed male Wistar rats with DDT, noted deleterious effects such as hepatomegaly, hepatocyte proliferation and focal necrosis.

However, an observational study in non-human primates has suggested that DDT may have a negligible effect on tumorigenesis (Thorgeirsson et al, 1994). The report covered a 32-year period of a chemical carcinogenesis study initiated by the National Cancer Institute in 1961, and suggested that the tumorigenic potential of DDT was negligible after dosing for 15–22 years.

Despite animal and cell studies demonstrating the tumorigenic nature of DDT, there is no evidence from human observational studies; no judgement is possible.

Vinyl chloride

There is evidence to show that occupational exposure to vinyl chloride monomer causes hepatic angiosarcoma in humans (Simonata et al, 1991; Ho et al, 1991; Wong et al, 1991; Lee et al, 1996). This relatively rare tumour constitutes only 2% of all primary tumours of the liver and is known to have a long latency period, which may be as great as 9 to 35 years after exposure (Lee et al, 1996). It is possible that human dietary exposure via packaging of foods exists but data are lacking.

The effects of ingestion of vinyl chloride have been studied in rats. One study demonstrated that the incorporation of polyvinyl chloride powder into the diet of Wistar rats at daily levels of 1.3mg/kg BW was sufficient to induce cancerous changes in the livers of both males and females. No other organs were affected (Til et al, 1991). Vinyl chloride is now known to be transformed to DNA-reactive chloroethylene oxide producing cyclic etheno adducts which are mutagenic (Whysner et al, 1996).

Amounts of vinyl chloride in food-grade packaging plastics are now controlled at low levels in order to prevent significant migration into foods.

Vinyl chloride monomer at high-level occupational exposures causes angiosarcoma of the liver. There are no data on the low levels of exposure associated with food packaging and no data on risk; no judgment is possible.

Polychlorinated biphenyls (PCBS)

Information on the effects of PCBs on humans after exposure to high doses of PCB- and PCDF-contaminated edible oil, and via transplacental/translactational routes (Williams and Horm, 1977; IARC, 1987). has been obtained principally from two large scale incidents which occurred in Japan in 1968 (the 'Yusho' episode) and in Taiwan (the 'Yu-Cheng' episode) in 1979. Epidemiological studies on those exposed revealed a number of non-carcinogenic effects, but have not provided convincing evidence of the carcinogenicity of these compounds in humans. However, large-scale mortality studies on workplace exposure indicated increased mortality from cancers of the liver and gall bladder and lymphoma in women (Bertazzi et al, 1987).

Three other large occupational cohort studies have shown an excess of liver and biliary tract cancer (Dalzell and Monson, 1982; Bernardinelli et al, 1987; Brown et al, 1987).

Several animal studies have been undertaken to evaluate the tumorigenic potential of PCBs. In one study in mice, liver tumours were initiated by administration of nitrosamine N-nitrosodimethylamine (NDMA) and the subsequent promotion of the hepatocarcinomas was enhanced by exposure to PCBs (Anderson et al, 1994). Similar results in mice have been documented by other researchers (Rumsby et al 1992; Beebe et al, 1993).

One meta-analysis of seven studies in which rats were fed PCB mixtures containing 42, 54, or 60% chlorine clearly indicated that the carcinogenic potential of these compounds depends heavily on the degree of chlorination (Moore et al, 1994). Another animal study has shown that administration of PCBs to male Sprague-Dawley rats decreased hepatic vitamin A and vitamin E levels, as well as lowering the activities of catalase and superoxide dismutase, leading the authors to suggest that PCBs may cause a long-lasting increase in rat oxidative stress with a concomitant decrease in antioxidant defence capabilities. In turn, this has to be linked to the ability of PCBs to act as tumour-promoting agents (Mantyla and Ahotupa, 1993).

Altered expression of 10 proto-oncogenes in rat liver at various times after exposure to PCBs has been noted (Jenke et al, 1991), and further studies with Chang liver cells have demonstrated that supplementing the growth medium with PCBs also results in interference of protooncogene expres-

sion (Hornhardt et al, 1994).

PCBs are a well established environmental pollutant and tumour promoter in animals. Evidence on low-level dietary exposure in humans is largely absent, as are data on any association with the risk of liver cancer; no judgement is possible.

Polybrominated biphenyls (PBBs)

Polybrominated biphenyls (PBBs) are chemically and toxicologically related to the PCBs.

Long-term studies on a commercial preparation of PBBs showed that this material induced hepatocellular carcinomas in rats and mice (Busby and Wogan, 1984). The lowest dose at which an increase in tumours occurred (mainly adenomas) was 0.5 mg/kg BW for two years.

A case report of a known human exposure to PBBs (Sherman, 1991) documents the history of a patient who was exposed to PBBs when animal feed was contaminated in Michigan (USA) in the early 1970s. He developed a liver cancer following chronic exposure to contaminated milk. Sherman's case report also lists several studies which have suggested that PBB exposure leads to carcinogenicity (Kimbrough et al, 1975, 1978, 1981; Moore et al, 1980; Blum and Ames, 1977); hepatotoxicity (Lee et al, 1975; Dent et al, 1976; Anderson et al, 1978) and enzyme induction (Dent et al, 1977; Safe et al, 1978).

Exposure to PBBs at high levels causes liver cancer in rodents and possibly in humans. There are few, if any, data on low-level dietary exposures in humans and no data on the relationship between such exposure and human liver cancer; no judgement is possible.

Polychlorinated dibenzodioxins (PCDDs) and dibenzofurans (PCDFs)

PCDDs and PCDFs are chlorinated aromatic compounds which are chemically stable, insoluble in water and highly soluble in fats and oils. TCDDs (tetrachlorodibenzo-p-dioxins) and HCDDs (hexachlorodibenzo-p-dioxins) are among the most toxic and carcinogenic of 'man-made' chemicals. Pharmacokinetic studies in laboratory animals indicate that 50–90% of dietary TCDD is absorbed and that it concentrates in adipose tissue and in the liver. In mammals, the TCDD present in the liver is slowly redistributed and stored in fatty tissue. Metabolism is slow as the biological half-life varies from weeks in rodents to years in humans. Elimination occurs via excretion of metabolites in the bile and urine and passively through the gut wall (Huff et al, 1991).

For people not occcupationally exposed, the daily intake of PCDDs and PCDFs via food consumption has been calculated to be 0.35 pg/kg BW for TCDD, and 2.3 pg/kg BW for TCDD equivalents. Food from animal sources contributes most, although human exposure begins with atmospheric emissions which deposit these compounds on plant surfaces (Beck et al, 1994). It has also been suggested that people who consume fish may have greater exposure.

One study investigated human exposure in relation to consumption of fish from the Baltic Sea (Svensson et al, 1991) which are known to contain high levels of PCDDs and PCDFs. Plasma levels of ten different dibenzofurans and seven dioxins were analysed in three groups of Swedish men: one group with a high intake of fish (almost daily consumption); one with a moderate intake (approximately once per week) and one with no consumption of fish. Median amounts of the most toxic dioxin studied (2,3,7,8-tetrachlorodibenzo-p-dioxin) were 8.0 pg/g of plasma lipid in the high-intake group; 2.6 pg/g in the moderate intake group and 1.8 pg/g in the non-consumers. The authors concluded that contaminated fish from sources such as the Baltic Sea are likely to be a significant source of exposure to PCDFs and PCDDs in people who eat fish regularly. The clinical consequences of dietary exposure to PCDDs and PCDFs in humans remain uncertain.

There are many studies based on occupational exposures (Fingerhut et al, 1991; Zober et al, 1990; Saracci et al, 1991; Hooiveld et al, 1996; Ott and Zober, 1996), but most of the information on the effects of dioxins on humans has been obtained from the large-scale incident that occurred in Italy (Seveso). Effects include hepatotoxicity and immunotoxicity observed principally in accidental exposures (after the Seveso incident) and other industrial exposures .

TCDD is known to act as a complete carcinogen in several animal species, causing both common and uncommon tumours at multiple sites. It has been shown to induce neoplasms in rat and mouse livers.

PCDDs and PCFDs at high levels of exposure cause liver damage in humans and liver cancers in rodents. There is evidence of low-level human intakes, but no data on the risk of liver cancer; no judgement is possible.

4.9.3.2 Microbial contamination

Aflatoxins

Many studies on diet and liver cancer have been concerned with the presence of the fungal metabolite aflatoxins, a generic term for a group of metabolites produced by the phylo-genetically related *Aspergillus flavus* and *Aspergillus parasiticus* (Busby and Wogan, 1984). A brief account of this generic group of metabolite(s) is given here because its hepatocarcinogenic activity appears to be strongly influenced by nutritional and other factors.

The most widely studied of the aflatoxin compounds is aflatoxin B_1 (AFB1) (Wogan, 1973). Aflatoxins were originally discovered in fungal-infested peanut meal that had been shown to be responsible for lethal toxicity in domestic farm animals, hatchery-reared trout, and experimental rodents (Ashley and Halver, 1961; Blount, 1961. In addition to the occurrence of tissue necrosis, hemorrhage, bile duct proliferation, and degeneration of the liver, aflatoxins were shown early to be potent hepatocarcinogens in certain experimental animal species (Ashley and Halver, 1961; Lancaster

et al, 1961; Carnaghan, 1965; Wogan et al, 1974). The widespread occurrence of aflatoxins in human food has been thought by many investigators to pose the possibility of cancer risk in humans (Goldblatt, 1969; Wogan, 1973; Campbell and Hayes, 1976).

That specific human populations are exposed to detectable levels of aflatoxins is indicated by discovery of an aflatoxin-bound guanine adduct in human DNA (Groopman et al, 1991); by the high correlation between urinary excretion of this adduct and AFB1 intake observed in studies in The Gambia (Groopman et al, 1992) and The Guangxi Autonomous Region of China (Groopman et al, 1992); and by the (somewhat weaker) correlations between aflatoxin intake and the urinary excretion of total oxidised aflatoxin metabolites (Groopman et al, 1992), aflatoxin serum albumin adducts (Gan et al, 1988; Sabbioni et al, 1990), and urinary AFB1 excretion (Groopman et al, 1992).

A number of ecological studies conducted in Africa, Thailand, and China have shown a relationship between aflatoxin exposure, based primarily on estimated intake, and the development of liver cancer. (IARC, 1976, 1987, 1993). A problem with most of these studies is potential confounding by chronic hepatitis infection and other risk factors for liver cancer.

In a few of these analyses, the correlation of liver cancer and HBsAg prevalence was also evaluated (Armstrong, 1980; Wang et al, 1983; Autrup et al, 1987; Peers et al, 1987). One study found that HBsAg positivity did not confound the relationship between the incidence of liver cancer and aflatoxin intakes (Peers et al, 1987); the remainder observed no significant or strong correlation between chronic hepatitis infection and liver cancer (Armstrong, 1980; Wang et al, 1983; Autrup et al, 1987). More recently, ecological studies in China (Campbell et al, 1990) and Thailand (Srivatanakul et al, 1991) have found no association between aflatoxin metabolites in urine (Campbell et al, 1990; Srivatanakul et al, 1991) or serum (Srivatanakul et al, 1991) and the risk of liver cancer.

Several analytical epidemiological studies have examined the association between aflatoxin exposure and the risk of liver cancer; the results of these studies are summarised in Table 4.9.3. Measurement of aflatoxin exposure was quite variable across these studies. In the first two cohort studies (Olsen et al, 1988; Yeh et al, 1989), the amount of aflatoxin ingested was based on the average for the particular 'exposed' group. In contrast, the study by Ross et al (1992) assessed adduct levels within individuals, but the follow-up time was rather short (<2 years on average), so it is possible that early disease may have affected aflatoxin metabolism. In the study in the Philippines (Bulatao-Jayme et al, 1982), average aflatoxin intake was determined from food-intake histories, whereas consumption of foods suspected to be contaminated by aflatoxin was the exposure of interest in the studies by Lam et al (1982) and Srivatanakul et al (1991) (this study also measured blood aflatoxin adducts).

Except for two case-control studies (Lam et al, 1982; Srivatanakul et al, 1991), a moderately strong association

TABLE 4.9.3 AFLATOXIN EXPOSURE AND THE RISK OF LIVER CANCER: COHORT AND CASE-CONTROL STUDIES

AUTHOR, YEAR, AND PLACE	SIZE OF COHORT: NO OF CASES	EXPOSURE	COMPARISON	RELATIVE RISK (95% CONFIDENCE INTERVAL)	ADJUSTMENT
Cohort studies					
Yeh et al, 1989, China	7,917 men	Aflatoxins	heavy vs light exposure	11.3 (nr)	
Olsen et al, 1988 Denmark	Livestock feed workers (men)	Contaminated dust	179 ng AFB_1/worker/day for ever having been exposed	1.39 (nr)	
			179 ng AFB_1/worker/day for $\geq$ 10 years prior to diagnosis	2.5 (1.08–4.86)	
Ross RK, 1992, China	18,244 men	Dietary aflatoxins	detectable urinary aflatoxins vs non detectable	3.8 (1.2–12.2)	Education, smoking, alcohol, HBsAg status
Qian G-S, 1994, China	18,244 men	Dietary aflatoxins	AFB_1-N^7 Gua adduct presence in urine	9.1 (2.9–29.2)	HBsAg positivity, smoking
Case-control studies					
Bulatao-Jayme et al 1982, Phillipines	90	Dietary aflatoxins	very heavy ($\geq$ 7µg)	17.0 (nr)	
Lam KC, 1982 Hong Kong	107	Dietary sources of aflatoxins	$\geq$ 1 per week vs less frequently		
			corn	1.0 (nr)	
			beans	0.9 (nr)	
			mung beans	1.0 (nr)	
			other grains	2.2 (nr)	
			peanuts	1.5 (nr)	
Srivatanakul et al 1991, Thailand	65	Aflatoxins	presence of albumin bound aflatoxin in blood not present	1.0 (0.4–2.7)	HBV infection

with aflatoxin was observed (Table 4.9.3). Misclassification of exposure may explain the relatively null findings of the studies in Hong Kong (Lam et al, 1982) and Thailand (Srivatanakul et al, 1991). The cohort study in Shanghai (Quin et al, 1994) did not find an association between dietary aflatoxin intakes and liver cancer incidence or with urinary aflatoxin levels. Most of these analytical studies adjusted for potential confounders, including chronic hepatitis B infection (Lam et al, 1982; Yeh et al, 1989; Srivatanakul et al, 1991; Ross et al, 1992; Quin et al, 1994). A strong interaction between HBsAg and the presence of urinary aflatoxin adducts on the risk of liver cancer was observed in the study by Ross et al (1992). High alcohol consumption and high aflatoxin intakes also appeared to enhance the risk of liver cancer in the case-control study in the Philippines (Bulatao-Jayme et al, 1982).

In experimental animal studies, aflatoxin has been demonstrated to cause a specific mutation, whose presence in humans is thought to be a 'footprint' of prior aflatoxin exposure (Bressac et al, 1991; Hsu et al, 1991; Ozturk et al, 1991; Scorsone et al, 1992). Specifically, this mutation results in the transversion of guanine to thymine in codon 249 of the *p53* tumour-suppressor gene. The association of this mutation with liver cancer cases is not entirely clear, however, because similar mutations have been observed in a high proportion of human liver cancer cases not known to involve aflatoxin exposure, as well as in human tumours at other sites where aflatoxin has not been shown to be causal (Nigro et al, 1989; Hollstein et al, 1991).

Aflatoxin contamination of food probably increases the risk of primary liver cancer.

4.10 Colon, rectum

Cancer of the colon and rectum is the fourth most common incident cancer and cause of death from cancer, throughout the world. An estimated 875,000 cases occurred in 1996, accounting for 8.5 per cent of all new cases of cancer.

Incidence of and deaths from this cancer are generally increasing, most of all in the developed world and urban areas of the developing world. Colorectal cancer is one of the two major cancers, the risk of which is commonly agreed to be modified mainly by food and nutrition.

The panel has reached the following conclusions. The evidence that diets high in vegetables decrease the risk of colorectal cancer, is convincing. The evidence that regular physical activity decreases the risk of colorectal

FOOD, NUTRITION AND COLORECTAL CANCERS

In the judgement of the panel, the dietary constituents and related factors, the foods and drinks, and the methods of food processing listed below, modify the risk of colon and rectal cancers, or else have no relationship with them. Judgements are graded according to the strength of the evidence.

EVIDENCE	DECREASES RISK	NO RELATIONSHIP	INCREASES RISK
Convincing	Physical activity[b] Vegetables[a]		
Probable			Red meat Alcohol
Possible	NSP/fibre Starch Carotenoids	Calcium Selenium Fish	High body mass[b] Greater adult height Frequent eating Sugar Total fat Saturated/animal fat Processed meat Eggs Heavily cooked meat
Insufficient	Resistant starch Vitamin C Vitamin D Vitamin E Folate Methionine Cereals Coffee		Iron

For an explanation of the terms used in the matrix, see chapter 3
[a] Not fruit — see text
[b] Colon only

cancer is also convincing. Alcohol, and consumption of diets high in red meat, probably increase the risk of this cancer.

The panel notes that a substantial number of dietary factors, and factors related to diet, possibly modify the risk of colorectal cancer. These are diets high in starch, non-starch polysaccharides (fibre) and carotenoids, all found in foods of plant origin, all of which possibly decrease risk. Obesity, greater adult height, frequent eating, and diets high in sugar, total and saturated fat, eggs, and processed meat, all possibly increase risk.

Established non-dietary causes of colorectal cancer include genetic predisposition, ulcerative colitis, infection with *Schistosoma sinesis* and smoking tobacco. Aspirin and other NSAIDs decrease risk.

The most effective ways of preventing colorectal cancer are consumption of diets high in vegetables and regular physical activity and low consumption of red and processed meat. Possible further means of preventing this cancer, are maintenance of body weight within recommended levels throughout life, and consumption of diets high in non-starch polysaccharides, starch and carotenoids and low in sugar, fat, and eggs.

COLORECTAL CANCER estimated rates of cancer incidence by sex and area

| 5.0 ↕ ▯ **Men** | | | | |
| 5.0 ↕ ▯ **Women** | | | | |

1. Eastern Africa	7. Central America	13. Eastern Asia: Other	19. Southern Europe
2. Middle Africa	8. South America (Temperate)	14. South Eastern Asia	20. Western Europe
3. Northern Africa	9. South America (Tropical)	15. Southern Asia	21. Australia/New Zealand
4. Southern Africa	10. North America	16. Western Asia	22. Melenesia
5. Western Africa	11. Eastern Asia: China	17. Eastern Europe	23. Micronesia/Polynesia
6. Caribbean	12. Eastern Asia: Japan	18. Northern Europe	24. USSR

INTRODUCTION

Colon and rectal cancers have different sex distributions, with essentially similar incidences between the sexes for colon, and a male predominance for rectum. Approximately 98% of malignant tumours of the colon and rectum are adenocarcinomas. Until recently, half of all colorectal cancers occurred in the rectum and rectosigmoid areas, one quarter in the sigmoid and the remaining quarter were equally distributed between the caecum, the ascending, transverse and descending colon. However, the left-sided dominance appears to be diminishing and rectal tumours now account for approximately 27%, while almost 50% occur proximal to the splenic flexure. Almost three-quarters of patients with a primary carcinoma will also have associated benign adenomas.

Although cancers of the colon and rectum differ somewhat in their descriptive epidemiology, the published data do not suggest that dietary risk factors are substantially different between the two cancer sites. Thus, they are reviewed together in this chapter.

Similarly, some differences exist in the descriptive epidemiology of cancers occurring at various subsites of the colon (higher proportions of proximal tumours in women and in low-risk countries; recent increase in right-sided tumours in developed countries) (Correa and Haenszel, 1978; McMichael and Potter, 1985; Muir et al, 1987; Parkin et al, 1992). However, there are only limited data indicating that dietary risk factors may differ by colonic subsites. When suggestive, these data are included in the review.

Adenocarcinomas are the focus of this review since they represent more than 90% of the cancers occurring in the large intestine. Studies on colonic adenomatous polyps, benign neoplastic lesions which are widely accepted as precursors of most colorectal cancers, are also included when they add to the weight of the evidence for an association with colorectal cancer.

Although smoking has not usually been regarded as a risk factor for colorectal cancer, it has consistently been associated with adenomatous polyps. Nonetheless, one study has suggested that smoking in the distant past is associated with colorectal cancer, whereas more recent smoking was not (Giovanucci et al, 1994). Data also suggest that prolonged use of aspirin or other non-steroidal anti-inflammatory drugs and, possibly, use of menopausal replacement oestrogens, may exert a protective effect against adenomatous polyps and colorectal cancer (Greenberg and Baron, 1993; Potter, 1995).

Other important non-dietary risk factors includes ulcerative colitis and infestation with *Schistosoma sinesis* (particularly important as a cause of rectal cancer in China). Colon cancer has long been known to occur more frequently in some families (Macklin, 1969) and there are several rare genetic syndromes which carry an excess risk of colon cancer (Gardner, 1951; Veale, 1965; Utsonomya and Lynch 1990).

INCIDENCE PATTERNS

Cancer of the colon and rectum is the fourth most common cancer in the world. In 1996, an estimated 875,000 new cases were diagnosed worldwide (WHO, 1997), accounting for 8.5% of all new cancers.

High risk areas include North America, Europe and Australiasia. The developed world accounts for over 63% (555,000 cases) of the total global incidence. Central and South America, Asia and Africa are areas of low risk. Incidence is now increasing in previously low-risk areas.

In both men and women, incidence of colon cancer occurs at a similar rate. However, cancer of the rectum is more common in men than women, with a 20–50% higher incidence.

Migrant and temporal trend studies suggest that colon and rectal cancers are determined largely by environmental exposures. Rates in migrants from low- to high-risk countries tend to increase to the rates of the host countries within one or two generations, or even as early as within the migrating generation itself.

Five-year survival rates are generally between 50–60%. In 1996, mortality attributable to colorectal cancer was estimated at 510,000 people, 7.2% of all cancer deaths (WHO, 1997).

PATHOGENESIS

The earliest model of pathogenesis of colorectal cancer – the adenoma–carcinoma hypothesis (Hill et al 1974), is now widely accepted. It proposes that the initial colorectal lesion arises as a benign adenomatous polyp that later undergoes further disorganisation of cellular and tissue phenotype. Some earlier stages in the process have also been proposed: hyperproliferation of the upper crypt cells leading to the formation of aberrant crypt foci and microadenomas (Bird et al 1987).

Vogelstein and colleagues (Baker et al, 1989; Vogelstein et al, 1989; Fearon et al, 1990; Fearon and Vogelstein, 1990; Kinzler et al, 1991) have provided a molecular basis for the adenoma/carcinoma sequence by describing the complex multistep process in which cells accumulate alterations of multiple genes that control cell growth and differentiation, resulting in the neoplastic phenotype.

Although this process involves cumulative rather than

BOX 4.10.1 ESTABLISHED NON-DIETARY FACTORS AND THE RISK OF COLORECTAL CANCER

The following factors increase the risk of colorectal cancer:
- Inheritance of mutations in specific genes including the APC genes and the HNPCC-related DNA mismatch-repair gene
- Ulcerative colitis
- Infestation: Schistosoma sinensis
- Smoking (increases the risk of colorectal adenomas and possibly cancer)

The following factor decreases the risk of colorectal cancer:
- Aspirin and other NSAIDs

Biological models at the biochemical and genetic levels have been proposed for colorectal cancer. These models provide useful frameworks for understanding the role of dietary factors in colorectal carcinogenesis and, ultimately, in controlling and preventing the disease (Potter, 1992; Greenwald et al, 1995).

The target cells of colon carcinogenesis are colonic crypt epithelial cells. Thus, attention has focused on the transition from normal cell to malignant cell and from the macroscopically normal colonic mucosa through adenomatous polyps to cancer. The adenoma/carcinoma sequence, as originally proposed by Hill, Morson and colleagues (Hill et al, 1974) is now a widely accepted description of this process and one that makes chemopreventive or dietary intervention studies in 'high risk' individuals with polyps an attractive substitute for very large cancer prevention trials in healthy subjects.

Cell proliferation is an important factor in carcinogenesis generally, and rectal mucosal proliferation has been used as an outcome measure for rapid tests of the anticarcinogenic potential of specific dietary agents (Lipkin, 1988). Another intermediate endpoint has been proposed – the aberrant crypt or microadenoma (Bird, 1987); it has been used in animal studies (Corpet et al, 1990), but its appropriateness for human studies is unclear.

Vogelstein and colleagues (Baker et al, 1989; Vogelstein et al, 1989; Fearon et al, 1990; Fearon and Vogelstein, 1990; Kinzler et al, 1991) have provided a molecular basis for the adenoma/carcinoma sequence by describing the complex multistep process in which cells accumulate alterations of multiple genes that control cell growth and differentiation, resulting in the neoplastic phenotype. There are, as yet, limited data linking diet to this accumulation of genetic events leading to neoplasia. Specific carcinogens in cooked food, particularly heterocyclic amines produced when meat is cooked at high temperatures for prolonged periods may interact with specific important genes including APC and K-ras, mutations which appear to occur early in colorectal cancer. Chronic folate and methionine deficiencies may produce the alteration in DNA methylation observed early in this process. Weinstein and colleagues have proposed that dietary fat is a source of diacylglycerol in the colon which may mimic and amplify cell replication signals (Guillem and Weinstein, 1990).

High rates of proliferation can occur in the colon as a result of mucosal damage (Kolonel and Le Marchand, 1986), or merely as a result of high intakes of food (Potter, 1992). Such compensatory proliferation of colonic epithelial cells could increase the opportunity for mutations to go unrepaired thus allowing the appearance of abnormal clones.

Diet would affect this model in several ways. High-fat and high-cholesterol diets may elevate risk by increasing bile acid production and the luminal concentration of free fatty acids. Dietary fiber may decrease risk by binding bile acids, as well as increasing stool bulk and, thus, diluting carcinogens. Bacterial fermentation of soluble fiber and resistant starch could be protective by increasing bulk, lowering pH (reducing the conversion of primary to the more toxic secondary bile acids) and producing short chain fatty acids that may be directly anticarcinogenic (Cummings, 1983), perhaps via induction of programmed cell death (apoptosis) (Hague et al, 1995). Intraluminal calcium ions could reduce the potentially promoting effect of bile acids and free fatty acids by converting them to insoluble calcium soaps (Wargovich et al, 1983). Additionally, calcium may reduce cell proliferation directly (Newmark et al, 1984), and influence the zone of proliferation (Bostick et al, 1995). Vegetables may be protective by providing the colon with fermentable fiber, as well as a number of anticarcinogenic compounds, such as carotenoids, vitamin C, folic acid, organosulfides, isothiocyanates, protease inhibitors, etc.

ordered sequential, somatic genetic and epigenetic changes, some events, including mutation or loss of the APC gene (a tumour-suppressor gene); mutation of K-ras (a proto-oncogene) and generalised disorganisation of DNA methylation occur relatively early, whereas loss of *p53* (a tumour-suppressor gene) is usually a late event.

There are two separate genetic syndromes that markedly increase the risk of colorectal cancer. Familial adenomatous polyposis (FAP), also called adenomatous polyposis coli, (Veale, 1965) is characterized by the development, sometimes from childhood, of multiple colonic adenomas, numbering from a few polyps to several thousand. The syndrome carries an almost 100% risk of colon adenocarcinoma but accounts for only a small proportion of colon cancer cases.

Localisation of the familial adenomatous polyposis gene was independently accomplished by Leppert et al (1987) and Bodmer et al (1987); the gene was mapped to chromosome 5q. The relevant gene is now sequenced and a variety of germline mutations in individuals with familial polyposis and Gardner syndrome have been described (Leppert et al, 1987; Nishiso et al, 1991; Groden et al, 1991; Kinzler et al, 1991; Joslyn et al, 1991).

The other form of colon cancer that runs in families is hereditary non-polyposis colorectal cancer (HNPCC) (Lynch and Lynch, 1985). This syndrome is not easily distinguished from 'sporadic' polyposis and cancer on physical examination (there is no tendency to extensive polyposis) but usually has an early onset and involves a particular pattern of other cancers – including endometrium, urinary tract, stomach, and biliary system (Lynch et al, 1989). HNPCC is more common than FAP.

The genes responsible are now established as DNA mismatch-repair genes: *MSH2; MLH1; PMS1; PMS2* (Aaltonen et al, 1991; Peltomaki et al, 1993; Thibideau et al, 1993; Papadopoulos et al, 1994). It seems plausible, in this group of patients, that the same environmental risk factors prevail as in the case of cancer in the general population; these individuals however, are unable to repair DNA damage with the same fidelity as those with intact mismatch repair genes.

JUDGEMENTS OF OTHER REPORTS

Diet has long been regarded as the most important environmental influence on colorectal cancer. The report of the

National Academy of Sciences, *Diet, Nutrition and Cancer* (NAS, 1982), implicated total fat and dietary fibre as causative and protective factors, respectively. Alcohol, and particularly beer, was also viewed as increasing the risk for rectal cancer. In the subsequent NAS report, *Diet and Health*, intakes of saturated fat and red meat, which are difficult to differentiate from that of total fat in the western diet, have also been regarded as risk factors, and fruit and vegetable consumption (highly correlated with dietary fibre intake) as a protective factor (NAS 1989).

The WHO report *Diet, Nutrition and the Prevention of Chronic Diseases* (WHO, 1990) concluded that an increased risk of cancer of the colon and rectum 'appears to be associated with high fat intake (particularly saturated fats) and low vegetable intake,' and that it was not clear whether the apparent protective effect of dietary fibre may be due to other food constituents. The report also stated that the consumption of beer may increase the risk of rectal cancer.

REVIEW

4.10.1   DIETARY CONSTITUENTS

4.10.1.1   **Energy and related factors**

Energy intake

It is difficult to distinguish between energy intake, and intake of fat (the most energy-dense constituent of the diet) when studying their relationship with disease. However, four cohort studies and numerous case-control studies have attempted to determine whether there are any associations between energy intake and colorectal cancer risk.

Of four cohort studies, two carried out in the USA found no relationship between total energy intake and risk of colon cancer (Willett et al, 1990; Giovannucci et al, 1994). A cohort study in the Netherlands reported that higher levels of total energy intake showed a protective association with colon cancer. However as the relative risks (men RR = 0.72; women RR = 0.75) were not statistically significant, it was concluded that total energy intake had little association with colon cancer risk (Goldbohm et al, 1994). One further prospective study of a cohort of Iowa (US) women found that risk of colon cancer decreased with increased energy intake. After multivariate adjusted analyses the authors reported a relative risk of 0.6 (0.4–0.9, p for trend = 0.05) (Bostick et al, 1994).

In contrast, many case-control studies that have examined total energy intake (Potter and McMichael, 1986; Lyon et al, 1987; Graham et al, 1988; Benito et al, 1990; Freudenheim et al, 1990; Gerhardsson de Verdier et al, 1990; Whittemore et al, 1990; Peters et al, 1992) have found that cases reported greater caloric intake than controls, suggesting an association between high energy intake and increased risk of colorectal cancer. This is somewhat puzzling because the evidence has strongly indicated a protective association with physical activity, which should lead us to expect reduced food intake among those who subsequently develop

colon cancer. It has subsequently been suggested that a methodological bias, due to some combination of selective participation or recall of past diet, has affected the relationship with energy intake in many of the case-control studies.

A large US multicentred case-control study noted an increase in risk associated with high energy intake, only at lower levels of lifetime vigorous physical activity and higher body mass. The association was seen almost exclusively in men (Slattery et al, 1997). (See below under High Body Mass and Physical Activity).

It is possible that total energy intake has no simple relationship with colorectal cancer risk, but its effect may be dependent on levels of obesity and physical activity. Whatever the reason, the data on energy intake and colorectal cancer are inconsistent; no judgement is possible.

Meal frequency

An association was first proposed between frequency of food intake and risk of colon cancer, in an Australian case-control study (Potter and McMichael, 1986). Eating increases the flow of bile acids, which are suspected to be carcinogenic to the colon, and triggers the gastroileal reflex, allowing digesta to enter the right colon. These effects make it plausible that meal frequency may be a risk factor for colorectal cancer. Subsequently, four case-control studies (LaVecchia et al, 1988; Young and Wolf, 1988; Benito et al, 1990; Gerhardsson de Verdier and Longnecker, 1992) have shown a small increase in risk (10 to 20%) associated with each daily eating occasion.

Frequent eating possibly increases the risk of colorectal cancer.

Adult height

Four cohort studies have found an increased risk in association with greater stature and colon cancer (Albanes et al, 1988; Chute et al, 1991; Bostick et al, 1994; Giovannucci et al, 1995). One study of a cohort of Iowa women (USA) found that taller women were at weakly increased risk of colon cancer (multivariate RR for highest versus lowest quintile of height = 1.23; p for trend < 0.05) (Bostick et al, 1994). Stronger associations between height and colon cancer were observed in the NHANES cohort in the USA. Men in the uppermost quantile for height had a relative risk of 2.1 (1.0–4.5) when compared with men in the lowest quantile. Taller women were also at a somewhat increased risk of colon cancer with a relative risk of 1.6 (0.8-3.0) (Albanes et al, 1988).

A prospective study of registered nurses in the USA also found that women in the tallest height category (greater than or equal to 168cm) were at significantly greater risk (RR = 1.6) of colon cancer than shorter women (Chute et al, 1991). In another cohort in the USA, men who were at least 73 inches tall were found to be at increased risk of colon cancer (multivariate adjusted RR 1.8, 1.1–2.7) when compared with men who were shorter than 68 inches (Giovannucci et al, 1995).

In contrast, the case-control studies have found no association between height and colorectal cancer (Dales et al, 1979; Jain et al, 1980; Young and Wolf, 1988; Peters et al, 1989).

It has been hypothesised that caloric restriction during childhood may reduce cell proliferation, thereby reducing cell number and organ size, or inhibiting early tumour events (Albanes et al, 1988). It has also been suggested that taller people simply have longer colons and therefore more cells at risk (Bostick et al, 1994).

Being tall as an adult possibly increases the risk of colorectal cancer.

High body mass

It has been suggested that people with excess body weight are at higher risk of colorectal cancer (Albanes and Taylor, 1990), but the data are not consistent.

Three cohort (Garland et al, 1985; Phillips and Snowdon, 1985; Nomura et al, 1985) and eight case-control studies (Graham et al, 1978; Wu et al, 1987; Peters et al, 1989; West et al, 1989; Benito et al, 1990; Gerhardsson de Verdier et al, 1990; Whittemore et al, 1990; Le Marchand et al, 1994) have found that men who are in the highest quantile for body size and who, thus, are likely to have a body mass index (BMI) classifiable as obese, are at as much as a twofold increased risk of colon cancer. However,one cohort (Thun et al, 1992) and four case control studies (Bjelke, 1973; Dales et al, 1979; Berry et al, 1986; Kune et al, 1990) in men have shown no association between BMI and colon cancer risk.

Data for women have been more inconsistent. Two cohort studies have reported no association between BMI and risk of colorectal cancer (Wu et al, 1987; Chute et al, 1991). However, another study of a cohort of Iowa women found that subjects who were in the uppermost quintile for BMI had a multivariate adjusted RR of 1.4 (p < 0.05) when compared with those in the lowest quintile (Bostick et al, 1994). Several case-control studies have also been suggestive of increased risk for women with increased body size. One case-control study in Stockholm reported that women who were in the uppermost quantile for body mass had weakly increased risks for cancers of the right colon and left colon but there was no association between BMI and rectal cancer (Gerhardsson de Verdier et al, 1990). One case-control study compared the colorectal-cancer risks associated with increased body size in Chinese women living in the USA and in China. Heavier Chinese women living in the USA had a weak increase in colon-cancer risk when compared to women who had lower BMI (< 20); however Chinese women living in China showed no association between BMI and risk of colon cancer (Whittemore et al, 1990). No associations were apparent for BMI and rectal cancer in the latter study. A further case-control study in the USA also found no association between BMI and rectal cancer risk (Freudenheim et al, 1990).

A large US multicentred case-control study (approximately 2000 cases and 2400 controls) noted that, while BMI was not associated with risk at higher levels of lifetime vigorous physical activity, at lower levels of such activity, risk appeared to be related both to total energy intake and BMI. The OR for those who were least active, had the highest energy intake and the highest body mass was 3.4 (2.1–5.4) compared with the opposite extreme. The association was explained by the findings for men, in whom the OR for a comparison of the extremes was 7.2 (3.4–5.2), (Slattery et al, 1997). There was little association in women.

Body fat distribution, expressed using waist-to-hip ratio (WHR), has been examined for its association with colon cancer in women in one US cohort study and no substantial association was found (Bostick et al, 1994). However in another cohort of US men, a larger WHR (> 0.99) was strongly associated with increased risk of colon cancer (RR = 3.4, 1.5–7.7; p = 0.01) even when adjusted for age, physical activity and total energy intake (Giovannucci et al, 1995).

The evidence suggests that obesity possibly increases risk of colon cancer, particularly in men, but perhaps not rectal cancer

Physical activity

Physical activity has consistently been associated with decreased risk of colon cancer in studies that have concentrated on occupational activity, leisure activity and total activity (Tables 4.10.1 and 4.10.2). Of nine prospective cohort studies (Gerhardsson de Verdier et al, 1986, 1988; Paffenbarger et al, 1987; Wu et al, 1987; Severson et al, 1989; Ballard-Barbash et al, 1990; Lee et al, 1991; Bostick et al, 1994; Giovannucci et al, 1995) only two (Bostick et al, 1994; Paffenbarger et al, 1987) have reported no substantial association between activity levels and risk of colon cancer.

Data from case-control studies are also strongly suggestive of a protective association with physical activity in both sexes. Of eleven studies (Garabrant et al, 1984; Vena et al, 1985; Slattery et al, 1988; Fredriksson et al, 1989; Gerhardsson de Verdier et al, 1990; Kato et al, 1990; Kune et al, 1990; Slattery et al, 1990; Whittemore et al, 1990; Brownson et al, 1991) only one, carried out in Australia, noted increased risks of colon cancer with higher total activity levels (Kune et al, 1990); the remainder all showed protective associations.

Occupational studies have largely examined usual lifetime occupation, while most other studies have examined activity levels two to three years prior to diagnosis. The period of life at which physical activity may have its greatest impact is not established, although some data exist. Marcus et al (1994) reported that physical activity during early adulthood (ages 14–22) was not associated with the risk of colon cancer. Lee et al (1991) showed that individuals who reported high levels of activity throughout their lives were at the lowest risk for developing colon cancer, whereas those who reported high levels of activity more recently were less

TABLE 4.10.1 PHYSICAL ACTIVITY AND COLORECTAL CANCER: COHORT STUDIES

AUTHOR, YEAR AND PLACE	SIZE OF COHORT; NO. OF CASES	SITE	EXPOSURE	COMPARISON	RELATIVE RISK (95% CONFIDENCE INTERVAL)	ADJUSTMENT SEX/AGE	OTHER VARIABLES
Gerhardson et al 1986, Sweden	1.1 million: 5,100	caecum and ascending	job activity	sedentary occupation vs active	1.5 (1.2–1.8)	Y	Y
		transverse and flexure	job activity	sedentary occupation vs active	1.6 (1.2–2.1)		
		descending	job activity	sedentary occupation vs active	1.3 (0.9–1.9)		
		sigmoid	job activity	sedentary occupation vs active	1.2 (1.0–1.4)		
Paffenberger et al 1987, USA	3,686: 21 deaths	colorectal	job activity	men light vs heavy work	0.85 (na)	Y	N
Wu et al, 1987 USA	11,888: 124	colorectal	physical activity	men > 2 hr/day vs < 1 hr/day	0.4 (0.2–0.8)	Y	N
		colorectal	physical activity	women > 2 hr/day vs < 1 hr/day	0.9 (0.5–1.6)	Y	N
Gerhardson et al 1988, Sweden	16,477: 53	colon	activity	sedentary occupation vs active	1.6 (0.8–2.9)	Y	N
		colon	activity	light/no recreational activity vs high recreational activity	1.6 (1.0–2.7)	Y	N
		colon	activity	totally sedentary lifestyle vs active lifestyle	3.6 (1.3–9.8)	Y	N
Severson et al 1989, Japan	8,006: 192 colon	colon	physical activity	men h vs l tertile	0.71 (0.5–0.99)	Y	Y
	95 rectum	rectum	physical activity	h vs l tertile	1.41 (0.84–2.36)	Y	Y
		ascending colon	physical activity	h vs l tertile	0.61 (0.31–1.21)		
		transverse and descending	physical activity	h vs l tertile	0.49 (0.20–1.22)		
		sigmoid	physical activity	h vs l tertile	0.79 (0.52–1.22)		
Ballard-Barbash et al, 1990, USA	1,906 men :73	colorectal	physical activity index	men l vs h tertile	1.8 (1.0–3.2)	Y	N
	2,308 women: 99	colorectal	physical activity index	women l vs h tertile	1.1 (0.6–1.8)		
Lee et al, 1991 USA	17,148: 225 colon	colon	physical activity index	highly active vs inactive	0.85 (0.64–1.12)	Y	N
	44 rectum	rectum	physical activity index	highly active vs inactive	1.43 (0.78–2.6)		
Bostick et al, 1994 Iowa, USA	35,215 women: 212	colon	general lifestyle	vigorous activity vs low activity	0.95 (0.68–1.39)	Y	N
Giovannucci et al 1995, USA	47,723: 203	colon	METs	h vs l quintile	0.53 (0.32–0.88)	Y	N

well protected. Studies of those who were in sedentary jobs for a larger part of their working life also indicate the importance of lifetime activity (Vena et al, 1985). Lifetime vigorous activity was also the best predictor in a large multicentred US study (Slattery et al, 1997).

Findings for specific associations with the various subsites are inconsistent (Gerhardsson de Verdier et al, 1986, 1990; Severson et al, 1989; Kato et al, 1990) but hint that the association may be stronger for distal colon tumours. Studies that have examined dietary intake and body size, as well as physical activity, have found that neither confounds the association with physical activity (Slattery et al, 1988; Gerhardsson de Verdier et al, 1990; Whittemore et al, 1990). However, as noted above, there is evidence that these factors may interact in a complex fashion such that the highest risk, particularly among men, is seen for those with the lowest physical activity, highest energy intake and highest body mass (Slattery et al, 1997).

There are several mechanisms by which physical activity may reduce the risk of colon cancer. One hypothesis is that physical activity stimulates colon peristalsis, thereby decreasing the time that dietary factors, endogenous secre-

tions such as bile acids, and carcinogens reside in the colon. Physical activity is also known to have favourable effects on T cells, B cells, natural killer cells and interleukin-1 levels (Simon, 1984). Furthermore, higher physical activity, especially in the presence of lower body mass, is associated with a general metabolic milieu (lower insulin, glucose and triacylglycerol levels, and possibly lower levels of other growth factors), that is less favourable to the growth of cancer in general, and perhaps colon cancer in particular (McKeown-Eyssen, 1994).

Evidence for a decreased risk of rectal cancer with increased physical activity is not as clear as that for colon cancer. Only two cohort studies have specifically examined risks for rectal cancer in association with physical activity, and both have reported that higher levels of activity are associated with weak increases in risk (Severson et al, 1989; Lee et al, 1991).

The seven case-control studies that have reported on the risk of rectal cancer have been somewhat equivocal. Four have reported no substantial association (Garabrant et al, 1984; Vena et al, 1985; Gerhardsson de Verdier et al, 1990; Brownson et al, 1991). A case-control study in Japan

TABLE 4.10.2 PHYSICAL ACTIVITY AND COLORECTAL CANCER: CASE-CONTROL STUDIES

AUTHOR, YEAR AND PLACE	NO. OF CASES	SITE	EXPOSURE	COMPARISON	ODDS RATIO (95% CONFIDENCE INTERVAL)	ADJUSTMENT SEX/AGE	OTHER VARIABLES
Garabrandt et al 1984	2,950 cases	colon	occupational activity	sedentary vs highly active	1.6†† (1.3–1.8)	Y	N
		rectum	occupational activity	sedentary vs highly active	0.9 (0.7–1.1)		
Veira et al, 1985 USA	210 colon cases	colon	occupational activity	> 20 years in sedentary work vs 0 years in sedentary work	2.05†† (na)	Y	N
	276 rectum cases	rectum	occupational activity	> 20 years in sedentary work vs 0 years in sedentary work	1.18 (na)		
Slattery et al 1988, USA	229	colon	total activity	men h vs l quartile	0.70 (0.38–1.29)	Y	Y
			intense	h vs l third	0.27 (0.11–0.65)	Y	Y
			non intense	h vs l quartile	1.25 (0.68–2.29)	Y	Y
			total activity	women h vs l quartile	0.48 (0.27–0.87)	Y	Y
			intense	any vs none	0.55 (0.23–1.34)	Y	Y
			non intense	h vs l quartile	0.53 (0.29–0.95)	Y	Y
Fredriksson et al 1989, Sweden	329 cases	appendix, caecum and ascending	physical activity	physical occupation vs sedentary	1.22 (0.63–2.4)		
		flexure	physical activity	physical occupation vs sedentary	0.66 (0.28–1.6)		
		descending and sigmoid	physical activity	physical occupation vs sedentary	0.49 (0.25–0.93)		
Kato et al, 1990 Japan	1,716 colon	colon	occupational activity	low vs high	1.9† (1.58–2.23)	Y	N
	1,611 rectum	rectum	occupational activity	low vs high	1.4† (1.17–1.62)	Y	N
Slattery et al 1990, Utah, USA	112	colon (men)	total activity	high vs low	0.7 (0.4–1.4)[b]	Y	Y
		colon (men)	occupational activity	intense vs light	0.6 (0.3–1.4)[b]		
	119	colon (women)	total activity	high vs low	0.5 (0.3–0.9)[b]		
		colon (women)	occupational activity	moderate vs light	1.5 (0.9–2.6)[b]		
Whittemore et al 1990, US and China	905	colon (US men)	sedentary vs active lifestyle	1 hr/day vs ≥ 5 hr/day vigorous	1.6 (1.1–2.4)		
		rectum (US men)	sedentary vs active lifestyle	1 hr/day vs ≥ 5 hr/day vigorous	1.5 (0.9–2.5)		
		colon (PRC men)	sedentary vs active lifestyle	1 hr/day vs ≥ 5 hr/day vigorous	0.85 (0.4–1.9)		
		rectum (PRC men)	sedentary vs active lifestyle	1 hr/day vs ≥ 5 hr/day vigorous	0.7 (0.3–1.6)		
		colon (US women)	sedentary vs active lifestyle	1 hr/day vs ≥ 5 hr/day vigorous	2.0†† (1.2–3.3)		
		rectum (US women)	sedentary vs active lifestyle	1 hr/day vs ≥ 5 hr/day vigorous	1.9 (1.0–3.6)		
		colon (PRC women)	sedentary vs active lifestyle	1 hr/day vs ≥ 5 hr/day vigorous	2.5 (1.0–6.3)		
		rectum (PRC women)	sedentary vs active lifestyle	1 hr/day vs ≥ 5 hr/day vigorous	0.7 (0.3–1.4)		
Brownson et al 1991, USA	1,838 colon cases	colon	occupational activity	low vs high	1.2* (1.0–1.5)	Y	Y
	812 rectum cases	rectum	occupational activity	low vs high	1.2 (0.8–1.7)		
Gerhardsson de Verdier et al, 1990 Sweden	352	colon	total activity	sedentary vs very active	1.8 (1.0–3.4)	Y	Y
		rectum	total activity	sedentary vs very active	0.9 (0.4–1.8)		
Kune et al, 1990 Australia	715	colorectal (men)	total activity	very active vs mostly sedentary	1.5 (0.9–2.7)	Y	Y
		rectum (men)	total activity	very active vs mostly sedentary	1.6 (0.8–3.2)	Y	Y
		colorectal (women)	total activity	very active vs mostly sedentary	0.9 (0.3–2.8)	Y	Y
		rectum (women)	total activity	very active vs mostly sedentary	1.9 (0.5–6.6)	Y	Y

*   p ≤ 0.05 for trend or highest vs lowest comparison

reported that lower levels of occupational activity were associated with a weak increase in the risk of rectal cancer (Kato et al, 1990) whereas a study in Australia found higher levels of total activity to be associated with moderate increases in the risk of rectal cancer (Kune et al, 1990). Furthermore, one study (Whittemore et al, 1990) that examined the risks of rectal cancer in Chinese men and women living in the USA and in China found that sedentary men in the USA had an increased risk of rectal cancer (OR=1.5, 0.9–2.5), whereas sedentary men in China had a decreased risk (OR=0.7, 0.3–1.6). The same pattern was apparent for women.

The evidence that physical activity, especially when lifelong, decreases the risk of colon cancer, is convincing.

However, the evidence relating to physical activity and the risk of rectal cancer is more limited and inconsistent; no judgement is possible.

4.10.1.2 Carbohydrate

Starch

One cohort study in a male population in the USA found that high carbohydrate intake was associated with a lower risk of colorectal adenomas (Giovannucci et al, 1992).

Higher polysaccharide intake was associated with a statistically significantly decreased risk of colon and rectal cancer in a Belgian case-control study, with an energy-adjusted odds ratio of around 0.6 (Tuyns et al, 1987). Most case-control studies, however, report no significant associations between colorectal cancer and intakes of starch (Haenszel et al, 1980; Slattery et al, 1988; Zaridze et al, 1993) or polysaccharides (Macquart-Moulin et al, 1986), with odds ratios between 0.8 and 1.2 for highest consumption levels.

Among studies of colorectal adenomas, four case-control studies have reported that high carbohydrate intake shows a protective association with colorectal adenomas (Hoff et al, 1986; Macquart-Moulin et al, 1987; Neugut et al, 1993; Sandler et al, 1993), although two of these found that the relationship was evident among women but not men (Neugut et al, 1993; Sandler et al, 1993). These relationships cannot, however, be assumed to reflect starch intake. Starch is the predominant carbohydrate in the diet, but sugars (and sometimes non-starch polysaccharides) are also classified as carbohydrates and may be independently associated with risk. Where it has been examined separately, however, intake of sugars appears to be associated with an increased risk of colorectal tumours (see below).

A correlational study which examined food intakes reported by individuals, rather than food balance sheet data, found a strong correlation (r = –0.7 to –0.8) between higher starch intakes and a decreased risk of both colon and rectal cancer in 12 countries; the relationship remained statistically significant after adjustment for fat and protein intakes (Cassidy et al, 1994).

In animal experimental studies, high-starch diets have been shown to reduce colonic cell proliferation (Caderni et

al, 1993), and inhibit the development of aberrant crypt foci and tumours (Caderni et al, 1991; 1994). These studies present interpretive difficulties, as the starch was fed in comparison to sucrose (Stamp et al, 1993). Further studies have demonstrated that the feeding of non-digestible, but fermentable, carbohydrates such as cereal bran or resistant starch, to rodents can result in reduced cellular proliferation and tumour development (Caderni et al, 1991; Boffa et al, 1992; Lupton and Kurtz, 1993; McIntyre et al, 1993), although this is not always true (Jacobs, 1987).

Evidence on diets high in starch and the risk of colorectal cancer is rather inconsistent. Several explanations can be postulated for this. For example, it may be that refined starchy foods (and sugars) increase risk by elevating plasma glucose and insulin levels. Insulin has recently been hypothesised to be related to colorectal cancer (McKeown-Eyssen, 1994; Giovannucci, 1995).

In contrast, some kinds of starch have been proposed as a protective component. Resistant starch was identified and characterised in the mid 1980s, but food-composition data on this constituent are currently incomplete. For this reason, epidemiological studies have yet to investigate resistant-starch intake in relation to cancer incidence. Resistant starch has, however, been proposed to have a protective role in colorectal cancer, primarily through its fermentation in the large bowel (Cummings and Bingham, 1987). There is evidence that fermentation of resistant starch produces butyrate (Englyst et al, 1987; Scheppach et al, 1988; Weaver et al, 1992), a short-chain fatty acid which may be a normal fuel for the colonic epithelium, and which inhibits the growth of colon cancer cell lines (Whitehead et al, 1986; Heerdt et al, 1994; Velazquez et al, 1996), perhaps by inducing apoptosis (Hague et al, 1995).

Human studies have established that a high resistant-starch intake has a number of potentially beneficial effects, including increased short-chain fatty acid and butyrate production, reduced faecal pH, increased faecal bile-acid excretion, reduced faecal cytotoxicity and reduced rectal proliferation; in contrast to wheat bran, however, it has only a modest faecal bulking and no effect on whole gut transit time (van Munster et al, 1994a, 1994b; Phillips et al, 1995; Cummings et al, 1996). Reflecting its lower digestibility in the small intestine, resistant starch also reduces plasma glucose, triacylglycerol and insulin levels, in comparison to readily digestible starch, in humans (Behall et al, 1989; Bornet et al, 1989; Raben et al, 1994) and animals (Morand et al, 1992; De Deckere et al, 1995).

In animals, resistant starch reduces aberrant crypt foci (Thorup et al, 1995) and adenomas, although not of tumours (Caderni et al, 1994) in comparisons with sucrose. In comparison to either a basic or a wheat-bran supplemented diet, however, raw potato starch has been shown to increase colonic proliferation as well as aberrant crypt foci and tumour formation (Young et al, 1996). Another study showed no effect on tumour incidence with a moderate or high resistant-starch diet (Sakamoto et al, 1996).

Consideration of the comparison diets in the animal studies may provide some explanation for these conflicting findings, and may suggest that the effects of resistant starch on colorectal cancer in experimental animals may be intermediate between the tumour-protection associated with wheat bran or cellulose and the tumour-promotion of sucrose. There is also evidence that the effects of resistant starch on experimental colorectal cancer could be similar to that of fermentable soluble fibres, which have been found to increase tumour incidence in rats (McIntyre et al,1994). Even so, the findings from these animal studies are difficult to interpret and of uncertain relevance.

While the data on cancer are inconsistent, the data on adenomas are less equivocal. Diets high in starch possibly decrease the risk of colorectal cancer.

Given that some of the inconsistency of the data arises from refined versus unrefined starch, any protective effect is more likely if starchy diets are relatively unrefined.

Notwithstanding the current lack of epidemiological evidence, there is some suggestion that diets high in resistant starch may reduce the risk of colorectal cancer but, currently, the evidence is insufficient.

Extrinsic sugars

Cleave originally proposed that refined sugars may increase a number of diseases of modern societies, but most research arising from this hypothesis has focused on the complementary notion that wholegrain, unrefined carbohydrates or dietary fibre were protective (Burkitt, 1969). Until recently, there has been comparatively little investigation into the possibility that extrinsic sugars increase the risk of any cancer.

One cohort study of women in the USA reported, after multivariate adjustment, a statistically significant relative risk for colon cancer (RR=2.0, 1.2–3.3), for highest versus lowest quintile of intake of non-dairy sucrose-containing foods (Bostick et al, 1994). In this study however, the associations for total sucrose-containing foods and sucrose as a macronutrient ranged between 1.2 and 1.8 and did not reach statistical significance (Table 4.10.3).

Eight case-control studies have shown that diets comparatively high in refined sucrose or sucrose-containing foods are associated with increased risk of colorectal cancer, with odds ratios between 1.3 and 3.6 (Miller et al, 1983; Pickle et al, 1984; Bristol et al, 1985; Tuyns et al, 1988; Benito et al, 1990; Bidoli et al, 1992; La Vecchia et al, 1993; Centonze et al, 1994). A further two studies reported an increased risk of adenomatous polyps (Macquart-Moulin et al, 1987; Benito et al, 1993). Five of these studies reported statistically significant associations (Bristol et al, 1985; Macquart-Moulin et al, 1987; Tuyns et al, 1988; La Vecchia et al, 1993; Centonze et al, 1994). Four further studies found no, or weak, associations between sucrose intake and colorectal cancer with ORs between 1.0 and 1.3 (Manousos et al, 1983; Macquart-Moulin et al, 1986; La Vecchia et al, 1988; Peters et al, 1992) (Table 4.10.4).

Most of the studies provide data on cancers of the colon and rectum combined, and there is evidence from several studies that sucrose intake may be associated with increased risk at both these sites (Tuyns et al, 1988; La Vecchia et al, 1993).

Seven studies have assessed, and adjusted for, calorie intake. Of these, five have reported a significantly increased risk associated with intake of sucrose (Macquart-Moulin et al, 1987; La Vecchia et al, 1993; Bostick et al, 1994; Centonze et al, 1994) or mono- and di-saccharide (Tuyns et al, 1987), while two have found no association (Macquart-Moulin et al, 1986; Peters et al, 1992).

Other factors also need consideration. In particular, individuals with high sucrose or sugar intakes (proportional to energy intake) tend to have lower intakes of a number of foods or dietary constituents which have probable or possible protective roles in colorectal cancer. These include vegetables, fruits, cereals, fibre, folate, carotenoids and other antioxidants (Baghurst et al, 1992; Bolton Smith and Woodward, 1995). Associations observed between sucrose intake and colorectal cancer could therefore, at least partly, be accounted for by low intake of such protective dietary constituents. Only one study has addressed this particular concern (Centonze et al, 1994) and reported a significantly increased risk of colorectal cancer, even after controlling for the intake of cereals, dairy products, vegetables, coffee and

TABLE 4.10.3 SUCROSE OR SUGAR INTAKE AND THE RISK OF COLON CANCER: COHORT STUDY

AUTHOR, YEAR AND PLACE	SIZE OF COHORT; NO. OF CASES	TYPE OF SUGAR	COMPARISON	RELATIVE RISK (95% CONFIDENCE INTERVAL)	SEX/AGE	ADJUSTMENT OTHER VARIABLES[a]	ENERGY INTAKE
Bostick et al,1994 USA	35,004: 212	Sucrose-containing foods	> 20.5/week vs < 5.5/week	1.74 (1.06–2.87)	Y	Y	Y
		Non-dairy sucrose-containing foods	> 20.5/week vs < 5.5/week	2.00* (1.21–3.30)	Y	Y	Y

* p ≤ 0.05 for trend or highest vs lowest comparison
a Also adjusted for the following: education, area of socio-economic status, ethnicity, body weight, smoking status, family history

TABLE 4.10.4 SUCROSE OR SUGAR INTAKE AND THE RISK OF RECTUM CANCER: CASE-CONTROL STUDIES

AUTHOR, YEAR	NO. OF CASES	SITE	TYPE OF SUGAR	COMPARISON	ODDS RATIO (95% CONFIDENCE INTERVAL)	SEX/AGE	ADJUSTMENT OTHER VARIABLES[a]	ENERGY INTAKE
Manousos et al 1983	100	colorectal	sugars and syrups	h vs l quartile of intake	nr[b] (nr)	Y	N	N
Miller et al, 1983	171 men	colon	sugar	> 17.7 vs < 17.7 g/day	1.4 (nr)	Y[c]	N	N
	177 women	colon	sugar	> 17.7 vs < 17.7 g/day	1.3 (nr)	Y[c]	N	N
	194	rectum	sugar	> 17.7 vs < 17.7 g/day	1.3 (nr)	Y[c]	N	N
Pickle et al, 1984	58	colon	sweets	above vs below 8.5 servings/week	1.4 (nr)	Y	Y	N
	28	rectum	sweets	above vs below 8.5 servings/week	1.6 (nr)	Y	Y	N
Bristol et al, 1985	50	colorectal	sugars depleted in fibre	> 99 g/day vs < 57 g/day	3.6* (1.2–10.9)	Y	Y	N
Macquart-Moulin et al, 1986	399	colorectal	sugar, honey, jam, jelly	h vs l quartile of intake	1.28 (nr)	Y	Y	Y
Macquart-Moulin et al, 1987	252	colorectal (polyps)	sugar and sweets	> 42.9 g/day vs < 14.3 g/day	1.98* (nr)	Y	Y	Y
La Vecchia et al 1988	339	colon	sugar	h vs l tertile of intake	1.22 (nr)	Y	N	N
	236	rectum	sugar	h vs l tertile of intake	0.51 (nr)	Y	N	N
Tuyns et al, 1988	435	colon	sugar	> 175 g/week vs 0 g/week	2.31* (nr)	Y	Y	N
	368	rectum	sugar	> 175 g/week vs	2.73* (nr)	Y	Y	N
Benito et al, 1990	286	colorectal	sugar, jam, honey	> 60/month vs 0/month	1.64 (nr)	Y	Y	N
Bidoli et al, 1992	123	colon	sugar	h vs l tertile of intake	1.6 (nr)	Y	Y	N
	125	rectum	sugar	h vs l tertile of intake	1.6 (nr)	Y	Y	N
Peters et al, 1992	123	colorectal		per 100 Kcal	1.0	Y	Y	N
La Vecchia et al 1993	953	colon	sugar added to hot beverages	≥ 3 teaspoons/cup vs none	2.0* (1.4–2.9)	Y	Y	Y
	633	rectum	sugar added to hot beverages	≥ 3 teaspoons/cup vs none	1.4* (0.9–2.1)	Y	Y	Y
Centonze et al 1994	119	colorectal	sugar and syrups	> 26 g/day vs < 7 g/day	2.75* (1.26–5.97)	Y	Y	N[d]

*   p ≤ 0.05 for trend or highest vs lowest consumption
nr   not reported
ns   not significant
a   Also adjusted for one or more of the following: education, area of residence, socio-economic status, ethnicity, body weight, smoking status, family history
b   Statistically significant heterogeneity but no significant trend
c   Adjusted also for saturated fat intake
d   Adjusted for intake of major food groups

wine. In this study, the ORs were 1.4 and 2.8 for the second and third tertile of consumption of foods containing refined sugars and syrups, which included sugar, sweet spreads, canned fruit and confectionery.

Fat and alcohol intake also vary inversely with sucrose consumption (Gibney et al, 1987; Baghurst et al, 1992; Lewis et al, 1992; Baghurst et al, 1994) and both these dietary components may be associated with increased risk of colorectal cancer. Such a relationship would inversely confound an association between sucrose intake and colorectal cancer, thus potentially strengthening the interpretation that the relationship with sugar is real. However, this cannot be verified using the currently published studies. Sucrose intake is also difficult to measure reliably and is prone to underreporting, particularly by overweight or obese individuals (Bingham and Nelson, 1991). As with fat and alcohol however, because obesity is possibly associated with increased risk for colorectal cancer, such recall bias would be more likely to obscure, rather than spuriously strengthen, any

association with sucrose intake.

Fructose was unrelated to the risk of colon cancer in a cohort study (Bostick et al, 1994). Such a finding may, however, reflect the fact that fructose is found mainly in fresh fruit and this group of foods contains a number of potentially protective constituents. Increased colorectal cancer risk has, nonetheless, been associated with consumption of dried fruit (Centonze et al, 1994), which raises the possibility that high intakes of sucrose or other sugars present naturally in foods may also be associated with increased risk with colorectal cancer.

Fructose, but not glucose, increased colon proliferation and the production of aberrant crypt foci in a similar fashion to sucrose in azoxymethane-treated mice (Stamp et al, 1993). Two other studies however, reported that fructose and glucose were both associated with lower colon proliferation than sucrose in rats (Caderni et al, 1996).

Several mechanisms have been postulated to explain the effects of sucrose consumption. When compared with other simple sugars or starch, sucrose is typically associated with greater colon proliferation as well as a greater number, or larger, aberrant crypt foci, adenomas or carcinomas in rodents treated with experimental carcinogens (Caderni et al, 1991, 1993, 1994; Stamp et al, 1993; Kristiansen et al, 1995; Luceri et al, 1996a). Only one study has reported that sucrose has no effect on such markers (Thorup et al, 1995).

The effect appears greater when sucrose is fed as a bolus rather than continuously (Caderni et al, 1996; Luceri et al, 1996a), which suggests that sugar may be affecting blood levels of glucose and/or triglycerides. These either directly or through hormones such as insulin, may influence colon proliferation and cancer development (Bruce et al, 1993; Stamp et al, 1993; McKeown-Eyssen, 1994; Giovannucci, 1995). Such a mechanism has yet to be investigated directly but is supported by a number of observations including associations between high blood levels of glucose or triglycerides and increased risk of colon cancer (as reviewed in McKeown-Eyssen, 1994 and Giovannucci, 1995). If such a mechanism is relevant, then the association may not be confined to refined sugars, but may extend also to other carbohydrates which produce large glycaemic responses, such as rapidly digestible starches. The findings from a number of early animal experimental studies that compared starch with sucrose were initially interpreted as evidence for a protective role of starch (Caderni et al, 1991, 1993, 1994) although, as noted by the authors and demonstrated in a later study (Luceri et al, 1996a), they could also reflect a deleterious effect of sucrose.

The second possible mechanism has arisen from findings that a diet containing cooked sucrose, in comparison to raw sucrose, promotes the formation of aberrant crypt foci in azoxymethane-induced rodents (Corpet et al, 1990). This has since been attributed to a thermolysis product of sucrose — 5-hydroxymethyl-2-furaldehyde (HMF) – which has been shown to be both an initiator and promoter of aberrant crypt foci in rodents (Archer et al, 1992; Zhang et al, 1993).

Lastly, diets high in refined sugar have been shown to be associated with slower gut transit times and faecal total and secondary bile excretion (Kruis et al, 1991) in humans.

Diets high in extrinsic (refined) sugars possibly increase risk of colo-rectal cancer. The evidence is strongest for sucrose.

Non-starch polysaccharide/ fibre

A role for dietary fibre in colon carcinogenesis was first proposed by Burkitt (1969) following the clinical observation that colon cancer was rare in Africans whose diet was high in unrefined foods. However, a belief in the beneficial effects of fibre can be traced back to the sixteenth century (Stubs, 1585).

Data from prospective studies is, at best, weakly supportive of the fibre hypothesis, with studies finding either no association (Willett et al, 1990; Giovannucci et al, 1994) or a weak protective association (Heilbrun et al, 1989; Steinmetz et al, 1994). It is notable that only one of the prospective studies (Heilbrun et al, 1989) provided data on

risks associated with rectal cancer; there was little evidence of an association with dietary fibre.

A combined analysis of 13 case-control studies provided evidence for a linear reduction in colorectal cancer risk with increasing intake of dietary fibre with odds ratios of 1.0, 0.8, 0.7, 0.6, 0.5 for each quintile of consumption from lowest to highest (p for trend <0.0001) (Howe et al, 1992). Similar findings have also been reported for a meta-analysis of 16 case-control studies, with an odds ratio of 0.6 for highest versus lowest intake of fibre (Trock et al, 1990).

Studies of colorectal adenomas are generally supportive of a protective association with dietary fibre. Intake of fibre from vegetables and cereals has been associated with a clear reduction in risk for colorectal adenomas in a prospective study, with a relative risk of 0.4 (0.2–0.6) for the highest versus the lowest quintile of total dietary fibre intake (Giovannucci et al, 1992). Other studies, using a case-control design, have found protective associations with total fibre (Neugut et al, 1993; Olsen et al, 1994; Almendingen et al, 1995; Martinez et al, 1996), fibre from cereals (Little et al, 1993) or fibre from vegetables and fruits (Benito et al, 1993; Sandler et al, 1993); several studies suggested that fibre is more protective in women than in men (Neugut et al, 1993; Sandler et al, 1993; McKeown Eyssen et al, 1994).

Overall, the epidemiology of fibre and colorectal cancer is somewhat inconsistent, perhaps because of the heterogeneous nature of fibre and differences in the way in which fibre is measured. Several investigators have attempted to distinguish effects by food source or type (soluble versus insoluble) of fibre. Meyer and White (1993) showed that fibre intake was different in colon cancer cases and controls but suggested that the source of this difference itself differed between the sexes – cereal fibre in men, fruit fibre in women. Benito et al (1991) found that the protective association with fibre was attributable to fibre from pulses. Freudenheim et al (1990) reported that the risk of colon cancer decreased with intake of cereal fibre for both sexes and with intake of fruit/vegetable fibre for men only. For the rectum, fruit/vegetable fibre was associated with decreased risk, whereas cereal fibre was not. Additionally, Freudenheim et al (1990) reported a greater protective association with colon cancer for insoluble cereal fibre than for soluble cereal fibre. In that study, no modification of the protective association with fruit/vegetable fibre by the soluble versus insoluble component was seen for rectal cancer. Thus, the limited data available do not clearly suggest a stronger effect for any food source or type of fibre.

In chemopreventive trials, supplements of wheat bran produced a small reduction in the incidence of rectal polyps among individuals genetically predisposed to these lesions (DeCosse et al, 1989), although they had no significant effect on the occurrence of new adenomas in individuals whose first 'sporadic' polyps had been removed (MacLennan et al, 1995).

Other human experimental trials demonstrated that wheat-bran supplementation favourably altered a number of other markers thought to be related to the risk of colorectal cancer, including faecal mutagenicity (Reddy et al, 1989), total and secondary faecal bile acid excretion (Reddy et al, 1992; Alberts et al, 1996) and rectal proliferation in high–risk individuals (Alberts et al, 1990). Although wheat bran is a rich source of fibre, it also contains other components that may contribute to colorectal cancer protection, notably phytate. Other mechanisms through which fibre may be beneficial include reduced exposure to carcinogens through dilution of the gut contents and fermentation to short-chain fatty acids.

In animal studies, insoluble fibres, such as wheat bran or cellulose, are typically associated with decreased incidence of tumours, while some soluble fibres, such as pectin, have been found to increase tumour incidence (Jacobs, 1987; Ma et al, 1996).

The particular components of a high-fibre diet that could contribute to the lowering of risk include not only the various subcategories of constituents that make up 'dietary fibre' but also other constituents of high-fibre foods – namely, vegetables, fruits, cereals, pulses and seeds. Despite this lack of clarity about which of many candidates and which of a number of mechanisms are central, the evidence suggests that diets high in fibre possibly decrease the risk of colorectal cancer.

4.10.1.3 Fat and cholesterol

Total fat

One early cohort study of colorectal cancers of Japanese men living in Hawaii (Stemmermann et al, 1984) showed decreased risk with higher intakes of total fat. This study used a single 24-hour recall to assess diet. Conversely, the great majority of the earlier case-control studies which reported specifically on fat and colorectal cancer found increased risks associated with higher intakes, with ORs ranging from 1.3–2.2 (Jain et al, 1980; Potter and McMichael, 1986; Kune et al, 1987; Lyon et al, 1987; Graham et al, 1988; Slattery et al, 1988; Gerhardsson de Verdier et al, 1990).

A number of these studies failed to adjust for total energy intake.

Of eleven studies that have attempted to distinguish the effect of fat from that of energy intake on the risk of colorectal cancer, four of the five cohort studies found no association (Bostick et al, 1994; Giovannucci et al, 1994; Goldbohm et al, 1994; Kampman et al, 1996). The other study, of US nurses (Willett et al, 1990) found that intake of total fat in the uppermost versus the lowest quintile was associated with a twofold increase in the risk for colon cancer. Results from five case-control studies that adjusted for energy intake were mixed. Three found no association between total fat intake and the risk of colorectal cancer (Tuyns et al, 1987; Benito et al, 1990; Meyer and White, 1993) while two others found statistically significant increases in risk (Freudenheim et al, 1990, rectal only; Peters et al, 1992).

Recently, Howe et al (1997) conducted a combined analysis of 13 case-control studies of colorectal cancer, involving 5,287 cases and 10,478 controls from various populations with differing cancer rates and dietary practices. There was no evidence of any increased risk with higher dietary fat after adjustment for total energy intake; the odds ratios were 0.9 (0.8–1.1), 1.1 (0.9–1.3), 0.9 (0.8–1.1), and 0.9 (0.8–1.0) for the uppermost quintiles of total, saturated, monounsaturated, and polyunsaturated fats, respectively. Further, there were no statistically significant associations for any type of fat in sub-group analyses by sex, age, or anatomic location of the cancer (right or left colon, or rectum).

Thus, recent cohort studies and the combined analysis of 13 case-control studies have failed to find clear evidence for the association of colorectal cancer with dietary fat observed in most early studies.

Three ecological studies examining mortality or incidence with per capita intakes found a high correlation between total fat and colon cancer (Drasar and Irving, 1973; Armstrong and Doll, 1975; Knox, 1977). A later analysis of mortality data identified animal fat, in particular, as the most strongly correlated factor (McKeown-Eyssen and Bright-See, 1984). In contrast, colon cancer mortality did not correlate with fat consumption by state in the USA, by region in the UK, or in temporal-trend comparisons in those two countries (Enstrom, 1975; Bingham 1979; McMichael 1979).

One case-control study in the USA reported on intake of total fat and the risk of rectal cancer (Freudenheim et al, 1990), and found a strongly increased risk of rectal cancer with increased total fat intake in men (RR=2.2,<0.01), although no association was apparent for women in the same study.

A large number of studies using a number of rodent strains and various carcinogens have shown that intestinal tumorigenesis is enhanced as the quantity of dietary fat is increased. The more enduring mechanism proposed invokes the increased excretion of bile acids in the gut, resulting from a high-fat diet, and consequent co-carcinogenic and trophic effects on the colonic epithelium (Hill and Aries, 1971). Attention has also focused on faecal mutagens in humans, (Reddy et al, 1980; Schiffman et al, 1989) and animals (Hinzman et al, 1987), with equivocal results. Alternatively, Guillem and Weinstein, (1990) have proposed that the interaction of fat, bile acids and bacteria produces excess intraluminal diacylglycerol, which may mimic and amplify cell-replication signals. Studies in experimental animals and humans have indicated that fat and fibre influence the colonic and concentrations of DAG (Pickering et al, 1995).

Taken together, the epidemiological and experimental evidence, supported by identification of mechanisms, suggests that diets high in total fat possibly increase the risk of colorectal cancer.

Saturated/animal fat

Five cohort studies have reported on saturated and/or animal fat. One early study of men of Japanese ancestry living in Hawaii, which employed 24-hour dietary recalls to estimate nutrient intake, reported that those men who consumed high levels of saturated fat had a strongly reduced risk of colon cancer but a moderately increased risk of rectal cancer (Stemmermann et al, 1984). Conversely, a much larger cohort study of women in the USA found that those with higher intakes of animal fat had a RR of 1.9 (1.1–3.2, p<0.05) for colon cancer when compared to those who consumed in the lowest quintile. Weak increases in risk were also apparent for those who were in the uppermost quintile for consumption of saturated fats (Willett et al, 1990). A weak increase in risk (RR = 1.4) for colon cancer was also reported for Dutch women who were in the uppermost quantile for saturated fat (Goldbohm et al, 1994), but no associations were apparent for males in the same study. No substantial associations between saturated and/or animal fat were apparent in another two cohort studies, with RRs ranging between 0.9 and 1.2 (Bostick et al, 1994; Giovannucci et al, 1994).

Fourteen case-control studies have examined associations between intakes of saturated and/or animal fat and the risk of colorectal cancer (Dales et al, 1979; Jain et al, 1980; Miller et al, 1983; Potter and McMichael, 1986; Tuyns et al, 1987; Lee et al, 1989; West et al, 1989; Gerhardsson de Verdier et al, 1990; Whittemore et al, 1990; Benito et al, 1991; Peters et al, 1992; Meyer and White, 1993; Sandler et al, 1993; Zaridze et al, 1993). Results from these studies are inconsistent. Six studies (Miller et al, 1983; Lee et al, 1989; Whittemore et al, 1990; Benito et al, 1991; Sandler et al, 1993; Zaridze et al, 1993) reported solely on colorectal cancer, without examining the effects for colon and rectum separately. Of these six, four found that higher intakes of saturated fat were associated with higher risks of colorectal cancer, with ORs ranging from 1.5 to 2.6 (Sandler et al, 1993; Miller et al, 1983; Whittemore et al, 1990; Zaridze et al, 1993). The other two studies found no substantial association with intakes of saturated fat (Lee et al, 1989; Benito et al, 1991).

Increases in risk were apparent with higher intakes of saturated fat in five (Dales et al, 1979; Jain et al, 1980; Potter and McMichael, 1986; West et al, 1989; Gerhardsson de Verdier et al, 1990) of nine (Tuyns et al, 1987; Lee et al, 1989; Peters et al, 1992; Meyer and White, 1993) case-control studies of colon cancer. However, the magnitude of risk estimates varied substantially between and within studies. For example, one case-control study in the USA noted an OR of 1.4 (0.8–2.7) for men who were in the uppermost quartile for saturated fats, and 1.7 (0.9–3.0) for women (West et al, 1989). In an Australian case-control study (Potter and McMichael, 1986), women in the uppermost quintile for saturated fats had a moderately increased risk of colon cancer (OR = 2.1, 0.9–4.8), whereas males in the uppermost quintile had no alteration in risk compared to men in the lowest quintile.

There are fewer studies of rectal cancer risk and saturated fat intake. Of five case-control studies (Jain et al, 1980; Potter and McMichael, 1986; Tuyns et al, 1987; Lee et al,

1989; Gerhardsson de Verdier et al, 1990), only one (Lee et al, 1989) suggested that higher saturated fat intakes may be weakly protective (OR = 0.64, 0.3–1.3). The remaining four found increased risks, with ORs ranging from 1.4 to 2.5.

In summary, 11 of the 19 studies conducted at the individual level show some element of elevated risk with higher intakes of saturated/animal fat and two show weak protective associations. Six show no association.

Diets high in saturated fat possibly increase the risk of colorectal cancer.

Monounsaturated fat

Four cohort studies have examined the risk of colorectal cancer in association with intakes of monounsaturated fatty acids (MUFA). Of these four (Willett et al, 1990; Bostick et al, 1994; Giovannucci et al, 1994; Goldbohm et al, 1994), only one (Willett et al, 1990) has reported an increased risk; women with the highest intake had a RR of 1.7 (1.0–2.9; p<0.05) compared to those in the lowest quintile. No substantial associations between MUFA intake and colorectal cancer were observed in the other three cohort studies, with RRs ranging between 0.9 and 1.3 (Bostick et al, 1994; Giovannucci et al, 1994; Goldbohm et al, 1994).

Of eight case-control studies, one USA study reported an OR of 2.1 (1.0–4.2) for higher intakes of MUFA in males and a OR of 1.3 (0.7–2.4) in females (West et al, 1989). Twofold increases in both colon and rectal cancer were observed in a Swedish case-control study (Gerhardsson de Verdier et al, 1990). Conversely, two studies, one in Russia (Zaridze et al, 1993) and one in the USA (Meyer and White, 1993), reported weakly protective associations. Four other case-control studies found no substantial associations between intakes of MUFA and the risk of colorectal cancer (Tuyns et al, 1987; Lee et al, 1989; Benito et al, 1991; Peters et al, 1992).

The evidence on monounsaturated fat and colorectal cancer is inconsistent; no judgement is possible.

Polyunsaturated fat

Three cohort studies have examined associations between polyunsaturated fat (PUFA) and the risk of colorectal cancer (Bostick et al, 1994; Giovannucci et al, 1994; Goldbohm et al, 1994). One USA cohort reported that women in the uppermost quintile for PUFA were at weakly decreased risk of colon cancer compared to those in the lowest quintile (Bostick et al, 1994). A US cohort of men reported that those in the uppermost quintile of intake had a weak decrease in risk for higher intakes after adjustment for energy (RR = 0.8, 0.5–1.2). Conversely, a study of a cohort of men and women in the Netherlands found that subjects with intakes in the uppermost quantiles had a weakly increased risk (Goldbohm et al, 1994).

Of seven case-control studies, two reported that higher levels of PUFA intake were associated with increased risk of both colon and rectal cancers (West et al, 1989; Gerhardsson de Verdier et al, 1990). A study of Singapore Chinese reported an increased risk of colon cancer with higher PUFA; and a decreased risk of rectal cancer (Lee et al, 1989). One study in Russia (Zaridze et al, 1993) reported an OR of 0.3 (0.1–0.6) for those whose intakes were in the uppermost compared to the lowest quartile. Decreased risks of colorectal cancer were apparent in a Belgian study (Tuyns et al, 1987) and a further US study found that PUFA had a protective association with colon cancer in women but no association in men (Meyer and White, 1993). One study reported no associations between PUFA intake and risk of colorectal cancer (Peters et al, 1992).

The evidence relating to diets high in PUFA and the risk of colorectal cancer is inconsistent; no judgement is possible.

Cholesterol

Two prospective cohort studies in the USA, one of men (Giovannucci et al, 1994) and the other of women (Bostick et al, 1994) have examined dietary cholesterol intake in relation to the risk of colon cancer. Neither found any association. In a combined analysis of 13 case-control studies of colorectal cancer, which involved 5,287 cases and 10,478 controls, a weak increase in risk with higher dietary cholesterol was reported; the energy-adjusted odds ratio was 1.3 (1.2–1.5) (Howe et al, 1997).

An international ecological study reported a positive correlation between cholesterol consumption and colon cancer mortality, after adjustment for consumption of fat and fibre ($r = 0.8$, $p < 0.001$) (Liu et al, 1979).

Egg consumption (see below) has been associated with the risk of colon cancer in nine of eleven epidemiological studies (statistically significant in three); and with rectal cancer in six of eight studies (statistically significant in two) (Steinmetz and Potter, 1994). Associations for eggs, which have a high cholesterol content, were generally stronger than those for cholesterol itself.

In animal studies, cholesterol-supplemented diets have been shown to promote experimentally-induced colon cancer (see Steinmetz and Potter, 1994).

The evidence suggests that dietary cholesterol may increase the risk of colorectal cancer but the overall picture is also consistent with no association; no judgement is possible.

4.10.1.4 Protein

Five cohort and 15 case-control studies have examined the relationship between protein intake and colorectal cancer risk. None of the five cohort studies found any association between intake of protein and the risk of colorectal cancer (Willett et al, 1990; Bostick et al, 1994; Giovannucci et al, 1994; Goldbohm et al, 1994; Kampman et al, 1996). All these studies adjusted for energy intake. Seven of the case-control studies found no association with the risk of colorectal cancer (Kune et al, 1987; Tuyns et al, 1987; Lee et al,

1989; Freudenheim et al, 1990; Whittemore et al, 1990; Peters et al, 1992; Meyer and White, 1993). One study found a protective association (Macquart-Moulin et al, 1986); in this study, higher intakes of animal protein showed a moderately decreased risk for colon cancer (OR = 0.53), but a statistically nonsignificant increase in risk for higher intakes of vegetable protein (OR = 1.5; ns).

Seven case-control studies found that higher total protein intakes were associated with increased risk of colon cancer (Jain et al, 1980; Potter and McMichael, 1986; Lyon et al, 1987; Slattery et al, 1988a, 1988b; Gerhardsson de Verdier et al, 1990; Benito et al, 1991). Strengths of associations have differed between studies. One case-control study in Stockholm (Sweden) reported strongly increased risk for colon (OR = 2.2) cancer in men and women combined (Gerhardsson de Verdier et al, 1990). In a case-control study in Australia, higher intakes of protein were associated with moderate to strong increases in risk for colon cancer in both men and women (Potter and McMichael, 1986). Sex differences were also apparent in a case-control study in the USA, in which the OR for men in the uppermost quintile for protein intake was 2.6 (1.3–5.37) and for women was 1.5 (0.7–3.0) (Slattery et al, 1988a) (adjusted for BMI, fibre and total activity), although the estimates were higher when adjusted additionally for calcium but not physical activity (Slattery et al, 1988b).

Benito et al (1981) found a strong direct association (OR = 2.5; p < 0.05) with colorectal cancer for men and women combined. A case-control study in Sweden (Gerhardsson de Verdier et al, 1990) reported strongly increased risk of rectal cancer for men and women combined (OR = 2.5). In ecological studies examining per capita consumption in relation to cancer mortality, protein was found to correlate strongly with the risk of colon cancer (Armstrong and Doll, 1975; IARC, 1977; Knox, 1977). The correlation was as strong as for dietary fat, as one might expect given the correlation between these two macronutrients.

The few experimental animal studies of dietary protein are consistent with a promoting effect on colon carcinogenesis (Reddy, 1992).

Dietary protein which escapes digestion and absorption in the small intestine is utilised by the gut microflora as a source of energy, nitrogen and carbon (Cummings and Macfarlane, 1991). A number of the metabolites that arise from the bacterial utilisation of protein may have a causative role in colorectal cancer. These include ammonia, a potential cancer promoter, and amines, which can be nitrosated, again by colonic bacteria, to N-nitroso compounds (Cummings et al, 1979; Macfarlane et al, 1995).

The epidemiological evidence for an association of protein with colorectal cancer is inconsistent. The data are not fully separable from data on calories and fat; no judgement is possible.

TABLE 4.10.5 ALCOHOL INTAKE AND THE RISK OF COLORECTAL CANCER: COHORT STUDIES

AUTHOR, YEAR	SIZE OF COHORT: NO. OF CASES	SITE	TYPE OF ALCOHOL/ CONSUMPTION	COMPARISON	RELATIVE RISK (95% CONFIDENCE INTERVAL)	SEX/AGE	OTHER VARIABLES[a]	ENERGY INTAKE
Garland et al 1985	2,107:49 men	colorectal	total alcohol		na			
Kono et al, 1986	5,135 men: 1,283 deaths	colorectal	total alcohol	≥ 2 g/day vs 0	1.4 (0.5–4.0)	Y	N	N
Wu et al, 1987	11,888: 126	colorectal	total alcohol	men ≥ 30 ml/day vs non-daily	2.4*	Y	N	N
				women ≥ 30 ml/day vs non-daily	1.5			
Klatsky et al 1988	106,203: 92 men 111 women	colon	total alcohol	men ≥ 3 drinks/day vs 0	1.2	Y	Y	N
				women ≥ 3 drinks/day vs 0	2.6*	Y	Y	N
	66	rectum	total alcohol	≥ 3 drinks/day vs 0	3.2	Y	Y	N
Hirayama et al 1989	265,118: 574 deaths	colon	total alcohol	men daily drinkers vs abstainers	5.42*	Y	N	N
				women drinkers vs abstainers	1.9*			
		rectum	total alcohol	men drinkers vs abstainers	1.39	Y	N	N
Stemmerman et al 1990	7,572: 211	colon	total alcohol	men ≥ 40/oz/month vs 0	1.4	Y	Y	N
	101	rectum	total alcohol	≥ 40/oz/month vs 0	1.9*	Y	Y	N
Giovannucci et al 1995	47,931: 205	colon	total alcohol	men > 2 vs < 0.25 drinks/day	2.07 (1.29–3.32)	Y	Y	Y
		proximal colon	total alcohol	high alcohol + low methionine + folate	1.95 (0.8–4.73)	Y	Y	Y
		proximal colon	total alcohol	high alcohol + low methionine + folate (non-aspirin users)	2.70 (0.88–8.34)	Y	Y	Y
		distal colon	total alcohol	high alcohol + low methionine + folate	3.88* (1.33–11.3)	Y	Y	Y
		distal colon	total alcohol	high alcohol + low methionine + folate (non-aspirin users)	7.44* (1.72–32.1	Y	Y	Y

* p ≤ 0.05 for trend or highest vs lowest consumption

a Also adjusted for one or more of the following: education, area of residence, socio-economic status, ethnicity, body weight, smoking status, family history

4.10.1.5 Alcohol

Of the six cohort studies that compared the cancer mortality of alcoholics with that of the general population (Sundby, 1967; Hakulinen et al, 1974; Monson and Lyon, 1975; Adelstein and White, 1976; Robinette et al, 1979; Schmidt and Popham, 1981), none found statistically significant associations with colon or rectal cancer (Table 4.10.5).

Of the five general population cohort studies conducted on colon cancer, four (Klatsky et al, 1988; Hirayama, 1989; Stemmermann et al, 1990; Giovannucci et al, 1995) found significant associations with alcohol intakes, as did all three cohort studies that reported on rectal cancer (Klatsky et al, 1988; Hirayama, 1989; Stemmermann et al, 1990), and two (Garland et al, 1985; Kono et al, 1986) of three cohort studies that did not distinguish between colon and rectal cancer. A particularly strong association was found in a study of Japanese adults (Hirayama, 1989), in which there was a fivefold increase in the risk of sigmoid colon cancer mortality (but no association with risk of proximal colon mortality) among men who drank alcohol daily compared to abstainers.

In a US cohort of men (Giovannucci et al, 1995), increased risk for colon cancer was seen among current drinkers and past drinkers. The association was particularly marked among, and indeed essentially confined to, those with a low intake of folate or methionine (Giovannucci et al, 1995) (Table 4.10.5)

Of eighteen case-control studies which examined the relationship between alcohol consumption and the risk of colon cancer, alcohol intake was associated with increased risk of colon cancer in nine (Wynder and Shigematsu, 1967; Williams and Horm, 1977; Pickle et al, 1984; Potter and McMichael, 1986; Tuyns et al, 1988; Longnecker, 1990; Hu et al, 1991; Peters et al, 1992; Meyer and White, 1993) as did nine of 17 studies of rectal cancer (Wynder and Shigematsu, 1967; Williams and Horm, 1977; Kabat et al, 1986; Potter and McMichael, 1986; Kune et al, 1987; Freudenheim et al, 1990; Longnecker, 1990; Choi and Kahyo, 1991; Hu et al, 1991). (Table 4.10.6)

Of the seven case-control studies on colon cancer that stratified on sex, four reported a positive association

TABLE 4.10.6 ALCOHOL INTAKE AND THE RISK OF COLORECTAL CANCER: CASE-CONTROL STUDIES

AUTHOR, YEAR	NO. OF CASES	SITE	TYPE OF ALCOHOL/ CONSUMPTION	COMPARISON	ODDS RATIO (95% CONFIDENCE INTERVAL)	SEX/AGE	ADJUSTMENT OTHER VARIABLES[A]	ENERGY INTAKE
Tuyns et al, 1982	142	colon	total alcohol	drinkers vs abstainers	1.4 (0.3–5.7)	Y	N	N
	198	rectum	total alcohol	drinkers vs abstainers	1.6 (0.5–5.5)	Y	N	N
Miller et al, 1983	348	colon	alcohol (not beer)	men ≥ 47.7 g/day vs 0	1.4 (nr)	Y	N	N[c]
		colon	alcohol (not beer)	women ≥ 47.7 g/day vs 0	1.0 (nr)			
	348	colon	beer	men ≥ 144 g/day vs 0	1.1 (nr)	Y	N	N[c]
		colon	beer	women ≥ 144 g/day vs 0	0.9 (nr)			
	194	rectum	alcohol (not beer)	men ≥ 47.7 g/day vs 0	1.3 (nr)	Y	N	N[c]
		rectum	alcohol (not beer)	women ≥ 47.7 g/day vs 0	0.8 (nr)			
	194	rectum	beer	men ≥ 144 g/day vs 0	1.1 (nr)	Y	N	N[c]
		rectum	beer	women ≥ 144 g/day vs 0	0.9 (nr)			
Pickle et al, 1984	58	colon	beer (commercial)	drinkers vs abstainers	2.7* (1.3–5.5)	Y	N	N
				men > 7/wk vs </1wk	5.3* (nr)			
		colon	wine (commercial)	> 7/wk vs </1wk	1.2 (0.3–2.3)	Y	N	N
	28	rectum	beer (commercial)	> 7/wk vs </1wk	1.4 (0.5–3.7)	Y	N	N
		rectum	wine (commercial)	> 7/wk vs </1wk	0.9 (0.3–2.3)	Y	N	N
Kabat et al, 1986	218	rectum	beer	men ≥ 32 g/day vs 0	3.5*	Y	Y	N
				women > 8 g/day vs 0	0.7	Y	Y	N
Potter & McMichael, 1986	220	colon	total alcohol	men > 12.9 g/day vs 0	1.0 (0.5–2.1)	Y	N	N
				women > 12.9 g/day vs 0	2.0 (0.9–4.5)	Y	N	N
	220	colon	beer	men glass/week	1.0 (0.99–1.01)	Y	N	N
				women glass/week	1.01 (0.95–1.06)			
	220	colon	wine	men glass/week	1.02 (0.98–1.06)	Y	N	N
				women glass/week	1.04 (0.98–1.11)			
	220	colon	spirits	men glass/week	1.08* (1.03–1.13)	Y	N	N
				women glass/week	1.13* (1.01–1.27)			
	199	rectum	total alcohol	men > 12.9 g/day vs 0	0.7 (0.4–1.5)	Y	N	N
				women > 12.9 g/day vs 0	1.5 (0.6–3.7)	Y	N	N
	199	rectum	beer	men glass/week	1.0 (0.98–1.01)	Y	N	N
				women glass/week	0.97 (0.92–1.03)			
	199	rectum	wine	men glass/week	0.98 (0.95–1.01)	Y	N	N
				women glass/week	1.11* (1.02–1.22)			
	199	rectum	spirits	men glass/week	1.04* (1.00–1.09)	Y	N	N
				women glass/week	1.05 (0.94–1.17)			
Kune et al, 1987	715	colorectal	total alcohol	men h vs l quartile	1.5	Y	N	N
				women h vs l quartile	0.9			
Tuyns et al, 1988	453	colon	beer	> 1.75 kg/week vs 0	1.4* (nr)	Y	Y	N
	365	rectum	beer	> 1.75 kg/week vs 0	1.2 (nr)	Y	Y	N

between one or more measures of alcohol exposure and colon cancer in men (Wynder and Shigematsu, 1967; Williams and Horm, 1977; Potter and McMichael, 1986; Meyer and White, 1993) and two reported similar findings in women (Potter and McMichael, 1986; Meyer and White, 1993). Of the nine studies of rectal cancer that stratified on sex, six reported a significant association with at least one type of alcoholic beverage in men (Wynder and Shigematsu, 1967; Kabat et al, 1986; Potter and McMichael, 1986; Kune et al, 1987; Freudenheim et al, 1991; Hu et al, 1991) and three reported a significant association in women (Williams and Horm, 1977; Potter and McMichael, 1986; Freudenheim et al, 1991). The greater inconsistency of the data in women may be due to their lower consumption of alcohol in many cultures.

Some case-control studies considered the potential modifying effect of diet on the association between alcohol and colorectal cancer. Longnecker (1990) reported that, in men,

the associations between consumption of five or more drinks per day (five years in the past) and cancer of the right colon and rectum were confined to those with low dietary calcium intake. He noted the same modifying effect with vitamin D.

Beer

Two cohort studies examined the association between alcohol and colon and rectal cancer in men employed in the beer industry (Dean et al, 1979; Jensen, 1979). In one study, there was an elevated rectal, but not colon, cancer mortality rate among male brewery workers in Dublin compared to that of skilled and unskilled workers in Dublin (standardised mortality rates = 1.6) (Dean et al, 1979). However, no association with either colon or rectal cancer was found in the other study (Jensen, 1979). The inconsistent results may suggest that there may be congeners in (Irish) stout beers (made from charred grain) that increase the risk of rectal cancer that are not present in lighter (Danish) beers.

Author, year	No. of cases	Site	Type of alcohol/ consumption	Comparison	Odds ratio (95% confidence interval)	Sex/age	Adjustment other variables[a]	Energy intake
Ferraroni et al 1988	455	colon	total alcohol	> 6 drinks/day vs < 3 drinks/day	1.2 (nr)	Y	Y	N
	295	rectum	total alcohol	> 6 drinks/day vs < 3 drinks/day	0.9 (nr)	Y	Y	N
Peters et al, 1989	106	colon	total alcohol	≥ 70 g/day vs ≤ 9 g/day	1.6 (0.6–3.7)	Y	Y	N
	41	rectum	total alcohol	≥ 70 g/day vs ≤ 9 g/day	1.4 (0.4–4.5)	Y	Y	N
Slattery et al 1990	231	colon	total alcohol	men > 15 g/week vs 0 women > 15 g/week vs 0	1.1 0.6	Y	Y	Y
Longnecker et al 1990	367	colon	total alcohol	> 5 drinks/day vs 0	1.8*	Y	Y	N
	251	rectum	total alcohol	> 5 drinks/day vs 0	1.5*	Y	Y	N
Hu et al, 1991	111	colon	total alcohol	≥ 10 kg/yr vs < 10 kg/yr	6.4* (nr)	Y	Y	N
	225	rectum	total alcohol	men ≥ 6 kg/yr vs < 6 kg/yr women ≥ 6 kg/yr vs < 6 kg/yr	2.1* (nr) na	Y	Y	N
Choi & Kahyo 1991	63	colon	total alcohol	men heavy vs non-drinker	0.8	Y	Y	N
	133	rectum	total alcohol	women heavy vs non-drinker	4.8*			
Peters et al, 1992	746	colon	beer	vs total alcohol	1.06	Y	Y	N
			liquor	vs total alcohol	1.11*	Y	Y	N
			white wine	vs total alcohol	1.35	Y	Y	N
			red wine	vs total alcohol	0.98	Y	Y	N
Bidoli et al, 1992	123	colon	wine	h vs l tertile	1.3 (nr)	Y	Y	N
			beer	h vs l tertile	1.4 (nr)	Y	Y	N
			spirits	h vs l tertile	1.6 (nr)	Y	Y	N
	125	rectum	wine	h vs l tertile	1.5 (nr)	Y	Y	N
			beer	h vs l tertile	1.1 (nr)	Y	Y	N
			spirits	h vs l tertile	1.0 (nr)	Y	Y	N
Meyer & White 1993	424	colon	total alcohol	men ≥ 30 g/day vs 0 women ≥ 30 g/day vs 0	2.6* 2.5*	Y Y	Y Y	N N

* p ≤ 0.05 for trend or highest vs lowest consumption

nr not reported

a Also adjusted for one or more of the following: education, area of residence, socio-economic status, ethnicity, body weight, smoking status, family history

b Men and women respectively

c Adjusted for saturated fat intake

Nonetheless, in a general population cohort study in Japan (Hirayama, 1989), daily beer consumers had a 12-fold elevated risk of sigmoid colon cancer mortality, compared to abstainers.

Stocks (1957) first reported an elevated, though not statistically significant, risk of colorectal cancer among daily beer drinkers compared to abstainers (OR = 1.4). Subsequently, a positive association between beer and rectal cancer was found in men in four (Wynder and Shigematsu, 1967; Kabat et al, 1986; Kune et al, 1987; Longnecker, 1990) of eight case-control studies (Wynder and Shigematsu, 1967; Williams and Horm, 1977; Miller et al, 1983; Kabat et al, 1986; Potter and McMichael, 1986; Kune et al, 1987; Longnecker, 1990; Bidoli et al, 1992). No association was found for women in any of these studies. Beer was also significantly associated with rectal cancer in men who consumed 15 litres of beer per month compared to abstainers (RR=3.0) in a cohort of Japanese in Hawaii (Stemmermann

et al, 1990).

Beer has been associated with colon cancer in some (Wynder and Shigematsu, 1967; Williams and Horm, 1977; Tuyns et al, 1982; Pickle et al, 1984; Longnecker, 1990) case-control studies but not in others (Miller et al, 1983; Potter and McMichael, 1986; Kune et al, 1987; Ferraroni et al, 1989; Peters et al, 1989, 1992; Bidoli et al, 1992; Meyer and White, 1993).

Wine

A prospective study reported an increased risk of colon cancer with higher intakes of wine (Giovannucci et al, 1994), but the data were more consistent with an overall effect of alcohol than with wine itself.

As shown in Table 4.10.6, three case-control studies of colon cancer have found a positive association with wine (Williams and Horm, 1977; Meyer and White, 1993; Centonze et al, 1994), whereas nine others found no association (Wynder and Shigematsu, 1967; Manousos et al, 1983; Pickle et al, 1984; Potter and McMichael, 1986; Kune et al, 1987; Ferraroni et al, 1989; Longnecker, 1990; Bidoli et al, 1992; Peters et al, 1992). Except for an Australian case-control study which reported a weak positive association in women only (Potter and McMichael, 1986), all other studies of rectal cancer showed no specific association with wine (Wynder and Shigematsu, 1967; Williams and Horm, 1977; Pickle et al, 1984; Kabat et al, 1986; Kune et al, 1987; Peters et al, 1989; Longnecker, 1990).

Spirits

Consumption of spirits has been positively associated with both colon (Williams and Horm, 1977; Potter and McMichael, 1986; Peters et al, 1992; Meyer and White, 1993) and rectal cancer (Potter and McMichael, 1986). Other studies found no association (Wynder and Shigematsu, 1967; Manousos et al, 1983; Kabat et al, 1986; Ferraroni et al, 1989; Peters et al, 1989; Longnecker, 1990; Bidoli et al, 1992), and one Australian case-control study found a protective association with rectal cancer in men (Kune et al, 1987).

Colon and rectal cancers have been positively correlated with alcohol, including beer, consumption in geographical and time-trend studies. No clear differences have been found between men and women (Breslow and Enstrom, 1974; Enstrom, 1977; McMichael, 1979; Potter et al, 1982).

Animal studies have shown that ethanol administered as part of the diet has cocarcinogenic effects. For example, alcohol enhances rectal carcinogenesis induced by dimethylhydrazine (DMH) in rats (Seitz et al, 1984).

Several mechanisms for the carcinogenic effect of alcohol have been advanced. A local action of ethanol on tissue has been proposed through a solvent or cytotoxic effect. However, this mechanism may be more relevant to the upper part of the alimentary tract where ethanol concentration would be greater (Baraona et al, 1974). Alcohol is also known to induce microsomal enzymes that convert pro-carcinogens to more active forms (Seitz et al, 1981) and to inhibit DNA repair (Farinati et al, 1985). Finally, alcohol consumption may have an indirect effect through associated deficiencies in nutrients, such as iron, zinc, riboflavin, pyridoxine, vitamin E and perhaps, particularly, folate (see below) (Garro and Lieber, 1990).

In summary, a majority of epidemiological studies have reported either an increased risk or no association between alcohol intake and colon and rectal cancer. Inconsistencies in results may be a consequence of the small number of cases in some studies or the result of differences in control groups, in methods of assessing consumption, and in preferred beverages across countries and between men and women. High alcohol consumption probably increases the risk of cancers of the colon and rectum. The effect generally seems to be related to total ethanol intake, irrespective of the type of drink.

4.10.1.6 Vitamins

Carotenoids

Studies of 'β-carotene' in foods have, until very recently, used food tables that included other carotenoids (particularly α-carotene) in their calculations of β-carotene intake. Below we have used the description chosen by the authors of the studies, but this inaccuracy should be borne in mind.

One prospective cohort study in the USA that examined total β-carotene intake (diet plus supplements) in association with the risk of colon cancer in women found no substantial association (RR = 0.8, 0.5–1.2) (Bostick et al, 1993).

Of eight case-control studies, five (La Vecchia et al, 1988; Lee et al, 1988; Freudenheim, 1990; Whittemore et al, 1990; Zaridze, 1993) reported that higher intakes of β-carotene were associated with a reduced risk of colorectal cancer, and three (Tuyns et al, 1987; Peters et al, 1992; Meyer and White, 1993) have found no relationship. Those studies that found reduced risks with higher intakes have been inconsistent in the degree of possible protection conferred. For example, one case-control study in northern Italy found that higher consumption of β-carotene showed a moderately protective association with both colon and rectal cancers (La Vecchia et al, 1988). A study of Chinese in Singapore found a moderate decrease in risk for rectal cancer but no relationship for colon cancer (Lee et al, 1989). A study of Chinese living in the USA reported that subjects who were in the uppermost quantile for β-carotene intakes had weakly decreased risk, but only for colon cancer (Whittemore et al, 1990). Sex differences were apparent in another USA study in which higher β-carotene intakes showed moderately protective associations with rectal cancer in men but only weakly protective associations in women (Freudenheim et al, 1990). The strongest protective association was observed in a case-control study in Russia which reported an OR of 0.2 (0.1–0.5; p=0.002) for subjects who were in the uppermost quantile for β-carotene intake (Zaridze et al, 1993). One other study in Spain also suggests lower risks with higher intake.

As with other microconstituents that are abundant in vegetables and fruits, it is unclear whether this association reflects the anticarcinogenic effects of β-carotene (or carotenoids) per se or those of other phytochemicals that are present in foods high in carotenoids.

High dietary carotenoid intake possibly decreases the risk of colorectal cancer.

Vitamin C

One cohort study has reported decreased risk of colon cancer with higher intakes of vitamin C (Stemmermann et al, 1984), but another cohort study did not confirm these findings (Bostick et al, 1993).

Of 11 case-control studies of colon or combined colorectal cancer seven were null (Bjelke, 1973; Jain et al, 1980; Pickle et al, 1984; Tuyns et al, 1987; La Vecchia et al, 1988; Graham et al, 1988; West et al, 1989), three showed statistically significantly reduced risks with higher dietary vitamin C (or an index) (Heilbrun et al, 1981; Macquart-Moulin, 1986; Kune and Kune, 1987) and one showed an increase in risk in women but not men (Potter and McMichael 1986).

Of eight case-control studies of rectal cancer that have examined vitamin C intake, three have observed statistically significant reductions in risk perhaps particularly in women (Kune and Kune, 1987; Potter and McMichael, 1986; Freudenheim, 1990); four studies were eventually null (Heilbrun et al, 1981; Pickle et al, 1984; Tuyns et al,1987; La Vecchia et al, 1988) and one suggested an increased risk (Jain et al 1990); in five, the association was statistically significant.

One case-control study of adenomatous polyps reported controls to have higher intakes of vitamin C than cases (Benito et al, 1993). Another found no association for vitamin C (Olsen et al, 1994).

A protective effect of vitamin C could result from its beneficial effect on the formation of faecal nitrosamines and other faecal mutagens (Bruce et al, 1977; Dion et al, 1982).

As with other microconstituents that are abundant in vegetables and fruits, it is unclear whether this association reflects the anticarcinogenic effects of vitamin C per se, or those of other phytochemicals that are present in foods high in vitamin C.

High dietary vitamin C intake may reduce the risk of colorectal cancer, but the evidence is, at present, insufficient.

Folate and methionine

Total folate intake and dietary folate were not associated with differences in risk of colon cancer in a cohort of men in the USA (Giovannucci et al, 1995). However, men in the highest versus lowest quantile of methionine intake had a weakly decreased risk (RR= 0.7; 0.4–1.0) of developing colon cancer. Increases in the risk of colon cancer were also apparent for men whose intakes of folate and methionine were low and whose alcohol intakes were high. The authors further noted that, among those with high folate intakes, there appeared to be little increase in risk with a higher alcohol intake.

Similar results were obtained by the same investigators for the relationship between folate, methionine, alcohol and adenomatous polyps in the same cohort study (Giovannucci et al, 1993). In a case-control study, the originators of the folate/colorectal cancer hypothesis (Freudenheim et al, 1991) found lower risks of both colon and rectal cancer in association with high folate intakes.

Mechanisms by which methyl donors may be involved in colorectal carcinogenesis have been proposed. Chronic methionine or choline deficiency results in alterations of DNA methylation and produces tumours in rats and mice (Hoffman, 1984). Folic acid deficiency may have related

effects (Yunis and Soreng, 1984). Both hypo- and hypermethylation of DNA are hallmarks of the early stages of the carcinogenic process (Feinberg et al, 1988; Hoffmann, 1984; Goelz et al, 1985).

The epidemiological evidence, together with a plausible biological role for methyl donors suggests that higher intakes of both folate and methionine may decrease the risk of colorectal cancer but is, as yet, insufficient.

Vitamin E

One prospective study of women in Iowa reported a strong protective association between total vitamin E and the risk of colon cancer (RR = 0.4 0.2–0.8); this, however, was almost entirely attributable to vitamin E from supplements, as opposed to that from diet (Bostick et al, 1993). The age-adjusted relative risk for the uppermost consumption level of dietary vitamin E alone was 0.7 (0.5–1.1); after additional adjustment for energy intake, height, parity, intake of vitamin A supplements, and intake of low-fat meats, the relative risk was 1.0. It was noted that the range of dietary vitamin E intake in this cohort was very narrow.

Two further cohort studies, one of colon cancer in American women and another of both colon and rectal cancers in Japanese-American men, found no association for vitamin E intake (Heilbrun et al, 1989; Willett et al, 1990).

Findings from case-control studies have not shown any clear or substantial association between dietary vitamin E and colorectal cancer (Lee et al, 1989; Freudenheim et al, 1990; Benito et al, 1991; Peters et al, 1992; Meyer and White, 1993).

Findings from five prospective studies suggested that the serum level of α-tocopherol, the predominant form of vitamin E in the blood, was lower in subjects who subsequently developed colorectal cancer than in control subjects. The data from these studies, when pooled, showed a relative risk of 0.6 (0.4–1.0) for the highest compared to the lowest quartile of serum α-tocopherol level (Longnecker et al, 1992).

Results of seven animal studies of vitamin E and carcinogen-induced colon cancer, as reviewed by Knekt in 1991, have been inconsistent, with studies showing tumour inhibition, tumour enhancement, or no effect of vitamin E. Possible antineoplastic effects of vitamin E (see Knekt, 1991) include its function as an antioxidant and free-radical scavenger.

Assessing vitamin E in diets is problematic, so measurement of prediagnostic blood levels is particularly relevant though, of course, these do not distinguish between dietary and supplement sources.

Evidence on diets high in vitamin E and the risk of colorectal cancer is relatively null but higher prediagnostic blood levels are associated with a lower risk of subsequent cancer. The evidence suggests that higher dietary vitamin E intake may reduce the risk of colorectal cancer but is, as yet, insufficient.

4.10.1.7 Minerals

Calcium, vitamin D

Of three cohort studies that have investigated the association between vitamin D and colorectal cancer, two suggested a protective association (Garland et al, 1985; Bostick et al, 1993), while the third was null (Willett et al, 1990; Kampman et al, 1994).

A nested case-control study showed a relative risk of 0.3 for colon cancer in individuals with a prediagnostic 25-OH vitamin D serum level greater than or equal to, compared to less than, 20 ng/ml (Garland et al, 1989).

Two case-control studies showed statistically non-significant reductions in risk (Benito et al, 1991; Peters et al, 1992).

Eight cohort studies (Garland et al, 1985; Wu et al, 1987; Stemmerman et al, 1990; Willett et al, 1990; Bostick et al, 1993; Kampman et al, 1994; Kearney et al, 1996; Heilbrun et al, 1985) have examined the association between calcium intake and colorectal cancer. Of 16 estimates of relative risk, only one was statistically significantly less than 1.0 (Garland et al, 1985).

Fifteen case-control studies have examined the association between calcium and colorectal cancer (Macquart-Moulin et al, 1986; Slattery et al, 1988; Lee et al, 1989; Whittemore et al, 1990; Peters et al, 1992; Meyer and White, 1993; Tuyns et al, 1987; Freudenheim et al, 1990; Negri et al, 1990; Benito et al, 1990; Kune et al, 1987; Graham et al, 1988; Kampman et al, 1994b; Zaridze et al, 1993; Arbman et al, 1992). Of 25 ORs presented, six showed statistically significant decreases in risk, one showed a statistically significant elevated risk and the remaining 18 were null.

Both studies reporting on polyps (Macquart-Moulin et al, 1986; Benito et al, 1993) showed null relationships with dietary calcium intake.

A meta-analysis by Bergsma-Kadijk et al, (1996) estimated a summary relative risk of 0.89 (0.79–1.01) for 24 studies.

Several ecological studies have demonstrated inverse correlations between calcium, vitamin D, and milk intake and colorectal cancer mortality (Sorenson et al, 1988; Emerson and Weiss, 1992).

In animal studies, calcium administration has a beneficial effect on colonic epithelial cell proliferation (Wargovich et al, 1983, 1984; Bird et al, 1986).

A mechanism by which vitamin D and calcium may protect against colorectal cancers has been proposed (Newmark et al, 1984) which involves both the binding of bile acids and fatty acids to form inert soaps, and direct effects on the cell cycle resulting in reduced proliferation and increased terminal differentiation of the colonic epithelial cells (Newmark et al, 1984). To date, clear human evidence for these effects is scant. Some (Lipkin et al, 1985; Lipkin et al, 1989; Wargovich et al, 1992; Bostick et al, 1995), but not all

(Bostick et al, 1993; Baron et al, 1995) clinical trials have shown that calcium supplementation may have some beneficial effect on colorectal epithelial cell proliferation. The proposed role for vitamin D is intimately related to its functions in calcium metabolism (Haynes and Murad, 1985); as with calcium, vitamin D has been shown to reduce cell proliferation in human colon cell lines in vitro (Lointier et al, 1987) and to colonic epithelial cell proliferation in rodents (Pence and Buddingh, 1988).

> The evidence suggests that Vitamin D may reduce the risk of colorectal cancer but is at present insufficient. The evidence on calcium suggests that there may be a very weak overall reduction in risk but the conservative judgement is that there is possibly no relationship.

Selenium

The majority of analytical epidemiological studies have been prospective studies relying on measurement of selenium in plasma or toenails. The findings of these studies, often based on a small number of cases, have provided no clear evidence of an association specifically with colorectal cancer (Nomura et al, 1987; Schober et al, 1987; Knekt et al, 1988, 1990; van der Brandt et al, 1993; Garland et al, 1995), though there are data suggesting associations between pre-diagnostic levels of selenium and cancer in general (Salonen et al, 1984).

Ecological studies of cancer mortality patterns have suggested a protective association between selenium intake and colorectal cancer (Schrauzer et al, 1977; Clark et al, 1991).

> These data suggest that dietary selenium is possibly unrelated to the risk of colorectal cancer.

Iron

Using data from the National Health and Nutrition Examination Study in the USA (NHANES) Stevens et al (1988, 1994) found an association between body iron stores (measured by TIBC and transferrin saturation levels) and overall cancer incidence rates in men. Further analysis of the NHANES data has since shown that risk of colon cancer associated with iron intake was increased for men and women, with an adjusted OR of 1.5 (1.4–1.6) for the proximal colon in women. They also confirmed that cases of colorectal cancer had higher serum iron levels although these were suggestive of differences by sex and subsite, perhaps largely due to small numbers for men or women (Wurzelmann et al, 1996).

Several case-control studies have generated some additional but inconsistent data. One study in California found a significant association between colon cancer risk and iron intakes in both men and women, but after adjusting for the effects of protein, this became statistically non-significant (Peters et al, 1992). However, a case-control study in Belgium found that cases had lower intakes of iron (Tuyns et al, 1987a), as did two studies of colorectal polyps (Macquart-Moulin et al, 1987; Hoff et al, 1992). One case-control study in the USA found that increased risk of rectal cancer in men was associated with high iron intakes (Freudenheim et al, 1990).

A case-control study in the USA that examined body iron stores found that serum ferritin levels were associated with increased adenoma risk (Nelson et al, 1994). A Finnish case-control study (Knekt et al, 1994) also reported increased colorectal cancer risk in persons whose transferrin saturation levels exceeded 60%. Relative risk adjusted for age, sex and smoking for colorectal cancer, compared to those with lower levels, was 3.0.

One ecological study in Germany, which investigated the correlation between regional mortality rates and nutrient intake data from a national survey, found significant correlations between the mortality rates from cancers of the colon and rectum in men and iron intakes (Boeing et al, 1985).

It has been suggested that high dietary intakes of iron can enhance the intracolonic generation of free radicals and that this might explain the association between high meat consumption and increased colon cancer risk (Babbs, 1990; Nelson, 1987). As part of this theory, it has also been suggested that phytates (found largely in grains) might be protective by chelating inorganic dietary iron and so reducing hydroxyl radical production (Nelson, 1987, 1992; Weinberg 1994).

The evidence suggests that iron intake may increase the risk of colorectal cancer, but is, as yet, insufficient.

4.10.2 FOODS AND DRINKS

4.10.2.1 Cereals
At the international level, the risk of colon cancer has been shown to be lower in those populations who eat traditional cereal-based diets, for instance in Asia and parts of Africa.

Only a small number of analytical studies have reported specifically on cereals and risk of colorectal cancer. As those studies that have examined the associations with cereals have included diverse dietary exposures including breakfast cereals, grains, wholewheat breads and, sometimes, starchy foods, the results are themselves diverse.

Five case-control studies have examined wholegrain intakes or a preference for wholegrain versus refined products and have found an association with reduced risk, but more so for colon than rectal cancer (La Vecchia et al, 1988; Tuyns et al, 1988; Peters et al, 1989; Bidoli et al, 1992; Thun et al, 1992). The magnitude of risk reduction varies from study to study. One case-control study in Belgium (Tuyns et al, 1988) reported that subjects whose consumption of meal and flour products was in the uppermost quartile had a moderately reduced risk of colon cancer (OR=0.7; p<0.05) when compared with those whose intakes were in the lowest quartile, but there was no substantial change in risk for rectal cancer. Weak reductions in risk of colon cancer were also observed in three further case-control studies (La Vecchia et al, 1988; Peters et al, 1989; Bidoli et al, 1992). In two of

these studies (La Vecchia et al, 1988; Peters et al, 1989), subjects whose wholegrain intakes were in the uppermost quantile showed no difference in relative risk compared to those who were in the lowest quantile. However, in the study by Bidoli et al (1992), risk of rectal cancer was significantly reduced (OR = 0.3; p = 0.002) in subjects who were in the uppermost tertile for consumption of wholegrain bread and pasta.

Five case-control studies found no association (Manousos et al, 1983; Miller et al, 1983; Kune et al, 1987; Centoze et al, 1994; Kampman et al, 1996). Three case-control studies of colorectal cancer reported increased risks with higher consumption of pasta and rice but no association with bread consumption (Macquart-Moulin et al, 1986); increased risks with both bread and polenta - but, as noted above, a protective association with wholegrain bread and pasta (Bidoli et al, 1992); and increased risks with cereals (Benito et al, 1990).

There is an inverse correlation between colon cancer mortality rates in both men and women and per capita cereal consumption (Armstrong and Doll, 1975).

The diversity of cereals and cereal products largely precludes a summary assessment of the association with colorectal cancer risk. There may be a difference in the effects of wholegrain and refined cereal products. Most of the risk estimates, nonetheless, are either less than 1.0 or null. The evidence suggests that cereals may reduce the risk of colorectal cancer but are currently insufficient.

4.10.2.2 Roots and tubers
One case-control study conducted in Belgium found a non-significant reduced risk (OR=0.86, p for trend = 0.44) associated with potato consumption (Tuyns et al, 1988). The OR for rectal cancer was statistically significant (0.7, p for trend = 0.61). Another case-control study in France reported that increased consumption of potatoes was associated with a weak reduction in risk of colorectal cancer (OR = 0.68, ns) (Macquart-Moulin et al, 1986). A similar reduction in colon cancer risk associated with higher consumption of potatoes (OR = 0.67, 0.4–1.2) was noted in a Dutch case-control study (Kampman et al, 1995). A case-control study in Argentina reported that subjects who were higher consumers of potatoes had a statistically significant lower risk of colon cancer when compared with subjects in the lowest quantile (Iscovich et al, 1992). Three other case-control studies found no substantial association between tuber consumption and colon cancer risk (La Vecchia et al, 1988; Bidoli et al, 1992; Steinmetz et al, 1993), although Bidoli et al (1992) did note that subjects who were in the uppermost tertile for potato consumption had a weakly increased risk of rectal cancer (OR = 1.5, ns). A case-control study in Spain reported that greater potato consumption was associated with a strongly increased risk (OR = 2.2; p < 0.05) of colorectal cancer (Benito et al, 1990).

The evidence on roots and tubers including, especially, potatoes is inconsistent; no judgement is possible

4.10.2.3 Vegetables and fruits

Vegetables and fruits – colon cancer

Four prospective studies in the USA have examined vegetable and fruit consumption in relation to colon cancer risk. The study of Seventh-day Adventists reported RRs of 0.7 (0.4–1.1) and 1.7 (0.9–3.4) for higher intakes of green salad for females and males respectively (Phillips and Snowdon, 1985). A large US cohort study reported RRs of 0.6 (0.5–0.9) and 0.8 (ns) for higher vegetable consumption for females and males respectively; protective associations were further reported with raw vegetables, green leafy vegetables, cruciferous vegetables and carrots, for both sexes (Thun et al, 1992). In a US cohort of elderly persons, protective associations were observed for various categories of vegetables and fruit in females, but higher intakes were associated with increased risk in males (Shibata et al, 1992). (Table 4.10.7.)

In the cohort of Iowa women, RRs of 0.7 (0.5–1.1) and 0.7 (0.5–1.0) were reported for higher intakes of vegetables and garlic respectively but less remarkable associations were reported for the other vegetable and fruit groups examined (Steinmetz et al, 1994).

Of 21 case-control studies of the association between vegetable and fruit consumption and colon cancer risk, 17 have found some degree of reduced risk with higher consumption of at least one category of vegetable or fruit (Table 4.10.8). Decreased risks of colon cancer have been particularly consistent for raw vegetables and green vegetables, for which three of four, and four of five studies, respectively, have shown protective associations. For cruciferous vegetables, 8 of 12 studies have shown decreased risks with higher consumption and findings from three of the remaining four studies were null. A meta-analysis of six case-control studies of vegetable consumption and risk of colon cancer, carried out by Trock et al (1990), calculated a combined OR of 0.48 (0.41–0.57) for highest versus the lowest quantiles of vegetable intake.

In the review by Steinmetz and Potter (1991) it is noted that the study by Lee et al (1989) hints at a greater beneficial effect of vegetable consumption at older ages, in that a protective effect of higher cruciferous vegetable consumption was found only in people greater than 60 years of age. However, the suggestion that age may play a role is not supported by the study of Young (1988) who reported that the lower colon cancer risk associated with greater consumption of cruciferous vegetables and lettuce salad was consistent across all ages.

Few studies have reported that higher consumption of vegetables and fruit increases risk of colon cancer. However, one study by Tajima et al (1985) in Japan found that higher intakes of many of the vegetables and fruits studied was associated with higher risk of colon cancer. For example, more frequent intakes of spinach, onions and pumpkin were associated with ORs of 2.6 (p < 0.05), 3.8 (p < 0.01) and 3.9 (p < 0.01) respectively. The authors offered no explanation of their unexpected findings but they did note that smoking, drinking, education, or intake of salty foods did not appear to be confounders in this hospital-based study.

Findings for fruit consumption and colon cancer risk are less abundant than those for vegetables. Moderate increases in risk with higher fruit intake (OR = 2.0) were found in the cohort study of Seventh-day Adventist men (Phillips and Snowdon, 1975). A case-control study in Australia reported that more frequent consumption of all fruit was associated with higher colon cancer risk in men (OR = 1.7, 0.9–3.5); no association was found in women (Steinmetz, 1993). Significant decreases in colon cancer risk associated with higher fruit consumption have been reported by Tuyns et al (1988) (OR = 0.3; p < 0.05) for apples; Slattery et al (1988) for fruit (OR = 0.3; p < 0.005); La Vecchia et al (1988) for melon (OR = 0.6; p < 0.05) and Modan et al (1975) for olives, melons and watermelons (OR not reported). However, for the majority of other fruits in other studies, no substantial associations with risk of colon cancer were found.

Vegetables and fruits – Rectal cancer

One prospective study reported on rectal cancer risk in Seventh-day Adventists; an RR of 0.7 (0.3–1.5) for higher consumption of green salad was found (Phillips and Snowdon, 1985).

Of thirteen case-control studies of rectal cancer, ten have reported on statistical significance and, of these, eight have shown a significant protective association for at least one vegetable and/or fruit category (Table 4.10.9). Of four studies that reported on vegetables as a broad category, two found protective associations and two found increased risk with increased consumption. Results have been most consistent for cruciferous vegetables, with each of five studies reporting protective associations. Of four studies that reported on fruit as a category, three reported protective associations.

Fruit intake generally has not been shown to be associated with the risk of rectal cancer. However, those few studies that did find associations were somewhat inconsistent. For example, Bjelke et al (1974) reported a reduced risk with increased consumption of fruit and berries. Another study in Belgium found a decreased risk with higher consumption of pears and apples, but an increased risk with greater consumption of stewed and canned fruit (Tuyns et al, 1988). La Vecchia et al (1988) reported a protective association with melon whereas apple consumption was associated with an increased risk of rectal cancer.

Vegetables and fruits – Colorectal cancer

Six case-control studies have reported on vegetable and fruit consumption and risk of combined colorectal cancer without presenting results for each site separately. One study in Japan (Haenszel et al, 1973), found that higher consumption of string beans, peas and carrots was associated with increased risk of large bowel cancer. Conversely, a study by Manousos et al (1983) in Athens found that colorectal can-

TABLE 4.10.7 VEGETABLE AND FRUIT CONSUMPTION AND THE RISK OF COLON CANCER: COHORT STUDIES

AUTHOR, YEAR AND PLACE	SIZE OF COHORT; NO. OF CASES	TYPE OF VEGETABLE OR FRUIT	COMPARISON	RELATIVE RISK (95% CONFIDENCE INTERVAL)	SEX/AGE	ADJUSTMENT SMOKING HISTORY	OTHER FACTORS
Phillips and Snowdon, 1985 USA	25,943 Seventh-day Adventists: 182	green salad	men ≥ 7/week vs < 4/week	1.7 (0.9–3.4)	Y	N	N
		green salad	women ≥ 7/week vs < 4/week	0.7 (0.4–1.1)	Y	N	N
Thun et al, 1992 USA	764,343 adults: 1,150 colon deaths, 5,746 matched non-cases	vegetables	men h vs l quintile	0.8 (0.6–1.0)	Y	N	N
		vegetables	women h vs l quintile	0.6 (0.5–0.9)	Y	N	N
		plants	men h vs l quintile	0.8 (0.6–1.0)	Y	N	N
		plants	women h vs l quintile	0.6 (0.5–0.9)	Y	N	N
Shibata et al, 1992 USA	11,580 elderly: 202	all vegetables and fruit	men ≥ 7.9/day vs < 5.5/day	1.5 (0.9–2.5)	Y	Y	N
		all vegetables and fruit	women 8.3/day vs < 5.9 day	0.6 (0.4–1.0)	Y	Y	N
		all vegetables	men ≥ 4.5/day vs < 3.0/day	1.4 (0.8–2.3)	Y	Y	N
		all vegetables	women ≥ 4.8/day vs < 3.2/day	0.7 (0.5–1.2)	Y	Y	N
		all fruit	men ≥ 3.2/day < 2.2 day	1.1 (0.7–1.8)	Y	Y	N
		all fruit	women ≥ 3.7/day vs < 2.4/day	0.5* (0.3–0.8)	Y	Y	N
		dark green vegetables	men ≥ 0.3/day vs < 0.1 day	2.3* (1.3–3.9)	Y	Y	N
		dark green vegetables	women ≥ 0.53/day vs < 0.13/day	1.0* (0.6–1.7)	Y	Y	N
Steinmetz et al 1994, USA	41,837 women: 212	all vegetables and fruit	> 47.0/week vs < 24.6 week	0.9 (0.6–1.4)	Y	N	Y
		vegetables	> 30.4/week vs <15.1 week	0.7 (0.5–1.1)	Y	N	Y
		green leafy vegetables	> 5.5/week vs < 1.5/week	0.9 (0.6–1.3)	Y	N	Y
		cruciferous vegetables	> 4.0/week vs < 1.5/week	1.1 (0.7–1.7)	Y	N	Y
		garlic	≥ 1.0/week vs 0/week	0.7 (0.5–1.0)	Y	N	Y
		carrots	≥ 3.0/week vs ≤ 0.5/week	1.1 (0.7–1.5)	Y	N	Y
		legumes	≥ 1.0/week vs 0/week	1.0 (0.7–1.4)	Y	N	Y

*   p < 0.05

cer cases reported significantly lower intakes of cabbage, beets, lettuce, spinach and vegetables than hospital controls. One of the earliest case-control studies reported that consumption of both vegetables and fruit showed protective associations with colorectal cancer (Bjelke et al, 1974).

Cruciferous vegetables, specifically, were identified as associated with reduced risk of colorectal cancer (OR=0.5; <0.01) in a case-control study in Spain (Benito et al, 1990), but a study in Russia found no association between cabbage intake and colorectal cancer risk (OR=1.0) (Zaridze et al, 1993). The Russian study, however, reported a moderate protective association with fruit (OR=0.5; <0.01).

Vegetables and fruits – Colorectal adenomatous polyps

One prospective study of adenomatous colorectal polyps in men reported an approximate halving of risk for greater intake of vegetable and fruit fibre; results for vegetables and fruits per se were not reported (Giovannucci et al, 1992).

At least six case-control studies of polyps have reported on vegetable and fruit consumption (Hoff et al, 1986; Macquart-Moulin et al, 1987; Kato et al, 1990; Kune et al, 1991; Benito and Cabeza, 1993; Sandler et al, 1993). Each of five studies that examined vegetables as a broad category found a protective association (not always statistically significant), as did three of four that examined fruit, and each of two that examined cruciferous vegetables.

One international ecological study of 30 countries found

an inverse correlation of –0.17 for females and a slightly positive correlation of 0.06 for males for vegetable availability and risk of colon cancer (Rose et al, 1986). Another study of 38 countries found no inverse correlations with consumption of vegetables, fruit, cruciferous vegetables or citrus fruit (McKeown Eyssen and Bright See, 1984). Conversely, a study within Great Britain reported strong inverse correlations between intakes of total and fresh green vegetables and mortality from cancer of the colon, but not rectum (Bingham et al, 1979, 1985).

Vegetables contain a large array of substances – both micronutrients, such as carotenoids, folate and ascorbate; and bioactive compounds, such as phenols, flavonoids, isothiocyanates, and indoles – with anticarcinogenic properties (Wattenberg, 1987a, 1987b; Steinmetz and Potter, 1991). Vegetables are also rich in fibre. Consumption of non-digestible fructo-oligosaccharides may selectively promote the growth and activity of potentially beneficial bacteria, such as Bifidobacterium and Lactobacillus (Kulkarni and Reddy, 1994; Gibson et al, 1995; Gibson and Roberfroid, 1996).

Evidence that diets rich in vegetables protect against cancers of the colon and rectum is convincing. The data on fruit are more limited and inconsistent; no judgement is possible.

TABLE 4.10.8 VEGETABLE AND FRUIT CONSUMPTION AND THE RISK OF COLON CANCER: CASE-CONTROL STUDIES

AUTHOR, YEAR AND PLACE	NO. OF CASES	TYPE OF VEGETABLE OR FRUIT	COMPARISON	ODDS RATIO (95% CONFIDENCE INTERVAL)	ADJUSTMENT AGE/SEX	OTHER VARIABLES
Bjelke, 1974 Norway		vegetables	na	decreased risk with increased intake		
		carrots	na	decreased risk with increased intake		
Modan et al, 1975 Israel	198	white beans	na	decreased risk with increased intake*		
		cabbage	na	decreased risk with increased intake*		
		cucumbers	na	decreased risk with increased intake*		
		fava beans	na	decreased risk with increased intake*		
		olives	na	decreased risk with increased intake*		
		melons	na	decreased risk with increased intake*		
		radishes	na	decreased risk with increased intake*		
		watermelon	na	decreased risk with increased intake*		
		kidney beans	na	decreased risk with increased intake*		
		other vegetables and fruit	na	decreased risk with increased intake		
Phillips, 1975 USA	41	green leafy vegetables	≥ 1/week vs < 1/week	0.5 (na)	na	na
		fresh fruit	≥ 1/day vs < 1/day	2.0 (na)	na	na
		vegetarian protein products	≥ 1/week vs < 1/week	0.4 (na)	na	na
		green beans	na	no assoc		
		dried beans	na	no assoc		
		dried fruits	na	no assoc		
		tossed salad	na	no assoc		
Graham et al, 1978 USA	470	raw vegetables	> 21/month vs 0–10/month	0.6** (na)	na	na
		vegetables	> 61/month vs 0–20 month	0.5* (na)	na	na
		cabbage	> 1/week vs never	0.3*** (na)	na	na
		sauerkraut	na	decreased risk with increased intake		
		coleslaw	na	decreased risk with increased intake		
		brussels sprouts	na	decreased risk with increased intake		
		broccoli	na	decreased risk with increased intake		
Miller et al, 1983 USA	348	cruciferous vegetables	men h vs l	0.9 (na)	Y	Y
			women h vs l	0.7* (na)	Y	Y
		citrus fruit	men h vs l	1.3 (na)	Y	Y
			women h vs l	0.9 (na)	Y	Y
		non-citrus fruit	men h vs l	0.7 (na)	Y	Y
			women h vs l	1.0 (na)	Y	Y
		all vegetables	men h vs l	0.8 (na)	Y	Y
			women h vs l	0.7 (na)	Y	Y
Tajima et al, 1985 Japan	42	spinach	> 4 vs < 1/week	2.6* (na)	Y	Y
		onion	> 4 vs < 1/week	3.8† (na)		
		pumpkin	> 1 vs < 1/week	3.9† (na)		
		mushrooms	> 4 vs < 1/week	1.6 (na)		
		carrots	> 4 vs < 1/week	1.4 (na)		
		green pepper	> 1 vs < 1/week	1.7 (na)		
		radishes	> 4 vs < 1/week	1.4 (na)		
		cabbage	> 4 vs < 1/week	2.1 (na)		
		lettuce	> 4 vs < 1/week	1.7 (na)		
		tomatoes	> 4 vs < 1/week	1.3 (na)		
		oranges	> 4 vs < 1/week	1.4 (na)		
		other fruit	> 4 vs < 1/week	1.1 (na)		
Macquart-Moulin 1986, France	399	low fibre vegetables	h vs l quartile	0.4 †† (na)	Y	Y
		medium fibre vegetables	h vs l quartile	0.6† (na)	Y	Y
Kune et al, 1987 Australia	715	cruciferous vegetables	> 425 g/week vs < 105 g/week	0.5 (na)	Y	N
Graham et al 1988, USA	428	tomatoes	na	decreased risk with increased intake*		
		peppers	na	decreased risk with increased intake*		
		carrots	na	decreased risk with increased intake*		
		onions	na	decreased risk with increased intake*		
		celery	na	decreased risk with increased intake*		
		cruciferous vegetables	na	decreased risk with increased intake*		

AUTHOR, YEAR AND PLACE	NO. OF CASES	TYPE OF VEGETABLE OR FRUIT	COMPARISON	ODDS RATIO (95% CONFIDENCE INTERVAL)	ADJUSTMENT AGE/SEX	OTHER VARIABLES
La Vecchia et al 1988, Italy	339	green vegetables	h vs l tertile	0.5† (na)	Y	Y
		melon	h vs l tertile	0.6† (na)	Y	Y
		peppers	h vs l tertile	0.7* (na)	Y	Y
		tomatoes	h vs l tertile	0.9 (na)	Y	Y
		cabbage	h vs l tertile	1.1 (na)	Y	Y
		carrots	h vs l tertile	0.8 (na)	Y	Y
		spinach	h vs l tertile	1.1 (na)	Y	Y
		lettuce	h vs l tertile	0.9 (na)	Y	Y
		citrus fruit	h vs l tertile	0.8 (na)	Y	Y
		fresh fruit	h vs l tertile	0.9 (na)	Y	Y
		apples	h vs l tertile	1.2 (na)	Y	Y
Slattery et al 1988, USA	229	cruciferous vegetables	h vs l quartile	0.3* (0.1–0.8)	Y	N
		fruit	h vs l quartile	0.3* (0.1–0.6)	Y	N
		vegetables	h vs l quartile	0.6 (0.3–1.3)	Y	N
Tuyns et al, 1988 Belgium	453	cooked vegetables	> 1375 vs < 800 g/week	0.7* (na)	Y	Y
		celery	> 0 vs < 0 g/week	0.2†† (na)	Y	Y
		leeks	> 0 vs < 0 g/week	0.3†† (na)	Y	Y
		carrots	> 0 vs < 0 g/week	0.8* (na)	Y	Y
		onions	> 0 vs < 0 g/week	0.2†† (na)	Y	Y
		string beans	> 0 vs < 0 g/week	1.1 (na)	Y	Y
		tomatoes	> 0 vs < 0 g/week	1.2 (na)	Y	Y
		tomato puree	> 0 vs < 0 g/week	0.8 (na)	Y	Y
		raw vegetables	> 268 vs < 80 g/week	0.4†† (na)	Y	Y
		chicory	> 0 vs < 0 g/week	0.6* (na)	Y	Y
		endive and lettuce	> 56 vs < 0 g/week	0.4†† (na)	Y	Y
		carrots	> 0 vs < 0 g/week	1.4 (na)	Y	Y
		tomatoes	> 100 vs < 0 g/week	1.2 (na)	Y	Y
		dry pod vegetables	> 0 vs < 0 g/week	1.7* (na)	Y	Y
		beans	> 0 vs < 0 g/week	4.7†† (na)	Y	Y
		fresh fruit	> 1538 vs < 300 g/week	0.9 (na)	Y	Y
		bananas	> 100 vs 0 g/week	1.1 (na)	Y	Y
		apples	> 560 vs < 0 g/week	0.3†† (na)	Y	Y
		pears	> 0 vs < 0 g/week	0.8 (na)	Y	Y
		citrus fruit	> 490 vs < 0 g/week	1.1 (na)	Y	Y
		stewed canned fruit	> 188 vs < 0 g/week	1.5* (na)	Y	Y
Young and Wolf 1988, USA	353	cruciferous vegetables	h vs l quartile	0.6 (0.4–0.9)	Y	N
		lettuce salad	h vs l quartile	0.4 (0.3–0.5)	Y	N
		cabbage	h vs l quartile	0.8 (0.6–1.1)	Y	N
		spinach	h vs l quartile	0.8 (0.6–1.2)	Y	N
		yellow vegetables	h vs l quartile	0.8 (0.5–1.1)	Y	N
		miscellaneous vegetables	h vs l quartile	0.7 (0.5–1.1)	Y	N
Lee et al, 1989 Singapore	203	cruciferous vegetables	h vs l tertile	0.5† (0.3–0.8)	Y	Y
		total vegetables	h vs l tertile	0.7 (0.5–1.3)	Y	Y
West et al, 1989 USA	231	cruciferous vegetables	men h vs l quartile	0.3 (0.1–0.8)	Y	Y
			women h vs l quartile	0.9 (0.4–1.8)	Y	Y
Benito et al, 1990 Spain	286	cruciferous vegetables	h vs l quartile	0.5 (na)	Y	Y
Hu et al, 1991 China	173	green vegetables	> 57 vs < 28.5 kg/yr	0.1† (0.03–0.4)		
		chives and celery	ever vs never	0.3 (0.1–0.8)		
		tomatoes	≥ 15 vs < 15 kg/yr	0.3 (0.1–0.5)		
		total fresh vegetables	≥ 193 vs < 75.5 kg/yr	0.2† (0.05–0.6)		
		dry vegetables	> 6 vs < 3 kg/yr	0.1† (0.03–0.3)		
		bean products	no assoc			
		garlic	no assoc			
		salted vegetables	no assoc			

Table 4.10.8 continues overleaf

TABLE 4.10.8 VEGETABLE AND FRUIT CONSUMPTION AND THE RISK OF COLON CANCER: CASE-CONTROL STUDIES

AUTHOR, YEAR AND PLACE	NO. OF CASES	TYPE OF VEGETABLE OR FRUIT	COMPARISON	ODDS RATIO (95% CONFIDENCE INTERVAL)	ADJUSTMENT AGE/SEX	OTHER VARIABLES
Bidoli et al, 1992 Italy	123	total vegetables	h vs l tertile	0.7 (na)	Y	Y
		cruciferous vegetables	h vs l tertile	0.6 (na)	Y	Y
		green peppers	h vs l tertile	1.0 (na)	Y	Y
		spinach	h vs l tertile	0.5† (na)	Y	Y
		carrots	h vs l tertile	0.8 (na)	Y	Y
		tomatoes	h vs l tertile	0.5† (na)	Y	Y
		total fresh fruit	h vs l tertile	1.0 (na)	Y	Y
		apples	h vs l tertile	1.3 (na)	Y	Y
		citrus fruit	h vs l tertile	0.9 (na)	Y	Y
		melon	h vs l tertile	0.8 (na)	Y	Y
		lettuce	h vs l tertile	0.5 (na)	Y	Y
		potatoes	h vs l tertile	0.8 (na)	Y	Y
Peters et al, 1992 USA	746	cruciferous vegetables	10 servings/month	1.0 (0.99–1.01)	N	Y
		non-cruciferous vegetables	10 servings/month	1.01 (0.97–1.04)	N	Y
		fruit	10 servings/month	1.0 (0.99–1.01)	N	Y
Iscovich et al 1992, Argentina	110	low fibre vegetables	> 318/yr vs < 69/yr	0.2* (0.1–0.4)		
		pulses	> 71/yr vs < 5/yr	0.5* (0.2–1.1)		
		green leafy vegetables	> 315/yr vs < 71/yr	0.2* (0.1–0.5)		
		other vegetables	> 326/yr vs < 92/yr	0.4* (0.2–1.0)		
Steinmetz & Potter 1993, Australia	220	men				
		all vegetables and fruit	≥ 59/week vs < 28/week	1.4 (0.7–2.7)	N	Y
		all vegetables	≥ 32/week vs < 15/week	1.3 (0.7–2.5)	N	Y
		all fruit	≥ 28/week vs ≤ 8/week	1.7 (0.9–3.5)	N	Y
		raw vegetables	≥ 3.6/week vs < 0.2/week	1.3 (0.6–2.6)	N	Y
		raw fruit	≥ 23/week vs < 6/week	1.2 (0.6–2.3)	N	Y
		cruciferous vegetables	≥ 5.8/week vs ≤ 1.7/week	1.1 (0.6–2.1)	N	Y
		onions	≥ 3.0/week vs < 0.5/week	0.9 (0.4–1.7)	N	Y
		green leafy vegetables	≥ 3.6/week vs ≤ 1.0/week	0.8 (0.5–1.5)	N	Y
		legumes	≥ 1.0/week vs 0/week	0.7 (0.4–1.5)	N	Y
		carrots	≥ 2.9/week vs ≤ 1.0/week	0.8 (0.5–1.4)	N	Y
		broccoli	≥ 0.5/week vs 0/week	0.9 (0.5–1.7)	N	Y
		cabbage	≥ 3.0/week vs ≤ 0.5/week	0.8 (0.4–1.6)	N	Y
		cauliflower	≥ 1.0/week vs ≤ 0.2/week	1.7 (0.9–3.3)	N	Y
		women				
		all vegetables and fruit	≥ 70/week vs ≤ 36/week	0.8 (0.3–1.8)	N	Y
		all vegetables	≥ 38/week vs ≤ 19/week	1.1 (0.5–2.5)	N	Y
		all fruit	≥ 34/week vs ≤ 12/week	0.9 (0.4–2.1)	N	Y
		raw vegetables	≥ 5.4/week vs < 0.7/week	1.3 (0.7–2.7)	N	Y
		raw fruit	≥ 30/week vs < 10/week	0.8 (0.3–1.9)	N	Y
		cruciferous vegetables	≥ 6.7/week vs ≤ 2.2/week	1.1 (0.5–2.5)	N	Y
		onions	≥ 2.6/week vs 0/week	0.4 (0.2–1.0)	N	Y
		green leafy vegetables	≥ 6.7/week vs ≤ 1.4/week	1.0 (0.5–2.2)	N	Y
		legumes	≥ 0.6/wk vs 0/week	0.4 (0.2–0.9)	N	Y
		carrots	≥ 3.4/wk vs ≤ 2.0/week	2.1 (1.1–4.0)	N	Y
		broccoli	≥ 0.4/wk vs 0/week	1.0 (0.5–2.0)	N	Y
		cabbage	≥ 3.0/wk vs ≤ 0.4/week	1.0 (0.4–2.3)	N	Y
		cauliflower	≥ 2.0/wk vs ≤ 0.4/week	1.4 (0.6–2.9)	N	Y
Kampman et al 1994, Netherlands	232	vegetables	> 247 g/day vs < 142 g/day	0.4† (0.2–0.7)	Y	Y
		fruit	> 269 g/day vs < 100 g/day	1.0 (0.5–2.0)	Y	Y
		fruit	> 327 g/day vs < 143 g/day	0.5† (0.2–1.3)	Y	Y

*   p < 0.05
†   p < 0.01
†† p < 0.001
na not available
a   Also adjusted for one or more of the following: fat, food group, smoking, education, area, province, race, occupation, BMI, energy intake, crude fibre, weight 10 years prior to interview, social status, protein, carbohydrate, alcohol, calcium, weight history, activity, cholecystectomy, urbanisation, family history

4.10.2.4 Pulses

No association between risk of colon cancer and intake of pulses was found in a cohort of Iowa women; in this population, consumption was low and homogeneous (Steinmetz et al, 1994). In a cohort study of Japanese men in Hawaii, mean consumption of pulses, seeds and nuts (as a group) was lower at baseline among cases than controls (24 versus 29grams per day), although the difference was not statistically significant (Heilbrun et al, 1989).

Of five case-control studies of colon cancer, two reported decreased risk with greater intake of pulses, one reported increased risk and two reported no association. A study in Argentina reported an odds ratio of 0.5(p < 0.05) for higher intakes (Iscovich et al , 1992) and another study in Australia reported odds ratios of 0.4 (0.2–0.9) and 0.7 (0.4–1.5) for higher intakes for males and females respectively (Steinmetz and Potter, 1993). On the other hand, an odds ratio of 4.7 (p < 0.05) was reported for higher consumption of beans in a study in Belgium (Tuyns et al, 1988). Findings from the remaining studies were less striking (La Vecchia et al, 1988; Bidoli et al, 1992).

An ecological study, in which colon cancer mortality among males was compared across 38 countries, reported an inverse correlation of –0.7 for consumption of pulses, (McKeown-Eyssen and Bright-See, 1984).

The Hawaiian–Japanese cohort reported a difference between rectal cancer cases and non-cases in mean consumption of pulses, seeds, and nuts and again the difference was not statistically significant. (Heilbrun et al, 1989)

Of five case-control studies of rectal cancer, two reported decreased risk with greater intake of pulses, one increased risk, and two reported no association. One case-control study in China reported an OR of 0.3 (0.2–0.7) for higher intake of bean products (Hu et al, 1991). Another in Japan reported an OR of 0.5 (0.2–1.1) for higher intake of beans (Kato et al, 1990). Conversely, a study in Belgium reported an OR of 5.9 (p < 0.05) for higher intake of beans (Tuyns et al, 1988). The remaining studies were null (La Vecchia et al, 1988; Bidoli et al, 1992).

A case-control study in Australia that presented data on colorectal cancer combined, but not on each site separately, reported ORs of 0.8 (ns) and 0.6 (p < 0.01) for higher intakes of pulses, nuts and seeds (as a group), for males and females respectively (Kune et al, 1987). Benito et al (1992) reported a similar reduction in risk for the highest quartile of intake of pulses in a study of colorectal cancer in Spain.

One further case-control study of colon cancer in Majorca, not included in the above paragraphs due to its reporting on fibre from pulses rather than pulses per se, found significantly decreased risk with increased intake with an OR of 0.4 for more than 1.1 versus less than 0.2g per day (Benito et al, 1991). Although fibre from pulses represented only 5% of total dietary fibre in this population, it was the only type of fibre for which a strong association was observed.

The evidence relating to pulses and the risk of colorectal cancer is inconsistent; no judgement is possible.

4.10.2.5 Nuts and seeds

As noted above, the Hawaiian Japanese cohort study reported that intake of pulses, nuts and seeds was statistically non-significantly lower in cases than non-cases (Heilbrun et al, 1989). A case-control study in Nebraska reported decreased risk of rectal, but not colon cancer, with higher intake of 'nuts and legumes'; ORs were 2.0 and 1.1 respectively for rectal and colon cancers for more than, versus less than 3.2 servings per week (Pickle et al, 1984).

A case-control study in Australia that reported also (as noted above) on combined colorectal cancer, but not on each site separately, found ORs of 0.8 (ns) and 0.6 (p < 0.01) for higher intakes of pulses, nuts and seeds, for males and females respectively (Kune et al, 1987).

The evidence relating to nuts and seeds and colorectal cancer is very limited; no judgement is possible.

4.10.2.6 Meat

Seven cohort studies have examined meat intake and the risk of colon and rectum cancer. A study of Seventh-day Adventists reported that meat intake was unassociated with risk of colorectal cancer in this generally low meat-eating population (Phillips et al, 1985). The Nurses Health study in the USA reported that subjects who consumed red meat frequently had an increased risk of colon cancer (RR 2.5, 1.2–5.0) compared with those women who rarely consumed red meat (Willett et al, 1990). Another USA study that examined colon cancer risk in a male cohort also reported that men who consumed five or more servings per week of beef, pork or lamb had a moderately increased risk (RR = 1.7; 1.2–2.6) of colon cancer when compared with men who consumed these products less than once per month (Giovannucci et al, 1994). (Table 4.10.10.)

The ACS cohort in the USA found no difference in risk between the uppermost and lowest quintiles of meat consumption in either men or women (Thun et al, 1992). The Netherlands cohort (Goldbohm et al, 1994) and the smaller Finnish study (Knekt et al, 1994) also showed no increase in risk with meat and fried meat consumption respectively. The Iowa women's study in the USA also reported no increase in risk with higher intakes of meat (Bostick et al, 1994).

Two of the four cohort studies showed statistically significant higher risks of colorectal cancer with higher consumption of processed meat (Willett et al, 1990; Goldbohm et al, 1994) and one showed a weakly elevated risk (Bostick et al, 1994). Only one study was null (Giovannucci et al, 1994). Of the 16 estimates of relative risk in Tables 4.10.10, eight were greater than 1.5 or statistically significantly greater than 1.0; eight were between 0.75 and 1.5; none was less than 0.75 or statistically significantly less than 1.0.

The results for the 26 case-control studies of colon or rectum or both (23 on cancer, 3 on adenomatous polyps) are shown in Table 4.10.11. As with the cohort studies, almost all estimates of risk (OR s) are increased or null with higher meat intake.

Each of 16 studies conducted in Greece, Canada,

TABLE 4.10.9 VEGETABLE AND FRUIT CONSUMPTION AND THE RISK OF RECTAL CANCER: CASE-CONTROL STUDIES

AUTHOR, YEAR AND PLACE	NO. OF CASES	TYPE OF VEGETABLE OR FRUIT	COMPARISON	ODDS RATIO (95% CONFIDENCE INTERVAL)	ADJUSTMENT SMOKING HISTORY	OTHER VARIABLES[A]
Bjelke 1974 Norway		fruit	na	decreased risk with increased intake		
		berries	na	decreased risk with increased intake		
Graham et al 1978, USA	512	raw vegetables	> 21 vs 0–10/month	0.6† (na)		
		cabbage	≥ 1/wk vs never	0.7* (na)		
		vegetables	≥ 61 vs 0–20/month	1.7 (na)		
Miller et al, 1983 Canada	194	cruciferous vegetables	men > 32 vs < 11 g/day	0.9 (na)	Y	Y
		citrus fruit	> 66 g/day vs never	0.8 (na)	Y	Y
		non-citrus fruit	> 169 vs < 69 g/day	1.4 (na)	Y	Y
		all vegetables	> 468 vs < 291 g/day	1.1 (na)	Y	Y
		broccoli	h vs l	1.0 (na)	Y	Y
		brussels sprouts	h vs l	1.6 (na)	Y	Y
		cabbage	h vs l	0.9 (na)	Y	Y
		cauliflower	h vs l	1.0 (na)	Y	Y
		turnip	h vs l	0.6* (na)	Y	Y
		fruit juices	> 187 vs < 81 g/day	1.4 (na)	Y	Y
Tajima et al, 1985 Japan	51	onion	> 4 vs < 1/week	3.0† (na)		
		pumpkin	> 1 vs < 1/week	2.6* (na)		
		mushrooms	> 4 vs < 1/week	0.9 (na)		
		carrots	> 4 vs < 1/week	1.1 (na)		
		spinach	> 4 vs < 1/week	1.5 (na)		
		green pepper	> 1 vs < 1/week	1.2 (na)		
		radishes	> 4 vs < 1/week	1.7 (na)		
		cabbage	> 4 vs < 1/week	1.0 (na)		
		lettuce	> 4 vs < 1/week	1.4 (na)		
		tomatoes	> 4 vs < 1/week	1.3 (na)		
		oranges	> 4 vs < 1/week	0.8 (na)		
		other fruit	> 4 vs < 1/week	0.8 (na)		
Macquart-Moulin 1986, France	399	low fibre vegetables	h vs l quartile	1.0 (na)	Y	Y
		medium fibre vegetables	h vs l quartile	0.6 (na)	Y	Y
Kune et al, 1987 Australia	715	cruciferous vegetables	> 425 g/week vs < 105 g/week	0.6 (na)	Y	N
La Vecchia et al 1988, Italy	236	green vegetables	h vs l tertile	0.5† (na)	Y	Y
		melon	h vs l tertile	0.6* (na)	Y	Y
		peppers	h vs l tertile	0.7 (na)	Y	Y
		tomatoes	h vs l tertile	0.8 (na)	Y	Y
		cabbage	h vs l tertile	0.9 (na)	Y	N
		carrots	h vs l tertile	0.7 (na)	Y	N
		spinach	h vs l tertile	1.1 (na)	Y	N
		lettuce	h vs l tertile	0.5 (na)	Y	N
		citrus fruit	h vs l tertile	0.8 (na)	Y	N
		fresh fruit	h vs l tertile	1.2 (na)	Y	N
		apples	h vs l tertile	1.6* (na)	Y	N
Tuyns et al, 1988 Belgium	365	cooked vegetables	> 1375 vs < 800 g/week	0.7 (na)	Y	Y
		celery	> 0 vs < 0 g/week	0.1†† (na)	Y	Y
		leeks	> 0 vs < 0 g/week	0.2†† (na)	Y	Y
		carrots	> 0 vs < 0 g/week	0.8 (na)	Y	Y
		onions	> 0 vs < 0 g/week	0.2†† (na)	Y	Y
		string beans	> 0 vs < 0 g/week	1.3* (na)	Y	Y
		tomatoes	> 0 vs < 0 g/week	1.0 (na)	Y	Y
		tomato puree	> 0 vs < 0 g/week	0.9 (na)	Y	Y

Australia (2), Italy (2), Belgium, the USA (5), Spain, Sweden, Argentina, and the Netherlands reported one or more statistically significant elevated ORs with higher consumption of meat (Manousos et al, 1983; Miller et al, 1983; Kune et al, 1987; La Vecchia et al, 1988; Tuyns et al, 1988; Young and Wolf, 1988; Wohlleb et al, 1990; Benito et al, 1990; Schiffman et al, 1990; Gerhardsson de Verdier et al, 1991; Kune et al, 1990; Bidoli et al, 1992; Iscovitch·et al, 1992; Neugut et al, 1993). Some of these elevated risks were specific to, or more marked in, one sex. For example, Miller et al, (1983); Neugut et al, (1993) and Kampman et al, (1995), all reported higher risk in women than in men. Further, some findings were more obvious for the rectum than the colon (e.g., Miller et al, 1983; Gerhardsson de Verdier et al, 1991). Two studies in Australia and the USA show weak increases in risk with higher intakes of meat (Steinmetz and Potter, 1993 and Sandler et al, 1993).

Seven of the 25 studies are essentially null (Macquart-Moulin et al, 1986, 1987; Lyon and Mahoney, 1988; Lee et al, 1989; Peters et al, 1989; Zaridze et al, 1992; Centonze et

AUTHOR, YEAR AND PLACE	NO. OF CASES	TYPE OF VEGETABLE OR FRUIT	COMPARISON	ODDS RATIO (95% CONFIDENCE INTERVAL)	ADJUSTMENT SMOKING HISTORY	OTHER VARIABLES[A]
		raw vegetables	> 268 vs < 80 g/week	0.5†† (na)	Y	Y
		chicory	> 0 vs < 0 g/week	0.4†† (na)	Y	Y
		endive and lettuce	> 56 vs < 0 g/week	0.5†† (na)	Y	Y
		carrots	> 0 vs < 0 g/week	0.9 (na)	Y	Y
		tomatoes	> 100 vs < 0 g/week	1.4† (na)	Y	Y
		dry pod vegetables	> 0 vs < 0 g/week	1.7* (na)	Y	Y
		beans	> 0 vs < 0 g/week	5.9†† (na)	Y	Y
		fresh fruit	> 1538 vs < 300 g/week	0.9 (na)	Y	Y
		bananas	> 100 vs 0 g/week	1.9†† (na)	Y	Y
		apples	> 560 vs < 0 g/week	0.2†† (na)	Y	Y
		pears	> 0 vs < 0 g/week	0.5† (na)	Y	Y
		citrus fruit	> 490 vs < 0 g/week	0.9 (na)	Y	Y
		stewed canned fruit	> 188 vs < 0 g/week	1.4* (na)	Y	Y
Lee et al, 1989 Singapore	203	cruciferous vegetables	h vs l tertile	0.5 (0.3–1.0)	Y	Y
		total vegetables	h vs l tertile	0.5 (0.3–1.0)	Y	Y
Freudenheim et al 1990, USA	277	broccoli	men na	decreased risk with increased intake		
		celery	women na	decreased risk with increased intake		
		lettuce	na	decreased risk with increased intake		
		carrots	na	decreased risk with increased intake		
		green peppers	na	decreased risk with increased intake		
		cucumbers	na	decreased risk with increased intake		
		tomatoes	na	decreased risk with increased intake		
		green beans	na	decreased risk with increased intake		
		tomatoes	na	decreased risk with increased intake		
Benito et al, 1990 Spain	130	cruciferous vegetables	h vs l quartile	2.3 (na)	Y	Y
Hu et al, 1991 China	225	chives and celery	men ≥ 7.5 kg/yr vs none	0.2† (0.04–0.6)		
		bean products	> 9 kg/yr vs < 2 kg/yr	0.3† (0.2–0.7)		
		green vegetables	women ≥ 30 kg/yr vs < 30 kg/yr	0.1 (0.02–0.5)		
		garlic	ever vs never	0.2 (0.1–0.8)		
Bidoli et al, 1992 Italy	125	total vegetables	h vs l tertile	0.6 (na)	Y	Y
		cruciferous vegetables	h vs l tertile	0.6 (na)	Y	Y
		green peppers	h vs l tertile	0.9 (na)	Y	Y
		lettuce	h vs l tertile	0.6† (na)	Y	Y
		potatoes	h vs l tertile	1.5 (na)	Y	Y
		spinach	h vs l tertile	0.6† (na)	Y	Y
		carrots	h vs l tertile	0.4† (na)	Y	Y
		tomatoes	h vs l tertile	0.4† (na)	Y	Y
		total fresh fruit	h vs l tertile	0.7 (na)	Y	Y
		apples	h vs l tertile	0.7 (na)	Y	Y
		citrus fruit	h vs l tertile	1.0 (na)	Y	Y
		melon	h vs l tertile	1.2 (na)	Y	Y

* p < 0.05
† p < 0.01
†† p < 0.001
na not available
a Also adjusted for one or more of the following: energy intake, energy, weight, education, area, 5 food groups, province, race, occupation, weight 10 years prior to interview, job activity trends, intake of other food groups, social status

al, 1994). Two of them were conducted in France, two in the USA, one in Russia and one in Singapore.

Among the 86 estimates of risk in Table 4.10.11, only five are statistically significantly less than 1.0; three of these are associated with pork intake in Australia and Belgium. These same studies showed statistically significantly increases in risk in association with higher beef consumption (Kune et al, 1987; Tuyns et al, 1988). The other two findings of reduced risk came from the study in China (Hu et al, 1991) and are seen for rectal, but not colon, cancer.

Five of the studies that reported on processed or cured meats found statistically significantly elevated risks (Young and Wolf, 1988; Wohlleb et al, 1990; Gerhardsson de Verdier et al; 1991; Bidoli et al 1992; Peters et al, 1992), whereas the other four showed no association (Peters et al, 1989; Benito et al, 1990; Steinmetz et al, 1993 and Centonze et al, 1994).

Both case-control studies that specifically explored the question of the role of cooking found statistically significant higher risks (Schiffman 1990, Gerhardsson de Verdier et al,

TABLE 4.10.10 MEAT INTAKE AND THE RISK OF COLORECTAL CANCER: COHORT STUDIES

AUTHOR, YEAR	SIZE OF COHORT: NO OF CASES	SITE	TYPE OF MEAT	COMPARISON	RELATIVE RISK (95% CONFIDENCE INTERVAL)	SEX/AGE	ADJUSTMENT OTHER VARIABLES[a]	ENERGY INTAKE
Phillips et al 1985	25,493: 182	colorectal	meat	≥ 4/week vs < 1/week	0.9 (0.6–1.5)	Y	N	N
Willett et al 1990	88,751: 150 women	colon	meat	≥ 134 vs < 59 g/day	1.77* (1.09–2.88)	Y	N	Y
			beef, pork or lamb as main dish	≥ 1/day vs < 1/month	2.49* (1.24–5.03)	Y	N	N
			processed meat	≥ 2/week vs < 1/month	1.86* (1.16–2.98)	Y	N	N
Thun et al, 1992	3,051: 611 men	colon	meat	h vs l quintile	1.21 (nr)	N	N	N
	2,695: 539 women	colon	meat	h vs l quintile	1.05 (nr)	N	N	N
Giovannucci et al 1992	7,284: 170 men	colorectal (adenomas)	meat	> 110g/day vs < 24 g/day	1.23* (0.7–2.14)	Y	Y	Y
Giovannucci et al 1994	47,949: 205 men	colon	meat	h vs l quintile: > 129.5 g/day vs < 18.5 g/day	1.71* (1.15–2.55)	Y	N	Y
			beef, pork or lamb as main dish	≥ 5/week vs 0	3.57* (1.58–8.06)	Y	N	Y
			processed meat	≥ 5/week vs 0	1.16 (0.44–3.04)	Y	N	Y
Goldbohm et al 1994	120,852: 215	colon	fresh meat (including chicken)	158 (145) g/day vs 54 (43) g/day[b,c]	0.84 (0.51–1.37)	Y	Y	Y[d]
			processed meat	h vs l quintile: > 20 g/day vs 0[b]	1.72* (1.03–2.87)	Y	Y	Y[d]
Knekt et al, 1994	9,990: 73	colorectal	fried meat	h vs l tertile	1.03 (0.56–1.90)	Y	Y	Y
Bostick et al 1994	35,212: 212 women	colon	meat	> 11/week vs < 1/week	1.04 (0.62–1.76)	Y	Y	Y
			beef, pork or lamb as main dish	> 3/week vs < 1/week	1.21 (0.75–1.96)	Y	Y	Y
			processed meat	> 3/week vs 0	1.51 (0.72–3.17)	Y	Y	Y

*   p ≤ 0.05 for trend or highest vs lowest consumption
nr   not reported
ns   not significant
a   Also adjusted for one or more of the following: education, area of residence, socio-economic status, ethnicity, body weight, smoking status, family history
b   Median intake of quintile
c   Intake for men and women respectively
d   Adjusted also for dietary fibre intake

1991) (see below).

Of the 86 ORs in Table 4.10.11, 47 are greater than 1.5 or statistically significantly greater than 1.0; 31 are between 0.75 and 1.5; and 8 are less than 0.75 or statistically significantly less than 1.0.

Mechanisms by which red meat and processed meat may increase the risk of colorectal cancer include the facilitating effect of fat on bile acid production, and the formation of carcinogens when meat is cooked or processed. Processed meats may contribute to the production of nitrosamines.

It is unclear whether the specific mechanisms of increased risk associated with meat intake involve animal fat, processing and cooking methods, or other factors. The evidence shows that red meat probably increases risk and processed meat possibly increases risk of colorectal cancer.

4.10.2.7 Poultry

Of three cohort studies, one of men in the USA found no substantial association between poultry consumption and risk of colon cancer (Giovannucci et al, 1994). A study of a cohort of women in Iowa (US) also reported no substantial associa-

tion with poultry without skin, but did find that women who were in the uppermost quartile for consumption of poultry with skin had a weakly increased risk of colon cancer (RR = 1.52; p = 0.07) (Bostick et al, 1994). In a cohort of USA women, consumption of chicken without skin, at least five times per week, was associated with a statistically significant decreased risk of colon cancer when compared with women whose frequency of consumption was less than once per month (Willett et al, 1990).

The majority of case-control studies have noted no relationship between poultry intake and colorectal cancer risk (LaVecchia et al, 1988; Tuyns et al, 1988; Lee et al, 1989; Bidoli et al, 1992; Peters et al, 1992; Centonze et al, 1994; Goldbohm et al, 1994; Kampman et al, 1996). However, a study in Canada that distinguished between men and women, and by colon versus rectum found that women who were in the highest tertile for poultry consumption had a moderately decreased risk of cancer of the rectum (OR = 0.5; p < 0.05). No associations were apparent for men or for colon cancer (Miller et al, 1983). Two other case-control studies have noted elevated risk with higher poultry consumption: in a study in Japan, high chicken consumption was associated with a twofold increase in risk (Tajima et al,

1985). The other study – conducted in Australia – reported an OR of 1.6 (0.8 – 3.2) for men who consumed more poultry. No such association was apparent for women, although some subsite differences were suggested (Steinmetz and Potter, 1993).

The data on poultry consumption are inconsistent; it may be that poultry has no relationship with colorectal cancer, but no judgement is possible.

4.10.2.8 Fish

In one cohort of women in the USA, there was no substantial association between the highest frequency of fish consumption (at least five times per week) and the risk of colon cancer (Willett et al, 1990). Two cohort studies, one in the USA and one in the Netherlands, have found no substantial associations (Giovannucci et al, 1994; Goldbohm et al, 1994).

Eight case-control studies have also found no association between fish consumption and risk of colorectal cancer (Tajima et al, 1985; Macquart-Moulin et al, 1986; Lee et al, 1989; Benito et al, 1991; Bidoli et al, 1992; Peters et al, 1992; Centonze et al, 1994; Kampman et al, 1996). However, four studies have suggested that higher fish intake may be associated with reduced risk. Bjelke (1973) suggested a statistically non-significant decrease in risk for higher fish intake. A study in Australia reported decreased risk for colon and rectal cancer for subjects who were in the uppermost quintile for fish consumption with ORs of 0.7 and 0.5 for colon and rectum respectively (Kune et al, 1987). Similar ORs for colon and rectum cancers were also reported in an Italian case-control study (La Vecchia et al, 1988). One Japanese case-control study reported that persons who ate shrimp at least once per month had a decreased risk of both colon cancer (OR = 0.6; p < 0.01) and rectal cancer (0.5; p < 0.01) compared to those who ate shrimp less than once per month (Haenszel et al, 1980).

Diets high in fish possibly have no relationship with the risk of colorectal cancer.

4.10.2.9 Eggs

A cohort of Seventh-day Adventists in the USA reported no substantial association between frequency of egg consumption and risk of rectal cancer among men and women together; however, men who consumed at least five eggs per week had an RR of 1.6 (0.8–3.4) for colon cancer when compared with men who ate less than two eggs per week. A cohort of women in Iowa reported no substantial association between frequency of egg consumption and the risk of either rectal or colon cancer. (RRs = 1.1, 0.2–4.5 and 1.3, 0.5–3.1, respectively) for more than seven per week compared to less than one per month).

Nine of 16 case-control studies have reported elevations in the risk associated with egg consumption. Sex differences were apparent in one Canadian case-control study (Miller et al, 1983); no substantial associations between egg consumption and colon cancer risk were apparent for men, whereas women who were in the uppermost tertile for egg consumption had a moderately increased risk of colon cancer. However, both sexes had strongly increased risks of rectal cancer with higher egg consumption (males OR = 2.2, p = 0.00; females OR = 2.0, p = 0.01). Similar findings have been reported in an Australian study, which showed no substantial association between egg consumption and colon cancer risk in men, but a strong increase in risk for women who consumed at least three eggs per week compared with those who ate less than or equal to 0.5 eggs per week (Steinmetz and Potter, 1993). A case-control study in Belgium found that higher frequency of egg consumption was associated with moderately increased risk of rectal cancer (OR = 1.6; p for trend = 0.008) but was not associated with risk of colon cancer (Tuyns et al, 1988). Conversely, a study in Italy reported a marginally stronger association between egg consumption and the risk of colon cancer (OR 2.5; p < 0.001) than rectal cancer risk (OR = 1.9; p = 0.01) (Bidoli et al, 1992). A case-control study in Spain noted that higher consumption of eggs was associated equally with increased risk of cancers of the colon (OR = 2.3; ns) and rectum (OR = 2.0; ns) (Benito et al, 1991).

The one case-control study which differentiated between cancers of the proximal and distal colon found that higher frequency of egg consumption was associated with a moderate increase in risk of proximal colon cancer, but that there was no substantial association between eggs and distal colon cancer (Young and Wolf, 1988).

The strongest association between egg consumption and colon cancer risk was found in an Argentinian study which reported that persons who ate at least 88 eggs per year had an OR of 4.7 (1.5-14.4) compared with those who consumed 11 or fewer eggs per year (Iscovich et al, 1992).

Two further case-control studies also noted increased risk of cancers of the large bowel (Martinez et al, 1979) and GI tract (Modan et al, 1981).

Seven of 16 case-control studies reported no substantial association between egg consumption and risk of colorectal cancer (Phillips et al, 1975; Tajima and Tominaga, 1985; Macquart-Moulin et al, 1986; Kune et al, 1987; LaVecchia et al, 1988; Centonze et al, 1994; Kampman et al, 1996).

Eggs are the top contributor of cholesterol to the western diet. Thus, an association with eggs may reflect an effect of cholesterol intake.

Animal studies have shown that metabolites of cholesterol in the colonic lumen may act to promote colon carcinogenesis. These include the colonic bacterial metabolites of cholesterol, coprostanol and cholestanone (Uchida et al, 1977; Cruse et al, 1979; Hiramatsu et al, 1983).

Based on this evidence, consumption of eggs possibly increases risk of colorectal cancers.

4.10.2.10 Milk and dairy products

Two cohort studies (Giovannucci et al, 1994; Phillips and Snowdon, 1985) and seven case-control studies (Manousos et al, 1983; Phillips and Snowdon, 1985; Tajima and

TABLE 4.10.11 MEAT INTAKE AND THE RISK OF COLORECTAL CANCER: CASE-CONTROL STUDIES

AUTHOR, YEAR AND PLACE	NO OF CASES	SITE	TYPE OF MEAT	COMPARISON	RELATIVE RISK (95% CONFIDENCE INTERVAL)	SEX/AGE	ADJUSTMENT OTHER VARIABLES[a]	ENERGY INTAKE
Manousos et al 1983, Greece	100	colorectal	beef	2/week vs 1/week	1.77* (nr)	Y	N	N
			lamb	2/week vs 1/week	2.61* (nr)	Y	N	N
Miller et al, 1983 Canada	171 men	colon	beef	> 110 g/day vs < 64.2 g/day	1.2 (nr)	Y	N	N
			pork	> 23.1 g/day vs < 6.9 g/day	1.1 (nr)	Y	N	N
	177 women	colon	beef	> 42.2 vs 0 g/day	1.0 (nr)	Y	N	N
			pork	< 14.0 g/day vs < 4.3 g/day	1.4 (nr)	Y	N	N
	114 men	rectum	beef	> 110 g/day vs < 64.2 g/day	1.7* (nr)	Y	N	N
			pork	> 23.1 g/day vs < 6.9 g/day	1.3 (nr)	Y	N	N
	80 women	rectum	beef	> 42.2 vs 0g/day	1.7* (nr)	Y	N	N
			pork	> 23.1 g/day vs < 6.9 g/day	2.7* (nr)	Y	N	N
Macquart-Moulin et al, 1986, France	399	colorectal	meat (including poultry)	h vs l quartile	0.89 (nr)	Y	Y	Y
Macquart-Moulin et al, 1986, France	252	colorectal (polyps)	meat (including poultry)	> 155.7 g/day vs <78.6 g/day	0.81 (nr)	Y	Y	Y
Kune et al, 1987 Australia	715	colorectal	beef	above vs below threshold	1.75* (1.20–2.44)	Y	N	N
			pork	above vs below threshold	0.55* (0.42–0.73)	Y	N	N
La Vecchia et al, 1988, Italy	339	colon	beef or veal	h vs l tertile	2.13* (nr)	Y	Y	N[b]
	236	rectum	beef or veal	h vs l tertile	2.26* (nr)			
Tuyns et al, 1988 Belgium	453	colon	beef	> 77 g/day vs < 32 g/day	2.09* (nr)	Y	Y	N
			pork	> 73 g/day vs < 28 g/day	0.39* (nr)	Y	Y	N
	365	rectum	beef	> 77 g/day vs < 32 g/day	0.71 (nr)	Y	Y	N
			pork	> 73 g/day vs < 28 g/day	0.70* (nr)	Y	Y	N
Lyon and Mahoney 1988, USA	246	colon	fried meat	men: ≥ 11.5/week vs ≤ 6/week	1.2 (0.8–1.9)	Y	N	Y
				women: ≥ 8.25/week vs ≤ 3.75/week	1.3 (0.8–2.1)	Y	N	Y
			broiled meat	men: ≥ 1.25/week vs ≤ 0.25/week	0.7 (0.5–1.0)	Y	N	Y
				women: ≥ 1.75/week vs ≤ 0.25/week	1.1 (0.7–1.7)	Y	N	Y
Young and Wolf 1988, USA	353	colorectal	lunchmeat	> 20/month vs < 1/month	1.85* (1.33–2.58)	Y	N	N
Lee et al, 1989 Singapore	203	colorectal	meat	h vs l tertile	1.29 (0.84–1.97)	Y	Y	N
Peters et al, 1989 USA	147 men	colorectal	fried bacon or ham	≥ 5/week vs ≤ 1/week	1.0 (0.4–2.4)	Y	Y	N
			barbecued or smoked meat	≥ 5/week vs ≤ 1/week	1.3 (0.6–2.7)	Y	Y	N
			beef	≥ 5/week vs ≤ 1/week	1.0 (0.6–1.6)	Y	Y	N
Wohlleb et al 1990, USA	43	colorectal	pork	≥ 1/week vs < 1/week	3.3* (1.3–8.1)	Y	N	N
			cured or smoked luncheon meat	≥ 1/week vs < 1/week	2.9* (1.2–7.1)	Y	N	N
			barbecued meat	≥ 1/week vs < 1/week	3.3* (1.2–9.2)	Y	N	N
			cured or smoked bacon	≥ 1/week vs < 1/week	5.0* (0.99–2.5)	Y	N	N
Benito et al 1990, Spain	156	colon	meat	> 32/month vs < 16/month	2.87* (nr)	Y	Y	N[c]
	130	rectum	meat	> 32/month vs < 16/month	2.42 (nr)	Y	Y	N
	286	colorectal	processed meat	> 22/month vs 0	1.36 (nr)	Y	Y	N
Schiffman, 1990 USA	50	colorectal	meat	well done vs rare to medium rare	3.5* (1.3–9.6)	N	N	N
Gerhardsson de Verdier et al 1991, Sweden	452	colon	bacon/smoked ham	> 1/week vs < 1/month	1.3 (0.8–1.9)	Y	N	N[d]
			beef/pork, fried	> 1/week vs < 1/month	1.1 (0.7–1.8)			
			beef/pork, roasted	> 1/week vs < 1/month	1.2 (0.8–1.8)			
			beef/pork, boiled	> 1/week vs < 1/month	1.8* (1.2–2.6)			

Author, year and place	No of cases	Site	Type of meat	Comparison	Relative risk (95% confidence interval)	Sex/age	Adjustment Other variables[a]	Energy intake
			sausage, fried	> 1/week vs < 1/month	1.0 (0.6–1.4)			
			sausage, roasted	> 1/week vs < 1/month	1.2 (0.5–2.8)			
			sausage, boiled	> 1/week vs < 1/month	1.4* (0.9–2.2)			
			brown gravy	> 1/week vs < 1/month	1.6* (1.1–2.3)			
	268	rectum	bacon/smoked ham	> 1/week vs < 1/month	1.7* (1.1–2.8)	Y	N	N[d]
			beef/pork, fried	> 1/week vs < 1/month	1.6 (0.9–3.0)			
			beef/pork, roasted	> 1/week vs < 1/month	1.8* (1.1–2.9)			
			beef/pork, boiled	> 1/week vs < 1/month	1.9* (1.2–3.0)			
			sausage, fried	> 1/week vs < 1/month	1.5 (0.9–2.3)			
			sausage, roasted	> 1/week vs < 1/month	2.1* (0.9–4.9)			
			sausage, boiled	> 1/week vs < 1/month	3.0* (1.8–4.9)			
			brown gravy	> 1/week vs < 1/month	1.9* (1.2–3.0)			
	452	colon	all meat	> 7/week vs < 1.6/week	1.9* (nr)			
			fried/roasted meat	> 5.25/week vs < 1/week	1.3 (nr)			
			boiled meat	> 2.5/week vs < 1/month	2.0* (nr)			
	268	rectum	all meat	> 7/week vs < 1.6/week	3.2* (nr)			
			fried/roasted meat	> 5.25/week vs < 1/week	2.1* (nr)			
			boiled meat	> 2.5/week vs < 1/month	3.0* (nr)			
Hu et al, 1991 China	116 men	rectum	meat	< 38 g/week vs > 96 g/week	0.3 (0.1–0.6)	Y	Y	N
	109 women	rectum	meat	< 38 g/week vs > 96 g/week	0.5 (0.3–0.9)	Y	Y	N
Kune et al, 1991 Australia	49	colorectal (adenomas)	beef (men)	above vs below threshold	2.42 (2.02–5.76)	?	?	?
			pork	above vs below threshold	0.69 (0.35–1.36)			
Bidoli et al, 1992 Italy	123	colon	meat	h vs l tertile	1.6 (nr)	Y	Y	N
			salami and sausages	h vs l tertile	1.8 (nr)	Y	Y	N
	125	rectum	meat	h vs l tertile	2.0* (nr)	Y	Y	N
			salami and sausages	h vs l tertile	1.9* (nr)	Y	Y	N
Iscovich et al 1992, Argentina	110	colon	meat	> 6/week vs < 3.4/week	0.82 (0.39–1.70)	Y	Y	N
				3.4 to 6/wk vs < 3.4/wk	2.29* (1.03–5.08)	Y	Y	N
Peters et al, 1992 USA	746	colon	meat	per unit	1.16* (1.09–1.26)	Y	N	N[e]
			processed meat	per unit	1.06* (1.01–1.12)	Y	N	N[e]
Zaridze et al 1992, Russia	217	colorectal	meat	h vs l quintile	1.02 (0.54–1.96)	Y	Y	Y
Steinmetz et al 1993, Austalia	121 men	colon	meat	≥ 8.3/week vs ≤ 3.9/week	1.59 (0.81–3.13)	Y	Y	Y[f]
			processed meat	≥ 7.7/week vs ≤ 2.2/week	1.03 (0.55–1.95)	Y	Y	Y
	99 women	colon	meat	≥ 7.2/week vs ≤ 3.4/week	1.48 (0.73–3.01)	Y	Y	Y
			processed meat	≥ 4.4/week vs ≤ 1.4/week	0.77 (0.35–1.68)	Y	Y	Y
Sandler et al 1993, USA	105 men	colorectal (adenomas)	beef	≥ 2.3/week vs < 0.5/week	1.59 (0.72–3.50)	Y	Y	Y
	131 women			≥ 2.6/week vs < 0.6/week	2.07 (0.82–5.19)	Y	Y	Y
Neugut et al 1993, USA	162 men	colorectal (adenomas)	meat to chicken ratio	> 2.16 vs < 0.43	1.3 (0.7–2.4)	Y	Y	Y
	124 women			> 1.33 vs < 0.34	1.9 (1.0–3.6)	Y	Y	Y
Centonze et al 1994, Italy	119	colorectal	fresh meat	≥ 132 g/day vs < 87 g/day	0.74 (0.37–1.45)	Y	Y	N
			processed meat	≥ 3 g/day vs ≤ 2 g/day	1.01 (0.57–1.69)	Y	Y	N
Kampmann et al 1995, Netherlands	130 men	colon	meat	> 102 g/day vs < 60 g/day	0.89 (0.43–1.81)	Y	Y	Y[e]
	102 women			> 83 g/day vs 38 g/day	2.35* (0.97–5.66)	Y	Y	Y[e]

*　p ≤ 0.05 for trend or highest vs lowest consumption
nr　not reported
ns　not significant
a　Including one or more variables such as education, area of residence, socio-economic status, ethnicity, body weight, smoking status, family history
b　Adjusted for other food items significantly related to risk (pasta, rice, vegetables, tomatoes, melons, coffee)
c　Adjusted for frequency of intake of cereals, potatoes, cruciferous vegetables, dairy products and eggs
d　Adjusted for fat intake
e　When adjusted for all calorie-bearing nutrients, ORs became non-significant
f　Adjusted for alcohol intake

Tominga, 1985; Lee et al, 1989; Peters et al, 1989; Bostick et al, 1993; Kampman et al, 1996) have reported no association between any dairy foods and risk of colorectal cancer.

However, results from 11 other case-control studies are equivocal. One study of Seventh-day Adventists in the USA reported that persons who consumed at least one serving of milk per day had a decreased risk of colon cancer (OR = 0.3) compared to those who consumed less than one portion per day (Phillips, 1975). Protective associations with milk were also observed in a French case-control study (OR = 0.7; p < 0.03) (Macquart-Moulin et al, 1986) and a case-control study in Italy (Centonze et al, 1994). High frequency of consumption of cultured milk was associated with a decreased risk in both proximal (OR = 0.5; 0.3–1.0) and distal (OR = 0.8; 0.45-1.3) colon cancers in a USA case-control study (Young and Wolf, 1988) but no associations were apparent for fresh milk. Another USA case-control study also noted an association with yoghurt (OR = 0.8; p < 0.05) but no association for milk (Peters et al, 1992).

Several studies have suggested that higher consumption of milk and/or dairy products may be associated with increased colorectal cancer risk. One of the earliest studies noted that, as milk consumption increased, risk of colorectal cancer increased (Haenszel et al, 1973). Two other case-control studies also found that higher milk intakes were associated with moderately increased risk of colorectal cancer (Kune et al, 1987; Tuyns et al, 1988). A case-control study in Canada that examined the intakes of a 'miscellaneous milk' category (cream, ice cream, desserts, milk) and risks of colon and rectal cancer reported that women in the uppermost tertile for consumption had a moderately increased risk of colon cancer, but that there was no apparent association in men. For rectal cancer, women in the uppermost tertile had a strongly increased risk whereas males had a more moderately increased risk (Miller et al, 1983). Although adjusting for saturated fat decreased the relative risks somewhat, higher consumption of milk products was still associated with an increased risk.

Cheese has been reported both to have no association with risk of colon and rectal cancer (Tuyns et al, 1988) and to be associated with an increased risk of colon (OR = 1.7; p = 0.03) and rectal (OR = 1.8; p = 0.01) cancers (Bidoli et al, 1992).

Finally, a case-control study in Spain found that persons in the uppermost quartile for dairy- product consumption had strongly increased risks of rectal cancer relative to those in the lowest quartile. However, in the same study, there was no association between dairy-product consumption and risk of colon cancer (Benito et al, 1991).

It seems plausible that, in relation to colorectal cancer, any increased risk associated with dairy products may be due to fat whereas any decreased risk may be a consequence of vitamin D and calcium content and possibly, for some dairy products, conjugated linoleic acid. As it stands, however, the evidence on the relationship between colorectal cancer and dairy products is inconsistent; no judgement is possible.

4.10.2.11 Coffee

Caffeine or coffee intake has been associated with approximately a twofold increased colon cancer risk in populations that are predominantly Mormon (Slattery et al, 1990) and Seventh-day Adventist (Phillips and Snowdon, 1985), and with a much smaller risk in one USA case-control study (Graham et al, 1978). In ten other studies, coffee intake has been associated with a decreased risk of colorectal cancer (risk estimates in the range of 0.6 to 0.7) (Haenszel et al, 1973; Jacobsen et al, 1986; Macquart-Moulin et al, 1986; LaVecchia et al, 1988, 1989; Tuyns et al, 1988; Lee et al, 1989; Rosenberg et al, 1989; Benito et al, 1991; Centonze et al, 1994). While two of these 10 studies (Haenzel et al, 1973; Rosenberg et al, 1989) were carried out in the USA, and the study by Lee (1989) in Singapore, the other seven were conducted in Europe. Four other studies have reported no association with coffee: one cohort study (Nomura et al, 1986); and three case-control studies (Graham et al, 1988; Bidoli et al, 1992; Peters et al, 1992); three of these four studies were conducted in the USA.

Some of these differences in findings could be a consequence of differences in the amount of coffee consumed. For instance, in the study of Bjelke (Bjelke, 1973, 1974) where a reduced risk was observed at the highest level of intake, those in the intermediate level of intake (2 to 3 cups a day) were at an increased level of risk similar to that observed in Mormons and Seventh-day Adventists where the upper level of intake was only two to three cups. In the study by Rosenberg et al (1989), the decrease in the risk of colon cancer was observed only for drinkers of more than four cups of coffee per day. No effect on risk was observed at lower levels of consumption. It is also possible that the increase in risk with coffee reported by Snowdon and Phillips (1984) and Graham et al (1978) reflects confounding from other dietary factors, such as fat or red meat, as detailed dietary data were collected in neither of these studies. As implied above, another major difference in studies showing increased or no change in risk versus those suggesting a protective association is that the majority of the increased/no risk studies were conducted in the USA (6 of 7) and the majority of the decreased risk studies were conducted in Europe (7 of 10). There are significant differences in coffee preparation between these populations.

Animal studies have shown no correlation between coffee consumption and tumor induction (Bauer et al, 1977; Palm et al, 1984). The mechanism by which coffee could affect colorectal cancer risk remains unclear. However, it has been proposed that coffee may decrease colon cancer risk by reducing excretion of bile acid and sterols into the bowel (Jacobsen and Thelle, 1987). Other possible mechanisms include the inhibition of chemical carcinogenesis by caffeine or other compounds in coffee (for example, kahweol and cafestol) (Nomura, 1974; Lam et al, 1982; Wattenberg and Lam, 1983). In contrast, coffee has been found to be mutagenic in the Ames test (Levin, 1982; Kosugi et al, 1983).

4.10.3 FOOD PROCESSING

4.10.3.1 Other residues

Chemical residues

Waterborne: chlorine

In 1991, IARC reviewed the relationship between chlorinated water and risk of cancers of the colon and rectum. One case-control study (Lawrence et al, 1984), showed no elevation in risk of colorectal cancer as a whole in the comparison between surface water and groundwater where the exposure data were collected at individual level. Four other case-control studies (Brenniman et al, 1980; Gottlieb et al, 1982; Young and Kanarek, 1983; Zierler et al, 1986), examined the risk of colon and rectal cancer separately using a community-based exposure definition and a variety of comparisons between chlorinated and otherwise treated or untreated water. Three of the fourteen estimates of risk were statistically significantly elevated, one for colon cancer in women (OR = 1.4, p< 0.05) (Young and Kanarek, 1983), and two for rectal cancer in men (OR = 3.2, 2.0–5.2) and women (OR= 1.7; 1.0–3.1)(Gottlieb et al, 1982). All of the other estimates of risk were not statistically different from 1.0. Six correlation studies have been undertaken (De Rouen and Diem, 1977; Kuzma et al, 1977; Bean et al, 1982; Cantor et al, 1978; Tuthill and Moore, 1980; Isacson et al, 1983). Of these six, only one (De Rouen and Diem, 1977) is consistent with an increased risk of colon cancer; the other five are essentially null. For rectal cancer, the results are more variable with both increased (De Rouen and Diem, 1977; Bean,1982) and decreased (Isacson et al, 1983) risks having been reported in association with chlorinated vs unchlorinated water. Tuthill and Moore (1980) reported a positive correlation with an estimate of trihalomethane exposure and the other two studies (Kurzma et al, 1977; Cantor et al, 1978) were null.

The data on the relationship between chlorinated drinking water and colorectal cancer are inconsistent; no judgement is possible.

4.10.3.2 Cooking

Broiling, grilling, barbecuing, frying

Sugimura and Sato (1983) originally proposed that specific heterocyclic amines, potent mutagens present in cooked food, were important in the aetiology of colon cancer. Several separate classes of these compounds have been identified (Jagerstad et al, 1986) and have been shown to be carcinogenic in animals (Ohgaki et al, 1986).

In the study of Gerhardsson de Verdier et al (1991) an odds ratio for colon cancer of 2.7 (1.4–5.9) was reported for the most frequent consumers of fried meat with a heavily browned surface (top 40% versus. lower 60% of consumption) and an even higher risk (OR= 6.0) for rectal cancer. Similarly Schiffman (1990) noted a 3.5-fold increase in risk

for those preferring well-done meat. Similar findings have been obtained in a case-control study of colorectal adenomas (Probst-Hensch et al, 1997). Subjects who ate red meat more than once a week, fried it more than 10% of the time, and ate it with a darkly browned surface were at a higher risk of adenomas than those who ate red meat once or less per week, fried it 10% or less of the time, and ate it with a lightly browned surface (OR = 2.2, 1.1–4.3). Adenoma risk also increased with frequency of frying red meat.

Heterocyclic amines from heavily-cooked meats are metabolised by the enzymes *N*-acetyltransferase and CYP_{1A2}, both of which show marked genetically-determined phenotypic variation in the population (Turesky et al, 1991; Kadlubar et al, 1992) but not all of the mechanisms and genetic data are consistent (Vineis and McMichael, 1996)

An increased risk of colon cancer has been observed in rapid acetylators in four of five studies; further in two of these, the association was found only in meat eaters (Lang et al, 1995; Roberts-Thomson et al, 1995).

Cooking meat at high temperatures possibly increases the risk of colorectal cancer.

4.11 Breast

Cancer of the breast is, in women, the most common incident cancer and cause of death from cancer, and is the third most common cancer overall, throughout the world. An estimated 910,000 cases occurred in 1996, accounting for nine per cent of all new cases of cancer.

Incidence of, and deaths from, this cancer are generally increasing throughout the world, mostly in developed societies.

The panel has reached the following conclusions. Some factors that affect the risk of breast cancer probably act early in life. In particular, evidence that rapid early growth and greater adult height increase risk is convincing.

In addition, diets high in vegetables and fruits probably decrease the risk of breast cancer; and alcohol and weight gain in adult life probably increase risk, as does high body mass after the menopause.

FOOD, NUTRITION AND BREAST CANCER

In the judgement of the panel, the dietary constituents and related factors, and the food and drinks listed below modify the risk of breast cancer, or else have no relationship to it. Judgements are graded according to the strength of evidence.

EVIDENCE	DECREASES RISK	NO RELATIONSHIP	INCREASES RISK
Convincing		Coffee	Rapid growth and greater adult height[b]
Probable	Vegetables and fruits[a]	Cholesterol	High body mass[c] Adult weight gain Alcohol
Possible	Physical activity NSP/fibre Carotenoids	Monounsaturated fat Polyunsaturated fat Retinol Vitamin E Poultry Black tea	Total fat Saturated/animal fat Meat
Insufficient	Vitamin C Isoflavones and lignans Fish		Animal protein DDT residues

For an explanation of the terms used in matrix, see chapter 3.
[a] In particular, the evidence is most abundant and consistent for vegetables, and particularly green vegetables
[b] Based upon studies of age at menarche and studies of height
[c] Postmenopausal

The panel notes that non-starch polysaccharides (fibre), regular physical activity, and carotenoids possibly decrease the risk of breast cancer, and that diets high in red meat, total fat, and animal/saturated fat, possibly increase risk.

The evidence that regular consumption of coffee does not affect the risk of breast cancer is convincing.

Established non-dietary causes of breast cancer include nulliparity, late age at first pregnancy, late menopause, ionising radiation and specific inherited genetic abnormalities.

The most effective dietary means of preventing breast cancer are the consumption of diets high in vegetables and fruits, avoidance of alcohol, and the maintenance of body weight within recommended levels by consumption of appropriate diets and by regular physical activity throughout life.

BREAST CANCER estimated rates of cancer incidence by sex and area

115.6

49.2

89.6

100.3

67.7

5.0		Women

1. Eastern Africa
2. Middle Africa
3. Northern Africa
4. Southern Africa
5. Western Africa
6. Caribbean
7. Central America
8. South America (Temperate)
9. South America (Tropical)
10. North America
11. Eastern Asia: China
12. Eastern Asia: Japan
13. Eastern Asia: Other
14. South Eastern Asia
15. Southern Asia
16. Western Asia
17. Eastern Europe
18. Northern Europe
19. Southern Europe
20. Western Europe
21. Australia/New Zealand
22. Melenesia
23. Micronesia/Polynesia
24. USSR

INTRODUCTION

INCIDENCE PATTERNS

Cancer of the breast is the third most common cancer in the world. In 1996, there were an estimated 910,00 new cases diagnosed worldwide (WHO, 1997), accounting for 9% of all new cancers. Breast cancer is the most common cancer in women.

Over 50% of breast cancer incidence (494,000 cases in 1996) occurs in the developed world. High risk areas include Europe and North America which, together, accounted for 400,000 cases in 1996. The lowest rates are reported in Africa and Asia. However, breast cancer is increasing in most countries, particularly in areas which have previously had low rates, although at least part of the increase is due to early detection of cases by screening (Doll et al, 1994).

Populations that migrate from low- to high-incidence countries develop rates of breast cancer which approximate those of the new host country, although the rapidity with which this occurs varies.

Of all cases diagnosed, approximately 50% will survive over a five-year period when given appropriate treatment. In 1996, mortality attributable to breast cancer was estimated at 390,000, 5.5% of all cancer deaths (WHO, 1997).

PATHOGENESIS

While some epidemiological risk factors for breast cancer have been identified, the events and/or factors that are responsible for the initiation and transformation of mammary epithelial cells are not clear. Numerous animal studies have identified chemical carcinogens that result in mammary tumors in rodents, but no known human carcinogens have been clearly established. There are some suggestions, nonetheless, that exposure to tobacco smoke – both active and passive – may be important (Morabia et al, 1996; Smith et al, 1994).

However, many chemical carcinogens are lipophilic substances, and may be stored in the adipose tissue of the breast (Obana, 1981; Morris, 1992). Work by Petrakis and colleagues showed that nipple fluid aspirate had mutagenic activity in an Ames Salmonella test that was sensitive to aromatic amines (Petrakis, 1980). Heterocyclic amines administered to nursing rat dams were found at high levels in the breast tissue, and were excreted in the milk (Ghoshal, 1993). In two recent studies, aromatic adducts (reactive metabolites of smoking-related compounds bound to DNA) were detected in breast tissue from cases and controls; adduct levels were significantly higher among cancer patients (Perera, 1995; Li, 1996). Thus, it is likely that chemical carcinogens do reach the breast. A role for chemical carcinogens in breast cancer is also supported by analysis of the mutational spectrum of the *p53* gene. The pattern of mutation in breast cancer is quite similar to that for lung cancer, in which chemical carcinogens are known to be aetiologically related (Biggs, 1993).

To date, the clearest risk factors found for breast cancer are those associated with hormonal and reproductive factors; however, the manner in which hormonal factors may affect breast carcinogenesis is unclear. It is thought that hormones play a promotional role in breast carcinogenesis, stimulating mitotic division of initiated cells. It has also become increasingly clear that a number of oncogenes and tumour suppressor genes are involved in the progression of breast cancer. It is estimated that the *p53* gene is mutated in 20–40% of breast tumours. Recent research has shown that *p53* abnormalities affect genomic instability, and appear to facilitate amplification of the *erbB2* oncogene, thought to be a growth factor receptor and associated with poorer prognosis (Eyfjord et al, 1995). *Hras* and *myc* are also frequently mutated in breast tumour cells. There is a strong familial

Whether breast-feeding children reduces a woman's risk of developing breast cancer has been a matter of debate for many years. Part of the confusion has been the distinction between childbearing, which clearly reduces the lifetime risk of breast cancer if the first completed pregnancy occurs before about 30 years of age, and breast-feeding itself.

Although not all studies have been consistent, the weight of evidence now indicates that breast-feeding does modestly reduce the risk of breast cancer, especially during the premenopausal years (Newcomb et al, 1994). The reduction in risk before menopause appears to be about 20–30% for women who breast-fed for approximately two years in total. Larger reductions have been observed in developing countries, where women may have a lifetime cumulative experience of breast-feeding of as many as ten years, as a result of bearing a greater number of children and of breast-feeding each for longer (Henderson et al, 1982).

component to breast cancer, and the identification of hereditary 'breast cancer genes', *BRCA-1* and *BRCA-2* and Ataxia Telangectasia gene (*ATM*), may elucidate other factors responsible for tumours both related and unrelated to the specific inherited mutations.

JUDGEMENTS OF OTHER REPORTS

The National Academy of Sciences report, *Diet, Nutrition and Cancer* (NAS, 1982) concluded that cancer of the breast might be associated with high calorie diets, the data being strongest for diets high in fat. The association, however, was thought to be be indirect, with diet 'possibly influencing cancer risk by its effect on hormones'. This was repeated in the subsequent report, *Diet and Health* (NAS, 1989), which additionally stated that the consumption of alcohol might also be a risk factor.

The WHO report *Diet, Nutrition and the Prevention of Chronic Diseases* (WHO, 1990) concluded that experimental and most epidemiological studies showed an increased risk of breast cancer with a higher consumption of total and saturated fats. It also noted that alcohol might also be a risk factor, but the epidemiological evidence was inconsistent.

REVIEW

4.11.1 DIETARY CONSTITUENTS

4.11.1.1 Energy and related factors

Growth and menarche

Early nutritional factors, in part, determine the rate of early growth and development in females, within a range of genetic potential. Rapid growth leads to earlier age at puberty, which is an established risk factor for breast cancer later in life – see below. Rapid growth and development are evidenced by greater height, in both childhood and adulthood; thus, studies of height provide data relevant to the role of rapid growth in breast cancer. Of course, height and, probably, age at menarche are in part genetically determined.

Three prospective studies have examined nutritional factors in girls as potential predictors of age at menarche. Two studies, in the USA and Canada, have found no material associations between dietary factors prior to onset of menarche and age at menarche (Moisan et al, 1990; Maclure et al, 1991). Both studies examined intakes of energy, total fat, saturated fat, protein and other nutrients; the latter study also examined intakes of food groups, such as milk, meat, pulses, vegetables and others. In the US study, risk estimates were adjusted for height and body mass index. In the third study, conducted in Germany, higher fat intake was associated with earlier menarche, with an energy-adjusted RR = 2.1 (1.1–4.0, p = 0.03 for trend) for the uppermost quartile after taking into account physical activity and body fatness (Merzenich et al, 1993). These three studies consistently reported that height, weight and body fatness (as determined by body mass index, various skin fold measurements, or various circumference measurements) were strongly associated with earlier age at menarche. The study in Germany further reported on level of physical activity and found that girls who performed more sports activity had a later age at menarche (Table 4.11.1).

Prior to these three well-designed cohort studies, few data existed on the relationship between diet and age at menarche. An earlier cohort study, utilising the 24-hour diet recall method to assess diet, found greater consumption of meat to be associated with earlier age at menarche (Kissinger and Sanchez, 1987). Another cohort study, involving fewer participants than the three described above, observed an association between higher energy intake and earlier age at menarche, after adjustment for weight (Meyer et al, 1987).

Ecological observations have shown that diets high in protein (Kralj-Cercek, 1956) or low in dietary fibre (Hughes and Jones, 1985) are correlated with early menarche. Another ecological study showed that girls who were vegetarians experienced menarche at a later age (Sanchez et al, 1981). In developed countries, the average age at menarche has declined throughout the twentieth century, while fat intake has increased (see Maclure et al, 1991).

Although some studies suggest a role for energy-, fat- or protein-dense diets in the determination of earlier menarche, two major cohort studies, while clearly showing a role for rate of growth, did not detect an association directly with diet as such. To the extent that total energy or fat intake contributes to greater fatness, these may affect the age of onset of menarche. As noted elsewhere (Willett, 1990), the lack of a direct association between energy intake and age at menarche in a free-living population is not surprising because energy intake is, to a large degree, determined by physical activity. To measure the difference between energy intake and energy expended by physical activity, which is the excess energy that would lead to accelerated growth or overweight, would require levels of precision in measurement that are not feasible in typical studies. Also, it is possible that intakes

TABLE 4.11.1 DIET, ANTHROPOMETRIC FACTORS, AND PHYSICAL ACTIVITY IN RELATION TO AGE AT MENARCHE: COHORT STUDIES

AUTHOR, YEAR AND PLACE	SIZE OF COHORT: NO OF CASES	VARIABLE	COMPARISON[a]	RELATIVE ESTIMATES (95% CONFIDENCE INTERVAL) FOR EARLIER AGE AT MENARCHE[b]
Kissinger & Sanchez 1987, California, USA	230 pre-menarcheal girls aged 9 to 15 years; followed for 44 months	Dietary energy	n	no assoc[m]
		Dietary fat	n	no assoc[m]
		Dietary protein	n	no assoc[m]
		Meat intake	o	positive assoc[m]
		Meal analogue intake	p	protective assoc[m]
		Grain intake	p	protective assoc[m]
		Bean intake	p	protective assoc[m]
Moisan et al, 1990 Quebec, Canada	2,299 pre-menarcheal girls in fifth grade; followed for an average 17 months	Dietary energy	h vs l quartile	1.1 (0.9–1.4)[ij]
		Dietary fat	h vs l quartile	1.1 (0.9–1.4)[ij]
		Dietary protein	h vs l quartile	1.1 (0.9–1.4)[ij]
		Body weight	h vs l quartile	5.8 (4.7–7.2)[j]
		Body mass index	h vs l quartile	3.4 (2.8–4.2)[j]
		Height	h vs l quartile	4.5 (3.7–5.6)[j]
Maclure et al, 1991 Massachusetts, USA	213 pre-menarcheal girls aged 10 years (± 9 months); followed for 4 years	Dietary energy	> 12,500 vs < 7,500 kJ/d	0.9 (0.5–1.8)**[ek]
		Dietary fat	> 100 vs < 70 g/day	0.6 (0.3–1.3)**[el]
		Dietary protein	> 110 vs <70 g/day	1.5 (0.6–3.8)**[el]
		Body weight	> 40 vs < 25 kg	2.5 (1.0–6.2)*
		Quetelet's index	> 19 vs < 15 kg/m²	2.1 (1.1–3.8)*
		Height	> 150 vs < 130 cm	2.0 (1.1–3.8)*
Merzenich et al, 1993 Germany, FRG	167 pre-menarcheal girls aged 8 to 12 years; followed for 2 years	Dietary fat	h vs l quartile	2.1 (1.1–4.0)*[cd]
		Body weight	h vs l quartile	3.0 (1.8–5.3)*
		Body mass index	h vs l quartile	2.5 (1.5–4.3)*
		% body fat	h vs l quartile	4.0 (2.1–7.5)**[g]
		Physical activity	h vs l quartile	0.3 (0.1–0.5)*[dh]

*   p ≤ 0.05 for trend

**   p > 0.05 for trend

a   cm = centimetres; g = grams; h = highest; kg = kilograms; kJ = kilojoules; l = lowest; m = metres

b   Risk estimates for earlier menarche defined as follows in different studies:

   Kissinger & Sanchez: Mean age at menarche compared for girls in uppermost and lowermost quartiles of intakes of nutrients and food groups. Positive association = earlier age at menarche with higher intakes. Protective association = later age at menarche with higher intakes

   Moisan et al: Incidence density ratio for onset of menarche during 17-month follow-up period

   Maclure et al: Relative risk of onset of menarche before age 12.5 years

   Merzenich et al: Relative risk of onset of menarche during 2-year follow-up period

c   Adjusted for energy intake, physical activity, and % body fat

d   Measured by 7-day food or activity record

e   Measured by questionnaire

f   Calculated from data obtained by questionnaire

g   Adjusted for energy-adjusted fat intake and physical activity

h   Adjusted for energy-adjusted fat intake and % body fat

i   Measured by 3-day food record

j   Adjusted for age at entry and mother's age at menarche

k   Adjusted for height and Quetelet's index

l   Adjusted or energy intake, height, and Quetelet's index

m   Measured by repeat 24-hour recalls over 1-year period

n   No statistically significant difference between mean age at menarche in girls in the uppermost quartile of intake compared to those in the lowest

o   Mean age at menarche lower for girls with intakes in uppermost quartile compared to lowermost (149 vs 156 months) (p < 0.025)

p   Mean age at menarche higher for girls with intakes in the uppermost quartile compared to lowermost (159 vs 149 months for meal analogues; 157 vs 151 months for cereals; 157 vs 152 months for beans (all p < 0.025)

of protein, and perhaps other nutrients, below those seen in North America could reduce growth rates and thus delay the onset of menarche.

In a review of the evidence regarding the relationship between reproductive factors and the risk of breast cancer, Kelsey et al (1993) concluded that 'the younger a woman's age at menarche, the higher her risk of breast cancer', based upon fifteen studies. It was also stated that, while some studies indicated that early age at menarche was a stronger risk factor for breast cancer before age 50, most of the evidence indicated it as a risk factor for breast cancer at all ages.

Although the relative risks associated with early menarche have often been modest, this is likely to be due to the limited range of age at menarche within single populations. For example, in the USA, the average age is between 12 and 13 years (Wyshak and Frisch, 1982), but in rural China the typical age is approximately 17–18 years (Chen et al, 1987). The strength of the association might well be greater if extremes of age at menarche were to be compared within any single study. In six case-control studies that compared age 11 or 12 or earlier to age 17 or 18 or later, statistically significant odds ratios of 1.3, 1.4, 1.7, 2.0, 2.0 and 5.0 were observed for early age at menarche. These studies were conducted in Slovenia, Greece, China, Japan, China (Shanghai) and Russia (Valaoras et al, 1969; Yuasa and MacMahon, 1970; Ravnihar et al, 1971; Yuan et al, 1988; Zaridze et al, 1991; Wang et al, 1992).

The average age at menarche has been declining worldwide for the last 200 years; thus, the increase in breast cancer rates that have generally occurred with industrialisation correlate with decreasing average age at menarche.

Support for a protective effect of nutritional restriction during early adolescence comes from a recent birth cohort analysis of breast cancer mortality rates in Norway, which experienced famine conditions during World War II (Tretli and Gaard, 1996). Women born in 1930 to 1932, who were thus exposed to famine at about the age of menarche, have experienced an overall 13% lower risk of breast cancer death. This reduction has been manifested at all ages as these women have subsequently passed through menopause. This finding provides strong support for an important role of diet during the period of sexual maturation, but cannot distinguish between effects of total energy, fat, meat, or other aspects of diet, as these were all greatly altered during the famine.

The biological pathway through which earlier age at menarche leads to increased risk of breast cancer probably involves earlier and longer exposure over a lifetime to the hormonal milieu that accompanies regular menstrual cycles. In addition, some studies have suggested that women who experience menarche at an earlier age have higher oestrogen levels for several years after menarche, and probably throughout their reproductive lives (Kelsey et al, 1993).

Each of eight prospective cohort studies are consistent in supporting a modest association between height and the risk of breast cancer. In a follow-up of 7,259 postmenopausal women in the Netherlands, de Ward and Banders-van Halewijn (1974) observed a more than twofold increase in risk across a 15 cm difference in height. Swanson et al, (1988), in a follow-up of the first National Health and Nutrition Examination Surveys (NHANES-I) population, in which women at risk for malnutrition had been over-sampled, observed a similar increase in risk. Among women in the Nurses' Health Study, a significant positive association was seen between height and breast cancer for postmenopausal women, but not for premenopausal women (London et al, 1989). Several large cohort studies have been conducted in Scandinavia; in all of these, significant associations have been observed with RRs ranging from 1.1 (for a 5 cm increment) to 2.0 (for a > 8 cm increment) (Tornberg et al, 1988; Tretli, 1989; Vatten and Kvinnsland, 1990, 1992). In the studies of Vatten and Kvinnsland (1990, 1992), the positive trend between height and risk of breast cancer was most linear in the birth cohort of women (1929–1932) who lived through their peri-pubertal period during the Second World War, a time in which food was scarce and average attained height was reduced. The Netherlands Cohort Study reported a doubling of risk in women > 175 cm compared with those < 155 cm and significant trend (p<0.001) (Van

der Brandt et al, 1997).

In the NHANES-I study, height was positively associated with later age at menarche (associated with reduced risk of breast cancer). Late age at first birth, low parity, higher socioeconomic status and the use of alcohol increased the risk of breast cancer, suggesting that the association with height may be confounded by other risk factors for breast cancer (Swanson et al, 1988). However, controlling for these variables (some of which may reflect diet) in multivariate analyses had little influence on the association between height and breast cancer.

Most of the case-control studies offer evidence of a modest positive association between attained height and the risk of breast cancer. This association is not confined to those countries in which energy restriction during growth might be expected; indeed, the two largest increases in risk were observed in studies conducted in the USA (Kalish, 1984; Whithead et al, 1985). In three studies conducted in western Europe, however, no elevation in risk was noted (Toti et al, 1986; Ewertz, 1988; Bouchardy and Hill, 1990).

Four studies have provided data for premenopausal and postmenopausal women separately; each observed a greater influence of height upon risk of postmenopausal than premenopausal breast cancer (Hislop et al, 1986; Ewertz, 1988; London et al, 1989; Hsieh et al, 1990). While these data are consistent with a cohort effect (older, postmenopausal women may have been more likely to have been energy-deprived during growth than younger women), more data are needed to assess whether this association differs by menopausal status.

A protective effect of energy and growth restriction on the risk of human breast cancer is strongly supported by animal experiments. Across a wide variety of tumour models, reduction of energy intake has consistently and substantially decreased the occurrence of mammary tumours (see reviews by Welsh, 1994 and Freedman, 1992). This reduction is independent of the fat intake. For example, in the study by Boissonneault et al (1986), energy restriction reduced the incidence of mammary tumours by 90%, even though the fat composition of the diet remained constant. The mechanisms by which energy restriction reduces mammary cancer probably include factors other than just delay of menstruation, because a reduction is seen in the incidence of a wide variety of tumours.

It is worth noting the teleological argument that there is a major survival advantage in delaying onset of fertility until a body size has been achieved that is adequate to carry a fetus to term. The increased risk of breast cancer much later in life, associated with the earlier onset of fertility will provide little to no selective pressure.

The evidence that rapid growth leads to earlier age at menarche, itself an established risk factor for breast cancer, and that greater height increases the risk of breast cancer is convincing. On this basis, the panel has concluded that evidence that rapid growth increases the risk of breast cancer is also convincing.

Body mass

The association between body mass index and breast cancer has been examined in numerous studies.

Data from the available prospective studies are somewhat anomalous; body mass index was not appreciably related to cancer among postmenopausal women, whereas body mass index was inversely significantly associated with breast cancer risk among premenopausal women. In the largest such study (Tretli 1989), a significant relative risk of only 1.2 was observed for a 10-unit increase in body mass index (which would correspond to a 50% gain in weight for a lean woman), suggesting that, if a positive association exists, it is weak. In the large Nurse's Health study, higher BMI at age 18 was associated with decreased risk of both pre- and postmenopausal breast cancer, whereas higher current BMI (updated every two years) was associated with decreased risk of premenopausal cancer, but increased risk of postmenopausal cancer, particularly in women who had never used oestrogen replacement therapy (Huang et al, 1996). In the Iowa Women's Health Study, the protective association between early higher BMI was also seen for postmenopausal women. Nonetheless, higher current body mass and weight gain were strong predictors of much of postmenopausal breast cancer (Barnes-Josiah et al, 1995). The investigators in the Iowa cohort also reported that central obesity was associated with increased risk of breast cancer, but only in women with a family history of breast cancer (Sellers et al, 1992).

A large number of case-control studies have examined body mass in relation to breast cancer risk (Tables 4.11.2, 4.11.3). When disaggregated by menopausal status the majority of case-control studies show an association between obesity and increased breast cancer risk in postmenopausal women: about 20 case-control studies have found an association between postmenopausal breast cancer risk and high BMI or relative body weight, whereas only three studies have found an association with increased risk of both pre- and postmenopausal breast cancer. Thus the available data suggest an interaction between body mass index and menopausal status.

There is some indication in these data that case-control studies of postmenopausal women indicate a higher relative risk for obese women than are seen in the prospective studies. The relatively consistent inverse association between body mass index and breast cancer risk among premenopausal women could be due to delayed detection of breast cancer among obese women, although analyses accounting for delay in detection suggest that this is unlikely (London et al, 1989).

It has also been hypothesised that the inverse association between BMI and premenopausal breast cancer could be related to an effect of obesity on anovulatory cycles. Fewer ovulatory cycles may be associated with a decreased risk of breast cancer (Henderson et al, 1985; Pike 1990), and obesity may result in frequent anovulation (Sherman et al, 1981). For postmenopausal women, obesity may increase breast cancer risk by affecting levels of endogenous oestro-gens, through the conversion of androstendione to oestrogens in adipose tissue.

Higher body mass probably increases the risk of breast cancer after menopause.

Adult weight gain

In a cohort study of postmenopausal women in Iowa, USA, weight gain between the ages of 18 and 50 was associated with increased risk of breast cancer (Barnes-Josiah et al, 1995). This increased risk was apparent for women who had low and high body mass at age 18, with RRs of 1.9 (1.5–2.5) and 1.6 (1.2–2.1) (both p < 0.001 for trend), respectively. In the Nurses' Health Study in the USA, the largest study to date involving 1,000 pre- and 1,517 postmenopausal cases, weight gain from age 18 was associated with decreased risk of premenopausal breast cancer, but increased risk of postmenopausal cancer, particularly in women who had never used oestrogen replacement therapy. An RR of 2.1 (p < 0.0001 for trend) was observed for a gain of more than 25 kg, compared to 2 kg or less, in women who had never used oestrogen replacement therapy (Huang et al, 1996). In another cohort study, a statistically significantly lower risk was observed for women who went from above to below the median body mass index over a 30-year period, although this was true only for the oldest of three birth cohorts and the number of women was small (Le Marchand et al, 1988). An additional advantage of this last study is that it was based on measurement of height and weight in adolescence and therefore did not depend on recall.

One case-control study found an 80% greater risk in women who had low body mass index at age 18, but who became overweight as adults (Chu et al, 1991). Another case-control study in Australia reported higher risk in women whose weight at age 25 was below the median, who then experienced high weight gain (Radimer et al, 1993).

Thus, three cohort and two case-control studies have consistently shown increased risk with higher adult weight gain, particularly for women with lower body mass index at young ages. One other study has shown decreased risk with weight loss.

Adult weight gain probably increases the risk of breast cancer.

Physical activity

At least three cohort studies have examined some aspect of physical activity in relation to breast cancer.

Frisch et al (1985) followed 2,622 former female college athletes and 2,776 non-athletes for subsequent risk of breast cancer. They reported that non-athletes had an 86% greater prevalence (0–347%) of breast cancer than athletes in multivariate analysis. Although the women who were former athletes were taller and leaner, the association with physical activity remained after controlling for BMI. Another study of college alumni found no association between participation in sports activities at college and later risk of breast cancer; in

TABLE 4.11.2 BODY WEIGHT AND THE RISK OF BREAST CANCER IN PREMENOPAUSAL WOMEN: CASE-CONTROL STUDIES

AUTHOR, YEAR AND PLACE	NO. OF CASES	MEASUREMENT	COMPARISON	ODDS RATIO (95% CONFIDENCE INTERVAL)	AGE	ADJUSTMENT REPRODUCTIVE HISTORY	FAMILY PRE-DISPOSITION	OTHER VARIABLES[a]
Paffenbarger et al, 1980, San Francisco USA	374	Quetelet	≥ 24.5% vs < 21.5%	0.7* (na)	Y	Y	N	Y
Helmrich et al, 1983 USA, Canada, Israel	465	BMI	> 40 vs < 30	0.5* (0.4–0.7)	Y	Y	Y	Y
Talamini et al, 1984 Northern Italy	89	BMI	> 30 vs < 25	1.3 (0.5–3.7)	Y	Y	N	Y
Hislop et al, 1986 British Columbia Canada	306	Obesity	≥ 27 vs ≤ 21	0.8 (0.5–1.4)	Y	na	na	na
Toti et al, 1986, Italy	446	Quetelet	≥ 27 vs 22	1.2* (0.8–1.7)	Y	Y	Y	Y
La Vecchia et al, 1987 Northern Italy	456	BMI	≥ 30 vs 20	1.9* (1.0–3.7)	Y	Y	Y	Y
Ewertz, 1988, Denmark	650	BMI	≥ 32 vs < 20	1.3 (0.6–2.5)	Y	N	N	Y
Marubini et al, 1988 Milano, Italy	106	Quetelet	> 28 vs < 20	0.6 (0.2–1.8)	na	na	na	na
Pryor et al, 1988 Utah, USA	99 whites[b]	BMI	≥ 24.7 vs < 20.5	0.4 (0.2–1.0)	Y	Y	N	Y
Rosenberg et al, 1990 Toronto, Canada	270	BMI	≥ 26 vs 21	0.8 (0.5–1.2)	Y	Y	Y	Y
Hsieh et al, 1990 Multinational	3,993[c]	Obesity	+4kg/m² diff.	1.0 (1.0–1.1)	Y	Y	N	Y
Chu et al, 1991, USA	2,053	BMI	≥ 32.3 vs < 20	1.3* (0.9–2.0)	Y	Y	Y	Y
Kato et al, 1992, Japan	459	BMI	≥ 24.1 vs ≤ 20.2	1.8 (1.2–2.7)	na	na	na	na
Radimer et al, 1993 Brisbane, Australia	135	Relative weight	≥ 35.9 vs ≤ 25.1	0.9 (0.4–2.0)	Y	Y	Y	Y

* p ≤ 0.05 for trend or as compared with lowest category

[na] not available

[a] Also adjusted for one or more of the following: race, alcohol and food intake, marital status, education, occupation, oral contraceptives, smoking history, methylxanthine consumption, residence, religion, dietary fat intake, study centre, history of benign breast disease, geographic area, socio-economic status

[b] Part of the Cancer and Steroid Hormone Study

[c] Includes postmenopausal cases

this study there was no disaggregation by menopausal status (Paffenbarger et al, 1987). A follow-up study of the NHANES-I cohort in the USA reported increased risk of post-menopausal breast cancer in women with occupations with low physical activity, with a relative risk of 1.7 (0.8–2.9) (Albanes et al, 1989).

At least two case-control studies have examined physical activity. In one study, higher physical activity was associated with decreased risk of breast cancer; an OR of 0.42 (adjusted for several potential confounding factors) (0.27–0.64) was reported for 3.8 or more hours of weekly physical activity, compared to inactive women; a dose–response relationship was also apparent (Bernstein et al, 1994). Among parous women, the protective association with physical activity appeared to be stronger, OR = 0.28 (0.16–0.50). Another case-control study, in New York (USA), in which the death-certificate description of occupation was used as an indicator of physical activity level, decreased risk of breast cancer was reported with higher levels of occupational physical activity (Vena et al, 1987).

Animal experimental studies have also demonstrated protective effects of exercise against mammary cancer (Cohen et al, 1992; Thompson, 1992).

Physical activity appears to be related to reproductive factors, such as age at menarche and age at menopause, possibly due to decreased oestrogen production with higher physical activity (Bernstein, 1987). Thus physical activity may act against the development of breast cancer, via a biological pathway involving decreased oestrogen levels.

Overall, two of three cohort studies, each of two case-control studies, and each of a few animal studies have found evidence of a protective effect of physical activity against breast cancer. Two epidemiological studies have suggested this effect to be stronger in parous women. Studies have suggested protective effects of both athletic and occupational physical activity. A plausible biological pathway has been identified.

Physical activity possibly decreases the risk of breast cancer, particularly postmenopausal breast cancer.

4.11.1.2 Carbohydrate
Starch
Three case-control studies have investigated the association

TABLE 4.11.3 BODY WEIGHT AND THE RISK OF BREAST CANCER IN POSTMENOPAUSAL WOMEN: CASE-CONTROL STUDIES

AUTHOR, YEAR AND PLACE	NO. OF CASES	MEASUREMENT	COMPARISON	ODDS RATIO (95% CONFIDENCE INTERVAL)	AGE	ADJUSTMENT REPRODUCTIVE HISTORY	FAMILY PRE-DISPOSITION	OTHER VARIABLES[a]
Lin et al, 1971, Taiwan	84 (aged 50+ yrs)	Weight	> 60kg vs < 45kg	2.8 (na)	na	na	na	na
Paffenbarger et al 1980, San Francisco USA	1,029	BMI	% > 24.5 vs % < 21.4	1.39* (na)	Y	Y	N	Y
Helmrich et al, 1983 USA, Canada, Israel	693	BMI	> 40 vs < 30	1.3 (1.0–1.8)	Y	Y	Y	Y
Talamini et al, 1984 Italy	275	BMI	> 30 vs < 25	1.9 (1.1–3.3)	Y	Y	N	Y
Lubin et al, 1985, Israel	699	BMI	> 27.1 vs < 19	2.38[c] (na) 2.53[d] (na)	Y	Y	Y	Y
Hislop et al, 1986 British Columbia, Canada	517	BMI	> 27 vs < 21	0.88 (0.59–1.32)	Y	na	na	na
Toti et al, 1986, Italy	1,107	BMI	> 27 vs < 22	1.50 (1.15–1.95)	Y	Y	Y	na
La Vecchia et al, 1987 Italy	646	BMI	> 30 vs < 20	1.43 (0.90–2.27)	Y	Y	Y	Y
Ewertz, 1988, Denmark	489	BMI	> 32 vs < 20	1.28 (0.62–2.65)	Y	na	na	Y
Marubini et al, 1988 Milan, Italy	107	BMI	> 28 vs < 20	1.5 (0.5–4.4)	Y	na	na	na
Pryor et al, 1989 Utah, USA	70	BMI	> 24.7 vs < 20.5	0.7 (0.3–2.2)	Y	Y	N	Y
Hsieh et al, 1990 Athens, Boston, Glamorgan, Sao Paulo, Slovenia, Taipei, Tokyo	3,993	BMI	+4kg/m^2	1.11 (1.07–1.16)	Y	Y	N	Y
Rosenberg et al, 1990 Toronto, Canada	329	BMI	> 26 vs < 21	1.2 (0.8–1.7)	Y	Y	Y	Y
Chu et al, 1991[b], USA	547	BMI	> 32.6 vs < 20	2.7* (1.4–5.4)	Y	Y	Y	Y
Graham et al, 1991 Western New York, USA	439	BMI	> 29 vs < 22	1.80* (1.23–2.63)	Y	Y	Y	Y
Kato et al, 1992, Japan	446	BMI	> 24.1 vs < 20.2	1.63* (1.11–2.40)	na	na	na	na
Radimer et al, 1993 Brisbane, Australia	185	Relative weight[e]	> 36.8 vs < 25.61	0.9 (0.5–1.7)	Y	Y	Y	Y
van den Brandt et al, 1993, Netherlands	448	BMI	> 27 vs < 22	0.90 (0.67–1.20)	na	na	na	na
Toniolo et al, 1994	98	BMI	> 26.6 vs < 21.7	2.10** (1.05–4.17)	Y	Y	Y	Y

* p ≤ 0.05 for trend
** log linear trend p < 0.005
na not available
a Also adjusted for one or more of the following: ethnicity, religion, education, area, diet, occupation, smoking, socio-economic class, study centre, fat intake, history of surgery, history of benign breast disease
b Data from the Cancer and Steroid Hormone Study
c Breast cancer patient compared with surgical control
d Breast cancer patient compared with neighbourhood control
e Relative weight calculated as weight (kg)/height (m)
f Data from the New York University Women's Health Study

between the risk of breast cancer and the intake of starch. Two studies reported little variation in risk associated with starch intake (Rohan et al, 1988; Katsouyanni et al, 1994). However, in a recent large case-control study conducted in an Italian population, high starch intake was associated with a statistically significant increase in the risk of breast cancer (Franceschi et al, 1996). The odds ratio for the highest quintile of starch intake (> 191 g/day) in this study was 1.4, after adjustment for possible confounding factors such as age, intake of energy and alcohol. The authors of this study offered no explanation for the increased risk, although they note that, in Italy, starch is predominantly consumed as refined products, such as white bread and pasta.

Ecological studies have shown negative correlations between mortality rates from breast cancer and per capita starch intakes (Hems and Stuart, 1975; Hems, 1978).

Starchy foods, as opposed to starch as such, have been associated with an increased risk of breast cancer in one cohort study (Rohan et al, 1993) and two case-control studies (Iscovich et al, 1989; Levi et al, 1993b), and with decreased risk in another case-control study (van 't Veer et al, 1990).

The evidence regarding starch and breast cancer is inconsistent. Two of the three case-control studies of starch as such showed no relationship and the other, increased risk; one cohort and two of three case-control studies that examined 'starchy foods' showed increased risk with higher intakes; ecological studies show protective associations.

The evidence relating to starch intake and the risk of breast cancer is inconsistent; no judgement is possible.

Non-starch polysaccharides/dietary fibre

It has been hypothesised that diets high in fibre may be protective against breast cancer, yet relatively few epidemiological studies have examined the association.

Three prospective cohort studies of breast cancer have examined fibre intake. In the largest study, the Nurses' Health Study (1,439 cases), the association between total dietary fibre intake and subsequent incidence of breast cancer was very close to null (Willett et al, 1992). Another study, in New York, with 344 cases, also reported no statistically significant association (Graham et al, 1992). A third study, in Canada, with 519 cases, reported a protective association: RR = 0.7 (0.5–1.0) for the uppermost quintile of dietary fibre intake (Rohan et al, 1993).

In a meta-analysis of ten case-control studies of breast cancer with data on dietary fibre intake, Howe et al (1990) reported a weak, but statistically significant protective association (OR = 0.85 for an increase in dietary fibre of 20 g/day). Several recent studies, not included in the meta-analysis, have similarly reported protective associations for various fibre-related components. A large case-control study, with 451 cases, reported highly statistically significant reductions in risk with increasing intake of a number of components of dietary fibre; for example, the odds ratio for the uppermost quintile of total non-starch polysaccharide intake was 0.46 (p < 0.05 for trend). Other case-control studies have found statistically significant protective associations with cellulose (Zaridze et al, 1991), crude fibre (Yuan et al, 1995) and fibre from vegetables and fruit, but not cereals (Freudenheim et al, 1996). A large study in Italy, however, reported no relationship for total dietary fibre (Franceschi et al, 1996).

In all of the studies in Western countries, intake of dietary fibre is quite low (approximately 5–20 g/day), when compared with the very high levels, 70–80 g/day, consumed in some parts of the world such as rural China (Chen et al, 1990). This may reduce the likelihood of finding an association.

In a recent animal experimental study (Cohen et al, 1991), a high-fibre diet was associated with reduced incidence of chemically induced mammary cancer.

Several biological mechanisms by which fibre may help prevent breast cancer have been proposed. Dietary fibre includes insoluble components that are excreted relatively unchanged, and many soluble fibre fractions that have varying biological effects. Fibre may reduce the intestinal reab-

sorption of oestrogen that is excreted via the biliary system (Goldin et al, 1982). In an experimental study of volunteers, a low-fat and high-fibre diet resulted in levels of serum oestrone sulphate 36% lower than a comparison 'Western diet' (Woods et al, 1989).

Fibre may also act more indirectly, through beneficial effects in reducing obesity or insulin sensitivity (Stoll, 1996), each of which may play a role in the aetiology of breast cancer. It is also recognised that other bioactive components of fibre-rich foods, such as carotenoids, isoflavones or lignans, may partly explain the epidemiological associations between fibre and the risk of breast cancer.

Based on the available epidemiological evidence and potential biological plausibility, NSP/dietary fibre possibly decreases the risk of breast cancer.

Sugar

Results from nine case-control studies of breast cancer that have examined sugar intake have been inconsistent. One large case-control study reported increased risk of breast cancer associated with sugar and confectionery intake (after control for energy intake) (Franceschi et al, 1995); other studies have reported statistically non-significant increases in risk (Katsouyanni et al, 1988; Toniolo et al, 1989), no association (Rohan et al, 1988; Iscovich et al, 1989; Ewertz and Gill, 1990; Ingram et al, 1991; Franceschi et al, 1996), or protective relationships (Zaridze et al, 1991).

International ecological studies have shown direct correlations between mortality rates for breast cancer and per capita sucrose and glucose consumption (Hems and Stuart, 1975; Seely and Horrobin, 1983).

It has been suggested that insulin may be involved in the development of breast cancer (Bruning et al, 1992; Yam, 1992; Kazer, 1995). Higher insulin levels have been associated with increased risk of breast cancer (independent of body weight or fat distribution) (Luceri et al, 1996b) and inhibition of insulin secretion or action has been shown to reduce the growth of mammary tumours in experimental animals (Yam, 1992).

The evidence regarding sugar and breast cancer is currently inconsistent; no judgement is possible.

4.11.1.3 Fat and cholesterol

Total fat

That diets high in fat increase the risk of breast cancer has long been the principal dietary hypothesis in relation to breast cancer. This hypothesis was generated originally by statistically strong correlations seen in international ecological studies, based upon food disappearance data (r = 0.7–0.9) (Armstrong and Doll, 1975; Rose et al, 1986; Hursting et al, 1990). The hypothesis that dietary fat plays a role in breast cancer has been the source of much scientific controversy and debate throughout the 1980s and 1990s.

Eleven prospective cohort and 23 case-control studies of breast cancer that have examined the relationship to fat and/or cholesterol consumption are shown in Tables 4.11.4 and 4.11.5.

Ten of the eleven prospective cohort studies examined total fat consumption; none of these reported any statistically significant increase in risk although, in one study with 99 cases, a strong statistically significant decrease in risk was observed for the lowermost quartile of fat intake (Jones et al, 1987). In the remaining nine studies, statistically non-significant relative risks ranged from 0.9 to 1.7 for the uppermost tertiles, quartiles or quintiles of total fat consumption (Knekt et al, 1990; Howe et al, 1991; Byrne et al, 1992; Graham et al, 1992; Kushi et al, 1992; Willett et al, 1992; van den Brandt et al, 1993; Toniolo et al, 1994; Gaard et al, 1995). In a tally of the relative risk estimates for the highest consumption level of total fat from these ten studies, without regard to statistical significance, five relative risks were between 0.8 and 1.2, four were between 1.3 and 1.5, one was 1.7 and one was 0.3. All of these studies were conducted in Western countries, including the USA, the Netherlands, Finland, Norway and Canada, in which mean fat intake is typically well above 30% total energy. About half of the prospective studies adjusted for reproductive history and familial predisposition to breast cancer; almost all adjusted for other factors, such as education, body mass or alcohol intake.

In the largest of these studies, which involved 1,439 cases of breast cancer in the USA, relative risks of 1.0 (0.7–1.3) and 0.9 (0.7–1.1) were observed for the uppermost decile of intake for premenopausal and postmenopausal breast cancer, respectively (Willett et al, 1992).

A meta-analysis of seven of these prospective studies was conducted by Hunter et al (1996). In total, 4,980 cases, from studies involving 337,819 women, were included in the analysis. The pooled analysis indicated no increase in risk of breast cancer with greater intake of total fat; the energy-adjusted relative risk for the highest quintile of fat intake was 1.1 (0.9–1.2). Although each of these seven studies was conducted in Western societies, the large number of cases in the combined analysis allowed the authors to determine that there was no evidence of decreased risk of breast cancer at intakes as low as < 20% total energy as fat.

Nineteen of the 23 case-control studies shown in Table 4.11.5 examined total fat intake; these have produced inconsistent results. Two of the studies, in the Netherlands and Denmark, reported statistically significant increases in risk for the uppermost consumption quantiles (Ewertz and Gill, 1990; Van't Veer et al, 1990); the remaining studies showed no statistically significant associations. In a tally of the 26 associations shown in the 19 studies, without regard to statistical significance, ten odds ratios for the uppermost intake levels were between 0.8 and 1.2, indicating no association, three were 0.7 or lower, nine were between 1.3 and 1.5, three were between 1.6 and 1.9, and one was 3.5. Thus, while several studies suggested weak to moderate increases in risk, strong associations were generally not observed, and as many studies indicated a null association. Several of these 19 studies adjusted for reproductive risk factors for breast cancer, a few adjusted for familial predisposition, and many

adjusted for various other factors, such as socioeconomic status, education, body mass index, history of benign breast disease or alcohol intake.

A meta-analysis of twelve case-control studies of breast cancer was conducted by Howe et al (1990), based upon 4,312 cases and 5,978 controls. Overall, for total fat, statistically significant positive associations were seen in four studies, statistically non-significant positive associations in six and protective associations in two. When the data were pooled, a significant increase in risk was observed for higher intake of total fat (OR = 1.35, p < 0.0001 for a 100 g increase in daily fat intake). The association was stronger for postmenopausal than premenopausal breast cancer, when examined separately (OR = 1.48, p < 0.0001, and OR = 1.1, ns, respectively). These authors proposed that, in North America, a reduction in total fat, to about 25–30% total energy, would lead to reductions in the incidence of breast cancer of 24 and 16% in post- and premenopausal women, respectively; these calculations were based upon the assumption that the associations observed in the meta-analysis were causal. The conclusion is clearly different from that derived from the prospective studies.

Another meta-analysis, in 1993, included 23 epidemiological studies of dietary fat and breast cancer, including seven cohort and sixteen case-control studies (Boyd et al, 1993). In contrast to the meta-analyses by Hunter et al and Howe et al, Boyd's study did not use the original data from each individual study, but averaged the relative risks for the highest level of intake in each study across the studies. This meta-analysis included nine of the twelve case-control studies included in the analysis by Howe et al. The summary relative risk of 1.12 (1.04–1.21) for total fat, based upon approximately 3,000 cases, signified a weak, but statistically significant, increase in risk with higher intake. Separate summary relative risks for cohort and case-control studies were 1.01 (0.90–1.13) and 1.21 (1.10–1.34), respectively. When only studies that had adjusted for energy intake and breast cancer risk factors were included, the summary relative risks were slightly stronger. When the analysis was restricted to eleven studies that met 90% or more of predetermined design criteria, the summary relative risk was 1.15 (1.05–1.27), i.e., similar to the overall summary estimate. When studies were stratified by geographical location, European studies tended to show stronger associations than North American or other studies, with summary relative risks of 1.45 (1.26–1.67), 1.00 (0.90–1.11) and 1.01 (0.85–1.20), respectively. The authors suggested that this geographical difference might be attributable to greater variation in fat intake in Europe.

The pattern of no relationship seen for dietary fat in combined analyses of cohort studies, as opposed to the increased risk seen in combined analyses of case-control studies, has been the focus of considerable debate among epidemiologists. Two studies have been conducted specifically to assess the possibility that recall bias, on the part of women who already have breast cancer, might lead to overestimation of fat intake by cases in case-control studies; this might

TABLE 4.11.4 DIETARY FAT AND CHOLESTEROL INTAKE AND THE RISK OF BREAST CANCER: COHORT STUDIES

AUTHOR, YEAR AND PLACE	SIZE OF COHORT: NO. OF CASES	TYPE OF FAT	COMPARISON (HIGHEST VS LOWEST QUANTILE)	RELATIVE RISK (95% CONFIDENCE INTERVAL)	AGE	ADJUSTMENT REPRODUCTIVE HISTORY	FAMILY PREDISPOSITION	OTHER VARIABLES[a]
Jones et al, 1987, USA	5,485[b]: 99	Total fat	h vs l quartile	0.3* (0.2–0.7)	Y	Y	Y	Y
		Saturated fat	h vs l quartile	0.3* (0.1–0.7)	Y	Y	Y	Y
		Polyunsaturated	h vs l quartile	0.7 (0.4–1.4)	Y	Y	Y	Y
		Monounsaturated	h vs l quartile	0.6 (0.3–1.1)	Y	Y	Y	Y
		Cholesterol	h vs l quartile	0.7 (0.4–1.4)	Y	Y	Y	Y
Miles et al, 1989 California	20,341[c]: 215	Animal fat	h vs l quartile	1.2 (0.8–1.8)	Y	Y	Y	Y
Knekt et al, 1990 Finland	3,988: 54	Total fat	h vs l tertile	1.7 (0.6–4.8)	Y	N	N	Y
		Saturated fat	h vs l tertile	1.4 (0.5–3.7)	Y	N	N	Y
		Monounsaturated	h vs l tertile	2.7* (1.0–7.4)	Y	N	N	Y
		Polyunsaturated	h vs l tertile	1.2 (0.6–2.8)	Y	N	N	Y
		Cholesterol	h vs l tertile	2.2 (1.0–5.0)	Y	N	N	Y
Howe et al, 1991	56,837[d]: 519	Total fat	h vs l quartile	1.3 (0.9–1.9)	na	na	na	Y
		Saturated fat	h vs l quartile	1.1 (0.7–1.6)	na	na	na	Y
		Monounsaturated	h vs l quartile	1.2* (0.8–1.9)	na	na	na	Y
		Polyunsaturated	h vs l quartile	1.3 (0.9–1.8)	na	na	na	Y
Kushi et al, 1992 Iowa, USA	34,388[e]: 459	Total fat	h vs l quartile	1.4 (0.9–2.2)	Y	Y	Y	Y
		Saturated fat	h vs l quartile	1.1 (0.7–1.7)	Y	Y	Y	Y
		Monounsaturated	h vs l quartile	1.1 (0.7–1.7)	Y	Y	Y	Y
		Polyunsaturated	h vs l quartile	1.5* (1.0–2.2)	Y	Y	Y	Y
Byrne et al, 1992, USA	6,122: 53	Total fat	h vs l quartile	1.0 (0.5–2.1)	N	N	N	N
Graham et al, 1992 New York, USA	18,586[e]: 395	Total fat	h vs l quintile	1.0 (0.7–1.4)	Y	N	N	Y
		Animal fat	h vs l quintile	1.1 (0.8–1.6)	Y	N	N	Y
		Vegetable fat	h vs l quintile	1.1 (0.8–1.5)	Y	N	N	Y
Willett et al, 1992 USA	89,494[f]: 1,439	Total fat	h vs l quintile	1.0 (0.7–1.3)[g]	Y	Y	Y	Y
		Saturated fat	h vs l quintile	0.9 (0.7–1.2)[g]	Y	Y	Y	Y
		Monounsaturated	h vs l quintile	1.0 (0.8–1.4)[g]	Y	Y	Y	Y
		Cholesterol	h vs l quintile	1.2 (0.9–1.6)[g]	Y	Y	Y	Y
		Total fat	h vs l quintile	0.9 (0.7–1.1)[e]	Y	Y	Y	Y
		Saturated fat	h vs l quintile	0.9 (0.7–1.1)[e]	Y	Y	Y	Y
		Monounsaturated	h vs l quintile	0.9 (0.7–1.8)[e]	Y	Y	Y	Y
		Cholesterol	h vs l quintile	0.9 (0.7–1.2)[e]	Y	Y	Y	Y
van den Brandt et al 1993, Holland	62,573[e]: 471	Total fat	h vs l quintile	1.1 (0.7–1.6)	Y	Y	Y	Y
		Saturated fat	h vs l quintile	1.4* (0.9–2.1)	Y	Y	Y	Y
		Monounsaturated	h vs l quintile	0.8 (0.5–1.1)	Y	Y	Y	Y
		Polyunsaturated	h vs l quintile	1.0 (0.6–1.4)	Y	Y	Y	Y
		Cholesterol	h vs l quintile	1.1 (0.7–1.6)	Y	Y	Y	Y
Toniolo et al, 1994 New York City, USA	14,291[h]: 180	Total fat	h vs l quintile	1.5 (0.9–2.5)	Y	Y	Y	Y
		Saturated fat	h vs l quintile	1.5 (0.9–2.5)	N	N	N	Y
Gaard et al, 1995 Norway	25,892	Total fat	h vs l quartile	1.3 (0.9–1.8)	Y	Y	N	Y
		Saturated fat	h vs l quartile	1.0 (0.8–1.6)	Y	Y	N	Y
		Monounsaturated	h vs l quartile	1.7* (1.2–2.5)	Y	Y	N	Y
		Polyunsaturated	na	no assoc	Y	Y	N	Y
		Cholesterol	na	no assoc	Y	Y	N	Y

* p ≤ 0.05 for trend or as compared with the lowest consumption level

na not available

a Also adjusted for one or more of the following: poverty index ratio, body mass index, history of benign breast disease, education, energy, other sources of calories, waist-to-hip ratio, alcohol intake, vitamin A intake, time period, oral contraceptives, Quetelet index, smoking history

b The National Health and Nutrition Examination Survey Epidemiologic Follow Up Study

c Seventh-Day Adventists (mostly postmenopausal)

d The Canadian National Breast Screening Study

e Postmenopausal women

f The Nurses' Health Study

g Premenopausal women

h The New York University Women's Health Study

have led to a false association in the direction of increased risk. These methodological studies involved two large cohorts, in which dietary data were collected from the same women, both before and after diagnosis of breast cancer. One study demonstrated a clear bias in the case-control approach, whereby an increase in risk with higher total fat intake was seen with the case-control, but not the cohort, approach; the resulting odds ratio and relative risk were 1.4 and 1.0, respectively (Giovannucci et al, 1993). The other study, however, showed no difference between associations

TABLE 4.11.5 DIETARY FAT AND CHOLESTEROL INTAKE AND THE RISK OF BREAST CANCER: CASE-CONTROL STUDIES

Author, year and place	No. of cases	Type of fat	Comparison (highest vs lowest quantile)	Relative risk (95% confidence interval)	Age	Reproductive history	Family predisposition	Other variables[a]
Miller et al, 1978	400	Total fat	h vs l tertile	1.1 (na)[b]	Y	N	N	Y
		Saturated fat	h vs l tertile	1.6 (na)[b]	Y	N	N	Y
		Cholesterol	h vs l tertile	1.3 (na)[b]	Y	N	N	Y
		Total fat	h vs l tertile	1.8 (na)[c]	Y	N	N	Y
		Saturated fat	h vs l tertile	1.2 (na)[c]	Y	N	N	Y
		Cholesterol	h vs l tertile	1.2 (na)[c]	Y	N	N	Y
Lubin et al, 1981 North Alberta, Canada	577	Animal fat	h vs l quartile	1.8* (na)	Y	N	N	N
		Cholesterol	h vs l quartile	1.2 (na)	Y	N	N	N
Graham et al, 1982 Buffalo, USA	2,024	Animal fats	h vs l quartile	0.9 (na)	na	na	na	na
La Vecchia et al, 1987 Northern Italy	1,108	Combined fat	h vs l tertile	1.3* (1.0–1.6)	Y	Y	Y	Y
Hirohata et al, 1987 Hawaii, USA	183 Japanese	Total fat	h vs l quartile	1.3 (0.6–2.7)[d]	Y	Y	Y	Y
		Saturated fat	h vs l quartile	1.3 (0.6–2.7)[d]	Y	Y	Y	Y
		Total fat	h vs l quartile	1.5 (0.8–2.9)[e]	Y	Y	Y	Y
		Saturated fat	h vs l quartile	2.2 (1.1–4.4)[e]	Y	Y	Y	Y
	161 Caucasian	Total fat	h vs l quartile	0.8 (0.4–1.7)[d]	Y	Y	Y	Y
		Saturated fat	h vs l quartile	1.0 (0.5–1.9)[e]	Y	Y	Y	Y
		Total fat	h vs l quartile	1.3 (0.6–2.6)[e]	Y	Y	Y	Y
		Saturated fat	h vs l quartile	2.0 (0.9–4.1)[e]	Y	Y	Y	Y
Katsouyanni et al 1988, Athens, Greece	120	Total fat	90th vs 10th centile	1.4 (0.7–2.7)[f]	Y	Y	N	Y
		Saturated fat	90th vs 10th centile	1.0 (0.5–2.2)[f]	Y	Y	N	Y
		Monounsaturated	90th vs 10th centile	1.5 (0.8–2.8)[f]	Y	Y	N	Y
		Polyunsaturated	90th vs 10th centile	1.1 (0.7–1.9)[f]	Y	Y	N	Y
		Cholesterol	90th vs 10th centile	1.2 (0.7–2.1)	Y	Y	N	Y
Rohan et al, 1988 Adelaide, Austrailia	451	Total fat	h vs l tertile	1.0 (0.5–1.9)[b]	Y	N	N	N
		Saturated fat	h vs l tertile	1.0 (0.5–1.9)[b]	Y	N	N	N
		Monounsaturated	h vs l tertile	0.9 (0.5–1.8)[b]	Y	N	N	N
		Polyunsaturated	h vs l tertile	0.8 (0.4–1.5)[b]	Y	N	N	N
		Cholesterol	h vs l tertile	2.1* (1.0–4.2)[b]	Y	N	N	N
		Total fat	h vs l quintile	1.1 (0.6–1.9)[c]	Y	N	N	N
Pryor et al, 1989 Utah, USA	172 white[g]	Total fat	h vs l quartile	0.7 (0.2–2.1)[b]	Y	Y	N	Y
		Total fat			Y	Y	N	Y
Toniolo et al, 1989 Vercelli, Italy	250	Total fat	h vs l quartile	1.8 (na)	Y	N	N	N
		Saturated	h vs l quartile	2.8* (na)	Y	N	N	N
		Monounsaturated	h vs l quartile	1.3 (na)	Y	N	N	N
		Polyunsaturated	h vs l quartile	0.9 (na)	Y	N	N	N
Iscovich et al, 1989 La Plata, Argentina	150	Animal fat	h vs l quartile	3.6* (na)[d]	Y	N	N	N
		Animal fat	h vs l quartile	2.6* (na)[e]	Y	N	N	N
Metzger et al, 1990 Colorado, USA	125	Total fat	na	0.8 (0.4–1.5)	Y	N	N	Y
Van't Veer et al, 1990 Holland	133	Total fat	h vs l quintile	3.5* (1.6–7.6)	Y	Y	Y	Y
Shun-Zhang et al, 1990, Shanghai	186	Total fat	h vs l quintile	1.7 (1.0–2.1)*	N	N	N	Y
		Saturated fat	h vs l quintile	0.9 (0.5–1.4)	N	N	N	Y
		Monounsaturated	h vs l quintile	1.9 (1.1–3.2)*	N	N	N	Y
		Polyunsaturated	h vs l quintile	1.2 (0.8–2.1)	N	N	N	Y
Ewert & Gill, 1990 Denmark	1,474	Total fat	h vs l quartile	1.5* (1.2–1.8)	Y	N	N	Y
Zaridze et al, 1991 Moscow, Russia	139	Total fat	h vs l quartile	0.5 (0.0–7.0)[c]	Y	Y	N	Y
		Saturated fat	h vs l quartile	1.7 (0.2–11.8)[c]	Y	Y	N	Y
		Monounsaturated	h vs l quartile	1.8 (0.2–16.7)[c]	Y	Y	N	Y
		Polyunsaturated	h vs l quartile	0.1* (0.0–0.7)[c]	Y	Y	N	Y

generated by the two different study designs (Friedenreich et al, 1993).

It has been suggested that the absence of statistically significant positive associations between dietary fat intake and breast cancer in cohort studies may be due to non-differential misclassification of dietary fat intake, leading to bias towards the null. However, an estimate of such a bias was provided by Willett et al (1992), who calculated a relative risk in the Nurses' Health Study for an increase of 24 g/day (an increase of 30% of total energy from fat to 44%), and found that measurement error could not account for the failure to find a strong positive association.

Neither cohort nor case-control studies have recorded childhood or adolescent fat intake, which may promote

AUTHOR, YEAR AND PLACE	NO. OF CASES	TYPE OF FAT	COMPARISON (HIGHEST VS LOWEST QUANTILE)	RELATIVE RISK (95% CONFIDENCE INTERVAL)	AGE	ADJUSTMENT REPRODUCTIVE HISTORY	FAMILY PRE-DISPOSITION	OTHER VARIABLES[a]
Ferraroni et al, 1991 Milano, Italy	214	Cholesterol	h vs l quartile	0.5 (0.2–2.0)[c]	Y	Y	N	Y
		Animal fat	h vs l quintile	1.1 (0.5–2.4)	Y	Y	Y	Y
		Vegetable fat	h vs l quintile	0.8 (0.3–1.7)	Y	Y	Y	Y
		Saturated fat	h vs l quintile	1.1 (0.4–2.8)	Y	Y	Y	Y
		Monounsaturated	h vs l quintile	1.1 (0.5–2.8)	Y	Y	Y	Y
		Polyunsaturated	h vs l quintile	1.3 (0.6–2.8)	Y	Y	Y	Y
Graham et al, 1991 Western New York, USA	439	Total fat	h vs l quartile	0.9 (0.6–1.4)[c]	Y	Y	Y	Y
		Saturated fat	h vs l quartile	1.0 (0.7–1.5)[c]	Y	Y	Y	Y
Richardson et al, 1991 Montpelier, France	409	Total fat	h vs l tertile	1.8 (1.0–3.3)[b]				
		Animal fat	h vs l tertile	1.8 (1.0–3.5)[b]				
		Saturated	h vs l tertile	1.7 (0.9–3.2)[b]				
		Monounsaturated	h vs l tertile	2.0* (1.1–3.7)[b]				
Lee et al, 1991 Singapore	200	Total fat	h vs l tertile	0.8 (0.4–1.4)[b]	Y	Y	N	N
		Saturated	h vs l tertile	0.9 (0.5–1.7)[b]	Y	Y	N	N
		Monounsaturated	h vs l tertile	1.0 (0.5–1.8)[b]	Y	Y	N	N
		Polyunsaturated	h vs l tertile	0.4* (0.2–0.7)[b]	Y	Y	N	N
		Cholesterol	h vs l tertile	0.9 (0.5–1.6)[b]	Y	Y	N	N
Ingram et al, 1991 Perth, Australia	99	Total fat	Median consump.	1.4 (0.8–2.5)	na	na	na	
		Saturated	Median consump.	1.0 (0.6–1.8)	na	na	na	
		Monounsaturated	Median consump.	1.6 (0.9–2.9)	na	na	na	
		Polyunsaturated	Median consump.	0.9 (0.4–1.7)	na	na	na	
Friedenreich et al 1991, Canada	325[h]	Total fat	75g unit	1.1 (0.8–1.7)	na	na	na	na
		Saturated	32g unit	0.9 (0.6–1.5)	na	na	na	na
		Cholesterol	320mg unit	1.1 (0.8–1.7)	na	na	na	na
Levi et al, 1993 Vaud, Switzerland	107[i]	Total fat	h vs l tertile	1.5 (na)	Y	N	N	N
Holmberg et al, 1994 Sweden	265	Total fat	h vs l quartile	1.3 (na)	Y	N	N	Y
		Saturated	h vs l quartile	1.3 (na)	Y	N	N	Y
		Polyunsaturated	h vs l quartile	1.0 (na)	Y	N	N	Y
Martin-Moreno et al 1994, Spain	762	Total fat	h vs l quartile	0.9 (0.5–1.4)[b]	Y	N	N	Y
		Saturated	h vs l quartile	0.8 (0.4–1.6)[b]	Y	N	N	Y
		Monounsaturated	h vs l quartile	0.7 (0.4–1.4)[b]	Y	N	N	Y
		Polyunsaturated	h vs l quartile	1.6 (0.9–2.7)[b]	Y	N	N	Y
		Total fat	h vs l quartile	1.1 (0.8–1.5)[c]	Y	N	N	Y
		Saturated	h vs l quartile	1.5 (0.9–2.6)[c]	Y	N	N	Y
		Monounsaturated	h vs l quartile	1.0 (0.6–1.6)[c]	Y	N	N	Y
		Polyunsaturated	h vs l quartile	1.1 (0.7–1.6)[c]	Y	N	N	Y

* p ≤ 0.05 for trend as compared with the lowest intake level

na not available

a Also adjusted for one or more of the following: marital status, residence, geographic area, socio-economic status, education, history of benign breast disease, body mass index, oral contraceptives, total fibre intake, smoking history, alcohol intake, Quetelet index, total caloric intake, month of mammography

b Premenopausal women

c Postmenopausal women

d Comparison with hospital controls

e Comparison with neighbourhood controls

f 90% confidence interval

g Adolescent fat intake

h Nested case-control study within the Canadian National Breast Screening Study

i Part of the SEARCH Programme of the International Agency for Research on Cancer

faster body growth and earlier onset of menarche, each of which are risk factors for breast cancer later in life. However, as noted above, in two of the three studies of diet and age at menarche, there was no relationship to the fat composition of the diet (see Table 4.11.1).

As mentioned above, international fat consumption (based upon disappearance data) is highly correlated with breast cancer rates. It has been demonstrated that this correlation remains statistically significant after controlling for per capita GNP and average age at menarche, two other factors associated with breast cancer at the population level (Prentice et al, 1988). However, other strong breast cancer risk factors, such as late age at first birth, low parity, high body mass and tall stature, are also more common in affluent societies and may confound the ecological association between dietary fat and breast cancer.

In a recent ecological study of 65 counties in China, in which diet was assessed in population samples by a standardised questionnaire, and in which per capita fat intake ranged from 6 to 25% total energy, that is, levels much lower than in Western cultures, a weaker statistically non-significant correlation was reported between fat consumption and breast cancer rates (r = 0.4, p < 0.10) (Marshall et al, 1992).

Rates of breast cancer in Japan have increased markedly in this century, as has fat consumption (Hirayama, 1978). However, this increase could be accounted for by an increased prevalence of reproductive risk factors, such as later age at first birth and decreased parity, as well as other dietary and public health changes associated with more rapid growth rates and a large increase in average adult height. Increases in breast cancer mortality rates in Japan show a birth cohort effect; little increase has occurred among women born before about 1925 (Aoki et al, 1992), suggesting that adult fat intake does not substantially influence the risk of breast cancer. Although it might be argued that older women have not changed their lifestyle and diet, dramatic increases in mortality due to colon cancer at all ages suggest that this explanation is unlikely (Aoki et al, 1992).

Over 50 years ago, Tannenbaum (1942) showed that diets high in fat increase the occurrence of mammary tumours in rodents. Since that report, a large number of laboratories have reported a stimulatory effect of high-fat diets on mammary tumorigenesis in mice and rats, using carcinogen-induced, transplantable, spontaneous and metastatic rodent mammary tumour models (Welsch, 1992).

Most of the experimental studies have used polyunsaturated fats derived from vegetable products (for example, corn oil, safflower oil, etc.). However, a number of studies have shown enhanced mammary tumorigenesis with increased quantities of saturated fats, such as lard and beef tallow. In general, the unsaturated vegetable oils are more potent and consistent than the saturated fats in promoting tumours, but there are also data that suggest that the growth of tumours in rats on saturated-fat diets may have been limited by marginal intake of essential fatty acids. Data from a number of experimental studies which examined high dietary levels of monounsaturated fats (for example, olive oil) have been inconsistent. Diets high in fish oil have been reported by several groups not to increase mammary tumours.

It should be pointed out that the stimulatory effect of a high-fat diet in rodents has been demonstrated consistently only when very high-fat diets (20–25% of fat by weight) have been compared with diets extremely low in fat (0.5–5.0% by weight). High-fat diets do not affect initiation, but act on promotion of mammary tumorigenesis.

Perhaps the most controversial aspect of the relationship between dietary fat and mammary tumorigenesis in experimental animals is the relative importance of energy intake. Because fat is the most energy-dense macronutrient, high-fat diets result in higher energy intake unless care is taken to hold energy constant. While the vast majority of studies that report enhanced mammary tumorigenesis by high-fat diets used isocaloric designs, the issue as to whether such diets actually were isocaloric remains controversial (Welsch, 1994). In a study designed specifically to separate the effects of fat and energy intakes on mammary tumorigenesis in rats, Ip et al (1991) found a considerably stronger association with energy intake. Similarly, Beth et al (1992) found a potent effect of caloric restriction in reducing mammary tumorigenesis in rats, but no independent effect of fat on weight gain or tumour incidence.

In a meta-analysis of experiments in mice on the relationship between diet and mammary tumours, Albanes (1987) observed a strong positive relationship with total energy intake, while fat composition, adjusted for energy, was not associated, or was weakly inversely associated, with the incidence of mammary tumours. In another meta-analysis of animal studies, however, Freedman et al (1992) reported a positive effect of fat, independent of a strong effect of energy. It is not clear how to resolve the apparent contradiction, but it does emphasise that, even in the literature, the association between fat and mammary tumours is unclear.

Most investigators have assumed that any observed tumour-enhancing effect of dietary fat needs to be adjusted experimentally for energy intake. However, this is not straightforward because a change in the fat composition of the diet may cause an alteration in the energy intake in humans, as well as in experimental animals. Thus, an increased energy intake, as a response to changes in fat composition, may be considered to be one of the mechanisms by which dietary fat affects tumour development.

Dietary fat may also play a role in the development of breast cancer via effects on hormone metabolism. Although empirical evidence is limited, endogenous oestrogen levels are thought to be related to the risk of breast cancer. Increased exposure to sex hormones, particularly oestrogen, may lead to an enhanced risk of breast cancer through the effects on mammary proliferation. Vegetarian women, who consume higher amounts of fibre and lower amounts of fat than non-vegetarians, have lower blood levels and reduced urinary excretion of oestrogens, apparently due to increased faecal excretion. (See also Goldin et al, 1982; Woods et al, 1989; Prentice et al, 1990; World Cancer Research Fund, Expert Panel, 1994.)

Alternatively, any mechanism for a role for dietary fat in breast cancer may be less direct. For example, high-fat diets may lead to higher body mass or obesity, a probable risk factor for postmenopausal breast cancer. Further, higher fat intake in childhood or adolescence may promote faster growth and earlier onset of menarche, both established risk factors for breast cancer, but such a relationship has not been established. If dietary fat intake early in life was most important, this might explain the inconsistent results of epidemiological studies in which only adult diet is measured. In some population groups, dietary patterns may have been relatively constant over a lifetime, whereas, in others, substantial dietary change may have occurred.

Analytical epidemiological studies conducted since the 1989 NAS report (which considered the data linking breast cancer and dietary fat to be convincing) do not strongly support an aetiological link between high dietary fat intake in adulthood and breast cancer. Most prospective studies show no relationship between fat intake and the risk of breast cancer. Results from case-control studies are somewhat inconsistent, but indicate a slight to moderate increase in risk with higher intake. While strong correlations between fat intake and breast cancer have been shown in international comparisons, these may be equally attributable to factors other than fat intake.

Increased risk is observed in animal experiments, and plausible direct and indirect biological mechanisms have been proposed.

Diets high in total fat possibly increase the risk of breast cancer.

Saturated/animal fat

In a pooled analysis of seven cohort studies of breast cancer, no material associations were seen for saturated or animal fats; the energy-adjusted relative risks for the uppermost quintiles of intake were 1.1 (1.0–1.2) and 1.0 (ns), respectively (Hunter et al, 1996).

On the other hand, a combined analysis of twelve case-control studies found an increased risk of postmenopausal breast cancer with higher saturated fat intake, with a combined OR = 1.57 (p < 0.0001) for the uppermost quintile of intake; this estimate was adjusted for total fat intake, which was also associated with increased risk (Howe et al, 1990).

The combined analysis by Boyd et al (1993) reported no material increase in risk with higher intake of saturated fat (summary RR = 1.10, 1.00–1.21), based upon six cohort and twelve case-control studies. A slightly stronger increase in risk was seen for case-control studies, when analysed separately, whereas no association was observed for cohort studies; the corresponding summary RRs were 1.36 (1.17–1.58) and 0.95 (0.84–1.08).

Nine of the prospective studies in Table 4.11.4 and 17 of the case-control studies in Table 4.11.5 examined intake of saturated or animal fat. Seven of the prospective studies showed no statistically significant association, with relative risks ranging from 0.9 to 1.7 for the uppermost tertiles, quartiles, or quintiles. One study, in the USA, showed a threefold statistically significant decrease in risk with higher consumption (Jones et al, 1987), and another, in the Netherlands, showed a weak increase in risk for the uppermost quintile of intake, with a statistically significant dose–response trend (Van den Brandt et al, 1993).

Five of the seventeen case-control studies that examined intake of saturated or animal fat, in Table 4.11.6, reported a statistically significant increase in risk for the highest consumption level or a statistically significant dose–response relationship; odds ratios ranged from 1.8 to 3.6 for the highest intake levels examined; these studies were conducted in Canada, Hawaii, Italy, Argentina and France (Lubin et al, 1981; Hirohata et al, 1987; Iscovich et al, 1989; Toniolo et al, 1989; Richardson et al, 1991). In a tally of 27 associations for saturated or animal fat (without regard to statistical significance), from the seventeen case-control studies in Table 4.11.6, twelve odds ratios were between 0.8 and 1.2, four were between 1.3 and 1.5, five were between 1.6 and 1.9, and six were 2.0 or greater. Thus, compared with the data on total fat, a greater proportion of the case-control data on saturated or animal fat suggest a strong increase in risk. No case-control studies indicated any protective association.

International ecological studies have reported positive correlations between consumption of animal fat and breast cancer (r = 0.6–0.8) (Rose et al, 1986; Hursting et al, 1990).

Several studies have examined the relationship of foods high in saturated fat, such as meat and dairy products, to breast cancer. Some studies have shown that higher meat intake is associated with increased risk of breast cancer, whereas others have not. Based upon the overall available evidence, the panel has judged that meat intake possibly increases the risk of breast cancer. It may be that observed associations for saturated fat in some studies are in fact a marker for a true increase in risk with higher meat consumption, due to some component of meat other than saturated fat, or due to some preparation method; on the other hand, observed associations for meat consumption may reflect a true effect of saturated fat. Data on the relationship between milk and dairy product consumption and the risk of breast cancer have been somewhat mixed, and the panel has concluded that there is possibly no relationship.

Overall, the somewhat inconsistent evidence regarding intake of saturated fat and the risk of breast cancer makes any conclusion difficult. Giving more weight to prospective studies for which a meta-analysis shows no relationship might suggest that there is no relationship between intake of saturated fat and the risk of breast cancer, at least not independent of that of total fat. On the other hand, the data, in sum, do not look a great deal different from the pattern seen in association with total fat.

Diets high in saturated fat possibly increase the risk of breast cancer.

Monounsaturated fat

In a pooled analysis of seven cohort studies of breast cancer, no relationship with monounsaturated fat intake was found; the combined energy-adjusted relative risk for the uppermost intake quintile was 1.0 (statistically non-significant) (Hunter et al, 1996).

On the other hand, a combined analysis of twelve case-control studies reported an increased risk of postmenopausal breast cancer with higher intake of monounsaturated fat (OR = 1.41, 1.19–1.67 per 45 g/day increase in intake); this estimate was not adjusted for total energy intake (Howe et al, 1990).

The combined analysis of cohort and case-control studies by Boyd et al (1993) showed a summary relative risk of 1.09 (0.99–1.21) for monounsaturated fat. A stronger increase in risk was observed from case-control studies when analysed separately (RR = 1.42, 1.19–1.69).

Seven of the prospective studies in Table 4.11.4 examined intake of monounsaturated fat. Three studies reported a statistically significant increase in risk at the highest consumption level examined, or a statistically significant dose–response trend; none reported a statistically significant decreased risk (Knekt et al, 1990; Howe et al, 1991; Gaard et al, 1995). In a tally of the eight associations presented in Table 4.11.4 for monounsaturated fat, one was lower than 0.75, five were between 0.75 and 1.5, and two were greater than 1.5.

One of nine case-control studies in Table 4.11.5 that examined intake of monounsaturated fat observed a statistically significant increase in risk for the highest tertile of intake (Richardson et al, 1991); none of the other studies reported any statistically significant association. In a tally of the eleven associations presented in Table 4.11.5 for monounsaturated fat, one was lower than 0.75, seven were between 0.75 and 1.5, and three were greater than 1.5.

An international ecological study found no correlation between consumption of monounsaturated fat and the incidence of breast cancer (r = 0.0) (Hursting et al, 1990).

Ecological and case-control studies that have examined olive oil, in which the fat is almost entirely monounsaturated oleic acid, have shown protective associations; see Box 4.11.4 on olive oil.

The results of experimental studies are inconsistent with regard to the intake of monounsaturated fat; some studies have found it to be protective against breast tumours, relative to other types of fat (Welsch, 1992).

Overall, the evidence regarding intake of monounsaturated fat and the risk of breast cancer is mixed, with a pooled analysis of cohort studies showing no relationship, but a combined analyses of case-control studies showing increased risk, although the results were not adjusted for total energy intake. The majority of individual epidemiological studies suggest no relationship. International ecological comparisons suggest no relationship, whereas epidemiological studies of olive oil, a concentrated source of monounsaturated fat, show decreased risk with higher intakes.

Diets high in monounsaturated fat per se possibly have no relationship with the risk of breast cancer, independent of that of total fat.

BOX 4.11.4 OLIVE OIL

Breast cancer is less common in Mediterranean than in North American and northern European countries and this difference has been hypothesised to be a consequence of more frequent consumption of olive oil in Mediterranean countries (Rose et al, 1986). Three case-control studies have reported significantly reduced risks associated with high consumption of olive oil (Martin Moreno et al, 1994; La Vecchia et al, 1995; Trichopoulos et al, 1995); these findings are consistent with research in experimental animals (Welsch, 1992).

Olive oil is a rich source of monounsaturated fatty acids, which the panel has concluded are possibly unrelated to breast cancer risk. Antioxidants present in olive oil, such as vitamin E, have also been suggested to be protective constituents (Martin-Moreno et al, 1994), although there is no direct evidence for this. The panel has concluded that vitamin E intake possibly has no relationship to the risk of breast cancer (see 4.11.1.7 on Vitamin E). Importantly, there are other antioxidants whose nature and relationship to the risk of breast cancer are not established. It may be that, if any protective effect of olive oil exists, it is due to the replacement of other fats that may increase breast cancer risk.

However, high consumption of olive oil may possibly decrease the risk of breast cancer, perhaps by mechanisms unrelated to monounsaturated fat.

Polyunsaturated fat

In a pooled analysis of seven cohort studies of breast cancer, no relationship with intakes of polyunsaturated or vegetable fats was found; the combined energy-adjusted relative risks for the uppermost intake quintiles were 1.1 (1.0–1.2) and 1.0 (ns), respectively (Hunter et al, 1996).

A combined analysis of twelve case-control studies reported no statistically significant association between the risk of postmenopausal breast cancer and the intake of polyunsaturated fat (OR = 1.25, 0.91–1.71, per 45 g/day increase in intake) (Howe et al, 1990). This estimate was not adjusted for energy intake, but when adjusted for intakes of the other two types of fat, the odds ratio was 0.78 (0.51–1.17).

The combined analysis of cohort and case-control studies by Boyd et al (1993) reported no association for polyunsaturated fat, with summary relative risk of 0.97 (0.88–1.07); this lack of association was apparent for both cohort and case-control studies, when analysed separately.

Of the seven prospective studies in Table 4.11.4 that examined intake of polyunsaturated or vegetable fat, one study reported a statistically significant dose–response relationship, indicating increasing risk with increasing intakes (Kushi et al, 1992); the remaining studies observed no statistically significant associations, with odds ratios ranging from 0.7 to 1.3. Nine case-control studies in Table 4.11.5 examined consumption of polyunsaturated or vegetable fat; two of these, including a study of postmenopausal women in Moscow (Russia) and a study of premenopausal women in Singapore, observed strong, statistically significant, protective associations; neither of these studies observed statistically significant associations for any other type of fat or for total fat (Lee et al, 1991; Zaridze et al, 1991). No statistically significant associations were reported in the other seven studies; odds ratios ranged from 0.8 to 1.3.

One international ecological study found a positive correlation between polyunsaturated fat consumption and the incidence of breast cancer (r = 0.5, p < 0.05) (Hursting et al, 1990), whereas another found no substantial correlation between consumption of vegetable fat and breast cancer mortality (r = 0.2) (Rose et al, 1986).

A tumour-promoting effect of polyunsaturated fat of the omega-6 series has been seen in numerous animal experiments; the effect has been observed primarily with diets very high in fat (about 45% total energy) (Hopkins and Carroll, 1979; Hopkins et al, 1981). To the extent that results from animals are relevant to humans, it should be noted that the meta-analyses did not examine the association for polyunsaturated fat at varying levels of total fat intake.

A conjugated dienoic derivative of linoleic acid (CLA), a mixture of isomers of linoleic acid that is a naturally occurring substance in food and is present at higher concentrations in products from animal sources, has been reported to be effective in inhibiting the development of mammary tumours induced by dimethylbenz(a)anthracene in rats; dose-dependent protection was observed at levels of 1% CLA and below (Ip et al, 1991).

Overall, a meta-analysis of seven cohort studies shows no relationship between intakes of polyunsaturated or vegetable fat and the risk of breast cancer risk; a combined analysis of twelve case-control studies also showed no statistically significant relationship for polyunsaturated fat; the majority of individual epidemiological studies also suggest no relationship. Ecological studies show either no relationship or increased risk with higher intake.

Diets high in polyunsaturated or vegetable fats possibly have no relationship with the risk of breast cancer, independent of any contribution to total fat intake.

Omega-3 fatty acids

An international ecological study has shown a weak protective correlation between consumption of omega-3 fatty acids from fish and breast cancer incidence (r = –0.3, ns) (Hursting et al, 1990).

Although no analytical epidemiological studies of breast cancer have examined omega-3 fatty acid intake per se, studies that have examined fish intake have found either decreased risk or no relationship with greater consumption; the panel has concluded that fish consumption may decrease the risk of breast cancer, but the evidence is, as yet, insufficient.

An experimental study has shown that a high-fat diet high in omega-3 fatty acids suppresses human breast cancer cell growth and metastases to the lungs in female athymic nude mice after human breast cancer cells have been injected into their mammary fat pad (Rose and Connolly, 1993).

Experimental work using rodent models generally supports a protective role of fish oil in breast tumorigenesis.

The evidence regarding omega-3 fatty acids and breast cancer is too sparse; no judgement is possible.

trans-Fatty acids

One cohort study of breast cancer in the USA examined trans-fatty acid intake and reported no association; the relative risk for the uppermost quintile of intake was 0.9 (ns) (Stampfer et al, 1987).

Based upon only one study, no judgement is possible.

Cholesterol

Five of the prospective studies of breast cancer in Table 4.11.4 have examined the relationship to cholesterol intake. None of these showed any statistically significant association; in four of the studies the relative risks were between 0.7 and 1.2 for the uppermost consumption levels; in the remaining study a relative risk of 2.2 was observed for the uppermost tertile (Knekt et al, 1990).

The pooled analysis of seven cohort studies of breast cancer by Hunter et al (1996) showed no material association with cholesterol intake; the combined energy-adjusted relative risk for the uppermost intake quintile was 1.08 (0.97–1.21). The degree of heterogeneity across studies was not statistically significant, with relative risks from the individual studies ranging from 0.97 to 1.12 per 100 mg increase in cholesterol intake.

Of the seven case-control studies in Table 4.11.5 that examined cholesterol intake, one study, in Australia, reported a statistically significant, approximately twofold increase in risk with higher consumption (Rohan et al, 1988). The remaining studies observed no statistically significant associations, with odds ratios ranging from 0.5 to 1.3 for the uppermost consumption levels.

Prospective and case-control studies have been fairly consistent in reporting no material relationship between cholesterol intake and risk of breast cancer.

Diets high in cholesterol probably have no relationship with the risk of breast cancer.

4.11.1.4 Protein

Total protein

Due to the focus on fat intake, data on protein intake have not generally been reported in case-control and cohort studies of breast cancer, even though these data may well exist. A recent prospective cohort study (Toniolo et al, 1994), which showed increased risk with increasing consumption of meat, showed no influence of protein intake, after adjustment for energy intake. A 1990 pooled analysis of 12 case-control studies similarly showed no effect of total protein intake on breast cancer risk, with a combined odds ratio of 0.97 (statistically non-significant); this estimate was adjusted for total fat intake (Howe et al, 1990).

As with dietary fat, strong positive ecological correlations have been seen between intake of total and animal protein and national mortality rates for breast cancer (r = 0.6 and 0.9, respectively) (Armstrong and Doll, 1975). The China Health Study did not find a correlation between breast cancer rates and protein intake (Chen et al, 1990). Levels of intake across the 65 counties included in this study were generally lower than in Western cultures; thus, if a threshold effect were to exist, such that only intakes above a certain, relatively high, level were to affect risk, then the true association might not be detectable within the Chinese populations studied.

> Because it is possible that there are differences between animal and plant proteins and their dietary sources, the panel has decided to make no judgement on total protein.

Animal protein

At least four case-control studies of breast cancer have examined animal protein intake. One study in Italy reported a strong increase in risk with higher intake, with energy-adjusted OR = 2.9 (p < 0.001) for the uppermost quartile; this association was apparent for both pre- and postmenopausal breast cancer, and also remained strong after adjustment for saturated fat intake (Toniolo et al, 1989). A study in Hawaii also reported increased risk (OR = 1.6, 1.0–2.6, p = 0.06 for trend for the uppermost quartile); this association was apparent among Japanese, but not Caucasian, women, and among women with early (before age 48), but not later, menopause (Goodman et al, 1992). A study in Singapore showed no association for the absolute amount of protein in the diet, but reported a strong increase in risk for animal protein as a proportion of total protein in pre-, but not postmenopausal, women (OR = 2.7, 1.5–4.9, p < 0.002 for trend) (Lee et al, 1991). The fourth study, in Japan, observed no relationship for animal protein (OR = 1.1, 0.7–1.9 for the uppermost compared to lowest quartile). An analysis restricted to postmenopausal cases also showed no association (Hirohata et al, 1985); further, intakes of animal protein from various food sources, including meat, poultry, eggs and milk products, were similar for cases and controls.

International correlations have been reported between the consumption of animal protein and the incidence of, and mortality from, breast cancer, as well as from other hormone-related cancers, such as ovarian, endometrial, and prostate cancers (Armstrong and Doll, 1975).

In a series of studies in which varying amounts of animal protein (casein, the major protein in cows' milk) were fed to female rats, both to mothers before conception and to their offspring, increased yield with increasing dietary animal protein was observed (Hawrylewicz, 1986). At 8% casein (by weight), body growth rates were reduced, sexual maturity was delayed, and tumour incidence was depressed, when compared with the more traditional level of 19.5% casein. The tumour-promoting effect of dietary animal protein appears to be most pronounced during early life, especially during sexual maturation and mammary gland development, when hormone activities are particularly significant (Huang et al, 1982).

Possible biological mechanisms relate to the effects of protein on endogenous hormone metabolism. In the above-mentioned experimental studies, the pre-oestrus surges in the hormones prolactin, oestrogen and progesterone were markedly inhibited in the animals fed lower levels of animal protein (Hawrylewicz, 1986). The finding of a direct association between the circulating levels of certain reproductive hormones and the incidence of mammary tumours in animals is reasonably consistent with some (Key et al, 1980; Goldin et al, 1986), but not all (Hayward et al, 1978), international comparisons of reproductive hormone levels and breast cancer incidence.

> The evidence suggests that diets high in animal protein may increase the risk of breast cancer but is, as yet, insufficient.

Plant protein

One case-control study in Italy reported a moderate decrease in risk with higher intake of vegetable protein: OR (energy-adjusted) = 0.7 (p < 0.001) for the uppermost quartile; this study reported a strong increase in risk with greater animal protein intake, as mentioned above (Toniolo et al, 1989). A case-control study in Singapore examined soya protein and found a strong protective association: OR = 0.4 (0.2–0.8) (p = 0.01 for trend) and 0.3 (0.2–0.6) (p < 0.001 for trend) for total soya protein and proportion of total protein as soya, respectively (Lee et al, 1991).

> Based upon these limited data, no judgement is possible.

4.11.1.5 Alcohol

Since the observation of an association with increased risk in two case-control studies in the late 1970s and early 1980s (Williams and Horm, 1977; Rosenberg et al, 1982), the hypothesis that alcohol consumption increases the risk of breast cancer has been vigorously pursued. In the 1980s and 1990s, many epidemiological studies examined the relationship. In a 1988 review of the evidence on alcohol consumption and cancer by an IARC Working Group, it was concluded that a 'significant positive association' was seen in each of four prospective and seven of thirteen case-control studies of breast cancer, and that a dose–response relationship with risks increased by 1.5–2.0 was generally apparent (IARC, 1988). It was further stated that confounding due to recognised risk factors for breast cancer was controlled for in most studies; however, a 'firm conclusion about a causal relationship' could not be made.

In a meta-analysis of 38 case-control and cohort studies up to 1992, Longnecker (1994) calculated summary relative risks

TABLE 4.11.6 ALCOHOL CONSUMPTION AND THE RISK OF BREAST CANCER: COHORT STUDIES

AUTHOR, YEAR AND PLACE	SIZE OF COHORT: NO. OF CASES	COMPARISON (HIGHEST VS LOWEST QUANTILE)	RELATIVE RISK (95% CONFIDENCE INTERVAL)	AGE	ADJUSTMENT REPRODUCTIVE HISTORY	FAMILY PRE-DISPOSITION	OTHER VARIABLES[a]
Gordon and Kannel 1984, Massachusetts, USA	5,209[b]: 28	na	no assoc	Y	N	N	Y
Hiatt and Bawol, 1984 California, USA	96,565[c]: 1,169	h vs l quartile	1.2 (na)	Y	Y	N	Y
Shatzkin et al, 1987 USA	7,188[d]: 121	h vs l quintile	2.0* (1.1–3.7)	Y	Y	Y	Y
Willett et al, 1987, USA	89,538[e]: 601	h vs l quintile	1.6 (1.3–2.0)	Y	Y	Y	N
Garfinkel et al, 1988 USA	581,321[f]: 2,933	h vs l octile	1.6* (1.0–2.6)	Y	Y	Y	Y
Hiatt et al, 1988 California, USA	68,674[c]: 303	h vs l sextile	3.3* (1.2–9.3)	Y	N	N	Y
Reynolds et al, 1988 California, USA	3,412[g]: 91	na	3.2* (na)	Y	Y	N	Y
Shatzkin et al, 1989 USA	2,636[h]: 143	h vs l quintile	0.6* (0.4–1.0)	Y	Y	N	Y
Simon et al, 1991 Michigan, USA	1,954[i]: 87	h vs l quintile	1.1 (0.3–5.0)	Y	Y	Y	Y
Gapstur et al, 1992 Iowa, USA	41,837[l]: 493	h vs l quintile	1.5* (1.0–2.0)	Y	Y	Y	Y
Friedenreich et al, 1993 Canada	56,837[m]: 519	h vs l quintile	1.9 (1.0–3.7)[n]	Y	Y	Y	Y
		h vs l quintile	0.9 (0.5–1.6)[g]	Y	Y	Y	Y

* p ≤ 0.05 for trend or as compared with the lowest consumption level

na not available

a Also adjusted for one or more of the following: race, education, smoking history, body mass, cholesterol levels, total dietary fat, meat consumption, skinfold measurements, total caloric intake, interaction smoking/menopausal status, Quetelet index, income, physical health status, blood pressure, lipoproteins

b Men and women from the Framingham Study

c Members of the Kaiser Foundation Health Plan of Northern California

d The National Health and Nutrition Examination Survey

e The Nurses' Health Cohort Study

f The American Cancer Society's Study

g Postmenopausal women

h The Framingham Heart Study

i The Tecumseh community Health Study

l Postmenopausal women from the Iowa Women's Health Study

m The Canadian National Breast Screening Study

n Premenopausal women

of 1.11 (1.07–1.16), 1.24 (1.15–1.34), and 1.38 (1.23–1.55) for increasing alcohol consumption, at levels of one, two and three drinks daily, respectively. Nineteen of these studies were conducted in the USA, five in Italy, and the remaining studies largely in other developed countries, including Greece and Argentina. The strongest associations were seen within countries with high average per capita alcohol intakes, predominantly western European countries, although these studies were not entirely responsible for the overall association. It was stated that, in the majority of the studies, the risk estimates were adjusted for established risk factors for breast cancer, such as reproductive factors. In an earlier 1988 meta-analysis, Longnecker et al (1988) calculated similar increases in risk with higher intake, with risk estimates of 1.4 (1.0–1.8) and 1.7 (1.4–2.2), for each 24 g/day of alcohol (about two drinks), for twelve case-control and four cohort studies, respectively.

In a combined analysis of six case-control studies in 1991, involving 1,575 cases, a moderate increase in risk was observed for alcohol intake of more than 40 g/day (about three drinks), compared with non-drinkers, with a summary odds ratio of 1.69 (1.19–2.40); consumption of 0–40 g/day was not associated with risk (Howe et al, 1991). This association was not attributable to confounding by other dietary factors, such as total energy, fat, fibre or vitamin C.

Eleven prospective studies of breast cancer that have examined alcohol consumption are presented in Table 4.11.6; these include the studies reviewed by IARC (1988) and Longnecker (Longnecker et al, 1988, 1994). The majority of these studies, each conducted within the USA or Canada, have reported some degree of increased risk with higher alcohol consumption. Six of these, including the largest with 2,933 cases (Garfinkel et al, 1988), have found statistically significant increases in risk at the highest consumption levels, or statistically significant dose–response associations. Relative risks ranged from 1.5 to 3.3 for higher intakes in these studies (Schatzkin et al, 1987; Willett et al, 1987; Garfinkel et al, 1988; Hiatt et al, 1988; Reynolds et al, 1988; Gapstur et al, 1992). In three other studies, two of which included only 28 and 87 cases respectively, the association with alcohol intake was essentially null (Gordon and Kannel, 1984; Hiatt and Bawol, 1984; Simon et al, 1991); another study suggested decreased risk (Shatzkin et al,

TABLE 4.11.7 ALCOHOL CONSUMPTION AND THE RISK OF BREAST CANCER: CASE-CONTROL STUDIES

Author, year and place	No. of cases	Comparison (highest vs lowest quantile)	Relative risk (95% confidence interval)	Age	Adjustment Reproductive history	Family predisposition	Other variables[a]
Williams and Horm 1977, USA	1,118[b]	h vs l tertile	1.6* (na)	Y	Y	N	Y
Byers and Funch 1982, New York, USA	1,314 whites[c]	h vs l sextile	1.1 (na)	Y	N	N	N
Rosenberg et al, 1982 USA, Canada, Israel	1,152	Ever vs never	1.4 (1.0–2.0)[d]	Y	Y	Y	Y
			1.9 (1.5–2.4)[e]	Y	Y	Y	Y
Begg et al, 1983 USA and Canada	572	h vs l tertile	1.4 (0.9–2.0)	Y	N	N	Y
Webster et al, 1983 USA	1,226[f]	h vs l septile	1.1 (0.6–1.8)	Y	Y	Y	Y
Paganini-Hill and Ross 1983, Los Angeles, USA	239	h vs l tertile	1.0 (na)	Y	N	N	Y
Le et al, 1984, France	1,010	h vs l quintile	1.2* (0.7–2.0)	Y	Y	Y	Y
Talamini et al, 1984 Italy	368	Ever vs never	2.5 (1.7–3.7)	Y	Y	N	Y
Katsouyanni et al 1986, Athens, Greece	120	h vs l quartile	no assoc	Y	Y	N	Y
Harvey et al, 1987 USA	1,524[g]	h vs l quintile	1.7* (1.2–2.4)	N	N	N	N
O'Connell et al, 1987 North Carolina, USA	276	h vs l half	1.5 (1.0–2.1)	Y	N	N	Y
Rohan & Michael, 1988 Adelaide, Australia	451	h vs l quartile	2.3 (0.9–6.4)[h]	Y	Y	Y	Y
		h vs l quartile	1.3 (0.7–2.3)[i]	Y	Y	Y	Y
Harris & Wynder, 1988 USA	1,467	h vs l quartile	0.9 (0.8–1.1)[l]	Y	N	N	Y
Adami et al, 1988, USA	422	h vs l quintile	0.5 (0.2–1.3)	Y	Y	Y	Y
La Vecchia et al, 1989 Milano, Italy	2,402	h vs l quintile	2.3* (na)[h]	Y	Y	Y	Y
		h vs l quintile	2.7* (na)[i]	Y	Y	Y	Y
Young, 1989 Wisconsin, USA	277	h vs l half	2.2 (1.4–3.5)[m]	Y	Y	Y	Y
		h vs l half	1.8 (1.3–2.6)[n]	Y	Y	Y	Y
Toniolo et al, 1989 Italy	250	h vs l sextile	1.9* (1.1–1.3)	Y	Y	N	Y
Iscovich et al, 1989 La Plata, Argentina	150	h vs l quartile	1.2 (na)[p]	Y	Y	Y	Y
		h vs l quartile	0.6 (na)[q]	Y	Y	Y	Y
Van't Veer et al, 1989 Holland	120	h vs l quintile	2.3* (0.3–19.0)[h]	Y	Y	Y	Y
			0.9 (0.2–4.5)[i]	Y	Y	Y	Y
Chu et al, 1989, USA	3,498[r]	h vs l quartile	0.9 (na)[h]	Y	Y	Y	Y
		h vs l quartile	1.0 (na)[i]	Y	Y	Y	Y
Richardson et al, 1989 Montpelier, France	349	h vs l quintile	3.5* (2.0–6.1)	N	N	N	N
Meara et al, 1989, USA	998[s]	h vs l quintile	0.7 (0.3–1.7)[h]	Y	Y	Y	Y
		h vs l quintile	1.1 (0.7–1.9)[i]	Y	Y	Y	Y
	118[t]	h vs l quintile	1.2 (0.1–9.4)[i]				
Rosenberg et al, 1990 Toronto, Canada	607	h vs l sextile	1.0 (0.7–1.5)	Y	Y	Y	Y
Sinnard et al, 1990 Canada	68	na	no assoc	Y	na	na	na
Metzger et al, 1990 Colorado, USA	125	na	1.7 (0.7–3.7)	Y	na	na	Y

1989). In the remaining study, an increase in risk of border-line statistical significance was observed for premenopausal, but not postmenopausal, breast cancer (Friedenreich et al, 1993). Among the eleven cohort studies, increased risk has been found with low (say 5 g/day), moderate (say 15 g/day), and heavy alcohol consumption (say 75 g/day). Almost all of the estimates of risk were adjusted for other potential risk factors for breast cancer, such as body mass index and reproductive factors.

Thirty-six case-control studies that have examined the relationship between alcohol consumption and breast cancer risk are shown in Table 4.11.7. Fifteen of these studies have reported a statistically significant increase in risk for the highest levels of consumption examined, or a statistically significant dose–response association, within at least one subgroup. Odds ratios ranged from 1.2 to 3.5 for higher intakes in these studies, which were conducted in the USA, Canada, Israel, France, Italy, the Netherlands, Switzerland, Spain and Sweden (Williams and Horn, 1977; Rosenberg et al, 1982; Le et al, 1984; Talamini et al, 1984; Harvey et al, 1987; La Vecchia et al, 1989; Richardson et al, 1989; Toniolo et al, 1989; Van't Veer et al, 1989; Young et al, 1989; Ferraroni et al, 1991; Levi et al, 1993; Martin-Moreno et al, 1993;

Author, year and place	No. of cases	Comparison (highest vs lowest quantile)	Relative risk (95% confidence interval)	Age	Adjustment Reproductive history	Family pre-disposition	Other variables[a]
Nasca et al, 1990	1,617	h vs l quintile	1.3 (1.0–1.6)	Y	Y	Y	Y
Ewertz, 1991, Denmark	1,486	h vs l tertile	0.6 (0.3–1.8)[h]	Y	Y	N	Y
		h vs l tertile	1.0 (0.4–2.1)[i]	Y	Y	N	Y
Sneyd et al, 1991 New Zealand	891	h vs l sextile	1.8 (0.9–3.8)	Y	Y	N	Y
Ferraroni et al, 1991 Milano, Italy	214	h vs l quintile	2.1* (1.1–3.9)	Y	Y	Y	Y
Zaridze et al, 1991 Moscow, Russia	139	h vs l quintile	8.0 (0.8–80.5)[h]	Y	Y	N	Y
		h vs l quintile	0.8* (0.1–8.9)[i]	Y	Y	N	Y
Kato et al, 1992, Japan	908	h vs l tertile	1.0 (0.7–1.3)	na	na	na	na
Levi et al, 1993 Vaud, Switzerland	107[u]	h vs l tertile	2.7* (na)	Y	N	N	Y
Martin-Moreno et al 1993, Spain	762	h vs l quintile	1.6 (0.9–2.8)[h]	Y	Y	Y	Y
		h vs l quintile	1.9* (1.3–2.8)[i]	Y	Y	Y	Y
Holmberg et al, 1994 Sweden	265	h vs l quartile	1.6* (1.0–2.4)	Y	N	N	Y
Longnecker et al 1995, USA	6,662	h vs l septile	1.8* (1.2–2.6)	Y	Y	Y	Y
Freudenheim et al 1995, New York, USA	740	h vs l quintile	0.9 (0.6–1.3)[v]	Y	Y	Y	Y
		h vs l quintile	0.7 (0.2–2.4)[w]	Y	Y	Y	Y

* p ≤ 0.05 for trend or as compared with the lowest consumption level

[na] not available

[a] Also adjusted for one or more of the following: race, geographic area, year of interview, previous hospital admissions, education, smoking history, religion, body weight, history of breast biopsy, origin, Quetelet index, food intake, marital status, occupation, oral contraceptives, socio-economic status, coffee consumption, residence, oestrogens, history of bilateral oophorectomy, practice of breast examination, dietary fat, total energy intake, history of benign cancer, intake of carotenoids, vitamin C, α-tocopherol, folic acid and dietary fibre, month of mammography

[b] The Third National Cancer Survey

[c] Mostly raised during the prohibition era

[d] Comparison with cancer controls

[e] Comparison with non-cancer controls

[f] Center for Disease Control's Cancer and Steroid Hormone Study

[g] The Breast Cancer Detection Demonstration Project

[h] Premenopausal women

[i] Postmenopausal women

[l] Stratified by body mass

[m] Early age

[n] Later age

[p] Comparison with hospital controls

[q] Comparison with neighbourhood controls

[r] The Cancer and Steroid Hormone Study

[s] Hospital study

[t] Screening study

[u] SEARCH Programme of the International Agency for Research on Cancer

[v] Two years earlier

[w] At 16 yrs of age

Holmberg et al, 1994; Longnecker et al, 1995). Most of these studies adjusted the risk estimates for alcohol consumption for reproductive and other recognised breast cancer risk factors.

Sixty-one associations from 47 epidemiological studies are described in Tables 4.11.6 and 4.11.7. Some studies reported more than one risk estimate, due to analyses stratified by type of control group; pre- compared with postmenopausal status; age at diagnosis; or diet at different stages of life. A tally of these 61 associations, without regard to statistical significance, shows that six of the risk estimates were lower than 0.75, 28 were between 0.75 and 1.5 (or there was said to be no association, but no risk estimate was given), and 27 were greater than 1.5. Thirteen risk estimates among this last group of 27 were 2.0 or greater, thereby suggesting a relatively strong increase in risk at the highest levels of alcohol consumption examined.

Of nine epidemiological studies that have examined the relationship of alcohol consumption to pre- and postmenopausal breast cancer separately, four studies suggested increased risk of premenopausal, but not postmenopausal, cancer (Rohan and McMichael, 1988; Van't Veer et al, 1989;

Zaridze et al, 1991; Friedenreich et al, 1993). On the other hand, two studies suggested increased risk for both types (La Vecchia et al, 1989; Martin-Moreno et al, 1993), and three suggested no relationship with either type (or possibly decreased risk of premenopausal cancer) (Chu et al, 1989; Meara et al, 1989; Ewertz, 1991). Thus, there is no clear evidence that any effect of alcohol consumption is modified by menopausal status.

Some European case-control studies have found that increased risk was confined to those women with the highest levels of alcohol consumption (Toniolo et al, 1989) The combined analysis of six case-control studies by Howe et al (1991) found that increased risk was significantly associated with consumption levels of more than 40 g/day (about three drinks), whereas there was no association with alcohol consumption at levels below that. On the other hand, the meta-analysis by Longnecker (1994) reported weak, but statistically significant, increases in risk with one and two drinks per day, and a dose–response pattern was apparent.

A few data are available linking age-specific drinking patterns with breast cancer risk. In the study of Harvey et al (1987) in the USA, women who consumed alcohol before age 30, and later stopped, experienced an elevation in risk similar to those who continued to drink. Similarly, in a California cohort, an increase in risk was observed among past drinkers, compared to women who never drank (RR = 2.2, 1.3–3.9); the age at quitting alcohol consumption was unspecified (Hiatt et al, 1988). On the other hand, one large case-control study reported recent consumption of three or more drinks per day to be associated with an OR of 2.2, while the OR for equivalent consumption at ages 16–29 was 0.9 (Longnecker et al, 1995). Two further case-control studies found no evidence that the association between alcohol consumption and breast cancer risk was confined to drinking in early adulthood (La Vecchia et al, 1989; Nasca et al, 1990). Thus, it is unclear whether alcohol consumption in middle life is more important than that in earlier life in determining breast cancer risk.

Although data are available from ecological correlation studies of national breast cancer rates and per capita alcohol consumption, such alcohol consumption data may not be a good indicator of intake in women; therefore, these data contribute little to the analytical epidemiological data discussed above (see Longnecker, 1994).

In animal experiments, alcohol has been shown to enhance the development of mammary cancer (Grubbs et al, 1988; Singletary et al, 1991). While alcohol alone has not been shown to induce cancer in animal models, it has been shown to alter the rate of cell proliferation in mammary gland cells (Longnecker, 1994).

The biological mechanisms by which alcohol may affect the development of breast cancer have not been well established. Several pathways have been proposed, including effects on the permeability of cell membranes in the breast, increased hepatic metabolism of carcinogens by ethanol-induced enzymes, and inhibition of DNA repair mechanisms. Another potential pathway involves effects on hormone

metabolism. Controlled feeding studies have shown that alcohol increases endogenous oestrogen levels among pre- and postmenopausal women (Reichman et al, 1993; Ginsburg et al, 1995). A further study showed elevated levels of oestrone sulphate, a long-term indicator of oestrogen levels, among women who regularly consume alcohol (Hankinson et al, 1995). Additionally, alcohol may induce P450 enzymes involved in the metabolism of oestradiol to more active metabolites.

One study of benign breast disease showed no association with alcohol consumption (Rohan and Cook, 1989).

Among the many hypothesised relationships between the risk of breast cancer and various nutrients, foods and drinks, increased risk with alcohol intake, along with decreased risk with vegetable and fruit consumption, are the most consistent findings. Data from numerous cohort and case-control studies have shown either increased risk with greater alcohol consumption, or sometimes no relationship. There is relative consistency of this association in studies from many countries, evidence of a dose–response relationship, evidence that alcohol increases endogenous oestrogen levels, and failure to find an alternative explanation for this relationship.

High alcohol intake probably increases the risk of breast cancer.

4.11.1.6 Vitamins

Carotenoids

Several different types of studies have assessed the relationship between carotenoids or β-carotene and the risk of breast cancer. Discussion of the different types of carotenoids, difficulties in measuring dietary intake and issues in the interpretation of studies of blood levels is presented chapter 5.6.

Four cohort studies of breast cancer have reported non-statistically significant odds ratios of 0.8–0.9 for higher carotenoid intake (Graham et al, 1992; Rohan et al, 1992; Shibata et al, 1992; Hunter et al, 1993). In a particularly large study of US nurses (1,439 cases), a relative risk of 0.9 (0.8–1.1) was reported for higher intake of carotenoids with vitamin A activity (Hunter et al, 1993).

Of fourteen case-control studies that have examined carotenoid intake, six studies have reported strong or moderate protective associations, with odds ratios ranging from 0.2 to 0.7 for higher intake (statistically significant in three studies); four studies have reported odds ratios of 0.8 (all statistically non-significant); and four have reported odds ratios ranging from 1.0 to 1.2 (all statistically non-significant) (see Garland et al, 1993). Particularly strong associations were reported from studies of premenopausal women in Singapore and postmenopausal women in Moscow (OR = 0.3, 0.2–0.7 and 0.2, 0.02–2.0, respectively); these associations were adjusted for energy or fat intake and for other breast cancer risk factors (Lee et al, 1991; Zaridze et al, 1991). In a combined analysis of eight case-control studies, involving over 6,000 cases, a weak, but statistically significant, protective association was found for β-carotene intake, with a collective odds ratio of 0.85 (p = 0.007) for the uppermost quintile, compared to the lowermost. This association appeared to be limited to postmenopausal breast cancer (Howe et al, 1990). This weak, but statistically significant, association is consistent with the statistically non-significant relative risks of 0.8–0.9 observed in the four cohort studies discussed above, which involved fewer cases and therefore less statistical power to detect true associations.

Two studies of breast cancer survival have reported that women with greater intakes of β-carotene were at lower risk of dying from their cancer. Odds ratios were 0.5 (0.2–1.0) and 0.7 (ns) for high versus low consumption (approximately > 8.0 vs < 3.5 mg/day in each study) (Rohan et al, 1993; Jain et al, 1994).

Levels of β-carotene in blood are thought to be a good indicator of recent dietary β-carotene intake. Studies of β-carotene levels in blood in relation to breast cancer were reviewed by Garland et al (1993). In three prospective studies, each of which, notably, included fewer than 60 cases, relative risks ranged from 0.5 to 3.3 for higher blood levels. In two studies, the possibility of an effect of preclinical disease on blood levels was addressed by excluding cases diagnosed within the first two years of follow-up. In the study reporting a relative risk of 0.5, the observed effect may have been artefactual, as blood samples were stored at −20˚C, a temperature at which considerable degradation occurred and, further, because degradation may have occurred to an unequal extent in cases compared with controls, due to more frequent thawing of case samples. (Garland et al, 1993).

Of the three case-control studies that reported odds ratios for quantiles of blood β-carotene level, one reported an odds ratio of 0.3 for the highest level; the other two reported odds ratios of 1.2. Two further case-control studies reported no significant difference between cases and controls; no odds ratios were reported in these studies. Interpretation of case-control studies is of course limited by the possibility that the disease or its treatment has affected blood nutrient levels (Garland et al, 1993).

Potential biological mechanisms by which carotenoids may protect against breast cancer include antioxidant and other activities; these mechanisms are relevant to other types of cancer, as well as to breast cancer, and are discussed more fully in chapter 5.6.

Taken together, the epidemiological studies of dietary carotenoids indicate a weak protective effect against breast cancer; biological pathways have also been proposed. The available studies on blood carotenoid levels cannot be weighted heavily due to various methodological limitations. Whether carotenoids (or β-carotene) specifically, as opposed to some other component of carotenoid-containing foods (mainly vegetables and fruits), are responsible for any protective effect remains unclear.

High dietary carotenoids possibly decrease the risk of breast cancer.

Vitamin C

Three recent prospective studies of breast cancer in the USA and Canada have examined dietary vitamin C intake. Of these, two studies, including the largest, with 1,439 cases, reported null associations, with relative risks of 1.0 (Hunter et al, 1993; Rohan et al, 1993). The other study also reported no material association, with a relative risk of 0.8 (0.6–1.1) for the uppermost quintile of intake (Graham et al, 1992).

Of six case-control studies that have reported odds ratios for quantiles of vitamin C intake, two reported moderate protective associations (OR = 0.3, 0.1–1.5, and 0.6, 0.4–0.9, for greater intake) (Graham et al, 1991; Zaridze et al, 1991), and four reported ORs ranging from 1.0 to 1.5 (all ns) (Graham et al, 1982; Katsouyanni et al, 1988; Toniolo et al, 1989; Ingram et al, 1991). In a pooled analysis of nine case-control studies involving a total of almost 7,000 cases, a statistically significant OR of 0.69 (p < 0.0001) was observed for the highest quintile of vitamin C intake. The nine studies included two of those mentioned above, as well as seven in which vitamin C intake was not reported, but obtained from the original food frequency data (Howe et al, 1990). In this combined analysis, vitamin C was the dietary factor most strongly related to the risk of breast cancer. The association for vitamin C persisted even after adjustment for intakes of [beta]-carotene and fibre, with an adjusted OR of 0.73 (p = 0.03).

Two studies of breast cancer survival reported women with greater intakes of vitamin C to be at lower risk of dying from their cancer: OR = 0.4 (0.2–0.9) and 0.7 (0.4–1.3) for the highest versus the lowest intakes (approximately > 210–230 vs < 70–110 mg/day in the two studies) (Rohan et al, 1993; Jain et al, 1994).

A case-control study of 48 cases of breast cancer reported the cases to have statistically significantly higher levels of vitamin C in leucocytes and statistically non-significantly higher levels of vitamin C in plasma, as compared to controls. These findings are not consistent with a protective association (see Garland et al, 1993).

In an experimental study, no effect was observed for vitamin C on the growth of transplanted or chemically induced breast tumours (Abdul-Hajj and Kelliher, 1982).

Potential biological mechanisms by which vitamin C may protect against breast and other cancers involve its roles as an antioxidant, in connective tissue protein synthesis and in immune surveillance; these pathways are discussed more fully in chapter 5.6.

Overall, three prospective studies have shown no relationship between vitamin C intake and breast cancer risk, whereas a combined analysis of nine case-control studies found a moderate decrease in risk with higher intake, even after adjustment for β-carotene and fibre intakes, two components of many vitamin C-containing foods that are also proposed to have cancer-protective effects. Biological pathways by which vitamin C may protect against breast cancer have been proposed.

The evidence suggests that high dietary vitamin C may decrease the risk of breast cancer but is, as yet, insufficient.

Retinol

Few prospective data are available on dietary retinol intake and the risk of breast cancer. Three cohort studies have found a weak reduction or no reduction in risk associated with higher retinol intakes, with RRs of 0.8–0.9 for intakes in the uppermost quintiles (Graham et al, 1992; Hunter et al, 1993; Rohan et al, 1993).

Most of the human studies of retinol and the risk of breast cancer have been case-control studies. In nine studies, ORs for higher intake ranged from 0.5 to 1.5. Four studies reported odds ratios of 1.0 or above and five reported 0.9 or less; none of these odds ratios were statistically significant (La Vecchia et al, 1987; Katsouyanni et al, 1988; Marubini et al, 1988; Rohan et al, 1988; Toniolo et al, 1989; Ingram et al, 1991; Richardson et al, 1991; Zaridze et al, 1991; London et al, 1992). In a combined analysis of seven case-control studies involving approximately 4,500 cases, Howe et al (1990) reported no association between retinol intake and the risk of breast cancer; the combined OR was 1.04 (ns). Thus, in contrast to decreased risk with higher β-carotene intake, this combined analysis did not show decreased risk with higher retinol intake.

An alternative to assessment of dietary retinol intake is the measurement of retinol-related compounds in blood. Unfortunately, most studies have assessed retinol in blood, which has been shown to be relatively unresponsive to retinol intake in well-nourished populations, because the liver stores over 90% of body retinol and maintains relatively constant blood retinol concentrations (Willett et al, 1984). Thus, studies of blood retinol in populations not deficient in retinol provide little information on retinol intake.

One case-control study in Italy reported higher levels of blood retinol in cases as compared with controls, even after adjusting for blood lipid levels (Marubini et al, 1988). In another case-control study, increased risk with increasing levels of blood retinol was observed for women with low β-carotene levels (Potischman et al, 1990). In both of these studies, circulating levels of β-carotene were associated with a statistically significantly decreased risk of breast cancer.

Retinol has been reported to reduce breast carcinogenesis in some rodent models (Moon et al, 1977; McCormick et al, 1981; Moon et al, 1983), perhaps because of its role in the regulation of epithelial cell differentiation (Sporn and Roberts, 1983).

Three prospective studies and a combined analysis of seven case-control studies have shown virtually no relationship between dietary retinol and the risk of breast cancer. Human studies of blood retinol levels can be largely discounted, in the context of judgements about dietary intake, because blood levels typically do not reflect dietary intake in most population studies.

Based mainly upon the dietary epidemiological studies, high dietary retinol intake possibly has no relationship with the risk of breast cancer.

Vitamin E

Several different types of studies have assessed the relationship between vitamin E and the risk of breast cancer. Discussion of the difficulties in measuring dietary intake, and issues in the interpretation of studies of blood levels, is presented in chapter 5.6.

Three prospective studies of breast cancer have reported essentially no association for dietary vitamin E, with relative risks of 0.9–1.0 (all statistically non-significant) for higher intake (Graham et al, 1992; Hunter et al, 1993; Rohan et al, 1993). In the largest of these, which involved 1,439 cases in the USA, an initially weak protective association with vitamin E disappeared entirely when adjusted for vitamin A intake (Hunter et al, 1993).

Of five case-control studies, three have reported weak protective associations with statistically non-significant ORs of 0.6–0.7 for higher intake (Graham et al, 1991; Lee et al, 1991; London et al, 1992). The other two studies reported ORs of 1.0 and 1.3 (both statistically non-significant) (Toniolo et al, 1989; Richardson et al, 1991).

One study of breast cancer survival reported that women with greater premorbid intakes of vitamin E were at lower risk of dying from their breast cancer (OR = 0.6, 0.3–1.2, for > 24 vs < 14 mg/day) (Jain et al, 1994).

Studies of vitamin E levels in blood in relation to the risk of breast cancer were reviewed by Garland et al (1993). In three small prospective studies, which ranged in size from 30 to 67 cases, relative risks ranged from 0.5 to 1.7 for the highest quantiles. The relative risk of 0.5 may have been biased by the storage conditions utilised in that study; the only study that utilised an optimal storage temperature of −70°C reported a relative risk of 1.7. The one study that adjusted for blood lipid levels reported a relative risk of 1.0; the need for adjustment for blood lipid levels is somewhat controversial among scientists in the field (see also chapter 5.6) (Garland et al, 1993).

Two case-control studies that have examined levels of vitamin E in blood have reported ORs of 0.8 and 4.2 for the highest quintile levels. Two other studies that reported case-control differences, but not odds ratios, found marginally to significantly higher levels of vitamin E in plasma, erythrocytes and leucocytes in cases, as compared to controls; these studies involved a small number of cases (Garland et al, 1993).

As mentioned in Box 4.11.5 on intervention trials of breast cancer using dietary supplements, two small short-term trials have reported no effect of vitamin E supplementation on prevalent benign breast disease (Ernster et al, 1985; London et al, 1985).

Knekt (1991) reviewed ten experimental studies that examined the effect of vitamin E on chemically induced (mainly DMBA-induced) breast cancer in rats or mice. Results were mixed in that six studies showed a protective effect and four showed no effect; no studies showed any harmful effect. One study showed that vitamin E inhibited breast cancer when the experimental diet was high in polyunsaturated fat, whereas another did not confirm this finding. Several studies showed that vitamin E potentiated the ability of selenium to inhibit the development of cancer.

Potential biological mechanisms by which vitamin E may protect against breast and other cancers involve its role as an antioxidant, which is discussed more fully in chapter 5.6.

None of three cohort or five case-control studies of dietary vitamin E and breast cancer have found a statistically significant association, although limitations to the accurate assessment of vitamin E intake in individuals may have made the detection of any true association difficult. Studies of blood levels of vitamin E have produced mixed results; each of these studies has entailed one or more methodological limitations that may have affected the validity of the results. Experimental studies have shown either protective effects or no effects.

High dietary vitamin E possibly has no relationship with the risk of breast cancer.

4.11.1.7 Minerals

Vitamin D

A prospective study found that high prediagnostic serum levels of vitamin D metabolites are associated with decreased risk of breast cancer (Corder et al, 1992).

The geographical variation in rates of breast cancer is similar to that of colon cancer, and it has been suggested that lack of exposure to solar radiation, which results in vitamin D deficiency, may be a risk factor for breast cancer (Gorham et al, 1990). One ecological study found regional breast cancer mortality rates to be correlated inversely with the intensity of local sunlight (Anon, 1990).

Limited experimental data support a possible role for both calcium and vitamin D in the aetiology of breast cancer (Carroll et al, 1991). Because human breast cells have vitamin D receptors, there is some biologically plausible basis for the hypothesis that vitamin D may help protect against breast cancer.

Evidence on vitamin D and the risk of breast cancer is limited; no judgement is possible.

BOX 4.11.5 INTERVENTION TRIALS OF BREAST DISEASE USING DIETARY SUPPLEMENTS

Breast cancer

The Women's Health Study (WHS), an intervention trial involving 40,000 US female heath professionals, is currently under way and is expected to provide information on which dietary changes or supplements, if any, lead to decreased risk of breast cancer and other common diseases in women. This will be the first large-scale intervention trial using supplements to provide results for breast cancer, as previous trials have either involved fewer women, or have been conducted in countries where breast cancer is less common. The β-carotene supplementation arm of the WHS was terminated in early 1996, following the release of the ATBCCPS (Finland), CARET and Physicians' Health Study results on lung cancer (see Box 4.5.4 on intervention trials of lung cancer using dietary supplements); the vitamin E, calcium and vitamin D supplementation arms of the WHS continued. The Women's Health Initiative (WHI), a large multi-centred US intervention trial, focused on reduction of breast cancer, and other diseases, includes a calcium supplementation arm as well as a dietary and hormone replacement therapy arm.

Benign breast disease

Two small intervention trials reported that vitamin E supplementation, at 150–600 IU/day for two months, had no effect on benign breast disease or serum hormone concentrations (Ernster et al, London et al, 1985).

In summary, no supplement intervention trial data are currently available with regard to breast cancer. The very limited evidence regarding vitamin E supplements and benign breast disease suggest no beneficial effect.

Selenium

No cohort or case-control studies have examined the relationship between selenium intake and the risk of breast cancer, because it is not feasible to measure accurately dietary selenium in individuals, due to the wide variation in the selenium content of foods grown in different geographical areas. (See also chapter 5.7.)

Some studies have employed blood or toenail levels of selenium as markers of selenium intake; these are thought to be valid indicators of dietary selenium (Hunter, 1990; Hunter et al, 1990). These studies were reviewed by Garland et al (1993). None reported any statistically significant associations; risk estimates varied widely.

In three prospective studies that examined selenium levels in serum or plasma, the RRs ranged from 0.5 to 3.4 for the uppermost quantiles (Coates et al, 1988; Knekt et al, 1990; Overvad et al, 1991). The RR of 0.5 was observed in Finland, where selenium levels are among the lowest in the world. This result perhaps suggests an increased risk for women with extremely low intakes. Two prospective studies of toenail selenium levels have observed essentially no association with the risk of breast cancer (Van Noord et al, 1987; Hunter et al, 1990). Toenail selenium is thought to be a more time-integrated measure of selenium status than serum selenium; these studies were thus less likely to have been biased by an effect of preclinical disease.

In two case-control studies that examined selenium levels

in various tissues, including erythrocytes, plasma and toenails, ORs ranged from 0.5 to 2.0 for the uppermost quantiles; none of these was statistically significant (Meyer and Verreault, 1987; Van't Veer et al, 1990). Of five studies that reported case-control differences, but not ORs, four studies found cases to have lower selenium levels in blood than controls (see Garland et al, 1993).

Thus, overall, no analytical epidemiological studies of tissue selenium levels have shown any statistically significant association with the risk of breast cancer, and the number of studies showing statistically non-significant decreased risk was roughly equivalent to the number showing increased risk. The largest study, involving 434 cases, showed no association (RR = 1.1, 0.7–1.7, for the uppermost quintile of toenail selenium concentration) (Hunter et al, 1990); almost all the remaining studies involved fewer than 100 cases.

Ecological studies have shown selenium exposure to be inversely correlated with rates of breast cancer, both internationally and within the USA (Shamberger et al, 1976; Schrauzer et al, 1977; Clark, 1985). These studies must be interpreted with caution because, for example, within the USA, high-selenium areas are generally sparsely populated rural areas, which differ in many respects from low-selenium urban areas.

In experimental studies, selenium supplementation has been particularly effective in inhibiting mammary carcinogenesis (Ip, 1986; Birt 1989). A review of numerous animal experiments has suggested that selenium is a potent inhibitor of virally and chemically induced tumours, in several organs, including the mammary gland (Fishbein, 1986). Selenium supplementation has been shown to inhibit mammary tumorigenesis in rats after administration of *N*-methyl-*N*-nitrosourea or 7,12-dimethylbenz(a)anthracene (Thompson and Becci 1980; Welsch et al, 1981; Thompson et al, 1982, 1984; Poirier et al, 1986). Results from one study of mice given 7,12-dimethylbenz(a)anthracene confirmed that selenium supplementation was effective in the prevention of both the initiation and post-initiation phases of carcinogenesis (Medina and Lane, 1983). Selenium supplementation at 2.5 mg/kg was shown to reduce the total mammary tumour yield in rats with adequate or low vitamin E intake (Poirier et al, 1986). In one study, selenium did not reduce lipid peroxidation, but was still an effective chemopreventive agent (Horvath and Ip, 1983). A novel organoselenium compound, 1,4-phenylenebis (methylene) selenocyanate (XSC), supplemented in the diet of rats, was shown to inhibit significantly 7,12-dimethylbenz(a)anthracene-induced mammary tumours, when compared to control rats fed the same diet without XSC (el-Bayoumy et al, 1992).

Biological pathways have been proposed in support of an anticarcinogenic effect of selenium. These include the role of selenium in antioxidation via maintenance of the enzyme glutathione peroxidase, suppression of cell proliferation when present at high levels, enhancement of the immune response, and alteration of the metabolism of carcinogens. These mechanisms are relevant to many cancer sites and are discussed in chapter 5.7. Some studies of mammary carcino-

genesis in animals have suggested that modulation of glutathione peroxidase activity is not the anticarcinogenic mechanism, because the selenium intakes required for inhibition are in excess of the amounts required for maximal enzyme activity (Ip, 1981; Ip and Simha, 1981; Lane and Medina, 1983). Results from one animal study suggest a mechanism whereby elemental selenium inhibits cell replication (Medina and Oborn, 1984).

Overall, although animal experiments have shown that high selenium intakes inhibit the development of breast tumours, human analytical studies have generally found no relationship or have been limited by methodological limitations, such as a small number of cases and therefore low statistical power, or a retrospective study design and therefore the possibility of tissue selenium levels being affected by the cancer.

The evidence on dietary selenium and breast cancer is limited by the discrepancies between the human and experimental data and by the serious difficulties in measuring human exposure; no judgment is possible.

4.11.1.8 Bioactive compounds

Isoflavones and lignans

The potentially preventive actions of isoflavones and lignans in breast cancer have been discussed by Adlercreutz (1990), Messina and Barnes (1991), Messina and Messina (1991), Adlercreutz et al (1993), Messina et al (1994), Barnes-Josiah et al (1994) and Adlercreutz et al (attributed in the journal as Herman et al) (1995). (See these papers for references to studies not individually cited in the following text.)

Isoflavones and lignans occur mainly in soybean and wholegrain products, various seeds and seed-containing berries. Isoflavones are heterocyclic phenols with structural similarities to oestrogens. Some specific isoflavones include daidzen, genistein, and the precursors formononetin and biochanin A; specific lignans include matairesinol, lariciresinol, isolariciresinol, and secoisolariciresinol. No analytical epidemiological studies have examined intakes of isoflavones or lignans per se; this is, in part, because the necessary extensive food composition analyses for these compounds have not been conducted.

Isoflavones and lignans have received scientific attention largely due to their actions as phyto-oestrogens. After consumption of lignan precursor and of the isoflavones themselves many metabolic conversions occur in the gut, which result in the formation of hormone-like compounds. One postulated anticarcinogenic mechanism involves the weak phyto-oestrogens activity of these compounds, which is about 0.1% of that of conjugated steroidal oestrogens. These phytoestrogens may bind to oestrogen receptors without eliciting a major response, and at the same time block the binding of more potent oestrogens. Phyto-oestrogens are structurally similar to the potent synthetic antioestrogen, tamoxifen, which has been successfully employed in breast cancer treatment and is presently undergoing evaluation as a prophylactic agent.

Limited cohort and case-control studies have examined the consumption of pulses (legumes), some of which, particularly soya beans, are concentrated sources of isoflavones. Results of these few studies have been inconsistent and the panel has concluded that no judgement is possible regarding any effect of pulses on the risk of breast cancer.

Human ecological observations indirectly support a cancer-protective effect of isoflavones. Vegetarians, for example, who often consume greater amounts of soya products, have a lower risk of many cancers, including breast cancer. Japanese women, who consume more soy foods, also have lower rates of breast cancer. Further, relatively low levels of urinary lignans have been observed in breast cancer patients and in omnivorous women (Herman et al, 1995).

Of 26 experimental studies that involved diets containing soya, 17 (65%) have reported protective effects against experimentally induced cancers of all types; no studies have reported increased tumours (Messina et al, 1994). Of eight studies of mammary tumours, five (63%) showed protective effects and the remaining three showed no effects. Another experimental study showed diets containing sesamin, a lignan in sesame, to decrease chemically induced breast carcinogenesis in rats (Hirose et al, 1992).

In a controlled human feeding trial, women fed moderate amounts of soy products, containing 45 mg isoflavones per day, experienced an increase in the length of their menstrual cycle, particularly of the follicular phase (Cassidy et al, 1993). Over a lifetime, longer and, therefore, fewer menstrual cycles would result in less exposure to the mid-cycle surge of endogenous oestrogens. The average menstrual cycle of Japanese women, who have a lower risk of breast cancer, is generally 4–6 days longer than that of Western women (see Cassidy et al, 1993).

In animal experiments, several isoflavonoids and lignans have been shown to compete with oestradiol for the rat uterine nuclear type II oestrogen-binding site (sometimes called the bioflavonoid receptor).

Phyto-oestrogens have also been shown to lead to an increase in the synthesis of serum hormone-binding globulin in the liver, and, thereby, to decrease the relative amount of free oestradiol and reduce the uptake and biological activity (Adlercreutz et al, 1992). Lignans have been shown to inhibit aromatase enzymes, and may reach sufficient concentrations in adipose cells to reduce the conversion of androstenedione to oestrone (Herman et al, 1995).

Other anticarcinogenic mechanisms have been proposed for a specific isoflavone, genistein, which has been shown to inhibit oestrogen receptor-negative breast cancer cells in vitro and may have a mechanism of action not directly related to the oestrogen receptor. In addition to possessing weak oestrogenic activity, genistein has been shown to inhibit protein tyrosine kinases (Herman et al, 1995), and to have antioxidant activity (Wei et al, 1995). In vitro, genistein has been shown to suppress the growth and stimulate the differentiation of a wide variety of cancer cells. Genistein

and an isoflavone precursor, biochanin A, have further been shown to induce apoptosis in tumour cells (Yanagihara et al, 1993).

Indirect evidence regarding a potential protective role for isoflavones and lignans comes from a human trial on oestrogen metabolism; ecological observations of vegetarians, Asians and breast cancer patients; and animal and in vitro studies.

Several biological mechanisms have been suggested. No human analytical studies of isoflavones and lignans per se are available, and studies of pulses, one major source of isoflavones, have been few and equivocal.

The evidence suggests that isoflavones and lignans may decrease the risk of breast cancer but is, as yet, insufficient.

Glucosinolates and indoles

Indoles, compounds formed from glucosinolates in cruciferous vegetables, have been hypothesised to be protective against breast cancer via their effect on oestrogen metabolism. In one human clinical trial, women given a dose of 500 mg/day (approximately 50 times the estimated average daily intake in the USA) were found to have a shift in oestrogen metabolism towards the production of a relatively less potent form of oestrogen (Michnovicz and Bradlow, 1990). Such a shift in metabolism might reduce oestrogen-promoted breast cancers. Studies in rats have shown similar effects on oestrogen metabolism.

Experimental studies have shown glucobrassicin and indole derivatives to inhibit the formation of chemically induced tumours of the breast (Wattenberg and Loub, 1978; Wattenberg et al, 1986). A further study showed increased breast tumours when indole-3-carbinol was given along with a diet high in cholesterol and beef tallow, and was administered after the chemical carcinogen (Pence et al, 1986). An in vitro study has shown indole-3-carbinol to inhibit the growth of an oestrogen-sensitive human breast cancer cell line, but not that of an oestrogen-insensitive cell line (Tiwari et al, 1994).

Based on these limited data, no judgement is possible.

4.11.2 FOODS AND DRINKS

4.11.2.1 Vegetables and fruits

Associations between fruit and vegetable consumption and the risk of breast cancer have been examined in three prospective and nineteen case-control studies (Tables 4.11.8 and 4.11.9).

One cohort study in California reported essentially null associations for all vegetables, all fruit, dark-green vegetables and yellow vegetables (Shibata et al, 1992). Another study in Canada reported no material associations for fruit or vegetables in general, but a statistically non-significant decrease in risk with higher intake of vegetables and fruits that are high in carotenoids and vitamins (p = 0.08 for trend) (Rohan et al, 1993). In the large Nurses' Health Study cohort, in the USA, an OR of 0.8 (0.7–1.0) was reported for higher vegetable intake; fruit intake was not associated with risk (Hunter et al, 1993).

Of the nineteen case-control studies of breast cancer that have examined some aspect of vegetable and fruit consumption, ten have found a statistically significant protective association for one or more vegetable and/or fruit categories (not all studies reported on level of statistical significance) (Katsouyanni et al, 1986; La Vecchia et al, 1987; Iscovich et al, 1989; Young et al, 1989; Simard et al, 1990; Pawlega et al, 1992; Kato et al, 1992; Levi et al, 1993; Trichopoulous et al, 1995; Freudenheim et al, 1996). These protective associations were observed in studies in Poland, Greece, Italy, Canada, Argentina, Japan, Switzerland and the USA.

Seventy associations from 21 epidemiological studies are shown in Tables 4.11.8 and 4.11.9; these relate to different types of vegetables and fruits, as well as, for some studies, results stratified according to diet at different ages, age at diagnosis, type of control group, country of origin of subjects, or pre-, compared with postmenopausal status. For the 70 associations presented, 37 of the risk estimates were lower than 0.75, thereby suggesting a protective association; 30 were between 0.75 and 1.5 (inclusive) (or there was said to be 'no association', but no risk estimate was given); and three were higher than 1.5.

Of eleven case-control and cohort studies that examined consumption of vegetables as a general category, eight observed decreased risk, with ORs from 0.3 to 0.8 for higher intakes (statistically significant in four studies) (only among women older than age 50 in one study) (Katsouyanni et al, 1986; Zaridze et al, 1991; Hunter et al, 1993; Rohan et al, 1993; Holmberg et al, 1994; Trichopoulous et al, 1995; Freudenheim et al, 1996); the remaining four studies reported no material associations (Toniolo et al, 1989; Van't Veer, 1990; Richardson et al, 1991; Shibata et al, 1992). Six studies examined consumption of green vegetables ('green vegetables', 'green leafy vegetables', 'dark-green vegetables', 'broccoli, spinach and green cabbage', 'green–yellow vegetables'). Of these, four studies observed statistically significant protective associations (ORs from 0.2 to 0.5 for higher intakes) (La Vecchia et al, 1987; Iscovich et al, 1989; Kato et al, 1992; Levi et al, 1993); the other two studies reported no association (Ewertz and Gill, 1990; Shibata et al, 1992). Three studies examined cruciferous vegetables, which are of particular interest in breast cancer due to the presence of indole compounds, which may effect oestrogen metabolism and, thereby, the risk of breast cancer. Two of these studies observed decreases in risk (OR = 0.6 in each for the highest consumption levels, statistically significant in one; borderline in the other) (Young et al, 1989; Levi et al, 1993); the third study reported no association (Graham et al, 1982). Three of four studies that examined carrot consumption sug-

gested decreased risk with higher intakes, although none of the risk estimates was statistically significant (Hislop et al, 1986; Katsouyanni et al, 1986; Ewertz and Gill, 1990; Levi et al, 1993). One study that examined onion consumption reported a statistically significant halving of risk for the highest intake level (Levi et al, 1993). A study that examined both raw and cooked vegetables reported a protective association for the former, but not the latter (Simard et al, 1990); conversely, another study reported a strong decrease in risk with higher intake of cooked vegetables (Pawlega et al, 1992).

Twelve of the studies in Tables 4.11.8 and 4.11.9 have examined consumption of 'fruit' or 'raw fruit'. Six of these studies reported essentially null associations (La Vecchia et al, 1987; Toniolo et al, 1989; Shibata et al, 1992; Hunter et al, 1993; Levi et al, 1993; Rohan et al, 1993); four reported decreased risk with higher intakes (statistically significant in one) (Katsouyanni et al, 1986; Van't Veer et al, 1990; Trichopoulous et al, 1995; Freudenheim et al, 1996). Two studies reported ORs of 0.7 or 0.8 for higher intakes among premenopausal women, and 1.7 or 1.8 among postmenopausal women (none was statistically significant) (Zaridze et al, 1991; Holmberg et al, 1994). For citrus fruit (or 'oranges'), three of four studies have reported no material association (Toniolo et al, 1989; Richardson et al, 1991; Levi et al, 1993); the other study observed a statistically non-significant protective association (Iscovich et al, 1989).

In a pooled analysis of case-control data from northern Italy, involving 2,860 cases of breast cancer, a moderate decrease in risk was reported with green vegetable consumption, with an odds ratio of 0.7 (0.6–0.8) (p < 0.01 for trend) for the uppermost tertile; an odds ratio of 1.1 (1.0–1.3) was observed for the uppermost tertile of fruit consumption (not shown in Table 4.11.9) (Negri et al, 1991).

One recent study examined the relationship of vegetable and fruit intake to cancer prognosis and survival in women who underwent surgery for early breast cancer; Those who had previously eaten more vegetables and fruits had tumours with more favourable prognostic characteristics, including smaller diameter, more normal cell differentiation, less vascular invasion, and positive oestrogen receptor status (Ingram et al, 1992).

Experimental studies have shown that inclusion of different vegetables in the diets of rats or mice results in a lower incidence of experimentally induced breast tumours (Wattenberg, 1983; Stoewsand et al, 1988, 1989; Wattenberg et al, 1989). These studies involved feeding cabbage, cauliflower, Brussels sprouts or broccoli, generally at levels of 5–20% of the diet. Another study showed that inclusion of 1 or 5% orange oil in the diet produced a lower tumour incidence and fewer tumours per animal (Wattenberg, 1983). A further study showed fewer metastases from transplanted mammary tumour cells, when cabbage or collards were fed at a level of 5 or 9% of the diet (Scholar et al, 1989).

TABLE 4.11.8 FRUIT AND VEGETABLE CONSUMPTION AND THE RISK OF BREAST CANCER: COHORT STUDIES

AUTHOR, YEAR AND PLACE	SIZE OF COHORT: NO. OF CASES	TYPE OF FRUIT OR VEGETABLE	COMPARISON (HIGHEST VS LOWEST QUANTILE)	RELATIVE RISK (95% CONFIDENCE INTERVAL)	AGE	ADJUSTMENT REPRODUCTIVE HISTORY	FAMILY PRE-DISPOSITION	OTHER VARIABLES[a]
Shibata et al, 1992 Los Angeles, USA	11,580[b]: 219	Vegetables and fruit	h vs l tertile	0.9 (0.6–1.2)	Y	N	N	Y
		Vegetables	h vs l tertile	1.0 (0.7–1.3)	Y	N	N	Y
		Fruit	h vs l tertile	0.8 (0.6–1.1)	Y	N	N	Y
		Dark green vegetables	h vs l tertile	0.9 (0.7–1.3)	Y	N	N	Y
		Yellow vegetables	h vs l tertile	1.0 (0.7–1.3)	Y	N	N	Y
Hunter et al, 1993 USA	89,494 female nurses: 1,439	Vegetables	≥ 2.2 vs < 0.9 servings/day	0.8 (0.7–1.0)*	Y	na	na	na
		Fruit	na	no assoc	Y	na	na	na
Rohan et al, 1993 Canada	56,837[c]: 519	Fruit	h vs l quintile	0.9 (0.6–1.2)	Y	Y	Y	Y
		Vegetables	h vs l quintile	0.7 (0.5–1.0)	Y	Y	Y	Y
		Vegetables rich in vitamins A and C	h vs l quintile	0.7 (0.5–1.1)	Y	Y	Y	Y

* p ≤ 0.05 for trend or as compared with the lowest consumption level
[na] not available
[a] Also adjusted for one or more of the following: smoking history, education, history of benign breast disease
[b] Cohort includes men and women
[c] The Canadian Breast Screening Study

A large amount of evidence has accumulated regarding vegetable and fruit consumption and the risk of breast cancer. Almost all of the data from epidemiological studies show either decreased risk with higher intakes or no relationship; the evidence is more abundant and consistent for vegetables, particularly green vegetables, than for fruits.

Diets high in vegetables and fruits probably decrease the risk of breast cancer.

4.11.2.2 Pulses (legumes)
In a Japanese cohort study, the risk of breast cancer was found to be decreased with a higher consumption of soya bean paste soup (Hirayama et al, 1986).

In a case-control study in Singapore, an OR of 0.4 (0.2–0.8) was reported for premenopausal breast cancer, for higher intake of total soya products, although no significant association was observed for postmenopausal cancer (Lee et al, 1991). In contrast, a case-control study in Argentina reported an OR of 3.3 (ns) for higher intake of pulses (Iscovich et al, 1989). Two further case-control studies in China reported no association for soya protein, with a combined OR of 1.0; further, there were no case-control differences in intakes of tofu or soy milk (Yuan et al, 1995).

One study in rats found that fewer rats fed a diet containing 50% soya beans developed breast tumours after irradiation, than rats fed a control diet (p < 0.01) (Troll et al, 1988). Another study showed dietary soya to decrease chemically induced breast tumours in rats (Barnes et al, 1990).

Soya beans have a high content of isoflavones; small quantities are also found in chickpeas. Isoflavones are phyto-oestrogens that may inhibit oestrogen-promoted cancers, such as breast cancer.

Evidence relating to pulses and the risk of breast cancer is limited and inconsistent; no judgement is possible.

4.11.2.3 Nuts and seeds
A case-control study of breast cancer in Argentina reported slightly increased risk of breast cancer with higher intakes of nuts, although the association was not statistically significant. Odds ratios were 1.2 and 1.7 for higher consumption in comparisons with neighbourhood and hospital controls, respectively (Iscovich et al, 1989).

In animal experiments, diets containing Brazil nuts, which are particularly high in selenium, have been shown to decrease chemically induced mammary tumours (Ip and Lisk, 1994).

Based on these very limited data, no judgement is possible.

4.11.2.4 Meat, poultry, fish and eggs
Meat
A recent cohort study of breast cancer in New York reported moderately increased risk with the consumption of red meat, with an energy-adjusted RR of 1.9 (1.1–3.2) for intake in the uppermost quintile, although no statistically significant relationship with total or any specific type of fat was observed (Toniolo et al, 1994). Increased risk has also been reported in cohort studies in Japan (Hirayama, 1986) and Norway (Vatten and Kvinnsland,1990; Gaard et al, 1995). However, in the Nurses' Health Study cohort, in the USA (Willett et al, 1992), as well as in British nuns (Kinlen, 1982) and post-

TABLE 4.11.9 FRUIT AND VEGETABLES CONSUMPTION AND THE RISK OF BREAST CANCER: CASE-CONTROL STUDIES

Author, year and place	No. of cases	Type of fruit or vegetable	Comparison (highest vs lowest quantile)	Odds ratio (95% confidence interval)	Age	Adjustment Reproductive history	Family predisposition	Other variables[a]
Graham et al, 1982 Buffalo, USA	2,024	Cruciferous vegetables	h vs l quartile	1.0 (na)	na	na	na	na
Zemla, 1984, Poland	328	Raw vegetables	h vs l tertile	0.7 (na)[b]	Y	N	N	N
			h vs l tertile	1.6 (na)[c]	Y	N	N	N
Katsouyanni et al 1986, Athens, Greece	120	Vegetables	h vs l quintile	negative assoc*	Y	N	N	Y
		Fruits	h vs l quintile	negative assoc	Y	N	N	Y
		Raw carrots	h vs l quintile	negative assoc	Y	N	N	Y
Hislop et al, 1986 British Columbia Canada	846	Yellow vegetables	h vs l quintile	0.8 (0.6–1.1)	Y	Y	N	N
		Carrots	h vs l quartile	0.6 (0.4–1.1)	Y	Y	N	N
		Other vegetables	h vs l quintile	0.8 (0.6–1.2)	Y	Y	N	N
		Yellow vegetables	h vs l quintile	0.7 (0.5–1.0)[d]	Y	Y	N	N
		Carrots	h vs l quartile	0.9 (0.5–1.6)[d]	Y	Y	N	N
		Other vegetables	h vs l quintile	1.0 (0.7–1.4)[d]	Y	Y	N	N
La Vecchia et al 1987, Italy	1,108	Green vegetables	h vs l tertile	0.4* (0.3–0.5)	Y	Y	Y	Y
		Fresh fruit	h vs l tertile	1.4 (1.0–1.9)	Y	Y	Y	Y
Isovich et al, 1989 La Plata, Argentina	150	Green leafy vegetables	h vs l quartile	0.3* (na)[e]	na	na	na	na
		All green vegetables	h vs l quartile	0.5* (na)[e]	na	na	na	na
		Citrus fruit	h vs l quartile	0.8 (na)[e]	na	na	na	na
		Other fruits	h vs l quartile	0.6 (na)[e]	na	na	na	na
		Green leafy vegetables	h vs l quartile	0.2* (na)[f]	na	na	na	na
		All green vegetables	h vs l quartile	0.4* (na)[f]	na	na	na	na
		Citrus fruit	h vs l quartile	0.6 (na)	na	na	na	na
		Other fruits	h vs l quartile	0.4* (na)[f]	na	na	na	na
Toniolo et al, 1989 Vercelli, Italy	250	Vegetables	h vs l quartile	1.2 (na)	Y	N	N	Y
		Oranges	h vs l quartile	1.3 (na)	Y	N	N	Y
		Fruit	h vs l quartile	1.1 (na)	Y	N	N	Y
Young, 1989 Wisconsin, USA	277	Yellow vegetables	na	0.7 (0.4–1.0)[g]	Y	Y	Y	Y
		Cruciferous vegetables	na	0.7 (0.4–1.0)[g]	Y	Y	Y	Y
		Yellow vegetables	na	0.6 (0.5–0.6)[h]	Y	Y	Y	Y
		Cruciferous vegetables	na	0.6 (0.4–1.0)[h]	Y	Y	Y	Y
Ewertz & Gill, 1990	1,474	Broccoli, spinach, green cabbage	h vs l half	0.9 (0.8–1.1)	Y	N	N	Y
		Carrots	h vs l quartile	1.0 (0.8–1.3)	Y	N	N	Y
		Tomatoes		1.0 (0.8–1.3)	Y	N	N	Y
Sinnard et al, 1990 Canada	68[i]	Raw vegetables	na	negative assoc*	Y	na	na	na
		Cooked vegetables	na	no assoc*	Y	na	na	na
Van't Veer, 1990 Holland	133	Vegetables	h vs l quartile	0.9 (na)	Y	Y	Y	Y
		Fruit	h vs l quartile	0.6 (na)	Y	Y	Y	Y
Richardson et al, 1991	409	Vegetables	h vs l tertile	no assoc	Y	Y	Y	Y

menopausal women in the Netherlands (van der Brandt et al, 1993), no significant association between meat consumption and breast cancer has been found. In two cohort studies of Seventh-day Adventists (Phillips and Snowdon, 1983; Mills et al, 1989), meat consumption has been shown to be unrelated to the risk of breast cancer; this population includes a high proportion of vegetarians and, among the meat eaters, consumption is relatively low and usually excludes pork.

A meta-analysis of seven case-control and cohort studies which recorded data for meat intake has reported a relative risk for high red meat intake of 1.54 (1.31–1.82) (Boyd et al, 1993). Case-control studies not included in this meta-analysis include a study in Uruguay, in which a fourfold statisti-cally significant increase in risk was reported with higher intake of red meat, after adjustment for energy intake; further analysis showed this increase in risk to be attributable to fried and broiled (grilled) meat and thus raised the question of the effects of cooking at high temperatures (Ronco et al, 1996). This study observed no association for processed meat. A case-control study in China reported a statistically significant increase in risk with meat intakes above 80 grams, although the relationship became weaker and statistically non-significant after adjustment for energy intake (Qi et al, 1994). Other case-control studies have reported increased risk with higher consumption of sausage (Goodman et al, 1992), processed meats (Iscovitch et al, 1989; Landa et al, 1994), or an undefined group of 'other

Author, year and place	No. of cases	Type of fruit or vegetable	Comparison (highest vs lowest quantile)	Odds ratio (95% confidence interval)	Age	Adjustment Reproductive history	Family predisposition	Other variables[a]
Montpelier, France		Citrus fruit	h vs l tertile	1.4 (1.0–2.0)	Y	Y	Y	Y
Zaridze et al, 1991	139	Vegetables	h vs l tertile	0.3 (0.0–3.7)[m]	Y	Y	N	Y
Moscow, Russia		Fruit	h vs l tertile	0.8 (0.1–5.3)[m]	Y	Y	N	Y
		Vegetables	h vs l tertile	0.7 (0.1–4.5)[n]	Y	Y	N	Y
		Fruit	h vs l tertile	1.8 (0.5–7.1)[n]	Y	Y	N	Y
Pawlega, 1992 Cracow, Poland	127	Cooked vegetables	h vs l tertile	0.4* (0.2–0.8)	Y	N	N	Y
Kato et al, 1992, Japan	908	Green-yellow vegetables	h vs l tertile	0.6 (0.4–0.9)	na	na	na	na
Levi et al, 1993 Vaud, Switzerland	107[l]	Green vegetables	h vs l tertile	0.5* (na)	Y	N	N	Y
		Cruciferous vegetables	h vs l tertile	0.6* (na)	Y	N	N	Y
		Carrots	h vs l tertile	0.7 (na)	Y	N	N	Y
		Tomatoes	h vs l tertile	0.9 (na)	Y	N	N	Y
		Onions	h vs l tertile	0.5* (na)	Y	N	N	Y
		Garlic	h vs l tertile	0.6 (na)	Y	N	N	Y
		Fresh fruit	h vs l tertile	0.8 (na)	Y	N	N	Y
		Citrus fruit	h vs l tertile	1.1 (na)	Y	N	N	Y
Holmberg et al, 1994 Sweden	265	Vegetables	h vs l quartile	0.8 (0.3–2.3)[p]	Y	N	N	Y
		Vegetables	h vs l quartile	0.6 (0.3–1.0)q	Y	N	N	Y
		Fruit	h vs l quartile	0.7 (0.3–2.1)[p]	Y	N	N	Y
		Fruit	h vs l quartile	1.7 (1.0–3.0)q	Y	N	N	Y
Trichopolou et al 1995, Athens, Greece	820	Vegetables	h vs l quintile	0.5* (0.4–0.7)	Y	Y	N	Y
		Fruit	h vs l quintile	0.7* (0.5–0.9)	Y	Y	N	Y
Freudenheim et al 1996, New York, USA	297[m]	Vegetables	h vs l quartile	0.5* (0.3–0.7)	Y	Y	Y	Y
		Fruit	h vs l quartile	0.7* (0.4–1.1)	Y	Y	Y	Y

* $p \leq 0.05$ for trend or as compared with the lowest consumption level

na not available

a Also adjusted for one or more of the following: education, interviewer, residence, marital status, socio-economic status, history of benign breast disease, body mass index, oral contraceptives, oestrogens, smoking history, alcohol consumption, size of household, total calories, energy intake, month of mammography

b Upper Silesians

c Migrants

d Childhood consumption

e Comparison with hospital controls

f Comparison with neighbourhood controls

g Age 18-35

h Age > 35

i Part of a cohort from the Canadian National Breast Screening Study

l Part of the SEARCH Programme of the International Agency for the Research on Cancer

m Premenopausal women

n Postmenopausal women

p Age ≤ 50

q Age > 50

meats' (Levi et al, 1993).

An early international ecological study reported strong correlations between meat consumption and breast cancer (r = 0.7–0.8) (Armstrong and Doll, 1975). In other ecological observations, Seventh-day Adventists in the USA, who consume relatively small amounts of meat, have only slightly lower mortality from breast cancer (about 10% lower), than US white women of similar socioeconomic status (Phillips et al, 1980). In a comparison of British nuns, who ate no or very little meat, to other single women, a slightly lower rate of breast cancer was observed in the vegetarian nuns (Kinlen, 1982).

The assessment of meat as a risk factor for breast cancer has focused primarily on its role as a source of dietary fat or animal protein. However, as noted, the study of Toniolo et al (1994) found that consumption of meat, but not total fat or protein, significantly increased the risk of breast cancer. It is possible that, if meat consumption does play a role in breast cancer aetiology, the risk may not be related to meat as a source of fat or protein, but, rather, as a source of mutagens and/or carcinogens, specifically heterocyclic amines (HAs), N-nitroso compounds, and polycyclic aromatic hydrocarbons (PAHs). Some HAs are powerful mammary carcinogens in rodents and may be breast cancer risk factors in humans. As reviewed by Snyderwine (1994), certain HAs are distributed to the mammary gland, form DNA adducts and cause mammary cancers in rats. Certain HAs are activated and form DNA adducts in cultured human mammary epithelial cells

(HMEC) (Pfau). *N*-nitrosamines are also rodent mammary carcinogens (Huggins, 1981; Zarbl, 1985; el-Bayoumy, 1992; Rivera, 1994), and cultured human mammary epithelial cells undergo unscheduled DNA synthesis following exposure to ethylmethanesulphonate (Eldridge et al, 1992), although transformation by *N*-nitroso compounds has not yet been shown (Calaf and Russo, 1993). Additionally, PAHs are known to be powerful mammary carcinogens in mice (Yuspa and Poirier, 1988), and are mutagenic to breast cell lines (Gould et al, 1986).

Three of eight prospective studies have reported an increased risk of breast cancer with higher meat intake; a meta-analysis of seven cohort and case-control studies has also shown increased risk, as have several case-control studies not included in this combined analysis.

Diets high in meat possibly increase the risk of breast cancer.

Poultry

In a meta-analysis of five case-control and cohort studies, poultry intake was shown to be unrelated to the risk of breast cancer, with a summary relative risk of 0.94 (0.78–1.13) (Boyd et al, 1993). Two cohort studies published after this meta-analysis also found no material association between poultry consumption and the risk of breast cancer (Toniolo et al, 1994; Tavani and La Vecchia, 1995).

Diets high in poultry possibly have no relationship with the risk of breast cancer.

Fish

A few epidemiological studies have investigated the association between fish (or fish oil) and breast cancer. Prospective studies report either no association (Toniolo et al, 1994; Willett et al, 1987) or a weak protective effect (Vatten et al, 1990). One case-control study in Japan has also reported a weak protective effect (Hirose et al, 1995).

Ecological studies have also reported either no association (Caygill and Hill, 1995) or protective associations (Kaizer et al, 1989).

Animal experiments generally support a protective role for fish oil in mammary tumorigenesis (Karmali et al, 1984; Rose et al, 1994).

The evidence suggests that diets high in fish may decrease the risk of breast cancer but is, as yet, insufficient.

4.11.2.5 Milk and dairy products

Many analytical epidemiological studies have examined the relationship between various milk products and the risk of breast cancer. For milk, nine studies have reported increased risk with higher intakes (Talamini et al, 1984; Hislop et al, 1986; Le et al, 1986; Pryor et al, 1989; Toniolo et al, 1989;

Ewertz and Gill, 1990; Kato et al, 1992; Levi et al, 1993; Gaard et al, 1995), ten have found no relationship (Lubin et al, 1981; Hirohata et al, 1987; La Vecchia et al, 1987; Mills et al, 1988a; Van't Veer et al, 1989; Ursin et al, 1990; Vatten et al, 1990; Ingram et al, 1991; Richardson et al, 1991; Tavani and La Vecchia, 1995), and four have reported decreased risk (Iscovich et al, 1989; Mettlin et al, 1990; Simard et al, 1990; Knekt et al, 1996). Specifically, among the six cohort studies, milk was associated with increased risk in one study, unrelated to breast cancer in four studies, and associated with decreased risk in one study. (Mills et al, 1988a; Ursin et al, 1990; Vatten et al, 1990; Gaard et al, 1995; Tavani and La Vecchia, 1995; Knekt et al, 1996).

With regard to cheese intake, four epidemiological analytical studies have reported increased risk with higher intakes (Le et al, 1986; Toniolo et al, 1989; Richardson et al, 1991; Levi et al, 1993), five have found no relationship (Lubin et al, 1981; Hirohata et al, 1987; Mills et al, 1988a; Iscovich et al, 1989; Knekt et al, 1996), and one has reported decreased risk (Van't Veer et al, 1989).

One cohort study examined dairy products as a general category and reported a moderate protective association, with an energy-adjusted RR of 0.6 (0.4–0.99, p = 0.10 for trend) for intake in the uppermost quintile (Toniolo et al, 1994).

In a 1993 meta-analysis of cohort and case-control studies, high consumption of milk and cheese was associated with very weak increases in risk for breast cancer, with summary relative risks of 1.20 (1.04–1.30 for milk and 1.02–1.40 for cheese) (Boyd et al, 1993).

Ecological studies have generally found positive correlations between the consumption of milk or dairy products and the incidence of breast cancer (Armstrong and Doll, 1975; Decarli and La Vecchia, 1986; Rose et al, 1986).

Fat, often present in milk and dairy products, possibly increases the risk of breast cancer risk (see section 4.11.1.3). On the other hand, milk and dairy products are good sources of calcium and conjugated linoleic acid, a fatty acid which has been shown to partially protect against chemically induced mammary tumours in animals (Ip et al, 1994,1995).

Evidence relating to diets high in milk and dairy products and the risk of breast cancer is inconsistent; no judgement is possible.

4.11.2.6 Coffee, tea and other drinks

Coffee

In 1979, interest in caffeine intake as a risk factor for breast cancer was generated when it was reported that elimination of caffeine from the diet led to relief of symptoms in women with benign breast disease (Minton et al, 1979). This led to the examination of coffee, a major contributor of caffeine in many diets, as a potential risk factor for breast cancer.

In 1991, an IARC Working Group reviewed seven case-control studies of breast cancer which had examined coffee consumption, and concluded that all the studies gave risk estimates that were close to 1.0 and none suggested the exis-

TABLE 4.11.10 COFFEE AND CAFFEINE CONSUMPTION AND THE RISK OF BREAST CANCER: COHORT STUDIES

AUTHOR, YEAR AND PLACE	SIZE OF COHORT: NO. OF CASES	COMPARISON (HIGHEST VS LOWEST QUANTILE)	RELATIVE RISK (95% CONFIDENCE INTERVAL)	AGE	ADJUSTMENT REPRODUCTIVE HISTORY	FAMILY PRE-DISPOSITION	OTHER VARIABLES[a]
Snowdon and Phillips 1984, California, USA	23,912[b]: 176	h vs l half	1.0 (0.7–1.3)	Y	N	N	Y
Jacobsen et al, 1986 Norway	2,891: 32	h vs l quartile	0.8 (na)	Y	N	N	N
Vatten, 1990, Norway	14,593: 152	h vs l quartile	0.8 (0.5–1.4)	na	na	na	na
Hunter et al, 1992 Harvard, USA	89,494[c]: 1,439	h vs l quintile	0.9 (0.8–1.1)[d]	na	na	na	na
		h vs l quintile	0.9* (0.7–1.0)[e]	na	na	na	na
Graham et al, 1992 New York, USA	18,586[f]: 395	na	no assoc	Y	N	N	Y
Folsom et al, 1993 Iowa, USA	34,388[g]: 580	h vs l quintile	1.0 (0.8–1.3)[d]	Y	Y	Y	Y
		h vs l quintile	1.0 (0.8–1.3)[e]	Y	Y	Y	Y

* p ≤ 0.05 for trend or as compared with the lowest consumption level
na not available
a Also adjusted for one or more of the following: smoking history, waist/hip ratio, education
b White Seventh-day Adventists (cohort includes men and women)
c Nurses' Health Study
d Coffee
e Caffeine
f Postmenopausal women
g Postmenopausal women from the Iowa Women's Health Study
h Education

tence of any association between the risk of breast cancer and the consumption of coffee. Further, no studies showed any association for instant or decaffeinated coffee, when results were presented separately for these. The Working Group further stated that there was no reason to believe that measurement error or confounding was responsible for the lack of an observed association. The final evaluation was that 'there was evidence suggesting lack of carcinogenicity of coffee drinking in the human female breast' (IARC, 1991).

Six prospective and nineteen case-control studies that have examined the relationship between the risk of breast cancer and coffee or caffeine consumption are presented in Tables 4.11.10 and 4.11.11; these include the studies reviewed by the IARC Working Group.

The six cohort studies were conducted in various parts of the USA and Norway. Only one statistically significant association was apparent in Table 4.11.10; this was a weak decrease in risk with higher consumption of caffeine in the Nurses' Health Study (USA) (RR = 0.9, 0.7–1.1, p = 0.04 for trend for the uppermost quintile of intake); the relative risk for the uppermost quintile of coffee consumption was similar, but the trend test was not statistically significant (Hunter et al, 1992). In the remaining studies, relative risks ranged from 0.8 to 1.0 for the highest consumption levels. In one of the cohorts of Norwegian women, while no substantial association was reported overall, an interaction with body mass was suggested, such that coffee consumption was associated with decreased risk in women with low body mass, but increased risk in those with high body mass (RR = 0.5, 0.3–0.9 and 2.1, 0.8–5.2, respectively) (statistically significant test for interaction) (Vatten et al, 1990).

The nineteen case-control studies shown in Table 4.11.11

were conducted in Canada, New Zealand, the UK, the USA, France, Israel, Italy, Greece, Australia, Argentina, Denmark, Singapore, Japan, Spain, Switzerland and Sweden. Only two of the nineteen studies reported any statistically significant association, with one reporting a weak increase in risk (Mansel et al, 1982), and another reporting a moderate decrease in risk (Le, 1985), with higher coffee intake.

Thirty-four associations from 25 epidemiological studies are presented in Tables 4.11.10 and 4.11.11; more than one risk estimate is shown for some studies due to: the examination of various types of coffee; examination of coffee and caffeine separately; examination of coffee intake at different ages; or stratified analyses by type of controls, or age or menopausal status at diagnosis. In a tally of these 34 associations (without regard to statistical significance), no risk estimates were greater than 1.5, 30 were between 0.75 and 1.5 (or there was said to be 'no association', but no risk estimate was given), and four were lower than 0.75. Thus, the epidemiological evidence, almost without exception, shows no material relationship between coffee consumption and the risk of breast cancer.

One international ecological study reported no correlation between breast cancer mortality and coffee consumption (Stocks, 1970); however, another study reported a moderate positive correlation between coffee consumption and breast cancer incidence (r = 0.4, ns) (Armstrong and Doll, 1975).

Caffeine is the component of coffee that has been most studied with regard to a potential role in the aetiology of breast cancer.

Experimental studies have shown caffeine to both stimulate and suppress breast tumours, depending upon the

TABLE 4.11.11 COFFEE CONSUMPTION AND THE RISK OF BREAST CANCER: CASE-CONTROL STUDIES

AUTHOR, YEAR AND PLACE	NO OF CASES	COMPARISON (HIGHEST VS LOWEST QUANTILE)	ODDS RISK (95% CONFIDENCE INTERVAL)	AGE	ADJUSTMENT REPRODUCTIVE HISTORY	FAMILY PRE- DISPOSITION	OTHER VARIABLES[a]
Lubin et al, 1981 North Alberta	577	h vs l half	1.2 (0.9–1.5)[b]	Y	na	na	na
Lawson et al, 1981 USA, Scotland, New Zealand	241	h vs l quartile	1.1 (0.6–1.8)[b,c]	Y	N	N	Y
Mansel et al, 1982 Cardiff, UK	na	h vs l tertile	1.3* (1.0–1.6)	na	na	na	na
Rosenberg et al, 1985 Eastern, USA	2,651	h vs l quartile	1.2 (0.9–1.6)[d]	Y	Y	Y	Y
			1.1 (0.7–1.6)[e]	Y	Y	Y	Y
Le, 1985, France	500	h vs l tertile	0.6* (na)	na	Y	Y	Y
Lubin et al, 1985 Tel Aviv, Israel	818	h vs l quartile	0.7 (0.4–1.1)	na	na	na	na
La Vecchia et al, 1986 Northern Italy	616	h vs l quartile	1.1 (0.7–1.7)	Y	Y	N	Y
Katsouyanni et al. 1986, Athens, Greece	120	h vs l tertile	no assoc	Y	N	N	Y
Schairer et al, 1987 USA	1,510[f]	h vs l sextile	1.0 (0.8–1.3)[g]	na	na	na	na
		h vs l sextile	0.7 (0.3–1.3)[h]	na	na	na	na
Rohan & Michael, 1988 Adelaide, Australia	451	h vs l tertile[i]	1.4 (0.6–3.0)[l]	Y	N	N	N
		h vs l quintile[i]	1.2 (0.7–2.0)[m]	Y	N	N	N
Iscovich et al, 1989 La Plata, Argentina	150	h vs l quartile[n]	1.1 (na)[p]	na	na	na	na
		h vs l quartile[n]	0.5 (na)[q]	na	na	na	na
Young, 1989 Wisconsin, USA	277	na	0.9 (0.7–1.3)[r]	Y	Y	Y	Y
		na	1.1 (0.9–1.5)[s]	Y	Y	Y	Y
Ewertz & Gill, 1990 Denmark	1,474	h vs l quartile	0.8 (0.6–1.2)	Y	N	N	Y
Simard et al, 1990	68[t]	na	no assoc[u]	Y	na	na	na
Lee et al, 1991 Singapore	200[l]	h vs l tertile	0.8 (0.4–1.4)[v]	Y	Y	N	N
		h vs l tertile	0.8 (0.4–1.4)[w]	Y	Y	N	N
Kato et al, 1992, Japan	908	h vs l tertile	0.9 (0.7–1.2)	na	na	na	na
Martin-Moreno et al. 1993, Spain	762	h vs l quartile	0.9 (0.7–1.2)	Y	N	N	Y
Levi et al, 1993	107[x]	h vs l tertile	0.9 (na)	Y	N	N	Y
Holmberg et al, 1994 Sweden	265	h vs l quartile	0.9 (0.3–2.4)[b,y]	Y	N	N	Y
		h vs l quartile	0.9 (0.6–1.6)[b,z]	Y	N	N	Y

* p ≤ 0.05 for trend or as compared with the lowest consumption level

na not available

a Also adjusted for one or more of the following: education, interviewer, oral contraceptives, marital status, smoking history, body mass index, residence, socio-economic status, total energy intake, Quetelet index, country, race, religion, tea consumption, alcohol consumption, hospital, hospitalizations, year of interview, geographic area, month of mammography

b Tea and coffee

c 90% confidence interval

d Comparison with non-cancer controls

e Comparison with cancer controls

f From the Breast Cancer Detection Demonstration Project

g Brewed coffee

h Instant coffee

i Total coffee

l Premenopausal women

m Postmenopausal women

n Caffeine-containing beverages

p Comparison with hospital controls

q Comparison with neighbourhood controls

r Age 18–35

s Age > 35

t Part of a cohort from the Canadian National Breast Screening Study

u Includes tea

v Total coffee

w Caffeine

x Part of the SEARCH Programme of the International Agency for Research on Cancer

y Age ≤ 50

z Age > 50

animal species and the tumorigenic phase (initiation/ promotion) of administration.

Six cohort studies and nineteen case-control studies have consistently shown no relationship between coffee intake and the risk of breast cancer.

Evidence that the consumption of coffee has no relationship with the risk of breast cancer is convincing.

Black tea

In 1991, an IARC Working Group reviewed the evidence on the relationship of tea consumption to cancer risk and concluded that none of five epidemiological studies of breast cancer showed any association (IARC, 1991). Subsequent to the IARC review, at least four prospective studies have examined this relationship. One study of postmenopausal women in Iowa (USA) reported no material association for black tea (RR = 1.1, 0.9–1.4, for two or more cups per day, compared to consumption either monthly or never) (Zheng et al, 1996). Another study of women in New York similarly found no association for tea intake (Graham et al, 1992). The Nurses' Health Study, a large study of USA women, reported a moderate protective association (RR = 0.7, 0.5–1.0, for four or more cups of tea per day, compared to one or fewer) (Hunter et al, 1992). A study in the Netherlands, where tea is more frequently consumed than in the USA, reported no statistically significant association (RR = 1.3, 0.9–2.0, for five or more cups per day, compared to non-consumption) (Goldbohm et al, 1996).

In addition to methylxanthines (caffeine, theobromine), tea also contains various antioxidant polyphenolic compounds which have been shown in experimental animal and in vitro models to have anticarcinogenic properties (Goldbohm et al, 1996). In black tea, some phenols are oxidised, thus reducing their potential for anticarcinogenic activity. Phenols and flavonoids are assessed in chapter 5.8.

The majority of nine epidemiological studies have shown tea intake to be unrelated to risk of breast cancer.

Consumption of tea possibly has no relationship to the risk of breast cancer.

4.11.3 FOOD PROCESSING

4.11 3.1 Contaminants

DDT residues

Wolff et al (1995) reported higher levels of the DDT metabolite DDE in sera of women with breast cancer and a fourfold increase in risk compared with controls. They concluded that organochlorine residues, particularly DDE, may be an important factor in breast cancer. However, a second study failed to confirm this finding. In a study by Unger et al (1984) of levels of DDT and other organochlorine compounds in human breast fat from deceased cases with and without breast cancer, and in biopsy samples from newly diagnosed breast cancer patients, no significant differences were observed.

The evidence suggests that dietary residues of DTT or its metabolites may increase the risk of breast cancer, but is, as yet, insufficient.

4.11.3.2 Cooking

Frying

A case-control study of breast cancer using 77 pairs of patients and controls, reported a 1.8-fold statistically non-significant increase in the risk among those with the highest consumption of fried foods and a 2.4-fold (p>0.05) increase with fried potatoes (Phillips, 1975). However, other dietary factors such as fat intake were not taken into account. More recently, studies in Finland (Knekt et al, 1994) and in Uruguay (Ronco et al, 1996) have reported associations between fried/red meat consumption and breast cancer independent of fat intake.

Based on this latest evidence, no judgement is possible.

4.12 Ovary

Cancer of the ovary is the seventh most common incident cancer in women. An estimated 191,000 cases occurred in 1996, accounting for 1.8 per cent of all new cases of cancer.

The panel has reached the following conclusions. There is as yet no convincing evidence that any dietary factors modify risk of ovarian cancer, nor evidence of any probable causal relationships with diet.

The panel notes that diets high in vegetables and fruits possibly reduce the risk of this cancer.

Established non-dietary causes of ovarian cancer are low parity and specific inherited genetic abnormalities.

The most effective dietary means of preventing ovarian cancer is, possibly, consumption of diets high in vegetables and fruits.

FOOD, NUTRITION AND OVARIAN CANCER

In the judgement of the panel, the dietary constituents and related factors and the food and drinks listed here modify the risk of ovarian cancer, or else have no relationship with it. Judgements are graded according to the strength of the evidence.

EVIDENCE	DECREASES RISK	NO RELATIONSHIP	INCREASES RISK
Convincing			
Probable			
Possible	Vegetables and fruits		
Insufficient	Carotenoids Fish		Total fat Saturated/animal fat Eggs

For an explanation of the terms used in the matrix, see chapter 3.

INTRODUCTION

Although not as common as breast cancer, ovarian cancer is an important contributor to cancer mortality in most affluent countries. Ovarian cancer is typically diagnosed at an advanced stage and has a high fatality rate.

INCIDENCE PATTERNS

Cancer of the ovary is the fifteenth most common cancer in the world. In 1996, an estimated 191,000 were diagnosed worldwide (WHO, 1997), accounting for 1.8% of all new cases. Ovarian cancer is the seventh most common cancer in women.

There are considerable variations in the incidence of ovarian cancer. Previous trends showed it was more common in developed countries. However, over half the global incidence

> **BOX 4.12.1 ESTABLISHED NON-DIETARY FACTORS AND OVARIAN CANCER**
>
> The following non-dietary factors increase the risk of ovarian cancer:
>
> - Inheritance of mutation in specific genes, such as the *BRCA-1* and *BRCA-2* genes
> - Low parity
>
> The following non-dietary factor decreases the risk of ovarian cancer:
>
> - Extended oral contraceptive use

of this cancer is now in the developing world (100,000 cases in 1996). Recent trends suggest there is a decline in those countries that previously had high rates, and increases in those that had low rates.

Ovarian cancer is thought to affect almost 2% of the

OVARIAN CANCER estimated rates of cancer incidence by sex and area

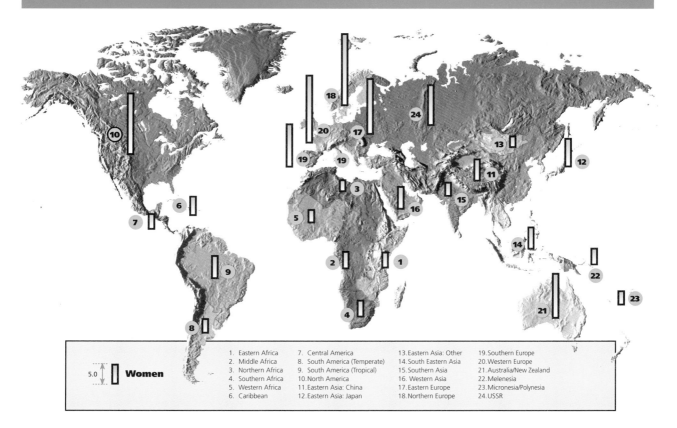

1. Eastern Africa	7. Central America	13. Eastern Asia: Other	19. Southern Europe
2. Middle Africa	8. South America (Temperate)	14. South Eastern Asia	20. Western Europe
3. Northern Africa	9. South America (Tropical)	15. Southern Asia	21. Australia/New Zealand
4. Southern Africa	10. North America	16. Western Asia	22. Melenesia
5. Western Africa	11. Eastern Asia: China	17. Eastern Europe	23. Micronesia/Polynesia
6. Caribbean	12. Eastern Asia: Japan	18. Northern Europe	24. USSR

5.0 **Women**

female population over their lifetimes. Five-year survival rates are less than 30%. In 1996, mortality attributable to cancer of the ovary was estimated at 124,000 women, 1.7% of all cancer deaths (WHO, 1997).

PATHOGENESIS

Little is known regarding aetiological factors and the natural history of ovarian cancer. Most of the known risk factors are related to hormonal and reproductive events, with higher parity, and oral contraceptive use significantly decreasing the risk of the disease. There are two main mechanisms proposed for ovarian carcinogenesis that are relevant to the effects of hormonal factors: excessive levels of circulating gonadotrophins, associated with fewer childbirths, could cause neoplastic changes in the ovary (Cramer and Welch, 1983), or the decreased number of ovulatory cycles experienced during pregnancy and breastfeeding, and with oral contraceptive use, could reduce mitotic events in the ovary, thereby reducing potential opportunities for mutations to be fixed (Casagrande et al, 1983).

The majority of ovarian cancers begin in a single layer of epithelial cells lining the surface of the ovary, and proliferation of cells in this surface occurs following every ovulation in order to repair damage produced by the rupture of mature follicles. Research has shown that repeated passage of rat ovarian surface epithelial cells in culture results in spontaneous transformation to a malignant phenotype in the absence of carcinogens (Godwin et al, 1992). It is not yet clear if this also occurs in the human ovary. It is likely that acquisition of the malignant phenotype occurs as a result of multiple genetic changes (i.e., loss or mutation of tumour-suppressor genes, and activation of proto-oncogenes). Mutations have been observed in the K-ras proto-oncogene, and this gene is mutated in about half of borderline ovarian tumours, suggesting it may be an early event in ovarian carcinogenesis (Mok et al, 1993). Other proto-oncogenes frequently mutated include fms (50%), a receptor for the growth factor–macrophage colony-stimulating factor, and c-erB-2 (86%), a transmembrane tyrosine kinase (Bast et al, 1992). The tumour-suppressor gene p53 is mutated in approximately 50% of ovarian cancers (Marks et al, 1991).

There is little evidence for a role of exogenous carcinogens in the initiation of ovarian cancer. It has been suggested that exogenous substances could ascend into the abdominal cavity via the genital tract, and the application of a polycyclic aromatic hydrocarbon (7, 12-dimethylbenz[a]anthracene) to mice resulted in ovarian tumour induction.

Additionally, talc granules have often been detected in ovarian tumours. Some studies have noted increased ovarian cancer risk among women who use talcum powder or are occupationally exposed to asbestos, while others have not confirmed such an association (see Dietl and Marzusch, 1993). There is also some support for an association between use of psychotropic medications (antidepressants, tranquillisers and antipsychotics) (Harlow and Cramer, 1995). These drugs induce microsomal enzymes that enhance oestrogen metabolism, and could mediate hormonally-associated carcinogenesis (Cramer and Welch, 1983; Feuer, 1983).

A family history of ovarian cancer increases the risk for ovarian cancer. Risk of ovarian cancer is more than four times greater among women with a family history of the disease (Kerber and Slattery, 1995). Several families with BRCA-1 and BRCA-2 mutations have members who have ovarian cancer (see for example, Feunteun et al, 1993; Easton et al, 1993).

JUDGEMENTS OF PREVIOUS REPORTS

The National Academy of Sciences report, Diet, Nutrition and Cancer (NAS, 1982) concluded that the 'evidence associating dietary factors, especially high fat diets, and ovarian cancer is largely indirect'. The subsequent report, Diet and Health (NAS, 1989) concluded that no dietary associations had been established for cancer of the ovary.

REVIEW

4.12.1 DIETARY CONSTITUENTS

4.12.1.1 Energy and related factors
Body mass
Six case-control studies have examined the relationship between ovarian cancer and body mass. Obesity, defined as a body mass index (BMI) of over 30, was found to be a risk factor for ovarian cancer in a US case-control study by Casagrande et al (1979), and a case-control study in Greece showed patients with ovarian cancer to be slightly taller and heavier than controls, but this difference was not significant (Tzonou et al, 1984). Obesity was associated with an OR of 1.7 (1.1–2.8) in a case-control study in the USA (Risch et al, 1983). In contrast, an earlier Japanese case-control study found no relationship between obesity and the risk of ovarian cancer (Wynder et al, 1969), while a case-control study in the USA (Byers et al, 1983) found a marginally significant trend (p < 0.10) for decreasing risk with increasing obesity in postmenopausal women (aged 50–79 years). A case-control study conducted in the USA (Slattery et al, 1989) found no increase in risk with a higher BMI (OR = 1.2).

On the basis of these somewhat inconsistent data, no judgement is possible.

4.12.1.2 Carbohydrate
Sugar
Galactose
Galactose is a component of the milk sugar, lactose and dietary intake of this sugar possibly has no relationship with ovarian cancer.

A case-control study in the USA by Cramer et al (1989) suggested that milk sugar or lactose, and, more specifically, its galactose component, may increase the risk of ovarian cancer by depleting ovarian germ cells and causing pituitary gonadotrophins to increase, thus inducing ovarian neoplasia. Cramer and colleagues found that women with ovarian cancer consumed more lactose, particularly in fermented forms, and had lower levels of a key enzyme, a galactose transferase, that metabolises galactose. Women with higher levels of lactose consumption and lower transferase activity had a high risk of ovarian cancer. However, there are limitations to this study as erythrocyte transferase activity was examined in patients who had received chemotherapy or radiation treatment. Three later case-control studies in the USA (Mettlin and Piver, 1990; Engle et al, 1991; Herrington et al, 1995) found little evidence to support the hypothesis of an association between lactose and galactose intake and ovarian cancer.

The evidence suggests that diets high in galactose have no relationship with the risk of ovarian cancer, but are too limited and inconsistent to make a judgement.

4.12.1.3 Fat and cholesterol

Total fat

Five case-control studies have examined total fat intake in relation to ovarian cancer. The ORs reported in two US studies were 1.2 (ns) and 1.3 (ns); in a Canadian study the OR of 1.2 (ns) was adjusted for energy intake (Slattery et al, 1989; Byers et al, 1993; Risch et al, 1994). A study of Chinese women reported a significant OR of 1.9 (p<0.05) (Shu et al, 1989). A case-control study in northern Italy reported an OR of 2.1 for fat intake, and this was largely attributable to higher butter consumption (La Vecchia et al, 1987).

Two international ecological studies of mortality rates for ovarian cancer and total fat consumption have shown an increase in risk from high intakes of total fat (Armstrong and Doll, 1975; Rose et al, 1986). In the study by Rose et al, of 30 countries, the risk (r = 0.67) was attributed to fats of animal origin; Armstrong and Doll observed a high correlation (r = 0.79) in 21 countries between ovarian cancer mortality rates and total fat consumption.

Overall, the evidence suggests that diets high in total fat may increase the risk of ovarian cancer but is, as yet, insufficient.

Saturated/ animal fat

Each of three case-control studies of ovarian cancer that have examined saturated fat have found some evidence of an increased risk with a higher intake. One study in Boston, USA reported a statistically nonsignificant increased risk (p < 0.10, no OR given), one in Utah, USA reported an OR of 1.3 (0.6–2.6), and another in Canada reported energy-adjusted ORs of 1.4–1.6 (some statistically significant) based upon various measures of saturated fat intake, including total grams, percentage of total fat, and percentage of energy (Cramer et al, 1984; Slattery et al, 1989; Risch et al, 1994).

Two case-control studies have reported increased risk

with greater consumption of animal fat, with ORs of 1.7 (p <0.05) and 1.8 (1.0–3.4); neither of these was adjusted for energy intake (Cramer et al, 1984; Shu et al, 1989).

An international ecological study has reported a positive correlation between consumption of animal fat and mortality from ovarian cancer (r = 0.8) (Rose et al, 1986).

The mechanism whereby animal fat may increase risk is not clear. A hormonal mechanism is consistent with findings of oestrogen receptors in epithelial ovarian tumours. It has been suggested that a diet high in animal fats can produce extragenital oestrogen via gut bacteria; oestrogen bioavailability is altered in vegetarian women (Shu et al, 1989).

The evidence suggests that diets high in saturated/ animal fat may increase the risk of ovarian cancer but is, as yet, insufficient.

Monounsaturated fat

Two case-control studies of ovarian cancer have examined monounsaturated fat intake and have reported ORs of 1.1 (ns, energy-adjusted) and 1.3 (0.7–2.3) for higher intake (Slattery et al, 1989; Risch et al, 1994).

The evidence on monounsaturated fat is very limited; no judgement is possible.

Polyunsaturated fat

Two case-control studies have examined the relationship between polyunsaturated fat intake and ovarian cancer. One in Canada reported an OR of 0.86 (ns, energy-adjusted) and the other in Utah, USA an OR of 1.2 (0.6–2.3) for higher intake (Slattery et al, 1989; Risch et al, 1994). A study in China reported an OR of 0.8 (ns) for plant fat (Shu et al, 1989), whereas a study in Boston, USA showed decreased risk (p < 0.05) (OR not given) with higher intakes of linoleic acid and vegetable fat (Cramer et al, 1984).

An international ecological study has reported no substantial correlation between consumption of vegetable fat and mortality from ovarian cancer (r = 0.2) (Rose et al, 1986).

The evidence on diets high in polyunsaturated or plant fat and the risk of ovarian cancer is limited; no judgement is possible.

Cholesterol

Two case-control studies of ovarian cancer, one in the USA and one in Canada, that have examined cholesterol intake found weak, statistically non-significant increases in risk (Cramer et al, 1984; Risch et al, 1994). In one of these studies, a stronger increase in risk was observed for egg cholesterol, with an energy-adjusted OR of 1.9 (1.4–2.7), than for total or non-egg cholesterol (Risch et al, 1994). Three studies have reported weakly increased risk or no association with higher consumption of eggs (Cramer et al, 1984; La Vecchia et al, 1987; Risch et al, 1994).

The evidence on diets high in cholesterol and the risk of ovarian cancer is limited and inconsistent; no judgement is possible.

4.12.1.4 Protein

Three case-control studies (two in the USA and one in China), have examined protein intake in relation to ovarian cancer risk: Byers et al (1983) and Slattery et al (1989) found no association, and Shu et al (1989) found little association when animal fat intakes were controlled.

In their international correlation study, Armstrong and Doll (1975) found positive correlations between animal protein intake and the incidence and mortality of ovarian cancer.

The panel has decided to make no judgement on total protein because of possible differences between animal protein and plant protein and their dietary sources.

4.12.1.5 Vitamins

Carotenoids

In three case-control studies in the USA, significant protective associations were observed with carotenoid intake. In the study by Byers et al (1983), this association was limited to premenopausal women (30–49 years). The study of Engle et al (1991) reported a decrease in risk (OR = 0.3) associated with high carotenoid intake; a limitation of the latter study was the absence of information on reproductive history. Slattery and co-workers (1989) observed a protective association with high carotene intake when reproductive history was accounted for. In the study by Shu et al (1989) in China a protective association was not observed with β-carotene.

The evidence suggests that high dietary carotenoids may decrease the risk of ovarian cancer but is, as yet, insufficient.

Vitamin C

The relationship between vitamin C intake and the risk of ovarian cancer has been examined in three case-control studies, two in the USA and one in China. Relative risks for highest versus lowest intakes in these studies were 1.1 (ns), 0.7 (0.3–1.4) and 0.9 (ns) (Byers et al, 1983; Shu et al, 1989; Slattery et al, 1989).

The evidence relating to high dietary vitamin C and the risk of ovarian cancer are very limited; no judgement is possible.

4.12.2 FOODS AND DRINKS

4.12.2.1 Vegetables and fruits

Six case-control studies in Italy, China, the USA and Canada have examined the relationship between vegetable and fruit consumption (or nutrients/fibre derived from vegetables and fruits) and ovarian cancer. Associations have mainly appeared protective, although not all are statistically significant and the specific dietary factors varied among studies. For example, in two studies more frequent vegetable consumption showed a protective association, OR = 0.6 (La Vecchia et al, 1987), OR = 0.8 (Shu, 1989). Another case-control study revealed vitamin A from fruit and vegetable sources had a significant protective association in premenopausal women (30–49 years) (OR = 0.43, p<0.01) (Byers et al, 1983). A protective association has been observed with green and raw salad vegetables (OR = 0.6) and carrots (OR = 0.3) (Engle et al, 1991), green and yellow vegetables (OR 0.6–0.8), (Slattery et al, 1989). In addition, consumption of vegetable fibre has been associated with a decrease in risk (OR = 0.6, p=0.0001) (Risch et al, 1994).

An international ecological study of 30 countries found an inverse correlation of –0.54 between vegetable availability and ovarian cancer (Rose et al, 1986).

Diets high in vegetables and fruits possibly decrease the risk of ovarian cancer.

4.12.2.2 Pulses (legumes)

One case-control study of ovarian cancer in Shanghai, China (Shu et al, 1989) reported that intake of pulses appeared to decrease risk (OR = 0.4 in higher middle quartile), although the trend was not statistically significant (p=0.22).

Based on only one study, no judgement is possible.

4.12.2.3 Meat, poultry, fish and eggs

Meat

The risk of ovarian cancer in association with high meat intake has been investigated in three case-control studies. In an Italian study (La Vecchia et al, 1987), women with ovarian cancer reported more frequent consumption of meat (OR = 1.6) than controls. In a study in China a high intake of red meat was associated with elevated risk, though it was not significant (OR = 1.4, p=0.19) (Shu et al, 1989). In a study in Japan there were no significant differences between cases and controls in meat consumption (Mori et al, 1988).

The evidence relating to meat and the risk of ovarian cancer is limited and inconsistent. No judgement is possible.

Fish

Four case-control studies in Italy, the USA, China and Japan examined the relationship between fish consumption and ovarian cancer risk. All associations appeared protective, though not all were statistically significant. For example, ORs of 0.7 (La Vecchia, 1987), 0.3, p<0.05 (Cramer et al, 1984), 0.9 (ns) (Shu et al, 1989) and 0.6 (p<0.05) (Mori et al, 1988) have been reported.

The limited evidence suggests that diets high in fish may decrease the risk of ovarian cancer, but is, as yet, insufficient.

Eggs

One cohort study in the USA found an increased risk of ovarian cancer with high egg consumption (Snowdon, 1985).

High egg consumption has been associated with a greater risk of ovarian cancer in one US case-control study (Cramer et al, 1984), but two other case-control studies, one in Italy (La Vecchia et al, 1987) and one in China (Shu et al, 1989) reported no increase in the risk of ovarian cancer with higher egg consumption (Shu et al, 1989). A case-control study in Canada (Risch et al, 1994) suggested a weak increase in risk (OR = 1.4).

An international ecological study (Rose et al, 1986) found a weakly positive, but not statistically significant, association with the consumption of eggs (r=0.3).

These data suggest that diets high in eggs may increase the risk of ovarian cancer, but are, as yet, insufficient.

4.12.2.4 Milk and dairy products

Milk

Milk and dairy products are the sole dietary sources of galactose. In these foods, galactose comprises part of the milk sugar, lactose. A case-control study found an increased risk of ovarian cancer with high consumption of lactose and low levels of galactase transferase, and suggested that galactose may be responsible (Cramer et al, 1989). Subsequent case-control studies have not confirmed these findings and report no increase in risk. Two case-control studies in New York,

USA (Mettlin and Piver, 1990; Engle et al, 1991) reported that the frequency of consuming milk and yoghurt was not associated with the risk of ovarian cancer in any category of consumption (OR = 1.2, 0.7–2.0; and OR = 0.9, 0.4–2.0, respectively). A case-control study in Washington (Herrinton et al, 1995) found no increase in risk in relation to galactose intake (OR = 0.9, 0.6–1.2).

The evidence relating to milk consumption and the risk of ovarian cancer is limited and inconsistent; no judgement is possible.

4.12.2.5 Coffee, tea and other drinks

Coffee

The 1991 IARC report reviewed a total of seven studies on the relationship between coffee consumption and ovarian cancer. Five of these (two with more than one report) showed no consistent association (Hartge et al, 1982; Byers et al, 1983; Miller et al, 1984, 1987; Trichopoulos et al, 1981, 1986; Tzonou et al, 1984; Cramer et al, 1984). In each study, there was neither a significant trend, nor any odds ratio with a 95% confidence limit that excluded 1.0. Some, but not all, of these studies controlled for smoking and other variables. Two of the seven studies showed higher risks with higher consumption – particularly when comparisons were made with hospital controls. Both studies controlled for smoking (La Vecchia et al, 1984; Whittemore et al, 1988)

These data are inconsistent; no judgement is possible.

4.13 Endometrium

Cancer of the endometrium (the lining of the womb) is the eighth most common cancer in women. An estimated 170,000 cases occurred in 1996, accounting for 1.6 per cent of all new cases of cancer.

In general, rates of this cancer are higher in economically developed societies.

The panel has reached the following conclusions. The evidence that high body mass increases the risk of endometrial cancer is convincing.

The panel notes that diets high in vegetables and fruits possibly reduce the risk of this cancer, and that diets high in saturated/animal fats and cholesterol possibly increase risk.

The most effective dietary means of preventing endometrial cancer is maintenance of body weight within recommended levels, by consumption of appropriate diets and by regular physical activity.

FOOD, NUTRITION AND ENDOMETRIAL CANCER

In the judgement of the panel, the dietary constituents and related factors, and the foods and drinks listed below modify the risk of endometrial cancer. Judgements are graded according to the strength of the evidence.

EVIDENCE	DECREASES RISK	NO RELATIONSHIP	INCREASES RISK
Convincing			High body mass
Probable			
Possible	Vegetables and fruits		Saturated/animal fat
Insufficient	Carotenoids		Total fat Cholesterol

For an explanation of the terms used in the matrix, see chapter 3.

INTRODUCTION

More clearly than for any other cancers, relatively high or prolonged exposure to oestrogens, whether endogenous or from external sources, increases the risk of this cancer, particularly when unopposed by progesterone. Thus, early age at menarche and late age at menopause increase the risk, whereas pregnancy and a having greater number of children reduce the risk of endometrial cancer.

Oestrogen replacement therapy after menopause definitely increases the risk of endometrial cancer, particularly among long-term users: for women who have used oestrogen for more than 10 years, the risk is elevated more than tenfold (Parazzini et al, 1991). When progesterone is added to the oestrogen replacement, this risk is reduced (Persson et al, 1989) but not eliminated, especially if oestrogen has previously been used alone.

BOX 4.13.1 ESTABLISHED NON-DIETARY FACTORS AND ENDOMETRIAL CANCER

The following non-dietary factors increases the risk of endometrial cancer:

- Low parity
- Exposures to prolonged endogenous oestrogen and to exogenous oestrogens (commonly used in HRT), particularly without concurrent progestogens.

INCIDENCE PATTERNS

Cancer of the endometrium is the sixteenth most common cancer in the world. In 1996, an estimated 170,000 new cases were diagnosed worldwide (WHO, 1997), accounting

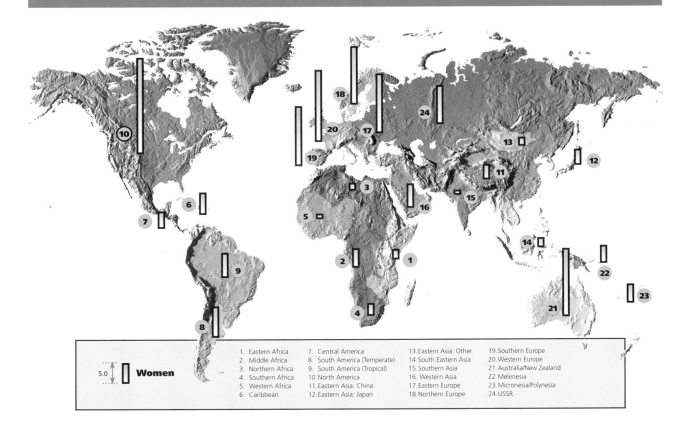

ENDOMETRIAL CANCER estimated rates of cancer incidence by sex and area

5.0 **Women**

1. Eastern Africa
2. Middle Africa
3. Northern Africa
4. Southern Africa
5. Western Africa
6. Caribbean
7. Central America
8. South America (Temperate)
9. South America (Tropical)
10. North America
11. Eastern Asia: China
12. Eastern Asia: Japan
13. Eastern Asia: Other
14. South Eastern Asia
15. Southern Asia
16. Western Asia
17. Eastern Europe
18. Northern Europe
19. Southern Europe
20. Western Europe
21. Australia/New Zealand
22. Melenesia
23. Micronesia/Polynesia
24. USSR

for 1.6% of all new cancers. Endometrial cancer is the eighth most common cancer in women.

The incidence rate of endometrial cancer varies greatly from country to country, and is highest in developed countries where over 100,000 cases were diagnosed in 1996 (WHO, 1997); the highest rates are found in the USA and Canada. In recent years however, a decline in incidence and mortality has become apparent. Africa and Asia have the lowest incidence.

Survival rates for cancer of the endometrium are generally good. In 1996, mortality attributable to endometrial cancer was estimated at 67,000 women, nearly 1% of all cancer deaths (WHO, 1997).

PATHOGENESIS

The central feature that characterises the risk factors for endometrial cancer is the presence of prolonged periods or high levels of unopposed oestrogen. Nulliparity, late menopause, unopposed postmenopausal oestrogen replacement therapy, postmenopausal obesity (which also results in an association between endometrial cancer and hypertension and adult-onset diabetes), polycystic ovary syndrome and feminising ovarian tumours, all share this central feature and all are associated with an elevated risk of endometrial cancer. Further, a number of these risks is moderated by endogenous or exogenous progestins.

High levels of unopposed oestrogens result in endometrial hyperplasia. Whether this elevated level of proliferation is sufficient to ensure that, sooner or later, a random mutation, perhaps as a result of endogenous oxidative damage to DNA, will not be repaired before the cell divides, is not known. What is established is that at least one inherited defect in DNA repair (mismatch repair) is associated with an elevated risk of endometrial cancer (see below).

The risk of endometrial cancer is greater for women with a family history of the disease, and is also doubled for women who report a family history of colorectal cancer (Gruber et al, 1996). Hereditary non-polyposis colorectal carcinoma (HNPCC) is an autosomal dominant condition characterised by early onset colorectal cancer and an increased risk of other cancers, especially endometrial (Vasen et al, 1990). To date, four genes which encode DNA mismatch-repair enzymes are known to be involved in HNPCC, as well as familial endometrial cancer (Peltomaki et al, 1993, Fishel et al, 1993; Bronner et al, 1994; Nicolaides et al, 1994). Mutations in these genes result in microsatellite instability, which has been noted in both colorectal and endometrial tumour tissue (Burks et al, 1994; Liu et al, 1995). The phenotype resulting from mutations in these genes (RER+) has also been detected in a significant proportion (20%) of sporadic endometrial tumours (Duggan et al, 1994). In these tumours, most of the alterations occured prior to clonal expansion, indicating that instability contributes to, and is not a result of, transformation. K-*ras* mutations appear to occur with similar frequencies in hyperplastic endometrial tissue as well as in carcinomas, indicating that

they may also be an early event (Saaski et al, 1993). Studies of alterations in tumour tissue have also observed mutations in c-*erB2* (10 – 15%) and *p53* (30%).

JUDGEMENTS OF OTHER REPORTS

The National Academy of Sciences report, *Diet, Nutrition and Cancer* (NAS, 1982), concluded that the evidence for an association between cancer of the endometrium and diet is indirect. This was repeated in the subsequent report, *Diet and Health* (NAS, 1989), which also stated that obesity, hypertension and adult-onset diabetes were associated with endometrial cancer.

The WHO report, *Diet, Nutrition and the Prevention of Chronic Diseases* (WHO, 1990) concluded that 'a strong association between endometrial cancer risk and excess weight has been reported in several studies, and a hormonal mechanism has been postulated for this association.'

REVIEW

4.13.1 DIETARY CONSTITUENTS

4.13.1.1 Energy and related factors
Body mass
Endometrial cancer has shown strong positive correlations with being overweight in both pre- and postmenopausal women. There is now persuasive evidence that body mass is associated with postmenopausal endometrial cancer. Results from epidemiological studies conducted over the last 30 years have consistently indicated that overweight women have a two–tenfold increased risk of endometrial cancer.

A number of recent studies have examined the relationship between the risk of endometrial cancer and body mass, weight gain and body fat distribution.

Four cohort studies carried out in Sweden, the USA and Norway support the hypothesis that obesity increases the risk of endometrial cancer (Folsom et al, 1989; Tretli and Magnus 1990; Le Marchand et al, 1991; Törnberg and Carstensen, 1994). (Table 4.13.1). Higher risk has been reported in older women in one study (Törnberg and Carstensen, 1994). A cohort study in Hawaii (Le Marchand et al, 1991) reported an increase in risk of endometrial cancer for women who had gained weight in adulthood.

Six case-control studies, three in the USA, one in Italy, one jointly in Switzerland and Northern Italy, and one in China, (Austin et al, 1991; La Vecchia et al, 1991; Levi et al, 1992; Shu et al, 1992; Swanson et al, 1992; Olsen et al, 1995) all found obesity to increase the risk of endometrial cancer. Increased risk for both pre- and postmenopausal women was reported in two studies (La Vecchia et al, 1991; Swanson et al, 1992); in one (La Vecchia et al, 1991) the association was stronger for postmenopausal women. Higher risk was seen in older women in one study (Levi et al, 1992). (Table 4.13.2.)

Three case-control studies all reported that obesity at

TABLE 4.13.1 BODY MASS (OBESITY) AND THE RISK OF ENDOMETRIAL CANCER: COHORT STUDIES

AUTHOR, YEAR AND PLACE	SIZE OF COHORT: NO OF CASES	COMPARISON (HIGHEST VS LOWEST QUANTILE)[a]	RELATIVE RISK (95% CONFIDENCE INTERVAL)	AGE	ENERGY INTAKE	ADJUSTMENT REPRODUCTIVE VARIABLES	OTHER VARIABLES[b]
Folsom et al, 1989, Iowa, USA	41,873: 63	BMI: h vs l tertile	1.8 (1.5–2.2)*	Y	N	Y	Y
Tretli and Magnus, 1990, Norway	569,281: 2,208	BMI: h vs l quintile	3.2 (2.6–3.9)[c]	Y	N	N	Y
Le Marchand et al, 1991, Hawaii, USA	30,266: 214	BMI: h vs l tertile	1.4 (0.9–2.2)	Y	N	Y	Y
Törnberg and Carstensen, 1994 Sweden	47,003: 412	BMI: h vs l quintile	2.6 (p for trend < 0.0001)[d]	Y	N	N	N

* p < 0.05
[a] h = high, l = low
[b] Adjusted for one or more of the following: education, area of residence, socio-economic status
[c] RR estimate for those in both highest quintile of BMI and highest quintile of height. There was a suggestion of an interaction between height and BMI in determining risk of endometrial cancer
[d] RR higher in older (3.2, p for trend < 0.0001) than younger (1.6, p for trend 0.33) women

early age (in childhood or many years prior to diagnosis of endometrial cancer) was not associated with the risk of endometrial cancer after adjusting for present weight (Levi et al, 1992; Shu et al, 1992; Swanson et al, 1992).

The distribution of body fat and its relationship to the risk of endometrial cancer has been examined in two cohort and four case-control studies, which looked at different measures including waist-to-hip ratio (WHR), waist-to-thigh ratio (WTR) and subscapular-to thigh-skinfold ratio (STR). A cohort study in the USA (Folsom et al, 1989) reported that body fat distribution did not seem to contribute additionally to the risk of endometrial cancer, and a cohort study in Sweden found no association between WHR and the risk of endometrial cancer after adjusting for BMI (Lapidus et al, 1988).

Schapira et al (1991) reported a mean WHR of 0.86 in cases versus 0.79 in controls (p < 0.001), while a case-control study in the USA (Swanson et al, 1993) reported an OR of 2.6 (1.5–4.5) for the highest versus the lowest quartile of WTR. Increased risk with higher STR was reported in two case-control studies: OR = 2.7 (1.5– 4.9, for highest vs lowest STR) (Austin et al, 1991) and OR = 1.7 (0.8–3.8, for highest vs lowest STR) (Shu et al, 1992). Three of these case-control studies, however, found no relationship between the risk of endometrial cancer and WTR (Shu et al, 1992); WHR (Austin et al, 1991); or STR (Swanson et al, 1993).

A plausible biological mechanism by which obesity may increase the risk of endometrial cancer is through increased aromatization of androstenodione to oestrone in adipose tissue (Key and Pike, 1988). Why this association exists for both pre- and postmenopausal endometrial cancer but only for postmenopausal breast cancer is not understood and the answer is not readily derivable from this possible mechanism.

> The evidence that high body mass (obesity) increases the risk of endometrial cancer is convincing. Obesity appears to be particularly important at older ages or when associated with marked weight gain at older ages.

4.13.1.2 Fat and cholesterol

Total fat

A case-control study in the USA reported that the risk of endometrial cancer increased as the percentage of energy derived from fat increased, with an odds ratio of 1.5 (0.9–2.4, after adjusting for obesity) for the uppermost quartile (Potischman et al, 1993). A case-control study carried out in Shanghai, China in the same year reported that the risk varied according to the source of energy. The highest quartiles of energy intake from fat were associated with an odds ratio of 3.9 (2.2–6.8, adjusted for obesity and total energy intake). The findings from this study do not support the hypothesis that energy intake per se affects risk, as carbohydrates, which are the major source of energy, were not related to risk (Shu et al, 1993). A case-control study in Hawaii, involving 341 cases and 710 controls, reported an increase in risk with a high intake of total fat, OR = 3.1 (Goodman et al, 1994).

Two case-control studies carried out jointly between northern Italy and Switzerland have reported strong increases in risk with higher consumption of added fats. The obesity-adjusted odds ratios from these two studies were 2.5 (p <0.01, adjusted for total energy intake) and 5.7 (2.8–11.6) respectively for the uppermost versus lowest tertiles (La Vecchia et al, 1986; Levi et al, 1993). The latter study did not isolate the effects of specific fat components. The odds ratios were not adjusted for total energy intake.

Four case-control studies that have compared associations for different types of fat have produced mixed results. One study in the USA reported a slightly stronger increase in risk

TABLE 4.13.2 BODY MASS (OBESITY) AND THE RISK OF ENDOMETRIAL CANCER: CASE-CONTROL STUDIES

AUTHOR, YEAR AND PLACE	NO OF CASES	COMPARISON (HIGHEST VS LOWEST QUANTILE)	ODDS RATIO (95% CONFIDENCE LIMIT)	AGE/SEX	ENERGY INTAKE	REPRODUCTIVE VARIABLES	OTHER VARIABLES
Austin et al, 1991 Alabama, USA	168	Quetelet's index: h vs l quartile	2.3 (1.3–3.9)	Y	N	N	Y
La Vecchia et al, Milan, Italy	562	BMI: h vs l quintile	3.4 (p for trend < 0.001)	Y	N	Y	Y
Levi et al, 1992 Switzerland and northern Italy	272	BMI: h vs l quartile	2.7 (1.4–5.1)[a]	N	N	N	N
Shu et al, 1992 China	268	BMI: h vs l quartile	2.5 (1.4–4.2)	Y	N	Y	Y
Swanson et al, USA	434	BMI: h vs l quartile	2.0 (1.2–3.3)	Y	N	Y	Y
Olsen et al, 1995 USA	231	BMI: h vs l tertile	3.2 (2.0–5.2)	Y	N	Y	Y

a   Crude OR calculated from presented data; multiply-adjusted age-specific data as presented suggest greater risk associated with obesity at older ages.

with saturated fat and oleic acid (monounsaturated) than with linoleic acid (polyunsaturated) (Potischman et al, 1993), whereas another study reported a somewhat stronger association for unsaturated (OR = 3.7) than saturated fat (OR = 2.0), (Goodman et al, 1994). One study in the USA reported only negligible associations for both animal and vegetable fat (ORs = 1.3 and 0.6, respectively) (Barbone et al, 1993), but did find a weak increase in risk with cholesterol intake (OR = 1.6). This association became more pronounced after controlling for obesity, total energy and protein intakes (OR = 1.9, p = 0.02).

An international ecological study found total fat consumption was the variable that correlated most highly with the incidence of endometrial cancer (r = 0.85) (Armstrong and Doll, 1975).

In addition to the role of dietary fat in increasing obesity, other mechanisms have also been suggested. Diets high in animal fat and protein may alter endogenous hormone production. This suggestion is supported by both dietary intervention studies (Hill et al, 1977; Rose et al, 1987; Bennett and Ingram, 1990) and comparisons of vegetarians and non-vegetarians (Hill et al, 1980; Armstrong et al, 1981; Barbosa et al, 1990). A change from a western diet to a vegetarian diet has been shown to lengthen the menstrual cycle and result in decreases in plasma prolactin and testosterone (Hill et al, 1977) and oestradiol levels (Bennet and Ingram, 1990; Rose et al, 1987). Postmenopausal vegetarian women have been found to have lower plasma levels of oestradiol and prolactin (Armstrong et al, 1981; Barbosa et al, 1990) and lower urinary levels of oestrogens (Armstrong et al, 1981) compared with non-vegetarian women. These differences appear not to be attributable to the effects of body weight (Shu et al, 1993).

A number of mutagens have been found in cooked beef and other meats, possibly as a result of prolonged cooking times and higher temperatures (Weisberger et al, 1989). Extensive frying and cooking may lead to formation of known mutagens including heterocyclic amines and aromatic hydrocarbons (Adamson et al, 1990, Shu et al, 1993). In a Chinese study (Shu et al, 1993) an elevated risk associated with deep-fried foods remained after adjustment for animal fat intake, suggesting that cooking practices may contribute to the association of increased endometrial cancer risk observed with animal fat consumption. Studies in humans and animals have also established that oestrogen reabsorption in the bowel is enhanced by diets high in beef or fat (Gorbach and Goldin, 1987).

The evidence suggests that diets high in total fat may increase the risk of endometrial cancer but is, as yet, insufficient.

Saturated/animal fat

Four case-control studies, three in the USA and one in China, have examined saturated or animal fat intake in relation to the risk of endometrial cancer. The two studies that have examined saturated fat intake reported an increased risk with higher intakes, ORs = 2.1 (1.2–3.7) and 2.0 for the highest versus lowest quantiles (Potischman et al, 1993; Goodman et al, 1994). The two studies that examined animal fat intake reported ORs of 1.3 (0.7–2.6, p = 0.75) and 3.5 (2.0–6.0, p <0.01), with the former adjusted for BMI and total energy intake and the latter for BMI (Barbone et al, 1993; Shu et al, 1993).

Overall, the evidence regarding saturated/animal fat and the risk of endometrial cancer, although not abundant, is consistently in the direction of a moderate increase in risk with higher intakes. This association appears to be independent of the effects of obesity and total energy intake.

Diets high in saturated/animal fat possibly increase the risk of endometrial cancer.

Monounsaturated fat

One case-control study of endometrial cancer in the USA has reported an increased risk with a greater intake of oleic acid. The energy- and obesity-adjusted odds ratio was 2.2 (1.2–4.0) for the uppermost quartile (Potischman et al, 1993).

> **Evidence relating to diets high in monounsaturated fats and the risk of endometrial cancer is limited; no judgement is possible.**

Polyunsaturated/vegetable fat

Four case-control studies of endometrial cancer (three in the USA and one in China) have examined some aspect of unsaturated fat and results have been inconsistent. Odds ratios of 3.7, 1.6 (0.9–2.8), 0.6 (0.3–1.1), and 1.2 (0.7–1.9), have been reported for the uppermost vs lowest quartiles of unsaturated fat, linoleic acid, vegetable fat and plant fat respectively. Each of these risk estimates was adjusted either for total energy intake or for obesity (BMI), or both (Goodman et al, 1994; Potischman et al, 1993; Barbone et al, 1993; Shu et al, 1993).

> **The available evidence relating to polyunsaturated vegetable fat and the risk of endometrial cancer is inconsistent; no judgement is possible.**

Cholesterol

Three case-control studies of endometrial cancer have examined cholesterol intake and each has reported an increased risk with higher intakes, with odds ratios of 1.9 (1.0–3.8) and 2.0 (1.2–3.3) for the uppermost quantiles versus lower (Barbone et al, 1993; Potischman et al, 1993; Goodman et al, 1994). There are also three studies that have examined egg consumption (see below).

> **The evidence suggests that diets high in cholesterol may increase the risk of endometrial cancer but is, as yet, insufficient.**

4.13.1.3 Protein

Animal protein

Potischman et al (1993) found a slightly increased risk of cancer of the endometrium associated with increasing calories derived from protein, but this largely disappeared when the odds ratios were adjusted for confounding by BMI (OR = 1.4, 0.7–2.7). Barbone et al (1993) found a slight protective association with animal protein (OR = 0.7, 0.3–1.3) which became more pronounced (OR = 0.5, 0.3–1.1) when intakes of both energy and cholesterol were included. Two other case-control studies, one in China and a collaborative study in Switzerland and northern Italy, have reported an increase in risk with increased intakes of animal protein. Odds ratios of 3.0 (1.7–5.1) (Shu et al, 1993) and greater than 2.0 (somewhat different for different types of meats including beef, pork and ham) (Levi et al, 1993) were reported for higher intakes. A case-control study conducted in Rome

(Italy) involving 388 cases found protein consumption to be elevated in cases relative to controls (t = 4.72, p = < 0.0001) (Villani et al, 1986).

> **The evidence on diets high in animal protein is limited and inconsistent; no judgement is possible.**

4.13.1.4 Vitamins

Carotenoids

Four case-control studies have examined carotene intake in relation to the risk of endometrial cancer. A Chinese case-control study did not find a protective association (OR = 1.3) for carotene (Shu et al, 1993). In contrast, a US case-control study observed carotene intake to be statistically significantly higher among controls than cases (OR = 0.4, 0.2–0.8, p = 0.007) (Barbone et al, 1993). These findings are consistent with those of La Vecchia et al (1986), who reported that high carotene intake was associated with a greater than threefold reduction in the risk of endometrial cancer (OR = 0.3, 0.12–0.6). A further analysis undertaken on data from Switzerland and northern Italy found the risk of endometrial cancer to be halved (OR = 0.5) in women in the highest versus lowest tertile of β-carotene intake (Levi et al, 1993).

A plausible role of carotenoids in the prevention of cancer is inactivation of oxygen radicals that have the potential to cause DNA damage and initiate other reactions including lipid peroxidation (Peto, 1983; Freudenheim and Graham, 1989).

> **The evidence suggests that high dietary carotenoids may decrease the risk of endometrial cancer, but is, as yet, insufficient.**

Vitamin C

Four case-control studies have examined the intake of vitamin C in relation to the risk of endometrial cancer. Two studies in the USA and China found no significant relationship with vitamin C intake; odds ratios were 0.7 (0.4–1.3; p = 0.45) and 1.1 (p = 0.78), (Barbone et al, 1993; Shu et al, 1993). A case-control study conducted in Switzerland and northern Italy involving 274 patients and 572 controls found a protective association with vitamin C. After adjusting for total energy intake, the OR was 0.5, p <0.01 (Levi et al, 1993). In a case-control study of 399 cases and 296 controls conducted in five areas of the USA, higher consumption of vitamin C was not associated with risk, OR = 1.3 (0.7–2.2). Further, no trends were observed either before or after adjustment for total energy (Potischman et al, 1993).

> **Evidence relating to dietary vitamin C intake and the risk of endometrial cancer is limited and inconsistent; no judgement is possible.**

4.13.2 FOODS AND DRINKS

4.13.2.1 Cereals (grains)
Wholegrain cereals

Two case-control studies, involving 274 and 206 cases respectively, have found a decreased risk associated with consumption of wholegrain bread and pasta, with odds ratios for highest versus lowest tertile of 0.5 (Levi et al, 1993) and 0.6 (La Vecchia et al, 1986). It has been suggested that the lignan and phyto-oestrogen content of wholegrains may have a protective effect against hormone-related diseases (Jacobs et al, 1995).

Evidence relating to wholegrain cereals and cereal products and the risk of endometrial cancer is very limited; no judgement is possible.

4.13.2.2 Vegetables and fruits

Five case-control studies have examined fruit and/or vegetable intake in relation to endometrial cancer and have reported both protective associations and null associations. Four studies have observed a protective association for one or more vegetable and/or fruit categories. In a study in the USA, more frequent consumption of selected vegetables was associated with a statistically significant decreased risk of endometrial cancer. ORs of 0.5 were observed for each of broccoli, cauliflower and spinach; an OR of 0.4 was observed for iceberg lettuce and 0.3 for carrots and tomatoes (Barbone et al, 1993). A case-control study in northern Italy and Switzerland observed ORs for the highest versus the lowest tertile of 0.6 (total vegetables); 0.6 (carrots); 0.5 (fresh fruit and artichokes); 0.6 (pears and melons). None of these protective associations were appreciably changed by adjusting for total energy intake (Levi et al, 1993).

A population-based case-control study in China found no association with the intake of vegetables after adjustment for total energy. However, fruit and allium vegetables (after adjustment for age, parity, BMI and total calories) were statistically non-significantly related to decreased risks with odds ratios of 0.7 (p = 0.12) and 0.7 (p = 0.25) respectively (Shu et al, 1993). A case-control study in Poland found more than a halving of risk at higher levels of vegetable consumption, with an odds ratio of 0.4 (p <0.001) for raw vegetables (Zemla et al, 1986). Another case-control study involving 399 cases and 296 controls and found no associations with fruits or vegetables (Potischman et al, 1993).

Diets high in vegetables and fruit possibly decrease the risk of endometrial cancer.

4.13.2.3 Pulses (legumes)
Two case-control studies have examined the relationship between pulses and the risk of endometrial cancer. A study in Switzerland and Italy reported a significantly elevated odds ratio of 2.0 (p < 0.01) for a higher intake of beans and peas which persisted after adjustment for total energy intake (Levi et al, 1993). A Chinese case-control study found an odds ratio of 1.4 (p = 0.25, ns) for pulses (Shu et al, 1993).

The evidence relating to pulses and the risk of endometrial cancer is limited; no judgement is possible.

4.13.2.4 Meat, poultry, fish and eggs
Fish

Three studies have examined fish consumption in relation to endometrial cancerand have reported mixed results. One study in Switzerland and northern Italy reported no association, OR = 0.9 (ns) for the uppermost versus lowest tertile (Levi et al, 1993). Another in northern Italy, reported lower fish consumption in cases than in controls (p = 0.05), suggesting a decreased risk with higher consumption (La Vecchia et al, 1986). A third study, in China, reported an increased risk with a higher consumption of fresh fish, OR = 1.7 (p for trend = 0.12) for the uppermost quartile (Shu et al, 1993).

Evidence relating to fish consumption and the risk of endometrial cancer is inconsistent; no judgement is possible.

Eggs

Three studies have examined egg consumption and the risk of endometrial cancer. Two of these reported an increased risk, both with odds ratios of 2.1 (p <0.01) for the uppermost quantiles (Levi et al, 1993; Shu et al, 1993). The remaining study reported no difference in mean egg consumption between cases and controls (La Vecchia et al, 1986).

Evidence relating to egg consumption and the risk of endometrial cancer is limited; no judgement is possible.

4.14 Cervix

Cancer of the cervix is the second most common cancer in women. An estimated 525,000 cases occurred in 1996, accounting for 5% of all new cases of cancer.

In general, rates of this cancer are higher in economically developing societies. Rates are declining in those parts of the developed world with widespread screening programmes.

The panel has reached the following conclusions. There is as yet no convincing evidence that any dietary factors modify the risk of cervical cancer, nor evidence of any probable causal relationships with diet.

The panel notes that diets high in vegetables and fruit, and in carotenoids, vitamin C and E, found in foods of plant origin, are possibly protective.

Established non-dietary causes of cervical cancer are infection with human papillomaviruses and smoking.

The most effective dietary means of preventing cervical cancer is, possibly, consumption of diets high in vegetables and fruits, with their associated microconstituents.

FOOD, NUTRITION AND CERVICAL CANCER

In the judgement of the panel, the dietary constituents and related factors, and the foods and drinks listed below modify the risk of cancer of the cervix or else have no relationship with it. Judgements are graded according to the strength of the evidence.

EVIDENCE	DECREASES RISK	NO RELATIONSHIP	INCREASES RISK
Convincing			
Probable			
Possible	Vegetables and fruits Carotenoids Vitamin C Vitamin E	Folate Retinol	
Insufficient			

For an explanation of the terms used in the matrix, see chapter 3.

BOX 4.14.1 ESTABLISHED NON-DIETARY FACTORS AND CERVICAL CANCER

The following non-dietary factors increase the risk of cervical cancer:

- Sexually transmitted viral infection: Human Papillomaviruses
- Smoking tobacco

INTRODUCTION

INCIDENCE PATTERNS

Cancer of the cervix is the seventh most common cancer in the world. In 1996, an estimated 525,000 new cases were diagnosed worldwide (WHO, 1997), accounting for 5% of all new cancers. Cervical cancer is the second most common cancer in women.

The highest incidence rates are seen in parts of sub-Saharan Africa, south-east Asia and Latin America. Developing countries account for 80% of cases. The lowest rates are found in North America, western Europe and a few nations in the Eastern Mediterranean. In developed countries, the incidence rates are declining, with age-standardised rates generally less than 15 per 100,000. This is

CERVICAL CANCER estimated rates of cancer incidence by sex and area

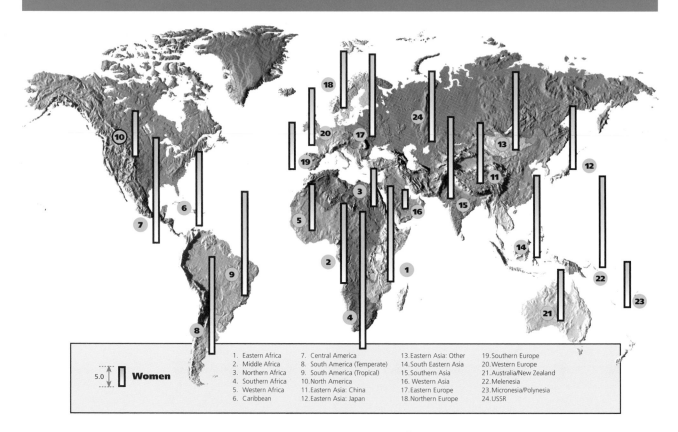

1. Eastern Africa	7. Central America	13. Eastern Asia: Other	19. Southern Europe
2. Middle Africa	8. South America (Temperate)	14. South Eastern Asia	20. Western Europe
3. Northern Africa	9. South America (Tropical)	15. Southern Asia	21. Australia/New Zealand
4. Southern Africa	10. North America	16. Western Asia	22. Melenesia
5. Western Africa	11. Eastern Asia: China	17. Eastern Europe	23. Micronesia/Polynesia
6. Caribbean	12. Eastern Asia: Japan	18. Northern Europe	24. USSR

5.0 ↕ Women

predominantly due to extensive screening programmes. Nonetheless, many Western countries also show an increase in incidence among young women, for example in the 20–29 age group. The long-established inverse socioeconomic gradient persists.

Survival rates for cervical cancer are generally good, with 90% of cases surviving five years after initial diagnosis. In 1996, mortality attributable to cancer of the ovary was estimated at 242,000 women, 3.4% of all cancer deaths (WHO, 1997).

PATHOGENESIS

In common with a few other cancers (for example, colon, oesophagus and stomach), cervical cancer has identifiable precursor abnormalities. This facilitates screening programmes. The preneoplastic stages are identified via the microscopically detected abnormalities of the cells alone (in contrast to colon cancer where the precursor lesions – adenomatous polyps – are detected macroscopically at endoscopy). Although the precursor cervical lesions are divided into grades of increasing dysplasia – cervical intraepithelial neoplasia grades I, II and III (CIN I, II, III) – there is, in reality, as with the stomach and the oesophagus, a continuum of cellular and, ultimately, tissue abnormality.

CIN I is the most benign of the cervical abnormalities, and appears often to revert to a normal cytological appearance. CIN III is also called carcinoma in situ (CIS); it is found in 10% of abnormal smears and current management usually involves surgical treatment. Because it is well established that these lesions are closely linked to cervical cancer, individuals with CIN II (the intermediate stage), as well as those with CIN I and CIN III, have been involved in studies aimed at preventing progression or inducing reversion of these precursor lesions.

The main causal factor for this cancer is thought to be sexually transmitted infectious agents – almost certainly the human papillomaviruses (HPVs) (Cuzick et al, 1992; Munoz and Bosch, 1992; Bosch et al, 1993; Schiffman et al, 1996). Human papillomavirus type 16 DNA is found in 60–70% of cervical cancers of high-grade precancerous lesions (Nuovo and Richart, 1990; Nuovo et al, 1990). Established risk factors for cervical cancer that are now thought to be mediated by HPV include age at first intercourse, number of sexual partners and number of partner's sexual partners (Bosch et al, 1994).

Regular direct screening for abnormal cervical cytology has proved to be an effective preventive strategy as it allows detection of early stages of the disease. Early detection, when followed by appropriate treatment, is associated with a very high cure and survival rate.

Invasive cervical cancer is preceded by dysplasia and carcinoma in situ, but only 30% to 40% of untreated patients will progress to invasive disease within ten years (Petersen, 1956; Clemmensen and Poulsen, 1971). It is likely that multiple genetic events are involved in this progression.

While cigarette smoking and infection with HPV are clearly associated with cervical cancer, the natural history of the disease and the mechanisms of action of smoking and HPV are not well understood. Nearly 100 variant genotypes for HPV have been identified, but only some are associated with cervical cancer. HPV-16 and HPV-18 have been identified in approximately 84% of cervical cancers (deVilliers). It is probable that HPV early proteins E6 and E7 interact with cellular proteins involved in growth control and apoptosis (Pillai et al, 1996), especially the retinoblastoma (*Rb*) and *p53* proteins. This complexing with tumour-suppressor proteins may prevent them from exerting their negative effects on cell growth. Inactivation of *p53* also results in suppression of bcl-2 expression, a protein that inhibits programmed cell death. In a recent study, the presence of the bcl-2 protein was strongly associated with invasive cervical disease, indicating that these events may distinguish dysplasia from invasive neoplasia (Pillai et al, 1996). It is unclear whether tobacco smoke and HPV infection act independently in the development of cervical cancer, or interact in affecting carcinogenesis. It is possible that components of tobacco smoke may allow HPV to persist in cevical epithelium (Barton et al, 1988, Burger et al, 1993). They may also independently damage DNA and, as elsewhere, provoke proliferation (Winkelstein, 1981; MacDonald, 1982; Holly et al, 1986; Schiffman et al, 1987; Schiffman et al, 1996).

Tobacco metabolites are found routinely in the cervical mucous of smokers (Schiffman et al, 1987; Holly et al, 1986).

Use of steroid oral contraceptives may also increase the risk of cervical cancer, with an increasing risk of adenocarcinoma associated with long-term use (Meisels et al, 1977; Wright et al, 1978; Vessey et al, 1983; Brinton et al, 1987; Ebeling et al, 1987; Schiffman et al, 1996).

JUDGEMENTS OF OTHER REPORTS

Neither of the National Academy of Sciences reports, *Diet, Nutrition and Cancer* (NAS, 1982) and *Diet and Health* (NAS, 1989), nor the WHO report *Diet, Nutrition and the Prevention of Chronic Diseases* (WHO, 1990) came to any conclusion about any relationship between dietary factors and the risk of cervical cancer.

REVIEW

Most of the analytical studies on cervical cancer have been conducted in the last 15 years. They have recently been comprehensively reviewed by Potischman and Brinton (1996). As with studies on several other epithelial cancers (for example, lung and upper aerodigestive cancers), early interest focused on retinol and antioxidants (notably carotenoids and later ascorbate and tocopherols). More recently, attention has been directed to folate.

Most of the studies have been case-control studies, with the majority of the cases having invasive cervical cancer, although some studies have focused on the precursor lesions. Most studies were conducted in the USA, with others in Australia, Italy, Netherlands and Central America. All studies examined the association with selected micronutrients, with the majority concentrating on the micronutrients, retinol, carotenoids, and vitamins C and E. Many of the studies examined major food groups, and a few examined macronutrients.

4.14.1 DIETARY CONSTITUENTS

4.14.1.1 Energy and related factors
Physical activity
A study of female college athletes found they had a significantly lower prevalence rate of cervical cancer (RR = 0.40, 0.18–0.85) and other cancers of the reproductive system, compared to non-athletes (Frisch et al, 1987, 1992). The follow-up of the United States NHANES-I cohort also found an association between occupational physical activity and decreased risk of cervical cancer (RR = 0.19, 0.07–0.7) (Albanes et al, 1989). In both of these studies the association remained after controlling for body mass index (BMI).

Lean athletes and underweight women have an altered neuroendocrine regulation of gonadotrophin secretion and consequently low levels of oestrogen (Vigersky et al, 1977; Veldhuis et al, 1988). It has been found that strenuous exercise delays menarche (Frisch et al, 1980; Warren, 1980; Frisch et al, 1981). The earlier age at menopause of athletes compared to non-athletes would also be expected because athletes are less fat. Fatness is associated with an increased extraglandular conversion of androgen to oestrogen and metabolism of oestrogen to more potent forms (Grodin et al, 1973; Fishman et al, 1975; Forney et al, 1981; Siiteri 1981) Excess body weight is linked with a decreased capacity of serum sex hormone-binding globulin and an increased level of serum oestradiol in the free state (Fishman et al, 1975). This is more likely to be relevant to the aetiology of breast and endometrial cancers (Moore et al, 1982) as the role of hormones in cervical cancer remains unclear.

Evidence on physical activity and the risk of cervical cancer, while suggestive of a protective association, is limited; no judgement is possible.

4.14.1.2 Carbohydrates
Complex carbohydrates
Complex carbohydrate intake was not found to be related to cervical cancer risk in two case-control studies conducted in the USA and four Latin American countries (Verreault et al, 1989; Herrero et al, 1991) and a study of CIN III (CIS) in the USA (Ziegler et al, 1991). However, Ziegler et al (1990) reported an elevated risk for higher complex carbohydrate intake in a study of invasive cervix cancer (CIN III) (OR = 2.2, p < 0.01).

Evidence on intakes of complex carbohydrates and the risk of cervical cancer is limited and inconsistent; no judgement is possible.

Non-starch polysaccharides/dietary fibre
Two case-control studies in the USA and the Netherlands have examined the association between fibre consumption and the risk of cervical cancer (Verreault et al, 1989) or the risk of CIN (de Vet et al, 1991). A weak protective association was associated with CIN III (OR = 0.64) (de Vet et al, 1991) while no relationship was reported for cervical cancer (Verreault et al, 1989).

Evidence on NSP/dietary fibre and the risk of cervical cancer, is limited; no judgement is possible.

4.14.1.3 Fat and cholesterol
Total fat
Four case-control studies, two in the USA, one in Latin America and one in Australia, have reported on fat intake in relation to cancer of the cervix. Three found no relation to risk (Brock et al, 1988; Verreault et al, 1989; Herrero et al, 1991), although the fourth study by Marshall et al (1983) in the USA found an elevated risk with fat intake (OR = 1.4, p < 0.05).

The evidence on fat is too limited and somewhat inconsistent; no judgement is possible.

4.14.1.4 Protein
Four case-control studies, two in the USA, one in Latin America and one in Australia which reported on protein intake in relation to cancer of the cervix, all found no association (Marshall et al, 1983; Brock et al, 1988; Verreault et al, 1989; Herrero et al, 1991).

Armstrong and Doll's international ecological study of dietary factors and cancer at many sites identified a significant inverse association between cervical cancer and protein intake (Armstrong and Doll, 1975).

The evidence on protein is too limited; no judgement is possible.

4.14.1.5 Alcohol
Two case-control studies of cervical cancer have examined alcohol consumption. One study in Australia found no association, while the other in the USA, conducted in a population with very low consumption levels, found that only beer had any association with risk (Marshall et al, 1983; Brock et al, 1988).

Evidence on high intakes of alcohol and the risk of cervical cancer is limited; no judgement is possible.

4.14.1.6 Vitamins
Carotenoids
Ten case-control studies in the USA, Latin America, Italy, the Netherlands and Australia have investigated the relationship between invasive cervical cancer or its precursors and intakes of different measures of carotenoids. In four studies, the link with total carotenoids suggests a protective associa-

tion between high dietary intake and the occurrence of invasive disease, with three of the studies showing decreased risk for higher intake (Marshall et al, 1983; LaVecchia et al, 1988; Verreault et al, 1989; Ziegler et al, 1990). Reported adjusted odds ratios were 0.5 (p < 0.05), 0.2 (p < 0.001), 0.6 (ns) and 1.0 (ns), respectively. In the four studies that examined precursor lesions, no significant reduction in risk was observed in three of the studies (ORs = 1.1, ns; 0.99, ns; and 0.7, ns) (La Vecchia et al, 1988; Slattery et al, 1990; Ziegler et al, 1991), while in the fourth study an increase in risk was associated with a high intake of β-carotene (OR = 2.3, 1.3–4.2) (DeVet et al, 1991). However, the findings by DeVet et al (1991) were obtained by questionnaires in which not all possible sources of β-carotene were covered.

A hospital-based case-control study carried out in four Latin America countries examined newly diagnosed cases of invasive cervical cancer and intake of β-carotene and other carotenoids separately. Odds ratios of 0.7 (p = 0.02) and 0.6 (p = 0.003) were reported for β-carotene and other carotenoids, respectively (Herrero et al, 1991).

There have been at least seven serological studies (six case-control studies with more than 100 cases and one nested case-control study), conducted to determine whether lower serum levels of β-carotene were associated with a higher risk of invasive and pre-invasive cervical cancer. Five of these studies, conducted in the UK, USA and Latin America, found inverse associations between the levels of β-carotene and the risk of cervical cancer (Harris et al, 1986; Palan et al, 1988, 1991; Potischman et al, 1991). Harris et al (1986) examined women with both invasive and pre-invasive disease, and observed a weak protective association between β-carotene levels and pre-invasive cancer (OR = 0.38, 0.14–1.0, p = 0.061), but no relationship was noted with invasive cervical cancer. Palan et al (1988, 1991, 1992) found significantly reduced plasma levels of β-carotene in women with histopathologically diagnosed cervical cancer (p < 0.0001). In addition, a protective association was noted between levels of plasma β-carotene and increasingly severe grades of neoplasia. Potischman et al (1991) also found mean serum levels of β-carotene to be lower in cases than controls. After adjustment, a trend toward decreasing risk was associated with higher levels of β-carotene (OR = 0.72, p = 0.05). Serum levels of β-carotene were similarly low in patients with both stage I and stage II disease compared with controls.

Two studies, in Australia and the USA, have investigated stage III neoplasia (CIN III/CIS) (Brock et al, 1988; Van Eenwyk et al, 1991). Brock et al (1988) found that unadjusted estimates of risk showed that women in the top quartile of total carotene intake had half the risk of CIS compared to those in the bottom quartile of consumption. However, when adjusted for known risk factors, the protective trend for total carotene disappeared (adjusted OR = 1.0, 0.3–2.9, p = 0.71). Further investigation of plasma levels revealed women in the top quartile of total carotenoid intake were at a 50% reduced risk compared to those in the lowest quartile but the trend was not significant (p = 0.82). However, after

adjustment, women in the top quartile of β-carotene intake had an 80% reduced risk with the trend significant (p = 0.02) (Brock et al, 1988). Van Eenwyk et al (1991) assessed a variety of carotenoids including α- and β-carotene, cryptoxanthin, lutein and lycopene. Adjusted ORs for lycopene were 0.2 (0.04–0.8); no association was noted for lutein intake. Elevated ORs were apparent for those in the lowest quartiles of serum cryptoxanthin (OR = 0.4) and α-carotene (OR = 0.55); however, after adjustment, the ORs were not statistically significant, with little evidence of a trend towards increasing odds with decreasing intake. Similarly, the halving of risk for those in the highest quartile of β-carotene intake was not statistically significant.

Butterworth et al (1992a) reported on total carotenoids in women with CIN I, II or III type disease. No association with levels of total plasma carotenoids was observed in this study (OR = 0.8, 0.7–2.2, p = 0.48).

Data from a serological cohort in Maryland (USA) shows that high levels of several of the individual carotenoids (except lutein) were associated with a reduced risk of CIS and invasive cancer (RR for total carotenoids = 0.4; p ≤ 0.05), this finding remained significant after adjustment for non-dietary risk factors including oral contraceptive use and smoking (Batieha et al, 1993).

The levels reported for controls in the study of Van Eenwyk et al (1991) are markedly lower than those seen in other populations; case levels, nonetheless, were lower still. As with some other measures, adjusting for sexual behaviour in this study attenuated the strength of association for all carotenoids except lycopene. Consistent with the possibility that disease may affect serological status, Potischman et al (1994) found lower levels at later stages of invasive disease. Two of the serological studies showed reciprocal trends of lower carotenoid concentrations accompanying an increasing level of dysplasia (Harris et al, 1986; Palan et al, 1991).

High dietary carotenoid intake possibly decreases the risk of cervical cancer.

Vitamin C

Six case-control studies and two ecological studies have investigated the relationship between vitamin C and the risk of cervical cancer. Three have reported a protective association with a decreased risk associated with an increased intake and ORs of 0.5 (p < 0.05), 0.7 (p < 0.01) and 0.7 (ns) (Verreault et al, 1989; Slattery et al, 1990; Herrero et al, 1991).

Two case-control studies, in Australia and in five areas of the USA, both found a statistically non-significant protective association. The study in the USA (Ziegler et al, 1990) found that the risk of invasive cervical cancer did not vary with intake of vitamin C (OR = 0.9). However, among heavy smokers (≥ 21 cigarettes a day) vitamin C intake appeared to be somewhat protective (OR = 0.5, p for trend = 0.27, for the highest compared to the lowest quartile of intake). Among the controls in this particular study, 54% had used a vitamin supplement, so an adjusted odds ratio for in situ cervical cancer by duration of vitamin C supplement use was calculated. An odds ratio of 0.45 (p = 0.03) was reported for longer duration of consumption (16 vs 0 years) (Ziegler et al, 1990). The case-control study conducted in Australia observed unadjusted estimates of risk which showed that intake in the highest quartile of vitamin C afforded a 60% lower risk of CIS; however, when adjusted, the protective trend, although still apparent, was not statistically significant, (OR = 0.5, 0.1–2.0, p = 0.2) (Brock et al, 1988).

Two case-control studies, in the USA and in the Netherlands, have reported on vitamin C intake and its relationship with cervical dysplasia or intraepithelial neoplasia. Protective associations were observed. Reported odds ratios for higher intake were 0.67 (p = 0.17) (DeVet et al, 1991) and 0.2 (0.0–0.7) (Van Eenwyk et al, 1992).

Two ecological studies and a serological study have reported no correlation between vitamin C intake and cervical cancer mortality in Hawaii (Kolonel et al, 1981), in a total of 41 countries (Correa, 1981) and in Alabama, USA (OR = 0.9, p = 0.77) (Butterworth et al, 1992a).

High intake of dietary vitamin C possibly decreases the risk of cervical cancer.

Folate

An early study by Whitehead et al (1973) observed megaloblastic features in cervical epithelial cells from a group of women using steroid hormones as oral contraceptives. Although the cytological changes were not associated with evidence of systemic folate deficiency, they disappeared with oral folate supplementation. This led to the suggestion that localised folate deficiency in the cervix occurred as a result of oral contraceptive use.

Butterworth et al (1982) tested whether folate supplementation influences the progression of cervical dysplasia. In a randomised controlled trial, 47 women with mild or moderate cervical dysplasia, each of whom was using oral contraceptives, were randomised to either 10 mg/day of supplemental folic acid (25 times the USA Recommended Daily Allowance (RDA)) or a placebo (10 mg/day of vitamin C). During the three-month trial, the severity of dysplasia decreased among the women who were using the folate, while the status of the placebo group was unchanged. Several methodological problems in this study, including the similarities between the cytological features of megaloblastosis seen with folate deficiency and the changes associated with dysplasia, make its interpretation difficult.

Butterworth et al (1992b) conducted another intervention trial of oral folic acid supplementation on the course of CIN I and CIN II cervical cancer. After six months, no significant differences were observed between supplemented and non-supplemented subjects (the placebo in this study was vitamin C). These findings are in agreement with a recent folate supplementation trial by Childers et al (1995) who also found no beneficial associations of oral folate supplementation in women with CIN I or CIN II disease.

There are at least six published case-control studies examining the relationship between dietary folate and cervical neoplasia, three of dysplasia or carcinoma in situ (Brock et al, 1988; Ziegler et al, 1991; Van Eenwyk et al, 1992), and three of invasive cancer (Verreault et al, 1989; Ziegler et al, 1990; Herrero et al, 1991). None of these studies has reported a statistically significant reduction of risk with higher dietary intakes after adjustment for various other factors, including sexual behaviour and smoking, although all but one estimate of risk was 1.0 or lower. Further, some studies may have over-adjusted in relation to other plant-related nutrients. It is clear, however, that adjustment for sexual behaviour and smoking often attenuates or eliminates the association with a variety of dietary and serum micronutrients (see, for example, Brock et al, 1988; Slattery et al, 1990; Herrero et al, 1991; Ziegler et al, 1991; Butterworth et al, 1992a, b; Van Eenwyk et al, 1992).

Three case-control studies have examined serum or erythrocyte levels of folate and CIN I–III (Butterworth et al, 1992a; Van Eenwyk et al, 1992) or invasive cancer (Potischman et al, 1991). One (Van Eenwyk et al, 1992) of the two studies of CIN is consistent with a lower level of folate in serum and erythrocytes, but the other is equivocal (Butterworth et al, 1992a). The case-control study by Potischman et al (1991a) found that mean serum levels in cases did not differ significantly from those in controls. Further, the mean folate levels were similar across stages of dysplasia.

Clearly, there is a major problem, when making biological measurements in case-control studies, that the disease itself may alter the serum/erythrocyte levels. This argues strongly for prospective studies to answer such questions. There is evidence from Butterworth's (1992a) study of an interaction between folate status and positivity for HPV-16: among women with both low erythrocyte folate (< 660 nmol/litre) and a positive Southern blot for HPV-16, the OR for abnormal cytology was about five times greater than that for those women with one or neither of these exposures (Butterworth et al, 1992b). Other less specific abnormalities of cervical cytology have also been reported among those oral contraceptive users (250 Los Angeles students) who also have a low erythrocyte folate (Harper et al, 1994). Inadequate folate could contribute to abnormal smears due to the megalocytic abnormalities specific to folic acid deficiency, and also because the immune system may fail to defend the host against HPV infection. A mechanism that supports a co-carcinogenic role for folate deficiency in cells has been suggested: with insufficient thymidylate, cells are arrested in the S-phase of the cell cycle, thus hindering the excision repair process and extending the period when critical sites on the DNA could be exposed to various mutagens and carcinogens. In addition, folate deficiency results in fragile chromosomes, chromosomal breaks and rearrangements. These may contribute to early events which predispose to cervical cancer (Kunz and Haynes, 1982; Everson et al, 1988).

There are hints that folate levels may be specifically abnormal in the cervix even with adequate blood and dietary levels. Whether this is related to HPV infection is unclear, but this may represent a localised metabolic process rather than evidence of dietary deficiency.

> Given the essentially null nature of the dietary data reviewed here, high dietary folate intake possibly has no relationship with the risk of cervical cancer.

Retinol

Retinoids were an early subject of studies aimed at establishing the possible role of dietary constituents that could protect against cancer. The idea evolved from evidence that retinoids could reduce the rate of cancer in animal studies; from data in human cohorts showing that cancer risk was higher in those with low serum retinol levels, and from studies demonstrating that retinols acted as differentiating agents (Bollag 1979; Peto et al, 1981). Studies noting that plant foods (particularly vegetables and fruit) were associated with lower risk were boldly interpreted as consistent with this retinoid story. Dietary vitamin A consists of retinol and that part of some carotenoids that can be converted into retinol in the human body. The dietary intake of retinol has almost no influence on the level of retinol in serum. This is because retinol is stored in the liver and released from it at essentially constant rates. It is biologically plausible therefore, that a high intake of retinol has no effect on cancer incidence, while an inverse effect has been noted for carotenoids, including those that are converted to retinol (see section on carotenoids, above).

Hirayama (1979), in a cohort study, reported a strong inverse relationship between per capita vitamin A intake and cervical cancer mortality in Japan.

Dietary intake of preformed vitamin A was unassociated with the risk of cervical cancer in nine of nine case-control studies (Lambert et al, 1981; Marshall et al, 1983; Harris et al, 1986; Brock et al, 1988; La Vecchia et al, 1988; Verreault et al, 1989; Slattery et al, 1990; Ziegler et al, 1990; Herrero et al, 1991; de Vet et al, 1991; Ziegler et al, 1991). Levels of serum or plasma retinol did not predict the risk of cervical cancer in seven of seven case-control studies (Lambert et al, 1981; Harris et al, 1986; Brock et al, 1988; Palan et al, 1988, 1991; Cuzick et al, 1990; Potischman et al, 1991), nor in the only cohort study (Batieha et al, 1993).

Four studies in Italy (La Vecchia et al, 1984), Japan (Hirayama, 1979) and the USA (Romney et al, 1981; Marshall et al, 1983) have all shown a protective association with the risk of cervical cancer for consumption of foods containing vitamin A, particularly those with a high β-carotene content. Romney et al (1981) found a deficiency of retinol and retinoic acid-binding proteins in cervical biopsy material from cases compared with controls.

Correa (1981) found no significant correlations with consumption of various dietary items and cervical cancer risk across 41 countries. Neither of these studies differentiates animal from plant sources of vitamin A.

Meyskens et al (1994) conducted a phase III randomised trial in the USA to investigate whether topically applied retinoic acid reversed moderate CIN II or severe CIN III. Over fifteen months, this therapy, in women with CIN II, produced a higher proportion with regression (43%) than among those receiving the placebo (27%) (p = 0.041). This was not seen among the women with CIN III. As the dietary, plasma and tissue levels are unrelated, the importance of this finding is unclear for dietary behaviour at population level, although it may be useful as clinical therapy, and again hints at local metabolic effects.

> High dietary retinol intake possibly has no relationship with the risk of cervical cancer.

Vitamin E

The cohort study of Batieha et al (1993) showed no association between vitamin E intake and the risk of cervical cancer with higher plasma levels. In a prospective study, from Finland, with up to ten years of follow-up of a population sample of 15,093 women, the number of cases of cervical cancer was small, and the inverse association (a 50–70% reduction in risk) was not statistically significant (Knekt, 1988).

At least seven case-control studies have examined the relationship of vitamin E and the risk of cervical cancer. Overall, the results have been more equivocal than for vitamin C. Of the two studies conducted in the USA on dietary vitamin E, Slattery et al (1990) found a statistically non-significant reduction of risk (OR = 0.7, 0.4–1.1, for highest vs lowest intake), while that of Verreault et al, (1989) reported a statistically significant OR of 0.4 (0.2–0.9). Of three serological case-control studies, in the UK, the USA and Latin America, those of Cuzick et al (1990) and Palan et al (1991) are consistent with a lower risk for higher levels; that of Potischman et al (1991) is not. Cuzick et al (1990) observed that the mean level of vitamin E decreased from controls to CIN I to CIN III (p = 0.04), and significant trends in vitamin E levels were found for both CIN I and CIN III with p = 0.01 and 0.003 respectively. Palan et al (1991) also noted an inverse association between plasma vitamin E levels and increasingly severe graded cancer (p = 0.005) which is consistent with the disease affecting the level of vitamin E in blood.

A case-control study of the incidence of invasive cervical cancer across five US states investigated the use of multivitamin supplements and cancer risk. An adjusted RR of 0.94 was noted among long-term (> 6 years) users of supplemental vitamin E relative to risks among non-users of the corresponding supplement (Ziegler et al, 1990).

> High dietary vitamin E intake possibly decreases the risk of cervical cancer.

4.14.2 FOODS AND DRINKS

4.14.2.1 Vegetables and fruits

The dietary micronutrient studies described above are a subset of the studies that measured self-reported intake of plant foods. As noted elsewhere in this report, specific micronutrient intakes are derived from dietary intake data as a whole, using food tables to impute typical intake of specific nutrients. In this section, we consider those studies that reported plant food intakes directly.

There are at least eight published studies of diet and cervical neoplasia. Of these, four (Marshall et al, 1983; Verreault et al, 1989; Ziegler et al, 1990; Herrero et al, 1991) focused on invasive cancer; three (Brock et al, 1988; de Vet et al, 1991; Ziegler et al, 1991) reported on CIN/CIS; and one (La Vecchia et al, 1988) studied both.

Of the five studies of invasive cancer, four reported a reduced risk in relation to one or more measures of vegetable or fruit intake. Marshall et al (1983) reported a reduced risk with higher intake of broccoli, carrots and tomatoes, but, a little inconsistently, an increase in risk with an index of cruciferous vegetable intake. There are some biochemical data that suggest that cruciferae could be protective in the colon, but increase risk in the lung or cervix (Gelboin, 1977). La Vecchia et al (1988) reported an inverse association with green vegetables and carrots; age-adjusted point-estimates for the highest versus lowest levels of consumption were 0.15 and 0.26, respectively. Verreault et al (1989), in a population-based case-control study in the USA, reported a protective effect with frequent consumption of dark-green and yellow vegetables (adjusted OR = 0.6); frequent consumption of fruit juices was also related to a reduced risk of cervical cancer (adjusted OR = 0.3), but consumption of fruits was not related to risk. Ziegler et al (1990), in a case-control study across five US metropolitan areas, found that risk was not associated with consumption of vegetables (highest vs lowest quartile of servings per week) (OR = 1.6), dark-green vegetables (OR=1.0), dark-yellow–orange vegetables (OR = 1.2) or fruits (0R = 1.4). Herrero et al (1991) found little reduction of risk (OR = 0.9, p < 0.01) with increasing consumption of fruit juices or vegetables.

Of the four studies of dysplastic lesions, La Vecchia et al (1988) found no associations; Brock et al (1988) noted a protective association with fruit juices (RR = 0.4, p = 0.07) and salad vegetables (RR = 0.4, p = 0.13); Ziegler et al (1991) found a significant protective association with highest intake of dark-yellow–orange vegetables (RR = 0.5, p = 0.02) and fruits (RR = 0.6, p = 0.09) for the highest vs lowest quartiles of weekly consumption; de Vet et al (1991) found a protective association with increased consumption of tomatoes (OR = 0.6, p = 0.01), fruits (OR = 0.3, p = 0.06) and orange juice (OR = 0.5, p = 0.06), but increased risks associated with cabbage, spinach and carrots (this study also found a positive association with β-carotene).

Fruits and fruit juices, tomatoes and green vegetables are the most consistent items associated with lower risk; there is one study reporting an increased risk with increased consumption of cruciferous vegetables. As with the plasma studies of folate and other micronutrients, controlling for sexual behaviour (with or without smoking) often markedly attenuated the inverse association with plant foods (Brock et al, 1988; Herrero et al, 1991; Ziegler et al, 1991).

An international ecological study (Armstrong and Doll,

1975) reported a modest positive correlation between frequency of fruit consumption and cervical cancer mortality.

A wide variety of mechanisms has been suggested to explain the probable reduction of risk associated with the higher consumption of plant foods (Steinmetz and Potter, 1991).

Overall the evidence on vegetables and fruits and the risk of cervical cancer is generally consistent. Diets high in certain vegetables and fruits possibly decrease the risk of cervical cancer and its precursor lesions.

4.14.2.2 Meat and fish

At least four studies have presented data on meat or a related variable such as liver or fish (La Vecchia et al, 1988; Ziegler et al, 1990, 1991; Herrero et al, 1991). None has shown any association with the risk of cervical neoplasia. La Vecchia et al (1988) examined intake of meat and liver separately for both invasive and intraepithelial neoplasia. The adjusted ORs in each case were not significant. In both studies by Ziegler et al (1990, 1991) meat and fish were examined collectively and then divided into two subgroups of expensive meat and fish and cheap meat and fish. The purpose of this was that the subgroups may be a marker of affluence. Again, all adjusted OR values were statistically non-significant, suggesting no association with cervical cancer. The Latin American case-control study (Herrero et al, 1991) examined a category called 'animal foods', which included meat, fish and dairy products; OR = 0.98 (0.7–1.3), after adjustment for non-confounding factors.

Evidence on meat and fish and the risk of cervical cancer is limited; no judgement is possible.

4.14.2.3 Milk and dairy products

At least four studies have reported on dairy products. Findings by La Vecchia et al (1988) who examined milk intake and Verreault et al (1989) who examined dairy products (OR = 0.7, p = 0.08) are consistent with a reduced risk in association with higher consumption. The two case-control studies of Ziegler et al (1990, 1991) found no association between the risk of cervical cancer and consumption of dairy products.

Evidence on milk or dairy products and the risk of cervical cancer is limited and somewhat inconsistent; no judgement is possible.

4.15 Prostate

Cancer of the prostate gland is, in men, the fourth most common incident cancer and the seventh most common cause of cancer death. An estimated 400,000 cases occurred in 1996, accounting for 3.9 per cent of all new cases of cancer, worldwide.

Incidence of, and deaths from, this cancer are generally increasing throughout the world. Rates are much higher in economically developed societies, in part because of more widespread screening and diagnosis.

The panel has reached the following conclusions. There is as yet no convincing evidence that any dietary factors modify risk of prostate cancer, nor evidence of any probable causal relationships with diet.

The panel notes that diets high in vegetables are possibly protective, and that regular consumption of fat, saturated/animal fat, red meat and milk and dairy products possibly increase risk.

Current evidence suggests that the most effective dietary means of preventing prostate cancer, is consumption of diets high in vegetables and low in fat and saturated/animal fat, red meat and milk and dairy products .

FOOD, NUTRITION AND PROSTATE CANCER

In the judgement of the panel, the dietary constituents and related factors, and the foods and drinks listed below modify the risk of prostate cancer, or else have no relationship with it. Judgements are graded according to the strength of the evidence.

EVIDENCE	DECREASES RISK	NO RELATIONSHIP	INCREASES RISK
Convincing			
Probable			
Possible	Vegetables	High body mass Alcohol Vitamin C Coffee Tea	Total fat Saturated/animal fat Meat Milk and dairy products
Insufficient			High energy intake

For an explanation of the terms used in the matrix, see chapter 3.

INTRODUCTION

Symptomatic carcinoma of the prostate is rare in men under 50 years of age, but its incidence increases almost exponentially beyond that age. Most prostatic cancers are adenocarcinomas which arise from the epithelial cells of the ducts or acini.

INCIDENCE PATTERNS

Cancer of the prostate is the ninth most common cancer in the world. In 1996, there were an estimated 400,000 new cases diagnosed worldwide (WHO, 1997), accounting for 3.9% of all new cancers. Prostate cancer is the fourth most common cancer in men.

Prostate cancer is much more common in developed than developing countries. Developed countries account for nearly 75% of all new cases (289,000 in 1996). The highest rates are found in Europe, North America and Australia. Within countries, substantial variations in incidence also occur; for example, among different ethnic groups in the USA (Parkin et al, 1992). The highest incidence rates in the world are reported among African-American men and the lowest among men in China (Whelan et al, 1990). Rates are much lower in Africa than among African-Americans (Waterhouse et al, 1976). Incidence increases particularly after 60–70 years of age.

The incidence rates of prostate cancer have been increasing in recent years in many parts of the world. Reasons for this increase are unclear, but, in the developed world, they are partly related to widespread screening for prostate cancer (Potosky et al, 1990). No change in dietary or other exposures has been identified that would account for this increase.

PROSTATE CANCER estimated rates of cancer incidence by sex and area

1. Eastern Africa	7. Central America	13. Eastern Asia: Other	19. Southern Europe
2. Middle Africa	8. South America (Temperate)	14. South Eastern Asia	20. Western Europe
3. Northern Africa	9. South America (Tropical)	15. Southern Asia	21. Australia/New Zealand
4. Southern Africa	10. North America	16. Western Asia	22. Melenesia
5. Western Africa	11. Eastern Asia: China	17. Eastern Europe	23. Micronesia/Polynesia
6. Caribbean	12. Eastern Asia: Japan	18. Northern Europe	24. USSR

5.0 **Male**

Cancer of the prostate is unusual in that a large number of undiagnosed tumours are often found post mortem (Guileyardo et al, 1980; Yatani et al, 1982). This prevalence increases markedly with age, with rates as high as 40% by the age of 80 (Breslow et al, 1977).

Survival rates for prostate cancer are high, with 70–90% surviving five years after diagnosis. In 1996, mortality attributable to prostate cancer was estimated at 204,000 men, nearly 3% of all cancer deaths (WHO, 1997).

PATHOGENESIS

About 70% of adenocarcinomas arise in the peripheral zone, 25% in the transitional zone and the remainder in the central zone of the gland. The tumours may have a multifocal origin. Prostate cancer spreads locally by direct invasion through the capsule into the seminal vesicles and the base of the bladder, and then often encircles and occludes the urethra. Bony metastases are a common secondary occurrence. The natural history of prostate cancer is variable and unpredictable. Some tumours have such great malignant potential that metastases occur before there are any local symptoms, whereas others are so indolent that they remain undetected until after death, as noted above.

A genetic contribution to the risk of prostate cancer is considered likely. Fathers and brothers of prostate cancer patients are at increased risk (Woolf, 1960; Cannon et al, 1982; Steinberg et al, 1990; Monroe et al, 1995; Whittemore et al, 1995), and several genes involved in the metabolism of androgens in the prostate gland are polymorphic in humans (Coetzee and Ross, 1994).

As a result of the similar rates of undiagnosed prostate cancer worldwide, initiation factors may be similar universally, but there could be variability in rate of promotion or progression (Pienta and Eser, 1993). As for progression of other solid tumours, it is believed that prostate carcinogenesis involves multiple genetic events, including those that result in an initiated cell, and those that promote growth. Most studies in American populations have shown that *ras* mutations are not common in either the initiation or the progression of prostate cancer (Isaacs et al, 1995). Studies in Japan have, however, found *ras* mutations present in 25% of both latent (K-*ras*) and clinical (H-*ras*) prostate tumours (Anwar et al, 1992; Konishi et al, 1993). c-*erb*B-2, frequently amplified in breast and ovarian cancer, is also over-expressed in prostate tumour tissue. Several tumour suppressor genes are commonly mutated or deleted in prostate cancer cells. These include the E-cadherin gene, which is important in cell adhesion, the retinoblastoma gene and the *p53* gene. The identification of a gene that appears to suppress prostate cancer metastasis, *KAI*1, may play a major role in the progression of latent prostate to a more aggressive form (Dong et al, 1995).

The contrasting international pattern for latent versus clinical prostate cancer, as well as observations in migrant populations, suggest that variability in risk may be a consequence of differences in exogenous exposures related to tumour promotion.

JUDGEMENTS OF OTHER REPORTS

The National Academy of Sciences report, *Diet, Nutrition and Cancer* (NAS, 1982) concluded that the evidence for a role of dietary fat in the aetiology of prostate cancer was limited but suggestive. In the subsequent report, *Diet and Health* (NAS, 1989) the panel concluded that the evidence for fat, especially animal fat, had strengthened somewhat.

REVIEW

4.15.1 DIETARY CONSTITUENTS

4.15.1.1 Energy and related factors

Energy intake

Few studies have evaluated the relationship between energy intake and the risk of prostate cancer. To date, only two cohort studies on prostate cancer have collected sufficiently comprehensive dietary data to enable the effects of energy intake to be examined. No association between energy intake and prostate cancer risk was found in either study (Severson et al, 1989b; Giovannucci et al, 1993).

Of four case-control studies that assessed energy intake in relation to prostate cancer risk, three reported increased risk with higher total energy intakes. Whittemore et al (1995) found that increased energy intake was associated with increased prostate cancer risk in three racial groups, but this was explained largely by saturated fat. West et al (1991) reported that men aged 68–74 years, who were in the uppermost quartile for energy intake, had a strongly elevated risk of aggressive tumours. Furthermore, a case-control study of Canadian men suggested that higher caloric intake was associated with increased prostate cancer risk: the risk for men in the uppermost quartile for energy intake was 75% greater than for those in the lowest quartile (Rohan et al, 1995). The low response rate reported in this study (51.4% of eligible cases; 39.4% of eligible controls) raises the serious possibility, however, of selection bias in the study participants. Only one case-control study, of Canadian men aged between 35 and 84 years, reported no association between energy intake and prostate cancer risk (Ghadirian et al, 1996).

It is difficult to determine whether any increased risk of prostate cancer with high energy intake results solely from caloric intake itself, or from the high intake of other dietary constituents or particular energy-dense foods.

The evidence suggests that high energy intakes may increase the risk of prostate cancer, but is, as yet, insufficient.

High body mass/Adult height

Nine cohort studies have examined the relationship between relative weight or percentage of desirable weight and the risk of prostate cancer. Two studies reported that increased body size strongly increased the risk of prostate cancer (Lew and Garfinkel, 1979; Snowdon et al, 1984). However, the seven other cohort studies found no consistent significant associations between body mass and the risk of prostate cancer (Greenwald et al, 1974; Nomura et al, 1985; Tulinius et al, 1985; Mills et al, 1989; Thompson et al, 1989; Le Marchand et al, 1994; Thune and Lund 1994).

Of eight case-control studies, only one study, among men in northern Italy, found that increased body mass index (BMI) was strongly associated with increased risk of prostate cancer (OR = 4.4, 1.9-9.9) (Talamini et al, 1986). The remaining eight case-control studies found no statistically significant associations between body mass and prostate cancer risk (Wynder et al, 1971; Graham et al, 1983; Ross et al, 1987; Kolonel et al, 1988; West et al, 1991; Rohan et al, 1995; Whittemore et al, 1995).

None of these studies distinguished between abdominal and peripheral obesity, although, in men, the former type greatly predominates. Body mass indices are not optimal measures of the degree of adiposity, especially in men, because greater muscle mass will also yield higher BMI values. One cohort study in Hawaii found that higher lean body mass (as assessed by mid-upper arm circumference) was more strongly associated with increased prostate cancer risk than BMI (Severson et al, 1988).

Nutritional factors in early life may also play an important role in the risk of prostate cancer in adulthood, as suggested by a recent report that a higher birthweight was associated with increased prostate cancer incidence (Tibblin et al, 1995). It has been suggested that adult height may be a useful indicator of childhood nutritional status. However, one cohort study in Hawaii found no association between adult height and risk of prostate cancer (Severson et al, 1988) and only one case-control study reported that height was associated with a moderately increased risk of prostate cancer (Le Marchand et al, 1994). Three other case-control studies found no association (Kolonel et al, 1988; La Vecchia et al, 1990; Whittemore et al, 1995).

Accurate assessment of body size and composition is difficult and problematic especially in large cohort studies.

However, the evidence suggests that high body mass possibly has no relationship with the risk of prostate cancer.

Physical activity

Five cohort studies and five case-control studies have examined physical activity in relation to the risk of prostate cancer. Results have been somewhat conflicting.

Of the cohort studies, one study of college alumni reported that students who had been athletes, and who had therefore been more physically active, were at significantly greater risk of developing prostate cancer than non-athletes (Polednak, 1976). However, another study of a cohort of Japanese men living in Hawaii reported no material association between physical activity levels and the risk of prostate cancer (Severson et al, 1989b). The three other cohort studies reported that increased levels of physical activity show a protective association with prostate cancer. Albanes et al (1989) found that men in the NHANES-I cohort who were active compared with those who took little or no recreational exercise had a moderately decreased risk of developing prostate cancer (RR = 0.6, p < 0.02). A Norwegian study found that men who walked during occupational hours and undertook regular recreational training had a significantly decreased risk of prostate cancer relative to sedentary men (RR = 0.45, p for trend = 0.03) (Thune and Lund, 1994). The protective association with increased physical activity levels was also observed by Lee et al (1992) in a cohort of college alumni.

Several of the case-control studies have also found that higher levels of physical activity protect against prostate cancer, but the results have not been consistent for all ages and ethnic groups. Brownson et al (1991) reported that men whose physical activity levels were classified as high had a significant moderate decrease in prostate cancer risk relative to those in the low-activity category. Furthermore, a case-control study in the USA reported that active white men had a weakly decreased risk of developing prostate cancer relative to those who seldom took physical exercise, but that there was no substantial association between physical activity and prostate cancer risk in black men (Yu et al, 1988). Whittemore et al (1991) found that risk of prostate cancer was not consistently associated with physical activity patterns. A case-control study in Utah (USA) reported no association between activity and prostate cancer risk in older men. However, younger men who were in the uppermost quantile for activity had a moderately increased risk for aggressive tumours (West et al, 1991). The finding that physical activity may be associated with increased prostate cancer risk is supported by another case-control study in Hawaii; men aged 70 years or over, who were in the lowest tertile for proportion of total life spent in sedentary or light occupations (that is the most active), had a weakly increased risk of prostate cancer (Le Marchand et al, 1991b).

As a result of the long latency period for prostate cancer, it is not clear at what point in life physical activity may be most relevant. Some of the studies that showed a protective association were based on activity in later life (Lee et al, 1992; Severson et al, 1989a), whereas one that showed an increased risk assessed physical activity in young adulthood (Polednak, 1976). The data are more difficult to interpret as a result of the different methods used to assess physical activity. Some studies have used an index based on lifetime occupation; others have combined recreational activity with occupational activity and still others have assessed time spent in physical training.

A plausible mechanism for a protective effect of physical activity would be through a reduction in circulating androgen levels. Several reports have shown that physically active or physically fit men have lower testosterone levels (Wheeler et al, 1984; Strauss et al, 1985; Hackney et al, 1988).

Given the limitations of the data relating to higher physical activity and the risk of prostate cancer, and the evidence of association between higher activity and both increased and decreased risk, no judgement is possible.

4.15.1.2 Fat and cholesterol

Total fat

The evidence on dietary fat and the risk of prostate cancer has been the topic of several reviews (Kolonel and Nomura, 1992; Rose and Connolly, 1992; Boyle and Zaridze, 1993; Pienta and Esper, 1993; Kolonel, 1996). Overall these authors have concluded that the data, although generally in the direction of increased risk with higher fat intake, are not entirely consistent.

Of several cohort studies that have studied the relationship between fat and prostate cancer risk, two obtained sufficient dietary data to enable the total fat intake to be calculated.

The cohort study by Giovannucci et al (1993), based on 3–4 years of follow-up of 51,521 professional men in the USA, found a statistically non-significant weak increase in the risk (RR = 1.7) of advanced prostate cancer with higher total fat intake, after adjusting for total energy intake. Another prospective study by Severson et al (1989b) studied a much smaller cohort of 7,999 men of Japanese ancestry living in Hawaii. Food-intake data, obtained using 24-hour recalls, showed no substantial association between total fat intake and the risk of prostate cancer. No adjustments were made for energy intake in this study.

Of nine case-control studies of prostate cancer that have reported on total fat, seven have reported increased risk of prostate cancer with higher intakes. In three studies, the moderate to strong associations were statistically significant, with odds ratios ranging from 1.9 to 2.9 for the uppermost quantiles of fat intake (Ross et al, 1987; West et al, 1991; Walker et al, 1992). Those studies that reported statistically non-significant increases in risk, reported ORs of between 1.5 and 1.9 (Graham et al, 1983; Heshmat et al, 1985; Kolonel et al, 1988; Whittemore et al, 1995). The most comprehensive of these case-control studies (Whittemore et al, 1995) included separate analyses for three different ethnic groups and found a weakly increased risk across all groups, even after adjustment for energy intake. Perhaps surprisingly, the study showed a much stronger trend in risk with higher fat intake among Asian-Americans than among men of other ethnicities, which could not be explained by differences in the slope of the regression line over different ranges of fat intake. The authors tentatively suggested that high-fat diets may be more accurately recalled by Asian-Americans because such diets vary so markedly from traditional cultural dietary behaviour.

Of the two studies that observed no association between total fat intake and the risk of prostate cancer, one was conducted in Japan where fat intake is usually considerably lower than in Western cultures (Ohno et al, 1988). If fat intake is important in the development of prostate cancer

only when above a certain threshold, then the lack of an association in this population might be expected. However, the other case-control study that reported no clear association between energy-adjusted total fat intake and prostate cancer risk was carried out in Canada (Rohan et al, 1995). The strong possibility of selection bias in this study as a result of low response rates has been described above.

Four international ecological studies (Howell 1974; Armstrong and Doll, 1975; Rose et al, 1986; Hursting et al, 1990) have shown positive correlations (r = 0.6–0.7) between per capita intake of fat and prostate cancer mortality. In one of these studies the correlation was attributed to animal, but not vegetable, fat (Rose et al, 1986; another attributed the positive correlation to saturated and monounsaturated but not polyunsaturated fat intake (Hursting et al, 1990). One further ecological study, which compared five ethnic groups in Hawaii, also found evidence of increased prostate cancer incidence with age-specific increased intakes of fat (r = 0.9). However, the highly positive correlation in the last study was attributed not to total fat itself, but to animal fat and saturated fat intake (Kolonel et al, 1981). Other ecological studies did not report on fat intake as such, but found positive correlations between intake of high-fat foods (Blair and Fraumeni, 1978) or added fats (Howell, 1974) and prostate cancer mortality.

Results concerning fat intake and the risk of prostate cancer from experimental studies have been somewhat conflicting. Spontaneous tumours of the prostate occur rarely except in humans and domesticated dogs (Nomura and Kolonel, 1991). Few suitable animal models for the study of diet and prostate cancer have been developed, and anatomical as well as physiological differences across species make extrapolations to humans difficult (Nomura and Kolonel, 1991).

In one animal study, a high-fat diet, fed under non-isocaloric conditions, increased the yield of prostate tumours in testosterone-treated Lobund Wistar rats (Pollard and Luckert, 1986). In another study (Wang et al, 1995), prostate tumours were induced in nude mice, on a 40.5% fat diet, by subcutaneous injection of human prostatic adenocarcinoma cells. After measurable tumours were formed, subgroups of these animals were assigned to diets with various degrees of fat reduction. Mice whose diets contained 21.2% or less of energy as fat had significantly lower tumour growth rates, final tumour weights and ratios of final tumour weights to animal weights, as well as correspondingly lower serum prostate-specific antigen (PSA) levels. (PSA is a marker used to screen for elevated risk of prostate cancer.) However, in another report, neither amount nor type of fat in the diet influenced the development of chemically induced prostate tumours in Wistar rats pre-treated with androgenic hormones (Kroes et al, 1986).

A possible mechanism for an effect of dietary fat on prostate cancer is through an influence on androgenic hormones, which are thought to be important determinants of the risk of prostate cancer. Although existing epidemiological data on hormonal patterns in men at different levels of risk are not entirely consistent (de Jong et al, 1991; Ross et al, 1992; Hsing and Comstock, 1993), dietary fat appears to influence endogenous androgen levels in men. In one study (Hill et al, 1979), for example, urinary levels of androgens and oestrogens decreased in a group of white and black American men when they were transferred from a customary Western diet containing 40% of calories from fat to a meat-free diet containing 30% of calories from fat. In another investigation (Key et al, 1990), male vegans were found to have significantly higher plasma levels of sex hormone-binding globulin (SHBG), but no differences in levels of total or free testosterone, compared with omnivorous men. Furthermore, SHBG was positively correlated with dietary fat and inversely correlated with alcohol intake in a subset of these men.

Ross and Henderson (1995) suggested that dietary fat may interact with androgens very early in life, possibly even *in utero*, and thereby influence prostate cancer occurrence in adult life. In their model, a high dietary fat intake by a pregnant woman would lead to higher circulating testosterone levels (low 'gonadostat' set point). High fat intake in childhood might advance the onset of puberty, thereby increasing the lifetime exposure of the prostate to circulating testosterone. In adulthood, high fat might lead to increased circulating testosterone levels more directly. All of these would have the common effect of increasing the activity of the enzyme 5-α-reductase (which converts testosterone to its bioactive form, dihydrotestosterone), which, in turn, would lead to cell proliferation in the prostate and ultimately to prostate cancer.

Other general mechanisms by which dietary fat might promote carcinogenesis in the prostate include effects on cell-membrane composition or prostaglandin synthesis (Ip et al, 1986; NRC, 1989).

The major limitation of the seven case-control studies that reported that higher intakes of total fat increase risk of prostate cancer is that only one adjusted the risk estimates for total energy intake. As fat contributes substantially to total energy, it is important that the effect of fat should be distinguished from that of energy. Despite the apparently consistent findings, caution must be exercised when interpreting the data.

Diets high in total fat possibly increase the risk of prostate cancer.

Saturated/animal fat

Four cohort studies have reported on saturated fat intake and the risk of prostate cancer. One relatively small prospective study of 7,999 men of Japanese ancestry living in Hawaii found no association between the risk of prostate cancer and intake of saturated fat. No adjustments were made for energy intake (Severson et al, 1988). The study of 51,521 men in the USA also reported no association between intake of saturated fat and the risk of advanced prostate cancer, even after adjustment for total energy intake. However a

statistically borderline increase (RR = 1.6, 1.0–2.8) in prostate cancer risk was observed for men who were in the uppermost quintile for animal fat intake (Giovannucci et al, 1993). Two further cohort studies carried out in Hawaii (n = 20,316) and the USA (n = 14,000) also reported statistically non-significant weak increases in risk with higher intakes of high fat animal products or with the percentage of energy derived from animal fat, with relative risks in the range 1.4–1.6 for higher intakes (Mills et al, 1989; Le Marchand et al, 1994).

Of seven case-control studies that reported associations between saturated/animal fat and prostate cancer risk (Graham et al, 1983; Heshmat et al, 1985; Kolonel et al, 1988; Mettlin et al, 1989; West et al, 1991; Rohan et al, 1995; Whittemore et al, 1995), six have reported increased risk with higher intakes. In four of these studies, the associations were statistically significant with ORs ranging from 1.7 to 3.2 (Graham et al, 1983; Kolonel et al, 1988; West et al, 1991; Whittemore et al, 1995). For one study carried out in Hawaii, an attributable risk of 13% (0–28%) was calculated for intakes of saturated fat above 26 g/day (the uppermost quartile), suggesting that about 13% of prostate cancer cases might be prevented if saturated fat intakes were reduced to less than 13 g/day (lowest quartile) (Hankin et al, 1992).

However, it is important to note that only two of the seven case-control studies that reported on saturated/animal fat intake and prostate cancer risk adjusted risk estimates for total energy intake. One of these studied saturated fat intake in three ethnic groups in the USA and Canada and found multivariate-adjusted ORs of 2.0 (p < 0.05) and 2.8 (p < 0.05) for risks of all tumours and advanced tumours, respectively. It should be noted that this study is unique in that the authors attempted to reduce misclassification bias resulting from the presence of subclinical cancers in the control group, by excluding men with elevated PSA levels (Whittemore et al, 1995). Conversely, the other study that adjusted for energy intake found that higher intakes of saturated fat and animal fat decreased prostate cancer risk, with ORs of 0.6 (p for trend = 0.01) and 0.7 (p for trend = 0.03), respectively (Rohan et al, 1995); as noted above, this study had poor response rates.

Several ecological studies that reported positive correlations between fat intake and incidence of, or mortality from, prostate cancer, attributed their findings to intakes of animal fat (Kolonel et al, 1981; Rose et al, 1986) and/or saturated fat (Kolonel et al, 1981; Hursting et al, 1991).

The relevant time period of exposure to dietary fat in relation to prostate cancer risk has not yet been established. As nearly all studies have measured adult diets, the positive findings suggest that relatively recent consumption affects the risk of this cancer. This is supported by one study (Slattery et al, 1990) which compared the effects of adolescent and adult diets (both obtained by recall in adulthood) on prostate cancer. These authors found that men who consumed a diet high in saturated fat as adults were at increased risk of prostate cancer, whereas men who consumed such a diet as adolescents were not. It is possible, however, that this null result might be explained by poor recall of adolescent diet.

The available data for saturated and animal fat intake and the risk of prostate cancer are similar to the pattern seen for total fat and similar caveats apply (see above).

Diets high in saturated and/or animal fat possibly increase the risk of prostate cancer.

Monounsaturated fat

Few studies have examined the association between monounsaturated fat intake and the risk of prostate cancer.

A cohort study in the USA reported a statistically non-significant increase in risk of advanced prostate cancer with higher intake of monounsaturated fat. When adjusted for energy intake, the relative risk for men in the upper quintile of intake was 1.6 (0.6–4.0) (Giovannucci et al, 1993).

Of three case-control studies that have examined monounsaturated fat intake in relation to prostate cancer risk, one found that higher intakes were associated with increased risk and two found no substantial association. One case-control study of prostate cancer in Utah (USA) reported a statistically significant strongly increased risk of aggressive tumours in older men (68–74 years) (OR = 3.6, 1.3–9.7 for men in the uppermost quintile of intake) (West et al, 1991). The OR was stronger than those seen for total (2.9), saturated (2.2) and polyunsaturated (2.7) fat (all p < 0.05) in the same study. However, risk estimates were not adjusted for total energy intake. One case-control study carried out in Canadian men, which did control for energy intake and age, found no significant association (OR = 0.8, 0.5–1.4) between intake of monounsaturates and the risk of prostate cancer (Rohan et al, 1995). Whittemore et al (1995) also reported no significant association between intake of monounsaturated fat and the risk of prostate cancer.

One international ecological study reported no correlation between consumption of monounsaturated fat and incidence of prostate cancer (r = 0.02) (Hursting et al, 1990).

Evidence on diets high in monounsaturated fat and the risk of prostate cancer is inconsistent; no judgement is possible.

Polyunsaturated/vegetable fat

A cohort study of professional men in the USA reported a strongly increased risk of advanced prostate cancer in men who had higher intakes of α-linolenic acid, a polyunsaturated essential fatty acid of the omega-3 series. The energy-adjusted relative risk was 3.4 (p = 0.002 for trend) for men whose intakes were in the uppermost quantile (Giovannucci et al, 1993). α-Linolenic acid is present in red meat, butter and vegetable oils; soya bean and rapeseed oils are a particularly rich source. In the same study, linoleic acid showed a statistically non-significant weakly protective association (energy-adjusted RR = 0.6, 0.3–1.3).

A cohort study that studied the risk of prostate cancer in association with plasma levels of individual fatty acids found a strongly increased risk with higher plasma levels of α-linolenic acid (RR = 2.1, 0.9–4.0, p = 0.03 for trend); for linoleic acid, the RR of 0.6 was not statistically significant. No substantial associations were found between prostate cancer risk and plasma levels of either arachidonic acid or eicosapentaenoic acid (Gann et al, 1994).

Evidence from three case-control studies is somewhat inconsistent. One case-control study of prostate cancer in Utah reported a statistically significant strongly increased risk of aggressive tumours for older men (68–74 years), for those whose intakes of polyunsaturated fat were in the uppermost quartile (OR = 2.7, 1.1–6.8). Two other case-control studies in the USA and Canada found no substantial associations between intakes of polyunsaturated fats and risk of prostate cancer (Rohan et al, 1995; Whittemore et al, 1995).

Two international ecological studies have examined polyunsaturated and vegetable fats in relation to prostate cancer risk. One study reported a positive correlation between consumption of polyunsaturated fat and incidence of prostate cancer (r = 0.5) (Hursting et al, 1990). The other found no substantial correlation between consumption of vegetable fat and prostate cancer mortality (r = 0.1) (Rose et al, 1986).

In an in vitro study, linoleic acid has been shown to stimulate the growth of a prostate cancer cell line (Rose and Connolly, 1992).

Overall, the evidence on diets high in polyunsaturated fat is inconsistent; no judgement is possible.

Omega-3 fatty acids

A cohort study in the USA reported no association between intake of omega-3 fatty acids from fish and risk of advanced prostate cancer (energy-adjusted RR = 0.9, 0.5–1.6) (Giovannucci et al, 1993). Another cohort study in the USA reported no association for plasma eicosapentaenoic levels (Gann et al, 1994).

Omega-3 fatty acids in the diet are obtained primarily from intake of fatty fish. Alaskan men who eat large quantities of fish are at low risk of prostate cancer; however, an international ecological study reported no correlation between consumption of omega-3 fatty acids from fish and incidence of prostate cancer (r = 0.04) (Hursting et al, 1990).

In an in vitro study, omega-3 fatty acids have been shown to inhibit the growth of a prostate cancer cell line (Rose and Connolly, 1992).

Evidence on diets high in omega-3 fatty acids and the risk of prostate cancer is limited: no judgement is possible.

Trans-fatty acids

A cohort study in the USA reported no association between

intake of *trans*-fatty acids and risk of advanced prostate cancer, after adjustment for other dietary factors (Giovannucci et al, 1993).

On the basis of a single study, no judgement is possible.

Cholesterol

Three case-control studies have examined dietary cholesterol in relation to prostate cancer risk. One study in Hawaii observed a statistically non-significant increase in risk of prostate cancer, with an OR of 1.6 for older men whose cholesterol intakes were in the uppermost quantile. No material association between dietary cholesterol and prostate cancer risk was seen in men younger than 70 years (Kolonel et al, 1988). In another case-control study in the USA, dietary cholesterol also showed no association with prostate cancer risk in younger men, whereas older men (68–74 years) in the uppermost quartile for cholesterol intake had a weakly increased prostate cancer risk (West et al, 1991). One other case-control study in Canada found no association between dietary cholesterol intake and prostate cancer risk (Rohan et al, 1995).

Given the equivocal nature of the limited evidence on cholesterol intake and the risk of prostate cancer, no judgement is possible.

4.15.1.3 Total protein

One prospective study of a cohort of men of Japanese ancestry living in Hawaii found no association between total protein intake and the risk of prostate cancer (Severson et al, 1989b). Another cohort study in the USA found that frequent consumption of vegetarian protein products (meat substitutes such as soy products and gluten) by Seventh-day Adventist men was associated with a statistically non-significant weak decrease (RR = 0.7, 0.4–1.1) in prostate cancer risk (Mills et al, 1989).

Two case-control studies have also examined the effects of protein intake on the risk of prostate cancer. One in Utah (USA) found a statistically significant moderate increase in risk for prostate cancer (all tumours) in 68- to 74-year-old men who were in the uppermost quartile for daily total protein intake (West et al, 1991). The other case-control study in Canadian men found that increased vegetable protein consumption was associated with decreased risk of prostate cancer (Fincham et al, 1990).

For prostate cancer, positive correlations between animal protein consumption and mortality rates have been reported at the international level (Armstrong and Doll, 1975), and between animal protein intakes and prostate cancer incidence at the national level (Kolonel et al, 1983).

Thus, two epidemiological studies of total protein have found either no association or increased risk of prostate cancer, two ecological studies of animal protein have found increased risk and two epidemiological studies of vegetable protein (or products) have reported decreased risk.

Based on the limited data, and the possible variation in the effects of different types of protein, no judgement is possible relating to total protein intake and the risk of prostate cancer.

4.15.1.4 Alcohol

Of four cohort studies that examined the relationship between alcohol intake and the risk of prostate cancer, two reported no association (Severson et al, 1989b; Hiatt et al, 1994). A cohort study of American men reported that increased consumption of beer was weakly associated with an increased risk of prostate cancer; smoking-adjusted relative risks for ex-users and current drinkers of beer were 1.7 and 1.2, respectively, whereas the risk for ex- and current drinkers of spirits were 0.7 and 1.0, respectively (Hsing et al, 1990b). A study of a cohort of men in Japan found an RR of 2.7 for men who were daily drinkers of alcohol but who were non-smokers (Hirayama 1992).

Four case-control studies also assessed effects of alcohol consumption on prostate cancer risk but none reported any substantial associations (Ross et al, 1987; Yu et al, 1988; Walker et al, 1992; Tavani et al, 1994).

Seven of eight studies are consistent with little or no increase in risk.

High alcohol intake possibly has no relationship with the risk of prostate cancer.

4.15.1.5 Vitamins

Carotenoids

Three cohort studies that have examined intakes of carotenoids in relation to prostate cancer have produced equivocal and inconsistent data. One study of a cohort of Lutheran men in the USA found that older men (≥ 75 years) had a strongly decreased risk of prostate cancer with higher β-carotene intakes (RR = 0.2, 0.1–0.6), whereas younger men (< 75 years) had a moderately increased risk of prostate cancer with higher intakes of β-carotene (Hsing et al, 1990a).

The two other cohort studies that examined β-carotene intake and risk of prostate cancer found no change in risk from lowest to uppermost quantiles of intake (Shibata et al, 1992; Giovannucci et al, 1995). The latter study also assessed intakes of four other carotenoids and no differences in risk were noted with intakes of α-carotene, β-cryptoxanthin and lutein. Only lycopene (obtained almost exclusively from tomato-based foods) showed a weakly protective association with prostate cancer (RR = 0.8, p < 0.05).

Case-control studies that have examined carotenoid intake with respect to the risk of prostate cancer are also somewhat equivocal. In one study in Hawaii, the investigators found that men aged 70 years or more who were in the uppermost quartile for intake of β-carotene and other carotenoids had statistically non-significant increases in the risk of prostate cancer, whereas no associations were apparent in younger men (Kolonel et al, 1987). The association was later attributed to one food item, papaya, which contains significant amounts of the carotenoid β-cryptoxanthin (Le Marchand et al, 1991a). Conversely, another case-control study in the USA which used a β-carotene index, based on 27 vegetables and fruits, to assess carotenoid intake found that higher levels of β-carotene showed a strong protective association with prostate cancer in younger men (≤ 68 years), but no association in older men (Mettlin et al, 1989). In a case-control study in Japan, Ohno et al (1988) found a protective association with prostate cancer for higher β-carotene intakes but this was significant only in men aged 70 years or over. Ross et al (1987) also found a protective association with β-carotene and prostate cancer but not in white men. Nevertheless, this association was apparent in both age groups for men whose fat intakes were below the median of the study population, suggesting an interaction between dietary fat and β-carotene and prostate cancer risk. A weakly protective association with β-carotene was observed in another case-control study in the USA (West et al, 1991), but only for younger men (45–67 years) and only for aggressive tumours. No substantial association between β-carotene and prostate cancer was observed for older men in the same study. A case-control study in Canadian men found no association between β-carotene intake and prostate cancer risk (Rohan et al, 1995).

Two cohort studies have examined serum levels of carotenoids and prostate cancer risk. One study in Finland reported an increased risk with elevated serum β-carotene levels (Knekt et al, 1990). In a prospective cohort in Maryland (USA), Hsing et al (1990a) found no association between serum β-carotene and prostate cancer. However, higher serum lycopene levels showed a moderately protective association in younger men (< 70 years) and a weakly protective one in older men.

One case-control study that investigated serum levels of β-carotene found no substantial association between increased serum β-carotene levels and the risk of prostate cancer (Hayes et al, 1988).

Both increased and decreased risk with higher carotenoid intake have been observed in various studies. Differences in the direction of the risk estimates for younger and older men are apparent in several studies, but some studies show decreased risk in older men and others show decreased risk in younger men. The evidence is not more consistent for any particular carotenoid than for other individual carotenoids or for carotenoids as a whole.

Based on the inconsistent nature of the available evidence on dietary carotenoids, no judgement is possible.

Vitamin C

Two cohort studies in the USA found no association between vitamin C intake from foods or from foods and supplements and risk of prostate cancer (Fincham et al, 1990; Shibata et al, 1992).

Of six case-control studies, five reported no significant associations between vitamin C intake and the risk of prostate cancer (Heshmat et al, 1985; Kolonel et al, 1988; Ohno et al, 1988; West et al, 1991; Rohan et al, 1995). Graham et al (1983) found a statistically significant strongly increased risk of prostate cancer for older men who were in the uppermost quantile for vitamin C intake (OR = 3.4). Although higher intakes of vitamin C were also weakly associated with elevated prostate cancer risk in younger men (< 70 years) in the same study, this was not statistically significant. A study by Kaul et al (1987) found that in men over 50 years of age, cases had higher intakes of vitamin C than controls, but the result was not statistically significant.

High dietary vitamin C possibly has no relationship with the risk of prostate cancer.

Retinol

Of five cohort studies that have assessed vitamin A and/or retinol in relation to risk of prostate cancer, two have been concerned with nutrient intakes and three have studied associations between serum levels and disease risk. The two cohort studies on dietary intakes of vitamin A/retinol and the risk of prostate cancer produced data that are somewhat confusing. One study of a cohort of Lutheran men in the USA found that higher total 'vitamin A' intakes were associated with a strongly increased risk of prostate cancer in men aged less than 75 years. However, in men aged 75 years or over, higher levels of total vitamin A intake were strongly protective against prostate cancer (Hsing et al, 1990a). The picture is confused further by results from another large American cohort (Giovannucci et al, 1995). Retinol from food sources alone was associated with a moderately elevated risk of prostate cancer, whereas retinol from supplements was not. However, this association was apparent only in men aged over 70 years. No association between retinol intake and the risk of prostate cancer was demonstrated for men aged 70 or younger.

Several case-control studies have also produced inconsistent results. One of the earliest case-control studies to report on vitamin A intake and the risk of prostate cancer suggested that intakes of vitamin A in the uppermost quantile were associated with a weakly increased risk of prostate cancer in men younger than 70 years, and with a moderately increased risk in men 70 years or older. However, vitamin A intake was assessed using a composite 'vitamin A index', which excluded rich dietary sources of preformed vitamin A, such as liver (Graham et al, 1983). Another case-control study in the USA, which also used a similarly limited 'vitamin A index', found no substantial association between vitamin A intake and risk of prostate cancer (Middleton et al, 1986).

More detailed approaches to the collection of vitamin A intake data in case-control studies have also produced confusing results. One study, which calculated total vitamin A from recalls of diets eaten when subjects were aged between 30 and 49 years, reported that prostate cancer cases had consumed significantly more (p < 0.007) vitamin A than controls (Heshmat et al, 1985).

Another case-control study in the USA reported a statistically non-significant weak decrease in incidence of aggressive tumours with higher vitamin A intakes in men aged 45–67 years (OR = 0.7, 0.3–1.9), but a non-significant weak increase in risk of all tumours (OR = 1.6) in men aged 68–74 years (West et al, 1991).

One study in Hawaii found that the risk of prostate cancer showed a statistically significantly moderate increase in men with higher intakes of total vitamin A (including supplements) in men aged 70 years or more (OR = 2.0, 1.3–3.1). However, there was no association apparent in men aged under 70 years (Kolonel et al, 1987).

A Canadian case-control study showed a weakly protective association with vitamin A for men who were in the uppermost quantile of intake (Rohan et al, 1995).

The three cohort studies that analysed serum levels of retinol have also produced confusing and inconsistent results. All three studies examined serum retinol levels; two in the USA reported that higher serum retinol levels were associated with significantly decreased risk of prostate cancer, with RRs of 0.3 and 0.45) (Hsing et al, 1990a; Reichman et al, 1990), but no association was found in a Finnish study (Knekt et al, 1990).

One case-control study also examined serum retinol levels and reported a statistically significant (p < 0.05) strong increase in risk for men whose serum retinol levels were in the lowest quintile (Hayes et al, 1988). However, an effect of the disease itself cannot be excluded in such an analysis.

It is important to note that serum retinol is not a good marker of dietary intake because blood levels of retinol are under tight homeostatic control and show little variation except in instances of extreme depletion of body stores.

Animal studies suggest that retinoids may inhibit chemically induced carcinogenesis at several different sites, including the prostate (NRC, 1989). The proliferation of human prostatic tissue in cell culture can be inhibited or enhanced, depending on the concentration of retinoid in the medium (Chaproniere and Webber, 1985).

A synthetic retinoid, fenretinide, reduced tumour incidence by 49% and the tumour mass by 52% in a mouse prostate model (Slawin et al, 1993).

As a result of the fact that measurement has varied so much across studies of 'vitamin A' and retinol intake, no clear picture regarding the risk of prostate cancer has yet emerged. The differences in direction in risk estimates between younger and older men, which are manifest in both cohort and case-control studies and noted above for carotenoids, only serves to confuse the evidence further.

Taking these factors into account, no judgement is

possible on 'vitamin A'/retinol and the risk of prostate cancer.

Vitamin E

One Canadian case-control study reported no alteration in risk of prostate cancer risk in association with intake of vitamin E (Rohan et al, 1995).

Two nested case-control studies within cohorts have examined serum tocopherol levels in relation to the risk of prostate cancer. The results of these studies are somewhat conflicting. One study in the USA, which analysed pre-diagnostic levels of serum tocopherol and subsequent prostate cancer incidence, found that younger men (< 70 years) in the uppermost quartile for serum tocopherol levels had a moderately decreased risk of prostate cancer. However, older men (≥ 70 years) in the uppermost quartile for serum tocopherol had a moderately increased risk of prostate cancer (RR = 2.5, p for trend = 0.38) (Hsing et al, 1990a). The other study, carried out in the Netherlands, reported a statistically non-significant decrease (RR = 0.6) in prostate cancer risk for men whose serum α-tocopherol levels were in the highest quintile (Hayes et al, 1988).

On the basis of the limited evidence for both dietary vitamin E intakes and serum levels and the risk of prostate cancer (and again the hint that risks are somewhat different by age), no judgement is possible.

4.15.1.6 Minerals

Calcium/vitamin D

No studies have presented data on calcium and prostate cancer. It has been hypothesised that vitamin D has a protective effect against cancer of the prostate (Schwartz and Hulka, 1990), but there are few studies that have specifically examined the relationship.

Two nested case-control studies within cohorts in the USA have analysed pre-diagnostic serum levels of 1,25-dihydroxy vitamin D3 (the active form of vitamin D in the body) and subsequent risk of prostate cancer. One found that low levels in older men were associated with increased prostate cancer risk (Corder et al, 1993), but the other found no association (Braun et al, 1995).

Administration of a 'non-calcaemic' vitamin D analogue, 1,25-dihydroxy-16-ene-23-yne-cholecalciferol resulted in a small increase in the proliferation of human prostate cancer cells after inoculation into nude mice (Schwartz et al, 1995).

The evidence on dietary vitamin D intakes and prostate cancer risk is limited; no judgement is possible.

Zinc

One case-control study in Hawaii (Kolonel et al, 1988) found a statistically significant increase in the risk of prostate cancer for older men whose zinc intakes were in the uppermost quantile (OR = 1.7). However, zinc intakes of this magnitude were obtained mainly from supplements, and no association between the risk of prostate cancer and zinc intake from food was observed. In the same study, neither total zinc nor zinc from food sources alone was associated with any alteration in prostate cancer risk in younger men (< 70 years). West et al (1991) found no association between dietary zinc intake and the risk of aggressive tumours in younger or older men.

One ecological study reported a direct linear correlation between zinc intake and prostate cancer mortality (Schrauzer et al, 1977).

Evidence relating to dietary zinc intake and the risk of prostate cancer is limited and inconsistent; no judgement is possible.

4.15.2 FOODS AND DRINKS

4.15.2.1 Vegetables and fruits

In contrast to evidence on most other cancer sites, where vegetables show consistently protective associations, the available data on the risk of prostate cancer are much less clear (see Tables 6.3.1 and 6.3.2).

Of seven cohort studies of vegetable and fruit intake, two reported no association between consumption of all vegetables and fruits and risk of prostate cancer (Snowdon et al, 1984; Shibata et al, 1992). The findings of the other five cohort studies have been somewhat equivocal. In Japan, Hirayama (1986) found that higher consumption of green and yellow vegetables showed a protective association (RR = 0.6) in men under 75 years of age. Among another cohort of Japanese men living in Hawaii (Severson et al, 1989), the risk of prostate cancer was weakly increased for men who were in the uppermost quantile of fruit intake (RR = 1.6, ns) and moderately increased in men who were in the upper-most quantile of seaweed intake (RR = 1.7, p < 0.05) (Severson et al, 1989b). In multivariate analyses based on a cohort of 14,000 Seventh-day Adventist men, Mills et al (1989) reported no association between the risk of prostate cancer and an index of fruit intake. However, greater frequency of consumption of raisins, dates and other dried fruits showed a weakly protective association, and tomato intake showed a moderately protective one (RR = 0.6, p = 0.02). A moderately protective association with tomatoes was also observed in another American cohort study (Giovannucci et al, 1995), but no substantial associations were found for either fruit or vegetable intake in the same study. A statistically non-significant weak protective association of vegetables was observed in another American cohort, and no substantial associations were observed with fruit and cruciferous vegetables (Hsing et al, 1990b).

Most case-control studies of prostate cancer reported no statistically significant associations for vegetable and fruit consumption. In fact, several studies have noted increases in prostate cancer risk for higher intakes in one or other categories of fruit. In one case-control study in Hawaii, an increase in risk with β-carotene intake, in men over 70 years of age, was largely explained by higher consumption of papaya (OR = 2.5, 1.6–4.0) (Le Marchand et al, 1991a).

In Japan, Ohno et al (1988) found that fruit consumption was associated with a moderate increase in prostate cancer risk, whereas consumption of green-yellow vegetables showed a moderately protective association. Multivariate analysis of data from a case-control study in northern Italy found no material association with either vegetable or fresh fruit intake (Talamini et al, 1992). An earlier paper from this group also reported no substantial association between intake of green vegetables and the risk of prostate cancer (Talamini et al, 1986).

Another American case-control study in Minneapolis reported that higher intakes of carrots showed a weakly protective association with prostate cancer (Schuman et al, 1982). Carrots showed a similar relation in a case-control study in South Africa; higher frequency of consumption of cabbage and spinach was shown to be moderately protective (OR = 0.6, p < 0.05) (Walker et al, 1992).

An international ecological study of 30 countries found an inverse correlation of –0.38 between vegetable availability and cancer of the prostate (Rose et al, 1986).

The pattern of association that emerges is not clear. Nevertheless, most studies found no association or even increased risk with some fruit categories and a marginally greater suggestion, but still with a number of null studies, of decreased risk with vegetables.

Diets high in vegetables possibly decrease the risk of prostate cancer.

Evidence on diets high in fruits is markedly inconsistent; no judgement is possible.

4.15.2.2 Pulses (legumes)

Two cohort studies have assessed the risk of prostate cancer in relation to intake of various pulses. One of these studies of Seventh-day Adventists in California reported an RR of 0.5 (0.3–0.9) for those men who consumed beans, peas and lentils more than three times per week (versus less than once per month) (Mills et al, 1989). The other study of a cohort of Japanese men in Hawaii reported an RR of 0.4 (0.4–1.4) for men who ate tofu five or more times per week versus those who consumed tofu less than four times per week (Severson et al, 1989b).

One case-control study in the USA reported a weak decrease in the risk of prostate cancer for men in the uppermost quantile for intake of peas and beans (Schuman et al, 1982).

Evidence on diets high in pulses is limited; no judgement is possible.

4.15.2.3 Nuts and seeds

Only one prospective cohort study carried out in Californian Seventh-day Adventists has examined nut consumption and the risk of prostate cancer. Men who consumed nuts five times a week or more were at decreased risk of prostate cancer (RR = 0.6, 0.4–0.8) compared with men who ate nuts less than once per week. This association was somewhat weakened by adjustment for other dietary factors (Mills et al, 1989).

Evidence on diets high in nuts and the risk of prostate cancer is very limited; no judgement is possible

4.15.2.4 Meat, poultry, fish and eggs

Meat

Of eight cohort studies that have examined meat intake and the risk of prostate cancer, three found no material association (Hirayama, 1974; Severson et al, 1989b; Hsing et al, 1990b). In a cohort of Seventh-day Adventist men in the USA, non-significant relative risks of between 0.8 and 1.2 were observed for frequency of consumption of beef and beef products, suggesting no material associations between beef intake and prostate cancer (Mills et al, 1989). Current intake of meat, poultry or fish (one food group) was reported in the same study as being associated with increased risk of prostate cancer, but the RR of 1.4 was not statistically significant. A statistically non-significant relative risk of similar magnitude was observed in another cohort of Seventh-day Adventists who consumed meat or poultry on three or more days per week compared with those who ate the same foods less than one day per week (Snowdon et al, 1984). Four of these five cohort studies were of Japanese men or Seventh-day Adventist men. In these populations, meat intake is substantially below that seen among the general population in North America and northern Europe.

In contrast, three cohort studies have found that the risk of prostate cancer increases substantially with higher meat consumption. A nested case-control analysis of a cohort of almost 15,000 male physicians in the USA found a moderate increase in the risk of prostate cancer with more frequent consumption of red meat, although the dietary data were somewhat limited. The RR of 2.5 for men who consumed red meat at least five times per week compared with those who ate red meat less than once per week was little changed by adjustment for α-linolenic acid, intake of which was associated with a strong increase in risk (Gann et al, 1994). Higher consumption of beef and high-fat animal products (including beef, pork, poultry, processed meats, milk and eggs) was associated with moderate increases in prostate cancer risk in about 20,000 men in Hawaii; the risk of prostate cancer in men whose intakes were in the uppermost tertile for beef intake was much stronger in men diagnosed at or before 72.5 years of age (RR = 2.2, p < 0.01) than in those diagnosed after 72.5 years (RR = 1.4, ns) (Le Marchand et al, 1994). The most comprehensive cohort study to date, based on 3–4 years of follow-up of almost 52,000 professional men in the USA, found a strong statistically significant association between higher intakes of red meat and the risk of prostate cancer. Further analysis in the same study found a relative risk of 2.6 specifically for fat from meat (Giovannucci et al, 1993).

Five case-control studies have examined meat intake in relation to the risk of prostate cancer. Only one American study reported no association between consumption of meat and risk of prostate cancer (Schuman et al, 1982). Two case-control studies in northern Italy (Talamini et al, 1986, 1992) and one in the USA (Mettlin et al, 1989) reported weak-to-moderate increases in the risk of prostate cancer with higher meat consumption. Another case-control study in South Africa found that men who consumed meat five or more times a week had a statistically significant moderate increase in the risk of prostate cancer when compared with those men who consumed meat less than once a week (Walker et al, 1992).

Two international ecological studies reported positive correlations (r = 0.6–0.7) between prostate cancer mortality and per capita intake of meat (Howell, 1974; Armstrong and Doll, 1975).

Among populations with a higher overall meat intake, three of four cohort studies and four of five case-control studies show an increased risk in association with higher consumption. Associations are not seen among the Japanese cohorts in Japan or Hawaii or among Seventh-day Adventist men.

Diets high in meat possibly increase the risk of prostate cancer.

Eggs

Of five cohort studies that examined egg intake and the risk of prostate cancer, four reported no substantial associations, with relative risks ranging from 0.8 to 1.0 (all statistically non-significant) (Snowdon et al, 1984; Mills et al, 1989; Hsing et al, 1990b; Le Marchand et al, 1994). One study of a cohort of Japanese men living in Hawaii reported a weak association (RR = 1.6, ns) between egg consumption and the risk of prostate cancer (Severson et al, 1989b).

However, of three case-control studies, only one reported no relationship between egg consumption and risk of prostate cancer (Talamini et al, 1992). One study of men in South Africa reported a strong statistically significant increase in risk of prostate cancer in men who consumed eggs five or more times a week (Walker et al, 1992). Statistically significant associations were also observed in a case-control study that separated men on the basis of ethnicity. African-American men who consumed eggs more frequently had an odds ratio for prostate cancer of 1.8 (p < 0.05); white men who ate eggs more often had an OR of 2.5 (p < 0.05) (Whittemore et al, 1995).

Two international ecological studies have reported no substantial correlations between egg consumption and prostate cancer mortality (Howell, 1974; Rose et al, 1986).

Most cohort data are derived from Japanese and Seventh-day Adventist men with low overall intake of eggs. The case-control data are consistent with increased risk. As there are differences between cohort and case-control designs that make recall and selection bias more likely in case-control studies, whether the differences that are seen between study designs are the result of a limited range of exposure in the cohort studies or of a greater likelihood of bias in the case-control design cannot be ascertained at this stage.

No judgement is possible.

4.15.2.5 Milk and dairy products

Two American cohort studies reported increased risk of prostate cancer with higher milk intakes (Snowdon et al, 1984; Le Marchand et al, 1994), although the multivariate-adjusted relative risk of 1.5 reported by Snowdon et al (1984) was statistically non-significant. Conversely, four other cohort studies that examined milk consumption did not find any substantial associations with the risk of prostate cancer. Daily milk consumption in a cohort of about 14,000 Seventh-day Adventist men in the USA was not associated with prostate cancer risk (Mills et al, 1989). In a cohort of Japanese men living in Hawaii, there was also no association between frequency of milk consumption and risk of prostate cancer. However, increased consumption of butter, margarine and cheese (one food group) was associated with increased risk (RR = 1.5, p = 0.05) (Severson et al, 1989b). In a large American cohort, fat from dairy products (with the exception of butter) was not associated with elevated risk of advanced prostate cancer (Giovannucci et al, 1993). Dairy products also showed no association with the risk of prostate cancer in the Lutheran Brotherhood cohort (Hsing et al, 1990b).

In contrast to most cohort studies, five case-control studies have suggested that dairy products are associated with increased risk of prostate cancer. One study in northern Italy found that higher consumption of milk/dairy products was strongly associated with increased risk of prostate cancer (OR = 2.5, p < 0.05). Increased risk was also observed in three other case-control studies (Mettlin et al, 1989; La Vecchia et al, 1990; Talamini et al, 1992). The last of these reported a strongly increased risk with milk consumption, but no association with cheese or butter intake. One further study also suggested that consumption of ice cream may be associated with a weakly increased risk (Schuman et al, 1982).

Milk consumption has been associated with an increased risk of prostate cancer mortality in four ecological studies with correlations ranging from 0.6 to 0.7 (Howell, 1974; Armstrong and Doll, 1975; DeCarli and La Vecchia, 1986; Rose et al, 1986).

It has been suggested that fat may be the constituent responsible for the possible increase in prostate cancer risk associated with dairy products, although this was not observed in the study by Giovannucci et al (1993).

As with eggs, the primary distinction in the data is between the cohort and case-control studies. Because the weight of the evidence is derived from the case-control studies with only modest support from the cohort data (some of which is, nevertheless, derived from Japanese who have low milk intake), the conservative judgement is that diets high in milk and dairy products possibly increase the risk of prostate cancer.

4.15.2.6 Coffee, tea and other drinks
Coffee

Of the three large cohort studies (Jacobsen et al, 1986; Nomura et al, 1986; Severson et al, 1989) which have examined coffee consumption and subsequent risk of prostate cancer, only one has reported any alteration in risk with increased consumption. This study, undertaken in 13,664 Norwegian men (260 prostate cancer cases), reported no substantial association between coffee consumption and prostate cancer when the crude data were analysed. However, after adjustment for age, residence and smoking, the authors demonstrated that increased coffee consumption was associated with a weak decrease in prostate cancer risk (RR = 0.7, ns) (Jacobsen et al, 1986).

An earlier cohort study in the USA noted no significant differences in prostate cancer mortality between men who drank at least two cups of coffee per day, compared with those who drank no coffee (Phillips and Snowdon, 1983). Another study of a cohort of US men which compared consumers of five or more cups of coffee per day with consumers of less than three cups per day also found no association with the risk of prostate cancer (Hsing et al, 1990).

The results from three case-control studies in Canada, Italy and the USA have also shown no substantial associations between coffee consumption and the risk of prostate cancer (Fincham et al, 1990; Talamini et al, 1992; Slattery and West, 1993).

High consumption of coffee possibly has no relationship with the risk of prostate cancer.

Tea

The majority of studies that have examined tea consumption in relation to the risk of prostate cancer have found no substantial associations. Of three cohort studies, only one noted an alteration in risk with increased tea consumption. This study, undertaken in a cohort of 7833 men of Japanese ancestry living in Hawaii (Heilbrun et al, 1986), found that men who consumed tea almost daily or more often had a moderately reduced risk (RR = 0.6, p for trend = 0.02) when compared with those who reported almost never drinking tea. The two other cohort studies (Kinlen et al, 1988; Severson et al, 1989) reported no substantial associations between tea consumption and the risk of prostate cancer.

High consumption of tea possibly has no relationship with the risk of prostate cancer.

4.15.3 FOOD PROCESSING

4.15.3.1 Contaminants
Cadmium

Cadmium has long been considered a potential risk factor for prostate cancer, primarily because of several reports based on occupational exposures. However, given the very high prevalence of prostate cancer in Western populations, the limited number of men exposed occupationally is unlikely to account for any more than a small proportion of the cancer burden.

Cadmium in food is generally considered to be a contaminant. It is found most often in seafood, especially shellfish. Few studies have reported on dietary cadmium exposure. Kolonel and Winkelstein (1977) found that a summary index of cadmium exposure (based on dietary, occupational and smoking exposure, but not dietary exposure alone) was positively associated with prostate cancer. Abd Elghany et al (1990) also found an increased risk from all these sources together, and a non-significant increase when diet alone was considered.

Cadmium is carcinogenic in animals, and produces localised tumours when injected subcutaneously or intratesticularly in rats (Haddow et al, 1964; Roe et al, 1964; Gunn et al, 1967). This effect can be blocked by simultaneous injection of zinc (Gunn et al, 1964). A mechanism for the carcinogenicity of cadmium could involve competition with zinc, an essential trace element more highly concentrated in the prostate than in any other organ in the body (Feustel et al, 1982; Hambridge et al, 1986).

Although the occupational association is clear, evidence relating to diets high in cadmium and the risk of prostate cancer is very limited; no judgement is possible.

4.16 Thyroid

Cancer of the thyroid is uncommon; accounting for only 1–2 % of all cancers.

Rates of this cancer are higher in women.

The panel has reached the following conclusions. Diets deficient in iodine probably increase the risk of this cancer. The panel notes that diets high in vegetables possibly decrease risk, and diets excessive in iodine, possibly increase risk.

Established non-dietary causes of thyroid cancer are goitre, and ionising radiation.

The most effective dietary means of preventing thyroid cancer are diets adequate in iodine, if necessary by fortification, and, possibly, diets high in vegetables.

NUTRITION AND THYROID CANCER

In the judgement of the panel, the dietary constituents and related factors, and the foods and drinks listed below modify the risk of thyroid cancer. Judgements are graded according to the strength of the evidence.

EVIDENCE	DECREASES RISK	NO RELATIONSHIP	INCREASES RISK
Convincing			
Probable			Iodine deficiency
Possible	Vegetables and fruits[a]		Iodine excess
Insufficient	Selenium		High body mass

For an explanation of the terms used in the matrix, see chapter 3.
[a] There is no evidence that vegetables rich in goitrogens increase the risk of thyroid cancer.

INTRODUCTION

Thyroid cancer is an uncommon tumour. The majority of thyroid cancers arise from the acinar cells. These cells are responsible for the production of thyroglobulin, the active transport of iodine within the cells, and the eventual formation of thyroxine (T_4). There is a wide variation in incidence among countries and regions, which suggests an influence of environmental factors. The incidence and proportion of histological subtypes of thyroid cancer also show geographical variations. Papillary cancer is the predominant histological type, generally comprising 60–70% of all cases, followed by follicular cancer (10–15%), anaplastic cancer (5–10%) and undifferentiated forms such as medullary cancer (2–8%). A mixed category that has papillary and follicular components was previously regarded as a separate histological type but is nowadays classified as a papillary carcinoma according to the World Health Organization criteria.

Inherited genetic abnormalities play a role in medullary thyroid cancer, but familial occurrence of the more common papillary type has been reported only rarely. Papillary cancer has the most favourable prognosis with the lowest likelihood of metastases.

INCIDENCE PATTERNS

Thyroid cancers are relatively rare (WHO, 1993) representing fewer than 2% of all recorded neoplasms worldwide (Goodman et al, 1988; Kolonel et al, 1990; Franceschi et al, 1991; Glattre et al, 1993; Omran and Ahmed, 1993; WHO, 1993). Thyroid cancer rates are among the highest in the world in Hawaii, and yet accounted for only 2.7% of all non-skin cancers there between 1973 and 1977 (Goodman et al, 1988; Kolonel et al, 1990). The World Bank (1993) does not list thyroid cancers among the world burden of diseases.

During the past two to three decades, a trend towards an increase in the incidence of thyroid cancer, but not its mortality (which has actually declined in a number of countries, such as Japan, Australia and Canada), has been apparent in may industrialised countries of the Americas, Europe, Asia and Oceania (WHO, 1993). Large increases in incidence and prevalence have occurred in Japan and Germany (WHO, 1993). Two major reasons seem to account for this trend (WHO, 1993): an increase in the number of asymptomatic benign lesions, especially in young women, as a result of improved detection; and improvements in survival due to better treatment. Five-year survival rates are typically in the range of 80%.

BOX 4.16.1 ESTABLISHED NON-DIETARY FACTORS AND THYROID CANCER

The following non-dietary factor increases the risk of thyroid cancer:

- Ionising radiation

However, some aspects of the international pattern of thyroid cancer do not fit this explanation. There has been a decline in the incidence of early thyroid cancer in Norway, and there is a wide difference in the rate of change of mortality between the sexes.

Incidence rates of thyroid cancer are two or three times higher among females than among males (Robbins et al, 1984). This striking sex difference suggests that hormonal factors influence its development. The difference in incidence rates between the sexes declines after middle age (Henderson et al, 1982; WHO, 1993), which perhaps implies an oestrogenic influence since levels of this hormone decline after the menopause. The combined data from all cancer registries reporting to the International Agency for Cancer Research (Henderson et al, 1982) show that, under the age of 10 years, the incidence is about equal between the sexes. This changes abruptly at around puberty, so that it is about three times higher in females than males in the 10–19 year age group. The ratio remains the same until menopause, when it starts to decline steadily, reaching 1.5 by the age of 65. This pattern seems to be constant worldwide.

The theory that a hormonal mechanism involving oestrogens is implicated in thyroid cancer is strengthened by studies which show that risk is approximately doubled in women with a high number of pregnancies, and a marked increase in risk is associated with a history of miscarriage (ORs = 4.0–100), particularly at first pregnancy, and for cancer at a young age (Ron et al, 1987; Goodman et al, 1992; Preston-Martin et al, 1993).

PATHOGENESIS

The aetiology of thyroid cancer is uncertain. Two major hypotheses have been proposed and each is supported by epidemiological and experimental data. The first, and more certain, is non-dietary, and implicates ionising radiation. The second involves a hormonal mechanism through which dietary and specific chemical agents exert their influences.

Ionising radiation, especially in childhood, is the only well-defined risk factor for thyroid cancer (Hirohata, 1976).

Irradiation of the head and neck, again particularly during childhood, is especially serious. This practice has now been abandoned apart from therapy for malignancy, but was formerly used widely in the treatment of trivial (for example, tinea capitis) and imaginary (for example, thymus enlargement) disorders.

The main epidemiological evidence linking irradiation to thyroid cancer comes from studies of children who received external X-irradiation for benign conditions, from the follow-up of the Japanese atomic bomb survivors (WHO, 1988; Department of Health, 1989) and, most recently, from the study of those exposed to fall-out from Chernobyl.

JUDGEMENTS OF OTHER REPORTS

Neither of the National Academy of Science reports, *Diet, Nutrition and Cancer* (NAS 1982) and *Diet and Health* (NAS1989), nor the WHO report *Diet, Nutrition and the Prevention of Chronic Diseases* (WHO, 1990) came to any conclusion about any relationship between dietary factors and the risk of thyroid cancer.

REVIEW

4.16.1 DIETARY CONSTITUENTS

4.16.1.1 Energy and related factors
Body mass
In a case-control study conducted in the state of Washington (USA), higher weight was found to be a strong risk factor for thyroid cancer, with the risk increasing significantly with increasing weight. Women who weighed 60 kg or more had a 2.5 times greater risk than women who weighed 52 kg or less (McTiernan et al, 1987). In a population-based case-control study in Hawaii, an increased risk was associated with greater weight and obesity (Kolonel et al, 1990). Odds ratios for BMI for above or equal to the median compared with below it, were statistically significant in men (OR = 2.7, 1.2–5.9) but not in women (OR = 1.4, 0.9–2.3). A greater dietary energy intake by cases relative to controls was consistent with their greater obesity, particularly in men. In contrast, a case-control study in Connecticut (USA) found an increase in risk with increasing BMI among women (OR = 1.5) but not among men (OR = 0.6) (Ron et al, 1987). In a hospital-based case-control study in Italy no trend of increasing risk with increasing average BMI was observed in either men or women (Franceschi et al, 1989). In a further analysis of the case-control study in Hawaii, an increased risk of thyroid cancer was observed with increasing body mass, particularly in later life (Goodman et al, 1992). The risk for thyroid cancer was significantly higher (OR = 4.3, 1.2–15.3) among women who had experienced a miscarriage or stillbirth at first pregnancy and who were above the 50th percentile for weight in early adulthood compared with women in the reference category (Goodman et al, 1992).

An association with weight or obesity may reflect hypofunctioning of the thyroid gland, especially as there is a positive association of thyroid cancer with prior benign thyroid disease. It is possible that excess adipose tissue in heavier women causes higher levels of circulating oestrogens, which may, in turn, increase the risk of thyroid cancer.

The evidence suggests that high body mass may increase the risk of thyroid cancer but, as yet, is insufficient.

4.16.1.2 Alcohol
Two case-control studies, one in the USA and one in Italy (Ron et al, 1987; Franceschi et al, 1989), did not detect any significant increase in risk with alcohol intake, with odds ratios of 0.9 and 0.7, respectively. Pooled analysis of four studies in Northern Italy and Switzerland found no increase in risk with alcohol intake. The results of the Third National Cancer Survey in the USA showed an increased risk of thyroid cancer with higher alcohol consuption.

Evidence on alcohol intake and the risk of thyroid cancer is limited; no judgement is possible.

4.16.1.3 Minerals
Selenium
Patients with thyroid cancer have repeatedly shown lower selenium concentrations than controls (Salonen et al, 1984, 1985; Kok et al, 1987). In a case-control study in Norway, serum from controls was found to be significantly higher in selenium than that from people who developed thyroid cancer (OR = 0.1, 0.02–0.8, for 1.65 mmol/l vs 1.25 mmol/l (Glattre et al, 1989).

The high concentrations of selenium in normal thyroids suggests an important function of selenium in this gland. A long-term experiment in 400 rats exposed to radiation showed that a selenium-enriched diet (started after the exposure) caused a longer average lifespan and a 1.5- to 3.5-fold decrease in thyroid cancer (Knizhnikow et al, 1996). As with iodine, selenium is concentrated and stored against a serum gradient (Glattre et al, 1989; Aaseth et al, 1990).

A possible mechanism to account for the apparent anti-cancerous effect of selenium is that the selenium-dependent functional antioxidant enzyme glutathione peroxidase may reduce tissue concentrations of toxic free radicals and hydroperoxides.

The evidence suggests that diets high in selenium may decrease the risk of thyroid cancer but is, as yet, insufficient.

Iodine
Both iodine deficiency and iodine excess have been implicated in thyroid tumour formation in humans and experimental animals (Henderson et al, 1982; Ward and Ohshima, 1986; Goodman et al, 1988; Franceschi et al, 1989, 1990, 1991; Kolonel et al, 1990; Yamashita et al, 1990; Kanno et al, 1992; Glattre et al, 1993; Wynford-Thomas, 1994). These may be related to different histological types of thyroid can-

cer, with deficient intakes increasing the risks of follicular cancer and excessive intakes increasing the risk of papillary cancer.

Iodine deficiency

Dietary iodine deficiency is associated with goitre in both humans and animals. Suboptimal levels of iodine influence thyroid function both directly, and indirectly as a reduction in the level of thyroid hormones leads to a consequent rise in thyroid-stimulating hormone (TSH). Chronic hypersecretion of TSH causes goitre, which appears to be related to carcinogenesis. An increased risk of thyroid cancer has been reported in humans with goitre and those living in some iodine-deficient areas of the world such as the Alps, the Andes and the Himalayas, where iodine-rich topsoil has been washed to the lowlands (Ingenbleek et al, 1980; ETA, 1985; Ward and Ohshima, 1986).

Associations have been found between the incidence of thyroid cancer and endemic goitre in Europe (Muir et al, 1987; Vigneri, 1988; Franceschi et al, 1989, 1990). A hospital-based case-control study in three areas of northern Italy observed that goitre was more commonly reported by cases than controls (OR = 5.6, 2.1–14.8), and that the risk of thyroid cancer increased significantly in those who had resided in endemic goitre areas for 20 years or longer (OR = 2.3, 1.2–4.3), or in childhood or adolescence (OR = 2.4, 1.3–4.3). Adjustments for history of benign thyroid disease reduced the OR estimate for ever having resided in an endemic goitre area during childhood or adolescence from 2.3 to 1.7 (0.9–3.1) (Franceschi et al, 1989). A case-control study conducted on the island of Sicily determined that the dietary supply of iodine was inadequate in the endemic goitre area (Vigneri, 1988). However, the severity of the iodine deficiency did not parallel the severity of goitre, sug-

gesting that some goitrogenic factors other than iodine deficiency may contribute to goitre prevalence. Franceschi et al (1990) examined European areas covered by cancer registries (Muir et al, 1987) and found support for the association between endemic goitre and thyroid cancer. However, high prevalence of goitre should not be regarded as a definite precondition for high rates of thyroid cancer.

Five case-control studies conducted in Italy, Switzerland, Sicily, China and Sweden found a significant association between iodine deficiency (indicated by endemic goitre or low intake of iodine-rich foods such as fish) and thyroid cancer (Vigneri, 1988; Franceschi et al, 1989, 1991; Preston-Martin et al, 1993; Wigren et al, 1993).

Two US population-based case-control studies conducted in Connecticut and Hawaii (both iodine-sufficient areas) noted a lower not higher risk to be associated with a higher intake of goitrogenic vegetables (cabbage, cauliflower, brussels sprouts and broccoli) (Ron et al, 1987; Kolonel et al, 1990).

The correction of iodine deficiency using iodised salt has proved successful in the control of goitre and, to some extent, cretinism, although the data are less clear for thyroid cancer. On the one hand, the steady and marked decline in thyroid cancer mortality reported in Switzerland since the 1920s has been largely attributed to salt iodisation (Levi et al, 1988; Franceschi et al, 1990). On the other hand, no evidence of reduction in incidence of thyroid cancer has been reported in the USA following the introduction of iodised salt, nor in Italy, the glacier-scoured highland areas of Asia, Africa or Latin America where iodine deficiency still persists (Franceschi et al, 1990; Hetzel, 1994). A recent review indicates that mild to moderate iodine deficiency persists in several European countries (ICCIDD, 1993).

First observed in 1821 (Coindent, 1821), it has been well

BOX 4.16.2 DIET, THYROID-STIMULATING HORMONE AND THYROID CANCER

Several epidemiological (Goodman et al, 1988; Kolonel et al, 1990; Franceschi et al, 1991; Glattre et al, 1989, 1990, 1993) and experimental studies (Ward and Ohshima, 1986; Yamashita et al, 1990; Kanno et al, 1992) have implicated dietary factors in the aetiology of thyroid cancer. These include iodine deficiency and excess; consumption of wine, beer and spirits (liquor) (Williams et al, 1977); and low consumption of vegetables.

Although the mechanisms by which diet may influence the development of thyroid cancer are poorly understood, there is evidence to suggest that a common pathway is through a hormonal mechanism. Suboptimal levels of dietary iodine influence thyroid function both directly and indirectly as a reduction in the level of thyroid hormones leads to a consequent rise in

TSH from the anterior pituitary gland. Excessive and prolonged secretion of TSH leads to increased thyroid follicular cell proliferation (hyperplasia) and an increase in the size of the cells (hypertrophy). The resulting enlargement of the gland is called a goitre. It is hypothesised that the prolonged TSH-induced growth stimulus to the thyroid gland ultimately selects for cells with a proliferative advantage, resulting in clonal expansion of a transformed phenotype (Hill et al, 1989; McLain, 1992).

Dietary conditions that increase TSH fall into three categories. First, because iodine is required as a substrate in the formation of thyroxine, chronic iodine deficiency results in a prolonged reduction in the production of thyroxine, and the feedback loop results in elevated TSH. Thus, diets that regularly (not sporadically) contain

sufficient iodine levels would be expected to be protective against thyroid cancer. Second, diets that contain constituents that interfere with iodine uptake by the thyroid gland (goitrogens) or increase renal loss will also elevate TSH levels. Third, it is possible for TSH to rise in response to conditions that stimulate its production directly, such as habitual alcohol intake. It appears that the critical step in the development of carcinoma is the increase in TSH secretion; the specific cause of this elevation is less important. A plausible path to carcinoma is: iodine deficiency results in elevated levels of TSH, thus compensating for the deficiency by ensuring that the thyroid gland takes up the maximal amount of the available iodine. High stimulation of thyroid follicles can result in clones of cells that are increasingly autonomous.

documented that the return of iodine sufficiency in the presence of autonomous nodules results in hyperthyroidism (Connolly et al, 1970). Iodine deficiency as such is not thought to be a direct risk factor for thyroid cancer, but acts indirectly via hormonally mediated pathways. Chronic deficiency leads to increased TSH secretion, which leads to growth stimulus of the thyroid. A highly stimulated thyroid gland will contain rapidly dividing cells, which may be more susceptible to fallible DNA-repair mechanisms following endogenous and/or radiation-induced DNA damage. Thus, prolonged iodine deficiency, or iodine deficiency followed by an excess of iodine beyond the levels recommended for the elimination of iodine deficiency, may result in malignancy (see Box 4.16.2).

Diets deficient in iodine probably increase the risk of thyroid cancer.

Iodine excess

Long-term intakes of excessive amounts of iodine (18–1,000 mg/day) can block the uptake of iodine by the thyroid gland and can lead to elevated TSH levels as observed in the 'coast iodide goitre' patients in Japan where the high consumption of seaweed results in iodine intakes of around 200 mg/day (Wolff, 1969). Very high intakes (over 100 times recommended daily allowances or intakes) are needed to achieve negative effects. Rapid changes in iodine status may also lead to the development of tumours; if autonomous nodules have developed during chronic iodine deficiency, the administration of a large dose of iodine can cause hyperthyroidism and increased cell replication, which, in turn, increases susceptibility to DNA damage.

The high incidence of thyroid cancer in iodine-rich Iceland and Hawaii is consistent with this observation that iodine excess may also lead to the development of goitre. Four case-control studies conducted in the USA (Hawaii and Connecticut), Norway and China examined iodine intake in relation to thyroid cancer (Ron et al, 1987; Kolonel et al, 1990; Glattre et al, 1993; Preston-Martin et al, 1993). Each of these studies found a high intake of iodine-rich foods, such as seafood, to be associated with an increased risk of thyroid cancer.

Iodine excess has been shown to be tumour-promoting in experimental animal studies (Yamashita et al, 1990; Kanno et al, 1992). In an experiment where male F344 rats were supplemented with 260 mg/l of potassium iodide to generate iodine excess, a condition of colloidal goitre together with normal thyroxine (T_4) and slightly decreased TSH was observed. These effects were directly proportional to the extent of iodine excess (Kanno et al, 1992).

In a study by Yamashita et al (1990), male Wistar rats were fed an iodine-rich diet (200 mg/kg iodine) that resulted in nodular proliferation of follicle cells. Nevertheless, the carcinoma that appeared in the iodine-rich group was papillary carcinoma; no follicular carcinoma was found. It is hypothesised that high-iodine treatment induces hyposecretion of TSH or may make follicle cells less sensitive

to the goitrogenic and/or promoting effects of TSH. The results from these two experimental studies may explain the observation that iodine added to food and drinking water inhibits the occurrence of goitre but not that of carcinoma (Costa et al, 1966). This may be because there are different tumour promotion mechanisms for excess and low intakes of iodine.

This evidence indicates that diets with an excessive intake of iodine possibly increase the risk of thyroid cancer.

4.16.1.4 Other bioactive compounds

Goitrogens

Several plants used as food, including wheat, maize, potatoes, pulses (legumes) and especially plants belonging to the cruciferous family (cabbage, brussels sprouts, cauliflower, broccoli and turnip), all contain cyanogenic glucosides (Wills, 1966). Degradation of such glucosides can lead to the endogenous production of thiocyanate, which can behave similarly to iodine (Ermans et al, 1980). At low concentrations, goitrogens inhibit iodine transport, and at high concentrations they inhibit the incorporation of iodide into thyroglobulin, thus causing the pituitary glands to increase TSH secretion. It has also been shown that thiocyanate can modify the interaction of thyroid hormones with their serum-binding protein (Langer et al, 1976).

Goitrogens have been shown to induce thyroid tumours in animals but only when iodine deficiency was present as a predisposing factor (Purves and Griesback, 1947). It was therefore hypothesised that cruciferous and other goitrogenic vegetables may contribute to the risk of thyroid cancer in humans. However, cruciferous vegetables contain not only thiocyanates but also indole components, phenols and other compounds that may inhibit the development of certain cancers (Palmer and Bakshi, 1983).

To date, there is no human evidence that goitrogens increase the risk of thyroid cancer. Four case-control studies conducted in Italy, the USA and Sweden have shown a decreased risk with increased cruciferous vegetable intake (Ron et al, 1987; Franceschi et al, 1989; Kolonel et al, 1990; Wingren et al, 1993) (see section 4.16.2.1).

Taken together, these data suggest that higher intakes of goitrogenic vegetables do not increase the risk of thyroid cancer.

4.16.2 FOODS AND DRINKS

4.16.2.1 Vegetables and fruits

Five case-control studies have reported a protective association for vegetables and/or fruits (Ron et al, 1987; Franceschi et al, 1989, 1991; Kolonel et al, 1990; Wingren et al, 1993). A case-control study in northern Italy found frequent consumption of green vegetables and fruits to be associated with a reduction in the risk of thyroid cancer, with ORs of 0.5 for all green vegetables and 0.2 (0.1–0.8) for all fresh fruits

(Franceschi et al, 1989). A subsequent pooled analysis of studies in Italy and the Swiss canton of Vaud also observed significant protective associations for carrots (OR = 0.6), green salad (OR = 0.6) and citrus fruits (OR = 0.7); intake of cabbage and other cruciferae showed a protective association (OR = 4.9, p<0.05) (Franceschi et al, 1991). In a Hawaiian case-control study, Kolonel et al (1990) examined intakes of potentially goitrogenic vegetables (cabbage, cauliflower, broccoli, brussels sprouts, turnips, beet greens and Swiss chard) only. Female cases reported a lower consumption of these vegetables relative to controls (OR = 0.6, 0.3–1.2, for the highest quartile of intake). A case-control study involving only women in south-east Sweden (Wingren et al, 1993) found a decrease in risk associated with a high intake of cruciferous vegetables. The OR for those in the highest vs lowest quartiles of consumption was 0.2 (0.1–0.8, p = 0.05). A case-control study in the USA noted that a decrease in the risk of thyroid cancer was associated with an increased consumption of all vegetables evaluated, although none reached statistical significance. The ORs for highest consumption (a few times weekly or daily) ranged from 0.5 to 0.8, potentially goitrogenic vegetables (cabbage, brussels sprouts, cauliflower and broccoli) showed an OR of 0.77 (ns) (Ron et al, 1987).

Diets high in vegetables and fruits possibly decrease the risk of thyroid cancer.

4.17 Kidney

Cancer of the kidney is relatively uncommon. An estimated 165,000 cases occurred in 1996, accounting for 1.6 per cent of all new cases of cancer.

In general, rates of this cancer are higher in economically developed societies.

The panel has reached the following conclusions. High body mass probably increases the risk of renal cancer.

The panel also notes that diets high in vegetables are possibly protective, and that regular consumption of red meat and of dairy products possibly increase the risk of this cancer.

Regular consumption of black tea and coffee probably do not affect risk. The panel notes that alcohol possibly does not affect risk.

Established non-dietary causes of renal cancer are smoking, and abuse of phenacetin.

The most effective dietary means of preventing renal cancer is maintenance of body weight within recommended limits by means of appropriate diets and by regular physical activity throughout life.

FOOD, NUTRITION AND RENAL CANCER

In the judgement of the panel, the dietary constituents and related factors, and the foods and drinks listed below modify the risk of renal cancer or else have no relationship with it. Judgements are graded according to the strength of the evidence.

EVIDENCE	DECREASES RISK	NO RELATIONSHIP	INCREASES RISK
Convincing			
Probable		Coffee Black tea	High body mass[a]
Possible	Vegetables	Alcohol Eggs	Meat Milk and dairy products
Insufficient			

For an explanation of the terms used in the matrix, see chapter 3.

[a] The association with obesity appears somewhat more consistent in women than in men (see text). This judgement is specific to renal cell carcinoma.

INTRODUCTION

Renal cancer is classified as either cancer of the parenchyma or cancer of the renal pelvis (the junction of the kidney and ureter). Renal cell adenocarcinoma is a predominant type of parenchymal cancer, although nephroblastoma occurs in children. Transitional cell carcinoma is the major type of cancer of the renal pelvis (Dayal and Kinman, 1983).

Cigarette smoking is an established cause of renal pelvic cancer (US Surgeon General, 1982; IARC, 1986), and appears to be causally related to renal cell carcinoma (US Surgeon General, 1982; Dayal and Kinman, 1983; IARC, 1986).

Abuse of phenacetin has been associated with cancer of the renal pelvis, particularly in Scandinavia (Carro-Ciampi, 1978; McCredie et al, 1993). Mechanistic studies in rodents (Johansson, 1981; Vaught et al, 1981) and humans (Veronese et al, 1985) appear to corroborate a bioactivation path-

BOX 4.17.1 ESTABLISHED NON-DIETARY FACTORS AND RENAL CANCER

The following non-dietary factors increase the risk of renal cancer:

- Smoking tobacco
- Drugs: phenacetin abuse

way that involves reactive intermediates that bind to DNA and could initiate the neoplastic process. Consequently, this drug has been withdrawn from the market in most countries. Renal papillary necrosis, which is the primary lesion of analgesic nephropathy, is believed to be caused by a variety of other compound analgesics that contain paracetamol, aspirin or a pyrazolone (Prescott, 1982). As paracetamol is the chief immediate metabolic product of phenacetin, there exists the possibility that this drug may yield the same direct carcinogens as phenacetin (Hinson, 1983).

RENAL CANCER estimated rates of cancer incidence by sex and area

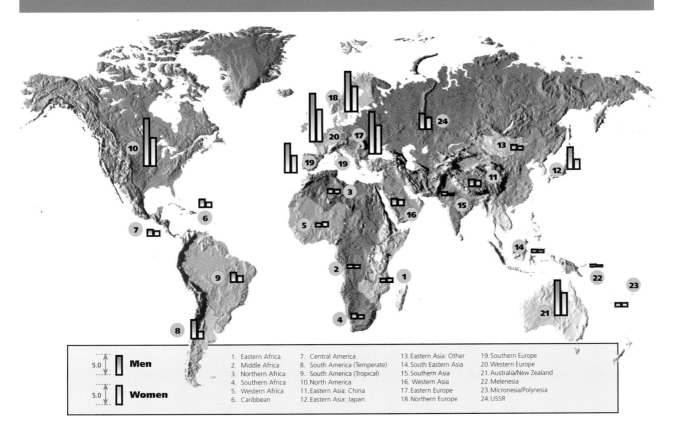

INCIDENCE PATTERNS

Cancer of the kidney is the seventeenth most common cancer in the world. In 1996, there were 165,000 new cases estimated to have been diagnosed worldwide (WHO, 1997), accounting for 1.6% of all new cancers.

Worldwide, there is at least a ten-fold difference in the incidence of renal cancer. The rates are highest in Europe especially Scandinavia and North America and are lowest in Asia and South America (Parkin et al, 1992).

The incidence rate of renal cancer is higher in men than in women in most countries (Parkin et al, 1992). In 1996, the number of male renal cancer cases was estimated to be nearly 60% (97,000 cases) of the total global incidence.

Over the past several decades, incidence and mortality rates have increased in many countries, but not universally (Coleman et al, 1993). In 1996, mortality attributable to renal cancer was estimated at 96,000 people, 1.3% of all cancer deaths (WHO, 1997).

PATHOGENESIS

The kidney is a complex organ composed of many different types of cells. The tumours which arise from this complex organ are themselves also diverse. They can be broadly classified into those of embryonal parenchymal or stromal origin. Embryonal tumours, nephroblastomas or Wilm's tumours are those most commonly found in children. They arise from embryonic cells that are the progenitors of the adult kidney. They generally have a good prognosis. Parenchymal tumours are usually found in adults. They can arise from various structures within the kidney, including the renal tubule, collecting duct, ureter, urethra and paraurethral gland and are usually of epithelial origin. Stromal tumours arise from mesenchymal cells of the kidney, such as fibroblasts, and are very rare.

The genes responsible for Wilm's tumour (nephroblastoma) and renal cell carcinoma (RRC), the two most frequent types of renal tumour, have now been identified. As expected, based on their different cellular origin and histological differences, the genes are very different. Two genes on human chromosome 11 and genes on chromosomes 16 and 1 are associated with the development of these tumours. One of the chromosome 11 genes, the Wilm's tumour-suppressor gene WT-1, has been identified. This gene is lost or mutated in a large proportion of Wilm's tumours.

RCC arises from epithelial cells and is composed of several histologically distinct types. Clear-cell RCC is known to arise as a result of mutations in the von Hippel-Lindau (VHL) tumour-suppressor gene, located on human chromosome 3. Inheritance of a mutation in this gene is responsible for hereditary RCC, and mutations in the VHL gene also occur in the vast majority of spontaneous RCC of the clear-cell type. Other types of RCC arising from epithelial cells such as papillary carcinoma do not contain mutations in this gene. As with other cancers involving the loss of a second copy of a tumour-suppressor gene, VHL genes are frequently mutated

in clear-cell carcinomas in individuals carrying the abnormal gene. In about 20% of cases, however, the second copy is silenced by methylation.

Renal cancers are also found in HNPCC-syndrome families where the known inherited defect is one of a family of DNA mismatch repair genes.

How, or whether, environmental and host risk factors, particularly obesity, interact with or provoke either the VHL mutations/deletions/hypermethylation or the DNA mismatch repair deficit is not known.

JUDGEMENTS OF OTHER REPORTS

Previous expert reports have not specifically made references to dietary factors and any association with cancer of the kidney, primarily because of limited epidemiological studies.

REVIEW

4.17.1 DIETARY CONSTITUENTS

4.17.1.1 Energy and related factors
Body mass
A Danish cohort study of obese women found a 2.7-fold (2.1–3.4) higher risk of renal parenchymal cancer than would have been expected from national rates, and obese men showed a statistically borderline relative risk of 1.5 (1.0–2.4) (Mellemgaard et al, 1991). This prospective study showed no appreciable association between obesity and renal pelvic cancer.

A 13-year cohort study of 750,000 women and men in the USA found a two-fold increase of dying of renal cancer among obese women (>40% above average RBW) compared with normal RBW (Lew and Garfinkel), 1979.

In eight case-control studies conducted in various countries (Table 4.17.1), an increase in the risk of cancer of the kidney (renal cell carcinoma) has been related to obesity as measured by body mass index (BMI) or relative weight. In four of the eight case-control studies (two in the USA, one in China and one in Canada), obesity was related to an equal increase in risk in both men and women (Yu et al, 1986; Maclure and Willett, 1990; McLaughlin et al, 1992; Kreiger et al, 1993). A greater increase was noted in women than men in three case-control studies (two in the USA and one in Denmark) (Wynder et al, 1974; McLaughlin et al, 1984; Mellemgaard et al, 1994), while in an Australian case-control study risk was more obviously elevated in men than in women (McCredie and Stewart, 1992). Even in the four case-control studies that reported differential risks for obesity by sex, the association was consistent with an increased risk in both men (Wynder et al, 1974; McLaughlin et al, 1984; Mellemgaard et al, 1994) and women (McCredie and Stewart, 1992). Odds ratios were adjusted for cigarette smoking in six of the studies (McLaughlin et al, 1984; Yu et al, 1986; Maclure and Willett, 1990; McLaughlin et al, 1992; Kreiger et al, 1993; Mellemgaard et al, 1994). The case-con-

TABLE 4.17.1 HIGH BODY MASS AND THE RISK OF RENAL CANCER: CASE-CONTROL STUDIES

AUTHOR, YEAR AND PLACE	NO. OF CASES	TIME PERIOD	SEX	COMPARISON (HIGHEST VS LOWEST QUANTILE)	ODDS RATIO (95% CONFIDENCE INTERVAL)	AGE/ SEX	ENERGY INTAKE	ADJUSTMENT REPRODUCTIVE VARIABLES	OTHER VARIABLES[a]
Wynder et al, 1974	202	2 years ago	men	< 95% vs > 125% relative weight	1.3[b] (0.6–2.9)	N	N	N	Y
			women		1.7[b] (1.6–8.5)				
McLaughlin et al, 1984	495	Usual adulthood	men	h vs l quintile BMI	1.3 (0.8–1.8)	Y	N	N	Y
			women		2.3 (1.3–4.1)				
Yu et al, 1986	160	10 years ago	men	h vs l quartile of Quetelet's index	1.8 (0.8–4.0)	Y	N	N	N
			women		2.7 (0.8–9.3)				
		1 year ago	men		2.5 (1.0–5.9)				
		1 year ago	women		3.3 (1.0–11.5)				
Maclure and Willett 1990	203		men	h vs l quintile of relative weight	1.7 (1.3–3.1)	Y	N	N	Y
			women		1.7 (0.9–3.2)				
Talamini et al, 1990	240	1 year ago	both	h vs l tertile BMI	0.74 (0.51–1.07)	Y	N	N	Y
McCredie and Stewart 1992	489	Usual adulthood	men	h vs l tertile BMI	1.6 (1.1–2.5)	Y	N	N	N
			women		1.3 (0.8–2.1)				
McLauglin et al, 1992	154	age 40	men	h vs l quartile BMI	3.6 (1.1–12.6)	Y	N	N	Y
		age 40	women		3.6 (0.9–14.7)				
		age 40	men		1.7 (0.5–5.7)				
		age 40	women		3.3 (0.7–15.1)				
Kreiger et al, 1993	518	age 25	men	h vs l quartile of Quetelet's index	1.3 (0.8–2.2)	Y	N	N	Y
		age 25	women		2.5 (1.4–4.6)				
		5 years ago	men		1.9 (1.2–3.1)				
		5 years ago	women		1.0 (0.5–1.8)				
Mellemgaard et al 1994	368	age 30	men	h vs l quartile BMI	1.4 (0.8–2.5)	Y	N	Y	Y
		age 30	women		2.3 (1.2–4.7)				
		age 50	men		1.1 (0.6–2.1)				
		age 50	women		2.4 (1.2–2.9)				

[a] Including one or more of: education, Quetelet's index, relative weight
[b] Calculated from distributions of cases and controls

trol study in Australia showed no appreciable association between obesity and renal pelvic cancer (McCredie and Stewart, 1992). In an Italian study that showed a decreased risk with obesity in men and no association in women (Talamini et al, 1990), the authors conceded that controls may have included patients admitted to hospitals for obesity-related diseases; the majority of controls were those with orthopaedic conditions such as low back pain, disc disorders, fractures and sprains.

The association between obesity and renal cell carcinoma appears to be more pronounced in females than in males, although there is controversy over the best way to measure the degree of obesity. Less is known about the importance of fat distribution and how age-related changes in adiposity may affect its relationship with risk in older populations. BMI or relative weight may not be as good an index of obesity in men, especially older men, as it is in women; measurements of body fat distribution may better predict risk in older men (Rimm et al, 1995). In fact, BMI in the remote past has been shown to be more predictive of renal cell carcinoma in men than more recent BMI measurements (Yu et al, 1986; McLaughlin et al, 1992; Kreiger et al, 1993; Mellemgaard et al, 1994). It has been hypothesised that obesity-related hormonal factors and altered lipid metabolism may be responsible for the increased risk associated with obesity (Wynder et al, 1974; Mellemgaard et al, 1994), but underlying mechanisms are essentially unknown. A plausible mechanism involves the generally growth-promoting environment of obesity (chapter 4.10).

High body mass probably increases the risk of renal cell carcinoma.

4.17.1.2 Fat and cholesterol
Total fat
Renal cancer is one of the cancers for which obesity has been identified as a probable risk factor (see above). To the extent that dietary fat leads to a positive energy balance and obesity, it may indirectly increase the risk of renal cancer.

No analytical epidemiological studies of renal cancer have reported on intake of total fat as such, although one case-control study reported an increased risk with higher intakes of saturated and animal fats (see below).

Two international ecological studies showed strong correlations between total fat intake and rates of kidney cancer (r = 0.77 men; 0.74, women) (Armstrong and Doll, 1975) (r = 0.8 for high animal fat intake) (Wynder et al, 1974).

Two experimental studies have investigated the effects of dietary fat on renal carcinogenesis. A study by Birt and Pour (1983) found that dietary fat (from corn oil) enhanced chemically-induced tumorigenesis in the kidneys of male Syrian hamsters (9% incidence), while a study by Clinton et al (1992) found no statistically significant relationship between the levels of dietary fat intake (from corn oil) and the occurrence of malignant lesions in the kidneys of male Sprague-Dawley rats.

Evidence relating to diets high in total fat and the risk of cancer of the kidney is limited; no judgement is possible.

Saturated/animal fat

A case-control study in the USA (Maclure and Willett, 1990) reported an increased risk with higher intake of saturated and animal fats, with odds ratios for the highest versus lowest quartiles of consumption of 1.3 (0.8–2.2) and 1.5 (0.9–2.5), respectively, adjusted for total calorie intake and other risk factors. A case-control study in Canada reported ORs of 1.0 (0.5–2.1) and 1.4 (0.6–3.3) for higher intakes of dairy fat for men and women, respectively (Kreiger et al, 1993).

In an ecological study of 15 countries (Wynder et al, 1974), mortality for male renal cancer was highly correlated with per capita consumption of animal fat (r = 0.83).

Meat and dairy products are considered to be major contributors to the amount of saturated fat in the overall diet. Some case-control studies have reported an increase in risk with higher consumption of meat and dairy products and these are reviewed separately below.

Evidence relating to diets high in saturated or animal fat and the risk of cancer of the kidney is limited; no judgement is possible.

Polyunsaturated/vegetable fat

A case-control study in Massachusetts (USA) reported no statistically significant association between the intake of vegetable fat and the risk of renal cancer (Maclure and Willett, 1990). In contrast, a hospital-based case-control study in northern Italy that reported on 240 cases of renal cell carcinoma found significant increases in risk of renal cell cancer with higher intakes of margarine (OR = 1.7) and oils (OR = 1.9) (Talamini et al, 1990).

Evidence relating to diets high in polyunsaturated/vegetable fat and the risk of renal cancer is limited and inconsistent; no judgement is possible.

Cholesterol

A case-control study involving 203 cases in the USA reported no statistically significant association between cholesterol intake and the risk of renal cancer (Maclure and Willett, 1990).

Egg consumption is considered to be a major contributor of cholesterol in the diet. Five case-control studies have examined egg consumption in relation to renal cancer risk and are reviewed below.

The information on cholesterol intake is based mainly on egg consumption. Based on the limited evidence on cholesterol as such, no judgement is possible.

4.17.1.3 Protein

Animal protein

High protein consumption has been related to the development of chronic renal conditions that may predispose to cancer.

In a case-control study in the USA, the intake of animal protein was related to a weakly increased risk; after adjustment for BMI, smoking, total energy intake and other non-dietary factors, an OR of 1.3 (0.8–2.1) was reported. However, the association with beef intake was stronger (OR = 3.4, 1.6–7.2) (Maclure and Willett, 1990).

An ecological study showed strong correlations between per capita consumption of animal protein and the international incidence and mortality rates for renal cancer (r = 0.81 for men and 0.83 for women) (Armstrong and Doll, 1975). A second study, using national food supply data from 15 countries, also reported a strong correlation in men (r = 0.80) (Wynder et al, 1974).

Experimental studies have not shown a direct effect of a high-protein diet on renal carcinogenesis. Low-protein diets fed during the initiation phase were associated with an increased risk of renal adenocarcinomas (p <0.001) in male Sprague-Dawley rats (Clinton et al, 1992) and in male Wistar rats of the Porton strain (McLean and Magee, 1970). In contrast, renal atrophy occurred in 13% of rats fed a high-protein diet compared with 4% of rats fed moderate-or low-protein diets (p = 0.023).

Evidence relating to diets high in animal protein and the risk of renal cancer is very limited; no judgement is possible.

4.17.1.4 Alcohol

Six case-control studies (conducted in the USA, the UK, Italy and Canada) have examined alcohol consumption and the risk of renal cancer. None found any significant increase in the risk of renal cell carcinoma with high alcohol consumption (wine, beer, spirits) (Wynder et al, 1974; Armstrong et al, 1976; McLaughlin et al, 1984; Maclure and Willett, 1990; Talamini et al, 1990; Kreiger et al, 1993). One study in the USA that involved 495 cases found beer consumption to show slightly elevated overall risk estimates but no clear trend in risk with increasing consumption (McLaughlin et al, 1984).

High alcohol consumption possibly has no relationship with the risk of renal cancer.

4.17.1.5 Vitamins

Carotenoids

Two case-control studies in the USA have investigated the relationship between carotene intake and renal cell carcinoma (McLaughlin et al, 1984; Maclure and Willett, 1990). In a population-based case-control study in Minneapolis involving 495 cases, a small decrease in risk with increasing carotene consumption was observed in men (OR= 0.8 for highest versus lowest quartile) but not in women

(McLaughlin et al, 1984). A case-control study in Boston involving 203 cases (Maclure and Willett, 1990) found that β-carotene intake was related to a moderate decrease in risk in both sexes combined (energy-adjusted OR = 0.6, 0.4–1.0, for highest versus lowest quartile).

No relevant experimental studies have been reported on carotenoids in renal carcinogenesis.

Evidence relating to high dietary carotenoids and the risk of renal cancer is very limited; no judgement is possible.

Vitamin C

Only one population-based case-control study of renal cell carcinoma has assessed intake of vitamin C. A small statistically non-significant decrease in risk was observed for a high intake of vitamin C (OR = 0.7) in men but not in women (McLaughlin et al, 1984).

Vitamin C supplementation has been shown to inhibit kidney carcinogenesis in animal models (Chen et al, 1988). In male Syrian hamsters, ascorbic acid reduced the frequency, but not the development and growth, of diethylstilboestrol-induced renal tumours (Liehr et al, 1989). The incidence of kidney tumours was lower (p < 0.05) in rats treated with a single dose of 1,2-dimethylhydrazine and fed 0.25% or 1.0% sodium ascorbate; such ascorbate treatment was not effective against multiple doses of the carcinogen (Reddy et al, 1982).

Evidence relating to high dietary vitamin C and the risk of renal cancer is very limited; no judgement is possible.

Retinol

Retinol intake was found to be unrelated to the risk of renal cell carcinoma in two case-control studies conducted in the USA, with odds ratios of 1.2–1.3 and 0.9 (0.5–1.5, p = 0.73), respectively (McLaughlin et al, 1984; Maclure and Willett, 1990).

No relevant experimental studies have been reported on the role of retinol in renal carcinogenesis.

Evidence relating to high dietary retinol and the risk of renal cancer is very limited; no judgement is possible.

4.17.2 FOODS AND DRINKS

4.17.2.1 Vegetables and fruits

There was no appreciable difference in the mortality rates from cancer of the kidney in relation to consumption levels of green–yellow vegetables in a Japanese prospective study (RR = 0.8) (Hirayama, 1990).

Five case-control studies (conducted in the USA, Italy and China) have examined whether consumption of vegetables and/or fruits is related to the risk of renal cell carcinoma (McLaughlin et al, 1984; Yu et al, 1986; Maclure and Willett,

1990; Talamini et al, 1990; McLaughlin et al, 1992). Three of these studies found a statistically significant protective association for at least one vegetable or fruit. Maclure and Willett (1990) found high consumption of vegetables to be generally related to a decreased risk, with spinach, cabbage and lentils showing statistically significant protective associations (ORs of 0.5, 0.6 and 0.8, respectively); Talamini et al, (1990) found a high intake of carrots to have a significant protective association (OR = 0.6, 0.4–0.9), and McLaughlin et al (1992) observed a statistically significant protective association between vegetables and the risk of renal cancer in men (OR = 0.3, 0.1–0.7) but not in women (OR = 1.6, 0.6–4.6). Of the remaining two studies, one showed statistically non-significant protective associations with cruciferous vegetables in men (OR = 0.8) and with fruits and vegetables combined in women (OR = 0.7) (McLaughlin et al, 1984), whereas the other (Yu et al, 1986) found no difference in the frequency of consumption of fresh fruits and vegetables between cases and controls.

Maclure and Willett (1990) found decreased risk to be associated with higher banana consumption (OR = 0.5), but no protective association was observed with a high consumption of stoned fruits. A study in China by McLaughlin et al (1992) demonstrated a significant protective association for fruits in men (OR = 0.2, 0.0–0.5), and a statistically non-significant association in women (OR = 0.7, 0.2–2.0). Two other case-control studies, one in the USA and one in Italy, found no association between fruit intake and the risk of renal cancer (Yu et al, 1986; Talamini et al, 1990).

In an international correlation study by Armstrong and Doll (1975), the per capita consumption of vegetables was weakly negatively correlated with renal cancer incidence in 23 countries and with renal cancer mortality in 34 countries.

Although not entirely consistent, the available epidemiological evidence suggests that diets high in vegetables possibly decrease the risk of renal cancer.

Evidence relating to diets high in fruit and the risk of renal cancer is limited; no judgement is possible.

4.17.2.2 Meat, poultry, fish and eggs

Meat

In a prospective study in Japan (Hirayama, 1990) those consuming meat daily had higher mortality from renal cancer than those eating meat less frequently.

Eight case-control studies have examined the relationship between meat consumption and renal cell carcinoma. Three of these studies found a statistically significant increase in risk with a high consumption of meat. In a study involving 495 cases in the USA, McLaughlin et al (1984) reported odds ratios of 1.5 (p < 0.05) for men and 1.6 (p < 0.05) for women. Another study in the USA (Maclure and Willett, 1990) also found that incident cases (both men and women) consumed more meat than controls; the adjusted odds ratio for an average intake of 85 g of beef per day was 3.4 (1.6–7.2), with ORs for other meat and related items (such

AUTHOR, YEAR AND PLACE	NO. OF CASES	SEX	COMPARISON	ODDS RATIO (95% CONFIDENCE INTERVAL)	AGE/ SEX	ENERGY INTAKE	ADJUSTMENT REPRODUCTIVE VARIABLES	OTHER VARIABLES[a]
Wynder et al, 1974	202	both	daily consumption between cases and controls	ns	N	N	N	Y
Armstrong et al, 1976	139	both	daily vs < daily	1.15[b] (0.51–2.65) 0.11[c] (0.00–0.8)	Y	N	N	Y
McLaughlin et al, 1984	495	men women	6+ cups vs 0 cups	1.0 (0.5–1.9) 1.2 (0.5–3.1)	Y Y	N	N	Y
McCredie et al, 1988	172	both	cases vs controls	ns				
Maclure and Willett, 1990	203	both	highest vs lowest intake	1.2 (ns) (0.63–2.2)	Y	N	N	Y
Talamini et al, 1990	240	both	highest vs lowest intake	1.4 (ns) (0.78–1.64)	Y	Y	N	N
McLaughlin et al, 1992	154	both	cases vs controls	ns				
Kreiger et al, 1993	518	men women	5+ cups daily vs < 1 cup daily	0.9 (ns) (0.5–1.6) 0.9 (ns) (0.5–1.5)	Y	N	N	Y
Yu et al, 1986	160	men women	5+ cups daily vs < 1 cup daily	0.9 (0.2–3.0) 4.3* (0.9–19.9)	Y	Y	N	Y

The table is titled: **TABLE 4.17.2 COFFEE CONSUMPTION AND THE RISK OF RENAL CANCER: CASE-CONTROL STUDIES**

* p < 0.06
[a] Including one or more of: education, Quetelet's index, relative weight
[b] Cancer of the parenchyma
[c] Cancer of the renal pelvis

as liver, pork, ham, chicken and fish) ranging from 0.6 to 1.5. The third case-control study to report an increase in the risk of renal cancer with high meat consumption was conducted in Shanghai, China (McLaughlin et al, 1992). This study examined 154 cases and 157 controls in an area with low rates for renal cell cancer. Among men, meat consumption was associated with a statistically significant increase in risk (OR = 4.0, 1.4–11.4; p = 0.005). In this study, as well as in two others (Armstrong et al, 1976; Kreiger et al, 1993), meat consumption was associated in women with small, statistically non-significant increases in risk, with ORs of 1.3, 1.3 and 1.6 respectively.

Three of the remaining studies (conducted in the USA, Australia and Italy) reported no relationship between meat consumption and renal cell carcinoma (Yu et al, 1986; McCredie et al, 1988; Talamini et al, 1990).

In the international correlation study by Armstrong and Doll (1975) renal cancer incidence was highly correlated with the per capita consumption of meat and milk (r = 0.70–0.74).

Animal protein and animal fat have been associated with cancer of the kidney in a small number of experimental studies (see above).

Diets high in meat possibly increase the risk of renal cancer.

Fish

Case-control studies in Canada and Italy have shown no statistically significant associations between the consumption of fish, a food high in omega-3 fatty acids, and the risk of renal cancer; odds ratios were in the range 0.7–1.0 (ns) for higher intakes (Talamini et al, 1990; Kreiger et al, 1992). A population-based case-control study in China (McLaughlin et al, 1992) observed decreased risk associated with higher

fish intakes in both men (OR = 0.4, 0.2–1.0) and women (OR = 0.7, 0.2–2.1).

Evidence relating to diets high in fish and the risk of renal cancer is limited and conflicting; no judgement is possible.

Eggs

Two case-control studies, one in the USA and one in Italy, have reported statistically non-significant odds ratios of 1.4 (0.7–3.0) (Maclure and Willett, 1990) and 1.2 (0.9–1.8) (Talamini et al, 1990) for the highest versus the lowest intake of eggs. A case-control study in England found no difference between controls and cases with parenchymal cancer in their frequency of consumption of eggs; however, patients with pelvic cancer showed a somewhat lower consumption of eggs (Armstrong et al, 1976). Two other case-control studies (conducted in Australia and the USA) found the risk of cancer of the renal parenchyma (McCredie et al, 1988) and the risk of cancer of the renal pelvis (Yu et al, 1986) to be unrelated to egg consumption.

Diets high in eggs possibly have no relationship with renal cancer.

4.17.2.4 Milk and dairy products

Daily milk users had an increased risk, relative to non-users, of 2.1 (1.4–3.3) in a Japanese prospective study (Hirayama, 1990).

Of seven case-control studies investigating the association of renal cancer with milk or dairy products, five reported ORs of 1.4 to 1.8 for the highest milk consumption (McLaughlin et al, 1984; McCredie et al, 1988; Maclure and Willett, 1990; Talamini et al, 1990; Kreiger et al, 1993), and one of these found a statistically significant increase in risk with the consumption of whole milk, (OR = 1.7, 1.1–2.8)

TABLE 4.17.3 TEA CONSUMPTION AND THE RISK OF RENAL CANCER: CASE-CONTROL STUDIES

Author, Year and Place	No. of Cases	Comparison	Odds Ratio (95% confidence interval)	Age/ Sex	Energy Intake	Adjustment Reproductive Variables	Other Variables[a]
Armstrong et al, 1976	139	Daily vs < daily	ns	Y	N	N	Y
McCredie et al, 1988	172	Cases vs controls	ns				
Maclure and Willett, 1990	203	2+ cups daily vs < 2 cups daily	0.93 (0.59–1.50)	Y	N	N	Y
Talamini et al, 1990	240	highest vs lowest intake	1.21 (0.81–1.82)	Y	Y	N	Y
La Vecchia et al, 1992	147	cases vs controls ≥ 1 cup daily	1.1 (0.7–1.7)	Y	N	N	Y
McLaughlin et al, 1992	154		ns				
Kreiger et al, 1993	518						
men		5+ cups daily vs	1.6 (ns) (0.8–2.9)	Y	N	N	Y
women		< 1 cup daily	1.1 (ns) (0.5–2.1)				

[a] Including one or more of: education, Quetelet's index, relative weight

(Maclure and Willett, 1990). Of the two remaining case-control studies, the association was not statistically significant in one (Yu et al, 1986) and null in the other (OR = 1.0, 0.5–2.0) (Armstrong et al, 1976).

Animal protein and animal fat have been associated with cancer of the kidney in a small number of experimental studies (see above).

Diets high in milk and dairy products possibly increase the risk of renal cancer.

4.17.2.5 Coffee, tea and other drinks
Coffee
A prospective study in Norway of 16,555 individuals reported a smoking-adjusted risk of cancer of the renal parenchyma of 0.3 (p = 0.008) with coffee consumption of seven or more cups per day compared with < 2 cups per day, in men only (Jacobsen et al, 1986).

Eight case-control studies have reported on coffee consumption and its relationship with the risk of renal cell carcinoma (Wynder et al, 1974; Armstrong et al, 1976; McLaughlin et al, 1984; McCredie et al, 1988; Maclure and Willett, 1990; Talamini et al, 1990; McLaughlin et al, 1992; Kreiger et al, 1993). All eight found there to be no relationship, and their results are summarised in Table 4.17.2. One case-control study in Los Angeles (Yu et al, 1986) reported a statistically significant increase in risk (p = 0.06) among women (but not men) who drank more than five cups of coffee daily.

In an ecological study, national per capita coffee consumption was shown to be moderately correlated with renal cancer mortality and incidence (Armstrong and Doll, 1975). However, adjustment for animal protein intake substantially reduced the magnitude of correlation between coffee and renal cancer incidence, from r = 0.62 to r = 0.31 in males, and from r = 0.40 to r = –0.18 in females.

Based on this fairly consistent evidence, high consumption of coffee probably has no relationship with the risk of renal cancer.

Tea
A cohort study conducted in Hawaii found no relationship between tea consumption and the risk of renal cancer (Heilbrun et al, 1986). A case-control study in Minneapolis (USA) (McLaughlin et al, 1984), reported an OR of 3.4 (1.4–8.9) in women consuming three cups or more of tea per day. A case-control study in Los Angeles (Yu et al, 1986) found an OR of 0.3 (0.1–0.9) in women drinking tea daily. There was no measurable association between tea and renal cell carcinoma in men in these studies, with ORs of 1.2 (0.6–2.3) (McLaughlin et al, 1984) and 0.7 (0.3–1.3) (Yu et al, 1986).

A further seven case-control studies have found tea to be unrelated to risk (Armstrong et al, 1976; McCredie et al, 1988; Maclure and Willett, 1990; Talamini et al, 1990; La Vecchia et al, 1992; McLaughlin et al, 1992; Kreiger et al, 1993). These studies are summarised in Table 4.17.3.

Although not specified directly in each study, tea is considered to be black tea in all of the studies except possibly the study in China (McLaughlin et al, 1992).

High consumption of (black) tea probably has no relationship with the risk of renal cancer.

4.17.3 FOOD PROCESSING

4.17.3.1 Microbial contamination
Mycotoxins
Among the naturally-occurring carcinogens, mycotoxins such as aflatoxin B_1 and aflatoxin G_1 are known to induce renal cell tumours in rats, with a 13–57% incidence (as well as a higher incidence of liver tumours). Other mycotoxins, including ochratoxin, citrinin and streptozotocin, also induce renal cell tumours (Shinohara et al, 1976; However, there has been no epidemiological evidence linking these mycotoxins with human renal cancer.

Evidence that mycotoxin contamination resulting from poor storage increases the risk of renal cancer is limited; no judgement is possible.

4.18 Bladder

Cancer of the bladder is the eleventh most common incident cancer. Three-quarters of all cases occur in men, among whom it is the eighth most common cancer. An estimated 310,000 cases occurred in 1996, accounting for 3% of all new cases of cancer.

Incidence of, and deaths from, this cancer are generally increasing, notably in economically developed societies.

The panel has reached the following conclusions. Diets high in vegetables and fruits probably protect against bladder cancer.

There is consistent evidence that a number of dietary factors are not associated with this cancer. The evidence that regular consumption of alcohol does not affect risk is convincing. Regular consumption of black tea and the sweetener saccharin probably does not affect risk. The panel also notes that cyclamates possibly do not affect risk.

Established non-dietary causes of bladder cancer are smoking; occupational exposure to carcinogenic chemicals; and infection with the *Schistosoma haematobium* parasite.

The most effective dietary means of preventing bladder cancer is consumption of diets high in vegetables and fruits.

FOOD, NUTRITION AND BLADDER CANCER

In the judgement of the panel, the dietary constituents and related factors, the foods and drinks and the methods of food processing listed below modify the risk of bladder cancer or else have no relationship with it. Judgements are graded according to the strength of the evidence.

EVIDENCE	DECREASES RISK	NO RELATIONSHIP	INCREASES RISK
Convincing		Alcohol	
Probable	Vegetables and fruits	Black tea Saccharin	
Possible		Eggs Cyclamates	Coffee[a]
Insufficient	Carotenoids Vitamin C Retinol		Total fat Chlorinated hydrocarbons Fried foods

For an explanation of the terms used in the matrix, see chapter 3.
[a] Risk appears to be elevated, if at all, only above 5 cups per day.

INTRODUCTION

INCIDENCE PATTERNS

Cancer of the bladder is the eleventh most common cancer in the world. In 1996, there were an estimated 310,000 new cases diagnosed worldwide (WHO, 1997), accounting for 3% of all new cancers.

Bladder cancer shows the highest incidence rates in North America, Europe, northern Africa and China. The incidence rates show an upward trend in the USA and most European countries, notably in men. Over 50% of cases are found in the developed world.

Incidence of bladder cancer is two to five times higher in men than in women (Parkin et al, 1992; Silverman et al, 1992); in 1996, approximately 75% of cases were male. In tropical and subtropical countries, where *Schistosoma*

> **BOX 4.5.1 ESTABLISHED NON-DIETARY FACTORS AND BLADDER CANCER**
>
> The following non-dietary factors increase the risk of bladder cancer:
> - ■ Smoking tobacco
> - ■ Specific occupational exposures
> - ■ Infestation: *Schistosoma haematobium*

haematobium is endemic, bladder cancer is the most common cancer in men, and second only to breast cancer in women, accounting for about 30% of all cancers (Badawi et al, 1995).

The predominant histological type of bladder cancer is transitional epithelial cell carcinoma (Silverman et al,

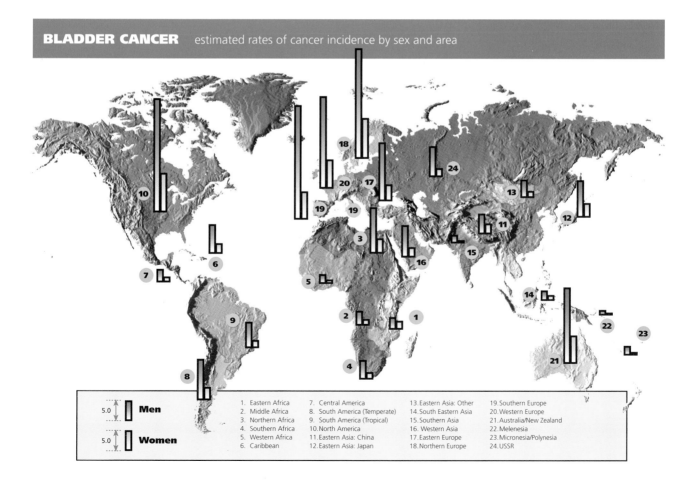

BLADDER CANCER estimated rates of cancer incidence by sex and area

1. Eastern Africa	7. Central America	13. Eastern Asia: Other	19. Southern Europe
2. Middle Africa	8. South America (Temperate)	14. South Eastern Asia	20. Western Europe
3. Northern Africa	9. South America (Tropical)	15. Southern Asia	21. Australia/New Zealand
4. Southern Africa	10. North America	16. Western Asia	22. Melenesia
5. Western Africa	11. Eastern Asia: China	17. Eastern Europe	23. Micronesia/Polynesia
6. Caribbean	12. Eastern Asia: Japan	18. Northern Europe	24. USSR

5.0 Men

5.0 Women

1992). However, squamous cell carcinoma is the major type in areas where urinary schistosomal infestation is prevalent (Badawi et al, 1995).

Survival among patients with cancer of the bladder is good, with a five-year survival of 90% for localised tumours. Mortality rates have recently declined in many countries (Coleman et al, 1993). In 1996, mortality attributable to bladder cancer was estimated at 144,000 people, 2% of all cancer deaths (WHO, 1997).

PATHOGENESIS

Of non-dietary factors, tobacco smoking is now regarded as the major cause of bladder cancer, accounting for at least 40–50% of all cases (IARC, 1986; Silverman et al, 1992). Occupational exposure to certain aromatic amines is another known cause of bladder cancer. However, the majority of these aromatic amine carcinogens are now either no longer used industrially or exposure of workers has been greatly minimised as a result of improved processing technology. It is estimated that about 19% of male and 6% of female bladder cancer cases can be attributed to occupational exposure to chemicals (IARC, 1980; Ward et al, 1991).

Although underlying mechanisms are not well understood, infestation with *Schistosoma haematobium* is undoubtedly the dominant cause of bladder cancer in certain areas (Badawi et al, 1995). Recent studies have shown that polymorphisms exist in the genes responsible for bioactivation and detoxification of carcinogenic aromatic amines (Kadlubar, 1994; Spruck et al, 1994); these compounds can be derived from tobacco smoke, occupational exposure and diet. Such susceptibility factors will need to be considered in future epidemiological studies on dietary factors and bladder cancer.

Some mutations and deletions in proto-oncogenes and tumour-suppressor gens have been described but the complete molecular pathogenesis remains unclear (Schulte, 1988)

JUDGEMENTS OF OTHER REPORTS

The National Academy of Sciences report, *Diet, Nutrition and Cancer* (NAS, 1982) concluded that coffee consumption had 'frequently been associated with cancer of the bladder', but that these relationships did not appear to be causal. Non-nutritive sweeteners (primarily saccharin) were not thought 'to be a significant risk factor'. The subsequent report, *Diet and Health* (NAS, 1989) noted that the risk of bladder cancer was clearly associated with the use of tobacco and various occupational exposures, and that the possible associations with the use of artificial sweeteners, consumption of alcohol, and coffee drinking, had not been confirmed.

REVIEW

4.18.1   DIETARY CONSTITUENTS

4.18.1 Fat and cholesterol

Total fat

One cohort study of Japanese men in Hawaii reported no association between total fat intake and the risk of bladder cancer, with a relative risk of 0.9 (0.5–1.4). The study assessed diet using a single 24-hour dietary recall (Chyou et al, 1993).

Four case-control studies of bladder cancer in Spain, New York, Washington State and Sweden have reported weak to moderate increases in risk with higher total fat intake (ORs ranging from 1.3 to 1.8, ns). In three studies the odd ratios were adjusted for total energy intake (Steineck et al, 1990; Riboli et al, 1991; Vena et al, 1992; Bruemmer et al, 1996).

An international ecological study showed substantial positive correlations between bladder cancer mortality and consumption of fats and oils (r = 0.7 for both males and females, p < 0.01 for females) (Armstrong and Doll, 1975).

One experimental study reported that neither saturated nor polyunsaturated fat had any promoting effect in bladder carcinogenesis (Kitano et al, 1995).

The evidence suggests that diets high in total fat may increase the risk of bladder cancer but is, as yet, insufficient.

Saturated/animal fat

One case-control study in Spain reported an increased risk of bladder cancer with higher intakes of saturated fat, OR = 2.3 (1.4–3.6) for the uppermost versus lowest quartile (Riboli et al, 1991). Another study, in Washington State (USA), reported a weaker increase in risk, with an odds ratio of 1.5 (0.7–3.2) for more than 41 g/day of saturated fat compared with less than 21 g/day (Bruemmer et al, 1996).

One experimental study reported no promoting effect of saturated fat in bladder carcinogenesis (Kitano et al, 1995).

Evidence relating to diets high in saturated/animal fat and the risk of bladder cancer is limited; no judgement is possible.

Cholesterol

One case-control study in Canada reported an increased risk of bladder cancer with higher cholesterol intake; the odds ratio for each 500 mg/day increase was 1.4; half of the cholesterol intake in this study was derived from eggs (Risch et al, 1988). (See also section 4.18.2 on Eggs.)

Evidence relating to diets high in cholesterol and the risk of bladder cancer amounts to only one study that examined cholesterol intake as such; no judgement is possible.

TABLE 4.18.1 ALCOHOL CONSUMPTION[a] AND BLADDER CANCER RISK: COHORT STUDIES

AUTHOR, YEAR AND PLACE	SIZE OF COHORT NO. OF CASES	ALCOHOL EXPOSURE FACTOR	COMPARISON[b]	RELATIVE RISK (95% CONFIDENCE INTERVAL)[c]	ADJUSTMENT		
					SEX/AGE	SMOKING HISTORY	OTHER FACTORS[c]
Mills et al, 1991 California, USA	34,198: 52 deaths	Alcohol	any vs none	1.3 (0.6–3.0) **	Y	Y	Y
Chyou et al, 1993 Hawaii, USA	8,006: 96 cases Japanese men[d]	Total alcohol	≥ 15 vs 0 g/day	1.2 (0.7–2.0) **	Y	Y	N

** p > 0.05 for trend and / or for comparison of highest vs lowest consumption level

[a] Table includes studies for which results for total alcohol intake or general alcohol consumption pattern were reported, and does not include studies for which only results on intake of specific alcoholic beverages were reported

[b] g = grams

[c] Adjusted for one or more of the following; rural residence; consumption of coffee, sweetened fruit juice, cooked green vegetables, meat/poultry/fish

[d] Cancer of the urinary tract; may include cancers of the ureter, renal pelvis and urethra in addition to cancer of the urinary bladder

4.18.1.2 Alcohol

In 1988, an IARC Working Group reviewing eight case-control studies, four cohort studies of alcoholics, one study of brewery workers and one cohort study of a general population group concluded that the evidence showed no association between alcohol drinking and the risk of bladder cancer. Many more studies have subsequently examined this relationship.

Two prospective and nineteen case-control studies are presented in Tables 4.18.1 and 4.18.2. These include the studies reviewed by the IARC Group, with the exceptions that studies with fewer than 20 cases, and studies of cohorts of alcoholics or brewery workers are not included.

Each of the two prospective studies shown in Table 4.18.1 reported an essentially null association for alcohol consumption; these cohorts were made up of Seventh-day Adventists in California and men of Japanese ancestry in Hawaii; the risk estimates for alcohol consumption were adjusted for smoking in both studies.

The 19 case-control studies shown in Table 4.18.2 were conducted in a variety of locations, including the USA, Canada, the UK, Denmark, Japan, Italy, Turkey, and France. Most often these studies examined alcohol consumption as a dichotomous variable, for example, 'ever', compared with 'never' consumption; 'yes', compared with 'no'; 'any' compared with 'none'; or 'user' compared with 'non-user'. Some studies, however, attempted to quantify intake and compared more than two consumption levels. Only one of the 19 studies reported any statistically significant association; this was a more than threefold higher risk for men in southern France who reported consuming more than 1,200 kg of alcohol over a lifetime, compared with less than 15 kg; this association was adjusted for smoking (Momas et al, 1994). Of the 27 statistically non-significant associations described in Table 4.18.2, relating to different measures of alcohol consumption, and presented separately for the two sexes in some studies, 20 odds ratios were between 0.75 and 1.5 (or there was said to be 'no association', but an odds ratio was not quoted), four were 0.75 or lower, and four were 1.5 or higher.

In nine of the 21 epidemiological studies in Tables 4.18.1 and 4.18.2, the risk estimates for alcohol consumption were adjusted for smoking habits. In eight studies, associations were presented separately for men and women, but no difference in the pattern of associations was apparent between the sexes; the majority of the associations were near null.

> Based on a large number of consistent epidemiological studies, the evidence that high alcohol intake has no relationship with the risk of bladder cancer is convincing .

4.18.1.3 Vitamins

Carotenoids

One cohort study of bladder cancer in elderly people in California (USA) reported a relative risk of 1.3 (ns) for men with a higher intake of β-carotene (Shibata et al, 1992).

Of seven case-control studies that have examined intakes of total carotene or β-carotene, two have reported strong or moderate protective associations, with ORs in the range 0.4–0.5 for higher intakes (in men younger than 65 years only in one study) (La Vecchia et al, 1989; Vena et al, 1992). Another study reported weak protective associations for both sexes (ORs of 0.5 (ns) and 0.7 (ns) for women and men, respectively) for the uppermost versus lowest quartile of intake (Nomura et al, 1991). The four other studies reported no material associations (ORs = 0.9–1.3, ns) for higher intakes (Risch et al, 1988; Steineck et al, 1990; Riboli et al, 1991; Bruemmer et al, 1996). Adjustment was made for smoking in all of these studies and for total energy intake in three (Riboli et al, 1991; Vena et al, 1992 ; Bruemmer et al, 1996).

In four prospective studies that examined serum β-carotene levels, no significant differences were noted

TABLE 4.18.2 ALCOHOL CONSUMPTION[a] AND BLADDER CANCER RISK: CASE-CONTROL STUDIES

AUTHOR, YEAR AND PLACE	CASES (NO.)	EXPOSURE	COMPARISON[b]	RELATIVE RISK (95% CONFIDENCE INTERVAL)[c]	ADJUSTMENT SEX/AGE	SMOKING HISTORY	OTHER FACTORS[d]
Dunham et al, 1968 New Orleans, USA	493	Alcoholic beverages	heavy vs occasional use	no assoc	Y/N	N	Y
Morgan & Jain, 1974	74 women	Alcohol	intake vs no intake	0.9 [f]	Y	Y	N
Toronto, Canada	158 men	Alcohol	intake vs no intake	0.4 [g]	Y	Y	N
Williams & Horn	73 women	Lifetime total alcohol	high vs low oz-yrs	0.8 **	Y	Y	Y
1977, USA	206 men	Lifetime total alcohol	high vs low oz-yrs	0.4 **	Y	Y	Y
Wynder & Goldsmith	158 women	Alcohol	high vs low	no assoc	Y	N	Y
1977, USA	574 men	Alcohol	high vs low	no assoc	Y	N	Y
Howe et al, 1980	152 women	Alcohol	ever vs never use	0.8 (0.4–1.4)	Y	N	N
Canada	480 men	Alcohol	ever vs never use	0.9 (0.6–1.2)	Y	N	N
Cartwright et al, 1981	210 women [e]	Alcohol	ever vs never	1.1 (0.7–1.7)	Y	N	N
West Yorkshire, UK	631 men [e]	Alcohol	ever vs never	1.1 (0.9–1.4)	Y	N	N
Sullivan, 1982 New Orleans, USA	82	Alcoholic beverages	[h]	no assoc	N	N	N
Mommsen et al, 1982 Aarhus, Denmark	165 men	Alcohol	user vs non-user	1.7	Y	Y	Y
Najem et al, 1982 New Jersey, USA	75	Alcohol	yes vs no	1.0 (0.6–1.9)	Y	N	Y
Mommsen et al, 1983 Aarhus, Denmark	47 women	Alcohol-drinking habits	na	no assoc	Y	N	Y
Thomas et al, 1983	725 women	Alcoholic drinks	≥ 42 servings/wk vs none	1.0**	Y	Y	Y
USA	2,226 men	Alcoholic drinks	≥ 42 servings/wk vs none	0.7**	Y	Y	Y
Ohno et al, 1985	66 women	Alcoholic beverages	ever vs never use	0.6 (0.3–1.1)	Y	Y	Y
Nagoya, Japan	227 men	Alcoholic beverages	ever vs never use	0.8 (0.6–1.2)	Y	Y	Y
Wynder et al, 1985 USA	194 men	Alcohol	na	no assoc	Y	na	Y
Brownson et al	823 men	Alcohol use	ex- vs never drinkers	0.9 (0.5–1.5)	Y	Y	N
1987, Missouri, USA			current vs never drinkers	1.1 (0.9–1.3)	Y	Y	N
Risch et al, 1988	826						
Canada	women	Total alcohol	per 20 ml/day	1.3 (1.0–1.8)	Y	N	Y
	men	Total alcohol	per 20 ml/day	0.97 (0.95–1.00)	Y	N	Y
Slattery et al, 1988 Utah, USA	332 men	Alcohol	any vs none	1.5 [i]	Y/N	N	N
La Vecchia et al 1989, Northern Italy	163	Alcohol	h vs l tertile	0.9 **	Y	N	N
Akdas et al, 1990 Turkey	194	Alcohol	ever- vs non-drinkers	1.7	Y	N	N
Momas et al, 1994 Southern France	219 men	Lifelong alcohol drinking	> 1,200,000 vs < 15,000 g/lifetime	3.1 (1.2–8.2)	Y	Y	Y

* p ≤ 0.05 for trend and / or for comparison of highest vs lowest consumption level

** p > 0.05 for trend and / or for comparison of highest vs lowest consumption level

[na] information not available or unclear from article

[a] Table includes studies for which results for total alcohol intake or general alcohol consumption pattern were reported, and does not include studies for which only results on intake of specific alcoholic beverages were reported

[b] g = grams; h = highest; l = lowest; ml = millilitres; oz = ounces; wk = week; yr = year

[c] 95% CI = 95% confidence interval; assoc = association

[d] Adjusted, matched and/or stratified for one or more of the following; race; hospital; type of case (prevalent vs incident); nocturia; prostatic surgery; cheroot smoking; socio-economic level; work with oil or gasoline; previous veneral disease; use of chewing tobacco; industrial work; work with petroleum or asphalt; symptoms of cystitis; work with chemical materials; geographic area; place of birth; residence; hazardous occupational exposure; year of interview; lifelong coffee-drinking; spice consumption; occupation at high risk for bladder cancer; residence in non-Mediterranean area; infrequent consumption of spinach, carrots, marrows; birthplace in Mediterranean area; saccharin intake

[e] Includes prevalent, as well as incident cases

[f] OR is for never smokers; OR = 1.7 for alcohol intake among ever smoking women

[g] OR is for never smokers; OR = 1.4 for alcohol intake among ever smoking men

[h] No statistically significant difference between cases and controls in average consumption

[i] OR = 2.2 (0.8–6.1) among never smokers

[j] This study was part of the collaborative study by Thomas et al, 1983, for which results are also given in the table

between subsequent bladder cancer cases and controls (Nomura et al, 1985; Wald et al, 1988; Helzlsouer et al, 1989; Knekt et al, 1990), although one study reported previously lower levels of serum lycopene in cases than in controls (p = 0.07) (Helzlsouer et al, 1989). Results from these studies were based on relatively small populations (fewer than 35 cases).

The majority of epidemiological studies of bladder cancer that have examined either dietary or serum carotenoids have reported no association, although a few suggest a reduced risk. The overall pattern of epidemiological associations is consistent with a marginally reduced risk, but is possibly the consequence of carotenoids being markers of the intake of plant foods, rather than being themselves the active agents.

The evidence suggests that high dietary carotenoid intake may decrease the risk of bladder cancer but is, as yet, insufficient.

Vitamin C

One prospective study of bladder cancer in California (USA) observed no material association for dietary vitamin C intake, RR = 0.9 (0.5–1.7) for the uppermost versus lowest tertile (Shibata et al, 1992).

Of six case-control studies that examined vitamin C intake, one in Washington State (USA) reported a moderate protective association (OR = 0.5, 0.3–0.9) for dietary vitamin C intakes of >156 mg/day, compared with 78 mg/day or less; this association was adjusted for smoking, total energy and other factors (Bruemmer et al, 1996). Another study, in Hawaii, reported a statistically non-significant protective association (OR = 0.6, 0.2–1.4) for higher intakes among women, but no association in men (Nomura et al, 1991). Results from the other four studies were essentially null, with odds ratios ranging from 0.9 to 1.2 for higher intakes (Risch et al, 1988; Steineck et al, 1990; Riboli et al, 1991; Vena et al, 1992). Overall, only one out of seven epidemiological studies has shown a statistically significant association between dietary vitamin C intake and the risk of bladder cancer.

The use of vitamin C supplements has been shown to be associated with some degree of reduced risk in one prospective study and three case-control studies. In the Californian cohort mentioned above, a relative risk of 0.6 (0.4–0.9) was reported for those who had used vitamin C supplements at least once per week, whereas no association was observed for dietary vitamin C (Shibata et al, 1992). In a case-control study in Washington State (USA) a strong protective association was reported for intakes greater than 502 mg/day from supplements compared with none (OR = 0.4, 0.2–0.8) (adjusted for smoking) (Bruemmer et al, 1996). In a Swedish case-control study, the odds ratio for high use of supplements was 0.7 (0.4–1.3) (Steineck et al, 1990); in a study in Hawaii, ORs were 0.5 (0.3–1.1) and 1.2 (0.8–1.8) for women and

men, respectively (Nomura et al, 1991).

Vitamin C has been shown to inhibit carcinogen-induced bladder tumours in some, but not all, experimental studies. In one experiment, the formation of 3-hydroxyanthranilic acid-induced urinary bladder tumours in mice was shown to be inhibited by ascorbic acid (Pipkin et al, 1969). Ascorbate has also been shown to have no effect on urinary bladder tumours induced by N-butyl-N(4-hydroxybutyl) nitrosamine in rats (Fukushima et al, 1984), or N-[4-(5-nitro-2-furyl)-2-thiazolyl] formamide in mice (Soloway et al, 1975). On the other hand, vitamin C actually increased the incidence of preneoplastic bladder lesions in mice treated with 2-acetyl-aminofluorene (Frith et al, 1980). Decreased water consumption may have contributed to the severity of these lesions. High dietary levels of sodium ascorbate have been shown to promote chemically induced bladder tumours in other experiments as well (Fukushima et al, 1983). However, it is recognised that sodium salts of organic and inorganic chemicals, such as sodium citrate and sodium bicarbonate, promote urinary bladder carcinogenesis (Fukushima et al, 1986a,b; Cohen et al, 1991) at high doses that are probably irrelevant to normal human usage. The high dietary sodium results in an increase in urinary pH and sodium ion concentration, which plays an important role in rat bladder carcinogenesis (Fukushima et al, 1986a,b; 1987).

Vitamin C inhibits the formation of nitrosamines, which are potential human bladder carcinogens (Preston-Martin and Correa, 1989) and may also exert an anticancer effect as an antioxidant that blocks oxidative DNA damage (Steinmetz and Potter, 1991).

The majority of the epidemiological data on vitamin C from diet shows no relationship with bladder cancer; some studies show a decreased risk with higher intakes. As with carotenoids, this pattern is consistent with vitamin C being a marker of intakes of vegetables and fruit without itself being a causal protective agent. However, several studies that examined the intake of vitamin C from supplements suggest a decreased risk with higher intakes. The results of experimental studies have been mixed; plausible biological mechanisms have been identified.

Evidence suggests that high dietary vitamin C intake may decrease the risk of bladder cancer but is, as yet, insufficient.

Folate

One case-control study in Washington State (USA) reported no material association between dietary intake of folate and the risk of bladder cancer (OR = 0.9, 0.5–1.6 for the uppermost versus lowest quartile). However, a protective association was reported for folate intake from diet and supplements combined (OR = 0.5, 0.3–0.9 for the uppermost quartile). Both associations were adjusted for smoking and total calorie intake (Bruemmer et al, 1996).

The evidence relating to high dietary folate and the risk of bladder cancer is very limited; no judgement is possible.

Retinol

Seven case-control studies of bladder cancer have examined the relationship between retinol intake and the risk of bladder cancer. Two have shown a moderate to strong protective association (OR = 0.4, p < 0.01 for trend) for the highest tertile in a study in Italy (La Vecchia et al, 1989), and OR = 0.5 (0.3–0.97, p = 0.03 for trend) for more than 3,338 IU/day compared with less than 1,163 IU/day in a study in the USA (Bruemmer et al, 1996). One study reported a statistically non-significant increase in risk with higher intake in men, but not in women (OR = 1.6, 0.9–2.7 and 1.0, 0.4–2.8, respectively) (Nomura et al, 1991). The four remaining studies reported no statistically significant associations (Risch et al, 1988; Steineck et al, 1990; Riboli et al, 1991; Vena et al, 1992).

Two prospective studies found no statistically significant difference in mean previous serum retinol levels between subsequent cases and controls (Nomura et al, 1985; Helzlsouer et al, 1989), whereas a third study suggested a protective association in males; the smoking-adjusted relative risk was not statistically significant at 0.1 (0.01–1.1) (Knekt et al, 1990).

Retinol and its analogues (retinoids) have been shown before, during or after carcinogen treatment to inhibit bladder carcinogenesis in experimental studies (Sporn et al, 1976; Murasaki et al, 1980; Moon and Mehta, 1986).

Based upon these somewhat inconsistent data, the evidence suggests that higher dietary retinol intake may decrease the risk of bladder cancer but is, as yet, insufficient.

Vitamin E

Of three case-control studies that examined dietary vitamin E intake and the risk of bladder cancer, one reported an odds ratio of 0.7 (0.5–1.1) for the highest intake level (Riboli et al, 1991), another an odds ratio of 0.7 (0.4–1.1) for more than 9 mg/day compared with 5 mg/day or less (Bruemmer et al, 1996), and the third found no statistically significant association (data not provided) (Vena et al, 1992).

Of the two prospective studies that have examined serum vitamin E levels, neither found a significant difference in values for cases compared with controls; these results were based upon relatively few cases (≤ 35) (Nomura et al, 1985; Helzlsouer et al, 1989).

One study in rats showed no effect of vitamin E on BBN-induced cancer of the bladder (see review by Knekt, 1991).

Based on these limited data, and the general problem of assessing dietary vitamin E intake with accuracy, no judgement is possible.

4.18.1.4 Minerals

Selenium

Three prospective studies have examined the relationship between serum selenium levels and the risk of bladder cancer. Two studies (Nomura et al, 1987; Helzlsouer et al, 1989) have reported a lower risk, RR = 0.5, p = 0.03 for trend for the uppermost tertile and RR = 0.3, p = 0.13 for trend for the uppermost quintile. The other study observed no difference between cases and controls (Knekt et al, 1990).

Evidence that high dietary selenium intake decreases the risk of bladder cancer is limited; no judgement is possible.

4.18.2 FOODS AND DRINKS

4.18.2.1 Vegetables and fruits

Five prospective studies have examined the relationship of bladder cancer to vegetable and fruit consumption, either as a group, or as individual vegetables or fruits; these are presented in Table 4.18.3. Studies in Sweden and Japan reported null associations with fruit and vegetables combined, and green–yellow vegetables, respectively (Steineck et al, 1988; Hirayama, 1990); these single, non-specific, collective variables were the only vegetable and/or fruit items queried in these studies and, might therefore be interpreted with caution. Within a cohort of Californian Seventh-day Adventists, higher intakes of cooked green vegetables and sweetened fruit juice were associated with a decreased risk, but no associations were noted for consumption of green salad or fresh citrus fruit (Mills et al, 1991). In another Californian cohort, no material associations were observed in males for consumption of vegetables or fruits as a whole, or for dark green or yellow vegetables, with the exception of a suggested decrease in risk with a higher intake of fruit in men (Shibata et al, 1992). A study in Hawaii reported statistically non-significant protective associations for a higher consumption of fruit and various types of seaweed; on the other hand, intakes of fried vegetables were associated with a more than twofold, but statistically non-significant, increase in risk (see also section 4.18.3 on Grilling, barbecuing and frying) (Chyou et al, 1993). The majority of these cohort studies were based on fewer than 100 cases of bladder cancer (Steineck et al, 1988; Mills et al, 1991; Shibata et al, 1992; Chyou et al, 1993).

Nine case-control studies of bladder cancer that have examined some aspect of vegetable and/or fruit consumption are presented in Table 4.18.4. An early US study, reported a moderate protective association with a higher consumption of carrots (Mettlin and Graham, 1979). A study in Germany reported a statistically non-significant decrease in risk in men, but not women, if fresh vegetables and fruit were eaten regularly (Claude et al, 1986). A study in Hawaii found some evidence of protective associations for dark green vegetables in men, and carrots in women; but each of these vegetables appeared to decrease the risk in only one sex, and higher intakes of papaya and tomatoes were unre-

TABLE 4.18.3 VEGETABLE AND FRUIT CONSUMPTION AND BLADDER CANCER RISK: COHORT STUDIES

AUTHOR, YEAR AND PLACE	SIZE OF COHORT: NO. OF CASES	TYPE OF VEGETABLE OR FRUIT	COMPARISON[a]	RELATIVE RISK (95% CONFIDENCE INTERVAL)[b]	ADJUSTMENT SEX/AGE	SMOKING HISTORY	OTHER FACTORS[c]
Steineck et al 1988, Sweden	16,477: 80	Fruit and vegetables	na	1.0 (0.6–1.6)	Y	N	N
Hirayama et al 1990, Japan		Green-yellow vegetables		no assoc			
Mills et al, 1991 California, USA	34,198 52 deaths	Sweetened real fruit juice	≥ 1 vs < 1/wk	0.3 (0.1–1.0) *	Y	Y	N
		Cooked green vegetables	≥ 1 vs < 1/day	0.5 (0.3–1.1) **	Y	Y	N
		Fresh citrus fruits	na	no assoc	N	N	N
		Green salads	na	no assoc[e]	N	N	N
Shibata et al, 1992 California, USA	71 cases	All vegetables and fruit	≥ 7.9 vs < 5.5 servings/day	0.9 (0.5–1.6)	Y	Y	N
		All vegetables	≥ 4.5 vs < 3.0 servings/day	1.1 (0.6–1.9)	Y	Y	N
		All fruit	≥ 3.5 vs < 2.2 servings/day	0.6 (0.3–1.1)	Y	Y	N
		Dark green vegetables	≥ 0.3 vs < 0.1 servings/day	0.9 (0.5–1.7)	Y	Y	N
		Yellow vegetables	≥ 0.7 vs < 0.3 servings/day	1.1 (0.6–1.4)	Y	Y	N
Chyou et al, 1993 Hawaii, USA	8,006: 96	Fruit	≥ 5 vs ≤ 1/wk	0.6 (0.4–1.1) *	Y	Y	N
		Nori, kobu & other seaweeds	≥ 5 vs ≤ 1/wk	0.4 (0.1–1.6)**	Y	Y	N
		Fried vegetables	≥ 5 vs ≤ 1/wk	2.6 (0.6–10.4) **	Y	Y	N

* p ≤ 0.05 for trend and/or for comparison of highest vs lowest consumption level

** p > 0.05 for trend and/or for comparison of highest vs lowest consumption level

na information unclear or not available from article

a wk = week

b assoc = association

d Cancer of the urinary tract; may include cancers of the ureter, renal pelvis, and urethra in addition to cancer of the urinary bladder

e RR < 1.0 (statistically non-significant)

lated to risk (Nomura et al, 1991). A study in Italy reported strong to moderate protective associations for higher intakes of carrots, green vegetables and fruit (La Vecchia et al, 1989; Negri et al, 1991). In a study in Washington State (USA) a statistically significant protective association was observed for fruit; less striking associations were observed for vegetables as a whole or tomatoes (Bruemmer et al, 1996).

Another case-control study, in France, reported that more cases than controls consumed carrots, spinach and marrows (combined) infrequently, although intake of other vegetables was not found to differ between cases and controls (Momas et al, 1994). In Uruguay, protective associations were observed with a higher consumption of green and yellow vegetables and raw fruit (DeStefani et al, 1991). In a study in New York, a statistically significant decrease in risk was reported for a greater consumption of several vegetable and fruit items, including celery, lettuce, carrots, green peppers, squash, peas, bananas and oranges (Vena et al, 1992). Contrary to much of this evidence, a study in Spain reported no association with either higher intakes of vegetables or fruits in general, or of carrots, tomatoes, or green and red peppers in particular (Riboli et al, 1991).

The vast majority of the associations in Tables 4.18 3 and 4.18.4 suggest a decreased risk of, or no relationship to, bladder cancer for higher vegetable and/or fruit consumption; almost all of the risk estimates are 1.0 or lower; no statistically significant increase in risk was reported in any study. Of the 14 analytical epidemiological studies, three examined vegetables as a collective grouping and each found no asso-

ciation (Riboli et al, 1991; Shibata et al, 1992; Bruemmer et al, 1996). Six studies examined fruit or raw fruit as a grouping (DeStefani et al, 1991; Negri et al, 1991; Riboli et al, 1991; Shibata et al, 1992; Chyou et al, 1993; Bruemmer et al, 1996). Five of these reported some degree of decreased risk with higher consumption (in men only, in one study) (DeStefani et al, 1991; Negri et al, 1991; Shibata et al, 1992; Chyou et al, 1993; Bruemmer et al, 1996). Odds ratios ranged from 0.4 to 0.6 in the four of these studies reporting risk estimates (not all were statistically significant). Seven studies reported on leafy vegetables, such as dark green vegetables, cooked green vegetables, green and yellow vegetables, or various types of seaweed; five of these reported some degree of decreased risk with higher intakes in one or both sexes, with risk estimates ranging from 0.3 to 0.6 (not all were statistically significant) (DeStefani et al, 1991; Negri et al, 1991; Nomura et al, 1991; Mills et al, 1991; Chyou et al, 1993). In the other two studies, both prospective, no association was reported for consumption of green vegetables (Hirayama, 1990; Shibata et al, 1992). Four out of the five studies that examined carrot consumption reported protective associations (in women, but not in men, in one study) (Mettlin and Graham, 1979; Negri et al, 1991; Nomura et al, 1991; Riboli et al, 1991; Vena et al, 1992); these were statistically significant in three studies.

In many of the epidemiological studies shown in Tables 4.18.3 and 4.18.4, the vegetable and/or fruit associations were adjusted for smoking, which is recognised to be the most important risk factor for bladder cancer (Claude et al,

TABLE 4.18.4 VEGETABLE AND FRUIT CONSUMPTION AND BLADDER CANCER RISK: CASE-CONTROL STUDIES

Author, year and place	No. of cases	Type of vegetable or fruit	Comparison[a]	Odds ratio (95% confidence interval)[b]	Sex/Age	Adjustment Smoking history	Other factors[c]
Mettlin & Graham 1979, New York, USA	569	Carrots	> 2/wk < 1/m	0.6 *	Y	N	N
		Cruciferous vegetables	≥ 15 vs ≤ 4/m	0.7 **	Y	N	N
Claude et al, 1986 Northern Germany	91 women [d]	Fresh fruits and vegetables	regularly vs not	0.9 (0.4–2.2)	Y	N	N
	340 men [d]	Fresh fruits and vegetables	regularly vs not	0.6 **	Y	Y	Y
La Vecchia et al 1989 Northern Italy	365	Green vegetables	h vs l tertile	0.3 (0.2–0.4) *	Y	Y	Y
		Fruit	h vs l tertile	0.4 (0.3–0.6) *	Y	Y	Y
Negri et al, 1991	163	Carrots	high vs low (3 groups)	0.6 *	Y	Y	Y
Nomura et al, 1991 Hawaii, USA	66 women [d]	Carrots	h vs l quartile	0.5 **	Y	Y	Y
		Papaya	h vs l quartile	1.3 **	Y	Y	Y
		Tomatoes	h vs l quartile	0.9 **	Y	Y	Y
		Dark green vegetables	h vs l quartile	0.8 **	Y	Y	Y
	195 men [d]	Carrots	h vs l quartile	1.0 **	Y	Y	Y
		Papaya	h vs l quartile	1.2 **	Y	Y	Y
		Tomatoes	h vs l quartile	0.7 **	Y	Y	Y
		Dark green vegetables	h vs l quartile	0.6 *	Y	Y	Y
De Stefani et al, 1991 Montevideo, Uruguay	111	Green & yellow vegetables	non-infrequent	protective assoc	Y	N	N
		Raw fruit	non-infrequent	protective assoc	Y	N	N
Riboli et al, 1991 Spain	432 men	Vegetables	h vs l quartile	1.0 (0.7–1.5) **	Y	Y	Y
		Fruit	h vs l quartile	1.0 (0.7–1.4) **	Y	Y	Y
		Carrots	na	no assoc	Y	na	na
		Tomatoes	na	no assoc	Y	na	na
		Green & red peppers	na	no assoc	Y	na	na
Vena et al, 1992 New York, USA	351 men	Lettuce	[e]	protective assoc	Y	N	Y
		Carrots	[e]	protective assoc	Y	N	Y
		Peas	[e]	protective assoc	Y	N	Y
		Celery	[e]	protective assoc	Y	N	Y
		Green peppers	[e]	protective assoc	Y	N	Y
		Squash	[e]	protective assoc	Y	N	Y
		Bananas	[e]	protective assoc	Y	N	Y
		Oranges	[e]	protective assoc	Y	N	Y
Momas et al, 1994 Southern France	219 men	Carrots, spinach, marrows	not infrequent vs infrequent	0.6 (0.4–0.9)	Y	Y	Y
Bruemmer et al, 1996 Washington State, USA	262	Fruit	> 2.7 vs ≤ 0.9/day	0.5 (0.3–0.9) *	Y	Y	Y
		Vegetables	> 3.6 vs ≤ 1.3/day	0.9 (0.5–1.5)	Y	Y	Y
		Tomatoes	> 0.29 vs ≤ 0.07/day	0.7 (0.4–1.3)	Y	Y	Y

* p ≤ 0.05 for trend and/or for comparison of highest vs lowest consumption level

** p > 0.05 for trend and/or for comparison of highest vs lowest consumption level

[na] Information not unavailable or unclear from publication

[a] h = highest; l = lowest; m = month; wk = week

[b] assoc = association

[c] Adjusted or matched for one or more of the following: high-risk industries; high-risk occupational exposures; bladder infection; consumption of beer, coffee, spirits; daily fluid intake; canned food eaten often; fatty meals eaten often; familial bladder cancer; social class; area of residence; education; ethnic group; total calories; neighbourhood of residence; lifelong coffee-drinking; spice consumption; occupation at risk for bladder cancer; residence in non-Mediterranean area; lifelong alcohol-drinking; birthplace in a Mediterranean area; saccharin intake

[d] Cancer of the lower urinary tract; may include cancers of the ureter, renal pelvis, and urethra in addition to cancer of the urinary bladder

[e] Cases consumed less on average than controls (statistically significant)

1986; La Vecchia et al, 1989; Mills et al, 1991; Negri et al, 1991; Nomura et al, 1991; Riboli et al, 1991; Shibata et al, 1992; Chyou et al, 1993; Momas et al, 1994; Bruemmer et al, 1996). Protective associations for specific vegetables or fruits were apparent in some studies after such adjustment (Mills et al, 1991; La Vecchia et al, 1989; Negri et al, 1991; Nomura et al, 1991; Momas et al, 1994; Bruemmer et al, 1996).

There are 14 individual-level epidemiological studies of vegetable and fruit consumption and the risk of bladder cancer. Almost all studies have reported either a decreased risk or no relationship with higher consumption for a variety of specific vegetable and/or fruit categories. Some studies have observed decreased risk after adjustment for cigarette smoking. The evidence has been most abundant and consistent for fruit, green vegetables, and carrots.

Diets high in vegetables and fruits probably decrease the risk of bladder cancer.

4.18.2.2 Pulses (legumes)

Two cohort studies of bladder cancer have reported results for pulses. No association was found for beans, peas, and lentils in a Seventh-day Adventist cohort (Mills et al, 1991), nor was an association found for tofu in a study in Hawaii (Chyou et al, 1993).

Evidence relating to diets high in pulses and the risk of bladder cancer is very limited; no judgement is possible.

4.18.2.3 Meat, poultry, fish and eggs

Meat

Four prospective studies have examined the relationship between bladder cancer and meat consumption. A study in Sweden reported a 2.2-fold (1.1–4.4) increase in risk with a higher intake of pork and beef (Steineck et al, 1988). A prospective study of Seventh-day Adventists in California also observed an increased risk with consumption of meat, poultry, and fish combined; the relative risk was 2.4 (1.2–4.6) for consumption three or more times per week compared with less often (Mills et al, 1991). A relative risk of 1.5 (0.8–3.2) (p for trend = 0.33) was noted when meat was consumed five or more times per week, compared with once or less often, in a prospective study in Hawaii (Chyou et al, 1993). A Japanese prospective study observed a relative risk of 1.0 for the daily consumption of meat compared with less frequent consumption (Hirayama, 1990).

Four case-control studies have examined meat consumption. A study in Sweden reported an essentially null association for weekly consumption of meat, pork and sausages (not fried) (OR = 0.8, 0.3–1.9). However, the odds ratio was 1.4 (0.6–3.3) for almost daily, compared with less than weekly, consumption of these same meats in fried form (Steineck et al, 1990). Two studies, in Italy and Germany, reported no material associations for the uppermost versus lowest tertile of meat intake or 'meat eaten frequently', respectively, with statistically non-significant odds ratios ranging from 1.0 to 1.5 for different subgroups (Claude et al, 1986; La Vecchia et al, 1989). Another study in Spain observed a statistically significant decrease in risk for meat consumption in the uppermost quartile (OR= 0.7) (Riboli et al, 1991).

These epidemiological data, particularly those derived from the cohort studies, suggest if anything increased risk with higher meat consumption. However, the pattern is different between the cohort and the case control studies. On the basis of these conflicting data, no judgement is possible.

Eggs

Three prospective studies of bladder cancer have shown essentially no association with egg consumption (Steineck et al,1988; Mills et al, 1991; Chyou et al, 1993).

A case-control study in Sweden reported a null associa-

tion with weekly consumption of boiled eggs, but an increased risk with fried eggs, OR = 1.0 (0.6–1.6) and 1.8 (1.0–3.1), respectively (Steineck et al, 1990). Another case-control study noted a statistically significant increase in risk associated with egg consumption, although the relevant data were not provided (Vena et al, 1992). A study in Italy reported a statistically non-significant odds ratio of 0.8 for the highest level of egg consumption (La Vecchia et al, 1989). In a study showing a strong positive association with cholesterol intake, half the calculated cholesterol intake was derived from eggs, but the association with egg consumption itself was not reported (Risch et al, 1988).

High egg consumption possibly has no relationship with the risk of bladder cancer.

4.18.2.4 Milk and dairy products

Of three prospective studies that have examined milk consumption, two have shown essentially no relationship with bladder cancer (Steineck et al, 1988; Mills et al, 1991) whereas the third study, in Hawaii, reported a decreased risk, for consumption more than five times per week compared with less than once (RR= 0.6, 0.4–1.0; p = 0.07 for trend) (Chyou et al, 1993).

Of four case-control studies that investigated milk consumption, one found an odds ratio of 0.6 (p < 0.01) for those consuming three or more cups per day (Mettlin and Graham, 1979). Another study reported an OR of 1.5 (1.0–2.2) for the highest consumption level of milk and dairy products combined (Riboli et al, 1991); the remaining two studies found no association with milk consumption (Risch et al, 1988; La Vecchia et al, 1989).

Four out of seven epidemiological studies have shown no relationship between milk or dairy product consumption and the risk of bladder cancer, two have shown a decreased risk with greater consumption, and one has shown an increased risk.

The evidence relating to diets high in milk and dairy products and the risk of bladder cancer is inconsistent; no judgement is possible.

4.18.2.5 Herbs and spices

A case-control study of bladder cancer in the Mediterranean region of France reported an increased risk with spice consumption in general (OR = 3.6, 2.2–6.0) for higher consumption of spices including anise, curry powder, ginger, mustard, paprika, peppers, pimento, and harissa collectively; the association was adjusted for smoking and for consumption of alcohol, vegetables, and coffee, as well as other factors (Momas et al, 1994). The authors suggested that spices may irritate and modify the bladder epithelium.

Evidence relating to high dietary intakes of herbs and spices and the risk of bladder cancer is very limited; no judgement is possible.

TABLE 4.18.5 COFFEE CONSUMPTION AND BLADDER CANCER RISK: COHORT STUDIES

AUTHOR, YEAR AND PLACE	SIZE OF COHORT, NO. OF CASES	COFFEE EXPOSURE FACTOR	COMPARISON[a]	RELATIVE RISK (95% CONFIDENCE INTERVAL)[b]	ADJUSTMENT SEX/AGE	SMOKING HISTORY	OTHER FACTORS[c]
Snowdon & Phillips 1984, California USA	23,912: 27 deaths	Coffee	≥ 2 cups/day vs no consumption	1.9	Y	Y	Y
Whittemore et al 1985, USA	51,477: 106	Coffee consumption	yes vs no in college	no assoc **	Y	N	N
Jacobsen et al, 1986 Norway	16,555: 94	Coffee	≥ 7 vs ≤ 2 cups/day	1.0 **	Y	N	Y
	13,644: 65 men	Coffee	≥ 7 vs ≤ 2 cups/day	1.0 **	Y	Y	Y
Mills et al, 1991 California, USA	34,198: 52 deaths	Regular coffee Coffee	≥ 2 cups/day vs never yes vs no	2.0 (0.9–4.3) **[d] 0.9 (0.5–1.9) **	Y Y	Y Y	N Y
Chyou et al, 1993 Hawaii, USA	8,006: 96	Coffee	≥ 5 vs 1/wk	2.1 (0.8–5.1) **	Y	Y	N
Zheng et al, 1996 Iowa, USA	35,369:148	Caffeinated coffee	≥ 4 cups/day vs never/ monthly	0.8 (0.5–1.3)	Y	Y	Y

* P ≤ 0.05 for trend and/or for comparison of highest vs lowest consumption level
** p > 0.05 for trend and/or for comparison of highest vs lowest consumption level
[a] wk = week
[b] assoc = association
[c] Adjusted for one or more of the following: meat consumption, alcohol consumption; rural residence; consumption of sweetened fruit juice, cooked green vegetables, and meat, poultry, or fish; residence, education; physical activity; all fruit and vegetable intake; total energy intake; waist/hip ratio; family history of cancer; prior history of blood transfusion
[d] Positive association was observed in never smokers, but not in past or current smokers
[e] Cancer of the urinary tract; may include cancers of the ureter, renal pelvis and urethra in addition to cancer of the urinary bladder

4.18.2.6 Coffee, tea and other drinks

Coffee

In 1971, a case-control study that reported an unexpected increase in the risk of bladder cancer with coffee drinking generated interest in coffee intake as a possible risk factor (Cole, 1971). Since then, a multitude of case-control studies and several prospective studies have examined this relationship. In 1991, an IARC Working Group reviewed results from 22 case-control and two prospective studies, published up to 1989, and concluded that the evidence was consistent with a weak positive association, but that bias and confounding could not be completely ruled out as explanations for the association. The overall evaluation was that 'there was limited evidence in humans that coffee drinking is carcinogenic in the urinary bladder' (IARC, 1991).

Subsequently, 35 case-control studies published up to 1992 were reviewed by Viscoli et al (1993). In a meta-analysis of a subset of seven studies that met rigid prespecified methodological criteria (histologically confirmed incident cases, measurement of coffee consumption prior to the onset of disease, and adjustment for smoking) no statistically significant association was observed for drinking at least one cup of coffee per day; odds ratios were 1.07 (1.00–1.14) for men and 0.91 (0.81–1.03) for women. For heavier consumption, defined as at least four to five cups per day, a minimal, but statistically significant, increase in risk was seen in men; odds ratios were 1.16 (1.05–1.28) and 0.94 (0.79–1.13) for men and women, respectively. The authors concluded that 'the best available evidence does not suggest a clinically important association between the regular use of coffee and development of cancer of the lower urinary tract in men or women'.

TABLE 4.18.6 COFFEE CONSUMPTION AND BLADDER CANCER RISK: CASE-CONTROL STUDIES

AUTHOR, YEAR AND PLACE	NO. OF CASES	EXPOSURE	COMPARISON[a]	ODDS RATIO (95% CONFIDENCE INTERVAL)[B]	SEX/ AGE	ADJUSTMENT SMOKING HISTORY	OTHER FACTORS[c]
Dunham et al, 1968 New Orleans, USA	493 [d]	Coffee	drinkers vs non-drinker	no assoc [t]	Y/N	N	Y
Cole, 1971 Massachusetts, USA	100 women	Coffee	drinker vs non-drinker	2.6 (1.3–5.1)	Y	Y	N
			≥ 4 vs <1 cups/day	2.2 [s]	Y	Y	N
	345 men	Coffee	drinker vs non-drinker	1.2 (0.8–1.9)	Y	Y	Y
			≥ 4 vs < 1 cups/day	1.3 [s]	Y	Y	Y
Bross & Tidings, 1973 New York, USA	120 women	Coffee	≥ 4 vs < 1 cups/day	0.8	Y	Y	N
	360 men	Coffee	≥ 4 vs < 1 cups/day	1.6	Y	Y	N
Morgan & Jain, 1974 Toronto, Canada	74 women	Coffee	≥ 5 vs 0 cups/day	1.1	Y	N	N
	158 men	Coffee	≥ 5 vs 0 cups/day	1.0	Y	N	N
Simon et al, 1975 Massachusetts & Rhode Island, USA	134 women [d]	Coffee	≥ 1 vs < 1 cups/day	2.1 (1.1–4.3) [z]	Y	N	Y
Wynder & Goldsmith 1977, USA	158 women	Coffee	≥ 7 cups/day vs none/occasional	1.3 (0.2–7.8)	Y	Y	Y
	574 men	Coffee	≥ 7 cups/day vs none/occasional	2.0 (0.8–4.9)	Y	Y	Y
Miller et al, 1978 Ottawa, Canada	72 women	Coffee	ever vs never	1.6 *	Y	N	N
	183 men	Coffee	ever vs never	1.3**	Y	N	N
Mettlin & Graham 1979, New York USA	111 women	Coffee	> 3 vs < 1 cup/day	0.8 **[e]	Y	Y	N
	353 men	Coffee	> 3 vs < 1 cup/day	1.6 **[f]	Y	Y	N
Howe et al, 1980 Canada	152 women	All types of coffee	≥ 5 vs 0 cups/day	1.3**	Y	Y	Y
		Regular coffee	≥ 5 vs 0 cups/day	0.7**	Y	Y	Y
		Instant coffee	≥ 5 vs 0 cups/day	1.2 *	Y	Y	Y
	480 men	All types of coffee	≥ 5 vs 0 cups/day	1.5**	Y	Y	Y
		Regular coffee	≥ 5 vs 0 cups/day	1.8**	Y	Y	Y
		Instant coffee	≥ 5 vs 0 cups/day	1.5**	Y	Y	Y
Cartwright et al 1981, West Yorkshire, UK	210 women [m]	Any type of coffee	drinker vs never drinker	0.8 (0.6–1.2) **	Y	Y	N
		Instant coffee	drinker vs never drinker	0.8 (0.6–1.2) **	Y	Y	N
		Ground coffee	drinker vs never drinker	0.8 (0.5–1.3) **	Y	N	N
	631 men [m]	Any type of coffee	drinker vs never drinker	1.1 (0.9–1.4) **	Y	Y	N
		Instant coffee	drinker vs never drinker	1.2 (0.9–1.5) **	Y	Y	N
		Ground coffee	drinker vs never drinker	0.7 (0.5–1.0) **	Y	N	N
Morrison et al, 1982 Boston, USA; Manchester, England; & Nagoya, Japan	1,417 [d]	Coffee	> 1 vs < 1 cup/day	1.0 (0.8–1.2)	Y	Y	Y
Mommsen et al, 1982 Aarhus, Denmark	165 men	Coffee	na	no assoc	Y	N	Y
Najem et al, 1982 New Jersey, USA	75	Coffee	yes vs no	1.8 (0.1–10.0)	Y	N	Y
Sullivan , 1982 New Orleans, USA π	82	Regular instant coffee	‡	no assoc	N	N	N
		Regular ground coffee	‡	no assoc	N	N	N
		Decaffeinated instant coffee	‡	no assoc	N	N	N
		Decaffeinated ground coffee	‡	no assoc	N	N	N
		Coffee and chicory	‡	no assoc	N	N	N
		Espresso	‡	no assoc	N	N	N
		Duration of coffee consumption	‡‡	no assoc	N	N	N
Marrett et al, 1983 Connecticut, USA π	117 women	Coffee	> 7 vs ≤ 7 cups/wk	1.0 **	Y	Y	N
		Ground coffee	> 7 vs ≤ 7 cups/wk	0.8 **	Y	Y	N
		Instant coffee	> 7 vs ≤ 7 cups/wk	1.1 **	Y	Y	N
		Regular coffee	> 7 vs ≤ 7 cups/wk	0.8 **	Y	Y	N
		Decaffeinated coffee	> 7 vs ≤ 7 cups/wk	1.7 **	Y	Y	N
		Duration of coffee consumption	per year	1.0 **	Y	Y	N
	295 men	Coffee	> 7 vs ≤ 7 cups/wk	1.5 * [l]	Y	Y	N
		Ground coffee	> 7 vs ≤ 7 cups/wk	1.3 **	Y	Y	N
		Instant coffee	> 7 vs ≤ 7 cups/wk	1.2 **	Y	Y	N
		Regular coffee	> 7 vs ≤ 7 cups/wk	1.6 * [l]	Y	Y	N
		Decaffeinated coffee	> 7 vs ≤ 7 cups/wk	0.8 **	Y	Y	N
		Duration of coffee consumption	per year	1.0 **	Y	Y	N
Hartge et al, 1983 USA	710 women	Coffee	ever vs never drank	1.2 (0.8–1.7) [g]	Y	Y	Y
		Coffee	> 63 vs ≤ 7 recent cups/wk	0.8 (0.4–1.4) [h]	Y	Y	Y
		Duration of coffee drinking	≥ 40 vs < 10 yrs	0.8 (0.4–1.5) [h]	Y	Y	Y
	2,197 men	Coffee	ever vs never drank	1.6 (1.2–2.2) [i]	Y	Y	Y
		Coffee	> 63 vs ≤ 7 recent cups/wk	1.5 (1.1–1.9) [h]	Y	Y	Y
		Duration of coffee drinking	≥ 40 vs < 10 yrs	1.1 (0.7–1.6) [h]	Y	Y	Y

Table 4.18.6 continues overleaf

TABLE 4.18.5 COFFEE CONSUMPTION AND BLADDER CANCER RISK: CASE-CONTROL STUDIES, continued

AUTHOR, YEAR AND PLACE	NO. OF CASES	EXPOSURE	COMPARISON[a]	ODDS RATIO (95% CONFIDENCE INTERVAL)[B]	SEX/ AGE	ADJUSTMENT SMOKING HISTORY	OTHER FACTORS[c]
Mommsen et al, 1893 Aarhus, Denmark	47 women	Coffee	yes vs no	3.6	Y	Y	Y
Ohno et al, 1985 Nagoya, Japan	66 women	Coffee	≥ 4 cups/day vs none	0.6 (0.1–2.9)	Y	Y	Y
	227 men	Coffee	≥ 4 cups/day vs none	1.8 (0.7–4.2)	Y	Y	Y
Rebelakos et al, 1985 Athens, Greece	50 women	Coffee	> 2 vs 0-1 cups/day	1.6 (0.8–3.2)	Y	Y	N
	250 men	Coffee	> 2 vs 0-1 cups/day	1.7 (1.2–2.4)	Y	Y	N
González et al, 1985 Mataro, Spain	58	Coffee	drinkers vs non drinkers	0.6 ** u	Y	N	Y
Wynder et al, 1985 USA	194 men	Caffeinated coffee	na	no assoc	Y	na	Y
Claude et al, 1986 Lower Saxony, Germany	91 women [d]	Ground coffee	> 4 vs < 1 cup/day	2.2 **	Y	Y	N
		Decaffeinated coffee	drinker vs non-drinker	1.0**	Y	Y	N
	340 men [d]	Ground coffee	> 4 vs < 1 cup/day	2.3 *	Y	Y	N
		Decaffeinated coffee	drinker vs non-drinker	1.6 **	Y	Y	N
Jensen et al, 1986 Copenhagen Denmark	91 women	Coffee	≥ 1.5 vs 01/day	2.7 (0.7–10.9) **	Y	Y	N
	280 men	Coffee	≥ 1.5 vs 01/day	1.0 (0.5–2.1) **	Y	Y	N
Kabat et al, 1986 USA	76 women [w]	Brewed coffee	≥ 7 cups/day vs none/occasional	2.4 (0.4–14.3)	Y	Y	Y
		Decaffeinated coffee	≥ 5 cups/day vs none/occasional	0.6 (0.03–11.8)	Y	Y	Y
	76 men [w]	Brewed coffee	≥ 7 cups/day vs none/occasional	0.5 (0.03–8.5)	Y	Y	Y
		Decaffeinated coffee	≥ 5 cups/day vs none/occasional	0.3 (0.02–4.1)	Y	Y	Y
Piper et al, 1986 New York, USA	173 women	Coffee	≥ 100 vs < 100 cups ever	0.7 (0.4–1.5)	Y	Y	Y
			> 100 cup-yrs vs non-drinker	2.1 (0.7–6.3)**	Y	Y	Y
Bravo et al, 1987 Madrid, Spain	406	Years of coffee consumption	na	positive assoc	N	N	N
Isovich et al, 1987 La Plata, Argentina	117	Coffee	≥ 3 vs 0 cups/day	12.0 (4.3–33.1)	Y	Y	N
Risch et al, 1988 Canada	826						
	women	Total coffee	ever regular vs no usage	1.9 (1.0–3.4)[j]	Y	Y	Y
			≥ 6 vs ≤1 cup/day	1.1 (0.5–2.7)	Y	Y	Y
		Ground coffee	ever regular vs no usage	1.2 (0.8–1.8)	Y	Y	Y
		Instant coffee	ever regular vs no usage	1.0 (0.7–1.5)	Y	Y	Y
		Instant decaffeinated coffee	ever regular vs no usage	1.5 (0.9–2.5)	Y	Y	Y
		Espresso	ever regular vs no usage	1.5 (0.6–3.8)	Y	Y	Y
	men	Total coffee	ever regular vs no usage	0.9 (0.6–1.3) [k]	Y	Y	Y
			> 6 vs ≤ 1 cup/day	0.9 (0.6–1.4)	Y	Y	Y
		Ground coffee	ever regular vs no usage	1.0 (0.8–1.3)	Y	Y	Y
		Instant coffee	ever regular vs no usage	1.1 (0.8–1.5)	Y	Y	Y
		Instant decaffeinated coffee	ever regular vs no usage	1.1 (0.8–1.5)	Y	Y	Y
		Espresso	ever regular vs no usage	1.6 (0.96–2.8)	Y	Y	Y
Ciccone & Vinels 1988, Torino, Italy	55 women	Current coffee consumption	≥ 4 cups/day vs non-drinkers	0.8 (0.2–2.6) [o]	Y/N	N	N
		Past coffee consumption [n]	≥ 4 vs ≤ 1 cup/day	1.4 (0.6–3.5) [p]	Y/N	N	N
	512 men	Current coffee consumption	≥ 4 cups/day vs non-drinkers	0.8 (0.5–1.2) [q]	Y/N	N	N
		Past coffee consumption [n]	≥ 4 cups/day vs non-drinkers	1.1 (0.6–1.8) [r]	Y/N	N	N
Slattery et al, 1988 Utah, USA	332 men	Caffeinated coffee	> 30 cups/wk vs non-users	1.3 (0.8–2.2)	Y/N	Y	N
Akdas et al, 1990 Turkey	194	Turkish coffee	‡‡‡	positive assoc *	Y	N	N
Nomura et al, 1991 Hawaii, USA	66 women [d]	All types of coffee	≥ 110 cup-yrs vs non-drinkers	0.5 (0.1–2.1) **	Y	Y	Y
		Regular ground coffee	≥ 90 cup-yrs vs non-drinkers	0.3 (0.1–1.0) *	Y	Y	Y
		Regular instant coffee	≥ 15 cup-yrs vs non-drinkers	1.6 (0.6–4.0) **	Y	Y	Y
		Decaffeinated instant coffee	≥ 5 cup-yrs vs non-drinkers	0.6 (0.2–1.6) **	Y	Y	Y
	195 men [d]	All types of coffee	≥ 110 cup-yrs vs non-drinkers	1.0 (0.4–2.7) **	Y	Y	Y
		Regular ground coffee	≥ 90 cup-yrs vs non-drinkers	1.0 (0.4–2.3) **	Y	Y	Y
		Regular instant coffee	≥ 15 cup-yrs vs non-drinkers	1.2 (0.8–1.9) **	Y	Y	Y
		Decaffeinated instant coffee	≥ 5 cup-yrs vs non-drinkers	1.1 (0.6–1.9) **	Y	Y	Y
Clavel & Cordier, 1991 France	91 women	Coffee	> 3 vs 0 cups/day	2.3 (0.6–8.9) ** ¶	Y	Y	Y
	599 men	Coffee	> 7 vs 0 cups/day	2.9 (1.1–8.2)	Y	Y	Y
D'Avanzo et al, 1992 Northeastern Italy	555	Coffee	drinkers vs non-drinkers	1.3 (1.0–1.8) x	Y	Y	Y
			≥ 4 cups/day vs non-drinkers	1.4 (0.9–2.2)**	Y	Y	Y
		Decaffeinated coffee	drinkers vs non-drinker	1.5 (0.9–2.4)	Y	Y	Y
		Duration of coffee drinking	≥ 30 yrs vs non-drinkers	1.4 (0.9–2.2) * y	Y	Y	Y
Kunze et al, 1992 Northern Germany	144 women [d]	Coffee	≥ 5 vs < 1 cup/day	2.7 (0.9–7.8)	Y	Y	N
	531 men [d]	Coffee	≥ 5 vs < 1 cup/day	2.0 (1.2–3.3) *	Y	Y	N
Momas et al, 1994 Southern France	219 men	Lifelong coffee-drinking	> 60,000 vs < 365 cups/lifetime	4.1 (1.7–10.0)	Y	Y	Y

* p ≤ 0.05 for trend and/or for comparison of highest vs lowest consumption level.

** p > 0.05 for trend and/or for comparison of highest vs lowest consumption level

na information not available or unclear from article

a l = litres; yr = year; wk = week

b assoc = association

c Adjusted, matched or stratified for / on one ore more of the following; race; occupation; urban / rural domicile; hospital status; high-risk industry – a priori; high risk industry – dust or fumes; use of nonpublic water supply; history of diabetes; grades of school; aspirin use; artificial sweeteners; smoking status; kidney infection; type of case (prevalent vs incident); study area; geographic area; place of birth; cheroot smoking; saccharin consumption; use of oestrogen; work in industry; work with chemical materials; borough of residence; source of selection; year of interview; hospital; education; use of phenacetin; history of bladder infection; history of iodine-131; telephone area code; date of admission to hospital; area of residence; social class; consumption of liver, carrots, green vegetables, tea; ethnic group; alcohol drinking; lifelong alcohol drinking; spice consumption; occupation at high risk for bladder cancer; residence in non-Mediterranean area; infrequent consumption of spinach, carrots, marrows; birthplace in Mediterranean area

d Cancer of the lower urinary tract; may include cancers of the ureter, renal pelvis, and urethra, in addition to cancer of the urinary bladder

e OR = 3.0 (ns) for smokers of half a pack per day or more

f OR = 2.1 (0.8–5.6) for smokers of half a pack per day or more

g ORs = 0.9 (0.6–1.5) for non-smokers and 1.3 (0.6-1.3) for smokers, among women

h Among coffee drinkers only

i ORs = 1.5 (0.9–2.5) for non-smokers and 2.1 (1.2–3.9) for smokers, among men

j OR = 2.1 (0.7–6.2) for non-smokers among women

k OR = 1.7 (0.3–9.6) for non-smokers among men

l ORs similar for smokers and non-smokers among men, but statistically significant only for smokers

m Includes prevalent, as well as incident cases

n Ten years prior to interview

o ORs = 1.4 (0.2–7.5) for current smokers and 0.5 (0.1–1.5) for non-smokers, for current coffee consumption among women

p ORs = 0.9 (0.1–6.6) for current smokers and 1.5 (0.6–3.5) for non-smokers, for past coffee consumption among women

q ORs = 0.7 (0.4–1.2) for current smokers, 0.6 (0.2–1.9) for ex-smokers, and 4.4 (0.8–25.1) for non-smokers, for current coffee consumption among men

r ORs = 1.0 (0.5–1.9) among current smokers, 0.8 (0.3–2.3) for ex-smokers, and 4.9 (0.8–31.6) for non-smokers, for past coffee consumption among men

s OR = 2.6 among non-smokers who never had a high-risk occupation, for both sexes combined

t Statistically significant positive association seen for coffee drinking among black women, but no association observed among the other three race-sex groups examined

u OR calculated from data in original publication

w Non-smokers

x OR = 1.9 (1.0–3.4) among 105 non-smoking cases

y OR = 2.3 (1.2–4.5) (p < 0.05 for trend) among 105 non-smoking cases

z ORs = 1.7 (0.8–3.5) among non-and light smokers and 3.7 (0.6–23.6) among moderate-to-heavy smokers

‡ No statistically significant difference in average cups/week in cases compared to controls

‡‡ No statistically significant difference in average years of consumption in cases compared to controls

‡‡‡ More cases than controls drank Turkish coffee (p = 0.01)

π This study was part of the collaborative study by Hartge et al, 1983, which is also included in the table

¶ OR is for non-smokers; OR = 1.1 (0.6–8.9) among smokers

Six prospective and 36 case-control studies of bladder cancer that have examined coffee consumption are presented in Tables 4.18.5 and 4.18.6. These include the studies reviewed by the IARC Working Group (1991) and Viscoli et al (1993) as well as a few subsequent studies.

Of the six prospective studies in Table 4.18.5, none showed any statistically significant association; four of the studies included fewer than 100 cases, and thus had limited statistical power to detect associations. Of the six cohort studies, three reported no material associations. The other three studies reported statistically non-significant increases in risk with higher consumption, with odds ratios ranging from 1.9 to 2.1 for two or more cups per day or at least five cups per week. All three of these studies adjusted for smoking; in one study of Seventh-day Adventists the association was limited to 'never smokers' (Mills et al, 1991). The two largest studies, with 106 and 143 cases, respectively, reported no association for coffee consumption during college, and no association for at least four cups of coffee per day compared with consumption monthly or less often (Whittemore et al, 1985; Zheng et al, 1996).

The 36 case-control studies in Table 4.18.6 exhibit a wide variety in the measures used to categorise coffee consumption. Some studies queried daily consumption, whereas others attempted to assess lifetime consumption; some examined coffee consumption as a dichotomous variable (e.g. drinker versus never) whereas others compared several levels of consumption. Various types of coffee were examined in different studies (e.g., caffeinated, decaffeinated, instant, espresso, all types combined), and some studies reported the associations separately for the two sexes or for smokers and non-smokers.

Overall, of the 36 case-control studies, 14 have reported a statistically significant increase in risk with some measure of coffee consumption (Cole, 1971; Simon et al, 1975; Miller et al, 1978; Howe et al, 1980; Hartge et al, 1983; Marrett et al, 1983; Rebelakos et al, 1985; Claude et al, 1986; Iscovich et al, 1987; Akdas et al, 1990; Clavel and Cordier, 1991; D'Avanzo et al, 1992; Kunze et al, 1992; Momas et al, 1994). While the majority of these studies adjusted for smoking, the most important known risk factor for bladder cancer, and a strong correlate of coffee consumption in most cultures, a few did not (Simon et al, 1975; Miller et al, 1978; Akdas et al, 1990). In some studies, the increase in risk was apparent only among men (Howe et al, 1980; Hartge et al, 1983 Marrett et al, 1983;) or only among women (Miller et al, 1978). In one study, the association was found for regular, but not for ground, instant or decaffeinated, coffee, nor for the duration of consumption (Marrett et al, 1983). The strongest association was observed in a study in Argentina, with a 12-fold higher risk for consumers of three or more cups of coffee per day compared with none, although the 95% confidence interval was quite wide (Iscovich et al, 1987). A study of men in southern France reported a more than fourfold increase in risk with lifelong consumption of more than 60,000 cups of coffee, compared with fewer than 365 (Momas et al, 1994). Only one study in Table 4.18.6

reported a statistically significant decrease in risk; this was for regular ground coffee, but not instant or decaffeinated, in females but not males, in a study in Hawaii (Nomura et al, 1991).

Of the total of 112 associations shown in Table 4.18.6, relevant to different aspects of coffee drinking, and for different subgroups in some studies, 40 odds ratios were 1.5 or higher (or there was said to be a 'positive association', without an odds ratio being quoted), 61 were between 0.75 and 1.5 (or there was said to be 'no association'), and 11 were 0.75 or lower. In a tally limited to the 75 associations that were adjusted for smoking, and excluding those for decaffeinated coffee, 31 odds ratios were at least 1.5 (or there was said to be a 'positive association', without an odds ratio being quoted), 39 were between 0.75 and 1.5 (or there was said to be 'no association'), and five were 0.75 or lower.

Seven of the case-control studies that adjusted for smoking in Table 4.18.6 compared relative extremes of consumption, such as five or more cups of coffee per day with fewer than one or 'occasional or never' consumption. Four of these studies reported statistically significant increases in risk with higher consumption (Howe et al, 1980; Hartge et al, 1983; Clavel and Cordier, 1991; Kunze et al, 1992), although the increase was only apparent for males in two studies, and only for regular (not decaffeinated) coffee in one. One study showed no relationship (Risch et al, 1988); results of the other two studies were variable between the sexes and for different types of coffee, and were not statistically significant (Wynder and Goldsmith, 1977; Kabat et al, 1986).

None of the seven case-control studies in Tables 4.18.6 that have examined consumption of decaffeinated coffee have reported any statistically significant association (Sullivan, 1982; Marrett et al, 1983; Claude et al, 1986; Kabat et al, 1986; Risch et al, 1988; Nomura et al, 1991; D'Avanzo et al, 1992).

Twenty-nine of the 42 epidemiological studies in Tables 4.18.5 and 4.18.6 adjusted the associations with coffee consumption for some measure of smoking habits. Nine of the studies examined associations between risk and coffee consumption within strata by smoking status; the results were varied and no pattern emerged for differences in risk between smokers and non-smokers (Cole, 1971; Simon et al, 1975; Mettlin and Graham, 1979; Hartge et al, 1983; Marrett et al, 1983; Ciccone and Vineis, 1988; Risch et al, 1988; Mills et al, 1991; D'Avanzo et al, 1992). Different studies have suggested stronger increases in risk with coffee consumption for either smokers (Simon et al, 1975; Mettlin and Graham, 1979) or non-smokers (Risch et al, 1988; Ciccone and Vineis, 1988; D'Avanzo et al, 1992; Mills et al, 1991). Seven studies that reported risk estimates for coffee consumption among non-smokers generally observed statistically non-significant increases in risk with higher consumption or no relationship (Cole, 1971; Hartge et al, 1983; Kabat et al, 1986; Risch et al, 1988; Ciccone and Vineis, 1988; Mills et al, 1991; D'Avanzo et al, 1992) (see footnotes to Table 4.18.6). Most of these analyses were limited by the relatively small number of bladder cancer cases

that were non-smokers. One study in Italy reported a more than twofold increase in risk (statistically significant for trend) among 105 non-smokers for a duration of coffee consumption of 30 years or more compared with non-consumers (D'Avanzo et al, 1992).

There is no evidence that coffee itself has any initiating or promoting effect in animal carcinogenesis (IARC, 1991). Likewise, caffeine has also been found to have no promoting activity on rat bladder carcinogenesis (Nakanishi et al, 1987). It is possible that high coffee consumption may simply be related to levels of liver cytochrome CYP1A2. This enzyme not only catalyses the bioactivation of aromatic amines but also catalyses caffeine 3-demethylation, which is the rate limiting step in caffeine biotransformation and plasma clearance (Butler et al, 1989). The ability to metabolise caffeine, and thus to consume higher amounts, may signal only the capacity to oxidise aromatic amines more rapidly, and thereby higher exposure to carcinogenic metabolites.

Overall, the evidence regarding coffee consumption and bladder cancer shows a very slight increase in risk with higher intakes and variation across studies; the panel has decided that these findings may be explained by residual confounding, most probably by cigarette smoking, or may represent different proportions of susceptible individuals in different populations. The panel acknowledges that uncertainty about the relationship stems from a large amount of evidence (rather than a paucity of data), but there may be a slight excess of risk at high intakes (say more than five cups per day).

High consumption of coffee possibly increases the risk of bladder cancer at high levels of intake, but is probably not associated with risk at consumption below 5 cups/day.

Both of the recent extensive reviews of the literature on coffee and bladder cancer (IARC, 1991; Viscoli et al, 1993) concluded that there was a weak positive association while also concluding that the small magnitude of the relationship made it of little practical importance.

Tea

Reviewing data from two prospective studies and 12 case-control studies, an IARC Working Group concluded in 1991 that the overall evidence indicated neither an increased nor decreased risk of bladder cancer risk with tea consumption; this evidence was exclusively concerned with black tea, except for one study in Japan (IARC, 1991).

Five prospective and 18 case-control studies of bladder cancer have examined tea consumption and these are presented in Tables 4.18.7 and 4.18.8. These include the studies reviewed by the IARC Working Group in 1991. With few exceptions, these studies reported on consumption of black tea, or tea as a whole which, in many areas where these stud-

TABLE 4.18.7 TEA CONSUMPTION AND BLADDER CANCER RISK: COHORT STUDIES

AUTHOR, YEAR AND PLACE	SIZE OF COHORT NO. OF CASES	TEA EXPOSURE FACTOR	COMPARISON[a]	RELATIVE RISK (95% CONFIDENCE INTERVAL)[b]	ADJUSTMENT SEX/AGE	SMOKING HISTORY	OTHER FACTORS[c]
Whittemore et al 1985, USA	51,477: 106 cases	Tea consumption	yes vs no in college	no assoc **	Y	N	N
Kinlen et al, 1988 London, England	20,000 men: 71 deaths	Tea	$\geq$ 10 cups/day	1.4 ** [d]	Y	N	N
Mills et al, 1991 California, USA	34,198: 52 deaths	Black tea	na	protective assoc **	N	N	N
Chyou et al, 1993 Hawaii, USA	8,006: 96[e]	Green tea	ever vs almost never	1.0 (0.8–2.3)	Y	Y	N
		Black tea	ever vs almost never	1.3 (0.9–2.0)	Y	Y	N
Zheng et al, 1996 Iowa, USA	35,369: 73	Tea	$\geq$ 2 cups/ day vs never/ monthly	0.3 (0.1–1.4) **	Y	Y	Y

** $p > 0.05$ for trend and/or for comparison of highest vs lowest consumption level

na information not available or unclear from original publication

b assoc = association

c Adjusted for one or more of the following; region; place of residence; ethnic origin; blood glucose level; coffee consumption; diabetes under treatment; race; examination site; date of first check up

d Age–adjusted standardized mortality ratio (SMR) reported rather than relative risk

e Cancer of the urinary tract; may include cancers of the ureter, renal pelvis and urethra in addition to cancer of the urinary bladder

ies were conducted, can be presumed to consist mainly of black tea. These studies were undertaken in a variety of geographical areas, including areas where tea consumption is common (e.g., Japan and the UK) and relatively infrequent (Iowa and France).

None of the five cohort studies in Table 4.18.7 observed any statistically significant association for tea consumption; the number of cases in these studies was generally small, ranging from 52 to 106 cases. The largest study, involving a cohort of college alumni, reported no association with consumption of tea during college (Whittemore et al, 1985). The next largest study, involving 96 cases among a cohort of men of Japanese ancestry in Hawaii, similarly found no relationship for consumption of either black or green tea with the risk of bladder cancer (adjusted for smoking) (Chyou et al, 1993). A study of men in England, where tea consumption is very common, reported a 40% greater risk among drinkers of 10 or more cups per day (none of the other cohort studies examined consumption at this high level), although this was neither statistically significant nor adjusted for smoking (Kinlen et al, 1988). A protective association (adjusted for smoking) was suggested within a cohort of post-menopausal women in the USA, but the 95% confidence interval was quite wide (Zheng et al, 1996).

Eighteen case-control studies of bladder cancer have examined tea consumption and these are presented in Table 4.18.8. Only one of these studies reported a statistically significant association. A study in Denmark reported a smoking-adjusted odds ratio of 1.5 ($p < 0.05$ for trend) for male drinkers of at least 1litre per day compared with none; no relationship was observed among females (Jensen et al, 1986). None of the remaining studies reported any statistically significant association; nor did they report any risk estimate that suggested a more than twofold increase or decrease in risk with higher tea consumption. Twelve of these case-control studies adjusted for some measure of smoking, which may be either directly or inversely correlated with tea consumption in various populations. Three of the studies that adjusted for smoking examined consumption of at least four cups of tea per day compared with none; these studies all suggested increases in risk in men, with odds ratios ranging from 1.4 to 1.9 (statistically significant for trend in one study) (Claude et al, 1986; Jensen et al, 1986; Kunze et al, 1992), whereas only one suggested any increase in risk in women (Claude et al, 1986). Two studies calculated lifetime tea consumption. One in Canada reported no association with each increase of 100 serving-years; another in Hawaii reported odds ratios of 0.5 and 0.7

TABLE 4.18.8 TEA CONSUMPTION AND BLADDER CANCER RISK: CASE-CONTROL STUDIES

AUTHOR, YEAR AND PLACE	NO. OF CASES	EXPOSURE	COMPARISON[a]	ODDS RATIO (95% CONFIDENCE INTERVAL)[B]	SEX/AGE	SMOKING HISTORY	OTHER FACTORS[c]
Morgan & Jain, 1974	74 women	Tea	≥ 5 vs 0 cups/day	0.5 [e]	Y	N	N
Toronto, Canada	158 men	Tea	≥ 5 vs 0 cups/day	0.5 [e]	Y	N	N
Simon et al, 1975 Massachusetts & Rhode Island, USA	134 women [d]	Tea	≥ 3 vs 0 cup/day	0.8	Y	N	Y
Miller et al, 1978	72 women	Tea	ever vs never	0.9 **	Y	N	N
Ottawa, Canada	183 men	Tea	ever vs never	1.1 **	Y	N	N
Howe et al, 1980	152 women	Tea	ever vs never	0.5 (0.2–1.0)	Y	N	N
Canada	480 men	Tea	ever vs never	1.0 (0.7–1.4)	Y	N	N
Sullivan, 1982	82	Hot tea	[g]	no assoc	N	N	N
New Orleans, USA [f]		Iced tea	[h]	no assoc	N	N	N
Hartge et al, 1983	710 women	Tea	≥ 14 vs 0 cups/wk	1.2 (0.7–2.0)[i]	Y	Y	Y
USA	2,197 men	Tea	≥ 14 vs 0 cups/wk	1.0 (0.7–1.4)[i]	Y	Y	Y
Ohno et al, 1985	66 women	Black tea	ever vs not used	0.6 (0.3–1.0)	Y	Y	Y
Nagoya, Japan	227 men	Black tea	ever vs not used	0.95 (0.7–1.3)	Y	Y	Y
		Matcha (powdered green tea)	ever vs not used	1.1 (0.7–1.5)	Y	Y	Y
Claude et al, 1986	91 women [d]	Black tea	≥ 4 vs 0 cups/day	1.9 **	Y	Y	N
Lower Saxony, Germany	340 men [d]	Black tea	≥ 4 vs 0 cups/day	1.9 **	Y	Y	N
Jensen et al, 1986	91 women	Tea	1–1.5 vs 0 litres/day	1.0 (0.4–2.5) **	Y	Y	N
Copenhagen, Denmark	280 men	Tea	1–1.5 vs 0 litres/day	1.5 (0.7–3.2) *	Y	Y	N
Kabat et al, 1986 USA	152 [j]	Tea	[k]	no assoc	Y	Y	Y
Iscovich et al, 1987 La Plata, Argentina	117	Tea	≥ 3 vs 0 cups/day	1.4	Y	Y	N
Risch et al, 1988 Canada	826						
	women	Tea	3/day [l]	0.98 (0.8–1.2)	Y	Y	Y
		Tea	100 serving-yrs [l]	0.97 (0.8–1.2)	Y	Y	Y
	men	Tea	3/day [l]	1.04 (0.9–1.2)	Y	Y	Y
		Tea	100 serving-yrs [l]	1.03 (0.9–1.1)	Y	Y	Y
Slattery et al, 1988 Utah, USA	332 men	Tea	≥ 3 cups/wk vs non-users	1.5 (0.98–2.4)	Y/N	Y	N
Akdas et al, 1990 Turkey	194	Tea	na	no assoc	Y	N	N
Nomura et al, 1991	66 women [d]	All types of tea	≥ 31 cup-yrs vs non-drinkers	0.5 (0.2–1.8) **	Y	Y	Y
Hawaii, USA		Black tea	≥ 11 cup-yrs vs non-drinkers	0.7 (0.3–1.7) **	Y	Y	Y
	195 men [d]	All types of tea	≥ 31 cup-yrs vs non-drinkers	0.7 (0.4–1.3) **	Y	Y	Y
		Black tea	≥ 11 cup-yrs vs non-drinkers	0.7 (0.4–1.2) **	Y	Y	Y
Clavel & Cordier	91 women	Tea	> 1 vs 0 cups/day	1.0 (0.3–3.6) [m]	Y	Y	Y
1991, France	599 men	Tea	> 1 vs 0 cups/day	0.5 (0.1–4.6) [n]	Y	Y	Y
D'Avanzo et al, 1992 Northeastern Italy	555	Tea	drinkers vs non-drinkers	0.9 (0.6–1.2)	Y	Y	Y
Kunze et al, 1992	144 women [d]	Black tea	≥ 5 vs <1 cups/day	0.7 (0.2–2.3) **	Y	Y	N
Northern Germany	531 men [d]	Black tea	≥ 5 vs <1 cups/day	1.4 (0.7–3.1) **	Y	Y	N

* p ≤ 0.05 for trend and/or for comparison of highest vs lowest consumption level

** p > 0.05 for trend and/or for comparison of highest vs lowest consumption level

na Information not available or unclear from article

[a] l = litres; yr = year; wk = week

[b] assoc = association

[c] Adjusted or matched for one or more of the following: urban/rural domicile; race; geographic area; history of coffee drinking; residence; hospital; year of interview; history of diabetes; area of residence; ethnic group; alcohol drinking; occupation at risk

[d] Cancer of the lower urinary tract; may include cancers of the ureter, renal pelvis and urethra in addition to cancer of the urinary bladder

[e] Odds ratio calculated from data in original publication

[f] This study was part of the collaborative study by Hartge et al, 1983, which is also included in the table

[g] No statistically significant difference in average cups/week for cases compared to controls (2.1 vs 2.5)

[h] No statistically significant difference in average glasses/week for cases compared to controls (4.3 vs 2.7)

[i] Among subjects who drank no more than 7 cups of coffee per week

[j] Non-smokers

[k] No difference in average intake for cases compared to controls

[l] Continuous variable

[m] OR is for non-smokers; OR = 0.2 (0.04–0.8) among cigarette smokers

[n] OR is for non-smokers; OR = 1.5 (0.3–7.6) among current smokers and inhalers of black tobacco cigarettes

(statistically non-significant) for women and men, respectively, for all types of tea at a level of 31 or more cup-years (Nomura et al, 1991).

In a tally of all 41 associations in Tables 4.18.7 and 4.18.8 (without regard to statistical significance and excluding footnotes), to which different studies contributed different numbers of associations (due to sex-specific analyses and the examination of different types of tea and different levels of consumption), five of the risk estimates were 1.5 or greater, 26 were between 0.75 and 1.5 (or there was said to be no association), and 10 were 0.75 or lower.

Two studies have examined consumption of green tea specifically. A cohort study of Japanese men in Hawaii reported no association (Chyou et al, 1993) whereas a case-control study in Japan observed a 50% lower risk among women but not men who were ever-users of matcha (powdered green tea), compared with non-users (Ohno et al, 1985).(Matcha is a rare form of green tea preparation in Japan.)

An international ecological study comparing bladder cancer death rates between 1964 and 1965 and annual consumption of tea in 20 countries found no statistically significant correlation (Stocks, 1970).

Neither tea solution nor tea extract has been shown to be carcinogenic or cancer-promoting to the bladder in animals (IARC, 1991).

Polyphenol extracts of green tea have been shown to be anticarcinogenic in animals, but their effects in bladder carcinogenesis are unknown (IARC, 1991; Fujiki et al, 1992).

Overall, there is a large amount of epidemiological data on tea consumption and the risk of bladder cancer, the majority on black tea.

High intake of black tea probably has no relationship with the risk of bladder cancer.

The evidence related to green tea consumption and the risk of bladder cancer is limited; no judgement is possible.

Maté

A case-control study in Argentina reported no material association with consumption of maté after adjustment for cigarette smoking, OR = 0.8 for 20 or more containers per day compared with none (Iscovich et al, 1987).

Based on only one study, no judgement is possible.

Total fluid intake

At least one prospective study and six case-control studies of bladder cancer have examined total fluid intake. In a cohort of Seventh-day Adventists in California, in which 52 cases of bladder cancer occurred, no statistically significant association was observed for total fluid intake (Mills et al, 1991).

In three out of six case-control studies, an increase in risk was seen with higher total fluid or beverage consumption for

at least one subgroup. In a study in Denmark, a stronger increase in risk was seen for men than women, with smoking-adjusted odds ratios of 3.3 (1.4–7.4) (p < 0.05 for trend) and 1.8 (0.4–7.4) (statistically non-significant for trend), respectively, for 4 litres/day or more compared with less than 1 litre/day (Jensen et al, 1986). Similarly, in Germany, a study reported an increased risk in men, but not women, with smoking-adjusted odds ratios of 4.9 (2.0–12.3) and 0.9 (0.3–2.5), respectively, for 3 litres/day or more of fluid compared with less than 2 litres/day. However, adjustment for consumption of coffee and beer, as well as other factors, greatly attenuated the association for total fluid intake in men (Kunze et al, 1992). A further, very large, study in the USA also reported a statistically significant increase in risk with greater total beverage consumption (no risk estimate given); this association appeared to be mainly attributable to the intake of chlorinated tap water (Cantor et al, 1987).

Three other case-control studies have reported no statistically significant relationships between total fluid intake and the risk of bladder cancer. A study in Utah (USA) reported a smoking-adjusted odds ratio of 1.4 (0.9–2.1) for more than 653 oz of total fluid per day, compared to 289 oz or less (Slattery et al, 1988a). Another study, in Canada, reported odds ratios of 1.0 (0.9–1.1) and 1.3 (0.98–1.6) for 1 litre/day increase in total liquid for men and women, respectively (Risch et al, 1988). A study in New Orleans (USA) reported no major differences in the frequency distribution of total fluid consumption for cases compared with controls (Dunham et al, 1968).

Various hypotheses have been put forward to explain the increase in risk with higher total fluid intake observed in some epidemiological studies. One is that greater fluid intake leads to bladder distension, with flattening of the urothelium, which might result in more prolonged and intensive contact of basal cells (known to be the target cells for neoplastic transformation) with any urine-borne cancer-causing agents (Claude et al, 1986; Kunze et al, 1992). Experimental studies have shown an increased incidence of chemically-induced urothelial hyperplasias and papillomas in rats with distended bladders due to augmented fluid intake (see Kunze et al, 1992).

Alternatively, the associations for total fluid intake observed in epidemiological studies may be attributable to intakes of specific beverages that contribute greatly to total fluid intake. For example, two studies have shown total fluid intake to be correlated with intakes of coffee (r = 0.4–0.6) and water (r = 0.5) (Jensen et al, 1986; Slattery et al, 1988a). In fact, in two studies that reported definite increases in risk with higher total fluid intake, the associations were largely attributable to specific beverages, including chlorinated tap water (Cantor et al, 1987) and beer and coffee (Kunze et al, 1992). It is generally not possible in epidemiological studies to determine whether constituents in specific, commonly consumed beverages are responsible for associations observed for total fluid intake, or whether the most commonly consumed beverages are implicated only because of their impact on the volume of total fluid consumed.

> Overall, epidemiological studies of bladder cancer that have examined total fluid intake have found either increased risk with higher intakes or no relationship. At least one biological mechanism has been hypothesised to explain any increase in risk. However, it remains unclear whether it is fluid volume as such, or factors inherent to specific, commonly consumed beverages that are responsible for any true increase in risk.

> Based on this evidence, no judgement is possible.

4.18.3 FOOD PROCESSING

4.18.3.1 Additives

Colours

The aromatic amines benzidine and 2-naphthylamine are known to be human bladder carcinogens. This conclusion is derived from epidemiological data on workers in the dye industry and is supported by experimental verification in animals, notably the dog (tumours appeared at sites other than the bladder in several other species) (Kadlubar et al, 1991). No dyestuffs are now manufactured using these raw materials, but they may arise as unintentional by-products in some processes and contaminate the product at low concentrations. Trace levels have been detected in some batches of the azo dyes, tartrazine and sunset yellow FCF. Accordingly, specifications for food-grade materials have addressed this issue and their presence is now limited. In view of the low levels of these amines in the dyestuff and the low concentration of the dyes in foods (typically 100–200 ppm) the contaminating levels in food are very low. (Note that the major source of human exposure to these aromatic amines is cigarette smoke, where they are present at levels of 1–100 ppb (US Surgeon General Report, 1987).)

> Based on this limited evidence, no judgement is possible

Artificial sweeteners

The principal artificial sweeteners include saccharin, cyclamate, aspartame and acesulfame K. It has been a matter of controversy whether artificial sweeteners play a role in human bladder cancer. This concern was first raised by experimental studies that reported an elevated incidence of bladder tumours in rats exposed to high doses of saccharin both *in utero* and in later life (National Research Council, 1989).

Saccharin has been used for many decades; cyclamates were introduced in the early 1960s, but were banned soon afterwards in some countries. Aspartame is a relatively new artificial sweetener; it was introduced in the early 1980s in the USA (National Research Council, 1989). Given the latency period for the development of bladder cancer, epidemiological data are primarily relevant to saccharin or the

mixture of saccharin and cyclamate, as cyclamate is usually formulated as a mixture with saccharin. Major sources of artificial sweeteners, include low calorie/dietetic soft drinks, sweeteners added directly to food and drink (hereafter called table-top sweeteners) and a variety of foods designed for diabetics or for slimmers, in toothpaste, and coatings on pharmaceuticals.

The literature on artificial sweeteners and bladder cancer has been extensively reviewed; it has been concluded that numerous epidemiological studies have not substantiated any increase in risk as a result of the use of artificial sweeteners in humans (Matanoski and Elliott, 1981; National Research Council, 1989; Silverman et al, 1992). Reviews by IARC, WHO, and JECFA have concluded that 25 human studies have shown no overall association between saccharin use and human cancer (IARC, 1980, 1987; WHO, 1993). Also, no excess risk of bladder cancer has been observed among diabetics who often use artificial sweeteners.

Thirty case-control studies of bladder cancer are presented in Table 4.18.9; each of these examined some aspect of artificial sweetener consumption, such as intake of saccharin, cyclamate or both combined; intake from table-top sweeteners, dietetic beverages, or dietetic foods; daily or lifetime consumption; or duration of use or time of first use. The table includes the studies encompassed in the above reviews, as well as a few subsequent studies.

Three of the studies in Table 4.18.9 have shown a statistically significant increase in risk with use of at least one type of artificial sweetener in at least one subgroup. A study in Canada reported increased risk with use of artificial sweeteners but not dietetic drinks, for men, but not women (Howe et al, 1980). A very large study in the USA, including 3,010 cases from different geographic areas, reported increased risk with heavy and prolonged use of table-top artificial sweeteners and diet drinks among non-smoking women not in high-risk occupations, and among male heavy smokers (Hoover and Strasser, 1980). Another study, in the UK, reported increased risk for 'takers' of saccharin, compared with 'non-takers', but only among male non-smokers (Cartwright et al, 1981).

On the other hand, three of the 30 studies in Table 4.18.9 have shown statistically significant protective associations. A study in Japan observed a decreased risk among both sexes with a history of sugar substitute use (Morrison et al, 1982), whereas studies in Canada and Denmark reported a decreased risk in women only with prolonged use of any type of artificial sweetener, and in men only with use of diet drinks (Morgan and Jain, 1974; Moller-Jensen et al, 1983).

Of the many data in Table 4.18.9, 72 of the risk estimates concern the intake of artificial sweeteners as such (e.g. 'artificial sweeteners', 'sugar substitutes', 'table-top sweeteners', 'saccharin' and 'cyclamate') rather than the intake of foods or drinks containing artificial sweeteners; the fact that other constituents might explain any association with bladder cancer cannot be ruled out. Of these 72 associations, which pertain to usage status, level of intake, or duration of use, 10 odds ratios were 1.5 or higher (or there was said to be a

TABLE 4.18.9 ARTIFICIAL SWEETENER CONSUMPTION AND BLADDER CANCER RISK: CASE-CONTROL STUDIES

AUTHOR, YEAR, AND PLACE	NO. OF CASES	EXPOSURE	COMPARISON[a]	ODDS RATIO (95% CONFIDENCE INTERVAL)[b]	SEX/AGE	SMOKING HISTORY	OTHER FACTORS[c]
Morgan & Jain, 1974 Toronto, Canada	74 women	Any type of artificial sweetener [k]	prolonged regular use vs non-use	0.4 *	Y	N	N
	158 men	Any type of artificial sweetener [k]	prolonged regular use vs non-use	1.0 **	Y	N	N
Simon et al, 1975 Massachussetts & Rhode Island, USA	134 women [d]	Cyclamate	users vs non-users	1.2 (0.5–2.6) [m]	Y	N	Y
		Saccharin	users vs non-users	1.0 (0.5–1.7)	Y	N	Y
Wynder & Goldsmith 1977, USA	158 women	Artificial sweeteners	≥ 15 yrs vs non-users	0.9 (0.1–15.4)	Y	N	Y
	574 men	Artificial sweeteners	≥ 15 yrs vs non-users	0.9 (0.1–14.8)	Y	N	Y
Miller et al, 1978 Ottawa, Canada	77 women	Artificial sweeteners	regular vs no regular use	0.9 **	Y	N	N
	188 men	Artificial sweeteners	regular vs no regular use	1.1 **	Y	N	N
Connolly et al, 1978 Ontario, Canada	100 women	Artificial sweeteners	ever vs never use	0.7 [r]	Y	N	Y
	248 men	Artificial sweeteners	ever vs never use	0.9 [r]	Y	N	Y
Kessler & Clark, 1978 Baltimore, USA	154 women	Saccharin	use vs non-use	0.8 (0.5–1.4)	Y	Y	Y
		Cyclamate	use vs non-use	0.6 (0.3–1.1)	Y	Y	Y
		Table sweeteners	high vs low	0.9 (0.4–1.9)	Y	Y	Y
		Carbonated diet sodas	high vs low	0.7 (0.3–1.7)	Y	Y	Y
		Any diet beverages	high vs low	0.8 (0.3–2.0)	Y	Y	Y
		Any diet foods	high vs low	0.9 (0.3–2.6)	Y	Y	Y
		Any non-nutritive sweetener product	high vs low	0.7 (0.3–1.5)	Y	Y	Y
	365 men	Saccharin	use vs non-use	1.1 (0.8–1.6)	Y	Y	Y
		Cyclamate	use vs non-use	1.2 (0.8–1.7)	Y	Y	Y
		Table sweeteners	high vs low	1.3 (0.7–2.4)	Y	Y	Y
		Carbonated diet sodas	high vs low	0.9 (0.5–1.7)	Y	Y	Y
		Any diet beverages	high vs low	1.0 (0.6–1.9)	Y	Y	Y
		Any diet foods	high vs low	0.7 (0.4–1.6)	Y	Y	Y
		Any non-nutritive sweetener product	high vs low	1.0 (0.6–1.7)	Y	Y	Y
Howe et al, 1980 Canada	152 women	Artificial sweeteners	≥ 7 vs 0/day	1.2 **	Y	Y	Y
		Dietetic drinks	ever vs never use	0.9 (0.2–3.0)	Y	N	N
	480 men	Artificial sweeteners	≥ 9 vs 0/day	2.8 **	Y	Y	Y
		Dietetic drinks	ever vs never use	0.8 (0.2–3.3)	Y	N	N
Morrison & Buring 1980, Boston, USA	155 women [d]	Sugar substitutes	history of use vs no use	1.9 (1.0–3.6)	Y	Y	N
		powder	≥ 3 packets/day vs no current use	1.3	Y	N	N
		tablets	use vs no current use	0.8	Y	N	N
		Dietetic beverages	history of use vs no use	1.8 (1.0–3.3)	Y	Y	N
			≥ 2 drinks/day vs no current use	0.5	Y	N	N
		Dietetic foods	≥ 3 servings/wk vs no current use	1.4	Y	N	N
	422 men	Sugar substitutes	history of use vs no use	0.9 (0.6–1.3)	Y	Y	N
		powder	≥ 3 packets/day vs no current use	1.0	Y	N	N
		tablets	≥ 5 tablets/day vs no current use	1.3	Y	N	N
		Dietetic beverages	history of use vs no use	0.9 (0.7–1.2)	Y	Y	N
			≥ 2 drinks/day vs no current use	1.9	Y	N	N
		Dietetic foods	≥ 3 servings/wk vs no current use	0.9	Y	N	N
Hoover & Strasser 1980, USA	3,010	Any form of artificial sweetener	ever vs never use	1.0 (0.9–1.1) [s]	N	Y	Y
		Diet drinks	ever use vs never use of any artificial sweetener	1.0 (0.9–1.1) [s]	N	Y	Y
		Table-top artificial sweeteners	ever use vs never use of any artificial sweetener	1.0 (0.9–1.2) [s]	N	Y	Y
		Diet foods	ever use vs never use of any artificial sweetener	1.1 (0.9–1.2) [s]	N	Y	Y
		Table-top artificial sweeteners + diet drinks	heavy [t] vs no use	1.5 (1.0–2.1) [s]	Y	Y	Y
	563 women	Table-top artificial sweeteners	≥ 6 uses/day vs never use of any artificial sweetener	1.4 * [u]	Y	Y	Y
		Diet drinks	≥ 3 servings/d vs never use of any artificial sweeteners	1.4 [v]	Y	Y	Y
	1,828 men	Table-top artificial sweeteners	≥ 6 uses/day vs never use of any artificial sweetener	1.1 [w]	Y	Y	Y
		Diet drinks	≥ 3 servings/day vs never use of any artificial sweetener	1.0 [x]	Y	Y	Y
Wynder & Stellman 1980, USA	65 women	Artificial sweeteners	use vs never use	0.6 (0.3–1.4)	Y	N	Y
		Diet beverages	use vs never use	0.6 (0.3–1.3)	Y	N	Y
	302 men	Artificial sweeteners	use vs never use	0.9 (0.7–1.3)	Y	N	Y

Table 4.18.9 continues overleaf

TABLE 4.18.9 ARTIFICIAL SWEETENER CONSUMPTION AND BLADDER CANCER RISK: CASE-CONTROL STUDIES, continued

AUTHOR, YEAR, AND PLACE	NO. OF CASES	EXPOSURE	COMPARISON[a]	ODDS RATIO (95% CONFIDENCE INTERVAL)[b]	ADJUSTMENT SEX/AGE	SMOKING HISTORY	OTHER FACTORS[c]
		Diet beverages	use vs never use	0.9 (0.6–1.2)	Y	N	Y
Cartwright et al, 1981 West Yorkshire, UK	210 women [f] 631 men [f]	Saccharin Saccharin	takers vs non-takers takers vs non-takers	1.6 (1.3–3.2) ** [g] 2.2 (1.3–3.8)** [h]	Y Y	Y [g] Y [h]	N N
Mommsen et al, 1982 Aarhus, Denmark	165 men	Artificial sweeteners	na	no assoc	Y	N	Y
Najem et al, 1982 New Jersey, USA	75	Saccharin	yes vs no	1.3 (0.6–2.8)	Y	N	Y
		Diet beverages	yes vs no	1.2 (0.6–2.1)	Y	N	Y
		Duration of saccharin consumption	[I]	no assoc	Y	N	Y
Sullivan, 1982 New Orleans, USA [y]	82	Artificially sweetened beverages	[n]	no assoc	N	N	N
		Duration of artificially sweetened beverage consumption	[o]	no assoc	N	N	N
		Age began usage of artificially sweetened beverages	[p]	no assoc	N	N	N
Morrison et al, 1982 Manchester, UK	142 women [d]	Sugar substitutes	history of use vs no use	1.1 (0.7–1.7)	Y	Y	N
			≥ 10 tablets/day vs no use	2.3	Y/N	N	N
		Time of first use	30–39 yrs prior to interview vs no use	0.8 (0.4–1.5)	Y/N	N	N
		Duration of use of sugar substitutes	≥ 15 yrs vs no use	0.9	Y/N	N	N
	382 men	Sugar substitutes	history of use vs no use	0.9 (0.7–1.3)	Y	Y	N
			≥ 10 tablets/day vs no use	0.6	Y/N	N	N
		Time of first use	30–39 yrs prior to interview vs no use	0.9 (0.6–1.3)	Y/N	N	N
		Duration of use of sugar substitutes	≥ 15 yrs vs no use	0.9	Y/N	N	N
Morrison et al, 1982 Nagoya, Japan	66 women [d]	Sugar substitutes	history of use vs no use	0.5 (0.2–0.9)	Y	Y	N
		Time of first use	30–39 yrs prior to interview vs no use	0.4 (0.2–0.8)	Y/N	N	N
		Duration of use of sugar substitutes	≥ 6 yrs vs no use	0.6	Y/N	N	N
	223 men [d]	Sugar substitutes	history of use vs no use	0.7 (0.5–0.9)	Y	Y	N
		Time of first use	30–39 yrs prior to interview vs no use	0.6 (0.4–0.8)	Y/N	N	N
		Duration of use of sugar substitutes	≥ 9 yrs vs no use	0.5	Y/N	N	N
Marrett et al, 1983 Connecticut, USA	117 women 295 men	Artificial sweeteners Artificial sweeteners	high vs low high vs low	1.1 (0.7–1.8) 0.7 (0.5–1.0)	Y/N Y/N	N N	N N
Moller-Jensen et al 1983, Copenhagen Denmark	98 women	Artificial sweeteners	ever vs never use	1.0 (0.6–1.8)	Y/N	Y	N
			≥ 15 tablets/day vs never use	1.5 (0.3–6.8)	Y/N	N	N
		Saccharin	users vs non-users	1.0 (0.5–2.1)	Y/N	N	N
		Cyclamates	users vs non-users	1.3 (0.2–8.1)	Y/N	N	N
		Duration of artificial sweetener use	≥ 15 yrs vs never use	0.8 (0.3–2.5)	Y	N	N
		Diet drinks	users vs non-users	0.7 (0.2–2.4)	Y/N	N	N
		Food with artificial sweeteners	users vs non-users	1.7 (0.6–5.3)	Y/N	N	N
	290 men	Artificial sweeteners	ever vs never use	0.7 (0.5–1.0)	Y/N	Y	N
			≥ 15 tablets/day vs never use	1.0 (0.5–2.0)	Y/N	N	N
		Saccharin	users vs non-users	0.7 (0.5–1.0)	Y/N	N	N
		Cyclamates	users vs non-users	0.7 (0.3–2.0)	Y/N	N	N
		Duration of artificial sweetener use	≥ 15 yrs vs never use	0.5 (0.2–0.98)	Y	N	N
		Diet drinks	users vs non-users	0.3 (0.1–0.8)	Y/N	N	N
		Food with artificial sweeteners	users vs non-users	1.5 (0.7–2.9)	Y/N	N	N
Mommsen et al 1983, Aarhus Denmark	47 women	Saccharin	yes vs no	7.5	Y	Y	Y
Wynder et al, 1985 USA	194 men	Saccharin	na	no assoc	Y	na	Y

Author, year, and place	Cases (No.)	Exposure	Comparison[a]	OR (95% Confidence Interval)[b]	Adjustment Sex/Age	Smoking History	Other Factors[c]
Kabat et al, 1986 USA	76 women [i]	Artificial sweeteners	[j]	no assoc	Y	Y	Y
		Diet drinks	[j]	no assoc	Y	Y	Y
	76 men [i]	Artificial sweeteners	[j]	no assoc	Y	Y	Y
		Diet drinks	[j]	no assoc	Y	Y	Y
Piper et al, 1986 New York, USA	173 women	Artificially sweetened beverages and/or tabletop sweeteners	≥ 100 vs < 100 uses ever	1.1 (0.7–1.7)	Y	N	Y
Bravo et al, 1987 Madrid, Spain	406	Artificial sweeteners	na	positive assoc	N	N	N
		Artificially sweetened beverages [e]	na	positive assoc	N	N	N
Iscovich et al, 1987 La Plata, Argentina	117	Saccharin	na	no assoc	Y	N	N
Risch et al, 1988 Canada	826						
	women	Table-top artificial sweeteners	ever regular vs no use	1.2 (0.8–1.8)	Y	Y	Y
		Saccharin	> 3 uses/day vs no use	1.3 (0.6–2.6)	Y	Y	Y
		Cyclamate	> 1 uses/day vs no use	1.2 (0.3–4.5)	Y	Y	Y
		Diet soda	> 4 uses/day vs no use	1.9 (0.7–5.4)	Y	Y	Y
	men	Table-top artificial sweeteners	ever regular vs no use	1.0 (0.7–1.3)	Y	Y	Y
		Saccharin	> 3 uses/day vs no use	0.8 (0.5–1.3)	Y	Y	Y
		Cyclamate	> 1 uses/day vs no use	1.4 (0.6–3.8)	Y	Y	Y
		Diet soda	> 4 uses/day vs no use	0.7 (0.3–1.2)	Y	Y	Y
Slattery et al, 1988 Utah, USA	419 w + m	Artificially sweetened beverages	≥ 7 vs 0 lifetime servings/ wk	1.1 (0.7–1.6)	Y	Y	Y
Akdas et al, 1990 Turkey	195 w + m	Artificial sweeteners	[q]	positive assoc	Y	N	N
Nomura et al, 1991 Hawaii, USA	66 women [d]	Saccharin	≥ 6 serving-yrs vs non-user	0.9 (0.3–2.9)**	Y	Y	Y
		Diet beverages	> 3 can-yrs vs non-user	0.4 (0.1–1.7)**	Y	Y	Y
	195 men [d]	Saccharin	≥ 6 serving-yrs vs non-user	1.1 (0.6–1.9)**	Y	Y	Y
		Diet beverages	> 3 can-yrs vs non-user	1.3 (0.7–2.5)**	Y	Y	Y
Vena et al, 1992 Western New York USA	351 men	Saccharin	na	no assoc	Y	na	Y
Momas et al, 1994 Southern France	219 men	Saccharin	high vs low	1.5 (0.8–3.0)	Y	Y	Y

* p ≤ 0.05 for trend and/or for comparison of highest vs lowest consumption level

** p > 0.05 for trend and/or for comparison of highest vs lowest consumption level

na information not available or unclear from article

[a] wk = week; yr = year

[b] assoc = association

[c] Adjusted, matched, or stratified for one or more of the following; urban/ rural domicile; hospital status; race; residence; occupation; diabetes mellitus; marital status; education; overweight; dieting; memory; high-risk industry – a priori; high-risk industry – dust or fumes; use of nonpublic water supply; bladder infection; grades of school; aspirin use; coffee consumption; smoking status; kidney infection; instant coffee consumption; occupational exposure; region; hospital; hospital-room status; type of case (prevalent vs incident); geographic area; place of birth; cheroot smoking; use of oestrogen; work in industry; work with chemical materials; year of interview; telephone area code; date of admission to hospital; neighbourhood of residence; lifelong coffee-drinking; spice consumption; occupation at high risk of bladder cancer; residence in non-Mediterranean area; infrequent consumption of spinach; carrots, marrows; birthplace in Meditteranean area; lifelong alcohol-drinking

[d] Cancer of the lower urinary tract; may include cancers of the ureter, renal pelvis and urethra in addition to cancer of the urinary bladder

[e] The most commonly consumed artificially sweetened beverage in the area where the study was conducted is wine mixed with "gaseosa", which is carbonated water mixed with saccharin and cyclamates

[f] Includes prevalent, as well as incident cases

[g] OR is for women non-smokers only; OR = 1.2 (0.5–2.6) for women smokers

[h] OR is for men non-smokers only; OR = 0.9 (0.6–1.3) for men smokers

[i] Non-smokers

[j] Percentage of never users in cases was similar to that in controls

[k] Includes sugar substitutes, diet desserts, sugar-free soft drinks

[l] Average numbers of years of saccharin consumption were 6.4 for cases and 6.3 for controls

[m] OR is for coffee drinkers only; OR = 1.2 (0.5–2.7) for tea drinkers

[n] No statistically significant difference between cases and controls in average number of glasses/week

[o] No statistically significant difference between cases and controls in average number of years of usage

[p] No statistically significant difference between cases and controls in average age at beginning of usage

[q] Numbers of cases using artificial sweeteners as a sugar substitute was different between cases (19) and controls (8) (p < 0.05)

[r] OR calculated from data in original publication

[s] ORs similar for women and men in stratified analysis

[t] ≥ 3 servings of table-top sweeteners and ≥ 2 diet drinks per day or ≥ 6 servings of table-top sweeteners and at least some diet drinks per day

[u] OR = 2.7 (p < 0.01) among non-smoking women not in high-risk occupations for ≥ 2 uses for ≥ 10 years

[v] OR = 3.0 (p < 0.05) among non-smoking women not in high-risk occupations for ≥ 2 uses for ≥ 10 years

[w] OR = 1.9 (p < 0.01) among men who smoked more than 40 cigarettes daily

[x] OR = 2.6 (p < 0.01) among men who smoked more than 40 cigarettes daily

[y] This study was part of the collaborative study by Hoover et al, 1980, also reported in the table

'positive association'), 49 were between 0.75 and 1.5 (or there was said to be 'no association'), and 13 were 0.75 or lower.

At least four studies have attempted to examine associations for saccharin and cyclamates separately. These were conducted in the USA shortly after the ban of cyclamates or were conducted in countries where cyclamates were not banned (Simon et al, 1975; Kessler and Clark, 1978; Moller-Jensen et al, 1983; Risch et al, 1988). No relationship to bladder cancer was apparent for either substance in any of these studies. Three studies have examined the duration of artificial sweetener use; odds ratios have ranged from 0.5 to 0.9 (generally statistically non-significant) for at least fifteen years of use, compared to non-users (Wynder and Goldsmith, 1977; Morrison et al, 1982; Moller-Jensen et al, 1983). Companion studies in the UK and Japan examined time of first use of sugar substitutes. In the UK, no association was observed with first use 30 to 39 years prior to interview compared with no use, whereas in Japan, early first use was associated with a decreased risk (Morrison et al, 1982). Many of the studies in Table 4.18.9 presented results for men and women separately, although no pattern of stronger associations (in either direction) for either sex is evident.

An ecological study in Denmark focused upon *in utero* exposure to saccharin. No increase in bladder cancer incidence was observed among a cohort of people born between 1941 and 1945, a time of increased saccharin consumption due to the scarcity of sugar during the second World War, compared with people born between 1931 and 1940, a pre-war period, when saccharin consumption was many times lower (Jenssen and Kamby, 1982).

Concern about saccharin arose because dietary administration of high doses (5% or 7%) to rats over two generations resulted in a significant increase in the frequency of bladder cancer, particularly in males (IARC, 1980). Saccharin is not mutagenic in most short-term assays (IARC, 1980; 1987; Cohen and Ellwein, 1994), but has been shown to be co-carcinogenic in an in vitro cell transformation assay (West et al, 1994).

Saccharin binds to urinary protein, thus enhancing precipitation and crystallisation that occasionally occur in control male rats. It has been suggested that the silicate crystals have cytotoxic effects on urothelial cells (Cohen and Ellwein, 1994). Because human urine has very little protein and has less sodium than rat urine, it is considered highly unlikely that silicate crystals would form under normal sodium saccharin ingestion (Cohen and Ellwein, 1994). Thus, positive carcinogenicity and tumour promotion in rats, but not in mice or hamsters, appear to be the result of changes in urinary pH and sodium levels that specifically alter rat urinary tract physiology (Fukushima et al, 1986 ; Cohen et al, 1991). However, saccharin can replace insulin as a growth factor in cultured human skin cells, and so its biological activity cannot be completely disregarded (West et al, 1994).

On the basis of data reviewed to date, JECFA stated that it is inappropriate to consider the bladder tumours induced in male rats by sodium saccharin consumption to be relevant to the assessment of a toxicological hazard to humans (WHO, 1993).

Cyclamates were originally associated with bladder cancer in male rats following studies involving mixtures of cyclamate and saccharin. Subsequently, several carcinogenicity studies in rats have failed to confirm this observation, and no increase in bladder tumours has been observed in mouse carcinogenicity studies. Following oral administration to two strains of mice, an increased incidence of lymphosarcomas was observed in females of one strain only. IARC (1987) classified cyclamates as Group 3 based on inadequate evidence of carcinogenicity in humans and limited evidence in experimental studies.

JECFA concluded that the data did not indicate that cyclamate was a carcinogenic risk to humans and allocated an ADI of 0–11 mg/kg based on a no-effect level for a non-carcinogenic end-point, testicular atrophy. However, under the Delaney Clause, the US Food and Drug Administration (FDA) was required to ban the use of cyclamates in the USA. Under the same legislation, the FDA would have banned the use of saccharin also; however, the US Congress passed legislation imposing a moratorium on the banning of saccharin as a food additive.

Based on the large amount of epidemiological data, the evidence shows that consumption of saccharin probably has no relationship with the risk of bladder cancer in the amounts obtainable from normal diets.

The evidence based on consistent, but less numerous, epidemiological data shows that consumption of cyclamates possibly has no relationship with the risk of bladder cancer.

Evidence relating to the consumption of aspartame or acesulfame K and bladder cancer is limited; no judgement is possible.

4.18.3.2 Contaminants
Waterborne residues
Chlorinated hydrocarbons
In 1991, IARC reviewed the relationship between chlorinated water and risk of cancers of the bladder. One cohort study (Wilkins and Comstock, 1981) reported statistically non-significantly elevated risks in both men (RR=1.8; 0.8–4.8) and women (RR=1.6; 0.5–6.3). Two case-control studies, using measures of individual levels of exposure, noted elevated risks of bladder cancer in women (OR=3.2; 1.2–8.7), but not men (Cantor et al, 1987), and in both sexes together (OR=1.6; 1.2–2.1) (Zierler et al, 1988). Four case-control studies, using a community-based definition of exposure, showed no associations between chlorinated water and bladder cancer risk, using a variety of comparison exposures (Brenniman et al, 1980; Gottlieb et al, 1982; Young and Kanarek, 1983; Zierler et al, 1986). Six correlation studies showed no relationship (Bean et al, 1982; Tuthill and Moore, 1980; Isaacson et al, 1983) or weakly elevated risks

(DeRouen and Diem, 1977; Kuzma et al, 1977; Cantor et al, 1978) in various comparisons of chlorinated with unchlorinated water.

The evidence suggests that chlorinated drinking water may increase the risk of bladder cancer but is, as yet, insufficient.

4.18.3.3 Cooking

Fried foods

A prospective study in Hawaii reported a relative risk of 2.6 (0.6–10.4) among men consuming fried vegetables five times or more per week, compared with once or less per week ($p = 0.06$ for trend) (Chyou et al, 1993).

A case-control study in Sweden (Steineck et al, 1990) that measured intakes of various fried food found elevated risks not only for fried meat but also for fried eggs, fried potatoes and gravy; subjects with the highest intake of these foods, combined, had an OR of 2.4 (1.4–4.2). The association did not change after adjustment for fat intake. A case-control study in Washington State (USA) similarly observed a strong increase in risk with greater consumption of fried foods, OR = 2.2 (1.3–4.0) ($p = 0.006$ for trend) for consumption more than twice per week compared to none (Bruemmer et al, 1996). A case-control study in New York (USA) (Vena et al, 1992) also noted a statistically significant increase in risk with gravy consumption, but showed no relevant data.

If high consumption of fried foods confers increased risk, heterocyclic amines are the most plausible candidate. Heterocyclic amines are potent carcinogens, and are found in fried or grilled (broiled) meats (Wakabayashi et al, 1992) (see chapter 7.7 for a detailed discussion). A recent experimental study demonstrated carcinogenicity of heterocyclic amine in the urinary bladder in male rats but not in females (Takahashi et al, 1995).

The evidence suggests that the consumption of fried foods may increase the risk of bladder cancer but is, as yet, insufficient.

PART III

NUTRITION, FOOD AND CANCER

CHAPTER FIVE

Dietary constituents

People consume foods and drinks: it is overall dietary patterns, rather than individual chemical compounds found in food, that should probably be seen as the key factors affecting the risk of major chronic diseases such as cancer, particularly when the context is recommendations to policy-makers and the public.

However, much, if not most, research on diet and cancer focuses on component parts of foods and drinks. Accordingly, this chapter assesses dietary constituents, some of which, such as carbohydrates, fats, protein, and various vitamins and minerals, are well-known. Carbohydrates include starches, sugars and fibre (or non-starch polysaccharides). There are many types of fat. Various vitamins and minerals have been studied, as have other bioactive compounds found mostly in foods of plant origin; these latter constituents are not usually classified as nutrients.

This chapter is derived from, but does not repeat, the literature reviews in chapter 4. To avoid repetition, data on each constituent and its relation to specific cancers are briefly summarised; in some cases, evidence for a dose–response relationship is presented. Each section of this chapter begins with a summary of the panel's judgements, in words and matrices. The dietary constituents, where they are found in the diet, their physiological functions, and the requirement for the constituents, are described. Patterns of consumption in different parts of the world are presented, and issues about the interpretation of the data are outlined. Judgements of previous reports, and public health considerations other than for cancer, are summarised. Finally the panel makes its recommendations for future research.

The evidence that was extensively reviewed in chapter 4 is then summarised, in a set format. Consistent with a policy agreed by the panel, evidence of protection against cancer is assessed first. Assessments are placed in order of confidence in their causality: thus, an assessment that evidence of protection against a specific cancer is convincing will be placed first. In this way, the role of nutrition in the prevention of cancer is emphasised, and possible patterns whereby a dietary constituent may consistently modify risk across a number of cancer sites can most readily be discerned.

The sequence of the chapter broadly follows nutritional convention and, begins with macroconstituents. Energy intake itself is assessed, together with factors necessarily connected with energy balance: growth, age at menarche, and stature, body mass and physical activity. Starch, fibre (non-starch polysaccharides) and sugar are assessed in the second section. The third section assesses the evidence not only on total fat in diets, but also of saturated and animal fats, and on unsaturated and vegetable fats. Protein is assessed in the fourth section. The fifth section assesses alcoholic drinks.

The final three sections deal with dietary microconstituents. Vitamins include carotenoids, vitamins C and E, and folate. Minerals include selenium, calcium, iodine, and iron. The chapter ends with reviews of the evidence on bioactive compounds mostly found in plant foods.

Other key issues are addressed. In this chapter, these include energy intake and its relationship with body mass; the role of relative degrees of refinement of starch; the relationship between diets high in fat, high body mass (obesity), energy density and cancer risk; the relevance of the antioxidant properties of various dietary microconstituents; the possibility that some cancers may be caused by multiple nutrient deficiencies; the evidence derived from intervention trials using dietary supplements; methyl donors; hydrogenated fats and deficiency diets.

5.1 Energy and related factors

In common with all other animals, humans need energy from food. The energy intake of adults in energy balance (neither losing nor gaining weight) varies as a function of height, body mass and physical activity.

Deficiency of energy remains a major public health problem within Africa and Asia. In the developed world, and also in urban areas of the developing world, energy-dense diets, together with physical inactivity, lead to overweight and obesity, which in turn increase the risk of many chronic diseases.

ENERGY AND RELATED FACTORS AND CANCER

In the judgement of the panel, energy intake and factors related to energy intake modify the risk of cancers of various sites as shown below, or else have no relationship with them. Judgements are graded according to the strength of the evidence.

EVIDENCE	DECREASES RISK	NO RELATIONSHIP	INCREASES RISK
Convincing	*Physical activity:* Colon		*Rapid growth, greater adult height:* Breast *High body mass:* Endometrium
Probable			*High body mass:* Breast[a] Kidney
Possible	*Physical activity:* Lung Breast	*High body mass:* Pancreas Prostate	*High energy intake:* Pancreas *Greater adult height:* Colon, rectum *Frequent eating:* Colon, rectum *High body mass:* Gallbladder Colon
Insufficient			*High energy intake:* Prostate *High body mass:* Thyroid

For an explanation of the terms used in the matrix, see chapter 3.
High body mass may usually be equated with obesity (defined as BMI >30)
[a] Post-menopausal

The panel has reached the following conclusions. A number of interrelated factors connected with energy balance may affect cancer risk. These include level of energy intake itself; rates of childhood growth and age at puberty; adult body mass and amount of physical activity.

The applicability to humans of animal experiments that show that energy restriction itself decreases the risk of cancer of some sites, is difficult to assess directly. The more relevant factors are body mass and physical activity, rather than energy intake itself.

The evidence that rapid growth in infancy and childhood, and early menarche, themselves both diet-related, increase the risk of breast cancer, is convincing.

The evidence that high body mass, itself caused by a combination of energy-dense diets, excess energy intake, and lack of physical activity, increases the risk of endometrial cancer, is convincing. Obesity probably increases the risk of postmenopausal breast cancer, and renal cancer. The panel notes that obesity also possibly increases the risk of colon cancer and cancer of the gallbladder.

Evidence that regular physical activity protects against colon cancer is convincing. The panel notes that physical activity possibly decreases the risk of lung cancer and breast cancer.

INTRODUCTION

Energy here refers to the energy (measured as calories or joules) derived from food that is needed by the body as fuel.

SOURCES

Dietary macroconstituents – carbohydrate, fat, protein and alcohol – which are reviewed and assessed in chapters 5.2 – 5.5, all provide energy. Energy values are about 4 kcal/g (16 kJ/g) for carbohydrate (starch and sugar) and protein, 9 kcal/g (37 kJ/g) for fat, and 7 kcal/g (29 kJ/g) for alcohol.

Because foods of plant origin are bulky, usually containing substantial volumes of water and fibrous material as well as carbohydrates and other dietary constituents, diets that are made up mainly of starchy staples, vegetables and fruits are likely to have a low content of energy per unit of food. Because fat contains the most energy, diets with a high fat content are likely to be energy-dense, which is to say that they have a high content of energy per unit of food. Dietary bulk and energy density are inversely related.

RELATED FACTORS

Factors related to energy intake itself include growth in childhood; weight; height; body mass; and physical activity. The effect of total energy on human health can be assessed fully only by also taking these factors into account.

FUNCTIONS

Energy is required by all living organisms to support life. Plants use the energy of sunlight to create complex carbohydrate, fat and protein. All animals, including humans, then consume and digest the constituents to extract energy.

REQUIREMENTS

Human energy requirement is defined as the energy intake that will balance energy expenditure when the individual has a body size, composition and level of physical activity consistent with long-term good health (FAO/WHO/UNU, 1985). Energy requirements therefore vary according to body size, body mass, nature of diets, age, sex, state of health, and climate, as well as genetic differences. Basal metabolic rate (BMR) and physical activity together account for the greater part of the energy expenditure of individuals.

Thus, the energy requirements of individuals in good health can vary from about 1,450 kcal/day (6 MJ/day) for small sedentary women, to 4,250 kcal/day (18 MJ/day) for large very active men.

The requirements of population groups vary from 1,900 kcal/day (8 MJ/day) in some African countries to 2,150 kcal/day (9 MJ/day) in some Asian countries, to 2,300–2,350 kcal/day (9.6–9.8 MJ/day) in Europe and North America. These variations are largely a reflection of average body size. In this report, the 'reference figure' of 2,000 kcal/day is used as a basis for calculating the dietary recommendations in chapter 8.1.

Expressed as kilocalories per kilogram of body weight, the requirements of the more active populations in the developing world are greater than those of typically sedentary people in the developed world. Figures are approximately 38 kcal/kg (160 kJ/kg) in Africa, 40 kcal/kg (170 kJ/kg) in Asia, and 33 kcal/kg (140 kJ/kg) in Europe and North America.

Absolute and relative energy requirements in the developed world have decreased remarkably in the second half of the twentieth century, reflecting the increased use of machines to replace human physical effort at work, at home and for transport. In the UK, recommended daily allowances (RDAs) for men were reduced from 38 kcal/kg (160 kJ/kg) in the 1930s to 33 kcal/kg (140 kJ/kg) in 1991. With increasing urbanisation in the developing world, this reduction of energy needed is now being repeated.

Human energy metabolism includes energy intake and energy output. Energy balance (intake minus output) can be in a state of equilibrium, negative (where energy intake is less than energy output), or positive (where energy intake is more than energy output). Positive energy balance, leading to weight gain as excess energy intake is converted to adipose and lean tissue, may be caused by high energy intake, by low levels of energy output, or by a combination of the two. Chronic energy deficiency leads to negative energy balance and weight loss as body tissues are broken down (catabolised) to meet the body's requirement for energy.

CONSUMPTION PATTERNS

Many people live in a state of approximate energy balance, and are neither greatly underweight nor overweight at any time in their lives. Public health problems associated with energy intake and its consequences are different in different parts of the world. Until the 1970s and 1980s, this contrast corresponded fairly reliably with differences in the nature of food supplies in the developing world and the developed world. Public health problems associated with energy intake and output have been identified as problems of deficiency in the developing world and problems of excess in the developed world.

Historically, most people in the developing world (Africa, Latin America and Asia) have consumed bulky low-energy diets and have been necessarily physically active throughout their lives. In some developing countries and regions, energy deficiency in infants can be caused by weaning diets (cereal-based gruels or porridges) that are so watery and low in energy that a sufficient quantity for energy needs cannot be consumed. In childhood, chronic severe energy deficiency, caused either by lack of food or by very bulky diets, can slow growth rates and lead to a permanent deficit in height. Other factors, notably infectious diseases and a low intake of nutrients such as protein, also affect growth. Infection interacting with chronic energy deficiency is known as the malnutrition–infection complex.

By contrast, since industrialisation, most people in the developed world (western and northern Europe, North America, Australasia) have consumed increasingly energy-dense diets and have become increasingly physically inactive. Chronic energy excess caused by energy-dense diets, such as those rich in fat, readily induce or allow an excess intake of energy (see chapter 5.3). This leads to overweight and obesity. In children, accelerated growth caused by diets dense not just in energy but also in other dietary constituents, including protein, also leads to early menarche. This is relevant to cancer because both accelerated growth in childhood and early menarche are established risk factors for breast cancer.

The relatively clear-cut distinction between the developing and the developed world has become confused since the 1970s and 1980s by two coincident secular shifts. The developing world is becoming industrialised with accelerating speed. Diets in urban areas and to some extent in rural areas in Africa, Latin America and Asia have also become more energy-dense at the same time as populations have become increasingly physically inactive. By contrast, in the developed world, a significant minority of health-conscious people are choosing to consume relatively bulky, low energy-dense diets and may also engage in physically active recreation.

INTERPRETATION OF THE DATA

The relationship of dietary energy to cancer risk is complex. The degree of energy intake may itself affect the cancer risk, and both human and animal studies have produced evidence on the relationship between levels of energy intake and cancer risk.

However, what is apparently a link between energy intake or output and cancer may actually be an effect of other factors that are related to energy balance rather than to energy intake alone. Such factors, as noted above, include the rate of childhood growth and age at puberty, which are the result not just of energy intake but also of levels of specific dietary constituents, notably protein. Other factors related to energy include body mass, which is determined by the net balance or imbalance between energy intake and output throughout life. The degree of physical activity, which itself affects energy input and body mass, may also affect the body's metabolism, independent of its effect on energy output or intake.

Further, there is often a strong collinearity between energy intake and fat consumption, which provides the most energy-dense component of diet. Hence, any effect ascribed to energy may in fact be caused by the fat contribution (see chapter 5.3).

Correlations between energy availability and cancer rates in different populations (Armstrong and Doll, 1975) should be interpreted with caution. Energy intakes in developed countries are substantially overestimated in food balance sheets because, generally speaking, the more affluent a nation, the more food is wasted or fed to pets. Nevertheless, the absolute energy intake may still be higher in developed countries than in developing countries, because of the heavier weight and taller stature of adults in the developed world. Energy intake relative to body weight is, however, generally higher in developing countries, because of higher levels of physical activity. Few human studies have examined energy intake in relation to overall energy balance, so it is difficult to determine the independent effects of energy intake as such.

Measurements of total energy expenditure are also difficult to make and are prone to error. The most accurate techniques (calorimetry and doubly-labelled water) have not been used (and are unlikely to be used) in epidemiological studies of cancer. A further problem is that most people in developed countries and regions lead sedentary lives. If they are conscious of gaining weight, they may restrict their energy intake; this will tend to obscure analyses that would otherwise show a relationship between either physical activity or the energy content of diets on the one hand, and body mass on the other.

For these reasons, the impact of energy intake and output on cancer risk in epidemiological studies may be best assessed by means of related factors such as rates of growth, relative body mass, or levels of physical activity (Willett, 1990).

Rates of childhood growth, age at puberty and attained adult height are sometimes used as indicators of energy intake in early life. However, growth rates are not a function only of energy intake but also of many dietary constituents, particularly protein. Nor are they functions solely of diet: in the developing world, growth and the height attained in adulthood can be compromised by repeated infections in early life.

Findings on relative body mass also need careful interpretation. Evidence that high body mass increases the risk of some cancers is relatively clear. Evidence on low body mass

is not straightforward, however, because smokers are, on average, thinner than non-smokers, and also because the cancer process itself may cause loss of weight, perhaps even before the cancer is evident. Any evidence that thin people seem to be at higher risk of cancer is therefore liable to be confused in any studies that do not control for current or previous exposure to smoking, and for chronic diseases other than cancer. By their nature, it is usually not possible to control for undiagnosed cancers except, in some cases, by excluding those that occur in the first few years of a long-term study.

The ratio of waist and hip circumferences (the waist-to-hip ratio or WHR) provides a useful measure for identifying subjects with abdominal or gluteal adiposity. Abdominal adiposity, also called android adiposity, is generally more common in men, but can also be found in women, and is associated with a higher risk of diabetes mellitus and cardiovascular disease. Body weight is partly a function of height, so various indices have now been developed to assess body mass and relative leanness or fatness. Early studies have not always used readily interpretable terms. Quetelet's index or the body mass index (BMI), which is $weight/height^2$, is now the one most commonly used. This is a measure of body weight adjusted for height. It correlates well with degrees of leanness or fatness for men, but somewhat less well for women, for whom $weight/height^{1.5}$ may be more accurate. Relative body weight (RBW) is also used. This is measured body weight for a given height compared with what is considered the desirable weight for that height. Neither of these indices discriminates between adipose and lean body tissue, so very muscular people will be misclassified as more overweight (fatter) than they are.

Findings on physical activity similarly need careful interpretation. In affluent societies, adults who are physically active are those who usually engage in strenuous leisure-time pursuits rather than in hard physical work. These individuals tend to be particularly health conscious and so are also usually non-smokers and consume a more healthy diet. Similarly, cross-cultural studies show that physically active societies generally have lower cancer rates at many sites, but these rates may also reflect the very different dietary patterns of these active communities.

Finally, most studies that have examined physical activity in relation to cancer risk have not assessed energy intake as well; however, those that also examined body mass have found that physical activity may interact with it, such that those at highest risk are those with a high body mass and low physical activity (Slattery et al, 1997a).

JUDGEMENTS OF PREVIOUS REPORTS

In *The Causes of Cancer*, Doll and Peto (1981) stated: 'over-nutrition should perhaps come first rather than last on a list of aspects of diet which may affect the incidence of cancer'. Their review also concluded that early menarche is diet-related and increases the risk of breast cancer.

The National Academy of Sciences report, *Diet, Nutrition*

and Cancer (NAS, 1982), noted that animal experiments consistently showed a reduction in the incidence of tumours as a result of caloric restriction. The report commented that this effect was not necessarily a result of a reduction in energy intake as such, but perhaps a result of a reduction in fat intake. In human studies, the report concluded that evidence on the role of energy intakes, as such, in carcinogenesis was 'slight and largely indirect'.

Nutrition and Health (Surgeon General, 1988) summarised more recent evidence showing that obese men and women were, respectively, 33% and 55% more likely to die from cancer than people of average weight. It concluded 'overweight individuals are at increased risk of … some types of cancer'. Any role of physical activity in cancer was not mentioned.

Diet and Health, the 1989 report of the National Academy of Sciences (NAS, 1989), noted a lack of human studies, and mentioned more recent experimental studies showing that energy restriction inhibited mammary and intestinal cancers, even when the restricted diets were high in fat.

SIGNIFICANCE FOR OTHER DISEASES

Chronic energy deficiency is common in many developing countries where, among children, protein-energy malnutrition causes increased morbidity and mortality. In developed countries on the other hand, public health problems are largely associated with chronic energy excess, together with physical inactivity, leading to overweight and obesity.

Elevated levels of body fat, caused by a combination of physical inactivity and chronic energy excess, increases the risk of a number of disorders and diseases other than cancer, including gallstones, high blood pressure, adult-onset diabetes mellitus, and coronary heart disease, and reduces life expectancy (WHO, 1990).

Regular physical activity maintains or improves regulation of energy balance, the metabolism of food, cardiovascular function, strength of the musculo-skeletal system, and hormone function, and increases life expectancy. Correspondingly, lack of regular physical activity, typical in industrialised countries and regions, is identified as increasing risk of obesity, other metabolic disorders, muscle wasting, bone disease, and adult-onset diabetes (WHO, 1990).

Between 1961 and 1991, 100 expert reports were published that were principally concerned with diet and cardiovascular disease or with diet and other chronic diseases. Most referred to developed countries and regions. The tendency of these reports was to recommend more physical activity rather then fewer calories. A total of eight recommended that whole populations should consume fewer calories (energy), whereas 33 recommended fewer calories only for population sub-groups at high risk of cardiovascular disease or for those who were already overweight or obese. Correspondingly, 45 recommended more physical activity for whole populations, and a further 16 for those at high risk: 61 in all, with none disagreeing (Cannon, 1992).

FUTURE RESEARCH

The panel made the following recommendations for future research:

- Studies of nutritional status early in life and its effect on growth, age at menarche, and the risk of cancer should be undertaken.
- Studies of the mechanisms whereby obesity and physical activity influence cancer risk should continue.
- The relative risks of cancers at different levels of BMI, physical activity level and with different patterns of fat distribution, need to be better established.

ASSESSMENT

The evidence on which this assessment is based is reviewed in the relevant sections of chapter 4.

Much of the epidemiological evidence on energy and related factors focuses on the relationship between high energy intake, high body mass and low levels of physical activity, and on cancers that are more common in developed countries and urban areas of developing countries: colorectal and breast cancer, in particular, and, to a lesser extent, cancers of the pancreas, endometrium, prostate and other sites.

5.1.1 ENERGY INTAKE

Epidemiological data on energy intake, as such, in relation to cancer risk are not extensive. Experimental studies show that low (restricted) energy intake reduces the risk of cancer at specific sites. Obversely, there is some evidence from epidemiological studies that high energy intake is a factor in an increased risk of cancers of some sites.

Evidence of decreased risk

Any data suggesting that high energy intake decreases the risk of cancer of any site probably reflects a protective effect of high levels of physical activity which in turn increases energy requirements, rather than any protective effect of high energy intake itself.

Evidence of increased risk

CONVINCING	PROBABLE	POSSIBLE	INSUFFICIENT
		Pancreas	Prostate

Pancreas (4.7). Ecological and animal data suggest that high energy intake, in itself, increases the risk of cancer of the pancreas. On balance, the data are supported by findings from case-control studies. The panel judged that high energy intake possibly increases the risk of pancreatic cancer. For assessment of high energy intake leading to energy imbalance, see 'body mass', below.

Prostate (4.15). Two cohort and four case-control studies have examined high energy and the risk of prostate cancer. It is difficult to determine from the evidence whether the apparently increased risk of prostate cancer with increased energy intake is due solely to caloric intake per se or to high intake of other dietary constituents or particularly energy-dense food groups. Taking this limitation into consideration, the panel judged the evidence as insufficient.

There are data suggesting that high energy intake may increase the overall risk of cancer. In international correlation study (Armstrong and Doll, 1975) found a relationship between the level of dietary energy supply and an increase in the overall incidence of cancer and mortality rates in the population. Correlations were also shown between energy intake and the incidence of, and mortality from, cancers of the breast, colon, rectum, uterus and kidney in women, and cancers of the colon, rectum, kidney and central nervous system in men.

Human correlation studies are supported by data from other experimental studies, which, since the early years of this century, have shown the obverse relationship, namely that low total energy intake results in reduced cancer risk. Since the early 1990s, experimental studies have demonstrated that underfeeding inhibits the development of cancers in general, and of the lung, mammary gland and skin in particular, as well as sarcoma and leukaemia (Rous, 1914; Tannenbaum, 1949, 1959; Carroll 1975; Kritchevsky and Klurfeld, 1986).

It had, at one point, been thought that fat, as the most energy-dense dietary constituent, might be the key factor. However, more recent work (Kritchevsky et al, 1984; Kritchevsky, 1985; Albanes, 1987; Klurfeld et al, 1989a, b) showed that not only did animals that were fed diets low in fat and low in energy produce fewer chemically induced tumours, but so also did those fed diets high in fats and low in energy. This suggested that energy itself was the key factor, at least in animals and for mammary cancer. There was increasing protection as energy was restricted by 10%, 20%, 30% and 40%. A meta-analysis of 100 rodent studies (Freedman et al, 1990) however, has shown an effect of fat independent of energy.

The mechanisms that would explain any possible effect of energy restriction on tumour growth include reduced stimulation of tumour cell growth (Ames and Shigenaga, 1992); a drop in plasma insulin (Klurfeld et al, 1989a, b); reduced cell proliferation and enhanced apoptosis (programmed cell death) (James and Muskhelishvili, 1994); enhanced maintenance of DNA repair (Weraarchakul et al, 1989); and reduced free radical damage (Yu, 1994).

The significance of the data on energy intake and cancer risk in humans remains unclear. The epidemiological data mostly do not distinguish any effect of energy as such from that of other dietary constituents.

In the view of the panel, the effect of energy intake on cancer is best assessed by examining the data on related factors: rate of growth, body mass, and physical activity.

5.1.2 GROWTH AND HEIGHT

Rapid rates of growth and early menarche are established factors for increased risk of breast cancer, a cancer common particularly in developed countries and the urban areas of developing countries. Tall adult stature, when it is a consequence of rapid growth, is also an established marker for a relatively high breast cancer risk. There are also some very limited data on birth weight, not reviewed here. It follows that slow rates of growth in infancy and early childhood, and late menarche, are associated with a relatively low breast cancer risk.

Evidence of increased risk

CONVINCING	PROBABLE	POSSIBLE	INSUFFICIENT
Breast[a]		Colon, rectum[b]	

a Rapid growth and greater adult height
b Greater adult height

Colon, rectum (4.10). Four cohort studies suggest that tall adults are at greater risk of colon cancer, although the majority of case-control studies showed no association. Possible mechanisms have been suggested. greater adult height possibly increases the risk of colorectal cancer.

Breast (4.11). Six cohort and ecological studies have examined the relationship between diet and early growth and/or age at menarche. Eight cohort studies and a number of case-control studies assessed height and the overall risk of breast cancer. Evidence that rapid growth leads to earlier age at menarche, itself an established risk factor for breast cancer, and that greater height increases the risk of breast cancer, is convincing.

5.1.3 BODY MASS

There is abundant evidence that relative body mass affects the risk of cancer of a number of sites. Evidence that obesity increases risk is strongest for cancers of the endometrium, breast and colon. Evidence on low body mass and cancer risk is liable to be confounded by the effects of smoking and possibly by undiagnosed cancer.

Evidence of no relationship

CONVINCING	PROBABLE	POSSIBLE	INSUFFICIENT
		Pancreas	
		Prostate	

Pancreas (4.7). Prostate (4.15). The balance of epidemiological evidence, from one cohort and four case-control studies on the pancreas and from nine cohort and nine case-control studies on the prostate, indicates that there is little or no association between high body mass and risk of pancreatic or prostate cancer. High body mass possibly has no relationship with the risk of pancreatic and prostate cancers.

Evidence of increased risk

CONVINCING	PROBABLE	POSSIBLE	INSUFFICIENT
Endometrium	Breast[a]	Gallbladder	Thyroid
	Kidney	Colon	

[a] post-menopause

Endometrium (4.13). Five case-control and six cohort studies have examined high body mass and the risk of endometrial cancer. The evidence that obesity (measured by elevated BMI or RBW) increases the risk of endometrial cancer, is convincing.

Figure 5.1.1 shows that the relative risk of endometrial cancer increases over about a threefold range as BMI increases from around 20 to 35. Each study included in Figure 5.1.1 (selected using the criteria described in chapter 3) shows that a BMI of greater than 30 is associated with a greater risk than a BMI of 23 or less.

Breast (4.11). Nineteen case-control and three cohort studies examined high body mass and the risk of breast cancer in postmenopausal women. The evidence from most case-control and a balance of cohort studies shows that high body mass (measured by elevated BMI or RBW) probably increases the risk of breast cancer after the menopause.

The relationship between body mass and the risk of breast cancer is summarised in Figure 5.1.2. This figure suggests that the relative risk of postmenopausal breast cancer increases over about a 1.8-fold range as BMI increases from 17 to 37. This is a modest but steady increase and all of the

Figure 5.1.1 Endometrial cancer and BMI, cohort and case-control studies with population controls

Relative risk vs Body mass index (kg/m²)

Swanson et al, 1993, CC
Olson et al, 1995, CC
Törnberg et al, 1994, Cohort
Shu et al, 1992, CC
Le Marchand et al, 1991, cohort pre and postmenopausal
Regression: −1.340 + 0.108x, p=0.0004

This figure shows the dose–response relationship between body mass index and the risk of endometrial cancer. The fitted regression line shows that the relative risk of endometrial cancer increases over about a threefold range as BMI increases from around 20 to about 35. A BMI greater than 30 is always associated with a higher risk than a BMI of 23 or less.

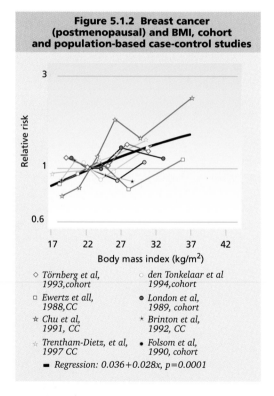

Figure 5.1.2 Breast cancer (postmenopausal) and BMI, cohort and population-based case-control studies

Relative risk vs Body mass index (kg/m²)

Törnberg et al, 1993, cohort
den Tonkelaar et al 1994, cohort
Ewertz et all, 1988, CC
London et al, 1989, cohort
Chu et al, 1991, CC
Brinton et al, 1992, CC
Trentham-Dietz, et al, 1997 CC
Folsom et al, 1990, cohort
Regression: 0.036+0.028x, p=0.0001

This figure shows the dose–response relationship between body mass index and the risk of postmenopausal breast cancer. The fitted regression line shows that the relative risk increases about 1.8-fold from a BMI of 17 to 37. A BMI of greater than 30 is associated with higher risk than a BMI of 23 or less.

studies in Figure 5.1.2 (selected using the criteria described in chapter 3) show that a BMI greater than 30 is associated with an elevated risk over that experienced by women with a BMI of 23 or less.

Kidney (4.17). The evidence from eight out of nine case-control studies is that obesity (usually measured as a BMI of 30+) probably increases the risk of renal cancer. The relationship between body mass and renal cancer is summarised in Figure 5.1.3. This figure suggests that the relative risk of renal cancer increases over about a 2.4-fold range from a BMI of less than 20 to a BMI of around 35. There is clear evidence from each study illustrated (which were selected according to the criteria described in chapter 3) that a BMI of greater than 30 is associated with a higher risk than a BMI of 23 or less.

Gallbladder (4.8). One large cohort study and a case-control study both found increased risk of gallbladder cancer

associated with obesity, particularly in women. In addition to this direct evidence, obesity is an established risk factor for gallstones, themselves a risk factor of gallbladder cancer. Obesity possibly increases the risk of gallbladder cancer.

Colon (4.10). Over twenty studies have examined the relationship beteen high body mass and colon cancer. A number of case-control studies do not find an association between high BMI or RBW and an increased risk of colon cancer. Other case control studies and most cohort studies, however, do find an association, although it is less consistent for women. High body mass possibly increases the risk of colon cancer, perhaps particularly in men.

Thyroid (4.16). Case-control studies tend to show an increased risk but the data are insufficient to make a judgement.

The relationship between energy intake, body mass and the overall risk of cancer has been extensively assessed (Albanes, 1987; NAS, 1989; Surgeon General, 1988). In a large cohort study, the lowest overall cancer mortality was found in men whose body weights ranged from 10% below to 20% above average. In women, the lowest overall risk was found for body weights ranging from 20% below to 10% above average. Non-smoking males showed a relationship between RBW and cancer mortality that was nearly linear (Lew and Garfinkel, 1979). In the USA, obese men (defined as more than 40% overweight) have been found to be at 33% greater risk of dying from cancer, compared with men of average weight. Obese women (defined in the same way) have been found to be 55% more likely to die from cancer. These data are supported by studies of differences in energy intake and obesity in animals (Pariza and Boutwell, 1987).

Suggested biological pathways are that the level of energy intake, and its supply to cells, controls cell growth, and that an excess of energy may increase cell replication and thus cancer risk; or, possibly, that obesity makes it more likely that higher amounts of chemical carcinogens are stored in body fat. In the case of breast cancer, excess energy intake leading to obesity may increase the risk by higher conversion of androstenedione into oestradiol which, after menopause, is produced solely in adipose tissue.

5.1.4 PHYSICAL ACTIVITY

Evidence consistently shows that high levels of physical activity reduce the risk of colon cancer, the third most common cancer of both men and women worldwide. High levels of physical activity possibly also protect against breast cancer.

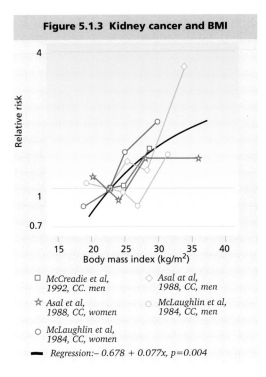

Figure 5.1.3 Kidney cancer and BMI

Relative risk

Body mass index (kg/m²)

☐ McCreadie et al, 1992, CC. men
◇ Asal at al, 1988, CC, men
★ Asal et al, 1988, CC, women
○ McLaughlin et al, 1984, CC, men
○ McLaughlin et al, 1984, CC, women
— Regression:– 0.678 + 0.077x, p=0.004

This figure shows the dose–response relationship between body mass index and the risk of kidney cancer from five case-control studies. The fitted regression line shows that the relative risk increases about 2.4-fold from a BMI of less than 20 to one of 35. A BMI of greater than 30 is always associated with higher risk than a BMI of 23 or less.

Evidence of decreased risk

CONVINCING	PROBABLE	POSSIBLE	INSUFFICIENT
Colon		Lung	
		Breast	

TABLE 5.1.1 PHYSICAL ACTIVITY AND THE RISK OF COLON CANCER IN MEN*

STUDY	HIGH ACTIVITY	ORs/RRs FOR MODERATE ACTIVITY	LOW ACTIVITY	HOURS AT DAILY JOB FOR MINIMUM RISK	HOURS AT SPORTS ACTIVITY FOR MINIMUM RISK	POPULATION STUDIED
Albanes et al, 1989	1.0	1.2	1.6			USA, NHANES I
Ballard-Barbash et al, 1990	1.0	1.4	1.8	>4		USA, Framingham
Brownson et al, 1991	1.0	1.1	1.2	>2		USA, Missouri
Garabrant et al, 1984	1.0	1.6	1.8	6.4		USA, California
Gerhardsson et al, 1986	1.0	-	1.3	4		Sweden
Gerhardsson et al, 1988	1.0	-	1.5	_a		Sweden
Giovannucci et al, 1995	1.0	1.8	1.9	–	4/week vigorous sport	USA
Kato et al, 1990	1.0	1.7	1.8	> 6		Japan
Lee et al, 1991	1.0	-	2.0	_b		USA, Harvard
Paffenbarger et al, 1987	1.0	-	1.2	–	5/week sports	USA
Peters et al, 1989	1.1	1.0	1.7	>6		USA, California
Severson et al, 1989	1.1	0.8	1.4	_c		Hawaii/Japanese
Slattery et al, 1990	1.0	-	1.4-1.6	_d		USA, Utah
Thun et al, 1992	1.0	-	1.6	ns		USA, all states
Vena et al, 1985	1.0	-	2.0	_e		USA, New York & Washington State
Wu et al, 1987	1.0	2.2	2.5	>2[f]		USA, California

*There are some data available for women but women tend to spend less time in vigorous activities, and so the range of activity levels tends to be inadequate to reveal a significant difference in risk.

[a] Including activity in both leisure time and at work increased RR to 2.5 for the most sedentary
[b] 500 kcal per week activity (stair climbing) associated with lowered risk
[c] Similar relative risk with leisure activity
[d] Relative risk values expressed as odds ratios; greater for coded job activity than for self-report activity
[e] Double risk for >20 year in light activity job. Lower risk seen with jobs
   with frequent lifting and carrying of weights >22.5 kg
[f] Current activity in retired people over 64 years old
[ns] Not significant

Colon (4.10). Eleven case-control studies and nine cohort studies have examined physical activity and the risk of colon cancer. Strong and consistent evidence that regular physical activity protects against colon cancer is convincing. Plausible, though not established, biological pathways have been identified. Evidence on rectal cancer alone is less impressive.

Most studies on physical activity and colon cancer have used methods that cannot readily be assessed together in a dose–response figure. The results of such studies are summarised in Table 5.1.1.

Taken together, these show that, at high physical activity levels, there is a reduction of the risk of colon cancer to about 60% of that of sedentary people.

Many of the earlier studies cited in the table are based on occupational activity in men. Some studies also take into account leisure-time activity, but this is not available for all studies. Some uncertainty remains in relation to the protective value of the intensity and duration of physical activity and some studies (Lee et al, 1991) suggest that lifelong activity levels are necessary for protection. Those studies that have recorded both energy intakes and body size as well as activity levels suggest that it is the activity itself that is protective (Slattery et al, 1988; Gerhardsson de Verdier et al, 1990; Whittemore et al, 1990), but later data are consistent with an interaction between body mass and activity such that

the highest risk is seen in those with the highest BMI and lowest level of physical activity (Slattery et al, 1997a).

The study of Slattery et al (1997b) is used for illustrative purposes in deriving a dose–response relationship. Figure 5.1.4 shows that a lifetime vigorous activity level of greater than 700kcal/week is associated with a risk of colon cancer that is approximately 60% that of both men and women who have no lifetime history of vigorous activity. Unlike most of the dietary variables and BMI, exercise has been measured in varying and sometimes study-specific ways, making a composite dose–response figure difficult to construct (see chapter 3). It is clear from Table 5.1.1 that there is a marked consistency in strength and direction of the association across a wide variety of studies of exercise and colon cancer.

Lung (4.5). Somewhat conflicting data on lung cancer inclines towards a protective association with regular physical activity.

Breast (4.11). A relatively small amount of epidemiological evidence (three cohort and two case-control studies), supported by animal data, indicates that regular physical activity possibly decreases the risk of breast cancer.

High levels of physical activity may be generally protective against the overall risk of cancer. In the first USA NHANES study, physical inactivity at work and low levels of recreational activity were related to an increased overall cancer risk in men and women (Albanes et al, 1989). Other cohort studies have found an increase in the overall cancer mortality risk associated with low levels of work activity, college sports activities and leisure time activities (Paffenbarger et al, 1987), and physical fitness (Blair et al, 1989).

More specifically, rates of hormone-related cancers of women may generally be reduced by physical activity. Apart from breast cancer, assessed above, a study of women who were college athletes also found that they had a reduced risk of cancers of the ovary, endometrium, cervix and vagina (Frisch et al, 1992). Associations remained similar after controlling for BMI. One case-control study has found physical activity to be associated with a decreased risk of endometrial cancer risk (Sturgeon et al, 1993).

In the NHANES study (Albanes et al, 1989), the association between cancer and work inactivity was greater among adults of moderate or lower BMI, and a relationship was difficult to discern on the basis of recreational exercise alone. When both work and leisure activities were taken into

account, the risk of cancer increased in men when activity levels were below what is estimated in this report (see chapter 8) as a PAL of perhaps 1.8. Women showed a less clear-cut increase when PAL values fell below moderately active levels that correspond to a PAL of 1.68 in FAO/WHO/UNU calculations (1985).

A review of the literature on exercise and experimental tumorigenesis in rats showed that, among ten studies of forced activity, seven showed inhibition, one found no change and two observed an increase in tumour growth. Every one of six studies involving voluntary exercise resulted in inhibition of tumour growth (Cohen et al, 1992).

In the case of colon cancer, plausible protective mechanisms may include reduced transit time; alteration of endogenous steroid hormone metabolism; and possibly beneficial effects on the immune system. The physiological effect of physical activity on the risk of cancer in general may depend on the maintenance of a higher ratio of lean tissue to body fat; a more favourable insulin/growth factor milieu; or simply that the physically active individual is able to consume more food and thus more protective dietary constituents.

Plausible mechanisms by which physical inactivity and obesity might increase risk of colorectal cancer and female hormone-related cancers have been proposed (McKeown-Eyssen, 1994; Giovannucci, 1995): energy imbalance leading to high body mass may result in a series of metabolic abnormalities; these include high plasma triglyceride, glucose and insulin levels, and insulin resistance. These features are part of what is known as 'syndrome X'. The result may be a physiological milieu that promotes growth generally and of tumour cells specifically, both because of a differential capacity to use glucose (by way of anaerobic metabolic pathways) and upregulation of receptors for growth factors, including insulin and insulin-like growth factors.

This mechanism may unify a variety of risk factors for colorectal cancer, including high body mass, low physical activity, high-fat diets, high alcohol intake, low plant food intake and elevated bile acids.

Other diseases, such as hypertension, diabetes and coronary heart disease, share overlapping subsets of these risk factors. A large number of diseases may therefore be consequences of an underlying metabolic profile caused by lifestyles characteristic of the developed world and urban areas of the developing world, reinforced, perhaps by specific genetic profile that may have had survival value in leaner times.

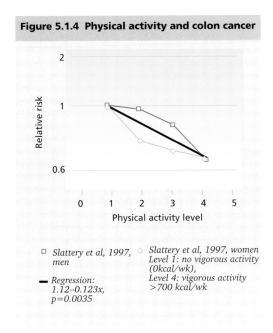

Figure 5.1.4 Physical activity and colon cancer

Relative risk / Physical activity level

□ Slattery et al, 1997, men

◇ Slattery et al, 1997, women
Level 1: no vigorous activity (0kcal/wk),
Level 4: vigorous activity >700 kcal/wk

— Regression: 1.12–0.123x, p=0.0035

This figure shows the dose–response relationship between physical activity and the risk of colon cancer from a single large case-control study (approximately 2,000 cases, 2,500 controls). This shows the steady decline in risk with higher lifetime levels of activity such that those with a history of lifetime expenditure of greater than 700 kcal/week have a risk that is approximately 60% of that for those with no history of vigorous activity.
The rationale for the use of a single study to illustrate the dose–response relationships is given in chapter 3 and the text above. The reader can examine Table 5.1.1 and note the very marked consistency both in direction and strength of the association across a wide variety of studies of colon cancer and physical activity.

5.2 Carbohydrate

Carbohydrate is the main source of dietary energy in most countries in the world. It is made up of starches, non-starch polysaccharides (NSP, the major component of dietary fibre), and sugars; these are chemically similar but vary in their physiological effects. Starchy and sweet foods may be consumed in whole form, as wholegrain bread and other cereal products, for example, or whole roots, tubers and plantains, and as fruits; or in refined or finely milled form, as white rice or pasta, for example, and extrinsic (refined) sugar. Almost all starchy foods are processed or cooked in some way before consumption.

In most parts of the developing world, 50–80 per cent total energy traditionally comes from carbohydrate, from starchy staple foods. With economic development, the proportion of energy from carbohydrate typically drops to 40–50 per cent of dietary energy, of which an increasing amount comes from refined sugar. The amount of NSP/ fibre in diets also drops, as less carbohydrate and starch is consumed and foods are increasingly refined.

CARBOHYDRATE AND CANCER

In the judgement of the panel, carbohydrate modifies the risk of cancers of various sites as shown below, or else has no relationship with them. Judgements are graded according to the strength of the evidence.

EVIDENCE	DECREASES RISK	NO RELATIONSHIP	INCREASES RISK
Convincing			
Probable			
Possible	*Starch[a]:* Colon, rectum *NSP/fibre:* Pancreas Colon, rectum Breast	*Sugar:* Stomach	*Starch[a]:* Stomach *Sugar:* Colon, rectum
Insufficient	*Resistant starch:* Colon, rectum *NSP/fibre:* Stomach		*Sugars:* Pancreas

For an explanation of the terms used in the matrix, see chapter 3.
[a] Data suggest that any increase in risk is due to very high-starch diets that are monotonous and deficient in various protective factors, or else high-starch diets where the starch is relatively highly refined. Such diets, when associated with an increased risk of stomach cancer, are also high in salt. In the case of colorectal cancer, relatively unrefined starch may be associated with decreased risk.

The panel has reached the following conclusions. There is a consistent pattern, suggesting that diets high in NSP/fibre possibly decrease the risk of pancreatic, colorectal and breast cancers, and diets high in starch possibly decrease the risk of colorectal cancer; diets high in refined starch possibly increase the risk of stomach cancer, and diets high in refined sugar possibly increase the risk of colorectal cancer.

INTRODUCTION

Carbohydrates may be divided into monosaccharides and disaccharides (glucose, fructose, sucrose, and other sugars); oligosaccharides; and polysaccharides (mainly starch, including resistant starch; and non-starch polysaccharides (NSP), which constitute a high proportion of dietary fibre).

SOURCES

Starch is found mainly in cereals (grains), pulses (legumes), roots, tubers and plantains: the starchy staples that supply most energy in the diets in many countries, most of all in the economically developing world. Resistant starch, so called because it resists digestion in the small intestine, is found in foods that enclose starch within a structure (such as whole grains and pulses), those that have cooled after cooking (such as bread, potatoes and rice), and certain raw starchy foods such as bananas.

Oligosaccharides are found in onions, leeks, beans and other plant foods, and are also used as ingredients by food manufacturers. Many, such as fructo-oligosaccharides, are non-digestible.

NSP/dietary fibre is the principal component of plant cell walls and is found in cereals (most of all in whole grains), and in vegetables and fruits. In Europe, cereals typically contribute 36–65% of dietary fibre intake; vegetables 22–47%;

and fruits 6–24% (Bingham, 1993; Cummings and Frølich, 1993).

Sugar can be described as either intrinsic (contained within the cell walls of plant foods, particularly fruits); or extrinsic (such as glucose, fructose, sucrose and syrups, refined from cane, beet, corn and other sources; these are used in manufactured food, in cooking or at table). Lactose is milk sugar. Most sugar is consumed in refined form.

COMPOSITION

Carbohydrates are polymers composed primarily of carbon, hydrogen and oxygen. The building blocks or basic units of these polymers are the monosaccharides. These and the disaccharides (two monosaccharides linked together) comprise simple carbohydrates, also called simple sugars. Oligosaccharides are short-chain carbohydrates composed of the monosaccharides galactose, glucose and fructose.

Polysaccharides, also known as complex carbohydrates, are large molecules composed of many monosaccharides: these include starch, formed from multiple glucose units; and non-starch polysaccharides. NSP is the primary constituent of dietary fibre; subclasses of NSP include cellulose, hemicellulose, pectin and gums. Dietary fibre consists primarily of NSP, but also includes lignin. Measurement of plant cell wall NSP is the most useful index of dietary fibre (Englyst et al, 1995).

FUNCTIONS

In addition to providing energy, dietary carbohydrate has many other functions. For example, carbohydrate is an important regulator of blood glucose and insulin, and may alter lipid and bile acid metabolism.

The relative digestibility and absorbability of carbohydrate is important in gut function. On the whole, complex carbohydrates are absorbed relatively slowly. Non-starch polysaccharides, resistant starch, many oligosaccharides, and lactose in some individuals and groups escape digestion and reach the large intestine. Here they are metabolised by bacteria and cause proliferation of the bacterial gut flora, increased stool bulk and weight, and short-chain fatty acid (SCFA) production; the last of these in particular, can regulate colonic epithelial cell turnover, perhaps by the influence of butyrate (one SCFA) on apoptosis (Hague et al, 1993). Recent research has shown that some carbohydrates can selectively stimulate the growth of specific bacteria in the colon (Gibson et al, 1995).

Since the colonic flora may be viewed as a vital body organ, with a flexibility and potential for metabolic transformation comparable with, if not greater than, that of the liver, the effect of carbohydrate of different types and quality on gut function is likely to be important in human health.

By contrast, sugars are absorbed in the small intestine and result in the release of glucose into the bloodstream relatively quickly. In addition, methods of processing and preparation of all forms of carbohydrate vitally affect their digestion and absorption (Jenkins et al, 1981). The way in which starch is processed and prepared both by manufacturers and in the home determines the amount that enters the colon. Fine milling of starch products disrupts the plant cell walls, and starch is often gelatinised during food processing, so that it becomes similar in its metabolic effects to sugar. It has been suggested that the human digestive system has not evolved to deal with diets high in refined starch and sugar (Englyst and Hudson, 1997).

REQUIREMENTS

No specific requirements for carbohydrate have been established, but because diets comprising mainly fat and protein are undesirable on many grounds, carbohydrate should be considered the principal staple of the diet. Diets containing 85% or more, or 40% or less, of total energy in the form of carbohydrate have both been identified as undesirable extremes (Englyst and Kingman, 1993).

CONSUMPTION PATTERNS

Grains are milled to various degrees before they are cooked in the home or used by the food industry. An exception is rice, which is usually refined, but mostly consumed in whole form. Corn (maize) may also be consumed as such, although it is also made into flour. In general, most starches and sugars are processed industrially or by cooking before they are eaten, and much starch and most sugar is eaten in refined form.

Tubers and roots, including those eaten as staples in Africa and other parts of the developing world, are usually processed domestically before cooking. Grains are usually eaten as staple foods in more economically developed societies in refined forms such as white rice, white bread, pastas and other foods made from white flour. Many manufactured foods include some, often a predominance of, refined carbohydrates. Refined sugar is used as an important ingredient in very many manufactured foods such as cakes, biscuits (cookies), chocolate, confectionery, and in soft drinks.

Carbohydrate consumption varies greatly throughout the world. Broadly, and with important exceptions, the less economically advanced the country, the higher is the consumption of carbohydrates, and particularly of starchy staples. Consumption of starches from cereals, roots and tubers and other staples in least-developed countries in Africa and Asia may amount to as much as 70–80% total energy, whereas in Europe and North America, starch intakes have dropped since industrialisation and now may supply as little as 20–25% total energy. In Western Europe, intakes are low (for example, around 22% total energy in The Netherlands) but are high in Eastern Europe (around 46% total energy) (Bright-See and Jazmaji, 1991).

Few data on resistant starch intake are available. A figure of 2–3 g/day has been suggested for the UK (Tomlin and Read, 1992), but no population-based studies have been undertaken in any country. Experimental studies show that intakes of up to 35 g/day are easily achieved (Silvester et al, 1995).

Dietary fibre intake, measured as NSP, varies from 10–13 g/day in Japan and the UK, to 15–20 g/day or more in Africa and India. Intake among individuals in a population may vary between 7 and 25 g/day (Bingham, 1993).

Consumption of intrinsic sugar largely reflects consumption of fruits, and varies from 1–3% within the UK (Department of Health, 1994). In Europe and the USA, consumption of refined sugar increased with industrialisation during the nineteenth century and now amounts to an average of around 14–17% of total energy (MAFF, 1994), with some subpopulations, notably children, consuming higher amounts of around 17–20% (Hinds and Gregory, 1995). This pattern is now being repeated in other parts of the world with industrialisation and urbanisation.

INTERPRETATION OF THE DATA

Few epidemiological studies to date have quantified intakes of carbohydrates, starches, fibre or sugars as such, but have instead investigated intakes of relevant foods. Consumption of cereals and cereal products such as rice, bread and pasta, and of roots and tubers have commonly been used as indices of starch intake, and consumption of cereals, vegetables and fruits as indices of fibre intake. Comparisons are thus really of the intakes of these foods, and it is impossible to be certain whether any observed differences in cancer risk are associated with starch or NSP/fibre, or some other component of these foods, or with some related aspect of the diet.

Refining of cereals and cane or beet to produce white rice, flour, bread, sugar and other products removes NSP/fibre and microconstituents that may protect against cancer; refined sugar, as such, contributes only energy (see chapters 5.6 and 5.7). Therefore, the degree to which starch is refined in diets, particularly when the intake of starch is high, may itself be an important factor in cancer risk, as may the volume of refined starches and sugars in diets. Epidemiological studies have not, however, generally distinguished between degrees of refining or processing of starches, and there are, as yet, no reliable epidemiological data specifically on the effects of refining on cancer risk.

Non-starch polysaccharides are measured precisely by the Englyst method (Englyst and Kingman, 1993), but there are, as yet, few epidemiological data on NSP as such. Instead, the data concern fibre, itself defined and measured in a number of different ways. Various analytical techniques used to assess the fibre content of foods give widely different results for some foods, making comparison across studies problematic.

Intakes of total carbohydrate and of fat vary inversely; data showing associations between fat intake and cancer risk therefore tend to show the reverse association between carbohydrate intake and risk. The levels of starches in the diet do not show the same correlation with fat and other macroconstituents as do levels of carbohydrate as a whole, although, in industrialised societies, there is an inverse correlation between fat and sugar intake (Hill and Prentice, 1995).

JUDGEMENTS OF OTHER REPORTS

Carbohydrates have been less studied than energy, fat and alcohol in the context of cancer. The National Academy of Sciences report, *Diet, Nutrition and Cancer* (NAS, 1982), noted that some studies had found associations between intakes of starch or starch-rich foods and an increased risk of cancers of the oesophagus and stomach, and between sugar and an increased risk of cancers of the pancreas and breast. These data were judged to be meagre. The report also noted associations between fibre intake and a decreased risk of colorectal cancer, but found these data to be inconclusive. The dietary guidelines issued as part of the report did, however, emphasise the value of wholegrain cereals.

Diets high in fibre have been thought to be protective against colorectal cancer since the 1960s (Burkitt, 1975). *Nutrition and Health* (Surgeon General, 1988) summarised evidence published in the 1980s that suggested that fibre-rich foods protected against colon cancer. The report recommended increased consumption of wholegrain foods and cereal products partly because of these data, which were, however, identified as inconclusive. *Diet and Health*, the 1989 report of the National Academy of Sciences (NAS, 1989), noted human and animal data that suggested a relationship between sugar and breast/mammary cancer. It also

noted that data on fibre and colon cancer were somewhat conflicting. It recommended consumption of more starches, complex carbohydrates, breads and cereals, and limitation of sugar consumption, deriving this recommendation from data on diseases other than cancer.

The World Health Organization (WHO, 1990) recommended that 50–70% total energy in diets should come from complex carbohydrates, noting that such diets 'seem to favour a lower incidence of a variety of cancers', and also recommended that consumption of dietary fibre (expressed as NSP) be between 16 and 24 g/ day.

SIGNIFICANCE FOR OTHER DISEASES

In the developing world, starches are the most available and most economical means of supplying total energy; as noted, diets are generally more sugary and fatty in the developed world. Starchy diets are commonly recommended as a better alternative to high-fat diets. Refined sugars are identified as a major cause of tooth decay, and reduction in the consumption of sugar is commonly recommended in developed countries as part of a diet for losing weight (Royal College of Physicians, 1983; Department of Health, 1991). Diets rich in wholegrain cereals and fibre are also recommended for the health of the intestinal tract (Royal College of Physicians, 1980).

Most expert reports distinguish between starches and dietary fibre on the one hand, and refined sugars on the other. Of 100 such reports published between 1961 and 1991, mostly concerned with diet and cardiovascular disease or diet and other chronic diseases generally in the developed world, 62 recommended more starch or complex carbohydrates, with none disagreeing; 61 recommended more fibre, and 74 recommended less refined sugar, with none disagreeing (Cannon, 1992).

FUTURE RESEARCH

The panel made the following recommendations for future research:

■ When undertaking studies relating dietary intake to cancer risk, starch, non-starch polysaccharides/dietary fibre and sugar should be regarded as separate dietary constituents; the degree of processing (including cooking) of starch and sugar should be considered; and intrinsic and refined sugars should be distinguished.

■ Better methods of quantification of intake, including biological markers, of each of these separate constituents should be developed.

■ Further studies of mechanisms of action – including feeding studies – whether increasing or decreasing risk, are crucial.

BOX 5.2.1 STARCH: QUANTITY AND QUALITY, AND CANCER RISK

There are a number of possible reasons why epidemiological studies tend to indicate that diets high in starch possibly increase the risk of stomach cancer while possibly decreasing the risk of colorectal cancer.

It may be that starch affects different organs of the body differently; that the nature of starch eaten varies in different parts of the world; or that starch may have different effects depending on its volume in diets, which in turn affects overall patterns of dietary intake. It is also possible that some factor other than starch is the agent.

It is biologically plausible that diets high in starch and in resistant starch and NSP protect against colon cancer. Resistant starch and NSP are fermented in the colon by bacteria to produce short-chain fatty acids; this, in turn, leads to an increase in faecal weight, dilution of colonic contents, decreased transit time (Stephen and Cummings, 1980) and possible control of cell proliferation and apoptosis (Hague et al, 1993). This protective mechanism may be attenuated when most starch in the diet is

refined, and is probably not relevant in the case of other cancers.

There are some reasons to believe that starch, as such, is not the factor increasing the risk of stomach cancer. Starchy diets associated with increased risk are also high in salt (Joossens et al, 1996), and starchy diets that are low in salt are associated with a low incidence of stomach cancer (Holcombe, 1992).

Diets that are very high in starch are, for that reason, low in vegetables, fruits and other foods that may protect against stomach cancer (see chapter 6.3 in particular). Further, refined starchy foods may themselves be poor sources of protective dietary constituents, depending on the nature of the starchy staple consumed and the degree of refining. The evidence that diets high in fibre possibly decrease the risk of stomach and breast cancer (see below) reinforces the reasoning that the quality of starchy diets rather than the starch itself is the relevant factor.

There are also data from studies carried out in southern Europe, where intakes of

starch are lower than in Africa and Asia, that show relationships between high-starch diets and an increased risk of stomach cancer (see chapter 4.6). This may, again, be because of the general quality of the diet as a whole and of the starchy staples themselves. Refined starchy foods such as white rice, white flour and white pasta are relatively poor sources of dietary fibre, as well as of microconstituents that may protect against cancer, compared with less processed starchy foods, including those made from whole grains (Holland et al, 1988). If such diets are also low in vegetables and fruits and other protective foods, as well as relatively salty, these factors also may increase the risk of stomach cancer.

In the view of the panel, any effect on cancer risk of diets high in starch is likely to be a function of the quality of such diets as a whole and not just the result of consumption of the starch itself.

The panel also notes, in the case of stomach cancer, that high-starch diets associated with increased risk are also high in salt.

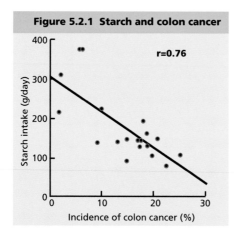

Figure 5.2.1 Starch and colon cancer

r=0.76

This figure shows the relationship between the intake of starch and the risk of colon cancer, from an international correlation study of 12 populations, using data on actual intakes, and adjusted for intakes of fat and protein. The usual caveats about ecological data apply (see chapter 3).

(Reproduced from Cassidy et al, 1994)

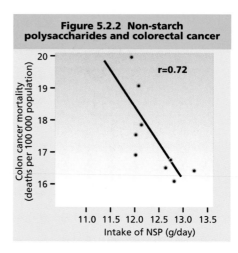

Figure 5.2.2 Non-starch polysaccharides and colorectal cancer

r=0.72

This figure shows the ecological relationship between the intake of non-starch polysaccharides and the risk of colorectal cancer across regions of the UK between 1969 and 1973. There is evidence that increased intakes of NSP are associated with a lower risk of colon cancer. The usual caveats about ecological data apply (see chapter 3).

(Reproduced from Bingham, 1988).

ASSESSMENT

The evidence on which this assessment is based is reviewed in the relevant sections of chapter 4.

5.2.1 TOTAL CARBOHYDRATE

Given the nutritional and biochemical differences between complex and simple carbohydrates, and between unrefined and refined starches and sugars, the panel did not assess the data on carbohydrate as a whole, but assessed starch, NSP/fibre and sugar separately.

5.2.2 STARCH

Diets high in starch are unusual in terms of cancer risk as there is evidence derived from epidemiological studies of a possible decreased risk of one major cancer (colorectal) and a possible increased risk of another (stomach). For the panel's judgement on these findings, see Box 5.2.1.

Evidence of decreased risk

CONVINCING	PROBABLE	POSSIBLE	INSUFFICIENT
		Colon, rectum[a]	

[a] Data suggest that any decreased risk may be associated with relatively unrefined starch

Colon and rectum (4.10). Most case-control studies find no relationship with cancer, but some find an inverse association with the risk of colorectal adenomas, as do experimental studies. Cross-cultural correlational data show a strong inverse association and a linear dose–response (see Figure 5.2.1). Animal and other experimental studies, as yet not supported by epidemiological data, suggest that resistant starch may be protective, but the evidence on resistant starch as such is, as yet, insufficient.

The somewhat conflicting data may be explained by studies indicating that relatively unrefined starch may protect against colorectal cancer by various mechanisms, whereas refined carbohydrate (including refined starch) may increase risk. Diets high in starch possibly protect against colorectal cancer. Any protective effect is likely to be from relatively unrefined starchy diets.

Evidence of increased risk

CONVINCING	PROBABLE	POSSIBLE	INSUFFICIENT
		Stomach[a]	

[a]Data suggest that any increase in risk is due to refined starch, usually in the context of monotonous diets deficient in various nutrients (see Box 5.5.2)

Stomach (4.6). Epidemiological data show a fairly consistent association between high starch intake and an increased risk of stomach cancer. Given the evidence that diets high in NSP/fibre do not increase stomach cancer risk (see below),

the panel judges that starch, as such, may increase stomach cancer risk only when diets are very high in starchy staples and are therefore likely to lack other important protective components, such as vegetables and fruits. An increased risk is unlikely if starchy diets are relatively unrefined (see Boxes 5.2.1 and 5.2.2).

5.2.3 NON-STARCH POLYSACCHARIDES/DIETARY FIBRE

Evidence from correlation studies and experimental and biological studies, on the whole supported by analytical epidemiological evidence, shows that diets high in non-starch polysaccharides/dietary fibre possibly decrease the risk of colorectal cancer. The evidence is similar for the risk of pancreatic and breast cancers. Evidence for other cancer sites is unimpressive.

Evidence of decreased risk

CONVINCING	PROBABLE	POSSIBLE	INSUFFICIENT
		Pancreas	Stomach
		Colon, rectum	
		Breast	

Pancreas (4.7). Six case-control studies have examined the relationship between pancreatic cancer and fibre intake. Five of these, and a combined analysis, showed protective

---

BOX 5.2.2 DEFICIENCY DIETS

'Poverty' or 'deficiency' diets notably those consumed by populations in the developing world, are monotonous and usually deficient in micronutrients such as antioxidant vitamins and minerals, iron and iodine, and bioactive compounds; other deficiencies are likely to be present. Such diets are very different from those consumed by impoverished people in the developed world and urban areas of the developing world: these diets tend to be high in fat and possibly protein and to be energy-dense. In contrast, poverty diets in the developing world are almost always low in fat and protein and very bulky; they are mostly made up of one starchy staple, which itself may be relatively refined or otherwise lacking in microconstituents.

The panel has taken the view that, in interpreting the data showing a correlation between starchy staples and/or complex carbohydrates or starch, and the risk of cancer of the oesophagus and other sites, that the likely causal factor is gross deficiency of specific essential constituents of the diet, rather than the carbohydrate/starch itself. This view is strengthened by the evidence reviewed in chapter 6.1, that wholegrain cereals, which are comparatively high in fibre, vitamins and minerals and other dietary constituents are, if anything, protective against cancer at some sites.

This view has important public health implications. It implies that balanced diets mostly made up of starchy staples, notably including the traditional diets eaten in many parts of the developing world, are themselves without risk, as long as they include a variety of other foods such as vegetables, fruits, pulses, and nuts and seeds, with or without meat, fish and dairy produce.

associations, and a steady decrease in risk with increasing consumption. Diets high in NSP/dietary fibre possibly decrease the risk of pancreatic cancer.

Colon and rectum (4.10). On the whole, case-control studies, including, especially, the meta-analysis of Howe et al (1992), suggest that diets high in non-starch polysaccharides/dietary fibre (from vegetables and fruits as well as cereals) protect against colorectal cancer, and this evidence is supported by a clear dose–response effect in the setting of ecological comparisons (see Figure 5.2.2), by correlation studies, experimental studies, and by identification of highly plausible biological pathways. Somewhat conflicting results from analytical epidemiological studies are not surprising because of the heterogeneous nature of dietary fibre. Taking these data together, and given the problem of confounding, the panel concluded that diets high in non-starch polysaccharides/dietary fibre possibly protect against colorectal cancer.

As shown in Figure 5.2.2, at a regional level in the UK, a higher non-starch polysaccharide intake is associated with a decreased risk of colon cancer. The advantage of this study over, say, a meta-analysis of case control studies of fibre and colon cancer (see Howe et al, 1992) is that the NSP was measured consistently across the region. Nonetheless, the usual caveats about ecological studies apply, most importantly that differences in other variables that might also contribute to the regional variation in colon cancer mortality (age differences, differences in socioeconomic status, differences in physical activity, etc) were not measured. These dose–response data, however, contribute to, and illustrate, the panel's judgement that NSP/dietary fibre is possibly protective against colon cancer.

Breast (4.11). Three cohort studies and at least fifteen case-control studies have examined NSP/fibre intake and breast cancer. The epidemiological, experimental and other data on the whole suggest a weak protective effect of fibre against breast cancer, which is biologically plausible. High intakes of NSP/fibre therefore possibly protect against breast cancer.

Stomach (4.6). Relatively limited and therefore insufficient data (from five case-control studies) are consistent with a protective effect of diets high in NSP/fibre.

5.2.4 SUGAR

With refined sugar, evidence points in the opposite direction from that seen for NSP/fibre. Epidemiological and experimental evidence shows that diets high in refined sugars (sucrose in particular) possibly increase the risk of colorectal cancer. Evidence on pancreatic cancer is less substantial.

Evidence of no relationship

CONVINCING	PROBABLE	POSSIBLE	INSUFFICIENT
		Stomach	

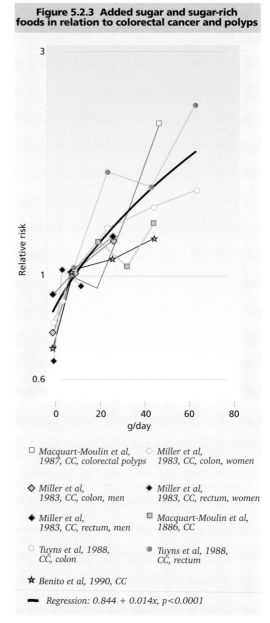

Figure 5.2.3 Added sugar and sugar-rich foods in relation to colorectal cancer and polyps

□ *Macquart-Moulin et al, 1987, CC, colorectal polyps*

◇ *Miller et al, 1983, CC, colon, women*

◇ *Miller et al, 1983, CC, colon, men*

◆ *Miller et al, 1983, CC, rectum, women*

◆ *Miller et al, 1983, CC, rectum, men*

▪ *Macquart-Moulin et al, 1886, CC*

○ *Tuyns et al, 1988, CC, colon*

● *Tuyns et al, 1988, CC, rectum*

★ *Benito et al, 1990, CC*

— *Regression: 0.844 + 0.014x, p<0.0001*

This figure suggests a steady increase in colon cancer, rectal cancer and, in one case, colorectal polyps in the presence of higher intakes of sugar and foods high in sugar. The fitted regression line is consistent with a greater than twofold increase in risk for those consuming about 60 g/day of sugar and sugar-rich foods compared with those consuming none. The figure shows that all studies are consistent with an elevated risk for those consuming above 30 g/d compared with those consuming less than 10 g/day.

Stomach (4.6). Eight case-control studies have examined intakes of simple carbohydrates, or sugar-rich products, or sugar use. Rather inconsistent data, some not independent of other dietary factors, suggests that diets high in sugar possibly have no relationship with the risk of stomach cancer.

Evidence of increased risk

CONVINCING	PROBABLE	POSSIBLE	INSUFFICIENT
		Colon, rectum[a]	Pancreas[a]

[a] Refined sugar

Colon and rectum (4.10). The evidence from 14 case-control studies and one cohort study supports data from correlation studies that show an association between diets high in refined sugars, notably sucrose, and an increased risk of colorectal cancer. There is also evidence from case-control studies of increased risk of adenomatous polyps. Experimental studies are supportive. Plausible mechanisms have been identified. Some studies did not control for possible confounding factors, and evidence for increased risk was sometimes not found and, when found, was not always statistically significant. On balance, the panel judged the evidence to show a possible causal relationship between refined sugars and colorectal cancer.

Data from five case-control studies are shown in Figure 5.2.3. These studies were selected according to the criteria described in chapter 3. They are consistent with a greater than twofold increase in risk across intakes of sugar and sugar-rich foods from 0 to 60 g/day. Each of the subgroups studied shows an elevated risk for those consuming 30 g or more per day compared with those eating less than 10 g/day.

Pancreas (4.15). A relatively small amount of evidence from analytical studies on balance supports data from correlation studies that show associations between diets high in refined sugars and an increased risk of pancreatic cancers. These data are judged to be insufficient evidence of causation.

5.3 Fat and cholesterol

Fat is the most energy-dense constituent of the diet. Its contribution to dietary energy rises with industrialisation and urbanisation. Meat from domesticated animals has a high fat-content, and many manufactured foods contain oils and fats of plant and animal origin. Such oils and fats are also added in cooking and at table. Most unsaturated fat is of plant origin. Some polyunsaturated fatty acids are essential nutrients. Most saturated fat is of animal origin, and cholesterol (not a fat but included here because of its related biology) is solely of animal origin.

FAT, CHOLESTEROL AND CANCER

In the judgement of the panel, fat and cholesterol modify the risk of cancers of various sites as shown below, or else have no relationship with them. Judgements are graded according to the strength of the evidence.

EVIDENCE	DECREASES RISK	NO RELATIONSHIP	INCREASES RISK
Convincing			
Probable		*Cholesterol* Breast	

Possible		*Monounsaturated fat:*
		  Breast
		Polyunsaturated/
		vegetable fat:
		  Breast
			Total fat:
			  Lung
			  Colon, rectum[a]
			  Breast[a]
			  Prostate
			Saturated/animal fat:
			  Lung
			  Colon, rectum
			  Breast
			  Endometrium
			  Prostate
			Cholesterol:
			  Lung
			  Pancreas

Insufficient			*Total fat:*
			  Ovary
			  Endometrium
			  Bladder
			Saturated/animal fat:
			  Ovary
			Cholesterol:
			  Endometrium

For an explanation of the terms used in the matrix, see chapter 3.
[a] Risk of these cancers is convincingly (endometrium), probably (post-menopausal breast) or possibly (colon) increased by high body mass, risk of which is increased by diets high in fat (see Box 5.3.1).

In most parts of the developing world, most fat consumed is of plant origin, and fat intake on a population basis varies between less than 15 to 25–30% total energy. Consumption of total fat, saturated fat and cholesterol tends to vary as a function of the amount and type of foods of animal origin consumed. In the developed world and in urban areas of the developing world, fat intake, on a population basis, varies from 30% to over 40% total energy, and much fat comes from foods of animal origin containing substantial amounts of saturated fat.

The panel has reached the following conclusions. There is a consistent pattern, suggesting that diets high in total fat possibly increase the risk of lung, colorectal, breast and prostate cancers; and that diets high in animal fat and/or saturated fat possibly increase the risk of lung, colorectal, breast, endometrial and prostate cancers. The panel notes that diets high in cholesterol possibly increase the risk of lung and pancreatic cancers.

Diets high in fat increase the risk of obesity; therefore, high-fat diets are an indirect risk factor for cancers, the risk of which is increased by obesity. As already noted, the evidence that obesity increases the risk of endometrial cancer is convincing, and obesity probably also increases the risk of postmenopausal breast and renal cancers.

INTRODUCTION

Fats may be classified by their chemical composition, as containing varying proportions of saturated, monounsaturated and polyunsaturated fatty acids. Some polyunsaturated fats are essential, meaning that, like vitamins, they must be supplied from food. Fats may also be classified as of plant or of animal origin. Cholesterol is a fatty substance found only in foods of animal origin.

SOURCES

Oils and fats are present in most foods in variable amounts. The amount of fat in foods of animal origin is generally greater than that in most foods of plant origin. In manufac-

tured fats and oils that are added in cooking or at table, such as vegetable oils, clarified butter), lard, shortenings, margarines, and butter, practically all the total energy content is fat. In red meat (defined here as beef, lamb and pork from domesticated animals, see chapter 6.6) and meat products, fat constitutes 40–75% of the total energy content. The fat content of non-domesticated land animals is generally lower. Approximately 65% of the total energy content of eggs comes from fat, and about 50% of that of whole cow's milk.

About 25–50% of the total energy of poultry is supplied by fat, especially in the meat found immediately under the skin; duck and goose are generally more fatty than chicken. Between 5% and 60% of the total energy content of fish is fat. Vegetables and fruits generally contain only small amounts of fat, although avocados and olives are exceptions. About 80–90% of the total energy content of nuts comes from fat. The intrinsic fat content of cereals (grains) ranges from 0.5% (white rice) to 8% (oats); of pulses (legumes) from 1.5% (black-eyed beans and black gram) to 5% (chickpeas). Cereal products such as traditional sweet cakes and biscuits and other baked goods are often high in fat. A variety of savoury crackers may be lower in fat. There are increasing numbers of very low/no fat products, but these tend to be high in sugar.

Saturated fat comes mostly from animal foods. Coconut and palm oils are important exceptions. For most populations these oils constitute a negligible proportion of fat intake. In palm oil and cow's milk, the fat is about 80% and 65% saturated, respectively. In meat, butter, lard, coconut oil, and hard margarines, approximately 45–50% of the fat is saturated. The fat in poultry and eggs is roughly 30–35% saturated. In vegetable oils about 10–20% of the fat is saturated; in soft margarines, about 20–30%. The fat in fish is approximately 10–25% saturated.

Monounsaturated fats, mainly oleic acid, come from a wide variety of foods. The most concentrated food source is olive oil, in which 70–90% of the fat is monounsaturated; rapeseed oil also contains a relatively high proportion. In avocados, 60–70% of the fat is monounsaturated. In meat, poultry, eggs, milk, butter, lard, nuts, and other vegetable oils and margarines, 10–50% of the fat is monounsaturated.

Polyunsaturated fat is also found in a wide variety of foods. The most concentrated sources are oils derived from safflower, sunflower, wheat germ, corn, soya bean, and cottonseed. These contain around 50–75% polyunsaturated fat, mostly linoleic acid. Margarines and shortenings made from vegetable oils generally contain 15–45% polyunsaturated fat, as do various types of nuts. Meat, poultry, eggs and dairy products contain relatively little polyunsaturated fat, although the proportion of polyunsaturated to saturated fat in wild land animals is much higher than in domesticated animals.

Fatty fish such as tuna, mackerel, salmon, herring, anchovies, lake trout, scad and whitefish contain large amounts of omega-3 fatty acids, a type of polyunsaturated fat.

Trans-fatty acids are mainly found in hydrogenated vegetable oil products such as margarines and shortenings, and in baked goods such as biscuits, and may constitute up to 35% of the fat in these foods. Trans-fatty acids also occur naturally in small amounts in milk and butter.

Cholesterol is found only in animal foods. Egg yolks (around 1%) and organ meats (0.4%) contain substantial amounts of cholesterol, and meat (0.07–0.09%) and some shellfish (0.08–0.2%) also contain significant amounts. Other sources are poultry, fish and whole-fat dairy products such as butter, cheese, and whole milk.

COMPOSITION

Dietary fat consists mostly of fatty acids esterified to glycerol and other alcohols. Fatty acids are chains of several carbon atoms, with hydrogen atoms attached, and an acidic (carboxyl) group at one end. About 90% of the fat in foods is as triacylglycerols (also known as triglycerides); these have one molecule of glycerol bound to three fatty acids. Mono- and diacylglycerols also occur in nature, as do free fatty acids. Phospholipids are compounds that resemble triacylglycerols except that a phosphorus-containing unit occurs in the place of one of the fatty acids.

Fatty acids differ in chain length and in their degree of saturation. Fatty acids usually have carbon chains of from 4 to 22 in length. Saturation refers to the number of hydrogen atoms attached to the carbon skeleton of a fatty acid. A saturated fatty acid contains as many hydrogen atoms as it can accommodate; an unsaturated fatty acid does not, and some carbons are therefore connected by double bonds. A fatty acid with one double bond is termed monounsaturated, whereas one with more than one double bond is called polyunsaturated. Saturated fatty acids (including hydrogenated fats and oils) are usually solid at room temperature; unsaturated fatty acids are usually liquid.

Fatty acids may be described in shorthand with a notation depicting first the chain length, and then the number of double bonds. For example, linoleic acid, which has 18 carbon atoms and two double bonds, is described as 18:2. Butyric (4:0), myristic (14:0), palmitic (16:0), and stearic (18:0) acids are examples of saturated fatty acids. The predominant monounsaturated fatty acid is oleic acid (18:1). Polyunsaturated fatty acids are divided into the omega-3 and omega-6 series according to the distance of their first double bond from the methyl end of the carbon chain. Linoleic (18:2) and arachadonic (20:4) acids are omega-6 fatty acids, whereas eicosopentanoic (20:5), decosahexanoic (22:6), and alpha-linolenic (18:3) acids are omega-3 fatty acids.

Almost all naturally occurring unsaturated fatty acids have a 'cis' configuration, meaning that the two hydrogen atoms attached to the double-bonded carbon atoms are on the same side of the chain. Trans-fatty acids, in which the hydrogen atoms are on opposite sides of the chain, are produced by hydrogenation, a manufacturing process that increases the degree of saturation of an unsaturated fat and thereby makes it more solid.

Cholesterol is a sterol compound that, like fat, is insoluble in water. Sterols consist of carbon, hydrogen, and oxygen atoms arranged in a ring structure, with any of a variety of side chains attached. Cholesterol is similar in structure to bile acids, sex hormones, adrenal hormones, and vitamin D, and is an important precursor (raw material) in their production by the body. It is produced by animals, including humans, but not plants.

FUNCTIONS

Digestion of dietary fat takes place primarily in the small intestine, where triacylglycerols mix with bile produced in the liver. Bile salts act as detergents and help to split large droplets of triacylglycerols into smaller droplets, making them more available to digestive enzymes. Lipases, produced by the pancreas, break triacylglycerols down to monoacylglycerols, glycerol, and fatty acids; cholesterol esters are also split into cholesterol and fatty acids. These individual components are then incorporated into aggregates called micelles, which ferry the lipid fragments closer to the intestinal wall, where they are released for absorption. If sufficient bile salts are present, 95–99% of all dietary fat is absorbed by a healthy small intestine, whereas, on average, only about 30–70% of dietary cholesterol is absorbed.

Once absorbed, short- and medium-chain fatty acids are transported to the liver in the blood. Long-chain fatty acids and cholesterol, which are water insoluble, are reassembled in the intestinal wall into lipoproteins called chylomicrons. These then flow through the lymphatic system, and eventually join the bloodstream. As lipoproteins move through the body, many give up their triacylglycerols to fat cells and muscles along the way. Fats and cholesterol remaining in the bloodstream pass through the liver, where they are reorganised into various lipoproteins; these are returned to the bloodstream, through which they deliver their components to various tissues.

REQUIREMENTS

The only specific requirement for fat in the diet is that for essential fatty acids. These include linoleic acid (18:2) and alpha-linolenic acid (18:3), an omega-3 fatty acid not synthesised by humans. Linoleic, arachadonic, eicosapentanoic, and related fatty acids are precursors to prostaglandins, which are hormone-like compounds with diverse effects, including roles in blood vessel dilation/constriction, blood clotting, and transmission of nerve impulses.

Dietary fat serves as a transport vehicle for fat-soluble vitamins, allowing them to be more readily absorbed. A large portion of body fat is stored in the adipose tissue as a concentrated form of reserve energy. Subcutaneous fat (adipose fat immediately under the skin) provides thermal insulation; the remaining adipose tissue surrounds and provides cushioning for internal organs. Fat in various forms is also a necessary component of cell membranes and nerve coverings.

Cholesterol, which is produced in the liver and comes from diet, is an important component of cell membranes and a precursor of steroid hormones and bile acids.

CONSUMPTION PATTERNS

The quantity and quality of fat consumed varies greatly in different parts of the world. As a general rule, consumption of total fat and of saturated fat increases with economic development. This is because people in developed countries generally eat more meat, meat products, dairy products, table fat, and baked goods, such as biscuits, pastries and cakes, which contain hydrogenated fats and oils. In low- and middle-income Asia, fat supplies less than 15–22% total energy. In the developed countries of Europe and North America, fat supplies from 30% to 45% total energy.

In the richer developed countries, fat consumption as a percentage of total energy is now decreasing. This is a result partly of dietary advice to consume less fat, largely in the context of cardiovascular disease, and more recently cancer. This in turn has led to changes in packaged and prepared foods. In the USA, for example, estimated average fat intake has dropped from 41% total energy in 1977, to 34% in 1993–94.

Consumption of saturated/animal fat is lowest in Africa and low income Asia, at 5–7% total energy, and highest in Europe and Australasia, at 15% or more. Consumption of polyunsaturated/vegetable fat as a percentage of total energy intake is lowest in sub-Saharan Africa and the Pacific Islands and highest in North America and Europe.

Fat consumption has changed markedly in the twentieth century in many areas of the world. In Japan since the 1950s, and in China and Korea since the 1970s, intake of meat and, thereby, of total fat, has increased markedly, particularly in large cities and urban areas. In areas of the developing world that are now rapidly becoming urbanised, intakes of total and saturated fat are increasing rapidly.

The intake of total and saturated/animal fat in the diets of developed countries generally increases as the availability and consumption of fatty meat, dairy products, added fats and oils increases. Fats and oils are extracted from a variety of plant and animal sources. Vegetable oils are derived from the storage lipids in plant seeds or nuts. Animal-fat products include butter and ghee made from milk fat, as well as lard (from pigs), tallow or suet (from cattle or sheep) and drippings (from cooked meat).

Since the early twentieth century, the hydrogenation process has been used to convert oils of vegetable and animal origin into hardened, variably saturated fats for use as table fats (margarine) and in commercially baked goods and many processed foods. Hydrogenation increases the amount and proportion of saturated/animal fat and trans-fatty acids in the diets of people living in industrialised parts of the world.

Added fats and oils account for 10–15% total energy in the Middle East and North Africa, 10% in Central and South America, and 5–10% in Asia and sub-Saharan Africa. In all these regions, vegetable oils predominate over animal fats. In Europe and North America, added fats and oils contribute 15–20% total energy. In Europe, vegetable oils and animal fats contribute equally, with the exception of the Mediterranean region where olive oil predominates. In North America, soya bean and corn oil are the predominant types of added fats.

On average, worldwide, added fats and oils make up around 40% total dietary fat, with the remainder derived from fats in meat, fish, poultry, milk and milk products.

Worldwide, the intake of added fats and oils (as well as total fat intake) contributed 50% more to total energy intake in the mid-1990s than it did in 1961. This trend has been most marked in areas with previously low or moderate dietary fat intake, such as parts of Asia, Africa and South America, where consumption of added fats has typically increased by 50–100%. A 100–200% increase in the contribution to total energy intake made by added fat has been recorded in some sub-Saharan African nations and several high-income east Asian countries, including Malaysia and Japan. Consumption of added fat has recently increased only modestly, from a high baseline, in Europe and North America.

INTERPRETATION OF THE DATA

The intake of total fat is correlated with the intake of other components of diet. There is a possible inverse relationship between the intake of fat and that of vegetables and fruits (Ziegler et al, 1992), and a strong direct relationship with consumption of meat, meat products and dairy products.

In developed societies, a substantial amount of fat from meat and table fats and oils may be discarded, so that household or supply data may overestimate fat intake, particularly that of total fat and saturated/animal fat. However, weight-conscious and food-conscious individuals may underestimate their fat intake in answers to dietary questionnaires. These opposite tendencies bias estimates of fat in different directions in different types of study.

Individual-level epidemiological studies vary in their ability to quantify total fat intake. Some studies have attempted to assess diet as a whole, whereas others have included only a short list of relevant foods. Various studies have examined different types of dietary fat in ways that also make comparison among studies problematic. For example, studies have investigated some or all of the following categories: total fat; saturated and unsaturated fat; monounsaturated and polyunsaturated fat; omega-3 and trans-fatty acids; oleic, linoleic, and other individual fatty acids; animal and vegetable fat; and meat, fish, and dairy fat.

Within the populations of most cohort and case-control studies, variation in fat intake is not broad enough to allow comparison of extremes of intake. Thus, if fat intakes below 20–25% total energy are protective against cancer, few of the studies conducted so far in Europe or North America would produce findings to this effect as not enough individuals with this level of intake are in the studies.

Despite the fact that diets consumed in developed countries typically contain 30 – 45% total energy as fat, and that a high proportion of fats and oils in these diets are extracted or hydrogenated, there are no reliable data specifically on the effects of these food processes on cancer risk.

The relationship between the risk of cancer and fat intake is often adjusted for total energy intake, so that fat is assessed not absolutely but as a proportion of total dietary energy (Willett et al, 1997).

Adjustment for total energy intake may also better simulate many dietary intervention studies, when such studies alter the composition of the diet while holding total energy intake constant. However, data from experimental studies are complicated by this relationship between total energy and fat intake. If the treatment diet is high-fat, then the low-fat control diet may be isocaloric, and therefore necessarily higher in other energy-providing macroconstituents that may themselves be relevant to cancer risk. Alternatively, the control diet may be equivalent in carbohydrate and protein, and therefore lower in total energy content and in the proportion of total energy from fat. Although isocaloric models have generally been preferred, these may not be the appropriate model for humans in real life. The rise of body mass with age, and the prevalence of overweight and obesity in sedentary populations consuming high-fat diets, suggest a general tendency for such populations to be in positive energy balance. See also Box 5.3.2.

JUDGEMENTS OF OTHER REPORTS

Fat has been studied extensively in the context of those cancers that are more common in the developed world, including those associated with obesity. The National Academy of Sciences report, *Diet, Nutrition and Health* (NAS, 1982), concluded that, of all the dietary components it reviewed, the epidemiological evidence from correlation and some case-control studies, supported by experimental evidence, was strongest and most suggestive for a causal relationship between dietary fat and cancer, particularly cancers of the breast and colon. One of that report's six dietary guidelines recommended reduction of total fat intake to 30% total energy, adding 'the scientific data do not provide a strong basis for establishing fat intake at precisely 30% total calories. Indeed, the data could be used to justify an even greater reduction'.

Nutrition and Health (Surgeon General, 1988) and *Diet and Health*, the 1989 report of the National Academy of Sciences (NAS, 1989), both recommended a reduction in intakes of total and saturated fat and cholesterol, primarily in the context of prevention of coronary heart disease and obesity and the maintenance of overall good health. However, the National Academy of Sciences report concluded that the weight of evidence supported a relationship between high-fat diets and cancers of the colon, prostate and breast. *Diet, Nutrition, and the Prevention of Chronic Diseases* (WHO, 1990) also concluded that diets containing large amounts of total fat were associated with an increased risk of cancers of the colon, prostate and breast, in order of the strength of evidence, and that obesity was associated with endometrial cancer.

SIGNIFICANCE FOR OTHER DISEASES

Below a certain level of fat intake, diets based on starchy staples such as those consumed in some countries of Africa and Asia are liable to become so bulky that it is difficult to eat enough for the body's needs. The World Health Organization (WHO) has set a lower limit of 15% total energy from fat to

BOX 5.3.1 FAT, ENERGY DENSITY, OBESITY AND CANCER

High body mass, commonly known as obesity, is related to an increased risk of a number of cancers. Evidence is strongest for cancers of the endometrium, breast (post-menopause) and kidney. Obesity possibly also increases the risk of cancer of the colon. See chapter 5.1 and relevant sections of chapter 4.

In the view of the panel, energy imbalance leading to increasing rates of obesity in both children and adults occurs, in part, because physical activity has been declining with industrialisation and urbanisation and this fall is accentuated by the usual reduction in physical activity with age. In the physically inactive, diets dense in energy, such as fat-rich diets, are particularly conducive to a positive energy balance and weight gain. Thus, young adults confined to sedentary activities remain in energy balance only if a bulky diet, such as one comprising only 20% fat, is available (Stubbs et al, 1995). Passive overconsumption of fat-rich diets readily occurs (Green and Blundell, 1996), fat having a lower satiety effect than carbohydrate or protein (Weststrate, 1992). The behavioural responses to the normal physiological attempt to limit intake to match low energy expenditure are many (James, 1995), with high-fat meals in the evening failing to induce a fall in intake the next day. Alcohol consumption promotes fat deposition (Suter et al, 1992; Trembalay et al, 1996) and dietary fat is readily stored in the body at minimal cost (Flatt, 1995). Animal studies consistently demonstrate the propensity to obesity when high-fat diets are fed.

The epidemiological evidence linking the fat content of diets with obesity has been reviewed by Lissner and Heitmann (1995). Cross-cultural correlation studies show associations between the fat content of diets and the body mass index (BMI) of populations: in general, the higher the proportion of fat in the diet, the greater the incidence of obesity and vice versa (Keys, 1970). Analytical studies within single populations do not, however, show consistent relationships between fat consumption and BMI, not only because intake measures are unreliable in the overweight (Prentice et al, 1986) but individual differences in energy needs and responses differ (Astrup, 1996) and also because only those from obese families may finally show weight gain unequivocally. Conscious dieting also limits the display of physiological links.

Fat is the most energy-dense constituent of diet and it is generally accepted that diets high in fat increase the risk of obesity and therefore of obesity-related diseases, including cardiovascular disease and adult-onset diabetes (Royal College of Physicians, 1983; NAS, 1989; WHO, 1990; Department of Health, 1994). It is therefore reasonable to conclude that high-fat diets increase the risk of obesity-related cancers.

While it is true that low-fat diets have been rather poor instruments for the reversal or control of obesity (see Dr Willett's comments on p 391), this in no way provides evidence that high-fat diets are not a major influence on the *initial* accumulation of adipose tissue. There are many pathophysiological processes that have a causal pathway that differs from the pathways that are the means of maintaining, controlling, or treating them; consider for instance, various addictions, diabetes, and the cancer process itself. These all include some irreversible changes in homeostatic mechanisms and other means have to be found to reverse or control the resulting pathological changes. As already noted, and probably originally for reasons of survival in harsh conditions, adipose tissue is gained readily, but loss is difficult because the new homeostasis is strongly defended.

The body's physiological systems respond more readily to underfeeding (Blundell et al. 1993) and as weight gain occurs there seems to be a progressive entraining of appetite control; attempts to slim, e.g. on lower fat diets, induce metabolic and behavioural responses to defend the existing weight (Kendall et al, 1991; Liebel et al, 1995). Thus, intervention studies with low fat diets may be ineffective for physiological reasons and/or because the diet's energy density is insufficiently reduced.

Although there are some data to show that replacement of dietary fat by carbohydrate reduces HDL and increases triglycerides (see Dr Willett's comments on p 391), there are, as far as we know, no data to suggest that low-fat diets increase the risk of coronary artery disease.

The quantitative relationship between the energy density or fat content of a diet and the usual activity levels of different population groups is undefined, but obesity is emerging as a public health problem in increasingly sedentary populations in China, Japan and the Caribbean on diets with intakes of 25–30% fat. Adult physical activity levels (PALs) of less than 1.8 increase the rate of obesity (Ferro-Luzzi and Martino, 1996), so the panel advocate maintaining physical activity levels at greater than 1.75 PAL and limiting fat intake to 30% at most.

---

allow for this; it is especially important for growing children (WHO, 1990).

Linoleic acid is required at a level of 1–2% total energy to prevent a chronic deficiency state with poor growth. Higher intakes modulate the responsiveness of the liver's control of lipid metabolism. Deficiency is rare.

Between 1961 and 1991, 100 expert reports were published that were principally concerned with diet and cardiovascular diseases or diet and chronic diseases generally, including obesity. Most referred to developed countries and regions, and 94 commented on cancer. Of those, 85 recommended reducing total fat intake for whole populations and another eight recommended its reduction for vulnerable groups, including the obese; one report disagreed. Of the 85 that mentioned saturated fat, a total of 81 recommended lower saturated fat intake for whole populations, and another four for vulnerable groups; none disagreed. Of the 62 that mentioned polyunsaturated fats, a total of 51 recommended more polyunsaturated fats (usually relative to saturated fats) for whole populations, and another five for vulnerable groups, with six disagreeing. Of the 49 that mentioned dietary cholesterol, a total of 42 recommended less dietary cholesterol for whole populations and another five for vulnerable groups, with two disagreeing. Of the 48 that mentioned butter, all recommended less butter, with none disagreeing.

For total fat, an upper limit of 30% total energy is commonly recommended; sometimes, in industrialised countries, a higher limit, of up to 35% total energy, is chosen pragmatically. The recommendation for saturated fat is commonly a maximum of 10% total energy, and for dietary cholesterol, an upper limit of 300 mg/day is commonly recommended (Cannon, 1992).

Two reports on obesity (Royal College of Physicians, 1983; Department of Health, 1995) specified that energy-dense diets in general, and fatty diets in particular, increase the risk of obesity, and recommended lower-fat diets as a means of preventing or controlling obesity.

Diet, Nutrition and the Prevention of Chronic Diseases (WHO, 1990) set upper limits of 30% total energy from total fat and 10% from saturated fat on a global basis. An FAO/WHO report (FAO/WHO, 1994) recommended an upper limit of 35% total energy from total fat and a maximum of 10% from saturated fat.

FUTURE RESEARCH

The panel made the following recommendations for future research:

■ Studies of fats and oils and cancer risk should be designed so as to enable distinctions to be made between total energy intake and total fat intake, and between saturated fat, fat of animal origin, and meat fat.
■ Studies of fats and oils and cancer risk should also enable distinctions to be made among relationships associated with diets of different fatty acid composition, and across fats and oils produced by different methods of processing. This has clear implications for needs in relation to food analysis and food tables.

ASSESSMENT

The evidence on which this assessment is based is reviewed in the relevant sections of chapter 4.

Much of the evidence on fat and the risk of cancer is derived from studies of diets high in total fat, or specific types of fat, and cancers of the colon and rectum, pancreas, breast, ovary, endometrium, and prostate – the cancers more common in societies where diets are relatively high in fat.

In this section, evidence on total fat is assessed first. Next, evidence on saturated fat and animal fat is taken together; followed by evidence on monounsaturated fat; then that on polyunsaturated fat together with plant (vegetable) fat.

The grouping of saturated with animal fat, and polyunsaturated with plant fat in this report allows a reasonable assessment of the evidence without excessive fragmentation of the data. Most epidemiological studies that have reported on saturated fat have not reported on animal fat; the converse is also true. While saturated and animal fat are neither interchangeable nor synonymous, they can be viewed as markers for one another. The majority of saturated fat in most diets comes from animal foods, although a significant

portion may come from tropical oils in some diets. Also, while saturated fat is a key component of animal fat, between one- and two-thirds of the fat in most animal foods is unsaturated. Polyunsaturated and plant fat are similarly not synonymous. While many plant oils are made up predominantly of polyunsaturated fat, some oils are very high in monounsaturated fat (for example olive oil) or saturated fat (for example coconut and palm oils).

5.3.1 TOTAL FAT

A great deal of research has been conducted on the association of total fat, and on types and fractions of fat, with cancer risk. Evidence on high-fat foods, notably meat and dairy products, are reviewed in chapter 4 and discussed in chapters 6.6 and 6.7.

Evidence of increased risk

CONVINCING	PROBABLE	POSSIBLE	INSUFFICIENT
		Lung	Ovary
		Colon, rectum	Endometrium
		Breast	Bladder
		Prostate	

Lung (4.5). Three cohort and four case-control studies have examined total fat intake and lung cancer and there are a number of ecological studies. Overall, the evidence regarding total fat and lung cancer is more abundant than for some other sites, but is somewhat inconsistent. Ecological studies show a clear pattern of higher rates of lung cancer with higher fat consumption, an effect largely independent of tobacco consumption. Analytical studies show either increased risk or no relationship. Experimental studies show a tumour-enhancing effect of high-fat diets, which may be due to increased energy intake. High-fat diets possibly increase the risk of lung cancer, but any effect is minor compared to that of cigarette smoking.

Colon, rectum (4.10). The majority of early case-control studies reported increased risk of colorectal cancer with higher fat intakes, results not supported by the majority of more recent cohort and case-control studies (including a meta-analysis) which adjusted for energy intake and which failed to find an association. Three ecological studies, however, found a high correlation between colon cancer incidence and mortality and total fat intake. This is supported by animal studies. Possible biological mechanisms have been proposed. The evidence suggests that high-fat diets possibly increase the risk of colorectal cancer.

Breast (4.11). Eleven cohort and twenty-three case-control studies have examined total fat intake and the risk of breast cancer. Analytical studies conducted since 1989 do not strongly support an aetiological link between high dietary fat intake and breast cancer. Most prospective studies show no relationship between fat intake and breast cancer. Results for case-control studies are somewhat inconsistent, but indicate a slight to moderate increase in risk with higher intake. International ecological studies have shown strong correlations. Results from animal studies are somewhat mixed, but a meta-analysis of such studies suggested a modest increase in risk for both higher total energy and higher fat, neither of which is explained by differences in body weight. The effect of fat on human breast cancer may occur at levels below those found in developed countries, where most epidemiological studies have been carried out, although the most recent data from a meta-analysis of the cohort studies does not support this interpretation. One mechanism that has been proposed is that fat may affect hormone metabolism and thus promote breast cancer. The main dietary determinants of breast cancer may have their effect during growth and breast development.

High fat diets possibly increase the risk of breast cancer. Also, high-fat diets increase the risk of obesity, and this, in turn, probably increases the risk of post-menopausal breast cancer (see Box 5.3.1).

Prostate (4.15). Several cohort studies and nine case-control studies have examined total fat intake and the risk of prostate cancer. The majority of these studies showed increased risk with higher intakes, but most did not adjust for total energy intake. Positive correlations between fat intake and prostate cancer mortality have been reported in four of five ecological studies. Results for animal studies are mixed. Possible mechanisms have been suggested. Diets high in total fat possibly increase the risk of prostate cancer.

Ovary (4.12). Limited epidemiological evidence, from five case-control studies and two ecological studies, tend to support a link between high-fat diets and an increased risk of ovarian cancer. Evidence on high-fat diets and the risk of ovarian cancer is, as yet, insufficient.

Endometrium (4.13). A relatively small amount of evidence from case-control studies supports data from correlation studies. Further, high-fat diets increase the risk of obesity, and the evidence that obesity increases the risk of endometrial cancer is convincing (see Box 5.3.1). Other possible mechanisms include a risk for endogenous hormone production or the mutagens in cooked foods. Evidence on high-fat diets and the risk of endometrial cancer is, as yet, insufficient.

Bladder (4.18). One cohort, four case-control and one ecological study have examined total fat intake and the risk of bladder cancer. The evidence tends to support a link between high-fat diets and an increased risk of bladder cancer. Evidence on high-fat diets and the risk of bladder cancer is, as yet, insufficient.

One member of the panel, Dr Willett, disagreed with the analysis above, and made the following statement:

> While fully in support of the rest the panel in all other respects, I do not agree that the data provide good evidence that the percentage of energy from dietary fat is an important cause of obesity as proposed in Box 5.3.1.
>
> For this reason, and because the panel did not find evidence that dietary fat was a probable or convincing

cause of cancer, I also do not agree with the dietary recommendation on fats and oils included in chapter 8.1. Indeed, if the reasoning in box 5.3.1 were correct, a clear relationship should be seen between dietary fat and obesity-related cancers, but the panel did not find such evidence.

A usual argument is that populations of countries with low fat intake are lean; but such observations are severely confounded by poverty, availability of food, and differences in physical activity. In regions where these factors vary less, such as within China or Europe, populations with higher fat intake are not fatter (Chen et al, 1987; Lissner and Heitmann, 1995), and within the USA a reduction in the percentage of calories from fat has been accompanied by a massive increase in obesity. Moreover, long-term randomised trials, the most rigorous form of study for evaluating this relationship, have consistently shown that reducing the percentage of energy from fat in the diet has little or no effect on body weight. The rationale for dietary fat being a cause of obesity rests largely on the fact that pure fat has a higher energy density than pure carbohydrate or protein. However, the studies of energy density have lasted only a few hours or days; long-term trials are lacking. If energy density is the important factor in obesity, a recommendation based on percentage of calories from fat is misleading because the modern food industry has provided a plethora of foods that are low in fat but high in energy density from refined carbohydrates. Further, healthy foods with a moderate to high percentage of calories from fat but low in energy density, such as salads with oil dressings, vegetables sautéed in vegetable oils, or soya bean products, may be unnecessarily avoided.

If reductions in dietary fat intake had no adverse effects, it might be reasonably argued that recommendations to reduce fat consumption are at least harmless, even if the evidence of benefit is not convincing. However, many carefully controlled metabolic studies have consistently shown that replacing unsaturated fats (which comprise about half the fat in most western diets) with carbohydrate reduces blood levels of HDL cholesterol and increases levels of triglycerides, and does not reduce total or LDL cholesterol (Willett, 1994; Mensink and Katan, 1992). These changes are characteristic of the atherogenic lipid pattern seen with obesity and insulin resistance, and suggest that replacement of unsaturated fats with carbohydrate may actually increase the risk of heart disease. These adverse effects of high-carbohydrate diets are not likely to be problematic for rural populations of developing countries that are extremely active and lean, or for athletes with high levels of physical conditioning, but they are seen among nonobese people with activity patterns typical of urbanised populations. Also, in many diets, vegetable oils are the primary source of vitamin E, which may play a role in the prevention of coronary disease (Kushi et al, 1996).

Abundant evidence indicates that replacing saturated and trans fats with unsaturated fats will reduce the risk of coronary heart disease, which is the leading cause of death in Western countries and is rapidly becoming so in many developing countries. An emphasis on reducing total fat intake distracts from this and other effective preventive strategies, including increasing physical activity, and has encouraged the promotion of food products that are high in energy-dense carbohydrates with little nutritional value.

5.3.2 SATURATED/ANIMAL FAT

Most foods of animal origin are relatively high in saturated fats, but almost all foods, including those of animal origin, also contain unsaturated fats. However, the epidemiological data do not allow a separation of evidence on saturated fats from evidence on animal fats, and these are assessed together here.

Evidence of increased risk

CONVINCING	PROBABLE	POSSIBLE	INSUFFICIENT
		Lung	Ovary
		Colon,rectum	
		Breast	
		Endometrium	
		Prostate	

Lung (4.5). Breast (4.11). Ovary (4.12). Endometrium (4.13). Prostate (4.15). Epidemiological evidence on saturated/animal fat and cancers at these various sites comes from: for lung cancer, two cohort, four case-control and an ecological study; for breast cancer, nine cohort, seventeen case-control and two ecological studies; for ovarian cancer, three case-control and an ecological study; for endometrial

---

BOX 5.3.2 HYDROGENATED FATS AND CANCER

In the view of the panel, inasmuch as extraction and hydrogenation have the effect of increasing availability of fat and saturated fats in diets, these processes possibly have an adventitious effect on cancer risk.

Oils and fats obtained by extraction or hydrogenation make up most of the added-fat content of the diets of developed countries and urban areas of developing countries. Hydrogenation has the effect of changing unsaturated oils into variably saturated fats. These are used as cooking and table fats and as an ingredient in very many manufactured foods.

Together with fatty meat, meat products and dairy products, consumption of these extracted and hydrogenated fats and oils in manufactured foods is the reason that the diets of developed countries and urban areas of developing countries are relatively high in total fat, particularly saturated fat.

---

cancer, from four case-control studies; for prostate cancer, from six cohort studies, seven case-control studies and three ecological studies. The balance of evidence from case-control and cohort studies suggests that diets high in saturated fat and/or animal fat possibly increase the risk of these cancers, with the exception of ovary, for which the evidence is suggestive, but currently insufficient.

Colon,rectum (4.10). Five cohort and 14 case-control studies have examined saturated fat intake and the risk of gallbladder cancer. 11 of the 19 studies found evidence of increased risk with higher intakes; 6 showed no association, and the one other study reported a decrease in risk. Diets high in saturated/animal fat possibly increase the risk of colorectal cancer.

5.3.3 MONOUNSATURATED FAT

There is a small amount of evidence to suggest that monounsaturated fat, as such, might influence cancer risk.

Evidence of no relationship

CONVINCING	PROBABLE	POSSIBLE	INSUFFICIENT
		Breast	

Breast (4.11). Overall, evidence regarding intake of monounsaturated fat and the risk of breast cancer is mixed: a pooled analysis of cohort studies showed no relationship, but a combined analysis of case-control studies showed increased risk. Ecological studies suggest no relationship. Diets high in monounsaturated fat possibly have no relationship with the risk of breast cancer.

5.3.4 POLYUNSATURATED/ PLANT (VEGETABLE) FAT

Most foods of plant (vegetable) origin (with the important exceptions of palm and coconut oils) tend to be relatively high in unsaturated, including polyunsaturated, fats, but almost all foods, including those of plant origin, also contain saturated fats. However, the epidemiological data do not allow a separation of the evidence on polyunsaturated fats from that on plant/vegetable fats, and these are assessed together here.

Evidence of no relationship

CONVINCING	PROBABLE	POSSIBLE	INSUFFICIENT
		Breast	

Breast (4.11). A meta-analysis of seven cohort studies and a combined analysis of twelve case-control studies consistently found no relationship between polyunsaturated fats or vegetable fats and breast cancer. An ecological study reported a positive correlation with breast cancer incidence. This epidemiological evidence largely contradicts data from experimental studies that suggests an increased risk with diets high in linoleic acid as well as in total fat. Polyunsaturated and vegetable fats possibly have no relationship with breast cancer.

5.3.5 CHOLESTEROL

Dietary cholesterol has for many years been identified as a risk factor for coronary heart disease, notably in the USA. For this reason, it has been studied in the context of cancers that are more common in the developed world.

Evidence of no relationship

CONVINCING	PROBABLE	POSSIBLE	INSUFFICIENT
		Breast	

Breast (4.11). Seven prospective and seven case-control studies have been fairly consistent in reporting no material relationship between cholesterol intake and the risk of breast cancer. Diets high in cholesterol possibly have no relationship with breast cancer.

Evidence of increased risk

CONVINCING	PROBABLE	POSSIBLE	INSUFFICIENT
		Lung	Endometrium
		Pancreas	

Lung (4.5). The evidence regarding dietary cholesterol and lung cancer is somewhat mixed. One of four cohort studies and three of five case-control studies showed increases in risk with higher intakes. The evidence is supported by ecological and experimental data.

Pancreas (4.7). Evidence from four out of seven case-control studies reported an increased risk of pancreatic cancer with higher intakes of cholesterol; the remaining studies were null.

Endometrium (4.13). Three case-control studies each reported increased risk of endometrical cancer with increased intake of cholesterol.

5.4 Protein

In order to manufacture its own proteins, the body requires an adequate supply of amino acids (the building blocks of proteins). These essential amino acids are found in cereals (grains) and pulses (legumes) and also in meat, fish and other foods of animal origin.

Protein intake on a population basis generally varies between 10 and 18% total energy. In the developing world, most protein consumed is of plant origin; in the developed world, most is of animal origin. Protein–energy malnutrition in early life remains a major public health problem within Africa and Asia. People living in industrialised countries and urban areas of developing countries typically consume more than adequate amounts of protein.

PROTEIN AND CANCER

In the judgement of the panel, protein modifies the risk of cancer of the sites as shown below. Judgements are graded according to the strength of the evidence.

EVIDENCE	DECREASES RISK	NO RELATIONSHIP	INCREASES RISK
Convincing			
Probable			
Possible			
Insufficient			*Animal protein:* Breast

For an explanation of the terms used in the matrix, see chapter 3.

INTRODUCTION

Protein may be classified as of plant or animal origin, or by its constituent amino acids. In this report, protein is classified as of plant or animal origin; the data do not allow for finer distinctions to be made.

SOURCES

Protein makes up 20–36% by weight of pulses (legumes), 8–25% of nuts and seeds, 8–16% of cereals, 10–20% of meat and fish, 15% of eggs, 3.5% of milk and 1–3% of vegetables.

Plant protein sources provide 65% of the world supply of edible protein (Young and Pellett 1994), of which cereals (grains) (47% of total protein supply) and pulses, nuts and oil seeds (8%) are the major sources. Intakes of plant protein vary little with economic development. Intakes of animal protein generally increase with increasing economic prosperity.

COMPOSITION

Protein is an essential human nutrient. Specifically, certain of its constituent amino acids are identified as essential, meaning that, like vitamins, the body is unable to manufacture them from other dietary constituents.

Proteins are complex molecules containing up to several thousand amino acids. Twenty-one amino acids are distinct; others are chemically modified during protein synthesis. Structural or fibrous insoluble proteins provide the framework for animal tissues and organs (hair, skin, cartilage, bone and tendons). Others include the semi-soluble contractile proteins of muscle, enzymes, peptide hormones, proteins of blood (including haemoglobin and albumin), milk (casein and whey proteins), cell membrane proteins, the plasma lipid-transport system, other transport proteins, and proteins involved in DNA replication, transcription, and repair.

FUNCTIONS

The characteristic functions of proteins are determined by the relative amounts and sequence of their constituent amino acids. All proteins turn over, that is they break down to constituent amino acids and are then resynthesised, although for the structural proteins this process is slow or minimal.

Individual amino acids also serve as precursors for a range of metabolites such as neurotransmitters, pigments, amines, nucleic acids and various cellular metabolites. Many amino acids can be easily interconverted, and are dispensible and replaceable by other amino acids or nitrogen sources. However eight (in adults) or nine (in infants) have structures that cannot be synthesised by humans; these are the essential amino acids.

REQUIREMENTS

Humans require dietary protein to provide amino acids both for the synthesis of proteins during tissue growth and turnover and for conversion to the various metabolites that are derived from amino acids. Dietary amino acids need not match the composition of tissue proteins exactly. However, diets must provide the essential amino acids as well as sufficient amino acids or nitrogen sources to allow synthesis of the non-essential ones.

Traditionally, the nutritional value (quality) of dietary proteins has been classified in terms of their ability to provide for tissue growth in rapidly growing rats; marked differences are observed between most animal proteins and individual plant-protein sources. With the exception of gelatin (from collagen), most animal dietary protein sources have an amino-acid composition similar to that of tissue protein. Cereal proteins tend to have lower levels of the amino acids lysine and tryptophan, and pulses contain lower levels of sulphur-containing amino acids. In combination, these differences tend to cancel each other out, so that mixtures of plant proteins allow similar body growth rates as animal proteins through provision of the appropriate balance of essential amino acids.

Human growth is very much slower than animal growth, so the nutritional demand for essential amino acids is much lower; moreover, contrary to the older view, there is little if any difference between the quality of protein of animal origin and that from plant sources when these include both cereals and pulses.

There are currently no generally agreed values for the requirements for essential amino acids in the human diet (FAO/WHO, 1991). National agencies now stress that, in most mixed, nutritionally balanced diets, sufficient essential amino acids will be provided irrespective of the relative amounts of plant or animal protein sources (Department of Health, 1991).

Recommendations for adults are specified as 0.75 g/kg in the UK (the RNI) and 0.8 g/kg in the USA (RDA), which is equivalent to about 9% total energy intake, with an upper limit recommended at 1.5 g/kg (about 18% total energy).

CONSUMPTION PATTERNS

The amount and type of protein consumed varies widely in different parts of the world. The most notable difference is in the ratio between protein of plant origin and protein of animal origin.

Throughout the world, protein intake varies between 10% and 18% total energy. The average in Africa is 58 g (10% total energy) of which 79% is of plant origin. Consumption in Japan is 79 g (15.5% total energy), of which 47% is of animal origin. In a UK nutrition survey, intakes were 73.2 g (13% total energy), of which 64% came from meat, milk, eggs and fish, and 31% from cereals and vegetables. Consumption in North America is 110 g (16–17% total energy), of which 66% is of animal origin.

Intakes of total protein above 2 g/kg are rare, although some athletes consume up to 3 g/kg (30% total energy). Low intakes of protein are more common among vegetarians. For example, in the UK, 32% of female and 20% of male vegetarians, compared with only 5.8% of female and 3.0% of male omnivores, consume less protein than the RNI of 9% total energy (Jackson and Margetts, 1993). The amino-acid composition of mixed lacto-ovovegetarian diets is not markedly different from that of meat eaters.

INTERPRETATION OF THE DATA

The effects of protein on cancer risk are difficult to disentangle from those of other dietary macroconstituents and foods. In industrialised societies, the collinearity of intakes of protein with intakes of animal fat, meat, animal foods in general and, to a somewhat lesser extent, total energy, makes interpretation of epidemiological studies of cancer risk and protein intakes problematic.

Even when protein intakes have been measured, the interdependence of animal protein, meat, and even plant foods still precludes complete disentanglement of associations. For example, as reviewed in the relevant sections of chapter 4 and assessed in chapters 5.8, 6.3 and 7.7, the risk of stomach and colorectal cancer is possibly increased by diets high in meats cooked at very high temperatures, and there is evidence that various constituents of foods of plant origin decrease the risk of various cancers.

In animal studies, low protein intake inhibits cancer and high intake promotes cancer of various sites. But animal data on protein and cancer should be interpreted cautiously. Most laboratory animals grow at a much faster rate than humans and their responses to reduced intakes are much more marked than in humans. Almost all human diets include protein at levels higher than any physiological requirement; a diet with protein levels sufficiently low to induce metabolic responses similar to those in rats fed low protein diets would be hard to construct.

As far as cancer risk and individual amino acid intakes is concerned, the similarity of the amino acid composition of mixed vegetarian and omnivore diets means that studies of populations with different dietary patterns probably could not detect any effects of individual amino acids.

JUDGEMENTS OF OTHER REPORTS

The National Academy of Sciences report, *Diet, Nutrition and Cancer* (NAS, 1982), reviewed the existing evidence available for six cancer sites (pancreas, colon and rectum, breast, endometrium, prostate and kidney). It concluded that although there was some evidence to suggest a role for protein as consumed in the USA in the causation of these cancers, it was not sufficient to draw any firm conclusions. This was because the epidemiological data were limited and inconsistent, and the collinearity between protein, particularly animal protein, intakes and fat intake made it difficult to identify independent effects on cancer risk.

Diet and Health, the 1989 report of the National Academy of Sciences (NAS, 1989), concluded that the findings remained inconsistent for colon cancer. For breast cancer, the report concluded that although intakes of protein, especially animal protein, were correlated with increased risk, case-control studies revealed no convincing association. For other cancers there were only limited data.

SIGNIFICANCE FOR OTHER DISEASES

Malnutrition (shortage of both energy and protein) in early life remains a major public health problem in parts of the developing world, notably in Africa and Asia. The amount and type of protein has generally not been identified as relevant to risk of chronic diseases (WHO, 1990; Cannon, 1992) apart from those of the kidney.

ASSESSMENT

The evidence on which this assessment is based is reviewed in the relevant sections of chapter 4.

5.4.1 TOTAL PROTEIN

The panel assessed the data on protein of plant origin and protein of animal origin separately, not that on protein as a whole. As noted above, there are no substantial data on individual amino acids and cancer risk.

5.4.2 PLANT PROTEIN

Evidence that diets high or low in plant protein modify the risk of cancer of any site is largely insubstantial. No judgement is possible for any site.

5.4.3 ANIMAL PROTEIN

Correlation studies and experimental studies both suggest that high intakes of animal protein might increase the risk of a number of cancers, largely those that are more common in the developed world. Apart from colorectal, breast and

endometrial cancers, these findings are generally not supported by analytical epidemiological studies.

Evidence of increased risk

Breast (4.11). Correlation studies showing associations
between high protein and animal protein intakes and an
increased risk of these cancers are only marginally supported
by data from case-control four studies. Overall, the evidence
suggests that high animal protein intakes may increase the
risk of breast cancer but is , as yet, insufficient.

5.5 Alcohol

There is no physiological need for alcohol, and alcohol is an addictive drug.

Consumption of alcohol differs in different parts of the world and within countries. Intake on a population basis varies between zero (in parts of the world where drinking alcohol is prohibited) or almost zero, to around 10% total energy. Individuals may consume far more, and alcohol abuse is a major public health problem in many parts of the world. Alcoholic drinks in general are identified by the International Agency for Research on Cancer as carcinogenic.

The panel has reached the following conclusions. The evidence that alcohol increases the risk of mouth and pharyngeal, laryngeal and oesophageal cancers is convincing; the risk is greatly increased if drinkers also smoke. The evidence that alcohol increases the risk of primary liver cancer, probably by way of alcoholic cirrhosis, is convincing. Alcohol probably increases the risk of colorectal cancer, and probably also of breast cancer, even at very low levels of consumption. In general, risk is a function of the amount of alcohol consumed.

ALCOHOL AND CANCER

In the judgement of the panel, alcohol modifies the risk of cancers of various sites as shown below, or else has no relationship with them. Judgements are graded according to the strength of the evidence.

EVIDENCE	DECREASES RISK	NO RELATIONSHIP	INCREASES RISK
Convincing		Bladder	Mouth and pharynx Larynx Oesophagus Liver[a]
Probable		Stomach Pancreas	Colon, rectum Breast
Possible		Prostate Kidney	Lung
Insufficient			

For an explanation of the terms used in the matrix, see chapter 3.
[a] The evidence is that this is by way of alcoholic cirrhosis.

INTRODUCTION

SOURCES

Alcohol is produced by the fermentation of sources of carbohydrate, including grapes and other fruits, grains, roots, and cacti. Very many different types of alcoholic drinks are made and consumed around the world, but most fall into the three broad categories of beers, wines and spirits (liquor).

Various ingredients and processes yield beers containing 4–7% alcohol by volume. Grapes generate various types of wine, which usually contains 10–13% alcohol. Distilled alcoholic drinks contain up to 30–50% alcohol. In addition, alcoholic drinks may contain carcinogenic contaminants such as nitrosamines, polycyclic aromatic hydrocarbons, and mycotoxins, as well as a wide variety of esters, phenolic and other compounds derived from the interaction between the original plant material and the production processes.

COMPOSITION

In chemical terms, there are different types of alcohol, but the type of alcohol drunk by humans is almost exclusively ethanol or ethyl alcohol (CH_3CH_2OH). In this report, the term alcohol is used synonymously with ethanol.

METABOLISM

Ethanol is metabolised, primarily in the liver, to acetaldehyde and then to acetic acid by several enzyme systems that demonstrate considerable variation among individuals. There are also non-oxidative metabolic pathways.

REQUIREMENTS

There is no physiological requirement for alcohol.

CONSUMPTION PATTERNS

The world average for alcohol consumption is 3% total energy, equivalent to 9 g of ethanol per person per day. This average masks great regional and national variations, as well as cultural and other variations within countries.

The consumption of alcohol is prohibited by Islam, some schools of Buddhism and Hinduism, and by some Christian denominations such as Seventh-day Adventists, fundamental Protestants, and members of the Church of Jesus Christ of the Latter-day Saints (sometimes called Mormons).

The lowest consumption is recorded in low-income Asia, the Middle East and North Africa, with less than 1% total energy and even zero consumption recorded in many countries. North Africa is one of the few regions where alcohol consumption has declined substantially, dropping by more than 60% in the past 30 years. In Asia, consumption levels are low or zero in many countries, but in some, such as Japan, Korea and certain areas of China, consumption levels are similar to those in Europe, North America and Australasia at 4 – 5% total energy. The highest levels of consumption occur in France, Portugal, Luxemburg and Italy, at 9–10% total energy.

In any population, most alcohol is drunk by men, and consumption by population subgroups varies between zero and 10–15% or more of total energy. Heavy drinkers, whether identified as alcoholics or not, may consume 25% or more of total energy in the form of alcohol. 25% total energy is equivalent to around 2 litres of beer, one bottle (750 ml) of wine, or 200 ml of spirits (liqor); it is about 70 g of ethanol per day in a 2,000 kcal/day diet.

Analysis of time trends shows increasing consumption levels in most countries, especially those in transition to urban-industrial societies.

INTERPRETATION OF THE DATA

Consumption of alcohol necessarily affects intake of other macroconstituents of diet. In particular, heavy drinkers who are in energy balance will have markedly lower intakes of other macroconstituents, and may have a diet that is poor in other respects; they may, for example, eat only small amounts of vegetables and fruits. Alcoholics and heavy drinkers often also smoke.

Because high alcohol consumption, especially among women, has a social stigma in many societies, it is often under-reported, in which case the risks at higher levels of consumption can be underestimated. Differences in the ways in which alcohol intakes have been both assessed and expressed make it difficult to summarise findings across studies.

The data available on specific types of alcoholic drinks mostly concern commercially made beers, wines and spirits (liquor). There are few data on the many other kinds of drinks, such as those traditionally drunk in Africa, Asia and Latin America (e.g., palm wine, pulque).

Studies may express alcohol intake in terms of volume (millilitres or fluid ounces) or weight (grams or ounces), or in terms of 'drinks'. Different countries have different measures for the size of a 'drink' and therefore for the amount of alcohol in a 'drink'. For example, a standard measure of spirits in the UK is 25 ml (8 g) while in the USA it is 45 ml (14 g). Additionally, different beers, wines and spirits vary in their alcohol content.

JUDGEMENTS OF OTHER REPORTS

Alcohol has been known to be related to cancer risk for many years. It was observed in the nineteenth and early twentieth centuries that many patients with cancers of the oesophagus were alcoholics or worked in the alcohol trade (Clemmesen, 1965).

Expert reports on diet and cancer generally specify alcohol as a risk factor for cancers of various sites when alcohol is counted as part of diet. Doll and Peto (1981) concluded that alcohol accounted for 3% of cancer deaths in the USA, adding 'it is most implausible that the true percentage lies outside the range of 2–4%', and 'the totality of the evidence suggests that the principal effect is due to the alcohol itself and is largely independent of the form in which it is drunk'. However, given the synergistic effect on upper aerodigestive cancers of smoking with drinking, they further stated: 'Most of the 3% of cancer deaths now caused by alcohol could have been avoided by the absence of smoking, even if alcohol consumption remained unchanged.'

The National Academy of Sciences report, *Diet, Nutrition and Health* (NAS, 1982), recommended that 'if alcoholic beverages be consumed, it be done in moderation', having reviewed the evidence then available on alcohol and cancers of the upper aerodigestive tract (synergistic with smoking), colorectal cancer (mentioning a possible link between beer and rectal cancer) and liver cancer (as a consequence of cirrhosis).

In 1988, the International Agency for Research on Cancer (IARC, 1988) concluded that while experimental studies did not show a carcinogenic effect for ethanol as such, the epidemiological data were so strong that alcoholic drinks as a whole were classified as group 1 carcinogens in humans for cancers of the mouth and pharynx, larynx, oesophagus and liver. For an explanation of IARC classifications, see chapter 3, Box 3.4. The report also concluded that there was 'suggestive but inconclusive' evidence of a causal link with cancer of the rectum. On breast cancer the report concluded 'the modest elevation in relative risk that has been observed is potentially important because of the high incidence of breast cancer in many countries. Although the available data indicate a positive association between drinking of alcoholic beverages and breast cancer in women, a firm conclusion about a causal relationship cannot be made at present'. The report also concluded that there was little or no indication that the effects of alcohol on the risk of cancer of any site were dependent upon the type of drink.

Diet and Health, the 1989 report of the National Academy of Sciences (NAS, 1989) concluded, after reviewing the evidence on alcohol and cancer as well as other diseases, 'the committee does not recommend alcohol consumption' and

proposed an upper limit of less than 1 oz (28 g) of pure alcohol a day.

A report of the UK Committee on Carcinogenicity of Chemicals in Food, Consumer Products and the Environment (Department of Health, 1996) concluded, on upper aerodigestive cancer generally, that alcohol was an independent risk factor, stating: 'on balance, the data support the view that there is convincing evidence of an increase in relative risk at intakes above 40 g ethanol/day. The evidence is less convincing at intakes between about 20–40 g ethanol/day. It is not possible to exclude a small increase in relative risk at lower intakes of alcohol below 20 g/day.' On cancer of the colon, the report concluded that the evidence of any causal association was insufficient; and on cancer of the rectum, that the evidence was inconclusive. On cancer of the breast, the report reviewed current epidemiological studies and meta-analyses, noted that the relative risk associated with consumption of between 1 g and 60 g of ethanol/day ranged between 1.2 and 3, and concluded: 'while there is no decisive evidence that breast cancer is causally related to drinking alcohol, the potential significance, for public health, of even a weak association between alcohol and breast cancer is such that we recommend, in particular, that this matter is kept under review.' In general, the report did not find evidence of any threshold level and concluded that epidemiological data were consistent with the view that 'the carcinogenic risk associated with the consumption of alcohol is proportional to ethanol consumption'.

A report of a working group convened by the World Health Organization (WHO) European region (WHO, 1997) identified alcohol as increasing the risk of cancers of the upper aerodigestive tract, liver and breast. The 1996 report of the American Cancer Society (ACS, 1996) noted that alcohol increased the risk of cancers of the mouth and pharynx, larynx and oesophagus, that the cancer risk rises at levels of intake as low as two drinks a day, and that the risk is markedly increased by smoking. The report also noted the association between alcohol and an increased risk of breast cancer, with the risk increasing at an intake of just a few drinks a week. It recommended people to 'limit consumption of alcoholic beverages, if you drink at all' and also suggested that 'women with an unusually high risk for breast cancer might reasonably consider abstaining from alcohol'.

SIGNIFICANCE FOR OTHER DISEASES

Consumption of alcohol at low levels is believed to reduce the risk of coronary heart disease. The WHO working group (WHO, 1997) concluded that 'the reduced risk for coronary heart disease has been found at the level of one drink every second day and there is little additional reduction of risk beyond consumption levels of about one drink a day'.

Alcohol (ethanol) has a range of metabolic, physiological and behavioural effects. Assuming energy balance, the more alcohol that is drunk, the fewer nutrients are consumed. Alcohol also interferes with metabolism of some nutrients. Persistent heavy drinking may damage the liver, digestive tract, central nervous system and cardiovascular system. It has been estimated that one in five hospital beds is occupied as a result of diseases or disorders in which alcohol plays a major contributory role.

There is a linear dose–response relationship between alcohol consumption and the risk of death from homicide, suicide, and traffic and other accidents (English et al, 1995). Alcohol is a drug of addiction. A substantial proportion of violent crime, including rape and murder, is committed under the influence of alcohol. Additionally, a substantial proportion of accidents in the home, at work, and on roads are alcohol-related (WHO, 1997). The figure in France, for example, is 40%.

The 1990 WHO report, *Diet, Nutrition and the Prevention of Chronic Diseases* (WHO, 1990), proposed that the greatest public health challenge with alcohol was to bring down average consumption in industrialised societies to 4% total energy, and to eliminate alcohol abuse. The report also recommended: 'in countries where alcohol is not an established social behaviour or is not acceptable, it is desirable that abstinence be maintained'.

Of 100 expert reports published between 1961 and 1991, mostly concerned with diet and cardiovascular diseases or diet and chronic diseases generally in developed countries and regions, 52 commented on cancer. Of these, 44 recommended less alcohol for whole populations and another eight less for vulnerable subpopulations. None disagreed (Cannon, 1992). No recommendations for an increase of alcohol consumption have ever been made.

FUTURE RESEARCH

The panel made the following recommendations for future research:

- Further work to establish the mechanisms by which alcohol and alcoholic drinks affect cancer risk should be carried out.
- Continue efforts to develop effective progress to reduce consumption among adults and to prevent onset of consumption among children and adolescents.

ASSESSMENT

The evidence on which this assessment is based is reviewed in the relevant sections of chapter 4.

Research on alcohol and the risk of cancer has mostly concentrated on the upper aerodigestive tract, which is exposed directly to alcohol; on primary liver cancer, given the relationship between alcoholic cirrhosis and liver cancer; on colorectal cancer; and, more recently, on breast cancer. There is also a substantial amount of data on specific alcoholic drinks, including beer.

While this chapter is concerned with dietary constituents, specific alcoholic drinks, as well as alcohol itself, are assessed in this section, for convenience.

Evidence of no relationship

CONVINCING	PROBABLE	POSSIBLE	INSUFFICIENT
Bladder	Stomach	Prostate	
	Pancreas	Kidney	

Bladder (4.18). Two cohort and 18 of 19 case-control studies that have examined alcohol consumption and bladder cancer found essentially null associations. In eight studies, no differences were apparent between the sexes. The evidence that high alcohol intake has no relationship with the risk of bladder cancer is convincing.

Stomach (4.6). Six cohort studies and 26 case-control studies examined alcohol consumption and the risk of stomach cancer. Four of the cohort studies and 17 of the case-control studies reported no material association. However, recent studies suggest that alcohol increases the risk of cancer of the gastric cardia. High alcohol intake probably has no relationship with stomach cancer.

Pancreas (4.7). Four of the six cohort studies and 20 case-control studies all reported no statistically significant association with alcohol consumption. An ecological study on pancreatic cancer mortality also found alcohol consumption not to be an important correlate. Animal studies reported similar results. No relationship has been demonstrated for different aspects of alcohol consumption, including average and lifetime consumption and duration, frequency, and history of consumption. High alcohol intake probably has no relationship with pancreatic cancer.

Prostate (4.15). Three of four cohort studies and four case-control studies report little or no increase in the risk of prostate cancer with high alcohol intake. High alcohol intake possibly has no relationship with the risk of prostate cancer.

Kidney (4.16). None of six case-control studies that examined alcohol consumption and the risk of renal cancer found any significant increase in the risk of renal cell carcinoma with high alcohol intake. High alcohol intake possibly has no relationship with the risk of renal cancer.

Evidence of increased risk

CONVINCING	PROBABLE	POSSIBLE	INSUFFICIENT
Mouth, pharynx	Colon, rectum	Lung	
Larynx	Breast		
Oesophagus			
Liver[a]			

[a] By way of alcoholic liver cirrhosis

Mouth and pharynx (4.1). Oesophagus (4.4). The relationship between alcohol consumption and the risk of cancers of the mouth and pharynx and oesophagus, has been examined in eleven cohort and nineteen case-control studies, and ten cohort and twenty-one case-control studies, respectively. Strong and consistent epidemiological data amount to convincing evidence that alcohol and alcoholic drinks are independent risk factors for oral and pharyngeal cancers and for oesophageal cancer. The risk is markedly increased among drinkers who are also smokers. Animal data are limited. Plausible biological pathways have been proposed.

Figure 5.5.1 shows six case-control studies selected according to the criteria described in chapter 3; there may be as much as a 20-fold increase in the relative risk of oesophageal cancer across the very wide range of intakes that have been reported, particularly in men.

Larynx (4.3). Data on the larynx are less extensive (from six cohort studies and 17 case-control studies) and are limited mainly to the parts of the laryngeal area that are directly exposed to alcohol; they do, however, amount to convincing evidence that alcohol and alcoholic drinks are independent

risk factors for laryngeal cancer. As with the other upper aerodigestive sites (above), the risk is increased among drinkers who are also smokers.

Figure 5.5.2 shows a fivefold increase in risk between those with an intake of zero alcohol and those consuming greater than 120 g/day of alcohol. The four studies were selected using the criteria described in chapter 3.

Liver (4.9). Data from 19 case-control and 18 cohort studies are consistent and amount to convincing evidence that very high and persistent alcohol consumption increases the risk of primary liver cancer, probably by way of alcoholic liver cirrhosis, although a number of studies did not control for important risk factors for liver cancer.

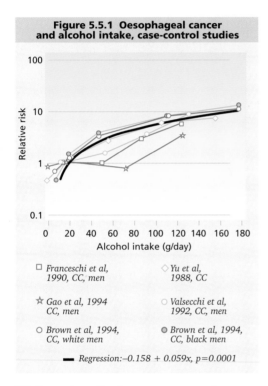

This figure shows the dose-response curve for alcohol intake and oesophageal cancer. The fitted regression line is consistent with a 20-fold difference in relative risk between those consuming 10 grams of alcohol or less per day and those consuming more than 160 grams per day.

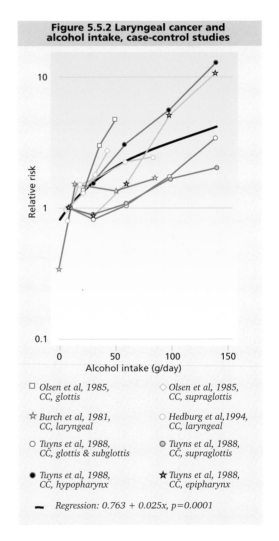

This figure shows the dose–response relationship between alcohol intake and risk of laryngeal cancer. The four case-control studies show a consistent elevation of risk above 50 g/day, even for the glottis and epipharynx. The fitted regression line suggests that there is an approximate fivefold increase in the relative risk across the range of alcohol intake from 0 to more than 120 g/day.

Colon and rectum (4.10). Eleven cohort studies and more than 20 case-control studies have examined alcohol consumption and colorectal cancer. Results of these studies are not quite as consistent as for the sites above, but case-control and cohort studies generally support time-trend and animal studies that show an increased risk. Plausible mechanisms have been identified. The data are consistent with as much as a 1.5- to twofold increase in risk for those consuming more than 30–50 g of alcohol per day compared with non-drinkers. Alcohol probably increases the risk of cancers of the colon and of the rectum.

Breast (4.11). Eleven cohort studies and 36 case-control studies have examined alcohol consumption and the risk of breast cancer. Evidence from both case-control and cohort studies, supported by identification of plausible biological pathways, shows a relationship between alcohol and alcoholic drinks and an increased risk of breast cancer. In animal studies, alcohol has been shown to enhance the development of mammary cancer.

Figure 5.5.3 suggests that the relative risk of breast cancer increases approximately twofold across the range of 0–80 g per day. Although one or two studies are consistent with a declining risk up to 20 g per day, the overall evidence is consistent with an approximately 25–30% increase at 20 g per day. The studies were selected using the criteria described in chapter 3. The regression line was fitted conservatively without the data point at 80 g/day from the study of Hiatt et al (1995) as this is based on small numbers. Alcohol and alcoholic drinks possibly increase the risk of breast cancer.

Figure 5.5.3 suggests that the risk of breast cancer increases at levels of intake of one drink a day. This finding is supported by a meta-analysis of 38 studies (Longnecker, 1994), which found evidence for an increased risk of breast cancer with alcohol consumption at all levels of intake. The relative risks associated with one, two and three drinks daily were respectively 1.1, 1.2 and 1.4. Strongest associations were seen in countries with high average alcohol intakes. Overall, the type of alcoholic drink was not important.

Lung (4.5). The balance of six cohort studies of lung cancer is consistent with increased risk with higher alcohol intake, but several case-control studies are not. The possibility of residual confounding remains. Biological mechanisms have been proposed. High alcohol intake possibly increases the risk of lung cancer, but any impact of alcohol consumption is minor compared with that of cigarette smoking.

Alcohol has not been shown to be a complete carcinogen in animal models, although cocarcinogenic activity in the liver of rats has been demonstrated, and acetaldehyde can induce DNA damage. Alcohol may act as a cocarcinogen, or as a promoting agent. A number of mechanisms have been suggested for this. These include both the direct effects of alcohol on specific organs and tissues, and indirect effects by way of the systemic effects of alcohol. Direct effects, notably on cancers of the upper aerodigestive and respiratory tract, and of the colon and rectum, may include altered mucosal cell permeability to carcinogens and/or altered carcinogen metabolism. Indirect effects may include alcohol-induced nutritional deficiencies, for example of folate; altered liver function; and changes in oestrogen levels.

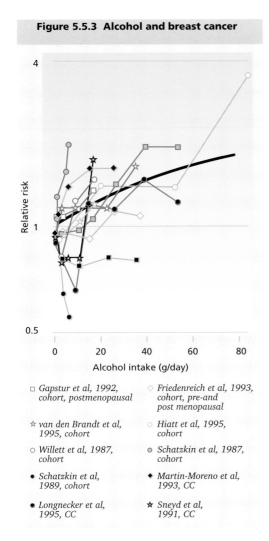

Figure 5.5.3 Alcohol and breast cancer

Relative risk

Alcohol intake (g/day)

□ *Gapstur et al, 1992, cohort, postmenopausal*

☆ *van den Brandt et al, 1995, cohort*

○ *Willett et al, 1987, cohort*

● *Schatzkin et al, 1989, cohort*

● *Longnecker et al, 1995, CC*

◇ *Friedenreich et al, 1993, cohort, pre-and post menopausal*

○ *Hiatt et al, 1995, cohort*

◉ *Schatzkin et al, 1987, cohort*

◆ *Martin-Moreno et al, 1993, CC*

★ *Sneyd et al, 1991, CC*

This figure shows the dose–response relationship between intake of alcohol and risk of breast cancer. The fitted regression line suggests an approximately two-fold increase in relative risk across the range of 0 to 80 g of alcohol per day.

5.6 Vitamins

The vitamins assessed here are carotenoids, which include the plant precursors of vitamin A; vitamin C; folate (also known as folic acid); vitamin B$_{12}$; retinol (pre-formed vitamin A); and vitamin E.

Intakes of carotenoids, vitamin C and folate tend to increase with intake of foods of plant origin, particularly vegetables and fruits. Retinol is found solely in foods of animal origin. The richest common source of vitamin E is oils of plant origin.

The panel has reached the following conclusions. The evidence that high intakes of carotenoids and vitamin C, as found in foods and drinks, decrease the risk of cancers of various sites is substantial and consistent. However, the possibility of confounding with other dietary constituents is considerable. High intakes of carotenoids from foods and drinks probably decrease the risk of lung cancer; high intakes of vitamin C from foods and drinks probably decrease the risk of stomach cancer.

Diets high in carotenoids possibly decrease the risk of oesophageal, stomach, colorectal, breast, and cervical cancers; and diets high in vitamin C possibly decrease the risk of mouth and pharyngeal, oesophageal, lung, pancreatic and cervical cancers.

The relationship between supplements of these nutrients and the risk of cancer is less clear.

Evidence on folate, vitamin E and cancer is less substantial. The panel notes that diets high in vitamin E possibly decrease the risk of lung and cervical cancers.

VITAMINS AND CANCER

In the judgement of the panel, the vitamins assessed here modify the risk of cancers of various sites as shown below, or else have no relationship with them. Judgements are graded according to the strength of the evidence.

EVIDENCE	DECREASES RISK	NO RELATIONSHIP	INCREASES RISK
Convincing			

Probable	*Carotenoids*:
	  Lung
	Vitamin C:
	  Stomach		

Possible	*Carotenoids :*
	  Oesophagus
	  Stomach
	  Colon, rectum
	  Breast
	  Cervix
	
	Vitamin C:
	  Mouth and pharynx
	  Oesophagus
	  Lung
	  Pancreas
	  Cervix
	
	Vitamin E:
	  Lung
	  Cervix
		Vitamin C
		  Prostate
		
		Retinol:
		  Lung
		  Stomach
		  Breast
		  Cervix
		
		Vitamin E:
		  Stomach
		  Breast
		
		Folate:
		  Cervix	

Insufficient	*Carotenoids*:
	  Larynx
	  Ovary
	  Endometrium
	  Bladder
	
	Vitamin C:
	  Larynx
	  Colon, rectum
	  Breast
	  Bladder
	
	Retinol:
	  Bladder
	
	Vitamin E:
	  Colon, rectum
	
	Folate and methionine
	  Colon, rectum		

For an explanation of the terms used in the matrix, see chapter 3.
Evidence based solely on intervention trials using supplements has been omitted. (See text and Box 5.6.2)

INTRODUCTION

The vitamins considered here are the carotenoids, vitamin C, folate (folic acid), vitamin B12, retinol and vitamin E.

SOURCES

β-carotene is the most abundant carotenoid and is found notably in orange vegetables and fruits, and in dark green leafy vegetables, such as carrots, sweet potatoes, pumpkin, winter squash, cantaloupe, apricots, mangoes, kale, spinach, collard greens, and chicory. Carrots are a rich source of α-carotene, and avocado and pumpkin also contain appreciable amounts. The predominant carotenoids in spinach, kale, and other greens are the xanthophylls; lutein is the major xanthophyll carotenoid. Lycopene is found in tomatoes and tomato products, as well as in watermelon, pink grapefruit and guava (Mangels et al, 1993). Cryptoxanthin is found in large amounts in mangoes, pawpaw, persimmon, red peppers and pumpkin. In countries where consumption of oranges and orange juice is common, these foods contribute a large proportion of dietary cryptoxanthin (see Mackerras, 1995). Unrefined red palm oil is the richest known source of carotenoids, of which α- and β-carotene are the major carotenoids. Although some populations consume unrefined palm oil, most of the carotenoid content is destroyed by refining processes that produce the lighter coloured oils that are usually consumed (Cottrell, 1991).

Vitamin C is present in vegetables, tubers, fruits and milk (including breast milk). Specific food sources include broccoli, cabbage and other green leafy vegetables, peppers, tomatoes, pumpkin, potatoes, cassava, yams, citrus fruits, mangoes, papaya, banana, strawberries and melon. Vitamin C is heat labile and prone to oxidation by ascorbic acid oxidase. As vitamin C is water soluble, it leaches out of food if cooked in a large quantity of water. Vitamin C is added to some foods (for example, bread) as an antioxidant preservative or as fortification.

Folate (folic acid) is so-called because it is abundant in foliage (green leafy vegetables) as well as in wholegrain cereals and other foods. Vitamin B_{12} is synthesised by human colonic flora but is found primarily in foods of animal origin. Traces are sometimes found in plant foods.

Retinol is found only in foods of animal origin, such as liver, milk and dairy products, egg yolks and fish-liver oils.

Vitamin E is found notably in vegetable oils (including safflower, corn, cottonseed and soya bean oils) and the products made from them, such as margarine, shortening and mayonnaise. Other sources include whole grains, nuts, seeds and wheat germ. α-tocopherol is the most widely distributed form in nature although, in industrialised diets, the gamma isomer is more abundant due to its prevalence in some corn and soya bean oils and margarines. α-tocopherol predominates in olive, canola, sunflower and safflower oils, as well as in animal foods. Significant losses of vitamin E from food can occur during processing, storage, and preparation.

COMPOSITION

Carotenoids are pigments synthesised by plants but not by animals and are widespread in nature – from algae to autumn leaves. β-carotene is the main percursor of vitamin A from plant sources; other carotenoids that have vitamin A activity are cryptoxanthin and α-carotene. Carotenoids are fat-soluble compounds classifiable as xanthophylls (carotenoids containing oxygen), carotenes (hydrocarbon carotenoids), or lycopene. Over 600 carotenoids occur in nature. Carotenoid absorption in the small intestine is relatively inefficient (10–30%), and decreases with increasing carotenoid intake or with decreasing fat intake. Human plasma contains only a fraction of the total carotenoids that have been identified in foods; lycopene is the carotenoid found most often at the highest concentrations. Reduction of dietary carotenoids is associated with a relatively rapid depletion of plasma levels.

Vitamin C is a water-soluble vitamin. Its two forms are L-ascorbic acid (the reduced form) and dehydroascorbic acid (the oxidised form). It is destroyed or lost from food as a result of heat, oxidation, or cooking in large amounts of water.

Folic acid (pteroyl glutamic acid) is the parent molecule for a large number of derivatives collectively known as folates. Free pteroyl glutamic acid is not present in food or human tissues unless used as a dietary supplement, and is physiologically inactive until it is reduced to dihydrofolic acid. In this form, it can enter the body's folate pool. The main naturally occuring forms are tetrahydrofolate, 5-methyl tetrahydrofolate, and 10-formyltetrahydrofolate, each with side chains of up to 11 glutamic acid residues. Polyglutamate forms, based mainly on 5-methyl tetrahydrofolate, predominate in fresh foods, but break down, with storage, to less available forms. The main circulating form is the monoglutamate 5-methyl tetrahydrofolate, although polyglutamates are the forms that are active within cells.

Retinol and vitamin E are fat-soluble vitamins. Vitamin E includes at least eight naturally occurring tocopherol and tocotrienol compounds with different biological activities. These include α-, β-, γ- and δ-tocopherol and tocotrienol.

FUNCTIONS

Some carotenoids are converted to vitamin A, which is required for growth and the normal development and differentiation of tissues. It has also been suggested that carotenoids act as antioxidants in tissues, deactivating free radicals. See Box 5.6.1.

Vitamin C is an important component of the antioxidant defence system and protects against damage from free radicals. Vitamin C facilitates the use of calcium for the building of bones and blood vessels. It also enhances the absorption of non-haem iron. Vitamin C has a number of biochemical functions linked to the immune system. It is involved in the acceleration of the hydroxylation reactions required for the formation of collagen; collagen is the essential component of basement membranes, which serve as the attachment for epithelial cells lining the digestive, respiratory, urinary and reproductive tracts.

Folates are involved in a number of single carbon transfer reactions, especially in the synthesis of purines, pyrimidines, glycine and methionine.

Vitamin E is an antioxidant. It is necessary for neurological and immune function and for prevention of red blood cell haemolysis. Only α and γ-tocopherol appear to be absorbed and retained to any appreciable extent. α-tocopherol has the highest biological activity among vitamin E compounds (as determined by animal assays), and is also superior in antioxidant activity; γ-tocopherol exhibits about 10–20% of the vitamin E activity of α-tocopherol and has about 30% of the antioxidant capability.

Retinol (preformed vitamin A) is involved in a number of functions in the body, including normal cell differentiation, the maintenance of epithelial tissues, night vision and immune responses. It does not have any antioxidant functions.

REQUIREMENTS

The WHO safe level (upper end of the normative storage requirement) for vitamin A for men aged 15–50+ years is 600 µg/day; for women aged 11–50+ years it is 500 µg/day (FAO/WHO, 1988). There is, as yet, no separate recommendation for carotenoids.

The WHO recommended nutritional intake (RNI) for vitamin C, for 11–50+ year olds is 30 mg/day (WHO, 1974). A maximum body pool of vitamin C is thought to be reached with intakes of about 100 mg/day; at intakes above this, and certainly above 200 mg/day, a large proportion of vitamin C is excreted in the urine.

The WHO safe level for folate (based on a normative storage requirement with 15% coefficient of variation) for men aged 15–50+ years is 200 µg/day; for women aged 11–50+ years it is 170 µg/day (FAO/WHO, 1988).

There are, as yet, no WHO recommendations for vitamin E. The European PRI (population reference intake) for α-tocopherol, for men aged 11–50+ years is at least 4 mg/day; for women, it is at least 3 mg/day (Commission of the European Community, 1993).

CONSUMPTION PATTERNS

In the USA, mean daily carotenoid intakes for adults in 1985 and 1986 were estimated to be 2.6 mg for men and 2.1 mg for women (United States Department of Agriculture, 1986, 1987). In China, mean daily intake of carotenoids was recently estimated to be about 1.6 mg (Chen and Gao, 1993). In other parts of Asia, average daily consumption of β-carotene is about 3.3 mg/day. Mean intakes worldwide range from 2.1 mg in South Asia to 4.5 mg in the Middle East.

In the USA, the estimated mean daily intake of vitamin C is around 80 mg (United States Department of Agriculture, 1987). In Asia, overall mean daily intake has been estimated

to be about 76 mg, with average intakes ranging from about 37 mg in India to 140 mg in China. In Italy, average daily is around 120 mg/day.

In the UK, median folate intakes from food have been estimated at 300 µg/day in men and 209 µg/day in women (Gregory et al, 1990).

In the USA, mean daily intakes of vitamin E are estimated to be 9.8 and 7.1 mg α-tocopherol for adult men and women, respectively (United States Department of Agriculture, 1986, 1987). In China, the average daily intake was recently estimated to be 8.9 mg α-tocopherol, with intakes varying widely by region; intakes are generally lower in southern China (Chen and Gao, 1993).

INTERPRETATION OF THE DATA

The intake of the vitamins considered here is highly correlated with intake of other components of the diet; this is a particular issue with the carotenoids and vitamin C which, as a result of their plant origin are correlated with their primary sources – particularly vegetables and fruits – and with the many other microconstituents that are found in these foods. Similar considerations apply to the correlation between grains and oils and vitamin E.

Until recently, few data were available on the amount of carotenoids in foods. Food composition databases using carotenoid values determined by high performance liquid chromatography (HPLC) now permit greater accuracy in assessment of carotenoid intakes (Chug-Ahuja et al, 1993; Mangels et al, 1993). Cigarette smokers have been shown to consume significantly lower amounts of carotenoids (Margetts and Jackson, 1993), and vegetables and fruits than non-smokers (Morabia and Wynder, 1990; Margetts and Jackson, 1993; McPhillips et al, 1994), so control for smoking must be adequate in epidemiological studies of carotenoids and smoking-related cancers. Lower blood levels of carotenoids in smokers may be caused by this lower carotenoid intake, or smoking may have an effect on carotenoid metabolism or absorption; one study showed smokers to have plasma β-carotene levels that were about 70–80% of those of non-smokers, even at similar carotenoid intakes (Stryker et al, 1988). Studies of blood levels may provide the best available measure of cellular exposure to carotenoids. However, a potential limitation of nested case-control studies of cancer using stored samples is that β-carotene degradation occurs at the temperatures of the level often used to store such samples; light exposure is perhaps more important.

Vitamin C intake may be underestimated, partly because food composition tables generally include only L-ascorbic and not dehydroascorbic acid, and partly because the vitamin C added to processed foods as a preservative is not included in food tables. Vitamin C in the blood is rapidly oxidised and degraded, thus prospective studies in which blood is collected and stored until incidence or mortality is determined are problematic; a few studies have analysed blood samples soon after they were drawn. Blood concentration of vitamin C reaches a plateau at intakes above about 90–150 mg/day; thus, blood levels do not accurately reflect intakes above this level. Leucocyte vitamin C levels are thought to be a reasonable measure of longer-term intake.

As with carotenoids, smokers generally have lower intakes than non-smokers of vitamin C, and vegetables and fruits (Morabia and Wynder, 1990; McPhillips et al, 1994; Margetts and Jackson, 1993); they also generally have lower plasma and leucocyte levels of vitamin C. These differences are only partly explained by the lower intakes. Again, as with carotenoids, data analysis adjusting for smoking may be important, but must be interpreted correctly. Extrapolation of the results of experimental studies of vitamin C to humans is hindered by the fact that, unlike most other animals, humans do not have the ability to synthesise vitamin C endogenously; the guinea-pig, the fruit-eating bat and primates share this lack of ability. The relevance to humans of studies in other animal models is questionable.

Although gross deficiency states are well described (including both neurological and haemotological consequences), there are relatively few data on the intake of and need for folate and B_{12}. The reasons for this are partly historical – the first evidence of the pathological effects of lipotrope deficiency states came with choline in rats and folate in humans – and partly biological – humans are often folate deficient but rarely choline deficient, whereas rodents can easily be made choline deficient but not folate deficient. Care thus has to be taken in assessing the relevance of experimental studies to human health.

Many older studies have not differentiated between retinol and carotenoids. More recent studies have distinguished between retinol and carotenoids, but few have examined the food sources of retinol separately. Mayne et al (1991) have suggested that there could be confounding with other constituents of retinol-rich foods, such as liver. Some of the more recent studies have also used serum retinol levels as a biomarker of exposure, but caution is needed when interpreting these studies because there is no dose-response relation between retinol intakes and serum retinol levels.

Intake of vitamin E is difficult to quantify since much comes from the vegetable oils used in food preparation. Further, intakes within populations are usually homogeneous because of the widespread occurrence of vitamin E in commonly consumed foods; such homogeneity makes it difficult or impossible to study the risks associated with high intakes compared with low intakes. Like carotenoids, substantial degradation of vitamin E can occur when blood samples are stored at $-20\,°C$ or $-70\,°C$.

JUDGEMENTS OF OTHER REPORTS

The evidence on carotenoids, retinol and vitamin A, and vitamin C was considered by the 1982 and 1989 reports of the National Academy of Sciences (NAS 1982, 1989) and the 1988 report of the Surgeon General (Surgeon General, 1988). Broadly, these reports concluded that there was evidence for protective effects in the cases of some cancers, but the possibility of confounding with other dietary constituents made it difficult to make any definite judgements. On folate and vitamin E, both the 1982 and 1989 NAS reports noted a lack of human data that might support experimental evidence of a protective role.

SIGNIFICANCE FOR OTHER DISEASES

High levels of β-carotene in the diet or blood have been associated with a decreased risk of coronary heart disease in men in at least three prospective studies in the USA (Rimm et al, 1993; Morris et al, 1994; Pandey et al, 1995). Carotenoids are not toxic, even when ingested in very large amounts for weeks, although very high intakes may cause the skin to become yellow.

Vitamin C is involved in wound healing, the immune response and other functions, and helps to facilitate the absorption of iron, which may help to prevent iron-deficiency anaemia. An adequate intake of vitamin C is essential to prevent scurvy. Vitamin C may help prevent coronary heart disease by reducing the degree of oxidation of serum cholesterol. Two out of three prospective studies in the USA have shown a decreased risk of coronary heart disease with higher intakes of vitamin C (Enstrom et al, 1992; Rimm et al, 1993; Pandey et al, 1995). The use of megadoses of vitamin C to prevent and treat the common cold, in general, show no clear benefit either in cold prevention or in shortening the duration (Third Conference on Vitamin C, 1987). At doses greater than 1,500 mg, more than 50% may remain unabsorbed in the intestine. Such intakes may be associated with adverse health effects, including renal tract stone formation, gastrointestinal disturbances, altered vitamin B_{12} metabolism, and iron overload, although such effects are disputed (Sestili , 1983).

Diets typically consumed in industrialised countries and regions are low in folate; low maternal intakes during pregnancy cause neural tube defects in children.

Clinical deficiency of vitamin B_{12} is rare. Vegans have been advised to take supplements but suffer from deficiencies in only a minority of instances (Geizel, 1993).

Vitamin A deficiency is the leading cause of blindness in developing countries and affects about 500,000 children worldwide each year (ACC/SCN, 1992). Poor vitamin A status also decreases resistance to infections such as measles, and increases the morbidity and mortality rates from these diseases in children. Excessive intakes of retinol from overuse of supplements are toxic and can cause damage to the liver and cell membranes.

Vitamin E deficiency is rare, although marginal deficiency may be more prevalent and can lead to a concomitant vitamin A deficiency (Meydani, 1995). Manifestations of vitamin E deficiency are exacerbated by selenium deficiency. High intakes of vitamin E are relatively safe; few side-effects have been reported, even at doses as high as 3,200 mg per day (Meydani, 1995). Vitamin E may be a factor in the prevention of coronary heart disease, because its capacity to reduce oxidative stress may prevent atherogenesis. Numerous

BOX 5.6.1 ANTIOXIDANTS

Antioxidants are microconstituents of diet that are involved in DNA and cell maintenance and repair. They specifically protect DNA and cell membranes against oxidative damage, including that induced by carcinogenic agents. It is therefore biologically plausible that diets rich in antioxidants protect against cancer.

Overall, there is no good evidence that antioxidant nutrients in the amounts that can be obtained from diet have any deleterious effects. There is conflicting evidence from chemoprevention trials in which antioxidants are taken in amounts or combinations not normally found in food. Some of these trials show protective effects; others show no effect. Some major trials using β-carotene supplements with smokers and other groups have shown an increased cancer incidence after supplementation (Box 5.6.2).

The provisional conclusion from such findings is that the quasipharmacological use of antioxidants currently shows no overall benefits and may be inadvisable. Supplements containing a mixture of antioxidants in physiological amounts that are no higher than can be found in diets may be beneficial, but are not a substitute for a varied diet. It is clear that no formulated supplement matches the complexity of the mixture of microconstituents achieved with the consumption of a diet rich in plant foods.

Certain microconstituents of diet have antioxidant properties. These include β-carotene, other carotenoids, vitamins C and E, and the trace element selenium. Other bioactive microconstituents of food also have antioxidant properties; some of these are reviewed and assessed in chapter 5.8.

Antioxidants help protect cell membranes, DNA and other macromolecules from damage by reactive oxygen molecules, which are formed as a consequence of normal metabolic reactions and following exposure to carcinogenic environmental agents in cigarette smoke and foods and drinks (see chapter 6). Oxidative potential can be elevated by infection and chronic inflammation. Reactive oxygen species can damage proteins and nucleic acids in DNA and RNA and saturate the double bonds of fatty acids in cell membranes, in each case altering structure and function. Any of these processes may increase the risk of cancer. Oxidative damage to DNA occurs at a daily rate of about 10^4 hits per cell in humans. Most, but not all, damage is corrected by internal surveillance and repair systems.

Individual and population requirements for antioxidants are determined by the level of exposure to oxidative stressors. Without continuous and abundant antioxidant and radical-scavenging capability, survival would be impossible. Each cell has an antioxidant defence system that includes various enzymes, antioxidants, and iron- and copper-binding proteins. Carotenoids and vitamins C and E scavenge reactive oxygen or interrupt oxidative chain reactions, as do mineral-dependent enzymes such as selenium-dependent glutathione peroxidase. Other bioactive compounds that have antioxidative properties include, but are not limited to, some phyto-oestrogens, glutathione, some phenols and some flavonoids (see chapter 5.8).

Selenium is found in plant foods such as cereals and seeds in amounts proportional to the selenium content of the soil in which they were grown. It is also found in offal, notably liver and kidney, and in seafood.

Diets high in a variety of vegetables and fruits protect against cancers of many sites. However, disentangling which constituents of vegetables and fruit are responsible for this decreased risk is more difficult. Further, specific nutrients such as antioxidants that receive attention in studies of diet are, in part, selected because they are measurable in foods; other constituents, for which few or no data on levels in foods are available, cannot be studied directly.

Data from the 1987 National Health Interview Survey in the USA showed that intakes of carotenoids and vitamin C were highly correlated with intakes of vegetables and fruit (Ziegler et al, 1992); thus, these nutrients may serve as markers for the overall anticarcinogenic potential of the myriad constituents of vegetables and fruit, or for other individual constituents that have been less studied. For these reasons, the panel has decided that, in general, evidence on the relationship between antioxidants (and other dietary constituents) and the risk of cancer should be seen as less strong than that on foods and drinks. Intakes of antioxidants may themselves be highly correlated with each other. For example, correlations of 0.78 between intakes of β- and α-carotene, and 0.81 between intakes of cryptoxanthin and vitamin C (Le Marchand et al, 1993) have been reported.

Only experimental studies and human intervention trials, in which specified amounts of antioxidants are given as supplements, allow any observed effect to be attributed confidently to the individual or combined antioxidants themselves, and these quasipharmacological interventions have important limitations particularly because both dose and the exact chemical structure of the agents do not, in general, match those of the comparable dietary constituents (see chapters 3 and 4.5, and box 5.6.2 for further discussion).

In addition to a role in the initiation, promotion, and progression of cancer, long-term oxidative stress has been linked to cardiovascular disease, because oxidised low-density lipoproteins appear to be involved in atherogenesis. Oxidative stress has further been suggested to contribute to diabetes mellitus (Oberly, 1988; Wolff, 1993), age-related eye diseases (Christen, 1994; Hodge et al, 1995), neurodegenerative diseases, such as Parkinson's disease (Shapira, 1995), and the ageing process in general. Because antioxidants combat oxidative stress in the body, these diseases may be prevented by antioxidants.

Compounds considered primarily as antioxidants may also have non-antioxidant properties that protect against cancer.

BOX 5.6.2 INTERVENTION TRIALS USING ANTIOXIDANT SUPPLEMENTS

Recent intervention trials using antioxidant nutrients in differing doses and combinations have produced variable results. Given popular attention to antioxidant supplements as potential 'magic bullets' against cancer and other diseases, the findings of these trials are of considerable interest. Data from the 1987 National Health Interview Survey in the USA showed that 8% of the adult population was using daily supplements of vitamin C, and 4% supplements of vitamin E, respectively (Subar and Block, 1990).

Trials may provide information about whether the individual antioxidant is responsible for protection against cancer. However, the doses employed in these trials have generally been above those found in most diets, and a nutrient consumed quasi-pharmacologically, separately from food, may have different biological effects from those consumed within a food, especially when the exact chemical structure of the nutrient does not match that of the dietary constituent.

Large-scale intervention trials using antioxidant nutrient supplements include the Physicians' Health Study (PHS), involving 22,000 US male physicians; the Alpha-Tocopherol, Beta-Carotene Cancer Prevention Study (ATBCCPS), involving 29,000 Finnish male smokers; the Beta-Carotene and Retinol Efficacy Trial (CARET), involving 18,000 US male and female smok-

ers and asbestos workers; the Women's Health Study (WHS), involving 40,000 US female health professionals; and intervention trials in Linxian, China, involving 30,000 rural Chinese males and females.

The comments that follow relate to trials such as these, involving antioxidant supplements in combinations not found in foods. It should not be taken to apply to antioxidants found in foods.

Trials in well-nourished populations have shown no beneficial effects of β-carotene or vitamin E in preventing cancer; if anything, β-carotene supplementation may be harmful. One trial in a less well-nourished population showed supplements containing β-carotene, vitamin E, and selenium, but not vitamin C, to be associated with a decreased cancer risk.

Evidence from intervention trials with pre-cancerous conditions suggests that supplementation with β-carotene and vitamins C and E possibly has no effect on the recurrence of colorectal adenomas, and that supplementation with vitamin E possibly has no effect on benign breast disease. A probable effect of supplementation with β-carotene and vitamin E in reducing oral leucoplakia is supported by the evidence.

β-carotene

Four large trials involving β-carotene supplementation, notably within well-nourished populations, have provided no

evidence of a protective effect against cancer; indeed, two have shown an increased risk of lung cancer and overall mortality.

One arm of ATBCCPS involved daily supplementation with 20 mg of β-carotene; the results, published in 1994 after five to eight years of supplementation, showed an 18% higher incidence of lung cancer (p = 0.01) and an 8% higher overall mortality (p = 0.02) in the group taking β-carotene supplements (The Alpha-Tocopherol Beta-Carotene Cancer Prevention Study Group, 1994).

One arm of the PHS involved supplementation with 50 mg of β-carotene on alternate days. No effect on disease or death had been observed at the conclusion of supplementation in 1995 (Hennekens et al, 1996).

CARET, which involved supplementation with 30 mg of β-carotene plus 25,000 IU of retinol, was terminated ahead of schedule in early 1996 after preliminary results showed a 28% increase in lung cancer and a 17% increase in overall deaths in the supplemented group (Omenn et al, 1994; Rowe, 1996)

WHS also terminated the β-carotene arm of its supplement interventions in early 1996, directly following the release of the CARET and PHS results (Rowe, 1996).

A smaller trial, of 1,800 participants with prior non-melanoma skin cancer, involved supplementation with 50 mg of β-

BOX 5.6.3 LIPOTROPES OR METHYL DONORS

The lipotropes are bioactive compounds involved in DNA and cell membrane synthesis, as well as in lipid metabolism. It is therefore biologically plausible that the lipotropes, analogously with the antioxidants, together have a role in protection against cancer. Human research on the role of lipotropes is at an early stage and there are few data on protective effects of diets rich in lipotropes.

Methionine and choline act as methyl donors (see chapter 2) and synthesise lipoproteins in the liver. The term 'lipotrope' derives from this function. A choline-deficient diet leads to a fatty liver in rats. Folate and B_{12} are crucial to the syn-

thesis of nucleic acids and thus to normal cell replication. Lipotrope metabolism is complex; there are many interactions, both between the different lipotropes and with other microconstituents such as vitamin E and selenium.

Because of their involvement in DNA methylation, liptropes may modify cancer risk. Abnormalities of DNA methylation are characteristic of cancer and may result in over- or underexpression of specific genes involved in growth control, cell cycle control etc.

So far, limited human data show that low intakes of some lipotropes are associated with an increased risk of some cancers.

Folate and methionine have recently become the focus of some interest. Green leafy vegetables, in particular, are important dietary sources of folate in many populations, and this may, in part, help to explain why low intakes of these foods have been consistently associated with an increased risk of various cancers (Steinmetz and Potter, 1991).

The data reviewed below, showing associations between low intake or deficiency of lipotropes and an increased risk of cancer, could be taken to suggest that high intakes are protective, but the panel has decided that this inference is inappropriate until more is known about dose-response.

carotene and showed no effect on the recurrence of non-melanoma skin cancer after five years, nor on total mortality after seven years (Greenberg et al, 1990).

Vitamin E

In the ATBCCPS, daily supplementation with 50 mg of α-tocopherol was associated with a 34% lower incidence of prostate cancer, but with no effect on lung cancer (the primary focus of the study) or overall mortality (The Alpha-Tocopherol Beta-Carotene Cancer Prevention Study Group, 1994). The WHS includes a vitamin E supplementation arm that was still continuing at the time this report went to press (Rowe, 1996).

Combinations

In the Linxian trials, supplements were given to adults in rural areas where micronutrient deficiencies and cancers of the oesophagus and proximal stomach (cardia) are common. The supplements included 15 mg of β-carotene, 30 mg of α-tocopherol and 50 µg of selenium; or 120 mg of vitamin C and 30 µg of molybdenum; or other combinations not involving antioxidant nutrients (Blot et al, 1993). The amounts given were somewhat lower than those given in most other trials. Overall mortality, mortality from all cancer and mortality for stomach cancer were lower in the participants taking β-carotene, α-toco-

pherol and selenium combined. Relative risks for supplementation were 0.87 (0.75–1.00) and 0.79 (0.64 –0.99) for all and stomach cancer mortality, respectively. No effect was found for supplementation with vitamin C and molybdenum.

PRECANCEROUS CONDITIONS

Oral leucoplakia

Four studies in the USA, Canada, and Italy have shown that β-carotene, as a single agent, completely or partially reduces oral leucoplakia in 44–71% of patients. Another study, in India, reported that 14% of patients responded completely to β-carotene; the percentage with partial improvement was not given. β-carotene was supplemented at levels of 30, 60, or 90 mg/day in these studies. Vitamin E, at 400 IU twice daily for 24 weeks, resulted in complete or partial disappearance of the abnormal tissue in 65% of evaluable patients in another study. In yet another study, combined supplementation with β-carotene, vitamin E and vitamin C resulted in a response in 60% of patients. The extent to which a reduction in oral leucoplakia will lead to a reduction in the incidence of oral cancer is unknown. See review by Garewal (1994).

Colorectal adenoma

Several intervention trials have used antioxidant supplements in patients with prior

colorectal adenomas or familial polyposis coli. The largest and most recent trial, involving 864 US patients with prior adenomas, showed no effect of either 25 mg of β-carotene, 1 g of vitamin C plus 400 mg vitamin E, or of all three nutrients given together on polyp recurrence after four years (Greenberg et al, 1994). A study in Italy showed a significant reduction in polyp incidence in a group of 70 patients who received supplemental vitamins C and E plus retinol (Ronccucci et al, 1993), whereas three earlier studies showed no major significant effects of vitamins C and E (Bussey et al, 1982; McKeown Eyssen et al, 1988; DeCosse et al, 1989).

Benign breast disease

Two small intervention trials have shown that vitamin E supplementation at 150 to 600 IU per day for two months has no effect on mammary dysplasia or benign breast disease (Ernster et al, 1985; London et al, 1985).

Cervical dysplasia

One intervention trial, which involved supplementation of 10 mg of β-carotene for three months of women with cervical dysplasia, showed no statistically significant effect on progression or regression of the dysplasia (de Vet et al, 1991)

studies, mostly experimental and in vitro, have examined the role of vitamin E in ageing, immune function and wound healing.

FUTURE RESEARCH

The panel made the following recommendations for future research:

■ Given the animal data and biological plausibility of a relationship between lipotropes (folate, B_{12}, methionine, choline – see Box 5.6.3) and carcinogenesis, research priority should be given to human studies of high as well as low lipotrope intakes and cancer risk, and lipotropes should be studied not in isolation but in appropriate combination.

■ Given the problem of measurement of exposure to specific vitamins and the problem of confounding among the many microconstituents in plant foods, research priority should be given to the development of more complete dietary databases and to the development of additional and better methods of measurement using biological samples.

ASSESSMENT

The evidence on which this assessment is based is found in the relevant sections of chapter 4.

The following assessments are of carotenoids, vitamin C, folate, vitamin B_{12}, retinol (pre-formed vitamin A) and vitamin E. Many epidemiological studies have reported associations for 'vitamin A' but have not reported results for carotenoids and retinol separately. Only studies with data specifically for carotenoids are included in the section on carotenoids (5.6.1). For retinol, see section 5.6.4.

5.6.1 CAROTENOIDS

The hypothesis that β-carotene may decrease the risk of cancer is relatively recent (Peto et al, 1981). Earlier attention was focused on retinol, because of its role in cell differentiation and also because animal studies showed that high doses inhibited induced carcinogenesis. There is abundant evidence that carotenoids affect the risk of cancer of a number of sites. Evidence that high intakes of carotenoids decrease the risk of cancer is strongest for cancer of the lung.

Evidence of decreased risk

CONVINCING	PROBABLE	POSSIBLE	INSUFFICIENT
	Lung	Oesophagus	Larynx
		Stomach	Ovary
		Colon, rectum	Endometrium
		Breast	Bladder
		Cervix	

Lung (4.5). Five cohort studies and 18 case-control studies of lung cancer have reported on dietary carotenoid intake. All but two studies found a protective association overall or for either males or females, although not all the associations were statistically significant. All the studies adjusted for tobacco smoking. There is evidence to support a protective effect in both men and women, in non-smokers and smokers, and against each of the four histological types of lung cancer. In prospectively collected blood samples, each of five nested case-control studies has consistently shown a protective association. Experimental studies in animals have supported an anticarcinogenic role for β-carotene against lung cancer. Carotenoids probably decrease the risk of lung cancer.

Oesophagus (4.4). Five case-control studies have reported a protective association for higher intakes of carotene or β-carotene. These data on the whole show that dietary carotenoids possibly decrease the risk of oesophageal cancer.

Stomach (4.6). Two cohort studies and six of eight case-control studies have shown a protective association between higher levels of intake of total dietary carotenoids or β-carotene from vegetables and fruits and stomach cancer. Four prospective studies that measured serum β-carotene found, after several years of follow-up, that stomach cancer cases tended to have lower levels of serum β-carotene at baseline. A correlation study reported a moderate protective association between stomach cancer and serum levels of β-

carotene. Experimental studies have shown that β-carotene inhibits carcinoma of the stomach in rats treated with a known carcinogen. These data show that carotenoids possibly decrease the risk of stomach cancer.

Colon, rectum (4.10). One cohort study and nine case-control studies have examined colorectal cancer and carotenoid intake. Six of the nine case-control studies reported a reduced risk of colon cancer with higher intakes of dietary carotenoids; the cohort study and the other three case-control studies showed no association. A case-control study of rectal cancer has shown a protective association for carotenoids. Four out of five studies of pre-diagnostic levels of serum β-carotene found lower levels in subsequent colon cancer cases than in controls. For rectal cancer, levels were lower in cases in two out of four studies. In two studies that examined colon and rectal cancers combined, levels were lower in cases. A few experimental studies that considered the effect of β-carotene against chemically-induced colon cancer have produced mixed results. These data, on the whole, show that dietary carotenoids possibly decrease the risk of colorectal cancer.

Breast (4.11). Four cohort studies have reported non-significant protective associations for higher dietary carotenoid intake in relation to breast cancer. Of 14 case-control studies that examined carotenoid intake, ten reported a protective association with high intakes. In a meta-analysis of eight case-control studies, a weak but significant protective association was found for β-carotene intakes in postmenopausal women. Two studies of breast cancer survival have reported women with greater intakes of β-carotene to be at a lower risk of dying from their cancer. Results from three cohort and five case-control studies of serum β-carotene levels in relation to breast cancer are mixed. Overall, the epidemiological studies indicate a weak protective effect. These data, on the whole, show that dietary carotenoids possibly decrease the risk of breast cancer.

Cervix (4.14). Of ten case-control studies that examined dietary carotenoids in relation to cervical cancer, five reported protective associations for higher intakes; the other studies reported essentially null association or increased risk. Twelve serological studies have been conducted; the majority have reported a protective association between cervical cancer and blood carotenoid levels. These data, on the whole, show that carotenoids possibly decreases the risk of cervix cancer.

Larynx (4.3). Ovary (4.12). Endometrium (4.13). Four, three and four case-control studies, respectively, have examined dietary carotenoid intake and the risk of cancer at these three sites. This relatively small amount of epidemiological evidence shows, on balance, a protective association between these cancers and dietary or serum carotenoid levels. Evidence for a protective effective is, as yet, insufficient.

Bladder (4.18). One cohort study has reported a non-significant increase in the risk of bladder cancer for men with a higher dietary intake of β-carotene. However, of the seven case-control studies that have examined intake of total carotene or β-carotene, three have reported protective associations and the other four no association with the risk of bladder cancer for higher intakes. In four prospective studies that examined serum β-carotene levels, no significant differences were noted between cases and controls. The evidence that diets high in carotenoids protect against bladder cancer is insufficient.

There is also some evidence to suggest that diets high in carotenoids protect against cancer as a whole. Two prospective studies have examined carotenoid intake and the risk of all cancers combined. In one cohort of elderly people in the USA, RRs of 1.0 and 0.8 (0.7–1.0) were reported for males and females, respectively, for the highest tertile of β-carotene intake (Shibata et al, 1992). In a cohort of male Western Electric employees in the USA, an RR of 0.8 (p = 0.07 for trend) was found for those consuming the most β-carotene (4.1–15.9 vs 0.5–2.9 mg per day); this association appeared strongest among current smokers (Pandey et al, 1995).

Studies in Finland, the UK, Switzerland, and the USA of pre-diagnostic serum beta-carotene levels, in relation to subsequent cancer at ten sites, were reviewed in 1992 by Comstock et al. Cancers of the stomach, colon, rectum, pancreas, lung, breast, skin (basal cell cancer), prostate, and bladder were included. In over 70% of the reports, cases had lower levels of β-carotene than controls; the case-control differences were greater than 20% in over one-third of the reports. In large part, studies that did not adjust for smoking were intentionally chosen for this review.

A prospective study of Swiss men that was included in the review by Comstock et al (1992) found, after 12 years of follow-up, baseline plasma carotene levels were 21% lower (p < 0.01) in those who had subsequently died of any type of cancer than in those who had not (Stahelin et al, 1991). In this study, analysis for vitamin levels was conducted immediately after the blood was collected, thus avoiding the problem of degradation during storage.

Several mechanisms have been proposed by which carotenoids may protect against cancer. Perhaps most important is their antioxidant capability: carotenoids are efficient quenchers of singlet oxygen and can directly scavenge free radicals. Individual carotenoids have been shown in vitro to vary in their antioxidant activity; for example, lycopene exhibits superior antioxidant ability to β-carotene or lutein.

A second possible mechanism involves the formation of retinol and its subsequent role in the regulation of epithelial cell differentiation. Because lack of proper differentiation is a feature of cancer cells, adequate vitamin A (from either carotenoids or retinol) may allow normal cell differentiation and thus avoid the development of cancer.

Another potential mechanism involves an up-regulation of gap junctional intracellular communication, which may be mediated by carotenoid-induced gene expression. This effect appears to be independent of the pro-retinol and antioxidant capacities of carotenoids, and has been shown for β-carotene, canthaxanthin, lutein, lycopene, and α-carotene (Zhang et al, 1991, 1992). In addition, β- and α-

carotene may inhibit cell proliferation (Murakoshi et al, 1989; Phillips et al, 1993), and β-carotene may enhance aspects of immunological function (Krinsky, 1991). Each of these biological activities may also be important in cancer prevention.

Evidence of increased risk

While a few individual studies have reported a relationship between diets high in carotenoids and an increased cancer risk, there is no cancer site for which the overall evidence suggests that diets high in carotenoids increase cancer risk. For evidence on β-carotene supplements used in chemoprevention trials, see Box 5.6.2.

5.6.2 VITAMIN C

There is a considerable amount of evidence that vitamin C affects the risk of cancer of a number of sites. Evidence that high dietary intakes of vitamin C decrease the risk of cancer is strongest for stomach cancer.

Evidence of decreased risk

CONVINCING	PROBABLE	POSSIBLE	INSUFFICIENT
	Stomach	**Mouth and Pharynx**	**Larynx**
		Oesophagus	**Colon, rectum**
		Lung	**Breast**
		Pancreas	**Bladder**
		Cervix	

Stomach (4.6). Two cohort studies and 13 case-control studies have examined the risk of stomach cancer and high dietary intakes of vitamin C. One of the cohort studies and 12 of the case-control studies reported protective associations for higher intakes (statistically significant in nine of the studies). In a study of prospectively collected serum, those who died from stomach cancer had plasma vitamin C levels that were lower at baseline than those without cancer. A geographical correlation study has reported a weak protective correlation between serum vitamin C levels and stomach cancer. In animal studies, vitamin C inhibits tumour formation. One case-control study of chronic atrophic gastritis, showed a reduced risk with higher vitamin C intake. A few studies have shown that people with chronic atrophic gastritis have lower concentrations of vitamin C in their gastric juice. Diets high in vitamin C probably decrease the risk of stomach cancer.

Mouth and pharynx (4.1). Five case-control studies have examined the relationship between vitamin C intake and cancers of the mouth and pharynx. Very generally, intake in the uppermost quartile or so of vitamin C consumption has been associated with an approximately 50% lesser risk. Diets high in vitamin C possibly decrease the risk of cancer of the mouth and pharynx.

Oesophagus (4.4). Five case-control studies reported significant protective associations for high levels of vitamin C intake. The majority of these studies involved only men.

Diets high in vitamin C possibly decrease the risk of oesophageal cancer.

Lung (4.5). Six cohort and eleven case-control studies have examined the relationship between vitamin C intake and the risk of lung cancer. All but one of the cohort studies adjusted for tobacco smoking or was conducted among non-smokers. Protective associations were found overall or for specific sub-groups in four of the cohort studies. Seven of the case-control studies reported decreased risk with higher intakes, the remaining four found no association. One study found a weak increase in risk for men only. One cohort study found no differences in baseline levels of plasma vitamin C between those who subsequently died of lung cancer and those who did not. Diets high in vitamin C possibly decrease the risk of lung cancer.

Pancreas (4.7). Each of seven case-control studies has shown a weak to moderate protective association with higher vitamin C intake. No association was found in one cohort study. Experimental studies have shown vitamin C to modulate the development of pancreatic cancer. Diets high in vitamin C possibly decrease the risk of cancer of the pancreas.

Cervix (4.14). Of six case-control studies of cervical cancer that examined dietary vitamin C, five reported protective associations, although only three were statistically significant. In one study, a protective association was observed in smokers. Two ecological studies have reported no correlation between vitamin C intake and cervical cancer mortality. Diets high in vitamin C possibly decrease the risk of cervical cancer.

Larynx (4.3). Four case-control studies, including a European multi-centre study, each found a protective association between higher vitamin C intake and the risk of laryngeal cancer, although not all the associations were statistically significant.

Colon, rectum (4.10). Two cohort studies and eleven case-control studies have examined vitamin C intakes and the risk of cancers of the colon and rectum. One of the two cohort studies found a protective association. Of the case-control studies of colon or combined colorectal cancer, three reported protective associations for vitamin C, one reported an increased risk, and seven reported no association. Three of eight case-control studies of rectal cancer that have examined vitamin C intake have observed results in the protective direction, while four were null. Evidence that vitamin C decreases the risk of colorectal cancer is, as yet, insufficient.

Breast (4.11). All three cohort studies that examined dietary vitamin C intake and the risk of breast cancer reported no association. Of six case-control studies that have reported on vitamin C intake, two reported protective associations for greater intakes and four statistically non-significant increases in risk. In a pooled analysis of nine case-control studies, a statistically significant protective association was observed for the highest quintile of intake. Two studies of breast cancer survival reported that women with greater intakes of vitamin C were at a lower risk of dying from their cancer. Cases were reported to have signifi-

cantly higher levels of leucocyte vitamin C and non-significantly higher levels of plasma vitamin C than controls: these findings are not consistent with a protective effect of vitamin C. In an experimental study, no effect was observed for vitamin C on the growth of transplanted or chemically-induced breast tumours. Evidence for a protective effect of vitamin C is, as yet, insufficient.

Bladder (4.18). Of six case-control studies on vitamin C intake and the risk of bladder cancer, two reported protective associations, one of these, only for women, with no association for men. Results from the other four studies were essentially null. One cohort study showed no association. In experimental studies, vitamin C has been shown to inhibit some, but not all, carcinogen-induced bladder tumours. Vitamin C also inhibits the formation of nitrosamines and acts as an antioxidant. Evidence for a protective effect of vitamin C and the risk of bladder cancer is, as yet, insufficient.

A cohort study of plasma antioxidant levels in Swiss men showed levels of vitamin C to be about 10% lower at baseline ($p < 0.01$) in those who subsequently died from any type of cancer than in those who survived (Stahelin et al, 1991). In this study, blood samples were analysed immediately after collection, thereby avoiding the problem of degradation during storage.

Several biological pathways have been suggested as anti-carcinogenic mechanisms for vitamin C. Firstly, and perhaps most importantly, vitamin C is the most abundant water soluble antioxidant in the body and is unique in that it can be regenerated when oxidised. Via this antioxidant action, vitamin C is able to detoxify carcinogens and block damage to DNA. Vitamin C has also been shown to scavenge and reduce nitrite, thus reducing substrate availability for the formation of *N*-nitroso compounds, which are known to be carcinogenic in animals. Further, vitamin C plays a role in the synthesis of connective tissue proteins such as collagen. In this respect, a deficiency of vitamin C might affect the integrity of intracellular matrices and thus have a permissive effect on tumour growth, or inhibit tumour encapsulation. Vitamin C may also have beneficial effects on immune function, which may enhance tumour surveillance by the immune system.

Evidence of no relationship

CONVINCING	PROBABLE	POSSIBLE	INSUFFICIENT
		Prostate	

Prostate (4.15). Two cohort studies and five of six case-control studies reported no association between the risk of bladder cancer and vitamin C intake. One case-control study found an increased risk with higher intakes in both older and younger men. Vitamin C possibly has no relationship with the risk of prostate cancer.

5.6.3 FOLATE

There is a small amount of evidence suggesting that folate might affect cancer risk.

Evidence of decreased risk

Colon, rectum (4.10). One case-control and one cohort study have found decreased risks of colon cancer with higher folate intakes; the case-control study also found a protective association for rectal cancer. The risk of colorectal adenoma was found to be associated with low intakes of folate and methionine in the Health Professionals Follow-up Study cohort. The increased risk of colorectal cancer with low intakes of folate and methionine appears to be exacerbated by high alcohol intakes. Evidence suggests that diets high in folate and methionine may decrease the risk of cancer of the colon and rectum, but is insufficient.

5.6.4 RETINOL

Because of its role in cell differentiation, there has been much interest in the role of retinol in human cancer. A large number of epidemiological studies have examined the relationship between vitamin A intakes and cancer risk. Many studies have not distinguished between retinol and carotenoids. There is a considerable amount of evidence pertaining to the relationship between retinol and the risk of cancer of a number of sites. Evidence that retinol has no relationship with cancer is strongest for melanoma of the skin.

Evidence of decreased risk

Bladder (4.18). Of seven case-control studies that have examined the risk of bladder cancer and retinol intake, four found no association, two decreased risk and one non-significant increased risk. Two prospective studies found no association with serum levels in cases, with a third cohort study showing a protective association. This somewhat inconsistent data suggests higher dietary retinol may decrease the risk of bladder cancer, but is insufficient.

Evidence of no relationship

CONVINCING	PROBABLE	POSSIBLE	INSUFFICIENT
		Lung	
		Stomach	
		Breast	
		Cervix	

Lung (4.5). Of two prospective studies on total vitamin A and the risk of lung cancer, one found no association, the other a decrease in risk. Three of nine case-control studies found no association, and six found moderate to strong protective associations either overall or in a subgroup. Three cohort studies and eleven case-control studies on retinol or 'preformed vitamin A' have shown inconsistent results; six have shown no statistically significant association.

Stomach (4.6). One cohort and six of seven case-control studies reported no statistically significant relationship between retinol intake and the risk of stomach cancer. Studies of serum and plasma retinol levels also show no relationship. In a ecological study, serum retinol levels were not correlated with stomach cancer mortality.

Breast (4.11). Three cohort studies and a combined analysis of seven case-control studies have shown virtually no relationship between dietary retinol and the risk of breast cancer. Human studies of blood retinol levels can be largely discounted. In some experimental studies, retinol has been reported to reduce breast carcinogenesis.

Cervix (4.14). All of nine case-control studies that have reported on dietary retinol intake found no association with the risk of cervical cancer. Seven case-control studies of serum or plasma retinol showed no association. An ecological study found a strong inverse correlation between vitamin A intake and cervical cancer mortality. Five clinical intervention studies observed that topically-applied retinol reduced dysplasia of the uterine cervix. High dietary retinol intake possibly has no relationship with the risk of cervical cancer.

5.6.5 VITAMIN E

There is a small amount of evidence suggesting that vitamin E might influence cancer risk.

Evidence of decreased risk

CONVINCING	PROBABLE	POSSIBLE	INSUFFICIENT
		Lung	Colon,
		Cervix	rectum

Lung (4.5). One cohort study has reported no differences in baseline dietary vitamin E intake between those who subsequently developed lung cancer and a selected control group. One case-control study of dietary vitamin E and lung cancer found a protective association, whereas another showed no association. Pre-diagnostic serum levels of vitamin E have been shown to be lower in subsequent cases of lung cancer than in controls in four out of six populations studied, and null in the remaining populations. Out of five case-control studies of lung cancer that reported on blood levels of vitamin E, four studies observed lower levels among cases than controls. Diets high in vitamin E possibly decrease the risk of lung cancer.

Cervix (4.14). One cohort study and two of three case-control studies of cervical cancer reported protective associations for high dietary vitamin E intakes. One prospective serological study and one case-control study reported no association between plasma levels of vitamin E and the risk of cervical cancer, while three case-control studies found protective associations for higher levels. These studies also reported a trend of lower vitamin E concentrations with higher grades of cervical lesion. Diets high in vitamin E possibly decrease the risk of cervical cancer.

Colon, rectum (4.10). Three cohort studies each found no association between colon and colorectal cancer and vitamin E intake. Five case-control studies of colon cancer similarly reported no association. A pooled analysis of five prospective studies of serum α-tocopherol levels and colorectal cancer reported a protective association. Results of seven experimental studies of vitamin E and chemically-induced colon cancer have been conflicting. Evidence that diets high in vitamin E reduce the risk of colorectal cancer is relatively null but suggests a lower risk with higher intake.

A 1992 review of pre-diagnostic serum vitamin E levels examined the subsequent risk of cancer at ten sites. Comstock et al showed that, in 19 out of 30 reports involving ten study populations, cases had somewhat lower values than controls although in only four reports were the case-control differences greater than 10%. Results that were not adjusted for blood lipid levels were specifically selected for Comstock's review. In a 1991 review of the same topic, Knekt reported that 16 nested case-control studies of cancer at various sites showed an overall average 3% lower serum vitamin E level for cases than controls. (These studies were also included by Comstock et al, 1992).

A cohort study of plasma antioxidant levels in Swiss men (also included in Comstock's review), showed that levels of

---

BOX 5.6.4 MULTIPLE DEFICIENCIES OF VITAMINS AND MINERALS, AND CANCER

The 'poverty' or 'deficiency' diets consumed by populations in some regions of the developing world are mostly made up of one starchy staple, often itself not a good source of nutrients, and are correspondingly deficient in many microconstituents, including B vitamins, iron, iodine, various trace elements, antioxidants and other bioactive microconstituents (see chapter 5.2).

The panel has taken the view that data showing a relationship between the deficiency of an array of microconstituents and an increased risk of cancer do not necessarily reveal a specific role for the constituents that happen to be the subject of study so much as indicating that cancer risk may be increased by a deficiency of a combination of protective microconstituents, some relatively well understood, others as yet little known or unknown.

The implication of this view is that future research should be less concerned with studying specific microconstituents singly or in combination, and more concerned with the relative balance of foods and drinks and the wide variety of nutrients in such diets.

Most studies that show an association between multiple deficiencies and an increased risk of cancer involve upper aerodigestive cancers, particularly oesophageal cancer. The results of case-control studies are few and inconsistent (Ziegler et al, 1981; Brown et al, 1988; Graham et al, 1990; Hu et al, 1994; Thurnham et al, 1982; van Rensburg et al, 1983). The results of intervention studies conducted in regions of high risk (China and Uzbekistan) are not entirely clear and have tended not to find any effect of supplementation with non-antioxidant micronutrients (Munoz et al, 1985; Blot et al, 1993; Li et al, 1993; Zaridze and Evstifeeva, 1993).

It is possible that riboflavin and zinc have specific roles. An increase in cell proliferation has been observed to occur in riboflavin and zinc deficiency, which may enhance the carcinogenicity of nitrosamines (Craddock, 1992).

---

vitamin E, adjusted for serum cholesterol and triglyceride levels, were no different in those who subsequently died from any type of cancer than in those who survived cancer-free (Stahelin et al, 1991). A strength of this study was that blood samples were analysed immediately after collection, thereby avoiding the limitation of degradation during storage.

Following the discovery of vitamin E in 1922, early experimental studies involving chemically-induced cancers were carried out in the 1930s and 1940s; these studies produced inconsistent and contradictory results (see Knekt, 1991).

The major function of vitamin E is as an intracellular antioxidant; it is the most important antioxidant found within lipid membranes in the body. As such, it protects polyunsaturated fatty acids in cell membranes from oxidation by scavenging oxygen radicals and terminating free radical chain reactions. Oxidation results in the production of malondialdehyde, which is possibly mutagenic, and free radicals, which can induce damage in DNA, cell membranes etc. Following interaction with free radicals, the active form of vitamin E can be regenerated by reduced glutathione, ubiquinol, or possibly vitamin C.

Another potential mechanism involves the ability of vitamin E to keep selenium and carotenoids in a reduced state, thereby enhancing their antioxidant capacity. Further, vitamin E has been shown to inhibit the formation of nitrosamines, which possibly increase the risk of stomach cancer (see chapter 4.6). However, note below that there appears to be no relationship between vitamin E and stomach cancer.

Evidence of no relationship

CONVINCING	PROBABLE	POSSIBLE	INSUFFICIENT
		Stomach	
		Breast	

Stomach (4.6). Of two prospective studies that examined the relationship between vitamin E intake and stomach cancer, one found no significant association and the other a decreased risk (statistically non-significant). Out of six case-control studies, two have shown significant protective associations for higher intakes, the other four reported no association. Neither of two prospective studies of serum or plasma concentrations of vitamin E and stomach cancer found significantly lower levels among cases than non-cases. Experimental studies have shown that vitamin E can inhibit forestomach carcinogenesis in rats. Men (but not women) with gastric dysplasia have been shown to have lower levels of serum vitamin E than healthy controls. Taken together the evidence suggests that diets high in vitamin E possibly have no relationship with stomach cancer.

Breast (4.11). None of three cohort or five case-control studies of dietary vitamin E and breast cancer risk have found a statistically significant association. Studies of blood levels of vitamin E have produced mixed results, probably a result of methodological limitations. Experimental studies have shown either protective effects or no association.

5.7 Minerals

The minerals and trace elements assessed here are calcium (together with vitamin D), selenium, iodine and iron. Evidence on the relationship of other minerals and trace elements with the risk of cancer is insubstantial.

Intakes of calcium and iron largely reflect the patterns of intake of foods that are good dietary sources. Intakes of selenium and iodine are largely determined by the amounts of these trace elements present in the soil where food is grown, although the food supply may be supplemented with iodine in iodine-poor areas.

The panel has reached the following conclusion. Diets deficient in iodine probably increase the risk of thyroid cancer. The panel notes that diets high in selenium possibly decrease the risk of lung cancer. However, the possibility of confounding with other dietary constituents is considerable.

MINERALS AND CANCER

In the judgement of the panel, the minerals assessed here modify the risk of cancers of the various sites as shown below. Judgements are graded according to the strength of the evidence.

EVIDENCE	DECREASES RISK	NO RELATIONSHIP	INCREASES RISK
Convincing			
Probable			*Iodine deficiency*: Thyroid
Possible	*Selenium*: Lung	*Calcium/*: Colon, rectum *Selenium* Colon, rectum	*Iodine excess*: Thyroid
Insufficient	*Vitamin D*: Colon, rectum *Selenium*: Stomach Liver Thyroid		*Iron*: Liver Colon, rectum

For an explanation of the terms used in the matrix, see chapter 3.

INTRODUCTION

The minerals and trace elements assessed here are calcium (together with vitamin D), selenium, iron and iodine. They are all essential nutrients.

SOURCES

Calcium is found in foods of both plant and animal origin. Rich sources are dairy products such as milk, cheese and yoghurt, and small fish (when eaten with their bones). Various plant foods are also rich sources but may also contain substances such as oxalates (found in cocoa, rhubarb and spinach) and phytates (found in cereals (grains) such as wheat), which reduce somewhat calcium absorption.

Selenium is found in cereals, meat and fish. Cereals provide about 50% of the selenium in the diet. The selenium content of plant foods varies with the selenium content of the soil.

Haem iron (somewhat more readily absorbed) is found only in foods of animal origin, such as meat and meat products, fish and blood products. Non-haem iron is found in plant foods, such as vegetables, cereals, and legumes (pulses).

Seafoods and seaweed are the only reliable dietary sources of iodine, although plant foods take up iodine in a manner related to soil concentration. In some countries, salt is iodised to make up possible deficiencies.

COMPOSITION

Calcium is the major mineral constituent of bones. Selenium is often present in biological systems as an amino acid compound, such as selenomethionine or selenocysteine (essential for the enzyme glutathione peroxidase). Iodine is a component of the hormones tri-iodothyronine (T3) and thyroxine (T4), which are synthesised by the thyroid gland. Iron is a component of haemoglobin and myoglobin, which carry oxygen in the blood and muscles.

FUNCTIONS

Calcium is central to a variety of functions in the body, such as nerve and muscle activity, as well as bone metabolism. It has a variety of roles in the control of cell proliferation and differentiation. Calcium metabolism is controlled by various factors, including vitamin D. Because of its role in regulating calcium and phosphate metabolism, vitamin D is better considered as a hormone.

Often identified as an antioxidant, selenium has no antioxidant capacity of its own, but functions as a co-factor for glutathione peroxidase, an enzyme that protects against oxidative tissue damage.

Iodine forms part of the hormones which are involved in the maintenance of the metabolic rate, cellular metabolism and the integrity of connective tissue. In the fetus, iodine is needed for the development of the nervous system; severely

deficient mothers are likely to give birth to infants who suffer from cretinism and other neuromuscular manifestations collectively called iodine deficienty disorders.

Iron has a central role in cell metabolism and growth. It is also involved in oxidative metabolism within cells, and is a component of a number of enzymes with diverse roles. Iron can also catalyse the generation of free radicals, which cause oxidative damage to specific cell components including DNA, protein and membrane lipids. Iron metabolism is strictly regulated to reduce in the likelihood of oxidative damage; most iron in living tissues is bound to proteins, such as transferrin and ferritin, which prevent its involvement in free radical generation.

REQUIREMENTS

The World Health Organization reference nutrient intake (RNI) for calcium, for 19–50+ year olds, is 400–500 mg/day (WHO, 1990). The RNI for vitamin D for 11–65 year olds is 2.5 µg/day. The RNI for selenium, for men aged 15–50+ years is 40 µg/day; for women, aged 11–50+ years it is 30 µg/day. The RNI for iodine for 11–50+ year olds is 120–150 µg/day. The WHO median basal requirement for iron, for males aged 15–50+ years, on an intermediate bioavailability diet, is 9 mg/day; for women, aged 15–50 years, it is 12.5 mg/day.

The body's requirement for iron depends on its bioavailability in the diet; this varies with the proportion of haem- and non-haem-iron (that is, animal versus plant sources).

CONSUMPTION PATTERNS

In the UK, the average dietary intake of calcium has been shown to be 940 mg/day for men and 730 mg/day for women (Gregor et al, 1990). In Japan, the average daily intake of calcium was 545 mg/day in 1994; in China, average daily intake of iron was 582 mg/day in 1983, while in the Netherlands, average daily intake of iron was 1,032 mg/day in 1990.

In China, dietary intakes of selenium of less than 12 µg/day have been observed in areas where Keshan disease (selenium responsive cardiomyopathy) is endemic (Levander, 1987). More generally, however, average daily intake of selenium in China has been estimated to be about 42 µg (Chen and Gao, 1993). In Southern England, dietary intakes of selenium are approximately 65 µg/day (Bunker et al, 1988). In the USA, the average dietary intake of selenium for men was 108 µg per day between 1974 and 1982.

The amount of iodine in foods depends mostly on the geophysical environment in which those foods are grown. Environments that are typically low in iodine are mountainous areas and flood plains – where glaciation and/or rivers have leached the water-soluble mineral out of the soil.

In the UK, the average dietary intake of iron was 14.0 mg/day for men and 12.3 mg/day for women (Gregory et al, 1990). In Japan, the average daily intake of iron was 11 mg/day in 1994, and in China it was 34 mg/day in 1983.

INTERPRETATION OF THE DATA

Assessment of the calcium and iron available in a diet is complicated, because of the wide variation in the amount absorbed from different diets, although these diets may contain similar calcium/iron levels when measured chemically.

Assessment of selenium intake is problematic as published tables of the selenium content of food apply, strictly, only to the area where the food was actually grown. Ecological studies indicate that the risk of some cancers varies as a function of soil selenium content; these are difficult to interpret, because other relevant factors also vary geographically, and because many of the foods consumed in one area have been grown in another.

Blood and toenail levels of selenium are thought to be fairly accurate measures of intake and have been used in several studies. Smokers have been shown to have lower levels of blood and toenail selenium (Hunter et al, 1990), so some studies have adjusted for smoking. However, it is not known whether selenium levels are lower in smokers because of a lower intake or an effect of smoking on selenium metabolism so such an adjustment may or may not be appropriate. Experimental studies have mostly involved very high doses of selenium such as would not normally be obtainable from food alone.

JUDGEMENTS OF OTHER REPORTS

Evidence on the relationship between minerals and trace elements and cancer risk was considered by the 1982 and 1989 reports of the National Academy of Sciences (NAS 1982, 1989) and the 1988 report of the Surgeon-General (Surgeon-General, 1988) to be too limited to allow any firm conclusions.

SIGNIFICANCE FOR OTHER DISEASES

Osteoporosis is seen by some as an outcome of calcium deficiency, in that deficiency may lead to the development of a lower peak bone mass. Dietary calcium, however, is only one factor in the accumulation and loss of bone mass throughout life. Deficiencies in vitamin D are usually caused by lack of exposure to sunlight; this can lead to rickets in children and osteomalacia in adults.

Selenium deficiency plays a role in Keshan disease, a cardiomyopathy that occurs in China and primarily affects children and young women. Selenium poisoning is known to occur with high doses, although the exact level needed to cause toxicity is not certain; levels of 5 mg per day may be toxic.

Over a billion people live in iodine-deficient areas. Deficiency causes a range of clinical symptoms now collectively called the iodine deficiency disorders (IDD). These include goitre (global incidence about 225 million) and cretinism, as well as other physical and mental ill-effects. Iodine deficiency is identified by the WHO as a major global public health problem.

Iron deficiency anaemia is common throughout the world, particularly among children and women of childbearing age, and is identified by the WHO as a major global public health problem.

ASSESSMENT

The evidence on which this assessment is based is in the relevant sections of chapter 4.

5.7.1 CALCIUM AND VITAMIN D

There is some epidemiological evidence relating to diets high in calcium, and in vitamin D, for the colon and rectum. Data for other cancer sites are inconclusive.

Calcium
Evidence of no relationship

CONVINCING	PROBABLE	POSSIBLE	INSUFFICIENT
		Colon, rectum	

Colon, recrum (4.10). Eight cohort and 15 case-control studies have examined calcium intake and the risk of colorectal cancer. Only one of 16 relative risk estimates was significantly lower than 1.0, and . 18 of 25 odds ratios from the case-control studies were null. A meta-analysis estimated a summary relative risk of 0.89 (0.79–1.01). The evidence suggests there may be a weak overall reduction in risk with higher calcium intakes, but the conservative judgment is that there is possibly no relationship.

Vitamin D
Evidence of decreased risk
Colon rectum (4.10). Three cohort and two case-control studies on vitamin D intake and the risk of colorectal cancer, on balance, show a decrease in risk for higher intakes. This is supported by a study of vitamin D serum levels. High intakes of vitamin D may decrease the risk of colorectal cancer, but the evidence is, at present, insufficient.

5.7.2 SELENIUM

There is some evidence that diets high in selenium might protect against lung cancer. Data for other cancer sites are limited and inconclusive.

Evidence of decreased risk

CONVINCING	PROBABLE	POSSIBLE	INSUFFICIENT
		Lung	Stomach
			Liver
			Thyroid

Lung (4.5). Thirteen cohort studies and three case-control studies have examined the relationship between tissue selenium levels and the risk of lung cancer. Although the evidence is constrained by a number of factors, two cohort studies found strong protective associations, and most of the other data are consistent with decreased risk. Ecological studies have also shown a protective association between estimated selenium intake and the risk of lung cancer. Diets high in selenium possibly decrease the risk of lung cancer.

Stomach (4.6), thyroid (4.16). A relatively small amount of evidence from epidemiological studies (three cohort and one ecological study of stomach cancer, and three case-control studies, of thyroid cancer) shows, on balance, a protective association between these cancers and serum selenium levels. These data are, however, judged to be insufficient.

Liver (4.9). A chemoprevention trial and one of two cohort studies showed a protective association of higher selenium serum levels with the risk of primary liver cancer. Selenium deficiency increases hepatocarcinogenesis in experimental animals.

There is also some evidence that selenium protects against the overall risk of cancer, but it is not strong, and it does not all point in the direction of protection. A review has shown pre-diagnostic serum selenium levels to be lower in cases than controls in 17 out of 24 reports involving ten cancer sites in ten study populations, but case-control differences were greater than 10% in only two reports (Comstock et al, 1992). In vitro, selenium has been shown to decrease the mutagenicity of many carcinogenic compounds, as determined by the Ames test. However, selenium compounds such as selenites have been shown to damage DNA.

Any potential anticarcinogenic mechanism of selenium may relate to its antioxidant properties, which are a function of its role in maintaining the enzyme glutathione peroxidase, which prevents cellular damage by catabolising organic peroxides. In addition to its role in antioxidation, selenium has been shown to suppress cell proliferation, when present at high levels; to enhance the immune response; and to alter the metabolism of carcinogens so as to produce less toxic compounds.

Evidence of no relationship

CONVINCING	PROBABLE	POSSIBLE	INSUFFICIENT
		Colon, rectum	

Colon, rectum (4.10). Seven analytical studies of serum selenium and the risk of colorectal cancer have reported no clear evidence of an association.

5.7.3 IODINE

Most of the evidence on iodine and cancer risk relates to thyroid cancer. There is evidence that both iodine excess and deficiency may increase the risk of this cancer.

Evidence of increased risk

Both very low and very high intakes of iodine are associated with an increased risk of thyroid cancer. These may be related to different histological types of thyroid cancer: deficient intakes may increase the risk of follicular cancer, and excessive intakes increase the risk of papillary cancer.

CONVINCING	PROBABLE	POSSIBLE	INSUFFICIENT
	Thyroid (iodine deficiency)	Thyroid (iodine excess)	

Thyroid (4.16). Five case-control studies have found an association between iodine deficiency and an increased risk of thyroid cancer. In countries where salt iodisation programmes have been implemented, the incidence of, and mortality rates from, thyroid cancer show contrasting trends: rates have declined in Switzerland, but not other areas. Iodine deficiency is thought to act indirectly via hormonally mediated pathways. Diets deficient in iodine probably increase the risk of thyroid cancer.

Excessive long-term intakes of iodine (over 100 times the recommended daily allowance (RDA)/RDI)) can block the uptake of iodine by the thyroid, leading to goitre. In four case-control studies, high intakes of iodine-rich foods, such as seafood, have been associated with an increased risk of thyroid cancer. Ecological and experimental data also support this association. Diets excessively high in iodine possibly increase the risk of thyroid cancer.

5.7.4 IRON

There is some evidence that diets high in iron may possibly increase the risk of liver and colorectal cancers. Evidence on other sites is inconclusive
.

Evidence of increased risk

Colon, rectum (4.10). One cohort and one ecological study found an increase in risk with high body iron stores and higher iron intakes. Data from case-control studies, five on colorectal cancer and two on polyps, are inconsistent. High iron intake may increase the risk of colorectal cancer, but the evidence is, as yet, insufficient.

Liver (4.9). Two ecological studies found no association between biochemical markers of iron status and liver cancer mortality. Experimental studies found that iron deficiency in rats inhibited the development of liver tumours, while iron overload enhanced carcinogenesis in mice. In humans, however, dietary-induced iron overload is rare. Data are as yet insufficient.

5.8 Other bioactive compounds

Cereals (grains), vegetables, fruits, pulses (legumes) and other plant foods contain many microconstituents, other than vitamins and minerals, that are known to be biologically active.

These bioactive compounds include allium compounds, dithiolthiones, isothiocyanates, terpenoids, isoflavones, protease inhibitors, phytic acid, polyphenols, glucosinolates and indoles, flavonoids, plant sterols, saponins, and coumarins.

Currently, although plausible biological pathways have been identified, the lack of epidemiological evidence to support existing experimental evidence means that it is not possible to come to any definite judgement about the role of these compounds in cancer risk. Nonethless, the panel notes that high intakes of allium compounds possibly decrease the risk of stomach cancer.

It is likely that further research will produce evidence indicating that diets high in various bioactive compounds protect against a number of cancers.

BIOACTIVE COMPOUNDS AND CANCER

In the judgement of the panel, bioactive compounds modify the risk of cancer of various sites as shown below. Judgements are graded according to the strength of the evidence.

EVIDENCE	DECREASES RISK	NO RELATIONSHIP	INCREASES RISK
Convincing			
Probable			
Possible	*Allium compounds*: Stomach		
Insufficient	*Isoflavones*: Breast		

For an explanation of the terms used in the matrix, see chapter 3
While the bioactive compounds listed above might protect against cancers of other sites, no judgement to that effect is yet possible. Other compounds for which no judgement is yet possible are phenols, glucosinolates and indoles, flavonoids, plant sterols, saponins, coumarin, limonoids and lectins.

INTRODUCTION

Foods of plant origin contain many bioactive compounds in addition to those microconstituents that are conventionally identified as nutrients, such as vitamins and specific minerals. Until fairly recently, these compounds have been generally assumed to be irrelevant to human health, probably in part, because, until the 1980s, vitamins and minerals were thought to be relevant to human health only inasmuch as they protected against deficiency diseases.

The concept that intakes of vitamins or minerals at levels above (perhaps well above) those that prevent clinically observable deficiency diseases might protect against chronic diseases began to emerge at that time. Further, the concept that some other microconstituents may be protective against chronic disease, even in the absence of a known deficiency state, is more recent still. Because such constituents are not yet considered essential nutrients, the term 'bioactive compounds' is used here. The terms 'phytochemicals' or 'phytoprotectants' have also been used.

SOURCES

The bioactive compounds assessed here are found in plant foods, particularly in cereals (grains), vegetables, fruits and pulses (legumes).

Allium compounds are found in the allium vegetables which include onions, garlic, scallions and chives. It is these compounds that account for the distinctive flavour and aroma of allium vegetables, as well as for the many reported medicinal effects.

Dithiolthiones are found in cruciferous vegetables, as are the isothiocyanates, benzyl isothiocyanate, phenethyl isothiocyanate and sulforaphane. Isothiocyanates are also found in other vegetables and in spices and are produced synthetically.

D-limonene, the most studied terpenoid, is the major component of the oil of citrus fruit peel. It is also used as a flavouring agent in non-alcoholic beverages, ice cream, sweets, baked goods, gelatins, puddings and chewing gum. In the USA D-limonene has GRAS (generally regarded as safe) status for use as an added flavouring agent.

Phytoestrogens, including isoflavones and lignans, are found in foods of plant origin. Cereals and pulses, including sorghum, millet, and particularly soya beans, contain isoflavones; the content varies depending on the time and location of the harvest. The main dietary sources of lignans are wholegrain products, seeds, fruits and berries. In cereals, the precursors of lignans occur in the fraction that is often eliminated by modern milling techniques. Mammalian forms of lignans are produced by bacteria in the colon from the ingested precursors.

Flavonoids are found in fruits, vegetables, coffee, tea, cola, and alcoholic beverages. Quercetin, kaempferol and myricetin are flavonols widely distributed in vegetables and fruits. The richest sources of quercetin are berries, tomatoes, potatoes, broad beans, broccoli, Italian squash and onions (Hertog et al, 1993; Leighton et al, 1993). Radishes, horseradish, kale and endive are relatively high in kaempferol (Hertog et al, 1993). Other flavonoids (tangeretin, nobiletin and rutin) are found in citrus fruits.

Other phenolic compounds are found in freshly harvested vegetables and fruits, relatively large amounts in teas and wines. Ellagic acid is found in high concentrations in fruits and nuts (Birt and Bresnick, 1991; Hollman and Venema, 1993), specifically in strawberries, raspberries, blackberries, walnuts and pecans.

Protease inhibitors are widely distributed in plants; cereals and pulses are particularly rich sources. In cereals, including barley, wheat, oats, and rye, protease inhibitors make up 5–10% of the water-soluble protein. Soya beans, kidney beans, chickpeas and other pulses contain protease inhibitors, some of which survive canning and processing, including that involved in making tofu.

Phytic acid (inositol hexaphosphate) is particularly found in cereals, nuts, seeds and pulses. Typical phytic acid contents of cereals and vegetables are 0.1–2.0 % and 0.01–0.1% of dry weight, respectively. Phytic acid occurs in high amounts in sesame seeds, lima beans, peanuts and soyabeans with levels of 5.4%, 2.5%, 1.9% and 1.4 % of dry weight, respectively.

Glucosinolates are found in cruciferous vegetables. Glucobrassicin makes up about 30% of the glucosinolates found in these vegetables. The glucobrassicin content of vegetables is influenced by genetics, growing conditions and maturity at the time of harvest. During cooking and chewing, glucosinolates are metabolised by the plant enzyme, myrosinase, to produce isothiocyanates and indoles.

Plant sterols, including β-sitosterol, campesterol, and stigmasterol, are found in vegetables, and together make up about 20% of the sterols in most diets.

Saponins are found in various foods of plant origin. They are abundant in soya beans, accounting for approximately 5% of their dry weight.

Coumarins are found in vegetables (particularly cassava), citrus fruit and some herbs.

Nitrate is present in large quantities in many foods of plant origin, to some extent as a function of the amount of NPK fertiliser used in their growing. It is also found in processed food (see chapters 6.1, 6.8 and 6.14).

COMPOSITION

Allium compounds contain sulphur. In garlic, the amino acid allin is enzymatically converted to allicin when garlic cloves are crushed. Allicin is unstable and converts rapidly to sulphide compounds, such as diallyl sulphide and allyl methyl trisulphide. An average clove of garlic contains several milligrams of sulphide. Garlic also contains allixin, a phenolic compound.

Dithiolthiones, too, are sulphur-containing compounds. Their structure is a pentacyclic ring, including two sulphur atoms, with a further sulphur atom and an aromatic ring attached (Jirousek and Starka, 1958).

Terpenoids, including D-limonene, geraniol, menthol, and carvone, are all members of a large group of compounds made up of a simple repeating unit, the isoprenoid unit. This unit, when condensed into ring structures, gives rise to compounds such as rubber, carotenoids, steroids and to simple terpenes.

Phytoestrogens, including the isoflavones and the mammalian lignans are diphenolic compounds with a variety of structures.

Flavonoids are a group of organic compounds ubiquitously distributed in vascular plants; over 2,000 individual flavonoids have been described. The structure of flavonoids includes two benzene rings linked via a heterocyclic pyrane ring. The flavonoid class includes flavones, flavonols, flavonones, methylated flavones, and O-glycosides of the flavonols and flavonones. Most flavonoids occur in nature as glycosides.

Other phenolic compounds include caffeic, ferulic, and ellagic acids. Many are present in foods as glycosides and are widely distributed in plants. Other phenolic compounds have been discussed elsewhere in the report, including α-tocopherol (chapter 5.6) and flavonoids.

Most protease inhibitors are proteins of 70–90 amino acids in length.

Phytic acid, or inositol hexaphosphate, is a phosphoric acid ester of inositol.

More than 20 glucosinolates have been isolated from edible plants. The hydrolysis of the glucosinolate glucobrassicin by the plant's own enzymes leads to the formation of various indoles, including indole-3-carbinol, indole-3-acetonitrile, and 3,3'-diindoylmethane. The ultimate amount of indoles is affected by storage and handling after harvest.

Plant sterols have a structure similar to the animal sterol, cholesterol.

Saponins are amphiphilic glycosides, characterised by their surfactant property, namely the ability to form a durable foam when shaken in solution.

Coumarins are lactones with a variety of anticoagulatory and anti-inflammatory properties.

Nitrates are salts or esters of nitric acid, and are relatively inert. They can be reduced by nitrate reductase in the human gastrointestinal tract, to nitrites, which are more reactive compounds.

FUNCTIONS

Allium compounds may have anticarcinogenic mechanisms involving the induction of enzymatic detoxification systems. Allium vegetables have also been hypothesised to protect against cancer by inhibiting the bacterial conversion of nitrate to nitrite in the stomach. They have antibiotic properties and may act against *Helicobacter pylori*.

Dithiolthiones are thought to protect against cancer by inhibiting enzymes that activate carcinogens or by inducing detoxifying enzymes.

Isothiocyanates have been defined as being both blocking and suppressing agents. More specifically, they also induce detoxifying enzymes and suppress the expression of neoplasia in cells that have undergone some steps towards cancer. Some isothiocyanates have goitrogenic effects.

Terpenoids such as D-limonene are believed to protect against cancer by inducing the family of enzymes called glutathione transferases.

Phytoestrogens have numerous biological effects. They are antiviral, antiproliferative and growth inhibiting. Phytoestrogens are weakly oestrogenic and can compete with steroid hormones for various enzymes and receptors. They also stimulate production of sex-hormone-binding globulin in the liver. In these ways, they may alter steroid hormone metabolism and, by inhibiting growth and proliferation of hormone-dependent cancer cells, may alter cancer risk.

In plants, flavonoids function as potent antioxidants and metal chelators, and as repellents to keep certain viruses, fungi and animals from feeding on the plant (see Birt and Bresnick, 1991). Unlike plant alkaloids, flavonoids are generally considered to be non-toxic.

Phenolic compounds are also involved in the induction of the detoxification systems. Some phenolic compounds have been found to inhibit N-nitrosation reactions by trapping nitrate to form C-nitrosophenolic compounds.

Protease inhibitors competitively inhibit proteases by the formation of complexes that block the enzyme's catalytic site. Proteases may be an important part of the invasive capacity of some cancer cells.

Phytic acid forms insoluble salts with specific cations, thus altering both intestinal absorption of specific minerals and redox potential. While it has been shown to be anticarcinogenic in experimental studies, the mechanisms are unclear but may involve control of cell proliferation.

Glutathione is probably the most important intracellular antioxidant, possibly evolving as a molecule that protects cells against oxygen toxicity (Fahey and Sundquist, 1991).

Indole-3-carbinol has been shown to increase microsomal mixed function oxidase activity. The effect of increased mixed function oxidase activity is not straightforward, as it can both activate and detoxify a variety of carcinogenic compounds. More specifically, indoles increase hepatic 2-hydroxylation of oestradiol. This shift from 16-hydroxylation to 2-hydroxylation of oestradiol represents a reduction in oestrogenic activity and may be protective against oestrogen-related cancers.

Although a high proportion of plant sterols pass through the gastrointestinal tract almost completely unabsorbed, they influence both cholesterol absorption and metabolism and possibly steroid hormone metabolism.

Saponins, although non-toxic, can generate adverse physiological responses in animals that consume them. They exhibit cytotoxic effects and growth inhibition against a variety of cells. They bind bile acids and reduce their recirculation. They have known tumour-inhibiting activity in animals.

Dicumarol, a coumarin, inhibits the synthesis of other vitamin K-dependent coagulation factors. A number of the derivatives of coumarins are used widely as anticoagulants in the treatment of disorders such as thrombophlebitis, pulmonary embolism and certain cardiac conditions.

Inorganic nitrate salts are believed by some to have therapeutic properties in the treatment of kidney stones and urinary tract infections. Organic nitrate esters have been used to relieve the symptoms of angina. Nitrates are reduced to nitrites in the acid environment of the stomach. Subsequent nitrosation of amines, amides and proteins can give rise to *N*-nitroso compounds some of which are known to be carcinogenic in animals.

REQUIREMENTS AND CONSUMPTION PATTERNS

Requirements for the bioactive compounds assessed here are not known. Data on consumption patterns of some compounds are imprecise and do not have much meaning, given the lack of estimates for requirements. As a generality, the richer a diet is in a variety of foods of plant origin, the higher will be the consumption of the bioactive compounds. It may be that intake of the more important compounds will eventually be measured, and requirements proposed, as with vitamins and minerals.

INTERPRETATION OF THE DATA

Interpretation of the data on bioactive compounds is more problematic than with other dietary constituents. First, there is, as yet, little human evidence. Second, it is difficult to quantify intakes in individuals, because the amount of these compounds in most foods has not been well determined. Third, the content, in foods, of these compounds can vary with plant genetics, with growth and storage conditions, as well as with food preparation methods.

In general, there is currently a lack of human data on these compounds. Most of the evidence comes from experimental studies, in which cancer has been induced largely by various chemical carcinogens. The animals in these studies were fed specific amounts of these compounds at known intervals and in known relation to the time of exposure to the carcinogen used. None of these conditions applies to humans and their normal intake. Further, the compounds are often found at levels far higher than could be obtained from human diets.

As with all other aspects of diet, the panel has decided that, when the evidence from human studies is insufficient, as is the case with most of the bioactive compounds assessed here, supportive data from animal studies can at most justify a conclusion that decreased human cancer risk is possible, even when plausible biological mechanisms have been identified. In cases where the human or animal data are fragmentary, confused or minimal, the panel has concluded that no judgement can currently be made.

JUDGEMENTS OF OTHER REPORTS

The National Academy of Sciences report *Diet, Nutrition and Cancer* (NAS, 1982), reviewed experimental studies of phenols, indoles, isothiocyanates, flavones, protease inhibitors, and the plant sterol β-sitosterol. It concluded that a number of bioactive compounds in vegetables inhibit carcinogenesis in laboratory animals, but that this evidence, in itself, did not mean that such compounds protect against human cancers.

SIGNIFICANCE FOR OTHER DISEASES

Some bioactive compounds may play roles in health in addition to their potential ability to protect against cancer. For example, allyl sulphides in garlic may decrease the tendency for blood clots to form and reduce total and LDL cholesterol levels, thereby protecting against heart disease. Flavonoids may protect against heart disease by protecting LDL cholesterol from oxidation and by inhibiting platelet aggregation. The prospective Zutphen study in The Netherlands showed higher flavonoid intake to be associated with decreased mortality from heart disease (Hertog et al, 1996). Of course, there are a wide variety of other plant-related compounds that might explain this finding, but it does illustrate the wider relevance of plant foods (and perhaps their constituent bioactive compounds) in the prevention of chronic disease.

FUTURE RESEARCH

The panel made the following recommendation for future research:

■ Where animal data and identification of biological pathways suggest that specific bioactive compounds have a role in modification of cancer risk, the presence of these compounds in foods and drinks should be measured and appropriate human studies be carried out. Studies of populations with contrasting intake are likely to be particularly fruitful.

ASSESSMENT

The evidence on which this assessment is based is found in the relevant sections of chapter 4.

The selection of bioactive constituents discussed in this section is not comprehensive. Judgements made here reflect the present state of science and are likely to become firmer in future.

While human studies are as yet lacking, evidence from experimental studies and identification of biological pathways suggests that some of the bioactive compounds reviewed here might protect against cancer of various sites or even against cancer in general. It is possible that further research will produce good evidence to this effect, but in the present state of science no such judgement can be made.

5.8.1 ALLIUM COMPOUNDS

There is some evidence that diets high in allium compounds may protect against stomach cancer. Data from other cancer sites is inconclusive.

Evidence of decreased risk

CONVINCING	PROBABLE	POSSIBLE	INSUFFICIENT
		Stomach	

Stomach (4.6). Nine out of 11 case-control studies found evidence that allium vegetables were protective for stomach cancer. Two ecological studies showed that, in areas where garlic or onion production is very high, mortality rates for stomach cancer were very low. Experimental studies have shown allium compounds to have anticarcinogenic effects at various sites, including the stomach. The antibacterial properties of allium compounds against *H. pylori* may provide another anticarcinogenic mechanism. Diets high in allium compounds possibly decrease the risk of stomach cancer.

5.8.2 ISOFLAVONES

Most of the evidence on phytoestrogens and cancer risk relates to breast cancer. The data are, as yet, insufficient.

Evidence of decreased risk
Breast (4.11). Indirect evidence for a potential protective role for isoflavones (and possibly lignans) comes from a human trial on oestrogen metabolism; from ecological observations of vegetarians, Asians and breast cancer patients, and from experimental studies. The probable role of lifetime oestrogen exposure in the risk of breast cancer suggests that isoflavones and lignans may protect against breast cancer. No human analytical studies of isoflavones and lignans per se are available, and evidence for a protective association with pulses, particularly soya beans, is limited and equivocal. Evidence that isoflavones and lignans may reduce the risk of breast cancer is, currently, insufficient.

5.8.3 POLYPHENOLS

Reviews of the effects of polyphenols in carcinogenesis were written in 1984 by Stich and Rosin and in 1991 by Birt and Bresnick. In experimental studies, ellagic, ferulic, and caffeic acids have been found to inhibit the chemical induction of lung tumours (Castonguay, 1993); ellagic and caffeic acids were also found to inhibit chemically-induced tumours of the tongue completely (Tanaka et al, 1993). Ellagic acid has also been shown to inhibit chemically-induced oesophageal tumours (Barch and Fox, 1989; Daniel and Stoner, 1991), and to inhibit promotion of skin tumours when applied topically.

Each of these compounds has been shown to increase the activity of phase II conjugation enzymes and to inhibit *N*-nitrosation reactions by trapping nitrite, thereby providing two potential anticarcinogenic mechanisms. Other effects on the metabolism of various carcinogens have also been shown. For example, ellagic acid may interact with benzo(a)pyrene in the gastrointestinal tract, thereby reducing its bioavailability (Stavric et al, 1992).

In vitro, various phenolic compounds have been shown to inhibit mutagenicity in the Ames test; ellagic acid was found to be an extremely potent inhibitor. (See Stich and Rosin (1984), Fiala et al (1985); Birt and Bresnick and Dragsted et al (1993) for references to specific animal and in vitro studies not individually cited here.)

Human studies on vegetables and fruits, and experimental and in vitro studies on polyphenols, suggest that these bioactive compounds might possibly protect against human cancer, and biological pathways for a protective effect have been suggested. However, without human studies specifically of phenolic compounds, no judgement can yet be made.

5.8.4 GLUCOSINOLATES AND INDOLES

Cruciferous vegetables probably protect against cancers of the colon, rectum and thyroid and, as part of a diet high in vegetables generally, against cancers of most sites (see chapter 6.3).

It has been suggested that indoles may protect against breast cancer by way of their effect on oestrogen metabolism. In one human clinical trial, women were given a massive daily dose of 500 mg (approximately 50 times the estimated average daily intake in the USA), resulting in a shift in oestrogen metabolism towards the production of relatively more of a less potent form of oestrogen, and less of a more potent form (Michnovicz and Bradlow, 1990). Such a shift in metabolism might reduce oestrogen-promoted breast and other cancers. Studies in rats have shown similar effects on oestrogen metabolism.

The early studies involving indoles produced results that were quite mixed, showing both inhibition and induction of tumorigenesis at various sites (see Birt and Bresnick, 1991). Studies on indole derivatives, such as indole-3-carbinol and indole-3-acetonitrile, were precipitated by the observation that these constituents were largely responsible for the induction of the mixed function oxidase system by cruciferous vegetables (Loub et al, 1975). Further animal studies showed that the effects of indole-3-carbinol on mixed function oxidase activity, and also on glutathione-S-transferase activity, varied with experimental conditions (see Birt and Bresnick, 1991). The mixed function oxidase system can either activate or detoxify carcinogens depending on the specific carcinogen involved and the specific enzymes induced; whereas glutathione-*S*-transferase conjugates various carcinogens and other xenobiotics for excretion.

Experimental studies have shown glucobrassicin or indole derivatives to inhibit the formation of chemically-induced tumours in the liver (Tanaka et al, 1990), breast, lung and forestomach of rats (Wattenberg and Loub, 1978; Wattenberg et al, 1986). Another study showed indole-3-carbinol to reduce tumorigenesis in the lung and nasal cavity, but to potentiate tumorigenesis in the liver in rats (Morse et al, 1988).

Other studies have shown indole-3-carbinol to potentiate carcinogenesis when administered during the promotion phase. One study in trout showed decreased aflatoxin-induced tumorigenesis when indole-3-carbinol was given prior to the administration of aflatoxin, but tumour response was increased when indole-3-carbinol was fed afterwards (Bailey et al, 1987). Another study showed increased breast tumours when indole-3-carbinol was given along with a diet high in cholesterol and beef tallow, administered after the chemical carcinogen (Pence et al, 1986). Experimental studies have shown indole-3-carbinol to have no effect or to decrease binding of aflatoxin to DNA (Salbe and Bjeldanes, 1986; Dashwood et al, 1989).

The protective effect of cruciferous vegetables, together with proposed biological pathways for cancer in general and hormone-related cancers in particular, suggest that that glucosinolates and indoles might protect against cancer, as might other bioactive compounds. But animal studies have shown these compounds both to decrease and increase tumorigenesis. These rather conflicting data are not a basis for any judgement.

5.8.5 FLAVONOIDS

In vitro, quercetin and other flavonoids have been found to be mutagenic in Ames assays. On the other hand, quercetin has been shown to inhibit the growth of certain leukaemia cells in vitro.

Because of the positive findings in Ames assays, quercetin was suspected as a potential carcinogen and carcinogenicity testing in animals followed. Only one of several of these studies has shown a carcinogenic effect (see Birt and Bresnick, 1991).

Several animal experiments have shown quercetin, when applied topically, to inhibit the promotion phase in two-stage skin cancer models; dietary quercetin, however, had no effect. One experimental study showed decreased colonic tumours, whereas another showed increased bladder and intestinal tumours. A further study showed quercetin, robinetin and myricetin to decrease lung tumours induced by diol epoxide-2, but not those induced by benzo(a)pyrene. Quercetin has also been shown to decrease colonic cell proliferation (Deschner et al, 1991). (See Brown (1980), Birt and Bresnick (1991) and Dragsted et al (1993) for references to studies not individually cited here.)

Flavonoids have differing antioxidant properties depending upon the degree of hydroxylation of the benzene rings; this property may provide one anticarcinogenic mechanism. In addition, flavonoids have been shown to increase the pump-mediated efflux of certain carcinogens from cells (Phang et al, 1993).

Some flavonoids have been shown to induce mixed function oxidase activity, which, as noted above, may either thwart or enhance carcinogenesis depending upon the carcinogen involved. Some experimental studies have shown

methoxylated flavonoids, including tangeretin and nobiletin, to induce the activity of benzo(a)pyrene hydroxylase, an enzyme that may inhibit benzo(a)pyrene-induced tumours. On the other hand, polyhydroxylated flavonoids, including kaempferol and myricetin, have been shown to inhibit the activity of this enzyme.

Quercetin has been shown to inhibit the activity of several carcinogens and tumour promoters (see Leighton et al, 1993). Quercetin may also interact with specific carcinogens in the gastrointestinal tract, thereby reducing their bioavailability (Stavric et al, 1992).

A recent analysis from the Seven Countries Study, an ecological study involving sixteen cohorts, found intake of antioxidant flavonoids not to be correlated with cancer mortality (Hertog et al, 1995).

Human studies on vegetables and fruits show that these foods protect against cancer, but there is little human evidence on flavonoids as such, and experimental and in vitro studies have produced conflicting results. As yet, these data are not a basis for any judgement.

5.8.6 PLANT STEROLS

Vegetarians, who experience lower rates of cancer of many sites, have been shown to have higher levels of the plant sterol, β-sitosterol, in their faeces, as might be expected. One study in rats showed that inclusion of 0.2% β-sitosterol in the diet decreased the occurrence of chemically-induced tumours in the colon. (See Raicht et al (1980), Fiala et al (1985) and Messina and Barnes (1991) for specific references and more discussion.) These data are not yet a basis for any judgement.

5.8.7 SAPONINS

The possible role of saponins as anticarcinogenic agents has been discussed by Messina and Barnes (1991) and Oakenfull and Sidha (1989). Experimental and in vitro studies have shown saponins to reduce colonic cell proliferation rates and to decrease growth and the rate of DNA synthesis of various tumour cells. The suggested anticarcinogenic mechanism of saponins involves their ability to bind bile acids and cholesterol.

However, human evidence on pulses (legumes), including soya beans, a rich source of saponins, is as yet equivocal. Taken together, these data are not yet a basis for any judgement.

5.8.8 COUMARINS

No human studies investigating the effects of coumarins have been undertaken. In a limited number of experimental studies they have been shown to inhibit chemically-induced cancer of the forestomach and breast (Wattenberg, 1987).

Any protective mechanism of coumarins may involve the induction of detoxification enzymes; the induction of glutathione transferase activity has been shown in the liver and small intestine in mice (Sparnins et al, 1982).

Human studies on vegetables and citrus fruit, and experimental studies on coumarins, suggest that these bioactive compounds might protect against human cancer, and a biological pathway for a protective effect has been suggested. This data is not yet a basis for any judgement.

CHAPTER SIX

Foods and drinks

It is now generally agreed that recommendations designed to reduce the risk of chronic diseases such as cancer should, whenever possible, be expressed in terms of foods and drinks. Only secondarily should recommendations address dietary constituents.

This policy, which allows more practical recommendations, may be of special importance for cancer. There is increasing reason to believe that many foods of plant origin contain bioactive compounds that may protect against cancers of various sites, and perhaps that microconstituents may protect against cancer not as single agents, but in the combinations as found in foods.

Accordingly, this chapter moves towards the panel's recommendations in chapter 8. Here, broadly conventional groupings of foods and drinks are followed.

The first two sections in this chapter assess starchy staple foods, the most readily available sources of energy in most parts of the world: cereals, and then roots, tubers and plantains. The next section assesses vegetables and fruits which, like starchy foods, are sources of fibre but also of many microconstituents. The next two sections assess other plant foods: pulses (legumes), which are important sources of protein in many parts of the world, and nuts and seeds, which are high in unsaturated fats and contain protein.

Two sections assess foods of animal origin: first meat, poultry, fish and eggs, then milk and dairy products. These foods are important sources of protein and of various vitamins and minerals; their fat content varies depending on methods of animal rearing, manufacture and preparation. In developed countries, principal meals tend to be based on meat or poultry; generally, fish is eaten less often.

The next section assesses some herbs and spices. Coffee and tea are assessed in the final section.

This chapter is derived from, but does not repeat, the literature reviews in chapter 4. A summary is presented, as well as more information about the relationship of particular foods and drinks to the risks of diseases other than cancer. Each section begins with a summary of the panel's judgements. Individual foods, their nutrient content, and consumption patterns throughout the world. Issues relating to interpretation of the data, judgements of other reports, and public health considerations for diseases other than cancer are then presented. Recommendations for future research are listed. Evidence reviewed in chapter 4 is then summarised. Evidence of protection against cancer is presented first. Assessments are placed in order of confidence: first causal associations, then probable associations, etc. In this way, primary prevention of cancer is emphasised, and possible consistent patterns across cancer sites can most readily be discerned.

Other key issues include the possible importance of cereal foods in wholegrain form. There has been substantial research on the diets of people who do not eat meat (vegetarians) and this evidence is assessed as a counterpoint to the evidence on meat itself.

6.1 Cereals (grains)

The major types of cereals (grains) are wheat, rice, maize (corn), millet, sorghum, barley, oats and rye. They are the staples in most diets everywhere. Generally, in the developing world, cereals (and other starchy foods) make up most of dietary volume and energy. As societies become industrialised, diets generally become less bulky and more energy-dense, cereals supply less of the total energy, and cereals and cereal products become more refined and processed in other ways.

On a population basis, consumption of cereals and cereal products varies between 20% and 70% of total energy.

Cereals, and foods made up mostly of cereals, are starchy and supply variable amounts of protein. The amount of other dietary constituents in cereals and cereal foods depends largely on the degree of refinement and other forms of processing. The fibre, fats, vitamins, minerals and other bioactive compounds in cereals are largely concentrated in the germ and husk of cereals, and so are reduced with refinement.

The panel has reached the following conclusions. Evidence on cereals and cereal foods and the risk of cancer is inconsistent, probably because studies have often not considered degree of refinement of cereals, or the extent to which diets very high in cereals may be deficient in other respects.

CEREALS AND CANCER RISK

In the judgement of the panel, cereals modify the risk of cancers of various sites as shown below, or else have no relationship with them. Judgements are graded according to the strength of the evidence.

EVIDENCE	DECREASES RISK	NO RELATIONSHIP	INCREASES RISK
Convincing			
Probable			
Possible	*Wholegrain cereals* Stomach		*Refined cereals*[a] Oesophagus
Insufficient	*Cereals* Colon		

For an explanation of the terms used in the matrix, see chapter 3.

[a] The factor may not be cereals as such, but deficiency of microconstituents, either in the context of deficiency diets (see chapter 5.2) or in the degree of refinement.

The panel notes that diets high in wholegrain cereals possibly decrease the risk of stomach cancer. Diets high in refined cereals possibly increase the risk of oesophageal cancer.

Given the importance of cereals in most diets, and the evidence that starchy diets protect against chronic diseases other than cancer, more research on the relationship between cereals and cancer risk is needed.

INTRODUCTION

Cereals (grains) are the seeds of cultivated grasses, thought to have originated in the Fertile Crescent of the Middle East. The rise in importance of cereals as a food group is associated with the neolithic revolution – the transition of our ancestors from gatherer–hunters to settled agriculturalists, which happened around 10,000–15,000 years ago.

The main varieties of cereals are wheat, rice, maize (corn), millet, sorghum, barley, oats and rye. Historically, each of these was grown and eaten in the particular region or regions of the world to which it is suited by climate and terrain.

Some varieties of cereal are now cultivated far from their region of origin and have become important new food crops. In addition, new high-yield varieties of wheat and rice have been developed, and these are replacing older varieties, as well as traditional cereals, such as millet, in many parts of Africa and Asia.

Because of the importance of cereals in most diets, and because one of the principal constituents of cereals is starch, they are sometimes called starchy staples. Other members of this food group are starchy roots and tubers; these are assessed in chapter 6.2.

NUTRIENT CONTENT

Cereals contain an average of 70% starch by weight. They also provide varying amounts of non-starch polysaccharide (NSP)/dietary fibre, protein, B vitamins, vitamin E, iron and various trace elements, and bioactive compounds. The nutrient content of cereals is greatly affected by the ways in which they are processed; most of the non-starch nutrients are concentrated in the outer parts of the cereal grain, which are removed during processing. The way they are cooked and how they are consumed can also influence the digestibility of the carbohydrates and the glycaemic response of the individual. Cereal-based diets tend to be bulky with a low energy density.

CONSUMPTION PATTERNS

Cereals and the many foods made from them are the most important single food group in the world. They form the basis of diets in many different countries. As described in chapter 1, their contribution to overall food intake shows considerable regional variation in both the amount and types consumed. Their contribution to total energy ranges from nearly 70% in many parts of Asia, to not much more than 20% in North America and Europe.

The few populations for whom cereals are not an important food group are pastoralist peoples, such as the Masai; hunters, including the Inuit and other arctic populations, who maintain their traditional way of life and diet; and populations in some regions of Oceania and sub-Saharan Africa where there is a high reliance on starchy roots, plantains and tubers.

Rice is the main cereal eaten, followed by wheat and maize (corn). More wheat is grown than rice on a global basis, but much wheat goes into animal feeds. Other cereals important in particular regions include millet and sorghum, eaten in parts of sub-Saharan Africa, South America and Asia, and rye, eaten in eastern and central Europe.

The importance of starchy staples, including cereals, in the diet is broadly correlated with economic/industrial development. There has been a long-term decline in their consumption in industrialised countries and in the world as a whole. A decline in the consumption of traditional staple foods is also associated with urbanisation in developing countries and the substitution of maize and wheat for the traditional cereals. An important exception is rice consumption in Asia.

Cereals are eaten in very many forms. None is eaten in an unprocessed raw state; even rice eaten as boiled grains has been milled to some degree, with its outer husk and bran removed. Many cereals are milled into flours of varying degrees of extraction of husk and germ, and then made into a vast variety of foods. Widely eaten cereal-based foods include leavened and unleavened breads (such as chapatti, tortilla and pitta), noodles, pasta, dumplings and gruels or porridges. Cereal flours are also used as ingredients in a huge variety of composite manufactured foods and home-made dishes.

INTERPRETATION OF THE DATA

Epidemiological data on the consumption of particular foods in relation to cancer risk are difficult to interpret because, as noted in chapter 3, there are many factors, both dietary and non-dietary, that could confound any observed association. Where associations are found to exist, these cannot be attributed simply to a single dietary constituent of that food, as all foods contain more than one dietary constituent. Nutrient content can vary according to the way in which a food is processed and eaten, and processing and preparation practices can greatly affect the composition of cereals and cereal products. In addition, the rest of the diet of which these foods are a part will also differ and, hence, so will the overall intake of constituents. This point applies to all foods assessed in chapter 6.

The consumption of cereal-based diets tends to be inversely related to the consumption of animal foods and fat, as well as to socioeconomic status. Deficiency diets (defined in chapter 5.2) are mostly made up of one starchy staple food. However, the panel judges that any diet-related causal link to the increased risk of cancer is more likely to be due to the absence of micronutrients and the lack of overall dietary diversity, than to the presence of complex carbohydrates and cereals as such.

In many epidemiological studies, intakes of wholegrain versus refined cereals have often been used as an indicator of NSP/dietary fibre intakes. However, differences in content of other constituents may well be more significant than the presence or absence of dietary NSP/fibre. In industrialised countries, high intakes of wholegrain cereal products tend to be associated with other dietary differences. These factors tend to confound any observed associations between cancer risk and cereal consumption. Finally, the ways in which cereals are eaten varies in different cultures. This disparity among the actual foods measured makes it difficult to aggregate the results of studies carried out in different countries.

Cereal consumption has been investigated mainly in relation to NSP fibre intakes and the risk of colon cancer. Recently, interest has grown in other carbohydrate fractions, particularly different types of starch, which, as discussed in chapter 5.2, vary in their digestibility and the glycaemic response they produce. It has also been suggested that other components of wholegrains, such as vitamin E, may possibly be important (Jacobs et al, 1995).

JUDGEMENTS OF OTHER REPORTS

In the National Academy of Sciences report, *Diet, Nutrition and Cancer* (NAS, 1982), a high consumption of wholegrain products was tentatively linked with a reduced risk of colorectal cancer, and a high starch intake derived from cereals with an increased risk of stomach cancer. The report's guidelines emphasised the importance of including wholegrain cereals in the daily diet.

SIGNIFICANCE FOR OTHER DISEASES

Consumption of diets based on polished white rice with little dietary diversity can cause beriberi due to thiamine deficiency, and maize-based diets can cause pellagra due to niacin deficiency. These deficiency diseases are not very common today, but do sometimes occur in populations eating a very restricted diet.

The World Health Organization report, *Diet, Nutrition and the Prevention of Chronic Diseases* (WHO, 1990), recommended the consumption of a diet that derived between 50% and 70% of total energy from complex carbohydrates

---

BOX 6.1.1 WHOLEGRAIN CEREALS AND CEREAL PRODUCTS

Cereal foods may be eaten in wholegrain form, although consumption in refined forms such as white rice, and bread and pasta made from white flour, is now generally more common. Despite considerable attention to dietary fibre, few epidemiological studies have specifically investigated the association between wholegrain cereals and cereal products and cancer risk.

The composition of wholegrain cereals such as brown rice, and cereal products such as wholemeal bread and pasta, is different from that of refined versions such as white rice, flour, bread and pasta. Much or most of the NSP/fibre and the essential fats, vitamins and minerals are removed in refining. Of these, NSP/fibre possibly protects against colorectal cancer (see chapter 5.2).

Refined cereal products such as bread may also contain substantial amounts of salt, and may be used as vehicles for fat or sugary spreads. Manufactured cereal-based products such as breakfast cereals, and baked goods such as biscuits and cakes, generally contain substantial amounts of fat and sugar. Salt, hardened fats and sugar have no known benefits in the context of cancer.

There is little if any evidence that wholegrain cereals and cereal products as such increase the risk of cancer of any site; the evidence generally points to a protective effect.

Panel recommendations
Given the significant differences in the composition of wholegrain cereals and cereal products compared with the refined versions, dietary recommendations designed to reduce cancer risk should specify that wholegrain and minimally refined cereals and cereal products are to be preferred.

Studies of cereals and cereal products should specify when these are wholegrain, and when refined and preferably in the degree of refinement.

and provided 16–24 g/day of NSP.

Of 100 expert reports published between 1961 and 1991, mostly concerned with diet and cardiovascular diseases or chronic diseases generally, in developed countries and regions, 62 recommended an increased intake of starch or complex carbohydrates. Of 64 that recommended increased cereal intake, 46 specified wholegrains. Of the 52 that recommended an increased intake of bread, 41 specified wholegrain bread. No report disagreed with this general pattern of recommendations (Cannon, 1992).

RECOMMENDATION FOR FUTURE RESEARCH

The panel makes the following recommendation:

■ Given the importance of cereals and cereal products in most diets, the remarkable and recent decline of these foods in industrialised diets, the nutritional differences between wholegrain and refined cereals, and the current lack of clear data, priority should be given to epidemiological and experimental studies of cereals and cereal foods and cancers of the digestive system and other sites, in which clear distinctions are made between degrees of refinement and relative nutritional content.

ASSESSMENT

Investigation of the consumption of cereals and cereal products in relation to cancer risk has mostly been in relation to cancers of the stomach, and colon and rectum.

Evidence of decreased risk

CONVINCING	PROBABLE	POSSIBLE	INSUFFICIENT
		Stomach (wholegrain cereals)	Colon

Stomach (4.6). Evidence from six case-control studies conducted in Europe and the USA consistently showed a protective association for consumption of wholegrain cereals and cereal products.

Colon rectum(4.10). The results of 13 case-control studies on cereals are inconsistent, around half finding decreased risk and half no association. One international study has shown that people eating a traditional cereal-based diet have a lower risk of colon cancer, and that there is an inverse correlation between colon cancer mortality rates and cereal consumption. The evidence that cereals may protect against colon cancer is, as yet, insufficient.

It has also been observed that increased risk is associated with high consumption of some cereal foods, such as rice and pasta, and a hypothesis to account for this is discussed in chapter 5.2.

Given that diets high in fibre probably protect against colorectal cancer, it is reasonable to judge that wholegrain cereals and cereal products may also protect against cancer of the colon.

Evidence of increased risk

CONVINCING	PROBABLE	POSSIBLE	INSUFFICIENT
		Oesophagus (refined cereals)	

Oesophagus (4.4). Nine case-control studies have examined cereals and oesophageal cancer. An association between increased risk and cereals such as maize (corn), wheat and millet has been observed. The suggestion that this association may result from fungal contamination of stored grain has received support from one case-control study in China and from animal studies which found fungal contaminants to have a carcinogenic effect in laboratory mice. As noted in chapter 4.4, the panel judges that any relationship between cereal consumption and oesophageal cancer is probably not with cereals as such, nor with starches, but with diets that are deficient in a number of protective microconstituents.

6.2 Roots, tubers and plantains

Roots (such as cassava), tubers (such as potatoes) and plantains (and bananas) are non-cereal starchy foods that are important in diets in some parts of the world. They are variable in their nutrient content.

On a population basis, consumption of these foods varies from small amounts only (where diets are almost wholly grain-based) to 15–20% total energy.

The panel has reached the following conclusions. While there are theoretical reasons to believe that diets high in roots, tubers and/or plantains might protect against some cancers, evidence is currently very limited.

Given the importance of starchy foods, more research on the relationship between roots, tubers, plantains and cancer risk is needed.

ROOT, TUBERS AND PLANTAINS AND CANCER RISK

In the judgement of the panel, roots, tubers and plantains are not known to modify the risk of cancers at any site.

EVIDENCE	DECREASES RISK	NO RELATIONSHIP	INCREASES RISK
Convincing			
Probable			
Possible			
Insufficient			

INTRODUCTION

Roots, tubers and plantains are starchy foods that are staples in some parts of the world.

Both roots and tubers are the underground storage organs of plants. Tubers include potatoes, sweet potatoes, yams and taro. Globally the most important starchy root is cassava or manioc. Like potatoes, cassava originated in Latin America, but is now an important food crop in many tropical countries because it is easy to cultivate and is drought-resistant. In botanical terms, plantains are fruits, although plantains, as well as some varieties of green banana, are eaten as vegetables in some countries. Other starchy plant foods include breadfruit and sago. Non-starchy root vegetables such as turnips, swedes, carrots and parsnips are assessed in chapter 6.3.

NUTRIENT CONTENT

Roots and tubers contain various amounts of starch: sweet potatoes about 12%, potatoes about 20%, yams about 30%, and cassava 25–50%, by weight.

Although different types of roots, tubers and plantains have different nutrient profits, they are, generally, good sources of NSP/fibre, carotenoids, vitamin C, potassium, other vitamins and minerals and other bioactive compounds.

CONSUMPTION PATTERNS

Parts of the world where starchy roots and tubers form a large proportion of the diet are the Pacific islands, where they contribute a regional average of about 20% total energy, and sub-Saharan Africa, where they contribute a regional average of about 15% total energy.

The potato is now the most important starchy food in the temperate regions of America and Europe. They are a staple food in parts of the Andes. Plantains and other cooking bananas are a staple food in some parts of sub-Saharan Africa, and bananas are eaten as a fruit in most countries.

INTERPRETATION OF THE DATA

Problems in interpreting the data are similar to those noted in relation to cereals (chapter 6.1) and to starch (chapter 5.2).

JUDGEMENTS OF OTHER REPORTS

The National Academy of Sciences reports, *Diet, Nutrition and Cancer* (NAS, 1992) and *Diet and Health* (NAS, 1989), made no recommendation on the consumption of roots, tubers and plantains.

SIGNIFICANCE FOR OTHER DISEASES

The World Health Organization report, *Diet, Nutrition and the Prevention of Chronic Diseases* (WHO, 1990), made no specific recommendation for consumption of roots, tubers or other non-cereal starchy staples except to classify these as suppliers of starch.

Of 100 expert reports published between 1961 and 1991, that were mostly concerned with diet and cardiovascular diseases or chronic diseases generally, in developed countries and regions, 34 recommended higher consumption of potatoes and other tubers (and 62 recommended higher con-

sumption of starchy foods or of complex carbohydrates) with none disagreeing (Cannon, 1992).

RECOMMENDATION FOR FURTHER RESEARCH

The panel recommends that:

■ Given the nutritional content of roots, tubers and plantains, and their importance in plant-based diets, particularly in poorer parts of the world, priority should be given to epidemiological and experimental studies in which these foods are carefully identified and their nutritional and health consequences studied.

ASSESSMENT

Few epidemiological studies have examined the consumption of starchy roots and tubers in relation to cancer risk. What epidemiological data there are almost all concern potatoes and bananas, perhaps because consumption of most of the other members of this food-group is relatively low in those countries where most studies have been conducted, that is North America and Europe.

6.3   Vegetables and fruits

Vegetables and fruits form a variable part of diets throughout the world.

On a population basis, vegetables (which here exclude roots and tubers, and pulses) and fruits, supply less than 5% total energy in most countries. Consumption is higher where, for climatic reasons, there is abundant supply, and lower where there is short or seasonal supply, and in parts of Africa and Asia where diets are impoverished. Consumption overall does not greatly vary as a function of economic development.

Generally, vegetables and fruits are low in energy and are good sources of non-starch polysaccharides (fibre) and of vitamins, minerals, and other bioactive microconstituents.

The panel has reached the following conclusions. There is a strong and consistent pattern showing that diets high in vegetables and fruits decrease the risk of many cancers, and perhaps cancer in general. The evidence that such diets decrease the risk of mouth and pharyngeal, oesophageal, lung and stomach cancers, is convincing, and they probably also protect against laryngeal, pancreatic, breast, and bladder cancers. The evidence that diets high in vegetables decrease the risk of colorectal cancer is convincing. The panel notes that such diets possibly protect against ovarian, cervical, endometrial and thyroid cancers, and that diets high in vegetables possibly protect against primary liver, prostate and renal cancers.

On the whole, the evidence for a protective effect of vegetables is rather stronger than that for fruits, perhaps reflecting the fact that vegetables are generally consumed in greater quantities than fruits, and thus in more variable quantities within populations.

In the present state of science it is probably best to consider vegetables and fruits collectively. However, different types of vegetables and fruits, such as dark green leafy vegetables, cruciferous vegetables, allium vegetables, and citrus fruits, have been investigated separately, as have some individual vegetables and fruits. The evidence that diets high in green vegetables protect against lung and stomach cancers is convincing, and they probably protect against mouth and pharyngeal cancer. Diets high in cruciferous vegetables probably protect against colorectal and thyroid cancers. The evidence that diets high in allium vegetables, and in tomatoes, and in citrus fruits protect against stomach cancer is convincing. Diets high in carrots probably protect against lung, stomach and bladder cancers.

VEGETABLES AND FRUITS AND CANCER RISK

In the judgement of the panel, vegetables and fruits modify the risk of cancers of various sites as shown below. Judgements are graded according to the strength of evidence.

EVIDENCE	DECREASES RISK	NO RELATIONSHIP	INCREASES RISK
Convincing	*Vegetables and fruits* Mouth and pharynx Oesophagus Lung Stomach *Vegetables* Colon, rectum		
Probable	*Vegetables and fruits* Larynx Pancreas Breast Bladder		
Possible	*Vegetables and fruits* Cervix Ovary Endometrium Thyroid *Vegetables* Liver Prostate Kidney		
Insufficient			

For an explanation of the terms used in the matrix, see chapter 3.
Evidence on specific vegetables and fruits is as follows. All judgements signify decreased risk with higher intake. These judgements are derived directly from Table 6.3.2.
Raw vegetables: convincing for stomach.
Green vegetables: convincing for lung and stomach; probable for mouth and pharynx; possible for oesophagus, colon and breast.
Cruciferous vegetables: probable for colon, rectum and thyroid.
Allium vegetables: convincing for stomach; possible for colon.
Carrots: probable for lung, stomach and bladder; possible for oral and rectum.
Tomatoes: convincing for stomach; possible for lung.
Citrus fruit: convincing for stomach; possible for oral and oesophagus.

INTRODUCTION

Vegetables and fruits are plant foods. Botanically, a vegetable is any part of a plant not involved in the sexual reproduction of the plant. Vegetables are typically the cultivated or gathered leaves, roots, stalks, bulbs and flowers of plants. Some foods that are culinary vegetables are botanically classified as fruits; these include avocados, cucumbers, aubergines (egg plant), peppers, tomatoes, pumpkins (winter squash) and courgettes (zucchini). Vegetables include artichokes, asparagus, beets, broccoli, Brussels sprouts, cabbage, carrots, cauliflower, chard, endive, fennel, garlic, kohlrabi, leeks, lettuce, mushrooms, okra, onions, parsley, parsnips, radishes, rhubarb, swede (rutabaga), spinach, turnips and various green leafy vegetables.

Vegetables may be grouped into categories that are either botanically or culinarily meaningful, for example: 'green leafy', 'cruciferous', 'allium'. Cruciferous vegetables include broccoli, cauliflower, kohlrabi, Brussels sprouts and cabbage. Allium vegetables include onions, garlic, scallions, chives and leeks.

Botanically, a fruit is any seed-containing part of the plant. Fruits include apples, apricots, blueberries, cherries, cranberries, figs, grapefruits, grapes, kiwi fruits, lemons, limes, mangoes, melons, nectarines, oranges, papayas, peaches, pears, pineapples, plums, raspberries and strawberries. Citrus fruits include oranges, grapefruits, lemons and limes. A few fruits are sometimes consumed in dried form, these include grapes, apricots, plums, apples, dates and figs.

NUTRIENT CONTENT

Vegetables and fruits are relatively rich in vitamins, minerals and other bioactive compounds compared with other food groups. Although different types have different nutrient profiles, they are, generally, good sources of NSP/fibre, carotenoids, vitamin C, folate, potassium and other vitamins, minerals and bioactive compounds. Some specific vegetables are good sources of B vitamins, calcium and iron. Dried fruits are concentrated sources of energy, sugar, dietary fibre and iron.

CONSUMPTION PATTERNS

Vegetables and fruits provide less than 5% total energy in most areas of the world. In some areas of China, Oceania, and the Caribbean, vegetables and fruits provide over 10% total energy; in southern Europe they provide about 6% total energy. Industrialised diets average about 5% total energy from vegetables and fruits. Consumption is lowest in parts of eastern Europe and in the poorer countries of Africa and Asia.

INTERPRETATION OF THE DATA

Most epidemiological studies on vegetables, fruits and cancer risk have been case-control studies but the number of cohort studies has recently grown. A few ecological studies, mostly based on food balance data, provide additional evidence. Some experimental studies have entailed the feeding of vegetables and fruits as such (not just individual micronutrients or other bioactive compounds) and have examined the resultant tumour incidence or some intermediate cancer-related matter. To date, no human feeding trials in which cancer incidence was the measured outcome have been undertaken using vegetables and fruits, because of the length of time and number of participants necessary to accrue enough cases for assessing the effect with appropriate statistical power.

One problem with the measurement of vegetable and fruit consumption is a tendency towards overestimation of intake with self-report; in many of the case-control and cohort studies, reported vegetable and fruit intakes appear higher than supposed true intakes (Steinmetz and Potter; 1993; Steinmetz et al, 1993, 1994). This may be due to 'social desirability bias', perhaps particularly in societies where vegetables and fruits are deemed 'healthy foods'. It is further possible that a selection bias occurs in some studies so that both cases and controls are of higher socioeconomic status than the general population and, therefore, have an actual intake that is somewhat higher than the population average.

Some problems of interpretation apply to other foods and are specified here only because of the very large number of studies of vegetables and fruits published, and the need to keep such issues in mind while interpreting this substantive literature.

Difficulty arises in summarising studies on vegetables and fruits because of the wide variation in the groupings used. Some studies have reported results only for broad categories (for example, 'all vegetables' or 'all fruits'), whereas others have reported results for more narrowly defined categories (for example, 'raw vegetables', 'green vegetables', 'citrus fruit') or for individual food items (for example, 'spinach', 'carrots', 'tomatoes'). Further, within the studies that have reported only on broad categories, some have based this broad exposure variable upon one question on a dietary questionnaire (for example, one question about total vegetable consumption), whereas others have compiled consumption frequencies of many different vegetable items to form this broad category.

Inconsistencies in vegetable and fruit classification schemes also make a summary of the data, as a whole, complicated. In some studies, vegetables and fruits have been categorised according to botanical classification; in others, categorisation has been according to culinary usage. Some studies have included pulses as vegetables, whereas others have classified these as a separate entity, or not at all. (Pulses are assessed in chapter 6.4.)

Some studies have included cereals such as corn, and tubers, such as potatoes, as vegetables, and plantains and banana as fruit. These starchy staples are reviewed in chapters 6.1 and 6.2. Further, as noted there, some bananas are cooked starchy staples while some are eaten raw as fruit. The variance in subjectively defined categories, such as 'green vegetables' or 'yellow–orange vegetables', is also great across studies, for example, broccoli and green peppers are included as 'green vegetables' in some studies, whereas only leafy greens are included in this category in others; tomatoes are considered 'yellow–orange vegetables' in some, but not in others. Vegetable and fruit products (for example, juices, jams and tomato sauce) have been included in vegetable and fruit categories in some studies, but not in others; the same is true for mixed dishes (for example, vegetable soups, stews, casseroles). Botanical fruits such as olives, avocados and coconut have generally not been included in vegetable and fruit categories, either because of their high fat content or because of infrequent consumption in a given population.

Another difficulty in data interpretation arises from the lack of reporting of null findings; some studies that have reported results for only a few vegetable and fruit items have probably also found null associations for other items, but have not included these results in their publication. Further, some studies have analysed data for a large number of vegetable and fruit items, thus increasing the probability of finding a significant association for one or a few items due to chance alone. In evaluating the contribution of multiple comparisons to the consistent evidence for a protective effect of vegetables and fruit, it should be noted that, as a point of reference, multiple comparisons have also been made in many studies for other food groups, perhaps particularly for cereal (grain) products, and it is noteworthy that far fewer significant associations have been observed than is true for vegetables and fruits.

Most case-control and cohort studies of vegetable and fruit consumption have been conducted within populations that have relatively homogeneous diets; this makes discussion of wider ranges of intake speculative. However, odds ratios or relative risks representing weak protective associations for vegetables and fruits from these studies may in fact be signalling stronger associations for greater differences in intakes. Ecological studies (across countries or cultures) are useful for making comparisons across a wider range of intakes, although attention must be given to the many potentially confounding factors that also vary across populations.

Potential confounding factors must also be adequately considered in the interpretation of results from case-control and cohort studies. Levels of certain known cancer risk factors may vary systematically with vegetable and fruit consumption (at least in some cultures), and the possibility that observed associations are not causal, but rather explained by other associated factors, must be evaluated. In particular, smokers have been documented to consume fewer vegetables and fruits than non-smokers (Morabia and Wynder, 1990; McPhillips et al, 1994). Further, dietary fat intake has been shown to be inversely correlated with vegetable and, particularly, fruit intake in the USA (Ursin et al, 1993). Evaluation of the degree to which these factors are responsible for observed associations for the consumption of vegetables and fruits is important in studies of cancers thought to have tobacco- or dietary fat-related aetiologies. Most recent studies of the effects of fruits and vegetables in cancers

thought to be caused by smoking have attempted to control for the effect of smoking. Physical activity, age, socioeconomic status and alcohol intake are other factors that may correlate with intakes of vegetable and fruits, and the role of these should likewise be evaluated.

Although the issue of confounding must be considered seriously, it is impressive to note that some 200 epidemiological studies have been conducted in quite diverse populations, in which health-related behaviours do not always cluster in the same way. Thus, no single correlate of vegetable and fruit consumption is likely to explain the consistent finding of protective associations across many sites and many populations.

JUDGEMENT OF OTHER REPORTS

Although the very earliest epidemiological studies of diet and cancer suggested a lower risk with higher intake of vegetables and fruits, the concept that diets rich in vegetables and fruits protect against cancer did not receive much consideration until the 1980s. The 1982 National Academy of Sciences report, *Diet, Nutrition and Cancer* (NAS, 1982), included a guideline emphasising 'the importance of including fruits, vegetables… in the diet'. The report reviewed the evidence on various micronutrients, including β-carotene, vitamin C, vitamin E and selenium, but did not summarise the literature on vegetables and fruit as such.

The later NAS report, *Diet and Health* (NAS, 1989), concluded that diets high in plant foods, including vegetables and fruits, 'are associated with lower occurrence of coronary heart disease and cancers of the lung, colon, oesophagus, and stomach' and, referring in particular to the evidence on vegetables and fruits and cancer, recommended five or more daily servings of a combination of vegetables and fruits, especially green and yellow vegetables and citrus fruits.

In 1992, the *5 A Day – For Better Health* programme was launched by the National Cancer Institute in the USA, with the goal of increasing average vegetable and fruit consumption to at least five servings per day by the year 2000 (Subar et al, 1992).

SIGNIFICANCE FOR OTHER DISEASES

There is good evidence that diets high in vegetables and fruits protect against a number of diseases other than cancer. Carotenoids, vitamin C and perhaps other antioxidants protect against cataracts. They also decrease the oxidation of cholesterol in the arteries and thus protect against cardiovascular disease. Vitamin C may help maximise intestinal iron absorption and thus help prevent iron-deficiency anaemia. In some developing countries, where food is scarce or diets are monotonous, the inclusion, in the diet, of even small amounts of vegetables and fruits containing β-carotene and vitamin C help prevent xerophthalmia and scurvy.

Many vegetables and fruits are high in NSP/fibre, and most are high in potassium. NSP/fibre may help control dia-

TABLE 6.3.1 VEGETABLE AND FRUIT CONSUMPTION AND THE RISK OF CANCER AT DIFFERENT SITES: CASE-CONTROL STUDIES

CANCER SITE	TOTAL STUDIES No.	STUDIES SHOWING A STATISTICALLY SIGNIFICANT[a] PROTECTIVE ASSOCIATION FOR ONE OR MORE VEGETABLE AND/OR FRUIT CATEGORIES		STUDIES SHOWING NO STATISTICALLY SIGNIFICANT[A] PROTECTIVE ASSOCIATIONS FOR ANY VEGETABLE AND/OR FRUIT CATEGORIES		STUDIES IN WHICH STATISTICAL SIGNIFICANCE IS NOT REPORTED No.
		No.	(%)[b]	No.	(%)[b]	
Stomach	31	28	(93%)	2	(7%)	1
Colon	21	15	(79%)	4	(21%)	2
Oesophagus	18	15	(83%)	3	(17%)	0
Mouth, oral cavity, and pharynx	15	13	(87%)	2	(13%)	0
Lung	13	11	(85%)	2	(15%)	0
Rectum	13	8	(80%)	2	(20%)	3
Breast	12	8	(67%)	4	(33%)	0
Pancreas	11	9	(82%)	2	(18%)	0
Larynx	8	6	(100%)	0	–	2
Bladder	8	6	(86%)	1	(14%)	1
Cervix	6	4	(80%)	1	(20%)	1
Colon/rectum combined[c]	6	3	(60%)	2	(40%)	1
Prostate	6	1	(17%)	5	(83%)	0
Endometrium	5	4	(80%)	1	(20%)	0
Thyroid	5	3	(60%)	2	(40%)	0
Kidney	5	3	(60%)	2	(40%)	0
Nasal cavity, paranasal sinuses, and nasopharynx	4	2	–	2	–	0
Ovary	4	3	–	1	–	0
Skin[d]	3	2	–	0	–	1
Vulva	1	1	–	0	–	0
Mesothelium	1	0	–	1	–	0
Leukemia[e]	1	0	–	-	–	1
All sites combined	**196**	**144**	**(78%)**	**40**	**(22%)**	**13**

[a] $p < 0.05$ for test for trend, $p < 0.05$ for odds ratio for uppermost consumption level, or 95% confidence interval excluding 1.0 for uppermost consumption level
[b] Percentage of total studies that reported on statistical significance
[c] Refers to studies in which cancers of the colon and rectum were studied together and not separately
[d] One study each of malignant melanoma and nonmelanocytic skin cancer
[e] Study of chronic myeloid leukemia

betes and high serum cholesterol levels, and protects against diverticular disease and other digestive disorders. Potassium may help prevent or control hypertension and thereby reduce the subsequent risk of stroke and heart disease.

Vegetables and fruits contain very little fat, and are low in calories. (Avocados are one exception, and drying of course increases the energy content of fruits.) Diets high in vegetables and fruits therefore protect against obesity and thus against the risk of cardiovascular disease, as well as against those cancers associated with overweight and obesity.

The World Health Organization report, *Diet, Nutrition, and the Prevention of Chronic Diseases* (WHO, 1990), recommended a goal of at least 400 g of vegetables and fruits daily (in addition to potatoes) including, within that, at least 30 g of legumes, nuts and seeds.

Of 100 expert reports published between 1961 and 1991 that were mostly concerned with diet and cardiovascular diseases or diet and chronic diseases, 66 recommended higher consumption of vegetables and 66 recommended higher consumption of fruits, with none disagreeing (Cannon, 1992).

RECOMMENDATIONS FOR FUTURE RESEARCH

The panel recommends that:

■ In future research on vegetables, fruits and cancer risk, special attention be paid to issues of measurement, both of overall intake and of individual foods; and that work on biological measures of intake also receive special attention.

■ Future studies make more use of large cohorts with heterogeneous patterns of intake.

■ That special attention be paid to the issue of the patterns of behaviour associated with high and low intakes of vegetables and fruits and the confounding that results from such patterns.

ASSESSMENT

At least 37 cohort, 196 case-control and 14 ecological studies have investigated the relationship between vegetable and fruit consumption and the risk of cancer. The case-control evidence is most abundant and consistent for cancers of the stomach, oral cavity, lung, oesophagus, pancreas, and rectum: 80% of studies have shown a statistically significant protective association for each of these sites for one or more vegetable and/or fruit category (Table 6.3.1).

Although fewer studies have focused on cancers of the larynx, bladder, cervix, and endometrium, more than 80% have shown at least one protective association.

Overall, when studies of all cancer sites are taken together, 78% have shown a significant decrease in risk for higher intake of at least one vegetable and/or fruit category examined. The general picture is not altered when allowance is made for the fact that some apparently significant protective associations may be due to chance alone, and that some studies have reported non-statistically significant protective associations.

The literature on vegetables, fruits and the prevention of cancer has been reviewed in several scientific papers, including those by Steinmetz and Potter (1991 a, b, 1996), Block et al (1992), and Ziegler (1991). In 1991, Steinmetz and Potter examined 137 epidemiological studies and concluded that 'consumption of higher levels of vegetables and fruit is associated consistently, although not universally, with a reduced risk of cancer at most sites', and that the association was 'most marked for epithelial cancers – particularly those of the alimentary and respiratory tracts…'.

In a 1992 review, Block et al (1992) found 'a statistically significant protective effect of fruit and vegetable consumption … in 128 of 156 dietary studies in which results were expressed in terms of relative risk'. The possible role of many bioactive constituents of vegetables and fruit in protecting against cancer is assessed in chapter 5.8 (Table 6.3.2).

Results from 196 case-control and 21 cohort studies for all cancer sites combined are summarised, with reference to different types of vegetables and fruits, in Table 6.3.3.

Evidence of decreased risk

CONVINCING	PROBABLE	POSSIBLE	INSUFFICIENT
Vegetables and fruits	*Vegetables and fruits*	*Vegetables and fruits*	
Mouth and pharynx	Larynx	Ovary	
Oesophagus	Pancreas	Endometrium	
Lung	Breast	Cervix	
Stomach	Bladder	Thyroid	
Vegetables		*Vegetables*	
Colon, rectum		Liver	
		Prostate	
		Kidney	

Mouth and pharynx (4.1). Oesophagus (4.4). Smoking (or other tobacco habits) and high alcohol consumption are thought to be of major importance in causing cancer in these sites, and many studies have performed appropriate statistical adjustments to allow for these factors. Protective associations for fruit and vegetable consumption remained in the great majority. For cancer of the mouth and pharynx , the evidence of a protective effect is most consistent for carrots, citrus fruit and green vegetables, but the evidence for vegetables and fruits in general is convincing.

For oesophageal cancer, the evidence for a protective

TABLE 6.3.2 CASE-CONTROL STUDIES OF CANCER AT DIFFERENT SITES[a] SHOWING INVERSE, NULL, OR POSITIVE ASSOCIATIONS FOR CONSUMPTION OF VARIOUS TYPES OF VEGETABLES AND FRUIT

CANCER SITE	RELATIONSHIP TO CANCER RISK[b] (NUMBER OF STUDIES, INVERSE–NULL–POSITIVE)								
	ALL VEGETABLES	ALL FRUIT	RAW VEGETABLES	CRUCIFEROUS VEGETABLES	ALLIUM VEGETABLES	GREEN VEGETABLES	CARROTS	TOMATOES	CITRUS FRUIT
Stomach	11–0–0	14–3–0	10–0–0	–[c]	9–1–1	8–0–0	7–1–1	9–1–1	11–1–0
Colon	8–0–1	5–2–1	3–0–1	8–3–1	4–1–1	4–1–0	4–1–2	4–0–2	2–1–3
Oesophagus	5–0–0	6–3–1	3–0–1	–	0–4–0	5–2–0	–	3–0–0	4–0–0
Mouth and pharynx	5–2–0	8–1–1	2–1–0	2–3–0	–	7–0–1	4–0–0	2–0–1	4–1–0
Lung	7–0–0	8–0–0	–	–	–	9–0–0	6–1–0	4–0–0	–
Rectum	2–0–2	3–0–1	–	5–0–0	2–0–1	–	4–0–1	3–2–1	4–1–0
Breast	–	3–0–1	–	–	–	5–1–0	3–1–0	–	1–0–2
Pancreas	6–1–0	7–1–0	2–1–0	–	–	–	–	–	1–2–0
Larynx	4–0–1	5–0–0	–	–	–	–	–	–	–
Bladder	–	1–2–0	–	–	–	3–0–0	5–0–0	–	–
Cervix	–	2–0–1	–	–	–	2–1–0	–	–	–
Prostate	–	–	–	1–0–2	–	1–0–2	–	–	–
Endometrium	–	3–0–1	–	–	–	–	2–1–0	–	–
Thyroid	–	–	–	5–0–0	–	–	–	–	–

[a] Table summarises results for the 196 case-control studies listed in Table 6.3.1. No entries are present for cancers of the kidney, nasal cavity, ovary, skin, vulva, mesothelium, colon/rectum combined, or leukemia because fewer than three studies reported on each category for these sites.
[b] Tallied results include both statistically significant and non-significant associations
[c] – = less than three studies investigated this category for this site

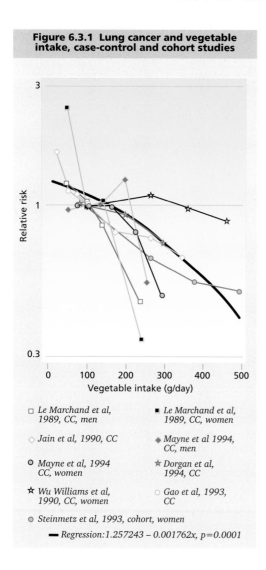

Figure 6.3.1 Lung cancer and vegetable intake, case-control and cohort studies

□ *Le Marchand et al,*
1989, CC, men

◇ *Jain et al, 1990, CC*

○ *Mayne et al, 1994*
CC, women

☆ *Wu Williams et al,*
1990, CC, women

■ *Le Marchand et al,*
1989, CC, women

◆ *Mayne et al 1994,*
CC, men

★ *Dorgan et al,*
1994, CC

○ *Gao et al, 1993,*
CC

● *Steinmetz et al, 1993, cohort, women*

━ *Regression:1.257243 – 0.001762x, p=0.0001*

This figure shows the dose–response relationship between vegetable intake and the risk of lung cancer. The fitted regression line shows that the relative risk decreases by about 50% as intake increases from 150 g/day to 400 g/day. An intake of > 400 g/day is always associated with a lower risk than 100 g/day or less.

effect for vegetables in general, and for tomatoes and citrus fruits, has been entirely consistent in one cohort and 22 case-control studies, and statistically significant protective associations have been found for at least one vegetable/fruit category in 18 studies. Overall, the evidence that vegetables and fruits protect against oesophageal cancer is convincing.

Lung (4.5). Lung cancer is one of the sites for which the most prospective data are available; six cohort studies and 13 case-control studies have examined consumption of vegetables and fruits. In these studies, the associations with intake of vegetables and fruit were appropriately adjusted for cigarette smoking. This reduces the possibility of observing a false protective association as a result of non-smokers consuming more vegetables and fruit than smokers, a phenomenon that has been documented in various populations (Morabia and Wynder, 1990; McPhillips et al, 1994).

Protective associations have been consistently shown for vegetables and fruits together and separately, and with individual items in both categories, in both cohort and case-control studies. The evidence for vegetables, fruit, green vegetables and tomatoes is convincing; six out of seven studies have also found inverse associations for carrots.

Stomach (4.6). Stomach cancer is the cancer most studied with respect to the consumption of vegetables and fruits. Six prospective cohort studies and 32 case-control studies have focused upon this site; specific findings of these studies are detailed in Tables 4.6.5 and 4.6.6 (vegetables) and 4.6.7 and 4.6.8 (fruit).

Protective associations with vegetables and fruits collec-

TABLE 6.3.3 CASE-CONTROL AND COHORT STUDIES OF ALL TYPES OF CANCER[a] SHOWING INVERSE, NULL, OR POSITIVE ASSOCIATIONS FOR CONSUMPTION OF DIFFERENT CATEGORIES OF VEGETABLES AND FRUIT

| | RELATIONSHIP TO CANCER RISK[b] | | | | | |
| | NUMBER OF STUDIES | | | % OF TOTAL STUDIES | | |
VARIETY OR FRUIT CATEGORY	**INVERSE**	**NULL**	**POSITIVE**	**INVERSE**	**NULL**	**POSITIVE**
Vegetables	59	6	9	80%	8%	12%
Fruit	36	15	5	64%	27%	9%
Raw vegetables	40	4	2	87%	9%	4%
Cruciferous vegetables	38	9	8	69%	16%	15%
Allium vegetables	27	4	4	77%	11%	11%
Green vegetables	68	6	14	77%	7%	16%
Carrots	59	7	7	81%	10%	10%
Tomatoes	36	5	10	71%	10%	20%
Citrus fruit	27	8	6	66%	20%	15%

[a] Table summarises results from 217 case-control and cohort studies
[b] Tallied results include both statistically significant and non-significant associations
[c] Percentages may not add to 100% due to rounding

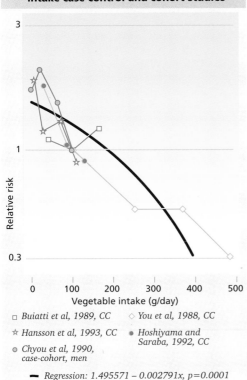

Figure 6.3.2 Stomach cancer and vegetable intake case control and cohort studies

Relative risk / Vegetable intake (g/day)

□ Buiatti et al, 1989, CC ◇ You et al, 1988, CC

☆ Hansson et al, 1993, CC ● Hoshiyama and Saraba, 1992, CC

◉ Chyou et al, 1990, case-cohort, men

— Regression: 1.495571 – 0.002791x, p=0.0001

This figure shows the dose–response relationship between vegetable intake and the risk of stomach cancer. The fitted regression line shows that the relative risk decreases by about 60% as intake increases from 100 g/day to 350g/day.

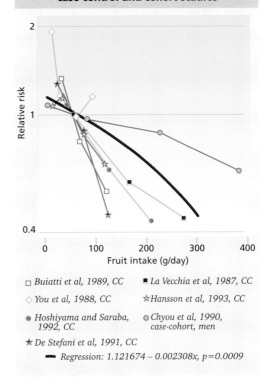

Figure 6.3.3 Stomach cancer and fruit intake, case control and cohort studies

Relative risk / Fruit intake (g/day)

□ Buiatti et al, 1989, CC ■ La Vecchia et al, 1987, CC

◇ You et al, 1988, CC ☆ Hansson et al, 1993, CC

● Hoshiyama and Saraba, 1992, CC ◉ Chyou et al, 1990, case-cohort, men

★ De Stefani et al, 1991, CC

— Regression: 1.121674 – 0.002308x, p=0.0009

This figure shows the dose–response relationship between fruit intake and the risk of stomach cancer. The fitted regression line shows that the relative risk decreases by about 50% as intake increases from 50 g/day to 300 g/day. An intake of > 150 g/day is always associated with a lower risk than 100 g/day or less.

tively and separately and with at least one fruit and/or vegetable category have been consistent. Most studies adjusted for potential confounding factors.

Time-trend studies in Japan, Poland, and the USA have shown decreasing mortality for stomach cancer with increasing consumption of vegetables or fruit.

Evidence that vegetables and fruits protect against stomach cancer is convincing.

Colon, rectum (4.10). Evidence from four prospective studies which examined consumption of vegetables and fruits in relation to the risk of colon cancer is particularly consistent for vegetables. Evidence of a protective association is stronger for women than men. A majority of case-control studies have shown a significant inverse association for at least one vegetable and/or fruit category, and such associations have been particularly consistent for raw and green vegetables.

Findings for fruit consumption and colon cancer risk are less abundant; two studies found increased risk with higher intakes and one decreased risk, while the majority showed no association.

There is only one prospective study on rectal cancer, but evidence from case-control studies is most consistent for cruciferous vegetables, carrots and citrus fruit, which all appear to be protective against rectal cancer. Overall, evidence on vegetables showed protective associations, while risk for fruits was somewhat inconsistent. There is also some evidence that consumption of vegetables and fruits may decrease the risk of developing adenomatous colorectal polyps. Evidence that vegetables decrease the risk of colon and rectal cancer is convincing.

Larynx (4.3). Evidence from case-control studies generally suggests that increased consumption of vegetables and fruits is linked with decreased risk of cancer of the larynx. Most studies controlled for tobacco smoking and alcohol. However, the number of studies overall is limited, not all have shown statistically significant findings, and there are few data on specific vegetables and fruit. Vegetables and fruits probably protect against laryngeal cancer.

Pancreas (4.7). The three prospective cohort studies of pancreatic cancer showed both increased and decreased risks for vegetables or fruit, although none of the

A large number of epidemiological studies have produced results on vegetables and fruits that apply to cancer as a whole, rather than to specific cancer sites.

Three cohort studies have examined the relationship between vegetables and fruits consumption and cancer of all sites combined. In a cohort of elderly persons in Massachusetts, (USA), odds ratios were 0.3 (0.1–1.0) for green and yellow vegetables, 0.3 (0.1–0.7) for strawberries, 0.5 (0.3–0.8) for tomatoes, and 0.6 (0.3–1.4) for dried fruit; odds ratios for broccoli, salads, and carrots or squash were less remarkable (Colditz et al, 1985). In another cohort of elderly persons in California, (USA), weakly inverse associations ORs=0.8 (some statistically significant) were seen for women for all vegetables, all fruit, and dark green vegetables, whereas associations for males were essentially null (Shibata et al, 1992). In a cohort of Japanese adults, an inverse association was observed for green and yellow vegetables (Hirayama, 1986).

associations was statistically significant.

Evidence from ten case-control studies is more consistent, with nine reporting a statistically significant association for one or more vegetable and/or fruit categories. Data on specific types of vegetable and fruit categories are limited. All the studies used some surrogate respondents, due to the very short survival time of the disease. Notably, many of the studies did not adjust for tobacco smoking. Vegetables and fruits probably protect against pancreatic cancer. More prospective data would be helpful.

Breast (4.11). Two out of the three prospective cohort studies have reported lower relative risk for higher vegetable consumption and one found a similar result for fruit intake. While evidence from 19 case-control studies was more consistent, with ten finding a statistically significant protective association for one or more vegetable and/or fruit categories, the majority of these studies did not adjust the associations for fat intake. Eight of eleven studies on vegetables as a general category but only four of twelve studies of fruits, found protective associations. Six of the studies on fruits found null associations. A study that examined women after surgery for early breast cancer found more favourable prognostic tumour characteristics in those who had previously eaten more fruit and vegetables. Vegetables and fruits probably protect against breast cancer.

Bladder (4.18). Five cohort studies that reported on vegetables and fruits and the risk of bladder cancer found either decreased risk or no association for vegetables and fruits combined or various categories of vegetables or fruits.

Of nine case-control studies that reported on statistical significance, eight found inverse associations for one or more vegetable and/or fruit categories. Carrots and green vegetables are the specific categories that have been most often examined and results have consistently shown a protective association. The majority of the studies adjusted for cigarette smoking (or found equivalent associations within both smokers and non-smokers), which is recognised to be the most important risk factor for bladder cancer. Vegetables and fruits probably protect against bladder cancer.

Ovary (4.12). Six case-control studies have reported inverse associations for one or more vegetable and/or fruit group. While most studies have investigated only a limited number of vegetable or fruit categories, associations have mainly appeared protective. An international ecological study of 30 countries found an inverse correlation between vegetable availability and ovarian cancer. The evidence indicates that vegetables and fruits possibly protect against ovarian cancer.

Endometrium (4.13). Five case-control studies of vegetable and fruit intake and endometrial cancer have been reported. Of these, four have observed inverse associations for one or more vegetable and/or fruit categories. Three have reported inverse associations for fruit, and two for carrots; data are not abundant for other specific types of vegetables or fruit. Odds ratios of 0.5 or lower have been reported for various vegetables or fruit in four of the five studies. Vegetables and fruits possibly protect against endometrial cancer.

Cervix (4.14). While a prospective cohort study in Japan reported an inverse association between green and yellow vegetable consumption and the risk of cervical cancer, evidence from case-control studies is less clear-cut. Four found inverse associations for one or more vegetable and/or fruit categories but few data are available on any individual category of vegetables or fruit. Such findings as there are tend to be inconsistent.

Three out of four case-control studies of women with in situ cervical cancer or cervical dysplasia have not produced clear-cut evidence of a protective role for vegetables and fruit, although associations have been found for some specific items. Vegetables and fruits possibly protect against cervical cancer.

Thyroid (4.16). Five case-control studies of cancer of the thyroid have reported statistically significant inverse associations for one or more vegetable and/or fruit categories. All five studies reported protective associations for cruciferous vegetables, although in one study, this applied to women only.

It is interesting that, as well as containing several potentially anticarcinogenic substances, cruciferous vegetables carry compounds which may promote goitre development and which have been shown to cause thyroid cancer in animal experiments. While there is no good evidence that goitrogenic compounds are harmful in iodine-sufficient areas of the world, they may contribute to goitre in areas where iodine deficiency occurs. Vegetables and fruits possibly decrease the risk of thyroid cancer.

Liver (4.9). Three cohort studies and five case-control studies have examined vegetable intake and liver cancer. All three cohort and the majority of case-control studies found decreased risk with higher intakes. A cohort study in Japan has shown decreased risk of liver cancer with greater green and yellow vegetable intake. Evidence relating to fruit consumption is limited. Diets high in vegetables possibly

BOX 6.3.2 ANIMAL STUDIES AND POSSIBLE MECHANISMS

At least 20 studies have been conducted in which cancer has been experimentally induced (usually via a chemical carcinogen or irradiation) in mice, rats, or hamsters. Animals were fed specified amounts of certain vegetables and fruits (most often cabbage, cauliflower, broccoli, brussels sprouts, carrots, citrus oils, or oils from allium vegetables) (Sparnins et al, 1982; Rieder et al, 1983; Stoewsand et al, 1988; Bresnick et al, 1990; Wattenberg, 1971; Boyd et al, 1979; Boyd et al, 1983; Wattenberg, 1983; Ansher et al, 1986; Stohs et al, 1986; Birt et al, 1987; Temple and Basu, 1987; Scholar et al, 1989; Wattenberg et al, 1989; Vang et al, 1991; Belman, 1983; Stoewsand et al, 1989; Maltzman et al, 1989; Wattenberg and Coccia, 1991). In the great majority of these studies, it was found that the animals fed vegetables or fruit experienced fewer tumours, smaller tumours, fewer metastases, less DNA damage, higher levels of enzymes involved in the detoxification of carcinogens, or other outcomes indicative of a lower risk of cancer. In most studies, the relative amounts of vegetables included in the animal diets were well above those typically consumed by humans. The extrapolation of results from animal studies to humans is further hampered by species differences, the use of administered carcinogens, and the use of genetically susceptible animals.

In one in vitro study, juice extracts from several vegetables were shown to reduce the mutagenicity of beef tallow, as determined by the Ames test (Munzner, 1986). Extracts that reduced mutagenicity included those from brussels sprouts, white cabbage, kohlrabi, red cabbage, and paprika (in order from greatest to least effect). Another study showed several vegetables, including onion, cabbage, cauliflower, turnip, and radish, to inhibit both a direct-acting mutagen and one requiring metabolic activation in vitro (Badria, 1994). In a further study, peas, grapefruit, red pepper, and some cruciferous vegetables were shown to induce quinone reductase activity (Tawfiq et al, 1994). In two in vitro studies, extracts of garlic showed antibiotic activity against *Helicobacter pylori* (Simm et al, 1996). It is biologically plausible that diets high in vegetables and fruits protect against cancers. Vegetables and fruits all contain a great number of constituents thought to protect against cancer. Some of these are conventionally defined as nutrients; others have only recently been identified as bioactive. Many vegetables and fruits are high in dietary fibre, which may protects against cancers of the stomach, pancreas, colon and rectum and breast, and perhaps other sites as well (see chapter 5.2).

Microconstituents in vegetables and fruits likely to protect against cancers include the antioxidant vitamins and minerals (see chapters 5.6 and 5.7). These include β-carotene, vitamins C and E, and selenium. β-carotene is found in the greatest amounts in orange vegetables and fruits, such as carrots, sweet potatoes, pumpkin, winter squash, cantaloupe, mango, and papaya. Carotenoids other than β-carotene also have antioxidant or other potentially anticarcinogenic actions, or both; these include lutein (a xanthophyll pigment in green vegetables), lycopene (the red pigment in tomatoes), and α-carotene (in orange vegetables). Vitamin C is found notably in citrus fruits and juices, leafy green vegetables. broccoli, green pepper, tomatoes, strawberries, and melon, as well as potatoes; vitamin E is found in vegetables, although in greater quantity in vegetable oils; selenium is found in plant foods in amounts proportional to the selenium content of soil.

Green leafy vegetables and citrus fruits are also rich in folic acid; see chapter 5.6.

Cruciferous vegetables, such as broccoli, cauliflower, cabbage, and brussels sprouts, contain several potentially anticarcinogenic bioactive microconstituents (see chapter 5.8). These include dithiolthiones, isothiocyanates, and indole-3-carbinol. Allium vegetables such as onions, garlic, scallions, leeks, and chives, contain the allium compounds, diallyl sulfide and allyl methyl trisulfide (see chapter 5.8). Citrus fruits contain coumarins (also found in some vegetables) and D-limonene (specifically found in oil from the skin of the fruit). Many vegetables and fruits contain the potentially anticarcinogenic flavonoids quercetin and kaempferol (which are also found in tea and wine). (See chapter 5.8).

---

decrease the risk of primary liver cancer.

Prostate (4.15). Evidence from epidemiological studies on vegetables and fruits and the risk of prostate cancer is less consistent than for other sites. Two of seven cohort studies found no association for all vegetables and fruits, the other five studies reported various associations for different categories of fruits and vegetables and most were protective or null. Most case-control studies reported null associations for vegetable and fruit consumption, with a few studies showing increased risk with increased consumption of fruits. An international ecological study found an inverse correlation with vegetable availablility. Vegetables possibly decrease the risk of prostate cancer.

Kidney (4.17). One cohort study found no association between renal cancer mortality and vegetable consumption. The five case-control studies of renal cell carcinoma that have examined vegetable and fruit consumption controlled for cigarette smoking and obesity. Three studies found a statistically significant inverse association for at least one vegetable and/or fruit category and weak inverse associations were found for the majority of vegetable and fruit categories examined. An ecological study found a negative correlation between renal cancer mortality and vegetable consumption.

The available evidence suggests that vegetables possibly protect against renal cancer.

Evidence of increased risk

There is no cancer site for which the evidence, taken as a whole, supports an overall increase in risk with higher intakes of vegetables and fruits.

As far as cancer as a whole is concerned, there is a theoretical possibility that consumption of vegetables and fruits might increase risk because of the presence of certain microconstituents or contaminants. These may include goitrogens (see chapters 4.16 and 5.8), nitrates from fertiliser residues as well as contained naturally (see chapters 5.8 and 7.1), pesticide residues (see chapter 7.1) and aflatoxin contamination (see chapter 7.3).

Nitrate is present in large quantities in vegetables. However, concomitant intake of various antioxidants in fresh vegetables probably prevents oxidation of nitrate to nitrite and counteracts any risk of cancer (Oshima et al, 1981). There is no good evidence that nitrate from vegetables increases cancer risk. (See Box 4.6.4).

Some pesticides are known to be toxic. In most developed countries use of pesticides believed to be harmful is regulated, but this is much less true in the developing world. In any case, all foods of animal and plant origin include contaminant residues; vegetables and fruits are not especially problematic in this respect. The question of fertiliser and pesticide residues is considered in chapter 7.1.

There is no evidence at present that any vegetables and fruits, properly stored and cleaned, have any significant adverse health effects.

6.4 Pulses (legumes)

Pulses, also known as legumes, are the most important plant sources of protein, and are also good sources of fibre and many vitamins, minerals and other bioactive compounds. With cereals, they are the staple protein source for populations that consume little or no food of animal origin.

On a population basis, consumption of pulses varies between very small amounts (where food of animal origin is the main source of protein) to 10% or more of total energy.

The panel has reached the following conclusions. While there are theoretical reasons to believe that diets high in pulses might protect against some cancers, evidence is currently very limited.

PULSES AND CANCER RISK

In the judgement of the panel, pulses are not known to modify the risk of cancers at any site.

EVIDENCE	DECREASES RISK	NO RELATIONSHIP	INCREASES RISK
Convincing			
Probable			
Possible			
Insufficient			

INTRODUCTION

Pulses (legumes) are derived from the fruits and seeds of a number of leguminous plants. They include beans, peas, lentils and groundnuts (peanuts). Those that have matured and dried on the plant are perhaps the most commonly consumed; pulses include adzuki beans, black beans, black-eyed peas, broad beans (also called fava beans), chickpeas (also called garbanzo or ceci beans), flageolets, kidney beans, lentils, mung beans, peanuts (also known as ground-nuts), pinto beans, soya beans, split peas and white beans (includes Great Northern, cannellini, navy and pea beans). Immature pulses, including fresh green peas, are picked before maturation and drying. Sprouts, the result of the germination of a wide variety of dried beans and, indeed, other seeds, are also consumed.

NUTRIENT CONTENT

Dry pulses are the richest plant source of protein and contain 6–11% protein by cooked weight. In this regard, they are comparable to meat. They are typically rich in NSP/dietary fibre as well as a number of dietary microconstituents and bioactive components such as isoflavones (found particularly in soya beans). They are low in fat, and the fat they do contain is mostly polyunsaturated. Immature pulses lack the concentrated levels of nutrients of dry legumes.

CONSUMPTION PATTERNS

Pulses are a dietary staple in some parts of the world, providing a significant portion of total protein intake. In societies with high meat intakes, pulses are usually consumed infrequently or in small amounts.

Pulses are consumed in a wide variety of ways; examples include Japanese and Chinese bean curd (tofu), Chinese mung bean sprouts, Mexican chilli and refried beans, Indian dahl, Middle Eastern falafel and humus, Indonesian cultured soya bean cakes (tempeh), Cuban black beans and rice, Boston baked beans, Italian minestrone, Swedish pea soup, and US peanut butter. Soya foods include soya milk and flour, tofu, tempeh, textured vegetable protein, and the many products that can be prepared from these items.

Pulses, together with nuts and seeds, have been estimated to provide about 5.6% total energy in economically developing countries, and 2.4% in developed countries (WHO, 1990). Pulses make the greatest contribution to dietary energy supply in some areas of sub-Saharan Africa, where 11–17% total energy is derived from them, followed by the Middle East, Asia and North Africa. In some areas of China, they provide as much as 10% total energy. In Central America, they are also a relatively important part of the diet. In Brazil, they are usually eaten with rice and provide 5% total energy. Consumption is lowest in Europe, Australia, New Zealand and North America.

INTERPRETATION OF THE DATA

Most of the evidence on pulses comes from human epidemiological studies in which either diet as a whole, or some aspect of diet other than pulses in particular, was the main concern. Typically, an item termed 'beans' or 'legumes' has been included on a food frequency questionnaire and an odds ratio or relative risk calculated. Many, but not all, of these studies were conducted in Western populations whose intakes of pulses are low and homogeneous. In many studies, the cutpoints used to define high and low intake groups were not given. In studies where only a small proportion of the study population has a higher intake, statistical power to detect any true association is limited. Some studies among non-Western or vegetarian populations have been able to consider a wider range of consumption. The human data currently available may well be insufficient for the purpose of determining the effect of relatively high consumption on cancer risk.

Other evidence comes mainly from experiments showing certain constituents of pulses to prevent experimentally induced cancer in animals and to have biological properties that may protect against cancer.

JUDGEMENTS OF OTHER REPORTS

Neither of the National Academy of Sciences reports (NAS, 1982, 1989) reviewed literature on the relationship between pulses and cancer, and neither report made any recommendation on consumption of pulses.

SIGNIFICANCE FOR OTHER DISEASES

Perhaps the most important role of pulses is as a provider of inexpensive dietary protein, since most animal protein sources, such as meat, poultry, milk and eggs, are generally far more expensive. When animal protein is unavailable, unaffordable or unwanted, pulses can provide appropriate protein–energy nutrition. In cultures with diets higher in animal foods and fat, regular consumption of pulses may help prevent or control diabetes, obesity and coronary heart disease. In clinical trials, soya foods have been shown consistently to lower total and LDL cholesterol and triglyceride levels in people with elevated levels (Carroll, 1991; Anderson et al, 1995).

The World Health Organization report, *Diet, Nutrition and the Prevention of Chronic Diseases* (WHO, 1990), recommended consumption of a daily minimum of 30 g of pulses together with nuts and seeds. This was included within its recommendation for consumption of vegetables and fruits at a minimum of 400 g/day, and was focused on some types of cancer as well as coronary heart disease. The report noted that the recommended intake of pulses, nuts and seeds was above the amounts typically consumed in developed countries. Otherwise, pulses have generally not been a focus of attention in expert reports on diet and public health (Cannon, 1992).

RECOMMENDATIONS FOR FUTURE RESEARCH

The panel makes the following recommendation:

■ Given the nutritional content of pulses and their importance in plant-based diets as rich sources of protein and of bioactive microconstituents that may protect against cancer, high priority should be given to epidemiological and experimental studies in which pulses are carefully identified and measured and their relation to disease risk established. Particular attention should be given to those populations where consumption is higher and more varied than has usually been the case in the studies to date.

ASSESSMENT

Few epidemiological studies have investigated the relationship between the consumption of pulses (legumes) and the risk of various cancers. Some evidence is available in respect to cancers of the mouth and pharynx, nasopharynx, larynx, oesophagus, stomach, pancreas, endometrium and prostate, but is either limited or too inconsistent for any judgement to be made.

Evidence of decreased risk

An ecological study showed per capita consumption of pulses, nuts and seeds to be inversely correlated with the incidence of cancers of the breast, endometrium, ovary, testis, kidney, and the central nervous system. Consumption was positively correlated with incidence of cancers of the liver and nose. (Armstrong and Doll, 1975). However, since consumption of pulses was positively correlated with that of

BOX 6.4.1 PULSES AND CANCER AT ALL SITES

A substantial number of studies have produced data on specific pulses or pulses in general, and cancer as a whole.

To date, 58 epidemiological studies have been identified that have reported results for pulses (K.A. Steinmetz, personal communication) (Kvale et al, 1983; Hirayama, 1982; Hirayama, 1986; Mills et al, 1988; Mills et al, 1991; Koo, 1988; Modan et al, 1975; Phillips, 1975; Tuyns et al, 1988; Cook-Mozaffari et al, 1979; McLaughlin et al, 1988; Risch et al, 1985; Trichopoulos et al, 1985; You et al, 1988; Schuman et al, 1982; Ziegler et al, 1990; Iscovich et al, 1989; Lee et al, 1991; Herrero et al, 1991; Hu et al, 1991; Iscovich et al, 1992; Steinmetz et al, 1993; Benito et al, 1990; Shu et al, 1993; Levi et al, 1993; Hu et al, 1994; Zheng et al, 1992; Zheng et al, 1992; Gridley e al, 1990; Zheng et al, 1992; Zheng et al, 1993; Bueno de Mesquita et al, 1991; Buiatti et al, 1989; Gonzalez et al, 1991; Tuyns et al, 1992; Ramon et al, 1993; Kune et al, 1992; Sturgeon et al, 1991; Nomura et al, 1990; Steinmetz et al, 1994; Chyou et al, 1993) (Yu et al, 1988; Sammon, 1992; Wang et al, 1992; Pickle et al, 1991; Kato et al, 1991; Mills et al, 1989; Severson et al, 1989; Maclure and Willett, 1990; Hirayama, 1988; Shu et al, 1992; Swanson et al, 1992; Li et al, 1989; Heilbrun et al, 1989; La Vecchia et al, 1988; Notani and Jayant, 1987; Kune et al,

1987). Thirty-six of these studies were summarised in a review by Steinmetz and Potter (1996).

These 58 studies reported results for food categories entitled 'legumes', 'pulses', 'seeds and legumes', 'nuts and legumes', 'legumes, nuts, and seeds', 'beans', 'beans and dry pod vegetables', 'dried beans', 'dried peas', 'peas and beans', 'beans, lentils, and peas', 'kidney beans', 'soybeans', 'soybean products', 'bean products', 'fermented bean products', 'tofu', 'bean curd', or 'soybean paste soup'. These studies were tallied with regard to the direction of the reported associations, without regard to statistical significance; none of the tallied data specifically involved bean sprouts or peanuts. Studies with results for more than one cancer site were counted more than once.

The results of these studies are somewhat conflicting. Of 58 studies, 29 (50 per cent) reported decreased risk with higher consumption, 22 (38 per cent) reported increased risk, and 7 (12 per cent) reported no association.

In a review specifically on the topic of soya intake and cancer risk, Messina et al (1994) concluded that the epidemiological data were inconsistent; consumption of non-fermented soy-products, such as soya milk and tofu, tended to be either not asso-

ciated with risk or to be associated with decreased risk, whereas no pattern was evident for fermented soya products, such as miso. Protective associations were observed for hormone-, as well as non-hormone-related cancers.

Of 26 experimental studies in which diets contained soya or soybean isoflavones, 17 (65%) reported protective effects, and no study reported increased tumours

It is biologically plausible that diets high in pulses protect against cancers. They are particularly high in NSP/fibre, which may protect against cancers of the stomach, pancreas, colon and rectum, and breast, and perhaps other sites as well (see chapter 5.2). They contain folic acid, which may protect against colorectal and cervical cancers (see chapter 5.6). They further contain a number of biologically active microconstituents, including protease inhibitors, saponins, phytosterols, and inositol hexaphosphate phytic acid each of which has been shown to inhibit carcinogenesis in animals or in vitro (see chapter 5.8). As already mentioned, soya beans have a high content of isoflavones, weak phyto-oestrogens that may not only inhibit oestrogen-promoted cancers, such as breast cancer, but may also inhibit non-hormone-related cancers by other mechanisms (see chapter 5.8).

---

vegetables and cereals, and inversely correlated with consumption of fat, animal protein, potatoes, and sugar, differences in cancer incidence between countries cannot be directly attributed to differences in the consumption of pulses.

Evidence of increased risk

A number of studies reported increased cancer risk with higher intakes of pulses. Studies reporting statistically significant increased risk, or a two-fold or greater increase in risk with higher intake, were examined more closely. The 10 studies meeting these criteria were of various cancers, including those of the nasopharynx, stomach (two studies), pancreas, colon (two studies), rectum (two studies), breast, and endometrium. They were conducted in both Western and non-Western cultures. In most studies that reported cutpoints for consumption categories, intakes in the uppermost group remained infrequent; for example, 'twice per week', or even 'ever', as opposed to 'never'.

In two of the studies, the associations were for fermented bean pastes, or soup made from them. In one study, associa-

tions for fermented bean pastes were found only with regard to diet in infants and not for diet at 20 years of age.

Three of the ten studies were conducted by one research group in Belgium, which found a more than four-fold increase in risk for consumption of more than, versus less than, zero grams of beans per week, for cancers of the colon, rectum, and stomach. No explanation for these findings is apparent.

When the evidence is considered for each individual cancer site, it is never suggestive of an overall judgement that pulses increase risk for any site.

6.5 Nuts and seeds

Nuts and seeds, common in the diets of pre-agricultural peoples, are dense in energy and are good sources of unsaturated fats, protein, NSP/fibre and microconstituents.

There are no good data on consumption of nuts and seeds on a population basis.

The panel has reached the following conclusion. While there are theoretical reasons to believe that diets high in nuts and seeds might protect against some cancers, evidence is currently lacking.

NUTS AND SEEDS AND CANCER RISK

In the judgement of the panel, nuts and seeds are not known to modify the risk of cancers at any site.

EVIDENCE	DECREASES RISK	NO RELATIONSHIP	INCREASES RISK
Convincing			
Probable			
Possible			
Insufficient			

INTRODUCTION

Nuts are the dried fruits of trees; most are enclosed in hard shells. Examples of nuts consumed in human diets include walnuts, hazelnuts (also known as filberts), almonds, chestnuts, ginkgo nuts (also known as ginan), pine nuts (also known as pignoli or Indian nuts), pistachio nuts and pecans. Some other foods thought of as nuts, including Brazil nuts, macadamia nuts and cashews, are actually seeds. Peanuts (also known as ground-nuts) are not tree nuts but pulses (legumes), and are considered in chapter 6.4.

Seeds come from the fruits of plants and contain the embryo and food supply for the next plant generation. Most seeds have hulls or shells that are softer than those of nuts; in some cases the shells can be eaten. Seeds commonly consumed in human diets include sunflower, sesame, pumpkin, poppy and squash seeds.

NUTRIENT CONTENT

Nuts and seeds are important sources of protein, particularly in diets that do not contain meat. The protein content of nuts and seeds ranges from 10 to 25% by weight. Nuts and seeds have a very high fat content and are therefore energy dense; for nuts, typically, 70–90% total energy comes from fat. Nuts and seeds are also rich sources of unsaturated oils. The NSP/dietary fibre content of nuts and seeds is high, more so when eaten with their skins or hulls; fibre content is typically 5–15% by weight. Nuts and seeds are also rich in vitamins and minerals.

CONSUMPTION PATTERNS

Nuts and seeds were an important part of the human diet before the advent of agriculture. They can be consumed whole, or ground into pastes, butters or spreads. Acorns were an important contributor to the diet in medieval Europe and used to augment flour for making bread.

There are no good data on consumption of nuts and seeds as a separate class of food, on a population basis.

INTERPRETATION OF THE DATA

There are few studies of nuts and seeds and cancer risk. Any search for such studies is made more difficult by 'nuts' and 'seeds' not often being used as key words, reflecting the practice in the studies themselves of coupling nuts and seeds with pulses. In some studies, items termed 'nuts' or 'seeds', or even individual items, such as 'walnuts', were included on a food frequency questionnaire, but most studies combined nuts or seeds with pulses on the dietary questionnaire or in the reporting of the data. For example, an item such as 'legumes, nut, and seeds' would be typical.

JUDGEMENTS OF PREVIOUS REPORTS

Neither of the two National Academy of Sciences reports, *Diet, Nutrition and Cancer and Diet and Health* (NAS, 1982,1989), reviewed literature on the relationship between nuts or seeds and cancer, and neither report made any recommendation on consumption of nuts or seeds.

SIGNIFICANCE FOR OTHER DISEASES

One prospective study among a Californian Seventh-day Adventist population showed an approximate halving of the risk of coronary heart disease with a higher intake of nuts (Fraser et al, 1992); in this study, ground-nuts were included as a 'nut' item; other nuts often eaten in this population were almonds and walnuts. The fatty acid profile of nuts was offered as a possible explanation for the observed association.

The World Health Organization report, *Diet, Nutrition and the Prevention of Chronic Diseases* (WHO, 1990), recommended that a minimum of 30 g/day of a combination of nuts, seeds and pulses be included within its recommendation of a minimum intake of 400 g/day of vegetables and fruits. This recommendation was focused on some types of cancer as well as on coronary heart disease. The report

noted that most people in developed countries consumed less than the recommended amount each day.

RECOMMENDATIONS FOR FUTURE RESEARCH

The panel makes the following recommendation:

■ Given the nutritional content of nuts and seeds, the panel recommends that human studies identify nuts and seeds as separate dietary items, so that their relevance to cancer risk can be assessed.

ASSESSMENT

Eight epidemiological studies have been identified that have examined nuts, seeds, or both. Of the eight, in only four was an association between nuts and cancer risk reported separately from that of pulses, and no studies reported on seeds alone.

These studies do not provide a basis for any judgement as to whether there might be a relationship between nuts and seeds and any type of cancer.

BOX 6.5.1 NUTS, SEEDS AND CANCER AT ALL SITES

While there are as yet no useful epidemiological data on nuts and seeds, it is biologically plausible that diets high in specific nuts and seeds or these foods as whole, protect against cancers. Nuts and seeds are high in vitamins, minerals and other bioactive compounds, including vitamin E and selenium (see chapter 5.6 and Brody, 1985; Fraser et al, 1992; and Ravai, 1995.) Brazil nuts are exceptionally high in selenium (Ip and Lisk, 1994). Nuts and seeds also contain inositol hexaphosphate (phytic acid), which may be protective against cancer. Walnuts, pecans, and perhaps other nuts, contain ellagic acid (Ravai, 1995), a phenolic compound that may reduce the risk of cancer. Seeds contain lignans, which may plausibly reduce the risk of breast and other cancers. Sesame exclusively contains sesamin, a lignan which may have anticarcinogenic properties. (See chapter 5.8).

6.6 Meat, poultry, fish and eggs

Meat, poultry, fish and eggs make up variable amounts of most diets. Red meat (from beef, lamb and pork) is central in most diets in developed societies, as are poultry (notably from chickens, as well as ducks, turkeys, and other birds). Meat from non-domesticated animals and birds is generally now less significant in most diets. Consumption of fish and of seafood is highly variable.

On a population basis, consumption of some or all of these foods varies between nothing (in vegetarian societies) to negligible amounts (in low-income societies) to 20% or more of total energy (notably in some richer developed countries).

Meat, poultry, fish and eggs are good sources of protein and various vitamins and minerals. The fat content of meat and poultry varies widely; meat from domesticated animals typically contains substantial amounts of fat, particularly saturated fats. Fatty fish are good sources of essential polyunsaturated fats. Eggs are a source of protein.

MEAT, POULTRY, FISH AND EGGS AND CANCER RISK

In the judgement of the panel, meat, poultry, fish and eggs modify the risk of cancers of various sites as shown below, or else have no relationship with them. Judgements are graded according to the strength of the evidence.

EVIDENCE	DECREASES RISK	NO RELATIONSHIP	INCREASES RISK
Convincing			
Probable			*Meat* Colon, rectum

Possible		*Poultry*
		  Breast
		Fish
		  Colon, rectum
		Eggs
		  Kidney
		  Bladder
			Meat
			  Pancreas
			  Breast
			  Prostate
			  Kidney
			Eggs
			  Colon, rectum

Insufficient	*Fish*
	  Breast
	  Ovary
			Eggs
			  Pancreas
			  Ovary

For an explanation of the terms used in the matrix, see chapter 3.
See chapters 7.4, 7.5 and 7.6 for assessments of the effects of various methods of preservation and preparation such as salting, curing, grilling, (broiling) and frying.

The panel has reached the following conclusions. Diets containing substantial amounts of red meat probably increase the risk of colorectal cancer. The panel also notes that such diets possibly increase the risk of pancreatic, breast, prostate and renal cancers.

The panel further notes the evidence, sometimes confounded by other lifestyle factors and problems of definition, indicating that varied vegetarian diets may decrease the risk of oral, nasopharyngeal, stomach, pancreatic, colorectal, breast, ovarian and bladder cancers.

Evidence on poultry, fish and eggs is less substantial. The panel notes that diets high in eggs possibly increase the risk of colorectal cancer.

Evidence that the fat in red meat increases the risk of cancer is assessed in chapter 5.3. Meat, poultry and fish are normally eaten prepared or cooked in some way. Evidence that some methods of preservation or preparation themselves modify cancer risk, is assessed in chapters 7.4, 7.5 and 7.6.

INTRODUCTION

The word 'meat' has no precise usage. It is sometimes used to refer to all non-fish and non-poultry flesh food; sometimes it also includes poultry. This ambiguity can present difficulties when comparing results from different studies. In the present report, the term 'meat' is used in a more restricted sense, to refer only to 'red meat' and essentially to beef, lamb and pork from farmed domesticated cattle, sheep and pigs in both fresh and preserved states. It does not refer to poultry or to fish.

Non-domesticated animals such as deer and rabbit are also killed for meat. Non-domesticated animals are a significant source of meat among some populations in extreme northern climates, in North Africa, in Islamic countries and the Eastern Mediterranean and in some rural areas of the USA. However, most of the evidence associating meat with cancer is derived from studies in which beef, lamb or pork are the predominant types of meat consumed. There are important differences, particularly in fatty acid content and composition, between meats from domesticated animals and 'wild' meats, that is, meats from non-domesticated or free-ranging species. The evidence presented here can be taken to apply only to meat from domesticated animals. Offal is also a form of meat, but there is little epidemiological evidence specific to this group of meats.

NUTRIENT CONTENT

Meat, poultry and fish contain around 20% protein, by weight. The fat content of meat, poultry and fish ranges from a low of less than 4% fat for lean poultry and some types of fish, to 30–40% fat by weight for fatty meat from domesticated farmed animals fed on cereals (grains) and pulses (legumes). Wild meat is typically low in fat.

Saturated fatty acids make up around 40–50% of the total fatty acids in meat. In the USA, these meats have been reported to contribute around one-third of saturated fat intake (Block et al, 1985). Poultry contains a somewhat lower proportion of saturated fatty acids (35%) and a higher proportion of polyunsaturated fatty acids (15–30% as compared with 10%). Fat from fish contains even less of saturated fatty acids (20–25%) and oily fish are a rich source of omega-3 fatty acids. Intensively reared poultry and farmed fish contain more fat than free-ranging or wild equivalents.

Meat and poultry are rich sources of the B vitamins B_6 and B_{12}, and of readily absorbable iron, zinc, selenium and fatty acids.

Fish contains relatively lower levels of B vitamins and iron and zinc than meat and poultry, but oily fish are a rich source of retinol and vitamin D; fish are a good source of calcium when the bones are eaten. Eggs are moderate sources of protein and fat. The yolks of eggs are high in dietary cholesterol.

CONSUMPTION PATTERNS

Worldwide, the consumption of meat, poultry and fish varies greatly. A substantial proportion of the world's population does not eat one or more of these groups of foods at all and, among those who do, consumption levels vary widely according to cost and preference. Meat and poultry intake is low in most African countries, India and other low-income Asian countries, typically contributing less than 3% total energy. Worldwide, meat and poultry contribute, on average, 9% total energy. The highest intakes are in Denmark, where meat and poultry contribute 24% total energy, and in Australia, New Zealand, Argentina and Bermuda, where these foods provide around 20% of total energy. Consumption of fish and seafood also varies widely in different parts of the world.

As a general rule, meat consumption increases with economic development. For example, between 1980 and 1987, meat intake in Japan rose from around 18 g/day to 71 g/day per person (WHO, 1990). Between the 1960s and the 1990s, poultry consumption has risen in almost every country, with a worldwide average increase of 50%.

Egg consumption has been reported to be around six eggs per person per week in the USA. Egg consumption has increased by 100–200% in Asia over the past 25 years but is still lower in most Asian countries than in the USA.

INTERPRETATION OF THE DATA

Improved methods of dietary assessment in epidemiological studies and evidence from experimental models are helping to identify, more precisely, what factors in meat, poultry and fish modify cancer risk. Nevertheless, many of the data reviewed here are not easy to interpret.

Although meat and fish can be eaten raw, virtually all of the evidence on these foods and the risk of cancer relates to these foods after they have been processed in some way. It is not possible to judge the relationship between raw meat, poultry or fish and cancer risk. However, while the assessment in this section is inevitably of meat, poultry and fish that have been prepared or cooked in some way, an attempt has been made to assess the evidence relating to these foods as such. Evidence on processing is assessed in chapter 7.

Diets containing substantial amounts of meat may well be energy-dense, and high in fat as well as protein of animal origin. Since energy, fat and protein may modify the risk of cancer severally and jointly, the interpretation of data on meat, as such, is problematic.

It is also difficult to assess the contribution of meat and poultry to fat intake. The fat content of these foods varies widely, even within the same cut, and is dependent on how the animal was raised (for example, grass or cereal-fed, free-range or factory-farmed) and the extent of fat trimming at the point of supply or in the home, among other factors. The greater availability of leaner products over recent years in some countries has also made it more difficult to characterise the fat composition of these foods.

JUDGEMENTS OF OTHER REPORTS

Meat was first identified as a possible cause of cancer in the mid-1970s, with reports of a strong correlation with cancers of the colon and rectum, stomach, breast and kidney. Later investigations using other study designs have not consistently reproduced these initial findings, but there is still great interest in the possible role of meat in cancer.

The NAS report, *Diet, Nutrition and Cancer* (NAS, 1982), made little specific comment on meat. Mutagens formed during the cooking of meat were concluded to be of unknown significance. Meat was noted to be an important source of saturated fat which, along with total fat, was the macroconstituent of food then identified as being most strongly associated with cancer.

The subsequent NAS report, *Diet and Health* (NAS, 1989), essentially confirmed these conclusions. Substitution of fatty meats with lean meat, the consumption of poultry without skin, and the consumption of fish was recommended because of the possible association between fat and certain cancers, cardiovascular disease and obesity. No report has made any recommendations on eggs in relation to cancer.

SIGNIFICANCE FOR OTHER DISEASES

Meat, poultry, fish and eggs are valuable foods in those parts of the world where diets are otherwise marginal or deficient in protective microconstituents, although they are likely to be more expensive to produce than cereals and pulses which, eaten in combination, are comparably nutritious.

Meat is an especially rich source of absorbable haem iron. Iron-deficiency anaemia is widespread in developing countries where iron losses are associated with intestinal parasitism and an estimated 15% of women have high menstrual iron losses. Zinc deficiency has been reported to limit the growth of children in affluent societies that consume inappropriate, highly processed diets and in the Middle East, where excessive intakes of unleavened phytate-rich cereals tend to impair zinc absorption. With the recent recognition of its important role in maintaining thyroid metabolism, selenium may be more relevant to iodine deficiency disorders which affect nearly one thousand million people worldwide, particularly in areas such as central Africa and China.

Recommendations concerned with reducing the risk of cardiovascular disease in industrialised countries commonly specify less fat from meat and the substitution of poultry and fish for meat.

Of 100 expert reports published between 1961 and 1991, that were mostly concerned with diet and cardiovascular diseases or with diet and chronic diseases in developed countries and regions, 47 recommended substitution of lean for fatty meat, and 48 recommended lower consumption of fatty meats and meat products. One report disagreed. A total of 36 recommended higher consumption of poultry, and 49 recommended more fish, with two disagreeing. The general purpose of these recommendations was to reduce total and saturated fat intake, and to maintain or increase the intake of unsaturated fats. Reports that recommend consumption of fewer eggs or egg yolks were concerned with the possible effect of dietary cholesterol on risk of cardiovascular disease (Cannon, 1992).

RECOMMENDATIONS FOR FUTURE RESEARCH

The panel makes the following recommendations:

■ In order to provide a better understanding of the relationship between consumption of meat, poultry, fish and eggs and cancer risk that future studies should pay special attention to methods by which the animals have been raised, their complete constituent nutritional profile (macronutrients, micronutrients, residues, etc.), and, in particular, actual measured, not assumed, fat content.

■ Studies should distinguish clearly between meat from intensively reared animals, and from non-domesticated animals, and among meat, poultry and fish.

ASSESSMENT

6.6.1 MEAT

Evidence indicates that diets containing substantial amounts of meat increase the risk of cancers of certain sites.

Evidence of increased risk

CONVINCING	PROBABLE	POSSIBLE	INSUFFICIENT
	Colon, rectum	Pancreas	
		Breast	
		Prostate	
		Kidney	

Colon, rectum (4.10). Seven cohort studies and twenty-six case-control studies have examined meat and the risk of colorectal cancer. The cohort studies showed either increased risk or no association. Two-thirds of the better conducted studies showed an increased risk of colon or colorectal cancer with higher meat intake. Meat intake is likely to be similarly associated with rectal cancer, although fewer studies have investigated this condition as distinct from colon cancer.

Early ecological studies in the 1970s reported correlations of around 0.7 and 0.9 between the intake of meat and the worldwide incidence of cancers of the colon, although later studies have shown less consistency.

Meat probably increases the risk of cancers of the colon and rectum for a combination of reasons. Fat is a possible risk factor, and other constituents in meat which may be associated with colorectal cancer include protein and iron. There is also evidence from human metabolic studies that meat increases the production of the potentially carcinogenic *N*-nitroso compounds in the large bowel (Bingham et al, 1996). This probably involves the bacteria in the large bowel and may relate to the protein and/or iron present in meat. Possible relationships between the risks associated with meat consumption and methods of preservation and cooking are discussed in Chapter 7.

Genetic factors also appear to be relevant to the risks associated with meat intake and colorectal cancer or polyps. The association with meat consumption is greatest among individuals characterised as having rapid rather than slow activity of specific metabolising enzymes (Lang et al, 1994; Roberts-Thomas et al, 1996). These enzymes include the N-acetyltransferases and CYP_{1A2} which catalyse the activation of compounds, such as the heterocyclic amines found in meat, to more active carcinogens.

Diets high in red meat probably increase the risk of colorectal cancer.

Pancreas (4.7). In three cohort studies and a number of case-control studies, a high meat intake has been associated with increased risk of pancreatic cancer. Other case-control studies found no association. No particular type of meat specifically contributed to this. The apparent association may reflect meat as a source of fat, which has been linked with increased risk in both epidemiological and experimental studies. The involvement of carcinogens formed during the cooking of meat in pancreatic cancer is unclear but under investigation.

These data show that diets containing substantial amounts of meat possibly increase the risk of pancreatic cancer.

Breast (4.11). Epidemiological studies of meat and breast cancer present a somewhat inconsistent picture, although a meta-analysis of seven case-control and cohort studies reported a relative risk for high meat intake of 1.5.(1.3–1.8). Three of eight cohort studies reported increased risk with higher meat intake, while the others found no association. Early ecological studies reported a strong correlation between meat intake and the incidence of

BOX 6.6.1 VEGETARIAN DIETS AND CANCER

A variety of vegetarian diets contain little or no meat or other foods of animal origin. Some are relatively simple adaptations of omnivorous diets. Others are more restrictive. Some vegetarian diets are followed by choice, for religious, cultural, or ethical reasons. Diets may also be virtually vegetarian not from choice but poverty. Vegetarian diets based upon a wide variety of plant foods should be distinguished from poverty vegetarian diets, which may be inadequate in both energy and nutrient content.

The term 'semi-vegetarian' is sometimes applied to people who exclude only selected kinds of meat, poultry or fish; sometimes red meat only is avoided. Many people who describe themselves as vegetarian may, in fact, eat any or all types of flesh occasionally as a feast, treat, or lapse. Vegetarians proper may follow lacto-ovo, lacto, or vegan diets. Lacto-ovo vegetarian diets exclude flesh foods, but include dairy products and eggs. Lacto-vegetarian diets exclude eggs, but include dairy products. Some semi-, lacto-ovo-, and lacto-vegetarian diets have nutrient profiles similar to that of omnivorous diets. Vegan diets exclude all foods of animal origin.

Macrobiotic regimes are predominantly vegetarian and emphasise natural, minimally-processed foods lower on the food chain. Meals are largely centred around plant foods; the preferred animal foods are fish and seafood, although no food is proscribed.

Perhaps one billion persons in the world are vegetarian, or virtually vegetarian. This includes largely the vegetarian population of India, which is vegetarian due to religious beliefs. It also includes the large number of Chinese who eat little or no flesh foods, mostly as a matter of poverty rather than choice or culture.

Meat accounts for only about 1% of total energy intake in India (see chapter 1.1) and 25–30% of the Indian population can be considered completely vegetarian, with the percentage being higher in central and southern states, and lower in the north (Achaya, 1994). The coastal areas have fewer vegetarians due to the availability of fish. Most vegetarians in India (90%) are in the habit of consuming milk, with the exception of the Jains, a religious group, who are vegans (1 to 2% of the population).

The proportions of most western populations that are vegetarian are relatively low, although interest in vegetarianism has recently increased in the USA and Europe. According to a Gallup poll, 5% of Americans considered themselves vegetarians, although a stricter poll, in which respondents were asked whether they ever ate meat, fish, or poultry, showed only 0.8% of adults and 1.9% of teenagers to be true vegetarians. Until recently, most North American vegetarians followed such a diet out of concern for animal welfare, whereas the recent upsurge in interest is more due to concern for health.

Studies of the effects of vegetarian diets on cancer risk must be interpreted carefully. People who are vegetarian from choice tend to differ from omnivores in ways other than diet. In developed countries, when personal, family or community good health is a motive for vegetarianism, for example, individuals may well drink little or no alcohol. They may also be non-smokers and have higher levels of physical activity. These factors must be taken into account when interpreting studies of vegetarians, so that a difference in risk due to some non-dietary factor, such as non-smoking, is not falsely attributed to the vegetarian diet. People who are semi-vegetarian other than from choice also differ from omnivores. If the reason for their diet is chronic poverty, they are likely also to be at high risk of infectious diseases, and their diets may be deficient in energy, as well as in essential nutrients.

Vegetarian diets may affect the risk of diseases other than cancer. Vegetarian groups have been shown to have lower overall mortality, lower risk of cardiovascular disease, lower rates of obesity, and longer life expectancy than general population comparison groups (Berkel and Waard, 1983; Fonnebo, 1992; Frenzel-Beyme and Chang-Claude, 1994; Thorogood et al, 1994; Key and Davey, 1996; Key et al, 1996). Lower prevalence of smoking is likely to be partly responsible for the lower rates of cardiovascular disease and overall mortality.

Nonetheless, there is evidence that various vegetarian diets decrease the risk of cancers of a number of sites. Most of this evidence comes from comparisons of cancer rates within vegetarian groups, such as Seventh-day Adventists, with general population rates.

Seventh-day Adventists are an evangelical religious denomination with about 2.5 million members world-wide. About half follow a lacto-ovo vegetarian diet and virtually all abstain from pork. Only a small proportion are vegans. Most avoid the use of alcohol, coffee, tea, hot condiments, and spices; smoking is proscribed.

Early data from 1958-65 on cancer mortality for Californian Seventh-day Adventists showed that rates were 53 per cent of general population rates for males and 67 per cent for females, for all cancer sites combined (Phillips, 1975). Rates were less than 50 per cent of general population rates for cancers related to tobacco and alcohol (cancers of the mouth and pharynx, oesophagus, and bladder). For cancers classified by the authors as unrelated to smoking or alcohol consumption (stomach, pancreas, colon, breast, and ovary), rates were generally in the range of 50–70% of general population rates.

In Norwegian Seventh-day Adventists, rates for 1962–86 for all-cancer mortality were 78% (p ≤ 0.05) of general population rates for men below age 75 years of age (Mills et al, 1994), but were not significantly different from general population rates for older men or for women of either age group (Fonnebo, 1992).

In Seventh-day Adventists in the Netherlands, mortality rates for 1968–77 for all cancers were 50% (p < 0.01) of general population rates (Berkel and Waard, 1983). Rates for cancers of the lung, stomach, colorectum and breast, were between 43 and 59% of general population rates. Smoking was virtually non-existent, which would largely explain the lower rate of lung cancer.

In Japanese Seventh-day Adventists, mortality rates for 1975–81 for all cancers combined were 30 per cent (p ≤ 0.05) and 78% (ns) of general population rates for men and women, respectively (Kuratsune et al, 1986). For both men and women, rates for stomach cancer were significantly lower than general population rates; these were 32 and 26% respectively.

Cancer incidence data for Californian Seventh-day Adventists for all sites combined for 1976–82 showed rates that were 73% (p ≤ 0.05) of the general population rate for men and 92% (ns) for women (Mills et al, 1994). For specific sites, rates for men were statistically significantly lower for cancers of the stomach (16% of the general population rate), oesophagus (no cases), colon (76%), rectum (61%), bronchus and lung (25%), bladder (59%), kidney (37%), and biliary passages and liver (24%); whereas the rate was statistically significantly higher for prostate cancer (126% of the general population rate). For women, rates were lower for cancers of the stomach (50%), colon (64%), rectum (71%), bronchus and lung (36%), breast (91%), bladder (59%) and kidney (38%); whereas the rate for cancer of the endometrium was significantly higher (191%).

In addition to comparisons made with external populations, studies within the Californian Seventh-day Adventist population have evaluated the association of specific cancers with various dietary and lifestyle factors. Seventh-day Adventists are, in some ways, a very useful population for internal comparison because of the wide range of dietary habits. For example, within this population there are a large number of both vegetarians and non-vegetarians, whereas random samples of most Western populations contain too few vegetarians for meaningful comparisons. Within the Californian Adventist population, meat consumption was shown not to be related to risk of prostate cancer (Mills et al, 1994); likewise, neither consumption of animal products (Mills et al, 1994), nor age at first exposure to a vegetarian lifestyle (Mills et al, 1989), was significantly associated with risk of breast cancer. On the other hand, higher consumption of soy-based products, which are a common component of vegetarian diets in this population, was associated with markedly lower risk of pancreatic cancer (Mills et al, 1994).

A study of approximately 6,000 British vegetarians, followed for twelve years, reported an all-cancer mortality rate that was 41% of the general British population rate (Thorogood et al, 1994). Further, the rate was 61% ($p \leq 0.05$) of that of a comparison group of meat-eating controls, even after adjustment for smoking, body mass index, and social class. The meat-eating controls included friends or relatives of the vegetarians; in both groups, smoking rates were low, obesity was uncommon, and a high proportion of participants were of high socioeconomic status. In a comparison limited to non-smokers, the all-cancer mortality rate for vegetarians was 56% ($p \leq 0.05$) of that of the meat-eating controls.

Another study, involving 11,000 British men and women recruited through health food shops, vegetarian societies, and magazines, found all-cancer mortality rates in men to be 50% of general population rates; in women, all-cancer rates were 76% of population rates (Key et al, 1996). For specific sites, cohort rates in men were statistically significantly lower than population rates for cancers of the stomach (37%), colon and rectum (64%) and lung (27%); in women, mortality rates were statistically significantly lower for cancer of the lung (37%). The lower risk of lung cancer in this cohort was attributed mainly to the lower proportion of smokers (19%). Within the cohort, persons described themselves as 'vegetarian' but were not at lower risk of cancer. In fact, in women, being vegetarian was associated with increased risk of dying from breast cancer (RR = 1.7, 1.01–2.7). The authors hypothesised that this finding might be due to chance, or due to differences in parity between vegetarian and non-vegetarian women.

An 11-year cohort study, of 1,904 self-identified German vegetarians, found lower all-cancer mortality rates, compared with the general German population; rates were 48%

($p \leq 0.05$) of expected rates for men, and 74% (ns) for women (Frentzel-Beyme and Claude, 1988; Frentzel-Beyme and Chang-Claude, 1994). The rate for lung cancer in men was only 8% ($p \leq 0.05$) of the expected rate. For other specific cancer sites, too few cancers occurred to assess differences from expected rates with any certainty, although rates for total intestinal system cancers were 57% (ns) of expected rates for men, and 49% ($p \leq 0.05$) for women. More than 20 years of a vegetarian diet was associated with approximately half the risk of all-cancer mortality, as compared with less than 20 years. The vegetarians making up this cohort were generally from higher socio-economic groups and almost all were non-smokers, which would explain the extremely low rate of lung cancer. They also tended to have lower body weight and be more physically active than non-vegetarians.

Plausible biological mechanisms have been identified for ways in which vegetarian diets may affect risk of cancers of the colon, breast, and prostate.

Colon. Several aspects of colonic metabolism have been shown to be different in vegetarians (Dwyer, 1988). Faecal excretion of neutral sterols (cholesterol and its metabolites) and bile acids is lowest in vegans, intermediate in lacto-vegetarians, and highest in non-vegetarians. Excessive excretion of cholesterol and its metabolites is common among persons with increased colon cancer risk. Vegans have also been shown to exhibit a low ratio of faecal secondary to primary bile acids; this ratio was shown to be higher in lacto-vegetarians and highest in non-vegetarians. Secondary bile acids are possible tumour promoters. Vegetarians have further been shown to excrete higher concentrations of faecapentaenes, strongly mutagenic compounds produced by anaerobic bacteria in the colonic lumen, although the implications of increased excretion are unclear (de Kok et al, 1992). Vegetarians have quiescent levels of colonic cell proliferation, whereas more rapid growth, and proliferative abnormalities are common among groups at high risk for colon cancer. (Lipkin and Newmarch; 1988)

Breast. In vegetarian women, sex hormone profiles may be altered. Vegetarian women have been shown to have lower levels of plasma oestrone and 17 β-oestradiol, lower levels of urinary oestrogens, higher levels of faecal oestrogens, lower levels of plasma prolactins, higher levels of plasma sex hormone-binding globulin, decreased metabolism to 16-hydroxylated oestrogen compounds, and more frequent menstrual irregularity (Barbosa et al, 1990; Pederden et al, 1991; and see Dwyer, 1988); each of these

may lead to decreased risk of breast cancer. One study that compared plasma hormones levels in vegetarians, non-vegetarians, and breast cancer patients found the lowest levels of androgens (androstenedione, testosterone, and free testosterone) in vegetarians and the highest levels in breast cancer patients (Adlercreutz et al, 1989).

Prostate. Hormone levels in male vegetarians have been shown to be different from those in non-vegetarians. It is suspected that exposure of prostate tissue, over time, to elevated levels of sex hormones may lead to hyperplasia and eventually carcinoma. Lower fat content of some vegetarian diets may decrease the enterohepatic circulation of steroid hormones, and a higher fibre intake may lead to binding and subsequent excretion of greater amounts of steroid hormones. Studies have found lower plasma levels of steroid hormones in middle-aged and older vegetarian men, but not younger vegetarian men, compared to non-vegetarian men of similar age (Pusateri et al, 1990). One study within a Seventh-day Adventist population found lower plasma prolactin levels and higher faecal oestrogen excretion in vegans, compared with lacto-ovo- and non-vegetarians (Pusateri et al, 1990). Another study reported higher levels of plasma sex-hormone-binding globulin and a lower free-androgen index (i.e. less testosterone available for androgenic action) in male vegetarians, compared to non-vegetarians (Belanger et al, 1989).

In conclusion, various studies have shown that groups following lacto-ovo, lacto-vegetarian, and vegan diets have decreased incidence of cancers in general, as well as of cancers at several specific sites. Plausible biological mechanisms have been identified by which vegetarian diets may specifically reduce the risk of cancers of the colon, breast, and prostate. Any effect of vegetarian diets is likely to be due not only to the exclusion of meat, (which has been judged by the panel to increase the risk probably of colorectal cancer and possibly of cancers of the pancreas, prostate, kidney and breast), but also due to the inclusion of a larger number and wider range of plant foods containing an extensive variety of potential cancer-preventive substances. Any beneficial effects of vegetarian diets may also be gained from semi-vegetarian diets containing small amounts of meat and other foods of animal origin. Extremely limited vegetarian diets, such as fruitarian regimes, and, more importantly, poverty diets, are probably not beneficial to overall health due to monotony and imbalance and an inadequate supply of some essential dietary constituents.

breast cancer. Although inconsistent, overall the evidence suggests that high meat intake possibly increases the risk of breast cancer.

Prostate (4.15). Three of four cohort studies and four of five case-control studies show an increased risk of prostate cancer with higher meat consumption. Two ecological studies found positive correlations with prostate cancer mortality.

These data show that diets containing substantial amounts of meat possibly increase the risk of prostate cancer.

Kidney (4.17). Cancer of the kidney has been associated with higher meat intake in one international correlational study, and in three out of eight case-control studies. The remaining case-control studies report mostly statistically non-significant increased risks associated with meat consumption, as does the one cohort study which has investigated meat consumption. An ecological study also shows similar findings. Diets containing substantial amounts of meat possibly increase the risk of cancer of the kidney.

6.6.2 POULTRY

A relatively small amount of evidence on poultry suggests no relationship with breast cancer. Although there are a number of studies of colorectal cancer, the results of these are inconsistent. Evidence for other sites is weaker.

Evidence of no relationship

CONVINCING	PROBABLE	POSSIBLE	INSUFFICIENT
		Breast	

Breast (4.11). A meta-analysis of five case-control and cohort studies concluded that the risk of breast cancer has no relationship with poultry intake and was confirmed by two later prospective studies. This evidence suggests that poultry possibly has no relationship to breast cancer.

6.6.3 FISH

What evidence there is suggests that fish may possibly be protective against cancers of the colon, rectum, breast and ovary. As with poultry, it is not clear whether any protective effect is from fish as such or because fish might substitute for other foods (such as red meat).

Evidence of decreased risk
Breast (4.11). Only a few epidemiological studies have investigated the association between fish (or fish oil) and breast cancer, but their findings show both no association and weak protective associations. Experimental models generally support a protective role of fish oil in mammary tumorigenesis. Evidence that fish decreases the risk of breast cancer is insufficient.

Ovary (4.12). Four case-control studies have each

reported decreased risk of ovarian cancer with higher intakes of fish, but not all were statistically significant. Evidence that fish decreases the risk of ovarian cancer is insufficient.

Evidence of no relationship

CONVINCING	PROBABLE	POSSIBLE	INSUFFICIENT
		Colon, rectum	

Colon, rectum (4.10). Three cohort studies and nine case-control studies have all found no relationship between the risk of colorectal cancer and fish consumption. Three further case-control studies found evidence of decreased risk. Fish possibly has no relationship with the risk of colorectal cancer.

6.6.4 EGGS

There is a moderate amount of information on eggs and cancer, perhaps in part prompted by the investigation of relationships between diets containing substantial numbers of eggs and cardiovascular disease.

Evidence of no relationship

CONVINCING	PROBABLE	POSSIBLE	INSUFFICIENT
		Kidney	
		Bladder	

Kidney (4.17). Three case-control studies report increased risk for high consumption of eggs and another three case-control studies find no association. Eggs possibly have no relationship with the risk of renal cancer.

Bladder (4.18). Three cohort studies show essentially no association between egg consumption and bladder cancer while four case-control studies show an association both with increased and decreased risk. Eggs possibly have no relationship with the risk of bladder cancer.

Evidence of increased risk

CONVINCING	PROBABLE	POSSIBLE	INSUFFICIENT
		Colon, rectum	Pancreas
			Ovary

Colon, rectum (4.10). One cohort and sixteen case-control studies have examined the risk of colorectal cancer and egg consumption. Nine of the case-control studies show that eggs are associated with increased risk, while the cohort study and seven of the case-control studies showed no association. The evidence is not consistent for women and men. Eggs possibly increase the risk of colorectal cancer.

Pancreas (4.7). Two case-control studies and one cohort study reported a statistically significant increase in risk of pancreatic cancer in association with high consumption of eggs. Four other case-control studies and one cohort study found no association with egg consumption. These data suggest that diets containing substantial numbers of eggs may increase the risk of pancreatic cancer, but are, as yet, insufficient.

Ovary (4.12). Egg consumption has been associated with increased risk of ovarian cancer in one case-control study and one cohort study. Two other case-control studies report no association. The evidence that eggs increase the risk of ovarian cancer, is, as yet, insufficient.

6.7 Milk and dairy products

Milk from domesticated animals is consumed both by infants and adults in many cultures. Dairy products such as butter and cheese make up variable amounts of most diets.

On a population basis, consumption of milk and dairy products varies between zero or practically zero, to 10 per cent or more of total energy.

Milk and dairy products can be good sources of protein, vitamin D and calcium. Milk and dairy products from domesticated animals typically have a high fat and saturated fat content. Some or most of this fat may be removed in processing.

The panel notes that diets high in milk and dairy products possibly increase the risk of prostate and kidney cancer.

MILK AND DAIRY PRODUCTS AND CANCER RISK

In the judgement of the panel, milk and dairy products modify the risk of cancer of various sites as shown below. Judgements are graded according to the strength of the evidence.

EVIDENCE	DECREASES RISK	NO RELATIONSHIP	INCREASES RISK
Convincing			
Probable			
Possible			*Milk and dairy products* Prostate Kidney
Insufficient			

For an explanation of the terms used in the matrix, see chapter 3.

INTRODUCTION

Milk from a variety of animals has been used by humans as post-weaning food throughout history. Cows' milk is most popular in European countries; goat, sheep and camels' milk are common in the Middle East. Water buffalo are used as a source of milk within Asia. As well as being consumed fresh, milk is also commonly processed into a wide variety of foods including cheese, fat products such as butter and ghee, and fermented products such as yoghurt.

This chapter is concerned with milk and its products when used as non-infant foods. It does not consider human or infant formula milks.

NUTRIENT CONTENT

Cows' milk contains just over 3 g protein, around 4 g fat and 4.6 g lactose per 100 g. Around two-thirds of the fatty acids in milk are saturated. Polyunsaturated fatty acids make up less than 4% of milk fat.

Milk, cheese and yoghurt are rich sources of calcium. High-fat dairy products, such as butter and cream, contain little calcium. Milk, cheese and yoghurt are also good sources of riboflavin and vitamin B$_{12}$. Full-fat dairy products such as whole milk and butter are important sources of retinol.

A wide variety of processes, including separation of fat and protein, drying and fermenting, are used to preserve and modify milk, and may alter its basic characteristics. Milk and its products are also amenable to the addition of other ingredients, such as sugar to make ice cream, and may be enriched, for example as in vitamin A- and D-enriched milks.

CONSUMPTION PATTERNS

As with meat, fish and poultry, milk and dairy products are not consumed universally and several population groups avoid or restrict some or all of these foods for religious, philosophical or health reasons.

On a worldwide basis, milk and dairy products contribute about 5% total energy. Consumption is higher among traditional pastoral peoples in Africa, India and China, and people living in or originating from northern Europe. In these populations, milk and dairy products typically contribute around 10% total energy and provide around 15–25% dietary protein and fat intake.

In the past 30 years, marked decreases in consumption have been seen in only a few countries in Central America, Africa and the Middle East. The increase in milk and dairy product consumption has been particularly marked in Japan and Korea.

INTERPRETATION OF THE DATA

Despite wide differences in composition between products, most studies do not distinguish among the various types of milks and dairy products. The majority of epidemiological studies provide data which are specific to cows' milk, and not to that from other species such as goats or sheep.

JUDGEMENTS OF OTHER REPORTS

There has been relatively little research interest in the role of milk and dairy products in cancer, and dairy products have generally been associated with cancer only indirectly.

The 1982 NAS report, *Diet, Nutrition and Cancer* (NAS 1982), made no recommendations on milk or dairy products. The later NAS report, *Diet and Health* (NAS 1989), recommended low- or non-fat dairy products on the basis of the relationship between fat, saturated fat and some cancers. The same report also recommended the consumption of low-

or non-fat dairy products in order to maintain adequate calcium intake.

SIGNIFICANCE FOR OTHER DISEASES

Like meat, poultry, fish and eggs, milk and dairy products are valuable foods in those parts of the world where diets are otherwise marginal or deficient in protein and, in particular, in vitamin D and calcium.

Recommendations concerned with reducing the risk of cardiovascular disease in industrialised countries commonly specify low-fat milk and dairy products. Of 100 expert reports published between 1961 and 1991, that were mostly concerned with diet and cardiovascular disease, or chronic diseases, in developed countries and regions, 52 recommended consumption of less full-fat milk, with five disagreeing, and 31 recommended consumption of less cheese or other dairy products, with none disagreeing (Cannon, 1992).

ASSESSMENT

Evidence of increased risk

CONVINCING	PROBABLE	POSSIBLE	INSUFFICIENT
		Prostate	
		Kidney	

Prostate (4.15). Six cohort studies and five case-control studies have examined prostate cancer risk and the intake of milk and dairy products. Two of the cohort studies reported increased risk with higher intakes of milk while the other four found no association. All five case-control studies reported increased risk with higher consumption of milk and dairy products. Milk consumption is correlated with increased risk of cancer mortality in four ecological studies. Milk and dairy products possibly increase the risk of prostate cancer.

Kidney (4.17). One cohort study showed increased risk for daily milk users compared to non-users. Five case-control studies report that high consumption of milk and dairy products increases the risk of kidney cancer. Two other case-control studies find no clear association.

Both animal protein and animal fat have been associated with cancer of the kidney in ecological studies and a small number of animal studies.

These data suggest that diets high in milk and dairy prod-

6.8 Herbs, spices and condiments

Herbs, spices and condiments are part of diets worldwide. Many of them have known pharmacological and therapeutic properties relevant to human health, and most contain potentially potent bioactive compounds.

The panel has reached the following conclusions. The evidence on the effect of any herb, spice or condiment, apart from salt (assessed in chapter 7.5), on the risk of any cancer is currently very limited.

HERBS, SPICES AND CONDIMENTS[a] AND CANCER RISK

In the judgement of the panel, various herbs, spices, and condiments modify the risk of cancer of the site shown below. Judgements are graded according to the strength of the evidence.

EVIDENCE	DECREASES RISK	NO RELATIONSHIP	INCREASES RISK
Convincing			
Probable			
Possible			
Insufficient	*Garlic* Stomach		

For an explanation of the terms used in the matrix, see chapter 3.
[a] Salt is not treated here as a condiment but is discussed in chapter 7.4.

INTRODUCTION

Practically all diets include seasonings, flavourings, savours and sauces made from herbs, spices and other edible substances that have aromatic, pungent or other flavours, aromas and colours.

NUTRIENT CONTENT

Various herbs contain high levels of carotenoids and vitamin C. Herbs and spices also contain very variable amounts of a number of bioactive compounds, whose relevance to human health is not yet fully understood. General knowledge of the therapeutic qualities of many herbs and some spices suggests that further human studies may yield evidence of a relationship with cancer. The fact that herbs, spices and condiments, by their nature, normally make up only a very small part by volume and weight of any diet is not in itself a reason to dismiss them as insignificant.

CONSUMPTION PATTERNS

Consumption of herbs, spices and condiments varies greatly in different parts of the world. Consumption probably varies inversely with consumption of salt, which here is not classified as a condiment. Many traditional cuisines are typified by the use of herbs, spices and condiments, singly or in combination, mixed into food in cooking or at the table.

Herbs, spices, and condiments may have specific functions. For example, they may make dull, distasteful or decaying food palatable. They may make otherwise ordinary food delicious. They may be preservatives. Many herbs and spices are believed to have medicinal or tonic value and, in some societies, are mixed into meals in various combinations and quantities to prevent or treat common diseases. Many pharmaceuticals are derived from herbs and other plants, and traditional therapies typically make use of herbs as medicines.

INTERPRETATION OF THE DATA

The limited data on herbs, spices and condiments come mainly from a few human case-control studies and some experimental animal studies. Human studies are limited by difficulties in quantifying intakes of individual items that are typically consumed in small quantities. Further, most case-control studies are conducted within populations that have a relatively similar use of herbs, spices and condiments; consumption generally varies much more between populations,

as a result of varying culinary traditions, than within them.

Some experimental studies have examined topical administration of spices or spice extracts; the relevance of such studies to spices as consumed is unknown. Even when a cancer-modifying effect of a particular herb or spice is observed, the complex chemical composition of these natural products makes it difficult to know which, if any, of their constituents are relevant.

PREVIOUS JUDGEMENTS

The 1982 and 1989 NAS reports, *Diet, Nutrition and Cancer and Diet and Health* (NAS, 1982, 1989), had little to say about herbs, spices or condiments, with the exception of salt.

SIGNIFICANCE FOR OTHER DISEASES

Similarly, expert reports on diet and public health that were largely concerned with diseases other than cancer have had little if anything to say about herbs, spices and condiments, except occasionally to point out that herbs are a good substitute for salt in cooking (WHO, 1990; Cannon, 1992).

RECOMMENDATION FOR FUTURE RESEARCH

Traditional beliefs that many herbs and spices have therapeutic value have not infrequently been verified by identification of pharmacological and other qualities.

The panel recommends that:

- More human studies of the relationship between herbs, spices and condiments and cancer risk be undertaken, preferably focusing on those culinary traditions where use is widespread, high and variable.

ASSESSMENT

This review first assesses herbs and spices in general and as mixtures, and then a number of individual herbs, spices and condiments where there is some evidence to suggest an effect on human cancer risk. It is conceivable that some herbs and spices may affect cancer risk as a whole. Further research may yield more definite results.

6.8.1 HERBS AND SPICES IN GENERAL

A few studies have provided results relevant to herbs and spices in general. These include epidemiological studies and in vitro and animal experiments. The epidemiological studies measured intake in a variety of ways: collectively as a combination of many individual herbs and spices, or as intake of a commonly consumed mixture.

A large case-control study of stomach cancer in Italy reported a protective association for greater intake of spices in general, including chilli, cloves, cinnamon, nutmeg, and peppers collectively. A case-control study of bladder cancer in the Mediterranean region of France reported an association with increased risk for spice consumption in general, including anise, curry powder, ginger, mustard, paprika, peppers, pimento, and harissa collectively; the association was adjusted for smoking and consumption of alcohol, vegetables, and coffee, as well as other factors. The authors suggested that spices may irritate and modify the bladder epithelium.

Garam masala is a food seasoning mixture commonly used in several oriental countries; it typically contains black pepper, clove, cinnamon, mace, nutmeg, bay leaf, cardamom, cumin and ginger. An animal study showed that garam masala reduced the incidence of tumours at multiple sites in the offspring of pregnant or lactating mice given dimethylbenz[a]anthracene (DMBA) (Rao and Hashim, 1995). Garam masala has further been shown to increase the activity of certain hepatic detoxification enzymes, including glutathione-S-transferase and cytochrome P450s (Singh and Rao, 1992).

Eugenol, a component of several herbs and spices, including nutmeg, mace, bay leaf, and clove, has been shown to increase the activity of detoxification enzymes in the liver in animals (Yokota et al, 1988).

Myristicin, a volatile aroma constituent of several herbs and spices, including parsley, dill, mace, and nutmeg, has been shown to inhibit chemically-induced tumours of the lung and forestomach in mice and to increase the activity of glutathione-S-transferase (Zheng et al, 1992).

6.8.2 Garlic

Evidence of decreased risk

Stomach (4.6). Nine of eleven epidemiological studies that examined the relationship between allium vegetables as a group and stomach cancer reported a protective association (see Table 6.3.3). One cohort and four case-control studies have examined the relationship between garlic intake and stomach cancer. The cohort study and two of the case-control studies found no association, while the other two studies found decreased risk with higher intakes. Garlic extracts have been found to kill *H.pylori* in vitro in concentrations that are achievable in vivo. The evidence that high garlic intakes decrease the risk of stomach cancer is, as yet, insufficient.

Garlic is often eaten cooked or raw as a vegetable or herb. It is also used as a condiment or nutritional supplement in var-

ious guises, including: dehydrated garlic powder, pickled garlic and garlic oil, juice and extract.

Many epidemiological studies have examined intake of allium vegetables – garlic, onions, scallions, leeks and chives. Twenty-seven of 35 case-control and cohort studies of cancer at any site have reported a protective association for allium vegetables.

Allium vegetables are unique in that they contain sulphur-containing allium compounds, which have been shown to inhibit experimentally-induced cancer of various sites in animal studies, to increase the activity of detoxification enzymes, and to exhibit antibacterial properties that may reduce the formation of nitrosamines in the stomach. These compounds are discussed in more detail in chapter 5.8.

It is conceivable that garlic protects against cancer of other sites, but further studies need to be carried out on garlic specifically.

6.8.3 TURMERIC

Turmeric is derived from the rhizome of a plant in the ginger family, native to south and south-east Asia. It is generally used as a spice in powdered form; is bright to dull yellow in colour and a major ingredient in curry powders. India is the largest producer. Turmeric is commonly used in Indian and Middle Eastern cooking and oleoresin, an extract of turmeric, is becoming more widely used in developed countries in food processing.

A review of turmeric as a potential protective against cancer was written by Krishnaswamy in 1993. In a controlled human study, turmeric was shown to decrease the urinary excretion of mutagens in human smokers; no change was apparent in non-smokers who took the same amount of turmeric (Polasa et al, 1992).

In animal experiments, turmeric has been shown to decrease tumour development and also to reduce the mutagenicity of the ubiquitous pollutant, benzo(a)pyrene in animals. Krishnaswamy (1993) showed that the active component of turmeric in this respect is curcumin. On the other hand, another study has shown no effect on the development of certain chemically-induced cancers in mice and rats.

In mice, turmeric has been shown to increase the activity of glutathione-S-transferase and to suppress chemically-induced aberrations in bone marrow cells; and in rats, to decrease levels of chemically-induced DNA adducts in the liver. These studies suggest several potential cancer-protective mechanisms.

In an attempt to extrapolate the doses of turmeric used in animal studies to humans, Krishnaswamy (1993) calculated that an intake of about 500 to 1,000 mg/day of turmeric in humans would correspond to the dose that has been found to decrease mutagenesis, carcinogenesis and DNA damage in animals. However, human consumption at this level would be considerably above that approved by FAO/WHO for daily intake of turmeric and curcumin as food additives.

In vitro, turmeric has been shown to inhibit growth of various tumour cells and to inhibit the effects of a variety of mutagens.

Curcumin, the principal active compound and the major yellow pigment in turmeric and curry, has been studied independently. In animal experiments, it has been shown to inhibit tumour promotion, ornithine decarboxylase activity, and inflammation in mouse skin and the development of certain tumours in mice.

In vitro, curcumin has been shown to be cytotoxic to various cancer cells and to thwart the effects of environmental mutagens.

Curcumin is a phenolic compound and is a strong antioxidant, a free radical scavenger, and a potent inhibitor of nitrosation. Additionally, it may inhibit reverse transcriptase activity or inhibit carcinogenesis via its potent non-steroidal anti-inflammatory properties.

Turmeric also contains a bioactive peptide, turmerin, which makes up 0.1% of its dry weight. Turmerin has been shown, in vitro, to be a strong antioxidant, a DNA-protectant against oxidative injury, an anti-mutagen, and an inhibitor of pro-oxidant-induced arachadonic acid release. It has also been shown to decrease arachadonic release, which may be an important event in membrane-mediated chromosomal damage.

The evidence on turmeric consistently suggests a protective effect, and it is conceivable that it protects against cancer as a whole, as yet, no judgement can be made for any site.

6.8.4 SAFFRON

Saffron is a strongly aromatic spice that imparts a bright yellow colour to foods; it is also used specifically as a food colour. It is used to treat various diseases in traditional Azerbaijani and Indian medicine.

The biological effects of saffron have been reviewed in a 1993 paper by Abdullaev. In studies of mice, saffron extract has been shown to increase the life span of tumour-bearing mice and to decrease a variety of induced tumours.

In vitro, saffron extract has been shown to be cytotoxic to various types of tumour cells and to decrease colony formation of tumour cells, but not normal cells; it has thus been suggested that saffron may contain some growth inhibiting substance(s) that are specific for tumour cells. Saffron has also been shown to inhibit DNA synthesis in leukaemia cells and various other malignant cells in vitro; this effect has likewise been found to be specific for cancer cells.

Saffron has been shown to elevate the level of glutathione-S-transferase in tumours cells when incubated in vitro.

The evidence on saffron so far suggests a protective effect for cancers of some sites but no judgement can be made.

6.8.5 CUMIN

Cumin is a strongly aromatic spice; the seeds are used whole or ground in cooking in Latin America, North Africa, the Middle East, Asia and Spain. Yellow-brown cumin seeds, sometimes referred to as white cumin, are used in Indian cuisine. Black cumin grows in Iran and Kashmir and is also used in Indian cooking.

A case-control study of bladder cancer in Israel observed decreased risk with greater intake of cumin. (Bitterman et al, 1991).

In animal studies, cumin seeds have been found to decrease chemically-induced tumours of the stomach in mice and hepatomas in rats.

An in vitro study showed cumin oil to suppress the formation of DNA adducts with aflatoxin B_1; this effect appeared to be due to inhibition of microsomal enzymes that activate aflatoxin B_1.

In support of a cancer-protective pathway for cumin, cumin seeds have been shown in mice to increase the activity of glutathione-S-transferase and to suppress chemically-induced aberrations in bone marrow cells.

The evidence on cumin so far suggests a protective effect for various sites but as yet no judgement can be made.

6.8.6 GINGER

Fresh ginger is a knobby brown tropical root native to south east Asia; it has a papery skin and yellow interior. Fresh ginger is typically used in grated form; powdered ginger is also used, primarily in baking. Pickled ginger is a Japanese condiment; crystallised ginger is a common ingredient in Chinese confections.

One animal experiment showed ginger extract to have no effect on the lifespan of mice transplanted with Ehrlich ascites tumours.

Ginger oil was shown to elevate glutathione-S-transferase and aryl hydrocarbon hydroxylase activities in an animal experiment, thus suggesting potential cancer-protective mechanisms. Further, an in vitro study showed ginger oil to suppress the formation of DNA adducts with aflatoxin B_1; this effect appeared to be due to inhibition of microsomal enzymes that activate aflatoxin B_1.

Ginger also contains gingerol, shogaol, and zingerone, each of which are antioxidants.

The evidence on ginger so far suggests a protective effect, but as yet no judgement can be made for any site.

6.8.7 PEPPER

Pepper comes from the berry of the tropical vine *Piper nigrum*; these peppercorns may be black, green, or white depending on when picked and how they are processed. Green peppercorns are unripe and have a fresh non-hot taste. Black peppercorns are unripe berries that turn black when dried; they become quite pungent when ground, as they are when used as a common condiment in some industrialised regions, such as the UK and USA. White peppercorns are ripened berries, whose seed is used as white pepper, and whose taste is less aromatic than black.

While a case-control study of bladder cancer observed a

protective association for greater intake of pepper (Bitterman et al, 1991), studies of oral and oesophageal cancer showed no significant association. (Cheng et al, 1992.) Animal studies have shown that black pepper induces detoxification enzymes, including glutathione-S-transferase; black pepper was also associated with decreased malondialdehyde, which signifies decreased lipid peroxidation. An in vitro study has shown oil from black pepper to suppress the formation of DNA adducts with aflatoxin B_1; this effect appeared to be due to an inhibition of microsomal enzymes that activate aflatoxin B_1. These findings suggest three possible cancer-protective mechanisms for black pepper.

Evidence on pepper and human cancer risk is interesting but fragmentary and conflicting. No judgement is as yet possible for any site.

6.8.8 CHILLI PEPPER

Chillies are the pungent fruit pods of the annual pepper plant, native to the Americas; their flavour varies in intensity from mild to very hot. Chillies are used fresh and also as a powder made from dried ripe chillies.

Intake of red chilli powder was shown to be statistically significantly associated with increased risk of oral, pharyngeal, oesophageal, and laryngeal cancers in a case-control study in India (Notani and Jayant, 1987). A case-control study of oesophageal cancer in Hong Kong, showed no significant association with the use of chilli or pepper.

A large case-control study of stomach cancer in Italy found higher consumption of chillies to be associated with decreased risk of stomach cancer, whereas another in Mexico found increased risk with high consumption. A case-control study of lung cancer in Hong Kong showed no significant association for fresh chillies and chilli sauces.

Animal studies have shown ingestion of red chilli powder to both increase, and have no effect on, chemically-induced colon cancer.

Dried chillies, but not fresh chillies or chilli sauces, have been shown to contain volatile nitrosamines, which may be carcinogenic (Tricker et al, 1988).

Capsaicin is the pungent component of chilli peppers; it has been shown to be mutagenic and carcinogenic, and has to have a tumour-promoting effect in some animal experiments (Toth et al, 1984; Agrawal et al, 1986). On the other hand, however, other studies have suggested possible pathways by which capsaicin might actually protect against gastric cancer.

Evidence on chillies as such, and as sauces and powder, and human cancer risk suggests increased risk with stomach cancer, but no judgement is possible. Evidence on other sites is fragmentary and conflicting and no judgement is possible.

6.8.9 HARISSA

The fiery condiment harissa, made up of red pepper, olive oil, garlic, caraway and salt, is consumed in north Africa.

A case-control study of nasopharyngeal cancer in Tunisia observed increased risk with higher childhood consumption of harissa; increased risk was also observed for a stewing mixture composed of red and black pepper, garlic oil, caraway, and coriander. Direct weaning from breast milk to the typical adult diet including harissa was an additional risk factor, (Jeannel et al, 1990). These data are not yet the basis for any judgement.

6.8.10 OTHER HERBS, SPICES, AND CONDIMENTS

Isolated animal and in vitro studies of solanum leaves, afternanthera leaves, drumstick leaves, poppy seeds, kandathpili, basil, asafoetida, neem flowers, manathakkali leaves, ponnakanni leaves, wasabi, rosemary, sesame, *Nigella sativa* seeds, shepherd's purse, nutmeg, cardamom seed, celery seed, coriander seed, tarragon, black and white mustard seed, thyme, and cinnamon are consistent with these herbs and spices being protective or at least harmless (Kuroda et al, 1983; Aruna and Sivaramakrishnan, 1990; Unnikrishnan and Kuttan, 1990; Tanida et al, 1991; Salomi et al, 1991; Aruna and Sivaramakrishnan, 1992; Hirose et al, 1992; Dragsted et al, 1993; Bianchi-Santamaria et al, 1993; Banerjee et al, 1994; Tawfiq et al, 1994; Huang et al, 1994; Badria, 1994; Hashim et al, 1994). No judgement is, as yet, possible for any of these.

6.9 Coffee, tea, and other drinks

The drinks assessed here are coffee, tea, maté and very hot drinks. Coffee and tea are drinks common throughout the world. Maté is an infusion commonly drunk in some regions of Latin America.

The panel has reached the following conclusions. Most evidence suggests that regular consumption of coffee and/or tea has no significant relationship with the risk of cancer of any site. The panel notes that regular drinking of green tea possibly reduces the risk of stomach cancer; and that the regular drinking of maté possibly increases the risk of mouth and pharyngeal and oesophageal cancers, perhaps because it is usually drunk very hot.

COFFEE, TEA AND OTHER DRINKS AND CANCER RISK

In the judgement of the panel, coffee, tea and other drinks modify the risk of cancer of various sites as listed below, or else have no relationship with them. Judgements are graded according to the strength of the evidence.

EVIDENCE	DECREASES RISK	NO RELATIONSHIP	INCREASES RISK
Convincing		*Coffee* Breast	
Probable		Coffee Stomach Pancreas Kidney *Tea* Stomach (black) Kidney (black) Bladder (black)	
Possible	*Tea* Stomach (green)	*Coffee* Prostate *Tea* *Pancreas* Breast (black) Prostate	*Coffee* Bladder *Maté*[a] Mouth and pharynx Oesophagus *Very hot drinks* Oesophagus
Insufficient	*Coffee* Colon, rectum		*Tea* Oesophagus

For an explanation of the terms used in the matrix, see chapter 3

[a] Perhaps because maté is usually drunk very hot.

INTRODUCTION

Coffee is made from coffee beans, the dried seeds of the berries of coffee trees. Coffee beans are grown primarily in Latin America, Africa and Indonesia. Tea is made from the leaves of tea plants which are grown in the largest quantities in Asia. Both black and green tea are made from the same plants. Maté is a type of herbal tea. Other teas made from various herbs or fruits are not considered here. Soft drinks are carbonated beverages containing sugar or sweeteners and flavourings. Some soft drinks, such as colas, contain caffeine.

NUTRIENT CONTENT

Coffee and tea contain mostly trivial amounts of a few vitamins and minerals as well as other substances, including caffeine, that are biologically active. Soft drinks are devoid of nutrients except for sugar; some soft drinks are caffeinated.

CONSUMPTION PATTERNS

Tea is the most commonly consumed drink in the world, after water. The areas where the most tea is consumed include India, China, Russia, Turkey, the UK, north Africa, Japan, the USA and Indonesia. The UK has the highest per capita tea consumption of any country. Worldwide, black tea is the type most commonly consumed; green tea is more commonly drunk in Japan, China and Taiwan. Maté, consumed mostly in Latin America, is often drunk very hot.

Green coffee beans are roasted by one of several methods, then ground. The coffee drink is then produced by boiling, brewing or brewing under pressure (espresso) with water. For boiled coffee, the grounds are often consumed in addition to the liquid. Coffee is consumed at different strengths and is often drunk with added sugar, milk or cream. Coffee beans can be decaffeinated by various processes.

To produce black tea, the leaves are first withered at a warm temperature, then rolled and allowed to ferment, and finally roasted at a high temperature. Green tea is produced by the brief exposure of fresh tea leaves to a very high temperature, only long enough to deactivate enzymatic fermentation. Oolong tea is a semi-fermented tea. All teas are then prepared by infusion with hot water. Tea is often drunk with combinations of sugar, milk, honey, lemon or spices.

INTERPRETATION OF THE DATA

In interpreting the results of epidemiological studies of coffee, tea, maté and soft drinks, confounding by other aspects of lifestyle must be considered. How much is consumed may vary according to other habits, such as smoking or alcohol consumption. Such potential confounders vary according to the cancer site and population under study.

Different kinds of coffee beans, teas and soft drinks are consumed in different cultures. The ways in which tea and coffee are prepared and drunk vary similarly: for example,

for coffee, the degree of roasting, the methods of brewing, and the strength at consumption differ, as do the substances added. Associations seen in one population, but not another, may reflect some aspect of the particular type of coffee, tea or soft drink consumed in that population rather than the beverages themselves.

JUDGEMENTS OF PREVIOUS REPORTS

The National Academy of Sciences report, *Diet, Nutrition and Cancer* (NAS, 1982), did not review evidence on tea or other drinks, and no recommendations were made on coffee or tea. The later NAS report, *Diet and Health* (NAS, 1989), noted that any evidence on coffee and cancer was weak and inconsistent and that tea drinking was not associated with the increase of any chronic disease in humans.

SIGNIFICANCE FOR OTHER DISEASES

The World Health Organization report, *Diet, Nutrition and Chronic Diseases* (WHO, 1990), and a review of 100 expert reports mostly concerned with diet and chronic diseases in developed countries and regions (Cannon, 1992), did not mention coffee or tea drinking, except to record that regular coffee drinking is associated with raised blood LDL (low-density lipoprotein) cholesterol and thus increased risk of heart disease.

ASSESSMENT

6.9.1 COFFEE

Most evidence on coffee suggests that coffee drinking has no relationship with cancer risk.

Evidence of decreased risk
Colon,rectum (4.10). Two cohort and fifteen case-control studies have examined the relationship between coffee and colorectal cancer. Ten studies showed decreased risk for higher consumption, three increased risk and four no association.

Differences appear to relate to the amount of coffee consumed, with a protective effect being seen only at the highest levels, and also to the method of preparation: seven out of the ten studies which showed a protective effect were conducted in Europe where the method of brewing is different from that in other parts of the world. The evidence is, however, as yet, insufficient.

Evidence for no relationship

CONVINCING	PROBABLE	POSSIBLE	INSUFFICIENT
Breast	Stomach	Prostate	
	Pancreas		
	Kidney		

Breast (4.11). An early report that caffeine could be associated with symptoms of benign breast disease triggered a number of case-control studies on caffeine as a risk factor for breast cancer.

Six cohort and 19 case-control studies have examined the relationship between coffee intake and breast cancer. No statistically significant associations were found except in one cohort and two case-control studies. An international ecological study found no association with breast cancer mortality. Such animal studies as exist support the judgement that coffee consumption does not affect breast cancer risk. The panel judges that the evidence that there is no relationship between coffee drinking and breast cancer is convincing.

Stomach (4.6). None of the two cohort and eight case-control studies that examined coffee intake and the risk of stomach cancer reported a statistically significant association. Coffee consumption probably has no relationship with the risk of stomach cancer.

Pancreas (4.7). Although early evidence suggested a possible link between coffee intake and pancreatic cancer and stimulated much investigation, a review in 1990, and a further review by an IARC working group in 1991, did not confirm this association.

Nine of ten cohort studies and 20 of 26 case-control studies reported no association with coffee consumption. For decaffeinated coffee, none of eight case-control studies found a statistically significant association. Two ecological studies and one time-trend study, however, all found a positive correlation between mortality from pancreatic cancer and coffee consumption.

It is likely that smoking and other dietary variables may be confounding factors. The panel judges that there is probably no relationship between coffee drinking and pancreatic cancer.

Kidney (4.17). One cohort study reported a decreased risk of renal cancer with increased coffee consumption, but none of eight case-control studies found any significant association. An ecological study found a weak positive correlation with renal cancer mortality. The panel judges that there is probably no relationship between coffee drinking and renal cancer.

Prostate (4.15). Two of three cohort studies and three case-control studies, all found no association between coffee consumption and the risk of prostate cancer. The other cohort study found a weak decrease in risk. Coffee consumption possibly has no relationship with the risk of prostate cancer.

Evidence of increased risk

CONVINCING	PROBABLE	POSSIBLE	INSUFFICIENT
		Bladder	

Bladder (4.18). Since a 1971 finding of an association between coffee drinking and increased risk of bladder cancer, many case-control studies and a few prospective studies have examined this relationship. A review by an IARC working group in 1991 concluded that the evidence was consistent with a weak positive association, but that bias and confounding as explanations for the association could not be completely ruled out. A subsequent review concluded that the association was not clinically important.

Overall, the evidence shows a very slight increase in risk with higher intakes and variation across studies. The panel decided these findings may be explained by residual confounding, most probably by cigarette smoking, or may represent different proportions of susceptible individuals in different populations. Uncertainty about the relationship exists even though there is a large amount of data, but there may be a slight excess of risk at high intakes.

High consumption of coffee possibly increases the risk of bladder cancer at high levels of intake, but is probably not associated with risk at consumption below five cups/day.

A prospective study in Norway reported a somewhat decreased risk of cancer of all sites combined with increased coffee intake; the relative risk was 0.8 (p = 0.05) for seven or more, versus two or fewer cups per day (men only; adjusted for smoking; cancers occurring in first four years of follow-up excluded) (Jacobsen et al, 1986).

In a 1975 ecological study by Armstrong and Doll, in which incidence rates for 27 cancers in 23 countries were compared, correlations were seen between coffee consumption and increased risk of cancers of the colon, rectum, breast, ovary, endometrium, prostate, kidney, and also testis and nervous system, with simple correlation coefficients ranging from 0.40 to 0.62. The correlation for bladder cancer was less impressive (r = 0.17 to 0.39).

In vitro studies have shown coffee, in the brewed, instant, and decaffeinated forms, to be mutagenic to bacteria (see NAS, 1982).

Green coffee beans have been shown to increase the activity of glutathione-S-transferase six- to seven-fold in animals; glutathione-S-transferase is an enzyme that helps to detoxify certain potential carcinogens. Considerably less induction of activity has been found for roasted coffee beans, commercial instant coffee, or instant decaffeinated coffee, therefore some destruction of the inducing compounds probably occurs during processing and, thus, the practical implications of these findings remain uncertain. (See NAS, 1982.)

6.9.2 TEA

The following review includes studies that have examined tea generally or black or green tea specifically. Few, if any, studies have looked at the relationship between herbal or fruit teas and cancer.

Evidence of decreased risk

CONVINCING	PROBABLE	POSSIBLE	INSUFFICIENT
		Stomach (green tea)	

Stomach (4.6). Four of five case-control studies in Japan and China found a decreased risk of stomach cancer with higher intakes of green tea. A clear dose–response relationship existed in one study. This evidence is supported by data from animal studies. Tea consumption possibly decreases the risk of stomach cancer.

Evidence of no relationship

CONVINCING	PROBABLE	POSSIBLE	INSUFFICIENT
	Stomach (black tea)	Pancreas	
	Kidney (black tea)	Breast (black tea)	
	Bladder	Prostate	

Stomach (4.6). Three cohort and 12 case-control studies have examined black tea consumption and the risk of stomach cancer. Two of the three cohort studies and nine of the 12 case-control studies found no statistically significant association, after controlling for potential confounding factors such as social class or education.

Kidney (4.17). In one cohort and seven case-control studies of the ten epidemiological studies that have examined black tea consumption, no significant association was observed; the two other case-control studies found both increased and decreased risk with greater tea intake in women, but not men. There is probably no relationship between tea consumption and renal cancer.

Bladder (4.18). In 1991, an IARC working group concluded that the data did not support any increased or decreased risk with consumption of black tea.

Five cohort and 18 case-control studies have examined consumption of black tea or tea as whole and the risk of bladder cancer. No association was reported in any of the cohort studies or 17 of the case-control studies. One case-control study showed an increase in risk with higher intakes for men, but not for women. An ecological study reported no association between bladder cancer mortality and tea consumption. There is probably no relationship between tea consumption and bladder cancer.

Pancreas (4.7). Four of six cohort studies and eight of eleven case-control studies have shown no relationship between tea consumption and the risk of pancreatic cancer. The remaining studies have shown mixed results, with most showing some degree of decreased risk, although these findings may be the result of residual confounding by smoking or vegetable and fruit consumption.

Breast (4.11). In 1991, an IARC Working Party concluded that no epidemiological study showed an association between tea consumption and the risk of breast cancer.

Of four subsequent cohort studies, three also showed no association, while one reported a moderate protective association. Experimental studies have shown polyphenols to be anticarcinogenic. Tea consumption possibly has no relationship with the risk of breast cancer.

Prostate (4.15). Two of three cohort studies that have examined the relationship between tea consumption and prostate cancer reported no association, while the third found a moderate protective association. Tea consumption possibly has no relationship with the risk of prostate cancer.

BOX 6.9.1 CAFFEINE, TANNIN, AND OTHER CONSTITUENTS OF COFFEE AND TEA

Coffee, tea, and some soft drinks contain various bioactive compounds, including methylxanthines, such as caffeine, theophylline, and theobromine. Caffeine is found at a level of about 100–150 g/150 ml in brewed coffee, 30–70 g/150 ml in brewed tea, and 30–60 g/360 ml in caffeine-containing soft drinks.

Caffeine has been shown in vitro to be mutagenic to bacteria, although the mutagenic activity observed for coffee is not fully attributable to its caffeine content, as decaffeinated coffee has also been shown to be mutagenic. Theophylline and theobromine have also been shown to be mutagenic to bacteria. One animal study showed no effect of caffeine on incidence of any type of tumours. In another animal study, caffeine was found to have no effect on promotion of bladder carcinogenesis

(Nakanishi et al, 1987). (See NAS, 1982 for references to studies not individually cited here.)

Caffeine is thought to inhibit repair of DNA damage caused by chemical mutagens (see NAS, 1982). A second mechanism by which caffeine may influence the cancer process involves a liver enzyme which, as well as helping to metabolise caffeine, also catalyses the bioactivation of aromatic amines, which are thought to be carcinogens (Butler et al, 1989).

Another mechanism which has been put forward to account for any possible protective effect which caffeine may have against colon cancer involves caffeine's ability to increase serum cholesterol levels by decreasing excretion of cholesterol. Low serum cholesterol levels have been associated with increased colon cancer risk in

some populations, although these it is not entirely clear whether these are an effect of the early undetected disease rather than a cause.

Two specific compounds with potent glutathione-S-transferase-inducing activity have been isolated from green coffee beans; these are kahweol palmitate and cafestol palmitate (see NAS, 1982).

Tannins are compounds that are widely distributed in plant foods and are naturally present in small amounts in coffee and tea. Animal studies of subcutaneously- and orally-administered tannins and different tumour sites have produced inconsistent results (see Heilbrun et al, 1987).

Coffee and tea contain flavonoids and phenols, also present in vegetables and fruit, which may have anticarcinogenic properties: see chapter 5.8.

Evidence of increased risk

Oesophagus (4.4). Four of five case-control studies reported an increased risk of oesophageal cancer was associated with intakes of very hot tea. No association was seen with frequency of intake. The fifth case-control study showed no association.

The evidence on increased risk with tea consumption appears to describe an association with temperature, rather than with tea drinking per se. (See discussion on maté and very hot drinks below.)

Results from a coordinated series of case-control studies in Italy showed odds ratios ranging from 0.4 to 1.4 for 16 different cancer sites for intake of one or more cups of tea per day, as compared with non-drinkers; these associations were adjusted for age, sex, area of residence, education, smoking, and coffee consumption (La Vecchia et al, 1992). For only three sites were the associations statistically significant; these were cancers of the larynx (decreased risk), rectum (increased risk), and endometrium (increased risk).

Many animal studies have shown black, green, or oolong, tea to inhibit experimentally-induced tumours at various sites (see Chen, 1992). Using a variety of in vitro mutagenicity tests, a number of studies have shown green or black tea to inhibit mutagenicity (see Chen, 1992).

6.9.3 MATÉ

Evidence that maté drinking increases risk of upper aerodigestive cancers may relate to maté as such, or alternatively to the fact that this drink is habitually drunk while very hot, which may cause thermal damage to epithelial tissue, thus predisposing to or promoting carcinogenesis.

Evidence for increased risk

CONVINCING	PROBABLE	POSSIBLE	INSUFFICIENT
		Mouth, pharynx Oesophagus	

Mouth, pharynx (4.1). Maté appears to be an independent risk factor for oral cancers, with regular drinkers having an approximately doubled risk. Because of its high prevalence in South America, mate drinking may account for up to 20% of cases of cancers of the mouth and pharynx in that part of the world. Regular maté drinking possibly increases risk of mouth and pharynx cancer.

Oesophagus (4.4). Consumption of maté appears to be an independent risk factor for cancer of the oesophagus, and a dose–response relationship has been shown in several studies. Risk increases significantly with duration of use. The temperature at which the maté is consumed appears to be important. Regular maté drinking possibly increases risk of oesophageal cancer, the effect being related to the temperature at which it is consumed.

6.9.4 VERY HOT DRINKS

As stated above, habitual consumption of very hot drinks may damage the lining of the upper aerodigestive tract: hence the hypothesis that such a habit may increase risk of upper aerodigestive cancers.

Evidence of increased risk

CONVINCING	PROBABLE	POSSIBLE	INSUFFICIENT
		Oesophagus	

Oesophagus (4.4). Nine case-control studies all reported increased risk of oesophageal cancer with beverages consumed at very high temperatures. Experimental studies show high temperatures to be associated with the development of precancerous lesions. Habitual consumption of very hot drinks possibly increases risk of oesophageal cancer.

CHAPTER SEVEN

Food processing

The processing of foods and drinks, including preservation and preparation, is a defining characteristic of civilisation. Conversion of primary products into palatable foods available all the year round is essential to sustain life out of the wild, and the preservation and cooking of food are both tasks and pleasures of life and an intrinsic part of all cultures.

In settled societies, agricultural or industrial, almost all food is eaten processed in some form. Gatherer-hunters and pastoralists, who eat more of their food raw or relatively unprocessed, nevertheless usually cook meat and fish. Methods of food processing, including methods of agriculture and manufacture, storage and preservation, and preparation, may affect cancer risk, directly, indirectly, or adventitiously.

This chapter assesses the evidence on aspects of food processing that may modify cancer risk. The sequence of the chapter follows the chain of production, manufacturing, storage, preservation and preparation, starting with a section assessing the relationship between agricultural and industrial chemical residues and cancer risk. (Manufacturing processes are assessed in other chapters, for example, grains and cereals are milled and refined to various degrees before consumption; sugar and oils are refined or processed into fats. The effects of refining on carbohydrates and fats is assessed in chapters 5.2, 6.2 and 5.3.)

The second section is on food additives. Processed foods and drinks usually contain additives, a number of which have been identified as carcinogens in experimental studies. For this and other reasons of potential toxicity they are subject to regulation.

The next three sections assess methods of food storage and preservation. Cereals, vegetables, fruits, pulses and other foods are stored to ensure continuity of supply throughout the year; preservation is often essential to storage. Traditional methods of preservation such as salting, smoking, curing and pickling are still used in many parts of the world to preserve common foods. In the developed world, where refrigeration is commonly used, traditionally preserved foods are eaten for their flavour.

The final section concerns cooking. Meat and fish may be cooked using water, fat, less or more fierce heat or direct flame, and in other ways.

Other key issues in this chapter include judging the role of residues and additives and the possible cancer risk posed by polycyclic aromatic hydrocarbons and heterocyclic amines formed by high-temperature cooking.

7.1 Contaminants

Many foods and drinks (including water) contain trace residues of chemicals used in agriculture, food manufacture, and other industry.

Soil has always been fertilised to increase crop yield. Synthetic fertiliser is an indispensable part of modern intensive agriculture. Consequently, the nitrate content of soil and water, and thus of foods and drinking water, has steadily increased.

Pesticides and herbicides are used extensively as a means to increase crop yields. Modern intensive farming methods depend upon the regular use of such chemicals, some of which are also used as a means to prevent communicable human diseases.

Drugs are used on farm animals raised by intensive methods, to treat and prevent disease. and to promote growth. Residues of these and other drugs may be present in food as eaten.

Chemicals used as food processing aids or in packaging may migrate into these foods as sold and eaten. Water supplies may contain fluoride or chlorine added for reasons of public health, and may be contaminated, both with organic by-products of chlorine and with residues of other chemicals.

Residues of some industrial chemicals accumulate in fatty foods at different stages in the food chain, and also accumulate in human fatty tissue. Some of these show hormonal (oestrogenic) activity.

A large number of these chemicals are known to be toxic, and some have been determined to be mutagenic or carcinogenic in experimental conditions. Consequently, the use of such chemicals is subject to evaluation and regulation by national and international bodies. Their presence as food

CONTAMINANTS AND CANCER

In the judgement of the panel, contaminants in food modify the risk of cancer of the site shown below. Pollution caused by misuse, spillage or industrial accidents is not included here. Judgements are graded according to the strength of the evidence.

	DECREASES RISK	NO RELATIONSHIP	INCREASES RISK
CONVINCING			
PROBABLE			
POSSIBLE			
INSUFFICIENT			*DDT residues* Breast *Chlorinated hydrocarbons* Bladder

For an explanation of the terms used in the matrix, see chapter 3.

contaminants is understandably a cause for public concern.
This section assesses the evidence that any such contaminants may
significantly modify human cancer risk, using the criteria for weighing the
evidence specified in chapter 3, and used in chapters 4 to 7. There is no
attempt at a comprehensive survey.

The panel has reached the following conclusions. There is no convincing
evidence that any food contaminant modifies the risk of any cancer, nor is
there evidence of any probable causal relationship. Indeed, there is
currently little epidemiological evidence that chemical contamination of
food and drink, resulting from properly regulated use, significantly affects
cancer risk. Evidence on other contaminants associated with diet is, at
most, insufficient.

The panel emphasises that its judgements do not apply to high-level
contamination of foods and drinks or to environmental pollution caused by
overuse or abuse, spillage, or industrial accidents; these are beyond the
scope of this report.

INTRODUCTION

Agricultural practices include the use of a broad spectrum of
chemicals, as fertilisers, pesticides, herbicides and veterinary
pharmaceuticals. Synthetic fertiliser is used in steadily
increasing amounts on farms all over the world, and is an
indispensable part of modern intensive agriculture. As a consequence, the nitrate content of soil and water, and thus of
vegetables and other foods and of drinking water, has
steadily increased. Pesticides and herbicides are used extensively as a means of increasing crop yields.

In addition, many veterinary pharmaceuticals are used on
farm animals raised by intensive methods, to treat disease,
to prevent disease, and to promote growth and output.
Residues of these veterinary and other drugs used on farms
can persist into the human food chain.

Industrial development involves massive use and disposal
of chemicals, and potential deposition of heavy metals;
many foods and drinks contain residues of chemicals that are
the by-products or waste products of industrial processes.
Some of these, notably a number of persistent chlorinated
biphenyls, the dioxins and related compounds, are known to

be highly toxic, and have been found to be carcinogenic in
animals. Foods are also liable to be contaminated with
traces of packaging materials and heavy metals. Water supplies may contain fluoride, added to protect against tooth
decay (or naturally occurring), and/or chlorine, added to
protect against microbial contamination; both of these
chemicals can be toxic at high doses. Additionally, sterilisa-
tion of drinking water with chlorine and other disinfectants
gives rise to other toxic contaminants such as chlorinated
and brominated organic compounds.

Concern centres on residues that can accumulate in fatty
foods and drinks such as meat, animal fat, milk and other
dairy products, and which may be present in relatively high
concentrations in fish and shellfish as a result of disposal in
rivers and at sea. Some residues also show hormonal
(oestrogenic) activity and may influence the risk of cancer in
hormonally-responsive tissues, such as the breast, endometrium, ovary and prostate. A number of polychlorinated
biphenyls (PCBs), polybrominated biphenyls (PBBs), and
polychlorinated dibenzodioxins (PCDDs) are of special concern due to their extreme stability against environmental
and biological degradation, and therefore their persistence,

accumulation, and toxicity. These contaminants accumulate in human fat tissue and in human milk.

There are currently very few epidemiological studies of the relationship between such contaminants actually present in foods and the risk of any cancer. However, because some contaminants have been shown, in experimental models, to be toxic, many of these substances are now subject to regulation. National and international regulatory bodies carry out toxicological assessments to determine safe levels of use, and to establish maximum levels of contaminants in food products or maximum allowable daily intakes.

In reviewing the literature in chapter 4, the panel applied the criteria explained in chapter 3, and has generally concluded that, in the absence of substantial epidemiological evidence, no judgement is possible on industrial and agricultural chemical contaminants in food products and the risk of cancer. Because of the established toxicity of a number of contaminants, and because epidemiological data on occupational exposure exist, some concerns remain (see Box 7.1.1)

There are currently very few epidemiological studies on the cancer risk associated with residues of agricultural chemicals in foods and drinks at levels consistent with use at or below regulated levels. There is a similar paucity of epidemiological evidence on anabolic hormone residues and antibacterials. Some epidemiological data are, however, available on DTT.

Epidemiological evidence relating to dietary residues of packaging materials, industrial chemicals, heavy metals, or waterborne residues is also essentially non-existent.

For information on the scale of use, residue content, toxicology and regulation of other potential contaminants, readers are referred to the IARC Monographs on the Evaluation of Carcinogenic Risks to Humans, particularly volume 52 (chlorinated drinking water), volume 53 (insecticides), volume 56 (aflatoxins and other mycotoxins), volume 69 (PCDDs, PCDFs)(IARC, 1991a, 1991b, 1993,1997).

The only contaminant on which the panel made a judgement is DDT, and the following sections provide informatiopn on its scale of use and residue content. Information about other contaminants is given in the assessment section.

SCALE OF USE

The organochlorine pesticide DDT (dichlorodiphenyltrichloroethane) was widely used between 1940 and 1960 as an insecticide for agricultural purposes and for the control of vector-borne diseases such as malaria. During the 1950s, DDT was used by the UN/WHO malaria control programme, resulting in spectacular reductions in the number of malaria deaths in over 120 countries, in which over a billion people were at risk.

The half-life of DDT in the environment is at least ten years and one of its metabolites, DDE, persists for decades. The environmental burden of DDT has been estimated at 500,000 tonnes.

Use of the more persistent chlorinated pesticides is increasingly restricted in many countries and residue levels of

DDT are now declining in Europe and North America. However, since decreases in the body burdens of these compounds takes several decades, consequent disease risks may continue for a long period after exposure. Hence, cancer with its generally long latency, has been of particular concern.

RESIDUE CONTENT

Pesticides, principally cyclic, aromatic, cyclodiene etc, organochlorine derivatives such as DDT, and its metabolites are persistent in the environment, have broad global dispersion and are readily bioaccumulated. Accumulation up the food chain has also been demonstrated.

WHO has allocated a maximum allowable daily intake for DDT as 0.02 mg/kg BW.

INTERPRETATION OF THE DATA

There are currently very few epidemiological data on the effects of pesticide residues in foods and drinks on cancer risk, apart from DDT.

There is a substantial body of experimental evidence on the carcinogenicity of a number of industrial, waterborne and other residues, and in some cases also a substantial body of epidemiological data from occupational and environmental exposures. As with other food contaminants, and additives, judgement of safety in use depends of establishment of tolerable daily intakes derived from toxicological studies which extrapolate from experimental doses or unusual levels of exposure caused by industrial accidents.

JUDGEMENT OF OTHER REPORTS

DDT was last evaluated by IARC in 1991 and assigned to Group 2B (possibly carcinogenic to humans) (IARC, 1991c). DDT is now banned or restricted in many countries because of its bioaccumulation and other biological effects.

In 1990, WHO judged that no confirmed ill effects have been reported due to residues of DDT in food (WHO, 1990).

The National Academy of Sciences report, *Carcinogens and Anticarcinogens in the Human Diet* concluded, of dietary exposure to chemical residues, that 'the great majority of individual naturally occurring and synthetic chemicals in the diet appear to present at levels below which a significant biologic effect is likely, and so low that they are unlikely to pose an appreciable cancer risk'. (NAS, 1996).

SIGNIFICANCE FOR OTHER DISEASES

Various chemicals, including DDT, are, or may be, toxic to various organ systems in animals, and as a result of environmental exposure, overuse and abuse, industrial accidents, spillage, and dumping. The relevance of these findings to exposure to residues in foods and drinks is unclear. The relevance to other diseases at levels found in diets is largely unknown.

BOX 7.1.1 CONTAMINANTS AND HUMAN CANCER RISK

It is commonly thought by the public that chemical contamination of food and drink is a significant cause of human cancer. This view, in part derived from the mistaken belief that cancer is typically caused by exposure to single carcinogenic agents, is reinforced by occasional media coverage, and is held by some consumer and environmental organisations and some scientists.

Public fear of chemical residues is understandable. They are not meant to be present in food. Some are very toxic in high concentrations or doses, and some are known to be mutagenic or carcinogenic in animal tests when administered in high doses far in excess of any amounts normally found in food. Some chemical residues are known to accumulate in fat-containing foods and in human adipose tissue and breast milk, and concentrations in fish and seafood as a result of dumping in rivers and seas can be quite high.

Judgement on residues in food is made more difficult by the evidence that occupational over-exposure can be hazardous, and that environmental pollution caused by improper use (as with pesticide spraydrift) or by industrial accidents (such as those in Seveso and Bhopal, for example) is a hazard to human health, and may increase cancer risk.

For these and other reasons of toxicity, many chemical inputs are assessed by international bodies such as the joint UNEP/FAO/WHO Food Contamination Programme, or GEMS/Food. a component of the Global Environment Monitoring System (GEMS), the Joint FAO/WHO Meeting on Pesticide Residues (JMPR), and the International Agency for Research on Cancer (IARC) and regulated by international bodies such as the UN Codex Alimentarius and national bodies such as the US Food and Drug Administration (FDA).

Over the years the use and disposal of a substantial number of industrial chemicals has been subject to increasingly stringent regulation on the basis of results of studies showing unusual toxicity.

However, problems remain. It is not possible to be complacent about the presence in food of any chemical known to be mutagenic or carcinogenic in experimental studies. Toxicology is in any case an inexact science. Substances known to be toxic to laboratory animals may have no effect on humans. The reverse is also true: other substances that do not harm animals may have toxic effects on humans. Moreover, paradigms for safety evaluations often are based on untested assumptions. Also, chemicals may interact with each other and thus be more toxic than the sum of individual chemicals, although clear evidence for this hypothesis has not been presented. The implications for the risk of cancer or other diseases of exposure over a lifetime are unknown.

Judgements made on the safety of chemical residues based on regulations issued by international and national bodies cannot be assumed to apply to parts of the world that do not recognise such regulations, or in cases of abuse, spillage or accidents.

Expert reports assessing the role of chemical residues in human cancer risk, compared with those assessing the risk of diets as a whole, food and drinks, dietary constituents and other methods of food processing, have generally come to the view that residues are relatively unimportant factors. Nonetheless, for the reasons summarised above, judgements on chemical residues cannot be unequivocal.

The panel recognises that the safety of residues of chemicals as found in foods and drinks is regulated by international and national bodies, and that exposure to residues of any regulated contaminant as found in food or drink is generally at levels thought to be safe. However, evidence on the carcinogenicity of chemical residues in the food chain is capable of various interpretations, is clouded by controversy, and is complicated by evidence on environmental pollution other than that found in food.

The panel has concluded that there is no substantial evidence that residues of chemicals as found in food and drink increase human cancer risk. Effects of chemical residues that are unregulated or used in amounts above those regulations, are not known. Occupational exposure and contamination of food caused by misuse, spillage, or by accidents, is outside the scope of this report.

RECOMMENDATION FOR FUTURE RESEARCH

The major issue that arises from this overview is that there is a marked scarcity of data on human exposure at the low levels associated with contamination of food by any of the above chemicals. Further, there is a similar lack of any data that assess the risk of cancer associated with such exposure. Recognising that the relevant studies are both logistically complex and expensive, but recognising also, that this is a major cause of concern in many parts of the world, the panel argues that, as a matter of some urgency, the relevant exposure/outcome studies be undertaken.

ASSESSMENT

The assessments here are of agricultural and other industrial chemicals known to be present as contaminants in foods and drinks, where there is some evidence to suggest effects on human cancer risk. There is no attempt at a comprehensive survey, and readers wishing to know more are referred to relevant IARC monographs. In general, toxicological data are not assessed because these are mostly concerned with the effects of contaminants in pharmacological doses in experimental settings. These are far in excess of any levels normally found in food, such studies are undertaken in order to guide regulations designed to ensure safe limits in food.

Contaminants are regularly reviewed and assessed by expert committees whose task is to ensure their safety in use, when appropriately regulated. These committees include various UN bodies that work within the Food and Agriculture

Organization and the World Health Organization, such as the Joint FAO/WHO Meeting on Pesticide Residues (JMPR) and the Joint Expert Committee on Food Additives (JECFA), and other international and national bodies, such as the Scientific Committee for Food of the European Union(SCF) and the US Food and Drug Administration (FDA). These committees determine ADIs (Allowable Daily Intakes), MRLs (Maximum Residue Limits) or TDIs (Tolerable Daily Intakes) for the presence of contaminants in food.

As already stated, unregulated use of contaminants, other overuse or abuse, dietary exposure as a result of accidents, and occupational or environmental exposure to chemicals, is beyond the scope of this report. Additionally, no judgement is possible on the interactions that might be produced by consumption of complex mixtures of contaminants as present in foods and drinks. Dietary items are already highly complex mixtures; the toxicology of natural constituents is largely unknown (IARC, 1990).

The evidence on which this assessment is based is in the relevant sections of chapter 4.

7.1.1 PESTICIDE RESIDUES

The only pesticide for which there is sufficient epidemiological and experimental evidence of the effects of residues in foods on which to make a judgement is DDT.

DDT

Breast (4.11). Evidence from three case-control studies suggest that dietary intakes of DDT may increase the risk of breast cancer, but is, as yet, insufficient.

Other pesticides

Pesticides have been used since the beginnings of agriculture to control living things that infest crops. With modern methods of agriculture, use of pesticides has greatly increased. Worldwide production in 1994–1995 of pesticides (including herbicides) has been estimated at 2.13 million tonnes. (US EPA, 1997).

Organochlorine pesticides other than DDT persist in the environment to a similar degree, and can accumulate in food and in human tissue. As with DDT, their use is generally restricted in countries where pesticide use is regulated. A number of these have been found to be carcinogenic in experimental settings. The pesticides commonly known as Lindane and Mirex are classified by IARC in group 2B (possible human carcinogens) and Aldrin, Endrin and Dieldrin are classified in group 3 (unclassifiable as to human cancer risk). JECFA and JMPR have ADIs set for a number of chlorinated pesticides.

Chlorinated pesticides are now largely being replaced in the EU and North America with organophosphorus and carbamate pesticides which, while often more acutely toxic, are much less persistent in the environment and have not been found to be carcinogenic in experimental settings.

In the absence of reliable data on dietary exposure, the panel notes that the relevant expert committees and regulatory bodies concerned with toxicity of pesticides, conclude that, in the current state of science, there is no direct evidence that residues of pesticides, with the possible exception of DDT, when regulated and monitored, significantly affect human cancer risk. Using the panel's own criteria, no further judgement is possible.

7.1.2 HERBICIDES

Use of herbicides has greatly increased in modern times. Of the various herbicides used to control weeds, 2,4-D and 2,4,5-T are chlorinated herbicides; 2,4,5-T, which is persistent in the environment, was a component of the defoliant Agent Orange used by the US forces in the Vietnam war. Both these herbicides are classified by IARC in group 2B (possible human carcinogens) (IARC, 1987).

In the absence of reliable data on dietary exposure, the panel notes that the relevant expert committees and regulatory bodies concerned with toxicity of herbicides, conclude that in the current state of science, there is no direct evidence that herbicide residues, when regulated and monitored, significantly affect human cancer risk. Using the panel's own criteria, no further judgement is possible.

7.1.3 FERTILISERS

Fertilisers have been added to soil to improve crop production since the beginnings of agriculture. The development of nitrogenous fertilisers in the nineteenth century, the mechanisation of agriculture especially in the second half of the twentieth century, and the development of new technologies needed to sustain growing populations, has meant increasing use of nitrogenous fertilisers. Global production increased from 15.8 million tonnes in 1961–62 to 42.3 million tonnes in 1974–76 (United Nations, 1976) and to 72 million tonnes in 1985 (Bumb, 1989).

As a consequence, nitrate concentrations in crops, especially vegetables, have increased, as has dietary intake of nitrates. Consumption of nitrates from foods is estimated to be in the range of 30–185 mg a day, and the average in the UK around 54 mg a day (Ministry of Agriculture, Fisheries and Food, 1992). The WHO recommended maximum level for nitrate in drinking water is 50 mg/litre. This level is infrequently exceeded, although well waters in agricultural regions may have high nitrate concentrations. (ECETOC, 1988).

As stated in chapter 4.6 (see Box 4.6.4) and elsewhere in this report, it is difficult to disentangle the separate effects on cancer risk that might be caused by nitrates as contained in relatively high amounts in food and in drinking water as a result of soil fertilisation; and as contained in foods with added nitrate and nitrite, or processed in ways that may increase the body load of nitrate, nitrate and their metabolites. Further, as stated, unregulated use of agricultural and other chemicals, other use and abuse, and occupational or environmental exposure, is beyond the scope of this report.

JECFA has concluded that nitrate is not carcinogenic and has set an ADI, which has been adopted by the Scientific Committee for Food of the European Union (see WHO, 1996).

The panel notes, firstly, that there are no reliable data on dietary exposure levels and secondly, that the relevant expert committees and regulatory bodies concerned with toxicity of fertilisers have concluded that, in the current state of science, fertiliser residues, when regulated and monitored, do not significantly affect human cancer risk. Using the panel's own criteria, no further judgement is possible.

7.1.4 VETERINARY DRUGS

Modern intensive methods of animal husbandry involve use of antibacterial drugs to treat and prevent infectious disease, and antibacterials are also used to promote growth in pigs and chickens.

Traces of antibacterials used in animal husbandry can be found in foods and drinks, normally at levels lower than JECFA MRLs. Some antibacterials found to be carcinogenic in animal settings have been withdrawn from use on animals. There are no epidemiological data on the effect of traces of antibacterials in food on human cancer risk.

Hormonal anabolic agents (IARC group 2A, probable human carcinogen) are used in animal husbandry in some countries, including the USA, to prevent and terminate pregnancy in cows, and to promote growth. Hormones designed to stimulate milk production include bovine somatotrophin (BST) and porcine somatotropin (PST) (WHO, 1992). Most oestrogens (IARC, group 1, human carcinogen) and progestins (IARC group 2B, possible human carcinogen), and also testosterone (IARC group 1, human carcinogen), have been found to be multi-site carcinogens in experimental settings. Traces found in foods and drinks are normally below hormonally active levels.

In the absence of data on dietary exposure, the panel notes that the relevant expert committees and regulatory bodies concerned with toxicity of veterinary drugs conclude that, in the current state of science, drug residues, when regulated and monitored, do not significantly affect human cancer risk. Using the panel's own criteria, no further judgement is possible.

7.1.5 PACKAGING

Many foods and drinks contain traces of chemicals used in packaging, and migration from food-contact materials can occur during the processing, storage and preparation of food. Use of polymeric packaging materials and of plastic containers for food and drink is increasing rapidly.

Polymeric materials used in packaging are inert, but their monomers, such as vinyl chloride and acrylonitrile, can and do migrate into foods, as do plasticisers such as phthalates. These are mutagenic or carcinogenic in animals .

Vinyl chloride has been classified by IARC in group 1 (human carcinogen).

Acrylonitrile and acrylamide have been classified by IARC in group 2A (probable human carcinogens). Industrial exposure to acrylonitrile is associated with increased risk of lung and prostate cancer.

Di-(2-ethylhexyl)-phthalate has been classified by IARC in group 2B (possible human carcinogen).

In the absence of data on dietary exposure, amd using the panel's own criteria, no further judgement is possible.

7.1.6 OTHER CHEMICALS

Many foods and drinks contain traces of industrial chemicals, some of which are highly toxic. These residues occur notably in fatty foods, and also in fish and seafood contaminated by effluent, and accumulate in human adipose tissue and in human milk.

The industrial chemicals concerned include polychlorinated biphenyls (PCBs); polybrominated biphenyls (PBBs); polychlorinated dibenzodioxins (PCDDs) including the congener 2,3,7,8-tetrachlorodibenzodioxin (TCDD); and dibenzofurans (PCDFs).

PCBs have been widely used in transformers, capacitors, inks, paper and paints for more than half a century. World production in 1980 was around 1 million tonnes. Until 1972, there was no restriction on their use or disposal, and several million tonnes have been released into the environment globally by leakage, disposal and incineration. Their use is now banned or restricted. They are very persistent in the environment. Some cause liver cancer in rodents. They are classified by IARC in group 2A (probable human carcinogen). Estimated intake in the USA is about two-thirds of the FDA TDI (WHO, 1996; Gorchev, 1985; Boyer, 1995).

PBBs are chemically and toxicologically related to the PCBs. One case-control study has shown that high serum PBBs were associated with increased breast cancer risk. (Henderson et al, 1995). Some PBBs cause liver cancer in rodents. They are classified by IARC in group 2B (possible human carcinogens).

PCDDs (including TCDD) and PCDFs are by-products of various industrial processes, notably of incineration of industrial wastes. Estimated intakes of PCDDs (including TCDD) and PCDFs, are about a fifth of the WHO TDI (WHO, 1993). They are teratogenic and carcinogenic in animals. 2,3,7,8-TCDD is exceptionally stable and persistent in fatty tissue. It causes cancer at several sites in animals. Occupational exposure has shown hepatotoxicity. TCDD is classified by IARC in group 1 (human carcinogen). PCDFs are classified by IARC as group3 (unclassifiable as to human risk). The panel notes that the relevant expert committees and regulatory bodies concerned with toxicity of industrial chemicals, conclude that, in the current state of science, residues of these chemicals, when regulated and monitored, do not significantly affect human cancer risk. Using the panel's own criteria, no further judgement is possible.

7.1.7 HEAVY METALS

Many foods and drinks contain traces of heavy metals such as lead, arsenic, and cadmium.

The main dietary source of exposure to lead is from soldered seams in canned foods, from lead piping and solder in plumbing, and from emissions. Residues from such sources are being reduced in developed countries. Lead as found in food is classified by IARC in group 2B (possible human carcinogen). Experimental studies show increased risk of kidney cancer as a result of oral administration of lead salts. There are no adequate epidemiological data on dietary exposure although consequences of acute chronic and low-level exposures are now well-known..

Arsenic residues in food and drink are largely as a result of agricultural, mining and industrial practices, or are naturally occurring. Arsenic is classified by IARC in group 1 (human carcinogen). Epidemiological studies in areas with exceptionally high concentrations of arsenic in drinking water show correlations with increased risk of lung, liver, colon, kidney and bladder cancers, but the broader applicability of these results is unclear.

Cadmium residues are largely a result of agricultural and industrial practices. This metal concentrates in organ meats, including liver and kidney. Cadmium is classified by IARC in group 2A (probable human carcinogen), based on industrial exposure. Experimental studies demonstrate carcinogenicity, but not by an oral route. There are no adequate epidemiological data on dietary exposure.

The panel notes firstly, that there are no reliable data on dietary exposure levels and secondly, that the relevant expert committees and regulatory bodies concerned with toxicity of residues of heavy metals in foods and drinks, conclude that in the current state of science, when regulated and monitored, these do not significantly affect human cancer risk. Using the panel's own criteria, no further judgement is possible.

7.1.8 WATERBORNE RESIDUES

Water supplies may contain chlorine, used as a disinfectant; fluoride, used to reduce risk of tooth decay; and nitrates, as a residue of fertilisers.

Evidence of increased risk

Bladder (4.18). In 1991, IARC concluded that the epidemiological evidence suggesting that chlorinated water increases the risk of bladder cancer was inadequate. On the basis of two cohort studies, four case-control studies and six correlation studies, evidence that chlorinated water may increase the risk of bladder cancer is, as yet, insufficient.

Chlorinated water is classified by IARC in group 3 (unclassifiable as to human cancer risk). Chloroform, a by-product of chlorinated water, is classified in group 2B (possible human carcinogen. The main by-products of chlorinated water of toxicological concern are the trihalomethanes and the halogenated acids. IARC has concluded that epidemiological evidence suggesting that chorinated water increases the risk of colorectal cancer, is inadequate. (IARC, 1991.

Fluoride causes bone cancer in rats, but over 50 epidemiological studies have found no relationship between fluoride and bone cancer risk. Fluoride is classified by IARC in group 3 (unclassifiable as to human cancer risk). The National Academy of Sciences has concluded that there is no evidence of human cancer risk from fluoridation (NAS, 1989).

There is an extensive literature on the relationship between nitrates, nitrites and *N*-nitroso compounds, and human cancer risk. Nitrates are found naturally in vegetables and fruits, and in preserved foods, as well as in water as a result of soil fertilisation (See Box 4.6.4.).

At present, the epidemiological evidence on the consequences of exposure to residues of water-borne chlorine is limited. Fluoride probably has no relationship with the risk of bone cancer. The evidence that *N*-nitroso compounds, formed in the body as a result of consumption of nitrates and nitrites in foods and drinks, increase risk of stomach cancer, is insufficient. (See Box 4.6.4.)

The panel notes that the relevant expert committees and regulatory bodies concerned with toxicity of waterborne chemicals, conclude that in the current state of science, residues of these chemicals, when regulated and monitored, do not significantly affect human cancer risk.

7.2 Food additives

Most manufactured foods and drinks contain chemicals added as a deliberate part of the manufacturing process.

Colours and flavours are used in manufactured foods to make them more appealing. Preservatives, including antioxidants, are designed to extend food shelf-life and/or to protect against microbial contamination. Emulsifiers, stabilisers, solvents, and sweeteners are used extensively, as are processing aids present as residues in food. Sugar and salt are not classified here as additives but are assessed in chapters 5.2 and 7.4; nitrates used as food preservatives are discussed in chapter 4.6.

As with chemical contaminants, a number of food additives are known to be toxic, and some have been determined to be mutagenic or carcinogenic in experimental conditions. Consequently, the use of such chemicals is subject to evaluation and regulation by national and international bodies.

This section assesses the evidence that any such additives may significantly modify human cancer risk, using the criteria for weighing the evidence specified in chapter 3. There is no attempt at a comprehensive survey.

The panel has reached the following conclusions. There is no convincing evidence that any food additive modifies the risk of any cancer, nor is there any evidence of any probable causal relationship. Indeed, there is currently little epidemiological evidence that the properly regulated use of food additives significantly affects cancer risk. There is probably no relationship between saccharin and bladder cancer, and the panel notes that there is possibly no relationship between cyclamates and bladder cancer. Evidence on other additives is, at most, insufficient.

FOOD ADDITIVES AND CANCER

In the judgement of the panel, food additives, as present in foods, modify the risk of cancers of the sites as shown below, or else have no relationship with them. Judgements are graded according to the strength of the evidence.

	DECREASES RISK	NO RELATIONSHIP	INCREASES RISK
CONVINCING			
PROBABLE		*Sweeteners* Bladder (saccharin)	
POSSIBLE		*Sweeteners* Bladder (cyclamates)	
INSUFFICIENT			

For an explanation of the terms used in the matrix, see chapter 3.

On the basis of current evidence, additives, when used, according to agreed good practice do not significantly modify the risk of human cancer. The panel emphasises that its judgements do not apply to contamination of foods and drinks caused by bad practice; this is beyond the scope of this report.

INTRODUCTION

Most manufactured foods and drinks contain chemicals that are added deliberately. Many additives have an aesthetic function: colours and flavours are used in manufactured food to make it more appealing. Some additives are antioxidants or preservatives, designed to extend food shelf-life and/or to protect against microbial contamination. Others have a variety of functions, including emulsifiers, stabilisers and solvents; processing aids are present as residues in food. Artificial sweeteners are also classified as additives. Sugar and salt are not classified as additives but are reviewed separately in chapters 5.2 and 7.5.

Classes of additives include colours and flavours, preservatives, antioxidants, solvents, sugar and fat substitutes, coatings, films, processing aids, surfactants and stabilising agents. Chemicals that migrate into foods from packaging are not generally regarded as additives but as contaminants; see chapter 7.1.

Experimental evidence has shown that a relatively small number of additives are mutagenic or carcinogenic. Generally, the doses used in such experimental studies have been far in excess of intakes likely to occur in normal human diets. However, concerns over potential carcinogenicity has led to regulation of the use of most classes of additives. National and international regulatory bodies carry out toxicological assessments to determine safe levels of additives in food products or preferred levels of daily intakes.

Other additives that have been in widespread use without direct evidence of significant harm are classified as 'generally regarded as safe' (GRAS) in the United States, or appear on permitted lists of additives without the large toxicological database required for evaluation of new substances. Human epidemiological evidence on additives is generally limited.

In reviewing the literature in chapter 4 the panel, applied the criteria explained in chapter 3 and has generally concluded that, because of the lack of epidemiological data, the evidence of relationships between most additives and cancer risk is currently insufficient or no judgement can be made. Nevertheless, concern remains because of the established carcinogenicity of a number of additives (see Box 7.2.1).

Evidence that any colours or flavours, or preservatives increase risk of any cancer is currently insubstantial. Conversely, experimental studies indicate that some additives with antioxidant properties (such as BHT) may be protective.

Significant epidemiological evidence exists only for artificial sweeteners which are discussed below.

For information on the scale of use, content in food and toxicology and evaluation of other additives readers are referred to the IARC Monographs on the Evaluation of Carcinogenic Risks to Humans, particularly volumes 8 and 16 (aromatic azo compounds), volume 22 (sweetening agents), volume 31 (food additives), volume 40 (food components), volume 51 (coffee, tea, etc), volume 56 (food items and constituents) and supplement 7 (IARC, 1975, 1978, 1980, 1983, 1986, 1991, 1993, 1987).

The only additives on which the panel make a judgement

are sweeteners, and the following sections provide information on its scale of use and residue content. Information about other additives is given in the assessment section.

SCALE OF USE

Artificial sweeteners are widely used in place of sugar and other naturally occurring sweetening agents. The synthetic sweeteners of potential concern are saccharin, cyclamate and aspartame.

Extensive studies into the mechanism and dose–response relationships now indicate that the carcinogenicity is a species- and sex-specific phenomenon (only male rats are affected), that a clear no-effect level can be established at about 1% of the rat diet, and that only the sodium salt is effective (not the free acid or the calcium salt). (Under similar circumstances, sodium ascorbate (the sodium salt of vitamin C) but not ascorbic acid (acid form of vitamin C) also produces bladder tumours).

Saccharin has now been banned in a number of countries (IARC, 1980), but is still used in more than 90 countries throughout the world. In 1997, the US FDA proposed banning the use of saccharin as possibly carcinogenic in humans, but the US Congress has declared a moratorium on enforcement of the ban by FDA, as is usually required by the Delaney Clause. The use of saccharin and its salts as sweetening agents in foods is generally permitted in baking products, pre-mixes, confectionery, and drinks.

Cyclamates are about 30 times as sweet as sucrose. Cyclamates were banned as a food or drink additive in the USA in 1970 because they were thought to be carcinogenic in humans, and were also banned in a number of other countries. They are widely used as additives in many products in another 50 countries. A re-evaluation of early data and later experimental evidence indicated that bladder tumours were only seen in studies on mixtures of cyclamate with saccharin; cyclamate per se did not produce tumours in rats or mice (NAS, 1982). Limited experimental data and inadequate evidence of carcinogenicity in humans has led IARC to classify cyclamates in group 3 (unclassifiable as to human cancer risk (IARC, 1987).

Aspartame has been approved for food, drink and table-top sweetener use in over 90 countries. Its application in low-calorie soft drinks means that it is a major sweetener in many countries.

CONTENT IN FOOD

Saccharin consumption, in those consuming high amounts largely from soft-drinks and table-top use, can approach the JECFA ADI of 5 mg/kg BW (300 mg/day for an average adult; equivalent in sweetness to about 60 g sugar) (WHO, 1993). In a survey in the UK, the highest user group was diabetic adolescent males, a small percentage of whom had intakes above the ADI.

Aspartame is the most widely used synthetic sweetener in the United States. Soft drinks may contain about 555 mg

aspartame/litre. Most studies indicate that daily human consumption of aspartame is below 10 mg/kg BW at the 90th percentile level. In a few individuals who consume large amounts of aspartame-sweetened foods and beverages, daily intake could be as high as 20–30 mg/kg BW.

INTERPRETATION OF THE DATA

Because of their nature as discrete chemical entities, it is comparatively easy to establish the relationship between individual additives and cancer risk in animals and mutagenicity in microbial models. It is, however, difficult to know how to extrapolate such results to humans in the absence of human data. For statistical and logical reasons, chemicals are typically tested in animals at levels far above those found in food. Data from animal studies may not always apply to humans; conversely, substances that have little or no effect when tested on animals may nevertheless increase human cancer risk (eg, alcohol, arsenic). Humans consume complex combinations of additives as part of their diets; any effects of lifetime consumption are not known.

JUDGEMENT OF OTHER REPORTS

Saccharin is classified by IARC in group 2B (possible human carcinogen) (IARC, 1987). Evaluations by JECFA concluded that saccharin does not pose a carcinogenic risk to humans under the conditions of dietary exposure. An ADI of 0–5 mg/kg BW has been set for saccharin as the free acid or the sodium or calcium salts (WHO, 1993). This evaluation is accepted by the SCF and many national regulatory agencies. In the US, an ADI for saccharin is not given, since it is regulated under the Delaney Clause which allows no safe level for any food additive inducing cancer in animals at any dose. However, as noted above the US Congress has imposed a moratorium on the implementation of a ban on the use of saccharin.

Cyclamates are classified by IARC as group 3 (unclassifiable as to human cancer risk). JECFA and SCF have concluded that the data does not indicate that this substance is a carcinogen in animals or in humans. An ADI of 0–11 mg/kg BW has been set, and cyclamate is now permitted in member states of the European Union.

SIGNIFICANCE FOR OTHER DISEASES

The use of artificial sweeteners has been promoted and accepted widely. They are used by individuals to reduce energy intake from sugar which may be relevant to the control of obesity, though substantive data are lacking. Among individuals with diabetes, use of artificial sweeteners may assist in the control of blood glucose levels. Other additives discussed below may be toxic to various organ systems in animals, or in humans possibly as a result of overuse. The relevance of these findings to exposure to the amounts normally found in foods and drinks, is unclear.

RECOMMENDATION FOR FUTURE RESEARCH

The major issue that arises from this overview is that there is a marked scarcity of data on human exposure at the low levels associated with food by any of the above chemicals. There is a lack of any data that assess the risk of cancer associated with such cumulative and complex exposures. Recognising that the relevant studies are both logistically complex and expensive but recognising also, that this is a major cause of concern in many parts of the world, the panel argues that, as a matter of some urgency, the relevant exposure/outcome studies be undertaken.

ASSESSMENT

The assessments here are of food additives for which there is some evidence to suggest effects on human cancer risk. There is no attempt at a comprehensive survey, and readers wishing to know more are referred to relevant IARC monographs (see above). In general, toxicological data are not assessed because these are mostly concerned with the effects of additives in pharmacological doses in animals, far in excess of any levels normally found in food, in order to guide regulations designed to ensure safe limits in food.

Additives are regularly reviewed and assessed by expert committees whose task is to ensure their safety in use, when appropriately regulated. These committees include the Joint Expert Committee on Food Additives (JECFA), the Scientific Committee on Food of the European Union (SCF) and, in the USA, the Food and Drug Administration (FDA). As a consequence, ADIs (Allowable Daily Intakes) are determined for the presence of additives in food.

As already stated, unregulated use of additives, other overuse or abuse, dietary exposure as a result of accidents, and occupational or environmental exposure to additives, is beyond the scope of this report. Additionally, no judgement can be made on the possible interaction produced by consumption of complex mixtures of additives as present in manufactured food. As noted in 7.1, food is itself a complex mixture of many chemicals and the toxicology of complex mixtures is essentially unexplored (IARC, 1990).

7.2.1 FLAVOURS

A vast number of flavours are added to manufactured food. Many are artificial, but most are natural, or chemically identical to colours found in nature. Up to 4,000 individual flavour compounds are used in the USA and other developed countries. (Ford, 1989). Like colours, flavours are sometimes identified as cosmetic additives, and many types of manufactured food are flavoured.

Alkenylbenzenes are naturally occurring flavours, some of which have been found to cause liver cancer in rodents at levels considerably higher than normal human intakes. Currently no ADI has been agreed for this class of flavours. In this case the panel judges that evidence that alkenylben-

zenes increase the risk of liver cancer is currently insufficient.

Limonene has been shown to cause renal cancer in rats by a mechanism believed to be species-specific. (Flamm and Lenihan-McKeeman, 1991). In contrast, D-limonene and citrus oils have been shown to reduce the occurrence of forestomach cancer in mice (Wattenberg, 1983)

The only additives on which the panel make a judgement are sweeteners, and the following sections provide information on its scale of use and residue content. Information about other additives is given in the assessment section.

The panel notes firstly, that there are no reliable data on dietary exposure levels and secondly, that the relevant expert committees and regulatory bodies concerned with toxicity of flavours have concluded that, in the current state of science, flavours, when regulated and monitored, do not significantly affect human cancer risk. Using the panel's own criteria, no further judgement is possible.

7.2.2 SWEETENERS

The principal sweeteners in use are saccharin, cyclamates, and aspartame. The major sources of exposure in the diet are low calorie/diabetic soft drinks, table top sweeteners, and a variety of other foods.

Evidence of no relationship

CONVINCING	PROBABLE	POSSIBLE	INSUFFICIENT
	Bladder (saccharin)	Bladder (cyclamates)	

Bladder (4.18) Over 25 epidemiological studies have shown no overall association between saccharin use and cancer in humans. Animal studies, however, have shown that the sodium salt of saccharin increases the incidence of bladder tumours in male rats. The mechanism by which this occurs almost certainly does not occur as a result of usual human intakes of saccharin. Overall, the evidence indicates there is probably no relationship between saccharin intake and the incidence of bladder cancer.

On the basis of more limited evidence cyclamates possibly have no relationship with the incidence of bladder cancer.

7.2.3 COLOURS

Many colours are added to manufactured food. Some are artificial, some are natural, and some are chemically identical to colours found in nature. Colours are sometimes identified as cosmetic additives, because they are used to make a very wide range of food look more attractive. Most types of manufactured food is coloured, including cereal products, baked goods, snack foods, meat, fish and poultry products, cheese, butter and other dairy products, and alcoholic and soft drinks. In industrialised countries, consumption of all colours taken together is substantial, amounting to around

BOX 7.2.1 ADDITIVES AND HUMAN CANCER RISK

It is commonly thought by the public that additives (which, unlike contaminants, are deliberately added to manufactured foods and drinks) are a significant cause of human cancer. As with contaminants (see Box 7.1.1), this view is, in part, derived from the mistaken belief that cancer is typically caused by exposure to single carcinogenic agents, is reinforced by occasional media coverage, and is held by some consumer representative organisations and some scientists.

Public fear of additives is understandable. They are almost ubiquitous in manufactured foods and drinks. Many are invisible. Most are artificial although many are derived from natural products or, if artificial, chemically related to products of nature. Mass manufacture and distribution of processed food at prices most people can afford would be impossible without the use of additives. In developed countries, there is a tension between the above concern and an increasing demand for food to be completely safe; there are thus trade-offs implicit in the use of some additives such as preservatives, which may inhibit microbial contamination.

Some classes and some specific examples of additives have been found to be mutagenic or carcinogenic in experimental studies. For this and other reasons of potential toxicity, additives are assessed by international bodies such as the FAO/WHO Joint Expert Committee on Food Additives (JECFA), and the International Agency for Research on Cancer (IARC) and regulated by international bodies such as the UN Codex Alimentarius and national bodies such as the US Food and Drug Administration (FDA). As a general rule, additives found to be mutagenic or carcinogenic in laboratory rodents, if permitted for use in food, are only at levels far below those at which any experimental toxic effect is detectable. Thus, ADIs (allowable daily intakes) are determined by regulatory agencies typically at 1/100th of the no-effect level in animals.

Faced with the vast number of additives now used in manufactured food, regula-tory bodies have concentrated on those believed most likely to be toxic to humans. Over the years, a substantial number of additives have been withdrawn from use on the basis of experimental studies showing unusual toxicity, including mutagenicity and carcinogenicity. Examples include a number of azo-dyes now no longer used in countries that have their own regulatory bodies or that accept the findings of international bodies. The use of other additives has been increasingly restricted: examples include nitrates and nitrites as used in curing meat. Additionally, many additives are not permitted for use in foods and drinks manufactured for babies and very small children.

However, problems remain. It is not possible to be complacent about the use of any additive known to be mutagenic or carcinogenic in experimental studies, and such substances have been generally prohibited in the USA. However, many additives are classified Generally Recognised as Safe (GRAS), without adequate toxicity testing on animals, simply because they have been used for many years with no established evidence of ill-effects on humans. The effects of other additives (notably most of the thousands of flavours now used) are unknown.

Toxicology is, in any case, an inexact science. Substances known to be toxic to laboratory animals may have no effect on humans. The reverse is also true: other substances that do not harm animals may have toxic effects on humans. Moreover, para-digms for safety evaluations often are based on untested assumptions.

Safety in use is to some extent a matter of judgement and some studies have shown that people who consume unusual amounts of certain foods or drinks (coloured products, for example) may at times exceed ADIs. Small children commonly consume adult food. A large number of additives consumed together in food and drink may interact with each other synergistically and thus be more toxic than the sum of the individual additives although clear evidence for this hypothesis has not been presented. The implications, for the risk of cancer or other diseases, of additives consumed over a lifetime are unknown.

Judgements made on the safety of additives based on regulations issued by international and national bodies cannot be assumed to apply to parts of the world that do not recognise such regulations, and where good manufacturing practice may not be followed in the production of processed foods.

Expert reports assessing the role of additives in human cancer risk, compared with those assessing the risk of diets as a whole, food and drinks, dietary constituents and other methods of food processing, have generally come to the view that additives are relatively unimportant factors. Nonetheless, for the reasons summarised above, judgements on additives as a whole, and on particular classes and examples of additives, cannot be unequivocal.

The panel recognises that use of additives is regulated by international and national bodies and that exposure to any regulated additive normally occurs at levels far lower than those found to be toxic in experimental studies. However, no judgement can be made on the cumulative lifetime effect on cancer risk of additives that are mutagenic or carcinogenic in laboratory conditions.

With this proviso, the panel has concluded that, when used in quantities that fall within the regulations for manufactured foods and drinks, there is no evidence that additives increase human cancer risk.

Effects of additives that are unregulated or used in amounts above those regulations, are not known.

100 mg/day (Winter et al, 1990).

Some azo and triarylmethane dyes were determined to be carcinogenic in experimental settings have been withdrawn from use. The dyes now used in countries where additives are regulated are believed not to be carcinogenic as found in food. The xanthene colour erythrosine has been found to produce thyroid adenomas and adenocarcinomas in rats given high oral doses, but JECFA has concluded that this effect has a threshold (that is, there is a level below which there is no effect) and does not indicate any carcinogenic risk at levels as found in food.

Caramels are a class of colours, amounting, in the USA and other developed countries, to over 90 per cent by weight of all colours used in food. Some studies have shown that class 3 caramel (ammonia caramel) causes severe leukopenia in rats, which has been allowed for in the current ADI for this caramel.

The panel notes, firstly, that there are no reliable data on dietary exposure levels and secondly, that the relevant expert committees and regulatory bodies concerned with toxicity of colours have concluded that, in the current state of science, colours, when regulated and monitored, do not significantly affect human cancer risk. Using the panel's own criteria, no further judgement is possible.

7.2.4 PRESERVATIVES

Preservatives are added to foods liable to microbial contamination and spoilage. Nitrates and nitrites are used in cured meats, fish and cheese. The antioxidants BHA and BHT are used extensively in packaged foods, notably breakfast cereals and snack foods.

There is an extensive literature on the relationship between nitrates, nitrites and *N*-nitroso compounds, and human cancer risk. These are found naturally in vegetables and fruits, and in relatively high amounts in various foods as a result of soil fertilisation, as well as in preserved foods. The panel judges that the evidence that *N*-nitroso compounds formed in the body as a result of consumption of nitrates and nitrites in foods and drinks, increases the risk of stomach cancer, is insufficient. See also Box 4.6.4, and chapter 7.5.

BHA and BHT are classified by IARC in group 2B (possible human carcinogen) and group 3 (non-classifiable) respectively (IARC, 1986, 1987), and ADIs have been set. It has been suggested that because BHA and BHT are antioxidants, it is theoretically possible that their use in food might reduce cancer risk. (Doll and Peto, 1982). There are no relevant human epidemiological data.

The panel notes, firstly, that there are no reliable data on dietary exposure levels and secondly, that the relevant expert committees and regulatory bodies concerned with toxicity of food preservatives have concluded that, in the current state of science, food preservatives, when regulated and monitored, do not significantly affect human cancer risk. Using the panel's own criteria, no further judgement is possible.

7.2.5 SOLVENTS

Solvents of various types are used in manufactured foods and drinks (IARC, 1987). Dichloromethane and trichloroethylene, which have been used for the decaffeination of coffee and tea, have been classified by IARC as a possible human carcinogen (group 2B) and unclassifiable (group 3), respectively, and currently no ADIs have been set. JECFA has recommended that use of these solvents be restricted and levels in food be as low as technologically possible. (WHO, 1992). They are now generally not used for decaffeination.

The panel notes, firstly, that there are no reliable data on dietary exposure levels and secondly, that the relevant expert committees and regulatory bodies concerned with toxicity of food solvents have concluded that, in the current state of science, when regulated and monitored, they do not significantly affect human cancer risk. Using the panel's own criteria, no further judgement is possible.

7.2.6 FAT SUBSTITUTES

Fat substitutes were first introduced into food supplies in 1993. They are regulated, not as additives, but as food ingredients or as novel foods. Since fat-soluble vitamins (particularly carotenoids, retinoids and vitamins D, E and K) are soluble in some fat substitutes, particularly sucrose polyester (Olestra) substantial consumption could, by depletion of blood levels of carotenoids, affect cancer risk. This theoretical possibility is currently not the basis for any judgement. The introduction of sucrose polyester into the USA food supply is being monitored in a series of epidemiological studies.

7.3 Microbial contaminants

The most important form of microbial contamination involves various types of mycotoxins, which are metabolites of moulds. This is most problematic in countries with hot damp climates, and with poor storage facilities; this results in foods being stored for prolonged periods at ambient temperatures.

The panel has concluded as follows. The evidence shows that aflatoxin, one type of mycotoxin, probably increases the risk of primary liver cancer.

MICROBIAL CONTAMINATION AND CANCER

In the judgement of the panel, microbial contamination of food increases the risk of cancers of the sites shown below. Judgements are graded according to the strength of evidence.

	DECREASES RISK	NO RELATIONSHIP	INCREASES RISK
CONVINCING			
PROBABLE			*Aflatoxins* Liver
POSSIBLE			
INSUFFICIENT			

For an explanation of the terms used in the matrix, see chapter 3.

INTRODUCTION

Mycotoxins are highly toxic secondary metabolites of a number of species of moulds. They are ubiquitous compounds that differ widely in their chemical, biological and toxicological properties.

While most food is stored for a relatively short period, some crops may be stored for long periods. In warm, damp areas of the world crops stored for long periods at ambient temperatures may become contaminated with aflatoxins produced by moulds, notably *Aspergillus flavus* and *A. parasiticus*.

Over 300 mycotoxins in foods and animal feeds have been identified worldwide, produced predominantly by three genera: *Aspergillus*, *Fusarium* and *Pencillium*.

Reduction in the levels of mycotoxin-producing organisms can be achieved through the use of synthetic and natural fungicides and insecticides (where insects play a major role as vectors for microbial contamination).

SCALE OF OCCURRENCE

In 1985, the Food and Agriculture Organisation estimated that approximately 25% of the world's food crops were contaminated annually with mycotoxins (WHO, 1992). Their occurrence varies greatly with geographical location, agricultural and agronomic practice and the susceptibility to fungal invasion during pre-harvest, storage and processing.

Crops that may be affected by mycotoxins include peanuts, tree nuts, cereals (maize, wheat, barley, rice and oats), beans and apples. Mycotoxins may also contaminate fish, animal feeds, and other foods that are allowed to ferment before being eaten.

Feedstuffs for farm animals may also be contaminated with aflatoxins, leading to the secretion of a metabolite, aflatoxin M_1, in the animal's milk.

Some mycotoxins such as aflatoxin-B_1 are highly carcinogenic in laboratory animals, suggesting that long-term, low-level consumption of foods contaminated with these toxins can pose a serious human health problem, notably in Africa and south-east Asia (Pohland and Wood, 1987; Hsieh, 1989; Van Rensburg et al, 1985; Peers et al, 1987; Yeh et al, 1989; IARC, 1987, 1993; Wild et al, 1990, 1993; Lutwick, 1994; Hall and Wild, 1993) and Latin America.

CONTENT IN FOOD

Aflatoxins

The levels of aflatoxins in food are highly variable. In one survey (Jelinek et al, 1989) covering nine countries, median levels in maize and maize products generally ranged from 0.1 to 80 μg/kg but maximum levels of 1920 and 700 μg/kg were found in Kenya and the USA, respectively. Groundnuts usually contained <20 μg/kg although 50% of samples of imports into the USA from India, the Sudan and Brazil contained over 26 μg/kg. Other nuts usually contained lesser amounts, although occasionally high levels were recorded in pistachio nuts, brazil nuts and pumpkin seeds (IARC, 1993). Occasionally, very high levels have been recorded in figs.

Fumonisins

The fumonisin mycotoxins, are less extensively studied than the aflatoxins. They are widely distributed in maize products from many regions including Europe and North America. Levels of contamination with fumonisin range from 0 to 330 mg/kg, the highest levels usually being found in animal feed, although human food products are also contaminated (IARC, 1993).

The trichothecene toxin, T_2 toxin, is produced by *Fusarium sporotrichoides*. It has been reported in cereals in many parts of the world and is a particular problem when there is prolonged wet weather at harvest. T_2 toxin is also found in groundnuts.

Ochratoxins

Ochratoxin A is produced mainly by *Penicillium viridicatum* and some *Aspergillus spp*. It has been reported as a contaminant in many commodities, including grains, pulses and coffee beans. Levels in grain destined for human consumption are usually low but levels of up to 5mg/kg have been recorded in barley in the UK. High levels have also been reported in wheat (up to 2.7 mg/kg) and, since ochratoxin is relatively stable during processing and unchanged in raw foodstuffs, it has been detected in bread. Ochratoxin accumulates in the kidney, so offal from animals fed contaminated feed may also be contaminated.

JUDGEMENTS OF OTHER REPORTS

IARC (1993) concluded that there is sufficient evidence for the carcinogenicity in humans of natural mixtures of aflatoxins, and of aflatoxin B_1 (Group 1). The milk metabolite, aflatoxin M_1 has been classified as a possible human carcinogen. JECFA have not been able to determine a tolerable intake of aflatoxins and have recommended that they should be reduced to the lowest levels achievable in food.

For aflatoxins, many countries have imposed limits of between 5 and 50 μg/kg, with 5 μg/kg most common (van Egmond, 1992). The limit established by FAO/WHO is 30 μg/kg in foods for human consumption.

IARC have classified the fumonisins as possible human carcinogens (2B) on the basis of evidence of carcinogenicity in animals and inadequate evidence in humans (IARC, 1993).

There are no generally agreed guidelines or limits for the fumonisins. An unofficial tolerance level of 01 mg/kg was established for T_2 toxin in the USSR in 1982 while existing or proposed limits for ochratoxin A range from 1 to 50 μg/kg in food and 100 to 1000 μg/kg in animal feed. In Denmark, levels of ochratoxin in kidney have been used to determine whether the whole carcass, or certain organs, can be used as food (van Egmond, 1991).

Ochratoxin A is classified as possibly carcinogenic to humans (2A) based on animal carcinogenicity (liver and kidney) and inadequate human evidence. JECFA have allocated a Provisional Tolerable Weekly Intake for ochratoxin A of 0–0.1 μg/kg BW.

SIGNIFICANCE FOR OTHER DISEASES

Food stored for long periods in hot, damp conditions is liable to be infested or infected with pathogenic organisms other than mycotoxins, and is therefore generally unsafe.

ASSESSMENT

The evidence on which this assessment is based is reviewed in chapter 4.

Evidence of increased risk

Convincing	Probable	Possible	Insufficient
	Liver (aflatoxins)		

Liver (4.9). Epidemiological data, mainly from Africa and south-east Asia, shows a strong association between the consumption of foods contaminated with alfatoxins and the geographical distribution of liver cancer, supported by experimental evidence that aflatoxins are extremely potent hepatocarcinogens in various animal species.

An additional factor is that the hepatitis B virus (and possibly hepatitis C) may increase the population's sensitivity to mycotoxins.

High aflatoxin contamination probably increases the risk of liver cancer.

7.4 Salt, salting and refrigeration

Foods have been preserved by salting, and by other processes including pickling and curing that may use salt, for thousands of years. Some traditional diets include salted foods as staples. Salt is also used extensively by industry as a preservative and flavour enhancer, and diets consumed in developed countries typically include salt in concentrations and volumes far in excess of requirements. Use of salt to preserve food has generally decreased as industrial and domestic use of refrigeration has increased.

The panel has reached the following conclusions. The evidence that regular refrigeration of food protects against stomach cancer, plausibly by reducing the need for salt and by facilitating year-round supply of fresh vegetables and fruits, is convincing. The evidence that diets high in Cantonese-style salted fish increase the risk of nasopharyngeal cancer, notably in early life, is convincing. Diets high in salted foods and in salt itself probably increase the risk of stomach cancer.

SALT, SALTING AND REFRIGERATION AND CANCER

In the judgement of the panel, diets containing substantial amounts of salt or salted foods, and the refrigeration process, modify the risk of cancers of the sites as listed below. Judgements are graded according to the strength of evidence.

	DECREASES RISK	NO RELATIONSHIP	INCREASES RISK
CONVINCING	*Refrigeration* Stomach		*Salted fish*[a] Nasopharynx
PROBABLE			*Salt and salted foods* Stomach
POSSIBLE			
INSUFFICIENT			

For an explanation of the terms used in the matrix, see chapter 3.
[a] Data apply to Cantonese-style salted fish. Risk increases when such foods are regularly eaten early in life.

INTRODUCTION

Salt (sodium chloride) has been used to preserve food for thousands of years. Salting is commonly used in combination with other methods of preservation like curing and smoking. To distinguish the effect of salting or salt itself from those of additional preserving methods, this section deals with salt intake and salted foods that are not additionally processed.

Refrigeration by means of natural ice has been traditionally available as a means of preservation only in winter or in cold climates. Natural ice refrigeration first developed on an industrial scale in the mid-nineteenth century. Freezing, chilling and domestic refrigeration on a mass scale is a phenomenon mostly of the second half of the twentieth century. Refrigeration reduces the need for, and use of, salt.

SOURCES

Foods in nature are generally poor sources of sodium and are generally much higher in potassium. It has been suggested that animals and humans have an inbuilt desire for salt as a compensatory mechanism: hence salt licks used by herbivorous animals and the value placed on salt; the word 'salary' derives from the Latin word for salt, because salt was sometimes part of the pay of Roman soldiers.

Salt from mines or the sea is now a cheap commodity. Salt in diets comes from salt added for preservation, in manufacture, in cooking or at table. Diets become salty only when salt is added as part of some process, designed to preserve food or to make it more attractive. Salt content per edible portion can be as high as 5–10 g/100 g in salted fish. Salt in processed meat such as bacon, ham and sausage is usually 2–6 g/100 g.

Salt is added to vast range of manufactured foods. The volume of salt in bread and other starchy processed foods may vary between 1.5 and 4 g/100 g. Breakfast cereals contain variable amounts of salt – up to 4 g/100 g. Savoury snacks such as potato crisps/chips, pretzels and peanuts can be as salty as foods preserved by salt and can contain up to 5 g/100 g of salt.

COMPOSITION

Salt is sodium chloride, which by weight is approximately 40% sodium and 60% chloride. Thus, 6 grams of salt contains about 2.4 grams of sodium.

FUNCTIONS

Sodium is the primary regulator of extracellular fluid volume. The body content of sodium and its concentration in body fluids is controlled homeostatically; excess sodium is secreted. Sodium also is involved in regulation of osmolarity, acid-base balance, and the membrane potential of cells.

REQUIREMENTS

Sodium is essential to normal function. On a population basis, a safe daily requirement has been estimated at 500 mg for adults. There is no evidence that intakes above such amounts have any benefit. A lower figure of 115 mg/day has been suggested for individuals who do not sweat much. (NRC, 1989). It has also been argued that average salt intake is around 20 times the requirement (Wrong, 1993).

CONSUMPTION PATTERNS

Salt intake varies substantially around the world. According to the Intersalt Study, daily salt intake, as determined by 24-hour urinary sodium excretion, ranged from a low of 12 mg in Yanomamo Indians to a high of 14 g in Tianjin, China. Average figures were around 8–10 g in most industrial countries and 10–12 g in Colombia, Japan, and Korea.

Salted foods are common in China, Korea, and Japan; the methods of salting vary. Salted fish is regularly eaten in southern parts of China. Salted foods are less commonly eaten outside Asia, although consumption is high in some countries in South America, and in Portugal. Salted vegetables such as sauerkraut and pickles are commonly eaten in Central and Eastern Europe and former USSR. About one-third of adult Italians are reported to consume salted or dried fish on average once a week (Buiatti et al 1989). In Japan, salt is usually used to pickle vegetables, and salted vegetables are eaten almost every day or several times per week. Condiments such as soy sauce and miso (fermented soybean paste), contribute to a large proportion of salt intake in the Far East; they presently account for approximately half of the salt intake in Japan.

This generally relatively narrow range for salt intake indicates that diets including salted food are often not much, if at all, more salty than diets whose salt comes mostly from manufactured foods. Very many processed foods contain substantial amounts of added salt: not only those foods that are obviously salty, such as cured and smoked meat and fish, but also cheese and butter, bread and many breakfast cereals. Foods that taste bland or even sweet may contain significant amounts of added salt. Most salt in diets is contained in manufactured foods, with 20–30% added in cooking or at table. (Sanchez-Castillo et al, 1987).

Nowadays much perishable processed food is frozen or chilled. Together with the growth of industrial refrigeration, the use of domestic refrigerators, commonly used in the USA, Australia and New Zealand since the 1920s, and Europe and Japan mostly since the 1950s, also has influenced the consumption of preserved foods, and is considered to have made an impact on the decline in stomach cancer (Hirayama, 1984; Joossens and Geboers, 1985; Howson, 1986). In Japan, households possessing refrigerators increased from 9% in 1960 to 91% in 1970.

INTERPRETATION OF THE DATA

Given that levels of salt in manufactured foods can be as high as those in salt–preserved foods, both are important to assess in establishing the overall salt in any diet.

JUDGEMENTS OF PREVIOUS REPORTS

The National Academy of Sciences report *Diet, Nutrition and Cancer* (NAS, 1982) recommended that the consumption of food preserved by salt-curing (including salt-pickling) be minimised. The later report of the National Academy of Sciences, *Diet and Health* (NAS 1989) further recommended that salty, highly processed salty, salt-preserved and salt-pickled foods should be consumed only sparingly. These recommendations were based on data concerning diet and cancer.

SIGNIFICANCE FOR OTHER DISEASES

Sodium deficiency is vary rare even among populations whose intake is very low. Individuals subject to heavy and persistent sweating may become depleted, as may individuals suffering chronic diarrhoea or renal disease.

Sodium is identified as an important cause of hypertension and stroke in the amounts present in those diets that include substantial amounts of salted or salty food. The National Academy of Sciences (NAS, 1989) recommended a goal of 6 g/day of salt (2.4 g/day of sodium) to prevent high blood pressure. This recommendation was repeated in the report *Diet, Nutrition and the Prevention of Chronic Diseases* (WHO, 1990). Of 100 expert reports published between 1961 and 1991, mostly concerned with diet and cardiovascular diseases or diet and the chronic diseases, generally in developed countries and regions, 70 recommended lower salt consumption; two disagreed (Cannon, 1992).

FUTURE RESEARCH

The panel made the following recommendations for future research:

■ In relevant populations, studies on diet should collect data on salt as generally contained in foods—either manufactured or added at table as well as salt-preserved foods

ASSESSMENT

The evidence on which this assessment is in the relevant sections of chapter 4.

7.4.1 SALT

Diets that contain few foods preserved by salting may nevertheless be high in salt, because salt is used extensively as a preservative and flavour enhancer throughout the world, mostly in manufactured food, and also in cooking and at table.

Evidence of increased risk

CONVINCING	PROBABLE	POSSIBLE	INSUFFICIENT
	Stomach		

Stomach (4.6). One cohort, sixteen case-control and one ecological study have estimated overall dietary salt or sodium intake. The majority of these reported statistically significant increases in risk of stomach cancer with higher intake. Experimental data and identification of well-understood biological pathways, involving damage to the mucosal layer and a role of *H.Pylori*; amounts to evidence that diets high in salt probably increase the risk of stomach cancer.

7.4.2 SALTING

Stomach cancer rates are highest in those parts of the world such as Japan, some parts of China and Latin America, (particularly Chile, Costa Rica and Colombia), where diets are traditionally very salty because meat, fish, vegetables and other foods preserved by salting are eaten regularly, as they are in Portugal, where stomach cancer mortality is the highest in Western Europe. Much data on salt and cancer risk, notably that from Japan and China, and Latin American countries, concern salted food as well as salt in the diet.

Evidence of increased risk

CONVINCING	PROBABLE	POSSIBLE	INSUFFICIENT
Nasopharynx[a]	Stomach		

[a] Cantonese-style salted fish. Risk increases further when eaten by babies and small children

Nasopharynx (4.3). Data from epidemiological studies, supported by identification of plausible biological pathways, amount to convincing evidence that regular consumption of Chinese-style salted fish increase the risk of nasopharyngeal cancer. Risk is further increased if such foods are eaten by infants and small children.

Stomach (4.6). Strong and consistent data from three cohort, 28 case-control and one ecological study show varying degrees of increased risk, or no association with higher intakes of a range of salted foods. Experimental data and well-understood biological pathways, amount to evidence that regular consumption of salted foods, including meat, fish, vegetables and other foods, probably increase the risk of stomach cancer. The concentration or, as well as the overall amount of, salt in the diet increases risk.

7.4.3 REFRIGERATION

Refrigeration, including industrial freezing and chilling as well as domestic refrigeration, has the effect of making fresh vegetables and fruits, as well as other perishable foods, available all the year round, and so can be said to protect against all those cancers the risk of which are reduced by diets high in vegetables and fruits (see relevant sections of chapter 4, and chapter 6.3). Refrigeration also delays spoilage and microbial contamination and so might theoretically protect against primary liver and other cancers (see chapter 4.8 and 7.4).

Refrigeration also has the effect of reducing need for and use of salt as a method of preservation, and therefore reduces the risk of stomach cancer (see chapter 4.6, and above in this section. Direct evidence to date is confined to the effects of refrigeration on risk of stomach cancer.

Evidence of decreased risk

CONVINCING	PROBABLE	POSSIBLE	INSUFFICIENT
	Stomach		

Stomach (4.6). Ten case-control studies consistently show associations between use of various methods of refrigeration and decreased risk of stomach cancer. The panel judges this as convincing evidence, given that refrigeration results in reduced use of salt in diets and also makes perishable foods available all year round. The panel also agrees that it is reasonable to suppose that for this reason refrigeration may protect against other cancers, the risk of which is reduced by diets high in vegetables and fruits.

7.5 Cured and smoked foods

Curing and smoking have been used as a means to preserve meat and fish for thousands of years, and cured foods are a common item in many diets. Cured and smoked foods are commonly also salted, and cured foods are the chief single source of nitrites in many diets.

The panel has reached the following conclusions. There is no convincing evidence that curing or smoking modifies the risk of any cancer, nor is there evidence of any probable causal relationship. The panel notes that diets high in cured meats possibly increase the risk of colorectal cancer.

CURED AND SMOKED FOODS AND CANCER

In the judgement of the panel, diets containing substantial amounts of cured and smoked foods modify the risk of cancers of the sites as shown below. Judgements are graded according to the strength of the evidence.

	DECREASES RISK	NO RELATIONSHIP	INCREASES RISK
CONVINCING			
PROBABLE			
POSSIBLE			*Cured meats* Colon, rectum

INSUFFICIENT			*Cured foods*
			  Stomach
			  Pancreas
			Smoked foods
			  Pancreas

For an explanation of the terms used in the matrix, see chapter 3.

INTRODUCTION

Curing has been used as a method of preserving meat and fish for thousands of years, and cured foods are a common item in many diets. Foods are cured by being injected with a solution of nitrate or nitrite, salt, and other condiments, or else by being immersed in such solutions. The nitrites and nitrates act as preservatives, protecting against anaerobic pathogens. They also colour the meat.

Meat and fish have been smoked by exposure to the smoke of a wood or coal fire for centuries. Cured meat may also have been smoked. Smoked foods are often also salted.

In the stomach particularly, nitrites may be converted into nitrosamines. These *N*-nitroso compounds could be a factor in stomach cancer risk and may increase risk of other cancers but, as indicated in chapter 4.6, carcinogenicity studies on nitrite in animals had been negative, suggesting that in vivo formation of *N*-nitroso compounds does not occur to a significant extent. Nonetheless, high levels of amines in the diets of animals, and of nitrite in their drinking water, were effective in inducing forestomach tumours. Probably of much more significance is the presence of carcinogenic pre-formed *N*-nitroso compounds in cured meats and fish. In addition, nitrates used to cure food may be reduced to nitrite during storage at room temperature and act as a further source of nitrosating agents.

SCALE OF USE

Consumption of cured and smoked foods is variable in diets around the world. These foods are not now, however, usually staples, but are eaten mostly as delicacies. Prior to refrigeration, consumption of cured and smoked foods formed a larger part of food intake.

CARCINOGENIC CONTENT

Cured meats are the main single dietary source of nitrite, with vegetables, baked goods and processed cereal products making a smaller contribution. Cured meats and fish are generally the greatest contributors of pre-formed *N*-nitroso compounds in the diet.

Surveys of nitrate and nitrite levels in cured meats have revealed a steady decrease from 1960 to the present (US Academy of Life Sciences, 1981; MAFF 1978; 1992) due to technological and legislative changes. In the most recent survey, average levels of nitrate in a range of cured meat products were reported to be between 9 and 43 mg/kg; nitrite levels ranged from 4 to 54 mg/kg.

The carcinogenic *N*-nitrosamines most commonly found in cured meats are *N*-nitroso-dimethylamine (NDMA) and *N*-nitroso-diethylamine (NDEA), *N*-nitrosopyrrolidine (N-Pyr) and *N*-nitrosopiperidine (N-Pip). There are few data on the occurrence of N-nitrosamides. In early studies, levels of N-Pyr in cured meats, sausages and fried bacon ranged from 1 to 200 mg/kg; but most commonly lower than 10 μg/kg. Levels of N-Pip, NDEA and NDEA range from non-detectable up to 100 μg/kg (Walker, 1990). Dietary surveys in the UK indicated mean intakes of 1 μg/week of dialkylnitrosamines and 3 μg/week of heterocyclic nitrosamines (excluding exposure through beer) (MAFF, 1987).

Since the recognition that carcinogenic *N*-nitroso compounds may be formed in cured meats, steps have been taken to reduce their formation by limiting the amount of nitrite used and by the use of inhibitors of nitrosation, such as ascorbic acid, in the curing solution. As a result of these actions, current exposure in developed countries are lower than in the past.

INTERPRETATION OF THE DATA

Cured meats and fish are often salted (see chapter 7.4) as well as containing added nitrites, making it difficult to judge which, if either, of these constituents might be a factor in cancer risk. A further complication is that cured foods such as bacon may be cooked a high temperature, which may result in the formation of heterocyclic amines, themselves known carcinogens (see chapter 7.6)

Data on smoked foods can be difficult to interpret because such foods are commonly also salted.

SIGNIFICANCE FOR OTHER DISEASES

Smoking and curing preserve food otherwise liable to microbial contamination. Inasmuch as smoking and curing involve salting, these processes contribute to the load of salt in diets: see chapter 7.4.

ASSESSMENT

7.5.1 CURED FOODS

Evidence of increased risk

Convincing	Probable	Possible	Insufficient
			Stomach (cured meats)
		Colon, rectum (cured meats)	Pancreas (cured meat and fish)

Colon, rectum (4.10). Of nine studies on processed and cured meats, five reported statistically significant increased risk with higher intake, the other four found no association. Cured meats possibly increase the risk of colorectal cancer.

Stomach (4.6). A cohort and six case-control studies, some on specific cured meats, others on groups of cured meats, examined both consumption and frequency of consumption. The data showed small increased risks of stomach cancer with higher consumption of cured meats. The evidence suggests that diets high in cured meats increase the risk of stomach cancer but is, as yet, insufficient.

Pancreas (4.7). One cohort study and three case-control studies have reported increased risk with higher intakes or more frequent consumption of a range of cured meats or fish. The evidence suggests that diets high in cured meat and fish may increase the risk of pancreatic cancer but is, as yet, insufficient.

7.5.2 SMOKED FOODS

Evidence of increased risk
Epidemiological studies on smoked foods have focused primarily on stomach cancer. High rates of mortality from stomach cancer are found in countries such as Iceland, Hungary and Latvia where diets include a regular intake of meat and/or fish preserved by smoking.

Pancreas (4.7). A cohort study and a case-control study found increased risk with higher consumption of some smoked food. The evidence suggests that diets high in smoked foods may increase the risk of pancreatic cancer but is, as yet, insufficient.

7.6 Cooking

Most foods are cooked before eating. Cooked meals are characteristic of most civilisations, and preparation and enjoyment of cooked food is intrinsic to social and family life.

Cooking food at very high temperatures, especially in flame, generates chemicals that are mutagenic or carcinogenic in experimental conditions.

The panel has reached the following conclusions. There is no convincing evidence that any method of cooking modifies the risk of any cancer, nor is there evidence of any probably causal relationship. The panel notes that diets high in meat cooked at high temperatures possibly increase the risk of stomach and colorectal cancers.

COOKED FOOD AND CANCER

In the judgement of the panel, certain types of cooking modify the risk of cancers of the sites as shown below. Judgements are graded according to the strength of the evidence.

	DECREASES RISK	NO RELATIONSHIP	INCREASES RISK
CONVINCING			
PROBABLE			
POSSIBLE			*Grilling and barbecuing* Stomach (meat and fish) *Grilling, barbecuing and frying (meat and other foods)* Colon, rectum
INSUFFICIENT			*Frying (various foods)* Bladder

For an explanation of terms used in the matrix, see chapter 3.
The common element that links each of these somewhat disparate cooking methods is probably the production of specific mutagenic compounds – see text.

INTRODUCTION

Some epidemiological studies have explored the relationship between cancer and the consumption of cooked foods; most have focused in particular on foods cooked at high temperature.

Different methods of cooking: expose foods to different temperatures; may or may not use direct flame; and may or may not involve the use of fats and oils.

Steaming, boiling and stewing expose food to heat not exceeding 100°C. *Baking, microwaving and roasting* expose food to temperatures up to 200°C, but not to direct flame. *Roasting* usually involves basting the food with oils or fats. *Grilling (broiling) and barbecuing* use temperatures up to 400°C and sometimes direct flame to cook food. *Frying* with a pan or wok normally uses high surface temperatures.

Grilling, known in the USA as broiling, and barbecuing have been the subject of extensive research because these methods of food preparation can often generate mutagens (polycyclic aromatic hydrocarbons (PAHs) and heterocyclic amines (HCAs)) (see Box 7.6.1), a number of which are known animal carcinogens. Frying has been of special research interest because of its use of added fat and because it, too, generates HCAs.

BOX 7.6.1 POLYCYCLIC AROMATIC HYDROCARBONS

Grilling (broiling) meat, fish or other foods with intense heat over a direct flame results in fat dropping on the hot fire and yielding flames containing a number of polycyclic aromatic hydrocarbons (PAHs) such as benzo[a]pyrene and dibenzo[a,h]anthracene. These chemicals adhere to the surface of the food. The more intense the heat, the more PAHs are present (Bogovski, 1983).

These foods also contain heterocyclic amines (HCAs) (see Box 7.6.2 below) which are also potent mutagens and animal carcinogens. A fairly consistent association between grilled (broiled), but not fried, fish and meat and stomach cancer suggests that dietary exposure to PAHs may be involved in human gastric carcinogenesis.

Many PAH derivatives are known to be carcinogenic in laboratory animals (Bogovski, 1983). They are present in tobacco smoke, and account for parts of tobacco-related cancers in human. Oral administration of such compounds in an oily base has been shown to induce squamous carcinoma of the stomach in mice and to a lesser extent in rats, cancer of the mammary gland in sensitive strains of rats, and lymphomas or leukaemias in certain strains of mice and rats.

In animals and humans, intake of PAHs induce enzymes of the cytochrome P450 type and phase II enzymes such as glucuronyl or glutathione transferases, altering the potential of metabolising these and other chemicals and drugs (Guengerich, 1993). The role of dietary exposure in human carcinogenicity remains to be clarified. New sensitive methods of measuring DNA adducts may be useful in future research (Strickland et al, 1993).

CONSUMPTION PATTERNS

Thorough cooking reduces or eliminates risk of various forms of microbial contaminants, some of which can be life-threatening.

CARCINOGENIC CONTENT

PAHs are present in grilled meat or fish in very variable amounts (0–130 ng/g). The content of the polycyclic aromatic hydrocarbon benzo[a]pyrene (B(a)P) in these foods ranges from 0.2 to 50 ng/g (IARC 1983). Grilled meat in general is estimated to contain around 10.5 ng/g B(a)P. Levels of total *N*-nitroso compounds in salt-dried fish grilled in city gas are approximately five times higher than the values in uncooked salt-dried fish (IARC, 1993).

Detailed analysis of grilled, fried and otherwise cooked meats or fish shows that heterocyclic amines occur in relatively small but very variable amounts, between 0.1 and 500 ng/g of meat (beef, chicken, pork, lamb) or fish, depending on the cooking method, degree of heat, and length of cooking. Barbecuing produces up to 500 ng/g (Sinha et al, 1995; Knize et al, 1995; Sinha et al, 1996).

For any cooking involving wood fires, the type of wood used can also be important. Hardwoods, such as oak and hickory, burn cleanly; whereas some woods such as mesquite, generate copious quantities of polycyclic aromatic hydrocarbons.

Grilling with sauces can often result in a burned meat surface.

Cooking methods involving grilling can produce marked differences in the levels of carcinogens. For example, fat dripping on hot surfaces can form PAHs and HCAs, while oven-grilling prevents reflux of pyrolysed drippings and results in much lower levels of PAHs and HCAs in the cooked food.

INTERPRETATION OF THE DATA

Interpretation of epidemiological data on cooked meat is made difficult by confounding with meat itself, with animal fat, and with animal protein.

In addition, the terminology used for different types of cooking varies around the world. In Japan, 'broiling' exposes foods directly to flame or other heat sources whereas 'grilling' may use a hot surface as well as direct exposure. 'Barbecuing' also has different meanings worldwide, ranging from grilling over direct flame to slow cooking near smoking embers. The results may therefore be confused, given that more carcinogenic compounds may be generated when direct flame is used.

SIGNIFICANCE FOR OTHER DISEASES

Grilling (broiling) may be recommended in the context of prevention of heart disease, inasmuch as this reduces the amount of fat and saturated fat in animal products as eaten.

BOX 7.6.2 HETEROCYCLIC AMINES

Sugimura and his colleagues (Sugimura et al, 1977; Nagao et al, 1977) demonstrated in 1977 that the charred surfaces of fish and beef, broiled over a direct flame or charcoal, were highly mutagenic in the Ames bacterial system; the mutagenic activities were far more potent than expected from the amount of benzo[a]pyrene contained in these materials. Commoner et al (1978) reported similar mutagenic activity in meats prepared by normal household cooking methods.

In the ensuing years heterocyclic amines (HCAs), a family of mutagenic compounds, have been isolated from various cooked meats and fish, as reviewed in detail by Skog (1993), Eisenbrand and Tang (1993), and Layton et al (1995). Of these, amino-imidazo-quinolines or amino-imidazo-quinoxalines (collectively called as IQ-type compounds) and amino-imidazo-pyridines such as PhIP are predominant classes of heterocyclic amines found in cooked meats and fish. However, when foods actually catch fire or burn, the aminocarbolines predominate.

IQ compounds and PhIP are formed from creatine or creatinine, certain amino acids, and sugars (Jägerstad et al, 1991). Since meats and fish are rich in creatine, the cooking of meats and fish at high temperature forms HCAs. (Jägerstad et al, 1991; Eisenbrand and Tang, 1993; Skog, 1993; Layton et al, 1995; Sinha et al, 1995). In general, grilling and frying produce high mutagenic activity and high yield of HCAs; boiling yields little or no mutagenic activity; and deep fat frying, roasting, and baking produce variable mutagenic activities. Specifically, it is the burning of meat juices that generates these carcinogens. Most fast-food hamburgers do not form high amounts of HAAs (Knize et al, 1995).

It has been found that brief pre-heating of raw meats by microwave greatly reduces the mutagenic activity and amount of heterocyclic amines in fried meats because such pre-treatment removes much of the crea-tine (Felton et al, 1994). Because PhIP is often the most abundant heterocyclic amine in cooked foods and because the oral administration of PhIP primarily induces both large-bowel and mammary cancers in animals (Wakabayashi et al, 1992; Minchin et al, 1993; Nagao and Sugimura, 1993), much research work has been devoted to investigation of exposure to this carcinogen and its relationship with these cancers in humans (Snyderwine, 1994).

Some people may be more vulnerable to HCAs than others. Supportive data have also been obtained from studies on polymorphic enzymes involved in the metabolism of heterocyclic amines, cytochrome P4501A2 (CYP1A2) and N-acetyltransferase type 2 (NAT2). Individuals possessing rapid CYP1A2 and rapid NAT2 phenotypes are considered to be more susceptible to colorectal cancer because they rapidly activate heterocyclic amines to reactive forms (Minchin et al, 1993; Nagao and Sugimura, 1993). In two (Lang et al, 1986; Ilett et al, 1987) of three reported studies (Lang et al, 1986; Ilett et al, 1987; Ladero et al, 1991), rapid acetylators determined by phenotype were more frequent in colorectal cancer patients than in control subjects. Minchin et al (1993) reported that rapid acetylators accounted for 47% (147/313) of colorectal cancer patients and 33% (94/286) of controls (p=0.001).

A case-control study of 75 cases and 205 controls demonstrated that presence of both the rapid CYP1A2 and rapid NAT2 phenotypes was associated with a 2.8-fold (p = 0.002) increase in the risk of colorectal cancer and polyps combined (Lang et al, 1994). However, a case-control study of colon adenomas found no measurable difference in the genetically determined NAT2 status between 447 cases and 487 controls (Probst-Hensch et al, 1995).

Heterocyclic amines so far tested have all been shown to be carcinogenic in various organs in mice, rats, and monkeys after long-term dietary administration: see reviews by Wakabayashi et al (1992), Nagao and Sugimura (1993), and Snyderwine (1994). In mice, IQ compounds induced tumours mainly in the liver but also in the lung, forestomach, and hematopoietic system. Rats developed tumours in the liver, large and small intestine, mammary gland, and other organs. PhIP induced primarily large-bowel cancer in rats, more frequently in male rats, mammary cancers in female rats, and lymphoma in mice. Heterocyclic amines of other amino acid pyrolysates mainly induced tumours in the liver and blood vessels in mice, and in the liver and intestines in rats and mice. The exposures in these experiments were, however, very much higher than exposures in humans from diets.

The overall estimates of cancer risk from these chemicals have so far been calculated, from two-year feeding studies, to be relatively small and insufficient to associate their presence directly with human cancers Layton et al, 1995; Gold et al, 1994; Stavric, 1994). However, carcinogenic HCAs have been detected in the urine of healthy subjects eating normal diets (Ushiyama et al, 1991), and evidence for the secretion of heterocyclic amines in the breast milk of lactating animals has also been noted (David et al, 1994). Moreover, recent studies now show that short-term feeding (6–12 weeks) is sufficient to induce tumours in experimental animals (Shirai et al, 1996; Snyderwine et al, 1996).

These data indicate that humans are exposed to HCAs in foods continuously from early life, even in utero. The effects of HCAs such as PhIP and IQ on the colon in male rats and on the mammary gland in female rats are powerfully promoted by a dietary fat level of 40 per cent of calories, the typical fat intake in many industrialised countries (Snyderwine, 1994; Weisburger et al, 1995).

ASSESSMENT

The evidence on which this assessment is based is reviewed in the relevant sections of chapter 4.

7.6.1 GRILLING (BROILING) AND BARBECUING; FRYING

Evidence of increased risk

CONVINCING	PROBABLE	POSSIBLE	INSUFFICIENT
		Stomach (meat and fish, grilled and barbecued) Colon, rectum (meat and other foods, grilled, barbecued and fried)	Bladder (various food, fried)

Stomach (4.6). A small number of epidemiological studies reviewing the frequency of consumption of grilled foods show increases in risk of stomach cancer for both meat and fish. One study reported increased mortality from stomach cancer with frequent consumption of grilled fish. Together with the experimental evidence and the biological pathways identified, this data suggests that the grilling of meat and fish possibly increase the risk of stomach cancer. It is also reasonable to assume that data on grilling apply to some forms of barbecuing.

Epidemiological evidence from nine studies on the relationship between stomach cancer and the level or frequency of consumption of fried meat, fried fish and other fried foods (alone or in combination) is inconsistent. Frying meat or fish results in the formation of HCAs. However, there is no experimental data linking HCAs to gastric cancer, and no judgement can be made.

Colon, rectum (4.10). Several case-control studies show an association between consumption of fried foods, broiled foods, or gravy and the risk of colorectal cancer. An increased risk is also shown to be associated with consumption of gravy and with the consumption of meat which is well-done or browned. Taken together with experimental evidence and plausible biological pathways, this evidence suggests that consumption of foods cooked at high temperature possibly increases the risk of colorectal cancer.

Bladder (4.18). One cohort and three case-control studies suggest that higher consumption of a range of fried foods including vegetables, fish, meat, eggs may increase the risk of bladder cancer but the data are, at present, insufficient.

PART IV

POLICY

CHAPTER EIGHT

Recommendations

It is now established that cancer is principally caused by environmental factors, of which the most important are tobacco; diet and factors related to diet, including body mass and physical activity; and exposures in the workplace and elsewhere. These interact with the differing vulnerability, both inherited and acquired, of individuals' constitutions. Much of the world's cancer burden could therefore be prevented if people did not smoke tobacco, by appropriate dietary and activity patterns, and by reducing other environmental exposures. This chapter sets out and explains the recommendations agreed by the panel, and puts them in a broad context of the prevention of disease.

Evidence of dietary protection against cancer is strongest and most consistent for diets high in vegetables and fruits. Evidence that physical activity protects against colon cancer is convincing. Evidence that alcohol increases the risk of cancers of the mouth and pharynx, larynx, oesophagus and liver, and that high body mass increases the risk of cancer of the endometrium, is convincing. Evidence that refrigeration of food protects against stomach cancer is convincing. Other aspects of diet probably or possibly modify the risk of cancers of various sites. There is essentially no evidence that dietary factors may decrease the risk of some cancers while increasing the risk of others. The recommendations in this chapter are therefore made with confidence of their probable impact on cancer in general.

Further, as shown in the third section of this chapter on other public health consequences, the recommendations made here are not only derived from, or generally supported by, the evidence on food, nutrition and the prevention of cancer but, also, are generally consistent with other dietary recommendations which have been designed to prevent infectious, deficiency, and other major chronic diseases and disorders. The panel's recommendations, therefore, should yield more benefit than solely the reduction of cancer incidence and mortality.

Fourteen dietary recommendations are made in the first section of this chapter. They are informed by the ten principles set out in the second section. They are specified both as goals for policy-makers, and as advice to the general public on achieving the goals. Most of the recommendations are food-based, and they are quantified wherever practicable. They cover foods and drinks, eating patterns, dietary supplementation, physical activity and obesity.

The first three recommendations concern food supplies and eating, the maintenance of body weight, and the maintenance of physical activity. The next five concern foods and drinks: specifically, vegetables and fruits, other plant foods, alcoholic drinks, meat, and fats and oils. Five further recommendations concern aspects of food processing: salt and salting, food storage and preservation, additives and residues, and food preparation. The final dietary recommendation concerns supplementation.

The recommendations are generally derived from convincing evidence of causal relationships with the risk of cancer, or else from evidence of probable causal relationships. The recommendations on other plant foods, additives and residues, and on food preparation, derive from less impressive evidence, but are included to enable the construction of complete diets derived from the recommendations, for reasons of prudence, or else in response to public concern.

The panel has also included a recommendation on not using tobacco. For some cancers, the effect of smoking tobacco can overwhelm any protective effect of following the recommendations presented here, and can interact strongly with the effects of consuming alcohol.

From the nutritional and culinary points of view, the recommended diets are similar to cuisines already well-established in various parts of the world, and are based on the regular consumption of a variety of vegetables, fruits and staple starchy foods.

FOOD, NUTRITION AND THE PREVENTION OF CANCER: AN OVERVIEW

This matrix summarises the judgements on dietary constituents, foods and drinks, and food processing, and the risk of cancer as shown in the individual matrices accompanying chapters 4, 5, 6 and 7 of this report. The methods used to reach the judgements are described in chapter 3.

This matrix is designed as a convenient reference: the rows specify the individual cancers reviewed in chapter 4; the columns on the left-hand page show aspects of diet that decrease the risk of cancer and those on the right-hand page those that increase the risk of cancer.

The strength of the current evidence is shown by the height of the blocks (see key). Evidence judged by the panel to be suggestive, but insufficient, is omitted, as are judgements on aspects of diet with no relationship to cancer risk.

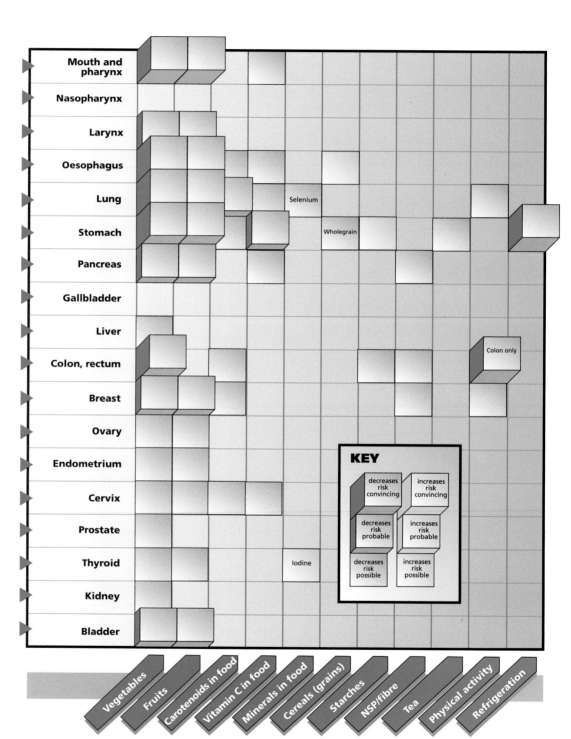

KEY

	decreases risk convincing	increases risk convincing
decreases risk probable	increases risk probable
decreases risk possible	increases risk possible

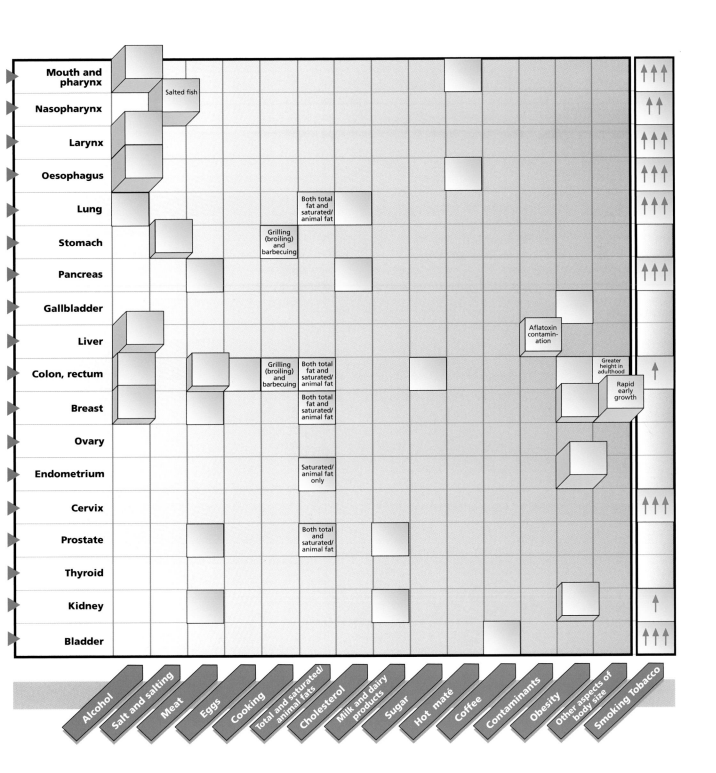

8.1 Goals for populations, advice for individuals

The panel's recommendations on foods and drinks, food processing, and other dietary and related factors designed to prevent cancer, are specified here. They are informed by the principles specified in chapter 8.2. For reviews and assessments of the evidence see the relevant sections of chapters 4–7.

The recommendations have an integrated structure and are designed to be implemented as a whole. It is not intended that individual recommendations be promoted or followed out of context.

The relative importance of the recommendations will vary in different parts of the world and for different populations. The goals are for policy-makers at international, national and local levels, and are also applicable to individuals. The advice to individuals, aged two years and above unless otherwise specified, includes weights of foods and portion sizes, and is designed for use by the general public.

Recommendations 1–3 concern the food supply, eating, the maintenance of body weight and physical activity. The panel judges that adequate and varied plant-based diets, avoidance of both obesity and weight gain, and regular physical activity are all protective against cancer.

BOX 8.1.1   PRINCIPLES

The recommendations here are based on the following principles, which are set out in detail in chapter 8.2:

- **QUANTIFICATION**: when possible, recommendations are quantified. Qualitative guidelines are also specified when appropriate.
- **RANGES OF INTAKE**: recommendations are usually expressed as ranges specifying lower and upper limits of intake.
- **ENERGY BASIS**: when appropriate, they are expressed as a percentage of total energy.
- **WHOLE POPULATION APPROACH**: they propose goals for whole populations, as well as for individuals within populations.
- **GLOBAL APPROACH**: they are designed to accommodate worldwide diversity.
- **CANCER IN GENERAL**: they are designed to accommodate the diversity of factors affecting most cancers, but especially those that are most common.
- **FOOD BASIS**: the recommendations are generally food-based rather than based on individual dietary constituents.
- **POSITIVE ADVICE**: the recommendations emphasise foods and drinks, methods of food processing, and dietary constituents that protect against cancer.
- **BIOLOGICAL PLAUSIBILITY**: they both rely on epidemiological data and take into account experimental data and plausible biological mechanisms.
- **CULTURE AND CUISINE**: they are designed to correspond to diets actually eaten in a variety of societies.

Recommendations 4–8 concern specific foods and drinks. The panel emphasises the value of diets high in vegetables and fruits, with little or no consumption of alcoholic drinks, with , at most, modest consumption of red meat, with modest consumption of fats and oils, and also, to ensure appropriate diets, with consumption of a variety of starchy or protein-rich foods of plant origin.

Recommendations 9–13 concern food processing in its broadest sense. The panel recommends diets that include only moderate amounts of salt, together with appropriate use of storage and preservation, careful regulation of chemicals, the residue of which may be found in foods and drinks, and the avoidance of charred food. Recommendation 14 emphasises the value of consuming diets that are adequate to protect agains cancer without the need of supplementation. Finally, the panel endorses the universal agreement that tobacco in all forms should be avoided.

8.1.1 FOOD SUPPLY, EATING AND RELATED FACTORS

RECOMMENDATION 1

FOOD SUPPLY AND EATING

PUBLIC HEALTH GOAL

Populations to consume nutritionally adequate and varied diets, based primarily on foods of plant origin

ADVICE TO INDIVIDUALS

Choose predominantly plant-based diets rich in a variety of vegetables and fruits, pulses (legumes) and minimally processed starchy staple foods

PLANT-BASED DIETS AND CANCER RISK

The evidence that diets high in vegetables and fruits protect against cancers of many sites is strong and consistent. The evidence is less strong for diets high in minimally processed starchy staple foods, which form the basis of generally healthy diets, but it shows a possible protective effect.

If plant-based diets consist of a variety of vegetables, fruits, pulses and minimally processed starchy staple foods, they are low in energy. These diets may prevent a variety of

cancers, either directly, because of their inclusion of constituents commonly found in foods of plant origin that are protective against cancer, or indirectly because of their exclusion of other constituents commonly found in foods of animal origin. Minimising the consumption of red meat possibly protects against cancer at several sites. Plant-based diets also may protect against obesity, which probably increases the risk of some cancers.

This does not, however, mean that the evidence shows that vegetarian diets (however defined) are more protective against cancer than other diets that are consistent with the recommendations of this report, that may include many protective foods and also modest amounts of meat. The recommendations also accommodate other foods of animal origin that may make an important nutritional contribution to the diets of vegetarians other than vegans.

RECOMMENDATION

In the judgement of the panel, diets should be based primarily on foods of plant origin, provided that such diets are also nutritionally adequate and varied.

This recommendation is similar to, but broader than, those of other expert reports, concerned either to prevent cancer specifically (ACS, 1996) or to do so in the context of other chronic diseases (NAS, 1989).

MAINTAINING BODY WEIGHT

PUBLIC HEALTH GOAL

Population average body mass indices throughout adult life to be within the range BMI 21–23, in order that individual BMI be maintained between 18.5 and 25

ADVICE TO INDIVIDUALS

Avoid being underweight or overweight and limit weight gain during adulthood to less than 5 kg (11 pounds)

The advice to individuals is equivalent to maintaining BMI between 18.5 and 25.0. In affluent, less physically active societies, lower average BMI levels may be desirable. For calculations of BMI for people of different heights and weights, see Figure 8.1.1.

BODY MASS AND CANCER RISK

In the view of the panel, energy-dense diets increase the risk of high body mass or obesity (defined here as body mass index, BMI, above 30), and risk is further increased in economically developed regions where populations are typically sedentary. The evidence that obesity increases the risk of cancer of the endometrium is convincing. Obesity also probably increases the risk of cancer of the breast in post-menopausal women and cancer of the kidney. It possibly increases the risk of cancer of the colon. (See chapters 4.10, 4.11, 4.13, 4.17 and 5.1.)

Overweight (BMI = 25–30) rather than obesity also increases the risk of cancer in general (Lew and Garfinkel, 1978; Goldstein, 1992; Williamson et al, 1995), and overweight children and adolescents are liable to become persistently obese in early adult life. Smoking tobacco may limit weight gain in itself, but causes and contributes to many types of cancer.

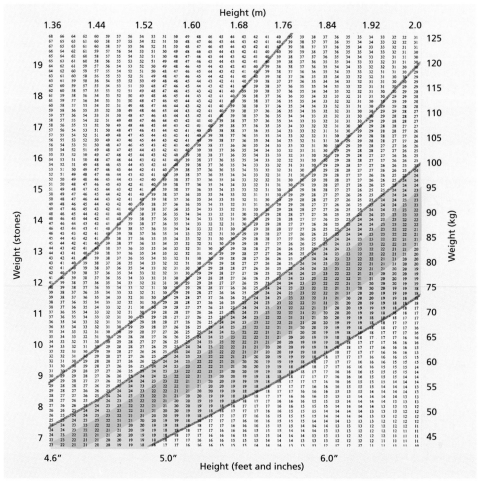

Adapted from SIGN, 1996.

Figure 8.1.1: Body mass indices

This shows BMI values for people of varying heights and weights. BMI between 18.5 and 25 is highlighted in the figure; the narrower band of BMI between 21 and 23 is shown in the darkest tint. The figure can be used as a ready reckoner for populations and for individuals.

RECOMMENDATION

The evidence reviewed in the relevant sections of chapter 4, and assessed in chapter 5.1, supports a goal of a BMI of 21–23 on a population basis; individuals should maintain a BMI of 18.5–25 throughout life. Figure 8.1.1 enables individuals to assess their own BMI.

These ranges are sufficiently wide to allow individuals with a small bone frame size and muscle mass to gain substantial weight before they exceed the recommended limit. Sedentary populations and individuals may gain further benefit from having BMIs towards the lower end of the recommended ranges (Manson et al, 1995). It is also important not to increase weight significantly during adult life, because excess weight gain itself is disadvantageous – insulin resistance and other risk factors become prominent during weight gain – and an upper limit of a 5 kg weight increase during adult life (age 18 years and above) is advised (Sonne-Holm et al, 1989).

An optimum weight can be maintained or achieved by adopting the other recommendations in this report, notably those on physical activity and foods of low energy density. (See Recommendations 3, 4 and 5.)

This recommendation is similar to those of other expert reports concerned either to prevent cancer specifically (European Code Against Cancer, 1995; ACS, 1996; Harvard Report on Cancer Prevention, 1996) or to do so in the context of other chronic diseases (NAS, 1989; WHO, 1990).

RECOMMENDATION 3
● ●

MAINTAINING PHYSICAL ACTIVITY

PUBLIC HEALTH GOAL

Populations to maintain, throughout life, an active lifestyle equivalent to a physical activity level (PAL) of at least 1.75, with opportunities for vigorous physical activity

ADVICE TO INDIVIDUALS

If occupational activity is low or moderate, take an hour's brisk walk or similar exercise daily, and also exercise vigorously for a total of at least one hour in a week

For equivalents of brisk walking and other vigorous exercise, see Table 8.1.1.

PHYSICAL ACTIVITY AND CANCER RISK

There is convincing evidence that regular physical activity, best expressed in terms of a relatively high physical activity level (PAL), protects against colon cancer. Regular physical activity possibly also protects against cancers of the breast, and lung. In addition, it protects against overweight and obesity and therefore against cancers for which the risk increases with obesity – see Recommendation 2. (See also chapters 4.10. and 5.1.)

TABLE 8.1.1 PHYSICAL ACTIVITY: WAYS TO SUSTAIN A PAL OF 1.75 OR MORE

This table is designed for individuals who are relatively sedentary, and whose physical activity level (PAL) is therefore likely to be around 1.55–1.60. Individuals whose occupation involves regular physical activity are likely to be at levels of PAL of 1.75 or more. The table shows ways in which PAL can be raised from 1.55–1.60 to 1.75 or more by an extra hour's moderate activity a day, plus an hour's vigorous activity a week. Physical activity can, of course, be adapted to suit national and local culture and custom and individual preference.

PAL values express energy expenditure per day as a multiple of basal metabolic rate (BMR), which allows adjustment for individuals of different sizes.

PAL values are a universally accepted way of expressing energy expenditure, and they also help to convey an easily understandable concept. In this report, moderate physical activity (for example, brisk walking) has been defined as exercise with an activity-to-resting metabolism of 4–5, and vigorous activity has been defined as exercise with a ratio of 7–8. All values are approximate. Individuals may prefer to spend less time performing a more strenuous activity; alternative times for activities with an activity ratio above 5 or 8 have therefore also been suggested to bring the overall average daily PAL up to 1.75.

Equivalent of 1 hour's moderate physical activity daily	Equivalent of 1 hour's vigorous physical activity weekly
1 hour (activity ratio 4–5) brisk walk (6 km/h) canoeing (5 km/h) cycling (12 km/h) gardening baseball volleyball	**1 hour (activity ratio 7–8)** brisk hillwalking (6 km/h) canoeing (7 km/h) swimming, breast stroke (40 m/min) running (8 km/hour) cross-country skiing (6.5 km/h) climbing stairs tennis
45 min (activity ratio 6–7) cross-country hiking cycling (15 km/h) skating (14 km/h) snowshoeing (4 km/h) water skiing dancing	**45 min (activity ratio 8–10)** mountain climbing cycling (21 km/h) running (10 km/h) squash swimming, crawl (50 m/min) cross-country skiing (8 km/h)
30 min (activity ratio 10–12) any 'vigorous' activity	**30 min (activity ratio 10–12)** basketball (competition) football (soccer) hockey running (13 km/h) rugby handball

To convert kilometres per hour (km/h) to miles per hour (mph) multiply by 5/8.
For example, 12 km/h equals 7.5 mph.
Adapted from McArdle et al, 1981; Shepherd, 1987; SIGN, 1996.

RECOMMENDATION

The evidence reviewed in the relevant sections of chapter 4 and assessed in chapter 5.1 provides the basis for the goal that populations should remain physically active throughout life at a PAL of 1.75 or more. Table 8.1.1 shows options for sedentary people to sustain such levels.

The goal corresponds broadly to the physical activity levels of people with active occupations (Ferro-Luzzi and Martino, 1996). People with sedentary occupations whose PAL may therefore average between 1.55 and 1.60 can achieve a PAL of more than 1.75 by physical activity amounting to an hour's brisk walking a day, plus another hour's vigorous physical activity during a week, or equivalent. Table 8.1.1 gives examples of how a PAL of more than 1.75 can be achieved through a variety of physical activities.

This recommendation is comparable with or similar to those of other expert reports concerned either to prevent cancer specifically (European Code Against Cancer, 1995; ACS, 1996; Harvard Report on Cancer Prevention, 1996) or to do so in the context of other chronic diseases (WHO, 1990; National Forum for Coronary Heart Disease Prevention, 1995; US Department of Health and Human Services, 1996).

8.1.2 FOODS AND DRINKS

RECOMMENDATION 4
• •
VEGETABLES AND FRUITS

PUBLIC HEALTH GOAL
Promote year-round consumption of a variety of vegetables and fruits, providing 7% or more total energy

ADVICE TO INDIVIDUALS
Eat 400–800 grams (15–30 ounces) or five or more portions (servings) a day of a variety of vegetables and fruits, all year round

Pulses (legumes), and starchy vegetables and fruits (tubers, starchy roots and plantains) are not included. (See Recommendation 5.)

VEGETABLES AND FRUITS, AND CANCER RISK

There is convincing evidence that diets high in vegetables and /or fruits protect against cancers of the mouth and pharynx, oesophagus, lung (in particular, the evidence is strongest for green vegetables), stomach (in particular, the evidence is strongest for raw vegetables, green vegetables, allium vegetables (the onion family), carrots, tomatoes and citrus fruit), and colon and rectum. Such diets probably also protect against cancers of the larynx, pancreas, breast and bladder, and possibly against cancers of the liver, ovary, endometrium, cervix, prostate, thyroid, and kidney. (See rel-

evant sections of chapters 4 and 6.3.)

Many vegetables and fruits are good sources of fibre and many vitamins, minerals and other bioactive compounds. Diets high in dietary fibre possibly protect against cancers of the pancreas, colon and rectum, and breast. Diets high in the naturally occurring carotenoids probably protect against cancer of the lung, and possibly protect against cancers of the oesophagus, colon and rectum, stomach, breast and cervix. Diets high in naturally occurring vitamin C probably protect against cancer of the stomach, and possibly against cancers of the mouth and pharynx, oesophagus, lung, pancreas, and cervix.

Many constituents found in plant-based foods have been identified as possibly protective against cancer and investigated since the 1970s. Although this research illustrates the ability of these constituents to prevent various cancers under restrictive experimental conditions, the panel believes that these findings should be interpreted in the form of whole foods containing these constituents, not in the form of nutrient supplements.

RECOMMENDATION

The evidence reviewed in the relevant sections of chapter 4, and assessed in chapter 6.3, supports a goal for policy-makers that populations should consume 7% or more of total energy from vegetables and fruits, and that individuals should consume 400–800 grams, that is, five or more portions (servings) per day of vegetables and fruits. In round figures, this is the equivalent of 15–30 ounces.

Table 8.1.2 is designed as a guide for planning food supplies and for individuals. On the basis that an average portion of vegetables or fruits may weigh 80 grams (Williams, 1995), a minimum consumption of 400 g/day amounts to at least five portions a day. A maximum of 800 grams is equivalent to ten portions of 80 g/day (although people who consume such amounts are actually likely to eat a lesser number of portions of larger size).

The recommendation to eat a variety of vegetables and fruits all year round is important because the carcinogenesis process (chapter 2) involves a recurrent and accumulative alteration of DNA in genes that control tissue growth; the protective benefits of vegetables and fruits are likely to depend on a variety of components with short- or medium-term storage times in the body, and seasonal shortages in vegetables and fruits may therefore contribute to the rate of progressive genetic change. Vegetables and fruits that are particularly valuable include green leafy vegetables and citrus fruits, but these should not be eaten to the exclusion of other vegetables and fruits.

Table 8.1.2 is not prescriptive. It simply suggests some possible combinations of vegetables and fruits, and shows that the recommended goal can readily be sustained by an average daily consumption of between four and six and a half portions of vegetables, plus between one and three and a half portions of fruits. Some fruits, such as a single orange or apple, may each be roughly the equivalent of one portion. The panel suggests that juices, which contain little if any non-starch polysaccharide (NSP)/dietary fibre, count as no more than one daily portion.

The average energy value of vegetables and fruits varies somewhat but can be taken as around 35 kcal/100 g (150 kJ/100 g). A few vegetables and fruits have higher energy density, notably olives and avocados. Starchy roots, tubers and plantains, including bananas, with an energy value of around 100 kcal/100 g (425 kJ/100 g), are counted as starchy staple foods (see Recommendation 5).

This recommendation is similar to, or consistent with, those of other expert reports concerned to prevent cancer specifically (NCI, 1994; ACS, 1996; Harvard Report on Cancer Prevention, 1996), but specifically encourages higher intakes. It also accords with recommendations for other chronic diseases (NAS, 1989; WHO, 1990).

RECOMMENDATION 5

OTHER PLANT FOODS

PUBLIC HEALTH GOAL

A variety of starchy or protein-rich foods of plant origin, preferably minimally processed, to provide 45–60% total energy. Refined sugar to provide less than 10% total energy

ADVICE TO INDIVIDUALS

Eat 600–800 grams (20–30 ounces) or more than seven portions a day of a variety of cereals (grains), pulses (legumes), roots, tubers and plantains. Prefer minimally processed foods. Limit consumption of refined sugar

Non-starchy roots are counted as vegetables (see Recommendation 4). In societies where diets are based on cereals, such as rice or millet, the weight of starchy and protein-rich foods of plant origin may be higher, say up to 1,000 g/day as served. Set portion (serving) sizes are not a meaningful concept in many societies, and those whose diets are cereal-based consume larger, rather than more frequent, portions.
This recommendation is consistent with, and generally supported by, but not primarily derived from, the data on cancer. (See chapter 8.3.)

TABLE 8.1.2 VEGETABLES AND FRUITS: WAYS TO SUSTAIN INTAKES OF 7% OR MORE OF TOTAL ENERGY

Recommendations for daily intake are expressed as a percentage of total energy intake, as grams and as portions (servings).

Energy values are for vegetables and fruits that are raw, or prepared or cooked and ready to eat, reconstituted with the addition of water if initially dried, but without any added fat or sugar. The recommendation can, of course, be achieved by limitless combinations of a variety of vegetables and fruits.

	Range for daily average intake		
	% total energy	grams	portions[a]
Total vegetables	5.6–9.1	320–520	4.0–6.5
green leafy	2.8–4.2	160–240	2.0–3.0
other	2.8–4.9	160–280	2.0–3.5
Total fruits	1.4–4.9	80–280	1.0–3.5
citrus	0.7–2.1	40–120	0.5–1.5
other	0.7–2.8	40–160	0.5–2.0
Total vegetables and fruits	**7.0–14.0**	**400–800**	**5.0–10.0**

[a]At higher levels of intake, portion sizes are likely to be larger. Any combination of a variety of vegetables and fruits is recommended: these figures are illustrative only.

Calculated on the basis of 2,000 kcal (8.4 MJ) daily energy intake, 80 grams per portion, average 35 kcal/100 g (150 kJ/100 g) for vegetables and fruits. Different bases for total energy intake and for portion sizes will produce different goals, for example, children's portions to be appropriately smaller. Pulses (legumes) and starchy vegetables are not included here but as part of Recommendation 5.

OTHER PLANT FOODS AND CANCER RISK

Diets high in wholegrain cereals possibly decrease the risk of cancer of the stomach. Diets high in starch possibly decrease the risk of cancer of the colon and rectum. In the view of the panel, the contrary epidemiological evidence that diets high in cereals possibly increase the risk of cancer of the oesophagus and diets high in starch possibly increase the risk of cancer of the stomach is likely to apply only when such diets are monotonous, or very high in processed carbohydrates, and thus deficient in protective dietary constituents.

Diets containing substantial amounts of NSP/fibre, found in cereals (grains) and pulses (legumes) as well as in vegetables and fruits, possibly decrease the risk of cancer of the colon, rectum, breast and pancreas; diets containing substantial amounts of refined sugar possibly increase the risk of cancer of the colon and rectum. Cereals, roots, tubers, plantains and pulses are relatively good sources of various microconstituents, for which there is evidence of probable and possible protection against cancers of some sites. These microconstituents include carotenoids, found in sweet potatoes, folate in pulses, vitamin E in wholegrain cereals, and vitamin C in potatoes, sweet potatoes and pulses. (See chapters 4.6, 4.7, 4.10, 4.11, 5.2, 5.6, 6.1, 6.2 and 6.4.)

RECOMMENDATION

The data reviewed in the relevant sections of chapter 4, and assessed in chapters 5 and 6, are consistent with the following recommendations: that 45–60% total energy comes from a variety of starchy and protein-rich foods of plant origin; that such foods are minimally refined; and that less than 10% total energy comes from refined sugar.

As in other reports, these recommendations are made

partly for practical reasons. First, starchy foods are staples in most parts of the world, and policy-makers and the public need to know that these foods are generally beneficial to health and an important source of energy. Second, diets high in a variety of starchy and protein-rich foods of plant origin are the prudent choice in the context of cancer prevention, in contrast to diets high in meat, fat, animal fat, sugar or alcohol.

Table 8.1.3 is designed as a guide for planning food supplies for populations as well as for individuals. On the basis that an average portion of any starchy or protein-rich food of plant origin may weigh around 80 grams, a recommendation of 600–800 g/day amounts approximately to more than seven portions per day. In practice, people are likely to eat larger amounts at any one meal. The concept of a portion of 80 grams is often less meaningful in societies in which diets are cereal-based and portions typically much larger.

Many cereals are a valuable source of protein. Pulses are rich sources of protein. The recommendation to eat a variety of starchy foods, preferably in a minimally processed form, is important. Variety ensures that intakes of various starches and other complex carbohydrates, each of which may have unique nutritional value, are more likely to provide better health. Whole grains, such as brown rice, wholegrain bread and brown pasta, are higher in essential fats, vitamins (notably B vitamins) and minerals, and also in fibre. Plantains, including bananas, are a good source of resistant starch. In areas where only one type of grain or tuber or root is available, varying the diet with other starchy foods, as well as with pulses, may be valuable.

No essential difference in the risk of cancer is evident between different forms of refined sugar added to foods and drinks (sucrose, glucose, high-fructose corn syrup, other syrups; white, brown and other sugars), and honey can be classified as a naturally refined sugar. There is no evidence that sugar contained as an intrinsic part of fruits and other foods affects cancer risk. Naturally sweet foods need not be restricted, and diets high in fruits are recommended (see Recommendation 4).

Table 8.1.3 is not prescriptive and allows for two types of diet. The first is for societies with cereal-based diets, where the goal is readily sustained by consumption of 600–800 g/day of grains such as rice. The second is for societies in which diets are based on cereal *products* such as pasta and breads, or tubers, such as cassava or potatoes, and where the goal is readily sustained by, say: three portions of pasta, three of bread, and two of cassava or potatoes; one portion of pasta, five of bread, and one of starchy roots or tubers; or two of cereals, four of bread, and one of plantain or banana. In either case, pulses are recommended.

The average energy value of starchy staple foods varies but can be taken as about 125 kcal/100 g (525 kJ/100 g) for grains, 200 kcal/100 g (850 kJ/100 g) for breads, 100 kcal/100 g (425 kJ/100 g) for starchy roots and tubers, and 100 kcal/100 g (425 kJ/100 g) for plantains, including bananas. Protein-rich foods of plant origin (that is, pulses) have an energy value of about 100 kcal/100 g (425 kJ/100 g).

Cereal-based foods with added fat and sugar, such as baked goods and breakfast cereals, have higher energy values of 250–500 kcal/100 g (1–2 MJ/100 g), as do pulses with added fat.

This recommendation on starchy and protein-rich foods of plant origin is similar to, although rather more specific than, those of other expert reports concerned either to prevent cancer specifically (ACS, 1996), or to do so in the context of other chronic diseases (NAS, 1989; WHO, 1990). The recommendation on sugar is similar to that of other expert reports concerned with chronic diseases (Freire et al, 1992).

TABLE 8.1.3 STARCHY AND PROTEIN-RICH FOODS OF PLANT ORIGIN: WAYS TO SUSTAIN INTAKES OF 45–60% TOTAL ENERGY

Recommendations for daily intake is expressed as a percentage of energy intake, as grams and as portions (servings).

Energy values are for cereals (grains), roots, tubers, plantains and pulses (legumes) prepared and ready to eat, with the addition of water as cooked, but without any added fat or sugar. This recommendation can, of course, be sustained by limitless combinations of a variety of starchy and protein-rich foods of plant origin.

	Range for daily average intake		
	% total energy	grams	portions[a]
Model 1: cereal-based diet			
Made up of a varied combination of any of the foods listed as, say			
Total	**45–60**	**750–1000**[a]	
Cereals	35–50	560–800	
Roots, tubers	5–10	100–200	
Plantains	0–4	0–80	
Pulses	2–4	40–80	
Model 2: bread or cereal product and/or tuber-based diet			
Made up of a varied combination of any of the foods listed as, say			
Total	**45–60**	**600–800**	**8–10**[b]
Cereals	5–10	80–160	1–2
Cereal products	0–20	0–320	0–4
Breads	16–40	160–400	2–5
Roots, tubers	8–24	160–480	2–6
Plantains	0–4	0–80	0–1
Pulses	2–4	40–80	0.5–1.0

[a] At higher levels of intake, portion sizes are likely to be larger. Any combination of an appropriate variety of starchy and protein-rich foods of plant origin is recommended; these figures are illustrative only. Set portion size of 80 grams is not a meaningful concept in Asian and other societies where diets are based on rice or other grains and portions are larger.

[b] Figures do not add up to total of 45–60% energy or eight to ten portions because consumption of different foods varies reciprocally: they may be almost exclusively from cereals with some pulses; include some roots and tubers; or be high in cereal products (such as pasta) with some pulses but relatively low in bread and potatoes, or vice versa.

Calculated on the basis of 2,000 kcal (8.4 kJ) daily energy intake, 80 grams per portion, average 125 kcal/100 g (525 kJ/100 g) for cereals and cereal products (such as rice, corn, oats, millet, pasta); 200 kcal/100 g (850 kJ/100 g) for breads (wholegrain and white); 100 kcal/100 g (425 kJ/100 g) for starchy roots and tubers (such as cassava, potatoes, sweet potatoes); 100 kcal/100 g (425 kJ/100 g) for plantains (including bananas) and 100 kcal/100 g (425 kJ/100 g) for pulses. Cereal products with added fat or sugar and pulses with added fat are more energy dense, at 250–500 kcal/100 g (1–2 MJ/100 g). Different bases for total energy intake and portion sizes produce different goals, for example, children's portions will be appropriately smaller. Non-starchy roots are not included here but as part of Recommendation 4.

ALCOHOLIC DRINKS

PUBLIC HEALTH GOAL

Consumption of alcohol is not recommended. Excessive consumption of alcohol to be discouraged. For those who drink alcohol, restrict it to less than 5% total energy for men and less than 2.5% total energy for women

ADVICE TO INDIVIDUALS

Alcohol consumption is not recommended. If consumed at all, limit alcoholic drinks to less than two drinks a day for men and one for women

Pregnant women, children and adolescents should not drink alcohol.

A drink is defined as 250 ml (one small glass) of beer, 100 ml (one glass) of wine, 25 ml (one measure) of spirits or equivalent.

Recommendation 6 is designed to take into account evidence that modest alcohol intake is protective against coronary heart disease. (See chapter 8.3.)

ALCOHOLIC DRINKS AND CANCER RISK

There is convincing evidence that alcoholic drinks increase the risk of cancers of the mouth and pharynx, larynx and oesophagus, and also primary cancer of the liver, this last is probably via alcoholic cirrhosis. The risk is increased if alcohol drinkers also smoke. Alcohol also probably increases the risk of cancers of the colon, rectum and breast.

The risk is increased by any alcoholic drink, irrespective of type and concentration. Alcoholic drinks have been adjudged as group 1 carcinogens (carcinogenic to humans) by the International Agency for Research on Cancer (IARC). (See chapters 4.1, 4.3, 4.4, 4.9, 4.10, 4.11 and 5.5.)

RECOMMENDATION

The evidence reviewed in the relevant sections of chapter 4, and assessed in chapter 5.5, does not support a recommendation that alcohol be consumed. Any recommendation on alcohol intake concerned solely with preventing cancer would recommend less than two drinks a day to prevent upper aerodigestive tract cancers and cancer of the colon and rectum, and complete abstinence to prevent cancer of the breast.

The advice for drinkers of alcohol to limit consumption to less than two drinks a day for men and less than one for women is designed to take into account the protective effect of a modest intake of alcoholic drinks on coronary heart disease, but also, on the other hand, the general ill-effects of alcohol (see chapter 8.3.) Pregnant women, children and adolescents should not drink alcohol. In the view of the panel, fruit juices, tea and coffee are preferable to alcoholic drinks.

This recommendation is similar to those made in other expert reports designed to prevent cancer (NAS, 1982; European Code Against Cancer, 1995; ACS, 1996).

MEAT

PUBLIC HEALTH GOAL

If eaten at all, red meat to provide less than 10% total energy

ADVICE TO INDIVIDUALS

If eaten at all, limit intake of red meat to less than 80 grams (3 ounces) daily. It is preferable to choose fish, poultry or meat from non-domesticated animals in place of red meat

'Red meat' refers to beef, lamb and pork, and products made from these meats. It does not refer to poultry or fish, or to game or meat from non-domesticated animals or birds, consumption of any or all of which is preferable to consumption of red meat.

MEAT AND CANCER RISK

Diets containing substantial amounts of red meat (beef, lamb and pork), and products made from these meats, probably increase the risk of cancers of the colon and rectum, and possibly increase the risk of cancers of the pancreas, breast, prostate and kidney.

Diets high in animal fat, of which red meat is an important source, possibly increase the risk of cancers of the lung, colon and rectum, breast, endometrium and prostate. Diets containing substantial amounts of grilled (broiled) or well-cooked meat and fish possibly increase the risk of cancer of the stomach; diets containing substantial amounts of grilled (broiled), barbecued or fried meat possibly increase the risk of cancer of the colon and rectum. (See chapters 4.5, 4.6, 4.7, 4.10, 4.11, 4.12, 4.13, 4.15, 4.17 and 6.6.)

RECOMMENDATION

The evidence reviewed in the relevant sections of chapter 4, and assessed in chapter 6.6, supports a goal for red meat consumption of no more than 10% total energy, which corresponds to advice that intake of red meat amounts to less than 80 grams daily.

The data apply only to red meat (beef, pork and lamb) and meat products made from beef, lamb and pork. They do not apply to other meats, such as that from non-domesticated animals and birds (the fat content and fatty acid composition of which are, in most cases, different from those of domesticated animals) to poultry or to any type of fish. Consumption of fish, poultry and of other meats as specified here is preferable to the consumption of red meat.

There is no essential lower limit of intake of any type of meat, and diets including no meat are not only compatible with good health and low cancer risk, but may be preferred in some settings, especially when plant foods are abundant, reliable and varied.

Table 8.1.4 is designed as a guide for planning food supplies and for individuals. On the basis that an average por-

TABLE 8.1.4 MEAT: WAYS TO LIMIT INTAKES TO 0–10% TOTAL ENERGY

Recommendations for daily intake are expressed as percentage of energy intake and as grams.

Energy values are in terms of meat and meat products cooked and ready to eat, without any added fat, and are for meat alone without bone and with most visible fat discarded. The main factor determining energy density of meat is its fat content.

| | Range for daily average intake | |
	% total energy	grams
Total meat	0–10	0–80

Calculated on basis of 2,000 kcal (8.4 MJ) daily energy intake, 80 grams per portion, average 250 kcal/100 g (1.0 MJ/100 g) for red meat (beef, lamb and pork). Meat products such as burgers and sausages have much the same energy value. The energy value of red meat of the type referred to is between 150 and 350 kcal/100 g (0.65–1.50 MJ/100 g), depending on its fat content. The energy value of organ meat (offal) is mostly within the same range. Cured meats such as bacon and salami and meat products with added fat, such as pies and pasties, are more energy dense, at 300–500 kcal/100 g (1.25–2.0 MJ/100 g). The energy value of meat from non-domesticated and free-ranging animals is typically much lower, at 100–200 kcal/100 g (425–850 kJ/100 g); of poultry, between 100 and 400 kcal/100 g (0.45 and 1.80 MJ/100 g), depending on fat content; of white fish around 100 kcal/100 g (425 kJ/100 g); and of fatty fish around 200 kcal/g (850 kJ/100 g). All energy values exclude bone. Different bases for energy intake and for portion sizes produce different goals, for example, children's portions are appropriately smaller.

tion of meat may weigh around 80 grams, a recommendation of less than 80 grams a day amounts to less than one portion a day. If meat is eaten occasionally, the figures can be adjusted accordingly.

This recommendation is comparable with, while more precise than those made in other expert reports concerned with prevention of cancer (Harvard Report on Cancer Prevention, 1996; ACS,1996).

RECOMMENDATION 8

PUBLIC HEALTH GOAL

Total fats and oils to provide 15% to no more than 30% total energy

ADVICE TO INDIVIDUALS

Limit consumption of fatty foods, particularly those of animal origin. Choose modest amounts of appropriate vegetable oils

The vegetable oils should be predominantly monosaturated with minimum hydrogenation. This point relates to the prevention of cardiovascular disease. (See chapter 8.3.)

FATS AND OILS, AND CANCER RISK

Diets high in fat possibly increase the risk of cancer of the lung, colon and rectum, breast, and prostate. Diets high in saturated or animal fat possibly increase the risk of cancer of the lung, breast, colon and rectum, endometrium and prostate. (See chapters 4.5, 4.10, 4.11, 4.13, 4.15 and 5.3.)

In the judgement of all but one member of the panel, diets high in fat increase the risk of obesity and therefore are an indirect risk factor for those cancers that demonstrate increased risk with excess body weight. Evidence that obesity increases the risk of cancer of the endometrium is convincing; it probably increases the risk of cancer of the kidney and postmenopausal cancer of the breast and possibly of the colon. (See chapters 4.10, 4.11, 4.13, 4.17 and 5.1.)

RECOMMENDATION

The evidence reviewed in the relevant sections of chapter 4, and assessed in chapters 5.1 and 5.3, supports a goal that total fats provide 15% to no more than 30% total energy. It also supports advice that consumption of fatty foods, particularly of animal origin, should be limited and that, when used as a source of added fat, vegetable oils should be preferred. The evidence on cardiovascular disease indicates that these should be predominantly monounsaturated with minimum hdrogenation. For populations currently consuming low-fat diets, limiting intake to 20% total energy as fat may be beneficial in maintaining their protection against cancer. One panel member disagreed with this view and considered the type rather than the amount of fat to be important.

The data on dairy products, and on nuts and seeds, do not generate any recommendation other than that relating to fats and oils.

This recommendation is similar to, or comparable with, those of other expert reports concerned either to prevent cancer specifically (NAS, 1982; European Code Against Cancer, 1995; ACS, 1996) or to do so in the context of other chronic diseases (NAS, 1989; WHO, 1990; FAO/WHO, 1994).

DR WILLETT'S NOTE OF DISAGREEMENT WITH RECOMMENDATION 8

Dr Willett fully supports the panel's other recommendations, but does not believe that the recommendation for restricting the intake of fats and oils is justified by current scientific evidence according to the criteria agreed upon by the panel. (See chapter 5.3 for a more detailed account of Dr Willett's views on this point.)

8.1.3 FOOD PROCESSING

RECOMMENDATION 9
SALT AND SALTING

PUBLIC HEALTH GOAL

Salt from all sources should amount to less than 6 g/day (0.25 ounces) for adults

ADVICE TO INDIVIDUALS

Limit consumption of salted foods and use of cooking and table salt. Use herbs and spices to season foods

Children should consume less than 3 g/1,000 kcal.
Salt supplies may be iodised (to prevent thyroid disorders).

SALT AND SALTING, AND CANCER RISK

Diets high in salted foods probably increase the risk of stomach cancer. This applies to diets that include substantial amounts of manufactured food that contain added salt. There is convincing evidence that diets high in Cantonese-style salted fish increase the risk of nasopharyngeal cancer. (See chapters 4.2, 4.6 and 7.4.)

RECOMMENDATION

The evidence reviewed in chapter 4.6, and assessed in chapter 7.4, supports the goal that salt from all sources should provide less than 6 g/day of salt (2.4 grams of sodium) for adults.

The specific recommendation of an upper limit of 3 g/1,000 kcal (3 g/4.2 MJ) per day for children corresponds to the recommendation of 6 g/day for the reference adult with an intake of 2,000 kcal (8.4 MJ), and is made to emphasise the importance of the upper limit for children.

A safe requirement of sodium has been estimated at 500 mg/day for adults (NRC, 1989). No lower limit has been set for salt intake, because diets corresponding to the recommendations in this report will include substantially more than the physiological requirement.

The use of salt as a method of preservation and in food manufacture commonly results in diets with comparable concentrations and volumes of salt. The panel recommends that consumption of food salted by any means be minimised and advises that consumption of salt in any form, as contained in manufactured food, or used in cooking and at the table, be limited. In developed societies most salt is contained in manufactured foods; however, foods prepared in the home can be seasoned and their flavour enhanced by the use of herbs and spices rather than salt. In the view of the

panel, consumption of salted foods as an occasional delicacy is unlikely to increase the risk of cancer significantly.

Expert reports designed to prevent cancer have previously recommended limitation of salted foods (NAS, 1982). The recommendation is similar to those issued by WHO and other expert groups concerned to prevent hypertension and stroke (WHO, 1982, 1990; NAS, 1989).

RECOMMENDATION 10
STORAGE

PUBLIC HEALTH GOAL

Store perishable food in ways that minimise fungal contamination

ADVICE TO INDIVIDUALS

Do not eat food which, as a result of long storage at ambient temperatures, is liable to contamination with mycotoxins

FOOD STORAGE AND CANCER RISK

Contamination of food with mycotoxins, including, especially, aflatoxins, probably increases the risk of primary cancer of the liver.

Various mycotoxins have been classified by IARC as either group 1 carcinogens (human carcinogens) or group 2A (probable) or 2B (possible) human carcinogens. (See chapters 4.9 and 7.3.)

RECOMMENDATION

The evidence reviewed in the relevant section of chapter 4, and assessed in chapter 7.3, supports advice not to eat foods liable to fungal contamination after long storage at ambient temperatures, especially if they become visibly mouldy.

This recommendation has special application in parts of Africa and Asia where primary cancer of the liver is common, and cereals (grains), pulses (legumes) and other crops may be stored for long periods in warm damp conditions. However, mycotoxin contamination is also present in crops grown in temperate climates and those exported from tropical and subtropical climates; levels of contamination in developed countries can approach those in developing countries. The goal, that perishable food be stored in ways that minimise fungal contamination, can be made more precise depending on local conditions and circumstances and the local economy.

This recommendation is comparable with those made in reports of regulatory and other expert bodies concerned to prevent cancer.

PRESERVATION

PUBLIC HEALTH GOAL

Perishable food, if not consumed promptly, to be kept
frozen or chilled

ADVICE TO INDIVIDUALS

*Use refrigeration and other appropriate methods to preserve
perishable food as purchased and at home*

FOOD PRESERVATION AND CANCER RISK

There is convincing evidence that refrigeration decreases the
risk of stomach cancer, by reducing the need for salt as a
preservative and enabling year-round availability of vegetables and fruits. (See chapters 4.6 and 7.4.)

RECOMMENDATION

The evidence reviewed in chapter 4.6, and assessed in chapter 7.4, supports the recommendation that, when possible,
perishable food should be preserved by means of freezing,
chilling or refrigeration. In the view of the panel, refrigeration is likely to protect against many cancers, inasmuch as it
has the effect of increasing availability and, therefore, consumption of vegetables and fruits.

ADDITIVES AND RESIDUES

PUBLIC HEALTH GOAL

Establish and monitor the enforcement of safety limits for
food additives, pesticides and their residues, and other
chemical contaminants in the food supply

ADVICE TO INDIVIDUALS

*When levels of additives, contaminants and other residues are
properly regulated, their presence in food and drink is not
known to be harmful. However, unregulated or improper use
can be a health hazard, particularly in economically
developing countries*

ADDITIVES AND RESIDUES, AND CANCER RISK

Epidemiological data on agricultural and other chemical
residues, and on food additives and cancer risk, generally
amount to no more than insufficient evidence of any relationship. Experimental data suggesting that agricultural and
other chemical residues, or food additives, increase the risk
of cancer of any site, derive almost entirely from animal
studies, using doses far in excess of any normally found in

food and drink. IARC has classified various chemicals, traces
of which may be found in food, as class 1 (carcinogenic to
humans) or 2A (probable human carcinogens) or 2B (possible human carcinogens). Given the extremely low doses normally found in food and drinks, the public health
implications of such judgements are currently unclear. (See
chapters 7.1 and 7.2.) As noted in these chapters, much
remains to be learnt about cumulative doses, synergism and
possible metabolic differences in the capacity to handle food
additives and residues.

RECOMMENDATION

The evidence reviewed in relevant sections of chapter 4, and
assessed in chapters 7.1 and 7.2, supports the advice to individuals that, when levels of additives, contaminants and
other residues are properly regulated, their presence in foods
and drinks is not known to affect cancer risk.

However, the panel emphasises that this advice only
applies when levels of additives, contaminants and other
residues are properly regulated. Therefore, the goal specified
by the panel is that enforcement of safety limits for additives
and residues be established and monitored. Occupational
exposure and contamination of food and drink caused by misuse, spillage or accidents is outside the scope of this report.

This recommendation is comparable with those made in
reports of regulatory and other expert bodies concerned to
prevent cancer.

PREPARATION

PUBLIC HEALTH GOAL

When meat and fish are eaten, encourage relatively low
temperature cooking

ADVICE TO INDIVIDUALS

*Do not eat charred food. For meat and fish eaters, avoid
burning of meat juices. Consume the following only
occasionally: meat and fish grilled (broiled) in direct flame,
cured and smoked meats*

PREPARATION AND CANCER RISK

As already noted, diets containing substantial amounts of
grilled (broiled) or heavily cooked meat and fish possibly
increase the risk of cancer of the stomach; diets containing
substantial amounts of grilled, barbecued or fried meat possibly increase risk of cancer of the colon and rectum. Diets
high in processed meats possibly increase the risk of cancers
of the colon and rectum.

Grilling (broiling) of foods (especially meat and fish) results
in the production of mutagenic compounds (heterocyclic aromatic amines). Despite the lack of data on the degree of risk that
these compounds pose for humans, several are carcinogenic in

experimental animals (IARC, 1986).

Volatile *N*-nitrosamines are found in foods treated with nitrites, such as bacon and cheeses. A causal relationship between exposure to *N*-nitroso compounds and carcinogenic risk to humans has not yet been established; however, many animal species and organs are susceptible to the carcinogenic action of these compounds (IARC, 1990).

Polycyclic aromatic hydrocarbons are produced largely as a result of the burning of wood and are found in smoked foods. Although epidemiological studies on the carcinogenicity to humans have been inconclusive, information from experiments in animals has been useful in establishing the carcinogenic risk of these compounds (IARC, 1990). (See chapters 4.6, 4.10, 6.6, 7.5 and 7.6.)

RECOMMENDATION

The data reviewed in chapters 4.6 and 4.10, and assessed in chapters 7.5 and 7.6, amount to no more than evidence of possible relationships with human cancer risk, because they come mostly from animal and in vitro studies.

However, in the judgement of the panel, in the present state of knowledge it is prudent to advise that, when meat and fish are eaten, the use of direct flame to cook these foods be minimised. The consumption of cured and smoked meats should also be minimised, the burning of meat juices avoided, and charred food should not be eaten.

In the view of the panel, consumption of meat and fish cooked in flame, and of cured and smoked meat, as occasional delicacies, is unlikely to increase the risk of cancer significantly. Also, relatively low-temperature cooking by steaming, boiling, poaching, stewing, braising, baking, microwaving or roasting should be the preferred methods of food preparation.

This recommendation is comparable with those made in reports of regulatory and other expert bodies concerned to prevent cancer.

8.1.4 DIETARY CONSTITUENTS

RECOMMENDATION 14
••••••••••••••••••••••••••
DIETARY SUPPLEMENTS

PUBLIC HEALTH GOAL
Community dietary patterns to be consistent with reduction of cancer risk without the use of dietary supplements

ADVICE TO INDIVIDUALS
For those who follow the recommendations presented here, dietary supplements are probably unnecessary, and possibly unhelpful, for reducing cancer risk

This recommendation is made in the context of cancer prevention. (See chapter 8.3.)

DIETARY SUPPLEMENTS AND CANCER RISK

The evidence that diets high in carotenoids and vitamin C possibly protect against cancer of a large number of sites should not be taken as suggesting that supplements of these or any other dietary microconstituents might reduce the risk of cancer. Evidence from intervention trials using supplements in varying combinations and doses is confused and, in some cases, has shown increased cancer rates in those being supplemented. (See relevant sections of chapters 4 and 5.6.)

RECOMMENDATION

Dietary supplements are probably unnecessary and possibly unhelpful, in the context of cancer prevention. The evidence reviewed in the relevant sections of chapter 4, and assessed in chapter 5.6 is consistent with this judgement.

This recommendation is similar to statements made in other expert reports concerned either to prevent cancer specifically (ACS, 1996) or to do so in the context of other chronic diseases.

8.1.5 TOBACCO

RECOMMENDATION 15
••••••••••••••••••••••••••
TOBACCO

PUBLIC HEALTH GOAL
Discouragement of production, promotion and use of tobacco in any form

ADVICE TO INDIVIDUALS
Do not smoke or chew tobacco

TOBACCO AND CANCER RISK

Tobacco is the chief cause of lung cancer. It is probably the most important single cause of cancers of the upper aerodigestive tract, and drinkers who also smoke greatly increase the risk of these cancers. It also contributes to cancers of the pancreas, cervix and bladder. Tobacco is a cause of cancer whether smoked, chewed or consumed in other ways.

RECOMMENDATION

Consideration of tobacco falls outside the terms of reference of this report. However, the panel judged that no set of recommendations designed to prevent cancer is complete unless it discourages the production, promotion and use of tobacco in any form.

This recommendation is similar to those made in other expert reports concerned to prevent cancer (Advisory Committee on Diet, Nutrition and Cancer Prevention, 1996; ACS, 1996; Harvard Report on Cancer Prevention, 1996)**.**

8.1.6 OTHER ASPECTS OF DIET

DIETARY CONSTITUENTS AND CANCER RISK

The recommendations made in this chapter are generally food based, and the panel has usually not made quantified recommendations on dietary constituents. Evidence on the relationship between dietary constituents and cancer risk is, with the exception of alcohol, less strong than that on relevant foods and drinks. For discussion of the interpretation of the evidence on dietary constituents and cancer risk, see chapter 3. (For reviews and assessments of the data, see chapters 4 and 5.) As elsewhere in this report, the term 'dietary constituent' is used rather than 'nutrient' because some items referred to are not usually classified as nutrients.

A number of dietary constituents related to cancer risk are not the subject of recommendations in this report. As already stated, diets high in fibre possibly decrease the risk of cancer of the colon, rectum, breast and pancreas; diets high in starch possibly decrease the risk of cancer of the colon and rectum. Diets high in carotenoids probably decrease the risk of cancer of the lung, and possibly of cancers of the stomach, colon and rectum, oesophagus, breast and cervix. Diets high in vitamin C probably decrease the risk of cancer of the stomach, and possibly of the mouth and pharynx, oesophagus, lung, pancreas, and cervix. Diets high in selenium possibly decrease the risk of cancer of the lung, and diets high in vitamin E possibly decrease the risk of cancer of the lung and cervix.

On the other hand, diets high in saturated/animal fat possibly increase the risk of cancers of the lung, breast, colon and rectum, endometrium, and prostate, those high in cholesterol possibly increase the risk of cancer of the lung, and pancreas. As already stated, epidemiological evidence that diets high in starch possibly increase the risk of cancer of the stomach is likely to apply only when such diets are monotonous and very high in processed carbohydrates.

The panel has decided not to include recommendations for dietary constituents for a number of reasons. First, the data generally do not enable a range of intake to be recommended with any confidence. Second, evidence on individual dietary constituents as contained in food should be treated with some caution. In particular, it is likely that any protective effect of specific vitamins, minerals and other bioactive compounds results from multiple nutrient combinations in proportions that are not well understood.

However, both policy-makers and individuals may wish to know what ranges of various dietary constituents are likely to be contained in the recommended diets. Such figures, which are not recommendations, but are derived directly from the overall recommendations on foods and drinks, are shown in Table 8.1.5. Estimates have been made using a number of food composition tables for different regions of the world; the ranges of estimated intakes are necessarily broad. A comparison is made with recommendations in other expert reports, and with estimated intakes in China, Japan, The Netherlands and Italy.

The ranges of intake for macroconstituents implied by recommendations in this report are broadly similar to those recommended in other reports concerned to prevent chronic diseases including cancer (NAS, 1989; WHO, 1990).

OTHER FOODS AND DRINKS AND CANCER RISK

The current evidence for causal relationships between a number of foods and drinks is weak or effectively non-existent. In such cases there are few if any data; or else what data exist are inadequate as the basis for any recommendation; or else the data indicate no relationship with cancer risk. For these reasons no dietary recommendations are made in this chapter.

These foods and drinks include nuts and seeds (no data); poultry (diets high in poultry possibly have no relationship with the risk of cancer of the breast); fish (diets high in fish possibly have no relationship with the risk of cancer of the colon and rectum, and conceivably may decrease the risk of cancer of the breast and ovary, although evidence here is insufficient); milk and dairy products (diets high in milk and dairy products possibly increase the risk of cancers of the prostate and kidney); coffee and tea (evidence that these drinks have no relationship with cancer risk is consistent for a number of sites).

The panel considers it prudent that if any or all of these foods and drinks are consumed, the diets of which they are a part should be varied and predominately plant-based, consistent with all the recommendations in this chapter, especially Recommendation 1.

TABLE 8.1.5 A DESCRIPTION OF THE RANGES OF INTAKE OF DIETARY CONSTITUENTS DERIVED FROM THE RECOMMENDATIONS IN THIS REPORT

The figures in this table are not recommendations. They are estimates of the probable ranges of dietary constituents consumed as a result of following the food-based recommendations made in this report.

The figures are compared with other figures and ranges of figures published in other reports on food, nutrition and the prevention of chronic diseases including cancer (NAS, 1989; WHO, 1990) and also with the amount of various dietary constituents recommended as population reference intakes (PRIs)[b] or ultimate goals[c] in the European Community (WHO, 1988; Commission of the European Community, 1993). They are also compared with estimated actual intakes in China, India, Japan, the Netherlands and Italy.

	Figures from other reports				Estimated actual intakes				
	Derived from this report	NAS 1989[a]	WHO 1990	European PRI[b] or goal[c]	Italy 1980–84	India 1990–92	China 1983	Netherlands 1990	Japan 1994
Carbohydrate, fat, protein, alcohol									
Carbohydrate (%)	55–75	> 55	55–75	45–55[c]	48	79	72	44	56
Starch (%)	50–70	–	50–70[f]	–	–	–	–	–	–
Sugar (%)[d]	**< 10[g]**	–	< 10	10[c]	–	–	–	–	–
NSP (g)	20–35	–	16–24	30[c]	21	–	8 (crude)*	6	–
Fat (%)	**15–30[g]**	< 30[h]	15–30	20–30[c]	36	10	15	40	26
Polyunsaturated/									
Vegetable (%)	2–10	≤ 10	3–7	2.5	6	–	–	18	13
Saturated/Animal (%)	0–10	< 10[h]	< 10	10[c]	12	–	–	16.6	13
Monounsaturated (%)	3–10	–	–	–	15	–	–	15.4	–
Cholesterol (mg)	100–130	< 300	< 300	–	348	–	–	297	–
Protein (%)	9–12	–	10–15	–	13	10	10	13	16
Vegetable (%)	6–12	–	–	–	8	–	9	–	7
Animal (%)	0–3	–	–	–	3	–	1	–	8
Alcohol (%)	**< 2[g]**	<2 drinks	–	–	4.6	–	–	2.8	–
Vitamins, minerals									
Carotenoids (mg)	9–18	–	–	–	–	–	5	–	–
Vitamin C (mg)	175–400	–	30	40–45	120	37	140	73	117
Folate (µg)	250–450	–	200	200	–	–	–	–	–
Vitamin D (µg)	0–10[i]	–	2.5	0–15[j]	–	–	–	–	–
Vitamin E (mg)[e]	4–7	–	–	> 4	–	–	–	–	–
Thiamine (mg)	1.10–1.65	–	0.9–1.2	0.9–1.1	1	1.1	2.3	1.06	1.21
Calcium (mg)	500–750[k]	–	400–500	700	940	494	582	1,032	545
Selenium (µg)	75–125	–	30–40	55	–	–	–	–	–
Iodine (µg)	125–150	–	120–150	130	–	–	–	–	–
Iron (mg)	15–25[k]	–	16	9–21[l]	15	25	34	12	11
Potassium (g)	1.6–3.2	–	–	3.1	–	–	–	–	–
Sodium (g)	**< 4[g]**	< 4[h]	< 4	0.58–3.50[m]	–	–	–	–	12.8
Zinc (mg)	11–13[k]	–	7.1–9.5	7.1–9.5	–	–	–	–	–

For macroconstituents values are expressed as percentages of total energy (%E) except cholesterol, expressed as milligrams per day (mg/day) and fibre, expressed as grams per day (g/day).
For microconstituents values are expressed as grams, milligrams or micrograms per day (g/day, mg/day or µg/day).

[a] NAS 1989 recommendations are for individuals. Other recommendations or numbers are for populations.
[b] PRI (population reference intake) ranges are for female/male (in that order) younger adults (aged 19–50 in Europe) (Commission of the European Community, 1993).
[c] Ultimate goal (James et al, 1988).
[d] Non-milk extrinsic sugars.
[e] Vitamin E as α-tocopherol.
[f] Expressed as complex carbohydrates.
[g] Specified as a recommendation in this report.
[h] Report also stated that more benefit from a further reduction is highly likely in relation to saturated fat, possibly beneficial for salt, and may be of more benefit if total fat falls.
[i] There is no requirement for vitamin D, in individuals aged 4–50 years, providing that there is sufficient exposure of skin to sunlight.
[j] European safe range.
[k] The bioavailability of calcium, iron and zinc from this recommended diet may be <10%.
[l] Bioavailability 15%.
[m] European acceptable range.

SUMMARY OF DIETARY RECOMMENDATIONS

Policy-makers should now recognise that the incidence of cancer throughout the world can be reduced by 30–40%, by feasible changes in diets and related lifestyles corresponding to the goals specified in chapter 8 and summarised here.

Individuals should also be aware that their own risk of cancer, and that of their families, can be substantially reduced by following the advice given here. The panel's 14 dietary recommendations, set out in detail in chapter 8, are based on the reviews and assessment of the literature in chapters 4–7, and on the method of interpreting the scientific evidence set out in chapter 3. The recommendations are governed by the principles and considerations specified in chapter 8, in particular:

- The recommendations are for those whole diets most likely to prevent cancer, and are consistent with the prevention of other diseases.

- They apply globally to all adults and to children aged two years and over, unless specified.

PUBLIC HEALTH GOALS AND ADVICE TO INDIVIDUALS

FOOD SUPPLY, EATING AND RELATED FACTORS

1 Food supply and eating
- Populations to consume nutritionally adequate and varied diets, based primarily on foods of plant origin
- *Choose predominantly plant-based diets rich in a variety of vegetables and fruits, pulses (legumes) and minimally processed starchy staple foods*

2 Maintaining body weight
- Population average body mass indices throughout adult life to be within the range BMI 21–23, in order that individual BMI be maintained between 18.5 and 25[a]
- *Avoid being underweight or overweight and limit weight gain during adulthood to less than 5 kg (11 pounds)*

3 Maintaining physical activity
- Populations to maintain, throughout life, an active lifestyle equivalent to a physical activity level (PAL) of at least 1.75, with opportunities for vigorous physical activity
- *If occupational activity is low or moderate, take an hour's brisk walk or similar exercise daily, and also exercise vigorously for a total of at least one hour in a week[b]*

FOODS AND DRINKS

4 Vegetables and fruits
- Promote year-round consumption of a variety of vegetables and fruits, providing 7% or more total energy
- *Eat 400–800 grams (15–30 ounces) or five or more portions (servings) a day of a variety of vegetables and fruits, all year round[c, d]*

5 Other plant foods[e]
- A variety of starchy or protein-rich foods of plant origin, preferably minimally processed, to provide 45–60% total energy. Refined sugar to provide less than 10% total energy
- *Eat 600–800 grams (20–30 ounces) or more than seven portions (servings) a day of a variety of cereals (grains), pulses (legumes), roots, tubers and plantains.[c, f] Prefer minimally processed foods. Limit consumption of refined sugar*

6 Alcoholic drinks
- Consumption of alcohol is not recommended. Excessive consumption of alcohol to be discouraged. For those who drink alcohol, restrict it to less than 5% total energy for men and less than 2.5% total energy for women
- *Alcohol consumption is not recommended. If consumed at all, limit alcoholic drinks to less than two drinks a day for men and one for women[g,h,i]*

7 Meat
- If eaten at all, red meat to provide less than 10% total energy
- *If eaten at all, limit intake of red meat to less than 80 grams (3 ounces) daily. It is preferable to choose fish, poultry or meat from non-domesticated animals in place of red meat[c, j]*

8 Total fats and oils
- Total fats and oils to provide 15% to no more than 30% total energy
- *Limit consumption of fatty foods, particularly those of animal origin. Choose modest amounts of appropriate vegetable oils [k]*

World Cancer Research Fund   American Institute for Cancer Research

■ They are designed to be the basis for both planning and education, and need to be made relevant to specific cultures and cuisines.

■ The relative importance of the recommendations will vary in different parts of the world and for different populations.

■ The goals are for policy-makers at international, national and local levels, but also apply to individuals.

■ The goals are quantified as numbers or ranges based on, or consistent with, current scientific evidence and judgement.

■ Policy goals are specified for populations; advice derived from the policy goals is for individuals.

■ The advice to individuals, which includes weights of foods and portion size , is designed for use by the general public.

FOOD PROCESSING

9 Salt and salting
● Salt from all sources should amount to less than 6 grams/day (0.25 ounces) for adults [1]
● *Limit consumption of salted foods and use of cooking and table salt. Use herbs and spices to season foods*

10 Storage
● Store perishable food in ways that minimise fungal contamination
● *Do not eat food which, as a result of prolonged storage at ambient temperatures, is liable to contamination with mycotoxins*

11 Preservation
● Perishable food, if not consumed promptly, to be kept frozen or chilled
● *Use refrigeration and other appropriate methods to preserve perishable food as purchased and at home*

12 Additives and residues
● Establish and monitor the enforcement of safety limits for food additives, pesticides and their residues, and other chemical contaminants in the food supply
● *When levels of additives, contaminants and other residues are properly regulated, their presence in food and drink is not known to be harmful. However, unregulated or improper use can be a health hazard, and this applies particularly in economically developing countries*

13 Preparation
● When meat and fish are eaten, encourage relatively low temperature cooking
● *Do not eat charred food. For meat and fish eaters, avoid burning of meat juices. Consume the following only occasionally: meat and fish grilled (broiled) in direct flame; cured and smoked meats*

DIETARY SUPPLEMENTS

14 Dietary supplements
● Community dietary patterns to be consistent with reduction of cancer risk without the use of dietary supplements
● *For those who follow the recommendations presented here, dietary supplements are probably unnecessary, and possibly unhelpful, for reducing cancer risk [m]*

TOBACCO

Tobacco
● Discourage production, promotion and use of tobacco in any form
● *Do not smoke or chew tobacco*

[a] The advice to individuals is equivalent to maintaining BMI between 18.5 and 25.0. In affluent, less physically active societies, lower average BMI levels may be desirable. For calculations of BMI for people of different heights and weights, see Figure 8.1.1.

[b] For equivalents of brisk walking and for types of vigorous exercise, see Table 8.1.1.

[c] Calculated on the basis of 2,000 kcal (8.4 MJ) daily energy intake, 80 grams per portion. Different bases for total energy intake and for portion sizes will produce different goals, for example, children's servings to be appropriately smaller.

[d] Pulses/legumes, and starchy vegetables and fruits (tubers, starchy roots and plantains) are not included. (See Recommendation 5.)

[e] This recommendation, is consistent with, and generally supported by, but not primarily derived from, the data on cancer. (See chapter 8.3.)

[f] In societies where diets are based on cereals, such as rice or millet, the weight of starchy and protein-rich foods may be higher, say up to 1,000 g/day as served. Set portions (serving) sizes are not a meaningful concept in many societies, and those whose diets are cereal-based consume larger, rather than more frequent, portions.

[g] Pregnant women, children and adolescents should not drink alcohol.

[h] A drink is defined as 250 ml (one small glass) of beer, 100 ml (one glass) of wine, 25 ml (one measure) of spirits, or equivalent.

[i] This recommendation is designed to take into account evidence that modest alcohol intake is protective against coronary heart disease. (See chapter 8.3.)

[j] 'Red meat' refers to beef, lamb and pork, and products made from these meats. It does not refer to poultry or fish, or to game or meat from non-domesticated animals or birds, consumption of any or all of which is preferable to consumption of red meat.

[k] The vegetable oils should be predominantly monounsaturated with minimum hydrogenation. This point relates to the prevention of cardiovascular disease. (See chapter 8.3.)

[l] Children to consume less than 3 g/1,000 kcal. Salt supplies may be iodised (to prevent thyroid disorders).

[m] This recommendation is made in the context of cancer prevention. (See chapter 8.3.)

8.2 Principles

The recommendations of this report are guided by ten general principles, some of which are discussed in chapter 3. First, recommendations are generally expressed as public health goals and as advice complementing the goals, quantified where appropriate. Second, recommendations are, where possible, quantified as ranges specifying lower and upper limits of optimum population intake, guided by dose–response data where these are available. Third, the goals are expressed in terms of the energy content of foods and drinks and so can be applied universally to different populations as well as to individuals.

Fourth, because the recommendations are designed, essentially, to be of universal benefit, they address both whole populations and individuals, and are especially important for vulnerable groups. Fifth, the recommendations can be adapted so as to have immediate relevance to policy-makers, health professionals, and the general public in specific regions, countries and circumstances. Sixth, they are primarily designed to reduce incidence of cancer in general, and have been devised paying particular attention to the most common cancers and evidence of the most persuasive relationships between diet and those cancers.

The strongest evidence linking cancers with diet relates to foods and drinks, rather than to specific constituents or aspects of diet; therefore, seventh, the recommendations are generally food-based. Eighth, in keeping with the general approach of the report, there is emphasis on positive recommendations for foods and drinks, methods of food processing and dietary constituents that can be expected to protect against cancer; prudent alternatives are recommended where the weight of evidence concerns aspects of diet likely to increase cancer risk.

Ninth, the panel's reviews and assessments do not rely exclusively on epidemiological data; indeed, recommendations take the totality of the evidence into account, and usually require identification of plausible biological mechanisms. Tenth, recommendations are designed to relate to whole diets actually eaten around the world; thus, they are not only nutritionally appropriate but also acknowledge and encompass the rich variety of international cuisines. Other public health consequences of the recommendations are summarised in chapter 8.3.

Principle 1
QUANTIFIED RECOMMENDATIONS

The recommendations made by the panel are quantified where possible and appropriate, as is the normal convention. Qualitative guidelines are also specified; these either provide advice on achieving the goals, or else are alternatives where goals are not immediately practical or appropriate.

The recommendations made in this report combine quantified goals as numbers, or ranges of numbers, for consumption of foods and drinks and related factors such as body mass and exercise, together with qualitative guidelines. Thus, for example, the panel recommends that over 7% total energy comes from vegetables and fruits (goal), and that charred food should not be eaten (guideline). Similarly, the panel recommends the goal of a minimum physical activity level (PAL) of 1.75, and the guideline to limit consumption of fatty foods, particularly of animal origin.

The combination of quantitative goals and qualitative guidelines is in keeping with recommendations made, since the early twentieth century, for the prevention of deficiency diseases and, in the second half of the twentieth century, for the prevention of chronic degenerative adult diseases.

During the 1920s to 1950s, the amounts of various nutrients needed to treat or avoid the 'classic' nutrient-specific deficiency diseases were estimated. Thus, the minimum intake of vitamin C needed to avoid scurvy was found to be around 8–10 mg/day. Recommended daily allowances (RDAs) for nutrients were then set. These took into account the estimated ranges of individual needs, and added an appropriate safety factor, or factors, to obtain an RDA which, if implemented, would protect practically all individuals (97–98%) within a population. Thus, the RDA for vitamin C has been determined by expert groups in different countries as 30, 45, 60 or 75 mg. Goals in the form of quantified RDAs for energy, protein, and various vitamins and minerals have become intrinsic to strategies for combating nutrient deficiencies throughout the world and are increasingly becoming standardised.

Industry commonly makes use of RDAs for vitamins and minerals on labels of manufactured food. Quantified goals are essential for planning the supply of food, whether on an international or national basis, or for institutions such as schools and canteens. In the 1990s, the four principal nutritional deficiencies of global public health significance have been confirmed as protein–energy malnutrition in children, and deficiencies of vitamin A, iron and iodine in children and adults. These are all recognised as being capable of remedy by public health programmes which take, as their points of reference, quantified goals for these dietary constituents.

Advice issued by governments and professional bodies may divide diets into 'food groups', with recommendations to eat specified amounts of foods in each group, expressed in terms of portions (servings) or weight. Such recommendations may include very general guidelines such as 'eat a variety of foods'. This report combines a goal with a guideline in the recommendation to 'eat 400 to 800 grams or five or more portions a day of a variety of vegetables and fruits'.

Starting in the 1950s, nutritional science developed in a new direction as coronary heart disease (CHD) emerged as a pandemic, first in developed countries and then in urban areas of developing countries. Assessment of the scientific evidence led expert panels to conclude, notably, that diets high in saturated fats increase the risk of CHD.

Authoritative reports issued by governments and expert bodies in countries where diets are high in saturated fats have, since the 1960s, set goals for whole populations, typically of less than 10% total energy from saturated fats, to prevent CHD. A maximum of 30–35% total energy from total fat is also often recommended as a means of limiting saturated fat intake, and in order to protect against other diseases. Similar reports, produced on a global basis or for countries where fat consumption is lower, have set lower goals, for example, 15–30% total energy from total fat (WHO, 1990). Guidelines are also used to prevent heart disease: thus, a report ratified by the Japanese Government in 1985, specified 'limit your eating of foods containing a large amount of fat and sugar' (Japan Dietetic Association, 1984), and a report issued by the US Government in 1988 recommended 'Reduce consumption of fat (especially saturated fat) . . . Choose foods relatively low in these substances, such as vegetables, fruits, wholegrain foods. . .' (Surgeon General, 1988).

Reports on diet and major chronic diseases other than coronary heart disease, such as obesity, adult-onset diabetes, intestinal disorders and a number of cancers, have also been published in many countries since the 1960s (Cannon, 1992). Their recommendations also tend to combine quantified goals with qualitative guidelines.

Principle 2
GOALS AS RANGES OF INTAKE

Quantified recommendations are usually expressed as ranges specifying lower and upper limits of intake,

guided by dose–response data where these are available.

Dietary goals issued by some expert committees have sometimes been expressed as single numbers, such as '10% total energy from saturated fat', when the purpose has been to encourage a decrease in saturated fat consumption in populations with an intake exceeding 10%. The panel has avoided use of single numbers. Such goals can be misinterpreted as suggesting that one should eat exactly this amount of saturated fat. Accordingly, a better strategy is to use expressions such as 'less than 10%' or 'at most 10%', which implies a range of intake. Similarly, a recommendation of five portions a day of vegetables and fruits could be misinterpreted to suggest a goal of no less, but also no more, than five portions and is therefore better expressed as 'five or more portions'.

Single-number goals imply an inappropriate precision. A preferable practice is to set goals as ranges of intake with specified lower and upper limits, such as '400–800 grams of vegetables and fruits', or '45–60% total energy from starchy staple foods'. Goals may specify only an upper limit when the evidence suggests either a safe lower limit of zero (as with alcohol) or a lower limit that cannot be reached in actual dietary practice. Goals may also specify only a lower limit when there is little scientific or practical reason to set an upper limit (as with physical activity).

As stated in chapter 3.4, the specification of goals as ranges of intake can be influenced by dose–response information, where these are available. Dose–response data for various characteristics of diet are shown as figures in chapters 5–7. A dose–response curve, showing the highest risk at zero intake and a progressively decreasing risk as intake increases, can for instance be used to support a goal giving a range of 400–800 grams/day of vegetables and fruits. The lower limit is associated with low risk; the higher limit, which may be above population but not individual ranges of intake, is likely to give even greater protection. In such cases an upper limit also takes into consideration the need for other foods.

Principle 3
ENERGY AS A BASIS FOR RECOMMENDATIONS

For universal application, recommendations where possible and appropriate are expressed as specified ranges, with reference to an population energy requirement of 2,000 kcal (8.4 MJ). Ranges of percentages of energy content of diets are also used.

Requirements for specific nutrients in foods and drinks are very approximately proportional to individual energy requirements. Specification of goals for foods and drinks in absolute terms does not take account of the different sizes of children, adults and indeed populations. Expressing the goal per 1,000 kcal (4.2 MJ), or to a reference requirement of 2,000 kcal (8.4 MJ), enables the recommendations to be applied not only to different populations with different energy needs but also, individually, to children as well as to

men and women of different sizes, and activity levels.

Recommendations in the form of advice to the public have sometimes also been specified in absolute terms, as recommended weights, volumes or numbers of portions. Such recommendations are easier for individuals to follow, but are illustrative only, in that they assume just a single overall energy requirement, which of course is not the case.

In giving advice on suitable amounts of foods and drinks in absolute terms, some principles have been used. First, the proposed intakes should allow for the nutrient needs for normal growth of children to be met. Second, corresponding to goals 2 and 3 in chapter 8.1, adults are assumed to be consuming enough food to maintain a body mass index (BMI) of 22.0, the approximate midpoint of the goal of a BMI of 18.5–25, and to sustain a physical activity level (PAL) of at least 1.75. Finally, a population 'reference' requirement of 2,000 kcal (8.4 MJ)/day is used where needed.

The advice to the general public given in absolute terms, as weights or servings, has been given in terms of broad ranges, to reflect not only upper and lower limits in terms of the recommended percentages of energy, but also to accommodate the different energy requirements of individuals.

To take an obvious example, tall people need to eat more to maintain an appropriate weight than shorter people with the same level of physical activity. This, in turn, means that the total amount of food consumed will be different. Small women in energy balance on, say, 1,750 kcal (7.35 MJ)/day, will receive perhaps 10% of their energy needs from 500 grams of vegetables and fruits per day, whereas tall men in energy balance on 2,750 kcal (11.55 MJ) per day, may require nearly 800 grams of vegetables and fruits per day to reach the same intake of energy.

In practice, the panel has specified ranges in both absolute and relative terms that are broad enough to accommodate almost all people. The requirements of very small people, or very tall people (especially if very active), may be close to the lower or the upper limits recommended by the panel. If required, advice can be made more precise by health professionals responsible for advising the general public, and by individuals themselves, using the tables that accompany the recommendations in chapter 8.1, with reference, if necessary, to food-composition information.

Principle 4
A WHOLE-POPULATION APPROACH

The recommendations address whole populations and individuals within populations, and are especially important for those groups most susceptible to cancer.

Cancer of one site or another is a relatively common life-threatening disease everywhere in the world. Therefore, the most rational approach to cancer prevention is on a population basis. The recommendations made in this report are, first, in the form of goals for policy-makers concerned with populations, and then as advice to individuals.

In the past, dietary recommendations designed to reduce the risk of chronic diseases have occasionally been targeted at 'at risk' groups within populations. Thus, some reports designed to prevent coronary heart disease have included dietary recommendations specifically for the obese or those with clinically diagnosed heart disease or a family history of heart disease, or those with identified intermediate risk factors such as raised blood pressure or raised blood cholesterol.

However, it is now recognised that such recommendations will be of limited value. Such a policy does not address the majority who will develop the disease; with heart disease, most cases occur among the large proportion of the population at apparently modest risk, with blood cholesterol levels around the average. Those at high risk are far fewer in number.

With cancer, the case for a whole-population approach is particularly strong, because there are, as yet, no established and readily measurable intermediate risk factors as there are with coronary heart disease. In the future, genetic tests may identify those with an increased vulnerability to specific cancers. However, such tests would have to allow the identification of those at risk of a majority of subsequent cancer cases if mass genetic screening, with all its economic and social implications, is to replace a population-based approach to prevention. Another argument in favour of the whole-population approach is that the dietary recommendations developed to prevent cancer are much the same as those most likely to prevent coronary heart disease and other diseases and disorders (see chapter 8.3).

Some groups of people can, however, be readily identified as at high risk of certain cancers, because of their lifestyle or medical condition. These include: smokers, ex-smokers and regular alcohol drinkers; the immunosuppressed and those with certain infections, notably with the hepatitis B and C viruses; and those with a personal or family history of cancer.

The panel has chosen not to make special recommendations for these high-risk groups, or for the nutritionally vulnerable, that is, very young children, pregnant women or elderly people. Those with a family history of specific cancers, for example, familial adenomatous polyposis, are very susceptible to developing cancer and should seek medical advice.

Principle 5
GLOBAL RECOMMENDATIONS

The recommendations are designed to accommodate worldwide diversity. They can be adapted by policy-makers and health professionals and developed for the general public in specific regions, countries and circumstances.

Although science is a universal endeavour, dietary recommendations designed to protect public health, other than those published by the World Health Organization and its agencies, are usually aimed at specific countries. Furthermore, resources for scientific research are generally much more substantial in the developed world. Most reviews and reports specifically on diet and cancer, despite drawing

on the world literature, have been commissioned by national governments and other national bodies, for their own populations, and have tended to focus on those cancers most prevalent in developed countries.

However, cancer is a disease that affects people everywhere. Some cancers are much more common in some regions and countries than in others, and analysis of the various environmental factors in areas of both high and low incidence provides an insight into the aetiological factors. It is not yet clear how important the genetic differences across races or groups are in determining cancer susceptibility. In the furure, when such data are available, local or regional results may, with prudence, be applied more globally. Thus, data on salted fish and nasopharyngeal cancer have special relevance in parts of China, but may be relevant universally wherever such food is eaten regularly. Data on diets rich in vegetables and fruit already seem universally valid and highly relevant to many cancers and to most, if not all, populations in the world.

Cancers are becoming more prevalent, if only because the world's population is both increasing and ageing. In the developing world, there is a pressing need to agree on, and apply, public health strategies designed to prevent existing diet-related cancers, because the social and economic costs will escalate rapidly. New epidemics of other diet-related cancers associated with urbanisation will add a further burden of unmet need. In the developed world, there is a clearly recognised need for strategies designed to prevent diet-related cancers. Thus, there are advantages in taking an integrated global approach and in drawing on the widest experience for both analysing the problem of cancer development and devising the best preventive strategies likely to be of most benefit (WHO, 1996).

The most coherent and ethical approach to cancer prevention is by means of universal recommendations. Nevertheless, there is a need to translate these recommendations into practical guides for national or special use. This is best done by appropriately qualified health professionals and food writers with local knowledge.

Principle 6
CANCER IN GENERAL

The need to reduce the overall burden of cancer leads to recommendations that are designed to account comprehensively for the diversity of factors affecting most cancers, but especially those that are most common.

Some cancers of adjacent sites or of specific systems of the body may have causes in common and be preventable in similar ways. For example, cancers of the upper aerodigestive tract (mouth and pharynx, larynx, oesophagus) can be broadly grouped together, as can female hormone-related cancers (of the breast, ovary and endometrium), and cancers of the urinary tract (kidney and bladder). Perhaps most importantly, virtually all aspects of diet relevant to cancer either consistently decrease or increase risk at specific sites of the body. With the possible exception of diets high in refined starch, which the panel has assessed as a special case in chapter 5.2, dietary recommendations designed to prevent cancer at specific sites can be made in the confident expectation that they will have a generally beneficial effect on cancer as a whole. However, although the dietary and other environmental factors affecting risk of cancers of sites within these groups have common features, they are not identical.

The term 'cancer' can also be misleading, inasmuch as it suggests one disease entity. Cancers of various types and sites have some features in common, but different cancers have different causes, and may be prevented in different ways. For example, ultraviolet sunlight is the chief cause of skin cancers, but has nothing to do with risk of lung or gastrointestinal cancers. The bacterium *Helicobacter pylori* is now believed to be an important factor in stomach cancer, but may be irrelevant to risk of any other cancer.

Similarly, some aspects of diet are important for some cancers but not for others. Alcohol increases the risk only of some cancers. Evidence that fungal contamination with mycotoxins increases cancer risk is much more impressive in the case of primary liver cancer than with any other site. Similarly, factors connected with energy intake affect some cancers and not others. There is good evidence that obesity increases the risk of a number of cancers but not others. The only factor that protects against cancers of most sites reviewed in this report is a diet containing substantial amounts of vegetables and fruits.

The panel, nevertheless, considers that devising a series of recommendations for different cancers would not be helpful. Common factors have allowed a coherent set of recommendations to be presented here.

Principle 7
FOOD-BASED RECOMMENDATIONS

The strongest evidence and the clearest advice on food, nutrition and cancer generally concern foods and drinks, so recommendations are generally food based rather than based on individual dietary constituents.

People eat food, not dietary constituents. The clearest advice to policy-makers and to the general public should ideally be in terms of foods and drinks and, indeed, dietary patterns. However, advice designed to reduce the risk of diet-related diseases other than cancer have, until recently, tended to focus mostly on dietary constituents because of the identifiable links between intakes of selected nutrients and specific pathological processes.

This conceptual framework is consistent with the earlier dietary advice designed to prevent classic deficiency diseases. Early in the twentieth century, the recognition that diseases then common in Europe were caused by deficiencies of specific dietary constituents led to nutritional advice designed to ensure that a sufficient intake of protein and various vitamins and minerals was achieved by balancing the intakes from different food groups. This provided the basis for the rather nebulous concept of a 'balanced and varied diet', a very general qualitative guideline originally developed from quantified goals specified as RDAs of specific constituents.

In the second half of the twentieth century, much advice, designed to prevent cardiovascular and other chronic diseases, has also taken the form of goals and guidelines for constituents of diet known to affect chronic disease risk. Saturated fats, for example, promote the development of atherosclerosis and thrombosis.

The tendency to make recommendations for dietary constituents rather than for foods and drinks has encouraged the misconception that the key factors in chronic diseases are usually single or, perhaps, several discrete nutrients.

For many years, public health professionals have been faced with the task of explaining the practical meaning of, say, a goal of 'less than 10% of total calories from saturated fat' to reduce the risk of coronary heart disease, to audiences who have no formal qualifications in nutritional biochemistry and cannot readily translate such concepts into choices about foods and drinks.

Clear dietary recommendations can, however, be expressed in terms of foods and drinks. The principal processes involved in the development of cancer are not yet clear. The resulting need to deal on the broader basis of foods and drinks, rather than dietary constituents, has a solid scientific rationale.

For example, it has been thought that the antioxidants β-carotene, vitamins C and E, and selenium were key factors protecting against several cancers. The data reviewed in the relevant sections of chapter 4, and assessed in chapters 5.6 and 5.7, do indeed show that carotenoids (not β-carotene specifically) and vitamin C may protect against a number of cancers. Yet attempts to test these conclusions, by selectively supplementing the diet with such antioxidants, singly or in combination, have not produced clear results. It is almost certainly a mistake, therefore, to single out the most researched, most easily measured or best known antioxidants as chemopreventive agents. It seems more appropriate, at present, to conclude that foods rich in antioxidants and other bioactive compounds, notably vegetables and fruits, protect against cancer, and that this effect is more powerful than that of any specific dietary constituent.

Another example is fat. The 1982 report of the National Academy of Sciences (NAS, 1982) concluded, on the basis of the data then available, that the evidence linking fat to increased risk of cancer was more persuasive than the evidence on any other aspect of diet. Although, as reviewed in chapter 4, and assessed in chapter 5.3, there is some evidence that diets containing substantial amounts of total fat possibly increase the risk of some cancers, the more recent evidence on (red) meat and meat products is rather stronger than the evidence on total fat or on specific fatty acid fractions. Meat contributes a substantial amount of animal fat, but the specific mechanisms by which meat increases cancer risk remain to be explored.

It is for this variety of reasons that the panel concludes that goals and guidelines designed to prevent cancer are best based on foods and drinks. They may, as in this report, also include recommendations on some dietary constituents and on methods of food processing, where the evidence is strong enough.

Principle 8
POSITIVE ADVICE

Where possible, the emphasis is on positive recommendations for foods and drinks and for methods of food processing that protect against cancer. Healthy alternatives are recommended where the strength of evidence concerns aspects of diet most likely to increase cancer risk.

This report is concerned with cancer prevention. Correspondingly, its recommendations consistently emphasise those aspects of diet that protect against cancer.

Recommendations designed to reduce the risk of cancer have been published by governments, authoritative organisations and experts in the field since the early 1980s. These are summarised in Appendix A. They have been designed mostly for developed countries and regions, including the USA, Canada, Europe as a whole and Japan. Policy analyses of diet and cancer have, from the beginning, attempted to make recommendations that emphasised dietary constituents involved in cancer risk, such as fat or specific carcinogens.

However, throughout the 1980s and 1990s, as evidence has mounted on the protective value of various foods, such as vegetables and fruits, more recent recommendations have given prominence to positive and generic food-based advice. This development in scientific research has proved helpful to health educators, in as much as health professionals and the general public are more responsive to positive advice. Emphasis on positive recommendations thus derives from the scientific data and is also more persuasive as public health messages.

Principle 9
BIOLOGICAL PLAUSIBILITY

The panel's reviews and assessments do not rely solely on epidemiological data; its recommendations also take experimental data and plausible biological mechanisms into account.

The panel's judgements on the strength of the evidence linking food and nutrition with cancer risk are not solely based on an assessment of the strength of epidemiological data. The panel had taken the view that coherent epidemiological evidence should, when possible, be buttressed by clear mechanistic arguments supported by clinical, physiological and molecular data.

As stated in chapter 3, epidemiological data, when strong and consistent, may amount to evidence of a convincing or probable causal relationship between a food and cancer risk. Data from experimental studies do not, of themselves, amount to evidence of a similar standing. On the other hand, an epidemiologically derived causal relationship between

foods and drinks and cancer risk is most persuasive when the evidence is corroborated by experimental data and evidence of biological plausibility.

Principle 10
CULTURE AND CUISINE

The recommendations are designed to correspond to those diets eaten in a variety of societies, modified to maximise protective effects while retaining the features of the rich variety of tried and tested cuisines.

The panel does not think it wise to make recommendations that are untried in human societies. Thus, the recommendation for a range of between 15% and 30% total energy from fat, corresponds to the known dietary patterns of most settled communities. (Only exceptionally and, largely, very recently has this upper limit been exceeded on a population basis.) Similarly, the recommended upper limit of 800 grams of vegetables and fruits is within the range of individual diets traditionally eaten in the Mediterranean region.

This does not mean that evolutionary pressure or breadth of choice has led to the diets of some societies having minimum potential for inducing cancer. Some diets traditionally eaten in various parts of the world, are known to be deficient or unbalanced. Nor is it suggested that food science and technology have little to offer. Many novel foods and drinks, and modern methods of processing, storage and preparation are beneficial to human health. At the same time, humans exposed to industrialised diets only in the last few generations have had little opportunity to adapt to this new environmental pressure.

In behavioural terms, many people living in the developed world and urban areas of the developing world may also have difficulty initially adapting to diets that minimise the risk of cancer and other diseases. Fat, sugar and salt are all highly palatable and alcohol can be addictive. Sensorial and behavioural adaptation to diets comparatively low in fatty, sugary and salty foods seems to take anything from one to six months, after which such foods may be sensed as more attractive and palatable.

Diets traditionally eaten in many parts of the world have a nutritional composition in accordance with the recommendations presented here. These include many celebrated cuisines from north and sub-Saharan Africa, Latin America, Asia and southern Europe, as well as cuisines now enjoyed in developed countries, devised both as adaptations of traditional cuisines and as new cuisines that make use of modern and time-honoured methods of processing and preparation

8.3 Significance for other diseases

The recommendations in this report are designed to prevent cancer. The panel has also been concerned that its recommendations should accord with those designed to prevent other diseases. It would not be helpful if recommendations designed to reduce the incidence of one disease increased the risk of others.

In practice, there is very little potential conflict between the panel's recommendations on cancer and those designed to prevent other diseases. Hence, they should contribute overall to improvement of child and general adult health, prevention of deficiency diseases, and therefore to increased resistance to infectious diseases and the prevention of other chronic diseases.

This chapter identifies consistency with recommendations designed to prevent other diseases and, where any inconsistency is apparent, proposes a means of reconciliation.

The recommendations of the panel are here compared with dietary recommendations designed to reduce the incidence of other diseases. Such recommendations are concerned with preventing childhood diseases (UNICEF, 1990), deficiency and infectious diseases (FAO/WHO, 1992), and other chronic diseases including coronary heart disease (NAS, 1989; WHO, 1990). Prevention of diseases other than cancer may require a different approach from those taken in this report, but if policy is to be coherent and universally applicable, an integrated approach is vital.

1 FOOD SUPPLY AND EATING

In recommending plant-based diets, the very different energy densities of diets in different parts of the world need to be recognised. In some African countries, babies and young children have difficulty meeting their energy needs because of the high water content of their very viscous, bulky diets. This has been allowed for by specifying that the recommendations apply only from the age of two years, and by recommending a maximum limit for starchy staple foods and a minimum limit for fat (see sections 5 and 8 below).

Bulky plant-based diets with a low energy density should generally be an advantage in developed countries and urban areas of developing countries. Under normal physiological conditions with low energy-dense diets and physical activity levels (PAL) of over 1.75, control of energy intake seems to be precise, as judged by an age-related stability in body weight (James and Ralph, 1994; Ferro-Luzzi and Martino, 1996), and such diets should also therefore reduce the risk of obesity, itself a risk factor for some cancers (see sections 2 and 3 below).

Diets high in foods of plant origin protect against major diseases and disorders of the cardiovascular, digestive and endocrine systems; such foods are notably vegetables and fruits and minimally processed cereals (grains), pulses (legumes), roots, tubers and plantains, which are relatively rich in protective dietary constituents (see sections 4 and 5 below).

Production of foods of plant origin requires less energy input than production of meat and other foods of animal origin. In addition, plant-based agriculture generally uses fewer resources, especially land and water; this is a consideration of increasing importance as the world population increases, and with mounting evidence of environmental and other ecological problems caused by resource-intensive livestock production and other agricultural activities. (See chapter 9.)

The panel's recommendation therefore is consistent with protection against the diseases and disorders mentioned above, and also implies a more economic and sustainable use of resources.

2 MAINTAINING BODY WEIGHT

Obesity (BMI > 30) is an increasing, major public health problem not only in developed countries, but also now in urban areas of developing countries. As well as increasing the risk of a number of cancers, obesity increases the risk of cardiovascular disease, adult-onset diabetes and other major chronic diseases, and reduces life expectancy (WHO, 1990). Overweight (BMI 25–30) also increases risk of disease. Underweight, defined as BMI below 18.5, lowers capacity for work and increases vulnerability to illness (James and Ralph, 1994).

The panel's recommendation therefore is consistent with protection against these diseases and disorders, and also promotes general good health.

3 MAINTAINING PHYSICAL ACTIVITY

Regular physical activity protects against coronary heart disease, adult-onset diabetes and osteoporosis, as well as overweight and obesity, and is associated with increased life expectancy.

The panel's recommendation therefore is consistent with protection against these diseases and disorders and also prolongs life.

4 VEGETABLES AND FRUITS

Diets high in vegetables and fruits are high in many dietary constituents, including vitamins, minerals and fibre found in vegetables and fruits. These protect against various deficiency diseases and also therefore against infections. Carotenoids and vitamin C may also protect against cataracts.

As already indicated, because vegetables and fruits are bulky and low in energy, such diets will also protect against obesity, itself a risk factor for some cancers. Diets high in vegetables and fruits are also recommended as protective against coronary heart disease (National Heart Forum, 1996).

Diets high in non-starch polysaccharide (NSP)/dietary fibre, found in vegetables and fruits, as well as in cereals/grains, protect against a variety of intestinal disorders and may help control adult-onset (non-insulinn dependent) diabetes.

There is no coherent or substantial evidence that pesticides or other chemical residues in vegetables and fruits are a significant public health problem when residues are within

agreed safety limits. Besides which, residues are found in food of animal as well as of plant origin.

The panel's recommendation therefore is consistent with protection against the diseases and disorders mentioned above.

5 OTHER PLANT FOODS

Monotonous diets that are very high in refined starchy foods can cause B vitamin deficiency leading to beri-beri or pellagra, although these diseases are now uncommon.

Diets high in a variety of starchy or protein-rich plant foods and therefore bulky and high in complex carbohydrates and NSP/dietary fibre, are commonly recommended as a means of preventing chronic diseases such as obesity, adult-onset diabetes, cardiovascular disease and intestinal disorders.

The frequent consumption of refined sugar is a major cause of tooth decay. Reduction of refined sugar intake is commonly recommended in developed countries for those seeking to lose excess weight. The nutrient density of diets necessarily varies inversely with the intake of sugar, other factors being constant. This may be an important factor especially for people whose diets are of marginal nutritional quality and for those on low energy intakes.

The evidence relating starchy and protein-rich foods of plant origin to reduction of cancer risk enables, at best, a judgement of possible causal relationships with starch and fibre. However, a problem would be created if no recommendation were made on starchy or protein-rich foods of plant origin as these are staple foods throughout the world. Further, starchy diets are generally preferable to diets high in fat and sugar. The recommendation is made to allow overall coherent dietary assessments to be made.

Other problems would be created if the recommendation were for too broad a range of starchy foods. At the highest level of a very broad-ranged recommendation, such diets could be too bulky to satisfy the energy needs of young children and could, if the starch was overly processed or refined, also be deficient in necessary nutrients and thus possibly increase the risk of stomach cancer (see chapter 5.2). This issue is resolved by specifying that the recommendations apply at and above two years of age, by specifying an upper limit of 60% total energy from such foods, and by recommending that they be minimally processed, so that they contain a relatively high content of microconstituents and NSP/fibre.

As with vegetables and fruits, there is no coherent or substantial evidence that pesticides or other chemical residues in other foods of plant origin are a significant public health problem when residues are within agreed safety limits. Residues are, as already noted, found in foods of animal as well as plant origin.

Resolving apparent contradictions:
> The upper limit of 60% total energy from starchy or protein-rich plant foods should avoid any possible problem arising from micronutrient-deficient high-starch diets, as should the recommendation that such foods be minimally processed.

6 ALCOHOLIC DRINKS

On a population basis, there is a linear dose–response relationship between average alcohol consumption per person and the death rate from domestic and traffic accidents, violence, suicide, homicide and other crimes. Heavy drinking may damage the liver, digestive tract, central nervous system and cardiovascular system, and leads to absenteeism, low productivity and family disruption. Women metabolise alcohol less rapidly than men, and women who drink during pregnancy are at increased risk of bearing infants with congenital defects.

Alcohol is an addictive drug. It interferes with the metabolism of some nutrients, and the nutrient density of diets necessarily varies inversely with the intake of alcohol, other factors being constant. This may be an important factor especially for people whose diets are of marginal nutritional quality and for small or inactive people with low total energy intakes.

There is no evidence that alcohol reduces the risk of any cancer at any level of intake, and the data on breast cancer are consistent with a recommendation that women should not drink alcohol at all. However, there is a potential conflict between a recommendation on alcohol designed to reduce cancer risk, and a recommendation designed to reduce the risk of coronary heart disease. Any recommendation not to drink alcohol at all in order to prevent cancer would conflict with the finding that modest alcohol intake protects men and, perhaps, women against coronary heart disease.

The advice for drinkers to limit consumption to a maximum of two alcoholic drinks a day for men and one drink a day for women is designed to take into account the protective effect of modest alcohol intake on coronary heart disease and, on the other hand, the consequences of alcohol-related accidents and social problems.

Resolving apparent contradictions:
> The upper limit, for those who do drink alcohol, of two drinks a day for men and one drink a day for women, should provide protection against coronary heart disease, which is also preventable by other means. One drink a day is associated with only a small increase in risk of breast cancer.

7 MEAT

Meat (of all types, not just red meat) is an important source of nutrients, such as iron, which is more readily absorbed from meat than from plant foods. In developing countries, iron-deficiency anaemia is common and iron losses associated with intestinal parasitism are prevalent and serious. Women also have especially high requirements for iron during the reproductive phase of their lives. Meat is also an important source of zinc and selenium, the intakes of which are marginal in many parts of the world.

A problem could be created if meat consumption were substantially reduced in the developing world. Although there is no need for meat if, optimally, diets include adequate mixtures of cereals (grains) and pulses (legumes), the readily available protein, iron and other micronutrients in meat ensure the longitudinal growth of children, infant and child brain development, and protection against iron-deficiency anaemia.

However, the data showing the relationships between diets high in meat and increased cancer risk concern only red meat (beef, lamb and pork) and meat products as cooked and eaten in developed countries and urban areas of developing countries. The recommendation is confined to those types of meat that are usually high in total and saturated fat. There are no data on meat from non-domesticated animals, which, in any case, is typically much lower in fat content and has a different fatty acid composition from that of red meat. The recommendation also does not include poultry, other birds or fish, or dairy products.

Resolving apparent contradictions:
> The recommendation for meat refers only to red meat (beef, lamb and pork) of the type eaten in developed societies. It does not refer to meat from non-domesticated animals. It also does not refer to poultry, or to other birds or fish.

8 FATS AND OILS

As fat is the most energy-dense dietary constituent, diets very low in fat can contribute to protein–energy malnutrition in young children. As already stated, a problem would be created if fat intake dropped to very low levels, making diets too bulky to supply sufficient energy needs for young children. It is for this reason that the goal specifies a lower limit of 15% total energy.

Diets high in fat are assessed as increasing the risk of obesity, itself a risk factor for a number of cancers. Diets high in saturated fat are assessed as increasing the risk of cardiovascular disease, so a problem could be created if no reference were made to saturated fat. However, the recommendation specifies that consumption of fatty foods, particularly those of animal origin, be limited and, with reference to cardiovascular disease, that vegetable oils should contain monounsaturates predominately with minimum hydrogenation.

The panel's recommendation should therefore reduce the likelihood of childhood protein–energy malnutrition, limit the development of obesity itself, as well as reducing the risk of obesity, related cancers and cardiovascular disease.

The panel's recommendation does not apply to young children under the age of two years. Infants should start their lives being breast-fed, with breast milk providing a fat intake amounting to 50–60% of the milk's energy content. As a child is weaned, it is important to sustain energy intake at a time when the capacity of the stomach is modest in relation to the high energy demand of the infant. Infants and young children should therefore maintain fat intake at 30–40% total energy between weaning and two years of age. In developing countries, this may require the addition of modest amounts of fats, oils and fatty foods to a young child's diet.

9 SALT AND SALTING

Salt (or more specifically the sodium and chloride in salt) is an essential nutrient but, in the view of the panel, it is practically impossible that any diet that follows the other dietary recommendations would have a sodium content below the minimum physiological requirement.

Diets high in salt and salted foods increase the risk of hypertension and therefore also of stroke. The panel's recommendation therefore is consistent with protection against these diseases.

A recommendation that would have the effect of reducing salt intake could create a problem in societies where salt supplies are or should be iodised to protect against iodine-deficiency disorders. To avoid any reduction in iodine in the food supply, the panel has recommended that salt supplies be iodised at appropriate levels.

Resolving apparent contradictions:
  The goal for salt and salting specifies that salt supplies should be iodised where necessary. The concentration of iodine should allow for a reduction in the amount of salt consumed.

10 STORAGE

Food stored inappropriately is liable to become spoiled and contaminated with microbes other than mycotoxins, and thereby cause various infections. The panel's recommendation therefore is consistent with protection against food-borne microbial diseases.

11 PRESERVATION

In as much as refrigeration reduces the need for the salting of foods, it will also reduce the risk of hypertension and stroke. Freezing, chilling and refrigeration also reduce spoilage and,

notably with foods of animal origin, the risk of mild to fatal food poisoning.

Implementation of the panel's recommendation will make perishable foods, including vegetables and fruits, last longer and be available out of season. Resulting increased consumption will protect against diseases, the risk of which are reduced by vegetables and fruits, as well as the diseases and infections mentioned in 4 above.

12 ADDITIVES AND RESIDUES

Many chemicals that enter the food chain as residues, or are contained in food as additives, are toxic in high doses and so are subject to regulation.

Implementation of the panel's recommendation will plausibly have the benefit of protecting against any ill-effects of additives, pesticides and other residues, while maintaining protection against fungal contamination and spoilage and without reducing the benefits of increased production and availability of food.

Individuals who remain concerned about unusually high levels of residues in food may choose to wash or scrub vegetables and fruits before eating them, to avoid fish and seafood from highly polluted waters, and to filter water containing high levels of chlorine or nitrates. The panel's recommendation also implies that individuals may wish to exercise their rights as citizens to encourage enforcement of appropriate safety limits.

13 COOKING

Grilled (broiled) meat and fish may be recommended in the context of the prevention of coronary heart disease, in preference to pan frying, because grilling (broiling) reduces the food's fat content, whereas pan frying is likely to use added fat or oil.

The panel recommends that, if grilling (broiling) meat and fish, the cooking should avoid burning/charring the food. The burning of meat should also be avoided and these recommendations could be a useful extension to the current emphasis in health promotion, in which coronary heart disease strategies involve the recommendation to grill (broil) rather than fry or roast.

Resolving apparent contradictions:
  Dietary recommendations to prevent heart disease should also take prevention of cancer into account, and should recommend that when grilling (broiling) meat, burning and charring should be avoided.

14 DIETARY SUPPLEMENTS

In many parts of the world, deficient diets are appropriately supplemented with vitamins and minerals and deficiency diseases, notably of vitamin A, iron and iodine, are prevented or treated by supplementation programmes.

A problem could therefore be created by a recommendation to avoid dietary supplements in all circumstances. This is why the recommendation states that dietary supplements are probably unnecessary and possibly unhelpful in the specific context of cancer prevention.

Resolving apparent contradictions:
The recommendation that dietary supplements are probably unnecessary and possibly unhelpful refers specifically to cancer prevention and not to the prevention of deficiency and other diseases.

15 TOBACCO

Tobacco is an addictive drug, and exposure to tobacco smoke is also a major cause of bronchitis, emphysema, other diseases of the respiratory tract, coronary heart disease, peripheral vascular disease, and other diseases of the cardiovascular system. The panel's recommendation therefore is also consistent with protection against these diseases.

DIETARY CONSTITUENTS

The panel has chosen not to make recommendations specifically on a number of dietary constituents, some of which are relevant to both prevention of cancer and prevention of other diseases.

The amount and balance of dietary constituents derived from the panel's recommendations, shown in Table 8.1.5, should protect against various diseases, and in the judgement of the panel are most unlikely to increase the risk of any disease. In general, as discussed in chapter 5, diets high in constituents that protect against cancers of various sites also reduce risk of other diseases. Similarly, diets high in constituents that increase risk of various cancers generally also increase risks of other diseases. This enables recommendations to be made designed to prevent cancer, with the confidence that these will be generally beneficial and have the general effect of increasing a healthy lifespan.

As shown in Table 8.1.5, the ranges of carbohydrate, starch, NSP/dietary fibre, cholesterol and protein derived from the recommendations, are similar to those recommended by the World Health Organization (WHO, 1990) and the National Academy of Sciences (NAS, 1989) for the prevention of chronic diseases and promotion of health. The panel considers that deriving most fat from plant sources is also likely to protect health, and deriving most protein from plant sources is unlikely to create any problems provided that the dietary protein is obtained from appropriate mixtures of cereals (grains) and pulses (legumes).

The recommendations therefore imply levels of intake of dietary constituents that should protect against a number of diseases other than cancer. As a whole, the recommended diets protect against protein–energy malnutrition. Diets high in NSP protect against intestinal disorders; those low in cholesterol may protect against coronary heart disease.

The ranges of folate and thiamine derived from the recommendations are somewhat higher, and those of vitamin C much higher, than those recommended to prevent deficiency diseases. In the case of vitamin C, the range is higher than amounts consumed in many populations but is within the range of individual intakes and other populations' average intakes. Ranges of retinol, carotenoids, vitamins D and E, calcium, potassium, iron, zinc, iodine and selenium derived from the recommendations are within, or in some cases higher than, ranges recommended or consumed on a population basis.

Diets high in vitamins and minerals protect against various deficiency diseases; those high in antioxidant vitamins and minerals may also protect against cardiovascular disease, and those high in folate protect against neural tube defects. Excessive intakes of dietary constituents known to be toxic in high amounts or doses could create a problem, but the recommendations imply intakes of fat-soluble vitamins, minerals and trace elements well within known safety limits.

In the light of these considerations, the panel recommends that expert groups set up to advise on intakes of dietary microconstituents should, where possible, assess ranges of intakes designed not only to prevent deficiency diseases, but also to prevent chronic diseases including cancer.

CHAPTER NINE

Policy implications

Policies adopted by governments, industry, international agencies and other influential organisations should rationally be based on expert advice. Such advice cannot be immutable; all public policies are subject to change in response to new knowledge. However, there comes a point where an issue is sufficiently important and urgent, and the arguments for action sufficiently cogent, that policy-makers and the public will wish to act. With food, nutrition and the prevention of cancer, such a point has already been reached.

This final chapter outlines the public policy requirements implied by the conclusions and recommendations of this report. It estimates the extent to which cancer may be prevented by means of diet; discusses global trends likely to affect cancer incidence and the prospects of prevention; provides a number of summary studies from different countries of the world; and suggests agenda for change worldwide.

All planning involves estimates based on current knowledge, and some of the issues in this chapter are very broad. It has been prepared with the support of organisations and individuals including some of those designated in this report as advisors and consultants. Its purpose is to provide not so much a blueprint as a portrait of the changes required to reduce incidence of cancer worldwide.

The first section estimates that the dietary recommendations made in this report have the potential of reducing cancer incidence and mortality worldwide, over time, by between 30 and 40 per cent. This estimate is consistent with those made in previous expert reports. In 1996, more than 10 million people in the world developed some form of cancer, and at least 6 million people died from cancer. Therefore, between three and four million cases of cancer could, in time, be avoided every year, by feasible dietary means. Consequently, the findings of this report have immense implications for global, international, and national policies and practices.

The second section looks into the near future and forecasts trends in the incidence of cancer and the costs of its treatment, against a background of vast and accelerating global societal and environmental change, and a corresponding change in disease patterns. Currently, about 12% of all deaths are from cancer. However, this proportion is higher in Europe, North America and Australasia and in urban areas of Africa, Latin America and Asia. With present trends, and with an increasing and ageing world population, these figures are liable to rise.

Experiences from ten countries in Africa, Latin America, Asia, Europe and North America form the third section of this chapter.

The fourth section identifies agents of change, by which both cancer incidence and mortality can be reduced. A global report can only make broad suggestions, and many of the issues touched on in this chapter can be turned into effective programmes for action only by competent agencies already working within specific countries and communities; however, these will be affected by broader international policies and may be stimulated by a suggested framework.

We call on policy-makers, worldwide, to make prevention of cancer an integral part of their work, and to build the prevention of cancer into all major programmes designed to improve the public health.

9.1 Prevention and its benefits

Cancer is largely a preventable disease. The role of tobacco as the overwhelming cause of lung cancer, now the most common cancer globally, is well known. A key message of this report is that between 30% and 40% of cancer incidence worldwide is preventable by the approach to eating, weight control and exercise recommended in this report. At current rates, this represents a figure of 3–4 million cases of cancer a year. The benefits of cancer prevention can be measured in terms of saved resources as well as saved lives. The cost of treating cancer is a burden on medical services and thus on national economies. In many parts of the world, cancers often remain untreated because medical services, treatment or palliative care are not available or cannot be afforded. The most practicable approach to cancer is prevention.

The estimates made by the panel, are consistent with previous estimates of the extent to which cancer may be prevented by appropriate diets. Realistic goals for effective global and national programmes for change should be set for short-, middle- and long-term periods.

9.1.1 THE SCALE OF BENEFIT

In 1996, over ten million people developed some form of cancer (WHO, 1997). The panel estimates that between 30% and 40% of cancer cases throughout the world are preventable by feasible dietary means. At current rates, this represents between 3 and 4 million cases of cancer a year that could be prevented by the dietary patterns recommended in this report. This worldwide estimate of the preventable fraction of cancers applies to most regions and countries. Some common cancers are probably largely preventable by means of diets and closely related factors. Diets containing substantial amounts of a variety of vegetables and fruits may on their own reduce the overall incidence of cancer by over 20%.

The conclusion that most cases of cancer are preventable has enormous implications for public health policy. This chapter concerns the public health policy implications of the dietary recommendations set out in the previous chapter. In this section, the panel quantifies the extent to which cancers of specific sites, and cancer in general, are preventable by appropriate diets and physical activity patterns. First, though, it is important to know what the concept of 'prevention' itself means.

THE CONCEPT OF PREVENTION

The phrase 'cancer prevention' refers, in general, to the process of reducing the age-specific incidence rate of cancer. With few exceptions, it is not meaningful to aim to eliminate cancer totally, that is to aim for a zero rate. Almost all types of cancer occur at a 'background rate' in nature, because of various random events or unidentified factors, although several rare types of cancer may be entirely prevented by elimination of very specific causal factors, for example, vinyl chloride polymerisation (an occupational exposure) in angiosarcoma of the liver, and respirable asbestos fibres in mesothelioma. Otherwise, 'cancer prevention' entails reducing the incidence of cancer at each age (especially at ages before about 75+ years), which often entails deferring clinically diagnosable cancer to an older age, rather than a life-long protection against the disease.

This is analogous to the situation referred to as the 'prevention of heart disease' (or stroke or diabetes, etc.), which means a slowing of the pathogenic processes that culminate, after several decades, in clinical disease. In ideal circumstances, it may be possible to prevent the onset of these long-latency non-infectious diseases, at least in some individuals. However, most prevention in heterogeneous populations, in which individuals are exposed to some 'risk factors' at some level (for example, excess total energy, environmental tobacco smoke, alcohol consumption), is the kind that defers, rather than precludes, the disease.

If the deferral of cancer occurrence, through slowing of the carcinogenic process, is for one or more decades (for example, from age 60 to 80 years), then the 'prevention' is very substantial and worthwhile. Indeed, given that many such individuals often die from some other non-cancer disease during these intervening years, then cancer can be truly prevented.

It is important to note that cancer is a strongly age-related disease. The overall cancer incidence rates increase markedly with age from around the sixth decade of life. Hence, as the average life expectancy increases in populations around the world, it is likely that an increased proportion of all deaths will be from cancer – even though the age-specific rates of cancer at ages 50–59, 60–69, etc., are falling. Cancer deaths occurring, on average, at substantially older ages as a result of cancer prevention strategies, contribute importantly to 'cancer prevention'.

Overall, 'cancer prevention' is made up of cancers avoided and those deferred. Most preventive strategies directed at other non-cancer diseases will also assist in the prevention of cancer, for example, changes in diet and physical activity directed at reducing cardiovascular disease and adult-onset diabetes, reduced smoking directed at prevention of a wide range of diseases, and reduced overall alcohol consumption in relation to both acute and chronic effects.

Death cannot be prevented, so the main task for dietary prevention of cancer is, first, to reduce the occurrence of premature cancers greatly, and, second, to seek to avert many of the cancers that are deferred to, or destined for, old age.

ASPECTS OF DIET

The scientific community and relevant organisations in the field agree, in general, that cancer is mostly a preventable disease and that the three main means of reducing cancer risk are the avoidance of tobacco use, the consumption of appropriate diets, and limiting exposure to occupational and other environmental carcinogens. This conclusion is endorsed by WHO, most relevant health organisations, and increasingly by governments throughout the world. 'Diets' are taken in this report to include alcoholic drinks and the closely associated factors of body mass and physical activity.

The strongest evidence for dietary aspects of cancer prevention relates to the benefits of eating substantial amounts of a variety of vegetables and fruits.

The epidemiological and experimental evidence showing that such diets reduce the risk of cancers of many sites is now very strong. The extent to which such diets may reduce cancer risk has been quantified by Dutch scientists (Jansen et al, 1995), for a projected increase in consumption from the then current intakes in the Netherlands of 242 g/day of vegeta-

TABLE 9.1.1 PREVENTION OF CANCER BY DIETS HIGH IN VEGETABLES AND FRUITS

SITE	PROPORTION OF TOTAL CANCER INCIDENCE[a] (%)	PROPORTION ATTRIBUTABLE TO ALCOHOL AND/ OR TOBACCO[b] (%)	RELATIVE RISKS[c] (VEGETABLE AND FRUIT CONSUMPTION)			PROPORTION OF TOTAL CANCER INCIDENCE PREVENTABLE[d]		
			Conservative	Best	Optimistic[e]	Conservative	Best	Optimistic
Mouth and pharynx	2.3	70	0.50	0.45	0.40	0.3	1.3	1.4
Larynx	1.2	85	0.50	0.45	0.40	0.1	0.7	0.7
Oesophagus	1.4	75	0.50	0.45	0.40	0.4	0.2	0.8
Lung:	15	–	0.55	–	–	1.4	–	–
Men	24	90	–	0.55	0.45	–	5.4	6.6
Women	5	60	–	0.55	0.45	–	1.1	1.4
Stomach	4.3	[f]	0.50	0.45	0.40	0.2	2.4	2.6
Pancreas	2.3	30	0.70	0.60	0.35	0.5	0.9	1.5
Colon/rectum	13	[f]	0.70	0.60	0.50	3.9	5.2	6.5
Breast	15	[f]	1.00	0.85	0.75	0.0	2.3	3.8
Ovary	2.1	[f]	1.00	0.85	0.55	0.0	0.3	1.0
Cervix	1.3	–	1.00	0.85	0.50	0.0	0.2	0.7
Prostate	7	[f]	1.00	0.90	0.75	0.0	0.7	1.8
Bladder	3.4	50	0.70	0.60	0.50	0.5	1.4	1.7
Other	32	[f]	1.00	1.00	1.00	–	–	–
Total	**100**					**7.0**	**22.7**	**30.5**

[a] Netherlands Cancer Registry (1990)
[b] Proportion of cancers related to tobacco and/or smoking (IARC, 1990)
[c] RR for a difference in vegetable and fruit consumption of 1.5 servings per day assuming a linear relationship between vegetable and fruit consumption and the risk of cancer
[d] Calculations: Best guess/optimistic estimates: (1–RR) x proportion of total cancers (%); Conservative estimate: (1–RR) x proportion of total cancers (%) x (100– proportion (%) contributed by alcohol and/or tobacco)/100
[e] Uses estimate from either Margetts (1994) or Block (1992)
[f] No value included in IARC (1990); set at 0% for calculations
na not applicable

Adapted from Jansen et al (1995)

bles and fruits (excluding potatoes and pulses) to a goal of 400 g/day (that is the lower end of the range recommended in this report). This increase equates to an extra 1.5 portions of vegetables and fruits per day.

Table 9.1.1 projects the extent to which overall cancer and those of specific sites might be prevented by diets rich in vegetables and fruits. The data for cancer incidence are from the Netherlands. Three approaches are proposed: 'conservative', 'best guess' and 'optimistic'.

Three estimates for potential prevention were envisaged and are projected in Figure 9.1.1 (Jansen et al, 1995). The data can be taken to apply to countries where the consumption of vegetables and fruits is similar to that in western and northern Europe.

The 'best guess' estimate, with the intermediate benefit of a 23% reduction in overall cancer incidence when average vegetable and fruit consumption increases from 250 to 400 g/day, is, in the opinion of the panel, a reasonable but modest estimate on the basis of the latest findings. The beneficial effects may not be expected immediately but may take one to two decades. Figure 9.1.1 also extrapolates the benefit of vegetables and fruits beyond 400 g/day up to 500 g/day, on the basis that intakes higher than 400 g/day confer additional protection. Such extrapolation is consistent with some of the dose–response data presented in this report. The panel estimates that diets high in vegetables and fruits (more than 400 g/day) could prevent at least 20% of all cancer incidence.

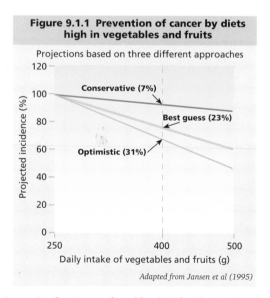

Figure 9.1.1 Prevention of cancer by diets high in vegetables and fruits

Projections based on three different approaches

Conservative (7%)

Best guess (23%)

Optimistic (31%)

Projected incidence (%)

Daily intake of vegetables and fruits (g)

Adapted from Jansen et al (1995)

'Best-guess' estimates use the mid-point of estimates developed by different authors. The 'optimistic' estimates use the data on relative risks from Block (1992) or Margetts (1994). The 'conservative' approach assumes that smoking and drinking alcohol should first be discounted without considering possible interaction with diet, and assumes that hormone-related cancers (for example, breast) were not affected by high intakes of vegetables and fruit. Figure 9.1.1 goes beyond the Jansen data by projecting a further reduction of risk above 400 g/day. Such a further extrapolation is consistent with some of the dose–response data presented in this report.

The 'optimistic' estimate projects a reduction of 31%, based on site-specific relative risks identified in the literature (Steinmetz and Potter, 1991; Block, 1992; Margetts, 1994). Block's analysis suggests benefits for all cancers, ranging from pancreatic cancer, with a potential benefit from consumption of high intakes of fruits and vegetables of about a 64% reduction in incidence, to breast cancer, with a benefit of 23%.

The 'conservative' projection assumes that the effect of smoking and drinking alcohol, as calculated by the IARC (1990), has an effect that is separate from any protective effect of vegetables and fruits. It also assumes that vegetables and fruits are not relevant to hormone-related cancers. Both these assumptions are, however, unduly cautious: as reviewed in chapter 4 and summarised below, vegetables and fruits protect against smoking-related cancers among smokers as well as in ex- and never-smokers, and the risk of some hormone-related cancers, for example, of the breast, is decreased by higher intakes of plant foods.

CANCER IN GENERAL

It is frequently suggested that about one-third of cancer deaths may be avoidable by practicable dietary means (NIH, 1986; Department of Health, 1991; NCI, 1996). This estimate has also been taken to refer to cancer incidence.

The most widely cited estimate is that made by Doll and Peto in their report to the US Congress (Doll and Peto, 1981). They estimated that diet (excluding alcohol) was responsible for about 35% of all cancer deaths in the USA, with a further 3% attributed to alcohol. However, they qualified this by also suggesting a range of acceptable estimates of between 10% and 70% attributable to diet and a further 2–4% to alcohol. It was later proposed that the evidence available up to the early 1990s involving diet with cancer had become stronger, and a narrower range of 20–60% was proposed (Doll, 1992).

By comparing age-standardised death rates from cancers of a large number of sites held at US registries with figures from the registry with the lowest recorded rates in the world, Doll and Peto estimated the avoidable proportion of specific cancers and therefore for cancer in general. For example, they found that the lowest rates of colon cancer (in Nigeria) were less than one-tenth of the rates found in the USA, and the lowest rates of breast cancer (among non-Jewish women in Israel) were less than one-fifth the US rates.

Given that specific cancers vary in incidence from country to country, then the extent to which cancers can be avoided depends on the cancer burden of the nation. For example, for stomach cancer, the extent to which it is preventable in the UK (with a low incidence of this cancer) is less than that in Japan (with a high incidence); however, for breast cancer, the potential for prevention in the UK (with a high incidence) is much higher than in Japan (which historically has a low incidence). If a study were undertaken, similar to that of Doll and Peto, in China for the prevalent nasopharyngeal cancer, the extent to which it may be prevented by environmental and dietary means would be high, whereas in the

USA reduction of the low rates by factors other than smoking (Nam et al, 1992) would be small.

On an international basis, a comparison of the highest and lowest rates of specific cancers from registries throughout the world (IARC, 1990), reveals that the theoretical extent to which cancers are preventable is higher than in the Doll and Peto study (1981), in which the figures from just one country were used as the baseline.

Doll and Peto also examined the relative risk associated with other exposures. Non-dietary exposures included tobacco, reproductive and sexual behaviour (including the effects of intercourse, pregnancy, childbirth and lactation), occupational and environmental exposures (including chemical and atmospheric pollution), infection (notably by specific viruses), medical procedures (including ionising radiation and exogenous hormones) and geophysical factors (including ultraviolet light). They also dealt with alcohol and food additives, which were considered separately from dietary factors. From these data, they were able to estimate, with varying degrees of confidence, the extent to which a number of cancers might be caused by diet.

In two later reports concerned with dietary prevention of chronic disease, the World Health Organization (WHO, 1988, 1990a) cited the estimates of Doll and Peto, or the rather higher earlier estimates based on cancer incidence in economically developed countries (Wynder and Gori, 1977). The 1989 report of the National Academy of Sciences (NAS, 1989) also cited the Doll and Peto estimates, stating that 'because few relationships between specific dietary components and cancer risk are well established, it is not possible to quantify the contribution of diet to individual cancers (and thus to total cancer rates) more precisely'. The 1990 report of the Chief Medical Officer in England to the Secretary of State for Health (Department of Health, 1991) cited the work of Doll and Peto as 'the best estimate' and, in effect, took their estimates as valid for the UK, adding that 'the potential scope for reducing the toll of cancer deaths related to diet is great'.

A task force of the European School of Oncology issued guidelines for Europe in 1994, concluding that at least 35% of cancer incidence might eventually be prevented by dietary modification (Miller at al, 1994). The 1996 guidelines of the American Cancer Society (ACS, 1996) were in line with the Doll and Peto estimates, noting that 'the evidence suggests that about one-third of the 500,000 cancer deaths that occur in the United States each year is due to dietary factors … therefore, for the large majority of Americans who do not smoke cigarettes, dietary choices, in association with physical activity, become the most important modifiable determinants of cancer risk'.

There are a number of issues that need to be considered when making calculations on modification of cancer risk by diet and other factors.

Interdependence

Environmental factors that modify cancer risk may not work independently of each other. They may act synergistically (as shown for drinking alcohol and smoking in relation to cancers of the upper aerodigestive tract). They may be co-factors, that is, two or more factors need to be present before cancer risk is modified (as seen with *Helicobacter pylori* infection and salt intake in inducing stomach cancer). They may be interdependent in other ways. Thus, although smoking causes most cases of lung cancer, diets high in vegetables and fruits protect a substantial proportion of smokers from lung cancer. This interdependence means that simply summing all published estimates of 'separate' effects caused by the factors capable of modifying cancer risk may, paradoxically, add up to more than 100%.

The induction time for cancer

There is often a latent period between exposure to a factor that modifies cancer risk and induction of the tumour itself. In addition, a further delay occurs before development of the tumour reaches the stage at which it is diagnosable; this varies with different factors and different sites. Thus, migrant studies suggest that the delay between exposure of migrants to urban–industrial diets and emergence of colorectal cancer may be 10–20 years. On the other hand, patterns of breast cancer may take longer to change with migration, often becoming evident only in the second generation; this suggests that the determinants of breast cancer risk have their effects early in life. It follows that appropriate diets may have their full impact in preventing cancer perhaps only decades after such diets were widely adopted. These delays need to be taken into account when setting realistic targets for cancer prevention in national plans.

Time needed for substantial dietary change

The dietary recommendations in this report apply to individuals as well as to populations. Those individuals who are able to change their diets immediately are more likely to reduce their cancer risk by the percentages indicated within a decade or so. At least one exception as stated is breast cancer, for which significant prevention may require dietary change before puberty. Stomach cancer may be another exception. Changes on a population basis will inevitably take longer simply because international and national changes in dietary patterns reflect the aggregate of individual changes. Policy-makers devising national goals would be wise to consider a 15- to 60-year period as the time-frame for benefits becoming evident.

Trends in patterns of diet and cancer

As set out in chapter 1 (and below), global and national trends in diet and in cancer rates are generally unfavourable, with specific important exceptions, such as stomach cancer. Urban–industrial diets and their associated lifestyles increase the incidence of many cancers. Furthermore, the burden of cancer is increasing because the population of the world is both increasing and ageing rapidly. Successful programmes of cancer prevention may therefore have the effect of slowing an upward trend or even reducing rates of cancer, but they may still not decrease the total number of cancer cases.

TABLE 9.1.2 CANCERS PREVENTABLE BY DIETARY MEANS

A global projection

Included as 'dietary factors' in this table are various foods, nutrients, alcoholic drinks, body weight and physical activity. The panel has estimated the extent to which specific cancers or cancer in general are preventable by the dietary and associated factors described in this report. The figures suggested are ranges consistent with current scientific knowledge as reviewed and assessed in chapters 4–7, and take established non-dietary risk factors, notably the use of tobacco, specific infections and occupational exposures to carcinogens, into account. The arrows represent either decreasing risk (↓) or increasing risk (↑).

	GLOBAL RANKING (INCIDENCE)	GLOBAL INCIDENCE (1,000s)	DIETARY FACTORS (CONVINCING OR PROBABLE)	NON-DIETARY RISK FACTORS (ESTABLISHED)	PREVENTABLE BY DIET			
					LOW ESTIMATE (%)	HIGH ESTIMATE (%)	LOW ESTIMATE (1,000s)	HIGH ESTIMATE (1,000s)
Mouth and pharynx / Nasopharynx	5	575	↓ Vegetables & fruits[a] ↑ Alcohol[a] ↑ Salted fish[b]	↑ Smoking[a] ↑ Betel[a] ↑ EBV[b]	33	50	190	288
Larynx	14	190	↓ Vegetables & fruits ↑ Alcohol	↑ Smoking	33	50	63	95
Oesophagus	8	480	↓ Vegetables & fruits ↑ Deficiency diets ↑ Alcohol	↑ Smoking ↑ Barrett's oesophagus	50	75	240	360
Lung	1	1,320	↓ Vegetables & fruits	↑ Smoking ↑ Occupation	20	33	264	436
Stomach	2	1,015	↓ Vegetables & fruits ↓ Refrigeration ↑ Salt ↑ Salted foods	↑ H. pylori	66	75	670	761
Pancreas	13	200	↓ Vegetables & fruits ↑ Meat, animal fat	↑ Smoking	33	50	66	100
Gallbladder	–	c	–	–	–	–	–	–
Liver	6	540	↑ Alcohol ↑ Contaminated food	↑ HBV and HCV	33	66	178	356
Colon, rectum	4	875	↓ Vegetables ↓ Physical activity ↑ Meat ↑ Alcohol	↑ Smoking ↑ Genes ↑ Ulcerative colitis ↑ S. sinensis ↓ NSAIDs	66	75	578	656
Breast	3	910	↓ Vegetables ↑ Rapid early growth ↑ Early menarche ↑ Obesity ↑ Alcohol	↓ Reproductive ↑ Genes ↑ Radiation	33	50	300	455
Ovary	15	190	–	↑ Genes ↓ Reproductive	10	20	19	38
Endometrium	16	170	↑ Obesity	↑ OCs ↑ Oestrogens ↓ Reproductive	25	50	43	85
Cervix	7	525	↓ Vegetables & fruits	↑ HPV ↑ Smoking	10	20	53	105
Prostate	9	400	↑ Meat or meat fat or dairy fat		10	20	40	80
Thyroid	–	100[d]	↑ Iodine deficiency	↑ Radiation	10	20	10	20
Kidney	17	165	↑ Obesity	↑ Smoking ↑ Phenacetin	25	33	41	54
Bladder	11	310		↑ Smoking ↑ Occupation ↑ S. haematobium	10	20	31	62
Other		2,355	–	–	10	10	236	236
Total (1996)		**10,320**					**3,022** **29.3%**	**4,187** **40.6%**

Figures on global ranking and incidence: Parkin et al (1993); WHO (1997)

[a] Mouth and pharynx; also chewing tobacco
[b] Nasopharynx
[c] Reliable worldwide data are not collected by IARC for this site
[d] Conservative estimate based on IARC, (1993)

Table 9.1.2 is a global projection of the percentage of cancers preventable by dietary means.

CANCERS OF SPECIFIC SITES

1 Mouth and pharynx

Smoking and other uses of tobacco and betel are important non-dietary causes of this cancer. Diets high in vegetables and fruits protect against this cancer whereas alcohol increases the risk.

The population-attributable risk or contribution of both alcohol drinking and smoking is well established and has been variously estimated at between 75% and 83% of all cases (Wynder et al, 1957; Rothman and Keller, 1972; IARC, 1990). It has been estimated that almost 87% of the incidence of this cancer can potentially be reduced by not smoking, reducing alcohol drinking and increasing consumption of vegetables and fruits (Zatonski et al, 1991).

Given the evidence of an independent protective effect of vegetables and fruits, the panel judges that diets high in a variety of vegetables and fruits, and the avoidance of alcohol, may prevent between 33% and 50% of the cases of cancer of the mouth and pharynx. The panel also notes the evidence that drinking very hot drinks may increase the risk.

2 Nasopharynx

Non-dietary causes of nasopharyngeal cancer include smoking tobacco (at least in the low-risk US white population) and infection (with the Epstein–Barr virus). The impact of diet on risk is so far confined to the role played by salted fish in increasing risk. It has been estimated that anything between 10% and 90% of the cases of nasopharyngeal cancer in south China could be prevented by avoiding the regular consumption of salted fish (Yu et al, 1988).

The panel judges that the avoidance of salted fish may prevent between 33% and 50% of cases of nasopharyngeal cancer.

3 Larynx

Smoking tobacco is an important non-dietary cause of this cancer. As with cancer of the mouth and pharynx, diets high in vegetables and fruits protect against this cancer; alcohol increases risk.

The attributable risk from drinking alcohol or smoking, or from both, is well established and has been variously estimated as between 80% and 90% of all cases of laryngeal cancer (Flanders and Rothman, 1982; IARC, 1990). Potentially, its development can be prevented by not smoking, reducing alcohol drinking and increasing consumption of vegetables and fruits. Their combined impact has been estimated to prevent almost 86% of this cancer (Zatonski et al, 1991). The risk attributable to a low intake of vegetables and fruits in Europe is estimated at 25–50% (Riboli et al, 1996) or 50–60% of all cases (Jansen et al, 1995).

Again, given the evidence of the independent protective effect of vegetables and fruits, the panel judges that varied diets high in vegetables and fruits, together with consump-

tion of little if any alcohol, may prevent between 33% and 50% of all cases of laryngeal cancer.

4 Oesophagus

Smoking is an important non-dietary cause of this cancer, as is Barrett's oesophagus. As with cancers of the mouth and pharynx and of the larynx, diets high in vegetables and fruits protect against this cancer; alcohol increases risk. Correspondingly, diets deficient in various dietary constituents increase risk.

The attributable risk of drinking alcohol and smoking is well established and has been estimated for various populations as equivalent to 75% of all cases (Wynder and Bross, 1961; Tuyns et al, 1988). Doll and Peto estimated that the total number of deaths from cancer of the aerodigestive tract in the USA could be reduced by 20% by practicable dietary means (Doll and Peto, 1981). Incidence of oesophageal cancer is potentially reduced by not smoking, reducing alcohol intake and increasing consumption of vegetables and fruits; this reduction has been estimated at almost 86% (Zatonski et al, 1991). Alternatively, it has been proposed that 'a substantial fraction' of cases could be prevented by a modest increase in consumption of vegetables and fruits (IARC, 1990). This has been quantified, in the Netherlands, as a reduction in overall incidence by between 50% and 60% as a result of increasing consumption of vegetables and fruits from about 250 to 400 grams/day (Jansen et al, 1995).

The panel judges that 50–75% of the cases of oesophageal cancer may be prevented by varied diets high in a variety of vegetables and fruits, together with consumption of little if any alcohol. The panel also notes that small amounts of meat may protect against the risk of this cancer, especially in parts of the world where microconstituent deficiencies are common, and that very hot drinks may increase risk.

5 Lung

Smoking is the most important cause of this cancer. Tobacco use, together with specific occupational exposures, is estimated to cause around 80% of the cases of this cancer (IARC, 1990). Diets high in vegetables and fruits are protective.

The extent to which mortality rates from lung cancer in the USA might be reduced by practicable dietary means has been estimated as 20% (Doll and Peto, 1981). Between 40% and 50% of the cases of this cancer have been estimated to be preventable by diets high in vegetables and fruits, whether in smokers, ex-smokers or never-smokers (Jansen et al, 1995; Ziegler et al, 1996).

The panel emphasises the importance of not smoking in the case of this (and other) cancers. At the same time, the panel judges that diets high in a variety of vegetables and fruits may prevent 20–33% of lung cancer cases in both smokers and non-smokers. The panel also notes the evidence that alcohol possibly increases the risk of this cancer.

6 Stomach

Stomach cancer has been considered, together with colorectal cancer, to be the cancer most related to diet. *Helicobacter pylori* infection is a non-dietary cause, but this infection may interact with dietary factors. Diets high in vegetables and fruits protect against this cancer, as does refrigeration of perishable foods. Diets high in salt and salted foods probably increase the risk of this cancer.

The extent to which the mortality rates from stomach cancer in the USA might be reduced by practicable dietary means has been estimated at 90% (Doll and Peto, 1981). It has been suggested that about 75% of the cases might be prevented by increasing vegetable and fruit consumption and decreasing intakes of cured meat and salt-preserved foods (Buatti et al, 1990). Daily consumption of several servings of vegetables and fruits is associated with a 50–60% reduction in incidence worldwide, that is, rates around one-half those seen in the lower-consuming individuals (IARC, 1990; Jansen et al, 1995).

The panel agrees that most cases of stomach cancer can be prevented by the dietary and related means recommended in this report. Although it is not yet clear whether *H. pylori* acts independently of dietary factors, the panel judges that diets high in a variety of vegetables and fruits, together with the use of freezing and refrigeration to preserve perishable food, and a low consumption of salt and salted foods, may prevent 66–75% of the cases of this cancer. The panel also notes the possible benefits of wholegrain cereals and other fibre-rich foods, and the possible role played by diets containing substantial amounts of cured foods and foods cooked in flame in increasing the risk of this cancer.

7 Pancreas

Smoking tobacco is an important non-dietary cause of this cancer. Diets high in vegetables and fruits probably decrease risk; diets high in either meat or cholesterol possibly increase risk.

The extent to which the mortality rates from pancreatic cancer in the USA might be reduced by practicable dietary means has been estimated at 50% (Doll and Peto, 1981). It has also been suggested that 70% of cases could be prevented by not smoking, and by increasing vegetables and fruits and reducing calories and dietary cholesterol (Howe et al, 1992).

Given the evidence that vegetables and fruits probably protect against this cancer, the panel judges that diets high in a variety of vegetables may prevent 33–50% of the cases of pancreatic cancer. The panel also notes that diets high in meat, cholesterol and total energy may increase the risk of this cancer.

8 Gallbladder

Gallstones are a cause of this cancer, with the risk of gallstones being increased by obesity.

The extent to which mortality rates from gallbladder cancer in the USA might be reduced by practicable dietary means has been estimated at 50% (Doll and Peto, 1981).

However, given that obesity is largely a risk factor for gallstones rather than for gallbladder cancer itself, and that the causes of gallstones vary in countries at high and low risk of gallbladder cancer, the panel could not estimate the extent to which this cancer might be prevented by dietary means alone.

9 Liver

Infection with the hepatitis B or C viruses, which could interact with dietary factors, including alcohol, is a non-dietary cause of this cancer. Contamination of food with aflatoxins and high consumption of alcohol increase risk.

Given the enormous differences in incidence throughout the world, it has been suggested that a halving of aflatoxin contamination could reduce incidence in Asia and Africa by 40%, and the avoidance of high levels of alcohol drinking could reduce the incidence by 13% (IARC, 1990).

Because viral infection can act synergistically with dietary factors, the panel judges that foods with little contamination with aflatoxin, together with consumption of little if any alcohol, may prevent 33–66% of cases of liver cancer. This rather wide range of values reflects the relative uncertainty about the ways in which dietary and viral causes of this cancer ultimately determine risk.

10 Colon and rectum

The main causes of colorectal cancer are believed to be diet and related factors, although much more is known about colon than about rectal cancer. Diets high in vegetables decrease risk, as does regular physical activity. Diets high in NSP/fibre possibly decrease risk; those high in meat and in alcohol probably increase risk. Non-dietary environmental risk factors include a possible increased risk of rectal cancer as a result of intestinal schistosomiasis. Family history is a risk predictor in a small but important number of individuals.

The extent to which mortality rates from these cancers in the USA might be reduced by practicable dietary means has been estimated at 90% (Doll and Peto, 1981). More specifically, it is suggested that up to a half of colorectal cancers could be prevented by diets high in vegetables and low in fat (Jain et al, 1980; IARC, 1990); others have estimated that between 30% and 50% of the cases could be prevented by diets high in vegetables and fruits (Jansen et al, 1995).

The panel agrees that the principal causes of colorectal cancer are dietary. It also emphasises the recent strong and consistent evidence that regular physical activity protects against colon cancer. The panel judges that diets high in vegetables, and therefore high in fibre, and low in meat, the avoidance of alcohol, and regular physical activity, may reduce the incidence of colorectal cancer by 66–75%. The panel also notes the evidence that obesity and diets high in fat, sugar, and overcooked and burnt meat, all possibly increase the risk of this cancer.

11 Breast

Hormonal events are central to the aetiology of breast cancer. Some of the main determinants of risk are probably related to diet, and may have most effect in early life. Rapid early growth and early menarche increase risk of this cancer. Diets high in vegetables and fruits probably decrease the risk; high body mass probably increases the risk after the menopause, and alcohol probably increases the risk. Family history is a predictor of risk in a small but important number of women.

The overall potential for prevention of breast cancer, based on data from registries recording the highest and lowest rates, has been estimated at about 80% (IARC, 1990). The extent to which mortality rates from breast cancer in the USA might be reduced by practicable dietary means has been estimated at 50% (Doll and Peto, 1981). Thirteen per cent of breast cancer cases in the USA have been attributed to alcohol (Longnecker et al, 1988).

Between 11% and 30% of breast cancer cases have been attributed to obesity (IARC, 1990). Diets high in a variety of vegetables and fruits have been estimated to prevent 10–20% of cases (Jansen et al, 1995).

The panel has found assessment of the evidence on breast cancer particularly difficult. It judges that plant-based diets, and the avoidance of alcohol, together with maintenance of recommended body mass and regular physical activity, may reduce the incidence of breast cancer by about 33–50%. However, the panel also judges, based on the present evidence, that such diets and related factors will have most benefit if established before puberty and then throughout life. The potential for prevention starting in adult life may be limited largely to that conferred by maintenance of a recommended body weight and the avoidance of alcohol; this may account for 10–20% of cases of this cancer. The panel also notes that greater physical activity may protect against this cancer, and that diets high in fat and meat may increase risk.

12 Ovary

Evidence on factors affecting the risk of ovarian cancer is unclear. It is possible that diets high in vegetables and fruits decrease risk and those high in animal fat and fat more generally increase risk.

It has been suggested that 66% of the cases could be prevented by diets low in fat (Miller at al, 1994).

The panel concludes that factors affecting the risk of ovarian cancer may be similar to those affecting other female hormone-related cancers; it judges that, following the overall recommendations of this report, diets high in vegetables and fruits and low in meat and other fatty foods of animal origin may, in adult life, reduce the incidence of ovarian cancer by 10–20%.

13 Endometrium

The chief cause of endometrial cancer is obesity. Certain types of hormone replacement therapy also increase risk.

The extent to which mortality rates from endometrial cancer in the USA might be reduced by practicable dietary means has been estimated at 50% (Doll and Peto, 1981). The risk attributable to obesity has been suggested to be 15–30%, and it is also suggested that a greater proportion might be prevented by weight control in younger women (Henderson et al, 1983; IARC, 1990).

Bearing in mind the lack of major non-dietary risk factors and the established risk factor of obesity, the panel judges that following the recommendations of this report, and in particular maintenance of recommended body mass, may prevent 25–50% of cases of endometrial cancer. The panel also notes that diets high in vegetables and fruits may protect against this cancer and those high in animal fat may increase risk.

14 Cervix

Infection with Human Papillomaviruses (HPVs) is the most important non-dietary cause of this cancer. Risk is also increased by smoking tobacco. Diets high in vegetables and fruits possibly protect against this cancer.

The very variable rates of cervical cancer suggest that 95% may be preventable (IARC, 1990). The extent to which mortality rates from cervical cancer in the USA might be reduced by practicable dietary means has been estimated at 20% (Doll and Peto, 1981).

Major reduction of risk of this cancer can be achieved by ceasing smoking and by protection against sexually transmitted HPVs. The panel judges that the recommendations in this report, including diets high in vegetables and fruits, may reduce the incidence of cervical cancer by 10–20%.

15 Prostate

The chief causes of prostate cancer may be related to diet. However, the only reasonably persuasive evidence shows that diets high in meat, or meat fat, or fat from other foods of animal origin possibly increase risk of this cancer.

It is suggested that diets high in a variety of vegetables and fruits may prevent between 10% and 20% of cases of this cancer (Jansen et al, 1995). Estimations of attributable risk for high saturated fat intake of between 6% and 24% in various US populations are possibly underestimates (Kolonel, 1996).

The panel judges that diets low in meat and other fatty foods of animal origin may prevent 10–20% of cases of prostate cancer.

16 Thyroid

Little is known about causes or prevention of this uncommon cancer. The panel judges that implementing the recommendations of this report will provide ample but not excessive intakes of iodine and this may prevent 10–20% of the cases of thyroid cancer. The panel also notes the evidence that diets high in vegetables and fruits may protect against this cancer.

17 Kidney

Smoking tobacco is a non-dietary cause of this cancer; obesity also increases the risk.

The panel judges that the recommendation to avoid obesity could reduce the incidence of kidney cancer by 25–33%.

The panel also notes evidence that diets high in vegetables possibly decrease the risk and those high in meat and other animal products possibly increase the risk of this cancer.

18 Bladder

Smoking tobacco is a non-dietary cause of this cancer, as are specific occupational exposures to carcinogens and parasitic infestation (schistosomiasis).

The extent to which mortality rates from cancer of the bladder in the USA might be reduced by practicable dietary means has been estimated at 20% (Doll and Peto, 1981). Specifically, it is estimated that diets high in vegetables could reduce incidence by 10–20% in Western populations (La Vecchia and Negri, 1996).

The panel judges that diets high in vegetables and fruits might reduce the incidence of bladder cancer by 10–20%.

Other

The panel judges that the diets recommended in this report may reduce the risk of other cancers not specified here by a notional 10%.

9.1.2 THE BENEFITS OF PREVENTION

In the case of chronic diseases such as cancer, which often involve years of patient care, prevention is usually cheaper than treatment. In economically developed countries with established social and medical infrastructures, and with health services and systems of medical insurance in place, the cost of treating cancer, to individuals, families and society, is substantial. In economically developing countries, with the existing burdens of endemic deficiency and infectious diseases, as well as endemic cancers, the impending burden of additional cancer epidemics related to urban–industrial diets and lifestyles will be unmanageable. For developing countries, prevention is therefore not only crucial, but is the only sensible approach in planning public health policies. In developed countries, the personal, social and health-care benefits of prevention should already be obvious.

THE COST OF TREATING CANCER

The cost of treating cancer is very much higher in developing than in developed countries. This is because the hospital procedures have a high foreign-exchange content, involving specialised training of staff and purchase of drugs and equipment. In Table 9.1.3, calculations are made for a lower-middle-income country with a per capita GNP (GNPN) of US$1,500. In making the calculations, it is assumed that the foreign exchange content of costs for the treatment of the early stages of oral, cervical, breast and rectal cancer, which involve largely surgical procedures is lower than for all other cancers where chemotherapy is more likely to be used on a long-term basis. Table 9.1.3 shows the estimated cost per case with treatment for lung cancer at the top of the scale

TABLE 9.1.3 COMPARISONS OF THE RELATIVE COST OF TREATING DIFFERENT CANCERS IN DEVELOPED AND DEVELOPING COUNTRIES

CANCER	RELATIVE COSTS PER CASE IN AN ECONOMICALLY DEVELOPED COUNTRY[a] (%)	COMPARABLE COSTS PER CASE IN AN ECONOMICALLY DEVELOPING COUNTRY[b] (% OF DEVELOPED COUNTRY AVERAGE)
Lung	122	782
Liver	113	727
Oesophagus	111	709
Leukaemia	109	700
Stomach	107	687
Colon & rectum	105	336
Mouth & pharynx	76	243
Breast	65	206
Cervix	54	174
Average	**100**	**641**

Calculations for developing countries are adjusted for their income and the economic burden of training, equipment and drugs
[a] Defined as 'high income' with gross national product per capita (GNPN)/year = US$21,500
[b] Defined as 'lower-middle-income' with GNPN/year = US$1,500
Sources: Cromwell and Gertman (1979); Barnum and Greenberg (1993); Rice et al (1985)

and for cervical cancer at the bottom. It shows that the real cost of treatment in a developing country in rapid transition is three to six times that in a developed country.

THE COST OF PREVENTING CANCER

The costs of preventive measures have not been calculated specifically for cancer. Table 9.1.4 compares the costs of a variety of public health packages (including education, information and communication, surveillance and monitoring) with the costs of some core primary-care clinical services for developing countries where the major needs are the treatment of trauma and acute and chronic infections. What emerges is a simple picture even for existing problems: prevention is a far more effective economic strategy for a country than the provision of treatment and palliation of disease.

Low-income developing countries do not have any resources to cope with measures other than public health and essential clinical services. In middle-income countries the costs of US$2,000–11,000 per cancer case treated mean that coping with the chronic diseases exceeds the cost of all other health needs.

Although the relevant prevention cost estimates in Table 9.1.4 will vary according to types of disease, cancer sites, local services and conditions, the scale of difference between treatment of cancer and any other health-care options is sufficiently massive to indicate that a strategy of prevention rather than treatment is the only logical course. The choice between options in low-income developing countries is even more stark. (See World Bank, 1993, pp 66–68.) The contrast is so marked, and the implications for health care costs so striking, that preventive measures need to become an overwhelming priority in the provision of health care; this applies

	CONTENTS OF HEALTH – RELATED PACKAGES	ALLOCATIONS* IN DEVELOPING COUNTRIES		
		PROPOSED	ACTUAL	COST PER DALY
Public health package	Expanded Programme on Immunisation (EPI) Plus; school health programmes; tobacco and alcohol control; health, nutrition, and family planning information; vector control; sexually transmitted disease prevention; monitoring and surveillance	5	1	25
Essential clinical services (minimum package)	Tuberculosis treatment; management of the sick child; pre-natal and delivery care; family planning; sexually transmitted disease treatment; treatment of infection and minor trauma; assessment, advice, and pain alleviation	10	4–6	25–75
Total, public health and minimum essential clinical services		15	5–7	50–100
Discretionary clinical services[c]	All other health services, including effective low-cost treatment of cancer, cardiovascular disease, other chronic conditions, major trauma, and neurological and psychiatric disorders	6	13–15	> 1,000
Total		**21**	**21**	

Current spending on essential clinical services is estimated to be 20–30% of total public expenditure on health on the basis of estimates in World Bank health sector reports. The numbers reported should be regarded as approximations.
* US $ per person per year
c Estimated as total cost of overall health package minus cost of public health and essential clinical services packages.

Source: World Bank (1993)

even more to developing countries than to developed nations. In the developed world, where the burden of health care is now emerging as a great concern, the advantages of resetting health priorities for prevention are clear for economic as well as social reasons.

In Table 9.1.2, the overall global cancer burden is considered in an integrated way; the table uses the estimates for the preventable component to derive the total number of cancers preventable by diet. The estimated rates of cancer in 1996 amount to 3–4 million preventable cancers per year; this figure will increase to perhaps 4.5–6 million by the year 2025 as a result of current trends in diet, population ageing and population growth (WHO, 1997).

To put this into perspective, similar calculations were undertaken for smoking-related cancers, using the maximum attributable risks set out for the impact of tobacco (Parkin et al, 1994). On this basis (Table 9.1.5), and recognising that smoking is easier to identify as a specific lifestyle feature that causes cancer, the global burden of preventable cancers from smoking involves almost 1.5 million individuals per year. This is between 37% and 50% of the numbers judged to be preventable by dietary and related measures; so perhaps twice as many cases of cancer may be prevented by dietary means as by ceasing smoking. This is not to set these as either/or strategies; it nevertheless re-emphasises the importance of including dietary issues as well as smoking cessation

in all programmes for the prevention of cancer. Given the combination of escalating smoking rates and the transition to urban-industrialised lifestyles in economically developing countries, a doubling of the world's cancer burden is likely

TABLE **9.1.5** THE RELATIVE IMPORTANCE OF SMOKING IN CAUSING CANCERS GLOBALLY

SITE	NUMBER OF CANCERS PER YEAR (1,000s)	PERCENTAGE OF ALL CANCERS ATTRIBUTED TO SMOKING	NUMBERS OF CANCERS THAT COULD BE PREVENTED BY NOT SMOKING (1,000s)
Mouth and pharynx	575	27	155
Larynx	190	61	116
Oesophagus	480	33	158
Lung	1,320	76	1,003
Pancreas	200	19	38
Bladder	310	31	96
Total			**1,566**

The cancers and the quantitative estimates of the impact of smoking are taken from Parkin et al (1994) with the global incidences as given in Table 9.1.2
Sources: Parkin et al (1994); WHO (1997)

unless determined action is taken.

ECONOMIC AND SOCIAL BENEFITS

The cost of effective strategies for maintaining or improving national dietary patterns has not yet been calculated. It is well recognised that smoking rates can be reduced by imposing heavy taxes on cigarette sales and tobacco imports. This is particularly effective in reducing the onset of smoking among young people. It is a comparatively simple means of making a major contribution to the health of a nation; the economic benefit of improving employment by allowing the inward investment of tobacco production and cigarette manufacture is comparatively short-lived compared with the huge national and individual costs of the resulting disease burden.

However, so far, expert groups have either neglected or simply hinted at the potential national and individual benefits of preventing cancer by dietary means. Further, the economic benefits of maintaining the dietary patterns of developing countries, in the face of culturally based aspirations to eat like people in affluent countries, have not been evaluated. The pressures of intense advertising and the lure for governments of inward investment by food and drink companies selling products which, from a health point of view, are inappropriate, have not been recognised or confronted. Some of these food and drink interests are now owned by transnational companies that also manufacture and sell tobacco products.

Cancer prevention has many more benefits than can readily be projected in simple analyses of costs and savings. A prevention strategy involving the whole family and community will have multiple benefits for general well-being and enhanced capacity to engage in worthwhile occupational and social activities. The costs of prevention are also likely to be less than those estimated here, because some of these costs presuppose that dietary patterns need to change rather than be maintained.

Furthermore, the prevention of several diseases may follow from a strategy aimed at one disease. For example, maintaining diets rich in vegetables and fruits, or increasing consumption of vegetables and fruits, will reduce not only cancer incidence but also incidence of coronary heart disease, nutritional blindness, child mortality and nutritional anaemia. Women can also be expected to have babies with fewer birth defects as a result of increased folate intake. Their children, if introduced to vegetables and fruits early in the weaning process, will also be far less liable to vitamin A deficiency with all its recognised effects on childhood morbidity and mortality.

Moreover, such a dietary strategy for prevention may be a better alternative to medical intervention. For example, well-intentioned programmes undertaken in Asia using injections of iodised oil as a means of preventing goitre, and repeated massive oral doses of vitamin A to prevent nutritional blindness and other vitamin A deficiency diseases, have been challenged: such medical approaches are expensive, often ineffective as prevention for the whole population, and dis-

---

BOX 9.1.1 A POLICY FRAMEWORK FOR CANCER PREVENTION

The panel invites international agencies and national governments, industry, the medical and health professions, consumer and public interest groups, the media, and all other organisations worldwide, to accept and to act on the following judgements, based on current scientific knowledge.

The scale of benefit

Cancer is mostly a preventable disease. The chief causes of cancer are use of tobacco, and inappropriate diets.

- Between 30% and 40% of all cases of cancer are preventable by feasible and appropriate diets and related factors
- On a global basis and at current rates, this means that appropriate diets may prevent 3–4 million cases of cancer every year
- Diets containing substantial and varied amounts of vegetables and fruits will prevent 20% or more of all cases of cancer
- Keeping alcohol intake within the recommended limits will prevent up to 20% of cases of cancers of the aerodigestive tract, the colon and rectum, and breast
- Cancers of the stomach and colon and rectum, are mostly preventable by appropriate diets and related factors
- A feasible intermediate target for the dietary prevention of cancer is the reduction of global incidence by 10% to 20% within 10–25 years

The need for prevention

- Prevention of cancer by dietary and associated means, and by prevention and cessation of smoking, are the most effective approaches
- Prevention benefits not only individuals, but also families, communities and national economies
- Prevention is the only sensible approach to cancer in the developing world; on a population basis, treatment and palliation of cancer are economically not feasible

---

tract from the primary need to iodise salt and ensure the adequate production and consumption of vegetables and fruits. Nutritional interventions involving injections are also dangerous because it is difficult to avoid the re-use of needles and syringes with all its risk of cross-infection with HIV and hepatitis (Gopalan, 1992).

9.2 Global trends

The world population is increasing. So is the incidence of cancer, whether measured in terms of the number of cases in populations of unchanging size and age; in relation to other diseases; or, given the ageing populations of the world, in terms of the public health burden that it represents. Global incidence of cancer is projected to rise from 10.3 million cases in 1996 to 14.7 million in 2020. Expanding populations amplify a number of adverse trends. Projections into the twenty-first century show that, in countries now in transition towards a developed economy, population-wide screening for, and treatment and palliation of, cancer are not feasible national policy options: the resources do not and will not exist.

Populations in Europe, Japan and North America are ageing, and the rates of ageing in China and other economically developing countries are dramatic. In Africa, Latin America and Asia, people are also moving away from rural areas into urban agglomerations, some of which are now vast and growing uncontrollably. World free trade involves the accelerating replacement of traditional agriculture, food systems and traditional diets with processed foods and drinks, either imported or manufactured locally.

These changes, reflecting external economic influences, are often not accompanied by commensurate increases in the wealth of developing countries, yet they are now faced with the prospect of new epidemics of cancer, and other chronic diseases that follow urbanisation, in addition to endemic infectious and deficiency diseases and pre-existing patterns of cancer. Many countries do not have the money, the trained personnel, the infrastructure or the facilities to screen for and treat cancer, or to provide palliative care.

With respect to diet-related diseases, the only feasible public health policy for many countries in Africa, Latin America, Asia, Oceania, eastern Europe and the former USSR is to ensure that populations preserve appropriate food patterns (primordial prevention) or to encourage people to change their diets before disease occurs (primary prevention).

These strategies require national programmes designed to protect both public health and economic stability and sustainability, using appropriate agriculture and food policies, combining the benefits of traditional diets and lifestyles with the benefits of current science and technology. In free-market economies, all sectors of society should benefit as public health improves, and as consumers come to understand the value, to health, of appropriate diets.

Such policies, together with integrated national programmes in which government, industry and non-governmental organisations are partners, are also needed in countries in other parts of Europe, North America and Australasia. These policies should become an integral part of multisectoral national programmes aimed at reducing the burden of chronic diseases. In general, policies designed to prevent cancer will prove to be complementary to, and supportive of, policies designed to prevent other chronic diseases, and diseases caused by nutrient deficiency and some infections.

9.2.1 THE SHIFT TO CITIES

By the year 2000, the world population will approach six billion people. Nonetheless, overall growth in global population, currently showing an increase of 80 million every year, is less significant than the shift throughout the economically developing world from rural areas into cities, many of which have now become vast. People living in cities depend on the products of industrialisation, including food and drink, and increasingly abandon old ways of life.

This demographic transition follows the one that took place in Europe and North America after the industrial revolution in the nineteenth century. However, there are fewer potential benefits for the mass of city dwellers in Africa, Latin America and Asia, who do not have the original European benefits of colonial wealth to support such transitions. The shift in population to the cities is unfortunately almost always accompanied by a disadvantageous change in dietary patterns.

This nutritional transition is taking place in countries likely to remain poor and to continue to suffer epidemic deficiency and infectious diseases as the new patterns of chronic diseases emerge. The extra demand for medical services for diseases that follow urbanisation may overwhelm many countries.

DEMOGRAPHIC TRANSITION

The process of global urbanisation has been extremely rapid. From the first century AD to 1800, it is estimated that perhaps one in twenty people lived in cities. By 1925, the figure was about one in five. By the year 2005, half the world's population will be urban, of which over 70%, more than two billion people, will be living in cities in developing countries. At that time, it is estimated that over 48 urban agglomerations, cities so large that their traditional geopolitical borders can no longer accommodate the mass of people who live and work in them, will each contain over five million inhabitants, of which 22 will contain more than 10 million people. Table

TABLE 9.2.1 PERCENTAGE OF POPULATION LIVING IN URBAN AREAS

REGION	1995		2025	
World	45.2		61.1	
Economically developing regions				
(average)	37.0		57.0	
Africa		34.4		53.8
Asia		34.6		54.8
Latin America and the Caribbean		74.2		84.7
Economically developed regions				
(average)	74.7		84.0	
Australia/New Zealand		84.9		89.1
Japan		77.6		84.9
Northern America		76.3		84.8
Europe		73.6		83.2

Source: UN World Urbanisation Prospects: The 1994 Revision

TABLE 9.2.2 POPULATIONS OF LARGE CITIES

Percentage of urban populations living in large cities – five million inhabitants or more

REGION	1990		2015	
Global total	13.9		17.7	
Economically developing regions	14.6		19.2	
Africa		8.1		18.8
Latin America and the Caribbean		18.0		17.8
Asia		16.9		20.5
Economically developed regions	12.7		12.9	
Northern America		16.3		17.8
Europe		7.1		6.5

Source: UN World Urbanisation Prospects: The 1994 Revision

9.2.1 shows that, by 2025, the total proportion of the world's population living in cities will have risen to 61% (UN, 1994).

A projection from 1990 to 2015 (Table 9.2.2) shows that, of these urban dwellers, an increasing proportion will be living in large cities with more than five million inhabitants. Populations of such mega-cities are now static or dropping in Europe and North America, and perhaps have nearly peaked in Asia and Latin America. However, rates in Africa are expected to triple, so that, whereas under 10% of the African urban population lived in cities of over five million inhabitants in 1990, nearly 20% are expected to do so in 2015.

People migrate from rural areas to the cities, typically because they cannot sustain life in the countryside. This pattern was evident in Europe between the seventeenth and nineteenth centuries, exemplified, for instance, by the enclosures in England and land clearances in Scotland. At that time, rural populations moved either to the new colonies elsewhere in the world, or else to cities whose prosperity depended on exploitation of the resources of colonised nations. As already noted, such resources are not available to the people who today live in the former colonies.

Other factors add to the burden of developing countries. Successive famines have created intolerable problems in many parts of sub-Saharan Africa. Elsewhere, land and irrigation systems have been degraded. Further, rural populations often move away from land as it deteriorates. Sustainable agriculture, in areas that are hilly, subject to erosion or flooding, or which are fragile or marginal in other respects, requires constant care without which the land can become permanently barren.

Many city dwellers are also impoverished. Hundreds of millions of people in Africa, Latin America and Asia migrate from rural areas in search of employment that they do not find. In Europe and North America, rates of long-term unemployment remain high in regions where older industries have become unprofitable. The poorest city dwellers have access to neither urban amenities nor rural subsistence. 'Food poverty', a consequence of inadequate money for, or access to, basic foods, affects large groups of people including students, unemployed and elderly people even in economically developed countries (Leather, 1996).

NUTRITIONAL TRANSITION

The concept of 'nutritional transition' is now used to identify the changes in dietary patterns that follow urbanisation, specifically in countries currently in rapid demographic transition (Popkin, 1994). This transition is from the diets deriving from peasant–agricultural and gatherer–hunter societies to an urban–industrial pattern: relatively low in starchy staple foods and fibre, and relatively high in foods of animal origin, and in fat, sugar and refined and processed foods.

This transition is a result of global societal, economic and political changes and runs parallel to demographic transition. Other related factors include accelerating industrialisation and development of technology, the globalisation of world markets and the dominance of free-trade ideology. Within the food system, transnational and multinational companies that manufacture and market standard branded goods are becoming increasingly influential. These trends are strengthened by the consequences of GATT (the General Agreement on Tariffs and Trade) which include global standards for food (the Codex Alimentarius) and by privatisation and the deregulation of markets. All these have the general effect of distancing people from processes of food production (McMichael, 1994, 1997).

In Europe, North America and Australasia, this nutritional transition is completed. Indeed, there is now some evidence that a proportion of the populations of such high-income Western countries are shifting again to diets high in vegetables and fruits and in starchy staples, with relatively low intakes of meat, dairy products and refined foods. These changes reflect consumer responses to recognition of the role of diet in the development of chronic diseases (Popkin et al, 1989, 1996).

The nutritional transition in some high-income, and economically developing countries has been very rapid. Between 1946 and 1987, consumption of fat in Japan more than tripled, and consumption of foods of animal origin greatly increased (Yamaguchi, 1991). Meat consumption has greatly increased in Asia: beef consumption more than doubled in Japan and Korea between 1980 and 1995. A similar pattern has now emerged in Thailand, the richer Arab countries (Musaiger and Miladi, 1996), and in the urban areas of Africa, Latin America, India, China and elsewhere in Asia (Gopalan, 1992; Bourne et al, 1993; Sanchez-Castillo et al, 1994). Alcohol consumption tends to increase in countries where alcohol is not prohibited.

Food supplies in cities can be more secure than in rural areas and people who live in cities may have access to more varied diets. Processed food may also be comparatively free from microbial contamination. But much of the readily available food in cities is energy dense; this factor, together with the typical urban sedentary lifestyle, increases obesity and other chronic diseases. Branded products become universally advertised and promoted: these include sweetened ready-to-eat breakfast cereals, fatty milk and dairy products, table fats, cakes, biscuits, chocolate, confectionery, packaged snacks, sweetened soft drinks, and 'fast food' usually eaten away from home, including burgers, high-fat chicken and deep-fried 'french fries'/chips (Lang, 1996).

In economically developed countries, almost everybody has enough to eat and most people can afford to eat well. Richer developed countries, where most of the rural population have cars and a quasi-urban lifestyle, can afford to screen for, treat and palliate epidemic chronic diseases because they have the infrastructure, technology, expertise and public as well as private funds. There are, however, signs that even the richest countries are becoming unwilling to pay for the cost of chronic diseases, especially when these develop many years before death. In Europe and in North America, national policies designed to improve public health tend to rely on education programmes that encourage consumers to make increasingly well-informed choices.

In North America, industry has responded to consumer demand and has changed the fatty-acid composition of many processed foods. There has been a reduction in coronary heart disease, but the prevalence of obesity and diabetes and the incidence of several cancers continue to increase. Elsewhere, for example in Scandinavia, systematic campaigns based on action by many sectors of society have led to better public health (Milio, 1986; Puska, 1985).

In most economically developing countries, the most important and urgent issues to do with food and health are security of the food supply, on the one hand, and the reduction of deficiency and infectious diseases, on the other (FAO/WHO, 1992). However, the demographic and nutritional transitions in urban areas in Africa, Latin America and Asia are having the effect of introducing new epidemics of chronic diseases, including the patterns of cancer generally more common in the developed world, without necessarily affecting the burden of other epidemic and endemic diseases, which include the pre-existing patterns of cancer. Examples are given in chapter 9.3.

9.2.2 PANDEMIC CANCER

It might be thought that cancer prevention cannot be a priority in many countries with so many other burdens. New analyses show, however, that the challenge of cancer as a preventable disease cannot sensibly be ignored. The dynamics of economic, demographic and nutritional change reveal the full human impact of current and expected rates of cancer, as well as the potential for reducing that impact.

Cancer develops slowly, typically taking many years before it becomes clinically evident; thus, immediate results from energetic public policies cannot be expected. Dietary prevention of cancer may take between 10 and 60 years to have an impact, the time scale depending, to some extent, on the type of cancer. Cancer incidence is set to increase markedly, particularly in the developing world, as populations increase and age, and this upward tendency may vitiate, to some extent, effects of programmes of prevention for at least 20 years.

The concept of 'epidemiological transition' describes the

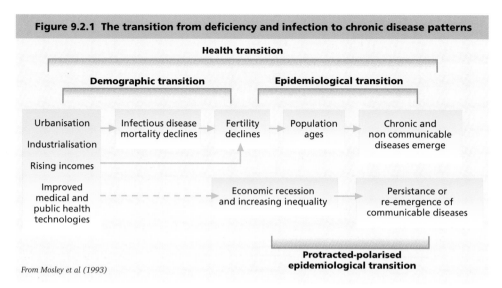

Figure 9.2.1 The transition from deficiency and infection to chronic disease patterns

From Mosley et al (1993)

et al, 1993). With urbanisation, industrialisation, rising incomes, expansion of education, and improved medical and public health technology, deaths from infectious and deficiency diseases decline, number of childbirths also decline, the population ages, and chronic diseases become epidemic.

As a general rule, the poorer the country, the greater the burden of emerging patterns of disease on the national economy and on the general health of the people. In many African

tendency towards a shift in disease patterns from dominant endemic and epidemic infectious and deficiency diseases to epidemic and eventually dominant chronic diseases. This transition has historically followed demographic and nutritional transitions which first occurred in western Europe and North America (Omran, 1971).

Variations on this transition are now a global phenomenon and many economically developing countries are changing rapidly. Figure 9.2.1 integrates these transitions (Mosley

countries, stagnation and indeed setbacks in health have been reflected in rising rates of childhood malnutrition. The widening disparity in the health conditions of different social classes creates yet another phenomenon: a polarisation where new patterns of cancer emerge and become epidemic in more affluent, usually urban, populations whereas old patterns of cancer, together with rampant infections and deficiency diseases, afflict the rural poor.

The burden on the state and on public services thus

TABLE 9.2.3 PATTERNS OF DISEASE IN DIFFERENT AGE GROUPS IN DEVELOPING COUNTRIES

AGE GROUP	POPULATION (MILLIONS)		DEATHS (MILLIONS)		IMPORTANT HEALTH PROBLEMS	
	1985	2015	1985	2015	CONTINUING PROBLEMS	EMERGING PROBLEMS
Young children (0–4 years)	490	626	14.6	7.5	Acute respiratory infection Diarrhoeal disease Learning disability Malaria Measles, tetanus, polio Micronutrient deficiencies Protein-energy malnutrition	Injury Learning disability
School-age children (5–14 years)	885	1,196	1.6	1.3	Helminth infection Micronutrient deficiencies Schistosomiasis	Learning disability
Young adults (15–44 years)	1,667	2,918	1.6	6.0	Excess fertility Malaria Maternal mortality Tuberculosis	AIDS Injury Mental illness Sexually transmitted diseases
Middle-aged (45–64 years)	474	1,131	5.9	10.4	Endemic infectious and other diseases	Cancers Cardiovascular disease Obstructive pulmonary disease Diabetes
Elderly (65+ years)	153	358	11.0	22.5	Endemic infectious and other diseases	Cancers Cardiovascular disease Cataracts Depression Disability
Total	**3,669**	**6,229**	**37.9**	**47.7**		

Note: many conditions in older age groups manifest themselves clinically long after the processes leading to the clinical condition have been initiated; preventive intervention will therefore need to be directed to younger populations
Source: Bulatao and Stephens (1990), Mosley et al (1993)

becomes exponentially heavy, because the more affluent and influential urban dwellers demand, and can pay for, treatment and care for their diseases. This demand drains resources from the rural poor. Worse, traditional disease patterns affect the young more than the old, as shown in Table 9.2.3, so children and young people, on whom any nation's future depends, are increasingly neglected simply because of a lack, either relatively or absolutely, of resources.

FUTURE TRENDS

The major current and future causes of death throughout the world are shown in Table 9.2.4. These estimates and projections are based on assumptions about changes in total mortality rates, built into the World Bank's demographic projections model, and on historically based assumptions about the relationship between mortality by cause and mortality level (Bulatao and Stephens, 1990; Mosley et al, 1993).

Major changes in disease patterns are expected in developing countries. Infections are projected to become no longer the main single causes of death, and the proportion of deaths from diseases of the circulatory system and from cancer is projected to approximate to proportions now found in developed countries. The proportion of deaths from cancer in developing countries is predicted to double; in addition, increases in population size mean that the actual number of deaths from cancer in these countries will more than double.

Reporting in 1997, the World Health Organization (WHO 1997) estimated an increase in the global incidence of cancer from 10.3 million cases in 1996 to 14.7 million in 2020.

Countries in the developing world cannot afford cancer. Table 9.1.3 (in chapter 9.1) showed that the current costs of treating cancer can be met only by rich countries. Given the relative costs of handling cancer patients effectively in a hospital setting in a developing country, the true cost is expected to escalate at least 25-fold between 1985 and 2015.

By the year 2015, without effective policies for prevention, the cost of cancer alone, in many developing countries, is likely to exceed the total national budget allocated to health care. As populations in the developing world age, it is clear that the only approach to the growing burden of cancer is primordial prevention designed to protect existing healthy dietary patterns, and to prevent deleterious national changes in diet. This is preferable to primary prevention where newly established diets need to be returned to a more appropriate composition. Reduction in the use of tobacco is also essential.

9.2.3 FOOD RESOURCES

Prevention of cancer implies new food, agriculture and fishery policies, and a reversal of current dietary trends in most parts of the world so that food supplies remain or become plant-based. Knowledge of the relationship between diet and cancer will not of itself create change. A recognition of the multiple factors affecting food consumption, and a new priority in national policies to consider the potential agricultural impact are needed.

This report's first dietary recommendation is that food supplies should be mainly of plant origin; this implies a reorientation of food, agriculture and fishery policies in most countries of the world. The recommendations also imply around a doubling of production of vegetables and fruits on a global scale, and further increases to keep up with world population growth. Vegetables and fruits, as well as cereals, should be perceived as staple human foods. Future world demands for food should no longer be considered solely in terms of cereal yields.

Another platform for the dietary recommendations is that diets centred on foods of land-animal origin increase the risk of cancer, as well as other chronic diseases and disorders. This, in turn, implies a reversal of currently influential policies based on ideas originating 150 years ago, which equated fast growth in children with good lifelong health. In the economically developed world, the implication is not only a shift to the production of leaner meat, but also the abandonment of feed-lot animal rearing in favour of a return to the use of pasture with its less intensive animal production. Further, there is need for a parallel change that ensures that cereal crops are grown primarily for human food rather than as animal feed. Traditional methods of agriculture that are the basis for adequate and varied diets should be preserved and protected.

FOODS OF PLANT ORIGIN

As part of this new thinking, the value of specific types of crops should be reassessed, taking account of their role in cancer protection, as well as their preventive role against other diseases.

Cereals (grains)

The main changes needed in cereal production are that a greater proportion should be for human food rather than ani-

TABLE 9.2.4 MAJOR CAUSES OF DEATH IN THE WORLD: 1985 AND 2015

CAUSE OF DEATH (AS PERCENTAGE OF ALL DEATHS)	ECONOMICALLY DEVELOPING COUNTRIES		ECONOMICALLY DEVELOPED COUNTRIES	
	1985 (%)	2015 (%)	1985 (%)	2015 (%)
Infection	36	19	9	7
Cancer	**7**	**14**	**18**	**18**
Circulation	19	35	50	53
Pregnancy, perinatal	9	6	1	1
Injuries	8	7	6	5
Other	21	19	15	16
Millions				
Total deaths from all causes	37.90	47.80	12.00	14.50
Total deaths from cancer	**2.65**	**6.69**	**2.16**	**2.61**

Adapted from Bulatao and Stephens (1990); Mosley et al (1993)

mal feed, that more cereals should be eaten in whole and otherwise minimally processed form, and that cereal varieties should be developed with a better nutritional composition.

Forty per cent of all cereals grown in the world is fed to livestock. In the USA, the figure is 90%. Much of the world's cereals, pulses such as soybeans, and fish-meal are used as feed for intensively reared livestock in rich countries (McMichael, 1993).

Asia produces and consumes 90% of the world's rice, which provides 35–80% of total energy in Asia. Management of water supplies is an important factor in the long-term sustainability of rice production. The green revolution contributed to breeding plants with increased yields and disease resistance, and substantial efforts are being made to improve the yields of the world's principal grain crops. Current projects of the International Rice Research Institute (IRRI) in the Philippines include developing new plant types for the five major rice ecosystems, genome studies, improving the sustainability and biodiversity of rice, and enhancing soil and integrated pest management.

Wheat is the most important cereal for breadmaking, because of its characteristic protein, gluten; it is also important for pasta and noodle products. Twenty per cent of the world's wheat harvest goes to feed livestock. If less wheat were grown for animal feed, more land could be made available to increase production of vegetables and fruits.

Two-thirds of the world's harvest of corn (maize) is used to feed livestock. Maize is a staple food in Africa and Latin America. Varieties higher in lysine and tryptophan are being developed. Cereal dwarfing and genetic engineering for other qualities have greatly increased the potential yields (Evans, 1997).

Roots and tubers

Roots and tubers such as potatoes and cassava are starchy staples, and provide minerals, vitamins and fibre; they are hardy, quick growing and productive; and they can be stored for long periods or left in the ground until required. Sweet potatoes are exceptionally good sources of carotenoids. Efficient cultivation practices in China increased the yields of sweet potato from 8 tonnes to 18 tonnes per hectare between 1961 and 1985, and yields of 37 tonnes per hectare have been reported in a dry season without irrigation. Sweet potatoes do not require high inputs of weeding or herbicides; pesticides are unnecessary, pH tolerance is wide and dry conditions are well tolerated. Both the tubers and the leaves of the plant can be eaten (Woolfe, 1992).

Vegetables and fruits

Dark-green leafy vegetables have been identified as especially protective against cancer. This protective effect is related probably to their rich content of many bioactive compounds, including their high content of carotenoids and vitamin C. They are also a valuable source of protein, folate, calcium and iron, and thus protect against deficiency and other diseases. They provide up to 90% of the carotenoids in the diets of rural people in parts of India (Rao, 1994); many

of these carotenoids, once consumed, are converted to vitamin A. They are the principal source of vitamin A in India and are invaluable in promoting resistance to infection and the avoidance of night blindness and eye diseases. Mangoes, oranges, papaya, carrots and tomatoes are also rich sources of carotenoids.

When deciding what varieties should be grown, the relevant nutritional profile, including microconstituents that may protect against cancer, should be considered; this varies considerably among varieties of one vegetable or fruit. The need for agricultural research to increase the yield, and pest- and disease-resistance of vegetables and fruits is poorly supported, in contrast to the current emphasis on cereals. The special preventive value of vegetables and fruits needs to be incorporated into agricultural policies.

Vegetables and fruits can also be grown in allotments, backyards and, indeed, in cities (National Food Alliance, 1996). In Asia, home-gardening schemes are promoted by UNICEF and agencies such as the Asian Vegetable Research Development Centre. Dark-green leafy vegetables can also be grown as inter-crops in paddy, sugar-cane and wheat fields (Gopalan, 1994). Where possible, horticulture should be appropriate to the region, requiring the minimum input of heating (in glass houses), irrigation, fertilisers and pesticides. Organic fertilisers and crop residues should be returned to the soil when possible.

Pulses (legumes)

The amino acid content of pulses complements that of cereals, so that consumption of wheat plus peas, maize plus beans or rice plus lentils improves the efficiency of protein use. Pulses are very productive and, as they fix their own nitrogen, need little fertiliser. The foliage of pulse crops is also good forage or green manure. The plants can be valuable in controlling soil erosion, improving the soil and providing food for wildlife (Greenwald, 1991).

FOODS OF ANIMAL ORIGIN

Meat and dairy products

Governments in Europe and North America have encouraged production and consumption of meat and dairy products since the nineteenth century for two reasons. First, these foods are high in animal protein, which promotes growth in childhood. Second, the terrain and climate in many parts of Europe and North America, as well as parts of Latin America and Australasia, support the profitable farming of cattle and sheep, so meat, meat products, milk, butter and cheese are readily produced in such countries and are comparatively cheap.

It is now known that protein of plant origin from suitable combinations of cereals and pulses is as healthy as protein of animal origin. Nonetheless, within the last 50 years, the trend has been to invest in the very resource-intensive rearing of animals in many parts of the world that are naturally unsuitable for this form of agriculture. The consumption of fatty meats and of meat, milk and other dairy products has also been promoted with the incorrect message that such foods are especially healthy.

Recently, as concern about fat, particularly in relation to heart disease, has grown in Europe and North America, much effort has been invested in the production of leaner animals (Wood and Fisher, 1991) but, for many years, subsidies have been given in those countries to the most fatty foods of animal origin, thereby limiting the effectiveness of new breeding policies.

The traditional use of draft animals, which can be bred on land unsuitable for crops, fed on crop residues and used to produce dung as fuel and fertiliser, remains a vital part of the economies of rural societies in many parts of the world. But the trend in Asian countries in rapid economic transition, such as China, Japan and Thailand, is towards mass animal breeding and/or the import of meat, meat products and dairy products. Thereby, the meat, animal fat and protein content of the diet is approaching that of Western economically developed countries. The consequences include less productive use of land, and increased incidence of many diseases such as those cancers now most common in the West.

Policy-makers in all parts of the world should be informed that increasing consumption of meat and fatty foods will lead to a massive increase in incidence of a large number of diseases that are expensive to treat. Given the centuries of experience out of which traditional diets have developed, the new dietary transition is neither a biological imperative nor a culinary advance. Rather, it reflects the impact of widespread perceptions of a cultural link between affluence and Western lifestyles. Traditional diets, when adequate and varied, are likely to be generally more healthy and more protective against many diseases than the diets typically eaten in urban–industrial societies.

Fish

Fish of all types are good sources of protein, vitamin A, iodine and omega-3 fatty acids. They do not increase cancer risk; indeed, there is some evidence to suggest that diets high in fish might protect against cancer, and such diets are also recommended as protective against heart disease (Department of Health, 1994). Ocean fisheries are now estimated to be at their annual yield limit of 100 million tonnes. However, much of the catch is not eaten as fish; it is made into raw materials for table and cooking fats, and fish in northern Europe is used extensively as animal feed.

Food policies should encourage preference for consumption of fish over land animals, and the maintenance of the quantity and quality of fish. Aquaculture has been practised in Asia for as long as there is a historical record; traditionally, small fish such as carp have been bred in paddy fields, but here, as well as in the ocean, fish stocks have been deteriorating. Pesticides, used to increase rice yields, kill the fish. Farmed fish tend to be more fatty and their fatty-acid composition is less desirable than that in wild fish, but polyculture, that is, the stocking of small lakes and ponds with several non-competitive species of each with a different feeding habit, gives good yields (Hulse, 1993).

9.2.4 ECOLOGICAL CHANGES

Current global trends in the use of land, water and energy may be unsustainable, and shifts in climate will create new challenges. Some examples are briefly considered. Rational food production policies that make more economic use of global resources should also have the effect of reducing cancer incidence.

LAND

Global food production exceeds consumption needs; nevertheless, currently, perhaps 800 million people are undernourished (FAO, 1996). An increasing global population, and the evidence that protection from many diseases including cancer requires development of varied plant-based diets, create new challenges for world agriculture. However, the land available for agriculture is decreasing. It is being lost to cities and roads, and it is being degraded by grazing, desertification, salination and the inappropriate use of agrochemicals. Much of the land in Africa is also very poor in nutrients and needs huge increases in inorganic and organic fertilisers to improve productivity.

Intensive agricultural methods originating in Europe and the USA, and now also used in other parts of the world, have led to irreversible degradation of much agricultural land. Much of this intensive land use has been to rear animals and to grow crops for animal feed. More appropriate ecological and nutritional use of the land would involve their use for plant-based food production for direct human consumption.

Traditional agricultural methods, together with careful use of relatively low-input modern technologies, are less destructive and can be indefinitely sustainable. If rural communities remain or become sustainable or even prosperous, the land and its inhabitants are preserved and farmers can support themselves and provide food for the cities. This requires initiatives in soil, water and soil-nutrient management. Soil conservation and restoration are priorities. Very little new land will become available, so increased food production will require better use of existing land and better yields from appropriate crops. Urban and rural development should proceed together, not at the expense of rural areas.

City populations currently produce little food and are almost totally dependent on imports of food produced in agricultural regions, usually at some distance if not in other countries or continents. The trend to urban gardening is gaining momentum and should be encouraged. As the developing world progresses economically, urban demand for appropriate foods requires that more land is used to grow crops for local markets. The relative values of these crops compared with cash crops for export, for example, coffee and tobacco, need to be considered from a public health as well as an economic standpoint.

Various estimates of biophysical limits to global food production have been made (Penning de Vries et al, 1995). They show that an affluent Western-style diet requires three times more biomass per head than a plant-based diet.

WATER

Water is a key constraint on agricultural production in many parts of the world. Deforestation, as well as desertification, salination and falling water tables, are making water an increasingly precious resource.

Land animal-based intensive agriculture systems demand relatively large amounts of water. Approximately 100 times more water is required to provide 1 kg of animal protein than 1 kg of plant protein. To raise 1 kg of beef requires about 10^5 litres of water, whereas to raise 1 kg of broiler chicken required 3,500 litres. Most of the water is used to produce the animal feed; the animals themselves consume very little water (Pimental, 1997). Table 9.2.5 summarises the water required to produce 1 kg of various foods. Skills required to conserve water in cereal-based agriculture have been learned over the centuries, for example, by the rice farmers of Asia who have also evolved methods of stocking fish in paddy fields.

The International Irrigation Management Institute has developed systems designed for rice production to support a diversity of crops in the dry season. These can save up to half the water required for irrigation and can also lead to substantial improvements in cropping intensity and farmers' net returns. Management of water resources is well studied and techniques and strategies should be widely communicated through organisations such as CGIAR (Consultative Group on International Agricultural Research) (Falkenmark, 1997; Wallace and Batchelor, 1997).

CLIMATE

Evidence of human-induced global warming is becoming clearer (IPCC, 1996; WHO, 1996). Food supplies could be affected by a gradual increase in world temperatures and by other accompanying climate changes in a number of ways. In response to warmer temperatures, changes in growing seasons, altered patterns of precipitation, and (in many rain-dependent regions) reduced soil moisture, the production of food-producing ecosystems would shift; agriculture and fisheries yields would thus change. Climatic influences on plant pests and pathogens could also occur.

Such trends may not be all bad; regions that now have a temperate or cold climate might benefit from increased temperature and be able to produce more food. However, many mid-continental and semi-arid regions now with marginal climatic conditions are vulnerable to even small increases in temperature. Altered conditions can lead to crop failure, leaving the soil exposed to wind erosion with steady loss of long-term productivity. In irrigation-dependent regions,

TABLE 9.2.5 FOOD AND DRINK	
LITRES OF WATER REQUIRED TO PRODUCE 1KG OF FOOD	
Potatoes	500
Wheat	900
Alfalfa	900
Sorghum	1,110
Maize	1,400
Rice	1,910
Soya beans	2,000
Chicken	3,500
Beef	100,000

From Pimental et al (1997)

ground-water availability and quality may be affected by altered rainfall and through increased demand as a result of population shifts. A rise in sea level would cause displacement of people both from low-lying urban centres and from fertile coastal regions. These trends will put more pressure on land and increase the need for plant-based agricultural systems that yield the most food per unit of resource.

ENERGY

Agriculture designed to grow crops for direct human consumption requires relatively less energy and other resources than animal husbandry. Although agricultural economists recognise the substantial costs of fossil fuel for producing the nitrogen needed to increase grain yields markedly, other long-term projections nevertheless assume that, with economic development, populations will shift to a meat-eating Western lifestyle (Dyson, 1996).

Such behavioural change is not to be recommended either for public health or for economic reasons, but economic projections rarely include either the long-term environmental or public health costs. This neglect by key national and international decision-makers emphasises policy-making in the context of a free-market ideology which, in practice, is distorted by many factors, including the involvement of only short-term market forces. People from nations in transition recognise that rich countries are very heavy consumers of energy, so it would be helpful if developing countries were provided with appropriately costed analyses of sustainable agricultural systems with the preservation of plant-based agriculture rather than animal rearing. Some trade-offs between agricultural development and environmental conservation are inevitable, but can, with care, be minimised, for example by use of integrated pest management (IPM) techniques (Alexandratos, 1995).

As shown in Table 9.2.6, it takes up to ten times less land to feed people on foods of plant origin than on animal products. The data come from analysis of temperate systems, but have a general application (Spedding, 1990).

9.2.5 SOCIAL

Prevention of cancer in the general context of improvement of public health involves reconsideration of all policies that impact on health. Agriculture, food and health policy are obviously important, but education and transport policies are also relevant.

EDUCATION

If cancer had no identified environmental causes, it would not have much relevance within education, except to students of medicine. But the fact that cancer is a disease largely preventable by appropriate diets and lifestyles, and that the seeds of cancer are often sown early in life, have profound implications for education policies and the circumstances of students.

TABLE 9.2.6 PRODUCTIVITY OF LAND FOR PLANT AND ANIMAL FOODS

The number of people supportable by the production from one hectare of land

	GROSS ENERGY OUTPUT MJ/HECTARE	NUMBERS OF PEOPLE FED[a]
Food of plant origin		
Wheat	69,534	15
Maize	75,905	17
Rice	87,768	19
Potatoes	102,080	22
Cabbage	105,000	23
Beans (field)	43,466	9
Peas	40,805	9
Food of animal origin		
Beef	4,796	1
Lamb	7,486	2
Bacon	14,438	3
Rabbit	13,251	3
Chicken	7,056	2
Eggs	4,118	1
Milk	8,770	2

[a] The 'people' column estimates number of people whose annual energy requirement could be met. Assumes energy requirements of 12.6 MJ/day (4,600 MJ/year) and that all energy is available

Source: Spedding (1990)

Education policy should identify nutrition and the relationship of foods to growth, development and well-being, as part of any core curriculum for boys and girls, not just as part of classes on biology or home economics. These concepts need to be integrated at primary and secondary level across subjects and topics, including science, geography, history, health, politics and economics.

The custom of protecting the health of schoolchildren, by means of free or subsidised provision of nourishing food in school and by physical recreation and sport within school hours, should be developed further in the light of modern knowledge of the causes of cancer and other chronic diseases.

Within schools, parents, teachers, administrators, pupils and caterers should all be involved in policies designed to protect the health of children and to teach them the benefits of healthy diets and lifestyles (Harvey and Passmore, 1994). In turn, this requires national policies and intersectoral collaboration among government, industry and non-governmental organisations to ensure that resources are adequate, that schools have access to appropriate materials and that the work of schools towards prevention is not undermined.

This report shows that regular physical activity helps to prevent cancer. The implications of establishing physical activity patterns in school have not been fully recognised. Pupils need to learn to enjoy a wide variety of non-competitive leisure time activities as well as competitive sports. With the decline in physically demanding work, involvement in leisure activity in adult life largely depends on people having acquired, at school, skills in, and knowledge of, sports and other physically active pursuits.

Most further education is specialist. Many courses within the medical, biological and social sciences can readily be developed to include teaching on prevention of disease and promotion of public health, at both an academic and practical level. Students in higher education also need provision of cooking, canteen, sporting and other recreational facilities.

TRANSPORT

The recommendations made in this report have two very different implications for international and national transport policies. First, globalisation of trade involves the transport of foods and drinks, sometimes across long distances, with uncalculated indirect environmental costs.

Public and private transportation and the infrastructure of railways and roads requires vast resources and use of energy. Within cities, lorries and trucks, many transporting food and drink, also use large amounts of fuel which contributes to urban pollution (itself sometimes carcinogenic). Incalculable amounts of energy are used on long-distance transportation of food. Freighting foods across continents and export of raw material to be processed abroad and then reimported back as processed products should be considered as an environmental cost (Paxton, 1994).

Second, the recommendations in this report imply a reorientation of the transport policies to protect or develop facilities for walking and cycling, especially in cities.

This report recommends that people should remain physically active throughout life and sustain a physical activity level (PAL) of 1.75 or more. In cities, typically sedentary people have a PAL of about 1.5–1.60 and PAL levels in industrialised societies, on a population basis, are drifting down.

Analyses of the energy cost of physical activities show that people who make extensive and increasing use of motorised transport, automated work and leisure may find it difficult to attain PAL levels at or above 1.75 simply by increasing leisure time activity (James, 1995; Ferro-Luzzi and Martino, 1996). Moving a PAL of 1.58 up to 1.72 involves an average of 20 minutes a day of vigorous exercise, say running or circuit training at a PAL of 11, a level of activity only achievable by an unusually physically fit person, or else an hour's extra walking every day. Moving up to a PAL of 1.76 requires an hour and a half of extra walking every day.

It follows that urban populations are likely to attain a PAL of 1.75 or more only if supported by vigorous national policies that encourage children to be physically active at play and school. These should involve traffic-free areas for safe play outside the home, together with extensive sports and recreation facilities at school which imply rewarding teachers for supervision out of school hours.

Adults should be able to walk and travel by safe means using physical effort. Specifically, there is a need to create urban environments in which walking and cycling become the most common means of travel to work and for short journeys and which therefore constrain the use of cars (National Forum for Coronary Heart Disease Prevention, 1995).

9.3 National experience

Global policy proposals can be useful as a general framework and as a means of generating ideas, but they cannot have detailed application to all countries and regions of the world. A report with a global perspective cannot also include policy proposals for individual countries.

Nevertheless, as a complement to the broad analysis and recommendations in earlier chapters, this section includes case studies from ten countries in Africa, Latin America, Asia, Europe and North America. These develop the discussion in chapter 1, and describe patterns of cancer and diet, together with current resources and future trends; they then go on to mention opportunities for and obstacles to prevention of cancer by dietary and associated means.

The case studies from Africa and Latin America are of the Gambia, a small predominately rural country, and Mexico, a country combining traditional diets and lifestyles with a rapid transition to life in vast cities. The four Asian studies consider China, Bangladesh, India and Japan. Three European countries with differing situations are outlined: Scotland, where high rates of diet-related cancers have not changed much despite local initiatives; Norway, where modern national public health policy dates back to the 1970s; and Bulgaria, one of the eastern European countries that was formerly a command economy. The final case study is of the USA.

These case studies may be useful, not only to readers from the countries and areas described, but also to readers who can identify analogies in their own societies.

The examples presented here are necessarily brief and provide only a sketch of information relevant to cancer and its prevention by diet. Public health strategies in most of the countries whose experience is outlined here, is largely limited to programmes designed to prevent epidemic infections and deficiency diseases or, in the case of economically developed countries, chronic diseases other than cancer. The perception that both endemic and epidemic cancers are preventable generally has not yet been fully understood or made into the basis for effective public health programmes.

9.3.1 AFRICA

THE GAMBIA

The Gambia has a population of just over one million, a population growth rate of 4%, and a gross domestic product (GDP) of US$360 per person. Most Gambians still live a traditional rural life, with 80% of the population engaged in agriculture. The Gambia therefore faces many of the problems associated with a poor, non-industrialised country.

Epidemiological trends

Average life expectancy is 45 years and infant mortality is 134 per 1,000 live births. Gastroenteritis and chronic diarrhoea are common causes of death, as are malaria and respiratory tract infections. Malnutrition is also a common cause of death, particularly among children and in rural communities before harvest time.

A National Cancer Registry was established in 1988, and figures published in 1990 show an overall age-standardised cancer incidence of 43.2 for men and 29.2 for women per 100,000 population. These rates are very low compared with other African countries or African-Americans.

For liver cancer, however, the incidence is 22.8 and 6.8 per 100,000 for Gambian men and women respectively (as against 3.5 and 1.0 for African-American men and women respectively). Liver cancer is caused, in considerable measure, by infection with hepatitis B and C viruses (HBV and HCV) (see chapter 4.9). In 1986, the Gambian government introduced an immunisation programme against HBV. By 1992, 90% of children had received all of their childhood immunisations, and preliminary studies suggest that, in children who complete the course, hepatitis B infection has fallen to less than 5%.

If this programme is maintained, the incidence of primary liver cancer should fall. However, other factors, notably aflatoxin contamination, are also important; rural children have aflatoxin metabolites in their blood and urine. Poorly stored ground nuts (peanuts) are a dietary source of this carcinogenic mould.

Gambian women also have a high incidence of cervical cancer (6.4 per 100,000). However, they have a low life-time exposure to endogenous oestrogens, given the late onset of menarche and high parity. This, coupled with high levels of work-related physical activity, and therefore a low prevalence of obesity, as well as a plant-based diet, offers protection against breast cancer.

The National Cancer Registry has not produced further cancer reports, but incidence of some cancers may increase if certain dietary trends in urban areas continue. Survey data are limited, but micronutrient deficiencies (including subclinical deficiencies) are likely to be common. Up to 45% of pregnant women and 15% of children under five are clinically anaemic. The incidence of goitre is high. Low daily intakes of riboflavin and calcium, and very large seasonal fluctuations in dietary vitamins A and C, have been reported.

Obesity is not a problem in rural areas but is increasing in urban areas, especially among women, and diabetes mellitus may be becoming more common. The diets of some urban groups are changing and sugar consumption is increasing.

Nutritional trends

Food intake varies greatly among population groups and between seasons. The commonly consumed staples are rice (for the relatively well-off), millet (for the poor), sorghum and maize. Ground nuts provide most dietary oil, and intake of meat, milk and fish tends to be low and infrequent. Only small amounts of green leafy vegetables, root vegetables and fruits are consumed, mainly during the rainy season.

Prospects for prevention

The Gambia is a poor country in conventional economic terms and appropriate technologies, involving only small amounts of capital, will need to be developed. These could be used, for example, to store and process ground nuts so as to minimise the risk of aflatoxin contamination. As with all economically developing countries, the nutritional transition among city dwellers is likely to increase the risk of those cancers associated with industrial–urban diets and lifestyles.

The success of the immunisation programme suggests that rates of primary liver cancer should fall, and augurs well for future public health projects. The National Cancer Registry has provided valuable baseline data, and further work to determine cancer trends will be important.

9.3.2 LATIN AMERICA

MEXICO

By the year 2000, Mexico's population is projected to grow to 100 million, with an estimated 26% of the country living in Mexico City. Dispossessed, rural people are moving to cities in huge numbers, and this demographic transition is so rapid that city services are not coping. The poverty that rural people sought to escape is being recreated, in different forms, in urban areas. GDP per person is US$3,872 and the economy is industrialising rapidly.

Epidemiological trends

Infectious and deficiency diseases remain acute public health problems, but improvements in infant mortality mean that the population is ageing. Cancer and cardiovascular diseases are already now the most common causes of morbidity and mortality. The epidemiological transition is so rapid that, within one family, young children may have chronic under-nutrition and infection, whereas adults have obesity, diabetes and cancers associated with urban–industrial diets and lifestyles.

The most common cancers are those that remain endemic, for example, stomach cancer, and those that have become epidemic, including cancers of the lung, colon and rectum, breast and prostate.

Nutritional trends

The traditional diet of Mexico is largely plant based, combining grains (corn), pulses (beans) and roots. Taste is added from indigenous products such as chillies, chocolate and vanilla. Meat and other animal foods are a comparative luxury. When food is available in adequate amounts, and when vegetables and fruits are also available, the diet is close to that recommended by international scientific reports (WHO, 1990). However, diets in poorer rural areas may be micronutrient-deficient.

In cities, consumption of fats and oils (some extensively recycled in cooking) tends to increase, as does consumption of higher-fat and lower-starch versions of traditional foods. Since the 1960s, corn consumption has declined by over 40%, and people are eating more refined cereals and cereal products. Alcohol, meat, fat and dairy-product consumption doubled between the 1960s and the 1990s, and sugar consumption also increased. At the same time, consumption of fruits rose and, on average, Mexicans eat more than 400 grams of vegetables and fruits a day. However, people are consuming far fewer garden vegetables and beans.

Prospects for prevention

Mexico spends about 5% of GNP on health care, but there is no effective national infrastructure of medical care for cancer patients. Typically, people living in rural areas present with cancer very late in the process. For most people, there are no social security services, no health insurance, no screening and no chance of early detection. Mexico has a national food and nutrition policy, which could offer advantages for a cancer prevention programme that was focused, in part, on diet.

The Pan American Health Organization supports over 70 non-government organisations (NGOs), and health campaigns have been effective when they involved international agencies, governments and NGOs with strong links in local communities. No advocacy groups with an interest in prevention of cancer have been identified. Some rural communities retain traditional ideas about the potential protective powers of food.

9.3.3 ASIA

CHINA

With over 1,200 million inhabitants, China is the most populous country on earth. Only 7% of the world's arable land is found in China, and yet the country feeds over 21% of the world's total population. Two-thirds of the Chinese people live in rural areas, and the GDP per head is US$435, although industrialisation and urbanisation are accelerating. There are distinct rural and urban differences, as well as dramatic geographical variations in dietary patterns and disease profiles.

Epidemiological trends

The rapid development of the national economy since the late 1970s has been accompanied by a rapid decline in infant mortality rates and increases in life expectancy at birth. Although nutritional deficiency diseases and infectious diseases have not been eradicated, these conditions are now largely confined to certain economic and age groups, and particular regions. Control of tuberculosis is increasingly thorough, immunisation cover is almost complete, and good progress is being made in immunisation programmes for other diseases such as hepatitis B.

As deficiency and infectious diseases have declined, deaths from cancer and cardiovascular diseases have increased. By 1994, 60% of all mortality was the result of chronic diseases, rising to 76% in urban areas. Obesity is now a public health problem in China.

The proportion of all deaths that result from cancer is about 22%, with cancers of the gastrointestinal tract accounting for 60% of those deaths and lung cancer for 20%. Lung cancer mortality is higher in urban areas (30%) than in rural areas (16%). Cancers of the colon and rectum have declined, but lung cancer has increased. Mortality rates for important specific cancers among women are lower than for men in the 1990s.

Over 70% of adults smoke and, despite the fact that some elderly people are quitting, younger people are starting to smoke earlier. Given these trends, and the fact that smoking is the major cause of lung cancer, lung cancer rates are predicted to continue to rise.

Nutritional trends

Patterns of food consumption have changed very substantially over the last 30 or 40 years. Meat consumption continues to increase, as does the contribution of fat to total energy. Some 75% of urban households consume over 30% of their energy from fat and, even in rural areas, energy from fat increased from 13% to 21% between 1990 and 1992 alone. Vegetable oil consumption has also increased markedly, and alcohol and salt intakes are high. In contrast, between 1982 and 1992 the contribution of cereals to dietary energy declined somewhat from 71% to 67%.

It will be a major challenge, given these dramatic dietary changes, to maintain traditional, plant-based, Chinese dietary patterns with cereals, vegetables and fruits as staple foods, and only limited amounts of animal-based foods.

Prospects for prevention

The Ministry of Public Health has established a number of steering committees to tackle the major chronic diseases such as diabetes, cardiovascular disease and cancers. In addition, Chinese health professionals have had some successes with health-promotion programmes in particular communities.

A community programme to improve management of hypertension, for example, also resulted in a significant reduction in smoking among adults. Similarly, some programmes have been able to halt an increase in alcohol consumption, and other interventions have reduced salt intake in some groups.

BANGLADESH

Bangladesh is one of the poorest countries in the world with a GDP per head of US$208. Half the population is below the national poverty line. With a population of over 120 million, Bangladesh is also one of the most densely populated countries in the world; there are 760 people per square kilometre. The population is growing at over 2% a year, and 83% of Bangladeshis live in rural areas. Over half of rural dwellers are landless, and urban growth, at over 5% per year, is one of the highest in Asia. About half the urban population live in slums and squatter settlements. The economy is based mainly on agriculture and industry accounts for only 10% of the GDP.

Epidemiological trends

Life expectancy at birth is now 51 years, 10 years more than in the 1960s. Nevertheless, infant mortality remains high at about 100 per 1,000 live births, and maternal mortality is 600 per 100,000 live births. About 60% of Bangladeshi children and half of the adults are undernourished. Infectious diseases, malnutrition and micronutrient deficiencies are endemic, and are worst in the lean and monsoon seasons. Infectious diseases and malnutrition are the leading causes of death.

By contrast, for the middle and upper classes in the cities, obesity is increasing as activity levels decrease and diets change. Although smoking rates are declining among the rich, this is from a very high level, and smoking rates among the poor and low middle classes are higher still. As a result of these trends, the incidence of cardiovascular diseases, diabetes and those cancers more common in developed economies is now beginning to rise.

Nutritional trends

The traditional Bangladeshi diet is largely plant-based, made up of rice, lentils, vegetables and fruits, and some fish, with small amounts of meat, fat and dairy products. If consumed in adequate quantities, this diet, like many in non-industrialised countries, largely meets World Health Organization recommendations for a healthy diet to avoid chronic diseases

(WHO, 1990). But among the urban and rural poor, under-nutrition and micronutrient deficiency are massive public health problems. Most mothers and their children have nutritional anaemias.

Since the 1960s, production and consumption of vegetables and fruits have decreased, whereas consumption of sweet foods, fats and animal products has increased. Urbanisation has brought major changes in food consumption patterns. A wide range of Western foods is available to the growing urban middle and upper classes, and bottle-feeding is now common among the urban elite. Street food vendors cater for the urban working poor, but the snacks and meals on sale are higher in fat, sugar and salt than traditional recipes. High relative prices of fruits and vegetables have led to a particularly high prevalence of micronutrient deficiency among the urban poor.

Prospects for prevention

A consortium of international donors and agencies has been working with the Bangladeshi government to develop a national nutrition strategy. This was incorporated into the 1991–1995 national development plan and focused on reducing infant, child and maternal mortality, and reducing malnutrition and micronutrient deficiency among women and children. A concurrent family planning strategy aims to reduce population growth.

The programme works across departmental boundaries and includes agriculture and fisheries development, infectious and micronutrient disease control, nutrition surveillance and rehabilitation, breast-feeding promotion, mass education campaigns on television and radio, and enhancement of women's status and independence. A national nutrition council has been established to co-ordinate activities, and consortium donors are providing financial and technical support and promoting the development of Bangladeshi institutions to continue the work in the long term.

Over 120 NGOs work in rural and urban areas to alleviate poverty and malnutrition, increasingly in collaboration with the government. Some of the largest NGOs are setting up research, advocacy and policy development departments to try to influence national policy, rather than simply providing basic services. Many NGO activities that tackle micronutrient deficiency may also help to prevent cancer. Recently, for example, NGOs have been working with the urban poor and landless people in rural areas to increase consumption of vegetables and fruits, in order to combat deficiency of vitamin A. Some NGOs are beginning to incorporate monitoring for chronic diseases into their primary health-care programmes, and there is also an established network of community health workers.

Reliable registration methods documenting causes of death have not yet been established. There are cultural obstacles to increasing consumption of vegetables and fruits, because, apart from imported oranges, apples and grapes, these are low status foods. Furthermore, obesity is commonly regarded as a sign of good health. Confidence in the public health service is low; it is perceived as offering poor quality care, and inadequate drug and other supplies, within a badly managed system. Bangladesh remains a very poor country and overcoming these problems, as well as the smoking epidemic, presents a major challenge.

Prevention of cancer and other chronic diseases, including by means of food and nutrition, is not yet a priority in Bangladesh, and does not figure in national action plans for the 1990s. The institutions and networks outlined above could be used to such ends as needs arise and are accepted by government and other agents of change.

INDIA

India's population was estimated at close to 950 million in 1995 and, with a growth rate of about 2%, will be about 1,000 million by the year 2000. Some 73% of Indians live in rural areas but urbanisation continues at about 3% each year. GDP per head is US$274 and almost 30% of the population live below the poverty line.

Epidemiological trends
Between 1970 and 1990, infant mortality decreased by 40% from 129 to 79 per 1000 live births. Life expectancy has also increased, although maternal mortality remains high at 570 per 100,000 live births. Despite the substantial increase in total energy intake since the 1960s, varying degrees of malnutrition in children and adults persist, affecting around 250 million people. Infectious and parasitic diseases, and diseases of the circulatory and respiratory systems, account for around half of all deaths.

In the last two decades, there has been a shift from infectious towards chronic diseases, such as cardiovascular and respiratory diseases, and cancer, as well as an increase in accidents. In the 1980s, cancer registries were established in some urban areas; their data show that overall cancer incidence rates are low, at 122 in men and 130 in women per 100,000 population. Head, neck and lung cancer in men, and cervical and breast cancer in women, account for about half of all cancer deaths. Chewing tobacco is responsible for around one-third of all cancers. Incidence rates for all cancers rose by 5.5% in men and 4.9% in women between 1982 and 1989 and are expected to rise further.

Nutritional trends
In the 20 years to 1991, overall food production in India increased, largely as a result of increased production of wheat and rice. Food availability per head increased only slightly for cereals, edible oils and sugar, and decreased for pulses. Consumption of cereals is close to recommended dietary intakes, but intakes of pulses, roots and tubers have decreased. There has been a marginal increase in intakes of green leafy vegetables. Richer Indians consume more milk, as well as more oils, sugar, fruits and pulses.

Dietary patterns have remained largely unchanged in rural areas, with no increase in protein and foods rich in micronutrients and phytochemicals. Deficiencies of vitamin A, iron and iodine, and of combinations of vitamins and minerals, are common.

The report produced by India for the FAO/WHO International Conference on Nutrition (Bagchi et al, 1992) pointed out that the food and agriculture policy that made India self-reliant in food grain, paid little attention to whole grains, pulses (legumes), oil seeds or vegetables, so that availability of these foods has declined, and prices have risen. This has made a substantial impact on the diets of economically impoverished people. In general, India has not yet successfully incorporated nutritional considerations into agriculture policy, or implemented a national nutrition policy that successfully targets the poorest and most vulnerable population groups.

A national agricultural policy is in place; one of its goals is to produce 200 million tonnes of food grains a year by the year 2000. There are also goals for oil seeds and pulses, and a wide ranging programme addressing productivity, research and development priorities. Horticultural projects are promoting the production and supply of vegetables and fruits.

Prospects for prevention
A national cancer control programme launched in 1975–1976 made funds available for the purchase of equipment to treat cancer. Several regional cancer research centres are currently concentrating on early detection and treatment programmes; these have also developed preventive strategies, including nutritional education, intervention projects and anti-tobacco campaigns.

In 1990, a national food and nutrition board was established. This undertakes a wide range of activities to promote production and consumption of nutritious foods and drinks. The national nutrition monitoring bureau collects and analyses data on diet. In 1993, a national nutrition policy was adopted to co-ordinate the short- and long-term policies required from various government departments to try to tackle the country's food and nutrition problems. A key focus of these policies is the health of women and children.

The report from India to the FAO/WHO International Conference on Nutrition (Bagchi et al, 1992) recognised the increasing incidence of diet-related chronic disorders and diseases such as obesity, coronary heart disease and cancer among relatively well-off people in India, but did not propose any plans to address this issue.

JAPAN

Like most industrialised countries, the Japanese population is now more or less static, but has reached over 125 million. Japan is among the wealthiest nations in the world with a GDP per person of US$29,497.

Epidemiological trends
Between 1950 and the early 1990s, there was a dramatic reduction in deaths from infectious diseases such as tuberculosis, and a rapid and continuing rise in deaths from cancers and cardiovascular diseases. In 1993, cancers accounted for 26.8% of deaths compared with 22.4% in 1980. When the

figures are adjusted for age, they show cancers to be rising mainly among men; rates are more or less static among women. Nevertheless, cancers were the first cause of death among men aged between 35 and 84, and among women aged 30–74.

Total cancer mortality is 190.4 per 100,000 (234.2 for men and 148.3 for women). Stomach cancer is the leading cause of death, but lung and liver cancers are also common.

Japan has an ageing population: the proportion of people aged 65 and over increased from 7.8% in 1980 to 11.7% in 1992 and is estimated to reach almost 15% by 2000. This will increase the overall burden of cancer.

Nutritional trends

Dietary patterns have changed dramatically, starting in the 1950s, strongly influenced by the USA. Average animal protein intake almost doubled and fat intake increased by almost two and a half times between 1952 and 1990. From 1975 to 1993, individual energy intakes declined from 2,226 kcal/day (9.35 MJ/day) to 2,034 kcal/day (8.54 MJ/day), and rice consumption fell so that carbohydrate intake dropped nearly 20% from 335 g to 285 g in the same period. Consumption of fruit and milk both increased during the 1960s and 1970s.

In the 1990s, energy intakes have continued to fall, but intakes of animal protein and fat have remained static; total fat makes up 25% of total energy intake and saturated fat 12% of total energy.

Prospects for prevention

Japan has a range of health bureaux under the direction of the Minister of Health and Welfare, including a health promotion and nutrition division. The government also maintains a school feeding programme which can be used for health promotion activities, including those in relation to nutrition. National nutrition surveys are conducted every year and so dietary changes and the impact of any health promotion activities can be closely monitored.

As early as 1984, the Japanese Dietetic Association (JDA) published dietary guidelines in order to address the problems of Japan's rapidly changing diet; these included guidelines to reduce the risk not only of cardiovascular diseases (coronary heart disease and stroke) but also of cancer. Guidelines to prevent cancer included: avoidance of foods containing a large amount of salt; moderation in intake of energy and fat; consumption of plenty of vegetables and fruits, unrefined cereals, pulses and seaweeds; moderate, if any, consumption of alcohol; and avoidance of very hot foods and drinks, and charred meat and fish. (Fujisawa and Itoh, 1984).

The resources devoted to screening for, and treatment and palliation of cancer, are at least as sophisticated in Japan as in other economically developed countries. The rapid changes in patterns of cancer, manifesting as a transition to those cancers hitherto more common in Western countries, has led to new advances in cancer epidemiology and treatment in Japan. The opportunities and resources for cancer prevention are very substantial.

9.3.4 EUROPE

SCOTLAND

Scotland's population, at 5.1 million, is static. The GDP per person of the UK as a whole is US$18,027, but is somewhat lower in Scotland. Agriculture is still an important industry, and Scottish farming communities are among the most cost-effective in the European Union. However, like the rest of the UK, Scotland is now largely industrialised and urbanised.

Epidemiological trends

Scotland has among the highest rates of incidences of coronary heart disease and cancer and premature mortality rates (death before 65 years of age) in the world. Cardiovascular diseases and cancer account, respectively, for 40% and 26% of premature deaths among men and 26% and 28% among women.

The dominant cancers in Scotland include those of the lung, colon and rectum, and prostate among men, and breast, lung, and colon and rectum among women; taken together these cancers account for over half the cancer incidence in both sexes. Cancers of the colon and rectum, breast and prostate are rising. Lung cancer is falling in men, but rising steeply among women. Lung cancer risk seems to be greater among Scottish smokers than elsewhere; this is probably because the Scottish diet is notoriously low in vegetables and fruits.

Nutritional trends

Major changes in the nature of the food supply in Scotland began as the country people in the highlands were driven off the land beginning in the eighteenth century, accelerated with industrialisation and urbanisation, and again more recently after World War II.

After the war, UK policy was to produce more food more cheaply, particularly meat, milk and dairy products. In Scotland, during the 1950s and 1960s, there were marked increases in consumption of confectionery, baked goods, meat and dairy products, whereas consumption of vegetables and fruits declined. In the 1990s, prepared foods, snacking and eating out have become an increasing feature of Scottish life. Diets are low in cereals, vegetables and fruits, and high in confectionery, fat-enriched meat products, sweet and salty snacks, baked goods and sugared drinks, and alcohol. As a result, the Scottish diet is high in total and saturated fat, refined sugars and salt, and low in non-starch polysaccharides (fibre) and various vitamins.

Recent surveys in all age groups indicate that harmful dietary habits start young. In some social groups, only 10% of infants are being breast-fed at one month. The diets of Scottish schoolchildren and of poor people in Scotland are thought to be among the most unhealthy in Europe.

Prospects for prevention

New agendas for change have been set in Scotland, in concert with developments in the UK and, more generally, in Europe as a whole. In 1993, as part of an overall series of policy initiatives aimed at improving Scotland's poor health record, *The Scottish Diet* was published.

This report broke new ground in the UK in that it developed dietary recommendations for the Scottish population for the prevention of cancer as well as coronary heart disease. Quantified nutrient targets were developed, including recommendations for consumption of vegetables and fruits.

Meeting the targets implied radical policy changes across all sectors of society, from agriculture and the food manufacturing and retailing industries, to the health and education sectors, the voluntary sector and the public. Examples of the types of initiatives required included: negotiation for transformation of the EU Common Agricultural Policy to incorporate public health criteria; major changes in food production and manufacture; changes in medical practice to incorporate dietary change in both primary and secondary prevention of disease; local alliances with industry, retailing and local authorities to achieve sustained change; and changes in cooking practices and catering policies.

In order to develop, co-ordinate, implement and audit the effectiveness of new initiatives appropriate to meeting the targets, a Scottish Food Council led by the Secretary of State for Scotland was recommended; it would include leaders from the farming and fishing industry, trade unions, food and retailing industries, local authorities, health, education, leisure, voluntary sector and consumers. The Council would also convene a number of working groups to develop concrete plans for each dimension of a co-ordinated strategy including: agriculture, food processing and retailing, educational services, catering and work place initiatives, medical services, social facilities, economic aspects of policy initiatives, and information technology and surveillance.

The Scottish Diet report was accepted by the Secretary of State for Scotland in 1994. Following the model of the English Nutrition Task Force, under the national 'Health of the Nation' programme, a Scottish Diet Group with a limited lifespan, rather than a permanent Scottish Food Council, has been set up and working groups established. One key constraint is limited funding. Nevertheless, these activities represent a major shift in agenda and potential for change.

Less positively, most of the medical profession and the public in Scotland have so far not been very responsive; one survey showed that 69% of Scots said that they believed they were consuming a healthy diet.

NORWAY

Norway shares some features with Scotland, having a static population of 4.3 million, but Norway's prosperity is similar to other Scandinavian countries; GDP per person is US$26,343. As a result of its hostile terrain and climate, less than 4% of the land can be used for agriculture, and yet Norway produces 55% of its own food supply.

Epidemiological trends

Cardiovascular disease and cancer are the main causes of premature mortality. Since the late 1970s, deaths from heart disease have declined sharply – for example, by about 40% in the 40–49 year age group. However, since 1970, there has been a more than 20% increase in deaths from cancer. The increase has occurred in people aged over 50 in both sexes, whereas cancer mortality in people under 50 years has declined. Stomach cancer has declined, whereas cancers of the breast, prostate, and colon and rectum have increased.

Nutritional trends

The two main elements of Norwegian agriculture have always been crops (notably grains and potatoes) and domestic animals. Traditionally, agricultural policy was preoccupied with self-sufficiency, and nutritional recommendations concentrated on milk and dairy foods as protective. Staple foods have therefore been cereals, milk and potatoes, with fish and meat being important for certain groups. Vegetables and fruits play a minor role in the diet; supply and consumption vary seasonally.

After the impact of World War II on food supplies, self-sufficiency became even more politically important and, in 1946, the National Nutrition Council (NNC) was set up to bring together policy-makers in agriculture, health and economics. In the post-war years there was increased production and consumption of meat, dairy products, cereals and sugars, and decreases in potatoes and fish. Fat consumption rose from 35% of total energy in 1945 to 42% in 1970, and at the same time total carbohydrate consumption fell, and with a higher proportion derived from sugars.

As a result, at least partly, of Norway's national nutrition and food policy, there have been some positive changes in the Norwegian diet. Low-fat milk, soya-based margarines and fish are all now consumed in substantially greater quantities, and full-fat milk and butter consumption has declined. There have been more modest increases in consumption of cereals, vegetables and fruits and, although meat consumption has remained stable, more poultry, veal, mutton and game are consumed with a decline in beef and pork. Since the mid-1970s, the proportion of fat in the diet has declined from 42% to 35% total energy in 1990.

Less positively, potato consumption has declined, aside from potatoes processed into chips (french fries) and crisps (chips). Similarly people are consuming more savoury snacks, sweets, cream, cheese and soft drinks. Thus the proportion of sugar in the diet has increased and, although people eat more vegetables and fruits, consumption levels remain low, at around 200 g/day.

Prospects for prevention

A collaborative and integrated approach to food, farm and nutrition policy is embedded in Norway's post-war history. As early as 1963, a joint farm, food and nutrition policy was recommended and, in 1968, Norway signed the Nordic collective agreement on diet. In 1974, the Norwegian government agreed to develop an integrated policy. This attempt to bring agricultural production into line with national nutrition and health goals and, with environmental considerations, remains unique in industrialised countries.

Nine ministries collaborate in the policy, and the National Nutrition Council provides independent scientific advice, co-ordinates nutrition campaigns and acts as a nutrition surveillance board. Dietary recommendations have focused on reducing total and saturated fat intake, and increasing consumption of cereals and vegetables. Policies to pursue these have included consumer and professional education, producer and consumer subsidies to encourage production and consumption of low-fat dairy products, cereals, potatoes, vegetables, grass-fed beef, poultry and fish, and regulations on food-product quality and labelling.

Despite its successes, funds to pursue the national nutrition and food policy have been limited. Norwegians are sensitive to the possibility that their pioneering policy may be under threat from the globalisation of food trade and the free-market system, which may push into their markets imported foods with a nutritional composition not permitted or encouraged under the Norwegian national plans. They choose to remain outside the European Union.

BULGARIA

Bulgaria's population is 8.8 million and is currently static. It is one of the countries in central and eastern Europe undergoing the transition from a command to a market economy. GDP per person is low at US$1,275. A predominantly agrarian country, agriculture was collectivised after 1945 and provides almost 20% of employment.

Epidemiological trends

Rates of chronic diet-related disorders and disease, including obesity and coronary heart disease, are high and are rising. Rates of coronary heart disease in Bulgaria are now among the highest in the world.

Similarly, age-adjusted and sex-specific death rates per 100,000 population as a result of cancer increased from 166.9 (in men) and 115.8 (in women) in 1957 to 221.8 (men) and 147.2 (women) in 1993. Cancer of the lung contributed disproportionately to mortality among men aged between 45 and 75 years. Cancers of the stomach, and colon and rectum were the next most common cause of male mortality. In women, breast cancer mortality accounted for more deaths up to age 45, whereas stomach cancer caused more deaths in older women.

Nutritional trends

In the post-war period, food prices were kept low to keep down labour costs and thereby encourage industrialisation. Deliberate steps were taken to exclude food imports and achieve self-sufficiency. Between 1970 and 1988, consumption of meat, milk and sugar, and products made from them, increased dramatically. Cereal consumption dropped, whereas vegetable consumption increased to some extent. Consumption of fat has risen and was 37% of total energy in 1989. Consumption of salt and alcohol is also high and rising.

Economic and social disruption after the introduction of free markets has caused a sharp decrease in consumption of vegetables and fruits, and also of pulses, traditionally an important part of the Bulgarian diet. Snack meals are increasingly eaten, and white bread is replacing the traditional dark breads.

Prospects for prevention

For over 30 years, the Bulgarian Institute of Nutrition has been involved in field studies and representative surveys. In 1984, a 'system for healthy nutrition of the Bulgarian people' was outlined. In 1987, a national programme was introduced designed to prevent chronic diseases such as cancer and coronary heart disease. Advice for the population included to reduce salt, animal fat and sugar, and to increase consumption of vegetables and fruits. The paper prepared by Bulgaria for the FAO/WHO International Conference on Nutrition (Petrova et al, 1992) concluded that this programme had been ineffective.

Recommendations aim to address groups at special risk of diet-related diseases, and also social and organisational dimensions of the diet and health issue by introducing, for example, legislation to ensure food safety, and a unified system of health education. The Bulgarian Medical Academy and the Ministry of Health and Social Welfare have made proposals to establish a Parliamentary Commission of Public Health to design, manage and implement programmes aimed at preventing major diseases causing premature deaths.

However, Bulgaria, like other countries in central and eastern Europe, faces a great many economic and social problems simultaneously. The pressure to deal with urgent public health problems means that chronic diseases such as cancer do not always feature high on the list of priorities.

9.3.5 NORTH AMERICA

UNITED STATES OF AMERICA

The USA, one of the richest countries in the world, has a static population of 263 million, and a GDP per person of US$23,197. Although farming remains an important industry, most Americans are employed in industrial or service occupations and live in towns and cities.

Epidemiological trends

Rates of cardiovascular diseases have been decreasing since the 1970s, but rates of cancer are generally increasing in the USA. In 1990, the age-adjusted death rate from all cancers was around 135 per 100,000 compared with 125 per 100,000 in 1950. Cancer is the second leading cause of death, accounting for around 22% of all deaths. Four cancers account for over half of all cancer-related illness and death: lung (28%), colon and rectum (12%), breast (9%) and prostate (6%).

Cancer incidence and mortality rates are higher among men than women, and among blacks than whites. In 1988,

BOX 9.3.1 THE 5 A DAY PROGRAMME

The National Cancer Institute (NCI) launched the national *5 A Day* programme in 1991. This is a major population-based public health initiative for nutrition and cancer. It is a national partnership between the NCI and the vegetable and fruit industry, represented by the Produce for Better Health Foundation (PBH).

The *5 A Day* programme aims to encourage Americans to eat five or more servings of vegetables and fruits daily, as recommended in this report. Distinguishing features are: the activation of government and the food industry at national, state and local levels; the creation of public/private and national/state/local partnerships; partnerships with the mass media and programmes that reach the public directly.

The national programme sets standards and establishes agreements with all partners participating in the programme. The NCI has licensed all 50 US states to organise state-level *5 A Day* programmes, and it has delegated to the PBH the authority to license industry partners such as supermarkets, restaurants, food services, merchandisers and suppliers.

By 1996, 1,200 industry partners, including retailers (with chains representing over 30,000 supermarkets nationwide), state and federal agricultural commodity boards, branded companies, wholesalers, merchandisers, suppliers, and food services were licensed to participate. The retailers and their suppliers participate in *5 A Day* by displaying promotional materials and the *5 A Day* logo on eligible products, incorporating the *5 A Day* message in print and broadcast advertisements, developing interactive events such as taste tests and store tours in supermarkets, and sharing with the community component through the state *5 A Day* coalitions. Restaurants and food service operators add to the point of sale component.

Initial funding for the *5 A Day* pro-

gramme came from PBH, which contributed US$500,000 to the programme in the first year and made media contributions (broadcast time and space for print advertising). In addition, NCI spent US$400,000 in the first year of the programme. Up to 1996 the vegetable and fruit industry has spent approximately US$150 million on the *5 A Day* programme, on advertising and on in kind donations to state and local coalitions. The NCI has spent an estimated US$25 million, primarily on behavioural change research and on media and communications.

The NCI serves as the programme's scientific voice to the public, to secure health and government partners, to conduct evaluation, and to advance intervention research. The PBH facilitates implementation of the programme in the food industry, working with the NCI to develop guidelines and programme direction, and to ensure that programme standards are maintained by industry partners.

Nationally, the NCI and PBH conduct market research, develop promotional themes and materials, and generate publicity to support the activities of all partners. At the state and local levels, partners can build on these to organise and run complementary interventions with regional or locally relevant 'hooks'. As the programme matures, additional collaborations with other national agents of change, such as the American Dietetic Association (ADA) are being established. In this case, the ADA will use its consumer hotline and media representatives to reach consumers, and will also urge its 65,000 members to implement *5 A Day* activities in their work settings.

Events to promote the *5 A Day* message involve the broadcast media, use of national spokespersons, print materials and media events. Special *5 A Day* events involve the local community and create media interest. Periodical promotional campaigns that focus on specific themes, such

as salads, fitness, entertaining, or microwaving, keep the programme fresh and visible in grocery stores. National *5 A Day* Week, held in September, allows all partners to join forces for a period of high visibility.

In 1995, the *5 A Day* Week theme of *'Take the 5 A Day Challenge'* aimed to move consumers beyond awareness towards behaviour change. Media efforts urged state and local opinion leaders such as athletes, disc jockeys, politicians and other celebrities to have fun and challenge each other to eat five servings each day for a week. The challenge was issued to the public nationally by astronauts using contemporary communications technology, in this case via a video news release transmitted by a satellite to television outlets across the nation.

Schools, supermarkets, workplaces, churches, food assistance programmes, restaurants, and civic and service organisations provide great opportunities for community interventions and provide consistency in the delivery of *5 A Day* messages.

The research component of *5 A Day* consists of nine community-based research studies, funded in 1993 initially for four years by NCI. The purpose of these grants is to implement and evaluate interventions aimed at increasing fruit and vegetable consumption among specific population groups in particular community channels, including workplaces, schools, churches, and food assistance programmes.

The NCI, with assistance from PBH, conducted a national survey to measure consumption in 1996 and a process evaluation of intervention activities by states. The NCI also funded, in 1994 and 1995, in coordination with the national Centers for Disease Prevention and Control (CDPC), eight grants to evaluate *5 A Day* activities implemented at the state level.

---

black men experienced a 19% higher risk of cancer compared with white men, and a 41% lower 5-year survival rate, reinforcing the evidence that access to treatment is lower among blacks. Similarly, among women, although breast cancer incidence was 17% lower for black than for white women, the 5-year relative survival rate was 24% lower among black women.

Since the late 1970s, increasingly sedentary lifestyles have contributed to the prevalence of obesity. Gross obesity is common in the USA.

Nutritional trends

Dietary patterns in the USA have changed greatly since the turn of the twentieth century, with increased consumption of meat (particularly beef and poultry), fish, dairy products, fats and oils, fruits, sugars and other sweeteners, and decreased consumption of vegetables, potatoes and cereals. In general, this trend is similar to the nutritional transition that accompanied increased urbanisation and industrialisation in economically developed countries throughout the twentieth century, and which is now accelerating in economically developing countries.

Fat intake increased steadily from about 30% of total energy at the turn of the century to over 40% in the mid-1980s; this has subsequently declined to around 37–38%, and lower among some groups with increased availability and promotion of low-fat milk and dairy products. Carbohydrate intake has declined from around 57% of total energy to about 46%, whereas the proportion of carbohydrate consumed as sugars has increased.

Major social developments since the 1970s led to major shifts in the pattern of food use within households. The traditional family meal has largely been replaced by snacking and casual and solitary eating; fast food and convenience foods have become the norm both outside and inside the home. At the same time, a significant minority of people have switched to diets that are plant-based and made up mostly of minimally processed foods, for health or environmental reasons.

The US food-manufacturing industry is innovative, introducing over 10,000 new food products each year. New products are typically promoted as convenient as well as nutritious. Low-fat and so-called no-fat products are increasingly common. New technologies have been developed to produce fat substitutes with low or no calorific value, and the market for micronutrient supplements has increased substantially.

Changes in the food supply have been driven, to some extent, by official acceptance and increasing public awareness of the links between diet and health. Many new products with specially formulated nutritional composition are sold at a premium price, thus placing them out of the reach of some low-income consumers.

Historically, the US view has been that market forces do and should shape the food patterns of the nation, and that what is needed for patterns to change is more information for consumers who, as individuals, can then change their food choices.

However, consumers in the USA, in common with consumers in other developed countries and indeed in developing countries, are saturated with information on food and health, much of which is confusing or even contradictory. For example, policies to increase demand for particular agricultural products have led to advertising programmes to promote dairy products, eggs, beef and pork, when dietary recommendations have been to reduce consumption. Federal assistance programmes for the poor have been explicitly used for market development and not nutrition. Given these contradictory signals, consumers are liable to reduce, say, fat or sugar from one food source, only to replace it from another. Aside from the recorded drop in fat consumption, the nutrient composition of the US diet overall has not changed greatly since the 1970s.

Prospects for prevention

Following publication by the National Academy of Sciences of *Diet, Nutrition and Cancer* (NAS, 1982), official policy in the USA, reflected in the work of government agencies and leading charities, has increasingly been to accept and promote the message that cancer is largely a preventable disease. A series of reports and position statements from the NAS (1989), the Department of Health and Human Services (DHHS, 1988a), the National Cancer Institute (NCI, 1994), and the American Cancer Society (ACS, 1996), have emphasised the role of food and nutrition in the prevention of cancer in the USA. The conclusions of these documents are summarised in Appendix A of the present report. (See also Box 9.3.1 on the National Cancer Institute's *5 A Day* programme.)

The Nutrition Policy Board, (NPB) a committee encompassed within the DHHS, advises on nutrition education, research, monitoring nutrition status, international nutrition issues and food safety. National policy objectives for nutrition are embodied in Dietary Guidelines for Americans issued jointly by the US Department of Agriculture and the Department for Health and Social Security every five years since 1980. Nutrition and cancer prevention is also a key focus of the Healthy People 2000 initiative (DHHS, 1988b).

9.4 Agents of change

Prevention of 30–40 per cent of cancers worldwide by dietary and associated means, is achievable. Success requires key sectors in society to work in collaboration to achieve the dietary goals recommended in this report. These agents of change include international organisations and national governments, industry, the medical and health professions, consumer and public interest groups, and the media.

This section describes briefly these agents of change, and suggests possible agenda that will promote multisectoral initiatives at international, national and local levels designed to prevent cancer, often in the general context of health promotion and disease prevention.

INTRODUCTION

The first step towards the prevention of cancer is acceptance that cancer is largely a preventable disease. The next step moves from acceptance to action, with appropriate initiatives that involve integrated thinking. Programmes for change will involve reconsideration of agriculture, of food and health policies, and of other policies that shape education and research, trade and industry, transport, water supply and other related areas.

In the economically developed world and urban areas of the economically developing world, the causes of epidemic cancers have much in common with the causes of cardiovascular and other chronic diseases. In the economically developing world, the underlying causes of endemic cancers have much in common with those that increase infectious and deficiency diseases. Strategies to reduce the incidence of cancer should complement and not compete with strategies to reduce incidence of other major diseases.

9.4.1 INTERNATIONAL AGENCIES AND NATIONAL GOVERNMENTS

The United Nations and other international agencies and national governments throughout the world can now identify reduction of the global burden of chronic diseases, including cardiovascular diseases and cancers, as of equal importance with the mission to reduce the global burden of infectious and deficiency diseases.

The United Nations and other international agencies promote co-operation on development, trade, agriculture, public health, child health and the environment, all of which bear on the prevention of epidemic diseases.

International agencies concerned with agriculture, food, nutrition and health include the Food and Agriculture Organization of the United Nations (FAO), the World Trade Organization (WTO) the World Bank, the World Health Organization (WHO), and its specialist agency, the International Agency for Research on Cancer (IARC), and the United Nations Children's Fund (UNICEF).

National governments, and, through them, the international agencies that have an increasing role in forming world food policies, are primary agents of change.

FAO

The Food and Agriculture Organization of the United Nations (FAO) assists rural populations, especially throughout the economically developing world, by encouraging greater food productivity and improved food security. FAO collects and analyses information on food and nutrition patterns throughout the world; data from FAO food balance sheets have been used in chapter 1 and elsewhere in this report.

FAO advises governments on agricultural policy and planning. In collaboration with the World Bank and other financial institutions, FAO helps to prepare agricultural development projects. Its field programmes include improvement of crop production and rural and livestock development, with special help for countries with major agricultural problems. FAO has been an official observer of the process that produced this report, and senior officials from the FAO Food Policy and Nutrition Division attended three panel meetings.

WORLD TRADE ORGANIZATION

The World Trade Organization (WTO) was set up following the closing of the eight-year Uruguay Round of the General Agreement on Tariffs and Trade (GATT) in 1994. The Uruguay Round of GATT was the first round to cover agriculture and food. The political context was a general agreement among the world's leading trading nations to promote free-market systems throughout the world.

WHO

The World Health Organization (WHO) is dedicated to attaining the highest possible level of health for all. Its 'Health For All' programme is aimed at achieving a level of health that allows the world's citizens to lead socially and economically productive lives.

The 1990 WHO report *Diet, Nutrition and the Prevention of Chronic Diseases*, (WHO, 1990) was the first global report to include dietary goals and guidelines designed to prevent cancer as well as other chronic diseases. Many of the recommendations and policy proposals made in this report proved to be consistent with the recommendations and proposals made in the WHO report. WHO has been an official observer of the process that produced this report, and senior officials from the WHO Nutrition and the Non-Communicable Diseases Divisions, and from IARC, attended four panel meetings.

UNICEF

The United Nations Children's Fund (UNICEF) works with other UN agencies, national governments, and directly with non-government organisations in over 140 developing countries. It is concerned with the health and welfare especially of mothers and children, with special reference to hygiene, nutrition, primary health care and basic education.

WORLD BANK

The World Bank (more formally, the International Bank for Reconstruction and Development) was set up to encourage economic growth in developing countries through the provision of loans and technical assistance.

The World Bank has given increased attention in recent years to improving nutrition in the context of food security, micronutrient deficiencies and child care and feeding. Its health sector is paying increased attention to non-communicable diseases; further, the nutritional contribution to non-communicable diseases is now emerging as a component in both its analytical studies and its lending programme.

TRANSNATIONAL GOVERNMENTS

In Europe, the European Community, in partnership with the EU member states, has devised a Europe Against Cancer campaign, and a 'Code Against Cancer'. This code is publicised for a week every year during a designated 'cancer week'.

NATIONAL GOVERNMENTS

In most countries, many government departments are necessarily involved in food and nutrition policy. These may include ministries of agriculture, fisheries, food, and health. They also include ministries of finance, foreign affairs, development, industry, trade, environment, urban and rural affairs, education, transport, and regions within nations. Some relevant experience of a number of countries throughout the world has been summarised in chapter 9.3. Successful national plans designed to improve public health are typically interdepartmental alliances in which government usually plays a key role, without necessarily controlling the process.

BOX 9.4.1 INTERNATIONAL AGENCIES AND NATIONAL GOVERNMENTS: SUGGESTIONS FOR POLICY INITIATIVES DESIGNED TO PREVENT CANCER

The panel invites national governments, supported by international agencies, to incorporate the prevention of cancer into relevant policies and programmes by initiatives such as those suggested here. These can be adapted to suit political, economic and local circumstances.

Such policies and programmes generally require government initiation and continued support. The suggestions are not comprehensive; they are designed to stimulate programmes of action that generally require collaboration between all the agents of change identified in this chapter.

General

■ Incorporate a strategic public health dimension into all relevant international and national political and economic policies
■ Identify the prevention of cancer as a key policy objective at global, regional, international, national, and local levels
■ Compile, update and disseminate case studies of international, national and local policies and experience relevant to the prevention of cancer
■ Sustain national food agencies or similar bodies with access to all ministries whose policies affect food, nutrition and public health
■ Ensure equitable representation on such agencies from representatives of industry and of health, medical, consumer and public interest groups
■ Enable such agencies to assess food supply systems 'from plough to plate' to ensure that typical diets protect against disease

Legislation

■ Examine, audit and revise existing and proposed legislation relevant to the prevention of diet-related diseases
■ Appoint ministers and senior officials with responsibility for public health and, in particular, for the prevention of cancer and chronic diseases

Economic

■ Assess the general effect of political and economic policies on public health and, where appropriate, use public sector investment to protect public health.
■ Estimate the economic impact of the burden of cancer, allowing for projected increases in population and changes in age distribution

■ Maintain and increase taxes on alcohol. Countries where alcohol is discouraged by a variety of means should maintain such policies
■ Ensure that adequate funding is available to ensure that publicly financed institutional catering can meet adequate nutritional standards

Development

■ Include the cost of policies to prevent cancer and other chronic diseases within international and national development plans
■ Address, as an integral part of public health strategies, the impact of urbanisation and industrialisation on patterns and incidence of cancer
■ Audit the impact of the globalisation of food trade on the projected incidence of cancer, internationally and nationally
■ Ensure that urban development and regeneration provides for and protects green belts, street markets, and inner city food-shopping facilities

Agriculture

■ Emphasise the production of foods of plant origin: vegetables and fruits, and cereals, tubers, roots and pulses for human consumption
■ Encourage sustainable and appropriate agriculture to produce foods important in diets that prevent chronic diseases, including cancer
■ Assess the land, water, energy, and all other resource needs for sustainable agriculture systems most likely to produce plant food
■ Reconsider the effects both of traditional and of modern agriculture on the nutritional adequacy and quality of the foods produced
■ Compare the relative benefits of cash crops grown for immediate economic return, and agriculture whose products protect public health
■ Encourage the market for foods of plant origin, especially vegetables and fruits, including, if appropriate, by price-support systems
■ Reconsider price support systems that create artificial markets for foods from land animals, in particular fatty foods
■ Review the ecological, public health and long-term economic impact of the rearing of land animals

Health

■ Integrate analyses of long-term public

health outcomes into strategies designed to sustain international and national economic growth
■ Recognise the economic benefits of primary health care, including prevention of and screening for cancer
■ Support cancer prevention proportionately to prevention and treatment of deficiency and infectious diseases, and other chronic diseases
■ Integrate cancer prevention into programmes to prevent deficiency, infectious, and other chronic diseases
■ Integrate cancer prevention into programmes to ensure food security and safety
■ Give increasing public funding to prevention of cancer up to appropriate levels in the general context of promotion of public health
■ Reconsider the proportions of public funding given to treatment of cancer, compared with funds designed to screen for and prevent cancer
■ Set targets for prevention of cancer over specified periods of time in a general framework of disease prevention
■ Establish programmes designed to achieve the dietary goals recommended in this report, in the short term and the longer term
■ Ensure that such programmes are effective, by means of multidisciplinary, multi-agency networks and alliances at all levels

Education

■ Ensure that school curricula include adequate teaching on food, nutrition and health, and on the importance of active living
■ Ensure that school children at all stages have proper access at school to healthy meals, and to recreation and sports facilities

Transport

■ Encourage local food production and distribution systems that minimise long-distance transportation of food and drink
■ Develop transport systems that encourage walking and cycling, and facilities that encourage physical activity throughout life
■ Allocate a proportion of transportation budgets for the development of bicycle and pedestrian facilities, notably in urban areas

9.4.2 INDUSTRY

The food industry has a special opportunity to ensure that the health of nations is protected by appropriate policies and practices, both old and new. Industrial policies and practices should be adapted in the light of reliable knowledge on the role of food and nutrition in the protection of public health and prevention of disease, including cancer. The food industry, itself increasingly global in nature, plays a major role in shaping food supplies, and thus diets, throughout the world.

AGRICULTURE

The recommendation that diets be plant-based has vast implications for agriculture. Since the mid-nineteenth century, agriculture has been shaped by the outdated belief that abundant consumption of protein of animal origin is necessary to ensure human health. By contrast, emphasis on horticulture and on the production of cereals and other plants foods principally for human consumption (with rearing of animals and production of meat and dairy products having a relatively minor role) corresponds to traditional patterns of agriculture in many parts of the world. In other parts of the world, a shift towards the production of foods of plant origin, with vegetables and fruits in effect considered as staple foods, and away from the production of foods of animal origin, implies substantial changes in policy and practice. Such change will necessarily involve consideration of climate and terrain, as well as the welfare of farmers.

The use of chemical inputs and the development of sophisticated food science and technology, designed to increase food production and to preserve processed foods or to make them more attractive, has become increasingly widespread, especially in the second half of the twentieth century. This has resulted in an increasing quantity and more complex combinations of food additives, including colours, flavours and processing aids. It is commonly supposed by the public that such practices significantly increase human cancer risk (Epstein, 1979). Conversely, it has been argued (Ames et al, 1987) that the chemicals used in agriculture may, on balance, have the effect of decreasing human cancer risk by helping to create secure and plentiful supplies of vegetables, fruits and other foods that protect against cancer. Similar arguments may apply to reduction of food spoilage by preservatives.

BOX 9.4.2 INDUSTRY: SUGGESTIONS FOR POLICY INITIATIVES DESIGNED TO PREVENT CANCER

The panel invites industry to incorporate the findings and recommendations of this report into relevant policies and practices, by methods such as those suggested here. These can be adapted to suit economic and other local circumstances.

The suggestions are not comprehensive; they are designed to stimulate programmes of action that generally require collaboration between all the agents of change identified in this chapter.

General policy
- Accept that food and nutrition are key means to prevent cancer and other chronic diseases as well as deficiency and infectious diseases
- Develop and sustain the promotion of foods and drinks recommended in this report as a means to increase both volume of sales and market share

Representative bodies
- Collaborate as members of national food agencies or equivalent bodies, with health, medical, consumer, and public interest groups
- Support the work of such agencies, with the declared policy of reducing the incidence of diet-related diseases including cancer

Agriculture
- Develop sustainable, appropriate-input methods of agriculture and horticulture that produce nourishing foods of plant origin
- Promote production, distribution and sale of a variety of vegetables and fruits and starchy staples for human consumption, if feasible, throughout the year

Manufacture
- Institute new policies of product formulation designed to increase availability of foods and drinks that protect against cancer
- Formulate and promote conveniently consumed foods and drinks the composition of which follows recommended nutritional standards
- Encourage new technology whose safety and benefits have been attested by official or other independent expert panels

Distribution and storage
- Develop and disseminate appropriate technology for control and minimisation of post-harvest losses and contamination
- Use benign technology such as vacuum packing and refrigeration, rather than salting, curing and smoking, to preserve perishable foods
- Favour those traditional methods of food processing that preserve fresh food without increasing the risk of cancer

Retailing
- Develop and maintain policies that promote and explain the value of foods and drinks that help to reduce the risk of cancer
- Shape markets by well-promoted policies that protect the health of customers and thus encourage their loyalty
- Specify composition of foods and drinks ordered from producers and manufacturers, so as to maximise their nutritional value
- Use and encourage appropriate and explicit labelling on manufactured and fresh food, in order to promote informed choice by customers

Catering
- Accept and use guidelines for institutional and commercial catering that incorporate prevention of cancer as a specific aim
- Promote, in all catering outlets, menus, foods and recipes that are devised to reduce risk of chronic diseases including cancer

Genetic engineering can also make foods of plant origin more plentiful and attractive, and can also be used to manipulate the genes of seeds, plants and animals in ways believed to benefit human health. Biotechnology can increase crop yield, help integrate pest management, produce plants resistant to viruses and fungi, and adapt them to marginal climatic and soil conditions.

MANUFACTURING

Economic development almost always involves increasing consumption of manufactured food: urban populations have less access to primary products and, instead, buy prepared and processed food and drinks in shops. Until recently, manufactured food has tended to make major use of components, such as hydrogenated fats, sugar and salt, designed to increase shelf-life. These are now known to be deleterious to human health when consumed in the amounts typical in the diets of industrialised and urbanised societies. Modern manufacturing methods, which use newer technology and take account of the cumulative effect of manufactured food on human health, may make less use of such components and instead make more use of minimal processing methods and better technologies.

The demographic and nutritional transitions described in chapter 9.2 are accompanied by rapid developments in food science and technology. Older methods of food preservation, notably salting, curing, and smoking, are being replaced by chilling, freezing and refrigeration, which have the effect of reducing salt in diets and increasing the availability of fresh vegetables and fruits.

Modification of traditional methods of preservation such as drying, and use of newer methods such as vacuum and gas packing, can preserve fresh foods, make local food supplies more secure, and benefit export markets.

A conspicuous aspect of economic development, is the growth of international and now transnational food and drink manufacturing companies, whose branded and other products tend to displace traditional foods. These products are energetically marketed and advertised, with names that have become well-known throughout the world, and their consumption is often associated with aspirations to the 'good life'. Such products tend to contain more added fat, sugar or salt than traditional foods and drinks. Alcoholic drinks are also energetically promoted in most countries.

Manufacturers prefer products already well-known to the public and likely to sell well. They are likely to reformulate existing products and formulate and promote new products only when they are convinced that evidence of the health benefits of such changes is solidly backed by governments and by leading scientific and medical organisations.

DISTRIBUTION AND STORAGE

Development of post-harvest systems is needed to minimise losses at all stages from harvesting, packaging, transportation, storage, distribution, sale and consumption.

Distribution systems can be adapted to local conditions,

to allow the efficient operation of wholesale and retail markets. For some crops, it may make most sense for the processing point to be close to the source of production; for others, it may be better for crops to be sent to a centralised processing centre near to a city.

Perhaps the most important aspect of food processing throughout the world likely to reduce risk of cancer is appropriate storage. General use of freezing, chilling and refrigeration has probably been a major contributor leading to the dramatic decline in incidence of stomach cancer during this century.

RETAILING

Food retailing also shapes food supplies and thus diets. In economically developed societies, large food retailers increasingly use their strength in the market place, and demand supplies from producers and manufacturers that are most likely to increase profit and market share. In many countries, retailers have become increasingly sensitive to pressure from consumers and consumer groups, and have adopted policies of purchase, availability, labelling and production that encourage sale of food and drink judged to be generally beneficial to human health.

CATERING

Meals served in workplace restaurants, canteens and cafeterias, nurseries, schools, colleges, hospitals, for the armed forces, and in prisons and homes for the elderly, are an important part of the diets of most people at some time in their lives, and perhaps most especially in early life.

The commercial catering sector includes restaurants, fast-food outlets, cafes, take-aways, hotels, bars, clubs, street vendors and eating and drinking facilities for travellers. Increased consumption of food outside the home is part of the nutrition transition. Much of this consists of branded foods and drinks controlled by transnational companies with national and local franchising. In many countries, regular shared meals in the home have been, and are being increasingly replaced by eating alone, inside and outside the home, and by regular snacking.

9.4.3 MEDICINE AND MEDICAL RESEARCH

Medical and health organisations generally have paid relatively little attention to the prevention of cancer, but work within a convention concerned mainly with diagnosis and treatment of disease, rather than its prevention and the promotion of public health. The evidence presented in this and other reports on food, nutrition and disease reinforces the need for an increasingly broad perspective.

Important agents of change include the medical and health professions, research organisations and cancer charities. The medical and allied professions in most societies form representative bodies in order to protect their interests, to promote good practice, to advise other constituencies

The panel invites the medical and health practitioners and organisations, including scientific research funding bodies, to incorporate prevention of cancer into their policies and programmes by means such as those suggested here. These can be adapted to suit relevant circumstances.

The suggestions are not comprehensive; they are designed to stimulate programmes of action that generally require collaboration between all the agents of change identified in this chapter.

Representative bodies
- Collaborate as members of national food agencies or equivalent bodies, in partnership with industry and with consumer and public interest groups
- Support the work of such agencies, with the declared policy of reducing incidence of diet-related diseases

including cancer
- Promote prevention and public health, by lobbying, media campaigns, and education of practitioners

Research support
- Devote an increasing proportion of funding to research into dietary modification of cancer risk, and prevention of cancer by diet
- Emphasise that prevention of cancer is as important and feasible as prevention of other major chronic and deficiency diseases

Medical training and practice
- Incorporate the concept of prevention into all branches of medical and other biological sciences as taught and practised.
- Make the study of food and nutrition

and their relation to health and disease an integral part of the training of medical students
- Make primary care teams the leaders in health centres and in the community in programmes designed to prevent cancer
- Ensure that the work of nutritionists, dietitians and other paramedical workers is based on the relevant research

Medical and health organisations
- Review and assess the findings of research and translate these into accessible messages for policy-makers and the general public
- Give increased emphasis to cancer as preventable by appropriate diets and lifestyles as well as by not smoking

within society including governments and the media, and to oversee training and research. These bodies may have very considerable influence on national policies.

RESEARCH SUPPORT

Organisations responsible for funding research, usually themselves funded with public money and sometimes also supported by industry, have a major role in setting the research priority agenda.

Private charities concerned with cancer have generally used most of their funds to support research into the cellular and molecular basis of cancer (in the hope of finding effective treatments) and clinical trials of cancer treatments. Some have specialised in palliative care for cancer patients. Funds devoted to research into the prevention of cancer, for cancer education and communication to the general public, have been far smaller.

By contrast, major heart disease organisations and charities, recognising the strength of the evidence linking diets and lifestyles with coronary heart disease and other vascular diseases, now tend to devote significant amounts of funding to prevention, public information campaigns, and health policy research.

MEDICAL TRAINING AND PRACTICE

Medical training usually includes very little education on nutrition, so physicians are seldom best qualified to give advice on healthy diets. However, the public generally respects the medical profession and is inclined to pay careful attention to physicians.

The primary care team in general practice may include

dietitians and practice nurses who can be trained in the basics of good nutrition. Primary care practitioners may also take advantage of post-qualification training in nutrition. In hospitals, there are special opportunities for giving advice to patients on diet and disease prevention.

Most work in the community that encourages people to choose healthy diets and lifestyles is done by local paramedical and health workers. Community dietitians take public health programmes into the community and identify what local factors affect dietary patterns and food choices.

Health education and promotion are tools used to improve public health at all levels. Health promotion is a relatively assertive enterprise, including self-empowerment, public agenda-setting and community action development, carried out in conjunction with, or by, consumer and public interest groups.

9.4.4 CONSUMER AND PUBLIC INTEREST GROUPS

Well-organised consumer and public interest groups may have deep roots in the community, special access to the media and politicians, and expert knowledge in their fields of interest. There is an increasing tendency for international and national policy agenda to be initiated by non-government organisations including public interest and consumer groups. Organisations independent both of government and industry, principally controlled by lay people, are, in most societies, a sector crucial to public health policy.

The consumer movement began in the USA and Europe in the 1950s and is now organised globally as well as nationally. Consumer organisations may be supported by govern-

---

BOX 9.4.4 CONSUMER AND PUBLIC INTEREST GROUPS: SUGGESTIONS FOR POLICY INITIATIVES DESIGNED TO PREVENT CANCER

The panel invites consumer and public interest groups to incorporate prevention of cancer into their policies and programmes, by methods such as those suggested here. These can be adapted to suit relevant circumstances.

The suggestions are not comprehensive. They are designed to stimulate programmes of action that generally require collaboration between all the agents of change identified in this chapter.

General

■ Form alliances of individual consumer and public interest groups, to develop consensus on major issues of food and nutrition policy

■ Ensure that advice that informs policies and programmes comes from reliable independent sources and is derived from current science

■ Create networks, nationally and internationally, whose programmes include prevention of cancer by appropriate diets and lifestyles

■ Incorporate prevention of cancer by means of appropriate diets into existing programmes on health promotion and disease prevention

■ Reconsider the balance of evidence for roles in modifying cancer risk as between nutrition, lifestyle, tobacco, occupational and environmental pollution

Representative bodies

■ Collaborate as members of national food agencies or equivalent bodies, in partnership with industry and with health and medical groups

■ Support the work of such agencies, with the declared policy of reducing incidence of diet-related diseases including cancer

Interface with the media

■ Supply the media with reliable information on food and health

---

ment, or may be wholly independent, relying on income from public subscriptions. Initially, consumer organisations tended to focus on campaigns to ensure that purchases were good value for money. More recently, they have been concerned with services as well as goods, and with public policy issues, including food policy.

Public interest groups, typically funded by public subscription or by grants, may have a relatively assertive style and may use direct action to get their messages across. Some are 'single interest' groups, being concerned, say, with campaigns on the genetic engineering of foods, the contamination of the environment by pesticides, or perceived questionable practices of the baby-formula milk industry. These groups are usually distrustful of government and industry.

Consumer and public interest groups can catalyse change. They may work as leading members of alliances including industry and health professionals to devise and promote healthy eating campaigns, and may encourage manufacturers and advertisers to promote healthy foods.

9.4.5 THE MEDIA

Communication of public health messages is most effectively done by networks of experts and advocates, working with the media so that reliable and interesting information is communicated to the public.

Public understanding of the relationship between food, nutrition and prevention of disease, and the translation of knowledge into action, depends on media involvement. Through the media very large audiences can be reached free or for little cost. Access can be gained to groups that are otherwise inaccessible to health professionals; messages can be amplified by means of influential role models; and a large proportion of the population can be reached simultaneously. Many people will recognise a new issue as affecting their lives

---

BOX 9.4.5 THE MEDIA: SUGGESTIONS FOR POLICY INITIATIVES DESIGNED TO PREVENT CANCER

The panel invites the media to communicate the prevention of cancer by methods such as those suggested here. These can be adapted to suit relevant circumstances

The suggestions are not comprehensive. They are designed to stimulate programmes of action that generally require collaboration between all the agents of change identified in this chapter

Journalism

■ Publicise the fact that primary prevention together with screening, rather than treatment and palliation alone, are now the crucial approaches to cancer

■ Appoint health correspondents whose brief incorporates coverage of public health, prevention and nutrition

■ Sponsor national, regional and community campaigns designed to encourage healthy diets and lifestyles

■ Make use of the findings of this report in developing coverage of food, nutrition and the prevention of cancer

Books

■ Promote textbooks that incorporate the reliable findings of current science on prevention of cancer and other chronic diseases

Electronic

■ Use electronic access to and retrieval of information in preparing stories on food, nutrition and public health and disease prevention

Advertising

■ Use advertising media to promote the consumption of healthy foods and to enhance public health campaigns

only when they see or hear it broadcast, or read about it.

The news media conventionally emphasise health disasters and medical 'breakthroughs'. Much 'health' coverage is written by medical or science correspondents, and the technology of medicine tends to dominate, with stories of transplants, body scanners, genes, and drug scares that emphasise risk, disease and treatment.

Scientific and popular publications influence thinking on public health. Textbooks tend, with some lag, to reflect contemporary science and some aspects of the diet and cancer story have developed rapidly in recent years. Medical textbooks often lack nutrition information and are mostly concerned with identifying and treating disease.

The medium of advertising also influences public opinion and choice. The major source of new information about food for most people is advertising. In some countries, foods and drinks are, in aggregate, more heavily advertised than any other product category.

Computers, together with networking and electronic mail services, have enabled the accumulation of information and global communication.

The Internet and the World Wide Web now allow the rapid and continuous exchange of information. The academic community, the defence industry and, more recently, the business community and legal professions, have created global networks that develop and review information and policies immediately without the need for face-to-face meetings, or conventional written or telephone communication. This has created widening circles of individuals with access to and input into the process, ranging from viewing only, equivalent to a reader of a book, to comment on-line, equivalent to an accredited correspondent, to the capacity to review (an electronic equivalent of a peer review), to the further facility to be a member of conference calls during which previously agreed positions are discussed and changed.

Appendix A: Other reports

This is a review of recommendations on diet and cancer prevention made by other organisations. It traces the evolution of dietary recommendations designed to reduce cancer risk in populations, and examines the rationales behind them. It focuses on recommendations made by governments and organisations such as health charities or professional associations (or their respective advisory committees), and not on recommendations made by individual scientists. The recommendations are summarised in Tables A1–A4.

INTRODUCTION

Many of the recommendations are from reports concerned with the prevention of chronic disease or the promotion of general health and well-being, but which have included a section on cancer prevention. The tables distinguish those recommendations that are based primarily on diet and cancer evidence and those on non-cancer evidence (marked with an asterisk). In many cases, a whole range of health and non-health factors underpins dietary recommendations (De Vet and Van Leeuwen, 1986), including the contribution that foods or dietary constituents make towards achieving a nutritionally balanced diet, as well as specific evidence relating to diet and chronic diseases. Reports usually do not spell out the precise scientific basis for a recommendation so judgments here are based on the conclusions described in the text of the reports.

Reports from government committees and expert organisations typically constitute part of the so-called 'grey literature'. They are usually not published in academic journals or listed in international abstracts or databases, and are consequently difficult to find. Most of the reports examined in this review come from the USA. This is not simply a reflection of the relative ease of finding information from the USA, but a result of the national importance given to diet and cancer prevention since the early 1980s. By contrast, nutrition and health promotion activities in Europe have been dominated by coronary heart disease prevention, and European cancer organisations have been relative late comers to dietary prevention activities.

The dietary recommendations summarised in the tables include guidelines and goals. Goals are numerical targets; guidelines offer more general, non-quantified advice. The setting of dietary goals indicates a belief in the need for dietary change, because goals allow direct comparison with current levels of intake. By comparison, guidelines such as 'eat more', 'limit' or 'increase' give no indication of the scale of change needed. Goals and guidelines may be given for dietary constituents or for foods, and can be directed at populations or individuals. Distinctions between these different types of recommendations are not always clear and can be further blurred when scientific recommendations are interpreted for the public in media articles and health education materials.

Until recently, when committees have devised quantified goals, these have tended to be for dietary constituents, and to refer to population average intakes. Recommendations on foods, and advice for individuals, have tended to be limited to more general guidelines. The predomination of goals for dietary constituents rather than foods is, in part, a legacy of the historical need to prevent deficiency diseases through the application of recommended daily allowances for dietary constituents. In Europe in the 1980s and early 1990s, however, such preference reflects the pressure on scientists to formulate recommendations acceptable within a political paradigm that promotes supremacy of consumer choice. This apparent reluctance to develop quantified advice about foods allowed a degree of complacency with existing levels of consumption among both public and policy makers alike (Williams, 1995). Recent reports, however, have begun to include goals for foods and for individuals.

REVIEW

Strategies for cancer prevention were initially focused on early detection so that treatment could be more effective. As more became known of some of the possible causes of cancers, the idea that environmental, and therefore modifiable, factors were involved began to be reflected in the recommendations of reports on cancer prevention. The 1964 World Health Organization Expert Committee (WHO, 1964), chaired by Sir Richard Doll, estimated that extrinsic factors were involved in three-quarters of all cancers. It advocated a health education strategy aimed at reducing tobacco smoking, the chewing of betel and tobacco, and the consumption of alcohol. The committee made no recommendations on diet (other than alcohol).

USA

The public health significance of an association between diet and cancer was given early recognition in the USA. The National Cancer Act of 1971 required the National Cancer

Institute (NCI), as a government agency, to investigate the relationship between nutrition and cancer. In 1975, the NCI held a joint symposium with the American Cancer Society (ACS and NCI, 1975) on nutrition in the causation of cancer. The symposium concluded that there was sufficient evidence to assume that nutrition and cancer were related and, although there were still many unanswered questions, there were opportunities for prevention which should not be missed. A diet with less fat, less meat, less energy and less cholesterol, and with more fruit, vegetables and cereals was recommended.

A report by a US Select Committee (US Congress, 1977) on nutrition and human needs produced the first comprehensive statement on risk factors in the American diet. This was followed in 1979 by a Surgeon General's report (US Department of Health, 1979) on health promotion and disease prevention. Both reports considered cancer prevention, promotion and disease prevention. Both reports considered cancer prevention, but most of the dietary recommendations were based on evidence for prevention of coronary heart disease, or provision of a nutritionally balanced diet. Both recommended reducing red meat consumption, as a means of reducing intakes of saturated fats and cholesterol, and to promote dietary patterns associated with low rates of coronary heart disease.

By 1980, the NCI was already investigating the roles of antioxidant vitamins, mineral and other bioactive constituents (Upton, 1979) and the National Academy of Sciences (NAS) was preparing its report, *Diet, Nutrition and Cancer*, commissioned by the NCI with specific instructions to develop recommendations for the public.

The NAS report, whose conclusions and recommendations are specified in detail within this report in chapters 4 – 7, served as the basis of subsequent recommendations from the American Cancer Society (ACS, 1984) and the NCI (Butrum et al, 1988). The ACS recommendations were stronger on antioxidant vitamins and other bioactive constituents, specifically advising the public to choose cruciferous vegetables, and foods rich in vitamins A and C. The NCI recommendations gave a quantified goal for fibre, but this was based on the advice of an expert panel on fibre, rather than the diet and cancer evidence. Both organisations advised avoidance of obesity (severe degree of overweight), but ACS modified this later as it became clear that any degree of overweight increased risk of cancer.

EUROPE

In contrast with the USA, health bodies in Europe in the 1980s did not make recommendations to the public on diet and cancer. The European health promotion agenda was dominated by coronary heart disease prevention. The report of the UK's National Advisory Committee on Nutrition Education (NACNE) on nutritional guidelines for health education in Britain barely mentions cancer (NACNE, 1983). A workshop on nutrition and cancer held by the International Union of Nutritional Sciences (IUNS) in 1980 in Cambridge, UK, concluded that it was not possible to make any recommendations to the public about diet and cancer prevention (Carroll, 1981).

In 1981, The European Cancer Programme (ECP) was established with a remit which included informing the public about cancer prevention. ECP held a joint symposium with the IUNS in 1985 in Aarhus, Denmark (ECP and IUNS, 1985) which produced a consensus statement on provisional dietary guidelines for cancer prevention. Although the recommendations are similar to those of the NAS report, they were justified on the basis that there was evidence that they were beneficial for reducing coronary heart disease risk, and only tentatively proposed that they might also lower rates of cancer. The exception is a recommendation to limit salt intake, based on salt and stomach cancer evidence.

A similar picture emerged in a report from the WHO's regional office for Europe in 1988 (WHO, 1988). This referred to the 1982 NAS report, but commented on how little was known about the links between diet and cancer, and echoed the conclusions of the ECP/IUNS conference that diets which prevented coronary heart disease would probably also reduce the risk of cancer. It pointed out that Sweden was the only European country to have conducted any official analysis of diet and cancer risk. The Swedish report concluded that diet had a substantial effect on determining total cancer incidence, and advised lowering fat intake and consuming more cereals, fruit and vegetables.

JAPAN

In 1984 in Japan, the Ministry of Health and Welfare (Fujisawa and Itoh, 1984) set up advisory panels to produce recommendations on preventing coronary heart disease, cancers and diabetes, and to make proposals for healthy eating habits. Cancers are the leading cause of death in Japan, and the overall proposals placed due emphasis on the conclusions of the panel on prevention of cancer. The panel's recommendations were broadly similar to those of the NAS, but additionally recommended eating more raw vegetables and avoiding consumption of foods or drinks at very high temperatures. Much emphasis was placed on the importance of variety, with a recommendation to eat more than 30 different foods per day.

DEFICIENCIES AND EXCESSES

Most reports examining prevention of chronic diseases at this time came from developed countries and, although their recommendations aimed to provide a nutritionally balanced diet, avoidance of dietary deficiencies was not necessarily a major consideration. In the late 1980s, the United Nations University and the Foundation Cavendes (Scrimshaw and Bengoa, 1988) convened a workshop in Caracas, Venezuela, with the aim of producing nutrition recommendations for preventing deficiencies and also reducing the risk of diet-related diseases. The intention was to develop quantitative dietary goals and practical dietary guidelines for health in Latin America which could be adopted, with appropriate modification, by individual Latin American countries. The 'metas nutricionales' that presented were primarily for dietary constituents that were not foods and, although cancer was considered, the diet and cancer evidence was not a major determining factor. However, they are one of the first examples of attempts to develop a single set of guidelines that apply equally to rich and poor. This approach was developed further by WHO (1990) and in the present report.

The Canadian Cancer Society was one of the first to introduce quantified dietary recommendations for cancer prevention (CCS, 1986). The CCS leaflet for the general public advised consuming 4–5 servings of fruits and vegetables per day (at least two of these to be vegetables), and 3–5 servings of bread and cereals. However, the figures were taken from Canada's food guide and were amounts designed to achieve a nutritionally balanced diet, rather than being specific to cancer prevention.

In 1989, the NAS Committee on Diet and Health (NAS, 1989) in the USA also devised quantified advice for the public. (These are specified in detail in this report in chapters 4 - 7.) It recommended eating five or more servings of fruit and vegetables, and six or more servings of a combination of breads, cereals and legumes per day; these figures are somewhat higher than those from the CCS. The NAS conclusions were based on 'experience in planning nutritionally balanced diets that would meet the committee's recommendations' – that is, achieving a balanced diet. For vegetables, fruits and starchy foods, this meant meeting nutrient requirements and substituting for fatty foods. These same goals continued to be used throughout the 1990s and, although the diet and cancer evidence is more frequently cited as a basis for recommending increased consumption, there has been scant attempt to justify scientifically the quantities (that is, number of servings or portions) recommended .

A report on chronic disease prevention (WHO, 1990) set quantified dietary goals for global application. To take account of the varying nutrition situation around the world, the goals set upper and lower limits. Populations with intakes between the upper and lower limits would avoid significant risks of inadequacy or excess. Countries with low intakes of fat, for example, would need to raise intakes to meet the lower limit, while more affluent countries would need to reduce intakes below the upper limit. WHO also set a quantified population target for vegetables and fruits, but no other foods. The target of a lower limit of 400 g of vegetables and fruits per day was based on intakes observed in populations in southern Mediterranean countries with low rates of coronary heart disease and cancers. Non-governmental organisations in the UK translated this 400 gram population goal into individual advice to eat five 'decent sized' portions of vegetables and fruits daily (Williams, 1995). Advice to 'eat at least five' was subsequently taken up by the media, major UK retailers and, in 1994, appeared in the Europe Against Cancer programme's annual promotion.

WHO recommended a high-carbohydrate, low-fat diet, rich in starchy foods and including a substantial intake of fruits and vegetables. The recommendations on vegetables and fruits, and total fat, were based on diet and cancer evidence. The report noted uncertainty over the range of fat intakes and their relationship with cancers, and proposed that it might be necessary to further reduce the upper limit from 30% energy to 20–25%. By contrast, a review of the diet and cancer evidence, carried out for the UK's Health Education Authority (Bingham, 1990), concluded that the balance of evidence was neither for nor against a causal role for fat. A reduction in total fat was still recommended in line with the long-standing strategy of coronary heart disease prevention advice in the UK, namely to reduce total fat because this in turn lowers intakes of saturated fats.

Reports in the late 1980s and early 1990s, showed a strong similarity in their recommendations, (US DHHS, 1988; ACS, 1991; CCS, 1992; Scottish Office, 1993; European School of Oncology, 1994). All made reference to the potential benefits of antioxidant vitamins and other bioactive constituents but, unlike some of the earlier recommendations, they made no specific reference to increasing consumption of particular vitamins. This reflected both the increasing complexity of the antioxidant and cancer evidence, and uncertainty over precisely which components are responsible for any beneficial effect, and concern about use of supplements. The CCS and European School of Oncology (ESO) specifically recommended avoidance of dietary supplements. The ESO described the dangers of false reassurance if people take supplements because they may be less inclined to make the other dietary changes recommended.

The USA's DHHS report, *Healthy People 2000*, was a health strategy document rather than an expert committee report. It included specific nutritional objectives to increase consumption of foods containing complex carbohydrates (fruits, vegetables and grains) and reduce consumption of fat and saturated fatty acids. Whereas *Healthy People 2000* clearly linked nutrition and cancer prevention objectives, England's health strategy *The Health of the Nation* (UK Department of Health, 1992) says virtually nothing on diet and cancer. Its two dietary targets, to reduce intakes of fat and saturated fatty acids, were firmly positioned within coronary heart disease reduction strategies and all publications from the Nutrition Task Force, charged with drawing up a programme for achieving the nutrition targets, were emblazoned with a bold heart-shaped logo.

LATEST REPORTS

Dietary recommendations made, in 1996, by the ACS (ACS, 1996), and from Harvard University (Harvard University, 1996) were most notable in that they recommended limiting meat consumption. The ACS and NCI symposium in 1975 recommended eating less meat, but with no clear scientific basis for such a recommendation based on diet and cancer evidence. Subsequent reports used diet and coronary heart disease evidence to recommend consuming less fatty meat as a means of reducing saturated fat and cholesterol intakes. The 1996 recommendations from ACS and Harvard University were concerned with a direct association between red meat consumption and cancers.

The Harvard University report also introduced a shift in advice about fat. It did not recommend a reduction in total fat; indeed, it proposed an increase in use of plant oils as added fats, and advised reducing intakes only of animal fats.

CONCLUSION

Overall, recommendations for cancer prevention between the 1970s and 1990s have been consistent, although direct evidence to support many of the recommendations has been available only recently. There has been an increasing move towards the quantification of dietary recommendations, for both the public and policy-makers. This is mainly a result of a greater realisation among scientific committees that quantification is a necessary part of achieving dietary change.

All of the above reports advocated greater consumption of vegetables and fruits, and most recommended grains or starchy foods. The recent strengthening of evidence to support a reduction in meat intake confirms the overall direction of recommendations on diet and cancer towards plant-based diets. Recommendations on saturated fatty acids began as measures that would prevent coronary heart disease and it was widely considered that total fat, rather than type of fat, was more important for cancer prevention. Table A2 illustrates how, gradually, the evidence against animal fats and cancers has accumulated.

Moderation in, or limiting alcohol consumption is another of the most consistent of the diet and cancer recommendations. Moderating consumption was the focus in the 1980s; most reports of the 1990s quantify maximum intakes.

SUMMARY TABLES OF DIETARY RECOMMENDATIONS FOR CANCER PREVENTION

Tables A1–A4 summarise dietary recommendations made by governments and professional organisations worldwide to reduce the risk of cancers. Some are from reports which deal exclusively with cancer prevention. Most are from reports that had a wider brief, such as prevention of chronic diseases in general, particularly coronary heart disease, and/or providing a healthy balanced diet meeting all nutrient requirements. These are marked in the tables with an asterisk. Recommendations that have no bearing on cancer prevention have been excluded. Recommendations from all reports not based on diet and cancer evidence are also marked with an asterisk.

Most recommendations take the form of advice to increase or decrease consumption of particular foods or dietary constituents based on existing national consumption patterns. To make the tables useful internationally, foods and dietary constituents have been grouped according to their general association with decreasing (Table A1) or increasing (Table A2) risk of cancers. These correspond with advice in most developed countries to 'eat more' or 'eat less' respectively. Recommendations on physical activity, energy balance and alcohol are presented in Tables A3 and A4. Where recommendations are contrary to most other reports or do not fit this classification, this is noted in the table.

KEY TO TABLES

nc No comment. Association of the food or dietary constituents with disease risk not discussed.

ns No specific recommendation. Association with disease risk is discussed (including insufficiency of evidence), but no conclusions are drawn on the benefits of choosing or limiting consumption.

ind Indirect recommendation. The benefits of choosing or limiting consumption are specifically mentioned, but there is no specific recommendation. This is common where a dietary strategy is recommended which will have the effect of altering consumption of specific dietary components in the right direction. It often indicates that the constituent panel were uncertain about the effects of the constituent but were happy to recommend changes in consumption patterns of foods containing the constituent, for example, fibre and fibre-rich foods, antioxidant vitamins and fruits and vegetables.

* With reference to a report: The report deals with chronic disease prevention or health promotion in general. Cancer prevention is a component, rather than the focus, of the report.
* With reference to a recommendation: the recommendation is based primarily on evidence for prevention of other diseases such as coronary heart disease and/or achieving dietary balance.

Wholegrains or cereals Recommendation specifies cereals and/or unrefined cereals, rather than starchy foods in general.

Meat Recommendation specifically advises choosing less meat. Does not include advice to choose leaner meats.

Pulses (legumes) Recommendations on pulses are included in the column on other plant foods unless the report specifically includes pulses in a vegetable food group.

TABLE A1 DIETARY RECOMMENDATIONS TO CHOOSE OR INCREASE FOODS OR DIETARY CONSTITUENTS ASSOCIATED WITH REDUCING RISK OF CANCERS

Reports of 1970s	Vegetables and fruits	Other plant foods (Starchy foods)	Vitamins and minerals	Other bioactive constituents	Dietary Fibre	Carbohydrate	Other recommendations
ACS and NCI 1977 USA Select Committee*	Yes*	cereals Yes* wholegrains	nc	nc	ns	Yes* 55–60% energy	Increase poultry and fish* Polyunsaturates –* 10% energy. Monounsaturates –10% energy
1979 USA Surgeon General*	Yes*	Yes* wholegrains and cereals	nc	nc	ind	Yes*	Increase poultry, poultry and legumes

Reports of 1980s	Vegetables and fruits	Other plant foods (Starchy foods)	Vitamins and minerals	Other bioactive constituents	Dietary Fibre	Carbohydrate	Other recommendations
1982 USA NAS	Yes	Yes – wholegrain cereals	ind	ind	ns	ns	
1984 USA ACS	Yes	Yes – wholegrain cereals	Yes – include foods rich in vitamins A and C in daily diet	Yes – include cruciferous vegetables in the diet	ind – eat more high fibre foods	nc	
1984 Japan*	Yes – raw, green or yellow vegetables once a day, and oranges	Yes – wholegrains, legumes, fungi and seaweed	Yes – eat fruit and vegetables rich in carotene and vitamin C	nc	ind	Yes* 55–60% energy	Eat a variety of foods. Take more than 30 food items a day. Eat soyabean products or fish once a day*
1985 Europe ECP/IUNS	Yes * – eat different types esp. green leafy and root vegetables and citrus fruits	ind* – wholegrains	ind	ns	Yes*	Yes*	Eat a varied diet. Use fresh or minimally processed foods
1986 Canada CCS	Yes – 4–5 servings/day, at least 2 servings vegetables	ind – 3–5 servings/day	ind – choose fruit and vegetables which are good sources of carotenes and vitamin C	ind	Yes – 30g/day	ns	
1987 USA NCI	Yes – include a variety of fruit and vegetables in the daily diet	ns	ind	ind	Yes – 20–30 g/day, 35 g/day upper limit*	nc	
1988 USA Surgeon General*	Yes	Yes – wholegrain foods and cereal products, dried beans and peas	ind	nc?	Yes	Yes	Choose fish and poultry
1988 Latin America. UNU/FC*	nc	ind * – wholegrains	nc	nc	Yes* – >8 g/ 1,000 kcal	Yes *– 60–70% energy	
1988 Europe WHO*	ns	ns	ns	nc	Yes* 30 g/day	Yes* – >40% energy (ultimately 45–55%)	
1989 USA NAS*	Yes – 5 or more servings/day, esp. green and yellow vegetables and citrus fruits	Yes *– 6 or more servings/day of bread, cereals and legumes	ind	ind	ind	Yes – >55% energy	Choose fish and poultry without skin

Reports of 1990s	Vegetables and fruits	Other plant foods (starchy foods)	Vitamins and minerals	Other bioactive constituents	Dietary fibre	Carbohydrate	Other recommendations
1990 Global WHO	Yes – 400 g/day lower population limit (incl. pulses)	ind*	ns	ns	Yes* – 16–24 g/day population limits	Yes* – 55–75% energy	
1990 UK HEA	Yes – esp. raw and lightly cooked green vegetables or salad	ind*	ns	ns	ind*	ns	
1991 USA ACS	Yes – include a variety of both vegetables and fruits in the daily diet	Yes – wholegrains and legumes	ns	ns	ind	nc	Eat a varied diet
1991 USA DHHS*	Yes – 5 or more servings/day (including legumes)	Yes – 6 or more daily servings grain products	ind	ind	ind	ind*	
1992 Canada CCS	Yes – choose dark green and orange–yellow vegetables and fruits	Yes – cereals, breads and other grain products.	ind	ind	ind	ns	Enjoy a variety of foods Choose foods not supplements
1993 Scotland SO*	Yes – >400 g/day (interim target – 3 portions/day)	ind	ind	ind	Yes – >16 g/day NSP	Yes – <40% energy	
1994 Europe ESO	Yes – 5 servings vegetables and fruit	ind – 6 servings wholegrain and cereal products	ind	ind	ind	ind	Avoid use of dietary supplements
1996 USA ACS	Yes – 5 or more servings/day	Yes – several times/day Including grain products with every meal Choose wholegrains	ns	ns	ns	nc	Choose beans as an alternative to meat
1996 USA HR	Yes – >5 servings/day (>3 servings vegetables) Vary from day to day	Yes – legumes and grains (Wholegrains ind)	ns	ns	ns	Partially – reduce consumption refined carbohydrates	Increase use of plant oils (e.g., olive oil) as added fats* Eat a varied diet

TABLE A2 DIETARY RECOMMENDATIONS TO LIMIT OR REDUCE FOODS OR NUTRIENTS ASSOCIATED WITH INCREASING RISK OF CANCERS

Reports of 1970s	Red meat	Protein	Fats and oils	Saturates	Salt	Refined sugar	Other recommendations
1975 USA ACS and NCI	Yes	nc	Yes	nc	nc	nc	
1977 USA Select Committee	Yes* – as *means to cut fat and cholesterol	nc	Yes* 30% energy	Yes*	Yes* 5 g/day	Yes* 15% energy	
1979 USA Surgeon General*	Yes*	ns	ns	Yes*	Yes*	Yes*	

Reports of 1980s	Red meat	Protein	Fats and oils	Saturates	Salt	Refined sugar	Other recommendations
1982 USA NAS	nc	ns	Yes – 30% energy	Yes	Salt-preserved foods only	ns	Minimise contamination of foods with carcinogens from any source
1984 USA ACS	nc	nc	Yes – endorses NRC 30% energy	ns	Yes – salt-preserved foods only	nc	Moderate consumption of smoked and nitrate cured foods
1984 Japan*	ind* – eat meat and fish equally (to reduce fat intake)	Take enough protein, 50% from plant sources	Yes – 20–25% energy*	nc	Yes – <10g/day	Yes*	Avoid foods and drinks of very high temperature. Avoid burnt fish and meats.
1985 Europe ECP/IUNS	nc	nc	Yes* – 30% energy	Yes*	Yes – <5 g/day*	ns	Avoid cured, pickled or traditionally smoked foods.
1986 Canada CCS	nc	nc	Yes – <30% energy	No	Yes – salt preserved foods only	nc	Minimise consumption smoked and nitrite cured foods
1987 USA NCI	nc	nc	Yes – <30% energy	No	Yes – salt preserved foods only	nc	Minimise consumption smoked foods
1988 USA Surgeon General*			Yes	Yes	Yes	Vulnerable groups only	
1988 Latin America UNU/FC*	ns	10–12% energy, >50% plant sources*	Yes* – 20–25% energy	Yes* – 6.3–8.1% energy	Yes* – <10 g/day	ind	Ratio saturated, poly and mono unsaturates 1:1:1
1988 Europe WHO*	ns	Yes* 12–13% energy	Yes* – 35% energy (ultimately 20–30%)	Yes* – 15% energy (ultimately 10%)	Yes* – 7–8 g/day (ultimately 5 g)	Yes* – 10% energy	
1989 USA NAS*	ns – choose lean meat	Maintain at moderate levels – < twice RDA (<1.6 g/kg BW adults)	Yes – <30% energy	Yes* – <10% energy	Yes – limit to <6 g/day	ind*	Avoid fibre supplements, and dietary supplements in excess of RDAs in any one day*

Reports of 1990s	Red meat	Protein	Fats and oils	Saturates	Salt	Refined sugar	Other recommendations
1990 Global WHO	ns	No – existing range population intakes 10–15% energy	Yes – 15–30% population limits	Yes* – 0–10% population limits	Yes* 6 g/day upper population limit	Yes* – 0–10% energy population limits	Polyunsaturates 3–7% population limits*
1990 UK HEA	ns	ns	Yes* – <35% energy	Yes* – <15% energy	ns	nc	Keep consumption of smoked, cured, pickled and barbecued food low
1991 USA ACS	nc	nc	Yes – <30% energy	nc	Yes – salt-preserved foods	nc	Limit consumption smoked and nitrite preserved foods
1991 USA DHHS*	nc	nc	Yes – <30% energy	Yes* – <10% energy	Yes	nc	
1992 Canada CCS	nc	nc	Yes – <30% energy	nc	Yes* – moderation	nc	Caffeine – moderation* Avoid charred meat. Use high temperature cooking methods occasionally, not regularly
1993 Scotland SO	ind – reduce consumption of meat products	nc	Yes – <35% energy	Yes* – <11% energy	Yes *– 70mmol/day	Yes* – <10% energy	
1994 Europe ESO	nc	nc	Yes – <30% energy	Yes – <10% energy	Yes – 6 g/day	ns	Polyunsaturates 6–8% energy Limit nitrite consumption
1996 USA ACS	Yes – limit consumption meats, esp high fat meats	ns	Yes	ind – limit consumption of high fat foods from animal sources	ns	nc	
1996 HR	Yes – <1 serving/week red meat	nc	No	ind – reduce consumption of animal fat	Yes	ind – reduce consumption refined carbohydrates	Don't blacken or char red meat, chicken or fish

TABLE A3 RECOMMENDATIONS ON ENERGY BALANCE

Reports of 1970s	Maintain healthy body weight	Maintain physical activity
1975 USA ACS and NCI	ind – consume less food	nc
1977 USA Select Committee*	nc	nc
1979 USA Surgeon General*	Yes*	Yes* 15–30 min exercise >3 times/week

Reports of 1980s	Maintain healthy body weight	Maintain physical activity
1982 USA NAS	ns	ns
1984 USA ACS	Yes – avoid obesity	ns
1984 Japan*	ind* – avoid too much energy intake	Yes*
1985 Europe. ECP/IUNS	Yes*	nc
1986 Canada CCS	Yes	ind
1987 USA NCI	Yes – avoid obesity	nc
1988 USA/ Surgeon General*	Yes	Yes
1988 Latin America UNU/FC*	Yes*	Yes*
1988 Europe WHO*	ns	ns
1989 USA NAS*	Yes	Yes

Reports of 1990s	Maintain healthy body weight	Maintain physical activity
1990 Global WHO	Yes	Yes*
1990 UK HEA	Yes*	nc
1991 USA ACS	Yes	ind
1991 USA DHHS	Yes	Yes
1992 Canada CCS	Yes	Yes
1993 Scotland SO	Yes	Yes*
1994 Europe ESO	Yes	Yes
1996 USA ACS	Yes	Yes – >30 min most days of the week
1996 USA HR	Yes (also reduce excess energy in early life to prevent early onset menstruation)	Yes

TABLE A4 RECOMMENDATIONS ON ALCOHOL

Reports of 1970s	Limit alcohol
1975 USA ACS and NCI	ns
1977 USA Select Committee*	nc
1979 USA Surgeon General*	nc – alcohol abuse only

Reports of 1980s	Limit alcohol
1982 USA NAS	Yes – moderation
1984 USA ACS	Yes – moderation
1984 Japan*	Yes – moderation
1985 Europe. ECP/IUNS	Yes – moderation if at all
1986 Canada CCS	Yes – <2 drinks/day, if at all
1987 USA NCI	Yes – moderation, if at all
1988 USA/Surgeon General*	Yes – moderation <2 drinks/day
1988 Latin America UNU/FC*	Yes – limit*
1988 Europe WHO*	ns
1989 USA NAS*	Yes – moderation

Reports of 1990s	Limit alcohol
1990 Global WHO	Yes – 4% energy in alcohol-consuming countries
1990 UK HEA	Yes – 14 and 21 units/week men and women.
1991 USA ACS	Yes – limit, if you drink at all
1991 USA DHHS	
1992 Canada CCS	Yes – moderation, <1 or 2 drinks/day
1993 Scotland SO	Yes – <24 g/day men, <16 g/day women
1994 Europe ESO	Yes – <2 small drinks/day if at all
1996 USA ACS	Yes – limit, if at all <2 drinks/day men, 1/day women.
1996 USA HR	Yes – moderation, especially smokers.

Appendix B: Note on method

Readers may wish to know the thinking behind the decision to commission this report and the selection of the panel responsible for its contents, and of the other scientists and experts who have supported the panel in its work. This appendix also includes an outline of the methods used to prepare and revise successive drafts and finally to approve the text for publication in this initial English language edition.

The education programmes of the World Cancer Research Fund (WCRF) and its affiliated organisation the American Institute for Cancer Research (AICR) have until now been based on the interim dietary guidelines issued by the US National Academy of Sciences (NAS) in its report *Diet, Nutrition and Cancer* published in 1982. Soon after the foundation of WCRF in the UK in 1990, it became apparent that a new report was needed, with conclusions and recommendations based on the world literature to date, and with a global scope.

Such a report, drawing on the work of international agencies, such as the Food and Agriculture Organization of the United Nations, the World Health Organization and the International Agency for Research on Cancer, would not only be a new foundation for the programmes of WCRF nationally and internationally, but also be a resource for policy-makers and health professionals throughout the world concerned with prevention of cancer in the general context of public health policy.

Throughout the 1980s and into the 1990s, much new scientific research into the relationship between food, nutrition and cancer has been undertaken. In 1992, the Board and Directors of AICR and WCRF, advised by Professor Colin Campbell, decided to commission this report, and invited Professor John Potter to chair the expert panel to be given responsibility for the report. It was agreed that panel members should include scientists who, like Professor Campbell, had worked with the NAS on its 1982 report, or else on the 1989 NAS report *Diet and Health*, and also members of the World Health Organization study group responsible for the 1990 WHO report *Diet, Nutrition and the Prevention of Chronic Diseases*.

Consequently Professor Laurence Kolonel, a member of the 1982 and 1989 NAS committees; Dr Sushma Palmer, previously Director of the Food and Nutrition Board responsible for both NAS reports, and also a member of the WHO study group, Professor WPT James, chairman of the WHO study group, and Professors AJ McMichael and Anna Ferro-Luzzi, members of the WHO study group, were invited to join the panel.

It was also decided that the panel should include leading scientists from Africa, Latin America, China, India and Japan, who, like the panel members from Europe, North America and Australasia, collectively had special knowledge of nutrition, food science, cancer epidemiology and relevant biomedical sciences, disease prevention and control, as well as insight into the circumstances of regions and countries with particular patterns of diet and of cancer. Consequently Dr Festo Kavishe, Dr Adolfo Chavez, Dr Junshi Chen, Dr Kamala Krishnaswamy, Professor Tomio Hirohata and Professor Suminori Kono were invited to join the panel. In addition, Dr Fred Kadlubar, Dr Lionel Poirier and Professor Walter Willett joined the panel, bringing between them additional special knowledge of the cancer process, assessment of scientific evidence, and of experimental and epidemiological studies of diet and cancer.

Throughout 1993, the secretariat to the report prepared background documents as a resource for the panel. A database, eventually containing over 4,000 scientific papers on diet and cancer published in peer-reviewed journals mostly since the early 1980s, was accumulated by means of literature searches and extensive consultation with panel members and other research scientists in the field.

The collective formal business of the panel was conducted conventionally, by means of a series of seven 3-day meetings at which successive drafts of text and key issues were discussed. Between meetings, text was drafted, developed, reviewed and revised.

At the first meeting, held in Washington in January 1994, the panel agreed the terms of reference of the report, its structure, its format and the process outlined here. First drafts of chapters 1–3, and of chapter 4 on cancer sites and their relationship with food and nutrition, were commissioned from panel members, with support from some other contributors.

Other panel members and some external contributors were commissioned to act as second and sometimes third authors of drafts of text. Additionally, the panel invited other scientists from around the world to review individual chapters and sections of the report in third or subsequent draft stage. Comments were invited from at least three reviewers for every chapter and section.

A special feature of the second panel meeting, held in London, in May 1994, was a seminar on the public policy implications of dietary recommendations to reduce the risk of chronic diseases such as cancer. The seminar was designed to guide the panel in preparation and assessment of chapter 9. This meeting also discussed the general balance and structure of text prepared thus far, nominated representatives of relevant UN agencies to be invited to attend future meetings as observers, and also identified representatives of other international and national organisations to be invited to advise the panel. At the third panel meeting, also held in London, in October 1994, the panel agreed the criteria to be used in assessing the scientific evidence, as specified in chapter 3.5.

The fourth meeting, held in Mexico City in April 1995, agreed or confirmed the uniform approach of the literature reviews in chapter 4. A feature of this meeting was parallel sessions followed by plenary sessions in which the panel assessed the strength of the evidence suggesting causal relationships between aspects of diet and cancer of specific sites, as shown in the matrices that introduce each section of chapters 4–7. The relationship of chapter 4, on cancer sites, and chapters 5, 6 and 7, designed to include more interpretive material on dietary constituents, foods and drinks, and food processing, was confirmed. The secretariat was charged with preparing drafts of chapters 5, 6 and 7, guided by the panel as a whole and specific panel members.

First outline drafts of chapters 8 and 9, and the general principles governing dietary recommendations designed to prevent cancer, as published in chapter 8.2, were also discussed at this meeting. The meeting was immediately followed by a symposium on diet and cancer in Mexico and elsewhere in Meso-America which was attended by experts in medicine, disease prevention, nutrition and public health from the region.

The fifth meeting, held in Rome in January 1996, was attended by observers from the United Nations (UN) agencies, the World Health Organization (WHO), and the Food and Agriculture Organization (FAO). This meeting focused on further discussion of chapters 1–4, by then in drafts incorporating comments from external peer reviewers, and on discussion of initial drafts of chapters 5–7. At this and other meetings, the panel also devoted time to discussion of key issues, such as the relationship of dietary fat and body mass; the role of what may be called 'deficiency diets' in cancers of certain sites; the significance of intervention trials using supplements of dietary microconstituents and assessment of agricultural residues. The issue of the weight to be given to different types of epidemiological evidence, and to epidemiology relative to experimental science and to identified plausible biological pathways (mechanisms), was kept under constant review.

Much of the meeting held in London in July 1996 was devoted to detailed discussion of the dietary recommendations specified in chapter 8.1. Most of the rest of the meeting was taken up with discussion of chapters 8 and 9, and with brief reviews of chapters 1–7. Dose–response analyses set out in chapters 5–7, designed to inform the quantified dietary goals and advice in chapter 8.1, were presented. The discussion on the dietary recommendations and their policy implications was attended by the WHO and FAO observers and also by an observer from the US National Cancer Institute. After the London meeting, further drafts of chapters 5–9

were prepared, taking into account comments by panel members, peer reviewers, and observer and adviser organisations.

The final panel meeting was held in Washington in November 1996. Observers from FAO, WHO and IARC were present. At this meeting the recommendations made by the panel were finally agreed.

In parallel with this editorial work, in 1993, the WCRF and AICR executive staff set up a process by which decisions on publication and promotion of the report were agreed. It was proposed, and accepted by the panel, that: the report should be a substantial document; that its main readership should be policy-makers, including experts in government and industry, in medical, health, consumer and public interest organisations and in the community, as well as senior scientists and that the findings and recommendations of the report would indeed form the foundation of the educational programmes of WCRF and AICR.

In 1983, AICR reprinted and distributed 50,000 copies of the 1982 National Academy of Sciences report throughout the USA to key opinion formers, including leaders in the scientific, medical and general health professional community, thus making the evidence of the relationship between diet and cancer widely available. Correspondingly, WCRF and AICR decided not only to publish this first, English language edition of *Food, Nutrition and the Prevention of Cancer: A Global Perspective*, but also to print more than 30,000 copies and distribute these to policy makers mostly in the English-speaking world. This first edition was launched in October and November 1997, in New Delhi, Washington, London and Brussels.

Appendix C:
The World Cancer Research Fund and
The American Institute for Cancer Research

The World Cancer Research Fund (WCRF) and the American Institute for Cancer Research (AICR) are affiliate organisations that share a common vision to reduce suffering and deaths due to cancer worldwide. WCRF is based in Europe with offices in London and the Netherlands. AICR is based in Washington, DC and is the third largest cancer charity in the USA.

Food, Nutrition and the Prevention of Cancer: A Global Perspective is a joint project of WCRF and AICR. Funded by both organisations, staff from Europe and the USA worked collaboratively to initiate, progress and publish the report of the expert panel. The recommendations of this report form the revised and updated scientific foundation for the organisations' own science and education programmes.

This report springs from the commitment of WCRF and AICR to reduce the risk of cancer worldwide. It provides the foundation for a series of initiatives to promote its findings to the scientific and health communities and to the general public throughout the world, and to encourage policy-makers to frame legislation and other measures designed to reduce the risk of cancer by means of appropriate diets and lifestyles.

The mission of WCRF and AICR is to increase scientific knowledge about the role of nutrition in the prevention of cancer, and to raise awareness that the risk of cancer can be reduced through good nutrition. Extensive research and education programmes throughout the USA and Europe help to fulfil this mission. WCRF and AICR believe that a dual commitment to scientific research and to education is the key to reducing the incidence of cancer around the world.

AMERICAN INSTITUTE FOR CANCER RESEARCH

The American Institute for Cancer Research is the only major American cancer organisation focusing exclusively on diet, nutrition and cancer. Founded in 1983, AICR's original dietary guidelines were based on the report, *Diet, Nutrition and Cancer* (NAS, 1982). AICR was the first organisation to promote dietary guidelines to reduce the risk of cancer, and the first to make these guidelines accessible to the general public.

AICR's grant programme, which supports research at universities, hospitals and research centres throughout the USA and elsewhere, has grown to a total commitment of almost $40 million up to 1997. This funding has enabled 280 researchers to undertake 405 research projects in diet, nutrition and cancer at 161 institutions in 40 US states and six

other countries. AICR research grants are awarded under a peer-review programme modelled on that of the US National Institutes of Health. In addition, AICR holds an annual research conference which draws international attendance.

AICR's education programmes span a wide range of media audiences. The AICR quarterly newsletter provides research news, healthy eating menus and recipes, and a variety of health-related information. Each issue reaches almost 1.5 million households across the USA. AICR also produces more than 45 booklets and brochures, with more than 12 million copies distributed nationwide.

Weekly newspaper health and nutrition columns produced by AICR are syndicated to more than 750 newspapers throughout the USA, and AICR provides educational public service advertising that has been aired on hundreds of television and radio stations. The Institute maintains a US-wide Nutrition Hotline in which Registered Dietitians provide consumers with personal answers to nutrition and health questions. AICR conducts a series of live seminars on reducing the risk of cancer in cities across the USA.

AICR's most recent education programmes have included the development of a web site (http://www.aicr.org). A new publication programme, *Cancer Resource*, provides information on a wide variety of resources for cancer patients, as well as descriptions of currently available cancer treatment protocols for those facing breast, lung, colon or prostate cancer.

AICR is a non-profit organisation whose programmes in cancer research and education have been made possible by the donations and support of more than 7 million Americans.

WORLD CANCER RESEARCH FUND

WCRF, founded in 1990, is the first international organisation to focus solely on the prevention of cancer through appropriate diets and lifestyles.

WCRF's research programme has grown to a commitment of almost £4 million up to 1997. The research grant programme has enabled 21 researchers to undertake over 30 research projects in the United Kingdom. All grant applications undergo peer review, overseen by a panel of leading scientists with a broad range of research experience. WCRF also funds the UK Women's Diet and Lifestyle Survey, a 10-year cohort study directed and managed by a team of research scientists, which explores the relationships between diet and cancer incidence and mortality.

WCRF's quarterly newsletter is sent to over 250,000

households in the UK and a Dutch language version to 40,000 in the Netherlands. A wide range of booklets, leaflets and health aids have been published in English and Dutch. These focus on a number of specific issues: dietary guidelines to reduce the risk of cancer, specific cancers (for example, breast and prostate), and nutritional needs for different stages of life (pregnancy, older age). These are widely distributed throughout the UK and the Netherlands. WCRF's policy is to provide clear statements on complex issues such as pesticides and the use of dietary supplements; to meet this need, fact sheets are produced for the general public.

WCRF maintains regular programmes for health professionals. Specialised leaflets on reducing cancer risk are distributed to over 4,000 UK general practitioners' surgeries and to over 1,000 physiotherapists' practices in the Netherlands. More than 15,000 dietitians, primary care practitioners and health workers in the UK, the Netherlands and other European countries are sent *Science News*, a quarterly digest of information on food, nutrition and cancer. WCRF's most recent programme, the Health Advisory Service, aims to take the prevention message into the heart of the community. Front-line health professionals (practice nurses and health visitors) are educated about nutrition and cancer and trained to deliver effective programmes in their communities.

WCRF works with schools to help children develop an interest in appropriate diets and lifestyles, and participates in a national programme which promotes study cards that meet curriculum standards to over 30,000 schools in the United Kingdom. In addition, a bi-annual newsletter, *The Great Grub Club*, develops these messages in a fun style for children and is offered as a free item through the quarterly newsletter.

WCRF is a registered charity and relies solely on donations from over 350,000 supporters in the UK and the Netherlands to fulfil its mission.

Glossary

10-formyltetrahydrofolate and 5-methyltetrahydrofolate: intermediate products in **folate** metabolism.

Abdominal adiposity: a measure of obesity in the abdominal or central part of the body. Part of the normal human variation in the distribution of body fat and one of the determinants of the **Waist-to-hip ratio.**

Absorbability: the degree to which a substance can be absorbed by the body after ingestion.

Acetylator: a molecule capable of introducing an acetyl group into an organic compound.

Acute effects: used in toxicology to refer to severe effects lasting for a short period of time.

Additives: chemicals added to a substance to improve or modify its characteristics. Typical examples are food additives such as emulsifiers, preservatives, artificial colours and flavours.

Adducts: the products of a chemical reaction in which a chemical compound or group is added to another compound. An important example involves the DNA adducts formed by the reaction of a chemical carcinogen with DNA, one of the early steps in the process of **Mutagenesis** and **Carcinogenesis.**

Adenomatous polyp: a precancerous lesion, particularly in the colon and rectum.

Adipose: related to fat tissue.

Aerodigestive cancer: cancer of the upper digestive and respiratory tracts.

Aetiology: The pattern of causes of a particular disease.

Aflatoxins: Toxic substances found in legumes and grains contaminated by the fungus *Aspergillus flavus*, as a consequence of warm and humid storage conditions. One subset of **Mycotoxins** which are caused by fungal contamination.

Age-specific death rate: the number of deaths, usually expressed per 100,000, in a defined period of time within a specific age-range.

Age-standardised death rate: the number of deaths, usually expressed per 100,000, over a defined period of time, taking account of the fact that the proportion of people in each age-group varies from country to country and over time. Allows for meaningful and useful comparisons of disease rates between countries with different age structures. Computed using **Age-specific death rates** and a standard set of weights.

Alpha-carotene: See **Carotenoids**.

Alpha-tocopherol: (α-tocopherol) the most common form of vitamin E.

Ames test: a test for mutagenicity of chemical compounds that uses special strains of the bacterium S*almonella typhimurium*. About 90-95% of demonstrated mutagens are also carcinogenic.

Androstenedione: A sex steroid hormone with masculinising activity.

Angiosarcoma: rare malignant tumour caused by the proliferation of endothelial and fibroblastic tissue in the blood vessels.

Antioxidants: substances capabls of protecting cell membranes and **Macromolecules** including lipids, DNA and RNA from the damage caused by oxidative reactions. Protective effects by these compounds against **Carcinogenesis** have been shown in experimental animals. Some **Vitamins, Phytochemicals** and food preservatives have antioxidant properties.

Apoptosis: a genetically controlled mechanism of cell death that is important in fetal development and may be important in protecting tissue and organs against cancer.

Aquaculture: farming of aquatic organisms such as fish, crustaceans or mussels.

Average life expectancy: number of years, based on population statistics, that a person may expect to live.

Basal metabolic rate: the amount of calories/hour/m^2 of body surface required to maintain the essential body functions in absolute resting and fasting conditions.

Beri-beri: a disease caused by thiamin deficiency.

Beta-carotene: see **Carotenoids.**

Bioactive compounds: constituents, particularly of vegetables, fruit and other plant foods, that are biologically active; these include vitamins, minerals and compounds collectively referred to as phytochemicals; may have anticarcinogenic, antioxidant, etc. properties.

Biomarkers: or biological markers, are molecular, biochemical, physiological changes that can be used as measures of susceptibility, as measures of exposure to dietary and environmental affects, as measures of ear]y pathological changes and as surrogates for screening and diagnosing disease.

Biomass: in ecology, all the living things, animal and vegetable, in a certain region.

Blind study: a study in which the subjects do not know whether they belong to the control group or to the group receiving treatment.

BMR: Basal metabolic rate.

Body mass index: body weight expressed in kilograms relative to the square of height expressed in metres (BMI=wt/ht^2). It is also called Quetelet's index.

BRCA- 1 gene: inherited mutations in this gene markedly increase the risk of breast and ovarian cancers in a small number of families.

BRCA-2 gene: like **BRCA- 1,** this gene, when inherited in a mutated form, is a cause of familial breast and ovarian cancer.

Broiling: see **Grilling.**

Caffeine: one of the xanthines soluble in water and alcohol, and obtainable from coffee, tea and maté. Caffeine stimulates the central nervous system, has a diuretic effect on the kidneys; stimulates striated muscle; and has a variety of effects on the cardiovascular system

Calcium: an essential mineral. A key constituent of bone; central to a very large number of biochemical pathways in the body.

Calorie: a measure of energy. Used to measure both dietary intake and physical activity. See also **Joule.**

Calorimetry: the measurement of the amount of energy produced or absorbed. Can be used to measure the energy content of food or the **Basal metabolic rate** of an animal or human.

Cancer risk: the probability of developing cancer during a stated period of time or as a consequence of a particular exposure or gene.

Carbohydrates: chemicals composed of carbon, hydrogen and oxygen. Key structural (e.g. fibre), energy storage (e.g. starch), and fuel (sugar) compounds in foods and living organisms.

Carcinogen: any cancer-producing substance: usually used to describe compounds that react directly with **DNA** and alter its structure.

Carcinogenesis: the multistep process of developing cancer.

Carcinoma: malignant tumour derived from epithelial cells, with the ability to spread into the surrounding tissue (**Invasion**) and produce secondary tumours (**Metastases**).

Carcinoma in situ: a neoplastic entity where the tumour cells are confined to the epithelium of origin, without invasion through into the basement membrane.

Carotenoids: pigments widespread in plants. Those found in vegetables and fruit include α-carotene, β-carotene, lycopene, cryptoxanthin and lutein which have important biological effects including antioxidant properties and, in some cases, the ability to be convened to retinol (**vitamin A**).

Case-control study: an epidemiological study in which a group of, say, cancer patients (cases) is compared to a similar but cancer-free population (controls) to help establish whether the past or recent history of a specific exposure such as smoking, alcohol consumption and dietary intake, etc. are causally related to the risk of disease.

Cell proliferation: increase in the number of cells, through the process of cell division. In some cases, uncontrolled proliferation can lead to cancer development.

Cellulose: a major non-digestible structural constituent of plants.

Cereals: Edible seeds of grain plants such as rice, wheat, maize, millet, sorghum, barley, oats and rye.

Cervical dysplasia: precancerous condition of the cervix (neck of the uterus).

Chemopreventive agents: chemical substances which inhibit or prevent the development of cancer. Certain vitamins and other constituents of fruit and vegetables have been shown to have chemopreventive properties.

Cholesterol: a molecule found in all animal tissues. It is an essential molecule in the biosynthesis of steroid hormones. Blood levels of cholesterol are often elevated (a risk factor for **Coronary heart disease**)in the presence of a high-fat diet.

Choline: basic constituent of lecithin. One of a group of compounds called methyl donors or **Lipotropes**.

Chronic disease: a disease that persists over a long period of time. Used to describe diseases such as cancer, cardiovascular disease and diabetes, but also applies to some infectious diseases such as tuberculosis.

Cirrhosis: disease of the liver characterised by chronic destruction of the normal structure of the organ. Prolonged high alcohol consumption is a common cause of liver cirrhosis.

Cohort study: follow-up study of a (usually large) group of people, initially disease-free. Differences in disease incidence within the cohort are calculated in relation to different levels of exposure to specific factors, e.g., smoking, alcohol consumption, diet and exercise, that were measured at the start of the study and, sometimes, at later times during the study.

Complex carbohydrate: large, structural and energy storage compounds made up of simple sugars.

Confounding variable: a variable that, within a specific epidemiological study, is associated both with the disease of interest and with the exposure of interest, thus distorting the relationship. An example is that age is related both to smoking history and to risk of lung cancer and thus must be accounted for (controlled) in studies of smoking as a cause of lung cancer.

Contaminants: substances or organisms that are found in food but which are neither natural constituents of the food nor deliberately added in processing.

Control group: the population in an epidemiological study or clinical trial who do not have the disease of interest or do not undergo the treatment being tested.

Controlled trial: a study in which a comparison is made between one treatment/prevention strategy and another. Sometimes one group receives an inactive agent: a placebo. Groups are usually randomised to one condition or the other. Both investigators and subjects usually do not know to which condition they have been randomised; this is called 'blinding'.

Coronary artery disease: a disease in which the blood vessels supplying the heart muscle itself become increasingly blocked by atherosclerotic plaque (fatty deposits). This is a major cause of disease and death in populations that consume high-fat diets and take little exercise. Also called coronary heart disease.

Correlation study: see **Ecological study**.

Cross-sectional study: a study that examines the relationship between diseases (or other health-related characteristics) and other variables of interest (e.g., age, smoking habits, exercise) as they exist in a defined population at one particular time.

Cryptoxanthin: see **Carotenoids**.

Dairy products: food products derived from milk.

Deficiency diets: diets, usually associated with extreme poverty that are characterised by the consumption, primarily, of a single staple, a low intake of foods rich in microconstituents, and generally a very restricted range of foods. (see Box 5.2.2)

Deficiency disease: any condition such as beri beri or scurvy, produced by a lack of **Vitamins** or other essential substances.

Dehydroascorbic acid: oxidised form of ascorbic acid, which has the same **Vitamin C** activity as ascorbic acid when reduced.

Demographic transition:the phenomenon of urbanisation whereby people move away from rural areas into cities, notably within Africa, Latin America and Asia. See also **Nutrition transition**, **Epidemiological transition**.

Dietary constituents: used in this report to describe all the components of the diet – macronutrients, micronutrients, **Phytochemicals**, etc.

Dietary fibre: fibrous substance in cereals, fruits, vegetables, seeds, etc. such as the structural polymers of cell walls: some fibres are fermented by bacteria in the colon.

Dietary supplements: these constitute a heterogeneous group of products which, as far as the consumer is concerned, fall at the boundary between foods and medicines. Include nutritional supplements, multivitamins, etc.

Dimethylhydrazine: used as a carcinogen in animal experiments.

Disaccharides: any of a class of sugars composed of two linked monosaccharides; most commonly used **Sucrose** and **Lactose.**

DNA: deoxyribonucleic acid: the carrier of genetic information; the nucleic acid in which the sugar is deoxyribose, with side chains composed of **Purine** (adenine, guanine) and **Pyrimidine** (cytosine, thymine) bases attached to the sugars. In double-stranded DNA, adenine forms two hydrogen bonds with thymine; and cytosine forms three with guanine; these are complimentary base pairs. The strands are twisted to form a double helix. DNA is duplicated by replication, and serves as a template for synthesis of ribonucleic acid (transcription).

DNA methylation: the addition of methyl groups to DNA; the process is found in many different gene types: in bacteria, viruses, fungi, vertebrates, and plants. It is involved in the protection of DNA against restriction enzymes, X-chromosome inactivation, imprinting, changes in DNA and chromatin structure, changes in the interaction of proteins with DNA, silencing viruses, and in embryogenesis and cancer.

Dose–response curve: graphical representation of the effects of a food, drug, chemical etc. The effect is plotted on the y-axis and the dose on the x-axis.

Double-blind study: see **Controlled trial.**

Ecological study: a study in which broad, between-population differences in patterns of exposure to a particular agent or consumption of a particular nutrient or food are compared with the population incidence rates of the disease of interest.

Epidemiological transition: the phenomenon whereby the nutrition transition and the demographic transition are followed by changes in the patterns of disease, a rise in chronic diseases, including cancers – particularly associated with an urban/industrial lifestyle, obesity, and coronary heart disease.

Exposure data: information, collected in epidemiological studies, on factors, including diet, alcohol, exercise, and occupation, to which the individual may have been exposed and which are of interest as possible causes or **Confounding factors.**

Exposure factors: the factors or conditions to which a population may have been subjected or exposed that may increase or decrease risk of disease.

False-positive results: outcome in a screening test (whether screening individuals for cancer e.g., mammography for breast cancer, or compounds for their carcinogenicity) where the initial screening test suggests a positive result (that is, there appears to be cancer present or the compound appears to be carcinogenic) but where the definitive test is negative (no cancer present or compound does not cause cancer).

False-negative result: outcome in a screening test where the initial screening test is negative but where, ultimately, the individual is found to have cancer. False-negative results are the ones most to be guarded against in screening because the individual is inappropriately reassured by the screening test and may ultimately have a cancer that is detected very late.

Familial adenomatous polyposis: growth of multiple precancerous polyps over the mucosa of the colon and occurring in several members of the same family. A dominantly inherited disorder characterised by the presence of a **Germline mutation** in the gene **APC,** found on the long arm of chromosome 5.

Fats or lipids: water-insoluble organic molecules with specific crucial functions in the cell, for example, as structural components of membranes and energy stores.

Fatty acids: long-chain molecules that combine to make **Fats** or **Lipids.**

Folate: an essential vitamin involved in a variety of crucial biochemical functions including growth and development, and the integrity of **DNA**.

Food balance sheets: provide a gross overall picture of food disappearance at country level; reasonable indicators of the consumption of foods; prepared by the FAO from data from individual countries.

Food processing: the conversion of primary products into foods. Includes milling of grains, removal of toxic compounds, preserving, adding of flavours or colours, freezing, cooking, etc. Can be done to improve edibility, to enhance shelf-life or to make products with higher profit-margins than the primary product. A domestic or manufacturing procedure.

Food-frequency questionnaire: questionnaire which includes a list of foods and a section to indicate how often each food is eaten. Sometimes includes questions on serving-size, on variation by season, etc. The food list is usually 50 –150 foods and is designed to cover the large majority of foods eaten in the population being studied. Used extensively in **Cohort** and **Case-control** studies of diet and cancer.

Foods of plant origin: foods derived from plants, such as fruit, vegetables, pulses, cereals, nuts and seeds.

Forage: feed for domesticated meat and dairy animals – largely grasses and cereals as consumed by free-ranging animals.

Free radicals: highly reactive, short-lived molecules which are thought to be involved in the process of carcinogenesis by reacting with cell constituents, particularly with **DNA**. Includes oxygen-containing molecules. Able to form **Adducts.**

Frying: cooking in fat heated to high temperatures. This process generates compounds that are mutagenic and carcinogenic.

Fructo-oligosaccharides: a sugar containing from two to ten units of the simple sugar, fructose.

Fructose: a simple sugar found in a large number of fruits as well as in honey.

Fungal contamination: food deterioration caused by moulds or fungi. Occurs in grains and legumes stored in warm and humid conditions. A major problem in the developing world. See **Aflatoxins** and **Mycotoxins.**

Galactose: simple sugar that, together with glucose, makes up the milk sugar, lactose.

Gallstones: concretions of organic material formed in the gallbladder or in the bile duct. In the developing world, these are comprised predominantly of bile pigments and may be related to recurrent infection. In the developed world, they are predominantly composed of cho]esterol and are associated with obesity.

Gamma- tocopherol: a form of vitamin E.

General Agreement on Tariffs and Trade (GATT): an international organisation comprising approximately 90 countries with the aim of promoting multilateral economic exchanges.

Genetic mutation: a change in the genetic material, i.e., in the basic structure of the DNA of a cell. Mutations can occur in the germline, ie., be present at birth and found in all cells, or can occur after birth in one or a few cells – somatic mutation. See **Germline, Mutation** and **Somatic mutation.**

Genetic susceptibility: an inherited predisposition to a disease, especially cancer. Used particularly to describe predispositions that are higher than the background risk in the population. Can apply to the likelihood of higher risk in the presence of specific exposures. See **Metabolic enzymes.**

Genome: the complete genetic material – both coding regions (exons) and non-coding regions (introns) of the **DNA** of an individual cell or organism.

Germline mutation: a change in the basic coding sequence of **DNA** that is inherited in all cells. Can be associated with an inherited disease (e.g., Huntington's chorea) including rather rare forms of cancer (e.g.,breast cancer occurring in

women that carry abnormal forms of the *BRAC-1* and *BRAC-2* genes).

Glucose: a simple sugar. The main source of energy for most living organisms.

Gluteal adiposity: accumulation of fat around the buttocks. Part of the normal human variation in the distribution of body fat and one of the determinants of the **Waist -to- hip ratio.**

Glycine: a non-essential amino acid – one of the building blocks of **Protein.**

Glycosylation: the addition of a simple sugar group to another molecule.

Grilling: cooking at high temperatures under or over a naked flame or other heat source . A common way of preparing meat without added fat. Usually, the intrinsic fat is allowed to drain off. The more usual term in the USA is broiling.

Group1 carcinogens: chemicals or industrial processes classified as 'carcinogenic to humans' by the International Agency for Research on Cancer.

Group 2a carcinogens: chemicals or industrial processes classified as 'probably carcinogenic to humans' by the International Agency for Research on Cancer.

Group 2b carcinogens: chemicals or industrial processes classified as 'possibly carcinogenic to humans' by the International Agency for Research on Cancer.

Group 3 carcinogens: chemicals or industrial process classified as 'unclassifiable as to carcinogenicity in humans' by the International Agency for Research on Cancer.

Gums: mucilagenous substances excreted by various plants. One of the components of dietary fibre. Can be used as food additives.

Helicobacter pylori: a bacterium which can infect the stomach. It has been recently identified as one of the possible causes of stomach cancer. It is the known cause of peptic ulcers.

Hemicellulose: complex carbohydrate found in the cell walls of plants and seaweeds. One of the components of dietary fibre.

Hepatitis B virus (HBV): cause of serious viral infection of the liver. Transmitted via body fluids, especially blood. A common infection in the developing world and the major known cause of primary liver cancer.

Hepatitis C virus (HBC): cause of serious viral infection of the liver. Transmitted via body fluids, especially blood. Recently recognised as an RNA virus involved in the development of liver cancer.

Heterocyclic amines: a family of mutagenic compounds formed from protein and sugars in meat, chicken and fish cooked at very high temperatures , i.e., by **Grilling (broiling)** or **Frying.**

Heterogeneous populations: groups of individuals with non-uniform characteristics, for example different ethnic origins, different dietary habits, different cultures.

High body mass: a general term for **Obesity**. See **Body mass index.**

High performance liquid chromatography (HPLC): an analytical technique which allows the separation, identification and quantitative measurement of different components of similar nature in a biological sample.

Hormone-related cancers: cancers whose risk is partly determined by endogenous hormones, such as oestrogens. Used to describe, collectively, breast, ovarian and endometrial (but usually not cervical) cancer in women, and prostate and testicular cancer in men.

Human papillomaviruses (HPV): a family of viruses involved in the causation particularly of cervical and anal cancers in humans.

Hydrocarbons: organic compounds containing on]y hydrogen and carbon. The simplest is methane (CH_4).

Hydrogenation: the addition of hydrogen across a double (or triple) carbon-to-carbon bond to produce an increasingly saturated compound; paiticularly in the manufacture of margarines etc.

Hydroxylation: a chemical reaction in which a hydroxyl group (-OH) is added to an organic compound. One of the key solubilising steps in the metabolism of ingested compounds. Also occurs to key **Macromolecules** as a result of oxygen **Free radicals**. Also see **Adducts.**

Hypermethylation: the (inappropriate) silencing of specific genes by DNA **Methylation.**

Hypertension: high blood pressure. A risk factor for **Coronary artery disease** and **Stroke**. Obese individuals are at higher risk.

Hypomethylation: of DNA is a nongenotoxic mechanism underlying the aberrant expression of oncogenes and other genes involved in carcinogenesis. (see **DNA methylation**).

In vitro study: a study performed outside of a living organism but using material derived from living organisms.

Incidence rate: the number of new cases of a certain disease appearing during a certain period of time expressed relative to the size of the population, e.g., 60 new cases of breast cancer per 100,000 women per year.

Infectious diseases: diseases caused by exposure to microscopic living organisms (e.g., viruses, bacteria) often transmitted from one individual to another or from one species to another (zoonoses).

Initiation: the early stgage of **Carcinogenesis** involving the alteration in the genetic make-up of a cell; in experimental systems using cells, the cell may later become neoplastic upon repeated exposure to the same carcinogen or by exposure to a promotor, but the process in the living organism is not as well defined.

Intervention study: see **Controlled trial.**

Intervention trial: see **Controlled trial.**

Intraepithelial neoplasia: a very early stage of cancer involving abnormal proliferation of cells which does not extend beyond the first barrier of the epithelium, namely the basement membrane – also called **Carcinoma in situ.**

Invasion: the spread of a primary cancer into surrounding tissues**.**

Iodine: an element in the same family as chlorine and fluorine. Essential to human growth and development. Intrinsic to the structure of the thyroid hormones.

Iron: an essential nutrient and a constituent of haemoglobin. Essential in the transport of oxygen to the cells of the organism. Widespread in foods both of animal (e.g., meat) and vegetable (e.g., green leafy vegetables) origin.

Irrigation: a method used in agriculture to bring water to plants. Can involve simple structures, e.g., ditches from local surface water, to very complex engineering schemes.

IU or **International Units:** units used to measure the activity of vitamins.

Joule (J): unit of measurement of energy – particularly energy supplied by food or expended during exercise.

Kilocalorie (kcal): unit of measurement of energy see **Joule.**
Kilojoule (kJ): 1000 joules.

L-ascorbic acid: chemical name for one form of **Vitamin C.**
Lactose: a sugar found in milk, comprised of the simple sugars, **Glucose** and **Galactose.**
Latency: used to describe the period of time between the beginning of a chronic disease process and its detection or clinical presentation.
Legumes: also known as pulses. This term includes beans, chickpeas, lentils and soya beans. Important sources of energy, protein and bioactive compounds.
Leucocyte: white blood cell.
Life expectancy: see **Average life expectancy.**
Lipotropes: compounds involved in the transport of methyl groups. Important in the structure and function of **DNA,** cell membranes and lipids. Include methionine, choline, folate and vitamin B_{12}. Also called methyl donors.
Lutein: a **Carotenoid** found particularly in leafy green vegetables.
Lycopene: a **Carotenoid** found particularly in tomatoes.

Macroconstituents: used in this report to refer to the components of the diet that provide the majority of the energy in the diet, e.g., carbohydrates, fats, and protein; and volume of the diet, e.g .fibre.
Macromolecules: large complex organic molecules. Usually refers to vital molecules such as **Proteins** (e.g., haemoglobin), **DNA** and **RNA.**
Malnutrition – infection complex: the combination of recurrent infection and malnutrition that impairs growth and development of infants and children; a major problem in the developing world.
Menarche: in adolescent girls, the onset or beginning of cyclic menstruation.
Menopause: cessation of menstruation usually around the age of 50.
Mesothielioma: a tumour derived from mesothelial tissue (peritoneum, pleura, pericardium). The malignant variety is usually the result of exposure to asbestos.
Metabolic enzymes: normal proteins that allow the body to metabolise (make use of or eliminate) ingested (or inhaled) compounds. Some of these are genetically variable (enzyme present versus absent; enzyme more efficient versus less efficient) and can partially determine whether exposures to particular compounds (in food, in

tobacco smoke, in the workplace, etc) increase the risk of cancer in an individual. See **Genetic susceptibility.**
Meta-analysis: the process of using statistical methods to combine the results of different studies.
Metastasis (plural: metastases): the spread of cancer to other tissues.
Methionlne: naturally occuring amino acid that is an essential component of the diet, furnishing both methyl groups and sulphur necessary for normal metabolism. See **Lipotropes.**
Migrant study: studies taking advantage of migration to one country by those from other countries with different environments and cultural backgrounds. Comparisons are made between the mortality and morbidity experience of the migrant groups with that of their current country of residence and their country of origin.
Minerals: the inorganic nutrients required for the structural composition of hard and soft body tissue and that participate in various essential biological functions. Minerals in the body are either major elements or trace elements. The major elements are calcium, phosphorus, magnesium, iron, sodium and potassium. The trace elements include copper, iodine, zinc, and selenium.
Molecular epidemiology: the use in epidemiological studies of techniques of molecular biology. See **Biomarkers**
Monosaccharides: simple sugars, includes **Glucose, Fructose, Galactose.**
Monotonous: in a dietary context, refers to an unvaried diet, particularly one that may lack specific nutrients and micronutrients.
Monounsaturated: of a chemical compound, containing one double (or triple) bond; used particularly of fatty acids, such as oleic acid.
Morbidity: the WHO Expert Committee on Health Statistics noted in its sixth report (1959) that morbidity could be measured in terms of three units: (1) persons who were ill; (2) the illnesses (periods or spells of illness) that these persons experienced; and (3) the duration (days, weeks etc) of these illnesses.
Mortality: the number of deaths within a population (see **Mortality rate).**
Mortality rate: an estimate of the proportion of a population that dies during a specitied period. The numerator is the number of persons dying during the period; the denominator is the number in the population.
Mutagenic compounds: compounds capable of inducing genetic mutations.
Mycotoxins: toxic compounds produced in food as a result of fungal contamination.

N-3 fatty acids: also called omega-3 fatty acids. A subset of unsaturated fatty acids, particularly found in cold-water fish.
NAS: National Academy of Sciences.
Neoplasm: see **Tumour; Carcinogenesis; Carcinoma** in which the growth is uncontrolled and progressive. Malignant neoplasms are distinguished from benign in that the former show a greater degree of anaplasia.
Nested case-control study: a case-control study

in which cases and controls are drawn from the population of a **cohort study;** often used for studies of prospectively collected biological samples.
Niacin: nicotinic acid: a B- complex vitamin.
Nitrite: any salt or ester of nitric acid; used as food preservatives.
Nitrosamines: any of a group of *N*-nitroso deriivitives of secondary amines (R_2-N-NO), formed by the combining of nitrites with amines; some nitrosamines are carcinogens.
Non-domesticated animals: wild animals hunted for food.
Non-starch polysaccharides (NSP): the principal and readily measurable component of dietary fibre. **NSP**s escape digestion in the small intestine and become available as fermentable substances for the colonic microflora.
Nutrition transition: the phenomenon whereby the demographic transition is followed by changes in dietary patterns, as people moving into cities become sedentary and shift to diets that are increasingly composed of processed and manufactured food.

Obesity: an increase in body weight beyond the limitation of skeletal and physical requirement, as the result of an excessive accumulation of fat in the body. A person is obese if he or she has a BMI > 30 kg/m^2.
Observational study: epidemiological study that does not involve any intervention, experimental or otherwise; includes case-control and cohort study designs.
Occupational carcinogens: cancer- causing substances found in the workplace.
Odds ratio: used as the outcome measure in case-control studies. Provides a very good approximation of the **Relative risk** of, say, cancer associated with exposure to the diet, behaviour, carcinogens etc., of interest.
Oestradiol: the most potent naturally occurring oestrogen (female sex hormone) in mammals.
Oligosaccharides: a **Carbohydrate** which is composed of from two to ten monosaccharides.
Oncogene: a gene capable, under certain conditions, of causing the initial and continuing conversion of normal cells into cancer cells. (see chapter 2)
Osteoporosis: a reduction in the amount of bone mass; a major cause of fractures and disability particularly in older women.
Overnutrition: consumption of more food than necessary to maintain health and weight.

Pandemic: an epidemic occurring over a very wide area, crossing intemational boundaries and usually affecting a large number of people.
Pathogenesis: the whole of a disease process and its pattern of causes from early to late stage.
Pectin: constituent of dietary fibre that forms gels.
Pellagra: a clinical syndrome caused by dietary deficiency of niacin and characterised by dermatitis, inflammation of mucous membranes, diarrhoea and psychotic episodes.
Physical activity level (PAL): Energy expenditure expressed as a function of **Basal**

metabolic rate (BMR); this is a useful measure of physical activity that can be universally compared.

Physiological requirement: minimal requirement of a nutrient for normal function.

Phyto-oestrogen: can be loosely defined as any plant-derived compound that can regulate gene expression in a manner comparable (or antagonistic) to 17 β-oestradiol, as a result of direct binding to an oestrogen receptor (er). Include lignans, derived from grains and berries and isoflavones from soya.

Plant-based diets: diets consumed in many parts of the world and recommended by this report – where the major focus is on a variety of foods of plant origin: cereals, vegetables, fruits, other starchy staples, nuts and seeds.

Polycyclic aromatic hydrocarbons: a family of **Hydrocarbons** that include cyclic structures and double bonds; includes known carcinogens.

Polymorphism: one of the varying forms of a gene; particularly important in the variation of cancer risk associated with different forms of **Metabolising enzymes.**

Polysaccharides: a carbohydrate made up of a large number of **Monosaccharides.**

Population: all the inhabitants of a given country or area considered together; also the group of people in a study.

Population attributable risk (PAR): the incidence of a disease in a population that is associated with (attributable to) exposure to a particular risk factor. It is often expressed as a percentage.

Potassium: potassium is the chief cation of muscle and most other cells (intracellular fluid); essential in electrolyte balance and cell osmolarity and function (e.g. nerve conduction).

Poultry: domestic fowls as a source of food.

Pre-cancerous state: early, usually reversible stage in the development of carcinoma.

Precursor lesion: an identifiable **Pre-cancerous state** used as an endpoint in clinical and epidemiological studies (examples include **Adenomatous polyps, Cervical intraepithelial neoplasia, etc).**

Prevalence rate: the number of existing cases of a given disease or other condition, at a designated point in time. Usually expressed per 100,000 population.

Procarcinogen: a chemical substance that becomes an active carcinogen only after it is altered by the body's metabolic processes.

Prospective study: see **Cohort study.**

Protective association: used in this report to identify a relationship between an exposure and disease in which higher levels of exposure are associated with a lower risk.

Protein: any of a group of complex organic compounds which contain carbon, hydrogen, oxygen, nitrogen and usually sulphur, the characteristic element being nitrogen; widely distributed in plants and animals. Proteins are of high molecular weight and consist of combinations of amino acids. Twenty different amino acids are commonly found in proteins, and each protein has a unique, genetically defined amino acid sequence, which determines its specific shape and function. They serve as enzymes,

structural elements, hormones, immunoglobulins etc., and are involved in oxygen transport, muscle contraction, electron transport, photosynthesis etc.

Protein–energy malnutrition: the shortage of both protein and total amount of food that is a major cause of mortality in infants in the developing world.

Pulses: see **Legumes.**

Purines: a group of compounds that include adenine and guanine, major components of DNA and **RNA.**

Pyrimidines: organic compounds that include major components of **DNA** and **RNA:** uracil, thymine and cytosine.

Quantiles: generic name for equal divisions of an exposure distribution – see **Tertiles, Quartiles, Quintiles**

Quetelet's index: see **Body mass index.**

Quintiles: five equal divisions of an exposure distribution – used extensively in epidemiological studies of diet.

Randomised control trial: see **Controlled trial.**

Recommended daily allowances (RDA): average daily intake of a nutrient, specified at levels appropriate to maintain good health.

Related factors: used in this report to describe factors related to diet, particularly obesity and physical activity.

Relative body weight (RBW): a measure of obesity, weight divided by height.

Relative risk: the ratio of the rate of disease or death among the exposed to the rate among the unexposed. Used as an outcome measure in **Cohort studies.** See **Odds ratio.**

Resistant starch (RS): the starch that resists digestion in the small intestine and therefore becomes available for fermentation in the large intestine in a manner analogous to dietary fibre; may be found in whole or partly-milled grains and seeds and in some very dense types of processed starchy foods.

Retinol equivalents: a measure of the intake of specific **Carotenoids** that derives from their **Vitamin A** activity.

Riboflavin: a B vitamin involved in oxidation–reduction reactions that are key to many metabolic pathways.

Risk factor: an aspect of personal behaviour or life-style, an environmental exposure, or an inborn or inherited characteristic, which on the basis of epidemiological evidence is known to be associated with a specific disease.

Saturated fats: fats made up of fatty acids without double bonds.

Selenium: an essential mineral, being a constituent of the enzyme glutathione peroxidase, and believed to be closely associated with vitamin E in its functions. Plant-food content is dependent on concentration in soil.

Servings: a portion or helping of food or drink - often specified in questionnaires used in epidemiological studies.

Sodium: the chief cation of the extracellular body fluids. Essential in cell function and osmolarity.

Somatic mutation: a change in the base coding sequence of **DNA** that occurs in one or just a few cells. If this mutation gives a growth or survival advantage to the cell (e.g., if it involves an oncogene, a tumour-suppressor gene, a DNA-mismatch repair gene, etc), such mutations can be an early step in the cancer process.

Staple: a major source of dietary energy, (usually starch) e.g. cereals.

Starch: composed of glucose units, occur widely in plant tissues in the form of storage granules.

Starchy staples: see **Staple.**

Sucrose: disaccharide (sugar) commonly used in the home: made up of **Fructose** and **Glucose.**

Supplements: additions designed to make up for a deficiency; can signify fortification of foods with vitamins or minerals; used to describe vitamins etc taken as pills (see **Dietary supplements).**

Tertiles: three equal divisions of an exposure distribution – used extensively in epidemiologcical studies of diet.

Thiamine: a B vitamin B central to **Carbohydrate** metabolism; deficiency leads to nervous system disorders and to the disease **Beri beri.**

Time-trend data: data on diseases, e.g. cancer, or exposures, e.g. diet, that show changes across time. (see chapter 1)

Tocopherol: any of a group of fat-soluble compounds with vitamin E activity that occur in wheatgerm oil, watercress, lettuce, egg yolks etc. (see **Alpha tocopherol**)

Tocotrienols: any of a series of structurally similar compounds derived from tocol, at Least some of which have biological vitamin e activity.

Total energy intake: the total number of calories consumed in a given time period.

Tumorigenesis: the whole process of the development of a **Tumour.**

Tumour: a new growth of tissue in which the multiplication of cells is uncontrolled and progressive; malignant tumours are called cancers.

Tumour progression: late stage of tumorigenesis (see chapter 2).

Tumour promotion: middle stage – clonal expansion of malignant cells – of **tumorigenesis** (see chapter 2).

Tumour-suppressor gene: gene involved in the control of cancer at the cellular level. Losses of tumour suppressor genes are key steps in carcinogenesis (see chapter 2).

Vegan: person who refrains from using any animal product, particularly as foods.

Vegetarian: person who eats no meat or fish; may eat eggs or dairy products.

Vitamin A: retinol or any of several realted fat-soluble compounds having similar biological activity; the vitamin acts in numerous capacities, particularly in the functioning of the retina, the growth of the bone, reproduction and immune response. Found in animal foods. Other major dietary sources are the provitamin A carotenoids found in plants. Deficiency is a major problem in the developing world.

Vitamin C: ascorbic acid, a water-soluble vitamin found in many fruits and vegetables. Ascorbic acid is required for the optimal function of a number of enzymes; antioxidant deficiency causes scurvy and poor wound repair.

Vitamin D: either of two fat-soluble compounds: cholecalciferol, which is synthesised in the skin and is considered to be a hormone, and ergocalciferol, which is the form generally used as a dietary supplement. Dietary sources includes some fish liver oils, egg yolks, and fortified dairy products. Deficiency of vitamin D can result in rickets in children and osteomalcalia in adults.

Vitamin E: see **Tocopherols and tocotrienols.**

Vitamins: derived from the phrase 'vital amines' a general term for a number of unrelated organic substances that occur in many foods in small amounts and that are necessary in trace amounts for the normal metabolic function of the body. They may be water-soluble or fat-soluble.

Waist-to-hip ratio: a measure of human body fat distribution. The ratio of waist circumference to hip circumference (the measurement positions are tightly defined and highly reproducible). A strong predictor of risk for particular chronic diseases, e.g., a high waist-to-hip ratio is associated with an elevated risk of diabetes mellitus, **Coronary artery disease** and, perhaps, breast cancer.

Whole-grain cereals: unrefined cereals; cereals from which the husk and germ has not been removed.

Xanthophylls: one group of oxygenated **Carotenoids** occurring along with carotenes in green leaves.

Zinc: necessary in trace amounts in the body (and hence in the diet); forms an essential part of many enzymes and plays an important role in protein synthesis and in cell division.

References

INTRODUCTION

AACR (1975) American Association for Cancer Research Nutrition in the Causation of Cancer: Symposium organised by the American Cancer Society and National Cancer Institute *Cancer Res* **35** 3221-3550

Anon (1903) Modern views of cancer *Med Press* 700-701

Bennett J (1849) *On Cancerous and Cancroid Growths* Edinburgh: Sutherland and Knox

Burkitt DP (1969) Related disease - related cause? *Lancet* **2** 1229-1231

Cheng KK, Day NE (1996) Nutrition and esophageal cancer *Cancer Causes* **7** 133-140

Davidson S, Passmore R, Brock, JF (1972) *Human Nutrition and Dietetics* Edinburgh: Churchill Livingstone

Doll R (1967) Prevention of Cancer *Pointers from Epidemiology* London: Nuffield Hospital Trust

Doll R, Peto R (1981) The causes of cancer *JNCI* **66** 1191-1308

Ferro-Luzzi A, James WPT (1994) The Mediterranean diet: the past and the present, but what for the future? *Proceedings of the Eugari meeting on Agriculture and Human Health* Koukoulakis PH, (ed) The Hague

Higginson J, Muir CS (1973) Epidemiology In: Holland JF, Frei E (eds) *Cancer Medicine* Philadelphia: Lee and Febiger

Hill HA, Austin H (1996) Nutrition and endometrial cancer *Cancer Causes Control* **7** 19-32

Hoffman F (1915) *The Mortality from Cancer Throughout the World* Newark, NJ: Prudential Press

Hoffman F (1931) Cancer and smoking habits In: *Adair F (ed) Cancer* London: Lippincott

Hoffman F (1937) *Cancer and Diet* Baltimore: Williams and Wilkins

Howard J (1811) *Practical Observations on Cancer* London: Hatchard

Howe GR, Burch JD (1996) Nutrition and pancreatic cancer *Cancer Causes Control* **7** 69-82

Hueper WC (1942) *Occupational Tumors and Allied Diseases* Springfield, Illinois: Charles Thomas

Hunter DJ, Willett WC (1996) Nutrition and breast cancer *Cancer Causes Control* **7** 56-68

IARC (1988) Alcohol drinking *IARC monograph on the evaluation of carcinogenic risks to humans* **44** Lyon:International Agency for Research on Cancer

Kearney J, Giovanucci E, Rimm EB et al (1995) Diet, alcohol, and smoking and the occurrence of hyperplastic polyps of the colon and rectum *Cancer Causes Control* **6** 45-56

Kolonel LN (1996) Nutrition and prostate cancer *Cancer Causes Control* **7** 83-94

Kono S, Hirohata T (1996) Nutrition and stomach cancer *Cancer Causes Control* **7** 41-55

La Vecchia C, Negri E, (1996) Nutrition and bladder cancer *Cancer Causes Control* **7** 95-100

Lambe W, (1815) *Additional Reports on the Effects of a Peculiar Regimen in Cases of Cancer, Scrofula, Consumption, Asthma, and other Chronic Diseases* London: Mawman

Longnecker MP, Berlin JA, Orza MJ, Chalmers TC (1988) A meta-analysis of alcohol consumption in relation to risk of breast cancer *JAMA* **260** 652-656

Longnecker MP et al (1994) Alcoholic beverage consumption in relation to risk of breast cancer: meta-analysis and review: *Cancer Causes Control* **5** 73-82

Loomis D, Wing S (1990) Is molecular epidemiology a germ theory for the end of the twentieth century? *Int J Epidemiol* **19** 1-3

Marshall JR, Boyle P (1996) Nutrition and oral cancer *Cancer Causes Control* **7** 101-112

Milton K (1993) Diet and primate evolution *Scientific American* August 1993 70-77

NAS (1982) National Academy of Sciences *Diet, Nutrition and Cancer* Washington: National Academy Press

Orr IM (1933) Oral cancer in betel nut chewers in Travancore: its aetiology, pathology and treatment *Lancet* **ii** 575-80

Park R (1899) A further enquiry into the frequency and nature of cancer *The Practitioner* **62** 385

Parkin M et al, (1987) Estimates of the worldwide frequency of sixteen major cancers in 1980 *International Journal of Cancer* **41** 184-187

Potischman N, Brinton LA, (1996) Nutrition and cervical neoplasia *Cancer Causes and Control* **7** (1) 113-126

Potter JD (1996) Nutrition and colorectal cancer *Cancer Causes and Control* **7** (1) 127-146

Proctor RN (1995) *Cancer Wars How politics shapes what we know and don't know about cancer* New York Basic Books

Riboli E, Kaaks R, Esteve J (1996) Nutrition and laryngeal cancer *Cancer Causes and Control* **7** (1) 147-156

Shaw J (1907) *The Cure of Cancer: and How Surgery Blocks the Way* London: Turney

Steinmetz KA, Potter JD (1991) A review of vegetables, fruit and cancer I epidemiology: *Cancer Causes Control* **2** 325-357

Steinmetz KA, Potter JD (1996) Vegetables, fruit, and cancer prevention: a review *JAn Dietetic Assoc* **96** 1027-1037

Stephen A, Cummings J (1980) Mechanism of action of dietary fibre in the human colon *Nature* **284** 283-4

Stewart GT (1968) Limitations of the germ theory *Lancet* **i** 1077-1081

Stocks P (1933) Cancer incidence in North Wales and Liverpool region in relation to habits and environment *British Empire Cancer Campaign 35th Ann Report*, Suppl to Part **2** 1-127

Tannenbaum A, Silverstone H (1957) *Nutrition and the genesis of tumours* In Raven R (ed) Cancer London: Butterworth

Trichopoulos D, Li F, Hunter DJ (1996) What causes cancer? *Scientific American*, September 1996 50-57

UICC (1965) *Cancer incidence in five continents* Berlin Germany: Springer-Verlag

UICC,(1970) *Cancer incidence in five continents* Berlin Germany: Springer-Verlag

Walshe W (1846) *The Nature and Treatment of Cancer* London: Taylor and Walton

Willett WC, Trichopoulos D (1996) Summary of the evidence: nutrition and cancer *Cancer Causes Control* **7** 178-180

Willett WC, Colditz GA, Mueller NE (1996) Strategies for minimizing cancer risk *Scientific American*, September 1996: 58-63

Williams W (1908) *The Natural History of Cancer, with Special Reference to its Causation and Prevention* London: Heinemann

Wiseman R (1676) *Several Chirurgicall Treatises* London: Flesher and Macock

Wolk A, Lindblad P, Adami HO (1996) Nutrition and renal cell cancer *Cancer Causes Control* **7** 5-18

Wynder EL, Shigematsu T (1967) Environmental factors of cancer of the colon and rectum *Cancer* **20** 1520-61

Wynder E, Gori G (1977) Contribution of the environment to cancer incidence: an epidemiological exercise *JNCI* **58** 825-832

Ziegler RG, Mayne ST, Swanson CA (1996) Nutrition and lung cancer *Cancer Causes Control* **7** 157-177

CHAPTER ONE
PATTERNS OF DIET AND CANCER

Bryceson DF (1989) Nutrition and the commodization of food in Sub-Saharan Africa *Soc Sci Med* **28** 425-440

Bulkley JL (1927) Cancer among primitive tribes *Cancer* 4 289-295

Coleman M, Estève J, Damiecki P (1993) Trends in Cancer Incidence and Mortality *IARC Sci Publ* No **121** Lyon: International Agency for Research on Cancer

Crawford M, Marsh D (1995) *Nutrition and Evolution* New Canaan Conneticut USA: Keats Publishing Inc

Dublin LI, Lotka AJ (1937) *Twenty-Five years of Health Progress* New York: Metropolitan Life Insurance

Eaton SB, Shostak M, Konner M (1988) *The Paleolithic Prescription* New York: Harper and Row

FAO/WHO (1991) Food and Agriculture Organisation/World Health Organization *Protein quality evaluation* (FAO food and nutrition paper 51) Rome: FAO

Gopalan (1997) *Diet Nutrition and Chronic Disease - Lessons from Contrasting Worlds* Shetty PS, McPherson K (eds)

Higginson J (1960) Population studies in cancer *Acta UICC* **16** 1667-1670

Kolonel LN, Hinds MW, Hankin JH (1980) Cancer patterns among migrant and native-born Japanese in Hawaii in relation to smoking, drinking, and dietary habits In: Gelboin HV et al (eds) *Genetic and Environmental Factors in*

Experimental and Human Cancer Tokyo:Japan Sci Soc Press pp 327-40

Le Conte J (1842) *On carcinoma in general, and cancer of the stomach* Lancet **ii** 284-287, 299-304

Maugh TH (1979) Cancer and environment: Higginson speaks out *Science* **205** 1363-1366

McMichael AJ, Giles GG (1988) Cancer in migrants to Australia extending the descriptive epidemiological data *Cancer Res* **48** 751-756

McMichael AJ, McCall MG, Hartshorne JM, Woodings TL (1980) Patterns of gastro-intestinal cancer in European migrants to Australia: the role of dietary change *Int J Cancer* **25** 431-437

National Academy of Sciences, National Research Council (US) (1989) *Committee on Diet and Health Diet and Health Implications for reducing chronic Disease risk* Washington DC: National Academy Press

Newman W (1896) Notes from registers of Market Deeping 1711-1723 *British Medical Journal* **1** 915-916

Park R (1899) A further inquiry into the frequency and nature of cancer *The Practitioner* **62** 385

Parkin DM, Muir CS, Whelan SL, Gao YT, Ferlay J, Powell J (eds) (1992) Cancer Incidence in Five Continents **VI** *IARC Sci Publ* 120 Lyon:International Agency for Research on Cancer

Piazza A (1986) *Food consumption and nutritional status in the PRC* Westview Press Inc pp 71-110

Popkin BM, Ge K, Zhai F, Xuguang G, Ma H, Zohoori N (1993) The nutrition transition in China a cross-sectional analysis *Eur J Clin Nutr* **47** 333-346

Proctor RN (1995) *Cancer War: How politics shapes what we know and don't know about cancer* New York: Basic Books

Roush G et al (1987) *Cancer risk and incidence trends: the Connecticut perspective* Washington DC: Hemisphere

Schweitzer A (1957) *Preface to* Berglas A *Cancer: Nature, Cause and Cure* Paris

Scotto J, Bailar JC (1969) Rigoni-Stern and medical statistics *J History Med* **24** 65 -75

Szostak WB, Sekula W (1991)Nutritional implications of changes in eastern Europe *Proc Nutr Soc* **50** 687- 693

Tanchou S (1843) Recherches sur la frequence du cancer *Gazette des hopitaux* July 6

Whelan SL, Parkin DM, Masuyer E (1990) Patterns of Cancer in Five Continents *IARC Sci Publ* **102** Lyon: International Agency for Research on Cancer

WHO (1995) *Annual epidemiological and vital statistics* Geneva: WHO

WHO (1997) *The World Health Report* Geneva: WHO

Williams WR (1908) *The Natural History of Cancer, with Special Reference to its Causation and Prevention* New York: William Wood

Wynder EL, Lemon F, Bross IJ (1959) Cancer and coronary artery disease among Seventh-day Adventists *Cancer* **12** 1016-1028

CHAPTER TWO
DIET AND THE CANCER PROCESS

Ames BN (1983) Dietary carcinogenesis and anticarcinogens, oxygen radicals, and degenerative diseases *Science* **221** 1256-1264

Anderson MW, Reynolds SH, You M, Maronpot, RM (1992) Role of proto-oncogene activation in carcinogenesis *Environ Health Persp* **98** 13-24

Bartsch H, Barbin A, Marion MJ, Nair J, Guichard Y (1994) Formation, detection, and role in carcinogenesis of ethenobases in DNA *Drug Metab Rev* **26** 349-371

Becci PJ, Thompson HJ, Grubbs CJ, Brown CC, and Moon RC (1979) Effect of delay in administration of 13-cis-retinoic acid on the inhibition of urinary bladder carcinogenesis in the rat *Cancer Res* **39** 3141-3144

Birt DF, Kris ES, Choe M, Pelling JC (1992) Dietary, energy, and fat effects on tumor promotion *Cancer Res* **52** (Suppl) 2035s-2039s

Chou MW, Pegram RA, Gao P, Allaben WT (1992) Effects of caloric restriction on aflatoxin B_1 metabolism and DNA modification in Fischer 344 rats In: Fishbein L (ed) *Biological Effects of Dietary Restriction* Springer-Verlag: Berlin 42-54

Christman JK, Chen M-L, Sheiknejad G, Dizik M, Abileah S, and Wainfan E (1993) Methyl deficiency, DNA methylation, and cancer: studies on the reversibility of the effects of the lipotrope-deficient diet *J Nutr Biochem* **4** 672-680

Doll R and Peto R (1981) *The causes of cancer* Oxford: Oxford University Press

Giovannucci E, Stampfer MJ, Colditz GA, Rimm EB, Trichopoulos D et al (1993) Folate, methionine, and alcohol intake and risk of colorectal adenoma *JNCI* **85** 875-883

Glynn SA and Albanes D (1994) Folate and cancer: a review of the literature *Nutr Cancer* **22** 101-119

Harris CC (1991) Chemical and physical carcinogenesis: advances and perspectives for the 1990's *Cancer Res* (Suppl) **51** 5023s-5044s

Harris CC (1993) p53: At the crossroads of molecular carcinogenesis and risk assessment *Science* **262** 1980-1981

Hass BS, Hart RW, Lu MH, Lyn-Cook BD (1993) Effects of caloric restriction in animals on cellular function, oncogene expression, and DNA methylation in vitro *Mutation Res* **295** 281-289

Hague, A, Elder, DJE, Hicks, DJ Paraskeva, C (1995) Apoptosis in colorectal tumour cells: induction by the short chain fatty acids butyrate, propionate and acetate and by the bile salt deoxycholate *Int J Cancer* **60** 400-406

Hemminki K, Dipple A, Shuker DEG, Kadlubar FF, Segerbäck D, Bartsch H (1994) DNA adducts Identification and biological significance *IARC Scientific Publ* **125** Lyon: International Agency for Research on Cancer

Hinrichsen LI, Floyd RA, Sudilovsky O (1990) Is 8-hydroxydeoxyguanosine a mediator of carcinogenesis by choline-devoid diet in the rat liver? *Carcinogenesis* **11** 1879-1881

Ho C-T, Osawa T, Huang M-T, Rosen RT (eds) (1994) *Food Phytochemicals for Cancer Prevention II Teas, Spices, and Herbs* ACS Symposium 547 Washington DC: American Cancer Society

Hu J-F, Chisari FV, Campbell TC (1994) Modulating effect of dietary protein in hepatitis B virus (HBV) transgenic mice *Proc Amer Assoc Cancer Res* **54** 104

Huang M-T, Osawa T, Ho C-T, Rosen RT, eds (1994) *Food Phytochemicals for Cancer Prevention I Fruits and Vegetables* ACS Symposium 546 Washington DC: American Chemical Society

Hursting SD, Perkins SN, Phang JM (1994) Calorie restriction suppresses spontaneous tumorigenesis in p53-knockout transgenic mice *Proc Amer Assoc Cancer Res* **54** 105

James SJ, Basnakian AG, Miller BJ (1994) In vitro folate deficiency induces deoxynucleotide pool imbalance, apoptosis, and mutagenesis in Chinese hamster ovary cells *Cancer Res* **54** 5075-5080

James SJ, Pogribny I, Basnakian A (1994) Increased frequency of DNA strand breaks within the P53 gene in livers from methionine/choline/folate-deficient rats *Proc Amer Assoc Cancer Res* **54** 105

James SJ, Yin L, Swendseid M (1989) DNA strand breaks, thymidylate synthesis and NAD levels in lymphocytes from methyl donor-deficient rats *J Nutr* **119** 661-664

Kadlubar FF, Beland FA (1985) Chemical properties of ultimate carcinogenic metabolites of arylamines and arylamides In Harvey RG (ed) *Polycyclic hydrocarbons and carcinogenesis* Washington, DC: American Chemical Society 341-70

Kritchevsky E, Klurfeld DM (1987) Caloric effects in experimental mammary tumorigenesis *Amer J Clin Nutr* **45** (Suppl) 236-242

Meuth M (1989) The molecular basis of mutations induced by deoxynucleotide triphosphate pool imbalances in mammalian cells *Exp Cell Res* **181** 305-316

Miller JA, Miller EC (1953) The carcinogenic aminoazo dyes *Adv Cancer Res* **1** 339-396

Newberne PM, Rogers AE (1986) The role of nutrients in cancer causation In: Hayashi Y(ed) *Diet, Nutrition, and Cancer* Tokyo:Japan Scientific Press 205-222

Newmark HL, Lipkin M (1992) Calcium, vitamin D and colon cancer *Cancer Res* **52** (Suppl) 2067s-2070s

Pariza MW (1987) Fat, calories, and mammary carcinogenesis: net energy effects *Amer J Clin Nutr* **45** (Suppl) 261-263

Parkin DM, Pisani P, Lopez AD, Masuyer E (1994) At least one in seven cases of cancer is caused by smoking Global estimates for 1985 *Int J Cancer* **59** 494–504

Pitot HC, Dragan, YP (1994) The multistage nature of chemically induced hepatocarcinogenesis in the rat *Drug Metab Rev* **26** 209-220

Pitot HC (1986) *Fundamentals of oncology* 3rd ed New York: Marcel Dekker,

Poirier LA, Newberne PM, Pariza MW (eds) (1986) *Essential Nutrients in Carcinogenesis* New York: Plenum Press

Poirier LA (1994) Methyl group deficiency in hepatocarcinogenesis *Drug Metab Rev* **26** 185-199

Poirier LA (1987) Stages in carcinogenesis: alteration by diet *Am J Clin Nutr* **45** 185

Radman M, Wagner R (1993) Missing mismatch repair *Nature* **366** 722

Randerath K, Randerath EA (1994) ^{32}P-postlabeling methods for DNA adduct detection: overview and critical evaluation *Drug Metab Rev* **26** 67-85

Rous P (1914) The influence of diet on transplanted and spontaneous mouse tumors *J Exp Med* **30** 433

Sawada N, Poirier LA, Moran S, Xu Y-H, Pitot HC (1990) The effect of choline and methionine deficiencies on the number and volume percentage of altered hepatic foci in the presence or absence of diethylnitrosamine initiation in rat liver *Carcinogenesis* **11** 273-281

Searle CE (1984) *Chemical carcinogens* 2nd ed ACS Monograph 182 Washington, DC: American Chemical Society

Shi CY, Chua S, Ong CN, Lee HP (1994) Dietary selenium inhibits DNA binding of aflatoxin B^1 in rats *Proc Am Assoc Cancer Res*; **34** 133

Simic MG, Bergtold DS (1991) Urinary biomarkers of oxidative DNA-base damage and human calorie intake In: Fishbein L (ed) *Biological Effects of Dietary Restriction*, Springer-Verlag: Berlin pp 217-225

Smith ML, Yeleswarapu L, Scalamogna P, Locker J, Lombardi B (1993) p53 mutations in hepatocellular carcinomas induced by choline-devoid diet in male F344 rats *Carcinogenesis* **14** 503-510

Steinmetz K, Potter JD (1991a) A review of vegetables, fruit, and cancer I: Epidemiology *Cancer Causes Control* **2** 325-357

Steinmetz K, Potter JD (1991b) A review of vegetables, fruit, and cancer II: Mechanisms *Cancer Causes Control* **2** 427-442

Stocks P, Karn M N (1933) A co-operative study of the habits, home life, dietary and family histories of 450 cancer patients and of an equal number of control patients *Ann Eugen Human Genet* **5** 30-33

Tannenbaum A, Silverstone H (1953) Nutrition in relation to cancer *Adv Cancer Res* **1** 451

Tannenbaum A (1940) The initiation and growth of tumors Introduction I Effects of underfeeding *Am J Cancer* **3** 335

Tomatis L, Aitio A, Day NE, Heseltine E, Kaldor J, Miller AB, Parkin DM, Riboli E (1990) *Cancer: causes, occurrence and control* IARC Scientific Publ **100** Lyon: International Agency for Research on Cancer

Wainfan E, Poirier LA (1992) Methyl groups in carcinogenesis: effects on DNA methylation and gene expression *Cancer Res* **52** (Suppl) 2071S-2077s

Wattenberg LW (1992) Inhibition of carcinogenesis by minor dietary constituents *Cancer Res* **52** (Suppl) 2085s-2091s

Wei Q, Matanoski GM, Farmer ER, Hedayati, MA, Grossman L (1994) DNA repair related to multiple skin cancers and drug use *Cancer Res*: **54** 437-440

Weinberg RA (1994) Oncogenes and tumor suppressor genes *Cancer J Clin* **44** 160-170

Weisburger JH, Yamamoto RS, Williams GM, Grantham PH, Matsushima T, Weisburger EK (1972) On the sulfate ester of *N*-hydroxy-*N*-2-fluorenylacetamide as a key ultimate hepatocarcinogen in the rat *Cancer Res* **32** 491-500

Wood AW, Chang RL, Huang MT, Uskokovic M, Conney AH (1983) 1-25-dihydroxy vitamin D3 inhibits phorvol ester-dependent chemical carcinogenesis in mouse skin *Biochem Biophys Res Commun* **116** 605-611

Yuspa SH (1994) The pathogenesis of squamous cell cancer: lessons learned from studies of skin carcinogenesis—thirty-third GHA Clowes Memorial award Lecture *Cancer Res* 1178-1189

Zeisel SH (1992) Choline an important nutrient in brain development, liver function, and carcinogenesis *J Am Coll Nutr* **11** 473-481

CHAPTER THREE
SCIENTIFIC EVIDENCE AND JUDGEMENT

Alpha-Tocopherol, Beta Carotene Cancer Prevention Study Group (1994) The effect of vitamin E and beta-carotene on the incidence of lung cancer and other cancers in male smokers *NEJM* **300** 1029-1035

Ames BN, Magaw R, Gold LS (1987) Ranking possible carcinogenic hazards *Science* **236** 271-280

Aoki K, Hayakawa N, Kurihara M, Suzuki S (1992) Death rates for malignant neoplasms for selected sites by sex and five-year age group in 33 countries, 1953-57 to 1983-87 In *International Union Against Cancer* Nagoya: University of Nagoya Coop Press

Armstrong B, and Doll R (1975) Environmental factors and cancer incidence and mortality in different countries, with special reference to dietary practices *Int J Cancer* **15** 617-631

Blot WJ, Li JY, Taylor PR, Guo W, Dawsey S, Wang GQ, Yang CS, Zheng SF, Gail M, Li GY, Yu Y, Liu B, Tangrea J, Sun Y, Liu F, Fraumeni JF Jnr, Zhang YH, Li B (1993) Nutrition intervention trials in Linxian, China: supplementation with specific vitamin/mineral combinations, cancer incidence, and disease-specific mortality in the general population *JNCI* **85** 1483-1492

Chen J et al (1990) *Diet, Lifestyle, and Mortality, A Study of the Characteristics of 65 Chinese Counties* Oxford: Oxford University Press

Correa P, (1992) Human gastric carcinogenesis: a multistep and multifactoral process *Cancer Res* **52** 6735-6740

Doll R, Peto R (1981) The causes of cancer *JNCI* **66** 1191-1308

Graham S, Dayal H, Swanson M, Mittelman A, Wilkinson G (1978) Diet in the epidemiology of cancer of the colon and rectum *J Natl Cancer Inst* **61** 709-714

Groopman JD, Wogan GN, Roebuck BD, Kensler TW (1994) Molecular biomarkers for aflatoxins and their application to human cancer prevention *Cancer Research* **54** (75) 1907S-1911S

Hill AB (1965) The environment and disease: association or causation? *Proc R Soc Med* **58** 295-300

Hoel DG, Haseman JK, Hogan MD, Huff J, McConnell EE (1988) The impact of toxicity on carcinogenicity studies: implications for risk assessment *Carcinogenesis* **9** 2045-2052

Hsu IC, Metcalf RA, Sun T, Welsh JA, Wang NJ, Harris CC (1991) Mutational hotspot in the p53 gene in human hepatocellular carcinomas *Nature* **350** 427-428

IARC (1990) Tomatis L, Aitio A, Day NE, Heseltine E, Kaldor J, Miller AB, Parkin M, Riboli E (eds) Cancer: Causes, Occurrence and Control Lyon: International Agency for Research on Cancer

IARC (1993) Monographs on the Evaluation of carcinogenic Risks to Humans, Volume 56 *Some Naturally Occurring Substances: Food Items and Constituents, Hetrocyclic Aromatic Amines and Mycotoxins* Lyon, pp 52

Kinlen LJ (1983) Fat and Cancer *Br Med J* **286** 1081-1082

McMichael AJ (1994) Invited commentary - 'Molecular Epidemiology': new pathway or new travelling companion? *Am Journal Epidemiol* **140** 1-11

Marmot M (1986) Epidemiology and the art of the soluble *Lancet* **i** 897-900

Multiple Risk Factor Intervention Trial Research Group (1982) Risk factor changes and mortality results *JAMA* **248** 1465-1477

NAS (1982) *Diet, Nutrition and Cancer* Washington, DC: National Academy Press

Peto R, Doll R, Buckley JD, Sporn MD (1981) Can dietary beta-carotene materially reduce human cancer rates? *Nature* **290** 201-208

Phillips RL, Garfinkel L, Kuzma JW, Beeson WL, Lotz T, Brin B (1980) Mortality among California Seventh-day Adventists for selected cancer sites *JNCI* **65** 1097-1107

Reichman ME, Judd JT, Longcope C, Schatzkin A, Clevidence BA, Nair PP, Campbell WS, Taylor PR (1993) Effects of alcohol consumption on plasma and urinary hormon concentrations in premenopausal women *JNCI* **85** 722-727

Roberts-Thomson I, Ryan P, Khoo KK, Hart WJ, McMicheal AJ, Butler RN (1996) Diet, acetylator phenotype and risk of colorectal neoplasia *Lancet* **347** 1372-3

Rose G (1992) *The Strategy of Preventive Medicine* Oxford: University Press

Schulte PA, Perera FP (eds) (1993) *Molecular Epidemiology* Academic Press

Vineis P, McMichael AJ (1996) Interplay between heterocyclic amines in cooked meat and metabolic phenotype in the aetiology of colon cancer *Cancer Causes Control* **7** 479-486

Wald N, Boreham J, Bailey A (1986) Serum retinol and subsequent risk of cancer *Br J Cancer* **54** 957-961

Wattenberg LW, Loub WD (1973) Inhibition of polycyclic aromatic hydrocarbon-induced neoplasia by naturally occurring indoles *Cancer Res* **38** 1410-1413

Willett WC (1990a) *Nutritional Epidemiology* New York: Oxford University Press

Willett WC (1990b) Total energy intake and nutrient composition: dietary recommendations for epidemiologists *Int J Cancer* **46** 770-71

Willett WC, Hunter DJ, Stampfer MJ, Colditz G, Manson JE, Spiegelman D, Rosner BA, Hennekens CH, Speizer FE (1992) Dietary fat and fiber in relation to risk of breast cancer: an eight-year follow-up *J Am Med Assoc* **268** 2037-2044

World Cancer Research Fund (1993) *Diet and Cancers: genetic, cellular and physiological mechanisms* London: WCRF

World Health Organization (1982) *Prevention of Coronary Heart Disease* Technical Report series no **678** Geneva: WHO

World Health Organization (1990) *Diet, Nutrition and the Prevention of Chronic Diseases* Technical Report series no **797** Geneva: WHO

CHAPTER 4 CANCERS

4.1 MOUTH AND PHARYNX

Adami HO, McLaughlin JK, Hsing AW et al (1992) Alcoholism and cancer risk: a population-based cohort study *Cancer Causes Control* **3** 419-425

Barone J, Taioli E, Herbert JR, Wynder EL (1992) Vitamin supplement use for oral and oesophageal cancer *Nutr Cancer*

Brugere J, Quenel P, Leclerc A, Rodriguez J (1986) Differential effects of tobacco and alcohol in cancer of the larynx, pharynx, and mouth *Cancer* **57** 391-395

Chyou P, Nomura AM, Stemmermann GN (1995) Diet, alcohol, smoking and cancer of the upper aerodigestive tract: a prospective study among Hawaii Jananese men *Int J Cancer* **60** 616-621

Day GL, Glot WJ, Shore RE, Schoenberg JB et al (1994) Second cancers following oral and pharyngeal cancers: patients' characteristics and survival patterns *Eur J Cancer B Oral Oncol* **30B** 381-386

De Stefani E, Correa P, Oreggia F et al (1988) Black tobacco, wine and mate in oropharyngeal cancer: a case-control study from Uruguay *Rev Epidemiol Sante Publique* **36** 389-94

Elwood JM, Pearson JC, Skippen DH and Jackson SM (1984) Alcohol, smoking, social and occupational factors with etiology of cancer of the oral cavity, pharynx and larynx *Int J Cancer* **34** 603-612

Franceschi S, Barro S, La Vecchia C, Bidoli E, Negri E, Talamini R (1992) Risk factors for cancer of the tongue and the mouth A case control study from Northern Italy *Cancer* **70** 2227-33

Franceschi S, Bidoli E, Baron AE et al (1991) Nutrition and Cancer of the oral cavity and pharynx in north-east Italy *Int J Cancer* **47** 20-25

Franco EL, Kowalski LP, Oliveira BV et al (1989) Risk factors for oral cancer in Brazil: A case control study *Int J Cancer* **43** 992-1000

Franscceschi S, Bidoli E, Baron AE, La Vecchia C (1990) Maize and risk of cancers of the oral cavity, pharynx and esophagus in northern Italy *JNCI* **82** 1407-11

Garewal HS (1995) Emerging role of beta-carotene and other antioxidant nutrients in prevention of oral cancer *Arch Otolaryngol Head Neck Surg* **121** 141-144

Graham S, Dayal H, Rohrer T et al (1977) Dentition, diet, tobacco and alcohol in the epidemiology of oral cancer *JNCI* **59** 1611-1618

Gridley G, McLaughlin JK, Block G, Blot WJ, Gluch M and Fraumeni JF Jr (1992) Vitamin supplement use and reduced risk of oral and pharyngeal cancer *Am J Epidemiol* **135** 1083-1092

Gridley G, McLaughlin JK, Block G et al(1990) Diet and oral and pharyngeal cancer among blacks *Nutr Cancer* **14** 219-225

Hakulinen T, Lehtimaki L, Lehtonen M et al (1974) Cancer morbidity among two male cohorts with increased alcohol consumption in Finland *JNCI* **52** 1711-1714

Hebert JR, Landon J, Miller DR (1993) Consumption of meat and fruit in relation to oral and esophageal cancer: A cross-national study *Nutr Cancer* **19** 169-179

Hirayama T (1985) A large scale cohort study on cancer risks by diet-with special reference to the risk reducing effects of green yellow vegetable consumption *Int Symp Princess Takamatsu Cancer Res Fund* **16** 41-53

Hirayama T (1966) An epidemiological study of oral and pharyngeal cancer in Central and South-east Asia *Bull Worls Health Org* **34** 41-69

Jacobson BK, Bjelke E, Kvale G (1986) Heuch I Coffee drinking mortality and cancer incidence, results from a Norwegian prospective study *JNCI* 76: 823-31

Jafarey NA, Mahmood Z, Zavidi SH (1977) Habits and dietary pattern of cases of carcinoma of the oral cavity and oropharynx *JPMA* **27** 340-43

Jensen OM (1979) Cancer morbidity and causes of death among Danish brewery workers *Int J Cancer* **23** 454-463

Keller AZ, Terris M (1965) The association of alcohol and tobacco with cancer of the mouth and pharynx *Am J Publ Hlth* **55** 1578-85

Knekt P, Aromaa A, Maatela J, Ritva-Kaarina A et al(1991) Vitamin E and cancer prevention *Am J Clin Nutr* **53** 283S-286S

Kono S, I Keda M, Ogata M, Tokudome S, Nishizumi M and Kuratsune M (1983) The relationship between alcohol and mortality among Japanese physicians *Int J Epidemiol* **12** 437-441

Kono S, Ikeda M, Tokudome S, Nishizumi M and Kuratsune M (1986) Alcohol and mortality : a cohort study of male Japanese Physicians *Int J Epidemiol* **15** 527-532

Kono S, Ikeda M, Tokudome S, Yoshimura T, Nishizumi M and Kuratsune M (1985) Alcohol and cancer in male Japanese Physicians *J Cancer Res Clin Oncol* **109** 82-85

Krinsky NI (1991) Effects of carotenoids in cellular and animal systems *Am J Clin Nutr* **53** 238S-246S

Krishnaswamy K, Prasad MPR, Krishna TP and Pasricha S (1993) Selenium in cancer - a case control study *Indian J Med Res* **44** 87-92

La Vecchia C, Negri E, D'Avanzo B et al (1991) Dietary indicators of oral and pharyngeal cancer *Int J Epidemiol* **20** 39-44

Lasserre O, Flamant R, Lellouch J et al(1967) Alcohol et cancer Etude de pathologie geographique portant sur les departements francais *Bull Inserm* **33** 53-60

Lemon FR, Walden RT, Woods RH (1964) Cancer of the lung and mouth in Seventh-Day adventists Preliminary report on a population study *Cancer* **17** 486-497

Marshall J, Graham S, Mettlin C, Shedd D, Swanson M (1983) Diet in the epidemiology of oral cancer *Nutr Cancer* **5** 96-106

Martinez I (1992) Factors associated with cancer of the esophagus, mouth, and pharynx in Puerto Rico *JNCI* **42** 1069-1094

McLaughlin JK, Gridley G, Block G et al(1988) Dietary factors in oral and pharyngeal cancer *J Natl Cancer Inst* **80** 1237-43

Middleton B, Byers T, Marshall J, Graham S (1986) Dietary vitamin A and cancer - multisite case control study *Nutr Cancer* **8** 106-115

Monson RR, Lyon JL (1975) Proportional mortality among alcoholics *Cancer* **36** 1077-1079

Nandakumar A, Thimmosetty KT, Sreeramareddy NM et al (1990) A population based case control investigation on cancers of the oral cavity in Bangalore, India *Br J Cancer* **62** 847-851

Notani PN and Jayant K (1987) Role of diet in upper aerodigestive tract cancers *Nutr Cancer* **10** 103-113

Olsen J, Sabroe S and Ipsen J (1985b) Effect of combined alcohol and tobacco exposure on risk of cancer of the hypopharynx *J Epidemiol Commun Health* **39** 304-307

Oreggia F, De Stefani E, Correa P and Fierro L (1991) Risk factors for cancer of the tongue in Uruguay *Cancer* **67** 180-183 Orr IM Oral cancer in betel nut chewers in Travancore Lancet 1933; ii:575- 80

Phillips RL, Garfincel L, Kuzmen JW et al(1980) Mortality among California Seventh Day Adventists for selected cancer sites *JNCI* **65** 1097-1107

Prasad MPR, Krishna TP, Pasricha S, Qureshi MA, Krishnaswamy K (1992) Diet and oral cancer - A case control study *Nutr Cancer* **18** 85-93

Prasad MPR, Mukundan MA, and Krishnaswamy K (1995) Micronuclei and carcinogen DNA adducts as intermediate end points in nutrient intervention study on oral precancerous lesions *European J Cancer B Oral Oncol* **31B** 155-159

Ramaswamy G, Rao VR, Kumaraswamy SV, Anatha N (1996) Serum vitamins' status in oral leucoplakias- a preliminary study *Oral Oncol, Eur J Cancer* **32B** 120-122

Robinette CD, Hrubec Z, Fraumeni JF (1979) Chronic alcoholism and subsequent mortality in World war II veterans *Am J Epidemiol* **109** 687-700

Rogers AE, Conner MW (1991) Interrelationship of alcohol and cancer In Alfin-Slater RB, Kritchevsky D (eds), Human Nutrition: a comprehensive treatise 7 *Cancer and nutrition* New York Plenum Press 321-336

Rogers MA, Thomas DB, Davis S, Vaughan TL, Nevissi AE (1993) A case-control study of element levels and cancer of the upper aerodigestive tract *Cancer Epidemiol Biomarkers Prev* 2 305-312

Rossing MA, Vaughan TL, McNight B (1989) Diet and pharyngeal cancer *Int J Cancer* **44** 593-97

Rothman K, Keller A (1972) The effect of exposure to alcohol and tobacco on risk of cancer of the mouth and pharynx *J Chronic Dis* **25** 711-6

Sankaranarayanan R, Duffy SW, Day NE, Nair MK, Padmakumary G (1989) A case control investigation of cancer of the oral tongue and the floor of the mouth in southern India *Br J Cancer* **44** 617-621

Schmidt W and Popham RE (1981) The role of drinking and smoking in mortality from cancer and other causes in male alcoholics *Cancer* **47** 1031-1041

Schmidt W, DeLint J (1972) Causes of death of alcoholics *Q J Stud Alcohol* **33** 171-85

Schwartz D, Lellouch J, Flammant R et al (1962) Alcool et cancer Resultats d'une enquete retrospective *Rev Franc Et Clin Biol* **7** 590-604

Spitz MR, Fueger JJ, Goepfert H, Hong WK and Newell GR (1988) Squamous cell carcinoma of the upper aerodigestive tract A case comparison analysis *Cancer* **61** 203-208

Steinmetz KA and Potter JD (1991a) Vegetables, fruit and cancer II Mechanisms *Cancer Causes and Control* **2** 427-442

Steinmetz KA and Potter JD (1991b) Vegetables, fruit, and cancer I Epidemiology *Cancer Causes and Control* **2** 325-357

Stich HF, Stich W, Rosin MP and Vallejera MO (1984) Use of micronucleus test to monitor the effect of vitamin A, beta-carotenes and canthaxanthin on the buccal mucosa of betelnut/tobacco chewers *Int J Cancer* **34** 745-750

Sundby P (1967) Alcoholism and mortality *Oslo, Universitetsforlaget*

Tuyns AJ, Esteve J, Raymond L et al (1988) Cancer of the larynx/hypopharynx, tobacco and alcohol : IARC international case-control study in Turin and Varese (Italy), Zaragoza and Navarra (spain), Geneva (Switzerland) and Calvados (France) *Int J Cancer* **41** 483-491

Tuyns AJ, Riboli E, Doornbos G et al (1987) Diet and esophageal cancer in Calvadas (France) *Nutr Cancer* **9** 81-92

Vincent RG, Marchetta F (1963) The relationship of the use of tobacco and alcohol to cancer of the oral cavity, pharynx or larynx *Am J Surg* **106** 501-505

WHO (1990) World Health Organization *Diet, Nutrition, and the Prevention of Chronic Diseases* Technical Report 797 Geneva: WHO

WHO (1997) World Health Organization *The World Health Report* Geneva:WHO

Winn DM, Ziegler RG, Pickle LW, Gridley G, Blot WJ and Hoover RN (1984) Diet in the etiology of oral and pharyngeal cancer among women from Southern United States *Cancer Res* **44** 1216-1222

Wynder EL, Bross IJ and Feldman RM (1957a) A study of etiological factors in cancer of the mouth *Cancer* **10** 1300-1323

Zheng T, Boyle P, Willett WC, Hu H, Dan J et alA case-control study of oral cancer in bejing, People's Republic of chiina; associations with nutrient intakes, foods, and food groups *Eur J Cancer* **29B** 45-55

Zheng TZ, Boyle P, Hu HF et al (1990) Tobacco smoking alcoholic consumption and risk of oral cancer A case control study in Beijing, People's Republic of China *Cancer Causes Control* **1** 173-179

Zheng W, Blot WJ, Shu XV et al (1992) Risk factors for oral and pharyngeal cancer in Shanghai, with emphasis on diet *Cancer Epidemiol Biomarkers Prov* **1** 441-448

4.2 NASOPHARYNX

Acheson ED, Cowdell RH and Rang EH (1972) Adenocarcinoma of the nasal cavity and sinuses in England and Wales *Br J Ind Med* **29** 21-30

Chen C-J, Chen J-Y, Hsu M-M et al (1988) Epidemiological characteristics and early detection of nasopharyngeal carcinoma in Taiwan In Wolf GT, Carey E (eds) *Head and Neck Oncology Research* Amsterdam-Berkelye: Kugler Publications, pp 505-513

Geser A, Charnay N, Day NE, de-The G and Ho JHC (1978) Environmental factors in the etiology of

nasopharyngeal carcinoma : report on a case control study in Hong Kong In *Nasopharyngeal Carcinoma : Etiology and control* G de-The, Ito Y (eds) IARC Scientific Publication No 20 Lyon: International Agency for Research on Cancer pp213-229

Henderson BE and Louie E (1978) Discussion of risk factors for nasopharyngeal carcinoma *IARC Scientific Publication 20* 251-260

Ho HC (1967) Nasopharyngeal carcinoma in Hong Kong In: Muir CS and Shanmugaratnam K (eds) *Cancer of the nasopharynx* (VIII monograph series no1), Copenhagen, Munksgaard pp 58-63

Ho HC (1971) Incidence of nasopharyngeal cancer in Hong Kong UICC Bull *Cancer* **9** 5

Huang DP, Ho JH, Webb KS et al (1981) Volatile nitrosamines in salt processed fish before and after cooking *Food Cosmet Toxicol* **19** 167-71

Huang DP, Ho JHC, Saw D, Teoh TB (1978) Carcinoma of the paranasal regions in rats fed Cantonese salted fish in G de-The and YIto (Eds) *Nasopharyngeal Carcinoma : Etiology and Control* IARC Sci Publ 20, Lyon: International Agency for Research on Cancerpp 315-328

IARC (1993) Monographs on the Evaluation of carcinogenic Risks to Humans, Volume 56 *Some Naturally Occurring Substances: Food Items and Constituents, Hetrocyclic Aromatic Amines and Mycotoxins*, Lyon, International Agency for Research on Cancer pp 52

Jeannel D, Hubert A, de Vaithaire F et al (1990) Diet, living conditions and nasopharyngeal carcinoma in Tunisia - a case control study *Int J Cancer* **46** 421-25

Nam JM, McLaughlin JK, Blot WJ (1992) Cigarette smoking, alcohol and nasopharyngeal carcinoma: a case control study among US Whites *JNCI* **84** 619-22

Ning JP, Yu MC, Wang QS, Henderson BE (1990) Consumption of salted fish and other risk factors for nasopharyngeal carcinoma (NPC) in Tianjin, a low risk region for NPC in the Peoples Republic of China *JNCI* **82** 291-296

Poirier S, Ohshima H, De-The G, Hubert A, Bourgade MC, Bartsch H (1987) Volatile nitrosamine levels in common foods from Tinisia, South China and Greenland, high-risk areas for nasopharyngeal carcinoma (NPC) *Int J Cancer* **39** 293-296

Shanmugaratnam K, Tye CY, Goh EH, Chia KP (1978) Etiological factors in nasopharyngeal carcinoma: a hospital-based, retrospective, case-control, questionnaire study In: de-The G, Ito Y (eds) *Nasopharyngeal Carcinoma Etiology and control* (IARC Scientific Publications No 20) Lyon, International Agency for Research on Cancer pp 199-212

Shao YM, Poirier S, Oshima H et al (1988) Epstein-Barr Virus activation in Raji cells by extracts of preserved food from high risk areas for nasopharyngeal carcinoma Carcinogenesis **9** 1455-57

Song PJ, Hu JF (1988) N-nitrosamines in Chinese foods Food Chem *Toxicol* **26** 205-208

Sriamporn S, Vatanasapt V, Pisani P, Yongchaiyudha S, Rungpitarangsri V (1992) Environmental risk factors for nasopharyngeal carcinoma: a case control study in north eastern Thailand *Cancer Epidemiol, Biomarkers and Prevention* **1** 345-48

Tannenbaum SR, Bishop W, Yu Mc et al (1985) Attempts to isolate N-nitroso compounds from Chinese-style salted fish *Natl Cancer Inst Monograph* **69** 209-11

Tricker AR, Preussmann R (1991) Carcinogenic N-nitrosamines in the diet : Occurrence, formation, mechanisms and carcinogenic potential *Mutation Res* **259** 277- 289

Yu MC, Ho JH-C, Henderson, BE and Armstrong RW (1985) Epidemiology of nasopharyngeal carcinoma in Malaysia and Hong Kong *Natl Cancer Inst Monogr* **69** 203-207

Yu MC, Ho JHC, Lai SH, Henderson BE (1986) Cantonese style salted fish as a cause of nasopharyngeal carcinoma: report of a case-control study in Hong Kong*Cancer Res* **46** 956-961

Yu MC, Huang TB, Henderson BE (1989) Diet and nasopharyngeal carcinoma: a case control study in Guangzhou, China *Int J Cancer* **43** 1077-1082

Yu MC, Mo CC, Chong WX et al (1988) Preserved foods and nasopharyngeal carcinoma : a case-control study in Guangxi, China *Cancer Res* **48** 1954-59

Zou XN, Lu SH and Liu B (1994) Volatile N-nitrosamines and their precursors in Chinese salted fish-a possible etilogical factor for NPC in China *Int J Cancer* **59** 155-158

4.3 LARYNX

Adami HO, McLaughlin JK, Hsing AW et al (1992) Alcoholism and cancer risk: a population-based cohort study *Cancer Causes Control* **3** 419-429

Brownson RC, Chang JC (1987) Exposure to alcohol and tobacco and the risk of laryngeal cancer *Arch Environ Health* **42** 192-96

Brugere J, Guenel P, Lecllerk A, Rodriguez J (1986) Differential effects of tobacco and alcohol in cancer of the larynx, pharynx, and mouth *Cancer* **57** 391-395

Burch JD, Howe GR, Miller AB, Semenciw R (1981) Tobacco, alcohol, asbestos and nickel in the etiology of cancer of the larynx: a case control study *JNCI* **67** 1219-24

De Stefani E, Correa P, Oreggia F et al (1987) Risk factors in laryngeal cancer *Cancer* **60** 3087-3091

Elwood JM, Person JCG, Skippen DH et al (1984) Alcohol, smoking and socioeconomic factors in the etiology of cancer of the oral cavity, pharynx and larynx *Int J Cancer* **34** 603-612

Esteve J, Riboli E, Pequignot G, Terracini G et al (1996) Diet and cancers of the larynx and hypopharynx: the IARC multi-center study in southwestern Europe *Cancer Causes Control* **7** 240-252

Flanders WD, Rothman KJ (1986) Interaction of alcohol and tobacco in laryngeal cancer *Am J Epidemiol* **115** 371-79

Freudenheim JL, Graham S, Byers TE et al (1992) Diet, smoking and alcohol in cancer of the larynx: a case control study *Nutr Cancer* **17** 33-45

Graham S, Mettlin C, Marshall J et al (1981) Diet in the epidemiology of cancer of the larynx *Am J Epidemiol* **113** 675-680

Hedberg K, Vaughan TL, White E, Thomas DB (1994) Alcoholism and cancer of the larynx: a case-control study in western Washington (United States) *Cancer Causes Control* **5** 3-8

Herity B, Moriarty M, Bourke GJ, Daly L (1981) A case control study of head and neck cancers in the Republic of Ireland *Br J Cancer* **43** 177-82

Herity B, Moriarty M, Daly L, Dunn J, Bourke GJ (1982) The role of tobacco and alcohol in the aetiology of lung and larynx cancer *Br J Cancer* **46** 961-64

Hinds MW, Thomas D, O'Reilly HP (1979) Asbestos, dental X rays, tobacco and alcohol in the epidemiology of laryngeal cancer *Cancer* **44** 114-20

La Vecchia C, Negri E, D'Avanzo B, Franceschi S, Decarli A, Boyle P (1990) Dietary indicators of laryngeal cancer risk *Cancer Res* **50** 4497-500

Mackerras D, Buffer PA, Randall DE et al (1988) Carotene intake and the risk of laryngeal cancer in coastal Texas *Am J Epidemiol* **128** 980-88

Maier W, Beck C (1992) Larynxkarzinom nach schussverletzung und paraffinenjektion *Laryngorhinootologie* **71** 83-5

Monson RR, Lyon JL (1975) Proportional mortality among alcoholics *Cancer* **36** 1077-1079

Notani PN and Jayant K (1987) Role of diet in upper aerodigestive tract cancer *Nutr Cancer* **10** 103-113

Olsen J, Sabroe S, Fasting U (1985) Interaction of alcohol and tobacco as risk factors in cancer of the laryngeal region *J Epidemiol Commun Health* **39** 165-68

Pintos J, Franco eL, Olivera BV, Kowalski LP, Curzo MP (1994) Mate, coffee and teaconsumption and rik of cancer of the aerodigestive tract cancer *Cancer epidemiology biomarkers and Prev*; **5** 583-590

Robinette CD, Hrubec Z, Fraumeni JF (1979) Chronic alcoholism and subsequent mortality in World war II veterans *Am J Epidemiol* **109** 687-700

Schmidt W, Popham RE (1981) The role of drinking and smokingin mortality from cancer and other causes in male alcoholics *Cancer* **47** 1031-1041

Spalajkovic M (1976) Alcoholism and cancer of the larynx and hypopharynx (Fr) *J fr Oto-rhinolaryngol* **25** 49-50

Splitz MR, Fueger JJ, Goepfert H, Hong WK, Newell GR (1988) Squamous cell carcinoma of the upper aerodigestive tract A case comparison analysis *Cancer* **61** 203-08

Sundby P (1967) *Alcoholism and Mortality* Oslo: Universitetsforlaget

Tavani A, Negri E, Franceschi S, La Vecchia C (1994) Risk factors for esophageal cancer in lifelong nonsmokers *Cancer Epidemiol Biomarkers Prev* **3** 387-392

Tuyns AJ, Estene J, Randall L et al (1988) Cancer of the larynx/hypopharynx tobacco and alcohol : IARC intervention case control study in Turin and Varese (Italy), Zaragoza and Navarra (Spain), Geneva (Switzerland) and Calvados (France) *Int J Cancer* **41** 483-91

WHO (1990) World Health Organization *Diet, Nutrition and the Prevention of Chronic Diseases* Technical Report no 797 Geneva: WHO

WHO (1997) World Health Organization *The World Health Report* Geneva: WHO

Wynder EL, Bross IJ, Day E (1956) A study of environmental factors in cancer of the larynx *Cancer* **9** 86-110

Wynder EL, Covey LS, Mabuchi K et al (1976) Environmental factors in cancer of the larynx A second look *Cancer* **38** 1591-601

Zagraniski RT, Kelsey JL, Walter SD (1986) Occupational risk factors for laryngeal carcinoma, Connecticut, 1975-1980 *Am J Epidemiol* **124** 67-76

Zatonski W, Becher H, Lissowska J, Wahrendorf J (1991) Tobacco, alcohol, diet and occupational exposure in etiology of laryngeal cancer - a population based case- control study

Cancer Causes Control **2** 3-10

Zemla B, Day N, Swiatnicka J, Banasik R (1987) Larynx cancer risk factors *Neoplasm* **34** 223-33

Zheng W, Blot WJ, Shu XU et al (1992) Diet and other risk factors for laryngeal cancer in Shanghai, China *Am J Epidemiol* **136** 178-91

4.4 OESOPHAGUS

Bashiron MS, Nugmanov SN, Kilycheva NI (1968) Epidemiological study of oesophageal cancer in the Akhtubinsk region of the Kazakh socialist Republic *Vopr Onkol* **14** 3-7

Blot WJ (1992) Alcohol and cancer *Cancer Res* **52(Suppl)** 2119-2123

Bradshaw E and Schonland M (1969) Oesophageal and lung cancers in natal African males in relation to certain socio-economic factors An analysis of 484 interviews *Br J Cancer* **23** 275-284

Bradshaw E and Schonland M (1974) Smoking, drinking and oesophageal cancer in African males of Johannesburg, South Africa *Br J Cancer* **30** 157-163

Breslow NE and Day N (1980) Statistical methods in cancer epidemiology, VolI *IARC Scientific Publications No32* Lyon: International Agency for Research on Cancer

Brown LM, Blot WJ, Schuman SH et al (1988) Environmental factors and high risk of esophageal cancers among men in coastal South Carolina *JNCI* **80** 1620-1625

Chang-Claude JC, Wahrendorf J, Liang QS et al (1990) An epidemiological study of precursor lesions of esophageal cancer among young persons in a highrisk population in Huixian, China *Cancer Res* **50** 2268-2274

Chen J, Geissler C, Parpia B, Li J and Campbell TC (1992) Antioxidant status and cancer mortality in China *Int J Epidemiol* **22** 625-635

Cheng KK, Day NE, Duffy SW, Lam TH, Fok M and Wong J (1992) Pickled vegetables in the aetiology of oesophageal cancer in Hongkong Chinese *Lancet* **339** 1314-1318

Cook-Mozaffari PJ, Azordegan F, Day NE et al (1979) Oesophageal cancer studies in the Caspian littoral of Iran: results of a case control study *Br J Cancer* **39** 293-309

Darby WJ, McNutt KW and Todhunter EN (1977) Niacin *Nutr Rev* **33** 289-297

De Carli A, Liati P, Negri E, Franceschi S and La Vecchia C (1987) Vitamin A and other dietary factors in the etiology of esophageal cancer *Nutr Cancer* **10** 29-37

De Jong UW, Breslow N, Goh EH et al (1974) Aetiological factors in oesophageal cancer in Singapore Chinese *Int J Cancer* **13** 291-303

De Stefani E, Manoz N, Esteve J, Vasallo A, Victora CG and Teuchmann S (1990) Mate drinking, alcohol, tobacco, diet and esophageal cancer in Uruguay *Cancer Res* **5** 426-431

Dean G, MacLennan R, McLoughlin H et al (1979) Causes of death of blue collar workers at a Dublin Brewety, 1954-73 *Br J Cancer* **40** 581-589

Dong J (1990) Effects of As203, MNNG and B(a) P on epithelia of human fetal tracheae and rat tracheae in organ culture (in Chinese) *Chung Kuo I Hsueh Ko Hsueh Yuan Hsueh Pao* **12** 380-384

Fong ZY, Ng WL and Newberne PM (1984) N-nitrosodimethyl amine induced forestomach tumours in male Sprague - Dawley rats fed a zinc-deficient diet *IARC Sci Publ* 543-546

Franscechi S, Bidoli E, Baron AE and La Vecchia C (1990) Maize and risk of cancers of the oral cavity, pharynx and oesophagus *JNCI* **82** 1407-1411

Gao YT, McLaughlin JK, Gridley G, Blot WJ, Ji BT, Dai Q and Fraumeni JF Jr (1994) Risk factors for esophageal cancer in Shanghai, II Role of diet and nutrients *Int J Cancer* **58** 197-202

Gopalan C and Rao KSJ (1975) Pellagra and amino acid imbalance *Vitam Horm* **33** 505-528

Graham S, Marshall J, Haughey B et al (1990) Nutritional epidemiology of cancer of the esophagus *Am J Epidemiol* **131** 454-467

Griciute L, Castegnaro M, Bereziat JC (1982) Influence of ethyl alcohol on the carcinogenic activity of N-nitrosodi-n-propylamine In: Bartsch H, Castegnaro M, O'Neill IK and Okada M (Eds) *N-nitroso compounds: Occurrence and biological effects* (IARC Scientific Publications No41), Lyon: International Agency for Research on Cancer, pp 643-648

Griciute L, Castegnaro M, Bereziat JC (1984) Influence of ethyl alcohol on carcinogenesis induced with N-nitrosodiethylamine In: Borzsonyi M, Day NE, Lapis K, Yamasaki H (eds) *Models, Mechanisms and Etiology of Tumor Promotion* (IARC Scientific Publications No56), Lyon, International Agency for Research on Cancer, pp 413-417

Guo WD, Li JY, Blot WJ et al (1990) Correlations of dietary intake and blood nutrient levels with oesophageal cancer mortality in China *Nutr cancer* **13** 121-127

Hirayama T (1985) A large scale cohort study on cancer risks by diet - with special reference to the risk reducing effects of green yellow vegetable consumption *Int Symp Princess*

Takamatsn Cancer Res Fund **16** 41-53

Hirayama T (1979) Diet and Cancer *Nutr Cancer* **1** 67-81

Hirayama T (1986) Nutrition and Cancer - a large scale cohort study *Prog Clin Biol Res* **206** 299-311

Hu J, Nyren O, Wolk Al et al (1994) Risk factors for oesophageal cancer in northeast China *Int J Cancer* **57** 38-46

International Agency for Research on Cancer (IARC) (1988) *Monographs on the evaluation of the carcinogenic risks to humans Vol 44: Alcohol drinking* Lyon: International Agency for Research on Cancer

International Agency for Research on Cancer IARC (1991) *Monographs on the evaluation of the carcinogenic risk of chemicals to humans Vol 51: Coffee, tea, mate, methylxanthines, and methylglyoxal* Lyon: International Agency for Research on Cancer

Jaskiewicz K, Marasas WF, Lazarus C, Beyers AD, Van Helden PD (1988) Association of esophageal cytological abnormalities with vitamin and lipotrope deficiencies in populations at risk for esophageal cancer *Anti Cancer Res* **8** 711-715

Jaskiewicz K (1989) Oesophageal carcinoma: cytopathology and nutritional aspects in aetiology *Anticancer Res* **9** 1847-1852

Jensen OM (1983) Cancer risk among Danish male Seventh-Day Adventists and other temperance Soceity members *JNCI* **70** 1011-1014

Kaufman BD, Liberman IS, Tyshetsky VI (1965) Some data concerning the incidence of oesophageal cancer in the Gurjev region of the Kazakh SSR (Russ) *Vopr Onkol* **11** 78-85

Krishnaswamy K, Prasad MPR, Krishna TP, Pasricha S (1993) A case control study of selenium in cancer *Indian Journal of Medical Research* **98** 124-128

La Vecchia C, Negri E (1989) The role of alcohol in oesophageal cancer in non-smokers and of tobacco in non-drinkers *Int J Cancer* **43** 784-785

Li JY, Ershow AG, Chen ZJ et al (1989) A case control study of cancer of the esophagus and gastric cardia in Linxian *Int J Cancer* **43** 755-761

Lu SH, Chui SX, Yang WX, Hu XN, Guo LP, Li FM (1991) Relevance of nitrosamines to esophageal cancer in China *IARC Sci Publ* **105** 11-17

Lu SH, Ohshima H, Bartsch H (1984) Recent studies on N-nitroso compounds as possible etiological factors in oesophageal cancer *IARC Sci Publ* **57** 947-953

Lu SH, Yang WX, Guo LP, Li FM, Wang GL, Zhang JS, Lin P (1987) Determination of nitrosamine in gastric juices and urine, and a comparison of endogenous formation of N-nitrosoproline and its inhibition in subjects from high- and low-risk areas of oesophageal cancer *IARC Sci Publ* **84** 538-543

Maqbool M, Ahad A (1976) Carcinoma of oesophagus in Kashmir *Indian J Otolaryngol* **28** 118-122

Martinez I (1969) Factors associated with cancer of the oesophagus, mouth and pharynx in Puerto Rico *JNCI* **42** 1069-1094

Mayne ST, Graham S, Zheng TZ (1991) Dietary retinol: prevention or promoting carcinogenesis *Cancer Causes Control* **2** 443-450

Mettlin C, Graham S, Priore R et al (1981) Diet and Cancer of the esophagus *Nutr Cancer* **2** 143-7

Middleton B, Byers T, Marshall J, Graham S (1986) Dietary vitamin A and cancer - a multisite case control study *Nutr Cancer* **8** 107-116

Mufti SI, Becker G, Siper IG (1989) Effect of chronic dietary ethanol consumption on the initiation and promotion of chemically-induced esophageal carcinogenesis in experimental rats *Carcinogenesis* **10** 303-309

Muir CS, McKinney PA (1992) Cancer of the oesophagus : a global overview *Eur J Cancer Prev* **1** 259-64

Munoz N, Wahrendorf J, Bang LJ, Gespi M, Grassi A (1988) Vitamin intervention on precancerous lesions of the esophagus in a high-risk population in China *Ann N Y Acad Sci* **534** 618-19

NAS (1982 *Diet, Nutrition and Cancer* Washington: National Academy Press

NAS (1989) *Diet and Health* Washington: National Academy Press

Nauss KM, Bueche D, Newberne PM (1987) Effect of vitamin A nutriture on experimental esophageal carcinogenesis *JNCI* **79** 145-147

Notani PN, Jayant K (1987) Role of diet in upper aerodigestive tract cancers *Nutr Cancer* **10** 103-113

Ohsima H, Bartsch H (1981) Quantative estimation of endogenous nitrosation in humans by monitoring N-nitrosoproline excretion in the urine *Cancer Res* **41** 3658-3662

Pearson JG (1966) The radiotherapy of carcinoma of the esophagus and postencoid region in south east Scotland *Clin Radiol* **17** 242-257

Pottern LM, Morris LE, Blot WJ et al (1981) Esophageal cancer among black men in Washington DC I Alcohol, tobacco and other risk factors *JNCI* **67** 777-783

Prasad MPR, Krishna TP, Pasricha S, Krishnaswamy K, Quereshi MA (1992) Esophageal cancer and diet - a case control study *Nutr Cancer* **18** 85-93

Ren A, Han X (1991) Dietary factors and oesophageal cancer: a case-contro study (in Chinese) *Chung Hua Liu Hsing Ping Hsueh Tsa Chih* **12** 200-204

Schottenfeld D (1984) Epidemiology of cancer of the oesophagus *Semin Oncol* **11** 92-100

Siddiqui M, Kumar R, Fazili Z, Spiegelhalder B, Preussmann R (1992) Increased exposure to dietary amines and nitrate in a population at high risk of oesophageal and gastric cancer in Kashmir (India) *Carcinogenesis* **13** 1331-1335

Singer G, Chuan J, Roman J, Li M, Lijinsky W (1986) Nitrosamines and nitrosamine precursors in foods from Linxian, China, a high incidence area for esophageal cancer *Carcinogenesis* **7** 733-736

Steinmetz K, Potter JD (1991) A review of vegetables, fruit, and cancer I: epidemiology *Cancer Causes Control* **2** 325-357

Tavani A, Negri E, Franceschi S, La Vecchia C (1994) Risk factors for esophageal cancer in lifelong nonsmokers *Cancer Epidemiol Biomarker Prev* **3** 87-92

Thurnham DI, Zheng SF, Munoz N, Crespi M, Grassi A (1985) Comparison of riboflavin, vitamin A, and zinc status in high and low risk regions for oesophageal cancer in China *Nutr Cancer* **7** 131-143

Tuyns AJ, Pequignot G, Abbatucci JS (1979) Oesophageal cancer and alcohol consumption: importance of type of beverage *Int J Cancer* **23** 443-447

Tuyns AJ, Pequignot G, Jensen OM (1977) Le cancer de L'oesophage in Ille-et-Villaine en fonction des niveauxde consommation d'alcool et de tabac Des risques qui se multiplient *Bull Cancer* **64** 45-60

Tuyns AJ, Riboli E, Doornbos G et al (1987) Diet and oesophageal cancer in Calvados (France) *Nutr Cancer* **9** 81-92

Tuyns AJ (1983) Oesophageal cancer in non-smoking drinkers and in non-drinking smokers *Int J Cancer* **32** 443-444

Umbenhauer D, Wild CP, Montesano R, Saffhill R, Boyle JM, Huh N, Kirstein U, Thomale J, Rajewsky MF, Lu SH (1985) Methyldeoxyguanosine in esophageal DNA among individuals at high risk of esophageal cancer *Int J Cancer* **36** 661-665

Valsecchia MG (1992) Modelling the relative risk of esophageal cancer in a case control study *J Clin Epidemiol* **45** 347-355

Van Helden PD, Beyers AD, Bester AJ, Jaskiewicz K (1987) Oesophageal cancer: vitamin and liptrope deficiencies in an at risk South Africa Population *Nutr Cancer* **10** 247-255

Van Rensburg SJ, Hall JM, du Bruyn DB (1985) Effects of various dietary staples on oesophageal carcinogenesis induced in rats by subcutaneously administered N-nitrosomethylbenzylamine *JNCI* **75** 561-566

Van Rensburg SJ, Hall JM, Gathercole PS (1986) Inhibition of oesophageal carcinogenesis in corn fed rats by riboflavin, nicotinic acid, selenium, molybdenum, zinc and magnesium *Nutr Cancer* **8** 163-170

Van Rensburg SJ (1981) Epidemiologic and dietary evidence for a specific nutritional predisposition to oesophageal cancer *JNCI* **67** 243-51

Vassallo A, Correa P, De Stefani E et al (1985) Oesophageal cancers in Uruguay : a case control study *JNCI* **75** 1005-1009

Victora CG, Munoz N, Day NE, Barcelos LB, Peccin DA, Braga N (1987) Hot beverages and oesophageal cancer in southern Brazil : A case control study *Int J Cancer* **39** 710-716

Wahrendorf J, Chang-Claude J, Liang QS et al (1989) Precursor lesions of oesophageal cancer in young people in a high risk population in China *Lancet* **2** 1239-1241

Wang LD (1992) Preliminary study on nutrition and precancerous lesions of the esophagus in the adolescents *Chung Hua Chung Liu Tsa Chih* **14** 94-97

Ward MH, Sinha R, Heinman EF, Rothman N, Markin R, Weisinburger DD, Correa P, Zahm SH (1997) Risk of adenocarcinoma of the stomach and esophagus with meat cooking method and doneness preference *Int J Cancer* **71** 14-19

WHO (1997) World Health Organization *The World Health Report* Geneva:WHO

Wu Y, Chen J, Oshima H, Pignatelli B, Boreham J, Li J, Campbell TC, Peto R, Bartsch H (1993) Geographic association between urinary excretion of N-nitroso compounds and oesophageal cancer mortality in China *Int J Cancer* **54** 713-719

Wynder EL, Hultberg S, Jacobsen R et al (1957) Environmental factors in cancer of the upper alimentary tract *Cancer* **10** 470-487

Wynder EL, Bross IJ (1961) A study of etiological factors in cancer of the esophagus *Cancer* **14** 389-413

Yamada Y, Weller RO, Kleihues P, Ludeke BI (1992) Effects of ethanol and various alcoholic beverages on the formation of O^6 methyldeoxyguanine from concurrently administered N-nitrosomethylbenzylamine in rats: a dose response study *Carcinogenesis* **13** 1171-1175

Yang CS (1980) Research on oesophageal cancer in China: a review Cancer Res **40** 2633-2644

Yang CS, Newmark HL (1987) The role of micronutrient deficiency in carcinogenesis *Crit Rev Oncol Hematol* **7** 267-287

Yioris N, Ivankovic S, Lehnert T (1984) Effect of thermal injury and oral administration of N-methyl N-nitro-N-nitrosoguanidine on the development of esophageal tumors in wistar rats *Oncology* **41** 36-38

Yu MC, Garabrant DH, Peters JM, Mack TM (1988) Tobacco, alcohol, diet, occupation and carcinoma of the esophagus *Cancer Res* **48** 3843-3848

Ziegler R, Morris L, Blot W et al (1981) Esophageal cancer among black men in Washington DC II Role of nutrition *JNCI* **67** 1199-1206

4.5 LUNG

Alavanja MC, Brown CC, Swanson C, Brownson RC (1993) Saturated fat intake and lung cancer risk among nonsmoking women in Missouri *JNCI* **85** 1906-1916

Albanes D, Blair A, Taylor PR (1989) Physical activity and risk of cancer in the NHANES I population *Am J Public Health* **79** 744–750

Ansher SS, Dolan P, Bueding E (1986) Biochemical effects of dithiolthiones *Food Chem Toxicol* **24** 405–415

Armstrong B, Doll R (1975) Environmental factors and cancer incidence and mortality in different countries, with special reference to dietary practice *Int J Cancer* **15** 617–631

Bandera E, Graham S, Freudenheim J (1991) Folate, alcohol consumption and the risk of lung cancer *FASEB* **5** A562

Bandera EV, Freudenheim JL, Graham S, Marshall JR, Haughey BP, Swanson M, Brasure J, Wilkinson G (1992) Alcohol consumption and lung cancer in white males *Cancer Causes Control* 361-369

Beems RB, van Beek L (1984) Modifying effect of dietary fat on benzo[a]pyrene-induced respiratory tract tumours in hamsters *Carcinogenesis* **5** 413-417

Bjelke E (1975) Dietary vitamin A and human lung cancer *Int J Cancer* **15** 561-565

Block G (1991) Vitamin C and cancer prevention: the epidemiologic evidence *Am J Clin Nutr* **53** 270s–280s

Bond GG, Thompson FE, Cook RR (1987) Dietary vitamin A and lung cancer: results od a case-control study among chemical workers *Nutr Cancer* **5** 305-12

Bratakos MS, Vouterakos TP, Ioannou PV (1990) Selenium status of cancer patients in Greece *Sci Total Environ* **92** 207-222

Brownson RB, Chang JC, Davis JR, Smith CA (1991) Physical activity on the job and lung cancer in Missouri *Am J Pub Health* **81** 639-642

Byers T, Vena J, Mettlin C, Swanson M, Graham S (1984) Dietary vitamin A and lung cancer risk: an analysis by histologic subtypes *Am J Epidemiol* **120** 769-776

Byers TE, Graham S, Haughey BP, Marshall JR, Swanson MK (1987) Diet and lung cancer risk: findings from the Western New York Diet Study *Am J Epidemiol* **125** 351-363

Candelora EC, Stockwell HG, Armstrong AW, Pinkham PA (1992) Dietary intake and risk of lung cancer in women who never smoked *Nutr Cancer* **17** 263-270

Carroll KK, Khor HT (1975) Dietary fat in relation to tumorigenesis *Prog Biochem Pharmacol* **10** 308-53

Chow W-H, Schuman LM, McLaughlin JK, Bjelke E, Gridley G, Wacholder S, Co Chien HT, Blot WJ (1992) A cohort study of tobacco use, diet, occupation, and lung cancer mortality *Cancer Causes Control* **3** 247-254

Chung F–L, Morse MA, Eklind KI, Xu Y (1993) Inhibition of the tobacco–specific nitrosamine–induced lung tumorigenesis by compounds derived from cruciferous vegetables and green tea *Ann NY Acad Sci* **686** 186–201

Chyou PH, Nomura AM, Stemmerman GN et al (1993) Lung cancer: a prospective study of smoking, occupation, and nutrient intake *Arch Environ Health* **48** 69-72

Coates RJ, Weiss NS, Daling JR, Morris JS, Labbe RF (1988) Serum levels of selenium and retinol and the subsequent risk of cancer *Am J Epidemiol* **128** 515-523

Comstock G, Bush T, Helzlsouer K (1992) Serum retinol, beta-carotene, vitamin E, and selenium as related to subsequent cancer at specific sites *Am J Epidem* **135** 115-121

Connet JE, Kuller LH, Kjelsberg MO et al (1989) Relationship between carotenoids and cancer The Multiple Risk Factor Intervention Trial (MRFIT) Study *Cancer* **64** 126-134

Dartigues JR, Dabis F, Gros N et al (1990) Dietary vitamin A, beta-carotene, and risk of epidemoid lung cancer in south-western France *Eur J Epidemiol* **6** 261-265

Dorgon JF, Ziegler RG, Schoenberg JB et al (1993) Race and sex differences in associations of vegetables, fruits, and carotenoids with lung cancer risk in New Jersey (USA) *Cancer Causes and Control* **4** 273-81

el-Bayoumy K, Upadhyaya P, Desai DH, Amin S, Hecht SS (1993) Inhibition of 4-(methylnitrosamino)-1-(3-pyridyl)-1-butanon e tumorigenicity in mouse lung by the synthetic organoselenium compound, 1,4-phenylenebis(methylene)selenocyanate *Carcinogenesis* **14** 1111-1113

Fontham ET, Pickle LW, Haenszel W, Correa P, Lin Y, Falk R (1988) Dietary vitamin A and C and lung cancer risk in Louisiana *Cancer* **62** 2267-2273

Gao C, Tajima K, Kuroishi T et al (1993) Protective effects of raw vegetables and fruit against lung cancer among smokers and ex-smokers: a case-control study in the Tokai area of Japan *Jpn J Cancer Res* **84** 594-600

Goldbohm RA, Hertog MGL, Brants HAM, van Poppel G, van den Brandt PA (1996) Consumption of black tea and cancer risk: a prospective cohort study *JNCI* **88** 93-100

Goodman MT, Hankin JH, Wilkens LR, Kolonel LN (1992) High-fat foods and the risk of lung cancer *Epidemiology* **3** 288–299

Goodman MT, Kolonel LN, Yoshizawa CN, Hankin JH (1988) The effect of dietary cholesterol and fat on the risk of lung cancer in Hawaii *Am J Epidemiol* **128** 1241–1255

Gordon T, Kannel WB (1984) Drinking and mortality: The Framingham Study *Am J Epidemiol* **120** 97-107

Gregor A, Lee PN, Roe FJC et al (1980) Comparison of dietary histories in lung cancer cases and controls with special reference to vitamin A *Nutr Cancer* **2** 93-97

Harris RW, J KT, Silcocks PB, Bull D, Wald NJ (1991) A case-control study of dietary carotene in men with lung cancer and in men with other epithelial cancers *Nutr Cancer* **15** 63-68

Heilbrun LK, Nomura AM, Stemmermann GN (1984) Dietary cholesterol and lung cancer risk among Japanese men in Hawaii *Am J Clin Nutr* **39** 375-379

Heimburger DC, Alexander CB, Birch R, Butterworth CE Jr, Bailey WC, Krumdieck CL (1988) Improvement in bronchial squamous metaplasia in smokers treated with folate and vitamin B12 *J Am Med Assoc* **259** 1525-1530

Hennekens CH, Buring JE, Manson JE, Stampfer M, Rosner B, Cook NR, Belanger C, LaMotte F, Gaziano JM, Ridker PM, Willett W, Peto R (1996) Lack of effect of long-term supplementation with beta carotene on the incidence of malignant neoplasms and cardiovascular disease *N Engl J Med* **334** 1145-1149

Herity B, Moriarity M, Bourke GJ, Daly L (1981) A case-control study of head and neck cancer in the Republic of Ireland *Br J Cancer* **43** 177–182

Hinds MW, Kolonel LN, Hankin JH, Lee J (1983) Dietary cholesterol and lung cancer risk in a multiethnic population in Hawaii *Int J Cancer* **32** 727–732

Hinds MW, Kolonel LN, Hankin JH, Lee J (1984) Dietary vitamin A, carotene, vitamin C and risk of lung cancer in Hawaii *Am J Epidemiol* **119** 227–237

Ho SC, Donnan SP, Martin WC, Tsao SY (1988) Dietary vitamin A, beta-carotene and risk of epidermoid lung cancer among Chinese males *Singapore Med J* **29** 213–218

Holst PA, Kromhout D, Brand R (1988) For debate: pet birds as independent risk factor for lung cancer *BMJ* **297** 1319–1321

Hunter DJ, Morris JS, Chute CG et al (1990b) Predictors of selenium concentration in human toenails *Am J Epidemiol* **132** 114-122

Hunter DJ, Morris JS, Stampfer MJ, Colditz GA, Speizer FE, Willett WC (1990a) A prospective study of selenium status and breast cancer risk *JAMA* **264** 1128-1131

Hursting SD, Thornquist M, Henderson MM Types of dietary fat and the incidence of cancer at 5 sites *Prev Med* 1990 **19** 242-253

Ip C, Lisk DJ, Stoewsand GS (1992) Mammary cancer prevention by regular garlic and selenium-enriched garlic *Nutr Cancer* **17** 279-286

Jacobsen BK, Bjelke E, Kvåle G et al (1986) Coffee drinking, mortality, and cancer incidence: results from a Norwegian prospective study *JNCI* **76** 823-831

Jain M, Burch JD, Howe GR, Risch HA, Miller AB (1990) Dietary factors and risk of lung cancer: results from a case- control study, Toronto, 1981-1985 *Int J Cancer* **45** 287-293

Kalandidi A, Katsouyanni K, Voropoulou N, Bastas G, Saracci R, Trichopoulos D (1990) Passive smoking and diet in the etiology of lung cancer among non-smokers *Cancer Causes Control* **1** 15-21

Katz EB, Boylan ES (1989) Effect of the quality of dietary fat on tumor growth and metastasis from a rat mammary adenocarcinoma *Nutr Cancer* **12** 343-350

Kinlen LJ, Willows AN, Goldblatt P, Yudkin J (1988) Tea consumption and cancer *Br J Cancer* **58** 397-401

Klatsky AI, Friedman GD, Siegelaub AB (1981) Alcohol and mortality: a ten year Kaiser-Permanente experience *Ann Intern Med* **95** 139–145

Knekt P, Aromaa A, Maatela J et al (1990) Serum selenium and subsequent risk of cancer among Finnish men and women *JNCI* **82** 864-868

Knekt P, Jarvinen R, Seppanen R, Rissanen A, Aromaa A et al (1991b) Dietary antioxidants and the risk of lung cancer *Am J Epidemiol* **134** 471-479

Knekt P, Seppanen R, Jarvinen R et al (1991a) Dietary cholesterol, fatty acids, and the risk of lung cancer among men *Nutr Cancer* **16** 267-275

Kolonel LN, Hankin JH, Lee J, Chu SY, Nomura AMY, Hinds MW (1981) Nutrient intakes in relation to cancer incidence in Hawaii *Br J Cancer* **44** 332-339

Kolonel LN, Hinds MW, Nomura AM, Hankin JH, Lee J (1985) Relationship of dietary vitamin A and ascorbic acid intake to the risk for cancers of the lung, bladder, and prostate in Hawaii *Natl Cancer Inst Monogr* **69** 137–142

Kono S, Ikeda M, Tokudome S, Nishizumi M, Kuratsune M (1986) Alcohol and mortality: a cohort study of male Japanese physicians *Int J Epidemiol* **15** 527-532

Koo LC (1988) Dietary habits and lung cancer risk among Chinese females in Hong Kong who never smoked *Nutr Cancer* **11** 155-172

Kromhout D (1987) Essential micronutrients in relation to carcinogenesis *Am J Clin Nutr* **45** 1361-1367

Kvale G, Bjelke E, Gart JJ (1983) Dietary habits and lung cancer risk *Int J Cancer* **31** 397-405

Le Marchand L, Hankin JH, Kolonel LN, Beecher GR, Wilkens LR, Zhao LP (1993) Intake of specific carotenoids and lung cancer risk *Cancer, Epidem, Biomarke and Prev* **2** 183-187

Le Marchand L, Yoshizawa CN, Kolonel LN, Hankin JH, Goodman MT (1989) Vegetable consumption and lung cancer risk: a population-based case-control study in Hawaii

JNCI **81** 1158-1164

Long-de W, Hammond EC (1985) Lung cancer, fruit, green salad and vitamin pills *Chin Med J* **98** 206-10

Lopez SA, Le Gardeur BY (1982) Vitamins A, C and E in relation to lung cancer incidence *Am J Epidem* **35** 851

Margetts BM, Jackson AA (1993) Interactions between peoples' diet and their smoking habits: the dietary and nutritional survey of British adults *BMJ* **307** 1381-1384

Mayne ST, Janerich DT, Greenwald P et al Dietary Beta Carotene and lung cancer risk in US nonsmokers *JNCI* 1994 **86** 33-38

McMichael AJ, Jensen OM, Karkin DM, Zardize DG (1984) Dietary and endogenous cholesterol and human cancer *Epidemiol Rev* **6** 192-216

McPhillips JB, Eaton CB, Gans KM, Derby CA, Lasater TM, McKenney JL, Carleton RA (1994) Dietary differences in smokers and nonsmokers from two southeastern New England communities *J Am Diet Assoc* **94** 287-92

Menkes MS, Comstock GW, Vuilleumier JP, Helsing KJ, Rider AA, Brookmeyer R (1986) Serum beta-carotene, vitamins A and E, selenium, and the risk of lung cancer *N Engl J Med* **315** 1250-1254

Mettlin C, Graham S, Swanson M (1979) Vitamin A and lung cancer *JNCI* **62** 1435-1438

Mettlin CJ (1989) Milk drinking, other beverage habits and lung cancer risk *Int J Cancer* **43** 608-612

Morabia A, Wynder EL, (1990) Dietary habits of smokers, people who never smoked, and exsmokers *Am J Clin Nutr* **52** 933-7

Morse MA, LaGreca SD, Amin SG, Chung F-L (1990) Effects of indole-3-carcbinol on lung tumorigeneisis and DNA methylation induced by 4-(Methylnitrosamine)-1-(3-pyridyl)-1-butanone (NNK) and on the metabolism and disposition of NNK in A/J mice *Cancer Res* **50** 2613–2617

Nachiappan V, Mufti SI, Chakravarti A, Eskelson CD, Rajasekharan R (1994) Lipid peroxidation and ethanol-related tumor promotion in Fischer-344 rats treated with tobacco-specific nitrosamines *Alcohol Alcohol* **29** 565-74

NAS (1982) *Diet, Nutrition and Cancer* Washington: National Academy Press

NAS (1989) *Diet and Health* Washington, National Academy Press

Nomura A, Heilbrun LK, Morris JS, Stemmermann N (1987) Serum selenium and risk of cancer by specific sites: case-control analysis of prospective data *JNCI* **79** 103-108

Nomura AM, Heilbrun LK, Stemmermann GN (1986) Prospective study of coffee consumption and the risk of cancer *JNCI* **76** 587–590

Nomura AM, Stemmermann GN, Heilbrun LK, Salkeld RM, Vuilleumier JP (1985) Serum vitamin levels and the risk of cancer of specific sites in men of Japanese ancestry in Hawaii *Cancer Res* **45** 2369–2372

Omenn GS, Goodman GE, Thornquist MD, Balmes J, Cullen MR, Glass A, Keogh JP, Meyskens FL, Valanis B, Williams JH, Barnhart S, Hamma S (1996) Effects of a combination of beta carotene and vitamin A on lung cancer and cardiovascular disease *N Engl J Med* **334** 1150–1155

Paffenbarger RS, Jr, Hyde RT, Wing AL (1987) Physical activity and incidence of cancer in diverse populations: a preliminary report *Am J Clin Nutr* **45** 312–17

Paganini Hill A, Chao A, Ross RK, Henderson BE (1987) Vitamin A, beta-carotene, and the risk of cancer: a prospective study *JNCI* **79** 443-448

Parkin DM, Muir CS, Whelan SL, Gao, YT, Ferlay J, Powell J (eds) (1992) *Cancer Incidence in Five Continents* **6** IARC: Lyon

Pastorino U, Pisani P, Berrino F et al (1987) Vitamin A and female lung cancer: a case-control study on plasma and diet *Nutr Cancer* **10** 171-179

Peleg I, Morris S, Hames CG (1985) Is serum selenium a risk factor for cancer? *Med Oncol Tumor Pharmacol* **2** 157-163

Pisani P, Berrino F, Macaluso M, Pastorino U, Crosignani P, Baldasseroni A (1986) Carrots, green vegetables and lung cancer : A case-control study *Int J Epidemiol* **15** 463-468

Pollack ES, Nomura AMY, Heilbrun LK, Stemmerman GN, Green SB (1984) Prospective study of alcohol consumption and cancer *N Engl J Med* **310** 617–621

Poole C (1989) Cancer and high selenium intake *Doctoral thesis, Harvard School of Public Health*

Potter JD (1996) Chemoprevention: pharmacology or biology? Invited commentary on: 'Chemoprevention of cancer: strategies for identification and clinical evaluation of promising agents' *Oncology* in press

Potter JD, McMichael AJ, Hartshorne JM (1982) Alcohol and beer consumption in relation to cancers of bowel and lung: an extended correlation analysis *J Chronic Dis* **35** 833-842

Potter JD, Sellers TA, Folsom AR, McGovern PG

(1992) Alcohol, beer, and lung cancer in postmenopausal women: the Iowa Women's Health Study *Ann Epidemiol* **2** 587-595

Ringstad J, Jacobsen BK, Tretli S, Thomassen Y (1988) Serum selenium concentration associated with risk of cancer *J Clin Pathol* **41** 454-457

Salonen JT, Alfthan G, Huttunen JK, Puska P (1984) Association between serum selenium and the risk of cancer *Am J Epidemiol* **120** 342-349

Salonen JT, Salonen R, Lappetelainen R, Meanpaa PH, Alfthan G, Puska P (1985) Risk of cancer in relation to serum concentrations of selenium and vitamins A and E: Matched case-control analysis of prospective data *Br Med J* **290** 417-420

Samet JM, Skipper BJ, Humble CG, Pathak DR (1985) Lung cancer risk and vitamin A consumption in New Mexico *Am Rev Respir Dis* **131** 198-202

Scholar EM, Violi LA, Newland J, Bresnic E, Birt DF (1989) The effect of dietary fat of metastasis of the Lewis lung carcinoma and the BALB/c mammary carcinoma *Nutr Cancer* **12** 109-119

Schrauzer GN, White DA, Schneider CJ (1977) Cancer mortality correlation studies - III: Statistical associations with dietary selenium intakes *Bioinorg Chem* **7** 23-31

Schwartz D, Lellouch J, Flamant R, Denoix PF (1962) Alcohol and cancer Results of retrospective study *Rev Fr Etud Clin Biol* **7** 590-604

Sellers TA, Bailey-Wilson J, Elston RC et al 1990 Evidence for Mendelian inheritance in the pathogenesis of lung cancer *JNCI* **82**: 1272-1279

Severson RK, Nomura AMY, Grove JS, Stemmermann GN (1989) A prospective analysis of physical activity and cancer *Am J Epidemiol* **130** 522-9

Shekelle RB, Lepper M, Liu S et al (1981) Dietary vitamin A and risk of cancer in the Western Electric Study *Lancet* **2** 1186-1190

Shekelle RB, Rossof AH, Stamler J (1991) Dietary cholesterol and incidence of lung cancer: the Western Electric Study *Am J Epidemiol* **134** 480-484

Shibata A, Paganini Hill A, Ross RK, Yu MC, Henderson BE (1992) Dietary [beta]-carotene, cigarette smoking, and lung cancer in men *Cancer Causes and Control* **3** 207–214

Stahelin HG, Gey KF, Eichholzer M et al (1991) Plasma antioxidant vitamins and subsequent cancer mortality in the 12-year follow-up of the prospective Basel Study *Am J Epidemiol* **133** 766-775

Steinmetz KA, Potter JD, Folsom AR: Vegetables, fruit, and lung cancer in the Iowa Women's Health Study Cancer Res 1993;53:536–543

Stocks P (1970) Cancer mortality in relation to national consumption of cigarettes, solid fuel, tea, and coffee *Br J Cancer* **24** 215–225

Swanson CA, Mao BL, Li JY et al (1992) Dietary determinants of lung-cancer risk: results from a case- control study in Yunnan Province, China Int *J Cancer* **50** 876-880

The alpha–tocopherol beta carotene cancer prevention study group (1994) The effect of vitamin E and beta carotene on the incidence of lung cancer and other cancers in male smokers *N Engl J Med* **330** 1029

Tominaga K, Saito Y, Mori K et al (1992) An evaluation of serum microelement concentrations in lung cancer and matched non-cancer patients to determine the risk of developing lung cancer: a preliminary study *Jpn J Clin Oncol* **22** 96-101

van den Brandt PA, Goldbohm RA, van't veer P et al (1993) A prospective cohort study on selenium status and the risk of lung cancer *Cancer Res* **53** 4860-4865

Virtamo J, Valkeila E, Alfthan G, Punsar S, Huttunen JK, Karvonen MJ (1987) Serum selenium and risk of cancer *Cancer* **60** 145-148

Wald NJ, Thompson SG, Densem JW, Boreham J, Bailey A (1988) Serum beta-carotene and subsequent risk of cancer: results from the BUPA Study *Br J Cancer* **57** 428-433

Wattenberg LW, Coccia JB (1991) Inhibition of 4-(methylnitrosamino)-1-(3-pyridyl)-1-butanone carcinogenesis in mice by D-limonene and citrus fruit oils *Carcinogenesis* **12** 115-117

WHO (1997) World Health Organization *The World Health Report* Geneva:WHO

Willett WC, Polk BF, Morris JS et al (1983) Prediagnostic serum selenium and risk of cancer *Lancet* **2** 130-134

Williams RR, Horn JW (1977) Association of cancer sites with tobacco and alcohol consumption and socioeconomic status of patients: Interview study from the Third National Cancer Survey *JNCI* **58** 525-547

Wu AH, Henderson BE, Pike MC, Yu MC (1985) Smoking and other risk factors for lung cancer in women *JNCI* **74** 747-751

Wu Y, Zheng W, Seller TA et al (1994) Dietary cholesterol, fat, and lung cancer incidence among older women: the Iowa Women's Health Study (United States) *Cancer Causes and Control* **5** 395-400

Wynder EL, Hofman D (1994) Smoking and lung cancer: scientific challenges and opportunities *Cancer Rei* **54** 5284-5295

Wynder EL, Hebert JR, Kabat GC (1987) Association of dietary fat and lung cancer *JNCI* **79** 631-637

Xie JX, Lesaffre E, Kesteloot H (1991) The relationship between animal fat intake, cigarette smoking, and lung cancer *Cancer Causes Control* **2** 79-83

Yang CS, Hong J-Y, Wang Z-Y (1993) Inhibition of nitrosamine-induced tumorigenesis by diallyl sulfide and tea *Food and Cancer Prevention: Chemical and Biological Aspects* 247-252

Zheng W, Doyle TJ, Kushi LH, Sellers TA, Hong C-P, Folsom AR (1996) Tea consumption and cancer incidence in a prospective study of postmenopausal women *Am J Epidemiol* **144** 175–182

Ziegler RG, Mason TJ, Stemhagen A et al (1984) Dietary carotene and vitamin A and risk of lung cancer among white men in New Jersey *JNCI* **73** 1429-1435

Ziegler RG, Subar AF, Craft NE, Ursin G, Patterson BH, Graubard BI 1(992) Does beta-carotene explain why reduced cancer risk is associated with vegetable and fruit intake? *Cancer Res* **52** 2060s-2066

4.6 STOMACH

Acheson ED and Doll R (1964) Dietary factors in carcinoma of stomach: a study of 100 cases and 200 controls *Gut* **5** 126-131

Adami HO, McLaughlin JK, Hsing AW, Wolk A, Ekbom A, Holmberg L et al (1992) Alcohol and cancer risk: a population-based cohort study *Cancer Causes Control* **3** 419-425

Agudo A, Gonzalez CA, Marcos G et al (1992) Consumption of alcohol, coffee, and tobacco, and gastric cancer in Spain *Cancer Causes Control* **3** 137-143

Ames BN, Gold LS (1990) Too many rodent carcinogens: motogenesis increases mutagenesis *Science* **249** 970-1

Anonymous (1992) Serum selenium concentrations in patients with intestinal metaplasia and in controls The ECP-EURONUT-IM study group *Eur J Cancer Prev* **1** 31-34

Ansher SS, Dolan P, Bueding E (1986) Biochemical effects of dithiolthiones *Food Chem Toxicol* **24** 405-15

Aoki K, Kurihara M, Hayakawa N, Suzuki S, editors (1992) *Death rates for malignant neoplasms for selected sites by sex and five-year age group in 33 countries, 1953-57 to 1983-87* University of

Nagoya Coop Press: Nagoya

Armstrong B and Doll R (1975) Environmental factors and cancer incidence and mortality in different countries, with special reference to dietary practices *Int J Cancer* **15** 617-631

Birt DF, Bresnick E (1991) Chemoprevention by nonnutrient components of vegetables and fruits, in Alfin-Slater RB, Kritchevsky D (eds): *Cancer and nutrition* New York, Plenum Press 221-260

Bjelke E (1974) Epidemiologic studies of cancer of the stomach, colon, and rectum; with special emphasis on the role of diet *Scand J Gastroenterol* **9** (suppl 31) 1-235

Blot WJ, Li JY, Taylor PR, Guo W, Dawsey S, Wang GQ et al (1993) Nutrition intervention trials in Linxian, China: Supplementation with specific vitamin/mineral combinations, cancer incidence, and disease-specific mortality in the general population *JNCI* **85** 1483-1492

Boeing H, Frentzel-Beyme R, Berger M, Berndt V, Gores W, Korner M et al (1991a) Case-control study on stomach cancer in Germany *Int J Cancer* **47** 858-864

Boeing H, Jedrychowski W, Wahrendorf J, Popiela T, Tobiasz-Adamczyk B and Kulig A (1991b) Dietary risk factors in intestinal and diffuse types of stomach cancer: a multicenter case-control study in Poland *Cancer Causes Control* **2** 227-233

Brown LM, Silverman DT, Pottern LM, Schoenberg JB, Greenberg RS, Swanson GM et al (1994) Adenocarcinoma of the esophagus and esophagogastric junction in White men in the United States: alcohol, tobacco, and socioeconomic factors *Cancer Causes Control* **5** 333-340

Buiatti E, Palli D, Decarli A, Amadori D, Avellini C, Bianchi S et al (1989) Case-control study of gastric cancer and diet in Italy *Int J Cancer* **44** 611-616

Buiatti E, Palli D, Decarli A, Amadori D, Avellini C, Bianchi S et al (1990) A case-control study of gastric cancer and diet in Italy II Association with nutrients *Int J Cancer* **45** 896-901

capsaicin protects against aspirin-induced lesion formation and bleeding in the rat gastric mucosa *Gastroenterology* **96** 1425-33

Charnley G, Tannenbaum SR (1985) Flow cytometric analysis of the effect of sodium chloride on gatric cancer risk in the rat *Cancer Res* **45** 5608-16

Chen LH, Boissonneault GA, Glauert HP (1988) Vitamin C, vitamin E and cancer (review) *Anticancer Res* **8** 739-748

Chen VW, Abu-Elyazeed RR, Zavala DE, Ktsanes VK, Haenszel W, Cuello C et al (1990) Risk factors of gastric precancerous lesions in a high-risk Colombian population I Salt *Nutr Cancer* **13** 59-65

Chyou PH, Nomura AMY, Hankin JH and Stemmermann GN (1990) A case-control study of diet and stomach cancer *Cancer Res* **50** 7501-7504

Coggon D, Barker DJP, Cole RB and Nelson M (1989) Stomach cancer and food storage *JNCI* **81** 1178-1182

Correa P (1988) A human model of gastric carcinogenesis *Cancer Res* **48** 3554-3560

Correa P (1992) Human gastric carcinogenesis: a multistep and multifactorial process—first American Cancer Society award lecture on cancer epidemiology and prevention *Cancer Res* **52** 6735-6740

Correa P, Cuello C, Fajardo L, Haenszel W, Bolanos O and de Ramirez B (1983) Diet and gastric cancer: nutrition survey in a high-risk area *JNCI* **70** 673-678

Correa P, Fontham E, Pickle LW, Chen V, Lin Y and Haenszel W (1985) Dietary determinants of gastric cancer in south Louisiana inhabitants *JNCI* **75** 645-654

Cuello C, Correa P, Haenszel W, Gordillo G, Brown C, Archer M et al (1976) Gastric cancer in Colombia I Cancer risk and suspect environmental agents *JNCI* **57** 1015-1020

De Sanjose S, Munoz N, Sobala G et al (1996) Antioxidants, Helicobacter pylori and stomach cancer in Venezuela *Eur J Cancer Prev* **5** 57-62

Demirer T, Icli F, Uzunalimoglu O and Kucuk O (1990) Diet and stomach cancer incidence: a case-control study in Turkey *Cancer* **65** 2344-2348

Dorant E, van den Brandt PA, Goldbohm RA and Sturmans F (1996) Consumption of onions and a reduced risk of stomach carcinoma *Gastroenterology* **110** 12-20

Dorant E, van den Brandt PA, Goldbohm RA, Hermus RJJ and Sturmans F (1993) Garlic and its significance for the prevention of cancer in humans: a critical review *Br J Cancer* **67** 424-429

Dragsted LO, Strube M, Larsen JC (1993) Cancer-protective factors in fruits and vegetables: biochemical and biological background *Pharmacol Toxicol* **72** Suppl (1)116-135

Elson CE, Yu SG (1994) The chemoprevention of cancer by mevalonate-derived constituents of fruits and vegetables *J Nutr* **124**(5) 607-14

Fontham E, Zavala D, Correa P, Rodriguez E, Hunter F, Haenszel W et al (1986) Diet and chronic atrophic gastritis: a case-control study *JNCI* **76** 621-627

Forman D (1987) Dietary exposure to N-nitroso compounds and the risk of human cancer *Cancer Surv* **6** 719-739

Forman D (1989) Are nitrates a significant risk factor in human cancer? *Cancer Surv* **8** 443-458

Forman D (1991) Helicobacter pylori infection: a novel risk factor in the etiology of gastric cancer *JNCI* **83** 1702-1703

Forman, DS, Al Dabbagh, S, Doll, R 1985a *Nature*, **313**, 620-625

Forman, DS, Al Dabbagh, S, Doll, R 1985b *Nature*, **317**, 676

Goldbohm RA, Hertog MGL, Brants HAM, van Poppel G and van den Brandt PA (1996) Consumption of black tea and cancer risk: a prospective study *JNCI* **88** 93-100

Gonzáles CA, Agudo A, Montes J, Riboli E and Sanz JM (1994a) Tobacco and alcohol intake in relation to adenocarcinoma of the gastic cardia in Spain *Cancer Causes Control* **5** 88-90

González CA, Riboli E, Badosa J, Batiste E, Cardona T, Pita S et al (1994b) Nutritional factors and gastric cancer in Spain *Am J Epidemiol* **139** 466-473

González CA, Sanz JM, Marcos G, Pita S, Brullet E, Saigi E et al (1991) Dietary factors and stomach cancer in Spain: a multi-centre case-control study *Int J Cancer* **49** 513-519

Gordon T and Kannel WB (1984) Drinking and mortality: the Framingham Study *Am J Epidemiol* **120** 97-107

Graham S, Haughey B, Marshall J, Brasure J, Zielezny M, Freudenheim J et al (1990) Diet in the epidemiology of gastric cancer *Nutr Cancer* **13** 19-34

Graham S, Lilienfeld AM, Tidings JE (1967) Dietary and purgation factors in the epidemiology of gastric cancer *Cancer* **20** 2224-2234

Graham S, Schotz W and Martino P (1972) Alimentary factors in the epidemiology of gastric cancer *Cancer* **30** 927-938

Haenszel W, Correa P, Cuello C, Guzman N, Burbano LC, Lores H et al (1976a) Gastric cancer in Colombia II Case-control epidemiologic study of precursor lesions *JNCI* **57** 1021-1026

Haenszel W, Correa P, López A, Cuello C, Zarama G, Zavala D et al (1985) Serum micronutrient levels in relation to gastric pathology *Int J Cancer* **36** 43–48

Haenszel W, Kurihara M, Locke FB, Shimizu K and Segi M (1976b) Stomach cancer in Japan *JNCI* **56** 265-278

Haenszel W, Kurihara M, Segi M and Lee RKC (1972) Stomach cancer among Japanese in Hawaii *JNCI* **49** 969-988

Hansson LE, Baron J, Nyrén O, Bergström R, Wolk A and Adami HO (1994) Tobacco, alcohol and the risk of gastric cancer A population-based case-control study in Sweden *Int J Cancer* **57** 26–31

Hansson LE, Nyrén O, Bergström R, Wolk A, Lindgren A, Baron J et al (1993) Diet and risk of gastric cancer A population-based case-control study in Sweden *Int J Cancer* **55** 181–189

Hansson LE, Nyrén O, Bergström R, Wolk A, Lindgren A, Baron J et al (1994) Nutrients and risk of gastric cancer A population-based case-control study in Sweden *Int J Cancer* **57** 638–644

Heilbrun LK, Nomura A and Stemmermann GN (1986) Black tea consumption and cancer risk: a prospective study *Br J Cancer* **54** 677-683

Hennekens CH, Buring JE, Manson JE et al (1996) Lack of effect of long-term supplementation with beta carotene on the incidence of malignant neoplasms and cardiovascular disease *N Engl J Med* **334** 1145-1149

Higginson J (1966) Etiological factors in gastrointestinal cancer in man *JNCI* **37** 527-545

Hirayama T (1971) Epidemiology of stomach cancer *Gann Monogr Cancer Res* **11** 3-19

Hirayama T (1975) Epidemiology of cancer of the stomach with special reference to its decrease in Japan *Cancer Res* **35** 3460-3463

Hirayama T (1986) A large-scale study on cancer risks by diet - with special reference to the risk reducing effects of green-yellow vegetable consumption In: Hayashi Y, Magao M, Sugimura T et al, ed *Diet, Nutrition, and Cancer* Tokyo:Japan Scientific Societies Press 41-53

Hirayama T (1990) Life-style and mortality: a large-scale census-based cohort study in Japan *Basel: Karger*

Hirohata T (1983) A case-control study of stomach cancer *Proceedings of the 21st General Congress of Japan Medical Association* 953-955 (in Japanese)

Hocman G (1989) Prevention of cancer: vegetables and plants *Comp Biochem Physiol* **93** 201-12

Hoey J, Montvernay C and Lambert R (1981) Wine and tobacco: risk factors of gastric cancer in France *Am J Epidemiol* **113** 668-674

Holcombe C (1992) Helicobacter pylori: the African enigma *Gut* **33** 429-431

Holzer D, Pabst MA, Lippe IT (1989) Intragastric

Honjo S, Kono S and Yamaguchi M (1994) Salt and geographic variation in stomach cancer mortality in Japan *Cancer Causes Control* **5** 285-286

Hoshiyama Y, Sasaba T (1992) A case-control study of single and multiple stomach cancers in Saitama Prefecture, Japan *Jpn J Cancer Res (Gann)* **83** 937-943

Howe GR, Harrison L and Jain M (1986) A short diet history for assessing dietary exposure to N-nitrosamines in epidemiologic studies *Am J Epidemiol* **124** 595-602

Howson CP, Hiyama T and Wynder EL (1986) The decline in gastric cancer: epidemiology of an unplanned triumph *Epidemiol Rev* **8** 1-27

Hu J, Zhang S, Jia E et al (1988) Diet and cancer of the stomach: A case-control study in China *Int J Cancer* **41** 331-335

IARC (1988) Alcohol drinking *IARC Monogr Eval Carcinogenic Risks Hum* **44** 194-207

IARC (1991) *Monographs on the evaluation of the carcinogenic risk of chemicals to humans*, volume **51** *Coffee, tea, mate, methylxanthines and methylglyoxal* International Agency for Research on Cancer, Lyon

IARC (1993) *Monographs on the Evaluation of carcinogenic Risks to Humans*, Volume **56** *Some Naturally Occurring Substances: Food Items and Constituents, Hetrocyclic Aromatic Amines and Mycotoxins* Lyon

Jacobs DR Jr, Slavin J, Marquart L (1995) Whole grain intake and cancer: a review of the literature *Nutr Cancer* **24** 221-229

Jacobsen BK, Bjelke E, Kvale G, Heuch I (1986) Coffee drinking, mortality, and cancer incidence: results from a Norwegian prospective study *JNCI* **76** 823-831

Jedrychowski W, Boeing H, Wahrendorf J, Popiela T, Tobiasz-Adamczyk B and Kulig J (1993) Vodka consumption, tobacco smoking and risk of gastric cancer in Poland *Int J Epidemiol* **22** 606-613

Jedrychowski W, Wahrendorf J, Popiela T and Rachtan J (1986) A case-control study of dietary factors and stomach cancer risk in Poland *Int J Cancer* **37** 837-842

Joossens JV and Geboers J (1981) Nutrition and gastric cancer *Nutr Cancer* **2** 250-261

Joossens JV, Hill MJ, Elliott P, Stamler R, Stamler J, Lesaffre E et al (1993) Stomach cancer, salt and nitrate in 24 countries *Proceedings of the Fifteenth International Congress of Nutrition* Sep 27 - Oct 2; Adelaide p381

Joossens JV, Kesteloot H (1996) *Nutrition in relation to stomach cancer and stroke mortality* In press

Kabat GC, Ng SKC and Wynder EL (1993) Tobacco, alcohol intake, and diet in relation to adenocarcinoma of the esophagus and gastric cardia *Cancer Causes Control* **3** 123-132

Kamiyama S, Ohshima H, Shimada A, Saito N, Bourgade MC, Ziegler P et al (1987) Urinary excretion of N-nitrosoamino acids and nitrate by inhabitants in high and low risk areas for stomach cancer in Northern Japan In *Relevance of N-nitroso compounds to human cancer: exposure and mechanisms* (Ed H Bartsch, IK O'Neill, R Schulte-Herman) IARC:Lyon pp497-502

Kato I, Tomimaga S, Ito Y, Kobayashi S, Yoshii Y, Matsuura A et al (1990) A comparative case-control analysis of stomach cancer and atrophic gastritis *Cancer Res* **50** 6559-6564

Kato I, Tominaga S and Matsumoto K (1992a) A prospective study of stomach cancer among a rural Japanese population: a 6-year survey *Jpn J Cancer Res* **83** 568-575

Kato I, Tominaga S, Matsumoto K (1992b) A prospective study of stomach cancer among a rural Japanese population: a 6-year survey *Jpn J Cancer Res* **83** 568-75

Kinlen LJ, Willows AN, Goldblatt P and Yudkin J (1988) Tea consumption and cancer *Br J Cancer* **58** 397-401

Knekt P, Aromaa A, Maatela J, Aaran RK, Nikkari T, Hakama M et al (1990) Serum vitamin A and subsequent risk of cancer: cancer incidence follow-up of the Finnish mobile clinic health examination survey *Am J Epidemiol* **132** 857-870

Knekt P, Aromaa A, Maatela J, Alfthan G, Aaran RK, Hakama M et al (1990) Serum selenium and subsequent risk of cancer among Finnish men and women *JNCI* **82** 864-868

Kneller RW, Guo WD, Hsing AW, Chen JS, Blot WJ, Li JY et al (1992) Risk factors for stomach cancer in sixty-five Chinese counties *Cancer Epidemiol Biomark Prev* **1** 113-118

Kneller RW, McLaughlin JK, Bjelke E, Schuman LM, Blot WJ, Wacholder S et al (1991) A cohort study of stomach cancer in a high-risk American population *Cancer* **68** 672-678

Kneller RW, You WC, Chang YS, Liu WD, Zhang L, Zhao L et al (1992) Cigarette smoking and other risk factors for progression of precancerous stomach lesions *JNCI* **84** 1261-1266

Kobayashi M, Kogata M, Yamamua M et al (1986) Inhibitory effect of dietary seleium on carcinogenesis in rat glandular stomach induced by N-methyl-N'-nitro-N-nitrosoguanidine *Cancer Res* **46** 2266-2270

Kolonel LN, Hankin JH, Lee L et al (1981) Nutrient intakes in relation to cancer incidence in Hawaii *Br J Cancer* **44**: 322-339

Kono S, Ikeda M and Ogata M (1983) Salt and geographical mortality of gastric cancer and stroke in Japan *J Epidemiol Community Health* **37** 43-46

Kono S, Ikeda M, Tokudome S and Kuratsune M (1988) A case-control study of gastric cancer and diet in northern Kyushu, Japan *Jpn J Cancer Res* **79** 1067-1074

Kono S, Ikeda M, Tokudome S, Nishizumi M and Kuratsune M (1987) Cigarette smoking, alcohol and cancer mortality: a cohort study of male Japanese physicians *Jpn J Cancer Res* **78** 1323-1328

La Vecchia C, Negri E, D'Avanzo B, Ferraroni M, Decarli A, Levi F, Franceschi S (1989) Coffee consumption and digestive tract cancer *Cancer Res* **49**: 1049-1051

La Vecchia C, Negri E, D'Avanzo B, Franceschi S (1990) Electric refrigerator use and gastric cancer risk *British Journal of Cancer;* **62**: 136-137

La Vecchia C, Negri E, D'Avanzo B, Franceschi S, Boyle P (1992) Tea consumption and cancer risk *Nutr Cancer* **17**: 27-31

La Vecchia C, Negri E, Decarli A, D'Avanzo B and Franceschi S (1987) A case-control study of diet and gastric cancer in northern Italy *Int J Cancer* **40** 484-489

Lee JK, Park BJ, Yoo KY and Ahn YO (1995) Dietary factors and stomach cancer: a case-control study in Korea *Int J Epidemiol* **24** 33-41

Li JY, Taylor PR, Li B, Dawsey S, Wang GQ, Ershow AG et al (1993) Nutrition intervention trials in Linxian, China: Multiple vitamin/mineral supplementation, cancer incidence, and disease-specific mortality among adults with esophageal dysplasia *JNCI* **85** 1492-2

Lopez-Carrillo L, Avila MH and Dubrow R (1994) Chili pepper consumption and gastric cancer in Mexico: a case-control study *Am J Epidemiol* **139** 263-271

Marquardt H, Rufino R and Weisburger JH (1977) On the aetiology of gastric cancer: mutagenicity of food extracts after incubation with nitrite *Food Cosmet Toxicol* **15** 97-100

Memik F, Nak SG, Gulten M, Ozturk M (1992) Gastric carcinoma in northwestern Turkey: epidemiologic characteristics *J Environ Path Toxicol Oncol* **11** 335-338

Mirvish SS (1983) The etiology of gastric cancer Intragastric nitrosamide formation and other theories *JNCI* **71** 629–647

Mirvish SS (1986) Effects of vitamins C and E on N-nitroso compound formation, carcinogenesis, and cancer *Cancer* **58** 1842-1850

Modan B, Lubin F, Barell V, Greenberg RA, Modan M and Graham S (1974) The role of starches in the etiology of gastric cancer *Cancer* **34** 2087-2092

Monsereenasorn Y, Kongsamut S, Pezella PD (1982) Capsaicin - a literature survey *CRC Crit Rev Tox* **10** 321-339

Montes G, Cuello C, Correa P et al (1985) *Journal Cancer Research Clinical Oncology* **109** 42-45

Myers,BM Smith,JL Graham,DY 1987 Effect of red pepper and black pepper on the stomach *Am J Gastroenterol*: **82**: 211-214

NAS (1982) National Academy of Sciences *Diet, Nutrition and Cancer* Washington: National Academy Press

NAS (1989) National Academy of Sciences *Diet and Health* Washington: National Academy Press

Nazario CM, Szklo M, Diamond E, Roman-Franco A, Climent C, Suarez E et al (1993) Salt and gastric cancer: a case-control study in Puerto Rico *Int J Epidemiol* **22** 790-797

Nomura A, Grove JS, Stemmermann GN and Severson RK (1990) A prospective study of stomach cancer and its relation to diet, cigarettes, and alcohol consumption *Cancer Res* **50** 627-631

Nomura A, Heilbrun LK, Morris JS and Stemmermann (1987) Serum selenium and the risk of cancer, by specific sites: case-control analysis of prospective study *JNCI* **79** 103-108

Nomura A, Yamakawa H, Ishidate T, Kamiyama S, Masuda H, Stemmermann GN et al (1982) Intestinal metaplasia in Japan: association with diet *JNCI* **68** 401-405

Nomura AM, Stemmermann GN, Chyou PH (1995) Gastric cancer among the Japanese in Hawaii *Jap J Cancer Res* **86** 916-923

Nomura AMY, Stemmermann GN, Heilbrun LK, Salkeld RM and Vuilleumier JP (1985) Serum vitamin levels and the risk of cancer of specific sites in men of Japanese ancestry in Hawaii *Cancer Res* **45** 2369-2372

Palli D, Bianchi S, Decarli A, Cipriani F, Avellini C, Cocco P et al (1992) A case-control study of cancers of the gastric cardia in Italy *Int J Cancer*

65 263-266

Parkin DM, Muir CS, Whelan SL, Gao YT, Ferlay J, Powell J, editors (1992) *Cancer incidence in five continents, Vol 6* IARC: Lyon

Puffer RR, Griffith GW (1967) Washington DC: PAHO

Ramon JM, Serra L, Cerdo C and Oromi J (1993a) Dietary factors and gastric cancer risk: a case-control study in Spain *Cancer* **71** 1731-1735

Ramon JM, Serra-Majem L, Cerdo C and Oromi J (1993b) Nutrient intake and gastric cancer risk: a case-control study in Spain *Int J Epidemiol* **22** 983-988

Risch HA, Jain M, Choi NW, Fodor JG, Pfeiffer CJ, Howe GR et al (1985) Dietary factors and the incidence of cancer of the stomach *Am J Epidemiol* **122** 947-959

Santamaria L, Bianchi A, Ravetto C, Arnaboldi A, Santagati G and Andreoni L (1985) Supplemental carotenoids prevent MNNG induced cancer in rats *Med Biol Environ* **13** 745-750

Santamaria L, Bianchi A, Ravetto C, Arnaboldi A, Santagati G and Andreoni L (1987) Prevention of gastric cancer induced by N'-methyl-N'-nitro-N-nitrosoguanidine in rats fed supplemental carotenoids *J Nutr Growth Cancer* **4** 175-181

Sierra R, Chinnock A, Ohshima H, Pignatelli B, Malaveille C, Gamboa C et al (1993) In vivo nitrosproline formation and other risk factors in Costa Rican children from high- and low-risk areas for gastric cancer *Cancer Epidemiol Biomarkers Prev* **2** 563-568

Silkoff R, Karmeli F, Goldin E et al (1988) Effect of substance P on rat gastrointestinal transit *Dig Dis Sci* **33** 74-77

Singh VN, Gaby SK (1992) Premalignant lesions: role of antioxidant vitamins and beta-carotene in risk reduction and prevention of malignant transformation *Department of Clinical Nutrition*

Sivam GP, Lampe JW, Ulness B, Swanzy SR, Potter JD (1997) Helicobacter pylori—in vitro susceptibility to garlic (Allium sativum) extract *Nutr Cancer* **27**(2) 118-21

Stähelin HB, Gey KF, Eichholzer M, Lündin E, Bernasconi F, Thurneysen J et al (1991) Plasma antioxidant vitamins and subsequent cancer mortality in the 12-year follow-up of the prospective Basel Study *Am J Epidemiol* **133** 766-775

Surgeon General of the United States (1982) The health consequences of smoking *United States Public Health Service*: Rockvill

Tajima K and Tominaga S (1985) Dietary habits and gastro-intestinal cancers: a comparative case-control study of stomach and large intestinal cancers in Nagoya, Japan *Jpn J Cancer Res* **76** 705-716

Takahashi M, Kokubo T, Furukawa F et al (1983) Effect of high salt diet on rat gastric carcinogenesis induced by N-methyl-N'-nitro-N-nitrosoguanidine *Jpn J Cancer Res* **74** 28-34

Takahashi M, Kokubo T, Furukawa F et al (1984) Effects of sodium chloride, saccharin, phenobarbital and aspirin on gastric carcinogenesis in rats after initiation with N-methyl-N'-nitro-N-nitrosoguanidine *Jpn J Cancer Res* **75** 494-501

Taylor PR, Li JY, Li B and Blot WJ (1994) Re: Nutritional intervention trials in Linxian, China: supplementation with specific vitamin/mineral combinations, cancer incidence, and disease-specific mortality in the general population [response] *JNCI* **86** 1647-1648

The Aplpha-Tocopherol, Beta-Carotene Cancer Prevention Study Group (1994) The effect of vitamin E and beta-carotene on the incidence of lung cancer and other cancers in male smokers *NEJM* **330** 1029-35

The Eurogast Study Group (1993) An international association between Helicobacter pylori infection and gastric cancer *Lancet* **341** 1359-62

Trichopoulos D, Ouranos G, Day NE, Tzonou A, Manousos O, Papadimitriou C et al (1985) Diet and cancer of the stomach: a case-control study in Greece *Int J Cancer* **36** 291-297

Tuyns AJ (1988) Salt and gastrointestinal cancer *Nutr Cancer* **11** 229-232

Tuyns AJ, Kaaks R, Haelterman M and Riboli E (1992) Diet and gastric cancer: a case-control study in Belgium *Int J Cancer* **51** 1-6

Van den Brandt PA, Goldbohm RA, Van 't Veer P, Bode P, Dorant E, Hermus RJ et al (1993) A prospective cohort study on toenail selenium levels and risk of gastrointestinal cancer *JNCI* **85** 224-229

Vaughan TL, Davis S, Kristal A and Thomas DB (1995) Obesity, alcohol, and tobacco as risk factors for cancers of the esophagus and gastric cardia: adenocarcinoma versus squamous cell carcinoma *Cancer Epidemiol Biomarkers Prev* **4** 85-92

Wald NJ, Thompson SG, Densem JW, Boreham J and Bailey A (1988) Serum beta-carotene and subsequent risk of cancer: results from the BUPA study *Br J Cancer* **57** 428-433

Wang ZY, Hong JY, Huang MT, Reuhl KR, Conney AH and Yang YS (1992) Inhibition of N-nitrosodiethylamine- and 4-(methylnitrosoamino)-1-(3-pyridyl)-1-butanone induced tumorigesis in A/J mice by green tea and black tea *Cancer Res* **52** 1943-1947

Ward MH, Sinha R, Heinman EF, Rothman N, Markin R, Weisinburger DD, Correa P, Zahm SH (1997) Risk of adenocarcinoma of the stomach and esophagus with meat cooking method and doneness preference *Int J Cancer* **71** 14-19

Wattenberg LW (1983) Inhibition of neoplasia by minor dietary constituents *Cancer Res* **43** (Suppl) 2448s-2453s

Wattenberg LW, Coccia JB (1991) Inhibition of 4-(methylnitrosoamino)-1-(3-pyridyl)-1-butanone carcinogenesis in mice by D-limonene and citrus fruit oils *Carcinogenesis* **12** 115-7

Wattenberg LW, Hanley AB, Barany G, Sparnins VL, Lam LKT, Fenwick GR (1986) Inhibition of carcinogenesis by some minor dietary constituents, in Hayashi Y (ed): *Diet, Nutrition, and Cancer* Tokyo: Japan Sci Soc Press 193-203

Weisburger JH, Marquardt H, Hirota N, Mori H and Williams GM (1980) Induction of cancer of the glandular stomach in rats by an extract of nitrite-treated fish *JNCI* **64** 163-167

WHO (1990) World Health Organization *Nutrition, Nutrition and Prevention of Chronic Diseases* Technical Report 797 Geneva: WHO

WHO (1997) World Health Organization *The World Health Report* Geneva:WHO

Wu-Williams AH, Yu MC and Mack TM (1990) Life-style, workplace, and stomach cancer by subsite in young men of Los Angels County *Cancer Res* **50** 2569-2576

Yamane T, Takahashi T, Kuwata K, Oya K, Inagake M, Kitao Y et al (1995) Inhibition of N-methyl-N'-nitro-N-nitrosoguanidine-induced carcinogenesis by (–)-epigallocatechin gallate in the rat glandular stomach *Cancer Res* **55** 2081–2084

Yang CS and Wang ZY (1993) Tea and cancer *JNCI* **85** 1038-1049

Yang D, Tannenbaum SR, Buch C and Lee GCM (1984) 4-Chloro-6-methoxyindole is the precursor of a potent mutagen that forms during nitrosation of fava beans (Vicia faba) *Carcinogenesis* **5** 1219-1224

You WC, Blot WJ, Chang YS, Ershow AG, Yang ZT, An Q et al (1988) Diet and high risk of stomach cancer in Shandong, China *Cancer Res* **48** 3518-3523

You WC, Blot WJ, Chang YS, Ershow G, Yang ZT, An Q et al (1989) Allium vegetables and reduced risk of stomach cancer *JNCI* **81** 162-164

Yu GP and Hsieh CC (1991) Risk factors for stomach

cancer: a population-based case-control study in Shanghai *Cancer Causes Control* **2** 169-174

Yu GP, Hsieh CC, Wang LY, Yu SZ, Li XL and Jin TH (1995) Green-tea consumption and risk of stomach cancer: a population-based case-control study in Shanghai, China *Cancer Causes Control* **6** 532-538

Zhang L, Blot WJ, You WC, Chang YS, Liu XQ, Kneller RW et al (1994) Serum micronutrients in relation to precancerous gastric lesions *Int J Cancer* **56** 650–654

Zheng W, Sellers TA, Doyle TJ, Kushi LH, Potter JD and Folsom AR (1995) Retinol, antioxidant vitamins, and cancers of the upper digestive tract in a prospective cohort study of postmenopausal women *Am J Epidemiol* **142** 955-960

4.7 PANCREAS

Adlercreutz H (1990) Western diet and western diseases: some hormonal and biochemical mechanisms and associations *Scan J Clin lab Invest* **50** (Suppl 201) 3-23

Alomoquera C, Shibata D, Forrester K et al (1988) Most human carcinomas of the exocrine pancreas contain mutant c-K-ras genes *Cell* **53** 549-554

American Cancer Society (1993) *Cancer Facts and Figures* - 1993 American Cancer Society: New York

Ammann RW and Schueler G (1984) Chronic pancreatitis, pancreatic cancer, alcohol, and smoking (Letter) *Gastroenterology* **87** 744-745

Ammann RW, Akovbiamtz A, Largiader F et al (1984) Course and outcome of chronic pancreatitis: longitudinal study of a mixed medical-surgical series of 245 patients *Gastroenterology* **86** 820-828

Anderson KE, Potter JD, Mack TM (1996) Pancreatic cancer In: *Cancer Epidemiology and Prevention* Schottenfeld D, and Fraumeni JF Jr, eds Oxford University Press, New York

Anderson LM, Souliotis VL, Chhabra SK, Moskal TJ, Harbaugh SD, Kyrtopoulos SA (1996) N-nitrosodimethylamine-0 (6) - methylguanine in DNA of monkey gastrointestinal and urogenital organs and enhancement by ethanol *Int J Cancer* **66** 130-134

Anderson,HA, Snyder J, Lewinson T, Woo C, Lilis R, Selikoff IJ (1978) Levels of CEA among vinyl chloride and polyvinyl chloride exposed workers *Cancer* **42**(3 Suppl) 1560-7

Aoki K, Hayakawa N, Kurihara M et al (eds) (1992) *Death Rates for Malignant Neoplasms for Selected Sites by Sex and Five-year Age Group in 33 countries 1953-57 to 1983-87* The

University of Nagoya Coop Press: Nagoya, Japan

Appel MJ, Roverts G and Woutersen RA (1991) Inhibitory effects of micronutrients on pancreatic carcinogenesis in azaserine-treated rats *Carcinogenesis* **12** 2157-2161

Armstrong B and Doll R (1975) Environmental factors and cancer incidence and mortality in different countries with special reference to dietary practises *Int J Cancer* **15** 617-631

Arnar DO, Theodors A, Isaksson HJ et al (1991) Cancer of the Pancreas in Iceland: an epidemiologic and clinical study 1974-85 *Scand J Gastroenterol* **26** 724-730

Axtell LM, Asire AJ and Myers MH (1976) *Cancer patient survival, Report* No **5** US Department of Health, Education, and Welfare: Bethesda

Baghurst PA, McMichael AJ, Slavotinek AH et al (1991) A case-control study of diet and cancer of the pancreas *Am J Epidemiol* **134** 167-179

Baker R, Arlauskas A, Bonin A et al (1982) Detection of mutagenic activity in human urine following fried pork or bacon meals *Cancer Lett* **16** 81-89

Beazley RM, McAneny, DB and Cohn I Jr (1991) *Progress in pancreatic cancer* American Cancer Society

Bernarde MA, Weiss W (1982) Coffee consumption and pancreatic cancer: temporal and spatial correlation *BMJ* **284** 400-402

Binstock M, Krakow D, Stamler J et al (1983) Coffee and pancreatic cancer: an analysis of international mortality data *Am J Epidem* **118** 630-40

Birt DF (1989) Effects of the intake of selected vitamins and minerals on cancer prevention *Magnesium* 8 17-30

Birt DF, Salmasi S and Pour PM (1981) Enhancement of experimental pancreatic cancer in Syrian golden hamsters by dietary fat *JNCI* **67** 1327-1332

Birt DF, Stepan KR and Pour PM (1983) Interaction of dietary fat and protein on pancreatic carcinogenesis in Syrian golden hamsters *JNCI* **71** 355-360

Blot WJ, Fraumeni JF Jr and Stone BJ (1978) Geographic correlates of pancreas cancer in the United States Cancer 42 373-380

Bos JL (1989) ras Oncogenes in human cancer: A review *Cancer Res* **49** 4682-4689

Bos JL (1990) ras Oncogenes in human cancer: A review (Erratum) *Cancer Res* **50** 1352

Bouchardy C, Clavel F, La Vecchia C et al (1990) Alcohol, beer and cancer of the pancreas *Int J Cancer* **45** 842-846

Boyle P, Hsieh C-C, Maisonneuve P et al (1989) Epidemiology of pancreas cancer *Int J Pancreatol* **5** 327-346

Breslow NE, Enstrom JE (1974) Geographic correlates between cancer mortality rates and alcohol-tobacco consumption in the United States *JNCI* **53** 631-639

Bueno de Mesquita HB *On the causation of cancer of the exocrine pancreas* (Thesis) Utrecht, The Netherlands

Bueno de Mesquita HB, Maisonneuve P, Moerman CJ et al (1991) Intake of foods and nutrients and exocrine carcinoma of the pancreas: A population-based case-control study in The Netherlands *Int J Cancer* **48** 540-549

Bueno de Mesquita HB, Maisonneuve P, Moerman CJ et al (1992) Lifetime consumption of alcoholic beverages, tea and coffee and exocrine carcinoma of the pancreas: A population-based case-control study in The Netherlands *Int J Cancer* **50** 514-522

Bueno de Mesquita, Moerman HB, Runia CJ and Maison-neuve P (1990) Are energy and energy-providing nutrients related to exocrine carcinoma of the pancreas? *Int J Cancer* **45** 435-444

Burch GE and Ansari A (1968) Chronic alcoholism and carcinoma of the pancreas *Arch Int Med* **122** 273-275

Burney PGJ, Comstock GW and Morris JS (1989) Serologic precursors of cancer: serum micronutrients and the subsequent risk of pancreatic cancer *Am J Clin Nutr* **49** 895-900

Challis BC, Bartlett CD (1975) Possible carcinogenic effects of coffee constituents *Nature* **254** 532-533

Clavel F, Benhamou D, Auquier A et al (1989) Coffee, alcohol, smoking and cancer of the pancreas: A case-control study *Int J Cancer* **43** 17-21

Comstock GW, Bush TL, Helzsouer K (1992) Serum retinol, beta-carotene, vitamin A and selenium as related to subsequent cancer od specific sites *Am J Epidem* **135** 115-121

Cubilla AL and Fitzgerald PJ (1978b) Pancreas cancer I Duct adenocarcinoma, a clinical-pathologic study of 380 patients In *Pathology Annual*, Part 1 Appleton-Century-Crofts: New York pp241-287

Cuckle HS, Kinlen LJ (1981) Coffee and Cancer of the Pancreas *Br J Cancer* **44** 760-761

Cuzick J and Babiker AG (1989) Pancreatic cancer, alcohol, diabetes mellitus and gall-bladder disease Int J *Cancer* **43** 415-421

Decarli A, La Vecchia C (1986) Environmental factors and cancer mortality in Italy: correlational exercise *Oncology* **43** 116-126

Dörken VH (1964) Einige daten bei 280 Patienten mit Pankreaskrebs *Gastroenterologia* **102** 47-77

Durbec JP, Chevillotte G, Bidart JM et al (1983) Diet, alcohol, tobacco and risk of cancer of the pancreas: A case-control study *Br J Cancer* **47** 467-470

Falk RT, Pickle LW, Fontham ET et al (1988) Lifestyle risk factors for pancreatic cancer in Louisiana: a case-control study *Am J Epidemiol* **128** 324-336

Farrow DC and Davis S (1990a) Risk of pancreatic cancer in relation to medical history and the use of tobacco, alcohol and coffee *Int J Cancer* **45** 816-820

Farrow DC and Davis S (1990b) Diet and risk of pancreatic cancer in men *Am J Epidemiol* **132** 423-431

Feinstein AR, Horwitz RI, Spitzer WO et al (1981) Coffee and pancreatic cancer: the problems of etiologic science and epidemiologic case-control research *JAMA* **246** 957-961

Felton JS and Knize MG (1991) Occurrence, identification and bacterial mutagenicity of heterocyclic amines in cooked food *Mutat Res* **259** 205-217

Fontham ETH and Correa P (1989) Epidemiology of pancreatic cancer *Surg Clin North Am* **69** 551-567

Friedman GD and van den Eeden SK (1993) Risk factors for pancreatic cancer: An exploratory study *Int J Epidemiol* **22** 30-37

Ghadirian P, Simard A and Baillargeon J (1991a) Tobacco, alcohol, and coffee and cancer of the pancreas *Cancer* **67** 2664-2670

Ghadirian P, Thouez J-P and PetitClerc C (1991b) International comparisons of nutrition and mortality from pancreatic cancer *Detect Prev* **15** 357-362

Go VLW, Garderner JD, Brooks FP et al (eds) (1986) *The Exocrine Pancreas: Biology, Pathobiology and Diseases* New York: Raven Press

Gold EB, Gordis L, Diener MD et al (1985) Diet and other risk factors for cancer of the pancreas *Cancer* **55** 460-467

Gordis L (1990) Consumption of methylxanthine-containing beverages and risk of pancreatic cancer *Cancer Lett* **52** 1-12

Gorham ED, Garland FC, Benenson AS Cottrell L (1988) Coffee and pancreatic cancer in a rural Californian county *West J Med* **148** 48-53

Goto R, Masuoko H, Yoshida K, Mori M and Miyake H (1990) A case-control study of cancer of the pancreas *Japanese J Cancer Clinics* **36** 344-350

Gumbmann MR, Dugan GM, Spangler WL et al (1989) Pancreatic response in rats and mice to trypsin inhibitors from soy and potato after short- and long-term dietary exposure *J Nutr* **119** 1598-1609

Haddock G and Carter DC (1990) Aetiology of pancreatic cancer *Br J Surg* **77** 1159-1166

Heilbrun LK, Nomura A and Stemmermann GN (1986) Black tea consumption and cancer risk: a prospective study *Br J Cancer* **54** 677-683

Heuch I, Kvale G, Jacobsen BK et al (1983) Use of alcohol, tobacco and coffee and risk of pancreatic cancer *Br J Cancer* **48** 637-643

Hiatt RA, Klatsky AL and Armstrong MA (1988) Pancreatic cancer, blood glucose and beverage consumption *Int J Cancer* **41** 794-797

Hirai H, Okabe T, Anruka Y et al (1985) Activation of the c-K-ras oncogene in a human pancreas carcinoma *Biochem Biophys Res Comm* **127** 168-174

Hirayama T (1989) Epidemiology of pancreatic cancer in Japan *Jpn J Clin Oncol* **19** 208-215

Hoffmann D, Rivenson A, Abbi R et al (1993) A study of tobacco carcinogenesis: Effect of the fat content of the diet on the carcinogenic activity of 4-(methylnitrosamino)-1-(3-pyridyl)-1-butanone in F344 rats *Cancer Res* **53** 2758-2761

Howard JM and Jordan GL (1977) Cancer of the pancreas *Curr Probl Cancer* **2** 1-52

Howe GR (1994) *Pancreatic cancer* In Trends in Cancer Incidence and Mortality Oxford: Imperial Cancer Research Fund, *Cancer Surveys* **19** 39-58

Howe GR and Burch JD (1996) Nutrition and pancreatic cancer *Cancer Causes and Control* **7** 69-82

Howe GR, Ghadirian P, Bueno de Mesquita HB et al (1992) A collaborative case-control study of nutrient intake and pancreatic cancer within the SEARCH program *Int J Cancer* **51** 365-372

Howe GR, Jain M and Miller AB (1990) Dietary factors and risk of pancreatic cancer: results of a Canadian population-based case-control study *Int J Cancer* **45** 604-608

Hsieh C-C, MacMahon B, Yen S et al (1986) Coffee and pancreatic cancer (Letter) *N Engl J Med* **315** 587-589

IARC (1988) *Monographs on the Evaluation of Carcinogenic Risks to Human: Alcohol Drinking* Lyon: International Agency for Research on Cancer Volume 44

IARC (1991) *Monographs on the Evaluation of the Carcinogenic Risk of Chemicals to Humans, vol 51, Coffee, Tea, Mate, Methylxanthines and Methylglyoxa l* Lyon: International Agency for Research on Cancer

Ishii K, Nakamura K, Ozaki H et al, (1968) Epidemiological problems of pancreas cancer *Jpn J Clin Med* **26** 1839-1842

Ishii K, Nakamura K, Takeuchi T et al (1973) Chronic calcifying pancreatitis and pancreatic carcinoma in Japan *Digestion* **9** 429-437

Jain M, Howe, GR, St Louis P et al (1991) Coffee and alcohol as determinants of risk of pancreas cancer: a case-control study from Toronto *Int J Cancer* **47** 384-389

Kessler II (1981) Coffee and cancer of the pancreas (letter) *N Engl J Med* **304** 1605

Kinlen LJ and McPherson K (1984) Pancreas cancer and coffee and tea consumption: A case-control study *Br J Cancer* **49** 93-96

Kinlen LJ, Willows AN, Goldblatt P, Yodkin J (1988) Tea consumption and cancer *Br J Cancer* **58** 397-401

Kise Y, Yamamura M, Kogata M et al (1990) Inhibitory effect of selenium on hamster pancreatic cancer induction by N'-nitrosobis (2-oxopropyl) amine *Int J Cancer* **46** 95-100

Kokkinakis DM, Scarpelli DG (1989) Carcinogenicity of N-nitroso (2-hydroxypropyl) (2-oxopropyl) amine, N-nitrosobis (2-hydroxypropyl) amine and cis-N-nitroso-2, 6-dimethylmorpholine administered continuously in the Syrian hamster, and the effect of dietary protein on N-nitroso (2-hydroxypropyl) (2-oxyopropyl) amine carcinogenesis *Carcinogenesis* **10** 699-704

Kono S and Ikeda M (1979) Correlation between cancer mortality and alcoholic beverage in Japan *Br J Cancer* **40** 449-455

Kuratsune M, Kochi S, Horie A et al (1971) Test of alcoholic beverages and ethanol solutions for carcinogenicity and tumor promoting activity *Gann* **62** 395

LaVecchia C, Liati P, Decarli A et al (1987) Coffee consumption and risk of pancreatic cancer *Int J Cancer* **40** 309-313

LaVecchia C, Negri E, D'Avanzo B et al (1990)

Medical history, diet and pancreatic cancer *Oncology* **47** 463-466

LaVecchia C, Negri E, Franceschi S, D'Avanzo B, Boyle P (1992) Tea consumption and cancer risk *Nutr Cancer* **17** 27-31

Lawson T, Birt DF (1983) Enhancement of the repair of carcinogen induced DNA damage in the hamster pancreas by dietary selenium *Chem Biol Interact* **45** 95

Lea AJ (1967) Neoplasms and environmental factors *Ann Royal Coll Surg Engl* **41** 432-438

Lemoine NR, Jain S, Hughes CM et al (1992) Ki-ras oncogene activation in preinvasive pancreatic cancer *Gastroenterology* **102** 230-236

Lin RS and Kessler II (1981) A multifactorial model for pancreatic cancer in man *JAMA* **245** 147-152

Livingston EH and Reber HA (1992) Cancer of the pancreas Current Opinion in *Gastroenterology* **8** 844-851

Longnecker D (1990) Experimental pancreatic cancer: role of species, sex and diet *Bull Cancer* **77** 27-37

Lowenfels AB (1984) Chronic pancreatitis, pancreatic cancer, alcohol, and smoking (Letter) *Gastroenterology* **87** 744

Lowenfels AB, Maisonneuve P, Cavallini G et al (1993) Pancreatitis and the risk of pancreatic cancer *New Engl J Med* **328** 1433-1437

Lowenfels AB, Patel VP and Pitchumoni CS (1985) Chronic calcific pancreatitis and pancreatic cancer (Abstract) *Dig Dis Sci* **30** 982

Lu LJ, Anderson KE, Gomez G, Nealon WH (1995) Decreased plasma levels of cholecystokinin in healthy males after chronic ingestion of a heat-treated soya product *Cancer Letters* **90** 149-55

Lyon JL, Egger MF, Robison LM et al (1992) Misclassification of exposure in a case-control study: The effects of different types of exposure and different proxy respondents in a study of pancreatic cancer *Epidemiology* **3** 223-231

Lyon JL, Slattery ML, Mahoney AW, Robinson LM (1993) Dietary intake as a risk factor for cancer of the exocrine pancreas *Cancer Epidemiol Biomarker Prev* **2** 513-518

Mack TM and Paganini-Hill A (1981) Epidemiology of pancreas cancer in Los Angeles *Cancer* **47** 1474-1483

Mack TM, Yu MC, Hanisch R et al (1986) Pancreas cancer and smoking, beverage consumption and past medical history *JNCI* **76** 49-60

MacMahon B, Yen S, Trichopoulos C et al (1981)

Coffee and cancer of the pancreas *N Engl J Med* **304** 630-633

Maruchi N, Aoki S, Tsuda K, Tanaka Y, Toyokawa H (1977) Relation of food consumption to cancer mortality in Japan with special reference to international figures *Gann* **68** 1-13

Mills PK, Beeson L, Abbey DE et al (1988) Dietary habits and past medical history as related to fatal pancreas cancer risk among Adventists *Cancer* **61** 2578-2585

Mizuno S, Watanabe S, Nakamura K et al (1992) A multi-institute case-control study on the risk factors of developing pancreatic cancer *Jpn J Clin Oncol* **22** 286-291

Nader CJ, Spencer LK and Weller RA (1981) Mutagen production during pan-broiling compared with microwave irradiation of beef *Cancer Let* **13** 147-151

Nagata Y, Abe M, Motoshima K et al (1990) Frequent glycine-to-aspartic acid mutations at codon 12 of c-Ki-ras gene in human pancreatic cancer in Japanese *Jpn J Cancer Res* **81** 135-140

National Research Council (1982) *Diet, Nutrition and Cancer* Washington DC: National Academy Press

National Research Council (1989) *Diet and Health* Washington DC: National Academy Press:

Norell SE, Ahlbom A, Erwald R et al (1986a) Diet and pancreatic cancer: A case-control study *Am J Epidemiol* **124** 894-902

O'Connor TP, Roebuck BD, Peterson FJ et al (1989) Effect of dietary omega-3 and omega-6 fatty acids on development of azaserine-induced preneoplastic lesions in rat pancreas *JNCI* **81** 858-863

Olsen GW, Mandel JS, Gibson RW et al (1989) A case-control study of pancreatic cancer and cigarettes, alcohol, coffee and diet *Amer J Publ Hlth* **79** 1016-1019

Pariza MW (1987) Dietary fat, calorie restriction, ad libitum feeding and cancer risk *Nutr Rev* **45** 1-7

Parkin DM, Pisani P and Ferlay J (1993) Estimates of the world wide incidence of eighteen major cancers in 1985 Int *J Cancer* **54** 594-606

Parsa I, Pour PM, Cleary CM et al (1988) Amplification of c-Ki-ras-2 oncogene sequences in human carcinoma of the pancreas *Int J Pancreatol* **3** 45-51

Paulino-Netto AP, Dreiling DA and Baronofsky ID (1960) The relationship between pancreatic calcification and cancer of the pancreas *Ann Surg* **151** 530-537

Pietri F and Clavel F (1991) Occupational exposure and cancer of the pancreas: A review *Br J Ind Med* **48** 583-587

Poston GJ, Gillespie J and Guillou PJ (1991) Biology of pancreatic cancer *Gut* **32** 800-812

Potter JD (1990) The epidemiology and prevention of pancreas cancer In *Cancer Prevention, Vital Statistics to Intervention* (Ed W Zatonski, P Boyle, J Tyczynski) PA Interpress: Warsaw

Pour PM and Birt DF (1983a) Modifying factors in pancreatic carcinogenesis in the hamster model IV Effects of dietary protein *JNCI* **71** 347-353

Pour PM, Tahahashi M, Conelly T et al (1983b) Modification of pancreatic carcinogenesis in the hamster model IX Effect of pancreatitis *JNCI* **71** 607-613

Prentice RI, Sheppard L (1990) Dietary fat and cancer: consistency of the epidemiologic data, and disease prevention that may follow from a practical reduction in fat consumption *Cancer Causes Control*; **1** 81-97

Raymond L and Bouchardy C (1990) Les facteurs de risque du cancer du pancréas d'après les études épidémiologiques analytiques *Bull Cancer* **77** 47-68

Raymond L, Infante F, Tuyns AJ et al (1987) Alimentation et cancer du pancréas *Gatroenterol Clin Biol* **11** 488-492

Riela A, Zinsmeister AR, Melton LJ et al (1992) Increasing incidence of pancreatic cancer among women in Olmsted County, Minnesota, 1940 through 1988 *Mayo Clin Proc* **67** 839-845

Roebuck BD (1992) Dietary fat and the development of pancreatic cancer *Lipids* **27** 804-806

Roebuck BD, Longnecker DS, Baumgartner KJ et al (1985) Carcinogen-induced lesions in the rat pancreas: effects of varying levels of essential fatty acid *Cancer Res* **45** 5252-5256

Roebuck BD, Yager JD Jr and Longnecker DS (1981a) Dietary modulation of azaserine-induced pancreatic carcinogenesis in the rat *Cancer Res* **41** 888-893

Roebuck BD, Yager JD Jr, Longnecker DS et al (1981b) Promotion by unsaturated fat of azaserine-induced pancreatic carcinogenesis in the rat *Cancer Res* **41** 3961-3966

Rutter WJ (1980) The development of the endocrine and exocrine pancreas In *The Pancreas* (ed PJ Fitzgerald, AB Morrison) Baltimore: Williams and Wilkinspp30-38

Segi M, Kurihara M (1972) Cancer Mortality for Selected Sites in 24 Countries No **6** (1966-1967)

Nagoya, Japan: Japan Cancer Society

Sener SF, Fremgen A, Imperato JP et al (1991) Pancreatic cancer in Illinois: a report by 88 hospitals on 2,401 patients diagnosed 1978-84 *Am Surg* **57** 490-495

Shibata A, Mack TM, Paganini-Hill A, Ross RK and Henderson BE (1994) A prospective study of pancreatic cancer in the elderly *Int J Cancer* **58** 46-49

Shibata D, Capella G and Perucho M (1990) Mutational activation of the c-K-ras gene in human pancreatic carcinoma *Baillière's Clin Gastroenterol* **4** 151-169

Spector T (1981) Coffee, Soya and pancreatic cancer *Lancet* **311** 474

Spingarn NE and Weisburger JH (1979) Formation of mutagens in cooked foods I Beef *Cancer Let* **7** 259-264

Steinmetz KA and Potter JD (1991) Vegetables, fruit, and cancer II Mechanisms *Cancer Causes and Control* **2** 427-442

Stocks P (1970) Cancer mortality in relation to national consumption of cigarettes solid fuel, tea and coffee *Br J Cancer* **24** 215-225

Sugimura T (1985) Carcinogenicity of mutagenic heterocyclic amines formed during the cooking process *Mutat Res* **150** 33-41

Sugimura T and Sato S (1983) Mutagens-carcinogens in foods Cancer Res 43 2415s-2421s (407231)

Sugimura T, Nagao M (1982) The use of mutagenicity to evaluate carcinogenic hazards in our daily lives In: Heddle JA, ed *Mutagenicity, new horizons in genetic toxicity* New York: Academic Press 73-88

Tada M, Yososuka O, Omata M et al (1990) Analysis of ras gene mutations in biliary and pancreatic tumors by polymerase chain reaction and direct sequencing *Cancer* **66** 930-935

Tanaka T, Barnes WS, Williams GM et al (1985) Multipotential carcinogenicity of the fried food mutagen 2-amino-3-methylimidazo[4,5-l]quinoline in rats *Jpn J Cancer Res (Gann)* **76** 570-576

Tannenbaum A (1959) Nutrition and Cancer In *The Physiopathology of Cancer* (Ed F Homburger) New York:Hoeber-Harper pp517-562

US Department of Health and Human Services (1990) *Cancer Statistics Review* 1973-1987 USDHHS, PHS, NCI, NIH publication No 90-2789

Velema JP, Walker AM and Gold EB (1986) Alcohol and pancreatic cancer, Insufficient

epidemiologic evidence for a causal relationship *Epidemiol Rev* **8** 28-41

Warshaw AL and Fernández-Del Castillo C (1992) Pancreatic carcinoma *N Engl J Med* **326** 455-465

Wattenberg LW (1985) Chemoprevention of cancer *Cancer Res* **45** 1-8

Whittemore AS, Paffenbarger RS, Anderson K et al (1983) Early precursors of pancreatic cancer in college men *J Chron Dis* **36** 251-256

WHO (1997) World Health Organization *The World Health Report* Geneva:WHO

Willett WC and MacMahon B (1984a) Diet and cancer - an overview (First of two parts) *N Engl J Med* **310** 633-638

Willett WC and MacMahon B (1984b) Diet and cancer - an overview (Second of two parts) *N Engl J Med* **310** 697-703

Williams RR and Horm JW (1977) Association of cancer sites with tobacco and alcohol consumption and socioeconomic status of patients: Interview study from the Third national Cancer Survey *JNCI* **58** 525-547

Woutersen RA and van Garderen-Hoetmer A (1988a) Inhibition of dietary fat promoted develpment of (pre)neoplastic lesions in exocrine pancreas of rats and hamsters by supplemental selenium and b-carotene *Cancer Lett* **42** 79-85

Woutersen RA and van Garderen-Hoetmer A (1988b) Inhibition of dietary fat promoted development of (pre)neoplastic lesions in exocrine pancreas of rats and hamsters by supplemental Vitamins A, C and E *Cancer Lett* **41** 179-189

Woutersen RA, van Garderen-Hoetmer A (1989) Modulation of dietary fat-promoted pancreatic carcinogenesis in rats and hamsters by chronic coffee consumption *Carcinogenesis* 10:311-316

Wynder EL, Dieck GS and Hall NEL (1986) Case-control study of decaffeinated coffee consumption and pancreatic cancer *Cancer Res* **46** 5360-5363

Wynder EL, Hall NEL and Polansky M (1983) Epidemiology of coffee and pancreatic cancer *Cancer Res* **43** 3900-3906

Yamada H, Sakamoto H, Taira M et al (1986) Amplification of both c-Ki-ras with a point mutation and c-myc in a primary pancreatic cancer and its metastatic tumors in lymph nodes *Jpn J Cancer Res (Gann)* **77** 370-375

Yanai H et al (1979) Multivariate analysis of cancer mortalities for selected sites in 24 countries *Environ Health Persp* **32** 83-101

Zatonski W, Boyle P, Przewozniak K et al (1993) Cigarette smoking, alcohol, tea and coffee consumption and pancreas cancer risk: a case-control study from Opole, Poland *Int J Cancer* **53** 601-607

Zatonski W, Przewozniak K, Howe GR et al (1991) Nutritional factors and pancreatic cancer: a case-control study from Opole, Poland *Int J Cancer* **48** 390-394

Zheng W, Doyle TJ, Kushi-LH, Sellers-TA, Hong-CP, Folsom-AR (1996) Tea consumption and cancer incidence in a prospective cohort study of postmenopausal women *Am J Epidemiol* **144**(2) 175-82

Zheng W, McLaughlin JK, Gridley G et al (1993) A cohort study of smoking, alcohol and dietary factors for pancreatic cancer (United States) *Cancer Causes and Control* **4** 477-482

4.8 GALLBLADDER

Arevalo JA, Wollitzer AO, Corporon MB et al(1987) Ethnic variability in cholelithiasis — an autopsy study *West J Med* **147** 44-47

Bennion LJ and Grundy SM (1978a) Risk factors for the development of cholelithiasis in man (first of two parts) *N Engl J Med* **299** 1161-1167

Bennion LJ and Grundy SM (1978a) Risk factors for the development of cholelithiasis in man (second of two parts) *N Engl J Med* **299** 1221-1227

Chow, WH, McLaughlin JK, Menck HR, Mack TH (1994) Risk factors for extrahepatic bile-duct cancers:Los Angeles County, California (USA) *Cancer causes control* **5** 267-272

Diehl AK (1983) Gallstone size and the risk of gallbladder cancer *JAMA* **250** 2323-2326

Heaton, KW (1973) The epidemiology of gallstones and suggested aetiology *Clin Gastroenterol* **2** 67-83

Kato K, Akai S, Tominaga S and Kato I (1989) A case-control study of biliary tract cancer in Niigata Prefecture, Japan *Jpn J Cancer Res* **80** 932-938

Kato I, Nomura AMY, Stemmermann GN, Chyou PH (1992) Prospective study of the association of alcohol with cancer of the upper aerdipertive tract and other sites *Cancer CausesControl* **3** 145-151

Kato I, Kato K, Akai S and Tominaga S (1990) A case-control study of gallstones: a major risk factor for biliary tract cancer *Jpn J Cancer Res* **81** 578-583

Lew EA and Garfinkel l (1979) Variations in mortality by weight among 750,000 men and women *J Chron Dis* **32** 563-576

Lowenfels AB (1978) Does bile promote extra-colonic cancer? *Lancet* **2** 2239-2241

Lowenfels AB, Llindstrom CG, Conway MJ et al(1985) Gallstones and risk of gallbladder cancer *JNCI* **75** 77-80

Lowenfels AB, Althaus DP, Townsend G and Domellof L (1989) Gallstone growth, size, and risk of gallbladder cancer: an interracial study *Int J Epidemiol* **18** 50-54

Maclure KM, Hayes KC, Colditz GA et al(1989) Weight, diet, and the risk of symptomatic gallstones in middle-aged women *N Engl J Med* **321** 563-569

Menck HR, Henderson BE, Pike MC et al(1975) Cancer incidence in the Mexican-American *JNCI* **155** 531-536

National Research Council (1989) *Committee on Diet and Health* Diet and Health, National Academy Press: Washington

Parkin DM, Muir CS, Whelan SL, Gao YT, Ferlay J and Powell J (eds) (1992) *Cancer Incidence in Five Continents, Volume VI* IARC Sci Publ No 120 International Agency for Research on Cancer: Lyon

Scragg RKR, McMichael AJ and Baghurst PA (1984) Diet, alcohol, and relative weight in gall stone disease: a case-control study *Br Med J* **288** 1113-1119

Thomas DB (1979) Epidemiologic studies of cancer in minority groups in the Western United States *Natl Cancer Inst Monogr* **53** 103-113

Tominaga S and Kato I Changing patterns of cancer and diet in Japan *Recent Progress in Research on Nutrition and Cancer* Wiley-Liss, Inc pp1-10

Young JL Jr, Ries LG and Pollack ES (1984) Cancer patient survival among ethnic groups in the United States *JNCI* **73** 341-352

Zatonski WA, La Vecchia C, Przewozniak K, Maisonneuve P, Lowenfels AB and Boyle P (1992) Risk factors for gallbladder cancer: a Polish case-control study *Int J Cancer* **51** 707-711

4.9 LIVER

Adami H-O, Hsing AW, McLaughlin JK, Trichopoulos D, Hacker D, Ekbom A and Persson I (1992) Alcoholism and liver cirrhosis in the etiology of primary liver cancer *Int J Cancer* **51** 898-902

Adelstein A and White G (1976) Alcoholism and mortality *Popul Trends* **6** 7-13

Anderson LM, Logsdon D, Ruskie S et al (1994) Promotion by polychlorinated biphenyls of lung and liver tumors in mice *Carcinogenesis* **15** 2245-2248

Anthony PP (1977) Cancer of the liver: Pathogenesis and recent aetiological factors *Trans Roy Soc Trop Med Hygiene* **71** 466-470

Armstrong B (1980) The epidemiology of cancer in the People's Republic of China *Int J Epidemiol* **9** 305-315

Armstrong B , Doll R (1975) Environmental factors and cancer incidence and mortality in different countries, with special reference to dietary practices *Int J Cancer* **15** 617-31

Ashley LM and Halver JE (1961) Hepatomagenesis in rainbow trout *Fed Proc* **20** 290 (abstract)

Austin H (1991) The role of tobacco use and alcohol consumption in the etiology of hepatocellular carcinoma In *Etiology, pathology, and treatment of hepatocellular carcinoma in North America* (Ed E Tabor, AM Di Bisceglie and RH Purcell) Gulf Publishing Co: Houston, TX pp57-75

Austin H, Delzell E, Grufferman S, Levine R, Morrison AS, Stolley PD and Cole P (1986) A case-control study of hepatocellular carcinoma and the hepatitis B virus, cigarette smoking, and alcohol consumption *Cancer Res* **46** 962-966

Autrup H, Seremet T, Wakhisi J and Wasunna A (1987) Aflatoxin exposure measured by urinary excretion of aflatoxin B1-guanine adduct and hepatitis B virus infection in areas with different liver cancer incidence in Kenya *Cancer Res* **47** 3430-3433

Beck H, Bross A, Mathar W (1994) PCDD and PCDF exposure and levels in humans in Germany *Environ Health Perspectives* **102** 173-185

Beebe LE, Kim YE, Amin S et al (1993) Comparison of trnsplacental and neonatal initiation of mouse lung and liver tumors by N-nitrosodimethylamine (NMDA) and 4-(methylnitrosoamino)-1-(3-Pyridyl)-Butanone (NNK) and promotability by a polychlorinated biphenyls mixture (Arochlor 1254) *Carcinogenesis* **14** 1545-1548

Bertazzi et al (1987) *AJIM* **11** 169-176

Best CH and Huntsman ME (1932) The effects of the components of lecithine upon deposition of fat in the liver *J Physiol* (London) **75** 405-412

Best CH, Huntsman ME and Ridout JH (1935) The effects of diets low in choline on normal rats and depancreatized dogs *Am J Physiol* **113** 11 (abstract)

Blount WP (1961) Turkey "X" Disease *Turkeys* March-April **52** 55-58, 61, 77

Blum A and Ames B (1977) Fire retardant additives as possible cancer hazards *Science* **195** 12-17

Bressac B, Kew M, Wands J and Ozturk M (1991) Selective G to T mutations of p53 gene in hepatocellular carcinoma from southern Africa *Nature* **350** 429-431

Bulatao-Jayme J, Almero EM, Castro MCA, Jardeleza MTR and Salamat LA (1982) A case-control dietary study of primary liver cancer risk from aflatoxin exposure *Int J Epidemiol* **11** 112-119

Busby WF Jr and Wogan GN (1984) Aflatoxins In *Chemical carcinogens* (Ed CE Searle) American Cancer Society: Washington DC pp945-1136

Cady B (1983) Natural history of primary and secondary tumors of the liver Seminars in *Oncology* **10** 127-134

Campbell TC and Hayes JR (1976) The role of aflatoxin in its toxic lesion *Tox Appl Pharm* **35** 199-222

Campbell TC, Chen J, Liu C, Li J and Parpia B (1990) Non-association of aflatoxin with primary liver cancer in a cross-sectional ecologic survey in the People's Republic of China *Cancer Res* **50** 6882-6893

Carnaghan RBA (1965) Hepatic tumours in ducks fed a low level of toxic groundnut meal *Nature* **208** 308

Carthew P, Nolan BM, Smith AG Edwards RE (1997) Iron promotes DEN initiated GST-P foci in rat liver *Carcinogenesis* **18** 599-603

Chandar M, Lombardi B, Locker J (1989) *Proc Natl Acad Sci USA* **86** 2703

Copeland DH and Salmon WD (1946) The occurrence of neoplasms in the liver, lungs, and other tissues of rats as a result of prolonged choline deficiency *Am J Pathol* **22** 1059-1079

Cordier S, Thuy LT, Verger P, Bard D, Dai LC, Larouze B, Dazza MC, Quinh HT and Abenheim L (1993) Viral infections and chemical exposures as risk factors for hepatocellular carcinoma in Vietnam *Int J Cancer* **55** 196-201

Crawford MA (1971) Epidemiological interactions In *Epidemiological interactions* (Ed IFH Purchase) Macmillan Press, Ltd: London pp231-244

Dauod AH and Griffin AC (1978) Effect of selenium and retinoic on the metabolism of N-acetylaminofluorene and N-hydroxyacetylaminofluorene *Cancer Letters* **5** 231-237

Dean G, MacLennan R, McLoughlin H and Shelley E (1979) Causes of death of blue-collar workers at a Dublin brewery, 1954-73

Br J Cancer **40** 581-589

Dent JG, Cagen SZ, McCormack KM, Rickert DE, Gibson JE (1977) Liver and mammary arylhydrocarbon hydroxylase and epoxide hydratase in lactating rats fed polybrominatedbiphenyls *Life Sciences* **20** 2075-2080

Dent JG, Netter KJ, Gibson JE (1976) The induction of hepatic microsomal metabolism in rats following acute administration of a mixture of polybrominated biphenyls *Toxicol Appl Pharmacol* **38** 237-249

Falk H, Herbert JT, Edmonds L, Heath J, CW, Thomas LB and Popper H (1981) Review of four cases of childhood hepatic angiosarcoma-elevated environmental arsenic exposure in one case *Cancer* **47** 382-391

Falk H, Telles NC, Ishak KG, Thomas LB and Popper H (1979) Epidemiology of Thorotrast-induced hepatic angiosarcoma in the United States *Environ Res* **18** 65-73

Farber E (1956) *Arch Pathol* **62** 445

Farber E (1963) *Adv Cancer Research* **7** 383

Feo F, PascaleR, Garcea R et al (1986) *Toxicol Appl Pharmacol* **83** 331

Fingerhut MA; Sweeney MH; Halperin WE; Schnorr TM (1991) The epidemiology of populations exposed to dioxin *IARC Sci Publ* **108** 31-50

Fukuda K, Shibata A, Hirohata I, Tanikawa K, Yamaguchi G and Ishii M (1993) A hospital-based case-control study on hepatocellular carcinoma in Fukuoka and Saga prefectures, Northern Kyushu, Japan *Jpn J Cancer Res* **84** 708-714

Gan L-S, Skipper PL, Peng A, JD, G, Chen J, Wogan GN and Tannenbaum SR (1988) Serum albumin adducts in the molecular epidemiology of aflatoxin carcinogenesis: Correlation with aflatoxin B1 intake and urinary excretion of aflatoxin M1 *Carcinogenesis* **9** 1323-1325

Garcea R, Pascale R, Daino L, Frasseto S, Cozzolino P et al (1987) *Carcinogenesis* **8** 595

Goldblatt LA (1969) *Aflatoxin* Scientific background, control and implications Academic Press: New York pp472

Goodman MT, Moriwaki H, Vaeth M, Akiba S, Hayabuchi H and Mabuchi K (1995) Prospective cohort study of risk factors for primary liver cancer in Hiroshima and Nagasaki, Japan *Epidemiology* **6** 36-41

Groopman JD, Hall AJ, Whittle H, Hudson GJ, Wogan GN, Montesano R and Wild CP (1992) Molecular dosimetry of aflatoxin-N7-guanine in human urine obtained in The Gambia, West Africa *Cancer Epi Biomarkers Prev* 1 221-227

Groopman JD, Sabbioni G and Wild CP (1991) *Molecular dosimetry of aflatoxin exposures In Molecular dosimetry of aflatoxin exposures* (Ed JD Groopman and P Skipper) CRC Press: Boca Raton, FL pp302-324

Groopman JD, Zhu J, Donahue PR, Pikul A, Zhang L, Chen J and Wogan GN (1992) Molecular dosimetry of urinary aflatoxin-DNA adducts in people living in Guangxi Autonomous Region, People's Republic of China *Cancer Res* **52** 45-52

Hadziyannis S, Tabor E, Kaklamani E, Tzonou A, Stuver S, Tassopoulos N, Mueller N and Trichopoulos D (1995) A case-control study of hepatitis B and C virus infections in the etiology of hepatocellular carcinoma *Int J Cancer* **60** 627-631

Hakulinen T, Lehtimaki L, Lehtonen M and Teppo L (1974) Cancer mortality among two male cohorts with increased alcohol consumption in Finland *JNCI* **52** 1171-1714

Han J (1993) Highlights of the cancer chemoprevention studies in China *Prev Med* **22** 712-722

Hann HWL, Stahlhut MW, Rubin R, Maddrey WC (1992) Antitumor effect of defeoxamine on human hepatocellular carcinoma growing in athymic nude mice *Cancer* **70** 2051-2056

Hardell L Bengtsson NO, Jonsson U, Eriksson S and Larsson LG (1984) Aetiological aspects on primary liver cancer with special regard to alcohol, organic solvents and acute intermittent porphyria — An epidemiological investigation *Br J Cancer* **50** 389-397

Harr JR, Exon JH, Whanger PD and Weswig PH (1972) Effect of dietary selenium on N-2-fluorenyl-acetamide(FAA)-induced cancer in vitamin E supplemented, selenium depleted rats *Clin Toxicol* **5** 187-194

Heilbrun LK, Nomura A, Stemmermann GN (l986) Black tea consumption and cancer risk: a prospective study *Br J Cancer* **54** 677–83

Hietanen E, Bartsch H, Bereziat JC et al (1990) Quantity and saturation degree of dietary fats as modulators of oxidative stress and chemically-induced liver tumours in rats *Int J Cancer* **46**(4) 640-7

Hirayama T (1989) A large-scale cohort study on risk factors for primary liver cancer, with special reference to the role of cigarette smoking *Cancer Chemother Pharmacol* **23** S114-S117

Hirayama T (1990) *Life-style and mortality* A large scale census-based cohort study in Japan Karger: Basel

Ho SF, Phoon WH, Gan SL (1991) Persistent liver dysfunction among workers at a vinyl chloride monomer polymerization plant *J Soc Occupational Med* **41** 10-16

Hollstein M, Sidransky D, Vogelstein B and Harris CC (1991) p53 mutations in human cancers *Science* **253** 49-53

Hornhardt S, Jenke HS, Michel G (1994) Polychlorinated biphenyls modulate protooncogene expression in Chang liver cells *FEBS Letts* **339** 185-188

Hsing AW, Guo W, Chen J, Stone BJ, Blot WJ and Fraumeni JF Jr (1991) Correlates of liver cancer mortality in China *Int J Epidemiol* **20** 54-59

Hsu IC, Metcalf RA, Sun T, Welsh JA, Wang NJ and Harris CC (1991) Mutational hotspot in the p53 gene in human hepatocellular carcinomas *Nature* **350** 427-428

Huff JE, Salmon AG, Hooper NK, Zeise L (1991) Long term carcinogenesis studies on 2,3,7,8-tetrachlorodibenzo-para-dioxin and hexachlorodibenzo-para-dioxins *Cell Biol Tox* **7** 67-94

IARC (1976) *Some naturally occurring substances* (Editor) International Agency for Research on Cancer: Lyon pp51-72

IARC (1987) *Hepatitis B, C, and D viruses* International Agency for Research on Cancer: Lyon pp45-221

IARC (1987) *Overall evaluations on carcinogenicity: An update of IARC monographs 1-42* International Agency for Research on Cancer: Lyon pp83-87, 96-99, 272-309

IARC (1988) *Monographs on the Evaluation of Carcinogenic risks to humans Alcohol drinking* International Agency for Cancer Research: Lyon

IARC (1993) *Monographs on the Evaluation of Carcinogenic risks to humans Some naturally occurring substances: Food items and constituents, heterocyclic aromatic amines and mycotoxins* International Agency for Research on Cancer: Lyon pp245-395

James SJ, Yin L, and Swendseid M (1989) DNA strand breaks, thymidylate synthesis and NAD levels in lymphocytes from methyl donor-deficient rats *J Nutr* **119** 661-664

Jenke HS, Michel G, Hornhardt S et al (1991) Protooncogene expression in rat liver by polychlorinated biphenyls (PCB) *Xenobiotica* **21** 945-960

Jensen OM (1980) Cancer morbidity and causes of death among Danish brewery workers *International Agency for Research on Cancer*: Lyon

Kew MC and Popper H (1984) Relationship between hepatocellular carcinoma and cirrhosis *Semin Liver Dis* **4** 136-146

Kimbrough RD, Burse VW, Liddle JA (1978) Persistent liver lesions in rats after a single oral dose of polybrominated biphenyls (Firemaster FF-1) and comcomitant PBB tissue levels *Environ Health Perspectives* **23** 265-273

Kimbrough RD, Groce DF, Korver MP et al (1975) Induction of liver tumours in female Sherman strain rats by polybrominated biphenyls *JNCI* **55** 153-1458

Kimbrough RD, Groce DF, Korver MP, Burse VW (1981) Induction of liver tumours in female Sherman strain rats by polybrominated biphenyls *JNCI* **66** 535-542

Kono S, Ikeda M, Tokudome S, Nishizumi M and Kuratsune M (1986) Alcohol and mortality: A cohort study of male Japanese physicians *Int J Epidemiol* **15** 527-532

Kostka G, Kopecszlezak J, Palut D (1996) Early hepatic changes induced in rats by two hepatocarcinogenic organohalogen pesticides - bromopropylate and DDT *Carcinogenesis* **17** 407-412

Krutoskikh VA, Mesnil M, Mazzoleni G, Yamasaki H (1995) Inhibition of rat liver gap junction intercellular communication by tumor promoting agents in vivo - association with aberrant localization of connexin proteins *Laboratory Investigation* **72** 571-577

La Vecchia C, Negri E, Decarli A, D'Avanzo B and Franceschi S (1988) Risk factors for hepatocellular carcinoma in Northern Italy *Int J Cancer* **42** 872-876

Lam KC, Yu MC, Leung JWC and Henderson BE (1982) Hepatitis B virus and cigarette smoking: Risk factors for hepatocellular carcinoma in Hong Kong *Cancer Res* **42** 5246-5248

Lancaster MC, Jenkins FP and Philp JM (1961) Toxicity associated with certain samples of groundnuts *Nature* **192** 1095-1096

Lapeyre JN, Becker FF (1979) *Biochem Biophys Res Commun* **87** 698

Lee DJ, Sinnhuber RO, Wales JH and Putnam GB (1977) Effect of dietary protein on the response of rainbow trout (Salmo gairdneri) to aflatoxin B1 *JNCI* **60** 317-320

Lee FI, Smith PM, Bennett B et al (1996) Occupationally related angiosarcoma of the liver in the United Kingdom 1972-1994 *Gut* **39** 312-318

Lee KP, Herbert RR, Sherman H et al (1975) Bromine tissue residues and hepatotoxic effects of octabromobiphenyl in rats *Toxicol Appl Pharmacol* **34** 115-127

Li WG, Gong HM, Xie JR, Yu SY, Zhu YJ, Gong XL, Hou C, Wu B and Cao LS (1986) Regional distribution of liver cancer and its relation to selenium level in Qidong county, China [Chinese] *Chin J Oncol* **8** 262-264

Lieber CS (1993) Herman Award Lecture, 1993: A personal perspective on alcohol, nutrition, and the liver *Am J Clin Nutr* **58** 430-442

Liver Cancer Study Group of Japan (1988) Survey and follow-up study of primary liver cancer in Japan—report 8 (in Japanese) *Acta Hepatol* **29** 1619-1626

London WT, McGlynn KA (1996) Liver Cancer in Scottenfeld D and Fraumeni JF Jr (eds) *Cancer Epidemiology and Prevention* 2nd Ed OUP New York 772-793

LSRO (Life Sciences Research Office) (1985) Summary of a report on assessment of the iron nutritional status of the United States population *Am J Clin Nutr* **42** 1318-1330

Lu SN, Chen CJ, Chen JS, Liaw YF, Chang WY and Hsu ST (1988) A case-control study of primary hepatocellular carcinoma in Taiwan *Cancer* **62** 2051-2055

Madhavan TV and Gopalan C (1968) The effect of dietary protein on carcinogenesis of aflatoxin *Arch Path* **85** 133-137

Maiorana A, Gullino PM, Goldman M et al (1980) Effect of retinyl acetate on the incidence of mammary carcinomas and hepatomas in mice *JNCI* **64** 655-663

Makk L, Delmore F, Creech JLJ, Ogden LLI, Fadell H, Songster CL, Clanton J, Johnson MN and Christopherson WM (1976) Clinical and morphologic features of hepatic angiosarcoma in vinyl chloride workers *Cancer* **37** 149-163

Mandel HG, Judah DJ and Neal GE (1992) Effect of dietary protein level on aflatoxin B1 actions in the liver of weanling rats *Carcinogenesis* **13** 1853-1857

Mantyla E and Ahotupa M (1993) Polychlorinated biphenyls and naththalenes - long lasting induction of oxidative stress in the rat *Chemosphere* **27** 383-390

Monson RR and Lyon JL (1975) Proportional mortality among alcoholics *Cancer* **36** 1077-1079

Munoz N and Bosch FX (1987) Epidemiology of hepatocellular carcinoma In *Neoplasms of the liver* (Ed K Okuda and KG Ishaki) Springer: Tokyo pp3-19

NAS (1982) National Academy of Sciences *Diet, Nutrition and Cancer* Washington DC: National Academy Press

NAS (1989) National Academy of Sciences *Diet and Health* Washington DC: National Academy Press

Newberne PM and Rogers AE (1971) *Aflatoxin carcinogenesis in rats: dietary effects In Aflatoxin carcinogenesis in rats: dietary effects* (Ed IFH Purchase) Macmillan Press Ltd: London pp195-208

Newberne PM and Zieger E (1978) Nutrition, carcinogenesis, and mutagenesis In *Nutrition, carcinogenesis, and mutagenesis* (Ed WG Flamm and MA Mehlman) John Wiley, Sons: New York pp53-84

Niederau C, Fischer R, Purschel A, Strmmel W, Haussinger D, Strohmeyer F (1996) Long-term survival in patients with hereditary hemochromatosis *Gastroenterology* **110** 1107-1119

Nigro JM, Baker SJ, Preisinger AC, Jessup JM, Hostetter R, Cleary K, Bigner SH, Davidson N, Baylin S, Devilee P et al (1989) Mutations in p53 gene occur in diverse human tumour types *Nature* (London) **342** 705-708

Okuda K (1991) Hepatitis C virus and hepatocellular carcinoma In *Etiology, pathology, and treatment of hepatocellular carcinoma in North America* (Ed E Tabor, AM Di Bisceglie and RH Purcell) Gulf Publishing Company: Houston TX pp119-126

Olsen JH, Dragsted L and Autrup H (1988) Cancer risk and occupational exposure to aflatoxins in Denmark *Br J Cancer* **58** 392-396

Orten JM and Neuhaus OW (1982) *Human Biochemistry* (Editor) pp984 CV Mosby Company: Toronto, Canada

Oshima A, Tsukuma H, Hiyama T, Fujimoto I, Yamano H and Tanaka M (1984) Follow-up study of HBsAg-positive blood donors with special reference to effect of drinking and smoking on development of liver cancer *Int J Cancer* **34** 775-779

Ott MG, Zober A (1996) Cause specific mortality and cancer incidence among employees exposed to 2,3,7,8-TCDD after a 1953 reactor accident *Occup Environ Med* **53**(9) 606-12

Ozturk M and Collaborators (1991) p53 hotspot mutation in hepatocellular carcinoma is geographically linked to aflatoxin exposure *Lancet* **338** 1356-1359

Pan W-H, Wang C-Y, Huang SM, Yeh S-Y, Lin W-G, Lin D-I and Liaw Y-F (1993) Vitamin A, vitamin E or beta-carotene status and hepatitis B-related hepatocellular carcinoma *Ann Epidemiol* **3** 217-224

Parkin DM, Srivatanakul P, Khlat M, Chenvidhya D, Chotiwan P, Insiripong S, L'Abbe KA and Wild CP (1991) Liver cancer in Thailand I A case-control study of cholangiocarcinoma *Int J Cancer* **48** 323-328

Pascale RM, Marras V, Simile MM, Daino L, Pinna G, Bennati S, Carta M, Seddaiu A, Massarelli G, Feo F (1992**)** *Cancer Res* **52** 4979

Peers FG, Bosch X, Kaldor J, Linsell A and Pluijmen M (1987) Aflatoxin exposure, hepatitis B virus infection and liver cancer in Swaziland *Int J Cancer* **39** 545-553

Poirier LA Methyl group deficiency in hepatocarcinogenesis Drug Metab Rev 1994;26:185–199

Qian G-S, Ross RK, Yu MC, Yuan J-M, Gao Y-T, Henderson BE, Wogan GN and Groopman JD (1994) A follow-up study of urinary markers of aflatoxin exposure and liver cancer risk in Shanghai, People's Republic of China *Cancer Epidemiol Biom Prev* **3** 3-10

Rivedal E, Yamasaki H, Sanner T (1994) Inhibition of gap junctional intercellular communication in Syrian Hamster embryo cells by TPA, retinoic acid and DDT *Carcinogenesis* **15** 689-694

Robinette CD, Hrubec Z and Fraumeni JF Jr (1979) Chronic alcoholism and subsequent morality in World War II veterans *Am J Epidemiol* **109** 687-700

Roseng LE, Rivedal E, Skaare JU et al (1994) Effect of 1,1'-(2,2,2-trichloroethylidene)-bis(4-chlorobenzene) DDT on gap junctional intercellular communication and morphological transformation of Syrian Hamster embryo cells *Chemico-Biological Interactions* **90** 73-85

Ross RK, Yuan J-M, Yu MC, Wogan GN, Qian G-S, Tu J-T, Groopman JD, Gao YT and Henderson BE (1992) Urinary aflatoxin biomarkers and risk of hepatocellular carcinoma *Lancet* **339** 943-946 (40959)

Rothman KJ (1980) The proportion of cancer attributable to alcohol consumption *Prev Med* **9** 174-179

Ruch RJ, Bonney WJ, Sigler K et al (1994) Loss of gap junctions from DDT treated rat liver epithelial cells *Carcinogenesis* **15** 301-306

Rumsby PC, Evans JG, Phillimore HE, Carthew P et al (1992) Search for H-ras codon 61 mutation s in liver tumors caused by hexachlorobenzene and arochlor 1254 in C57BL/10SCSN mice with iron overload *Carcinogenesis* **13** 1917-1920

Rushmore TH, Lim YP, Farber E et al (1984) *Cancer Lett* **24** 251

Sabbioni G, Ambs A, Wogan GN and Groopman JD (1990) The aflatoxin-lysine adduct quantified by high-performance chromatography from human serum albumin samples *Carcinogenesis* **11** 2063-2066

Safe, S, Hutzinger, O, Hill, TA *Polychlorinated dibenzo-p-dioxins and furans (PCDDs/PCDFs): sources and environmental impact, epidemiology, mechanisms of action, health risks* Berlin, Hedelberg: Springer-Verlag

Salmon WD and Copeland DH (1954) Liver carcinoma and related lesions in chronic choline deficiency *Ann NY Acad Sci* **57** 664-667

Saracci R, Kogevinas M, Bertazzi PA, Bueno de Mesquita BH et al (1991) Cancer mortality in workers exposed to chlorophenoxy herbicides and chlorophenols *Lancet* **338**(8774) 1027-32

Schmidt W and Popham RE (1981) The role of drinking and smoking in mortality from cancer and other causes in male alcoholics *Cancer* **47** 1031-1041

Schulsinger DA, Root MM and Campbell TC (1989) Effect of dietary protein quality on development of aflatoxin B1-induced hepatic preneoplastic lesions *JNCI* **81** 1241-1245

Scorsone KA, Zhou YZ, Butel JS and Slagle BL (1992) p53 mutations cluster at codon-249 in hepatitis-B virus-positive hepatocellular carcinomas from China *Cancer Res* **52** 1635-1638

Sherman JD (1991) Polybrominated biphenyl exposure and human cancer: report of a case and public health implications *Toxicol Industrial Health* **7** 197-205

Shibata A, Hirohata T, Toshima H and Tashiro H (1986) The role of drinking and cigarette smoking in the excess deaths from liver cancer *Jpn J Cancer Res (Gann)* **77** 287-295

Shinozuka H, Katyal SL, Lombardi B (1978) *Int J Cancer* **22** 36

Sigler K, Ruch RJ (1993) Enhancement of gap junctional intercellular communication in tumor promoter treated cells by components of green tea *Cancer Letts* **69** 15-19

Simonato L, Labbe KA, Anderson A et al (1991) A collaborative study of cancer incidence and mortality among vinyl chloride workers *Scand J Work Environ Health* **20** 317-334

Sirtori CR, Noseda G and Descovich GC (1983) Studies on the use of a soybean protein diet for the management of human hyperlipoproteinemias In *Studies on the use of a soybean protein diet for the management of human hyperlipoproteinemias* (Ed MJ Gibney and D Kritchevsky) Alan R Liss Inc: New York pp135-148

Smith AG, Carthew P, Clothier B et al (1995) Synergy of iron in the toxicity and carcinogenicity of polychlorinated biphenyls (PCBs) and related chemicals *Toxicol Letts* **82-83** 945-950

Smith ML, Yeleswarapu L, Scalamogna P et al (1993) *Carcinogenesis* **14** 503

Srivatanakul P, Parkin DM, Jiang Y-Z, Khlat M, Kao-Ian U-T, Sontipong S and Wild CP (1991) The role of infection by Opisthorchis viverrini, hepatitis B virus, and aflatoxin exposure in the etiology of liver cancer in Thailand A correlation study *Cancer* **68** 2411-2417

Srivatanakul P, Parkin DM, Khlat M, Chenvidhya D, Chotiwan P, Insiripong S, L'Abbe KA and Wild CP (1991) Liver cancer in Thailand II Case-control study of hepatocellular carcinoma *Int J Cancer* **48** 329-332

Stal P, Hultcrantz R, Moller L et al (1995) The effects of iron on the initiation and promotion in chemical hepatocarcinogensis *Hepatology* **21** 521-528

Stanford J, Thomas D and the WHO Collaborative Study of Neoplasia and Steroid Contraceptives (1991) Reproductive factors in the etiology of hepatocellular carcinoma *Cancer Causes Control* **2** 37-42

Stemhagen A, Slade J, Altman R and Bill J (1983) Occupational risk factors and liver cancer A retrospective case-control study of primary liver cancer in New Jersey *Am J Epidemiol* **117** 443-454

Sundby P (1967) Alcoholism and mortality *Universitetsforlaget*: Oslo

Suphakarn VS, Newberne PM, Goldman M (1983) Vitamin A and aflatoxin: effect on liver and colon cancer *Nutr Cancer* **5**(1) 41-50

Svensson BG, Nilsson A, Hansson M et al (1991) Exposure to dioxins and dibenzofurans through the consumption of fish *NEMJ* **324** 8-12

Szmuness W (1978) Hepatocellular carcinoma and the hepatitis B virus: Evidence for a causal association *Prog Med Virol* **24** 40-69

Tabor E and Kobayashi K (1992) Hepatitis C virus, a causative infectious agent of non-A, non-B hepatitis: Prevalence and structure - Summary of a conference on hepatitis C virus as a cause of hepatocellular carcinoma (1990) *JNCI* **84** 86-90

Tanaka K, Hirohata T, Koga S, Sugimachi K, Kanematsu T, Ohryohji F, Nawata H, Ishibashi H, Maeda Y, Kiyokawa H et al (1991) Hepatitis C and hepatitis B in the etiology of hepatocellular carcinoma in the Japanese population *Cancer Res* **51** 2842-2847

Tanaka K, Hirohata T, Takeshita S, Hirohata I, Koga S, Sugimachi K, Kanematsu T, Ohryohji F and Ishibashi H (1992) Hepatitis B virus, cigarette smoking and alcohol consumption in the development of hepatocellular carcinoma: A case-control study in Fukuoka, Japan **Int J Cancer 51** 509-514

Tannenbaum A and Silverstone H (1949) The genesis and growth of tumors IV Effects of varying the proportion of protein (casein) in the diet *Cancer Res* **9** 162-173

Tateno C, Ito S, Tanaka M et al (1994) Effect of DDT on hepatic junctional intercellular communication in rats *Carcinogenesis* **15** 517-521

Temcharoen P, Anukarahanonta T and Bhamarapravati N (1978) Influence of dietary protein and vitamin B12 on the toxicity and carcinogenicity of aflatoxins in rat liver *Cancer Res* **38** 2185-2190

Terpstra AHM, Hermus RJJ and West CE (1983) Dietary protein and cholesterol metabolism in rabbits and rats In *Dietary protein and cholesterol metabolism in rabbits and rats* (Ed MJ Gibney and D Kritchevsky) Alan R Liss Inc: New York pp9-18

Thomas DB (1988) Exogenous steroid hormones and hepatocellular carcinoma In: *Etiology, pathology, and treatment of hepatocellular carcinoma in North America* (Ed E Tabor, AM Di Bisceglie and RH Purcell RH)Gulf Publishing Co: Houston, TX pp77-89

Thorgeirsson UP, Dalgard DW, reeves J et al (1994) Tumor incidence ina chemical carcinogenesis study of nonhuman primates *Rgulatory Toxicol Pharmacol* **19** 130-151

Til HP, Feron VJ, Immel HR (1991) Lifetime (49 week) oral coarcinogenicity study of vinyl chloride in rats *Food Chem Toxicol* **29** 713-718

Trichopoulos D, Day NE, Kaklamani E, Tzonou A, Munoz N, Zavitsanos X, Koumantaki Y and Trichopoulou A (1987) Hepatitis B virus, tobacco smoking and ethanol consumption in the etiology of hepatocellular carcinoma *Int J Cancer* **39** 45-49

Trichopoulos D, Kremastinou J and Tzonou A (1982) Does hepatitis B virus cause hepatocellular carcinoma? In *Host factors in human carcinogenesis* (Ed B Armstrong and H Bartsch) International Agency for Research on Cancer: Lyon pp317-332

Tsukuma H, Hiyama T, Tanaka S, Nakao M, Yabuuchi T, Kitamura T, Nakanishi K, Fujimoto I, Inoue A, Yamasaki H and Kawashima T (1993) Risk factors for hepatocellular carcinoma among patients with chronic liver disease *New Engl J Med* **328** 1797-1801

Turlin B, Juguet F, Moirand R (1995) Increased liver iron stores in patients with hepatocellular carcinoma developed on a noncirrhotic liver *Hepatology* **22** 446-450

USDHHS (United States Department of Health and Human Services) (1988*) The Surgeon General's Report on Nutrition and Health* (Editor) Superintendent of Documents, US Government Printing Office: Washington DC pp727

Vall Mayans M, Calvet X, Bruix J, Brugera M, Costa J, Esteve J, Bosch FX, Bru C and Rodes J (1990) Risk factors for hepatocellular carcinoma in Catalonia, Spain *Int J Cancer* **46** 378-381

Wainfan E and Poirier LA·(1992) Methyl groups in carcinogenesis: effects on DNA methylation and gene expression *Cancer Res* **52** (Suppl) 2071S-2077s

Wainfan E, Dizik M, Stender M (1989) *Cancer Res* **49** 4094

Wang Y, Lan L, Ye B, Xu Y, Liu Y and Li W (1983) Relation between geographical distribution of liver cancer and climate—aflatoxin B1 in China *Sci sin* (Ser B) **26** 1166-1175

Wells P, Aftergood L and Alfin-Slater RB (1976) Effect of varying levels of dietary protein on tumor development and lipid metabolism in rats exposed to aflatoxin *J Am Oil Chem Soc* **53** 559-562

WHO (1997) World Health Organization *The World Health Report* Geneva:WHO

WHO, 1990 World Health Organization *Diet, Nutrition, and the Prevention of Chronic Diseases* Technical Report 797 Geneva: WHO

Whysner J, Conaway CC, Verna L (1996) Vinyl chloride mechanistic data and risk extrapolation *Pharmacology and Therapeutics* **71** 7-28

Williams RR and Horm JW (1977) Association of cancer sites with tobacco and alcohol consumption and socioeconomic status of patients: Interview study from the Third National Cancer Survey *JNCI* **58** 535-547

Wogan GN (1973) Aflatoxin carcinogenesis Meth *Cancer Res* **7** 309-344

Wogan GN, Paglialunga S and Newberne PM (1974) Carcinogenic effects of low dietary levels of aflatoxin B1 in rats Food Cosmet *Toxicol* **12** 681-685

Wong O, Whorton MD, Foliart DE, Ragland D (1991) An industry-wide epidemiologic study of vinyl chloride workers 1942-1982 *Am J Ind Med* **20**(3) 317-34

Yeh F-S, Yu MC, Mo C-C, Luo S, Tong MJ and Henderson B (1989) Hepatitis B virus, aflatoxins, and hepatocellular carcinoma in Southern Guangxi, China *Cancer Res* **49** 2506-2509

Yoshiji H, Nakae D, Mizumoto Y (1992) The inhibitory effect of dietary iron deficiency on inductions of putative preneoplastic lesions as well as 8-hydroxydeoxyguanosine in DNA and lipid peroxidation in the livers of rats acused by exposure to a choline -eficient L-amino acid defined diet*Carcinogeneis* **13** 1227-1233

Youngman LD (1990) *The growth and development of aflatoxin B1-induced preneoplastic lesions, tumors, metastasis, and spontaneous tumors as they are influenced by dietary protein level, type, and intervention* (Editor) Cornell University, PhD Thesis, Ithaca: NY pp203

Youngman LD and Campbell TC (1992) Inhibition of aflatoxin B1-induced gamma-glutamyl transpeptidase positive (GGT+) hepatic preneoplastic foci and tumors by low protein diets: Evidence that altered GGT+ foci indicate neoplastic potential *Carcinogenesis* **13** 1607-1613

Yu M-W and Chen C-J (1993) Elevated serum testosterone levels and risk of hepatocellular carcinoma *Cancer Res* **53** 790-794

Yu M-W, Hsieh H-H, Pan W-H, Yang C-S and Chen C-J (1995) Vegetable consumption, serum retinol level, and risk of hepatocellular carcinoma *Cancer Res* **55** 1301-1305

Yu MC, Mack T, Hanisch R, Peters RL, Henderson BE and Pike MC (1983) Hepatitis, alcohol consumption, cigarette smoking, and hepatocellular carcinoma in Los Angeles *Cancer Res* **43** 6077-6079

Yu MC, Tong MJ, Govindarajan S and Henderson BE (1991) Nonviral risk factors for hepatocellular carcinoma in a low-risk population, the non-Asians of Los Angeles County, California *JNCI* **83** 1820-1826

Zober-A, Messerer-P, Huber-P (1990) Thirty-four-year mortality follow-up of BASF employees exposed to 2,3,7,8-TCDD after the 1953 accident *Int Arch Occup Environ Health* **62**(2) 139-57

4.10 COLON, RECTUM

Adelstein A and White G (1976) Alcoholism and mortality *Population Trend* **6** 7-13

Albanes D and Taylor PR (1990) International differences in body height and weight and their relationship to cancer incidence *Nutr Cancer* **14** 69-77

Albanes D, Jones DY, Schatzkin A et al (1988) Adult stature and risk of cancer *Cancer Res* **48** 1658-1662

Alberts DS, Einspahr J, Rees McGee S, Ramanujam P, Buller MK, Clark L, Ritenbaugh C, Atwood J, Pethigal P, Earnest D et al (1990) Effects of dietary wheat bran fiber on rectal epithelial cell proliferation in patients with resection for colorectal cancers *Journal Natl Cancer Inst* **82** 1280-1285

Alberts DS, Ritenbaugh C, Story JA, Aickin M, Rees McGee S, Buller MK, Atwood J, Phelps J, Ramanujam PS, Bellapravalu S, Patel J, Bettinger L, Clark L (1996) Randomized, double-blinded, placebo-controlled study of effect of wheat bran fiber and calcium on fecal bile acids in patients with resected adenomatous colon polyps *JNCI* **88** 81-92

Alltonen LA, Peltomaki P, Leach FS et al (1993) Clues to the pathogenesis of familial colorectal cancer *Science* **260** 812-816

Almendingen K, Trygg K, Larsen S, Hofstad B, Vatn MH (1995) Dietary factors and colorectal polyps: a case-control study *Eur J Cancer Prev* **4** 239

Arbman G, Axelson O, Ericsson-Bedodzki AB, Fredricksson M Nilsson E, Sjodahl R (1992) Cereal fiber, calcium and colorectal cancer *Cancer* **69** 2042-2048

Archer MC, Bruce WR, Chan CC, Medline A, Stamp D and Zhang X-M (1992) Promotion of colonic microdenoma in rats by 5-hydroxymethyl-2-furaldehyde in thermolysed sugar *Proc Am Assoc Cancer Res* **33** 130

Armstrong B and Doll R (1975) Environmental factors and cancer incidence and mortality in different countries, with special reference to dietary practices *Int J Cancer* **15** 617-631

Babbs CF (1990) Free radicals and the etiology of colon cancer *Free Rad Biol Med* **8** 191-200

Baghurst KI, Baghurst PA, Record SJ (1994) Demographic and dietary profiles of high and low fat consumers in Australia *J Epidemiol Comm Health* **48** 26-32

Baghurst KI, Baghurst PA, Record SJ (1992) Demographic and nutritional profiles of people consuming varying levels of added sugars *Nutr Res* **12** 1455-1465

Baker S, Fearon E, Nigro J et al (1989) Chromosome 17 deletions and p53 gene mutations in colorectal carcinomas *Science* **244** 217-222

Ballard-Barbash R, Schatzkin A, Albanes D et al (1990) Physical activity and risk of large bowel cancer in the Framingham Study *Cancer Research* **50** 3610-3613

Baraona E, Pirola RC and Lieber CS (1974) Small intestinal damage and changes in cell population produced by ethanol ingestion in the rat *Gastroenterology* **66** 226-234

Baron JA, Tosteson TD, Wargowich MJ, Sandler R, Mandel J, Bond J, Haile R, Summers R, van Stolk R, Rothstein R and Weiss J (1995) Calcium supplementation and rectal mucosal proliferation: a randomized controlled trial *JNCI* **87** 1303-1307

Bauer AR Jr, Rank RK, Kerr R, Straley RL and Mason JD (1977) The effects of prolonged coffee intake on genetically identical mice *Life Sci* **21** 63-70

Bean JA, Isacson P, Hausler WJ, Kohler J (1982) Drinking water and cancer incidence in Iowa I Trends and incidence by source of drinking water and size of municipality *Am J Epidemiol* **116** 921-923

Behall KM, Scholfield DJ, Yuhaniak I, Canary J (1989) Diets containing high amylose vs amylopectin starch: effects on metabolic variables in human subjects *Am J Clin Nutr* **49** 337-44

Benito E, Cabeza E, Moreno V, Obrador A and Bosch FX (1993) Diet and colorectal adenomas: a case-control study in Majorca *Int J Cancer* **55** 213-166

Benito E, Obrador A, Stiggelbout A et al (1990) A population-based case-control study of colorectal cancer in Majorca I Dietary factors *Int J Cancer* **45** 69-76

Benito E, Stiggelbout A, Bosch FX et al (1991) Nutritional factors in colorectal cancer risk: A case-control study in Majorca *Int J Cancer* **49** 161-167

Bergsma-Kadijk JA, van't Veer P, Kampman E, Burema J (1996) Calcium does not protect against colorectal neoplasia *Epidemiol* **7** 590-597

Berry EM, Zimmerman J, Peser M et al (1986) Dietary fat, adipose tissue composition, and the development of carcinoma of the colon *JNCI* **77** 93-97

Bidoli E, Franceschi S, Talamini R et al (1992) Food consumption and cancer of the colon and rectum in north-eastern Italy *Int J Cancer* **50** 223-229

Bingham S, Williams DRR, Cummings JH (1985) Dietary fibre consumption in Britain: new estimates and their relationship to large bowel cancer mortality *Br J Cancer* **52** 399-402

Bingham SA, Nelson M (1991) Assessment of food composition and nutrient intake In: BM Margetts, M Nelson (eds) *Design Concepts in Nutritional Epidemiology* (pp 153-191) Oxford: Oxford Medical Publications

Bingham SA, Williams DDR, Cole TJ, James WPT (1979) Dietary fibre and regional large bowel cancer mortality in Britain *Br J Cancer* **40** 456-463

Bingham SA, Williams DRR, Cole TJ and James WPT (1984) Dietary fibre and regional large-bowel cancer moratlity in Britain *Br J Cancer* **40** 456-463

Bird RP (1987) Observation and quantification of aberrant crypts in the murine colon treated with a colon carcinogen; preliminary findings *Cancer Lett* **37** 147-151

Bird RP, Schneider R, Stamp D et al (1986) Effect of dietary calcium and cholic acid on the proliferative indices of murine colonic epithelium *Carcinogenesis* **7** 657-661

Bjelke E (1973) Epidemiologic studies of cancer of the stomach, colon and rectum Vol III *Case-control study of gastrointestinal cancer in Norway* Univ Microfilms: Ann Arbor, MI

Bjelke E (1973) Epidemiologic studies of cancer of the stomach, colon and rectum Vol IV *Case-control study of digestive tract cancers in Minnesota* Univ Microfilms: Ann Arbor, MI

Bjelke E (1974) Epidemiologic studies of cancer of the stomach, colon, and rectum; with special emphasis on the role of diet *Scand J Gastroenterol* **9** 124-229

Bodmer WF, Bailey CJ, Bodemr J et al (1987) Localization of the gene for familial adenopolyposis in chromosome 5 *Nature* **328** 614-616

Boeing H, Martinez L, Frentzel Beyme R, Oltersdorf U (1985) Regional nutritional pattern and cancer mortality in the Federal Republic of Germany *Nutr Cancer* **7** 121-130

Boffa LC, Lupton JR, Mariani MR, Ceppi M, Newmark HL, Scalmati A and Lipkin M (1992) Modulation of colonic epithelial cell proliferation, histone acetylation, and luminal short chain fatty acids by variation of dietary fiber (wheat bran) in rats *Cancer Research* **52** 5906-5912

Bolton Smith C Woodward, M (1995) Antioxidant vitamin adequacy in relation to consumption of sugars *Eur J Clin Nutr* **49** 124-133

Bonnett A, Dickman P, Roder D et al (1992) *Survival of Cancer Patients in South Australia* South Australian Cancer Registry: Adelaide

Bornet FRJ, Fontvieille AM, Rizkalla S, Colonna P, Blayo A, Mercier C, Slama, G (1989) Insulin and glycemic responses in healthy humans to native starches processed in different ways: correlation with in vitro alpha-amylase hydrolysis *Am J Clin Nutr* **50** 315-323

Bostick RM, Fosdick L, Wood JR, Grambsch P,

Grandits GA, Lillemoe TJ, Louis TA and Potter JD (1995) Calcium and colorectal epithelial cell proliferation in sporadic adenoma patients: a randomized, double-blinded, placebo-controlled clinical trial *JNCI* **87** 1307-1315

Bostick RM, Potter JD, Fosdick L et al (1993) Calcium and colorectal epithelial cell proliferation: Findings from a preliminary randomized double-blind placebo-controlled clinical trial *JNCI* **85** 132-141

Bostick RM, Potter JD, Kushi LH, Sellers TA, Steinmetz KA, McKenzie DR, Gapstur SM and Folsom AR (1994) Sugar, meat, and fat intake, and non-dietary risk factors for colon cancer incidence in Iowa women (United States) *Cancer Causes Control* **5** 38-52

Bostick RM, Potter JD, McKenzie DR, Sellers TA, Kushi LH, Steinmetz KA and Folsom AR (1993) Reduced risk of colon cancer with high intake of vitamin E: The Iowa Women's Health Study *Cancer Res* **53** 4230-4237

Bostick RM, Potter JD, Sellers TA, McKenzie DR, Kushi LH and Folsom AR (1993) Relation of calcium, vitamin D, and dairy food intake o incidence of colon cancer among older women: The Iowa Women's Health Study *Am J Epidemiol* **137** 1302-1317

Brenniam GR, Vasilomanolakis-Lagos J, Amsel J, Namekata T, Wolf AH (1980) Case-control study of cancer deaths in Illinois communities served by chlorinated or nonchlorinated water In: Jolley RL, Brungs WA, Cumming RB, Jacobs VA (eds) *Water Chlorination: Environmental Impact and Health Effects* vol 3 pp1043-1057 Ann Arbor: Ann Arbor Science

Breslow NW and Enstrom JE (1974) Geographic correlations between cancer mortality rates and alcohol-tobacco consumption in the United States *JNCI* **53** 631-639

Bristol JB, Emmett PM, Heaton KW, Williamson RC (1985) Sugar, fat, and the risk of colorectal cancer *Br Med J Clin Res Ed* **291** 1467-1470

Brownson RC, Chang JC, Davis JR and Smith CA (1991) Physical activity on the job and cancer in Missouri *Am J Public Health* **81** 639-642

Bruce WR, Archer MC, Corpet DE, Medline A, Minkin S, Stamp D, Yin Y, Zhang XM (1993) Diet, aberrant crypt foci and colorectal cancer *Mut Res* **290** 111-118

Bruce WR, Varghese AJ, Furrer R, Eng Z and Land TC (1977) A mutagen in the feces of normal humans In *Origins of Human Cancer* (Ed HH Hiatt HH, JD Watson JD, JA Weinsten) Cold Spring Harbor Laboratory: Cold Spring Harbor, New York pp1641-1646

Burkitt DP (1969) Related disease, related cause? *Lancet* **2** 1229-1231

Caderni G, Bianchini F, Mancina A, Spagensi MT and Dolara P (1991) Effect of dietary carbohydrates on the growth of dysplastic crypt foci in the colon of rats treated with 1,2-dimethyl hydrazine *Cancer Research* **51** 3721-3725

Caderni G, Dolara P, Spagnesi T, Lucerni C, Bianchini F, Mastrandrea V and Morozzi G (1993) Rats fed high starch diets have lower colonic proliferation and faecal bile acids than high sucrose-fed controls *Journal of Nutrition* **123** 704-712

Caderni G, Luceri C, Lancioni L, Dolara P (1996) Dietary sucrose, glucose, fructose, and starches affect colonic functions in rats *Nutr Cancer* **25** 179-186

Caderni G, Luceri C, Spagnesi MT, Giannini A, Biggeri A and Dolara P (1994) Dietary carbohydrates modify azoxymethane-induced intestinal carcinogenesis in rats *Journal of Nutrition* **124** 517-523

Cantor KP, Hoover R, Mason TJ, McCabe LJ (1978) Associations of cancer mortality with helomethanes in drinking water *JNCI* **61** 979-985

Cassidy A, Bingham SA and Cummings JH (1994) Starch intake and colorectal cancer - an international comparison *British Journal of Cancer* **69** 937-942

Centonze S, Boeing H, Leoci C, Guerra V and Misciagna G (1994) Dietary habits and colorectal cancer in a low risk area Results from a population-based case-control study in Southern Italy *Nutr Cancer* **21** 233-246

Choi SY and Kahyo H (1991) Effect of cigarette smoking and alcohol consumption in the etiology of cancer of the digestive tract *Int J Cancer* **49** 381-386

Chute CG, Willett WC, Colditz GA et al (1991) A propspective study of body mass, height, and smoking on the risk of colorectal cancer in women *Cancer Causes Control* **2** 117-124 (410115A)

Clark LC, Cantor K and Allaway WH (1991) Selenium in forage crops and cancer mortality in US counties *Arch Environ Health* **46** 37-42

Coleman MP, Esteve, Journal, Damiecki P, Arsalan A, Renard H (1993) *Trends in cancer incidence and mortality* IARC Sci Publ 121 International Agency for Research on Cancer: Lyon (4103B)

Cook MG and McNamara P (1980) Effect of dietary vitamin E on dimethylhydrazine-induced colonic tumors in mice *Cancer Res* **40** 1329-1331

Corpet D, Stamp D, Medline A et al (1990) Promotion of colonic microadenoma growth in mice and rats fed cooked sugar or cooked casein and fat *Cancer Res* **50** 6955-6958

Corpet DE, Stamp D, Medline A, Minkin S, Archer M, Bruce WR (1990) Promotion of colonic microadenoma growth in mice and rats fed cooked sugar or cooked casein and fat *Cancer Research* **50** 6955-6958

Correa P and Haenszel W (1978) The epidemiology of large bowel cancer *Adv Canc Res* **26** 2-141

Cruse P, Lewin M and Clark CG (1979) Dietary cholesterol is co-carcinogenic for human colon cancer *Lancet* **i** 752-755

Cummings J (1983) Fermentation in the human large intestine: evidence and implications for health *Lancet* **i** 1206-1209

Cummings JH (1981) Short chain fatty acid in the human colon *Gut* **22** 763-779

Cummings JH and Macfarlane GT (1991) The control and consequences of bacterial fermentation in the human colon *Journal Appl Bacteriol* **70** 443-459

Cummings JH, Beatty ER, Kingman SM, Bingham SA, Englyst, HN (1996) Fermentation properties of resistant starch in the human large bowel *Br J Nutr* in press

Cummings JH, Hill MJ, Bone ES, Branch WJ and Jenkins DJA (1979) The effect of meat protein and dietary fiber on colonic function and metabolism II Bacterial metabolites in feces and urine *American Journal of Clinical Nutrition* **32** 2094-2101

Cummings JH, Stephen AM and Branch WJ (1981) Implications of dietary fiber breakdown in the human colon In *Gastrointestinal cancer: endogenous factors Banbury Report No 7* Cold Spring Harbor Laboratory

Cummings, JH Bingham, SA (1987) Dietary fibre, fermentation and large bowel cancer *Cancer Surv* **6** 601-621

Dales LG, Friedman GD, Ury HK et al 1979 A case-control study of relationships of diet and other traits to colorectal cancer in American Blacks *Am J Epidemiol* **109** 132-144

De Deckere, EAM, Kloots, WJ, Van Amelsvoort, JMM (1995) Both raw and retrograded starch decrease serum triacylglycerol concentration and fat accretion in the rat *Br J Nutr* **73** 287-298

Dean G, MacLennan R, McLoughlin H and Shelley E (1979) Causes of death of blue-collar workers at a Dublin Brewery, 1954-73 *Br J Cancer* **40** 581-589

DeCosse, JJ, Miller, HH, Lesser, ML (1989) Effect of wheat fiber and vitamins C and E on rectal polyps in patients with familial adenomatous polyposis *JNCI* **81** 1290-1297

DeRouen TA, Diem JE (1977) Relationships between cancer mortality in Louisiana drinking-water and other possible causative agents In: Hiatt HH, Watson JD, Winsten JA (eds) *Origins of Cancer in Humans* book A *Incidence of Cancer in Humans* Cold Spring Harbor: CSH Press, 331-345

Dion PW, Bright-See EB, Smith CC, Furrer R, Eng Z and Bruce WR (1982) The effect of dietary ascorbic acid in alpha-tocopherol on fecal mutagenicity *Mutat Res* **102** 27

Drasar BS and Irving D (1973) Environmental factors and cancer of the colon and breast *Br J Cancer* **27** 167-172

Emerson JC and Weiss NS (1992) Colorectal cancer and solar radiation *Cancer Cause Control* **3** 95-99

Englyst HN, Hay S, Macfarlane GT (1987) Polysaccharide breakdown by mixed populations of human faecal bacteria *FEMS Microbiol Ecol* **95** 163-171

Enstrom JE (1975) Colorectal cancer and the consumption of beef and fat *Br J Cancer* **32** 432-439

Enstrom JE (1977) Colorectal cancer and beer drinking *Br J Cancer* **35** 674-683

Farinati F, Espina N, Lieber CS and Garro AJ (1985) In vivo inhibition by chronic ethanol exposure of methylguanine transferase activity and DNA repair *Ital J Gastroenterol* **17** 48-49

Fearon E, Cho K, Nigro J et al (1990) Identification of a chromosome 18q gene that is altered in colorectal cancers *Science* **247** 49-56

Fearon ER and Vogelstein B (1990) A genetic model for colorectal tumorigenesis *Cell* **61** 759-767

Fearon ER, Vogelstien B (1990) A genetic model for colorectal tumorigenesis *Cell* **61** 759-767

Feinberg AP, Gehrke CW, Kuo KC et al (1988) Reduced genomic 5-methylcytosine content in human colonic neoplasia *Cancer Res* **48** 1159-1161

Ferraroni M, Negri E, LaVecchia C et al (1989) Socioeconomic indicators, tobacco and alcohol in the aetiology of digestive tract neoplasms *Int J Epidemiol* **18** 556-562

Fredriksson M, Bengtsson NO, Hardell L and Axelson O (1989) Colon cancer, physical activity, and occupational exposures *Cancer* **63** 1838-1842

Freudenheim JL, Graham S, Horvath PJ, Marshall JR, Haughey BP and Wilkinson G (1990) Risks associated with source of fiber and fiber components in cancer of the colon and rectum

Cancer Res **50** 3295-3300

Freudenheim JL, Graham S, Marshall JR, Haughey BP and Wilkinson G (1990) A case-control study of diet and rectal cancer in western New York *Am J Epidemiol* **131** 612-624

Freudenheim JL, Graham S, Marshall JR, Haughey BP, Cholewinski S and Wilkinson G (1991) Folate intake and carcinogenesis of the rectum and colon *Int J Epidemiol* **20** 368-374

Garabrant DH, Peters JM, Mack TM and Bernstein L (1984) Job activity and colon cancer risk *Am J Epidemiol* **119** 1005-1014

Gardner EJ (1951) A genetic and clinical study of intestinal polyposis, a predisposing factor for carcinoma of the colon and rectum *Am J Human Genet* **3** 167-176

Garland C, Barrett-Connor E, Rossof AH et al (1985) Dietary vitamin D and calcium and risk of colorectal cancer: A 19-year prospective study in men *Lancet* **1** 307-309

Garland CF, Garland FC, Shaw EK et al (1989) Serum 25-hydroxyvitamin D and colon cancer: Eight-year prospective study *Lancet* **2** 1176-1178

Garland M, Morris JS, Stampfer MJ, Colditz GA, Spate VL, Baskett CK, Rosner B, Speizer FE, Willett WC and Hunter DJ (1995) Prospective study of toenail selenium levels and cancer among women *JNCI* **87** 497-505

Garro AJ and Lieber CS (1990) Alcohol and cancer *Annu Rev Pharmacol Toxicol* **30** 219-249

Gerhardsson de Verdier M and Longnecker MP (1992) Eating frequency-a neglected risk factor for colon cancer? *Cancer Causes and Controls* **3** 77-81

Gerhardsson de Verdier M, Broderus B and Norell SE (1988) Physical activity and colon cancer risk *Int J Epidemiol* **17** 743-746

Gerhardsson de Verdier M, Hagman U, Peters RK et al (1991) Meat, cooking methods and colorectal cancer: a case-referent study in Stockholm *Int J Cancer* **49** 520-525

Gerhardsson de Verdier M, Hagman U, Steineck G et al (1990) Diet, body mass and colorectal cancer: a case-referent study *Int J Cancer* **46** 832-838

Gerhardsson de Verdier M, Steineck G, Hagman U et al (1990) Physical activity and colon cancer: a case-referent study in Stockholm *Int J Cancer* **46** 985-989

Gerhardsson M, Norell SE, Kiviranta H et al (1986) Sedentary jobs and colon cancer *Am J Epidemiol* **123** 775-780

Gibney MJ, Maloney M, Shelley E (1987) The Kilkenny health project: patterns of food intake in individuals consuming low, moderate- and high-fat diets *Proc Nutr Soc* **46** 14

Gibson GR, Beatty ER, Wang X, Cummings JH (1995) Selective stimulation of bifidobacteria in the human colon by oligofructose and inulin *Gastroenterol* **108** 975-982

Gibson GR, Roberfroid MB (1996) Dietary modulation of the human colonic microbiota: introducing the concept of prebiotics *J Nutr* **125** 1401-1412

Giovannucci E, Ascherio A, Rimon E, Colditz G, Stampfer M and Willett WC (1995) Physical activity, obesity, and risk for colon cancer and adenoma in men *Ann Intern Med* **122** 327-334

Giovannucci E, Rimm EB, Ascherio A, Stampfer MJ, Colditz GA and Willett WC (1995) Alcohol, methyl-deficient diets and risk of colon cancer in men *JNCI* **87** 265-273

Giovannucci E, Rimm EB, Stampfer MJ, Colditz GA, Ascherio A and Willett WC (1994) Intake of fat, meat, and fiber in relation to risk of colon cancer in men *Cancer Research* **54** 2930-2997

Giovannucci E, Rimm EB, Stampfer MJ, Colditz GA, Ascherio A, Kearney J and Willett WC (1994) A prospective study of cigarette smoking and risk of colorectal adenoma and colorectal cancer in US men *JNCI* **86** 183-191

Giovannucci E, Stampfer MJ, Colditz G, Rimm EB and Willett WC (1992) Relationship of diet to risk of colorectal adenoma in men *JNCI* **84** 91-98

Giovannucci E, Stampfer MJ, Colditz GA, Rimm EB, Trichopoulos D, Rosner BA, Speizer FE and Willett WC (1993) Folate, methionine, and alcohol intake and risk of colorectal adenoma *JNCI* **85** 875-884

Goelz SE, Vogelstein B, Hamilton SR et al, (1985) Hypoemthylation of DNA from benign and malignant human colon neoplasms *Science* **228** 187-190

Goldbohm RA, van den Brandt PA, van 't Veer P, Brants HAM, Dorant E, Sturmans F and Hermus RJJ (1994) A prospective cohort study on the relation between meat consumption and the risk of colon cancer *Cancer Res* **54** 718-723

Gordon T and Kannel WB (1984) Drinking and mortality: the Framingham Study *Am J Epidemiol* **120** 97-107

Gottlieb MS, Carr JK Clarkson JR (1982) Drinking water and cancer in Louisiana A retrospective mortality study *Am J Epidemiol* **116** 652-667

Graham S, Dayal H, Swanson M, Mittelman A and Wilkinson G (1978) Diet in the epidemiology of cancer of the colon and rectum *J Nat Cancer Inst* **61** 709-714

Graham S, Marshall J, Haughey B et al (1988) Dietary epidemiology of cancer of the colon in western New York *Am J Epidemiol* **128** 490-503

Greenberg E and Baron JA (1993) Prospects for preventing colorectal deaths *JNCI* **85** 1182-1184

Greenwald P, Kelloff GJ, Boone CW and McDonald SS (1995) Genetic and cellular changes in colorectal cancer: Proposed targets of chemopreventive agents *Cancer Epidemiol Bionmarkers Prev* **4** 691-702

Groden J, Thliveris A, Samowitz W et al (1991) Identification and characterization of the familial adenomatous polyposis coli gene *Cell* **66** 589-600

Guillem JG and Weinstein IB (1990) The role of protein kinase C in colon neoplasia In *Familial Adenomatous Polyposis* (Ed L Herrera) Alan R Liss: New York pp325-332

Haenszel W, Berg JW, Segi M et al (1973) Large bowel cancer in Hawaiian Japanese *J Nat Cancer Inst* **51** 1765-1779

Haenszel W, Kurihara M, Locke FB et al (1976) Stomach cancer in Japan *J Nat Cancer Inst* **56** 265-278

Haenszel W, Locke FB and Segi M (1980) A case-control study of large bowel cancer in Japan *J Nat Cancer Inst* **64** 17-22

Haenszel W (1961) Cancer mortality among the foreign born in the United States *JNCI* **26** 37-132

Hague A, Elder DJE, Hicks DJ and Paraskeva C (1995) Apoptosis in colorectal tumour cells: induction by the short chain fatty acids butyrate, propionate and acetate and by the bile salt deoxycholate *International Journal of Cancer* **60** 400-406

Hakulinen T, Lehtimaki L, Lehtonen M and Teppo L (1974) Cancer morbidity among two male cohorts with increased risk of alcohol consumption in Finland *JNCI* **52** 1711-1714

Haynes RC and Murad F (1985) In *The Pharmacologic Basis of Therapeutics 7th ed* (Ed AG Gilman, LG Goodman, TW Rall, F Murad F) MacMillan Publishing: New York

Heerdt BG, Houston MA and Augenlicht LH (1994) Potentiation by specific short chain fatty acids of differentiation and apoptosis in human colonic carcinoma cell lines *Cancer Research* **54** 3288-3294

Heilbrun KL, Hankin JH, Nomura AM and Stemmermann GN (1986) Colon cancer and dietary fat, phosphorous and calcium in

Hawaiian-Japanese men *A J Clin Nutr* **43** 306-309

Heilbrun LK, Nomura A, Hankin JH, Stemmermann GN (1989) Diet and colorectal cancer with special reference to fiber intake *Int J Cancer* **44** 1-6

Heilbrun LK, Nomura AMY, Hankin JH, Stemmermann GN, (1985) Dietary vitamin D and calcium and risk of colorectal cancer *Lancet* i 925

Hill MJ and Aries VC (1971) Faecal steroid composition and its relationship to cancer of the large bowel *J Path* **104** 129-139

Hill MJ, Morson BC and Bussey HJR (1978) Aetiology of adenoma-carcinoma sequence in large bowel *Lancet* **I** 245-247

Hinzman MJ, Novotny C, Ullah A and Shamsuddin AM (1987) Fecal mutagen fecapentene-12 damages mammalian colon epithelial DNA *Carcinogenesis* **8** 1475-1479

Hiramatsu Y, Takada H, Yamamura M, Hioki K, Saito K et al (1983) Effect of dietary cholesterol on azoxymethane-induced colon carcinogenesis in rats *Carcinogenesis* **4** 553-558

Hirayama T (1981) A large-scale cohort study on the relationship between diet and selected cancers of digestive organs *Gastrointestinal Cancer: Endogenous Factors; Banbury report 7* (Ed WR Bruce, P Correa, M Lipkin et al) Cold Spring Harbor Laboratory: NY 409-426

Hirayama T (1989) Association between alcohol consumption and cancer of the sigmoid colon: observations from a Japanese cohort study *Lancet* 725-727

Hoff G, Moen IE, Mowinckel P, Rosef O, Nordbo E, Sauar J, Vatn MH, Torgrimsen T (1992) Drinking water and the prevalence of colorectal adenomas: an epidemiologic study in Telemark, Norway *Eur J Cancer Prev* **1** 423-428

Hoff G, Moen IE, Trygg K et al (1986) Epidemiology of polyps in the rectum and sigmoid colon Evaluation of nutritional factors *Scand J Gastroenterol* **21** 199-204

Hoffman RM (1984) Altered methionine metabolism, DNA methylation and oncogene expression in carcinogenesis *Biochem Biophys Act* **738** 49-87

Howe GR, Aronson KJ, Benito E, Castelleto R, Cornee J, Duffy S, Gallagher RP, Isovitch JM, Deng-ao J, Kaaks R, Kune GA, Kune S, Lee HP, Lee M, Miller AB, Peters RK, Potter JD, Riboli E, Slattery ML, Trichopoulos D, Tuyns A, Tzonou A, Watson LF, Whittemore AS, Wu-Williams AH, Shu Z (1997) The relationship bewteen dietary fat intake and risk of colorectal cancer: evidence from the combined analysis of 13

case-control studies *Cancer Causes Control* **8** 215-228

Howe GR, Benito E, Castellato, R et al (1992) Dietary intake of fiber and decreased risk of cancers of the colon and rectum: evidence from the combined analysis of 13 case-control studies *J Natl Canc Inst* **84** 1887-1896

Hu J, Liu Y, Yu Y et al (1991) Diet and cancer of the colon and rectum: a case-control study in China *Int J Epidemiol* **20** 362-367

IARC (1991) Clorinated drinking water; chlorination by-products; some other halogenated compounds; cobalt and cobalt compounds *IARC Monographs on the Evaluation of Carcinogenic Risks to Humans* vol 52 Lyon:International Agency for Research on Cancer

International Agency for Research on Cancer (IARC) (1990) *Cancer: causes, occurrence and control* (Ed Tomatis, L et al) IARC SCI Publications No 100 International Agency for Research on Cancer: Lyon (41019B)

International Agency for Research on Cancer (IARC) Intestinal Microecology Group (1977) Dietary fibre, transit time, faecal bacteria, steroids, and colon cancer in two Scandinavian populations *Lancet* **2** 207-211

Isacson P, Bean JA, Lynch C (1983) Relationship of cancer incidence rates in Iowa municipalities to chlorination status of drinking water In: Jolley RL, Brungs WA, Cotruvo JA, Cumming RB, Mattice JS, Jacobs VA (eds) *Water Chlorination: Environmental Impact and Health Effects* vol 4, book 2 pp1353-1364 Ann Arbor: Ann Arbor Science

Iscovich JM, L'Abbee KA, Castelleto R, Calzona A, Bernedo A, Chopita NA, Jmelnitzsky AC and Kaldor J (1992) Colon cancer in Argentina I: Risk from intake of dietary items *Int J Cancer* **51** 851-857

Jagerstad M, Reutersward AL, Grivas S et al (1986) Effects of meat composition and cooking conditions on the formation of Mutagenic Imidazoquinoxalines (MeIQx and its methyl derivatives In *Diet, Nutrition and Cancer* (Eds Hayashi Y et al) Japan Sci Soc Press: Tokyo pp87-96

Jacobs LR (1986) Relationship between dietary fiber and cancer: Metabolic, physiologic and cellular mechanisms *Proc Soc Exp Biol Med* **183** 2909-3110

Jacobs LR (1987) Effect of dietary fiber on colonic cell proliferation and its relationship to colon carcinogenesis *Prev Med* **16** 566-571

Jacobsen BK and Thelle DS (1987) Coffee, cholesterol, and colon cancer: is there a link? *Br Med J* **294** 4-5

Jacobsen BK, Bjelke E, Dvale G and Heuch I (1986) Coffee drinking, mortality, and cancer incidence: results from a Norwegian prospective study *JNCI* **76** 823-831

Jain M, Cook GM, Davis FG et al (1980) A case-control study of diet and colo-rectal cancer *Int J Cancer* **26** 757-768

Jain M, Miller AB, To T (1994) Premorbid diet and the prognosis of women with breast cancer *JNCI* **86** 1390-1397

Jensen OM (1979) Cancer morbidity and causes of death among Danish brewery workers *Int J Cancer* **23** 454-463

Joslyn G, Carlson M, Thliveris A et al (1991) Identification of deletion mutations and three new genes at the familial polyposis locus *Cell* **66** 601-613

Kabat GC, Howson CP and Wynder EL (1986) Beer consumption and rectal cancer *Int J Epidemiol* **15** 494-501

Kadlubar FF, Butler MA, Kaderlik KR et al (1992) Polymorphisms for aromatic amine metabolism in humans: relevance for human carcinogenesis *Environ Health Persp* **98** 69-74

Kampman E, Goldbohm A, van den Brandt PA and van 't Veer P (1994) Fermented dairy products, calcium, and colorectal cancer in the Netherlands cohort study *Cancer Res* **54** 3186-3190

Kampman E, Verhoeven D, Sloots L and van't Veer P (1996) Vegetable and animal products as determinants of colon cancer risk in Dutch men and women *Cancer Causes and Controls* **6** 225-234

Kato I, Tominaga S and Ikari A (1990) A case-control study of male colorectal cancer in Aichi Prefecture, Japan: with special reference to occupational activity level, drinking habits and family history *Jpn J Cancer Res* **81** 115-121

Kearney J, Giovanucci E, Rimm EB, Asherio A, Stampfer MJ, Colditz GA, Wing A, Kampman E, Willett WC (1996) Calcium, vitamin D and dairy foods and the occurrence of colon cancer in men *Am J Epidemiol* **143** 907-917

Kinzler K, Nilbert M, Vogelstein B et al (1991) Identification of a gene located at chromosome 5q21 that is mutated in colorectal cancers *Science* **251** 1366-1370

Klatsky AL, Armstrong MA, Friedman GD and Hiatt RA (1988) The relations of alcoholic beverage use to colon and rectal cancer *Am J Epidemiol* **128** 1007-1525

Knekt P (1991) Role of vitamin E in the prophylaxis of cancer *Ann Med* **23** 3-12

Knekt P, Aromaa A, Maatela J et al (1988) Serum vitamin E, serum selenium and the risk of gastrointestinal cancer *Int J Cancer* **42** 846-850

Knekt P, Aromaa A, Maatela J et al (1990) Serum selenium and subsequent risk of cancer among Finnish men and women *JNCI* **82** 864-868

Knekt P, Steineck G, Jaervinen R, Hakulinen T, Aromaa A Intake of fried meat and risk of cancer: a follow-up study in Finland *Int J Cancer* **59** 756-760

Knox EG (1977) Foods and diseases *Br J Prev Soc Med* **31** 71-80

Kolonel LN and Le Marchand L (1986) The epidemiology of colon cancer and dietary fat In *Progress in Clinical and Biological Research, vol 222: Dietary Fat and Cancer* (Ed C Ip, A Rogers, D Birt, C Mettlin) Alan R Liss Inc: NY pp69-91

Kono S, Ikeda M, Tokudome S, Nishizumi M and Kuratsune M (1986) Alcohol and mortality: a cohort study of male Japanese physicians *Int J Epidemiol* **15** 527-532

Kono S, Imanishi K, Shinchi K and Yanai F (1993) Relationship of diet to small and large adenomas of the sigmoid colon *Jpn J Cancer Res* **84** 13-19

Kosugi A, Nagoa M, Suwa Y et al (1983) Roasting coffee beans produces compounds that induce prophage in E cole and S typhimurium *Mutat Res* **116** 179-184

Kristiansen E, Thorup I, Meyer O (1995) Influence of different diets on development of DMH-induced aberrant crypt foci and colon tumor incidence in Wistar rats *Nutr Cancer,* **23** 151-159

Kruh, Journal (1982) Effects of sodium butyrate, a new pharmacological agent, on cells in culture *Molecular and Cellular Biochemistry* **42** 65-82

Kruis W, Forstmaier G, Sheurlen C and Stellard F (1991) Effect of diets low and high in refined sugars on gut transit, bile acid metabolism and bacterial fermentation *Gut* **32** 367-371

Kulkarni N Reddy BS (1994) Inhibitory effect of bifidobacterium longum cultures on the azoxymethane- induced aberrant crypt foci formation and fecal bacterial beta-glucuronidase *Proc Soc Expl Biol Med* **207** 278-283

Kune GA, Kune S (1987) The nutritional causes of colorectal cancer: an introduction to the Melbourne study *Nutr Cancer* **9** 1-4

Kune GA, Kune S and Watson LF (1990) Body weight and physical activity as predictors of colorectal cancer risk *Nutr Cancer* **13** 9-17

Kune GA, Kune S, Read A, MacGowan K, Penfold

C, Watson LF (1991) Colorectal polyps, diet, alcohol, and family history of colorectal cancer: a case-control study *Nutr Cancer* **16** 25-30

Kune S, Kune GA and Watson LF (1987) Case-control study of alcoholic beverages as etiologic factors: the Melbourne colorectal cancer study *Nutr Cancer* **9** 43-56

Kune S, Kune GM and Watson F (1987) Case-control study of dietary etiologic factors: The Melbourne colorectal cancer study *Nutr Cancer* **9** 21-42

Kuzma RJ, Kuzma CM, Buncher CR (1977) Ohio drinking water source and cancer rates *Am J Public Health* **67** 725-729

Lam LKT, Sparnins VL and Wattenberg LW (1982) Isolation and identification of kahweol palmitate and cafesol palmitate as active constituents of green coffee beans that enhance glutathione S-transferase activity in the mouse *Cancer Res* **42** 1193-1198

Lang NP, Butler MA, Massengill J et al (1994) Rapid metabolic phenotypes for acetyltransferase and cytochrome P4501A2 and putative exposure to food-borne heterocyclic amines increae the risk for colorectal cancer or polyps *Cancer Epidemiol Biomark Prev* **3** 675-682

LaVecchia C, Ferraroni M, Negri E et al (1989) Coffee consumption and disgestive tract cancers *Cancer Res* **49** 1049-1051

LaVecchia C, Franceschi A, Dolora P, Bidoli E and Barbone F (1993) Refined sugar intake and the risk of colorectal cancer in humans *Int Journal Cancer* **55** 386-389

LaVecchia C, Negri E, Decarli A et al (1988) A case-control study of diet and colo-rectal cancer in northern Italy *Int J Cancer* **41** 492-98

LaVecchia C, Negri E, Parazzini F et al (1990) Height and cancer risk in a network of case-control studies for Northern Italy *Int J Cancer* **45** 275-279 (410115B)

Lawrence CE, Taylor PR, Trock BJ, Reilly AA (1984) Trihalomethanes in driking water and human colorectal cancer *JNCI* **72** 563-568

Le Marchand L and Kolonel LN (1992) Cancer among Japanese migrants to Hawaii: Gene-environment interactions *Rev Epidemiol Santé Publique* **40** 425-430

Le Marchand L, Wilkens LR and Mi M-P (1994) Obesity in youth and middle age and risk of colorectal cancer in men *Cancer Causes and Control* **3** 349-354 (410144A)

Lee HP, Gourley L, Duffy SW et al (1989) Colorectal cancer and diet in an Asian popualtion - a case control study among Singapore Chinese *Int J Cancer* **43** 1007-1016

Lee IM, Paffenbarger RS and Hsieh C-c (1991) Physical activity and risk of developing colorectal cancer among college alumni *JNCI* **83** 1324-1329

Leppert M, Dobbs M, Scrambler P et al (1987) The gene for familial polyposis coli maps to the long arm of chromosome 5 *Science* **238** 1411-3

Levin RE (1982) Influence of caffeine on mutations induced by nitrosoguanidine in Salmonella typhimurium tester strains *Environ Mutagen* **4** 689-694

Lewis CJ, Park YK, Dexter PB, Yetley EA (1992) Nutrient intakes and body weights of persons consuming high and moderate levels of added sugars *J Am Dietetic Assoc* **92** 708-713

Lipkin M (1988) Biomarkers of increased susceptibility to gastrointestinal cancer: new application to studies of cancer prevention in human subjects *Cancer Res* **48** 235-245

Lipkin M and Newmark H (1985) Effect of added dietary calcium on colonic epithelial cell proliferation in subjects at high risk for familial colonic cancer *N Engl J Med* **313** 1381-1384

Lipkin M, Friedman E, Winawer SJ et al (1989) Colonic epithelial cell proliferation in responders and non-responders to supplemental dietary calcium *Cancer Res* **49** 248-254

Little J, Logan RF, Hawtin PG, Hardcastle JD, Turner ID (1993) Colorectal adenomas and diet: a case-control study of subjects participating in the Nottingham faecal occult blood screening programme *Br J Cancer* **67** 177-184

Liu K, Stamler J, Moss D et al (1979) Dietary cholesterol, fat and fibre, and colon cancer mortality *Lancet* **2** 782-785

Lointier P, Wargovich MJ, Saez S et al (1987) The role of vitamin D3 in the proliferation of a human colon cancer cell line in vitro *Anticancer Res* **7** 817-822

Longnecker MP (1990) A case-control study of alcoholic beverage consumption in relation to risk of cancer of the right colon and rectum *Cancer Causes Control* **1** 5-14

Longnecker MP, Martin-Moreno J-M, Knekt P, Nomura AMY, Schober SE, Stahelin HB, Wald NJ, Gey F and Willett WC (1992) Serum alpha-tocopherol concentration in relation to subsequent colorectal cancer: Pooled data from five cohorts *JNCI* **84** 430-435

Luceri C, Caderni G, Lancioni L, Aiolli S, Dolara P, Mastrandrea V, Scardazza F, Morozzi G (1996a) Effects of repeated boluses of sucrose on proliferation *Nutr Cancer* **25** 187-196

Luceri C, Caderni G, Lodovici M, Spagnesi MT,

Monserrat C, Lancioni L, Dolara P (1996b) Urinary-excretion of sucrose and fructose as a predictor of sucrose intake in dietary intervention studies *Cancer Epidemiol Biomark Prev* **5** 167-171

Lupton JR and Kurtz PP (1993) Relationship of colonic luminal short chain fatty acids and pH to in vivo cell proliferation in rats *Journal Nutrition* **123** 1522-1530

Lynch HT, Lynch JF, Cristofaro G (1989) Genetic epidemiology of colon cancer In: Lynch HT, Hirayama T (eds) *Genetic epidemiology of cancer* Boca Raton: CRC Press 251-277

Lyon JL, Mahoney AW, West DW et al (1987) Energy intake: its relationship to colon cancer risk *JNCI* **78** 853-861

Ma Q, Hoper M, Halliday I, Rowlands BJ (1996) Diet and experimental colorectal cancer *Nutr Res* **16** 413-426

Macfarlane GT, Gibson GR, Drasar BS and Cummings JH (1995) Metabolic significance of the gut microflora Ch 13 in *Gastrointestinal and oesophageal pathology* (Ed R Whitehead) Churchill Livingstone: London pp249-273

Macklin MT (1969) Inheritance of cancer of the stomach and large intestine in man *JNCI* **24** 551-571

MacLennan R, Macrae F, Bain C, Battistutta D, Chapuis P, Gratten H, Lambert J, Newland RC, Ngu M, Russell A, Ward, M, Wahlqvist ML (1995) Randomized trial of intake of fat, fiber, and beta carotene to prevent colorectal adenomas *JNCI* **87** 1760-1766

Macquart Moulin G, Riboli E, Cornee J, Kaaks R, Berthezene P (1987) Colorectal polyps and diet: a case-control study in Marseilles *Int J Cancer* **40** 179-188

Macquart-Moulin G, Riboli E, Cornee J, Kaaks R and Berthezene P (1987) Colorectal polyps and diet: a case-control study in Marseilles *Int J Cancer* **40** 179-188

Macquart-Moulin G, Riboli E, CornJe J et al (1986) Case-control study on colorectal cancer and diet in Marseilles *Int J Cancer* **38** 183-191

Manousos O, Day NE, Trichopoulos D et al (1983) Diet and colorectal cancer: A case-control study in Greece *Int J Cancer* **32** 1-5

Marcus PM, Newconmb PA and Storer BE (1994) Early adulthood physical activity and colon cancer risk among Wisconsin women *Cancer Epidemiol Biomarkers Prev* **3** 641-644 (410142A)

Martinez I, Torres R, Frias Z, ColCn JR and Fern<ndez N (1979) Factors assoicated with adenocarcinomas of the large bowel in Puerto Rico In *Advances in Medical Oncology,*

Research, and Education, Vol III Pergamon Press: Oxford pp45-52

Martinez ME, McPherson RS, Annegers JF, Levin B (1996) Association of diet and colorectal adenomatous polyps: dietary fiber, calcium, and total fat *Epidemiol* **7** 264-268

McIntyre A, Gibson PR and Young GP (1993) Butyrate production from dietary fibre and protection against large bowel cancer in a rat model *Gut* **34** 386-391

McKeown-Eyssen G and Bright-See E (1983) Relationship between colon cancer mortality and fibre consumption: An international study (abstract) *Fibre in Human and Animal Nutrition* Proceedings of a symposium New Zealand, May 1982 (Ed Wallace G, Bell L) Royal Society of New Zealand: Wellington **35**

McKeown-Eyssen GE and Bright-See E (1984) Dietary factors in colorectal: Internatinoal relationships *Nutr Cancer* **6** 160-170

McKeownEyssen GE, BrightSee E, Bruce WR, Jazmaji V, Cole LJ, Feinman SV, Myers ED, Newman A, Stern HS, Hamilton JD, Rudd WWH, Ruderman RL, Moore TL, Ottaway CA, Prokipuchuk EJ, Cohen Z, Greenberg GR, Jeejebhoy KN, McLeod RS et al (1994) A randomized trial of a low fat high fibre diet in the recurrence of colorectal polyps *J Clin Epidemiol* **47** 525-536

McKeownEyssen, G (1994) Epidemiology of colorectal cancer revisited: are serum triglyc rides and/or plasma glucose associated with risk? *Cancer Epidemiol Biomark Prev* **3** 687-695

McMichael AJ (1979) Alimentary tract cancer in Australia in relation to diet and alcohol *Nutr Cancer* **1** 82-89

McMichael AJ and Giles GG (1988) Cancer in migrants to Australia: Extending the descriptive epidemiological data *Cancer Res* **48** 751-756

McMichael AJ and Potter JD (1985) Host factors in carcinogenesis Certain bile-acid profiles that selectively increase the risk of proximal colon cancer *JNCI* **75** 185-191

McMichael AJ, Potter JD and Hetzel BS (1979) Time trends in colorectal cancer mortality in relation to food and alcohol consumption: United States, United Kingdom, Australia and New Zealand *Int J Epidemiol* **8** 295-303

Meyer F (1977) Relations alimentation-cancer en France *Gastroenterol Clin Biol* **1** 971-982

Meyer F and White E (1993) Alcohol and nutrients in relation to colon cancer in middle-aged adults *Am J Epidemiol* **13B** 225-236

Miller AB, Howe GR, Jain M et al (1983) Food items

and food groups as risk factors in a case-control study of diet and colorectal cancer *Int J Cancer* **32** 155-161

Modan B, Barell V, Lubin F et al (1975) Low-fiber intake as an etiologic factor in cancer of the colon *J Nat Cancer Inst* **55** 15-18

Modan B, Cuckle H and Lubin F (1981) A note on the role of dietary retinol and carotene in human gastro-intestinal cancer *Int J Cancer* **28** 421-424

Monson RR and Lyon JL (1975) Proportional mortality among alcoholics *Cancer* **36** 1077-1079

Morand C, Remesy C, Levrat MA, Demigne C (1992) Replacement of digestible wheat starch by resistant cornstarch alters splanchnic metabolism in rats Journal of Nutrition, 122, 345-354

Muir C, Waterhouse J, Mack T et al (1987) *Cancer Incidence in Five Continents, Vol 5* IARC Sci Publ 88 International Agency for Research on Cancer: Lyon

National Academy of Sciences, National Research Council (US), Committee on Diet, Nutrition and Cancer (1982) *Diet, Nutrition and Cancer* National Academy Press: Washington, DC

National Academy of Sciences, National Research Council (US), Committee on Diet and Health (1989) *Diet and Health: Implications for reducing chronic Disease risk* National Academy Press: Wasington, DC

Nauss KM, Jacobs LR and Newberne PM (1987) Dietary fat and relationship to caloric intake, body growth, and colon tumorigenesis *Am J Clin Nutr* **45** 243-251

Negri E, LaVecchia C, D=Avanzo B et al (1990) Calcium dairy products and colorectal cancer *Nutr Cancer* **13** 255-262

Nelson RL (1987) Dietary minerals and colon carcinogenesis (review) *Anticancer Res* **7** 259-269

Nelson RL (1992) Dietary iron and colorectal cancer risk *Free Rad Biol Med* **12** 161-168

Nelson RL, Davis FG, Sutter E, Sobin LH, Kikenhall JW and Bowen P (1994) Body iron stores and risk of colonic neoplasia *Journal of the National Cancer Institute* **86** 455-460

Neugut AI, Garbowski GC, Lee WC, Murray T, Nieves JW, Forde KA, Treat MR, Waye JD, Fenoglio Preiser C (1993) Dietary risk factors for the incidence and recurrence of colorectal adenomatous polyps: a case-control study *Ann Int Med* **118** 91-95

Newmark HL, Wargovich MJ and Bruce WR (1984)

Colon cancer and dietary fat, phosphate, and calcium: a hypothesis *JNCI* **72** 1323-1325

Nishisho I, Nakamura Y, Miyoshi Y et al (1991) Mutations of chromosome 5q21 genes in FAP and colorectal cancer patients *Science* **253** 665-669

Nomura A, Heilbrun LK and Stemmermann GN (1985) Body mass index as a predictor of cancer in men *JNCI* **74** 319-323

Nomura A, Heilbrun LK and Stemmermann GN (1986) Prospective study of coffee consumption and the risk of cancer *JNCI* **76** 587-590

Nomura A, Heilbrun LK, Morris JS and Stemermann GN (1987) Serum selenium and the risk of cancer, by specific sites: case-control analysis of prospective data *JNCI* **79** 103-108

Nomura T (1974) Diminution of tumorigenesis initiated by 4-nitro-quinoline-1-oxide by post treatment with caffeine in mice *Nature* **260** 547-549

Ohgaki H, Hasegawa H, Kato T et al (1986) Carcinogenicities in mice and rats of IQ, MeIQ, and MeIQx In: *Diet, Nutrition and Cancer* (Eds Hayashi Y et al) Japan Sci Soc Press: Tokyo pp97-105

Olsen GW, Mandel JS, Gibson RW, Wattenberg LW, Schuman LM (1989) A case-control study of pancreatic cancer and cigarettes, alcohol, coffee and diet *Am J publ Health* **79** 1016-1019

Olsen J, Kronborg O, Lynggaard J, Ewertz M (1994) Dietary risk factors for cancer and adenomas of the large intestine A case-control study within a screening trial in Denmark *Eur J Cancer* **30A** 53-60

Paffenbarger RS, Hyde RT and Wing AL (1987) Physical activity and incidence of cancer in diverse populations: a preliminary report *Am J Clin Nutr* **45** 312-317

Palm PE, Arnold EP, Nick MS, Valentine JR and Doerfler TE (1984) Two-year toxicity/carcinogenicity study of fresh-brewed coffee in rats initially exposed in utero *Toxicol Appl Pharmaco* **74** 364-382

Papadopoulos N, Nicolaides NC, Wei Y-F et al (1994) Mutation of a *mutL* homolog in heriditary colon cancer *Science* **263** 1625-1629

Parkin DM, Muir CS, Whelan SL et al (1992) *Cancer Incidence in Five Continents, Vol 6* IARC Sci Publ 120 International Agency for Research on Cancer: Lyon

Parkin DM, Pisani P and Feraly J (1993) Estimates of the worldwide incidence of eighteen major cancers in 1985 *Int J Cancer* **54** 594-606 (4103A)

Peltomaki P, Aaltonen LA, Sistonen P et al (1993)

Genetic mapping of a locus predisposing to human colorectal cancer *Science* **2 60** 810-812

Pence BC and Buddingh (1988) Inhibition of dietary fat-promoted colon carcinogenesis in rats by supplemental calcium or vitamin D3 *Carcinogenesis* **9** 187-190

Peters RK, Garabrant DH, Yu MC and Mack TM (1989) A case-control study of occupational and dietary factors in colorectal cancer in young men by subsite *Cancer Res* **49** 5459-5468

Peters RK, Pike MC, Garabrant D and Mack TM (1992) Diet and colon cancer in Los Angeles County, California *Cancer Causes and Control* **3** 457-473

Phillips J Muir JG, Birkett A, Lu ZX, Jones GP, Odea K, Young GP (1995) Effect of resistant starch on fecal bulk and fermentation-dependent events in humans *Am J Clin Nutr* **62** 121-130

Phillips R (1975) Role of life-style and dietary habits in risk of cancer among Seventh-day Adventists *Cancer Res* **35** 3513-3522

Phillips RL and Snowdon DA (1985) Dietary relationships with fatal colorectal cancer among Seventh-Day Adventists *JNCI* **74** 307-317

Pickering JS, Lupton JR and Chapkin RS (1995) Dietary fat, fiber, and carcinogen alter fecal diacylglycerol composition and mass *Cancer Research* **55** 2293-2298 (410217A)

Pickle LN, Greene MH, Ziegler RG et al (1984) Colorectal cancer in rural Nebraska *Cancer Res* **44** 363-369

Potter JD (1992) Colon cancer: reconciling the epidemiology, physiology, and molecular biology *JAMA* **268** 1573-1577

Potter JD (1995) Hormones and colon cancer *JNCI* **87** 1039-1040

Potter JD and McMichael AJ (1986) Diet and cancer of the colon and rectum: A case-control study *JNCI* **76** 557-569

Potter JD, McMichael AJ and Hartshorne JM (1982) Alcohol and beer consumption in relation to cancers of bowel and lung: An extended correlation analysis *J Chron Dis* **35** 833-842

Probst-Hensch NM, Sinha R, Longnecker MP, Witte JS, Ingles SA, Frankl HD, Lee ER, Haile RW (1997) Meat preparation and colorectal adenomas in a large sigmoidoscopy-based case-control study in California (United States) *Cancer Causes and Control* **8** 175-183

Raben, A, Tagliabue, A, Christensen, NJ, Madsen, J, Holst, JJ, Astrup, A (1994) Resistant starch: the effect on postprandial glycemia, hormonal response, and satiety *Am J Clin Nutr* **60** 544-551

Reddy B, Engle A, Katsifis S, Simi B, Bartram HP, Perrino P, Mahan C (1989) Biochemical epidemiology of colon cancer: effect of types of dietary fiber on fecal mutagens, acid, and neutral sterols in healthy subjects *Cancer Res* **49** 4629-4635

Reddy BS (1992) Animal experimental evidence on macronutrients and cancer In *Macronutrients: Investigating Their Role in Cancer* (Ed MS Micozzi and TE Moon) Marcel Dekker: New York pp33-54

Reddy BS, Engle A, Simi B, Goldman M (1992) Effect of dietary fiber on colonic bacterial enzymes and bile acids in relation to colon cancer *Gastroenterol* 1**02** 1475-1482

Reddy BS, Sharma C, Darby L, Laakso K and Wynder EL (1980) Metabolic epidemiology of large bowel cancer Fecal mutagens in high and low-risk populations for colon cancer *Mutation Research* **72** 511-522

Reddy BS, Simi B and Engle A (19??) Biochemical epidemiology of colon cancer: effect of types of dietary fiber on colonic diacylglycerols in women *Gastroenterology* **106** 883-889 (410217B)

Ries LAG, Hankey BF and Edwards BK (1990) Cancer Statistics Review 1973-87 *USDHHS NIH* Publication No 90-2789

Roberts-Thomson IC, Ryan P, Khoo KK, Hart WJ, McMichael AJ, Butler RN (1996) *Lancet* **347** 1372-1374

Robinette CD, Hrubec Z and Fraumeni JF (1979) Chronic alcoholism and subsequent mortality in World War II veterans *Am J Epidemiol* **109** 687-700

Roediger WE (1982) Utilisation of nutrients by isolated epithelial cells of the rat colon *Gastroenterology* **83** 424

Rose DP, Boyar AP, Wynder EL (1986) International comparisons of mortality rates for cancer of the breast, ovary, prostate, and colon, and per capita food consumption *Cancer* **58** 2363-2371

Rosenberg L, Werler MM, Palmer JR et al (1989) The risks of cancers of the colon and rectum in relation to coffee consumption *Am J Epidemiol* **130** 895-903

Rozen P, Horwitz C and Gilat T (1982) Can changes in dietary habits prevent coloectal cancer? *Colonic Carcinogenesis* Falk Symposium No 31 (Ed RA Malt, RCN Williamson) MTP Press Ltd: Boston

Sakamoto J, Nakaji S, Sugawara K, Iwane S, Munakata A (1996) Comparison of resistant starch with cellulose diet on 1,2-dimethylhydrazine-induced colonic carcinogenesis in rats *Gastroenterol* **110** 116-120

Salonen JT, Alfthan G, Huttunen JK and Puska P (1984) Association between serum selenium and the risk of cancer *Am J Epidemiol* **120** 342

Sandler RS, Lyles CM, Peipins LA, McAuliffe CA, Woosley JT, Kupper, LL (1993) Diet and risk of colorectal adenomas: macronutrients, cholesterol, and fiber *JNCI* **85** 884-891

Scheppach W, Fabian C, Sachs M, Kasper H (1988) The effect of starch malabsorption on fecal short-chain fatty acid excretion in man *Scand JGastroenterol* **23** 755-759

Schiffman MH, Andrews AW, van Tassell RL et al (1989) Case-control study of colorectal cancer and fecal mutagenicity *Cancer Research* **49** 3420-3424

Schmidt W and Popham RE (1981) The role of drinking and smoking in mortality from cancer and other causes in male alcoholics *Cancer* **47** 1031-1041

Schober SE, Comstock GW, Helsing KJ, Salkeld RM, Morris JS, Rider AA and Brookmeyer R (1987) Serologic Precursors of Cancer *Am J Epidemiol* **126** 1033-1041

Schrauzer GN (1976) Cancer mortality correclation studies II Regional associations of mortalities with the consumptions of foods and other commodities *Med Hypoth* **2** 39-49

Schrauzer GN, White DA and Schneider CJ (1977) Cancer mortality correlation studies: III Statistical associations with dietary selenium intakes *Bioinorg Chem* **7** 23-34

Seitz HK, Czygan P, Waldherr R, Veith S, Raedsch R, Kassmodel H and Kommerell B (1984) Enhancement of 1,2-dimethylhydrazine-induced rectal carcinogenesis following chronic ethanol consumption in the rat *Gastroenterology* **86** 886-891

Seitz HK, Garro AJ and Lieber CS (1981) Sex-dependent effect of chronic ethanol consumption in rats on hepatic microsome mediated mutagenicity of benzo(alpha)pyrene *Cancer Lett* **13** 97-102

Severson RK, Nomura AMY, Grove JS and Stemmermann GN (1989) A prospective analysis of physical activity and cancer *Am J Epidemiol* **130** 522-529

Severson RK, Nomura AMY, Grove JS, Stemmermann GN (1989) A prospective analysis of physical activity and cancer *Am J Epidemiol* **130** 522-529

Shibata A, Paganini Hill A, Ross RK, Henderson BE (1992) Intake of vegetables, fruits, beta-carotene, vitamin C and vitamin supplements and cancer icidence among the elderly: a prospective study *Br J Cancer* **66** 673-679

Siegers CP, Bumna D, Baretton G and Younes M (1988) Dietary iron enhances the tumor rate in dimethylhydrazine-induced colon carcinogenesis in mice *Cancer Letters* **41** 251-256

Simon HB (1984) The immunology of exercise; A brief review *JAMA* **252** 2735-2738

Slattery ML, Abd-Elghany N, Kerber R and Schumacher MC (1990) Physical activity and colon cancer: A comparison of various indicators of physical activity to evaluate the association *Epidemiology* **1** 481-485

Slattery ML, Edwards SL, Ma K-N, Friedman GD, Potter JD (1997) Physical activity and colon cancer: a public health perspective *Ann Epidemiol* **7** 137-145

Slattery ML, Schumacher MC, Smith KR et al (1988) Physical activity, diet, and risk of colon cancer in Utah *Am J Epidemiol* **128** 989-999

Slattery ML, Sorenson AW and Ford MH (1988) Dietary calcium intake as a mitigating factor in colon cancer *Am J Epidemiol* **128** 504-514

Slattery ML, West DW, Robison LM et al (1990) Tobacco, alcohol, coffee, and caffeine as risk factors for colon cancer in a low-risk population *Epidemiology* **1** 141-145

Snowden DA and Phillips RL (1984) Coffee consumption and the risk of fatal cancers *Am J publ Health* **74** 820-823

Sorenson AW, Slattery ML and Ford MH (1988) Calcium and colon cancer: A review *Nutr Cancer* **11** 135-145

Spalholz JE (1994) On the nature of selenium toxicity and carcinostatic activity *Free Radicals Biol Med* **17** 45-64

Stamp D, Zhang XM, Medline A, Bruce WR and Archer MC (1993) Sucrose enhancement of early steps of colon carcinogenesis in mice *Carcinogenesis* **14** 777-779

Steinmetz K and Potter J (1991) Vegetables, fruit, and cancer II Mechanisms *Cancer Causes Control* **2** 427-442

Steinmetz KA and Potter JD (1993) Food group consumption and colon cancer in the Adelaide Case-control Study I Vegetables and fruit *Int J Cancer* **53** 711-719

Steinmetz KA and Potter JD (1993) Food group consumption and colon cancer in the Adelaide Case-control Study II Meat, poultry, seafood, dairy foods, and eggs *Int J Cancer* **53** 720-727

Steinmetz KA and Potter JD (1994) Egg consumption and cancer of the colon and rectum *Eur J Cancer Prev* **3** 237-245

Steinmetz KA, Kushi LH, Bostick RM, Folsom AR and Potter JD (1994) Vegetables, fruit and colon cancer in the Iowa Women=s Health Study *Am J Epidemiol* **139** 1-15

Stemmerman GN, Nomura A and Chyou P-H (1990) The influence of dairy and non-dairy calcium on subsite large-bowel cancer risk *Dis Colon Rectum* **33** 190-194

Stemmermann GN, Nomura A, Chyou PH et al (1990) Prospective study of alcohol intake and large bowel cancer *Digest Dis Sci* **35** 1414-1420

Stemmermann GN, Nomura AMY and Heilbrun LK (1984) Dietary fat and the risk of colorectal cancer *Cancer Res* **44** 4633-4637

Stevens RG, Graubard BI, Micozzi MS, Neriishi K, Blumberg BS (1994) Moderate elevation of body iron level and increased risk of cancer occurrence and death *Int J Cancer* **56** 364-369

Stevens RG, Jones DY, Micozzi MS et al (1988) Body iron stores and the risk of cancer *N Engl J Med* **319** 1047-1052

Stocks P (1957) Cancer incidence in North Wales and Liverpool region in relation to habits and environment *Brit Emp Cancer Campaign 35th Annual Report* Suppl to Part 2 **1** 127

Stubs P (1980) The Anatomie of Abuses London 1585 Cited in *Royal College of Physicians: Medical Aspects of Dietary Fibre* Pitman Medical: Bath p61

Sugimura T and Sato S (1983) Mutagens-carcinogens in foods *Cancer Research* **43** 2415s-2421s

Sundby P (1967) *Alcoholism and Mortality* Universitetsforlaget: Oslo

Tajima K and Tominga S (1985) Dietary habits and gastro-intestinal cancers: A comparative case-control study of stomach and large intestinal cancers in Nagoya Japan *Jpn J Cancer Res* **76** 705-716

Thibideau SN, Bren G, Schald D (1993) Microsatellite instability in cancer of the proximal colon *Science* **260** 816-819

Thorup I, Meyer O, Kristiansen E (1995) Effect of potato starch, cornstarch and sucrose on aberrant crypt foci in rats exposed to azoxymethane *Anticancer Res* **15** 2101-2105

Thun MJ, Calle EE, Namboodiri MM et al (1992) Risk factors for fatal colon cancer in a large prospective study *JNCI* **84** 1491-1500

Trock B, Lanza E, Greenwald P (1990) Dietary fiber, vegetables, and colon cancer; critical review and meta-analyses of the epidemiologic evidence *JNCI* **82** 650-661

Trock BJ, Lanza E, Greenwald P (1990) High fiber diet and colon cancer: a critical review *Prog Clin Biol Res* **346** 145-157

Turesky RJ, Lang N, Butler MA et al (1991) Metabolic activation of carcinogenic heterocyclic aromatic amines by human liver and colon *Carcinogenesis* **12** 1417-1422

Tuthill RW, Moore GS (1980) Drinking water chlorination: a practice unrelated to cancer mortality *J Am Water Works Assoc* **72** 570-573

Tuyns AJ, Haelterman M and Kaaks R (1987) Colorectal cancer and the intake of nutrients: oligosaccharides are a risk factor, fats are not A case-control study in Belgium *Nutr Cancer* **10** 181-196

Tuyns AJ, Kaaks R and Haelterman M (1988) Colorectal cancer and the consumption of foods: a case-control study in Belgium *Nutr Cancer* **11** 189-204

Tuyns AJ, PJquignot G, Gignoux M and Valla A (1982) Cancers of the digestive tract, alcohol and tobacco *Int J Cancer* **30** 9-11

Uchida K, Nomura Y, Kadowaki M, Takeuchi N and Yamamura Y (1977) Effects of dietary cholesterol on cholesterol and bile acid metabolism in rats *Jpn J Pharmacol* **27** 193-204

Utsunomiya J and Lynch HT (1990) *Hereditary Colorectal Cancer* Springer-Verlag: New York

Van der Brandt PA, Goldbohm RA, van't Veer P, Bode P, Dorant E, Hernus RJJ and Sturmans F (1993) A prospective cohort study on toenail selenium levels and risk of gastrointestinal cancer *JNCI* **85** 224-229

van Munster IP, Tangerman A, Nagengast FM (1994) Effect of resistant starch on colonic fermentation, bile acid metabolism, and mucosal proliferation *Digest Dis Sci* **39** 834-842

Veale AMO (1965) *Intestinal Polyposis* Cambridge University Press: Cambridge

Velazquez OC, Lederer HM, Rombeau JL (1996) Butyrate and the colonocyte implications for neoplasia *Digest Dis Sci* **41** 727-739

Vena JE, Graham S, Zielezny M et al (1985) Lifetime occupational exercise and colon cancer *Am J Epidemiol* **122** 357-365

Vineis P, McMichael A (1996) Interplay between heterocyclic amines in cooked meat and metabolic phenotype in the etiology of colon cancer *Cancer Causes Control* **7** 479-486

Vogelstein B, Fearon E, Kern S et al (1989) Allelotype of colorectal carcinomas *Science* **244** 207-212

Wargovich MJ, Eng VWS and Newmark H (1984)

Calcium inhibits the damaging and compensatory proliferative effects of fatty acids on mouse colon epithelium *Cancer Lett* **23** 253-258

Wargovich MJ, Eng WWS, Newmark HL et al (1983) Calcium ameliorates the toxic effect of deoxycholic acid on colonic epithelium *Carcinogenesis* **4** 1205-1207

Wargovich MJ, Isbell G, Shabot M et al (1992) Calcium supplementation decreases rectal epithelial cell proliferation in subjects with sporadic adenoma *Gastroenterology* **103** 92-97

Wattenberg LW (1977) Inhibition of carcinogenic effects of polycyclic hydrocarbons by benzyl isothiocyanate and related compounds *JNCI* **58** 195-198

Wattenberg LW and Lam LKT (1984) Protective effects of coffee constituents on carcinogenesis in experimental animals In: *Coffee and Health, Banbury Report 17B* (Ed B MacMahon and T Sugimura) Cold Springs Harbor Laboratory: Cold Spring Harbor, NY pp232-237

Wattenberg, LW (1987) Inhibition of chemical carcinogenesis *JNCI* **60** 11-18

Weaver GA, Krause JA, Miller TL, Wolin MJ (1992) Cornstarch fermentation by the colonic microbial community yields more butyrate than does cabbage fiber fermentation; cornstarch fermentation rates correlate negatively with methanogenesis *Am J Clin Nutr* **55** 70-77

Weinberg ED (1994) Association of iron with colorectal cancer *Biometals* **7** 211-216

West DW, Slattery ML, Robison LM et al (1989) Dietary intake and colon cancer: Sex and anatomic site-specific associations *Am J Epidemiol* **130** 883-894

Whitehead RH, Young GP and Bhathal PS (1986) Effects of short chain fatty acids on a new colon carcinoma cell line (LIM 1215) *Gut* **27** 1457-1463

Whittemore AS, Wu-Williams AH, Lee M et al (1990) Diet, physical activity, and colorectal cancer among Chinese in North American and China *JNCI* **82** 915-926

WHO (1997) World Health Organization *The World Health Report* WHO: Geneva

Willett WC, Stampfer MJ, Colditz GA et al (1990) Relation of meat fat and fiber intake to the risk of colon cancer in a prospective study among women *N Engl J Med* **323** 1664-1672

Williams RR and Horm JW (1977) Association of cancer sites with tobacco and alcohol consumption and socioeconomic status of patients: interview study from the Third National Cancer Survey *JNCI* **58** 525-547

Wohlleb JC, Hunter CF, Blass B, Kadlubar FF, Chu DZJ, Lang NP (1990) Aromatic amine acetyltransferase as a marker for colorectal cancer: environmental and demographic associations *Int J Cancer* **46** 22-30

Wu AH, Paganini-Hill A, Ross RK and Henderson BE (1987) Alcohol, physical activity, and other risk factors for colorectal cancer: A prospective study *Br J Cancer* **55** 687-694

Wurzelmann JI, Silver A, Schreinmachers DM, Sandler RS and Everson RB (1996) Iron intake and the risk of colorectal cancer *Cancer Epidemiol Biomark Prev* **5** 503-507

Wynder EL and Shigematsu T (1967) Environmental factors of cancer of the colon and rectum *Cancer* **20** 1520-1561

Wynder EL, Kajitani T, Ishikana S et al (1969) Environmental factors of cancer of the colon and rectum II Japanese epidemiological data *Cancer* **23** 1210-1220

Xue S and Rao P (1981) Sodium butyrate blocks HeLa cells preferentially in early G_1 phase of the cell cycle *Journal of Cell Science* **51** 163-171

Young GP, McIntyre A, Albert V, Folino M, Muir JG, Gibson PR (1996) Wheat bran suppresses potato starch-potentiated colorectal tumorigenesis at the aberrant crypt stage in a rat model *Gastroenterol* **110** 508-514

Young TB and Wolf DA (1988) Case-control study of proximal and distal colon cancer and diet in Wisconsin *Int J Cancer* **42** 167-175

Young TB, Kanarek MS (1983) Matched pair case control study of drinking water chlorination and cancer mortality In: Jolley RL, Brungs WA, Cotruvo JA, Cumming RB, Mattice JS, Jacobs VA (eds) *Water Chlorination: Environmental Impact and Health Effects* vol 4, book 2, 1365-1380 Ann Arbor: Ann Arbor Science

Yunis JJ and Soreng AL (1984) Constitutive fragile sites and cancer *Science* **226** 1199-1204

Zaridze D, Filipchenko V, Kustov V et al (1993) Diet and colorectal cancer: results of two case-control studies in Russia *Eur J Cancer* **29A** 112-115

Zhang XM, Chan CC, Stamp D, Minkin S, Archer MC, Bruce WR (1993) Initiation and promotion of colonic aberrant crypt foci in rats by 5-hydroxymethyl-2-furaldehyde in thermolyzed sucrose *Carcinogenesis* **14** 773-775

Zierler S, Danley RA and Feingold L (1986) Type of disinfectant in drinking water and patterns of mortality in Massachusetts *Environ Health Perspect* **69** 275-279

4.11 BREAST

Abdul-Hajj YJ, Kelliher M (1982) Failure of ascorbic acid to inhibit growth of transplantable and dimethylbenzanthracene induced rat mammary tumors *Cancer Letters* **17** 67-73

Adami HO, Lund E, Bergstrom R, Meirik O (1988) Cigarette smoking, alcohol consumption and risk of breast cancer in young women *Br J Cancer* **58**(6) 832-7

Adlercreutz H (1990) Western diet and western diseases: some hormonal and biochemical mechanisms and associations *Scand J Clin Lab Invest* **50** (suppl 201) 3-23

Adlercreutz H, Hamalainen E, Gorbach S, Goldin B (1992) Dietary phytoestrogens and the menopause in Japan *Lancet* **339** 1233

Adlercreutz H, Markkanen H, Watanabe S (1993) Plasma concentrations of phyto-estrogens in Japanese men *Lancet* **342** 1209–10

Albanes D, Blair A, Taylor PR (1989) Physical activity and risk of cancer in the NHANES I population *Am J Public Health* **79** 744-750

Aoki K, Hayakawa N, Kurihara M, Suzuki S (1992) Death Rates for Malignant Neoplasms for Selected Sites by Sex and Five-year Age Group in 33 Countries 1953-57 to 1983-87 *International Union Against Cancer* Nagoya:University of Nagoya Coop Press

Armstrong B, Doll R (1975) Environmental factors and cancer incidence and mortality in different countries, with special reference to dietary practices *Int J Cancer* **15** 617-31

Barnes S, Grubbs C, Setchell KD, Carlson J (1990) Soybeans inhibit mammary tumors in models of breast cancer *Prog Clin Biol Res* **347** 239-253

Barnes-Josiah D, Potter JD, Sellers TA et al, (1995) Early body size and subsequent weight gain as predictors of breast cancer incidence *Cancer Causes Control* **6** 112-118

Barnes-Josiah D, Potter JD, Sellers TA, Himes JH (1994) Early body size and subsequent weight gain as predictors of breast cancer incidence (Iowa, United States) *Cancer Causes Control* **6** 112-118

Begg CB, Walker AM, Wessen B et al, (1983) Alcohol consumption and breast cancer *Lancet* **I** 293-294

Bernstein L, Henderson BE, Hanisch R et al, (1994) Physical exercise and reduced risk of breast cancer in young women *JNCI* **86** 1403-1408

Bernstein L, Ross RK, Lobo RA et al, (1987) The effects of moderate physical activity on menstrual cycle patterns in adolescence: implications for breast cancer prevention *Br J Cancer* **55** 681-685

Biggs PJ, Warren W, Venitt S, Stratton MR (1993) Does a genotoxic carcinogen contribute to human breast cancer? The value of mutational spectra in unravelling the aetiology of cancer *Mutagenesis* 8:275-283

Birt DF (1989) Effects of the intake of selected vitamins and minerals in cancer prevention *Magnesium* **8** 117-130

Boice JDJ, Monson RR (1977) Breast cancer in women after repeated fluoroscopic examinations of the chest *JNCI* **59** 823-832

Boissoneault GA, Elson CE, Pariza MW (1986) Net energy effects of dietary fat on chemically induced mammary acrcinogenesis in F344 rats *JNCI* **76** 335-338

Bouchardy C, Le MG , Hill C (1990) Risk factors for breast cancer according to age at diagnosis in a French case-control study *J Clin Epidemiol* **43** 267-275

Boyd NF, Martin LJ, Noffel M et al, (1993) A metaanalysis of studies of dietary-fat and breast-cancer risk *British Journal of Cancer* **68** 627-636

Bruning PF, Bonfrer JMG, Hart AAM, van Noord PAH, van der Hoeven H, Collette HJA, Battermann JJ, de Jong-bakker M, Nooijen WJ, de Waard F (1992) Body measurements, estrogen availability and the risk of human breast cancer: a case-control study *Int J Cancer* **51** 14-19

Byers T, Funch DP (1982) Alcohol and breast cancer *Lancet* **I** 799-800

Byrne C, Ursin G, Ziegler R (1992) Dietary fat and breast cancer in NHANES I continued follow-up *Am J Epidemiol* **136** 1024-1025

Calaf G, Russo J (1993) Transformation of human breast epithelial cells by chemical carcinogens *Carcinogenesis* **14** 483-492

Carroll KK (1991) Review of clinical studies on cholesterol lowering response to soy protein *J Am Diet Assoc* **91** 820-827

Cassidy A, Bingham S, Carlson J et al, (1993) Biological effects of plant oestrogens in premenopausal women *FASEB J* **7** A866

Caygill CP, HillMJ (1995) Fish, n-3 fatty acids and human colorectal and breast cancer mortality *Eur J Cancer Prev* **4**(4) 329-32

Chen J, Campbell TC, Junyao L , Peto R (1987) *The Diet, Lifestyles, and Mortality Characteristics of 65 Rural Populations in the People's Republic of China* Oxford:Oxford University Press

Chen J, Campbell TC, Li J , Peto R (1990) *Diet, life-style and mortality in China A study of the characteristics of 65 Chinese counties* Oxford,

UK; Ithaca, NY; Beijing, PRC:Oxford University Press; Cornell University Press; People's Medical Publishing House

Chu SY, Lee NC, Wingo PA et al, (1991) The relationship between body mass and breast cancer among women enrolled in the Cancer and Steroid Hormone Study *J Clin Epidemiol* **44** 1197-1206

Chu SY, Lee NC, Wingo PA, Webster LA (1989) Alcohol consumption and the risk of breast cancer *Am J Epidem* **130** 867-77

Clark LC (1985) The epidemiology of selenium and cancer *Fed Proc* **44** 2584-9

Claus EB, Risch NJ , Thompson WD (1990) Age at onset as an indicator of familial risk of breast cancer *Am J Epidemiol* **131** 961-972

Coates RJ, Weiss NS, Daling JR, Morris JS, Labbe RF (1988) Serum levels of selenium and retinol and the subsequent risk of cancer *Am J Epidemiol* **128**:515-23

Cohen LA, Boylan , Epstein M, Zang E (1992) Voluntary exercise and experimental mammary cancer *Adv Exp Med Biol* **322** 61

Cohen LA, Kendall ME, Zang E, Meschter C, Rose DP (1991) Modulation of N-nitrosomethylurea-induced mammary tumor promotion by dietary fiber and fat *JNCI* **83** 496-501

de Waard F , Baanders-van Halewijn EA (1974) A prospective study in general practice on breast-cancer risk in postmenopausal women *Int J Cancer* **14** 153-160

Decarli A, La Vecchia C (1986) Environmental factors and cancer mortality in Italy: Correlation exercise *Oncology* **43** 116-126

Doll R, Fraumeni Jr JF, Muir CS et al, (1994) eds: *Trends in cancer incidence and mortality* Cold Spring Harbor Laboratory Press

Easton DF (1994) The inherited component of cancer *Br Med Bull* **50** 527-535

el-Bayoumy K (1992) Enviromental carcinogenss that may be involved in human breast cancer etiology *Chem Res Toxicol* **5** 585-90

el-Bayoumy K, Chae Yh, Upadhyaya P et al (1992) Inhibition of 7,12-dimethylbenz (a) anthracene-induced tumors and DNA adduct formation in the mammary glands of female Sprague-Dawley rats by the synthetic organoselenium compound, 1,4-phenylenebis (methylene) selenocyanate *Cancer Res* **52**: 2402-2407

Elridge SR, Gould MN, Butterworth BE (1992) Genotoxicity of environemtal agents in human mammary epithelial cells *Cancer Res* **52** 5617-5620

Ernster VL, Goodson WH, Hunt TK et al, (1985) Vitamin E and benign breast "disease": a double-blind, randomized clinical trial *Surgery* **97** 490-494

Ewertz M (1988) Influence of non-contraceptive exogenous and endogenous sex hormones on breast cancer risk in Denmark *Int J Cancer* **42** 832-838

Ewertz M &Gill C (1990) Dietary factors and breast cancer risk in Denmark *Int J Cancer* **46** 779-84

Ewertz M (1991) Alcohol consumption and breast cancer risk in Denmark *Cancer Causes Control* **2**(4) 247-52

Eyfjord JE, Thorlacius S, Steinarsdottir M et al, (1995) p53 Abnormalities and genomic instabliity in primary human breast carcinomas *Cancer Res* **55** 646-651

Ferraroni M, Decarli A, Willett WC, Marubini E (1991) Alcohol and breast cancer risk: a case-control study from northern Italy *Int J Epidemiol* **20**(4) 859-64

Fishbein (1986) Perspectives in metal carcinogenesis **I** Selenium [Review] *Archiv fur Geschwulstforschung* **56** 53-78

Folsom AR, McKenzie DR, Bisgard KM et al, (1993) No association between caffeine intake and postmenopausal breast cancer incidence in the Iowa Women's Health Study *Am J Epidemiol* **138** 380-383

Franceschi S, Favero A, Decarti A, Negri E, La Vecchia C, Ferraroni M, Russo A, Salvini S, Amadori D, Conti E, Montella M, Giacosa A (1996) Intake of macronutrients and risk of breast cancer *Lancet* **347** 1351-1356

Franceschi S, Favero A, La Vecchia C et al (1995) Influence of food groups and food diversity on breast cancer risk in Italy *Int J Cancer* **63**(6) 785-9

Freudenheim JL, Marshall JR, Graham S et al (1995) Lifetime alcohol consumption and risk of breast cancer *Nutr Cancer* **23**(1) 1-11

Freudenheim JL, Marshall JR, Vena JE et al, (1996) Premenopausal breast cancer risk and intake of vegetables, fruits, and related nutrients *JNCI* **88** 340-348

Friedenreich CM, Howe GR, Miller AB et al, (1993) A cohort study of alcohol consumption and risk of breast cancer *Am J Epidemiol* **137** 512-520

Friedenreich CM, Howe GR, Miller AB, (1991) An investigation of recall bias in the reporting of past food intake among breast cancer cases and controls *Ann Epidemiol* **1** 439-453

Frisch RE, Wyshak G, Albright NL et al, (1985) Lower prevalence of breast cancer and cancers of the reproductive system among former

college athletes compared to nonathletes *Br J Cancer* **52** 885-91

Gaard M, Tretli S, Loken EB (1995) Dietary fat and the risk of breast cancer: a prospective study of 25,892 Norwegian women *International Journal of Cancer* **63** 13-17

Gapstur SM, Potter JD, Sellers TA , Folsom AR (1992) Increased risk of breast cancer with alcohol consumption in postmenopausal women *Am J Epidemiol* **136** 1221-1231

Garfinkel L, Boffetta P , Stellman SD (1988) Alcohol and breast cancer: a cohort study *Prev Med* **17** 686-93

Garland M, Willett-WC, Manson JE, Hunter-DJ (1993) Antioxidant micronutrients and breast cancer *J Am Coll Nutr* **12**(4) 400-11

Ghoshal A, Snyderwine EG (1993) Excretion of food-derived heterocyclic amine carcinogens into breast milk of lactating rats and formation of DNA adducts in the newborn *Carcinogenesis* **14** 2199-2203

Ginsburg ES, Walsh BW, Shea BF et al, (1995) The effects of ethanol on the clearance of estradiol in postmenopausal women *Fertility, Sterility* **63** 1227-1230

Giovannucci E, Stampfer MJ, Colditz GA et al, (1993) A comparison of prospective and retrospective assessments of diet in the study of breast cancer *Am J Epidemiol* **137** 502-511

Goldbohm RA, Hertog MGL, Brants HAM et al, (1996) Consumption of black tea and cancer risk: a prospective cohort study *JNCI* **88** 93-100

Goldin BR, Adlercreutz H, Gorbach SL et al, (1982) Estrogen excretion patterns and plasma levels in vegetarian and omnivorous women *N Engl J Med* **307** 1542-

Goldin BR, Adlercreutz H, Gorbach SL et al, (1986) The relationships between estrogen levels and diets of Caucasian American and Oriental immigrant women *Am J Clin Nutr* **44** 945-953

Goldin BR, Aldercreutz H, Gorbach SL et al, (1982) Estrogen excretion patterns and plasma levels in vegetarian and omnivorous women *N Engl J Med* **307**1542-7

Goodman MT, Nomura A, Wilkens A et al, (1992) The association of diet, obesity, and breast cancer in Hawaii *Cancer Epidem Bio Prev* **1** 269-75

Gorham ED, Garland FC, Garland CF (1990) Sunlight and breast cancer incidence in the USSR *Int J Epidemiol* **19**(4) 820-4

Gould MN, Grau DR, Seidman LA, Moore CJ (1986) Interspecies comparison of human and rat mammary epithelial cell-meditated mutagenesis by polycyclic aromatic hydrocarbons *Cancer Res* **46** 4942-4945

Graham S, Hellmann R, Marshall J et al, (1991) Nutritional epidemiology of postmenopausal breast cancer in western New York *Am J Epidemiol* **134** 552-556

Graham S, Marshall J, Mettlin C et al, (1982) Diet in the epidemiology of breast cancer *Am J Epidemiol* **116** 68-75

Graham S, Zielezny M , Marshall J et al, (1992) Diet in the epidemiology of postmenopausal breast cancer in a New York State cohort *Am J Epidemiol* **136** 1327

Grubbs CJ, Juliana MM, Whitaker LM (1988) Effect of ethanol on initiation of methylnitrosourea (MNU)- and dimethyl-benzanthracene (DMBA)-induced mammary cancers [abstract] *Proc Am Assoc Cancer Res* **29** 148

Hankinson SE, Willett WC, Manson JE et al, (1995) Alcohol, height, and adiposity in relation to estrogen and prolactin levels in postmenopausal women *JNCI*

Harris RE, Wynder EL (1988) Breast cancer and alcohol consumption A study in weak associations *JAMA* **259**(19) 2867-71

Harvey EB, Schairer C, Brinton (1987) Alcohol consumption and breast cancer *JNCI* **78** 657-661

Hawrylewicz EJ (1986) Fat-protein interaction, defined 2-generation studies In: *Dietary Fat and Cancer* (Ip, C, Birt, DF, and Rogers, AE, eds) Progress in Clinical and Biological Research Alan R Liss, Inc, New York**222**403-434

Hayward JL, Greenwood FC, Glober G et al, (1978) Endocrine status in normal British, Japanese and Hawaiian-Japanese women *Eur J Cancer* **14** 1221-1228

Helmrich SP, Shapiro S, Rosenberg L et al, (1983) Risk factors for breast cancer *Am J Epid* **117** 35-45

Hems G, Stuart A (1975) Breast cancer rates in populations of single women *Br J Cancer* **31**(1) 118-23

Hems-G (1978) The contributions of diet and childbearing to breast-cancer rates *Br J Cancer* **37**(6) 974-82

Henderson BE, Ross RK, Judd HL et al, (1985) Do ovulatory cycles increase breast cancer risk? *Cancer* **56** 1206-1208

Henderson BE, Ross RK, Pike MC , Casagrande JT (1982) Endogenous hormones as a major factor in human cancer *Cancer Res* **42** 3232-3239

Herman C, Adlercreutz T, Goldin BR et al, (1995) Soybean phytoestrogen intake and cancer risk *J*

Nutr **125** 757S-770S

Hiatt RA, Bawol RD (1984) Alcoholic beverage consumption and breast cancer incidence *Am J Epidemiol* **120** 676-683

Hiatt RA, Klatsky AL, Armstrong MA (1988) Alcohol consumption and the risk of breast cancer in a prepaid health plan *Cancer Res* **48** 2284-2287

Hirayama T (1978) Epidemiology of breast cancer with special reference to the role of diet *Prev Med* **7** 173-95

Hirayama T (1986) A large-scale study on cancer risks by diet - with special reference to the risk reducing effects of green-yellow vegetable consumption In: Hayashi Y, Magao M, Sugimura T et al, ed *Diet, Nutrition, and Cancer* Tokyo:Japan Scientific Societies Press 41-53

Hirohata T, Nomura AMY, Hankin JH, Kolonel LN, Lee J (1987) An epidemiological study on the association between diet and breast cancer *JNCI* **78** 595-600

Hirohata T, Shigematsu T, Nomura AM, Nomura Y, Horie A, Hirohata I (1985) Occurrence of breast cancer in relation to diet and reproductive history: A case-control study in Fukuoka, Japan *Nat Cancer Inst Monogr* **69** 187-190

Hirose K, Tajima K, Hamajima N et al (1995) A large-scale, hospital-based case-control study of risk factors of breast cancer according to menopausal status *Japanese Journal of Cancer Research* **86** 146-154

Hislop TG, Coldman AJ, Elwood JM et al, (1986) Childhood and recent eating patterns and risk of breast cancer *Cancer Detection Prevention* **9** 47-58

Holmberg L, Ohlander EM, Byers T et al (1994) Diet and breast cancer risk: results from a population-based, case- control study in sweden *Archives of Internal Medicine* **154** 1805-1811

Hopkins GJ, Carroll KK (1979) Relationship between amount and type of dietary fat in promotion of mammary carcinogenesis induced by 7, 12-dimethylbenzanthracene *JNCI* **62** 1009-1012

Hopkins GJ, Kennedy TG , Carroll KK (1981) Polyunsaturated fatty acids as promoters of mammary carcinogenesis induced in Sprague-Dawley rats by 7,12-dimethylbenz[a]anthracene *JNCI* **66** 517-522

Horvath PM, Ip C (1983) Synergistic effect of vitamin E and selenium in the chemoprevention of mammary carcinogenesis in rats *Cancer Res* **43** 5335

Howe GR, Friedenreich CM, Jain M , Miller AB

(1991) A cohort study of fat intake and risk of breast cancer *JNCI* **83** 336-40

Howe GR, Hirohata T, Hislop TG et al, (1990) Dietary factors and risk of breast cancer: combined analysis of 12 case-control studies *JNCI* **82** 561-9

Hsieh C-C, Trichopoulos D, Katsouyanni K et al, (1990) Age at menarche, age at menopause, height and obesity as risk factors for breast cancer: associations and interactions in an international case-control study *Int J Cancer* **46**:96-800

Huang HH, Hawrylewicz EJ, Kissane JQ , Drab EA (1982) Effect of protein diet on release of prolactin and ovarian steroids in female rats *Nutr Rpts Int* **26** 807-820

Huang Z, Hankinson S, Colditz G et al, (1996) mass index, weight change and risk of breast cancer among women *Am J Epidemiol* **143** S85 (abstract)

Huggins CB, Ueda N, Wiessler M (1981) N-nitroso-N-methylurea elicits mammary cancer in resistant and sensitive rat strains *Proc Natl Acad Sci USA* **78** 1185-1188

Hughes RE, Jones E (1985) Intake of dietary fibre and age of menarche *Ann Hum Biol* **12** 325-332

Hunter DJ (1990) Biochemical indicators of dietary intake In: Willett WC ed *Nutritional Epidemiology* pp 143-216 New York: Oxford University Press

Hunter DJ, Manson JE, Stampfer MJ et al (1992) A prospective study of caffeine, coffee, tea, and breast cancer *Am J Epidemiol* **136** 1000-1001 (Abstract)

Hunter DJ, Morris JS, Chute CG et al, (1990) Predictors of selenium concentration in human toenails *Am J Epidemiol* **132** 114-22

Hunter DJ, Morris JS, Stampfer MJ et al, (1990) A prospective study of selenium status and breast cancer risk *JAMA* **264** 1128-31

Hunter DJ, Spiegelman D, Adami HO et al, (1996) Cohort studies of fat intake and the risk of breast cancer-a pooled analysis *N Engl J Med* **334** 356-361

Hunter DJ, Stampfer MJ, Colditz GA et al, (1993) A prospective study of intake of vitamin C, E, and A and the risk of breast cancer *N Engl J Med* **329** 234-40

Hursting SD, Thornquist M, Henderson MM (1990) Types of dietary fat and the incidence of cancer at 5 sites *Prev Med* **19** 242-253

IARC (1988) *Monographs on the Evaluation of Carcinogenic Risks to Human: Alcohol Drinking* International Agency for Research on Cancer:

Volume **44** Lyon

IARC (1990) *Cancer: Causes, occurrence and control* (Ed L Tomatis) International Agency for Research on Cancer: Lyon

Ingram DM, Nottage E , Roberts T (1991) The role of diet in the development of breast cancer: a case-control study of patients with breast cancer, benign epithelial hyperplasia and fibrocystic disease of the breast *Br J Cancer* **64** 187-191

Ingram DM, Roberts A, Nottage EM (1992) Host factors and breast cancer growth characteristics *Eur J Cancer* **28A**(6-7) 1153-61

Ip C, Lisk DJ (1994) Bioactivity of selenium from Brazil nut for cancer prevention and selenoenzyme maintenance *Nutr Cancer* **21** 203-212

Ip C, Sinha D (1981) Anticarcinogenic effect of selenium in rats treated with dimethyl[a]benzanthracene and fed different levels and types of fat *Carcinogeneis* **2** 435-438

Ip C (1981) Modification of mammary carcinogenesis and tissue peroxidation by selenium deficiency and dietary fat *Nutr Cancer* **2** 136-142

Ip C (1986) The chemopreventive role of selenium in carcinogenesis *J Am Coll Tox* **5** 7-20

Ip C (1990) Quantitative assessment of fat and calorie as risk factors in mammary carcinogenesis in an experimental model - Recent Progress on Nutrition and Cancer - Wiley-Liss Inc 107-117

Ip C, Chin SF, Scimeca JA, Pariza MW (1991) Mammary cancer prevention by conjugated dienoic derivative of linoleic acid *Cancer* **51** 6118-6124

Ip C, Scimeca JA, Thompson H (1995) Effect of timing and duration of dietary conjugated linoleic acid on mammary cancer prevention *Nutr Cancer* **24**(3) 241-7

Iscovich JM, Iscovich RB, Howe J et al, (1989) A case-control study of diet and breast cancer in Argentina *Int J Cancer* **44** 770-77

Jacobsen BK, Bjelke E, Kvale G, Heuch I (1986) Coffee drinking, mortality and cancer incidence: results from a Norwegian prospective study *JNCI* **76** 823-831

Jain-M, Miller AB, To T (1994) Premorbid diet and the prognosis of women with breast cancer J Natl Cancer Inst **86**(18) 1390-7

Jones DY, Schatzkin A, Green SB et al, (1987) Dietary fat and breast cancer in the National Health and Nutrition Examination Survey I Epidemiologic follow-up study *JNCI* **79** 465-71

Kaizer L, Boyd NF, Kriukov V,, Tritchler D (1989) Fish consumption and breast cancer risk: an ecological study *Nutrition and Cancer* **12** 61-68

Kalish LA (1984) Relationships of body size with breast cancer *J Clin Oncol* **2** 287-293

Kampert JB, Whittemore AS , Paffenbarger RSJ (1988) Combined effect of childbearing, menstrual events, and body size on age-specific breast cancer risk *Am J Epidemiol* **128** 962-979

Karmali RA, Marsh J, Fuchs C (1984) Effect of omega-3 fatty acids on growth of a rat mammary tumor *JNCI* **73** 457-461

Kato I, Miura S, Kasumi F, Iwase T, Tashiro H, Fujita Y, Koyama H, Ikedo T, Fujiwara K, Sootome K, Asaishi K, Abe R, Nihei M, Ishida T, Yokoe T, Tamamoto H, Morata M (1992) A case-control study of breast cancer among Japanese women: with special reference to family history and reproductive and dietary factors *Breast Cancer Res Treat* **24** 51-59

Katsouyanni K, Trichopoulos D, Boyle P et al, (1986) Diet and breast cancer: a case-control study in Greece *Int J Cancer* **38** 815-20

Katsouyanni K, Trichopoulous A, Stuver S et al (1994) The association of fat and other macronutrients with breast cancer: a case-control study from Greece *Br J Cancer* **70** 537-541

Katsouyanni K, Willett W, Trichopoulos D et al, (1988) Risk of breast cancer among Greek women in relation to nutrient intake *Cancer* **61** 181-5

Kazer RR (1995) Insulin resistance, insulin-like growth factor I and breast cancer: a hypothesis *Int J Cancer* **62**(4): 403-6

Kelsey JL, Gammon MD, Esther MJ (1993) Reproductive factors and breast cancer *Epidem Rev* **15** 36-47

Key TJA, Chen J, Wang DY, Pike MC, Boreham J (1990) Sex hormones in women in rural China and in Britain *Brit J Cancer* **62** 631-636

Kinlen LJ (1982) Meat and fat consumption and cancer mortality: a study of strict religious orders in Britain *Lancet* **i** 946-9

Kissinger DG, Sanchez A (1987) The association of dietary factors and age at menarche *Nutr Res* **7** 471-479

Knekt P (1988) Serum vitamin E level and risk of female cancers *Int J Epidemiol* **17** 281-286

Knekt P, Albanes D, Seppanen R et al, (1990) Dietary fat and risk of breast cancer *Am J Clin Nutr* **52** 903-8

Knekt P, Aromaa A, Maatela J et al, (1990) Serum vitamin A and the subsequent risk of cancer: cancer incidence follow-up of the Finnish Mobile Clinic Health Examination Survey *Am J Epidemiol* **132** 857-870

Knekt P, Aromaa A, Maatela J et al, (1990) Serum selenium and subsequent risk of cancer among Finnish men and women *JNCI* **82** 864-8

Knekt P, Aromaa A, Maatela J, Ritva-Kaarina A et al, (1991) Vitamin E and cancer prevention *Am J Clin Nutr* **53** 283S-286S

Knekt P, Järvinen R, Seppänen R, Pukkala E, Aromaa A (1996) Intake of dairy products and risk of breast cancer *Br J Cancer* **73** 687-691

Kushi LH, Sellers TA, Potter JD et al, (1992) Dietary fat and postmenopausal breast cancer *JNCI* **84** 1092-1099

La Vecchia C, Decarli A, Parazzini F et al, (1987) General epidemiology of breast cancer in Northern Italy *Int J Epid* **16** 347-355

la Vecchia C, Negri E, Franceschi S, Decarli A, Giacosa A, Lipworth L (1995) Olive oil, other dietary fats, and the risk of breast cancer (Italy) *Cancer Causes Control* **6**(6) 545-50

La Vecchia C, Negri E, Parazzini F et al, (1989) Alcohol and breast cancer: update from an Italian case-control study *Europ J Cancer Clin Oncol* **25** 711-1717

La Vecchia C, Talamini R, Decarli A, Franceschi S et al (1986) Coffee consumption and the risk of breast cancer *Surgery* **100**(3) 477-81

Landa MC, Frago N, Tres A (1994) Diet and the risk of breast cancer in Spain *Eur J Cancer Prev* **3** 313-320

Lane HW, Medina DM (1983) Selenium concentrations and glutathione peroxidase activity in normal and neoplastic development of the mouse mammary gland *Cancer Res* **43** 1558-1561

Lawson DH, Jick H, Rothman KJ (1981) Coffee and tea consumption and breast disease *Surgery* **90**(5) 801-3

Le Marchand L, Kolonel LN, Earle ME, Mi MP (1988) Body size at different periods of life and breast cancer risk Am J Epidemiol **128** 137-152

Le MG (1985) Coffee consumption, benign breast disease, and breast cancer [letter] *Am J Epidemiol* **122**(4) 721

Le MG, Hill C, Kramer A et al, (1984) Alcohol beverage consumption and breast cancer in a French case-control study *Am J Epidem* **120** 350-357

Le MG, Moulton LH, Hill C et al, (1986) Consumption of dairy produce and alcohol in a case-control study of breast cancer *JNCI* **77** 633-36

Lee HP, Gourley L, Duffy SW et al, (1991) Dietary effects on breast cancer risk in Singapore *Lancet* **337** 1197-1200

Levander OA (1986) The need for a measure of selenium status *J Am Coll Toxicol* **5**:37-44

Levi F, La Vecchia C, Gulie C et al, (1993) Dietary factors and breast cancer risk in Vaud, Switzerland *Nutr Cancer* **19** 327-335

Li D, Wang M, Dhingra K, Hittleman WN (1996) Aromatic DNA adducts in adjacent tissues of breast cancer patients; clues to breast cancer etiology *Cancer Res* **56** 287-93

Lilienfeld AM (1996) The relationship of cancer of the female breast to artificial menopause and marital status *Cancer* **9** 927-934

Lin TH, Dhen KP, MacMahon B (1971) Epidemiologic characteristics of cancer of the breast in Taiwan *Cancer* **27** 1497-1504

London RS, Sundaram GS, Murphy L et al,(1985) The effect of vitamin E on mammary dysplasia: a double-blind study *Obstet Gynecol* **65** 104-106

London SJ, Colditz GA, Stampfer MJ,et al, (1989) Prospective study of relative weight, height and the risk of breast cancer *JAMA* **26** :2853-8

London SJ, Stein EA, Henderson IC et al, (1992) Carotenoids, retinol, and vitamin E and risk of proliferative benign breast disease and breast cancer *Cancer Causes Control* **3** 503-512

Longnecker MP (1994) Alcoholic beverage consumption in relation to risk of breast cancer: meta-analysis and review *Cancer Causes Control* **5** 73-82

Longnecker MP, Berlin JA, Orza MJ , Chalmers TC (1988) A meta-analysis of alcohol consumption in relation to risk of breast cancer *JAMA* **260** 652-6

Longnecker MP, Newcomb PA, Mittendorf R et al, (1995) Risk of breast cancer in relation to lifetime alcohol consumption *JNCI* **87** 923-929

Lubin F, Ruder AM, Wax Y , Modan B (1985) Overweight and changes in weight throughout adult life in breast cancer etiology A case-control study *Am J Epid* **122** 579-88

Lubin JH, Burns PE, Blot WJ, Ziegler RG, Lees AW, Fraumeni JFJ (1981) Dietary factors and breast cancer risk *Int J Cancer* **28** 685-689

Maclure M, Travis LB, Willett WC , MacMahon B (1991) A prospective cohort study of nutrient intake and age at menarche *Am J Clin Nutr* **54** 649-656

MacMahon B, Cole P, Lin TM et al, (1970) *Age at first birth and breast cancer risk* Bull World Health Organ **43** 209-221

Marshall JR, Yinsheng Q, Junshi C et al (1992) Additional ecological evidence: Lipids and breast cancer mortality among women aged 55 and over in China *Eur J Cancer* **28A** 1720-1727

Martin-Moreno JM, Boyle P, Gorgojo L, Willett WC et al (1993) Alcoholic beverage consumption and risk of breast cancer in Spain *Cancer Causes Control* **4**(4) 345-53

Martin-Moreno JM, Willett WC, Gorgojo L et al (1994) Dietary fat, olive oil intake and breast cancer risk *Int J Cancer* **58** 774-780

Marubini E, Decarli A, Costa A et al, (1988) The relationship of dietary intake and serum levels of retinol and beta-carotene with breast cancer Results of a case-control study *Cancer* **61** 173-80

McCormick DL, Burns FJ , Albert RE (1981) Inhibition of Benz(a)pyrene-induced mammary carcinogenesis by retinyl acetate *JNCI*t **66** 559-64

McGregor H, Land CE, Choi K et al, (1977) Breast cancer incidence among atomic bomb survivors, Hiroshima and Nagasaki 1950-69 *JNCI* **59**799-811

Meara J, McPherson K, Roberts M, Jones-L, Vessey M (1989) Alcohol, cigarette smoking and breast cancer *Br J Cancer* **60**(1) 70-3

Medina D, Lane HW (1983) Stage specificity of selenium mediated inhibition of mouse mammary tumorigenesis *Biol Trace Element Res* **5** 297

Medina D, Oborn CJ (1984) Selenium inhibition of DNA synthesis in mouse mammary epithelial cell line YN-4 *Cancer Res* **44** 4361-4365

Merzenich H, Boeing H , Wahrendorf J (1993) Dietary fat and sports activity as determinants for age at menarche *Am J Epidemiol* **138** 217-224

Messina M, Barnes S (1991) The role of soy products in reducing risk of cancer *JNCI* **83** 541-546

Messina M, Messina V (1991) Increasing use of soyfoods and their potential role in cancer prevention *J Am Diet Assoc* **91**(7) 836-40

Messina MJ, Persky V, Setchell KDR, Barnes S (1994) Soy intake and cancer risk: a review of the *in vitro* and *in vivo* data *Nutr Cancer* **21** 113-131

Mettlin CJ, Schoenfeld ER, Natarajan N (1990) Patterns of milk consumption and risk of cancer *Nutr Cancer* **13**(1-2) 89-99

Meyer F, Verreault R (1987) Erythrocyte selenium and breast cancer risk *Am J Epidemiol* **125** 917-9

Michnovicz JJ, Bradlow-HL (1990) Induction of estradiol metabolism by dietary indole-3-carbinol in humans *JNCI* **82**(11) 947-9

Miki Y, Swensen J, Shattuck-Eldens D et al, (1994) Isolation of BRCA1, the 17q-linked breast and ovarian cancer susceptibility gene *Science* **266** 66-7

Miller AB (1978) An overview of hormone-associated cancers *Cancer Research* **38** 3985-3990

Mills PK, Annegers JF, Phillips RL (1988) Animal product consumption and subsequent fatal breast cancer risk among Seventh-day Adventists *Am J Epidemiol* **127**(3) 440-53

Mills-PK, BeesonWL, Phillips RL, Fraser GE (1989) Dietary habits and breast cancer incidence among Seventh-day Adventists *Cancer* **64**(3) 582-90

Minton JP, Foecking MK, Webster DJ et al, (1979) Response of fibrocystic disease to caffeine withdrawal and correlation of cyclic nucleotides with breast disease Am J Obstet Gynecol **135** 157-158

Moisan J, Meyer F , Gingras S (1990) Diet and age at menarche *Cancer Causes Control* **1** 149-154

Moon RC, Grubbs CJ, Sporn MG et al, (1977) Retinyl acetate inhibits mammary carcinogenesis induced by N-methyl-Nnitrosourea *Nature* **267** 620-621

Moon RC, McCormick DL , Mehta RG (1983) Inhibition of carcinogenesis by retinoids *Cancer Res* **43** 2469

Morris JJ, seifter et al, (1992) The role of aromatic hydrocarbons in the genesis of breast cancer *Medical Hypotheses* **38** 177-184

NAS (1982) *Diet, Nutrition and Cancer* Committee on Diet, Nutrition and Cancer, Assembly of Life Science, National Academy Press: Washington DC

NAS (1989) *Diet and Health, Implications for Reducing Chronic Disease Risk* Committee on Diet and Health, National Academy Press: Washington DC

Nasca PC, Baptiste MS, Field NA et al (1990) An epidemiological case-control study of breast cancer and alcohol consumption *Int J Epidemiol* **19**(3) 532-8

Nasca PC, Baptiste MS, Field NA et al, (1990) An epidemiological case-control study of breast cancer and alcohol consumption *Int J Epid* **19** 532-538

Negri E, La Vecchia C, Franceschi S et al, (1991) Vegetable and fruit consumption and cancer risk *Int J Cancer* **48** 350-354

Newcomb PA, Storer BE, Longnecker MP et al, (1994) Lactation and a reduced risk of premenopausal breast cancer *N Engl J Med* 330:81-87

O'Connell DL, Hulka BS, Chambless LE et al (1987) Cigarette smoking, alcohol consumption, and breast cancer risk J Natl Cancer Inst **78**(2) 229-34

Obana H, Hori S, Kashimoto T, Kunita N (1981) Polycyclic aromatic hydrocarbons in human fat and liver *Bull Env Contam Toxicol* **27** 23-27

Overvad K, Wang DY, Olsen J et al, (1991) Selenium in human mammary carcinogenesis: a case-cohort study *Eur J Cancer* **27** 900-902

Paffenbarger RS Jr, Kampert JB , Chang HG (1980) Characteristics that predict risk of breast cancer before and after the menopause *Am J Epid* **112** 258-68

Paffenbarger RSJ, Hyde RT, Wing AL (1987) Physical activity and incidence of cancer in diverse populations: a preliminary report *Am J Clin Nutr* **45** (Suppl) 312-317

Paganini-Hill A, Ross RK (1983) Breast cancer and alcohol consumption *Lancet* **I** 626-7

Pawlega J Breast cancer and smoking, vodka drinking and dietary habits *Acta Oncologica* 1992 **31** 387-392

Pence BC, Buddingh F, Yang SP (1986) Multiple dietary factors in the enhancement of dimethylhydrazine carcinogenesis: main effect of indole-3-carbinol *JNCI* **77** 269-276

Perera FP, Estabrook A, Hewer A, Channing K, Rundle A, Mooney LA, hyatt R, Phillips DH (1995) Carcinogen-DNA adducts in human breast tissue *Cancer Epid Bio Prev* **4** 233-238

Petrakis NL, Maack CA, Lee RE, Lyon M (1980) Mutagenic activity in nipple aspirates of human breast fluid *Cancer Res* **40** 188-189

Pfau W, O'Hare MJ, Grover PL, Phillips DH (1992) Metabolic activation of the food mutaagens 2-amino-3-methylimidazo [4,5-f] quinoline (IQ) and 2-amino-3-4-dimethylimadazo [4,5-f] quinoline (MeIQ) to DNA binding in human mammary epithelial cells *Carcinogens* **13** 907-909

Phillips RL , Snowdon DA (1983) Association of meat and coffee use with cancers of the large bowel, breast, and prostate among Seventh-Day Adventists: Preliminary results *Cancer Res* **43**(s) 2403-8

Phillips RL, Garfinkel L, Kuzma JW, Beeson WL,

Lotz T , Brin B (1980) Mortality among California Seventh-day Adventists for selected cancer sites *JNCI* **65** 1097-1107

Pike MC (1990) Reducing cancer risk in women through lifestyle-mediated changes in hormone levels *Cancer Detect Prev* **14** 595-607

Pike MC, Krailo MD, Henderson BE, Casagrande JT , Hoel DG (1983) 'Hormonal' risk factors, 'breast tissue age' and the age-incidence of breast cancer *Nature* **303** 767-70

Poirier LA, Newberne PM, Pariza MW (eds) (1986) *Essential Nutrients in Carcinogenesis, Advances in Experimental Medicine and Biology*, Volume **206** Plenum Press, New York,

Potischman N, McCulloch CE, Byers T et al (1990) Bresat cancer and dietary and plasma concentrations of carotenoids and vitamin A *Am J Clin Nutr* **52** 909-915

Prentice RL, Kakar F, Hursting S, Sheppard L, Klein R , Kushi LH (1988) Aspects of the rationale for the Women's Health Trial *JNCI* 80 802-14

Pryor M, Slattery ML, Robison LM Egger M (1989) Adolescent diet and breast cancer in Utah *Cancer Res* **49**(8) 2161-7

Qi XY, Zhang A, Wu G, Pang W (1994) The association between breast cancer and diet and other factors *Asia Pac J Public Health* **7** 98-104

Radimer K, Siskind V, Bain C, Schofield F (1993) Relation between anthropometric indicators and risk of breast cancer among Australian women *Am J Epidemiol* **138** 77-89

Ravnihar B, MacMahon B, Lindtner J (1971) Epidemiologic features of breast cancer in Slovenia, 1965-1967 *Eur J Cancer* **7**(4) 295-306

Reichman ME, Judd JT, Longcope C et al (1993) Effects of alcohol consumption on plasma and urinary hormone concentration in premenopausal women *JNCI* **85** 722-7

Richardson S, de Vincenzi I, Pujol H, Gerber-M (1989) Alcohol consumption in a case-control study of breast cancer in southern France Int J Cancer **44**(1) 84-9

Richardson S, Gerber M , Cenee S (1991) The role of fat animal protein and vitamin consumption in breast cancer: A case-control study in Southern France *Int J Cancer* **48** 1-9

Rivera ES, Andrade N, Martin G et al (1994) Induction of mammary tumours in rats by intraperitoneal injection of NMU: histopathology and estral cycle influence *Cancer Let* **86** 223-228

Rohan TE, Cook MG (1989) Alcohol consumption and risk of benign proliferative epithelial disorders of the breast in women *Int J Cancer*

43 631-636

Rohan TE, Howe GR, Friedenreich CM et al (1993) Dietary fiber, vitamins A, C, and E, and risk of breast cancer: a cohort study *Cancer Causes Control* **4** 29-37

Rohan TE, McMichael AJ , Baghurst PA (1988) A population-based case-control study of diet and breast cancer in Australia *Am J Epidemiol* **128** 478-89

Ronco A, De Stefani E, Mendilaharsu M, Deneo-Pellegrini H (1996) Meat, fat and risk of breast cancer: A case-control study from Uruguay *Int J Cancer* **65** 328-331

Rose DP, Boyar AP, Wynder EL (1986) International comparisons of mortality rates for cancer of the breast, ovary, prostate, and colon, and per capita food consumption *Cancer* **58** 2263-71

Rose DP, Connolly JM (1993) Effects of dietary omega-3 fatty acids on human breast cancer growth and metastases in nude mice *JNCI* **85** 1743-1747

Rose DP, Rayburn J, Hatala MA, Connolly JM (1994) Effects of dietary fish oil on fatty acids and eicosanoids in metastasizing human breast cancer cells *Nutrition and Cancer* **22** 131-141

Rosenberg J, Miller DR, Helmrich SP et al (1985) Breast cancer and the consumption of coffee *Am J Epidem* **122** 391-9

Rosenberg L, Palmer J, Miller D, Clarke E , Shapiro S (1990) A case-control study of alcoholic beverage consumption and breast cancer *Am J Epid* **131** 6-14

Rosenberg L, Sloane D, Shapiro S et al (1982) Breast cancer and alcohol beverage consumption *Lancet* **i** 267-271

Sanchez A, Kissinger DG, Phillips RI (1981) A hypothesis on the etiological role of diet on age of menarche *Med Hypotheses* **7**(11) 1339-45

Schairer C, Brinton LA, Hoover RN (1987) Methylxanthines and the consumption of coffee *Int J Cancer*

Schatzkin A, Carter CL, Green SB et al (1989) Is alcohol consumption related to breast cancer? Results from the Framingham Heart Study *JNCI* **81** 31-35

Schatzkin A, Palmer JR, Rosenberg L et al (1987) Risk factors for breast cancer in black women *JNCI* **78** 213-217

Scholar EM, Wolterman K, Birt DF, Bresnick E (1989) The effects of diets enriched in collards on murine pulmonary metastasis *Nutr Cancer* **12** 121-126

Schrauzer GN, White DA , Schneider CJ (1977) Cancer mortality correlation studies - III: Statistical associations with dietary selenium intakes *Bioinorg Chem* **7** 23-31

Seely S, Horrobin DF (1983) Diet and breast cancer: the possible connection with sugar consumption *Med Hypotheses* **11**(3) 319-27

Sellers TA, Kushi LH Potter JD et al (1992) Effect of family history, bofy-fat distribution, and reproductive factors on the risk of postmenopausal breast cancer *NEMJ* **326** 1323-9

Shamberger RJ, Tytko SA, Willis CE (1976) Antioxidants and Cancer Part VI Selenium and age-adjusted human cancer mortality *Arch Env Health* **31** 231-5

Sherman B, Wallace R, BeanJ, Schlabaugh L (1981) Relationship of body weight to menarcheal and menopausal age: implications for breast cancer risk *Clin Endocrinol Metab* **52** 488-93

Shibata A, Paganini-Hill A, Ross RK et al (1992) Intake of vegetables, fruits, beta-carotene, vitamin C and vitamin supplements and cancer incidence among the elderly: a prospective study *Br J Cancer* **66** 673-679

Shun-Zhang Y, Rui-Fang L, Da-Dao X, Howe GR (1990) A case-control study of dietary and nondietary risk factors for breast cancer in Shanghai *Cancer Res* **50**: 5017-5021

Simard A, Vobecky J, Vobecky JS (1990) Nutrition and life-style factors in fibrocystic disease and cancer of the breast *Cancer Detection Prev* **14** 567-572

Simon MS, Carman W, Wolfe R , Schottenfeld D (1991) Alcohol consumption and the risk of breast cancer: a report from the Tecumseh Community Health Study *J Clin Epid* **44** 755-61

Singletary KW, McNary MQ, Odoms AM, Nelshoppen J, Wallig MA (1991) Ethanol consumption and DMBA-induced mammary carcinogensis in rats *Nutr Cancer* **16** 13-23

Sneyd MJ, Paul C, Spears GF, Skegg DC (1991) Alcohol consumption and risk of breast cancer *Int J Cancer* **48**(6) 812-5

Snowden DA, Phillips RL (1984) Coffee consumption and risk of fatal cancers *Am J Pub Health* **74** 820-3

Snyderwine EG (1994) Some perspectives on the nutritional aspects of breast cancer research: food-derived heterocyclic amines as etiologic agents in human mammary cancer *Cancer* **74** 1070-1077

Sporn MB , Roberts AB (1983) Role of retinoids in differentiation and carcinogenesis *Cancer Res* **43** 3034-40

Stocks P (1970) Cancer mortality in relation to national consumption of cigarettes solid fuel, tea and coffee *Br J Cancer* **24** 215-225

Stoewsand GS, Anderson JL, Munson L (1988) Protective effects of dietary brussels sprouts against mammary carcinogenesis in Sprague-Dawley rats *Cancer Lett* **39** 199-207

Stoewsand GS, Anderson JL, Munson L, Lisk DJ (1989) Effect of dietary brussels sprouts with increased selenium content on mammary carcinogenesis in the rat *Cancer Letters* **45** 43-48

Stoll BA (1996) Nutrition and breast cancer risk: can an effect via insulin resistance be demonstrated? *Breast Cancer Res Treat* **38** 239-46

Swanson CA, Jones DY, Schatzkin A, Brinton LA , Ziegler RG (1988) Breast cancer risk assessed by anthropometry in the NHANES I epidemiological follow-up study *Cancer Res* **48** 5363-7

Talamini R, La Vecchia C, Decarli A et al (1984) Social factors, diet and breast in a northern Italian population *Br J Cancer* **49** 723-29

Tannenbaum A (1942) The genesis and growth of tumors III: Effects of a high fat diet *Cancer Res* **2** 468-75

Tavani A, La Vecchia C (1995) Fruit and vegetable consumption and cancer risk in a Mediterranean population *American Journal of Clinical Nutrition* **61** 1374S-1377S

Thompson HJ (1992) Effect of treadmill exercise intensity on hepatic glutathione content and its relevance to mammary tumorigenesis *J Sports Med Phys Fitness* **32**(1): 59-63

Thompson HJ, Becci PJ (1980) Selenium inhibition of N-methyl-N-nitrosourea induced mammary carcinogenesis in the rat *JNCI* **65** 1299

Thompson HJ, Meeker LD, Becci PJ et al (1982) Effect of short term feeding of sodium selenite on 7,12-dimethylbenz (a) anthracene induced mammary carcinogenesisi in the rat *Cancer Res* **42** 4954

Tiwari RK, Guo L, Bradlow HL, Telang NT , Osborne MP (1994) Selective responsiveness of human breast cancer cells to indole-3-carbinol, a chemopreventive agent *JNCI* **86** 126-131

Toniolo P, Riboli E, Protta F, Charrel M , Cappa AP (1989) Calorie-providing nutrients and risk of breast cancer *JNCI* **81** 278-286

Toniolo P, Riboli E, Shore RE , Pasternack BS (1994) Consumption of meat, animal products, protein, and fat and risk of breast cancer - A prospective cohort study in New York *Epidemiol* **5** 391-397

Tornberg SA, Holm LE , Carstensen JM (1988) Breast cancer risk in relation to serum cholesterol, serum beta-lipoprotein, height, weight, and blood pressure *Acta Oncolog* **27** 31-37

Toti A, Agugiaro S, Amadori D et al (1986) Breast cancer risk factors in Italian women: a multicentric case-control study *Tumori* **72** 241-249

Tretli S (1989) Height and weight in relation to breast cancer morbidity and mortality A prospective study of 570,000 women in Norway *Int J Cancer* **44** 23-30

Tretli S, Gaard M (1996) Lifestyle changes during adolescence and risk of breast cancer: an ecologic study of the effect of World War II in Norway *Cancer Causes Control* **7**(5): 507-12

Trichopoulos A, Katsouyanni K, Stuver S et al (1995) Consumption of olive oil and specific food groups in relation to breast cancer risk in Greece *JNCI* **87** 110-116

Trichopoulos D, MacMahon B , Cole P (1972) Menopause and breast cancer risk *J NatlCancer Inst*; **48** 605-613

Unger M, Kiaer H, Blichert-Toft M, Olsen J Clausen J (1984) Organochlorine compounds in human breast fat from deceased with and without breast cancer and in a biopsy material from newly diagnosed patients undergoing breast surgery *Environ Res* **34**(1) 24-8

Ursin G, Bjelke E, Heuch I et al (1990) Milk consumption and cancer incidence A Norweigen prospective study *Br J Cancer* **61** 454-459

Valaoras VG, MacMahon B, Trichopoulos D (1969) Lactation and reproductive histories of breast cancer patients in greater Athens 1965 *International Journal of Cancer* **4**: 350-363

Van den Brandt PA, Van't Veer P, Goldbohm RA et al (1993) A prospective cohort study on dietary fat and the risk of postmenopausal breast cancer *Cancer Res* **53** 75-82

van Noord PA, Collette HJ, Maas MJ , de Waard F (1987) Selenium levels in nails of premenopausal breast cancer patients assessed prediagnostically in a cohort- nested case-referent study among women screened in the DOM project *Int J Epidemiol* **16** 318-22

Van't Veer P, Kalb CM, Verhoef P et al (1990) Dietary fiber, B-carotene and breast cancer: results from a case-control study *Int J Cancer* **45** 825-828

van't Veer P, Kok FJ, Hermus RJ, Sturmans F (1989) Alcohol dose, frequency and age at first exposure in relation to the risk of breast cancer *Int J Epidemiol* **18**(3) 511-7

Vatten LJ , Kvinnsland S (1990) Body mass index and risk of breast cancer A prospective study of 23,826 Norwegian women *Int J Cancer* **45** 440-444

Vatten LJ , Kvinnsland S (1992) Prospective study of height, body mass index and risk of breast cancer *Acta Oncologica* **31** 195-200

Vatten LJ, Solvoll K, Loken EB (1990) Coffee consumption and the risk of breast cancer A prospective study of 14,593 Norwegian women *Br J Cancer* **62** 267-270

Vena JE, Graham S, Zielezny M et al (1987) Occupational exercise and risk of cancer *Am J Clin Nutr* **45** 318-27

Wang QS, Ross RK, Yu MC et al (1992) A case-control study of breast cancer in Tianjin, China *Cancer Epidem Biomarkers Prev* **1** 435-9

Wattenberg LW (1983) Inhibition of neoplasia by minor dietary constituents *Cancer Res* **43** (Suppl) 2448s-2453s

Wattenberg LW, Hanley AB, Barany G, Sparnins VL, Lam LKT, Fenwick GR (1986) Inhibition of carcinogenesis by some minor dietary constituents, in Hayashi Y (ed): *Diet, Nutrition, and Cancer* Tokyo, Japan Sci Soc Press 193-203

Wattenberg LW, Loub WD (1978) Inhibition of polycyclic aromatic hydrocarbon-induced neoplasia by naturally occurring indoles *Cancer Res* **38** 1410-3

Wattenberg LW, Schafer HW, Waters L Jr, Davis DW (1989) Inhibition of mammary tumor formation by broccoli and cabbage *Proc Am Assoc Cancer Res* **30** 181

WCRF (1994) World Cancer Research Diet and cancers *A review of the literature on genetic, cellular, and physiological mechanisms* London: WCRF

Webster LA, Layde PM, Wingo PA et al (1983) Alcohol consumption and risk of breast cancer *Lancet* **ii** 724-26

Wei H, Bowen R, Cai Q, Barnes S, Wang Y (1995) Antioxidant and antipromotional effects of the soybean isoflavone genistein *Proc Soc Exp Biol Med* **208**(1) 124-30

Welsch CW (1992) Relationship between dietary fat and experimental mammary tumorigenesis: a review and critique *Cancer Res* suppl **7** 2040s-2048s

Welsch CW (1994) Interrelationship between dietary lipids and calories and experimental mammary gland tumorigenesis *Cancer* **74** (suppl) 1055-1062

Welsch EO, Goodrich-Smith M, Brown CK et al (1981) Selenium and the genesis of murine mammary tumors *Carcinogenesis* **2** 519

White E (1987) Projected changes in breast cancer incidence due to the trend toward delayed childbearing *Am J Public Health* **77** 495-497

WHO (1990) World Health Organization *Nutrition, Nutrition and Prevention of Chronic Diseases* Technical Report 797 Geneva: WHO

WHO (1997) World Health Organization *The World Health Report* Geneva:WHO

Willett WC, Hunter DJ, Stampfer MJ et al (1992) Dietary fat and fiber in relation to risk of breast cancer: An eight year follow-up *JAMA* **268** 2037-2044

Willett WC, Stampfer MJ, Colditz GA, Rosner BA, Hennekens CH, Speizer FE (1987) Dietary fat and the risk of breast cancer *N Engl J Med* **316** 22-8

Willett WC, Stampfer MJ, Colditz GA, Rosner BA, Speizer FE (1990) Relation of meat, fat, and fiber intake to the risk of colon cancer in a prospective study among women *N Engl J Med* **323** 1664-72

Willett WC, Stampfer MJ, Underwood BA et al (1984) Vitamin A supplementation and plasma retinol levels: a randomized trial among women *JNCI* **73** 1445-8

Williams RR and Horm JW (1977) Association of cancer sites with tobacco and alcohol consumption and socioeconomic status of patients: Interview study from the Third national Cancer Survey *JNCI* **58** 525-547

Wolff MS, Toniolo PG (1995) Environmental organochlorine exposure as a potential etiologic factor in breast cancer *Environ Health Perspect* **103** Suppl 7 141-5

Woods MN, Gorbach SL, Longcope C, Goldin BR, Dwyer JT (1989) Low-fat, high-fiber diet and serum estrone sulfate in premenopausal women *Am J Clin Nutr* **49** 1179-1193

Wyshak G , Frisch RE (1982) Evidence for a secular trend in age at menarche *N Engl J Med* **306** 1033-1035

Yam D (1992) Insulin-cancer relationships: possible dietary implication *Med Hypotheses* **38**(2) 111-7

Yanagihara K, Ito-A, Toge-T, Numoto-M (1993) Antiproliferative effects of isoflavones on human cancer cell lines established from the gastrointestinal tract *Cancer Res* **53**(23) 5815-21

Yong LC, Brown CC, Schatzkin A, Schairer C (1996) Prospective study of relative weight and risk of breast cancer: the Breast Cancer Detection Demonstration Project follow-up study, 1979 to 1987-1989 *Am J Epidemiol* **143**(10) 985-95

Yuan J, Wang Q, Ross RK, Henderson BE, Yu MC (1995) Diet and breast cancer in Shanghai and Tianjin, China *Br J Cancer*;**71**:1353-1358

Yuan JM, Yu MC, Ross RK et al (1988) Risk factors for breast cancer in Chinese women in Shanghai *Cancer Res* **48** 1949-53

Yuasa S, MacMahon B (1970) Lactation and reproductive histories of breast cancer patients in Tokyo, Japan *Bull WHO* **42** **195-204**

Yuspa SH, Poirer MC (1988) Chemical carcinogenesis: from animal models to molecular models in one decade *Adv Cancer Res* **50** 25-70

Zarbl H, Sukumar S, Arthur AV, Martin-Zanca D, Barbacid M (1985) Direct mutagenesis of Ha-ras-1 oncogenes by N-nitroso-N-methylurea during imitation of mammary carcinogenesis in rats *Nature* **315** 382-385

Zaridze D, Lifanova Y, Maximovitch D, Day NE , Duffy SW (1991) Diet, alcohol consumption and reproductive factors in a case-control study of breast cancer in Moscow *Int J Cancer* **48** 493-501

Zemla B (1984) The role of selected dietary elements in breast cancer risk among native and migrant populations in Poland *Nutr Cancer* **6** 187-195

Zheng W, Doyle TJ, Kushi LH, Sellers TA, Hong C-P, Folsom AR (1996) Tea consumption and cancer incidence in a prospective study of postmenopausal women *Am J Epidemiol* **144** 175-182

4.12 OVARY

Armstrong B and Doll R (1975) Environmental factors and cancer incidence and mortality in different countries, with special reference to dietary practices *Nit J Cancer* **15** 617-631

Bast RC, Jacobs I, Berchuck A (1992) Malignant transformation of ovarian epithelium *JNCI* **84** 556-558

Byers T, Marshall J, Graham S et al (1983) A case-control study of dietary and nondietary factors in ovarian cancer *JNCI* **71** 1299-1300

Byers T, Marshall J, Graham S et al (1983) A case-control study of dietary and nondietary factors in ovarian cancer *JNCI* **71** 681-686

Casagrande JT, Louie EW, Pike MC et al (1979) 'Incessant ovulation' and ovarian cancer *Lancet* **2** 170-2

Cramer DW, Welch AR, Hutchinson GB et al (1984) Dietary animal fat in relation to ovarian cancer risk *Obstet Gynaecol* **63** 833-838

Cramer DW, Welch WR (1983) Determinants of

ovarian cancer risk, II: inferences regarding pathogenesis *J Natl Cancer Inst* **71** 717-721

Cramer DW, Welch WR, Hutchison GB, Willett WC and Scully RE (1984) Dietary animal fat in relation to ovarian cancer risk *Obstet Gynecol* **63** 833-838

Cramer DW, Willett WC, Bell DA et al (1989) Galactose consumption and metabolism in relation to risk of ovarian cancer *Lancet* 66-71

Dietl J, Marzusch K (1993) Ovarian surface epithelium and human ovarian cancer *Gynecol Obstet Invest* **35** 129-135

Easton DF, Bishop DT, Ford D, Crockford GP, and the Breast Cancer Linkage Consortium (1993) Genetic linkage analysis in familial breast and ovarian cancer: results from 214 families Am *J Hum Genet* **52** 678-701

Engle A, Muscat JE and Harris RE (1991) Nutritional risk factors and ovarian cancer *Nutr Cancer* **15** 239-247

Feuer G (1983) Drug control of steroid metabolism by the hepatic endoplasmic reticulum *Drug Metab Rev* **14** 1119-44

Feunteun J, Narod SA, Lunch HT et al (1993) A breast-ovarian cancer susceptibility gene maps to chromosone 17q21 *Am J Hum Genet* **52** 736-742

Godwin AK, Testa JR, Handel LM et al (1992) Spontaneous transformation of rat ovarian surface epithelial cells: association with cytogenetic changes and implications of repeated ovulation in the etiology of ovarian cancer *JNCI* **84** 592-601

Harlow BL, Cramer DW (1995) Self-reported use of anti-depressants or benzodiazepine tranquilisers and risk of epithelial ovarian cancer: evidence from two combined case-control: evidence from two combined case-control studies (Massachusetts, United States) *Cancer Causes and Control* **6** 130-134

Hartge P, Leshner LP, McGowan L et al (1982) Coffee and ovarian cancer *Int J Cancer* **30** 531-532

Herrinton LJ, Weiss NS, Beresford SA et al (1995) Lactose and galactose intake and metabolism in relation to the risk of epithelial ovarian cancer *Am J Epidemiol* **141** 407-416

Kerber RA, Slattery ML(1995) The impact of family history on ovarian cancer risk The Utah Population Database *Arch Intern Med* **155** 905-912

La Vecchia C, Decarli A, Negri E et al (1987) Dietary factors and the risk of epithelial ovarian cancer *JNCI* **79** 663-669

La Vecchia C, Franceschi S, Decarli A et al (1984) Coffee drinking and the risk of epithelial ovarian cancer *Int J Cancer* **33** 559-562

Marks JR, Davidoff AM, Kerns BJ et al (1991) Overexpression and mutation of p53 in epithelial ovarian cancer *Cancer Res* **51** 2979-2984

Mettlin CJ and Piver MS (1990) A case-control study of milk-drinking and ovarian cancer risk *Am J Epidemiol* **132** 871-876 (41210)

Miller DR, Rosenberg L, Helmrich SP et al (1984) Ovarian cancer and coffee drinking In MacMahon B, Sugimura T (eds) *Coffee and Health* (Banbury Report 17), Cold Spring Harbor, NY, CSH press

Miller DR, Rosenberg L, Kaufman DW et al (1987) Epithelial ovarian cancer and coffee drinking *Int J Epidemiol* **16** 13-17

Mok, SC-H, Bell DA, Knapp RC et al (1993) Mutation of K-*ras* protooncogene in human ovarian epithelialtumours of borderline malignancy *Cancer Res* **53** 1489-1492

Mori M, Harabuchi I, Miyake H et al (1988) Reproductive, genetic, and dietary risk factors for ovarian cancer *Am J Epidemiol* **128** 771-777 (4126)

NAS (1982) Committee on diet, nutrition and cancer *'Diet, nutrition and cancer'* National Research Council, Washington DC: National Academy Press

NAS (1989) *Diet and health : 'Implications for reducing chronic disease risk'* National Research Council Washington DC: National Academy Press

Risch HA, Jain M, Marrett LD, Howe GR (1994) Dietary fat intake and the risk of epithelial ovarian cancer *JNCI*

Rose DP, Boyar AP and Wynder EL (1986) International comparisons of mortality rates for cancer of the breast, ovary, prostate, and colon, and per capita food consumption *Cancer* **58** 2263-2271

Shu XO, Gao YT, Yuan JM et al (1989) Dietary factors and epithelial ovarian cancer *Br J Cancer* **59** 92-96

Slattery ML, Schuman KL, West DW et al (1989) Nutrient intake and ovarian cancer *Am J Epidemiol* **130** 497-502 (4128)

Snowden DA, Phillips RL (1984) Coffee consumption and risk of fatal cancers *Am J Public Health* **74** 820-823

Snowdon DA (1985) Diet and ovarian cancer *J Am Med Assoc* **254** 356-357 (41213)

Trichopoulos D, Papapostolou M, Polychronopoulou A (1981) Coffee and ovarian cancer *Int J Cancer* **28** 691-693

Trichopoulos D, Papapostolou M, Polychronopoulou A, Day AE (1981) Coffee and ovarian cancer *Int J Cancer* **36** 291-297

Tzonou A, Day NE, Trichopoulos D et al (1984) The epidemiology of ovarian cancer in Greece: a case-control study *Eur J Cancer Clin Oncol* **20** 1045-1052

Tzonou A, Day NE, Trichopoulos D et al (1984) The epidemiology of ovarian cancer in Greece: a case-control study *Eur J Cancer Clin Oncol* **20** 1045-52

Whittemore AS, Wu ML, Paffenbarger RS et al (1988) Personal and environmental characteristics related to epithelial ovarian cancer *Am J Epidemiol* **128** 1228-1240

WHO (1997) World Health Organization *The World Health Report* WHO: Geneva

Wynder EL, Doko H, Barber HRK (1969) Epidemiology of cancer of the ovary *Cancer* **23** 352

4.13 ENDOMETRIUM

Adamson RH, Thorgeirsson UP, Snyderwine EG et al (1990) Carcinogenicity of 2-amino-3-methylimidazo[4,5-f]quinoline in nonhuman primates: induction of tumors in three Macaques *Jpn J Cancer Res (Gann)* **81** 10-14

Armstrong B, Doll R (1975) Environmental factors, cancer incidence, mortality in different countries, with special reference to dietary practices *Int J Cancer* **15** 617-631

Armstrong BK, Brown JB, Clarke HT et al (1981) Diet and reproductive hormones: a study of vegetarian and nonvegetarian postmenopausal women *JNCI* **67** 761-7

Austin H, Austin JM Jr, Partridge EE, Hatch KD, Shingleton HM (1991) Endometrial cancer, obesity,, body fat distribution *Cancer Res* **51** 568-572

Barbone F, Austin H, Partridge EE (1993) Diet, endometrial cancer: A case-control study *Am J Epidemiol* **137** 393-403

Barbosa JC, Shultz TD, Filley SJ, Nieman DC (1990) The relationship among adiposity, diet,, hormone concentrations in vegetarian, nonvegetarian postmenopausal women *Am J Clin Nutr* **51** 798-803

Bennett FC, Ingram DM (1990) Diet and female sex hormone concentrations: an intervention study for the type of fat consumed *Am J Clin Nutr* **52** 808-12

Bronner CE, Baker SM, Morrison PT et al (1994) Mutation in the DNA mismatch repair gene homologue hMLH1 is associated with hereditary non-polyposis colon cancer *Nature* **368**(6468) 258-61

Burks RT, Kessis TD, Cho KR, Hedrick L (1994) Microsatellite instability in endometrial carcinoma *Oncogene* **9** 1163-1166

Duggan BD, Felix JC, Muderspach LI et al (1994) Microsatellite instability in sporadic endometrial carcinoma *JNCI* **86** 1216-1221

Elliott EA, Matanoski GM, Rosenshein NB et al (1990) Body fat patterning in women with endometrial cancer *Gynecol Oncol* **39** 253-8

Fishel R, Lescoe MK, Rao MRS et al (1994) Human mutator gene homologue (hMSH-2_, its association with hereditary non-polyposis colon cancer *Nature* **368** 258-261

Folsom AR, Kaye SA, Potter JD, Prineas RJ (1989) Association of incident carcinoma of the endometrium with body weight, fat distribution in older women: early findings of the Iowa women's health study *Cancer Res* **49** 6828-6831

Freudenheim, JL, Graham, S (1983) Toward a dietary prevention of cancer *Epidemiol Rev* **11** 229-235

Goodman MT, Nomura AMY, Kolonel LN, Hankin JH (1994) Case-control study of the effect of diet, body size on the risk of endometrial cancer In *Proceedings of the International Cancer Congress* Rao RS, Deo MA, Sanghvi DA (eds) New Delhi, India: Monduzzi Editore pp2325-2328

Gorbach SL, GoldinBR (1987) Diet and the excretion and enterohepatic cycling of estrogens *Prev Med* **16** 525-31

Gruber SB, Thomson WD et al (1996) A population-based study of endometrial cancer, familial risk in younger women *Cancer Epidemiol Biomarkers Prev* **5** 411-417

Hill P, Chan P, Cohen-L et al (1977) Diet and endocrine-related cancer *Cancer* **39**(Suppl) 1820-6

Hill P, Garbaczewski L, Helman P, Huskisson J, Sporangisa E, Wynder EL (1980) Diet, lifestyle, and menstrual activity *Am J Clin Nutr*,; **33**: 1192-1198

Jacobs DR, Slavin J, Marquart L (1995) Wholegrain intake, cancer: a review of the literature *Nutr Cancer* **24** 221-229

Key TJ, Pike M (1988) The dose effect relationship between "unopposed" oestrogens, endometrial mitotic rate: its central role in explaining, predicting endometrial cancer risk *Br J Cancer* **57** 205-212

La Vecchia C, Decarli A, Fasoli M, Gentile A (1986) Nutrition, diet in the etiology of endometrial cancer *Cancer* **57** 1248-1253

LaVecchia FC, Parazzini F, Negri E et al (1991) Anthropometric indicators of endometrial cancer risk *Eur J Cancer* **27** 487-490

Le Marchand L, Wilkens LR, Mi M-P (1991) Early-age body size, adult weight gain, endometrial cancer risk *Int J Cancer* **48** 807-811

Levi F, Franceschi S, Negri E, La Vecchia C (1993) Dietary factors, the risk of endometrial cancer *Cancer* **71** 3575-3581

Liu B, Nicolaides NC, Markowitz S et al (1995) Mismatch repair gene defects in sporadic colorectal cancers with microsatellite instability *Nat Genet* **9** 48-55

NAS (1982) *Diet, Nutrition, Cancer* Washington DC: National Academy Press

NAS (1989) *Diet, Health* Washington DC: National Academy Press

Nicolaides NC, Papadopoulous N Liu B et al (1994) Mutations of two PMS homologues in hereditary non-polyposis colon cancer *Nature* **371** 75-80

Peltomaki P, Aaltonen LA, Sistonen P et al (1993) Genetic mapping of a locus predisposing to human colorectal cancer *Science* **260** 810-812

Potischman N, Swanson CA, Brinton LA et al (1993) Dietary associations in a case-control study of endometrial cancer *Cancer Causes Control* **4** 239-250

Rose DP, Boyar AP, Cohen C, Strong LE (1987) Effect of a low-fat diet on hormone levels in women with cystic breast disease I Serum steroids and ganodotropins *J Natl Can Inst* **78** 623-626

Sasaki H, Nishii, Takahasi H et al (1993) Mutation of the Ki-*ras* protooncogene in human endometrial hyperplasia, carcinoma *Cancer* ***Res*** **53** 1906-1910

Schapira DV, Dumar NG, Lyman GH (1991) Obesity, body fat distribution and sex hormones in breast cancer Cancer **67** 2215-2218

Shu XO, Brinton LA, Zheng W et al (1992) Relation of obesity, body fat distribution to endometrial cancer in Shanghai, China *Cancer Res* **52** 3865-3870 (41321)

Shu XO, Zheng W, Potischamn N et al (1993) A population based case-control of dietary factors, endometrial cancer in Shanghai, People's Republic of China *Am J Epidemiol* **137** 155-165

Swanson CA, Potischman N, Wilbanks GD et al (1993) Relation of endometrial cancer risk to past, contemporary body size, body fat distribution *Cancer Epidemiol Biomarkers, Prevention* **2** 321-327

Tornberg SA, Carstensen JM (1994) Relationship between Quetelet's index, cancer of breast, female genital tract in 47,000 women followed for 25 years *Br J Cancer* **69** 358-361

Tretli S, Magnus K (1990) Height, weight in relation to uterine corpus cancer morbidity, mortality A follow-up study of 570,000 women in Norway *Int J Cancer* **46** 165-172

Vasen HFA, offerhaus JA, den Hartog Jager GCA et al (1990) The tumour spectrum in hereditary nonpolyposis colorectal cancer: a study of 24 kindreds in the Netherlands *Int J Cancer* **46** 31-34

Weisburger JH, Jones RC (1989) Nutritional toxicology: on the mechanisms of inhibition of formation of potent carcinogens during cooking *Prog Clin Biol Res* **304** 377-90

WHO (1990) World Health Organization *Diet, nutrition, the prevention of chronic diseases* Report of a WHO study group Geneva: *(Technical report series 797)*

WHO (1997) World Health Organization *The World Health Report* Geneva: World Health Organization

4.14 CERVIX

Albanes D, Blair A, Taylor PR (1989) Physical activity and risk of cancer in the NHANES 1 population *American Journal of Public Health* **79** 744-750

Armstrong B, Doll, R: Environmental factors and cancer incidence and mortality in different countries, with special reference to dietary practices *Int J Cancer* 1975 **15** 617-632

Barton SE, Jenkins D, Cuzick J Maddox PH et al (1988) Effect of cigarette smoking on cervical epithelial immunity: a mechanism for neoplastic change? *Lancet* **II** 652-654

Batieha A, Armenian H, Norkus E et al (1993) Serum micronutrients and the subsequent risk of cervical cancer in a population-based nested case-control study *Cancer Epidemiol Biomarkers Prev* **2** 335-339

Bollag W (1979) Retinoids and cancer *Cancer Chemother Pharmacol* **3** 207

Bosch FX, Muñoz N, de Sanjosé S et al (1994) Importance of human papillomavirus endemicity in the incidence of cervical cancer: an extension of the hypothesis on sexual behaviour *Cancer Epidemiol Biomarkers Prev* **3** 375-379

Brinton L, Tashima K, Lehman H et al (1987) Epidemiology of cervical cancer by cell type *Cancer Res* **47** 1706-1711

Brock K, Berry G, Mock P et al (1988) Nutrients in diet and plasma and risk of in situ cervical cancer *JNCI* **80** 580-585

Burger MPM, Hollema H, Gouw ASH et al (1993) Cigarette smoking and humanpapillomavirus in patients with reported cervical cytological sbnormality *Br Med J* **306** 749-752

Butterworth C, Hatch K, Macaluso M et al (1992a) Folate deficiency and cervical dysplasia *JAMA* **267** 528-533

Butterworth C, Hatch K, Soong S-J et al (1992b) Oral folic acid supplementation for cervical dysplasia: a clinical intervention trial *Am J Obstet Gynecol* **166** 803-809

Butterworth CE, Jr, Hatch KD, Gore H et al (1982) Improvement in cervical dysplasia associated with folic acid therapy in users of oral contraceptives *Am J Clin Nutr* **35** 73-82

Childers J, Chu J, Voigt L et al (1995) Chemoprevention of cervical cancer with folic acid: a Phase III Southwest Oncology Group Intergroup Study *Cancer Epidemiol Biomarkers Prev* **4** 155-159

Clemmensen J, Poulsen H (1971) Report of the Ministry of the Interior Document **3** Copenhagen

Correa P (1981) Epidemiological correlations between diet and cancer frequency *Cancer Res* **41** 3685-3690

Cuzick J, De Stavola B, Russell J, Thomas B (1990) Vitamin A, vitamin E and the risk of cervical intraepithelial neoplasia *Br J Cancer* **62** 651-652

Cuzick J, Terry G, Ho L et al (1992) Human papillomavirus type 16 DNA in cervical smears as predictor of high-grade cervical cancer *Lancet* **339** 959-960

deVet H, Knipschild P, Grol M, Schouten H, Sturmans F (1991) The role of beta-carotene and other dietary factors in the aetiology of cervical dysplasia: results of a case-control study *Intl J Epidemiol* **20** 603-610

deVilliers EM (1992) Labatory techniques in the investigation of human papillomavirus *Genitourin Med* **68** 50-54

Ebeling K, Nischan P, Schindler C (1987) Use of oral contraceptives and risk of invasive cervical cancer in previously screened women *Int J Cancer* **39** 427-430

Everson RB, Wehn CM, Erexson GI, MacGregor JT (1988) Association of marginal folate depletion with increased human chromosomal damage in

vivo: Demonstration by analysis of micronucleated erythrocytes *JNCI* **80** 525-529

Fishman J, Boyar RM, Hellman L (1975) Influence of body weight on oestradiol metabolism in young women *J Clin Endocrinol Metab* **41** 989-991

Forney JP, Milewich L, Chen GT et al (1981) Aromatization of androstenedione to oestrogen by human adipose tissue in vitro Correlation with adipose tissue mass, age and endometrial neoplasia *J Clin Endocrinol Metab* **53** 192-199

Frisch R, Wyshak G, Albright N et al (1987) Lower lifetime occurrence of breast cancer and cancers of the reproductive system among former athletes *Am J Clin Nutr* **45** 328

Frisch RE, Gotz Welbergen AV, McArthur JW et al (1981) Delayed menarche and amenorrhea of college athletes in relation to age of onset of training *JAMA* **246** 1559-63

Frisch RE, Wyshak G, Albright NL et al (1992) Former athletes have a lower lifetime occurrence of breast cancer and cancers of the reproductive system *Adv Exp Med Biol* **322** 29-39

Frisch RE, Wyshak G, Vincent L (1980) Delayed menarche and amenorrhea in ballet dancers *NEMJ* **303** 17-9

Gelboin H (1977) Cancer susceptibility and carcinogen metabolism *New Engl J Med* **297** 384-385

Grodin JM, Siiteri PK, Mac Donald PC (1973) Source of oestrogen production in postmenopausal women *J Clin Endocrinol Metab* **36** 207-214

Harper J, Levine AJ, Rosenthal D et al (1994) Erythrocyte folate levels, oral contraceptive use and abnormal cervical cytology *Acta Cytol* **38** 324-330

Harris R, Forman D, Doll R et al (1986) Cancer of the cervix uteri and vitamin A *Br J Cancer* **53** 653-659

Herrero R, Potischman N, Brinton LA et al (1991) A case-control study of nutrient status and invasive cervical cancer 1 Dietary indicators *Am J Epidemiol* **134** 1335-1346

Hirayama T (1979) Diet and cancer *Nutr Cancer* **1** 67-81

Holly E, Petrakis N, Friend N et al (1986) Mutagenic mucus in the cervix of smokers *JNCI* **76** 983-986

Knekt P (1988) Serum vitamin E level and risk of female cancers *Int J Epidemiol* **17** 281-286

Kolonel LN, Hankin JH, Lee L et al, (1981) Nutrient intakes in relation to cancer incidence in Hawaii

Br J Cancer **44** 322-339

Kunz BA, Haynes RH (1982) DNA repair and the genetic associations of thymidylate stress in yeast *Mutat Res* **93** 353-375

La Vecchia C, Decarli A, Fasoli M et al (1988) Dietary vitamin A and the risk of intraepithelial and invasive cervical neoplasia *Gynecol Oncol* **30** 187-195

La Vecchia C, Declari A, Gentile A et al (1984) "Pap" smear and the risk of cervical neoplasia: quantitative estimates from a case control study *Lancet* **2** 779-782

Lambert B, Brisson G, Bielmann P (1981) Plasma vitamin A and precancerous lesions of cervix uteri: A preliminary report *Gynecol Oncol* **11** 136-139

MacDonald H (1982) Smoking and oral contraception in cancer of the cervix *Lancet* **ii** 989

Marshall J, Graham X, Byers T et al (1983) Diet and smoking in the epidemiology of cancer of the cervix *JNCI* **70** 847-851

Meisels A, Begin R, Schneider V (1977) Dysplasias of uterine cervix: epidemiological aspects: role of age at first coitus and use of oral contraceptives *Cancer* **40** 3076-3081

Meyskens F, Surwit E, Moon T et al (1994) Enhancement of regression of cervical intraepithelial neoplasia II (Moderate dysplasia) with topically applied all-*trans*-retinoic acid: a randomized trial *JNCI* **86** 539-543

Moore JW, Clark GM, Bulbrook RD et al (1982) Serum concentrations of total and non-protein-bound oestradiol in patients with breast cancer and in normal controls *Int J Cancer* **29** 17-21

Munoz N, Bosch FX (1992) Review of case-control and cohort studies In: Munoz N, Bosch FX, Shaliku Z, Meheus A (eds) *The Epidemiology of Cervical Cancer and Human Papillomavirus* IARC Scientific Publication No **119** Lyon: International Agency for Research on Cancer 251-60

Munoz,N, Bosch FX, de Sanjose S et al (1992) The casual link between human papillomavirus and invasive cervical cancer: A population based case control study in Colombia and Spain *Int J Cancer* **52** 743-749

NAS (1982) *Diet, Nutrition and Cancer* Washington DC: National Academy Press

NAS (1989) *Diet and Health* Washington DC: National Academy Press

Nuovo GJ, Friedman D, Richart RM (1990) In situ hybridization analysis of human papillomavirus DNA segregation patterns in lesions of the female genital tract *Gynecol Oncol* **36** 256-62

Nuovo GJ, Richart RM (1990) Human papillomavirus DNA in situ hybridization may be used for the quality control of genital tract biopsies *Obstet Gynecol* **75** 223-6

Palan P, Mikhail M, Basu J, Romney S (1991) Plasma levels of antioxidant b-carotene and a-tocopherol in uterine cervix dysplasias and cancer *Nutr Cancer* **15** 13-20

Palan P, Romney S, Mikhail M, Basu J (1988) Decreased plasma b-carotene levels in women with uterine cervical dysplasias and cancer *JNCI* **80** 454-455

Petersen O (1956) Spontaneous course of cervical pre-cancerous conditions *Am J Obstet Gynecol* **72** 1063

Peto, R, Doll, R, Buckley, J and Sporn, M (1981) Can dietary -carotene materially reduce human cancer rates? *Nature* **290** 201-208

Pillai MR, Halabi S, McKalop A et al (1996) The presence of human papillomavirus- 16/-18 ET AL6, p53, and Bcl-2 protein in cervicovaginal smears from patients with invasive cervical cancer *Cancer Epi Biomarkers Prev* **5** 329-335

Potischman N, Brinton L Nutrition and cervical neoplasia *Cancer Causes Control* **7** 113-126

Potischman N, Brinton L, Laiming V et al (1991) A case-control study of serum folate levels and invasive cervical cancer *Cancer Res* **51** 4785-4789

Potischman N, Herrero R, Brinton L et al (1991) A case-control study of nutrient status and invasive cervical cancer *Am J Epidemiol* **134** 1347-1355

Potischman N, Hoover R, Brinton L et al (1994) The relations between cervical cancer and serological markers of nutritional status *Nutr Cancer* **21** 193-201

Romney, SL, Palan, PR, Duttagupta, C et al (1981) Retinoids and prevention of cervical dysplasias *Am J Obstet Gynecol* **141** 890

Schiffman M, Brinton L, Fraumeni J, Devesa S (1996) Cervical cancer In: Schottenfeld D, Fraumeni JF Jr, eds *Cancer Epidemiology* New York: Oxford University Press

Schiffman M, Haley N, Felton J, Anderws A et al (1987) Biochemical epidemiology of cervical neoplasia: measuring cigarette smoke constituents in the cervix *Cancer Res* **47** 3886-3888

Siiteri PK (1981) Extraglandular oestragen formation and serum binding of oestradiol: Relationship to cancer *J Endocrinol* **89** 119-129

Slattery M, Abbott T, Overall J et al (1990) Dietary vitamins A, C, and E and selenium as risk factors for cervical cancer *Epidemiol* **1** 8-15

Steinmetz K, Potter J (1991) A review of vegetables, fruit and cancer II: Mechanisms *Cancer Causes Control* **2** 427-442

VanEenwyk J, Daivs F, Colman N (1992) Folate, vitamin C, and cervical intraepithelial neoplasia *Cancer Epidemiol Biomarkers Prev* **1** 119-124

VanEenwyk J, Davis F, Bowen P (1991) Dietary and serum carotenoids and cervical intraepithelial neoplasia *Int J Cancer* **48** 34-38

Verreault R, Chu J, Mandelson M, Shy K (1989) A case-control study of diet and invasive cervical cancer *Int J Cancer* **43** 1050-54

Vessey M, Lawless M, McPherson K, Yeates D (1983) Neoplasia of the cervix uteri and contraception: a possible adverse association of the pill *Lancet* **2** 930-934

Wassertheil-Smoller S, Romney SL, Wylie-Rosett J et al (1981) Dietary vitamin C and uterine cervical dysplasia *Am J Epidemiol* **114** 714-24

Whitehead N, Reyner F, Lindenbaum J (1973) Megaloblastic changes in the cervical epithelium; association with oral contraceptive therapy and reversal with folic acid *JAMA* **226** 1421-4

WHO (1990) *Diet, Nutrition and the Prevention of Chronic Diseases Report of a WHO study group* Technical report series 797 Geneva: WHO

WHO (1997) *The World Health Report* Geneva: World Health Organization

Winkelstein W (1981) Smoking and cancer of the cervix *Br J Cancer* **43** 736-737

Wright N, Vessey P, Kenward B et al (1978) Neoplasia and dysplasia of the cervix uteri and contraception; a possible protective association of the diaphragm *Br J Cancer* **38** 273-279

Ziegler R, Brinton L, Hamman R et al (1990) Diet and the risk of invasive cervical cancer among white women in the United States *Am J Epidemiol* **132** 432-445

Ziegler RG, Jones CJ, Brinton LA et al (1991) Diet and risk of in situ cervical cancer among white women in the United States *Cancer Causes Control* **2** 17-29

4.15 PROSTATE

Abd Elghany N, Schumacher MC, Slattery ML et al (1990) Occupation, cadmium exposure, and prostate cancer *Epidemiol* **1** l07–l5

Albanes D, Blair A, Taylor PR (1989) Physical activity and risk of cancer in the NHANES I

population *Am J Public Health* **79** 744–50

Anwar K, Nakakuki K, Shiraishi T, (1992) Presence of ras oncogene mutations and human papilloma virus DNA in human prostate carcinoma *Cancer Res* **52** 599

Armstrong B, Doll R (1975) Environmental factors and cancer incidence and mortality in different countries, with special reference to dietary practices *Int J Cancer* **15** 617–31

Blair A, Fraumeni JF (1978) Geographic patterns of prostate cancer in the United States *JNCI* **6l** l379–84

Boyle P, Zaridze DG (1993) Risk factor for prostate and testicular cancer *Eur J Cancer* **29A** 1048-1055

Braun MM, Helzlsouer KJ, Hollis BW, Comstock GW (1995) Prostate cancer and prediagnostic levels of serum vitamin D metabolites *Cancer Causes Control* **6** 235–9

Breslow N, Chan CW, Dhom G et al (1977) Latent carcinoma of prostate at autopsy in seven areas *Int J Cancer* **20** 680–8

Brownson RC, Chang JC, Davis JR et al (1991) Physical activity on the job and cancer in Missouri *Am J Public Health* **81** 639–42

Cannon L, Bishop DT, Skolnick M et al (1982) Genetic epidemiology of prostate cancer in the Utah Mormon genealogy *Cancer Surv* **1** 47–69

Chaproniere DM, Webber MM Dexamethasone and retinyl acetate similarly inhibit and stimulate EGF-or insulin-induced proliferation of prostatic epithelium *J Cell Physiol* **l22** 249–53

Coetzee GA, Ross RK (1994) Re: Prostate cancer and the androgen receptor *JNCI* **86** 872–3

Corder EH, Guess HA, Hulka BS et al (1993)Vitamin D and prostate cancer: a prediagnostic study with stored sera *Cancer Epidemiol Biomarkers Prev* **2** 467–72

de Jong FH, Oishi K, Hayes RB et al (1991) Peripheral hormone levels in controls and patients with prostatic cancer or benign prostatic hyperplasia: results from the Dutch-Japanese case-control study *Cancer Res* **5l** 3445–50

Dong J-T, Lamb PW, Rinker-Schaeffer CW et al (1995) KAI1, a metastasis suppressor gene for prostate cancer on human chromosome 11p112 *Science* **268** 884–6

Feustel A, Wennrich R, Steiniger D et al (1982) Zinc and cadmium concentration in prostatic carcinoma of different histological grading in comparison to normal prostate tissue and adenofibromyomatosis (BPH) *Urol Res* **10** 30l–3

Fincham SM, Hill GB, Hanson J, Wijayasinghe C (1990) (179) Epidemiology of prostatic cancer A case-control study *Prostate***17** 189-206

Gann PH, Hennekens CH, Sacks FM et al (1994) Prospective study of plasma fatty acids and risk of prostate cancer *JNCI* **86** 281–6

Ghadirian P, Lacroix A, Maisonneuve P et al (1996) Nutritional factors and prostate cancer: a case-control study of French Canadians in Montreal, Canada *Cancer Causes Control* **7**(4): 428-36

Giovannucci E, Ascherio A, Rimm EB et al (1995) Intake of carotenoids and retinol in relation to risk of prostate cancer *JNCI* **87** 1767–76

Giovannucci E, Rimm EB, Colditz GA et al (1993) A prospective study of dietary fat and risk of prostate cancer *JNCI* **85** 1571–9

Graham S, Haughey B, Marshall J et al (1983) Diet in the epidemiology of carcinoma of the prostate gland *JNCI* **70** 687–92

Greenwald P, Damon A, Krimss V et al (1974) Physical and demographic features of men before developing cancer of the prostate *JNCI* **53** 341–6

Guileyardo JM, Johnson WD, Welsh RA et al (1980) Prevalence of latent prostate carcinoma in two US populations *JNCI* l **65** 311–16

Gunn SA, Gould TC, Anderson WAD (1964) Effects of zinc on cancerogenesis by cadmium *Proc Soc Exp Biol Med* **115** 653–7

Gunn SA, Gould TC, Anderson WAD (1967) Specific response of mesenchymal tissue in cancerogenesis by cadmium *Arch Pathol* **83** 493–9

Hackney AC, Sinning WE, Bruot BC (1988) Reproductive hormonal profiles of endurance-trained and untrained males *Med Sci Sports Exerc* **20** 60–65

Haddow A, Roe FJC, Dukes CE et al (1964) Cadmium neoplasia: Sarcomata at the site of injection of cadmium sulphate in rats and mice *Br J Cancer* l**8** 667–73

Hambidge KM, Casey CE, Krebs NF (1986) Zinc In: Mertz W, Underwood EJ (eds) *Trace Elements in Human and Animal Nutrition* Vol **2** 5th ed Orlando FL: Academic Press Inc

Hankin JH, Zhao LP, Wilkens LR et al (1992) Attributable risk of breast, prostate, and lung cancer due to saturated fat *Cancer Causes and Control* **3** 17-23

Hayes RB, Bogdanovicz JFAT, Schroeder FH et al (1988) Serum retinol and prostate cancer *Cancer* **62** 2021–6

Heilbrun LK, Nomura A, Stemmermann GN (1986)

Black tea consumption and cancer risk: a prospective study *Br J Cancer* **54** 677–83

Heshmat MY, Kaul L, Kovi J et al (1985) Nutrition and prostate cancer: a case-control study *Prostate* **6** 7–17

Hiatt RA, Armstrong MA, Klatsky AL, Sidney S (1994) Alcohol consumption, smoking, and other risk factors and prostate cancer in a large health plan cohort in California (United States*) Cancer Causes Control* **5** 66–72

Hill P, Wynder EL, Garbaczewski L et al (1979) Diet and urinary steroids in black and white North American men and black South African men *Cancer Res* **39** 5101–5

Hirayama T (1979) Epidemiology of prostate cancer with special reference to the role of diet *Natl Cancer Inst Monogr* **53** 149–55

Hirayama T (1986) A large scale cohort study on cancer risks by diet – with special reference to the risk reducing effects of green–yellow vegetable consumption In: Hayashi Y et al (eds) *Diet, Nutrition and Cancer* Tokyo: Japan Science Society Press 41–53

Hirayama T (1992) Life-style and cancer: from epidemiological evidence to public behavior change to mortality reduction of target cancers *NCI Monogr* **12** 65–74

Howell MA (1974) Factor analysis of international cancer mortality data and per capita food consumption *Br J Cancer* **29** 328–36

Hsing AW, Comstock GW (1993) Serological precursors of cancer: serum hormones and risk of subsequent prostate cancer *Cancer Epidemiol Biomarkers Prev* **2** 27–32

Hsing AW, Comstock GW, Abbey H, Polk BF (1990a) Serologic precursors of cancer Retinol, carotenoids, and tocopherol and risk of prostate cancer *JNCI* **82** 941–6

Hsing AW, McLaughlin JK, Schuman LM et al (1990b) Diet, tobacco use, and fatal prostate cancer: results from the Lutheran brotherhood cohort study *Cancer Res* **50** 6836–40

Hursting SD, Thornquist M, Henderson MM (1990) Types of dietary fat and the incidence of cancer at 5 sites *Prev Med*; **19**: 242-253

Ip C, Birt DF, Rogers AE, Mettlin C (eds) (1986) *Dietary Fat and Cancer Progress in Clinical and Biological Research* Vol **222** New York Alan R Liss Inc

Isaacs WB, Bova GS, Morton RA et al (1995) Molecular biology of prostate cancer progression *Cancer Surveys* **23** 19–32

Jacobsen BK, Bjelke E, Kvale G, Heuch I (1986) Coffee drinking, mortality, and cancer

incidence: Results from a Norwegian prospective study *JNCI* **76** 823–31

Kaul J, Heshmat MY, Kovi J et al (1987) The role of diet in prostate cancer *Nutr Cancer* **9** 123–8

Key TJ, Roe L, Thorogood M et al (1990) Testosterone, sex hormone-binding globulin, calculated free testosterone, and oestradiol in male vegans and omnivores *Br J Nutr* **64** 111–1

Kinlen LJ, Willows AN, Goldblatt P, Yudkin J (1988) Tea consumption and cancer *Br J Cancer* **58** 397-401

Knekt P, Aromaa A, Maatela J et al (1990) Serum vitamin A and subsequent risk of cancer: cancer incidence follow-up of the Finnish Mobile Clinic Health Examination Survey *Am J Epidemiol* **132** 857–70

Kolonel LN, Winkelstein W Jr (1977) Cadmium and prostatic carcinoma *Lancet* ii 566–7

Kolonel LN, Hankin JH, Lee J et al (1981) Nutrient intakes in relation to cancer incidence in Hawaii *Br J Cancer* **44** 332–9

Kolonel LN, Hankin JH, Yoshizawa CN (1987) Vitamin A and prostate cancer in elderly men: enhancement of risk *Cancer Res* **47** 2982–5

Kolonel LN, Nomura AM (1992) Dietary intervention trials on prostate cancer in *Macronutrients: investigating their role in cancer* Micozzi M, Moon T (eds) Marcel Dekker Inc New York 423-436

Kolonel LN, Nomura AM, Hinds MW et al (1983) Role of diet in cancer incidence in Hawaii *Cancer Res* **43** 2397s-2402s

Kolonel LN, Yoshizawa CN, Hankin JH (1988) Diet and prostatic cancer: a case-control study in Hawaii *Am J Epidemiol* **127** 999–1012

Konishi N, Enomoto T, Buzard G et al (1992) K-ras activation and ras p21 expression in latent prostatic carcinoma in Japanese men *Cancer* **69** 2293

Kroes R, Beems RB, Bosland MC et al (1986) Nutritional factors in lung, colon, and prostate carcinogenesis in animal models *Federation Proc* **45** 136–41

LaVecchia C, Negri E, Parazzini F et al (1990) Height and cancer risk in a network of case-control studies from northern Italy *Int J Cancer* **45** 275–9

Le Marchand L, Hankin JH, Kolonel LN, Wilkens LR (1991a) Vegetable and fruit consumption in relation to prostate cancer risk in Hawaii: A reevaluation of the effect of dietary beta-carotene *Am J Epidemiol* **133** 215–19

Le Marchand L, Kolonel LN, Wilkens LR et al (1994)

Animal fat consumption and prostate cancer: a prospective study in Hawaii *Epidemiol* **5** 276–82

Le Marchand, L, Kolonel LN, Yoshizawa CN (1991) Lifetime occupational physical activity and prostate cancer risk *Am J Epidemiol* **133** 103–11

Lee I-M, Paffenbarger RS, Hsieh C-C (1992) Physical activity and risk of prostatic cancer among college alumni *Am J Epidemiol* **135** 169–79

Lew EA, Garfinkel L (1979) Variations in mortality by weight among 750,000 men and women *J Chron Dis* **32** 563–76

Mettlin C, Selenskas S, Natarajan N et al (1989) Beta-carotene and animal fats and their relationship to prostate cancer risk *Cancer* **64** 605–I2

Middleton B, Byers T, Marshall J et al (1986) Dietary vitamin A and cancer—a multisite case-control study *Nutr Cancer* **8** I07–I6

Mills PK, Beeson WL, Phillips RL et al (1989) Cohort study of diet, lifestyle, and prostate cancer in Adventist men *Cancer* **64** 598–604

Monroe KR, Yu MC, Kolonel LN et al (1995) Evidence of an X-linked or recessive genetic component to prostate cancer risk *Nature Med* **1** 27–9

Myers RB, Srivastaava S, Oelschlager DK et al Expression of p160 erbB-3 and p185 erbB-2 in prostatic intraepithelial neoplasia and prostatic adenocarcinoma *JNCI* **86** 1140–5

NAS (1982) *Diet, Nutrition and Cancer* Washington DC: National Academy Press

NAS (1989) *Diet and Health* Washington DC National Academy Press

Nomura A, Heilbrum LK and Stemmermann GN (1986) Prospective study of coffee consumption and the risk of cancer *JNCI* **76** 587-590

Nomura A, Heilbrun LK, Stemmermann Gn (1985) Body mass index as a predictor of cancer in men *JNCI* **74** 319-323

Nomura AMY, Kolonel LN (1991) Prostate cancer: a current perspective *Am J Epidemiol* **I3** 200–27

Ohno Y, Yoshida O, Oishi K et al , (1988) Dietary beta-carotene and cancer of the prostate: a case-control study in Kyoto Japan *Cancer Res* **48** I33I–6

Paffenbarger RS, Jr, Hyde RT, Wing AL (1987) Physical activity and incidence of cancer in diverse populations: a preliminary report *Am J Clin Nutr* **45** 312–17

Parkin DM, Muir CS, Whelan SL et al (eds) (1992) Cancer Incidence in Five Continents Volume **VI**

IARC Sci Publications No 120 Lyon: International Agency for Research on Cancer

Pienta KJ, Esper PS (1993) Risk factors for prostate cancer *Ann Int Med* **118** 793–803

Polednak AP (1976) College athletics, body size and cancer mortality *Cancer* **38** 382–7

Pollard M, Luckert PH (1986) Promotional effects of testosterone and high fat diet on the development of autochthonous prostate cancer in rats *Cancer Lett* **32** 223–7

Potosky AL, Kessler L, Gridley G et al, (1990) Rise in prostatic cancer incidence associated with increased use of transurethral resection *JNCI*

Reichman ME, Hayes RB, Ziegler RG et al (1990) Serum vitamin A and subsequent development of prostate cancer in the First National Health and Nutrition Examination Survey Epidemiologic Follow-up Study *Cancer Res* **50** 23II–I5

Roe FJC, Dukes CE, Cameron KM et al (1964) Cadmium neoplasia: Testicular atrophy and Leydig cell hyperplasia and neoplasia in rats and mice following the subcutaneous injection of cadmium salts *Br J Cancer* **I8** 674–8I

Rohan TE, Howe GR, Burch JD, Jain M (1995) Dietary factors and risk of prostate cancer: a case-control study in Ontario Canada *Cancer Causes Control* **6** 145–54

Rose DP, Boyar AP, Wynder EL (1986) International comparisons of mortality rates for cancer of the breast, ovary, prostate, and colon, and per capita food consumption *Cancer* **58** 2363-71

Rose RP, Connolly JM (1992) Dietary fat, fatty acids and prostate cancer *Lipids* **27** 798-790

Ross RK, Henderson BE (1995) Do diet and androgens alter prostate cancer risk via a common etiologic pathway? *JNCI* **86** 252–4

Ross RK, Bernstein L, Lobo RA et al (1992) 5-alpha-reductase activity and risk of prostate cancer among Japanese and USA white and black males *Lancet* **339** 887–9

Ross RK, Shimizu H, Paganini-Hill A et al (1987) Case-control studies of prostate cancer in blacks and whites in Southern California *JNCI* **78** 869–74

Schrauzer GN, White DA, Schneider CJ (1977) Cancer mortality studies - III: Statistical associations with dietary selenium intakes *Bioinorg Chem* **7** 23-34

Schuman LM, Mandel JS, Radke A et al (1982) Some selected features of the epidemiology of prostatic cancer: Minneapolis-St Paul, Minnesota case-control study, I976–I979 In: Magnus K (ed) *Trends in Cancer Incidence:*

Causes and Implications' Washington: Hemisphere Publishing Corp 345–54

Schwartz GG, Hill CC, Oeler TA et al (1995) 1,25-Dihydroxy-16-ene-23-yne vitamin D^3 and prostate cancer cell proliferation *in vivo Urology* **46** 365–9

Severson RK, Grove JS, Nomura AMY et al (1988) Body mass and prostatic cancer: a prospective study *Br Med J* **297** 713–15

Severson RK, Nomura AMY, Grove JS et al (1989a) A prospective analysis of physical activity and cancer *Am J Epidemiol* **130** 522–9

Severson RK, Nomura AMY, Grove JS et al (1989b) A prospective study of demographics, diet and prostate cancer among men of Japanese ancestry in Hawaii *Cancer Res* **49** I857–60

Shibata A, Paganini-Hill A, Ross RK, Henderson BE (1992) Intake of vegetables, fruits, beta-carotene, vitamin C and vitamin supplements and cancer incidence among the elderly: a prospective study *Br J Cancer* **66** 673–9

Slattery ML, Schumacher MC, West DW et all, (1990) Food-consumption trends between adolescent and adult years and subsequent risk of prostate cancer *Am J Clin Nutr* **52** 752–7

Slattery ML, West DW (1993) Smoking, alcohol, coffee, tea, caffeine, and theobromine: risk of prostate cancer in Utah (United States) *Cancer Causes Control* **4** 559-563

Slawin K, Kadom D, Park SH et al (1993) Dietary fenretinide, a synthetic retinoid, decreases the tumour incidence and the tumour mass of ras + myc-induced carcinomas in the mouse prostate reconstitution model system *Cancer Res* **53** 4461–5

Snowdon DA, Phillips RL, Choi W (1984) Diet, obesity, and risk of fatal prostate cancer *Am J Epidemiol* **I20** 244–50

Steinberg GD, Carter BS, Beaty TH et al, (1990) Family history and the risk of prostate cancer *Prostate* **17** 337–47

Strauss RH, Lanese RR, Malarkey WB (1985) Weight loss in amateur wrestlers and its effect on serum testosterone levels *JAMA* **254** 3337–8

Talamini R, Franceschi S, La Vecchia C et al (1992) Diet and prostatic cancer: a case-control study in Northern Italy *Nutr Cancer* **I18** 277–86

Talamini R, La Vecchia C, Decarli A et al (1986) Nutrition, social factors and prostatic cancer in a Northern Italian population *Br J Cancer* **53** 8I7–2I

Tavani A, Negri E, Franceschi S et al (1994) Alcohol consumption and risk of prostate cancer *Nutr Cancer* **2I** 25–3I

Thompson MM, Garland C, Barrett-Connor E et al (1989) Heart disease risk factors, diabetes and prostatic cancer in an adult community *Am J Epidemiol* **129** 511–17

Thune I, Lund E (1994) Physical activity and the risk of prostate and testicular cancer: a cohort study of 53,000 Norwegian men *Cancer Causes Control* **5** 549–56

Tibblin G, Eriksson M, Cnattingius S et al (1995) High birthweight as a predictor of prostate cancer risk *Epidemiol* **6** 423–4

Tulinius H, Sigfusson N, Sigvaldason H, Day NE (1985) Can anthropometric and biochemical measurements illustrate the diet-cancer connection? *Näringsforskning;* **29**: 17-22

Walker ARP, Walker BF, Tsotetsi NG et al (1992) Case-control study of prostate cancer in black patients in Soweto South Africa *Br J Cancer* **65** 438–4l

Wang Y, Corr JG, Thaler HT et al (1995) Decreased growth of established human prostate LNCaP tumors in nude mice fed a low-fat diet *JNCI* **87** 1456–62

Waterhouse J, Muir C, Correa P (1976) Cancer incidence in five continents Lyon: International Agency for Research on Cancer

West DW, Slattery ML, Robison LM et al (1991) Adult dietary intake and prostate cancer risk in Utah: a case-control study with special reference to aggressive tumors *Cancer Causes Control* **2** 85–94

Wheeler GD, Wall SR, Belcastro AN et al (1984) Reduced serum testosterone and prolactin levels in male distance runners *JAMA* **252** 514–16

Whelan SL, Parkin DM, Masuyer E (eds) (1990) Patterns of Cancer in Five Continents IARC Sci Publications No **102** Lyon: International Agency for Research on Cancer

Whittemore AS, Keller JB, Betensky R (1991) Low-grade, latent prostate cancer volume: predictor of clinical cancer incidence? *JNCI;* **83** 1231–5

Whittemore AS, Kolonel LN, Wu AH et al (1995) Prostate cancer in relation to diet, physical activity and body size in blacks, whites and Asians in the USA and Canada *JNCI* **87** 652–61

Whittemore AS, Wu AH, Kolonel LN et al (1995) Family history and prostate cancer risk in black, white and Asian men in the United States and Canada *Am J Epidemiol* **141** 732–40

WHO (1997) *The World Health Report* Geneva: World Health Organization

Woolf CM (1960) An investigation of the familial aspects of carcinoma of the prostate *Cancer* **3** 739–44

Wynder EL, Mabuchi K, Whitmore WF Jr (1971) Epidemiology of cancer of the prostate *Cancer* **28** 344–60

Yatani R, Chigusa I, Akasaki K et al (1982) Geographic pathology of latent prostatic carcinoma *Int J Cancer* **29** 6ll–l6

Yu H, Harris RE, Wynder EL (1988) Case-control study of prostate cancer and socioeconomic factors *Prostate* **13** 317–25

4.16 THYROID

Aaseth J, Frey H, Glattre E, Norhem G et al (1990) Selenium concentrations in human thyroid gland *Biological Trace Element Research* **24** 147-152

Coindet JF (1821) Nouvelle recherches sur l'effets de d'iodide et sur les precautions à suivre dans le traitement du goitre par le nouveau remede *Bibl Universelle Sci Arts, Geneve* **16** 320

Connolly RJ, Vidor GI and Stewart JC (1970) An increase in thyrotoxicosis in an endemic goitre area after iodization of bread *Lancet* **1** 500 (41628)

Costa A, Ferraris M, Buccini G, Ferrara C, Marocco F (1966) The relationship between endemic goitre and thyroid cancer In: *Tumor of the Thyroid Gland* Appaiz A (ed)) Basel and New York: Karger 197-214

Ermans, AM Mbulamoko, NM, Delange, F, Ahluwalia, R (1980) Role of cassava in the etiology of endemic goitre and cretinism Ottawa, Ontario: IDRC

Franceschi S, Fassina A, Talamini R et al (1989) Risk factors for thyroid cancer in northern Italy *Int J Epidemiol* **18** 578-584

Franceschi S, Levi F, Negri E, Fassina A, La Vecchia C (1991) Diet and thyroid cancer: A pooled analysis of four European case-control studies *Int J Cancer* **48** 395-398

Franceschi S, Talamini R, Fassina A, Bidoll E (1990) Diet and epithelia cancer of the thyroid gland *Tumori* **76** 331-338

Geneva: World Health Organization

Glattre E, Haldorsen T, Berg JP, Stensvold I, Solvoll K (1993) Norwegian case-control study testing the hypothesis that seafood increases the risk of thyroid cancer *Cancer Causes Control* **4** 11-16

Glattre E, Thomassen Y, Thoresen SO et al (1989) Prediagnostic serum selenium in a case-control study of thyroid cancer *Int J Epidemiol* **18** 45-49

Goodman MT, Kolonel LN, Wilkens LR (1992) The association of body size, reproductive factors and thyroid cancer *Br J Cancer* **66** 1180-1184

Goodman TM, Yoshizawa CN, Kolonel L (1988) Descriptive epidemiology of thyroid cancer in Hawaii *Cancer* **61** 1272-1281

Henderson BE, Ross RK, Pike MC, Casagrande JT (1982) Endogenous hormones as a major factor in human cancer *Cancer Res* **42** 3232-3239 August

Hetzel BS (1994) SOS for a Billion- The Nature and Magnitude of the Iodine Deficiency Disorders In: *SOS for a Billion: The Conquest of Iodine Deficiency Disorders* Hetzel BS and Pandav CS (eds) Oxford University Press pp3-26

Hill RN, Erdreich LS, Paynter OE et al (1989) Thyroid follicular cell carcinogenesis *Fund Appl Toxicolo* **12** 629-697

Hirohata T (1976) Radiation carcinogenesis *Semin Oncol* **3** 25-34

ICCIDD (1993) *Iodine Deficiency Persists in Europe: Review of the Brussels Conference* ICCIDD Newsletter **9** Feb

Ingenbleek Y, Luypaert B, De Nayer P (1980) Nutritional status and endemic goitre *Lancet* **i** 388-91

Kanno J, Onodera H, Furuta K, Maekawa A, Kasuga T and Hayashi Y (1992) Tumor promoting effects of both iodine deficiency and iodine excess in the rat thyroid *Toxicol Path* **20** 227-235

Knizhnikov VA, Komleva VA, Shandala NK (1993) Study of the anticarcinogenic characteristics of the trace element, selenium, sanitary-hygienic experiment *Gig Sanit* **7** 54-7

Kok FJ, De Bruijn AM, Hofman A et al (1987) Is serum selenium a risk factor for cancer in men only? *Am J Epidemiol* **125** 12-16

Kolonel LN, Hankin JH, Wilkens LR et al (1990) An epidemiologic study of thyroid cancer in Hawaii *Cancer Causes Control* **1** 223-234

Langer P, Kokoesova H, Gschwendtova K (1976) Acute redistribution of thyroxine after the administration of univalent anions, salicylate, theophylline and barbiturates in rats *Acta Endocrinal* **81** 516-524

McClain RM (1992) Thyroid neoplasia: nongenotoxic mechanisms *Toxicol Lett* **64/65** 397-408

McTieran A, Weiss NS, Daling JR (1987) Incidence of Thyroid Cancer in Women in Relation to Known or suspected Risk Factors for Breast Cancer *Cancer Res* **47**(1) 292-295

Muir C, Waterhouse J, Mack T, Powell J, Whelan S (eds) (1987) *Cancer Incidence in Five Continents*

Vol **V** IARC Scientific Publication No 88 Lyon: International Agency for Research on Cancer

NAS (1982) *Diet, Nutrition and Cancer* Washington DC: National Academy Press

NAS (1989) *Diet and Health* Washington DC National Academy Press

Omran M, Ahmed ME (1993) Carcinoma of the thyroid in Khartoum *E African Med J* **70** March

Plamer S, Bakshi K (1983) Diet, nutrition, and cancer: interim dietary guidelines *JNCI* **70** 1151-1170

Preston-Martin S, Jin F, Duda MJ, Mack WJ (1993) A case-control study of thyroid cancer in women under age 55 in Shanghai (People's Republic of China) *Cancer Causes Control* **4** 431-440

Purves HD, Griesback WE (1947) Studies on experimental goitre VIII: Thyroid tumours in rats treated with thiourea *Br J Exp Pathol* **28** 46-51

Robbins SL, Cotram RS, Kumar V (1984) Thyroid gland *Pathologic basis of disease* pp 1201-1225 Philadelphia: WB Saunders

Ron E, Kleinerman RA, Boice JD Jr et al (1987) A population-based case-control study of thyroid cancer *JNCI* **79** 1-12

Salonen JJ, Alfthan G, Huttanen JK, Paska, P (1984) Association between serum selenium and the risk of cancer *AmJ Epidemiol* **125** 12-16

Vigneri R (1988) Studies on the goitre endemia in Sicily *J Endocrinol Invest* **11** 831

Ward JM, Ohshima M (1986) The role of iodine in carcinogenesis *Adv Exp Med Biol* **206** 529-542

WHO (1988) *Guidelines for iodine prophylaxis following nuclear accidents*

WHO (1993) *Trends in Cancer Incidence and Mortality* Chapter 25: Thyroid IARC Scientific Publications No 121 Lyon: International Agency for Research on Cancer pp609-640

WHO (1997) World Health Organization *The World Health Report* WHO: Geneva

Wigren G, Hatschek T, Axelson O (1992) Determinants of papillary cancer of the thyroid *Am J Epidemiol* **138** 482-491

Wills, JH (1966) Goitrogens in food In: *Toxicants occurring naturally in foods* Washington DC: National Research Council pp 3-17

Wolff J (1969) Iodide goitre and the pharmacological effects of excess iodide *Am J Med* **47** 101-124

World Bank (1993) *World Development Report 1993 Investing in Health: World Development Indicators* Oxford University Press Tables B2 and B3 pp 216-219 (41648)

Wynford-Thomas D (1994) Thyroid Cancer In *Cancer: A Molecular Approach* Lemoine N, Neoptolemos J, Cooke T (eds) Oxford: Blackwell Scientific Publications

Yamashita H, Noguchi S, Murakami N et al , (1990) Effects of dietary iodine on chemical induction of thyroid carcinoma *Acta Pathologica Japonica* 705-712

4.17 KIDNEY

Armstrong B, Doll R (1975) Environmental factors and cancer incidence and mortality in different countries, with special reference to dietary practices *Int J Cancer* **15** 617-631

Armstrong B, Garrod A, Doll R (1976) A retrospective study of renal cancer with special reference to coffee and animal protein consumption *Br J Cancer* **33** 127-136

Birt DF, Pour PM (1983) Increased tumorigenesis induced by N-nitrosobis(2-oxopropyl)amine in Syrian golden hamsters fed high-fat diets *JNCI* **70** 1135-1138

Carro-Ciampi G (1978) Phenacetin abuse: a review *Toxicology* **10** 311-339

Chen LH, Boissonneault GA, Glauert HP (1988) Vitamin C, vitamin E and cancer (review) *Anticancer Research* **8** 739-748

Clinton SK, Imrey PB, Mangian HJ et al (1992) The combined effects of dietary fat, protein, and energy intake on azoxymethane-induced intestinal and renal carcinogenesis *Cancer Res* **52** 857-865

Coleman MP, Estève J, Damieki P et al (1993) *Trends in cancer incidence and mortality* IARC Sci Publ, No 121 Lyon: International Agency for Research on Cancer

Dayal H, Kinman J (1983) Epidemiology of kidney cancer *Semin Oncol* **10** 366-377

Heilbrun LK, Nomura A, Stemmerman GN (1986) Black tea consumption and cancer risk: a prospective study *Br J Cancer* **54** 677-683

Hinson JA (1983) Reactive metabolites of phenacetin and acetaminophen: a review *Environ Hlth Persp* **50** 37-49

Hirayama T (1990) *Life-style and mortality* Karger: Basel

IARC (1986) *IARC monographs on the evaluation of carcinogenic risk of chemicals to men Vol 38 Tobacco smoking* Lyon: International Agency for Research on Cancer

Jacobsen BK, Bjelke E, KvÜle G, Heuch I, (1986) Coffee drinking, mortality and cancer incidence: Results from a Norwegian Prospective Study *JNCI* **76** 823-831

Johansson SL (1981) Carcinogenicity of analgesics: long-term treatment of Sprague-Dawley rats with phenacetin, phenazone, caffeine and paracetamol *Int J Cancer* **27** 521-52

Kreiger N, Marrett LD, Dodds L, Hilditch S, Darlington GA (1993) Risk factors for renal cell carcinoma: results of a population-based case-control study *Cancer Causes Control* **4** 101-110

Liehr JG, Roy D,Gladek A (1989) Mechanism of inhibition of estrogen-induced renal carcinogenesis in male Syrian hamsters by vitamin C *Carcinogenesis* **10** 1983-1988

Maclure M, Willett W (1990) A case-control study of diet and risk of renal adenocarcinoma *Epidemiology* **1** 430-440

McCredie M, Stewart JH (1992) Risk factors for kidney cancer in New South Wales, Australia II Urologic disease, hypertension, obesity, and hormonal factors *Cancer Causes Control* **3** 323-331

McCredie M, Ford JM, Stewart JH (1988) Risk factors for cancer of the renal parenchyma *Int J Cancer* **42** 13-16

McCredie M, Stewart JH, Day NE (1993) Different roles for phenacetin and paracetamol in cancer of the kidney and renal pelvis *Int J Cancer* **53** 245-249

McLaughlin JK, Gao YT, Gao RN et al (1992) Risk factors for renal-cell cancer in Shanghai, China *Int J Cancer* **52** 562-565

McLaughlin JK, Mandel JS, Blot WJ et al (1984) A population-based case-control study of renal cell carcinoma *JNCI* **72** 275-284

McLean AE, Magee PN (1970) Increased renal carcinogenesis by dimethylnitrosamine in protein deficient rats *Br J Exp Pathol* **51** 587-590

Mellemgaard A, Engholm G, McLaughlin JK, Olsen JH (1994) Risk factors for renal-cell carcinoma in Denmark III Role of weight, physical activity and reproductive factors *Int J Cancer* **56** 66-71

Mellemgaard A, Moller H, Olsen JH, Jensen OM (1991) Increased risk of renal cell carcinoma among obese women *JNCI* **83** 1581–1582

NAS (1982) *Diet, Nutrition and Cancer* Washington DC: National Academy Press

NAS (1989) *Diet and Health* Washington DC National Academy Press

Parkin DM, Muir CS, Whelan SL et al (eds) (1992)

Cancer incidence in five continents Vol 6 Lyon: Internatioanl Agency for Research on Cancer

Prescott LF (1982) Analgesic nephropathy: a reassessment of the role of phenacetin and other analgesics *Drugs* **23** 75-149

Reddy BS, Hirota N, Katayama S (1982) Effect of dietary sodium ascorbate on 1,2-dimethylhydrazine- or methylnitrosourea-induced colon carcinogenesis *Carcinogenesis* **3** 1097-1099

Rimm EB, Stampfer MJ, Giovannucci E et al (1995) Body size and fat distribution as predictors of coronary heart disease among middle-aged and older US men *Am J Epidemiol* **141** 1117–1127

Shinohara Y, Aral M, Hirao K et al (1976) Combination effect of Citrinin and other chemicals on rat kidney tumorigenesis *Jpn J Cancer Res* **67** 147-155

Talamini R, Baron AE, Barra S et al (1990) A case-control study of risk factor for renal cell cancer in northern Italy *Cancer Causes Control* **1** 125-131

US Surgeon General (1982) *The health consequences of smoking Cancer* US Department of Health and Human Services, Public Health Service: Rockville, Maryland

Vaught JB, McGarvey PB, Lee MS et al (1981) Activation of N-hydroxyphenacetin to mutagenic and nucleic acid-binding metabolites by acyltransfer, deacylation, and sulfate conjugation *Cancer Res* **41** 3424-3429

Veronese ME, McLean S, D'Souza CA, Davies DW (1985) Formation of reactive metabolites of phenacetin in humans and rats *Xenobiotica* **15** 929-940

WHO (1997) *The World Health Report* Geneva: World Health Organization

Wynder E, Mabuchi K and Whitmore W Jr (1974) Epidemiology of adenocarcinoma of the kidney *JNCI* **53** 1619-1634

Yu MC, Mack TM, Hanisch R et al (1986) Cigarette smoking, obesity, diuretic use, and coffee consumption as risk factors for renal cell carcinoma *JNCI* **77** 351-356

4.18 BLADDER

Akdas A, Kirkali Z, Bilir N (1990) Epidemiological case-control on the etiology of bladder cancer in Turkey *Eur Urol* **17** 23-26

Armstrong B, Doll R (1975) Environmental factors and cancer incidence and mortality in different countries, with special reference to dietary practice *Int J Cancer* **15** 617–631

Badawi AF, Mostafa MH, Probert A, O'Connor PJ (1995) Role of schistosomiasis in human bladder cancer: evidence of association, aetiological factors, and basic mechanisms of carcinogenesis *Eur J Cancer Prev* **4** 45-5

Bean JA, Isacson P, Hausler WJ et al (1982) Drinking water and cancer incidence in Iowa I Trends and incidence by source of drinking water and size of municipality *Am J Epidemiol* **116** 912-923

Bravo MP, Del Rey-Calero J, Conde M (1987) Risk factors of bladder cancer in Spain *Neoplasma* **34** 633-637

Brenniman GR, Vasilomanolakis-Lagos J, Amsel J et al (1980) Case-control study of cancer deaths in Illinois communities served by chlorinated or nonchlorinated water In: Jolley RL, Brungs WA, Cumming RB et al (eds) *Water Chlorination: Environmental Impact and Health Effects*, **3** Ann Arbor, MI, Ann Arbor Science

Bross ID, Tidings J (1973) Another look at coffee drinking and cancer of the urinary bladder *Prev Med* **2** 445-451

Brownson RC, Chang JC, Davis JR (1987) Occupation, smoking, and alcohol in the epidemiology of bladder cancer *Am J Public Health* **77** 1298-1300

Bruemmer B, White-E, Vaughan TL et al (1996) Nutrient intake in relation to bladder cancer among middle-aged men and women *Am J Epidemiol* **144**485-95

Butler MA, Iwasaki M, Guengerich FP, Kadlubar FF (1989) Human cytochrome P-450PA (P-450IA2), the phenacetin O-deethylase, is primarily responsible for the hepatic 3-demethylation of caffeine and N-oxidation of carcinogenic arylamines *Proc Natl Acad Sci USA* **86** 7696-7700

Cantor KP, Hoover R, Hartge P et al (1987) Bladder cancer, drinking water source, and tap water consumption: a case-control study *JNCI* **79** 1269-1279

Cantor KP, Hoover R, Hartge P et al (1987) Bladder cancer, drinking water source, and tap water consumption: a case-control study *JNCI* **79** 1269-1279

Cantor KP, Hoover R, Mason TJ et al (1978) Associations of cancer mortality with halomethanes in drinking water *JNCI* **61** 979-985

Cartwright RA, Adib R, Glashan R, Grey BK (1981) The epidemiology of bladder cancer in West Yorkshire: a preliminary report on non-occupational aetiologies *Carcinogenesis* **2** 343-347

Chyou PH, Nomura AMY, Stemmermann GN (1993) A prospective study of diet, smoking, and lower urinary tract cancer *Ann Epidemiol* **3** 211-216

Ciccone G, Vineis P (1988) Coffee drinking and bladder cancer *Cancer Lett* **41** 45-52

Claude J, Kunze E, Frentzel-Beyme R et al (1986) Life-style and occupational risk factors in cancer of the lower urinary tract *Am J Epidemiol* **124** 578-589

Clavel J, Cordier S (1990) Coffee consumption and bladder cancer risk *Int J Cancer* **47** 207-212

Cohen SM, Ellwein LB, Okamura T et al (1991) Comparative bladder tumor promoting activity of sodium saccharin, sodium ascorbate, related acids, and calcium salts in rats *Cancer Res* **51** 1766-1777

Cohen SM, Ellwein,LB (1994) Cell proliferation in carcinogenesis *Science* **249** 1007-1011

Cole P (1971) Coffee-drinking and cancer of the lower urinary tract *Lancet* **ii** 1335-1337

Coleman MP, Esteve J, Damieki P et al (1993) *Trends in cancer incidence and mortality* IARC Sci Publ, No 121 Lyon: International Agency for Research on Cancer

Connolly JG, Rider WD, Rosenbaum L, Chapman J-A (1978) Relation between the use of artificial sweeteners and bladder cancer *Can Med Assoc J* **119** 408

D'Avanzo B, La Vecchia C, Franceschi S et al (1992) Coffee consumption and bladder cancer risk *Eur J Cancer* **28A** 1480-1484

De Stefani E, Correa P, Fierro L, Fontham E, Chen V, Zavala D (1991) Black tobacco, mate, and bladder cancer A case-control study from Uruguay *Cancer* **67** 536-40

DeRouen TA, Tiem JE (1977) Relationships between cancer mortality in Louisiana drinking-water source and other possible causative agents In Hiatt HH, Watson JD, Winsten JA (eds) *Origins of human cancer,* Book A, *Incidence of cancer in humans,* Cold Spring Harbor, NY, CSH Press

Dunham LJ, Rabson AS, Stewart HL et al (1968) Rates, interview, and pathology study of cancer of the urinary bladder in New Orleans, Louisiana *JNCI* **41**683-709

Frith CH, Rule J, Kodell RL (1980) The effect of ascorbic acid on the induction of urothelial lesions in mice by acetylamino-fluorene *Toxicol Lett* **6**:309

Fujiki H, Yoshizawa S, Horiuchi T et al (1992) Anticarcinogenic effects of (-)-epigallocatechin gallate *Prev Med* **21** 503-509

Fukushima S, Imaida K, Sakata T et al (1983) Promoting effects of sodium L-ascorbate on two-stage urinary bladder carcinogenesis in rats *Cancer Res* **43** 4454-4457

Fukushima S, Kurata Y, Shibata MA et al (1984) Promotion by ascorbic acid sodium erythrobate and ethoxyquin of neoplastic lesions in rats initiated with N-butyl-N-94-hydroxybutyl)-nitrosamine *Cancer Lett* **23** 29-37

Fukushima S, Shibata M, Shirai T et al (1986) Roles of urinary sodium ion concentration and pH in promotion by ascorbic acid of urinary bladder carcinogenesis in rats *Cancer Res* **46** 1623-1626

Fukushima S, Shibata M-A, Shirai T, Kurata Y, Tamano S, Imaida K (1987) Promotion by L-ascorbic acid of urinary bladder carcinogenesis in rats under conditions of increased urinary K ion concentration and pH *Cancer Res* **47** 4821-4824

Fukushima S, Thamavit W, Kurata Y, Ito N (1986) Sodium citrate: A promoter of bladder carcinogenesis *Jpn J Cancer Res* **77** 1-4

Gonzalez CA, Lopez-Abente G, Errezola M et al (1985) Occupation, tobacco use, coffee, and bladder cancer in the country of Mataro (Spain) *Cancer* **55** 2031-2034

Gottlieb MS, Carr JK, Clarkson JR (1982) Drinking water and cancer in Louisiana A retrospective mortality study *Am J Epidemiol* **116** 652-667

Hartge P, Hoover R, West DW, Lyon JL (1983) Coffee drinking and risk of bladder cancer *JNCI* **70** 1021-1026

Helzlsouer KJ, Comstock GW, Morris JS (1989) Selenium, lycopene, a-tocopherol, ß-carotene, retinol, and subsequent bladder cancer *Cancer Res* **49** 6144-6148

Hirayama T (1990) *Life-style and mortality* Karger Basel

Hoover RM, Strasser PH Artificial sweeteners and human bladder cancer Preliminary results *Lancet* **i** 837-840

Howe GR, Burch JD, Miller AB et al (1980) Tobacco use, occupation, coffee, various nutrients, and bladder cancer *JNCI* **64** 701-713

IARC (1980) Working Group An evaluation of chemicals and industrial processes associated with cancer in humans based on human and animal data IARC Monographs Vols 1-20 *Cancer Res* **40** 1-12

IARC (1986) *IARC monographs on the evaluation of carcinogenic risk of chemicals to men Vol 38 Tobacco smoking* Lyon: International Agency for Research on Cancer

IARC (1987) *Monographs on the evaluation of carcinogenic risks to humans Suppl 7 Overall evaluations of carcinogenic risks to humans: an updating of IARC monographs Vols1-42* Lyon: International Agency for Research on Cancer 83-87; 101-105; 152-154; 322-326; 350-354

IARC (1991) *IARC monographs on the evaluation of carcinogenic risks to humans Vol 51 Coffee, tea, mate, methylxanthines and methylglyoxal* IARC: Lyon

Isacson P, Bean JA, Lynch C (1983) Relationship of cancer incidence rates in Iowa municipalities to chlorination status of drinking water In: Jolley RL, Brungs WA, Cotruvo JA et al (eds) *Water Chlorination: Environmental Impact and Health Effects*, **4** Ann Arbor, MI, Ann Arbor Science

Jacobsen BK, Bjelke E, Kvale G, Heuch I (1986) Coffee drinking, mortality, and cancer incidence: results from a Norwegian prospective study *JNCI* **76** 823-831

Jensen OM, Kamby C (1982) Intra-uterine exposure to saccharine and risk of bladder cancer in man *Int J Caner* **29** 507-509

Jensen OM, Wahrendorf J, Knudsen JB, Sorenson BL (1986) The Copenhagen case-control study of bladder cancer **II** The effect of coffee and other beverages *Int J Cancer* **37** 651-657

Kabat GC, Dieck GS, Wynder EL (1986) Bladder cancer in nonsmokers *Cancer* **57** 362-367

Kadlubar FF (1994) Biochemical individuality and its implications for drug and carcinogen metabolism: recent insights from acetyltransferase and cytochrome P4501A2 phenotyping and genotyping in humans *Drug Metab Rev* **26** 37-46

Kadlubar FF, Talaska G, Lang NP et al (1988) *Assessment of exposure and susceptibility to aromatic amine carcinogens In Methods for Detecting DNA Damaging Agents in Humans: Applications in Cancer Epidemiology and Prevention* (Ed H Bartsch, K Hemminki, IK O'Neill) IARC Sci Pub No **89** Lyon: International Agency for Research on Cancer pp166-174

Kessler II, Clark JP (1978) Saccharin, cyclamate, and human bladder cancer No evidence of an association *JAMA* **240** 349-355

Kinlen LJ, Willows AN, Goldblatt P, Yudkin J (1998) Tea consumption and cancer *Br J Cancer* **58** 397-401

Kitano M, Mori S, Chen T, Murai T and Fukushima S (1995) Lack of promoting effects of -linoleic, linoleic or palmitic acid on urinary bladder carcinogenesis in rats *Jpn J Cancer Res* **86** 530-534

Knekt P, Aromaa A, Maatela J et al (1990) Serum vitamin A and subsequent risk of cancer: cancer incidence follow-up of the Finnish Mobile Clinic Health Examination Survey *Am J Epidemiol* **132** 857-70

Knekt P, Aromaa A, Maatela J, Ritva-Kaarina A et al (1991) Vitamin E and cancer prevention *Am J Clin Nutr* **53** 283S-286S

Kunze E, Chang Claude J, Frentzel Beyme R (1992): Life style and occupational risk factors for bladder cancer in Germany A case-control study *Cancer* **69**1776-1790

Kuzma RJ, Kuzma CM, Buncher CR (1977) Ohio drinking water source and cancer rates *Am J Pub Health* **67** 725-729

La Vecchia C, Negri E, Decarli A et al (1989) Dietary factors in the risk of bladder cancer *Nutr Cancer* **12** 93-101

La Vecchia C, Negri E, Franceschi S (1992) Tea consumption and cancer risk *Nutr Cancer* **17** 27-31

Marrett LD, Walter SD, Meigs JW (1983) Coffee drinking and bladder cancer in Connecticut *Am J Epidemiol* **117** 113-127

Matanoski GM, Elliott EA (1981) Bladder cancer epidemiology *Epidemiol Rev* **3** 203-229

Mettlin C, Graham S (1979) Dietary risk factors in human bladder cancer *Am J Epidemiol* **110** 255-263

Miller CT, Neutel CI, Nair RC et al (1978) Relative importance of risk factors in bladder carcinogenesis *J Chronic Dis* **31** 51-56

Mills PK, Beeson WL, Phillips RL, Fraser GE (1991) Bladder cancer in a low risk population: results from the Adventist health study *Am J Epidemiol* **133** 230-239

Moller-Jensen O, Knudsen JB, Sorensen BL et al (1983) Artificial sweeteners and absence of bladder cancer risk in Copenhagen *Int J Cancer* **32** 577-82

Momas I, Daures JP, Festy B et al (1994) Relative importance of risk factors in bladder carcinogenesis: some new results about Mediterranean habits *Cancer Causes Control* **5** 326-332

Mommsen S, Aagaard J, Sell A (1982) An epidemiological case-control study of bladder cancer in males from a predominantly rural district *Eur J Cancer Clin Oncol* **18** 1205-1210

Mommsen S, Aagaard J, Sell A (1983) A case-control study of female bladder cancer *Eur J Cancer Clin Oncol* **19** 725-729

Moon RC, Mehta RG (1986) Anticarcinogenic effects of retinoids in animals *Adv Exp Med Biol* **206** 339-411

Morgan RW, Jain MG (1974) Bladder cancer: smoking beverages, and artificial sweeteners *Can Med Assoc J* **111** 1067-1070

Morrison AS, Buring JE (1980) Artificial sweeteners and cancer of the lower urinary tract *NEJM* **302** 537-541

Morrison AS, Buring JE, Verhoek WG et al, (1982) Coffee drinking and cancer of the lower urinary tract *JNCI* **68** 91-94

Murasaki G, Miyata Y, Babaya K et al (1980) Inhibitory effect of an aromatic retinoic acid analog on urinary bladder carcinogenesis in rats treated with N-butyl-N-(4-hydroxybutyl)nitrosamine *Jpn J Cancer Res* **71** 333-340

Najem GR, Louria DB, Seebode JJ et al (1982) Life-time occupation, smoking, caffeine, saccharin, hair dyes and bladder carcinogenesis *Int J Epidemiol* **11** 212-217

Nakanishi K, Fukushima S, Shibata M et al (1987) Effect of phenacetin and caffeine on the urinary bladder of rats treated with N-butyl-N-(4-hydroxybutyl)nitrosamine *Jpn J Cancer Res* **69** 395-400

NAS (1989) *Diet and Health* Washington DC: National Academy Press

Negri E, La Vecchia C, Franceschi S et al (1991) Vegetable and fruit consumption and cancer risk *Int J Cancer* **48** 350-354

Nomura A, Heilbrun LK, Morris JS, Stemmermann GN (1987) Serum selenium and the risk of cancer, by specific sites: case-control analysis of prospective data *JNCI* **79** 103-108

Nomura AMY, Kolonel LN, Hankin JH, Yoshizawa CN (1991) Dietary factors in cancer of the lower urinary tract *Int J Cancer* **48** 199-205

Nomura AMY, Stemmermann GN, Heilbrun LK et al (1985) Serum vitamin levels and the risk of cancer of specific sites in men of Japanese ancestry in Hawaii *Cancer Res* **45** 2369-2372

Ohno Y, Aoki K, Obata K, Morrison AS (1985) Case-control study of urinary bladder cancer in metropolitan Nagoya *Natl Cancer Inst Monogr* **69** 229-234

Parkin DM, Muir CS, Whelan SL et al (eds) (1992) *Cancer incidence in five continents, Vol 6* Lyon: International Agency for Research on Cancer

Piper JM, Matanoski GM, Tonascia J (1986) Bladder cancer in young women *AJE* **123** 1033-1042

Pipkin GE, Schlegel JU, Nishimura R et al (1969) Inhibitory effect of L-ascorbate on tumour formation in urinary bladders implanted with 3-hydroxyanthranilic acid *Proc Soc Exp Biol Med* **131** 522

Preston-Martin, Correa P (1989) Epidemiological evidence for the role of nitroso compounds in human cancer *Cancer Surv* **8** 459-473

Rebelakos A, Trichopoulos D, Tzonou A et al (1985) Tobacco smoking, coffee drinking, and occupation as risk factors for bladder cancer in

Greece *JNCI* **75** 455-461

Riboli E, Gonzalez CA, Lopez-Abente G et al (1991) Diet and bladder cancer in Spain: a multi-centre case-control study *Int J Cancer* **49** 214-219

Risch HA, Burch JD, Miller AB et al (1988) Dietary factors and the incidence of cancer of the urinary bladder *Am J Epidemiol* **127** 1179-1191

Shibata A, Paganini-Hill A, Ross RK, Henderson BE (1992) Intake of vegetables, fruits, beta-carotene, vitamin C and vitamin supplements and cancer incidence among the elderly: a prospective study *Br J Cancer* **66** 673-679

Silverman DT, Hartge P, Morrison AS, Devesa SS (1992) Epidemiology of bladder cancer *Hematol Oncol Clin North Am* **6** 1-30

Simon D, Yen S, Cole P (1975) Coffee drinking and cancer of the lower urinary tract *JNCI* **54** 587-591

Slattery ML, Schumacher MC, West DW, Robison LM (1988) Smoking and bladder cancer: The modifying effect of cigarettes on other factors *Cancer* **61** 402-408

Slattery ML, West DW, Robison LM (1988) Fluid intake and bladder cancer in Utah *Int J Cancer* **42** 17-22

Snowdon DA, Phillips RL, Choi W (1984) Diet, obesity and risk of fatal prostate cancer *Am J Epidemiology* **120** 244-250

Soloway MS, Cohen SA, Dekernion JB et al (1975) Failure of ascorbic acid to inhibit FANFT-induced bladder cancer *J Urol* **113** 483

Sporn MB, Dunlop NM, Newton DL, Smith JM (1976) Prevention of chemical carcinogenesis by vitamin A and its synthetic analogs (retinoids) *Fed Proc* **35** 1332-1338

Spruck CH III, Ohneseit PF, Gonzalez-Sulueta M et al (1994) Two molecular pathways to transitional cell carcinoma of the bladder *Cancer Res* **54** 784-788

Steineck G, Hagman U, Gerhardsson M, Norell SE (1990) Vitamin A supplements, fried foods, fat and urothelial cancer A case-referent study in Stockholm in 1985-87 *Int J Cancer* **45** 1006-1011

Steineck G, Norell SE, Feychting M (1988) Diet, tobacco and urothelial cancer *Acta Oncologica* **27** 323-327

Steinmetz K, Potter JD (1991) Vegetables, fruits, and cancer **II** Mechanisms *Cancer Causes Control* **2** 427-442

Stocks P (1970) Cancer mortality in relation to national consumption of cigarettes, solid fuel, tea, and coffee *Br J Cancer* **24** 215-225

Sullivan JW (1982) Epidemiologic survey of bladder cancer in greater New Orleans *J Urol* **128** 281-283

Takahashi M, Toyoda K, Aze Y et al (1993) The rat urinary bladder as a new target of heterocyclic amine carcinogenicity: tumor induction by 3-amino-1-methyl-5H-pyrido[4,3-b]indole acetate *Jpn J Cancer Res* **84** 852-858

Thomas DB, Uhl CN, Hartge P (1983) Bladder cancer and alcoholic beverage consumption *Am J Epidemiol* **118** 720-727

Tuthill RW, Moore GS (1980) Drinking water chlorination: a practice unrelated to cancer mortality *J Am Water Works Assoc* **72** 570-573

US Department of Health and Human Services, Public Health Services (1988) *The Surgeon General's report on nutrition and health* Washington DC:US Government Printing Office (DHHS (PHS)PublNo88-50210)

Vena JE, Graham S, Freudenheim J et al (1992) Diet in the epidemiology of bladder cancer in western New York *Nutr Cancer* **18** 255-264

Viscoli CM, Lachs MS , Horwitz RI (1993) Bladder cancer and coffee drinking: a summary of case-control research *Lancet* **341** 1432-1437

Wakabayashi K, Nagao M, Esumi H, Sugimura T (1992) Food-derived mutagens and carcinogens *Cancer Res* **52** 2092S-2098S

Wald NJ, Thompson SG, Densem JW et al (1988) Serum beta-carotene and subsequent risk of cancer: results from the BUPA study *Br J Cancer* **57** 428-433

Ward E, Carpenter A, Markowitz S et al (1991) Excess number of bladder cancer in workers exposed to ortho-toluidine and aniline *JNCI* **83** 501-506

West CM, Scott D, Peacock JH (1994) The Association for Radiation Research First Workshop: report Normal cell radiosensitivity: clinical application in predicting response to radiotherapy and cancer predisposition 21-23 March 1994, Westlakes Research Institute, Cumbria, UK *Int J Radiat Biol* **66**(2) 231-4

Whittemore AS, Paffenbarger RS Jr, Anderson K, Lee JE (1985) Early precursors of site-specific cancers in college men and women *JNCI* **74** 43-51

WHO (1993) *Toxicological Evaluations of Certain Food Additives and Naturally Occurring Toxicants* Thirty-ninth Meeting of the Joint FAO/WHO Expert Committee on Food Additives (JECFA) WHO Food Additive Series: 30 Geneva: World Health Organization 3579

WHO (1997) *The World Health Report* Geneva: World Health Organization

Wilkins JR III, Comstock GW (1981) Source of drinking water at home and site-specific cancer incidence in Washington County, Maryland *Am J Epidemiol* **114** 178-190

Williams RR, Horm JW (1977) Association of cancer sites with tobacco and alcohol consumption and socioeconomic status of patients: Interview study from the Third national Cancer Survey *JNCI* **58** 525-547

Wynder EL, Dieck GS, Hall NE, Lahri H (1985) A case-control study of diesel exhaust exposure and bladder cancer *Environ Res* **37** 475-489

Wynder EL, Goldsmith R The epidemiology of bladder cancer: a second look *Cancer* **40** 1246-1268

Wynder EL, Stellman SD Artificial sweetener use and bladder cancer: a case-control study *Science* **207** 1214-1216

Young TB, Kanarek MS (1983) Matched pair case-control study of drinking water chlorination and mortality In: Jolley RL, Brungs WA, Cotruvo JA et al (eds) *Water Chlorination: Environmental Impact and Health Effects*, **4** Ann Arbor, MI, Ann Arbor Science

Zheng W, Doyle TJ, Kushi LH, (1996) Tea consumption and cancer incidence in a prospective study of postmenopausal women *Am J Epidemiol* **144** 175-182

Zierler S, Danley RA, Feingold L (1986) Type of disinfectant in drinking water and patterns of mortality in Massachusetts *Environ Health Perspect* **69** 275-279

CHAPTER FIVE
DIETARY CONSTITUENTS

ACC/SCN (1992) *Second report on the world nutrition situation* Volume **1** global and regional results Geneva: ACC/SCN

ACS (1996) American Cancer Society Dietary guidelines advisory committee *Guidelines on diet, nutrition and cancer prevention: Reducing the risk of cancer with healthy food choices and physical activity* Washington DC: American Cancer Society

Albanes D, Blair A, Taylor PR (1989) Physical activity and risk of cancer in the NHANES 1 population *Am J Public Health* **79** 744-750

Ames BN, Shigenaga MK (1992) Oxidants are a major contributor to ageing *Ann New York Acad Sci*, **663** 85-96

Armstrong B, Doll (1975) Environmental factors and cancer incidence and mortality in different countries, with special reference to dietary practice *Int J Cancer* **15** 617-631

Asal NR, Risser DR, Kadamani S et al (1988) Risk factors in renal cell carcinoma: I Methodology, demographics, tobacco, beverage use, and obesity *Cancer Detect Prev* **11** (3-6) 359-77

Astrup A (1996) Obesity and metabolic efficiency *Ciba Found Symp* **201** 159-68 discussion 168-73, 188-93

Bailey GS, Hendricks JD, Shelton DW et al (1987) Enhancement of carcinogenesis by the natural anticarcinogen indole-3-carbinol *JNCI* **78** 931-4

Ballard-Barbash R, Schatzkin A, Albanes D (1990) Physical activity and risk of large bowel cancer in the Framingham Study *Cancer Res* **50** 3610-3613

Barch DH, Fox CC (1989) Dietary ellagic acid reduces the esophageal microsomal metabolism of methylbenzylnitrosamine *Cancer Lett* **44** 39-44

Benito E, Obrador A, Stiggelbout A et al (1990) A population-based case-control study of colorectal cancer in Majorca I Dietary factors *Int J Cancer* **45** 69-76

Bingham S (1993) Patterns of dietary fibre consumption in humans In GA Spiller (ed) *Dietary Fibre in Human Nutrition* 2nd ed Boca Raton: CRC Press

Bingham SA (1988) Meat, starch, and nonstarch polysaccharides and large bowel cancer *Am J Clin Nutr* **48** 762-767

Bingham SA (1988) Meat, starch, and nonstarch polysaccharides and large bowel cancer *Am J Clin Nutr* **48** Suppl 762-7

Birt DF, Bresnick E (1991) Chemoprevention by nonnutrient components of vegetables and fruits In Alfin-Slater RB, Kritchevsky D (eds): *Cancer and nutrition* New York: Plenum Press 221-260

Blair SN, Kohl HW, Paffenbarger RS et al (1989) Physical fitness and all-cause mortality: a prospective study of healthy men and women *JAMA* **262** 2395-2401

Blot WJ, Li J-Y, Taylor PR et al (1993) Nutrition intervention trials in Linxian, China: supplementation with specific vitamin/mineral combinations, cancer incidence, and disease-specific mortality in the general population *JNCI* **85** 1483-1492

Blundell JE, Burley VJ, Cotton JR, Lawton CL (1993) Dietary fat and the control of energy intake: evaluating the effects of fat on meal size and postmeal satiety *Am J Clin Nutr* **57** Suppl: 772S-777S; discussion 777S-778S

Bright-See E, Jazmaji V (1991) Estimation of the amount of dietary starch available to different populations *Can J Physiol Pharmacol* **69** 56-59

Brinton LA, Swanson CA (1992) Height and weight at various ages and risk of breast cancer *Ann Epidemiol* **2** 597-609

Brown JP (1980) A review of the genetic effects of naturally occurring flavonoids, anthraquinones and related compounds *Mut Res* **75** 243-77

Brown LM, Blot WJ, Schuman SH et al (1988) Environmental factors and high risk of esophageal cancer among men in coastal South Carolina *JNCI* **80** 1620-1625

Brown LM, Hoover RN, Greenberg RS (1994) Are racial differences in squamous cell esophageal cancer explained by alcohol and tobacco use? *JNCI* **86** 1340-1345

Brown LM, Hoover RN, Greenberg RS (1994) Are racial differences in squamous cell esophageal cancer explained by alcohol and tobacco use? *JNCI* **86** 1340-5

Brown LM, Silverman DT, Pottern LM,et al (1994) Adenocarcinoma of the esophagus and esophagogastric junction in White men in the United States: alcohol, tobacco, and socioeconomic factors *Cancer Causes Control* **5** 333-40

Brownson RC, Chang JC, Davis JR, Smith CA (1991) Physical activity on the job and cancer in Missouri *Am J Public Health* **81** 639-642

Bunker VW, Lawson MS, Stansfield MF, Clayton BE (1988) Selenium balance studies in apparently healthy and housebound elderly people eating self-selected diets *Br J Nutr* **59** 171-80

Burch JD, Howe GR, Miller AB, Semenciw R (1981) Tobacco, alcohol, asbestos and nickel in the etiology of cancer of the larynx : a case control study *JNCI* **67** 1219-24

Burkitt DP (1975) Large-bowel cancer: an epidemiological jigsaw puzzle *JNCI* **54** 36

Bussey HJ, DeCosse JJ, Deschner EE et al (1982): A randomized trial of ascorbic acid in polyposis coli *Cancer* **50** 1434-1439

Cannon G (1992) *Food and Health: the Experts Agree* London: Consumers' Association

Carroll KK (1975) Experimental evidence of dietary factors and hormone-dependent cancers *Cancer Res* **35** 3374-3383

Cassidy A, Bingham SA, Cummings JH (1994) Starch intake and colorectal cancer risk: an international comparison *Br J Cancer* **69** 937-942

Castonguay A (1993) Pulmonary carcinogenesis and its prevention by dietary polyphenolic compounds *Ann N Y Acad Sci* **686** 177-185

Chen J, Gao J (1993): The Chinese Total Diet Study

in 1990 Part II Nutrients *J AOC Int* **76** 1206-1213

Christen WG (1994): Antioxidants and eye disease *Am J Med* **97**(Suppl):s14-s17

Chu SY, Lee NC, Wingo PA et al (1991) The relationship between body mass index and breast cancer among women enrolled in the cancer and steroid hormone study *J Clin Epidemiol* 44 1197-1206

Chug-Ahuja JK, Holden JM, Forman MR et al (1993) The development and application of a carotenoid database for fruits, vegetables, and selected multicomponent foods *J Am Diet Assoc* **93** 318-323

Clemmesen J (1965) Statistical studies in the aetiology of malignant neoplasms *J Copenhagen Danish Cancer Registry*

Cohen LA, Boylan E, Epstein M, Zang E (1992) Voluntary exercise and experimental mammary cancer *Adv Exp Med Biol* **322** 61

Commission of the European Community (1993) *Report of the Scientific Commission for Food (thirty-first series): Nutrient and energy intakes for the European Community* Director (Industry) Brussels: Commission of the EC

Comstock GW, Bush TL, Helzlsouer K et al (1992) Serum retinol, beta carotene, vitamin A and selenium as related to subsequent cancer of specific sites *Am J Epidemiol* **135** 115-121

Cottrell RC (1991) Introduction: nutritional aspects of palm oil *Am J Clin Nutr* **53** 989S-1009S

Craddock VM (1992) Aetiology of oesophageal cancer : some operative factors *Eur J Cancer Prevention* **1** 89-103

Cummings JH, Frolich W (1993) *Dietary fibre intakes in Europe* Survey by members of the management committee of cost 24 Directorate-General, Science, Research and Development Commission of the European Communities

Daniel EM, Stoner GD (1991) The effects of ellagic acid and 13-cis-retinoic acid on N-nitrosobenzylmethylamine-induced esophageal tumorigenesis in rats *Cancer Lett* **56** 117-124

Dashwood RH, Arbogast DN, Fong AT et al (1989) Quantitative inter-relationships between aflatoxin B1 carcinogen dose, indole-3-carbinol anti-carcinogen dose, target organ DNA adduction and final tumor response *Carcinogenesis* **10** 175-181

de Vet HC, Knipschild PG, Willebrand D et al (1991) The effect of beta-carotene on the regression and progression of cervical dysplasia: a clinical experiment *J Clin Epidemiol* **44** 273-83

DeCosse JJ, Miller HH, Lesser ML (1989) Effect of wheat fiber and vitamins C and E on rectal polyps in patients with familial adenomatous polyposis *JNCI* **81** 1290-1297

Department of Health (1991) *Dietary Reference Values for Food Energy and Nutrients for the United Kingdom* Report of the Panel on Dietary Reference Values of the Committee on Medical Aspects of Food Policy London: HMSO

Department of Health (1994)*National Food Survey* London: HMSO

Department of Health (1994) Nutritional Aspects of Cardiovascular Disease *Committee on Medical Aspects of Food Policy* London: HMSO

Department of Health (1995) Obesity - Reversing the Increasing Problem of Obesity in England *A report of the Nutrition and Physical Activity Task Forces* London: HMSO

Department of Health (1996) *Committees on Toxicity, Mutagenicity and Carcinogenicity of Chemicals 1995 Annual Report* London: HMSO

Deschner EE, Ruperto J, Wong G, Newmark HL (1991) Quercetin and rutin as inhibitors of azoxymethanol-induced colonic neoplasia *Carcinogenesis* **12** 1193-6

Doll R,& Peto R (1981) The causes of cancer *JNCI* **66** 1191-1308

Dragsted LO, Strube M, Larsen JC (1993) Cancer-protective factors in fruits and vegetables: biochemical and biological background *Pharmacol Toxicol* **72** Suppl 1:116-135

English D et al (1995) *The quantification of drug caused morbidity and mortality in Australia* Part 1 and 2 Commonwealth Department of Human Services and Health Australian Government Printing Office

Englyst HN, Hudson GJ (1997) *Starch and health* Proceedings of Conference on Starch: Structure and Function Donald Am, Frazier PJ, Richmond P (eds) London: Royal Society of Chemistry

Englyst HN, Kingman SM (1993) Carbohydrates In: Garrow JS, James WPT (eds) *Human Nutrition and Dietetics* 9th edn Edinburgh: Churchill Livingstone

Englyst HN, Quigley ME, Hudson GJ (1995) Definition and measurement of dietary fibre *Eur J Clin Nutr* **49** 48-62

Enstrom JE, Kanim LE, Klein MA (1992) Vitamin C intake and mortality among a sample of the United States population *Epidemiol* **3**194-202

Ernster VL, Goodson WH, Hunt TK et al (1985) Vitamin E and benign breast "disease": a double-blind, randomized clinical trial *Surgery* **97** 490-494

Ewertz M (1988) Influence of non-contraceptive exogenous and endogenous sex hormones on breast cancer risk in Denmark *Int J Cancer* **42** 832-838

Fahey RC, Sundquist AR (1991) Evolution of glutathione metabolism *Adv Enzymol* **64** 1-53

FAO/WHO (1991) Food and Agriculture Organisation/World Health Organisation *Protein quality evaluation (*FAO food and nutrition paper 51) Rome: FAO

FAO/WHO (1994) Food and Agriculture Organization/World Health Organization *Fats and Oils in Human Nutrition*: Report of a joint expert consultation FAO food and nutrition paper **57** FAO: Rome

FAO/WHO/UNU (1985) Food and Agriculture Organization, World Health Organization, United Nations University *WHO Technical Report Series* No: **724** WHO: Geneva

Ferro-Luzzi A, Martino L (1996) Obesity and physical activity In: *The Origins and Consequences of Obesity* Chichester: John Wiley

Fiala ES, Reddy BS, Weisburger JH (1985) Naturally occurring anticarcinogenic substances in foodstuffs *Annu Rev Nutr* **5** 295-321

Folsom AR, Kaye SA, Prineas RJ et al (1990) Increased incidence of carcinoma of the breast associated with abdominal adiposity in postmenopausal women *Am J Epidemiol* **131** 794-803

Franceschi S, Bidoli E, Baron AE, La Vecchia C (1990) Maize and risk of cancers of the oral cavity, pharynx, and esophagus in Northeastern Italy *JNCI* **82** 1407-1411

Franceschi S, Talamini R, Barra S et al (1990) Smoking and drinking in relation to cancers of the oral cavity, pharynx, larynx, and esophagus in northern Italy *Cancer Res* **50** 6502-7

Freedman LS, Clifford C, Messina M, (1990) Analysis of dietary fat, calories, body weight, and the development of mammary tumours in rats and mice: a review *Cancer Res* **50** 5710-5719

Friedenreich CM, Howe GR, Miller AB et al (1993) A cohort study of alcohol consumption and risk of breast cancer *Am J Epidemiol* **137** 512-520

Frisch RE, Wyshak G, Albright NL (1992) Former athletes have a lower lifetime occurrence of breast cancer and cancers of the reproductive system *Adv Exptl Med Biol* **322** 29-39

Gao YT, McLaughlin JK, Blot WJ et al (1994) Risk factors for esophageal cancer in Shanghai China I Role of cigarette smoking and alcohol drinking *Int J Cancer* **58** 192-6

Gao YT, McLaughlin JK, Gridley G et al (1994) Risk factors for esophageal cancer in Shanghai, China II role of diet and nutrients Int J Cancer **58** 197-202

Gapstur SM, Potter JD, Sellers TA, Folsom AR (1992) Increased risk of breast cancer with alcohol consumption in postmenopausal women Am J Epidemiol **136**1221-1231

Garabrant DH, Peters JM, Mack TM, Bernstein L (1984) Job activity and colon cancer risk Am J Epidemiol **119** 1005-1014

Garewal H (1994) Chemoprevention of oral cancer: beta-carotene and vitamin E in leukoplakia Eur J Cancer Prev **3** 101-107

Gerhardsson de Verdier M, Froderus B, Norell SE (1988) Physical activity and colon cancer risk Int J Epidemiol **17** 743-746

Gerhardsson de Verdier M, Norell SE, Kiviranta H, (1986) Sedentary jobs and colon cancer Am J Epidemiol **123** 775-780

Gibson GR, Beatty ER, Yang Xin, Cummings JH (1995) Selective stimulation of Bifido bacteria in the human colon by oligofructose and inulin Gastroenterol **108** 975-982

Giovannucci E (1995) Insulin and colon cancer Cancer Causes Control **6** 164-179

Giovannucci E, Ascherio A, Rimon E (1995) Physical activity, obesity, and risk for colon cancer and adenoma in men Ann Int Med **122** 327-334

Graham S, Marshall J, Haughey B et al (1990) Nutritional epidemiology of cancer of the esophagus Am J Epidemiol **131** 454-467

Green SM, Blundell JE (1996) Subjective and objective indices of the satiating effect of foods Can people predict how filling a food will be? Eur J Clin Nutr **50** 798-806

Greenberg ER, Baron JA, Stukel TA et al (1990): A clinical trial of beta carotene to prevent basal-cell and squamous-cell cancers of the skin NEJM **323** 789-795

Greenberg ER, Baron JA, Tosteson TD et al, (1994) A clinical trial of antioxidant vitamins to prevent colorectal adenoma NEJM **331**141-147

Gregory J, Foster K, Tyler H, Wiseman M (1990) The Dietary and Nutritional Survey of British Adults London: HMSO

Hague A, Manning AM, Hanlon KA, Hueschtchav L, Hart D, Paraskeva C (1993) Sodium butyrate induces apoptosis in human colonic tumour cell lines Int J Cancer **55** 498-505

Hague A, Manning AM, Hanlon KA et al (1993) Sodium butyrate induces apoptosis in human colonic tumour cell lines in a p53-independent

pathway: implications for the possible role of dietary fibre in the prevention of large-bowel cancer Int-J-Cancer **55**498-505

Heitman B, Irizarry A (1995) Hypothyroidism: common complaints, perplexing diagnosis Nurse Pract **20** 54-60

Heitman BL, Lissner L (1995) Dietary underreporting by obese individuals - is it specific or non-specific BMJ **311** 986-989

Hennekens CH, Buring JE, Manson JE et al (1996) Lack of effect of long-term supplementation with beta carotene on the incidence of malignant neoplasms and cardiovascular disease NEJM **334** 1145-1149

Hertog MG (1996) Epidemiological evidence on potential health properties of flavonoids Proc Nutr Soc **55** 385-97

Hertog MG, Feskens EJ, Hollman PC et al (1993)Dietary antioxidant flavonoids and risk of coronary heart disease: the Zutphen Elderly Study Lancet **342** 1007-11

Hertog MGL, Kromhout D, Aravanis C et al (1995): Flavonoid intake and long-term risk of coronary heart disease and cancer in the Seven Countries Study Arch Intern Med **155** 381-186

Hill JO, Prentice AM (1995) Sugar and body weight regulation Am J Clin Nut **62** (supplement 1): 264s-274s

Hinds K, Gregory JR (1995) National Diet and Nutrition Survey: children aged $1^1/_2$ to $4^1/_2$ years London: HMSO

Hodge WG, Whitcher JP, Satariano W (1995) Risk factors for age-related cataracts Epidemiol Rev **17** 336-346

Holcombe C (1992) Helicobacter pylori: the African enigma Gut **33** 429-431

Holland B, Unwin ID, Buss DH (1988) (eds) Cereals and Cereal Products The third supplement to McCance and Widdowson's The Composition of Foods London: Royal Society of Chemistry/ Ministry of Agriculture, Fisheries and Food

Hollman PCH, Venema DP (1993) The content of the potentially anticarcinogenic ellagic acid in plant foods In Waldron KW, Johnson IT, Fenwick GR (eds): Food and Cancer Prevention: Chemical and Biological Aspects Cambridge, England: The Royal Society of Chemistry pp202-208

Howe GR, Benito E, Castellato R et al (1992) Dietary intake of fiber and decreased risk of cancers of the colon and rectum: evidence from the combined analysis of 13 case-control studies JNCI **84**1887-96

Hu J, Nyren O, Wolk A et al (1994) Risk factors for

oesophageal cancer in northeast China Int J Cancer **57**38-46

Hunter DJ, Morris JS, Chute CG et al(1990)Predictors of selenium concentration in human toenails Am J Epidemiol **132** 114–122

IARC (1988) Alcohol drinking IARC monograph on the evaluation of carcinogenic risks to humans volume **44** Lyon: International Agency for Research on Cancer

Jackson AA, Margetts BM (1993) Protein intakes in the adult population in the UK Int J Food Sci Nut **44** 95-104

James SJ, Muskhelishvili L (1994) Rates of apoptosis and proliferation vary with caloric intake and may affect incidence of spontaneous hepatoma in C57BL/6X C3 HFI mice Cancer Res **54** 5508-5510

James WP (1995) A public health approach to the problem of obesity Int J Obes Relat Metab Disord **19** Suppl 3 S37-45

Jenkins DJA, Thomas DM, Wolever TMS et al (1981) Glycaemic index of foods: a physiological basis for carbohydrate exchanges Am J Clin Nutr **34** 362-366

Jirousek L, Starka J (1958) Uber das vorkommen von trithionen (1,2-dithiacyclopent-4-en-3-thione) in Brassicapflanzen Naturwiss **45** 386

Joossens JV, Hill MJ, Elliott P et al (1996) Dietary salt, Nitrate and stomach cancer mortality in 24 countries The Intersalt study Int J Epidemiol **25** 1-11

Kato I, Tominaga S, Ikari A (1990) A case-control study of male colorectal cancer in Aichi Prefecture, Japan: with special reference to occupational activity level, drinking habits and family history Jpn J Cancer Res (Gann) **81** 115-121

Keys A (1970) Coronary heart disease in seven countries Circulation **XLI** (Suppl 1): 1-191

Klurfeld DM, Welsch CB, Davis MJ, Kritchevsky D (1989a) Determination of degree of energy restriction necessary to reduce DMBA-induced mammary tumourigenesis in rats during the promotion phase J Nutr **119** 286-291

Klurfeld DM, Welsch CB, Lloyd CB, Kritchevsky D (1989b) Inhibition of DMBA-induced mammary tumourigenesis by caloric restriction in rats fed high-fat diets Int J Cancer **43**: 922-925

Knekt P (1991) Role of vitamin E in the prophylaxis of cancer Ann Med **23** 3-12

Krinsky N (1991) Effects of carotenoids in cellular and animal models Am J Clin Nutr **53** 238S-246S

Kritchevsky D (1985) Calories and chemically

induced tumours in rodents *Comp Therapy* **11** 35-39

Kritchevsky D, Klurfeld DM (1986) Influence of caloric intake on experimental carcinogenesis: a review *Adv Exp Biol* **206** 55-68

Kritchevsky D, Weber MM, Klurfeld DM (1984) Dietary fat versus caloric content in initiation and promotion of 7, 12-dimethyl benz(a)anthracene - induced mammary tumourigenesis in rats *Cancer Res* **44** 3174-3177

Kushi LH, Folsom AR, Prineas RJ et al (1996) Dietary antioxidant vitamins and death from coronary heart disease in postmenopausal women [see comments] N Engl J Med **334** 1156-62

Lam LKT, Zhang J, Hasegawa S et al (1994) : Inhibition of chemically induced carcinogenesis by citrus limonoids In Huang MJ, Osawa T, Ho C-T, Rosen RT (eds): *Food Phytochemicals for Cancer Prevention* **I** Fruits and Vegetables Washington DC, American Chemical Society pp 209-219

Le Marchand L, Hankin JH, Kolonel LN et al (1993) Intake of specific carotenoids and lung cancer risk *Cancer Epidemiol Biomarkers Prev* **2** 183-187

Le Marchand L, Wilkens LR, Mi MP (1991) Early-age body size, adult weight gain and endometrial cancer risk *Int J Cancer* **48** 807-11

Lee IM, Paffenbarger RS, Hseih C-C (1991) Physical activity and risk of developing colorectal cancer among college alumni *JNCI* **83** 1324-1329

Leighton T, Ginther C, Fluss L (1993) The distribution of quercetin and quercetin glycosides in vegetable components of the human diet In Waldron KW, Johnson IT, Fenwick GR (eds) *Food and Cancer Prevention: Chemical and Biological Aspects* Cambridge, England: The Royal Society of Chemistry pp 222-232

Levander OA (1987) Aglobal view of human selenium nutrition *An Rev Nutr* **7** 227-250

Lew EA, Garfinkel I (1979) Variations in mortality by weight among 750,000 men and women *J Chronic Dis* **32** 563-576

Li J, Taylor PR, Li B et al (1993) Nutrition intervention trials in Linxian, China: multiple vitamin/mineral supplementation, cancer incidence, and disease-specific mortality among adults with esophageal dysplasia *JNCI* **85** 1492-1498

Lissner L, Heitmann BL (1995) Dietary fat and obesity: evidence from epidemiology *Eur J Clin Nutr* **49** 79-90

London RS, Sundaram GS, Murphy L et al (1985):

The effect of vitamin E on mammary dysplasia: a double-blind study *Obstet Gyneco l* **65** 104-106

London SJ, Colditz GA, Stampfer MJ, Willett WC et al (1989) Prospective study of relative weight, height and the risk of breast cancer *JAMA* **262** 2853-8

Longnecker MP (1994) Alcoholic beverage consumption in relation to risk of breast cancer: meta-analysis and review *Cancer Causes Control* **5** (1) 73-82

Longnecker MP, Newcomb PA, Mittendorf R et al (1995) Risk of breast cancer in relation to lifetime alcohol consumption *JNCI* **87** 923-929

Loub WD, Wattenberg LW, Davis DW (1975) Aryl hydrocarbon hydroxylase induction in rat tissues by naturally occurring indoles of cruciferous plants *JNCI* **54** 985-8

Mackerras D (1995) Antioxidants and health - fruits and vegetables or supplements? *Food Australia* **47** (Supplement):s1-s24

Macquart-Moulin G, Riboli E, Cornee J et al (1986) Case-control study on colorectal cancer and diet in Marseilles *International Journal of Cancer* **38** 183-191

Macquart-Moulin G, Riboli E, Cornee J et al (1987) Colorectal polyps and diet: a case-control study in Marseilles *Int J Cancer* **40** 179-188

MAFF (1994) Ministry of Agriculture, Fisheries and Food *The Dietary and Nutritional Survey of British Adults - Further Analysis* London: HMSO

Mangels AR, Holden JM, Beecher GR, Forman MR, Lanza E (1993) Carotenoid content of fruits and vegetables: an evaluation of the analytic data *J Am Diet Assoc* **93** 284-296

Margetts BM, Jackson AA: Interactions between peoples' diet and their smoking habits: the dietary and nutritional survey of British adults (1993) *BMJ* **307** 1381-1384

Martin-Moreno JM, Boyle P, Gorgojo L et al (1993) Alcoholic beverage consumption and risk of breast cancer in Spain *Cancer Causes Control* **4** 345-53

Mayne ST, Graham S, Zheng TZ (1991) Dietary retinol: prevention or promotion of carcinogenesis in humans? [published erratum appears in *Cancer Causes Control* (1992) **3** 184] *Cancer Causes Control* **2** 443-450

McCredie M, Stewart JH (1992) Risk factors for kidney cancer in New South Wales, Australia II Urologic disease, hypertension, obesity, and hormonal factors *Cancer Causes Control* **3** 323-331

McKeown Eyssen G, Holloway C, Jazmaji V et al

(1988) A randomized trial of vitamins C and E in the prevention of recurrence of colorectal polyps *Cancer Res* **48** 4701-4705

McKeown-Eyssen G (1994) Epidemiology of colorectal cancer revisited: are serum triglycerides and/or plasma glucose associated with risk? *Cancer Epidemiol* **3** 687-695

McLaughlin JK, Mandel JS, Blot WJ (1984): A population-based case-control study of renal cell carcinoma *JNCI* **72** 275-284

McPhillips JB, Eaton CB, Gans KM et al (1994) Dietary differences in smokers and nonsmokers from two southeastern New England communities *J Am Diet Assoc* **94** 287-92

Mensink RP, Katan-MB (1992) Effect of dietary fatty acids on serum lipids and lipoproteins A meta-analysis of 27 trials *Arterioscler Thromb* **12** 911-9

Messina M, Barnes S (1991) The role of soy products in reducing risk of cancer *JNCI* **83** 541-546

Meydani M (1995) Vitamin E *Lancet* **345** 170-175

Michnovicz JJ, Bradlow-HL (1990) Induction of estradiol metabolism by dietary indole-3-carbinol in humans *J NCI* **82** 947-9

Miller AB, Howe GR, Jain M et al (1983) Food items and food groups as risk factors in a case-control study of diet and colorectal cancer *Int J Cancer* **32** 155-61

Morabia A, Wynder EL (1990) Dietary habits of smokers, people who never smoked, and exsmokers *Am J Clin Nutr* **52** 933-7

Munoz N, Lipkin M, Crespi M et al (1985) Proliferative abnormalities of the oesophageal epithelium of Chinese populations at high and low risk for oesophageal cancer *Int J Cancer* **36** 187-9

Munoz N, Wahrendorf J, Jian Bang L et al (1985) No effect of riboflavine, retinol, and zinc on prevalence of precancerous lesions of oesophagus *Lancet* 111-114

Murakoshi M, Takayasu J, Kimura O et al (1989) Inhibitory effects of alpha-carotene on proliferation of the human neuroblastoma cell line *JNCI* 1649-1642

NAS (1982) *Diet, Nutrition and Cancer* Washington DC: National Academy Press

NAS (1989) *Diet and Health* Washington DC: National Academy Press

Oakenfull D, Sidhu GS (1989) Saponins In Cheeke PR (ed): *Toxicants of Plant Origin* Boca Raton: CRC Press

Oberley LW (1988) Free radicals and diabetes *Free Radic Biol Med* **5**113-124

Olsen J, Sabreo S, Fasting U (1985) Interaction of alcohol and tobacco as risk factors in cancer of the laryngeal region *J Epidemiol Community Health* **39** 165-8

Olson SH, Trevisan M, Marshall JR et al (1995) Body mass index, weight gain, and risk of endometrial cancer *Nutr Cancer* **23**141-9

Olson SH, Trevisan M, Marshall JR, Graham S, Zielezny M, Vena JE, Hellman R, Freudenheim JL (1995) Body mass index, weight gain and risk of endometrial cancer *Nutrition and Cancer* **23** 141-149

Omenn GS, Goodman G, Thornquist M et al (1994) The beta-carotene and retinol efficacy trial (CARET) for chemoprevention of lung cancer in high risk populations: smokers and asbestos-exposed workers *Cancer Res* **54** 2038s-2043s

Paffenbarger RS, Hyde RT, Wing AL (1987) Physical activity and incidence of cancer in diverse populations: a preliminary report *Am J Clin Nutr* **45** 312-317

Pandey DK, Shekelle R, Selwyn BJ et al (1995) Dietary vitamin C and beta-carotene and risk of death in middle-aged men The Western Electric Study *Am J Epidemiol* **142**1269-1278

Pariza MW, Boutwell RK (1987) Historical perspective: calories and energy expenditure in carcinogenesis *Am J Clin Nutr* **45** 151-156

Pence BC, Buddingh F, Yang SP (1986) Multiple dietary factors in the enhancement of dimethylhydrazine carcinogenesis: main effect of indole-3-carbinol *JNCI* **77** 269-276

Peters RK, Garabrant DH, Yu MC, Mack TM (1989) A case-control study of occupational and dietary factors in colorectal cancer in young men by subsite *Cancer Res* **49** 5459-5468

Peto R, Doll R, Buckley JD et al (1981) Can dietary beta-carotene materially reduce human cancer rates? *Nature* **290** 201-208

Phang JM, Poore CM, Lopaczynska J, Yeh GC (1993) Flavonol-stimulated efflux of 7,12-dimethylbenz(a)anthracene in multidrug-resistant breast cancer cells *Cancer Res* **53** 5977-5981

Phillips RW, Kikendall JW, Luk GD et al (1993) beta-carotene inhibits rectal mucosal ornithine decarboxylase activity in colon cancer patients *Cancer Res* 3723-3725

Prentice AM, Black AE, Coward WA et al (1986) High levels of energy expenditure in obese women *Br Med J Clin Res Ed* **292** 983-7

Prentice AM, Black AE, Coward WA, Davies HL,

Goldberg GR, Murgatroyd PE, Ashford J, Sawyer M, Whitehead RG (1986) High levels of energy expenditure in obese women *BMJ* **292** 983-987

Raicht RF, Cohen BI, Fazzini EPet al (1980) Protective effect of plant sterols against chemically induced colon tumors in rats *Cancer Res* **40** 403-5

Rimm EB, Stampfer MJ, Ascherio A et al (1993) Vitamin E consumption and risk of coronary heart disease in men *NEJM* **328**1450-1456

Roncucci L, Di Donato P, Carati L et al (1993) Antioxidant vitamins or lactulose for the prevention of the recurrence of colorectal adenomas *Dis Colon Rectum* **36** 227-234

Rous P (1914) The influence of diet on transplanted and spontaneous mouse tumours *Journal of Experimental Medicine* **20** 433-451

Rowe PM (1996) Beta-carotene takes a collective beating *Lancet* 347:249

Royal College of Physicians (1980) *Medical Aspects of Dietary Fibre* Tunbridge Wells: Pitman

Royal College of Physicians (1983) Obesity *Journal of the Royal College of Physicians of London* **17** (1): 3- 58

Royal College of Physicians of London (1983) Obesity *Journal of the Royal College of Physicians of London* **17** 1 358

Salbe AD, Bjeldanes LF (1986) Effects of Brussels sprouts, indole-3-carbinol and in vivo DNA binding of aflatoxin B1 in the rat *Fed Proc* **45** 970

Schapira AHV (1995)Oxidative stress in Parkinson's disease - review *Neuropathy Appl Neurobiol* **21** 3-9

Schatzkin A, Carter CL, Green SB et al (1989) Is alcohol consumption related to breast cancer? Results from the Framingham Heart Study *JNCI* **81**:31-35

Schatzkin A, Palmer JR, Rosenberg L et al (1987) Risk factors for breast cancer in black women *JNCI* **78** 213-217

Sestili MA (1983) Possible adverse health effects of vitamin C and ascorbic acid *Semin Oncol* **10** 299-304

Severson RK, Nomura AMY, Grove JS, Stemmermann GN (1989) A prospective analysis of physical activity and cancer *Am J Epidemiol* **130** 522-529

Shibata A, Paganini Hill A, Ross RK, Henderson BE (1992) Intake of vegetables, fruits, beta-carotene, vitamin C and vitamin supplements and cancer incidence among the elderly: a

prospective study *Br J Cancer* **66** 673-679

Shu XO, Brinton LA, Zheng W et al (1992) Relation of obesity and body fat distribution to endometrial cancer in Shanghai, China *Cancer Res* **52** 3865-3870

Silvester KR, Englyst HN, Cummings JH (1995) Ileal recovery of starch from whole diets containing resistant starch measured in vitro and fermentation of ileal effluent *Am J Clin Nutr* **62** 403-411

Slattery ML, Edwards S, Ma KN et al (1997b) Physical activity and colon cancer: a public health perspective *Ann Epidemiol* (in press)

Slattery ML, Potter J, Caan B et al (1997a) Energy balance and colon cancer - beyond physical activity *Cancer Res* **57** 75-80

Slattery ML, Schumacher MC, Smith KR et al (1988) Physical activity, diet, and risk of colon cancer in Utah *Am J Epidemiol* **128** 989-999

Sneyd MJ, Paul C, Spears GF, SkeggDC (1991) Alcohol consumption and risk of breast cancer *Int J Cancer* **48** 812-5

Sparnins VL, Venegas PL, Wattenberg LW (1982) Glutathione S-transferase activity: enhancement by compounds inhibiting chemical carcinogenesis and by dietary constituents *JNCI* **68** 493-496

Stahelin HB, Gey FK, Eichholzer M et al (1991) Plasma antioxidant vitamins and subsequent cancer mortality in the 12 year follow up of the prospective Basel study *Am J Epidemiol* **133** 766-775

Stavric B, Matula TI, Klassen R, (1992) Effect of flavonoids on mutagenicity and bioavailability of xenobiotics in foods, in Huang M-T, Ho C-T, Lee CY (eds): *Phenolic compounds in food and their effects on health* **II** Antioxidants and cancer prevention ACS symposium series 507 Washington DC: American Chemical Society pp239-249

Steinmetz KA, Potter JD (1991) Vegetables, fruit, and cancer II Mechanisms *Cancer Causes Control* **2** 427-442

Stephen AM, Cummings JH (1980) Mechanism of action of dietary fibre in the human colon *Nature* **284** 283-284

Stich HF, Rosin MP (1984) Naturally occurring phenolics as antimutagenic and anticarcinogenic agents *Adv Exp Med* **177** 1-29

Stryker WS, Kaplan LA, Stein EA et al (1988) The relation of diet, cigarette smoking, and alcohol consumption to plasma beta-carotene and alpha-tocopherol levels *Am J Epidemiol* **127** 283-296

Stubbs RJ, Ritz P, Coward WA, Prentice A M (1995) Covert manipulation of the ratio of dietary fat to carbohydrate and energy density: effect on food intake and energy balance in free-living men eating ad libitum *Am J Clin Nutr* **62** 330-337

Sturgeon SR, Brinton LA, Berman ML et al (1993) Past and present physical activity and endometrial cancer risk *Br J Cancer* **68** 584-589

Subar AF, Block G (1990)Use of vitamin and mineral supplements: demographics and amounts of nutrients consumed *Am J Epidemiol* **132**1091-1101

Surgeon General (1988) *The Surgeon General's Report on Nutrition and Health* US Department of Health and Human Services: DHHS (PHS) Publication no 88-50210

Suter PM, Schutz Y, Jequier-E (1992) The effect of ethanol on fat storage in healthy subjects *N Engl J Med* **326** 983-7

Swanson CA, Potischman N, Wilbanks GD et al (1993) Relation of endometrial cancer risk to past and contemporary body size and body fat distribution *Cancer Epidemiol Biomarkers, Prevention* **2** 321-327

Tanaka T, Kojima T, Kawamori,T et al (1993)Inhibition of 4-nitroquinoline-1-oxide-induced rat tongue carcinogenesis by the naturally occurring plant phenolics caffeic, ellagic, chlorogenic and ferulic acids *Carcinogenesis* **14** 1321-5

Tanaka T, Mori Y, Morishita Y et al (1990) Inhibitory effect of sinigrin and indole-3-carbinol on diethylnitrosamine-induced hepatocarcinogenesis in male ACI/N rats *Carcinogenesis* **11** 1403-6

Tannenbaum A (1949) The role of nutrition in the origin and growth of tumours In: Moulton FR (ed): *Approaches to Tumour Chemotherapy* Washington DC: American Association for the Advancement of Science

Tannenbaum A (1959) Nutrition and cancer In: Homburger FF (ed): *The Physiopathology of Cancer* New York: Hoeber-Harper

The Alpha-Tocopherol Beta Carotene Cancer Prevention Study Group: The effect of vitamin E and beta carotene on the incidence of lung cancer and other cancers in male smokers *NEJM* **330**1029-1035

Third conference on vitamin (1987) *Ann NY Acad Sci* Volume **498** New York, New York Academy of Sciences

Thun MJ, Calle E E, Namboodiri MM et al (1992) Risk factors for fatal colon cancer in a large prospective study *JNCI* **84** (19) 1491-1500

Thurnham DI, Zheng SF, Munoz N et al (1985)Comparison of riboflavin, vitamin A, and zinc status in high and low risk regions for oesophageal cancer in China *Nutr Cancer* **7**131-143

Tomlin J, Read NW (1992) A comparison of the effect of 95 gram/day resistant starch and lactulose on colon function *Eur J Clin Nutr* **46** S139-S140

Tornberg S, Carstensen J (1993) Serum beta-lipoprotein, serum cholesterol and Quetelet's index as predictors for survival of breast cancer patients *Eur J Cancer* **29A** 2025-30

Tornberg SA, Carstensen JM (1994) Relationship between Quetelet's index and cancer of breast and female genital tract in 47,000 women followed for 25 years *Br J Cancer* **69** 358-361

Tornberg-SA, Carstensen-JM (1994)Relationship between Quetelet's index and cancer of breast and female genital tract in 47,000 women followed for 25 years *Br J Cancer* **69** 358-61

Tremblay A,St Pierre S (1996) The hyperphagic effect of a high-fat diet and alcohol intake persists after control for energy density *Am J Clin Nutr* **63** 479-82

Trentham-Dietz A, Newcomb PA, Storer BE et al (1997) Body size and risk of breast cancer *Am J Epidemiol* **145** 1011-9

Tuyns AJ, Estene J, Randall L et al (1988) Cancer of the larynx/hypopharynx tobacco and alcohol : IARC intervention case control study in Turin and Varese (Italy), Zaragoza and Navarra (Spain), Geneva (Switzerland) and Calvados (France) *Int J Cancer* **41** 483- 91

Tuyns AJ, Kaaks R, Haelterman M (1988) Colorectal cancer and the consumption of foods: a case-control study in Belgium *Nutr Cancer* **11**189-204

United States Department of Agriculture (USDA) (1986) *Nationwide Food Consumption Survey Continuing Survey of Food Intakes of Individuals Men 19-50 Years 1 Day 1985* Report No **85-3**, Hyattsville, Maryland, Nutrition Monitoring Service, Human Nutrition Information Service

United States Department of Agriculture (USDA) (1987) *Nationwide Food Consumption Survey Continuing Survey of Food Intakes of Indivuduals Women 19-50 Years and Their Children 1-5 Years 4 Days 1985* Report No **85-4,** Hyattsville, Maryland, Nutrition Monitoring Division, Human Nutrition Information Service

Valsecchi MG ,(1992) Modelling the relative risk of oesophageal cancer in a case control study *J Clin Epidemiol* **45** 347-355

van den Brandt PA, Goldbohm RA, van 't Veer P (1995) Alcohol and breast cancer results from The Netherlands Cohort Study *Am J Epidemiol* **141**907-15

van den Brandt PA, Ronckers C, van den Hoogen P, Goldbloom RA, Lurney LH (1995) Height, weight and breast cancer risk: results from the Netherlands cohort study *Am J Epidemiol* **141** 61A

van Rensburg SJ, Benade AS, Rose EF, du Plessis JP (1983) Nutritional status of African populations predisposed to esophageal cancer *Nutr Cancer* **4** 206-16

Vena JE, Graham S, Zielezny M, Swanson et al (1985) Lifetime occupational exercise and colon cancer *Am J Epidemiol* **122** 357-365

Waraarchakul N, Strong R, Wood RG, Richardson A (1989) The effect of ageing and dietary restriction on DNA repair *Exper Cell Res* **181** 197-204

Wattenberg LW (1987) Inhibition of chemical carcinogenesis *JNCI* **60** 11-18

Wattenberg LW, Hanley AB, Barany G et al (1986) Inhibition of carcinogenesis by some minor dietary constituents, in Hayashi Y (ed): *Diet, Nutrition, and Cancer* Tokyo, Japan Sci Soc Press pp193-203

Wattenberg LW, Loub WD (1978) Inhibition of polycyclic aromatic hydrocarbon-induced neoplasia by naturally occurring indoles *Cancer Res* **38** 1410-3

Whittemore AS, Wu Williams AH, Lee M et al (1990) Diet, physical activity, and colorectal cancer among Chinese in North America and China *JNCI* **82** 915-926

WHO (1975) World Health Organisation Report of the committee on international dietary allowances of the international union of nutritional sciences *Nutr Abstr Rev* **45** 89-111

WHO (1990) World Health Organization *Diet, Nutrition, and the Prevention of Chronic Diseases Technical Report 797* Geneva: WHO

WHO (1997) World Health Organization *The World Health Report* Geneva: WHO

Willett W C (1990) *Nutritional Epidemiology* New York: Oxford University Press

Willett WC (1994) Diet and health: what should we eat? *Science* **264** 532-7

Willett WC, Howe GR, Kushi LH (1997) Adjustment for total energy intake in epidemiological studies *Am J Clin Nutr* (in press)

Willett WC, Stampfer MJ, Colditz GA et al, (1987) Moderate alcohol consumption and the risk of breast cancer N Engl J Med **316** 1174-80

Wolff SP (1993) Diabetes and free radicals *Br Med Bull* **49** 642-652

Wu AH, Paganini Hill A, Ross RK, Henderson BE (1987) Alcohol, physical activity and other risk factors for colorectal cancer: a prospective study *Br J Cancer* **55** 687-694

Young VR, Pellett PL (1994) Plant proteins in relation to human protein and amino acid nutrition *Am J Clin Nutr* **59** (suppl) 1203S-1212S

Yu BP (1994) How diet affects the ageing process of the rat *Exper Biol Med* **205** 97-104

Yu MC, Garabrant DH, Peters JM, Mack TM (1988) Tobacco, alcohol, diet, occupation and carcinoma of the esophagus *Cancer Res* **48** 3843-3848

Yu MC, Garabrant DH, Peters JM, Mack TM (1988) Tobacco, alcohol, diet, occupation, and carcinoma of the esophagus *Cancer Res* **48** 3843-8

Zhang L-X, Cooney RV, Bertram JS (1991) Carotenoids enhance gap junctional communication and inhibit lipid peroxidation in C3H/10T1/2 cells: relationship to their cancer chemopreventive action *Carcinogenesis* **12** 2109-2114

Zhang L-X, Cooney RV, Bertram JS (1992): Carotenoids up-regulate Connexin43 gene expression independent of their provitamin A or antioxidant properties *Cancer Res* **52** 5707-5712

Ziegler RG, Morris LE, Blot WJ et al (1981) Esophageal cancer among black men in Washington DC II Role of nutrition *JNCI* **67** 1199-1206

Ziegler RG, Subar AF, Craft NE et al, (1992) Does beta-carotene explain why reduced cancer risk is associated with vegetable and fruit intake? *Cancer Res* **52** 2060s-2066s

CHAPTER SIX
FOODS AND DRINKS

Abdullaev FI (1993) Biological effects of saffron *BioFactors* **4** 83-86

Adlercreutz H, Hamalainen E, Gorbach SL et al (1989) Diet and plasma androgens in postmenopausal vegetarian and omnivorous women and postmenopausal women with breast cancer *Am J Clin Nutr* **49** 433-42

Adlercreutz H, Hamalainen E, Gorbach SL, Goldin BR, Woods MN, Dwyer JT (1989) Diet and plasma androgens in postmenopausal vegetarian and omnivorous women and postmenopausal women with breast cancer *Am J Clin Nutr* **49** 433-442

Agrawal RC, Wiessler M, Hecker E (1986) Tumour-promoting effect of chilli extract in Bald mice *Int J Cancer* **38** 689-95

Anderson J, Johnstone BM, Cook-Newell ME (1995) Meta-analysis of the effects of soy protein intake on serum lipids *Med* **333** 276-282

Ansher SS, Dolan P, Bueding E (1986) Biochemical effects of dithiolthiones *Food Chem Toxicol* **24** 405-15

Armstrong B, Doll R (1975) Environmental factors and cancer incidence and mortality in different countries, with special reference to dietary practice *Int J Cancer* **15** 617-631

Aruna K, Sivaramakrishnan VM (1990) Plant products as protective agents against cancer *Indian J Exp Biol* **28** 1008-1011

Aruna K, Sivaramakrishnan VM (1992) Anticarcinogenic effects of some Indian plant products *Food Chem Toxicol* **30** 953-956

Badria FA (1994) Is man helpless against cancer? An environmental approach: antimutagenic agents from Egyptian food and medicinal preparations *Cancer Lett* **84** 1-5

Banerjee S, Hawksby C, Miller S, Dahill S, Beattie A D and McColl K E L (1994) Effect of Helicobacter pylori and its eradication on gastric juice ascorbic acid *Gut* **35** 317-22

Banerjee S, Sharma R, Kale RK, Rao AR (1994) Influence of certain essential oils on carcinogen-metabolizing enzymes and acid-soluble sulfhydryls in mouse liver *Nutr-Cancer* **21** 263-9

Barbosa JC, Shultz TD, Filley SJ, Nieman DC (1990) The relationship among adiposity, diet, and hormone concentrations in vegetarian and nonvegetarian postmenopausal women *Am J Clin Nutr* **51** 798-803

Belanger A, Locong A, Noel C et al (1989) Influence of diet on plasma steroid and sex plasma binding globulin levels in adult men *J Steroid Biochem* **32** 829-833

Belman S (1983) Onion and garlic oils inhibit tumor promotion *Carcinogenesis* **4** 1063-5

Benito E, Obrador A, Stiggelbout A et al (1990) A population-based case-control study of colorectal cancer in Majorca I Dietary factors *Int J Cancer* **45** 69-76

Berkel J, de-Waard F (1983) Mortality and life expectancy of Seventh-day Adventists in the Netherlands *Int J Epidemiol* **12** 455-459

Bingham S (1996) Epidemiology and mechanisms relating diet to risk of colorectal cancer *Nutrition Research Reviews* **9**

Bingham SA (1988) Meat, starch, and nonstarch polysaccharides and large bowel cancer *Am J Clin Nutr* **48** (3 Suppl) 762-7

Birt DF, Pelling JC, Pour PM et al (1987) Enhanced pancreatic and skin tumorigenesis in cabbage-fed hamsters and mice *Carcinogenesis* **8** 913-7

Block G, Dresser CM, Hartman AM, Carroll MD (1985) Nutrient sources in the American diet:quantitative data from the NHANES II survey II Macronutrients and fats *Am J Epidemiol* **122** 27-40

Block G, Patterson B, Subar A (1992) Fruit, vegetables, and cancer prevention: a review of the epidemiological evidence *Nutr Cancer* **18** 1-29

Boyd JN, Misslbeck N, Stoewsand GS (1983) Changes in preneoplastic response to aflatoxin B1 in rats fed green beans, beets, or squash *Food Chem Toxicol* **21** 37-40

Boyd JN, Sell S, Stoewsand GS (1979) Inhibition of aflatoxin-induced serum alpha-fetoprotein in rats fed cauliflower *Proc Soc Exp Biol Med* **161** 473-5

Bresnick E, Birt DF, Wolterman K et al (1990) Reduction in mammary tumorigenesis in the rat by cabbage and cabbage residue *Carcinogenesis* **11** 1159-1163

Brody J (1985) Jane Brody's Good Food Book Living the High-Carbohydrate Way, New York, WW Norton, Company Inc pp112-121

Bueno de Mesquita HB, Maisonneuve P, Runia S, Moerman CJ (1991) Intake of foods and nutrients and cancer of the exocrine pancreas: a population-based case-control study in The Netherlands *Int J Cancer* **48** 540-54 9

Buiatti E, Palli D, Decarli A et al, (1989) A case-control study of gastric cancer and diet in Italy *Int J Cancer* **44** 611-616

Butler MA, Iwasaki M, Guengerich FP, Kadlubar FF (1989) Human cytochrome P-450PA (P-450IA2), the phenacetin O-deethylase, is primarily responsible for the hepatic 3-demethylation of caffeine and N-oxidation of carcinogenic arylamines *Proc Natl Acad Sci USA* **86** 7696-7700

Cannon G (1992) *Food and Health: the Experts Agree* London: Consumers' Association

Carroll KK (1991) Review of clinical studies on cholesterol lowering response to soy protein *J Am Diet Assoc* **91** 820-827

Chen J (1992) The antimutagenic and anticarcinogenic effects of tea, garlic and other natural foods in China: a review *Biomed Environ Sci* **5** 1-17

Chyou PH, Nomura AM, Hankin JH, Stemmermann GN (1990) A case-cohort study of diet and stomach cancer *Cancer Res* **50** 7501-7504

Chyou PH, Nomura AM, Stemmermann GN (1993) A prospective study of diet, smoking, and lower urinary tract cancer *Ann Epidemiol* 3 211-216

Colditz GA, Branch LG, Lipnick RJ et al (1985) Increased green and yellow vegetable intake and lowered cancer deaths in an elderly population *Am J Clin Nutr* **41** 32-36

Cook-Mozaffari PJ, Azordegan F, Day NE et al (1979) Oesophageal cancer studies in the Caspian Littoral of Iran: results of a case-control study *Br J Cancer* **39** 293-309

de Kok TMCM, van Faassen A, Bausch-Goldbohm RA et al (1992) Fecapentaene excretion and fecal mutagenicity in relation to nutrient intake and fecal parameters in humans on omnivorous and vegetarian diets *Cancer Lett* **62** 11-21

De Stefani E, Correa P, Oreggia F et al (1987) Risk factors for laryngeal cancer *Cancer* **60** 3087-3091

Dorgan JF, Schatzkin A (1991) Antioxidant micronutrients in cancer prevention *Hematology/Oncology Clinics of North America* **5** 43-68

Dragsted LO, Strube M, Larsen JC (1993) Cancer-protective factors in fruits and vegetables: biochemical and biological background *Pharmacol Toxicol* **72** Suppl 1:116-135

Dwyer JT (1988) Health aspects of vegetarian diets *Am J Clin Nutr* **48** 712-738

Fonnebo V (1992): Mortality in Norwegian Seventh-Day Adventists 1962-1986 *J Clin Epidemiol* **45** 157-167

Fraser GE, Sabate J, Beeson WL, Strohen TM (1992) A possible protective effect of nut consumption on risk of coronary heart disease: the Adventist health study *Arch Intern Med* **152** 1416-1424

Frentzel Beyme R, Chang Claude J (1994) Vegetarian diets and colon cancer: the German experience *Am J Clin Nutr* **59** 1143S-1152S

Frentzel Beyme R, Claude J, Eilber U (1988) Mortality among German vegetarians: first results after five years of follow-up *Nutr Cancer* **11** 17-126

Gao C, Tajima K, Kuroishi T et al (1993) Protective effects of raw vegetables and fruit against lung cancer among smokers and ex-smokers: a case-control study in the Tokai area of Japan *Jpn J Cancer Res* **84** 594-600

Gonzalez CA, Sanz JM, Marcos G et al (1991) Dietary factors and stomach cancer in Spain: a multi-centre case-control study *Int J Cancer* **49** 513-519

Gridley G, McLaughlin JK, Block G et al (1990) Diet and oral and pharyngeal cancer among blacks *Nutr Cancer* **14** 219-225

Hansson L-E, Nyren O, Bergstrom R et al (1993) Diet and risk of gastric cancer A population-based case-control study in Sweden *Int J Cancer* **55** 181-9

Heilbrun LK, Nomura A, Hankin JH, Stemmermann GN (1989) Diet and colorectal cancer with special reference to fiber intake *Int J Cancer* **44** 1-6

Heilbrun LK, Nomura A, Stemmermann GN (1986) Black tea consumption and cancer risk: a prospective study *Br J Cancer* **54** 677–83

Herrero R, Potischman N, Brinton LA et al (1991) A case-control study of nutrient status and invasive cervical cancer I Dietary indicators *Am J Epidemiol* **134** 1335-1346

Hirayama T (1982) Relationship of soybean paste soup intake to gastric cancer risk *Nutr Cancer* **3** 223-233

Hirayama T (1986): A large scale cohort study on cancer risks by diet with special reference to the risk reducing effects of green yellow vegetable consumption In Hayashi Y (ed) *Diet, nutrition and cancer* Tokyo, Sci Soc Press 41-53

Hirayama T (1988) Epidemiology of pancreatic cancer in Japan *Int J Pancreatol* **3** S203-S204

Hirose N, Doi F, Ueki T et al (1992) Suppressive effect of sesamin against 7,12-dimethylbenz[a]-anthracene induced rat mammary carcinogenesis *Anticancer Res* **12** 1259-66

Hoshiyama Y, Sosaba T (1992) A case-control study of stomach cancer and its relation to diet, cigarettes, and alcohol consumption in Saitama Prefecture, Japan *Cancer Causes Control* **3** 441-448

Hu J, Nyren O, Wolk A et al (1994) Risk factors for oesophageal cancer in northeast China *Int J Cancer* **57** 38-46

Hu JF, Liu YY, Yu YK et al (1991) Diet and cancer of the colon and rectum: a case-control study in China *Int J Epidemiol* **20** 362-367

Huang M-T, Ho C-T, Wang ZY et al (1994) Inhibition of skin tumorigenesis by rosemary and its constituents carnosol and ursolic acid *Cancer Res* **54** 701-8

IARC (1991) *IARC monographs on the evaluation of the carcinogenic risk of chemicals to humans, coffee, tea, mate, methylxanthines and methylglyoxal* volume **51** Lyon: International Agency for Research on Cancer

Ip C, Lisk DJ (1994) Bioactivity of selenium from Brazil nut for cancer prevention and selenoenzyme maintenance *Nutr Cancer* **21** 203-212

Iscovich JM, Iscovich RB, Howe G et al (1989) A case-control study of diet and breast cancer in Argentina *Int J Cancer* **44** 770-776

Iscovich JM, L'Abbee KA, Castelleto R et al (1992) Colon cancer in Argentina I Risk from intake of dietary items *Int J Cancer* **51** 851-857

Jacobs DR, Slavin J, Marquart L (1995) Wholegrain intake and cancer: a review of the literature *Nutr Cancer* **24** 221-229

Jacobsen BK, Bjelke E, Kvale G, Heuch I (1986) Coffee drinking, mortality and cancer incidence results from a Norwegian prospective study *JNCI* **76** 823-831

Jain M, Burch JD, Howe GR, Risch HA, Miller AB (1990) Dietary factors and risk of lung cancer: results from a case-control study, Toronto, 1981-1985 *Int J Cancer* **45** 287-293

Kampman E, Verhoeven D, Sloots L, van 't Veer P (1996) Vegetable and animal products as determinants of colon cancer risk in Dutch men and women *Cancer Causes Control* **6** 225-234

Key T, Davey G (1996) Prevalence of obesity is low in people who do not eat meat [letter] *BMJ* **313** (7060) 816-7

Key TJA, Thorogood M, Appleby PN, Burr ML (1996) Dietary habits and mortality in 11,000 vegetarians and health concious people: results of a 17 year follow up *BMJ* **313** 775-779

Koo LC (1988) Dietary habits and lung cancer risk among Chinese females in Hong Kong who never smoked *Nutr Cancer* **11** 155-172

Krishnaswamy K, Prasad MPR, Krishna TP, Pasricha S (1993) A case control study of selenium in cancer *Indian J Med Res* **98** 124-128

Kune GA, Bannerman S, Field B et al (1992) Diet, alcohol, smoking, serum beta-carotene, and vitamin A in male nonmelanocytic skin cancer patients and controls *Nutr Cancer* **18** 237-244

Kune S, Kune GA, Watson LF (1987) Case-control study of dietary etiological factors: the Melbourne Colorectal Cancer Study *Nutr Cancer* **9** 21-42

Kuratsune M, Ikeda M, Hayashi T (1986) Epidemiologic studies on possible health effects of intake of pyrolyzates of foods, with reference to mortality among Japanese Seventh-Day Adventists *Environ Health Perspect* **67** 143-146

Kuroda K, Terao K, Akao M (1983) Inhibitory effect of fumaric acid on 3-methyl-4'-

(dimethylamino)- azobenzene-induced hepatocarcinogenesis in rats *JNCI* **71** 855-857

Kvale G, Bjelke E, Gart JJ (1983) Dietary habits and lung cancer risk *Int J Cancer* **31** 397-405

La Vecchia C, Negri E, Decarli A et al (1988) A case-control study of diet and colo-rectal cancer in northern Italy *Int J Cancer* **41** 492-498

La Vecchia C, Negri E, Decarli A, D'Avanzo B, Franceschi S (1987) A case-control study of diet and gastric cancer in northern Italy *Int J Cancer* **40** 484-489

La Vecchia C, Negri E, Franceschi S et al (1992) Tea consumption and cancer risk *Nutr Cancer* **17** 27-31

Lang NP, Butler MA, Massengill J et al (1994) Rapid metabolic phenotypes for acetyltransferase and cytochrome P4501A2 and putative exposure to food borne heterocyclic amines increase the risk for colorectal cancer or polyps *Cancer Epidemiol Biomarkers Prev* **3** 675-82

Le Marchand L, Yoshizawa CN, Kolonel LN et al (1989) Vegetable consumption and lung cancer risk: a population-based case-control study in Hawaii *JNCI* **81** 1158–1164

Lee HP, Gourley L, Duffy SW et al (1991) Dietary effects on breast-cancer risk in Singapore *Lancet* **337** 1197-1200

Levi F, Franceschi S, Negri E, La Vecchia C (1993) Dietary factors and the risk of endometrial cancer *Cancer* **71** 3575-3581

Li JY, Ershow AG, Chen ZJ et al (1989) A case-control study of cancer of the esophagus and gastric cardia in Linxian *Int J Cancer* **43** 755-761

Maclure M, Willett W (1990) A case-control study of diet and risk of renal adenocarcinoma *Epidemiology* **1** 430-440

Maltzman TH, Hurt LM, Elson CE et al (1989) The prevention of nitrosomethylurea-induced mammary tumors by d-limonene and orange oil *Carcinogenesis* **10** 781-3

McLaughlin JK, Gridley G, Block G et al (1988) Dietary factors in oral and pharyngeal cancer *JNCI* **80** 1237-1243

McPhillips JB, Eaton CB, Gans KM et al (1994) Dietary differences in smokers and nonsmokers from two southeastern New England communities *J Am Diet Assoc* **94** 287-92

Messina MJ, Persky V, Setchell KD, Barnes S (1994) Soy intake and cancer risk a review of the in vitro and in vivo data *Nutr Cancer* **21** 113-131

Miller AB, Howe GR, Jain M et al (1983) Food items and food groups as risk factors in a case-control study of diet and colorectal cancer *Int J Cancer*

32 155-61

Mills PK, Beeson L, Phillips RL, Fraser GE (1989) Cohort study of the diet, lifestyle and prostate cancer in Adventist men *Cancer* **64** 598-604

Mills PK, Beeson L, Phillips RL, Fraser GE (1991) Bladder cancer in a low risk population Results from the Adventist Health Study *Am J Epidemiol* **133** 230-9

Mills PK, Beeson WL, Abbey DE et al (1988) Dietary habits and past medical history as related to fatal pancreas cancer risk among Adventists *Cancer* **61** 2578-2585

Mills PK, Beeson WL, Phillips RL, Fraser GE (1989): Dietary habits and breast cancer incidence among Seventh-day Adventists *Cancer* **64** 582-590

Mills PK, Beeson WL, Phillips RL, Fraser GE (1994) Cancer incidence among California Seventh-Day Adventists 1976-1982 *Am J Clin Nutr* **59** 1136S-1142S

Modan B, Barell V, Lubin F et al (1975) Low-fiber intake as an etiologic factor in cancer of the colon *JNCI* **55** 15-18

Morabia A, Wynder EL (1990) Dietary habits of smokers, people who never smoked, and exsmokers *Am J Clin Nutr* **52** 933-7

Munzner R (1986) Modifying action of vegetable juice extract on the mutagenicity of beef extract and nitrosated beef extract *Food Chem Toxicol* **24** 847-9

Nakanishi K, Fukushima S, Shibata M et al (1987) Effect of phenacetin and caffeine on the urinary bladder of rats treated with N-butyl-N-(4-hydroxybutyl)nitrosamine *Jpn J Cancer Res* **69** 395-400

NAS (1982) *Diet, nutrition and cancer* Washington DC: National Academy Press

NAS (1989) *Diet and Health* Washington DC: National Academy Press

Nomura A, Grove JS, Stemmermann GN, Severson RK (1990) A prospective study of stomach cancer and its relation to diet, cigarettes, and alcohol consumption *Cancer Res* **50** 1990 627-631

Notani PN, Jayant K (1987) Role of diet in upper aerodigestive tract cancers *Nutr Cancer* **10** 103-113

Notani PN, Jayant K (1987) Role of diet in upper aerodigestive tract cancers *Nutr Cancer* **10** 103-113

Oshima H, Bartsch H (1981) Quantitative estimation of endogenous nitrosation in humans by monitoring N-nitrosoproline

excreted in the urine *Cancer Res* **41** 3658-62

Pedersen AB, Bartholomew MJ, Dolence LA et al (1991) Menstrual differences due to vegetarian and nonvegetarian diets *Am J Clin Nutr* **53** 879-885

Phillips RL (1975) Role of life-style and dietary habits in risk of cancer among Seventh-day Adventists *Cancer Res* **35** 3513-3522

Phillips RL (1975): Role of life-style and dietary habits in risk of cancer among Seventh-day Adventists *Cancer Res* **35** 3513-3522

Polasa K, Raghuram TC, Krishna TP, Krishnaswamy K (1992) Effect of turmeric on urinary mutagens in smokers *Mutagenesis* **7** 107-109

Pusateri DJ, Roth WT, Ross JK, Shultz TD (1990) Dietary and hormonal evaluation of men at different risks for prostate cancer: plasma and fecal hormone-nutrient interrelationships *Am J Clin Nutr* **51** 371-377

Ramon JM, Serra L, Cerdo C, Oromi J (1993) Dietary factors and gastric cancer risk A case-control study in Spain *Cancer* **71** 1731-1735

Rao AR, Hashim S (1995) Chemopreventive action of oriental food-seasoning spices mixture Garam masala on DMBA-induced transplacental and translactational carcinogenesis in mice *Nutr Cancer* **23** 91-101

Ravai M (1995) California walnuts: the natural way to a healthier heart *Nutrition Today* **30** 173-176

Rieder A, Adamek M, Wrba H (1983) Delay of diethylnitrosamine-induced hepatoma in rats by carrot feeding *Oncology* **40** 120-123

Risch HA, Jain M, Choi NW et al (1985) Dietary factors and the incidence of cancer of the stomach *Am J Epidemiol* **122** 947-959

Roberts-Thomson I, Ryan P, Khoo KK et al (1996) Diet, acetylator phenotype and risk of colorectal neoplasia *Lancet* **347** 1372-3

Salomi MJ, Nair SC, Panikkar KR (1991) Inhibitory effects of Nigella sativa and saffron (Crocus sativa) on chemical carcinogenesis in mice *Nutr Cancer* **16** 67-72

Sammon AM (1992) A case-control study of diet and social factors in cancer of the esophagus in Transkei *Cancer* **69** 860-865

Scholar EM, Wolterman K, Birt DF, Bresnick E (1989) The effects of diets enriched in collards on murine pulmonary metastasis *Nutr Cancer* **12** 121-6

Schuman LM, Mandel JS, Radke A et al (1982) Some selected features of the epidemiology prostatic cancer: Minneapolis-St Paul, Minnesota case-control study, 1976-1979 In

Magnus K (ed): *Trends in cancer incidence: causes and practical implications* Washinton, DC: Hemisphere Publishing Corp pp345-354

Severson RK, Nomura AM, Grove JS, Stemmermann GN (1989) A prospective study of demographics, diet, and prostate cancer among men of Japanese ancestry in Hawaii *Cancer Res* **49** 1857-1860

Shibata A, Paganini Hill A, Ross RK, Henderson BE (1992) Intake of vegetables, fruits, beta-carotene, vitamin C and vitamin supplements and cancer incidence among the elderly: a prospective study *Br J Cancer* **66** 673-679

Shu XO et al (1992) Diet and other risk factors for laryngeal cancer in Shanghai, China *Am J Epidemiol* **136** 178-191

Shu XO, Zheng W, Potischman N et al (1993) A population-based case-control study of dietary factors and endometrial cancer in Shanghai, People's Republic of China *Am J Epidemiol* **137** 155-165

Singh A,Rao-AR (1992) Evaluation of the modulatory influence of food additive-garam masala on hepatic detoxication system *Indian J Exp Biol* **30** 1142-5

Slattery ML, Schumacher MC, Smith KR et al (1988) Physical activity, diet, and risk of colon cancer in Utah *Am J Epidemiol* **128** 989-99

Sparnins VL, Venegas PL, Wattenberg LW (1982) Glutathione S-transferase activity: enhancement by compounds inhibiting chemical carcinogenesis and by dietary constituents *JNCI* **68** 493-496

Steinmetz K, Potter JD (1991a) A review of vegetables, fruit, and cancer I: epidemiology *Cancer Causes Control* **2** 325-357

Steinmetz KA, Kushi LH, Bostick RM et al (1994)Vegetables, fruit, and colon cancer in the Iowa Women's Health Study *Am J Epidemiol* **139** 1-15

Steinmetz KA, Potter JD (1991b) Vegetables, fruit, and cancer II Mechanisms *Cancer Causes and Control* **2** 427-442

Steinmetz KA, Potter JD (1993) Food group consumption and colon cancer in the Adelaide case-control study I Vegetables and fruit *Int J Cancer* **53**711-719

Steinmetz KA, Potter JD (1996) Vegetables, fruit, and cancer prevention:a review *J Am Diet Assoc* **96** 1027-1037

Steinmetz KA, Potter JD, Folsom AR (1993) Vegetables, fruit, and lung cancer in the Iowa Women's Health Study *Cancer Res* **53** 536-543

Stoewsand GS, Anderson JL, Munson L (1988)

Protective effect of dietary brussels sprouts against mammary carcinogenesis in Sprague-Dawley rats *Cancer Lett* **39**199-207

Stoewsand GS, Anderson JL, Munson L, Lisk DJ (1989) Effect of dietary Brussels sprouts with increased selenium content on mammary carcinogenesis in the rat *Cancer Lett* **45** 43-8

Stohs SJ, Lawson TA, Anderson L, Bueding E (1986) Effects of oltipraz, BHA, ADT, and cabbage on glutathione metabolism, DNA damage, and lipid peroxidation in old mice *Mech Ageing Dev* **37**137-45

Sturgeon SR, Ziegler RG, Brinton LA et al (1991) Diet and the risk of vulvar cancer *Ann Epidemiol* **1** 427-437

Subar AS, Heimendinger J, Krebs-Smith SM et al (1992) *5 A Day for Better Health* A Baseline Study of Americans' Fruit And Vegetable Consumption, Rockville, Maryland: National Cancer Institute

Swanson CA, Mao BL, Li JY et al (1992) Dietary determinants of lung-cancer risk: results from a case- control study in Yunnan Province, China *Int J Cancer* **50** 876-880

Tanida N, Kawaura A, Takahashi A, Sawada K, Shimoyama T (1991) Suppressive effect of wasabi (pungent Japanese spice) on gastric carcinogenesis induced by MNNG in rats *Nutr Cancer* 16:53-58

Tawfiq N, Wanigatunga S, Heaney RK et al (1994) Induction of the anti-carcinogenic enzyme quinone reductase by food extracts using murine hepatoma cells *Eur J Cancer Prev* **3** 285-92

Temple LJ, Basu TK (1987) Selenium and cabbage and colon carcinogenesis in mice *JNCI* **79**1131-4

Thorogood M, Mann J, Appleby P, McPherson K (1994) Risk of death from cancer and ischaemic heart disease in meat and non-meat eaters *Br Med J* **308** 1667-1670

Toth B, Rogan E, Walker B (1984) Tumorigenicity and mutageniscity studies with capsaicin of hot peppers *Anticancer Res* **4** 117-20

Trichopoulos D, Ouranos G, Day NE et al (1985) Diet and cancer of the stomach: a case-control study in Greece *Int J Cancer* **36**291-297

Tricker AR, Preussmann R (1991) Carcinogenic *N*-nitrosamines in the diet: Occurrence, formation, mechanisms and carcinogenic potential *Mutation Res* **259** 277-289

Tuyns AJ, Kaaks R, Haelterman M (1988) Colorectal cancer and the consumption of foods a case-control study in Belgium *Nutr Cancer* **11** 189-204

Tuyns AJ, Kaaks R, Haelterman M, Riboli E (1992) Diet and gastric cancer A case control study in Belgium *Int J Cancer* **51** 1-6

Unnikrishnan MC, Kuttan R (1990) Tumour reducing and anticarcinogenic activity of selected spices *Cancer Lett* **51**85-89

Ursin G, Ziegler RG, Subar AF et al (1993) Dietary patterns associated with a low-fat diet in the national health examination follow-up study: identification of potential confounders for epidemiologic analyses *Am J Epidemiol* **137** 916-927

Vang O, Jensen H, Autrup H (1991) Induction of cytochrome P-450IAl1, IA2, IIB1, IIB2 and IIE1 by broccoli in rat liver and colon *Chem Biol Interact* **78** 85-96

Wang YP, Han XY, Su W et al (1992) Esophageal cancer in Shanxi Province, People's Republic of China: a case-control study in high and moderate risk areas *Cancer Causes Control* **3**107-113

Wattenberg LW (1971) Studies of polycyclic hydrocarbon hydroxylases of the intestine possibly related to cancer *Cancer* **28** 99-102

Wattenberg LW (1983) Inhibition of neoplasia by minor dietary constituents *Cancer Res* 43 (Supplement):2448s-53s

Wattenberg LW, Coccia JB (1991) Inhibition of 4-(methylnitrosoamino)-1-(3-pyridyl)-1-butanone carcinogenesis in mice by D-limonene and citrus fruit oils *Carcinogenesis* **12** 115-7

Wattenberg LW, Schafer HW, Waters LJr, Davis DW (1989) Inhibition of mammary tumor formation by broccoli and cabbage *Proc Am Assoc Cancer Research* **30**181

WHO (1990) Diet, nutrition, and the prevention of chronic diseases Report of a WHO study group Technical Report Series 797, Geneva, World HealthOrganization

Wu-Williams AH, Yu MC, Mack TM (1990) Life-style, workplace,and stomach cancer by subsite in young men of Los Angeles County *Cancer Res* **50** 2569-76

You WC, Blot WJ, Chang YS et al (1988) Diet and high risk of stomach cancer in handong, China *Cancer Res* **48** 3518-3523

Zheng W, Blot WJ, Shu XO et al (1992) Diet and other risk factors for laryngeal cancer in Shanghai, China *Am J Epidemiol* **136** 178-191

Zheng W, McLaughlin JK, Chow WH et al (1992) Risk factors for cancers of the nasal cavity and paranasal sinuses in Shanghai, with emphasis on diet *Cancer Epidemiol Biomarkers Prev* **1** 441- 448

Zheng W, McLaughlin JK, Chow WH et al (1993) Risk factors for cancers of the nasal cavity and paranasal sinuses among white men in the United States *Am J Epidemiol* **138** 965-972

Ziegler RG (1991) Vegetables, fruits, and carotenoids and the risk of cancer *Am J Clin Nutr* **53** 251S-259S

Ziegler RG, Brinton LA, Hamman RF et al (1990) Diet and the risk of invasive cervical cancer among white women in the United States *Am J Epidemiol* **132** 432-445

CHAPTER SEVEN
FOOD PROCESSING

Bogovski P (ed) (1983) Polycyclic aromatic compounds Part I *IARC Monogr Eval Carcinogenic Risks Hum*

Buiatti E, Palli D, Decarli A, Amadori D, Avellini C, Bianchi S et al (1989) Case-control study of gastric cancer and diet in Italy *Int J Cancer* **44** 611-6

Bumb B (1989) *Global fertiliser perspective 1960-95* The dynamics of growth and structural change Mussel Shoals, Alabama: International Fertiliser Development Center

Cannon G (1992) *Food and Health The Experts Agree* London Consumers Association

Commoner B, Vithayathil AJ, Dolara P, Nair S, Madyastha P, Cuca GC (1978) Formation of mutagens in beef and beef extract during cooking *Science* **201** 913-6

David CD, Ghoshal A, Schut HA, Snyderwine HG (1994) Metabolism of the food derived carcinogen 2-amino-1-methyl-6-phenylimidazo[4,5-b]pyridine by lactating Fischer 344 rats and their nursing pups *JNCI* **86**:1065-70

ECETOC (1988) Nitrate and drinking water Brussels European Chemical Industry Ecology and Toxicology Centre *Technical Report No27*

Eisenbrand G, Tang W (1993) Food-borne heterocyclic amines Chemistry, formation, occurrence and biological activities *Toxicology* **84**1-82

Felton JS, Fultz E, Dolbeare FA, Knize MG (1994) Effect of microwave pretreatment on heterocyclic aromatic amine mutagens/carcinogens in fried beef patties *Food Chem Toxicol* **32**897-903

Flamm WG, Lehinan-McKeeman L (1991) The human relevance of the tumor-inducing potential of d-limonene in male rats : implications for risk assessment *Regul Toxicol Pharmacol* **13** 70-86

Ford RA (1989) General principles of the regulation of flavors In: Middlekauf RD, Shubik P (eds) *International Food Regulation Handbook* New York and Basel: Marcel Dekker 241-51

Gold LS, Slone TH, Manley NB, Ames BN (1994) Heterocyclic amines formed by cooking food: comparison of bioassay results with other chemicals in the Carcinogenic Potency Database *Cancer Lett* **83** 21-9

Hall AJ, Wild CP (1993) The epidemiology of aflatoxin-related disease In: Eaton DL, Groopman JD (eds) *The Toxicology of Aflatoxins: Human Health, Veterinary and Agricultural Significance* New York Academic Press

Henderson AK, Rosen D, Miller GL (1995) Breast cancer among women exposed to polybrominated biphenyls *Epidemiology* **6** 544-546

Hirayama T (1984) Epidemiology of stomach cancer in Japan: with special reference to the strategy for the primary research *Jpn J Clin Oncol* **14** 159-68

Howson CP, Hirayama T, Wynder EL (1986) The decline in gastric cancer: epidemiology of an unplanned triumph *Epidemiol Rev* **8** 1-27

Hsieh DPH (1989) Carcinogenic potential of mycotoxins in foods in: Taylor SL, Scanlan RA (eds) *Food Toxicology* New York and Basel Marcel Dekker 11-30

IARC (1974) Monographs on the evaluation of the carcinogenic risk of chemicals to humans Vol **5** *Some organochlorine pesticides* Lyon: International Agency for Research on Cancer

IARC (1975) *Monographs on the Evaluation Of Cacinogenic Risks to Humans, Some Aromatic Azo Compounds* Vol **8** International Agency for research on Cancer, Lyon, France

IARC (1978) *Monographs on the Evaluation Of Cacinogenic Risks to Humans, Some Aromatic Amines and Related Nitro Compounds - Hair Dyes, Colouring Agents and Miscellaneous Industrial Chemicals* Vol **16** International Agency for research on Cancer, Lyon, France

IARC (1980) *Monographs on the Evaluation Of Cacinogenic Risks to Humans, Some Non-Nutritive Sweetening Agents* Vol **22** International Agency for research on Cancer, Lyon, France

IARC (1980) Monographs on the evaluation of the carcinogenic risk of chemicals to humans Vol **22** *Some Non- nutritive Sweetening Agents* Lyon: International Agency for Research on Cancer

IARC (1983) *Monographs on the Evaluation Of Cacinogenic Risks to Humans, Some Food Additives, Feed Additives and Naturally Occurring Substances* Vol **31** International Agency for research on Cancer, Lyon, France

IARC (1983) Monographs on the evaluation of carcinogenic risks to humans Vol **32** *Polynuclear Aromatic Compounds, Part:1 Chemical, Enviromental and Experimental Data* Lyon: International Agency for Research on Cancer

IARC (1986) *Monographs on the Evaluation Of Cacinogenic Risks to Humans, Some Naturally Occurring and Synthetic Food Components, Furocoumarins and Ultraviolet Radiation* Vol **40** International Agency for research on Cancer, Lyon, France

IARC (1987) Monographs on the evaluation of carcinogenic risks to humans Suppl 7 *Overall evaluations of carcinogenic risks to humans: an updating of IARC monographs* Vols **1-42** Lyon: International Agency for Research on Cancer 83-87; 101-105; 152-154; 322-326; 350-354

IARC (1987) *Overall Evaluations of Carcinogenicity: An Updating of IARC Monographs Volumes 1 to 42* Supplement **7** International Agency for research on Cancer, Lyon, France

IARC (1991) Monographs on the evaluation of carcinogenic risks to humans Vol **52** *Chlorinated Drinking-Water; Chlorination By-Products; Some other Halogenated Compounds; Cobalt and Colbalt Compounds* Lyon: International Agency for Research on Cancer

IARC (1991a) *Monographs on the Evaluation Of Cacinogenic Risks to Humans, Chlorinated Drinking-Water; Chlorination By-products; Some other Halogenated Compounds; Cobalt and Cobalt Compounds* Vol **52** International Agency for research on Cancer, Lyon, France

IARC (1991b) *Monographs on the Evaluation Of Cacinogenic Risks to Humans, Occupational Exposures in Insecticide Application, and Some Pesticides* Vol **53** International Agency for research on Cancer, Lyon, France

IARC (1993) *Monographs on the Evaluation Of Cacinogenic Risks to Humans, Some naturally occurring Substances: Food Items and Constituents, Heterocyclic Aromatic Amines and Mycotoxins* Vol **56** International Agency for research on Cancer, Lyon, France

IARC (1993) Monographs on the evaluation of carcinogenic risks of chemicals to Humans, Volume **56** *Some Naturally Occurring Substances: Food Items and Constituents, Hetrocyclic Aromatic Amines and Mycotoxins* Lyon: International Agency for Research on Cancer

IARC (1997) *Monographs on the Evaluation Of*

Cacinogenic Risks to Humans, Polychlorinated Dibezo-dioxins and Vol **69** International Agency for research on Cancer, Lyon, France

Ilet KF, David BM, Detchon P, Castleden WM, Kwa R (1987) Acetylation phenotype in colorectal carcinoma *Cancer Res* **47**1466-9

Jägerstad M, Skog K, Grivas S, Olsson K (1991) Formation of heterocyclic amines using model systems *Mutat Res* **259** 219-33

Jelinek CF, Pohland AE, Wood GE (1989) Worlwide occurrence of mycotoxins in foods and feeds and feeds-an update *J Assoc Off Anal Chem* **72** 223-230

Joossens JV, Kesteloot H (1996) Nutrition in relation to stomach cancer and stroke mortality (in press)

Kato T, Hasegawa R, Nakae D et al (1996) Dose-dependent induction of 8-hydroxyguanine and preneoplastic foci in rat liver by a food-derived carcinogen, 2-amino-3,8-dimethylimidazo[4,5-f]quinoxaline, at low dose levels *Jpn J Cancer Res* **87**127-133

Knize MG, Dolbeare FA, Cunningham PL, Felton JS (1995) Mutagenic activity and heterocyclic amine content of the human diet *Princess Takamatsu Symp* **23** 30-8

Ladero JM, González JF, Benítez J, Vargas E, Fernández MJ, Baki W et al (1991) Acetylator polymorphism in human colorectal carcinoma *Cancer Res* **51** 2098-100

Lang NP, Butler MA, Massengill J, Lawson M, Stotts RC, Hauer-Jensen M et al (1994) Rapid metabolic phenotypes for acetyltransferase and cytochrome P4501A2 and putative exposure to food borne heterocyclic amines increase the risk for colorectal cancer or polyps *Cancer Epidemiol Biomarkers Prev* **3** 675-82

Lang NP, Chu DZJ, Hunter CF, Kendall DC, Flammang TJ, Kadlubar FF (1986) Role of aromatic amine acetyltransferase in human colorectal cancer *Arch Surg* **121** 1259-61

Layton DW, Bogen KT, Knize MG, Hatch FT, Johnson VM, Felton JS (1995) Cancer risk of heterocyclic amines in cooked foods: an analysis and implications for research *Carcinogenesis* **16** 39-52

Lutwick-LI (1979) Relation between aflatoxin, hepatitis-B virus, and hepatocellular carcinoma *Lancet* **i** 755-7

Minchin RF, Kadlubar FF, Ilett KF Role of acetylation in colorectal cancer *Mutat Res* **290** 35-42

Ministry of Agriculture, Fisheries, Food (1992) Nitrate, nitrite and N-nitroso compounds in food *Food Surveillance Paper* No**32** London: HMSO

Nagao M, Honda M, Seino Y, Yahagi T, Sugimura T (1977) Mutagenicities of smoke condensates and the charred surface of fish and meat *Cancer Lett* **2** 221-6

Nagao M, Sugimura T (1993) Carcinogenic factors in food with relevance to colon cancer development *Mutat Res* **290** 43-51

NAS (1982) *Diet, Nutrition and Cancer* Washington DC: National Academy Press

NAS (1989) *Diet and Health* Washington DC: National Academy Press

NRC (1989) *Recommended dietary allowances*, National Academy Press, 10th edition Washington DC

Peers F, Bosch X, Kaldor J, Linsell A, Pluijmen M (1987) Aflatoxin exposure, hepatitis A virus infection and liver cancer in Swaziland *Int J Cancer* **39** 545-553

Pohland AE, Wood GE (1987) Occurrence of mycotoxins in food In: Krough P (ed) London: Academic Press pp 35-64

Probst-Hensch NM, Haile RW, Ingles SA, Longnecker MP, Han CY, Lin BK et al (1995) Acetylation polymorphism and prevalence of colorectal adenomas *Cancer Res* **55** 2017-20

Rothman N, Poirier MC, Baser ME et al (1990) Formation of polycyclic aromatic hydrocarbon-DNA adducts in peripheral white blood cells during consumption of charcoal-broiled beef *Carcinogenesis* **11** 1241-1243

Sanchez-Castillo CP, Warrender S, Whitehead TP, James WPT (1987) An assessment of the sources of dietary salt in the British population *Clin Sci* **72** 95-102

Sinha R, Rothman N, Brown ED et al (1995) High concentrations of the carcinogen 2-amino-1-methyl-6-phenylimidazo- [4,5-b]pyridine (PhIP) occur in chicken but are dependent on the cooking method *Cancer Res* **55** 4516-4519

Skog K (1993)Cooking procedures and food mutagens: a literature review *Food Chem Toxicol* **31** 655-75

Snyderwine EG (1994) Some perspective on the nutritional aspects of breast cancer research Food derived heterocyclic amines as etiologic agents in human mammary cancer *Cancer* **74**1070-1077

Stavric B (1994) Biological significance of trace levels of mutagenic heterocyclic aromatic amines in human diet: A critical review *Food Chem Toxicol* **32** 977-94

Strickland PT, Routledge MN, Dipple A (1993) Methodologies for measuring carcinogen adducts in humans *Cancer Epid Biomarkers Prev* **2** 607-19

Sugimura T, Nagao M, Kawachi T, Honda M, Yahagi T, Seino Y et al (1977) Mutagen-carcinogens in food, with special reference to highly mutagenic pyrolytic products in broiled foods In: Hiatt HH, Watson JD, Winsten JA (eds) *Origins of human cancer* NY: Cold Spring Harbor Laboratory 1561-77

United Nations (1976) Statistical Yearbook, 1975 New York: United Nations p 298

Ushiyama H, Wakabayashi K, Itoh H, Sugimura T, Nagao M (1991) Presence of carcinogenic heterocyclic amines in urine of healthy volunteers eating normal diet but not of inpatients receiving parenteral alimentation *Carcinogenesis* **12** 1417-22

Van Egmond HP (1996) Analytical methodology and regulations for ochratoxin A *Food Addit Contam* **13** Suppl 11-3

Van Rensberg SJ, Cook-Mozaffari P, Van Schalkwyk DJ, Van der Watt JJ, Vincent TJ, Purchase IF Hepatocellular carcinoma and dietary aflatoxin in Mozambique and Transkei *Br J Cancer* **51** 713-726

Wakabayashi K, Nagao M, Esumi H, Sugimura T (1992) Food-derived mutagens and carcinogens *Cancer Res* **52** 2092S-8S

Walker R (1990) Nitrates, nitrites and N-nitroso compounds: a review of the occurrence in food and diet and the toxicological implications *Food Add Contam* **5** 717-768

Weisburger JH, Rivenson A, Kingston DGI, Wilkins TD, Van Tassell RL et al (1995) Dietary modulation of the carcinogenicity of the heterocyclic amines In: Adamson RH, Gustafsson JA, Ito N, Nagao M, Sugimura T, Wakabayashi K, Yamazoe Y(eds) *Heterocyclic amines in cooked foods* Princeton, NJ Princeton Scientific Publishing

WHO (1982) *Prevention of Coronary Heart Disease Report of a WHO expert committee* Technical report series 678 Geneva: WHO

WHO (1990) *Diet, Nutrition and the Prevention of Chronic Diseases* Technical report 797 Geneva: World Health Organization

WHO (1990)*Public health impact of pesticides used in agriculture Geneva*: World Health Organization

WHO (1992) *Report on the panel on food and agriculture* Geneva: World Health Organization, 104-109

WHO (1992) World Health Organization Commission on Health and Environment *Report of the panel of food and agriculture* Geneva:

WHO

WHO (1993) Toxicological evaluation of certain food additives and contaminants Forty-first Meeting of the Joint FAO/WHO Expert Committee on Food Additives (JECFA) *WHO Food Additive Series:32 Geneva*: World Health Organization105-153

WHO (1996) World Health Organization *Climate change and human health* Geneva: WHO

Wild CP, Jansen LAM, Cova L, Montesano R (1993) Molecular dosimetry of aflatoxin exposure: contribution to understanding the multifactorial etiopathogenesis of primary hepatocellular carcinoma with particular reference to hepatitis B virus *Env Hlth Persp* **99**115-122

Wild CP, Jiang YZ, Allen SJ, Jansen LAM, Hall AJ, Montesano R (1990) Aflatoxin-albumin adducts in human sera from different regions of the world *Carcinogenesis* **11** 2271-2274

Winter CK, Seiber JN, Nuckton CF, editors (1990) *Chemicals in the human food chain* New York and Basel: Van Nostrand Reinhold117-126

Yeh FS, Yu MC, Mo CC, Luo S, Tong MJ, Henderson BE (1989) Hepatitis B virus, aflatoxins and hepatocellular carcinoma in Southern Guangxi, China *Cancer Res* **49** 2506-2509

CHAPTER EIGHT
RECOMMENDATIONS

American Cancer Society (1996) Advisory Committee on Diet, Nutrition, and Cancer Prevention 1996 Guidelines on diet, nutrition, and cancer prevention: reducing the risk of cancer with healthy food choices and physical activity *CA: A Cancer Journal for Clinicians* **46** 325–341

Cannon G (1992) *Food and Health: the Experts Agree* London: Consumers' Association

Commission of the European Community (1993) *Report of the Scientific Commission for Food (thirty-first series): Nutrient and energy intakes for the European Community* Director (Industry) Brussels: Commission of the EC

European Code against Cancer (1995) Boyle P, Veronesi M, Tubiana FE et al *Eur J Cancer* Vol **31A** No 9

FAO/WHO (1992) *International Conference on Nutrition Declaration and Plan of Action* Rome: FAO

Ferro-Luzzi A, Martino L (1996) Obesity and physical activity In: *The Origins and Consequences of Obesity CIBA Foundation Symposium 201* Chichester: Wiley

Goldstein DJ (1992) Beneficial effects of modest weight loss *Int J Obesity* **16** : 397–415

Harvard Report on Cancer Prevention (1996) *Cancer Causes Control* **7** (suppl): S3–S59

IARC (1986) *Cancer: Causes, Occurrence and Control* IARC Scientific Publications No 100 Lyon: International Agency for Research on Cancer

James WPT, Ralph A (eds) 1994 Functional significance of low body mass index (BMI) *Eur J Clin Nutr* **48** (Suppl 3) S1–S202

Japan Dietetic Association (1984) *Dietary guidelines and nutritional policies in Japan* Tokyo: Japan Dietetic Association

Lew EA, Garfinkel L (1978) Variations in mortality by weight among 750,000 men and women *J Chron Dis* **32** 563–576

McArdle WD, Katch FI, Katch VL (1981) *Exercise Physiology: Energy, Nutrition, and Human Performance* Philadelphia: Lea, Febiger

Manson JE, Willett WC, Stampfer MJ, Colditz GA, Hunter DJ, Hankinson SE, Hennekens CH, Speizer FE (1995) Body weight and mortality among women *NEJM* **333** 677–685

NAS (1982) *Diet, Nutrition and Cancer* Washington DC: National Academy Press

NAS (1989) *Diet and Health* Washington DC: National Academy Press

National Cancer Institute and Produce for Better Health (1994) *'5 a day' for better health* Bethesda, MA: NCI

National Forum for Coronary Heart Disease Prevention (1995) *Physical Activity: An Agenda for Action* London

SIGN (1996) *Obesity in Scotland* Scottish Intercollegiate guidelines Network Publication No **8**

Sonne-Holm S, Sorensen TA, Jensen G, Schnohr P (1989) Independent effects of weight change and attained body weight on prevalence of arterial hypertension in obese and non obese men *BMJ* **399** 767–770

Surgeon General (1988) *The Surgeon General's Report on Nutrition and Health* Washington DC: DHHS

UNICEF (1990) United Nations Children's Fund *First call for children: World declaration and plan of action from the world summit on children and convention on the rights of the child* New York: UNICEF

US Department of Health and Human Services (1996) *Physical Activity and Health: A Report of the Surgeon General* Atlanta: DHHS

WHO (1982) *Prevention of Coronary Heart Disease Report of a WHO expert committee* Technical report series 678 Geneva: WHO

WHO (1990) *Diet, Nutrition and the Prevention of Chronic Diseases* Report of a WHO study group Technical report series 797 Geneva: WHO

WHO (1996) *The World Health Report 1996* Geneva: WHO

WHO (1988) World Health Organization *Healthy Nutrition* European series 24 Copenhagen:WHO

Williams C (1995) Healthy eating: clarifying advice about fruit and vegetables *BMJ* **310** 1453–1455

Williamson DF, Pamuk E, Thun M, Flanders D, Byers T, Heath C (1995) Prospective study of intentional weight loss and mortality in never-smoking overweight US white women aged 40–64 years *Am J Epidemiol* **141** : 1128–1141

CHAPTER NINE   POLICY

ACS (1996) Dietary guidelines advisory committee Guidelines on diet, nutrition and cancer prevention: Reducing the risk of cancer with healthy food choices and physical activity Washington DC: American Cancer Society

Ames B N, Magaw R, Gold L S (1987) Ranking possible carcinogenic hazards *Science* **236** 271-280

Bagchi K, WHO, FAO (1992) International conference on nutrition case study *Impact of four decades of development on nutrition and health status in India* Rome: FAO/WHO1-126

Barnum H, Greenberg ER (1993) Cancers In: *Disease Control Priorities in Developing Countries* Jamison DT, Mosley WH, Measham AR, Bobadilla JL (eds) New York:Oxford University Press, Inc pp 529-559

Block G, Patterson, Subar A(1992) Fruit, vegetables, cancer prevention: a review of the epidemiological evidence *Nutr Cancer***18** 1-29

Bourne LT, Langenhoven L, Steyn K, Katzenllenbogen J, Jooste PL, Lombard CJ, Badenhorst CJ (1993) Urbanisation and diet: an atherogenic transition The BRISK study Presented at the 12th conference of he Epidemiological Society of South Africa Durban

Buatti E, Palli D, DeCarli A et al (1990) A case-control study of gastric cancer and diet in Italy II Association with nutrients *Int f Cancer* **45** 896-901

Bulatao RA, Stephens P (1990) *Estimates and Projections of Mortality by Cause: A Global*

Overview, 1970-2015 Population Policy and Advisory Service of the Director's Office of the Population and Human Resource Department World Bank, Washington, DC

Cromwell J, Gertman P (1979) The cost of cancer *Laryngoscope* **89** 393-409

Department of Health (1991) UK Department of Health *On the state of the public health for the year 1990* London: HMSO

Department of Health (1994) *Nutritional Aspects of Cardiovascular Disease: Report of the COMA Cardiovascular Review Group* London: HMSO (Report on Health and Social Subjects; No 46)

DHSS (1988) US Department of Health and Human Services *Healthy people 2000 : National health promotion and disease prevention objectives* Washington DC: Government Printing Office

DHSS (1988) US Department of Health and Human Services, Public Health Services *The Surgeon General's report on nutrition and health* Washington DC: US Government Printing Office, (DHHS (PHS)Publ No 88-50210)

Doll R (1992) The lessons of life Keynote address to the nutrition and cancer conference *Cancer Res* **52** 2024s-2029s

Doll R, Peto R (1981) *The Causes of Cancer* Oxford: University Press

Epstein SS (1979) *The politics of cancer* New York: Anchor Press

FAO/WHO (1992) Food and Agriculture Organization of the United Nations/ World Healh Organization Nutrition and development - a global assessment International conference on nutrition Rome: FAO

Ferro-Luzzi A, Martino L (1996) Obesity and physical activity In: *The Origins and Consequences of Obesity CIBA Foundation Symposium 201* Chichester: Wiley

Flanders WD, Rothman KJ, (1982) Interaction of alcohol and tobacco in laryngeal cancer *Am J Epidemiol* **115** 371-379

Fujisawa Y, Itoh R (1884) *Dietary Guidelines and Nutrition Policies in Japan* Tokyo: Japanese Dietetic Association

Gopalan C (1992) *Nutrition in developmental transition in South-East Asia* Regional Health Paper, SEARO, No21 New Delhi: WHO

Gopalan C (1994) *Trends in food consumption patterns: impact of developmental transition* In: Biswas MR, Gabr M (eds) Delhi: Oxford University Press 34 -54

Greenwald P (1991) The future of nutrition research in cancer prevention In: Laidlaw SA,

Swendseid ME (eds) *Vitamins and cancer prevention* New York: Wiley-Liss Inc, 111-127

Harvey J, Passmore S (1994) *School nutrition action groups (SNAGS)* A new policy for managing food and nutrition in schools Birmingham: Health Education Unit

Henderson BE, Casagrande JT, Pike MC MackT, Rosario I, Duke A (1983) The epidemiology of endometrial cancer in young women *Br J Cancer* **47** 749-756

Howe GR, Ghadirian P, de Masquita HBB et al (1992) A collaborative case-control study of nutrient intake with pancreatic cancer within the Search programme *Int J Cancer* **51** 365-372

Hulse JH (1993) Agriculture, aquaculture and nutrition In: Leathwood P, Horisberger M, James WPT (eds) *For a better nutrition in the 21st century* Vevey/New York: Nestec/Raven

IARC (1990) International Agency for Research on Cancer *Cancer: causes, occurrence and control* Lyon: International Agency for Research on Cancerr

Jain M, Cook GM, Davis FG et al (1980) A case-control study of diet and colo-rectal cancer *Int J Cancer* **26** 757-768

James WPT (1995) A public health approach to the problem of obesity *Int J Obes Relat Metab Disord* **19** Suppl 3 S37-45

Jansen MCJF, van't Veer P, Kok FK (1995) *Fruits and vegetables in chronic disease prevention* Wageningen: Landbouwuniversiteit

Kolonel L (1996) Nutrition and prostate cancer *Cancer Causes Control* **7** 83-94

La Vecchia C, Negri E (1996) Nutrition and bladder cancer *Cancer Causes Control* **7** 95-100

Leather S, (1996) *The making of modern malnutrition* The eighth Caroline Walker Lecture London: Caroline Walker Trust

Margetts BM, Thompson R, Duffy S (1994) On behalf of The Nutritional Epidemiology Working Group on diet and cancer *A review of the epidemiological literature linking fruit and vegetable consumption to risk of cancer*

McMichael AJ (1993) Planetary overload *Global environmental change and the health of the human species* Cambridge: Cambridge University Press

McMichael AJ (1994) Global environmental change and human health: new challenges to scientist and policy-maker *J Public Health Policy* **15** 407-19

Milio (1986) Promoting health through public policy Canadian Public Health Association

Miller AB, Berrino F, Hill M, Pietinen P, Riboli E, Wahrendorf J (1994) Diet in the aetiology of cancer: a review *Eur J Cancer* **30A** 207-220

Mosley WH, Bobadilla JL, Jamison DT (1993) The health transition: implications for health policy in developing countries In *Disease Control Priorities in Developing Countries* Jamison DT, Mosley WH, Measham AR, Bobadilla JL (eds) New York: Oxford University Press

Musaiger AO, Miladi SS (1996) *Diet-related Non-communicable Diseases in the Arab Countries of the Gulf* Cairo: Food and Agriculture Organization, Office of the Near East

Nam JM, McLaughlin JK, Blot WJ (1992) Cigarette smoking, alcohol, and nasopharyngeal carcinoma: a case-control study among US whites *JNCI* **84** 619-22

NAS (1982) *Diet, nutrition and cancer* Washington DC: National Academy Press

NAS (1989) *Diet and health* Washington DC: National Academy Press

National Food Alliance (1996) *Growing Food in Cities* London: NFA

National Forum for Coronary Heart Disease Prevention (1995) *Physical activity An agenda for action* London: NFCHDP

NCI (1994) National Cancer Institute and Produce for Better Health *'5 a day' for better health* Bethesda, Maryland

Netherland Cancer Registry (1989) *Incidence of cancer in the Netherlands 1989* Landelijk Overlegorgaan Kankercentra Utrecht

Omran AR (1971) The epidemologic transition: a theory of the epidemiology of population change *Milbank Mem Fund* **49** 509-538

Parkin D, Pisani P, Ferlay J (1993) Estimates of the world-wide frequency of eighteen major cancers in 1985 *Int J Cancer* **54** 594-606

Parkin DM, Pisani P, Lopez AD, Masuyer E (1994) At least one in seven cases of cancer is caused by smoking Global estimates for 1985 *Int J Cancer* **59** 494-504

Paxton A (1994) *The food miles report* London: Sustainable agriculture, food and environment (SAFE) alliance

Petrova S, Haralanova M, Milanova M, Ovcharova D, (1992*) Case study presentation: Bulgaria* Preparatory Meeting on ICN for Central and Eastern European Countries, Nitra, Czechoslovakia

Pimmentel D, Houser J, Preiss E (1997) Water Resources: Agriculture, the Enviroment, and Society *BioScience* **47** 97-106

Popkin BM (1994) The nutrition transition in low-income countries: an emerging crisis *Nutr Rev* **52** 285-298

Popkin BM, Haines PS, Reidy KC (1989) Food consumption trends of US women: patterns and determinants between 1977 and 1985 *Am J Clin Nutr* **49** (6) 1307-19

Popkin BM, Siega-Riz AM, Haines PS (1996) A comparison of dietary trends among racial and socioeconomic groups in the United States *NEJM* **335** 716-720

Puska P, Nissinen A, Tuomilehto J et al (1985) The community-based strategy to prevent coronary heart disease: conclusions from The 10 years of the North Karelia project *Annu Rev Public Health* **6** 147-193

Rao BSN (1994) Use of beta-carotene-rich foods for combating vitamin A deficiency In: Gopalen C, Kaur H (eds) *Towards better nutrition - problems and policies* New Dehli: Nutrition Foundation of India: 273 -282

Riboli E, Kaaks R, Esteve J (1996) Nutrition and laryngeal cancer *Cancer Causes Control* **7** 147-156

Rice DP, Hodgson TA, Kopstein AN (1985) The economic costs of illness: a replication and update *Health Care Financing Review* **7** 61-80

Rothman K, Keller A (1972) The effect of joint exposure to tobacco and alcohol on risk of cancer of the mouth and pharynx *J Chron Dis* **25** 711-716

Sanchez-Castillo CP, Graizbord B, Bourges H, Romero J, Gross R (eds) (1994) Nutritional challeges in urban areas in Latin America A biomedical and social sciences approach *Archivos Latinoamericanos de Nutricion* **44** (2) 1-199

Scottish Office (1993) *The Scottish diet : Scotland's health challenge to us all* Report of a working party to the chief medical officer for Scotland Edinburgh: Scottish Office Home and Health Department

Spedding CRW (1990) The effect of dietary changes on agriculture In: Lewis B, Assmann G (eds) *The social and economic contexts of coronary prevention* London: Current Medical Literature

Steinmetz K, Potter JD (1991) A review of vegetables, fruit, and cancer I: Epidemiology *Cancer Causes and Control* **2**:325-357

Tuyns AJ, Esteve, Raymond L, Berrino F et al (1988) Cancer of the larynx/hypopharynx, tobacco and cancer *Int J Cancer* **41** 483-491

UN (1995) United Nations *World Urbanisation Prospects: the 1994 Revision*

WHO (1988) World Health Organization *Healthy Nutrition* European series 24 Copenhagen: WHO

WHO (1990) World Health Organization *Diet, nutrition, and the prevention of chronic diseases* Technical series 797 Geneva: WHO

WHO (1996) World Health Organization *Climate change and human health* Geneva: WHO

WHO (1997) *The World Health Report* Geneva: WHO

Wood JD, Fisher AV (1991) *Reducing fat in meat animals* London: Elsevier

Woolfe JA (1992) *Sweet potato, an untapped food resource* Cambridge: University Press

World Bank World development report (1993) *Investing in health* New York: Oxford University Press

Wynder EL, Bross IJ, Feldman RM (1957) A study of the etiological factors in cancer of the mouth *Cancer* **10** 1300-1322

Wynder EL, Gori GB (1977) Contribution of the environment to cancer incidence: an epidemiological exercise *JNCI* **58** 825-832

Yamaguchi K (1991) Changes in nutritional and health status in Japan after the Second World War In: *Procedings of the International Symposium on Food, Nutrition and Social Economic Development Beijing: Chinese Academy of Preventive Medicine*

Yu MC, Mo CC, Chong WX et al (1988) Preserved foods and nasopharyngeal carcinoma: a case control study in Guangxi, China *Cancer Res* **48** 1954-59

Zatonski W, Becher H, Lissowska J, Wahrendorf J (1991) Tobacco, alcohol, diet and occupational exposure in etiology of laryngeal cancer - a population-based case-control study *Cancer Causes Control* **2** 3-10

Ziegler R, Mayne ST, Swanson CA (1996) Nutrition and lung cancer *Cancer Causes Control* **7** 157-177

APPENDICES

American Cancer Society (1991) Guidelines on diet, nutrition and cancer *CA-A Cancer J for Clinicians* **41** 335-38

American Cancer Society and National Cancer Institute (1975) Symposium on nutrition in the causation of cancer Key Biscayne, Florida, May 19-22 *Cancer Research* **35** 3231-3551

American Cancer Society Special Report (1984) Nutrition and cancer: cause and prevention *CA-A Cancer J for Clinicians* **32** 121-5

American Cancer Society Dietary guidelines advisory committee (1996) *Guidelines on diet, nutrition and cancer prevention:* Reducing the risk of cancer with healthy food choices and physical activity Washington DC: American Cancer Society

Bingham S (1990) *Diet and cancer : Briefing paper* London: Health Education Authority

Butrum RR, Clifford CK, Lanza E (1988) National Cancer Institute dietary guidelines: rationale *Am J Clin Nutr* **48** 888-95

Canadian Cancer Society (1986) *Facts on cancer and diet*: Your food choices may help you reduce your cancer risk Revision June 86 Toronto: Canadian Cancer Society

Canadian Cancer Society (1992) *Health eating*: Reducing your risk of cancer Toronto: Canadian Cancer Society

Carroll KK (1981) Introductory remarks Paper from a workshop on nutrition and cancer, Dunn Clinical Nutrition Centre, Cambridge, England,24-25 July 1980 *Nutr Cancer* **2** 197-8

de Vet WHC, van Leeuwen FE (1986) Dietary guidelines for cancer prevention: The etiology of a confused debate *Nutr Cancer* **8** 223-29

European Cancer Prevention Organisation (1991) *Public education on diet and cancer* ed BenitoE, Gicacosa A, Hill D Cleaver Adams

European Organisation for Cooperation on Cancer Prevention Studies (ECP) and International Union of Nutrition Scientists (IUNS) (1986) Proceedings of a joint workshop on diet and human carcinogenesis, Aarhus, Denmark; June 1985 *Nutr Cancer* **8** 1-40

European School Oncology Task Force Miller AB, Berrino F, Hill M, Pietnen P, Riboli E, Warendorf J (1994)Diet in the etiology of cancer: A review *Eur J Cancer* **30A** 207-20

Fujisawa Y, Itoh R (1984) Dietary guidelines and nutrition policies in Japan: current situation and trends Tokyo: Japan Dietetic Association

Harvard Report on Cancer Prevention (1996) Cancer Causes and Control **7** Supplement

James WPT (1988) *Healthy nutrition*: Preventing nutrition related diseases in Europe Copenhagen: WHO Regional Office for Europe

NAS (1982) *Diet, nutrition and cancer* Washington DC: National Academy Press

NAS (1989) *Diet and health* Washington DC: National Academy Press

National Advisory Committee on Nutrition Education (1983) *A discussion paper on proposals for nutritional guidelines for nutrition education in Britain* London; Health Education Council

Scottish Office (1993) *The Scottish diet : Scotland's health challenge to us all* Report of a working party to the Chief Medical Officer for Scotland Edinburgh: Scottish Office Home and Health Department

Scrimshaw NS, Bengoa JM (1988) *United Nations University and Foundation Cavendes Report of Caracas workshop Dietary goals and guidelines for health in Latin America Dietary guidelines: Proceedings of an international conference, Toronto, Canada,26-27 June* Ed Latham MC, Scott van Veen M Cornell International Monograph series **21**133-50

Secretary of State for Health (1992) *The health of the nation : A strategy for health in England* London: HMSO

Upton C (1979) Director of the National Cancer Institute Status of the diet, nutrition and cancer program *Statement before the subcommittee on nutrition, senate committee on agriculture, nutrition and forestry* Bethesda, Maryland: US Dept Health, Education and Welfare

US Congress (1979) Dietary goals for the United States Report of the Select Committee on nutrition and human needs Washington DC:US Government Printing Office (Also known as the McGovern Report after the committee's chair)

US Department of Health and Human Services (1988) Healthy people 2000 : *National health promotion and disease prevention objectives* Washington DC: Government Printing Office

US Department of Health and Human Services, Public Health Services (1988) *The Surgeon General's report on nutrition and health* Washington DC:US Government Printing Office, (DHHS (PHS)PublNo88-50210)

WHO (1988) World Health Organization *Healthy Nutrition* European series **24** Copenhagen: WHO

Williams C (1995) Healthy eating: Clarifying advice on fruit and vegetables *BMJ* **310** 1453-5

World Health Organization(1990) *Diet, nutrition and the prevention of chronic diseases* Report of a WHO study group Geneva:WHO (Technical report series 797)

World Health Organization (1964) *Prevention of cancer:* Report of a WHO expert committee Geneva:WHO (Technical report series 276)

Index